MW00790405

WILLIAM HARRIS MILLER

KATHERINE OLDHAM MILLER

ERRATTA

It would have been pleasing, indeed, to have finished without error, but perfection need not be expected of imperfection. If there are not more serious errors than here pointed to, we shall have cause to be glad.

In Part III, Chap. 4, Art. 1, subject, "Christopher Harris," appears the statement that "Two of his sons married 'daughters' ", when it should read " 'sisters' of the old pioneer, Higgason Grubbs." (See Supplement.)

In Part III, Chap. 6, Art. 1, subject, "Robert Harris," it is stated that "he married Nancy Grubbs, a 'daughter' ", when it should read " 'sister' of Higgason Grubbs." (See Supplement.)

In Part III, Chap. 12, Art. 1, subject, "Christopher Harris" (Rev.), the statement that he "married Elizabeth Grubbs, a 'daughter' ", should read " 'sister' of Higgason Grubbs." (See Supplement.)

In Part III, Chap. 3, Sec. 4, Sub-sec. 5, subject, "Lucy Harris," it appears that the subject, "Lucy Harris, married Thomas Grubbs, who in 1758 was in actual service against the Indians on the Virginia frontier," when the fact is, she married Higgason Grubbs, who came from Albemarle County, Virginia, to Kentucky among the early pioneers. (See Supplement.)

In the Supplement appended additional matter relative to families of this history will be found, which is divided into 9 paragraphs—the head-lines thereto indicate the subject matter of each paragraph, which is not otherwise indexed.

History and Genealogies

OF THE FAMILIES OF

MILLER, WOODS, HARRIS, WALLACE, MAUPIN, OLDHAM, KAVANAUGH, AND BROWN

(Illustrated)

WITH INTERSPERSIONS OF NOTES OF THE FAMILIES OF

DABNEY, REID, MARTIN, BROADDUS, GENTRY, JARMAN, JAMESON, BALLARD, MULLINS, MICHIE, MOBERLEY, COVINGTON, BROWNING, DUNCAN, YANCEY AND OTHERS

By W. H. MILLER

RICHMOND, KY.

1907

Copyright 1906, by W. H. Miller

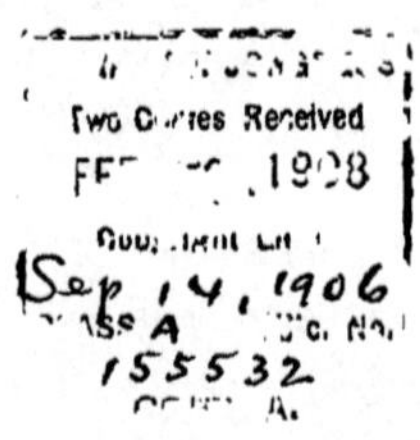

PRESS OF
TRANSYLVANIA CO.
LEXINGTON, KY.

PREFACE.

In the pages following, besides giving the lines of descent as far back as traced, are brief narratives, sketches, etc., of individual members of the families of Miller, Woods, Harris, Wallace, Maupin, Oldham, Kavanaugh, Brown, and others. The lineage running back to one Miller, of Anglo-Scotch-Irish-Franco-German blood; Woods, an English Trooper of Scoth-Irish blood; Maupin, a Frenchman; Harris of Wales; Overton, an English soldier; Wallace, of the Scottish Clan Wallace (Scotch-Irish); Dabney, of French origin; Kavanaugh, from Ireland; Oldham, Anglo-Welsh, and Brown, of English ancestry. By intermarrige these several bloods have intermingled and coursed into the veins of people who today are a prominent part of the best citizenship of our great country, and have all along, in the years gone by, held, and are now occupying, high positions of public trust in the body politic, and in the counsels of the nation their influences are felt, as well as filling prominent places in the marts of trade and commerce and agriculture and every otherwise, and have spread to the remotest portions of the globe.

Among the early mothers appear the names of Lynn, Worsop, Campbell, Overton, Walters, Clairbourne, Glenn, Anderson, McCord, Bratton, Rice, Mullens, and others of whom very little more than the mere name is known, and sometimes hardly that because the lines have not been run out—made very difficult to trace from the fact, as it seems, that the heads of the house pretty generally have been slow and careless in the making, preserving and handing down full and complete family records, and often when this was done reasonably well, by some mishap the same were lost or destroyed. Therefore, in many, if not most instances, only very meagre accounts can be obtained, especially of the maternal line, and often the little gathered does not satisfy, but only produces a desire to know more —there seems to be no stopping place.

The data at hand has been gotten from old family and court records, letters and testimony of creditable persons, and from every source considered reliable, within reach, by long and patient search and labor. An endeavor has been made to put the facts together in a clear and comprehensive shape. No doubt some errors occur. and should be noted and corrected when detected. In a work of this kind perfection need not be expected. All matters set forth as facts are known or believed to be true from substantial evidence.

The work is submitted to the kind and charitable judgment of the families and friends, and pardon is asked for shortcomings and imperfections. It is confidently hoped that the presentation may be interesting enough to cause some, at least, to overlook the faults, and that some good may result.

This book is divided into eight parts, and each part into chapters, and the chapters into sections, for convenience and easy reference. A genealogical table precedes each part.

Part I. The Miller Family.
Part II. The Woods Family.
Part III. The Harris Family.
Part IV. The Wallace Family.

Interspersed through the parts are brief notes of the families of Reid, Dabney, Martin, Gentry, Jarman, Jameson, Ballard, Mullins, Michie, Moberley, Covington, Browning, Duncan, Yancey, etc.

A general index to the whole is made, complete enough, it is thought, to enable the ready finding of any of the contents.

To the following named persons thanks are extended for material aid generously and kindly rendered, viz.:

Mrs. Joseph W. (Mattie Maupin) Bales, Lexington, Ky.
Mrs. (Susan Woods) Matt M. Bearden, of Elk River Mills, Fayetteville, Tenn.
A. R. Bentenstien, Esq., Clerk of Court, Warrenton, Va.
J. L. Bishop, Esq., attorney-at-law, Selma, Ala.
A. J. Broaddus, Esq., Moberley, Ky.
Hon. A. Rollins Burnam, attorney-at-law, Richmond, Ky.
Mrs. Bettie Harrish Bush, Stanford, Ky.
Col. and Mrs. James W. Caperton, Richmond, Ky.
Hon. A. T. Chenault, Richmond, Ky.
Mrs. Margaret O. Chenault, Mt. Sterling, Ky.
Jesse T. Cobb, Esq., Clerk County Court, Richmond, Ky.
Collins' History of Kentucky.
W. E. Coons, Esq., Clerk Court, Culpeper, Va.
Mrs. Sallie Harris Wallace Conroy, Irvine, Ky.
William Q. Covington, Esq., now deceased, Waco, Ky.
Joseph Collins, Esq., Richmond, Ky.
Mrs. Jacob S. Collins, Richmond, Ky.
Mrs. Margaret Oldham Doty, Richmond, Ky.
Mr. William Kavanaugh Doty, Richmond, Ky.
Mrs. Robert L. (Jane Arie) Doty, Richmond, Ky.
Dr. John Harris Duncan, St. Louis, Mo.
Mrs. Mary Duncan, Richmond, Ky.
Mrs. Brutus K. (Laura) Duncan, Richmond, Ky.
Leslie Evans, Esq., Richmond, Ky.
Thomas Geddy, Esq., Clerk Court, Williamsburg, Va.
Richard Gentry, Esq., Kansas City, Mo.
Miss Angeline Gentry, Richmond, Va.
Miss Sallie Gentry, New Hope, Va.
Mrs. Aileen, Kavanaugh Gilbert, Lawrenceburg, Ky.
Judge John D. Goodloe, Whites Station, Ky.
B. F. Golden, Esq., Richmond, Ky.
Charles D. Grubbs, Esq., Mt. Sterling, Ky.
Miss Martha Overton Harris, Fulton, Mo.
Overton Harris, Esq., Harris, Mo.
Clifford B. Harris, Esq., Harris, Mo.
John W. Harris, Esq., Nortonville, Kansas.
Mr. Harris, Clerk Court, Irvine, Ky.
Mrs. Wm. J. Hanna, Harrodsburg, Ky.
Thomas J. Hill, Jr., attorney-at-law, Stanford, Ky.
Archibald W. Kavanaugh, Esq., Vinton, Kansas.
Joseph Kennedy, Esq., Richmond, Ky.
Mrs. C. A. Lacey, Houston, Va.
Dulaney M. Lackey, Esq., Lancaster, Ky.
Frank N. Lee, Esq., Danville, Ky.
John Lipscomb, Esq., Beans Creek, Tenn.
Life of Bishop Kavanaugh, by Bedford.

Mrs. R. N. (Ellen Miller) McClain, Gallatin, Tenn.
A. H. Martin, Esq., Clerk Court Norfolk Co., Portsmouth, Va.
David G. Martin, Esq., Boone, Ky.
W. L. Martin, Esq., Clerk Court, Charlottesville, Va.
Mrs. Socrates (Anna T). Maupin, Lafollette, Tenn.
Leland D. Maupin, Esq., Waco, Ky.
Breckinridge Maupin, Esp., Kingston, Ky.
Julian H. Maupin, Esq., Waco, Ky.
Calumn Maupin, Esq., Richmond, Ky.
Christopher Harris Maupin, Esq., Moberley, Ky.
Mrs. Susan Chenault Miller, Ardmore, Indian Territory.
Col. Thomas W. Miller (now dead), late of Stanford, Ky.
Malcom Memmings Miller, Esq., Richmond, Ky.
Thomas Southworth Miller, Esq., Flat, Texas.
Mrs. Garland Burleigh Miller, Falfurrias, Texas.
Mr. and Mrs. James C. Miller, Esq., Moberley, Ky.
R. L. Mitchell, Esq., Clerk Supreme Court Caswell Co., Yanceyville, N. C.
E. Nelson, Esq., Clerk Court, Manassas, Va.
Rev. William Abner Oldham, Nortonville, Kansas.
Thompson B. Oldham, Esq., Burgin, Ky.
Samuel Oldham, Esq., Zanesville, Ohio.
Alf. V. Oldham, Clerk City Court, Louisville, Ky.
Abner Oldham, Esq., Lexington, Ky.
Thomas M. Oldham, Esq., (now dead), Brassfield, Ky.
William Dowell Oldham, Esq., Lexington, Ky.
Hon. John Samuel Owsley, Jr., attorney-at-law, Stanford, Ky.
William N. Prarott, Esq., Charlottesville, Va.
George W. Park, Esq., Speedwell, Ky.
Mrs. Dudley (Bettie Miller) Portwood, Ft. Worth, Texas.
Perriss, etc., History of Kentucky.
A. C. Quisenberry's History of Families.
Mrs. Miriam Reid, Red House, Ky.
Forrestus Reid, Esq., Danville, Ky.
Mrs. John J. (Jane Harris) Rogers, Lexington, Ky.
Hon. Charles H. Rodes, Danville, Ky.
Dr. Slaughter's Notes on Culpeper Co., Va., by Raleigh T. Green, by permission.
W. Rodes Shackelford, Esq., Richmond, Ky.
Mrs. Sallie Goodloe Smith, Richmond, Ky.
John Speed Smith, Esq., Washington, D. C.
Z. F. Smith's History of Kentucky.
Mrs. Pattie Harris Stone, Louisville, Ky.
Mrs. G. B. (Annie Maupn) Stevensoni Velardeno, Mexico.
Miss Helen Terrill, Terrill, Ky.
Robert B. Terrill, Esq., Deputy Clerk, Richmond, Ky.
Miss Annie Miller Tevis, Middlesborough, Ky.
O. T. Wallace, Esq., (chart), Point Levell, Ky.
Coleman C. Wallace, Esq., Richmond, Ky.
Mrs. John (Elizabeth Jane) Wallace, Irvine, Ky.
Mrs. Ann Wallace, Lexington, Ky.
Mrs. Ellen Tracey Wallace, Irvine, Ky.
Mrs. Jennie Walderschmidt, Vinton, Kansas.
Roy C .White, Esq., Circuit Clerk, Richmond, Ky.
Mrs. Sallie M. Williamson, Pulaski, Tenn.
Hon. Robert H. Winn, Mt. Sterling, Ky.
C. W. Woolfolk, Esq., Clerk Court, Orange, Va.
Mrs. John T. (Nannie) Woodford, Mt. Sterling, Ky.

G. M. Woods, Esq., Tullahoma, Tenn.

Woods-McAfee Memorial, by Rev. Neander M. Woods, by his kind permission.

Rev. Edgar Woods' History of Albemarle Co., Charlottesville, Va., by kind permission.

Mrs. Malinda Yates, Trenton, Mo.

Miss Lucy Miller, Paris, Ky.

Mrs. Charles (Mary Miller) Stephens, Paris, Ky.

Mrs. Lillian Curd Elliott, Kansas City, Mo.

C. D. Bailey, Esq., County Court Clerk, Clarksville, Tenn.

Mrs. Mary Eliza Crews, Glasgow, Mo.

Will M. Maupin, Esq., Lincoln, Neb.

B. F. Maupin, Esq., Pulaski, Ill.

Mrs. Anna P. Kavanaugh, Pine Bluff, Ark.

James Howard Boggs, Esq., Nicholasville, Ky.

Mrs. Barry (Minnie H.) Miller, Dallas, Texas.

Miss Sallie Yates, Trenton, Mo.

Miss Mary Brown Miller, Huntsville, Ala.

Mrs. T. E. (Mariam Othelia) Manning, Roswell, New Mexico.

D. R. Broaddus, Esq., Blue Springs, Mo.

American Encyclopedia, edited by Riply and Dana.

Mrs. Jane Redd Gentry Shelton, 4467 Lindell Bld., St. Louis, Mo.

Mrs. Oscar Williams, Trenton, Mo.

Dr. J. P. Oldham, San Antonio, Texas.

Edmund McKinney Oldham, Esq., Brymer, Burleson Co., Texas.

Robert E. Miller, Esq., Huntsville, Mo.

Rufus P. McGoodwin, Esq., Danville, Ky.

Mrs. Samuel E. Lackey, Gallatin, Tenn.

Mrs. Bessie Cale Broaddus, El Paso, Texas (Box 230).

Joe A. McMurray, Esq., Valley Mills, Texas.

Mrs. James Harrison (Estelle Moxley) Maupin, Edgerton, Mo., (R. R. No. 2).

Miss Lillye Oldham, Brymer, Burleson Co., Texas.

Joel E. Gates, Esq., City Clerk, St. Joseph, Mo.

Mrs. Dollie Smith Lutz, ———, Mo. (Letter fails to give P. O.)

Stephen Collins Oldham, venerable (old man), Austin, Texas.

Judge A. E. Wilkinson, Austin, Texas.

Judge W. Overton Harris, Louisville, Ky.

Appleton's Cyclopaedia.

Dictionary of U. S. History, by Jameson.

Mrs. Mary E. Grumbine, Richmond, Mo.

Prof. Grant B. Grumbine, Richmond, Mo. (Prin. Woodson Inst.)

Mrs. Mary Virginia Brown Osburn, Richmond, Mo.

Captain David McFadden, Waco, Texas.

Frank Ish, Waco, Texas.

Most respectfully,

WILLIAM HARRIS MILLER.

Richmond, Ky., May 1, 1906.

Atoms massed, make up the universe,
The many littles make at last the whole;
No man is great, but each created soul
Has, yet, within, the promise of perfection,
The image, and the stamp of the divine.
Adversity may hinder, dwarf and crush,
A chilling frost may blight the budding flower,
And years break down the growing tree of greatness
But, as the cycles roll, each passing life
Bequeaths its portion to the common good.
The generations piling, each on each,
Time writing still prosperity and failure,
And still recording effort and achievement,
And life and death, and shade and shine succeeding,
Bring on the world to that millenial age,
When every hill shall blossom with perfection,
The waters leap and dance for very joy,
And man regenerate stand great and good,
The statue and the fullness of a God.

K. O. M.

LIST OF ILLUSTRATIONS

LIST OF SOME AGED MEMBERS

Years

Mrs. ————(Garland) Basey......118
Magdalene Woods McDowell—Borden Bowyer, 1706-1810..........104
John Meadows 103
William Parrott 101
Hezekiah Rice and wife, Mary Bullock, lived together as man and wife 75 years.
Jane Dulaney Miller, 1751-1844..... 93
William B. Miller, 1807-1899........ 92
Amanda Reid McMurtry, 1811-1907, living at 96
Robert Harris, 1787-1883 96
Cornelius Dabney, Sr., over........ 90
Gabriel Maupin, 1700-1794.......... 94
Thomas Maupin, 1758-1855 97
Michie Maupin, 1779-1876 97
Mary Mullins Gillespie, over........ 90
Jane Mullins Clark, 1754-1844...... 90
Stephen Collins Oldham, 1815, living at 91
Sarah Thompson Brown, 1724-1815.. 91
Polly Thompson Brown 92
B. B. Parrott, living at............ 96
Bettie Early Chapman 96
Lucy B. Thompson 91
Bettie Thompson 93
Dr. Charles Brown 96
Lucy E. Parrott Brown............ 92
William T. Barrott, living at....... 94
Mourning Woods Thorpe, 1783-186- -
Col. Thos. Woods Miller, 1811-1891.. 80
Mary Jane Hocker Miller, 1825-1905, 80
Robert Miller, 1775-1861 86
Edna Elizabeth Miller Hill, 1823, living at 83
Samuel Lackey, Sr., 1746-1830...... 84
William Malcolm Miller, 1810-18—.. 8-
Archibald Woods, 1749-1836 89
Mary Woods Reid, 1746-1828....... 82
Hon. Curtis F. Burnam, 1820, living at 87
Thomas Thorpe, 1800-1885 85
Margaret Maupin Harris, 1767-1855, 88
Robert Harris, 1786-1868........... 82
Malinda Miller Harris Yates, 1822, living at 84
Pauline Rodes Harris, living at.... 80
Judge Christopher Harris, 1788-1871 83
Elizabetr Berry Harris, 1800-1884.. 84
James Anderson Harris, 1817-189—over 80
Susan Taylor Harris, living at..... 80
Mary Rice Woods Harris, 1795-1876, 81
Susan Harris Duncan, 1808-18—, over 80
Richard Gentry, 1763-1843 80
John Maupin, 1725-1806 81
Nicholas Hocker, 1782-1854 82
James Faris, 1822, living at........ 84
Annie Reid Wallace Maupin, 17—1880, over 80
Cabel Chenault, 1795-1881 86
David Chenault, 1771-1851 80
P. P. Ballard, 1818, living at....... 89
Jesse Oldham 89
Thompson B. Oldham, 1819, living at 88
Hezekiah Oldham, 1787-1868........ 81
Mary Kavanaugh Oldham.1798-1882, 84
Othniel Rice Oldham, 1817-1900.... 83
Caleb Oldham, 1789-1872............ 83
Elizabeth Oldham Fisher, 1795, over 80
Nancy Oldham Grubbs, 1797, over.. 80
Jane Miller Kavanaugh-Faulkner-Walker, 1809, over 80
Jael Ellison Harris, 1795-189—, over 80
Sarah Ann Kavanaugh Moore, over 80
Bishop Hubbard Hinde Kavanaugh, 1802-1884 82
Wm. Barbour Kavanaugh, 1807-1888 81
Robert Covington, 1760-1847 87
Wm. Covington, 1783-1869 86
Jeptha M. Covington, 1816-1903..... 87
Wm. Q. Covington, 1820-1906....... 86
Coleman Covington, 1800—, over... 80
Sarah Browning Duncan, 1742-1824, 82
Brightberry Brown 84
Bettie Thompson 80
Nathaniel Thompson 81
Parthenia Brown Hayden 82
George B. Brown 87
Sikie Ward 89
Garland Brown 84
Captain Jesse Early 80
Nancy Ward Thompson 80
Sarah Parrott Stephens 82
Richard P. Ward 83
Evaline Brown Fretwell 85
Thomas H. Brown 87
Lucy T. Brown 85
James D. Brown 80

SOLDIERS IN VARIOUS WARS

COLONIAL, INDIAN AND FRONTIER WARS

Bland Ballard, Virginia Frontier	5	13	Note
Capt. William Briscoe, Va. Frontier (died in Madison Co., Ky.)	4	18	
James Brown, Virginia Frontier	8	1	4
Lt. Abraham Buford, in battle of Point Pleasant	2	5	
Captain James Brown, Virginia Frontier	8	1	6
Major Brown, Virginia Frontier	8	1	12
John Buster, Virginia Frontier (died -820)	2	13	1
General Richard Gentry, Virginia Frontier	3	46	3
Thomas Grubbs, Virginia Frontier	3	3	4
Randolph Harris, Kentucky Frontier against Indians	3	1	1
Jeremiah Harris, Kentucky Frontier agains tIndians	3	1	11
Major Overton Harris, Black Hawk War	3	32	
James Harris, Black Hawk War	3	38	
Thomas Jameson, Virginia Frontier			
Alexander Jameson, Virginia Frontier			
Colonel Nicholas Miller, Kentucky Frontier	1	1	4
Henry Miller, General Wayne's Army	1	1	5
Christopher Miller, General Wayne's Army	1	1	5
Lt. William Miller, Kentucky Frontier at Estill's defeat	1	1	10
Maj. Anderson Miller, Kentucky Frontier at Estill's defeat	1	1	14
Ichabod B. Miller, Kentucky Frontier	1	1	12
Jacob Miller, Madison Co., Ky., Frontier	1	1	12
John McDowell, killed at Balcony Falls	2	5	1
John McDowell, Indian Wars	2	1	6
Joseph McDowell, Indian Wars	2	1	8
Thomas McDowell, killed in Madison Co., Ky., by Indians	2	1	10
William Maupin, Virginia Frontier	5	3	5
John Maupin, Virginia Frontier	5	4	
Daniel Maupin, Virginia Frontier	5	11	
William Mullins, Virginia Frontier	5	13	1
Matthew Mullins, Virginia Frontier	5	13	
Michael Woods, Jr., Virginia Frontier			
William Woods, Ensign, Virginia Frontier			
Lt. William Woods, Virginia Frontier			
Col. James Woods, Virginia Frontier	2	20	
Joshua Woods, Virginia Frontier			
Col. John Woods, Virginia Frontier, Indian and Colonial wars	2	19	
John Woods, Virginia Frontier			
John Woods, Virginia Frontier	2	1	11
Archibald Woods, Virginia Frontier, Dunmore War	2	8	
William Woods, Virginia Frontier	2	6	
John S. Wallace, Virginia and Kentucky Frontier	4	1	1
John Wallace, Virginia and Kentucky Frontier			
Sam'l Wallace, commanded at Ft. Young French and Indian War	4	15	2

REVOLUTIONARY WAR

Captain William Briscoe, died in Madison Co., Ky., 1830	4	18	
John Brown	1	1	22
Captain Tarleton Brown	1	1	42
Benjamin Brown, under Light Horse Harry Lee	8	2	

Captain Brightberry Brown, at Yorktown	8	2	
Captain Bezabel Brown	8	2	2
Bernard Brown, dispatch bearer from New York to Charleston	8	3	
John Buster, (died 1820)	2	13	1
Colonel Abraham Buford, Virginia line	2	5	1
Robert Covington, Virginia line (died in Madison Co., Ky.)	7	18	1
Wm. Chenault, Virginia line (died in Madison Co., Ky., 1803)	5	13	9
Edward Garland, Captan 14th Virginia			
Peter Garland, Captain 6th Virginia			
Nathaniel Garland, Lieutenant Virginia State Militia			
Richard Gentry, Captain Virginia Militia	3	16	
Benjamin Harris, Captain Virginia Militia	3		
Captain Robert Harris, Virginia Militia, went to Sunny Co., N.C.	3	3	9
William Harris, Virginia line			
John Jameson, Colonel of Dragoons			
Capt. John Jouett, Virginia line (died in 1802)	3	3	9
Capt. John Jouett, Virginia line (died in Kentucky)	3	3	9
Capt. Robert Jouett, Virginia line	3	3	9
Capt. Matthew Jouett, Va. line (died in Fayette Co., Ky., 1827)	3	3	9
Capt. Robert Jouett, 7th Virginia			
Adam Keblinger, Virginia line			
John Lapsley, wounded at Brandywine, died in Lincoln Co., Ky.	2	47	
Robert Miller, at Yorktown (died in Orange Co., Va., 1806)	1	4	
Robert Miller, Virginia line (died in the service			
Lt. Col. John Miller, at Yorktown (died in Madison Co., Ky., 1806)	1	14	
James McDowell	2	5	1
John McDowell	2	5	1
Samuel McDowell (settled in Mercer Co., Ky.)	2	5	1
Samuel McDowell (settled in Fayette Co., Ky.)	2	5	1
Judge William McDowell (moved to Kentucky 1784)	2	5	1
Thomas Marshall	2	5	1
William McKee (moved to Kentucky, 1793)	2	47	3
Lt. Hudson Martin	3	5	7
Capt. John Martin	3	5	7
Cornelius Maupin, at Yorktown	5	4	3
Daniel Maupin, at Yorktown	5	4	3
William Maupin, at Yorktown	5	4	4
Matthew Mullins, Sergeant 4th, 8th and 12 Va. Foot	5	13	
Matthew Mullins, Jr., (died in Madison Co., Ky., 1836)	5	13	4
John Martin, Captain State Militia			
Corporal Thomas Martin			
Lt. Col. Wm. Oldham (killed at St. Clair's defeat, 1791)	6	1	4
	6	2	
Capt. John Oldham, N .C. line (died in Estill Co., Ky., 1832)	6	13b	
Capt. John Oldham, Pennsylvania Rangers	6	40	
Jesse Oldham, N. C. line (died in Madison Co., Ky., 1814)	6	3	
Ready Money Richard Oldham, N. C. line (Capt.), died in Madison Co., Ky., 1836	6	1	
Major George Oldham, Lee's Legion	6	2	2
Moses Oldham, N. C. line (moved to Montgomery Co., Tenn.)	6	2	3
Conway Oldham, Virginia line	6	2	4
Conway Oldham, Virginia line (killed at Eutah Springs)	6	2	
James Oldham, North Carolina line	6	2	5
Richard Oldham, N. C. line, (died in Estill Co., Ky., 1834)	6	2	6
William Oldham, North Carolina line	6	2	8
Capt. Isaac Oldham	6	2	
	6	40	

Lt. Edward Oldham	6	2	
	6	40	
Col. Henry Pauling	4	5	
Capt. Nathan Reid, Virginia line	1	4	
	2	2	
Samuel Reid	2	29	
Capt. Robt. Rodes, captured at Charleston, S. C. (died in Madison Co., Ky.)	3	3	7
Capt. Clough Shelton, 10th Virginia			
Richard Snow, at Yorktown			
Capt. Roger Thompson	8	7	Note
Lt. John Thompson	8	7	Note
William Woods, Virginia line	2	6	
John Woods, Virginia line			
William Woods, Virginia line			
Capt. Michael Wallace, Virginia line	4	4	
Malcolm Wallace, under Gen. Morgan at Boston (died in ser. 1775)	4	15	1
Samuel Wallace, Va. (commanded at Ft. Young in F. & I. wars)	4	15	2
Jas. Wallace, Ensign 3d Va., (died in Philadelphia in 1776)	4	15	3
Capt. Adam Wallace, 10th Virginia (killed at Waxhaw, S. C.)	4	15	4
Capt. Andrew Wallace, 8th Virginia (killed at Guilford C.H. 1781)	4	15	5
Capt. Charles Yancey, Virginia line	7	2	
Lt. Layton Yancey, Virginia line	7	2	
Major James Yancey, Virginia line	7	2	
Col. James Woods, Virginia line	2	20	
Thomas Maupin, Virginia line (died in Madison Co., Ky., 1855)	5	2	B
Daniel Maupin, Va. line at Yorktown (died in Mad. Co., Ky. 1832)	5	12	

WAR OF 1812

Beverley Brown	8	1	1
General Jacob Brown	8	1	21
Colonel Barbee Collins, Madison Co., Ky.	4	20	1
William Fisher, Estill Co., Ky.	6	35	
Jesse Grubbs, Estill Co., Ky.	6	36	
Maj. Overton Harris, Madison Co., Ky. (Black Hawk campaign)	3	37	
James Harris, Madison Co., Ky. (Black Hawk campaign)	3	38	
Robert Harris, Madison Co., Ky. (died 188—)	3	14	
Archibald Kavanaugh, Madison Co., Ky.	7	8	7
Charles Kavanaugh, Madison Co., Ky. (died 186—)	7	11	
Nicholas Kavanaugh, Madison Co., Ky. (went to Lone Jack, Mo.)	7	12	
Philemon Kavanaugh, Madison Co., Ky.	7	16	
Lt. Thomas W. Kavanaugh, Kentucky	7	17	2
Major Samuel McDowell, Kentucky	2	5	1
Major James McDowell, Kentucky	2	5	1
Joseph McDowell, Kentucky	2	5	1
Col. James McDowell, Kentucky	2	5	2
Col. Walliam Williams, Kentucky	2	21	6
Gen. James Miller	1	1	21
William Miller	1	1	16
Moses Oldham, Tennessee line	6	39	
Thomas Moberley, Kentucky	6	34	
Maj. Richard Oldham (son of Lt. Col. Wm. Oldham)	6	2	
Maj. Richard Oldham (Ready Money)	6	4	
Michael Woods	2	7	
Maj. Charles Yancey, Virginia	7	2	
Col. Wm. B. Yancey, Virginia	7	2	
Col. John Yantis	2	47	

Col. John Miller, Commanding in Indiana and Ohio 1 1 20
William Kavanaugh, Kentucky 7 8 9
Asa Smith, Kentucky .... 5 2 B

MEXICAN WAR

Col. James C. Stone, Madison Co., Ky. 3 3 7
G. B. F. Broaddus, 1st Lt., Madison Co., Ky. .... 1 13 3 Note
Dr. Franklin Harris, Madison Co., Ky. 3 48 5
Humphrey Kavanaugh, Madison Co., Ky. 7 11 4
Dr. William J. Chenault, Madison Co., Ky. 5 13 9
David Waller Chenault, Madison Co., Ky. 5 13 9
Aaron Burr Richardson, Madison Co., Ky. (died) 3 13 1
Thomas Jefferson Richardson, Madison Co., Ky. (died) 3 43 1
General W. H. L. Wallace 4 2 7
Archibald Woods White, Tennessee 1 14 10 7
Milton Miller, Rockcastle Co., Ky. ....
Wm. (Big Foot) Wallace, Texas, (prisoner of Mier, 1842) 4 3 4
4 1 3 37

Maj. William Oldham, Texas, (Mier Expedition, 1842) 6 1 2 14
6 13a 1

Thomas Oldham, Texas, (Mier Expedition, 1842) 6 39 3
Thomas Staynor, Madison Co., Ky. .... 5 2 B

Other members of Captain James C. Stone's company:—William Guess, Corporal, John Lawrence, orderly serjeant, Thomas H. Barnes, 3rd lieutenant, Green Clay Smith, 2nd lieutenant, N. D. Burrus, Willis Garrison, Clifton Shifflett, James P. Denham, Philip Brakehill, James Simpson and brother, Alfred Williams, Bradford Dozier, David Amerine, George Amerine, Joe Perkins, William Prewitt, Harrison M. Taylor, Howard Land, Hiram Land, Merrill Roberts, and Bowen Denham.

CIVIL WAR

Federal Army

James L. Bishop, (killed at Memphis, Tenn.) 5 12 1
Dr. G. W. Evans 3 48 8
5 13 9

Col. John K. Faulkner, Garrard Co., Ky. 7 5 5
Maj. William Goodloe, Kentucky 2 11 6
Gen. W. J. Landrum, Kentucky 2 47 6
Gen. John Miller, Mad. Co., K. (killed in Richmond battle 1862) .. 1 7
Col. Samuel McKee, 1st Kentucky 2 47 8
Samuel McKee Lapsley (died in 1862) 2 47 9
Gen. John Franklin Miller 1 1 20
Col. Reuben Munday, Mardison Co., Ky. 5 13 9
Oscar Oldham, Kentucky 6 11 1
Capt. Wm. E. Simms, Kentucky 3 46 12
Andrew Wallace, Estill Co., Ky. 4 12
Gen. Llew. Wallace 4 2 9
Col. Charles J. Walker, Madison Co., Ky. 3 8 1
Col. William B. Woods 2 1 14
Col. Charles R. Woods 2 1 13
Capt. Uriah Wright Oldham, Oldham Co., Ky., Co. F, 9 Ky. Cav. 6 2
John M. Cole .... 5 2 B

Confederate Army

Joseph Emmerson Brown	8	1	26
Gen. Benjamin Gratz Brown	8	1	18
Tazewell Brown, Albemarle Co., Va.	5	4	13
James D. Brown, Albemarle Co., Va.	5	4	13
Allen Henry Brown, Albemarle Co., Va.	5	4	13
William A. Brown, Albemarle Co., Va.	5	4	13
Bernard Brown, Albemarle Co., Va.	5	4	13
George P. Bright, Tenn. troops (lives in Lincoln Co., Ky.)	3	31	2
James Howard Boggs, Gen. John H. Morgan	2	7	4
Jake Bronston, Capt. T. B. Collins, Gen. John H. Morgan	6	8	1
	5	13	7
Lt. R. C. H. Covington, Capt. T. B. Collins, Gen. John H. Morgon	3	29	1
Charles Covington, Capt. T. B Collins, Gen John H. Morgan	6	8	1
Serg. Jos. Collins, Capt. T. B. Collins, Gen. John H. Morgan	6	8	1
Capt. Thomas B. Collins, Gen. John H. Morgan	6	8	1
David Chenault, Col. D. W. Chenault, Gen. John H. Morgan	5	13	9
Anderson Chenault, Col. D. W. Chenault, Gen. John H. Morgan	5	13	9
Colby Chenault, Tennessee Army	5	13	9
David Chenault, Tennessee Army	5	13	9
James Chenault, Tennessee Army	5	13	9
Harvey Chenault, Tennessee Army	5	13	9
Col. David Waller Chenault, Gen. John H. Morgan	5	13	9
Jas. Cosby, Co. F afterward 11 Ky. Cav., Gen. John H. Morgan	6	8	1
Boyle Doty, Co. F afterward 11 Ky. Cav., Gen. John H. Morgan	7	7	1
Chas. K. Doty, Co.F afterward 11 Ky.Cav., Gen. John H. Morgan	7	7	1
A. J. Dudley, Co. F afterward 11 Ky. Cav., Gen. John H. Morgan	7	5	2
N. B. Deatherage, 11 Ky. Cav., Gen. John H. Morgan	6	17	3
Joel T. Embry, Co.F afterward 11 Ky.Cav., Gen. John H. Morgan	6	10	11
Henry Goodloe, Kentucky Cavalry	2	11	6
Robert Harris Hume, 11 Ky Cav., Gen. John H. Morgan	3	21	3
John M. Hume, Kentucky Cavalry	1	9	Note
Isham G. Harris, Gen. Johnston's staff, served in the West	3	1	13
John Miller Wallace Harris, Ky. Cav. under Morgan	3	33	
Ira Harris, Albemarle Co., Va.	5	4	2
William Harris, Albemarle Co., Va.	5	4	4
Anderson Harris, Madison Co., Ky., Gen. Morgan's Cav	6	8	1
William D. Jarman, Albemarle Co., Va.	5	4	13
John L. Jarman, Albemarle Co., Va.	5	4	13
Archibald W. Kavanaugh, Gen. John H. Morgan	7	7	3
Samuel E. Lackey, Gen. John H. Morgan	1	14	11
	7	7	1
Samuel R. Lapsley, Kentucky Cavalry	2	47	9
John W. McPherson, Gen. John H. Morgan's Cav	6	10	4
	7	6	8
James Miller, Lincoln Co.,Ky., Gen. John H. Morgan's Cav	1	8	6
John H. Miller, Lincoln Co.,Ky., Gen. John H. Morgan's Cav	1	8	5
Wm. H. Miller, Lincoln Co.,Ky., Gen. John H. Morgan's Cav	1	8	9
Robt. Dan. Miller, Madison Co.,Ky., Gen. John H. Morgan's Cav.	1	13	2
Jas. C. Miller, Madison Co.,Ky., Gen. John H. Morgan's Cav	1	13	3
Thomas Miller, Tennessee Troops	1	14	4
Garland Burleigh Miller, Tennessee troops	1	14	4
Thomas Garland Miller, Tennessee troops	1	14	10
Dr. William Jo Miller, Tennessee troops	1	14	10
C. B. Maupin, Albemarle Co., Va.	5	1	6
Isaac Maupin, Albemarle Co., Va.	5	4	13
Corporal David Maupin, Albemarle Co., Va.	5	1	6
Carson Maupin, Albemarle Co., Va.	5	1	6

Sergeant James R. Maupin, Albemarle Co., Va. 5 1 6
— —— Maupin (son of C. C.), Albemarle Co., Va. 5 3 5
William B. Maupin, Albemarle Co., Va. 5 1 1
Calumn Maupin, Madison Co., Ky. 5 6 3
Robert Maupin and brother, Missouri forces 5 7 3
——— Maupin, Missouri forces 5 7 3
Rice Maupin, Albemarle Co., Va. .... 5 11 Note
Gabriel Maupin, Albemarle Co., Va. .... 5 11 Note
J. R. Maupin, Albemarle Co., Va. .... 5 11 Note
John Rice Maupin, Albemarle Co., Va. .... 5 11 Note
David Maupin, Albemarle Co., Va. .... 5 11 Note
C. P. Maupin, Albemarle Co., Va. .... 5 11 Note
James H. Maupin, Albemarle Co., Va. .... 5 11 Note
Gabriel O. Maupin, Albemarle Co., Va. .... 5 11 Note
B. T. Maupin, Albemarle Co., Va. .... 5 11 Note
John D. Maupin, Albemarle Co., Va. .... 5 11 Note
G. N. Maupin, Albemarle Co., Va. .... 5 11 Note
Thomas R. Maupin, Albemarle Co., Va. .... 5 11 Note
B. P. Maupin, Albemarle Co., Va. .... 5 11 Note
Horace Maupin, Albemarle Co., Va. .... 5 11 Note
T. J. Maupin, Albemarle Co., Va. 5 1 4
N. J. Maupin, Albemarle Co., Va. .... 5 11 Note
Caldwell C. Maupin, Madison Co., Ky., Gen. Morgan's Cav...... 5 12 14
Archibald Maupin, Madison Co., Ky., Gen. Morgan's Cav........ 5 12 14
Lt. Seth W. Maupin, Madison Co., Ky. Gen. Morgan's Cav...... 5 12 14
George W. Maupin, Madison Co., Ky., Gen. Morgan's Cav....... 5 12 14
Corp. Joel W. Maupin, Madison Co., Ky., Gen. Morgan's Cav.... 5 12 14
Wm. King Maupin, Madison Co., Ky., Gen. Morgan's Cav....... 5 12 16
Sidney Maupin, Madison Co., Ky., Gen. Morgan's Cav.......... 5 12 16
Ed William Roberts, Madison Co., Ky., Gen. Morgan's Cav..... 5 12 21
George Daniel Shackelford, Price's Army, wounded in battle.... 1 11 1
T. Snow, Albemarle Co., Va. .... 5 11 Note
P. Snow, Albemarle Co., Va. .... 5 11 Note
Capt. William Tipton, Kentucky Cavalry 6 30 64
Harris Thorpe, Madison Co., Ky., Gen. John H. Morgan's Cav... 3 13 1
Thomas Thorpe, Kentucky 1 13 1
Lt. Jas. Tevis, Madison Co., Ky., Gen. John H. Morgan's Cav... 3 48 7
W. H. Terrill, Albemarle Co., Va. .... 5 11 Note
Capt. Robt. Bruce Terrill, Madison Co., Ky., Gen. Morgan's Cav. 5 12 17
John C. Terrill, Madison Co., Ky., Gen. Morgan's Cav.......... 5 12 17
John W. Via, Albemarle Co., Va. .... 5 11 Note
C. E. Via, Albemarle Co., Va. .... 5 11 Note
M. P. Via, Albemarle Co., Va. .... 5 11 Note
Durrett White, Madison Co., Ky., Gen. Morgan's Cav............ 5 13 1
Thomas K. Wallace, Mo., Price's Army, wounded in battle...... 4 16
John Woods, Albemarle Co., Va. .... 5 11 Note
Thomas Woods, Albemarle Co. .... 5 11 Note
Skidmore Woods, Albemarle Co., Va. .... 5 11 Note
Clifton Woods, Albemarle Co., Va. .... 5 11 Note
Alexander Woods, Madison Co., Ky., Gen. Morgan's Cav........ 6 8 1
Daniel White, Madison Co., Ky., Gen. Morgan's Cav............6 8 1
Lt. Joseph F. Oldham, Madison Co., Ky., Gen. Morgan's Cav.... 6 11 1
Thomas M. Oldham, Madison Co., Ky., Gen. Morgan's Cav...... 6 32
J. Presley Oldham, Madison Co., Ky. 6 31
Richard Oldham, Madison Co., Ky., Gen. Morgan's Cav.......... 6 11
James W. Oldham, Madison Co., Ky., Gen. Morgan's Cav....... 6 17 1
Othniel Rice Oldham, Madison Co., Ky., Gen. Morgan's Cav..... 6 17
Hezekiah Oldham, Madison Co., Ky., Gen. Morgan's Cav 6 17

Lt. Charles K. Oldham, Madison Co., Ky., Gen. Morgan's Cav...	6	28	
Abner Oldham, Madison Co., Ky., Gen. Morgan's Cav...........	6	29	
Lt. Robert J. Park, Madison Co., Ky., Gen. Morgan's Cav.......	6	11	1
W. N. Parrott, Pickett's Div., wounded at Hatcher's Run and at Gettysburg	8	7	7
C. B. Parrott, Pickett's Div., killed at Hatcher's Run 1865.......	8	7	7
Rev. Ben Taylor Kavanaugh, Chaplain, Surgeon and Physician..	7	17	2
Rev. Hubbard Hinde Kavanaugh, Jr., Chaplain	7	17	2
Lt. Robert Hord Kavanaugh	7	17	2
Samuel R. Lapsley, color bearer at battle of Shiloh.............	2	47	9
Lt. Col. Ccareleus (Crill) Miller, Indian Territory...............	I	14	5
Frank Leonard, died in the service.	I	14	5
Rush Williamson, Tenn., served through the war................	1	14	4
Thos. K. Miller, Tenn., served in Va. and under Gen. Forest....	1	14	4
Garland Burleigh Miller, Tenn., under Gen. Forest	1	14	4
Thomas Ross, Tennessee	I	14	4
Garland B. Lipscomb, Tennessee	I	14	10
Gen. Elijah Gates, Missouri, leg shot off in battle...............	5	2	B
Capt. William Maupin, Missouri, fell in battle.	5	2	B
Moses Oldham, Co. K, 15 Texas Infantry	6	39	3
Samuel Zerah Oldham, Missouri, Shelby's forces.................	6	40	4
Capt. Hilary V. Harris, killed at Sailor's Creek in 1865..........	3	49	
W. Overton Harris, corps of cadets Va. Military Institute......	3	49	
Larkin Jabes Cox, wounded in battle and died Nov. 1, 1862......	5	2	B
Coleman D. Pattie, Gen. John H. Morgan	6	5	2

PART I.

CHAPTER 1.

1. KENTUCKY AND MADISON COUNTY ITEMS, PIONEER FORTS AND STATIONS OF MADISON COUNTY AND ADJACENT THERETO. 2. SCHEDULE AND EXCERPTS OF DEPOSITIONS TAKEN TO PERPETUATE TESTIMONY, ETC., AS TO LAND BOUNDARIES AND CLAIMS IN MADISON COUNTY, KY., IN HER INFANT DAYS. 3. A BRIEF HISTORY OF ALBEMARLE COUNTY, VA., WHICH COUNTY FURNISHED MANY IMMIGRANTS INTO KENTUCKY; A BRIEF HISTORY OF CULPEPER COUNTY, VA. 5. GENEALOGICAL TABLE OF THE MILLER FAMILY. 6. EARLY MARRIAGES OF THE MILLER NAME IN MADISON COUNTY, KY. 7. MISCELLANEOUS MARRIAGES IN MADISON COUNTY, KY., CONNECTED WITH THE FAMILIES. 8. ITEMS CONNECTING THE MILLER NAME WITH EVENTS IN SECTIONS 1 TO 32.

Article 1—Kentucky and Madison County Items.

One of the three counties into which Fincastle County, Virginia, was divided, December 31, 1776, was Kentucky County, and Col. Richard Calloway and Col. John Todd were elected the first representatives of Kentucky County in the Virginia General Assembly. Afterwards Col. John Miller, Gen. Green Clay, Squire Boom, and Col. William Irvine, living in what was afterwards and is now Madison County, were members of the Virginia General Assembly from Kentucky County.

In May, 1780, the said county was divided and established into the three counties of Jefferson, Fayette and Lincoln.

In October, 1784, the part of Jefferson south of Salt River was established and named as the County of Nelson.

May 1, 1785, Bourbon County was formed out of the northern part of Fayette County.

August 1, 1785, out of Lincoln the counties of Madison and Mercer were carved (the county of Madison then embracing a much larger territory than it does at this day), extending and taking in the Goose Creek waters, Clay and many other eastern and southern counties.

May 1, 1788, Mason was carved out of Bourbon, and Woodford out of Fayette, making at this date nine counties into which the original Kentucky County had been carved, which comprised the Commonwealth of Kentucky, when admitted into the Union as a State, June 1, 1792, with General Isaac Shelby, of Danville, her first Governor; James Brown, Secretary of State; John Logan, Treasurer, and George Nicholas, Attorney General; her constitution at that time made no provision for a Lieutenant Governor.

The first village of Kentucky, and the only one within its borders prior to the settlement at Harrodsburg in 1774-5, was in what is now Greenup County, opposite the mouth of the Scioto River, built by the Shawanee Indians and some French traders years before the French War in 1753, where in 1805 stood the little village of Alexandria, about a mile below where Portsmouth, Ohio, is. In 1773, this Indian village consisted of about twenty log cabins with roofs, doors, windows and chimneys made of clap-boards, and some cleared ground around them.

Kentucky was the hunting ground of the northern and southern tribes of Indians on which different tribes often met and tried their rights in deadly combat. The six nations north of the Ohio River: the Mohawks, Tuscaroras, Oneidas, Onondagas, Cayugas, and Senecas, with the dependant or sub-tribes: the Shawanees, the Delewares, the Mingos, the Wyandotts, and others, and the tribes south of Kentucky: the Cherokees, the Chickasaws, and others, claimed Kentucky as their Hunting Ground, and not only fought one another, but harassed the white settlers for years, till about the year 1793. After this year there were only occasionally a few lurking, skulking marauders spying through the interior settlements.

At different periods from 1747 to 1772, Kentucky was visited by various parties of white men, adventurers and hunters, but the first that gave any promise of actual, permanent settlement and improvement was in 1773, when a large number of surveys were made.

Kentucky being the Hunting and Battle Ground of the various tribes of Indians was called the Dark and Bloody Ground.

The first fort in Kentucky was erected March 26, 1775, in what was afterwards and is now Madison County, about five miles south of the present city of Richmond, and a little over a mile in a southwest direction from Estill's old station, on a small branch of Taylor's Fork, and about a quarter of a mile west of Hart's Fork of Silver Creek, upon a little elevated ground, about one hundred yards from Bossie's Trace, and called Twetty's or the Little Fort. It was built of logs in a square, six or seven feet high, the day after the attack made by the Indians before the break of day upon the companies of Colonel Daniel Boone and Captain William Twetty, as a protection against further surprises and sudden attacks of the Indians. The wounded, Captain Twetty, who had been shot in both knees, and young Felix Walker, were removed into the fort and there nursed, and the third day after receiving the wound in said battle, and the second day after the fort was built, Captain Twetty died, and his body was buried inside the fort. A portion of the company remained at the fort to nurse Walker until April 6, 1775, when he was well enough to be moved, and was taken to Boonesborough, which latter fort, although commenced was not completed until June 14, 1775.

For several years Twetty's, or the Little Fort, was one of the best known and most noted places in what is now Madison County.

Boones Fort, or Boonesborough, was the second fort built and the first station fortified, and where Colonel Daniel Boone and his company arrived April 1, 1775, which fort was completed June 14, 1775.

William Bush, Jesse Oldham, Rev. Joseph Proctor, Peter Hackett and ten other men in their depositions describe the Indian attack and the Little Fort above mentioned.

Harrodsburg is reputed to be the oldest town in the State built by white settlers.

In order of formation, Madison County was the seventh, and

was carved out of Lincoln, and was established by act of the General Assembly of Virginia in 1785; the first court was organized and held by Justices of the Peace, holding commissions from Patrick Henry, Governor of Virginia, August 22, 1786, at the house of George Adams, and the first court house was erected at the place where Captain David Gass' path leaves the Great Road, near Taylor's Fork of Silver Creek; and it is claimed by some that the work was done under contract by William Golden, son-in-law of Daniel Maupin, Sr., (who died in Madison County in 1803). Mr. Golden lived to be 110 years old and died just about the beginning of or a short time before the Civil War.

This court house, or county seat, was called Milford, or Old Town. In 1798 the county seat was removed to Richmond, where the first settlement and improvement of the place had been made by Colonel John Miller, who granted 50 acres for the town, which was surveyed and laid off into lots and streets by the surveyor, John Crooke. (See Part 1, Chapter 1.)

At the residence of Colonel Charles Robertson, at the Sycamore Shoals, on the Watanga, a tributary to the Holston River, on March 17, 1775, a treaty known as the Treaty of Fort Stanwix with the chief warrior Oconostoto and other prominent chiefs, towit: Ataculacullah (or Little Carpenter) and Savanooko (or Coronoh) of the Overhill Cherokee Indians, was consummated by nine gentlemen from Granville and adjoining counties of North Carolina, towit: Colonel Richard Henderson, John Litterell, Nathaniel Hart, Thomas Hart, David Hart, William Johnston, John Williams, James Hogg, and Leonard Hendley Bullock, to whom, for 10,000 pounds lawful money of Great Britain, were deeded a large portion of the beautiful, fertile lands of Kentucky, between the Cumberland and the Kentucky (Chenoco or Louisa) Rivers, not less than seventeen million acres, which company was called the Henedrson Company, afterwards the Transylvania Company, or Colony, making them proprietors of a magnificent territory, and they organized a form of government for their colony called the Transylvania, and the House of Delegates, or representatives of this colony, assembled May 23, 1775, under a large spreading elm tree, at Boonesborough, on the Kentucky River, and held, on what is Madison County soil, the first legislative meeting west of the Allegheny Mountains.

After heated contest in the court and before the Virginia General Assembly, the treaty and government organization of this colony was nullified but a considerable tract of land was granted the company by the Virginia General Assembly.

Boonesborough was established as a town by act of said Assembly of Virginia in October 1779; twenty acres had already been laid off into lots and streets and fifty acres more directed to be so laid off, and five hundred and seventy acres, the balance of a section, were to be laid off for a common called Lick Common.

The first trustees appointed, Richard Calloway, Charles Minn Thruston, Levin Powell, Edmund Taylor, James Estill, Edward Bradley, John Kennedy, David Gass, Pemberton Rollins, and Daniel Boone, gentlemen, refused to act, and by act of 1787, Thomas Kennedy, Aaron Lewis, Robert Rodes, Green Clay, Archibald Woods, Benjamin Bedford, John Sappington, William Irvine, David Crews and Higgason Grubbs, gentlemen, were made trustees of the town.

The historic elm under which the first legislative council was held, and under which the first sermon preached in Kentucky was delivered, stood on the Lick Commons, and was, in about 1828, cut down for its wood by the servants of Samuel Holley—a very unthoughtful piece of work.

From its incipiency Boonesborough was the main object of Indian hostilities. Three days after it was begun—on the 6th of April, 1775—the Indians killed a white man of the fort. December 24, 1775, they killed another and wounded one. April 15, 1777, a simultaneous attack was made on Boonesborough, Harrodsburg and Logan's Fort by a large number of Indian warriors, in which Boonesborough suffered the loss of some men, some corn and some cattle, but the Indians were forced to retire. July 4 of the same year the fort was again attacked with fury, but without success, by about two hundred warriors; this seige lasted two days and nights. August 8, 1778, a third siege was made by five hundred armed and painted Indian warriors, led by Canadian officers, with the display of British colors, and a surrender of the fort demanded. At about the same time twenty-five Wyandotts made an attack on Estill's Station, and were chased by Col. Estill and his men, and led to the bloody battle of Little Mountain, near where Mount Sterling is, where Col. Estill and several of his men were killed and a number wounded.

In August, 1792, seven Indians made an attack on the dwelling house of Mr. Stephenson, in Madison County but were finally repulsed. Mr. Stephenson was badly wounded.

The last Indian incursion into the county of Madison was in 1793. After this date there were only a few prowling Indian thieves and vagabonds.

The Long Hunter's Road led from Pepper's Ferry, on New River, in Virginia, to Rockcastle River in Kentucky, distance 316 miles.

The Wilderness Road, from Philadelphia through the Valley of Virginia and Cumberland Gap, to the Falls of the Ohio (Louisville, Ky.), distance 826 miles, or 208 miles from Cumberland Gap onto the waters of Dick's River to the Falls, the great traveled road from Virginia to Kentucky, through Cumberland Gap, Hazel Patch, Crab Orchard, and Logan's Fort, to Danville, Harrodsburg and other interior settlements in Kentucky.

Boone's Trace was cut from the Long Island on the Holston River, not far from the place of Treaty of Fort Stanwix, at the Sycamore Shoals on the Watanga, a branch of the Holston, to Boonesborough, on the Kentucky (Louisa) River, by Colonel Daniel Boone under a bargain with the proprietors of the Transylvania or Henderson Company, to go before and open the road (233 miles).

At Big Moccasin Gap the three roads, the Long Hunter's Path, the Wilderness Road, and Boone's Trace, came together and continued the same to the Hazel Patch; here Boone's Trace branched off northward, through Boone's Gap in the Big Hill, to Boonesborough.

The Warrior's Path, traveled by the Indians through the Hunting Ground, traversed Kentucky from the villages of the southern tribes, across the Cumberland Mountains at its southern boundary near the mouth of Buffalo Creek, branching to the northern villages, Old Shawnee Town near the mouth of the Scioto River, the Mingo nation crossing the Ohio at the mouth of Cabin Creek, a fork taking down the Licking to its mouth, crossing there the Ohio to the Great and Little Miami towns, and other points in the northwest.

In the interesting and perilous pioneer days many of the immigrants from Virginia and North and South Carolina traveled these roads—the Wilderness, the Long Hunter's Path, and Boone's Trace. Others from Pennsylvania and northeasterly parts came down the

Monongahela and Ohio Rivers to Lees Town, the Falls of the Ohio and other points; thence different routes to the interior.

Pioneer Forts and Stations of Madison County and Adjacent Thereto.

Adams Station—Garrard County.

Bell's Station—One-half mile from Paint Lick Creek, enclosed one of the most remarkable springs in the world, about 12 feet square at the top and 100 feet deep, boiling up, pure, cold and fresh, and flowing off in a large and constant stream.

Boonesborough (Daniel Boone)—Established in 1775.

Boone's Station (Daniel)—In Fayette County, four or five miles Northwest of Boonesborough; established in 1783-4.

Boone's Station (Squire).

Boone's Station (George)—Two and a half miles northwest of where Richmond is.

Bush's Station (William)—In Clark County, near Boonesborough.

Crab Orchard Station—On the old pioneer road to Cumberland Gap, in Lincoln County.

Craig's Station—On Gilbert's Creek in Loncoln County.

Crew's Station (David)—One mile from Foxtown and one and a half miles from George Boone's Station in Madison County; established in 1781.

Estill's Station—On Little Muddy Creek in Madison County; established in 1782.

Estill's (new) Station—Five miles southeast of Richmond.

Grubbs' Station—Settled by Higgason Grubbs on Muddy Creek, in Madison County, prior to October, 1792.

Grubbs' Station (Higgason)—On Tates Creek, two miles west of Hoy's Station; established in 1781.

Hoy's Station—Six miles northwest of Richmond; established in 1781.

Hart's Station—One mile above Boonesborough, in the Kentucky River bottom, in Madison County; established in 1779.

Holder's Station (John)—Two miles below Boonesborough.

Irvine's Station—On headwaters of Tates Creek, two miles west of Richmond; established in 1781.

Kennedy's Station—In Garrard County.

Locust Thicket Fort—In Madison County; established prior to 1780.

Marble Creek Station—Seven miles below Boonesborough.

McGee's Station—On Cooper's Run, in Fayette County, three miles from Boonesborough. Aquilla White in his deposition states that he went to McGee's Station in the latter part of 1779 and moved away in the spring of 1780 to Grubbs' Station.

Paint Lick Station—Near the line between Madison and Garrard Counties.

Strode's Station—In Clark County, two miles from Winchester.

Scrivner's Station—In Madison County.

Shallow Ford Station—In Madison County, three miles from Foxtown.

Stephenson's Station—On Paint Lick Creek.

Twetty's, or the Little Fort—About five miles south of Richmond, on a small branch of Taylor's Fork; the first one built in Kentucky; erected in 1775.

Tanner's Station (John)—Six miles northwest of Richmond; established in 1781.

Warner's Station—On Otter Creek, in Madison County, one mile from Estill's.

Warren's Station (Thomas)—In Madison County.

Woods' Station (Archibald)—On Dreaming Creek, two miles northeast of Richmond.

The Dunmore war resulted in a treaty of peace with the six nations of Indians north of the Ohio, in which the Indians surrendered all claim to Kentucky. But on account of renegade Indians and traitorous whites, who unscrupulously violated the terms of peace, it was difficult to enforce the treaty with all the faithful efforts of the leading spirits on both sides of the question.

Colonel Daniel Boone was Deputy Surveyor of Madison County, Kentucky. In 1788 Aaron Lewis and William Calk were appointed by the court to examine Daniel Boone touching his capacity to execute the office of Deputy surveyor of Madison County, Kentucky.

Article 2—Schedule and Excerpts of Depositions Taken to Perpetuate Testimony as to Land Boundaries and Claims in Madison County, Kentucky, in Her Infant Days, etc.

(A, page 82) Deposition taken July 24, 1790, before George Adams and Joseph Kennedy, Commissioners of the Court.

Nathan Hawkins, deponent, 74 years old, sworn: "I was present 31 or 32 years ago, in the County of Spotsylvania, when John Hawkins married Elizabeth Ellis, daughter of William Ellis, of Spotsylvania." He tells of the promise of William Ellis to give John Hawkins certain negroes for marrying his daughter, etc. John Hawkins died and his widow married Robert Collins.

(A, page 150) Deposition taken on Silver Creek, March 3, 1787, before John Boyle, Commissioner of the Court.

Deponent, Ambrose Ross, sworn, testifies relative to land entered by John Kennedy on which old man Ross lived, and Kennedy was to give Ross part of it.

(C, page 669) Deposition taken on Muddy Creek, July 8, 1895, before Samuel Estill and James Hogan, Commissioners, and John Snoddy, Justice of the Peace.

Daniel Boone, deponent: "Agreeable to an order from the Worshipful Court of Madison to us, Samuel Estill and James Hogan, cased call Daniel Boone to appear before us on a certain tract of land, lying on Muddy Creek, and took the oath on a "sertain" track of land and saith that he made the Improvement in the year 1775 for James Wharton, and the Improvement tree, showed to us, and further saith he never made any other for the said Wharton, the bushes stand spliced this day before us. Given under my hand this 8th day of July, 1795. DANIEL BOONE.

Samuel Estill, James Hogan, Commissioners.

Madison, towit:

This day Daniel Boone appeared personally before John Snoddy, a Justice for the said county, on the above named Improvement made for James Wharton, and took the oath required by law, then testified the above is just and true, as it stands stated above my name, in the presence of Samuel Estill and James Hogan, Commissioners.

Sertified by JOHN SNODDY.

July the 3d day, 1795.

(D, page 76) Deposition taken on the west side of Silver Creek at the ford called St. Asaphs, April 29, 1796, before Robert Caldwell and John Kennedy, Commissioners of the Court.

Squire Boone, deponent, respecting the claim of the heirs of Andrew Hannah for 1,000 acres of land · the meeting place was Boone's Mill seat. He describes Gerusha's Grove, where Squire Boone built a cabin and began to work at a mill, bu found it not convenient to go on with it, and went into the settl ment to move his family out. This was in 1775. He gave George Smith Gerusha's Grove on Silver Creek. Boone made it his camping place with many others from Boonesborough to St. Asaph's Spring. St. Asaph's Ford is here at the upper end of a little island, at the place known as Boone's Mill Seat. The cabin is on the hill side close below the ford on the west side of the creek. He sold the cabin to Joseph Benny. Squire Boone, Col. Calloway, Maj. Hoy and others came to the place some time in August, 1775. He moved his family out in 1775. He made Gerusha's Grove in July, 1775. Within the distance of a mile about northeast course a black oak tree marked "S. & B." In answer to a question he said, "Before any person gave me any information I asked if it was not that course and distance, and they told me nearly. I believe it was James Harris on the road between Silver Creek and David Gasses."

(D. page 547) Depositions taken on Station Camp, in 1798, before James Berry, Robert Rodes, Philip Turner and Joseph Todd, Commissioners of the Court.

Samuel Estill, deponent, in matter of land on Station Camp running across Boone's Trace.

(D, page 548) Deponent, Joseph Long, in same case.

(D, page 549) Depositions taken on settlement of William Hancock, plantation of James Turner, on the dividing ridge between Tates Creek and Otter Creek, March 15, 1798, before James Berry, Robert Rodes, Philip Turner and Joseph Todd, Commissioners of the Court.

Stephen Hancock, deponent. Some time in 1776 he and William Hancock and Richard Taylor passed through the place and each marked their initials on different trees. Deponent blazed and marked his with powder; the others cut theirs in the bark.

James Turner, deponent. In 1782 he cleared the land described by Stephen Hancock.

John Weagle, deponent. In 1782 he settled with James Turner on this place.

William Chenault, deponent. In 1787 he passed by with Higgason Grubbs two different times.

(D, page 551) Deposition of Ambrose Coffee, taken at a spring near Joel Estill's fence, where stands a sugar tree marked "W. E. Sept. 22, 1798," before Asa Searcy, Thomas Collins and Robert Covington, Commissioners of the Court, January 2, 1799.

About 17 or 18 years ago he camped near this spring, the tree stood near the trace from Boonesborough to Station Camp.

(D, page 692) Deposition of Joseph Proctor, 45 years old, taken October 7, 1799, at David Trotter's, on Muddy Creek, and adjacent to what is called Debon's Run near by, before Thomas Collins, Daniel Miller and Samuel Gilbert, Commissioners of the Court.

There were people came out and built cabins three-fourths or one-half of a mile above here called Banta. I was there when the cabins were building 16 or 18 years ago. Always heard the branch called Bone's Run. Banta's cabins stand on this side of Muddy Creek, towards Boonesborough on the lower side, and the same side this branch runs in Muddy Creek.

(D, page 692) Frederick Referdam, age 50 years, same date, same case and same commissioners.

I was passing frequently through the woods in 1781. I saw a tree marked with the first letters of Joseph Deban's name standing about a mile up the branch from the mouth, on the north side. In the year 1779 he heard of the tree marked near 800 miles from this place on Muddy Creek waters. Since he came to Kentucky he always heard the branch called Deban's Run.

(D, page 694) Peter Hackett, same date, same case, same place and same Commissioners.

(D, page 694) Thomas Warren, same, about 55 years old.

About 18 or 19 years ago the Dutch Company came up, called Banta's Company, to build cabins above here, about one-half mile. Some years after he heard this branch called Deban's Run, which he expected took its name from some of that company. It was a general thing at Estill's Station to call the Bald Hills about here the Bald Hills, but some called them Bald Knobs. On the east side of the creek they begin about one-half mile from here and run very thick on the east side about 4 or 5 miles, and on the west side they begin about 4 or 5 miles from here, and that it is 4 or 5 miles to the Knobs as called at Estill's Station, but might decently be called mountains. Knew nothing of Banta's beginning.

(D, page 695) David Lynch, 38 years old, same date, case, place and soforth.

This branch is the only one he ever heard called Deban's Run. He has been in Kentucky as his home ever since 1777, on Christmas Eve, and from summer of 1780 until this time has been well acquainted with these woods as any place in the State; never heard it (the branch) called by any other name than Deban's Run. Saw a tree marked up the branch on the north side; he thinks a white oak. It is 8 or 10 miles to the Knobs, a south course. The Bald Hills near here some call Bald Hills, some Bald Knobs, begin on the east side of the creek within one-half mile of here or a mile, and extend up the east side 5, 6 or 7 miles with here and there a skirt of woods; between them and the nearest part of the mountains is 6 or 7 miles off from this place.

(Commissioner Daniel Miller's home was near this place, and near the mouth of a branch of what is called Hickory Lick, and near here in about 1782, as related by Ambrose Coffee, in his deposition below copied, Peter Duree, John Bullock and John Bullock's wife, who was a daughter of old man Duree, were killed by Indians. He didn't remember when old Mr. Duree died, but Henry Duree and Daniel Duree were killed at the White Ooak spring on an early date, and Copart was killed at Boonesborough on an early date.)

(E, page 135) Deposition of Joshua Barton, taken March 10, 1801, on land on Silver Creek adjoining David Barton, heir-at-law of Joshua Barton, dec'd before Joseph Kennedy, John Barnett and Samuel Campbell, Commissioners of the Court, on Pre-emption Warrant No. 811. 1,400 acres John C. Owens on Silver Creek to adjoin David Barton and to include 1,000 acres laid off for David Barton's father under Henderson in 1776. Was chain carrier at the survey made by John Kennedy for his father under Henderson, etc.

(E, page 158) David Maxwell. Knew the place by the ground, the little draining and from killing the buffalo.

(E, page 159) John Cochran. Settled in the neighborhood about 14 years ago; branch empties into Silver Creek above the Locust Bent.

(E, page 159) John Maxwell. Was here in April, 1780, with two sons, Bazil and David. They shot some buffalo at this place and Bazil made a location. Knew of no other claim near, except the Locust Bent and the Elk Garden. Been here many a time since. I showed it to Bazil Maxwell.

Witnesses to their signatures: Dudley Faris, Samuel Wallace.

(E, page 231) Deposition of Jesse Copher (Coffee) taken March 4, 1801, on Drowning Creek, on William Shelton's Claim, 1,000 and odd acres at beech tree. H. G., I. C., 1780, before John Harris, Daniel Miller and Thomas Collins, Commissioners of the Court.

In the fall of 1780 deponent and Higgason Grubbs came from the station where James Hendricks lives a buffalo hunting, and fell in upon Drowning Creek, killed a buffalo, then turned off the creek. Came up a clift nearly where Rich. Estill now lives, through the woods and camped at a beech tree, he believes to be the beech tree we are now at, and then tells why he believes it.

(E, page 230) Higgason Grubbs, same case. In 1780 he and Jesse Coffee camped at the root of the beech tree where we are now tonight, when they went out buffalo hunting, and made the letters H. G. I. C. and the figures 1780 at that time, also Oc for October, on this beech tree. After the location was made for William Shelton that he came to hunt for this tree, and Thomas Shelton and Peter Woods came with me, and found this tree very readily.

The witnesses were questioned by Archibald Woods.

(E, page 228) Littleberry Proctor, age 36 years, same occasion. Tells of Ambrose Coffee's, Old John Johnson's, James Reid's entry of 500 acres made by James Estill. Acquainted with the place 15 or 16 years.

(E, page 231) Joel Estes, same occasion. He claimed half of James Reid's entry.

Notice for these depositions published in John Bradford's Kentucky Gazette.

(E, page 232) Deposition of Humphrey Baker, 25 years old, taken February 7 and 8, 1801, on 4,000 acres in the name of William Mayo, on Station Camp, met at house of Joe Wells; adjourned to the 8th to house of Azariah Martin, farmer. Questioned by Green Clay. (Notice published in John Bradford's Gazette.) John Sappington, John Harris and Stephen Trigg, Commissioners of the Court.

Shortly after McMullins and Carpenter were killed on Drowning Creek, myself, Col. Estill, Elick Reid, Benjamin Estill, Benjamin Cooper, Braxton Cooper, Sharswell Cooper, Patrick Woods, Charles Shurley, Higgason Harris, Daniel Hancock, Jesse Noland and others were going to Station Camp, and as we came along Samuel Estill showed us an oak tree and spoke to Ben Estill and told him to take notice in case he should die that that tree was the beginning of James Estill's 1,000 acre entry, etc. On this trip was some distance up the creek of Station Camp. Alexander Reid killed a deer some distance before we crossed Station Camp Creek.

(E, page 234) Deposition of Colonel John Crooke, on same occasion, before John Sappington, John Harris and Stephen Trigg, Commissioners of the Court, at Azariah Martin's house, February 8, 1801.

The Old Trace from Estill's Station to Miller's Bottom went by the Mulberry Lick, Hoy's Lick, on a branch of Station Camp Creek, just below Harris Massie's crossing, main Station Camp, about a mile from the mouth. I know of six Licks on Station Camp or the main South Fork thereof. One about 1¼ miles below near Henton's, the second at this place, the third at the Long Ford on the

North Fork of Station Camp, the fourth the old lick on the east side of Station Camp, the fifth and sixth on the west side of the main South Fork of Station Camp, the uppermost one not more than four miles from this place.

(E. page 236) Azariah Martin, at the same time and place, before the same Commissioners; John White also present.

Deponent Martin. Locating Licks. One about 1¼ miles below here on the east side of Station Camp on the side a noll, the second at Hinton's about the same distance on the west side of the creek, the third this place, the fourth about a quarter west of this on a branch, the fifth on the bank of the creek about ¼ mile above here on the west side, the sixth about 1½ miles from here on the bank of the creek on the east, the seventh on the bank of the creek on the west side about 2½ miles, the eighth on the bank of the creek on the east about 4½ miles from this place, also the ninth on the War Fork, called the Salt Lick, besides a number of smaller deer licks too tedious for me to recollect and point out at present. In April, 1784, I came from Estill's Station in company with 2 Samuel Estill, 3 Harris Massie, 4 John Woods, 5 William Kavanaugh, 6 Nicholas Proctor, 7 John Mitchell, 8 William McCrary, and several others (the others were probably those named in Humphrey Baker's deposition, towit: 9 Humphrey Baker, 10 Cal. Estill, 11 Alex. Reid, 12 Benjamin Estill, 13 Benjamin Cooper, 14 Braxton Cooper, 15 Sharswell Cooper, 16 Patrick Woods, 17 Charles Shurley, 18 Higgason Harris, 19 Daniel Hancock, 20 Jesse Noland, which composes a company of twenty men) in pursuit of a * * Indian camp near the mouth of Station Camp Creek, and I was showed by some of the company at or near the Blue Banks, about two miles from this place, there was the War Road to our right hand. And some short time after I came the same way with William Cradlebough and passed by this lick along this trace, and he, also, informed me this was the War Path, and he showed me pictures made with both red paint and black, that he said was done by the Indians, and in particular showed me marks and pictures at this place, which are now some to be seen, and other trees that had them on it were cut down by my family.

The beginning tree, two or three feet from the ground, is about fourteen feet around. In my answer to Estill I knew nothing but by information. Now I say the same.

We on that scout did not follow this trace any, but on my traveling here the second time I traveled it perhaps between three and five miles up there, and up the West Fork to the Red Lick, thence to Estill's Station. But as to the size of the War Road, I can only answer it was a small path, and from where it came I know not.

Do you know that this lick is on the War Road?

I know this lick is on the same trace that was showed to me for the War Road.

William Cradlebough was alive, for all I know or ever heard, and was living on the head waters of Otter Creek two months ago in Madison County.

(E. page 240) Peter Hackett, on the same occasion, Feb. 5 and 6, 1801, at the house of Joseph Wells, on Station Creek, before Stephen Trigg and Joseph Boggs, Commissioners of the Court.

In the fall of 1780 was the first of my being acquainted with Station Camp Creek. The fall after James Estill was killed I was over on the east side of the creek passing to Miller's Bottom. We saw sign, thought to be Indian sign, on the east side of the creek, going down towards the Kentucky River, along a small path. Since that I was going up the river with Shelby on a campaign after Indians on the east side of Station Camp, nearly opposite the lower crossing on Station Camp, when I saw at a lick at a small distance, perhaps not more than ¼ mile from said crossing, a number of Indian pictures, which were generally marked with black. I thought that the War Path went up on the east side of said creek, from said Indian Picture Lick, along up the Fork which is now called the South Fork, but which is called the Main Station Camp Creek, and there was a path cross the North Fork, at an old lick above the forks of Station Camp, which I thought was the same path called the War Path, which path I think crossed the creek twice.

The Trace from Estill's Station to Miller's Bottom came out by the Mulberry Lick, from there to Hoy's Lick on the waters of Station Camp, about ½ mile below, where Harris Massie now lives, thence down Hoy's Lick Branch a small distance, thence leaving Hoy's Lick Branch on the right hand, and what is now called Crooked Creek on the right hand, thence down into Station Camp Bottom, thence the bottom to a ford, opposite to the Picture Lick, thence up the Kentucky River to Miller's Bottom. I was passing by from one lick to another about sixteen or eighteen years ago, and Samuel Estill showed me an old lick on the bank of a small branch, where Azariah Martin now lives, running into Station Camp on the west side, where Samuel Estill told me James Estill and himself had an entry of land of 1,000 acres beginning on a large oak standing on the bank of the lick, from this lick at which the tree stands that was the beginning to the crossing at what I thought was the War Road above the forks of Station Camp Creek. At the time I went on this campaign with Shelby I saw the pictures and they appeared to be fresh done. I did not examine whether they all were newly done, but my idea is now that the blazes on which the marks were had not been done a great while. But powder marks may appear to be newly done when they have been done a great while.

There was a trace that came down from Hoy's Lick to what is called Hinton's Lick on the waters of Station Camp, thence across some small ridges bearing up Station Camp by where Joseph Wells now lives, thence across Station Camp nearly opposite to where Joseph Wells now lives, thence to Miller's Bottom. It is about 2½ miles between the two crossings of Station Camp from Hoy's Lick to Miller's Bottom. There was a trace led past both the beginning lick showed me and the lick where Hinton lives. It was a common thing from my early settling in this country, and from my general knowledge of the woods, for buffalo traces to lead from one lick to another, and from licks much frequented by game for traces to lead from them, even several miles out into the range. I think in the fall of 1780 I was first acquainted with the lower trace across Station Samp to Miller's Bottom.

(E, page 242) Rev. Joseph Proctor, at the same place, Feb. 6, 1801, before the same Commissioners.

I have been in Kentucky ever since the big battle at Boonesborough, and obtained a pre-emption of 400 acres from the Commissioners.

The Indians that traveled the South Fork of Station Camp generally crossed the river above the mouth of Station Camp and came through the small Picture Lick, and so up the creek, passing opposite to where Azariah Martin now lives on the east side of the creek, through a large cany bottom to the South Fork of said creek, and I think the trace crossed about 1¾ or 2 miles above the mouth of the Red Lick Fork, at a small lick where there was a white oak stood on the east side of the creek painted with red paint; the trace then turned up on the west side of the creek, it then ran up the creek and crossed it several times to a ford now called the War Fork, and nearly out at the head of that fork. It was generally the opinion of the people in the country that that was the War Road, and this deponent's opinion for thinking it was the War Road was the frequency of their traveling of it and the camps along the road which he has seen. One in particular, a Bark Camp, which he thinks was nearly thirty yards long. He believes the trace was the most traveled in the years 1780 and 1781, from Estill's Station to Miller's Bottom, came out by the Mulberry Lick to Hoy's Lick, and he believes the one most frequently traveled from Hoy's Lick on the waters of Station Camp was from Hoy's Lick down Crooked Creek bottoms to the bottoms on Station Camp, leaving Crooked Creek on the right hand, thence down Station Camp Creek opposite to the Little Picture Lick, thence to Miller's Bottom. There was another trace we used to travel some times from Hoy's Lick on to Clear Creek and down Clear Creek to the crossing some distance above the mouth, thence cross the point of the ridge onto Station Camp Bottom, up the bottom to the above mentioned ford on the first trace. There was another trace that led from Hoy's Lick down Hoy's Lick for about a mile, thence cross Hoy's Lick Fork to Crooked Creek, thence through a large level white oak flat to a lick, thence to the top of a high ridge, the banks of the south side of the ridge was naked to the blue where the buffalos use to wallow, thence to a small creek to a lick on the bank of the creek on the south side, thence to a lick where Hinton now lives, thence it turned up on the ridge crossing several small ridges, along by where Joseph Wells now lives, thence to the lick where Azariah Martin now lives, thence cross Station Camp, thence over the mountains, through the woods to Miller's Bottom, or to the river, there being no trace from the crossing of Station Camp to the river.

Question by Samuel Estill: Do you recollect in the years 1780 and 1781, when George Adams came to range from Estill's Station with a company of men, that the said Adams applied to James Estill for a couple of pilots to show him all the suspected crossing places by the Indians, that James Estill ordered you and myself to pilot said Adams to Hinds Lick, as he thought it the most certain place for the Indians passing, and did not James Estill order us to pilot him over the river to the Picture Lick, and he refused to go, it being out of the county?

Ans. I remember of being out with Major Adams on the scout, and I think, as well as I remember, we came out to Hinds Lick and went down to the river, or nearly there. Major Adams would go no further; then we turned and came back till we struck the trace again, and some where about where Hinton now lives we came on the sign of the Indians, then followed them along by where Joseph Wells now lives, and so on by where Azariah Martin now lives, thence up the creek above the forks; then night came on us and we lost the trail of the Indians. The next morning we found the Indian trail where the trace crossed the Red Lick Fork.

That a free negro by the name of Hinds, with another man by the name of John Dumford, came to Hinds' Lick and the said Hinds was there killed at the lick, from whence that lick took its name.

Question by Samuel Estill. Was not the War Road on the west side of Station Camp as large as that on the east side at an early period?

Ans. There was a road that came up Hinds Lick branch by

Hinds Lick that came over cross Clear Creek to a small lick, thence cross a bald point to a small lick above Hoy's Lick, at the head of a little drain that emptied into Hoy's Lick Branch; there was a plain trace from the small lick to Hoy's Lick, from thence down the trace by a small lick about ¾ of a mile from Hoy's Lick which I did not mention before, and so along by Azariah Martin's as before mentioned, thence along by the Red Lick, and I believe the trace on the west side of the creek at an early period was as large as the trace on the east side of the creek; I mean from Hoy's Lick along up by here, or Martin's. I do not remember that there was a trace cross the Red Lick Fork where the Indians crossed when I was out with Adams. There was a trace led up on both sides of said creek.

Question by Green Clay. How many licks do you know of on the waters of Station Camp on the east side of the creek from the mouth up to the War Road Fork?

Ans. The Indian Picture Lick, the next is where the War Road the South Fork crossing of the creek the first.

Question by Clay. How many on the west side of the creek?

Ans. I remember of thirteen at and below Azariah Martin's on the waters of Station Camp. And above Azariah Martin's to the ford where the War Road crosses, I know of twelve. What I mean by the War Road is that that runs up the South Fork of Station Camp as above mentioned from the Indian Picture Lick and out at the head of the War Fork, and so out to the Wilderness Road. I don't know that the Indians have any particular crossing place or road that they traveled—one more than another. When out with Adams we did not see any Indians. My reason for believing that they were Indians was that, that I knew of no white man being out in the woods at that time but ourselves, and it was generally believed by the company at the time that it was Indians. I do not remember of any path from Hoy's Lick to Station Camp bottom at the time that Shelby and Logan went out on the campaign up the Kentucky River. When we came to the bottom there was no old trace to the ford of the creek until Shelby and Logan went out; they made a smart trace all the way to the ford of the creek; the path went through the said Picture Lick, then turned over the ridge to the head of a small branch that ran into the Kentucky and down the branch to the river bottom and up the river bottom, thence along on the hill sides next to the river, until it crossed a small creek that is called Doe Creek, thence still up the river on this side.

Joseph Proctor was not only a woodsman, Indian scout and spy, but a preacher of the Gospel.

(E, page 248) Ben. Cooper, at Joe Wells' house on Station Camp, Feb. 6, 1801, before Stephen Trigg and Joseph Boggs, Commissioners. Tells about coming from Mulberry Lick to Hinton's Lick with Samuel Estill, and stopped at Hinton's to eat breakfast, etc.

(E, page 248) Alexander Reid, at the same time and place, and before the same Commissioners.

This lick at Hinton's is on a branch that runs into Crooked Creek; the distance from the lick to Crooked Creek is between three and four hundred poles; from the lick to main Station Camp may be more or less than ¾ of a mile.

(E, page 296) Squire Boone, at house of John Reid, on Hart's Fork of Silver Creek, March, 1802, before John Harris and John Kincaid, Commissioners, on spring branch below Reid's house at two white oaks and honey locust—one of the oaks marked G. M.

1786 and J. E. D. and the white oak marked N. 1. 86. D. B. and an ash marked C 1.

Squire Boone being of lawful age in the presence of Yelverton Peyton and Israel Wilson, was sworn, etc.

Question by Basil Prather, who married one of the legatees of George Merewether: I was present when the survey of 1,000 acres was made for George Merewether, etc. He proves the marks and letters, etc.

(E, page 299) Nicholas Hawkins, on the same occasion, at the same place and before the same Commissioners, was sworn and examined on Merewether's claim.

(E, page 356) John Holliday, 1802, on the South Fork of the Kentucky River at the mouth of Meadow Creek, before Jacob Miller and James Moore, Commissioners, to perpetuate testimony on an entry of 1,000 acres.

(E, page 417) Joshua Barton, on Silver Creek, adjoining Barton entry of John Cochey of 1,000 acres, 4th Tuesday in November, 1802, before Jomes Anderson and John Reid, Commissioners. Sworn and examined.

(E, page 417) Squire Boone, on the same occasion, before the same Commissioners, being first sworn, deposeth and saith:

Ques. by Robert Caldwell. Was you a making a survey for Joshua Barton, deceased, under Henderson? Ans. I was, and acted as marker to mark a 1,000 acre survey, and this honey locust and ash was the beginning corner where we now are. Ques. by the same. When was the 1,000 acre survey made under Henderson? Ans. I believe it was in April in the year 1776. Ques. by Samuel Campbell. Who surveyed it? Ans. John Kennedy. Ques. by the same. What kind of a compass did he have to survey it with? Ans. A small compass which is called a pocket compass. Ques. by Robert Caldwell. Which way did you go when making the survey under Henderson from the beginning corner? Ans. The surveyor was ordered to run south, which I believe he did, and crossed one or two large branches of Silver Creek. 400 poles to the corner, a black walnut, and I think there was another tree marked for the corner, but do not remember what it was, thence west crossing Silver Creek four times to a walnut, hickory and mulberry, about one hundred yards from the creek, which is the corner we now are at, and from here we intended to run north, and I believe did, with a view to strike the southwest corner of the Stockfield tract of 1,000 acres, but did not find it, to my knowledge, at the time, nor did make a corner as I recollect, but concluded wherever the lines intersected should be the corner, thence with my line of 1,000 acres granted me under Henderson to the beginning corner. Ques. by Samuel Campbell. Do you recollect the length of the second line? Ans. I don't, but suppose it to be 400 poles. Ques. by the same. Do you know the length of your line from the southeast corner to the southwest corner? Ans. I called it 400 poles. Ques. by Caldwell. Did you hear John Kennedy say he had an entry on the waters of Silver Creek before he surveyed a tract of 1,000 acres for Joshua Barton, deceased? Ans. I know he had a claim called the Locust Bent, and I believe had one under Henderson for the same. Ques. by ditto. Did you understand, when being in company with Barton and Kennedy, that these two claims above mentioned would interfere?. Ans. No. I never heard any such thing and this deponent further saith not.

SQUIRE BOONE.

Test: James Anderson, John Reid, Commissioners.
This deposition was acknowledged before us.

JOHN ROSS,
YELVERTON PEYTON,

February 7, 1803. These depositions being returned were ordered to be recorded Attest. WILL IRVINE, C. M. C.

(E, page 594) Joseph Kennedy, at the dwelling house of Andrew Bogie, on Silver Creek, December 25, 1803, before Humphrey Jones, Robert Porter and William Green, Commissioners, on 300 acres entered in the name of John Kennedy. Surveyer in the name of Thomas Kennedy.

I have been acquainted with the place ever since the year 1780. Had often heard his brother, John Kennedy, say that he had an entry of 300 acres, that he withdrew his entry adjoining the Elk Garden. Had corn in the bottom below the spring. Don't know of any other spring on Silver Creek that would answer the description of this spring; nor of no long flat neither on the north nor on the south sides of the Silver Creek that would answer the description of this bottom betwixt this place and the mouth of the long branch. (Describes trees marked J. K., etc., and speaks of the spring.) I traveled the trace which crossed Silver Creek at the lower end of Bogie's farm the first time in the year 1779, and it was called at that time Boone's Trace, from Boones to Logans and from Logans to Boones. I knew of another trace leading from Boonesborough to Logans known by the name of Logan's Trace, at a place known by the name of the Cool Lick where McCormack's mill dam is now, down about 8 or 10 miles above this place. I think I heard of the trace from Logan's to Boone's which crossed Silver Creek near where Andrew Bogie now lives called Logan's Trace.

(E, page 596) James Anderson, in the same case, same place, same date, before the same Commissioners.

In an early date, or before the year 1786, he thinks, he was a this spring, and saw the walnut tree described by Joseph Kennedy, marked J. K., not exceeding 10, 15 or 20 yards from the head of the spring, and the bottom above and below said spring was cany. I knew the long branch and it runs into the creek about ¼ mile above the place on the west side of the creek. I was acquainted with the trace that crossed here called by some Boone's and by some Logan's as early as 1779, and heard of the trace that crossed Silver Creek at the Bull Lick near where William Dryden built a mill, now owned by James McCormack, called Logan's Trace.

(E, page 596) Ambrose Ross, on the same occasion, before the same Commissioners.

Some time in the year 1780 Samuel Bell and myself were about on this side of Silver Creek a hunting, and steering through to the creek came to this spring. Samuel Bell being on the speculative line, made marks upon the bank about the head of the said spring. The creek was so high we could not cross conveniently. We went up the creek and crossed. When I went to Kennedy's Station and was telling John Kennedy what a fine spring I had seen on Silver Creek, and gave Kennedy direction and description of the place, and the same year I was at the same spring and saw the first two letters of John Kennedy's name upon an elm or walnut. The back water of the creek came up that near the head of the spring that we had to go round the head of the spring as it was very cany, and we could not see ten yards through the cane. It appeared from the water and cane we had no chance of crossing. Ques. by Bogie. The spring that you were at and are now describing, is this the same spring that we are now at, that is now before my doors? Ans. Yes. I considered the spring to be in the bank of the creek from the appearance it then had.

(F, page 171) William Cradlebough, Monday, August 2, 1805. on the Middle Fork of the Kentucky River at Rock Back Encampment and adjourning from time to time to different places described in the deposition before James McCormack and William Bryant, Commissioners.

The Deposition of William Cradlebough, taken at the Rock Back Encampment the second Monday in August, on the Middle Fork of Kentucky, 1805.

William Cradlebough, in company with Thomas Brooks and John Calloway, camped at this place in the year 1780, in November or December, for several days and made a canoe at this place, which stump is now here, and on this beech is my letters thus W. C. 1780, which I then cut; also letters thus J. C. which John Calloway cut. This place is on the south side of the said Middle Fork, and nearly opposite where McWillard now lives, and I this day marked my letters on the same beech tree thus W. C. B. I never heard any other place called Rock Back Encampment. Thomas Brooks has often told me in his life time we were here together was the only time he was up here on the Middle Fork of Kentucky. The tree that stands about 4 miles above this place on the south side of this river at a buffalo lick, on a branch near the mouth marked thus T. Brooks, 1780, appears like Thomas Brooks' letters, and I do verily believe the letters were cut by him, and on the same beech tree letters cut thus J. C., which I take to be John Calloway's letters. I do not remember of seeing them cut the letters, but we were all about there often. The bottom which is about 4 miles above Williams Creek, being on the Middle Fork of Kentucky, he takes to be the same bottom where he, Brooks and Calloway did encamp and cut down several trees in the same year, but as the timber was young and not lasting wood, I cannot see my signs now, but the course of the river and the looks of the bottom looks so much like the bottom I do believe it to be the same bottom, which at the lower end of said bottom there is corner trees marked as corner trees, towit: three lynns, elm, beech and buckeye. I have here cut my letters thus W. C. B. And the deponent being on Cabin Creek, now called the Upper Twins, saith, that the creek was called in those days when T. Brooks and Calloway and himself was here Williams Creek, because he said deponent first found it when hunting, and that himself and Brooks and Calloway did build a cabin at this place, which is now called the Lower Twins, but called and known by us Cabin Creek. The cabin is rotten, but sign is in an oak tree and beech where we cut out cutlets and we cut our first letters of our names which is now here present, which place is about ¾ of a mile up said creek from the mouth which place I am confident to be the place.

Signed. WILLIAM CRADLEBOUGH.

This is to certify that agreeable to a commission from Madison Circuit Court we met at the Rock Back Encampment on the Middle Fork of Kentucky and swore William Cradlebough, to witness such things as he knew concerning several Encampments and marked trees, and we marked our letters and our names at the said Rock Back and adjourned to the tree marked T. Brooks, and the bottom where it was said to be trees fell, and to the Twins as is now called Cabin Creek and Williams Creek, and cut our letters of our names at the different places and did everything to the best of our knowledge according to law. JAMES McCORMICK,

August 12, 1805. WILLIAM BRYANT.

Deposition of James McCormick, taken on the Middle Fork of the Kentucky River. In the fall of 1798 James Trabue applied to me to survey for him on the Middle Fork of the Kentucky and furnished me with several entries. One calling for a buffalo lick at the mouth of the small creek on the north side, with a tree marked thus T. Brooks, 1780, which tree and lick I seen the same fall and the marks that was on the tree appeared to be very old, or old enough to have been marked at the same date. There was several entries that called for another encampment called the Rock Back Encampment, which by the direction of William Cradlebough I found at the same time with W. C. 1780 and I. C. 1780 cut on a small beech tree, which mark also appears to be old enough for that date, which rock and tree William Cradlebough this day swore in my presence. Also the bottom I surveyed for David Trabue, with the trees fell down, was so well described by William Cradlebough and the course of the river that I verily believe it to be the same bottom. Notwithstanding the trees is rotted and gone and being present with him in search of the bottom.

12 August, 1805. JAMES McCORMICK.

(F. page 201) John Boyle, on the Improvement John Boyle gave to John Mounce on Hay's Fork (made in 1779), Sept. 2, 1806, before William Miller and Richard Calloway, Commissioners of the Court.

I think it was in the year 1779, and in the month of May, and Hugh Seper was in company with me, when I made this improvement. In the month of June following I was here with John Mounce, Yelverton Peyton and David Miller. I gave it to John Mounce. I think he did mark some trees or sapplings. This is the same improvement I made for Black and afterwards gave to Mounce. It is about 25 or 30 steps from the mouth of the branch that we went up on our route to Boonesborough. I think there is appearance of the old improvement upon two trees. It is about ¼ mile below the Mounce improvement or Mounce's Fork below here. This is about ½ mile from Kincaid. John Kincaid's improvement was in a good smart bend in the creek in a flat bottom near the creek. The branch was the conditional line between Mounce's and Kincaid's. They both marked the two first letters of their names there. Mounce's was to run up the creek and Kincaid's down for quantity. I was with Mounce when he laid in his claim and obtained a certificate. I think the land he intended to hold was from Mounce's Fork up the creek. I should think this place from the intersection of the two forks was so remarkable that a man who was formerly acquainted with it might know it again. The branch that mouths in just above this improvement and comes down through John Kincaid's improvement or plantation is the branch that we went up on our way to Boonesborough.

(F. page 202) Yelverton Peyton, on the same improvement, at the same time, and before the same Commissioners.

In June, 1779, I was in company with John Boyle, John Mounce and John Kincaid at Mounce's improvement (described in John Boyle's deposition) on the way to Boonesborough. John Boyle had made the improvement in company with Hugh Seper for James

Black, which Boyle afterwards gave to John Mounce as a favor, because there was not room between Kincaid and Black for him.

(F, page 364) Samuel Estill, Feb. 28, 1807, on William Hickman's survey of 1,525½ acres on the Kentucky River, before Commissioners William Woods and Nathan Lipscomb.

I came to Kentucky in the last half of the year 1778, or the beginning of 1779. Was acquainted with Flint Creek in February or March, '79; acquainted with Drowning Creek and Muddy Creek since February or March, '79. Drowning Creek known by me to be a place of notoriety, and was a place well known to the inhabitants of Estill's Station, Boonesborough and the settlements adjacent thereto from my earliest acquaintance in the county till the present day.

(I, pages 10 to 19) The depositions of James Bingham, John Hendricks, Stephen Noland, Yelverton Peyton, David Gentry and James Anderson were taken Sept. 16, 1811, before Commissioners Joseph Barnett, James Anderson and William M. Morrison, on the claim of Godfrey Coradon and Susannah his wife, late Susannah Shelton, widow of David Shelton, deceased, and James Shelton, Mary Shelton, and Hannah Shelton, devisees of David Shelton, deceased.

(I, page 87) Aquilla White, in 1809, on 2,040 acres of Abraham Banta, assignee of Henry French, on Muddy Creek, at the mouth of Deban Run, before John Barnett, John Crooke, Joseph Barnett and Samuel Gilbert.

I heard of this place in 1779 and got fully acquainted with it in 1780 and 1781. He speaks of Banta's cabins, Duree's cabins, and old man Duree and James Estill when he got his arm broken by the Indians at the time they (the Bantas) brought their tools, etc. I came to Kentucky in April, 1779, and moved my family out that fall to Boonesborough, and lived at McGee's Station in the years 1780 and 1781. (He speaks of Viney Fork, Bald Hills and Bald Knobs, etc.) In the year 1779, about April 13, I came to this country. Old William Calk told me those was the knobs that went by their names, Blue Lick Knob, Joe's Lick Knob, and the Red Lick Knobs.

(I, page 22) Ambrose Coffee, at the same time and place, before the same Commissioners, in the same case.

I first became acquainted with this Muddy Creek that we are now at in the year 1777, and with Deban's Run in March, 1779. Old Mr. Duree, Peter Duree, Henry Duree, Peter Cossart came out in company with myself from Boonesborough. We came up the East Fork of Otter Creek to where the trace forked. Said old Mr. Duree, we will take the right hand fork, and we followed that trace or buffalo road it was, and blazed until we fell upon the Run that we are now at. So soon as we could come to this Run, old Mr. Duree, says he, there is Deban's Run, and says he, I gave it its name. His two sons, Peter Cossart that was with him, and myself, the other three said the same, and said they called it Deban's Run. In the spring of 1781, deponent and John Banta and Albert Bones came out a hunting from Boonesborough to Banta's cabins and killed some buffalos and returned to Boonesborough. These people, Durees and Cossart, were not all killed by the Indians in the year 1780, but I think Peter Duree and John Bullock and John Bullock's wife—a daughter of old man Duree—were killed in the year 1782, as well as I remember; but I kept no memorandum of it. Old Mr. Duree, I don't know when he died, but Henry

Duree and Daniel Duree were killed at the White Oak Spring in an early period. Cassart was killed at Boonesborough on an early date. Thirty-three years ago I came to Kentucky, in the year 1776, and landed at the town called Lee's Town, on the Kentucky; from thence Major Crittenden & Co. went near the head of Willis Lee's Run, waters of Elkhorn, and now known by Crittenden's Camp. There we cleared a piece of ground and planted corn in the same year, 1776, and in the fall of 1776 Major Crittenden & Co. went up the Ohio and I went to Harrodsburg, and there I continued part of that fall and the greater part of the winter; and report came that Colonel Boone was taken, from the Lower Blue Licks to Logan's Station, and to Harrodsburg the report came; and one Richard May raised a company to go to the Lower Blue Licks to see what was done. I was one of the company with Richard May. Some time in February, 1777, we arrived at Boonesborough, and there I continued till 1785 or 1786, and moved then out of Boonesborough into Bush's Settlement; stayed there a year or two; from that there were two of the Martin's built a mill on Lower Howard's Creek and there I attended that mill going upon two years, and then Colonel Solder bought her, and after he bought her I attended her near two years, and from that I moved up to the head of Spencer Creek, near old Nicholas Anderson's, and from that to State Creek, where I now live, near Myer's Mill. I knew no fields in 1781. I knowed Banta's Improvement. It was up here above the mouth of Deban's Run on the bank of Muddy Creek, and the Improvement where Peter Duree, John Bullock and John Bullock's wife were killed, on the branches of Muddy Creek. Ques. by Green Clay. When you came over the high seas were you sold in America as a servant? Who did you serve your time with? and who is there in this country that knew you in your servitude? Ans. Yes, I was sold as a servant. I served my time with John Huff, and I don't know that there is any person in this country that knew me in my servitude. (It was proved that he was sold for passage fare over the sea.)

William Buchanon got killed at Holder's defeat at the upper Blue Licks.

(I, page 113) Sept. 16, 1811, John Fluty, on the same case, before Joseph Barnett and John Crooke, Commissioners.

Was acquainted with Muddy Creek where we are at in 1781.

(I, Page 122) Jesse Hodges, a lengthy deposition on the same behalf.

(I, page 191-204) Frederick Reperdam, a lengthy deposition.

(I, page 197) Henry Banta, a lengthy deposition.

(I, page 207) Thomas Warren, a lengthy deposition.

Article 4—A Brief History of Albemarle County, Virginia, which Furnished many of the Early Settlers of Kentucky.

(The facts given in this article are taken, by his permission, almost entirely from Rev. Edgar Woods' History of Albemarle.)

In the early colonial days of Virginia, settlements commenced principally on the water courses, stretching along the fertile bottoms of the James River and the shores of the Chesapeake Bay, and the tributaries thereto. After the landing at Jamestown it was more than a century before white men passed the Blue Ridge to make settlements, and when the hardy, restless first settlers did cross over, and the news went abroad, a rapid stream came and the tide of population in the succeeding twenty years spread to the interior portions of the colony—one stream flowing westward from the seacoast and another up the Shenandoah Valley from the wilderness of Pennsylvania, which was urged on by the rage and boom of speculators.

The county of Goochland was formed in 1727, some ten years or more after Gov. George Spotswood's expedition to the Blue Ridge, and the first settlements included in the present bounds of Albemarle were then parts of Goochland and Hanover. These settlements extended along up the South Anne, the James, the Rivanna, and the Hardware, meeting others coming from the foot of the Blue Ridge made by immigrants who had come up the valley and crossed the mountain at Woods' Gap (where Michael Woods settled). The first land patents were taken out June 16, 1727, by George Hoomes (Hume) on the far side of the mountain called Chestnut, 3,100 acres, and Nicholas Merewether, 13,762 acres at the first ledge of mountains called Chestnut, including the present seat of Castle Hill. These were the first grants of the virgin soil within the present bounds of Albemarle, located in the line of the South Anne River, up which the population had been slowly creeping and increasing for a number of years. It was nearly two years later before the next patents were issued to lands on the James River. In 1730 a number were issued on the James and both sides of the Rockfish, on the Rivanna at its forks and up the north fork, on both sides of the Hardware, on the Great Mountain and the Hardware, in the forks of the James, called to this day Carter's Mountain, and on the branches of the Hardware, Rockfish and other creeks flowing into the James, and over the South West Mountain on Turkey Run. In 1731 patents were issued on the Rivanna, at the mouth of Buck Island Creek, on the west side of Carter's Mountain, on the back side of Chestnut Mountain, and along the Rivanna within the present limits of Fluvanna. In 1732 there were eight grants confined to the James and the western base of the South West Mountain, and four patents in 1733, none reaching farther west than the west bank of the Rivanna under the shadow of the South West Mountain, and thirteen grants in 1734, located mainly near the bases of the South West Mountain on the Rivanna and Mechunk. After this time there was a more rapid settlement of the county of Albemarle. In 1735 the number of patents were twenty-nine, the population was yet sparse. The whole Peidmont Region and the fertile valley were simultaneously opened and strong inducements held out to settlers and patents were taken out this year on the Green in the southern part, on the south fork of the Hardware near the cove, on the south fork of the Rivanna, on Meadow Creek, Icy Creek, Priddys and Buck Mountain Creeks; in the north on Naked, Fishing, Mountain Falls, Piney Mountain and Meadow Creeks, and in 1736 on the north fork of the Hardware in North Garden. In 1737, nineteen patents; among the patentees—Michael Woods, his son Archibald and his son-in-law William Wallace, more than 1,300 acres on Licking Hole, Mechum's River and Beaver Creek, embracing Blair Park and the present Mechum's Depot, and the same day Michael Woods purchased the 2,000 acre patent of Charles Hudson on Ivy Creek. These transactions took place at Goochland Court House and Williamsburg. It is believed that Michael Woods and his families were the first settlers in Western Albemarle, and perhaps anywhere along the east foot of the Blue

Ridge in Virginia. The first patent to lands on Moorman's River was in 1739, on the North Fork, to David Mills, 2,850 acres.

Albemarle County was established in 1744 by legislative enactment, its existence to begin the first of January, 1745; the reasons assigned for its formation was the divers inconveniences attending the upper inhabitants of Goochland on account of their great distance from the Court House and other places usually appointed for public meetings; the dividing lines were to run from the point of Fork of the James River (the mouth of the Rivanna, where Columbia now stands) N. 30 degrees E. to the Louisa line, and from the same point a direct course to Brooks' Mill; thence the same course to Appomattox River, which embraced the county of Buckingham, parts of Appomattox and Campbell and the counties of Amherst, Nelson and Fuvanna—the Blue Ridge being the western line, that portion of the present county of Albemarle north of a line running past the mouth of Iva Creek, with the course N 65 degrees W, remained in Louisa for sixteen years longer.

Albemarle was named in commemoration of the Governor General of the Colony, William Anne Keppel, second Earl of Albemarle. The organization took place the fourth Thursday of February, 1745, probably on the plantation of Mrs. Scott, near the present Scottsville, where the next court was ordered to be held; the commissioned Justices of the Peace present were Joshua Fry, Peter Jefferson, Allen Howard, William Cabell, Joseph Thompson, and Thomas Ballew. Howard and Cabell administered to Fry and Jefferson the oaths of a Justice of the Peace and of a Judge of a Court of Chancery, the Abjuration oath—renouncing allegiance to the House of Stewart, and the Test oath—affirming and receiving of the sacrament according to the Rite of the Church of England. Thereupon Fry and Jefferson administered the same oaths to the other commissioned Justices; the court was then held. William Randolph, by commission of Thomas Nelson, secretary of the council, was appointed Clerk; Joseph Thompson, Sheriff; Joshua Fry, Surveyor; Edmund Craig, King's Attorney by commission of William Gooch, Governor of the Colony, and all were duly qualified and took the oaths. The following May Benjamin Harris was sworn in as Deputy Clerk, John Harris, Constable. Andrew Wallace was appointed Surveyor for the opening of the road from the Davis Stockton Ferry to Mechum's River Ford and Archibald and Michael Woods, Jr., to assist in clearing it.

William Harris petitioned for a road from his plantation on Green Creek to the South River, that is the James, on the lower side of Ballinger's Creek. And Robert Rose, Clerk, petitioned for one from his place on Tye River to Leakes, in the neighborhood of William Harris. The hands of William Harris and others were ordered to clear a road from the Green Mountain road, near the head of Hog Creek, to the Court House road, below the Stith's Quarter.

The Browns of Brown's Cove, for whom the cove was named, began to obtain grants in Albemarle soon after its formation. They had, also, patented large areas of land in Louisa, both before and after its establishment in 1742. Benjamin Brown and his eldest son, Benjamin, from 1747 to 1760, entered more than 6,000 acres on both sides of Doyle's River, in Albemarle County. Benjamin Brown devised to his son, Bezaleel Brown, the Bear cornfield. In a deed of 1789, conveying land north of Stony point, one of the lines passed by "the Bear Spring on the road."

The Brown family, from their early settlement, their prominent part in public affairs, the high character generally prevalent among them, and the lasting impress they have made on the natural scenery of the county, is one of the most noted in its history. In 1805 William Jarman and Brightberry Brown undertook the construction of Brown's Turnpike, beginning at a point called Camping Rock, crossing the ridge at Brown's Gap, descending through Brown's Cove and terminating at Mechum's Depot. In 1819 James Jarman, eldest son of William Jarman, and Sarah Maupin, his wife, sold his share of the turnpike to Ira Harris.

In 1761 the territory on the south side of the James River was cut off to form the county of Buckingham. North of the James River and west of the Rockfish, from its mouth up to the mouth of the Green, thence west of line running directly to the house of Thomas Bell, continuing to the Blue Ridge, constituted the county of Amherst, and there was added to Albemarle the part of Louisa west of a line beginning at the boundary between Albemarle and Louisa on the ridge between Mechunk and Beaver Dam Swamp, and running along the ridge intersecting east course line from the Widow Cobb's plantation, thence a direct course to the Orange line opposite the plantation of Ambrose Coleman. These changes left the Court House on the extreme southern border, very inconvenient to the people of the northern section, and a new site was fixed on land purchased of Col. Richard Randolph, of Henrico, 1,000 acres, the town called and known as Charlottesville, established in 1762, named in honor of Princess Charlotte of Mecklenburg Strelitz, who had recently become Queen of England, as the wife of George III. It occupied almost the exact center of the county, in a fertile country, and a beautiful situation; a more suitable location could not have been chosen. The first sale of lots was in September, 1763, when fourteen lots were sold to seven purchasers; the next sale was in October, 1765, when twenty-three lots were disposed of, fourteen of which were at once purchased by Benj. Brown and David Ross.

Near the close of the Revolutionary War a great misfortune befell the country in the loss of the early records of the county by the wanton ravages of the British troops under Tarlton, causing a break in the records from 1748 to 1783, covering a most interesting period in the history of the county, which affects not only the county of Albemarle, but the whole country; and in 1794 a commission was appointed by the court to reinstate the lost or destroyed records. The transactions of the Commissioners were ordered to be recorded, but the result was far from making good the loss.

Tarlton's raid took place in June, 1781. The British commander, with two hundred and fifty horses, was passing Louisa at a rapid rate when espied by John Jouett, a temporary sojourner there, suspecting their object, he leaped on his horse and being familiar with the roads, he took the shortest cuts and soon left the enemy behind. Tarlton's detention at Castle Hill for breakfast was also advantageous, and meeting an acquaintance at Milton, Jouett dispatched him to Monticello to warn Mr. Jefferson, then Governor of the State, while he pressed on to Charlottesville to give the alarm, and the Legislature, which had just convened, was notified in time to adjourn and make a hurried retreat to Staunton. In a short while Tarlton and his troops entered the town; though disappointed, they remained a part of two days, and it is said destroyed 1,000 fire locks, 400 barrels of powder and a considerable quantity of clothing and tobacco; but the greatest loss, as well as the most useless waste, was the destruction of the public records.

In the diary of Thomas Lewis, 1746, he describes his journey to Orange County to join the surveyors to run the line between the Northern Neck and the rest of the colony, wherein he states that he crossed from Augusta at Woods' Gap and stopped with Michael Woods both on his departure and return.

As late as near the close of the Revolution, when Rockfish Gap was much used, the prisoners of the convention army were taken across the Blue Ridge at Woods' Gap. The Three Notched Road was the dividing line between the parishes of Fredericksville and St. Anne's.

The globe of St. Anne's was bought of William Harris in 1751 by Sam'l Jordon and Patrick Napier, church wardens of the parish.

The first Baptist Church of the county was organized in January, 1773, in Lewis Meeting House, which stood on old David Lewis' place, on the elevated ground south of the Staunton road, with a membership of forty-eight. It was several years without a pastor, but was occasionally supplied by such ministers as John Waller, Elijah Craig and Lewis Craig. It was variously called "Albemarle," "Buck Mountain" and "Chestnut Grove." Andrew Tribble was chosen her pastor in 1777 and was ordained by Elder Lewis Craig and others. He purchased a farm of one hundred and seventy-five acres a short distance below the D. S. Tavern, which he sold in 1785. He performed his pastoral duties till the time that he emigrated to Madison County, Kentucky, in about 1783. He became a noted pioneer preacher in Madison and adjoining counties of Kentucky. He preached to Howard's Creek (Providence) Church, in Clark County, during the great spiritual two years' revival which commenced there shortly after the church had been organized and the church house erected, in 1787, and was minister to Dreaming Creek (Mt. Nebo), Tates Creek and other churches in Madison county.

William Woods, distinguished as "Baptist Billy," was ordained a minister of the Gospel at Lewis Meeting House in 1780, by Elders Andrew Tribble and Benjamin Burgher, and became the pastor after the work of Elder Tribble ceased.

One hundred and forty pounds of tobacco were allowed for the scalp of an old wolf, and when tobacco ceased to be a medium of exchange, $6 and $12 were given as premiums, and scalps were reported in large numbers and continued for many subsequent years. The last on record, Isaac W. Garth was awarded $12 for killing an old wolf. The names appearing most frequently in this connection were Jonathan Barksdale, Samuel Jameson, William Ramsay and Ryland Rodes.

White Hall was an election precinct which went under the successive names of "Glenn's Store," "William Maupin's Store," "Maupin's Tavern," "Miller's Tavern," and "Shumate's Tavern," till given its present name about 1835.

The present location of the Barrack's Road, immediately west of Charlottesville, was fixed about the beginning of the 18th century. A contention respecting it arose between Isaac Miller and John Carr, Clerk of the District Court, owners of the adjoining lands. After several views and reports it was finally determined according to Mr. Miller's ideas, whose residence at the time was at Rose Valley, near the house of Mason Gordon.

Miller's School House stood on Mechum's River in 1781.

In 1803 Isaac Miller was one of the Commissioners appointed to draw up a plan for a new Court House and to solicit bids for its erection.

Under General Orders from England Lord Dunmore had, on the night of April 20, 1775, clandestinely removed from the magazine in Williamsburg all the powder of the colony. The alarm spread rapidly throughout the province and the people flew to arms. Seven hundred men assembled at Fredericksburg, but receiving assurance that the powder would be restored were disbanded. And the people of Albemarle County were not slow, but promptly acted and on the 2nd of May, 1775, eighteen volunteers, under Captain Charles Lewis, marched to Williamsburg to demand of Lord Dunmore satisfaction; and shortly after their return twenty-seven volunteers, under Lieutenant George Gilmer, 11th July, 1775, marched to Williamsburg on a similar mission.

Theodoric Bland, who was fourth in descent from Pocahontas through his grandmother, Jane Rolfe, at the outbreak of the Revolution enlisted in the contest and bore an active part throughout the war. He was one of a score of men who removed from Lord Dunmore's palace the arms and ammunition which that nobleman had abstracted from the public arsenal. Soon after, Bland published a series of bitterly indignant letters against the Governor under the signature of "Cassius." He was made Captain of the first troop of Virginia cavalry, but when six companies had been enrolled he became Lieutenant Colonel, with which rank he joined the main army in 1777. He was a citizen of Prince George County, but died in New York in 1790.

In 1818 William Harris and Henry T. Harris were Commissioners of Education.

In 1828 Dr. Harris was agent for the Albemarle Bible Society.

Soldiers of Albemarle, the 1st Virginia, were in the battles of Brandywine, Germantown, Guilford Court House, Ninety-six and Eutah Springs. The 14th Virginia, under Col. Charles Lewis, was in the battles of Long Bridge, King's Mountain, Ninety-six, Brandywine, Germantown and Monmouth. The 10th Virginia was in the battles of Guilford Court House, Eutah Springs and Yorktown.

The statute guaranteeing religious freedom having been enacted, the old law requiring all marriages to be solemnized by ministers of the established church was abolished and the courts authorized to license ministers of all denominations to perform the marriage ceremony. Under the new law William Irvine, a Presbyterian minister, was licensed in 1784; Matthew Maury, Episcopalian, William Woods, Benjamin Burgher, and Martin Dawson, Baptists, in 1785. The first Methodist minister receiving such license was Athanasias Thomas, who lived near the present site of Crozet, in 1793.

The convention which met July 17, 1775, following the second march to Williamsburg, to provide for soldiers, etc., formed sixteen districts in the colony. Albemarle was placed in the district with Buckingham, Amherst and East Augusta. The committee of this district met Sept. 8, 1775, at the house of James Woods, in Amherst; present from Albemarle, Charles Lewis and George Gilmer; from Amherst, William Cabell, John and Hugh Rose; from Buckingham, John Nicholas, Charles Patterson and John Cabell; and from Augusta, Sampson Matthews, Alexander McClannahan, and Samuel McDowell. Thomas Jefferson was the other delegate from Albemarle, but was absent attending the Continental Congress, of which he had been appointed a member the previous June.—History of Albemarle by Rev. Edgar Woods.

Article 4—A Brief History of Culpeper County, Virginia, whence Came Some of Our Ancestors. The Old Home of Kavanaugh, Duncan, Browning, Yancey, Covington, Phelps, Deatherage, etc.

The territory of Culpeper originally embraced what is now Culpeper, Madison and Rappahannock, and was the subject matter of a protracted controversy, involving the title to several million acres of land. All the land within the heads of Tappahannock (or Rappahannock) and Quivough (or Potomac), the courses of those rivers and the bay of Chesapayoak, etc., was granted at different times by King Charles I and II to Lord Hopton, the Earl of St. Albans, and others, and subsequently by King James to Lord Culpeper, who had purchased the rights of the other parties. Thomas the Fifth Lord Fairfax, had married Catherine, the daughter of Lord Culpeper, and become the proprietor of this princely domain, commonly known as the Northern Neck. In 1705 Gov. Nott, of Virginia, in the name of the King, granted 1,920 acres of land to Henry Beverley, in the forks of the N. and S. branches of the Rappahannock. Robert Carter, known as King Carter, Fairfax's agent, objected to the grant as being within the limits of Lord Fairfax's grant. Virginia's Governor and Council appointed Commissioners to meet Fairfax's commissioners and survey the rivers and report whether the south (the Ripidan) or the north branch of the Rappahannock was the chief stream. In 1706 the commissioners jointly reported that the streams seemed to be of equal magnitude.

In 1733 Fairfax complained to the King that patents had been granted in the name of the Crown in the disputed territory. Other commissioners were appointed by the Governor and Council of Virginia, and for Fairfax, to survey and measure the S. branch (the Rapidan) from the fork to the head spring and return an exact map of same, and describe all the tributaries. The King's commissioners met at Williamsburg Aug. 3, 1736. The commissioners of the Crown and of Fairfax made their report Dec. 14, 1736, to the Council for plantation affairs; Lord Fairfax took the report of his commissioners to England and had the matter referred to the Lords of Trade, to report all the facts and their opinion to the Lords of the Committee of Council. The Council for Plantation affairs, the 6th of April, 1745, confirmed the report, and afterwards by the Lords and the King, who ordered the appointment of commissioners to run and mark the dividing line. This was done in 1746, and made the branch of the Rapid Anne, called the Conway, the head stream of the Rappahannock, and the southern boundary of the Northern Neck—thus confirming to Lord Culpeper the original county of Culpeper or to the proprietor of Lord Fairfax.

Fairfax was the first town, established by act of assembly in 1759, since changed to Culpeper.

Culpeper was named in honor of Thomas Lord Culpeper, Governor of Virginia 1680-3, was formed in 1748 from Orange County—Orange was taken from Spotsylvania, which had been cut from Essex.

On October 21, 1765, the sixteen Justices of the Peace for Culpeper County drew up and signed a protest to Gov. Fanquier against the imposition of the stamp act, emphasizing their protest by resigning their commissions, and same was recorded in Deed Book E, page 138, by Roger Dixon, the first Clerk of the Court of the County.

The present limits of the county comprise an average length o twenty miles, with a breadth of about eighteen miles, drained b the Rappahannock and its branches along the northeast and th Rapid Anne and its branches along the southeast and southwes boundaries. The Great Southern Railway runs through the county

Culpeper minute men distinguished themselves in the Revolu tion. The brilliant John Randolph, of Roanoke, in the U. S. Senate said: "They were raised in a minute, armed in a minute, marche in a minute, fought in a minute, and vanquished in a minute."

The earliest County Court held for Culpeper, as shown by th Deed Book (the first Minute Book having been lost) was 18th o May, 1749.

Brandy Station was the great battle ground between the cavalr of the armies of Northern Virginia and of the Potomac during th war between the States. It was the scene of quite a number o pitched battles, in which thousands of cavalrymen met in deadl conflict.

Other engagements in the county were the battle of Cedar Ru and minor ones, the battles of near Culpeper C. H., July 12, 1862 Brandy Station, Aug. 20, 1862; Kelley's Ford, Aug. 21, 1862, an March 17, 1863; Rappahannock's Station, Kelley's Ford and Brand Station, Aug. 1-3, 1863, and Kelley's Ford, Nov. 7, 1863.

(From Dr. Slaughter's Notes on Culpeper, by R. T. Green, b the kind, courteous permission of Mr. Green.)

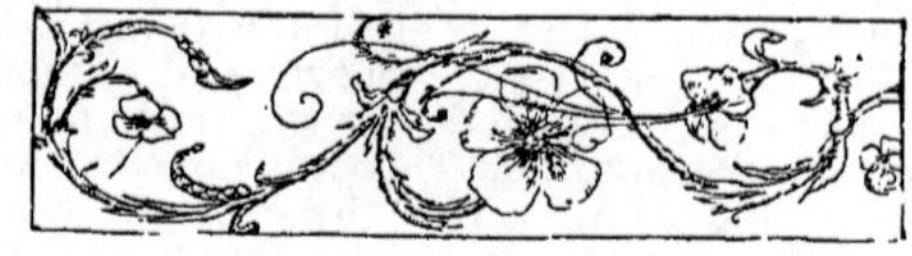

Article 5—Genealogical Table.

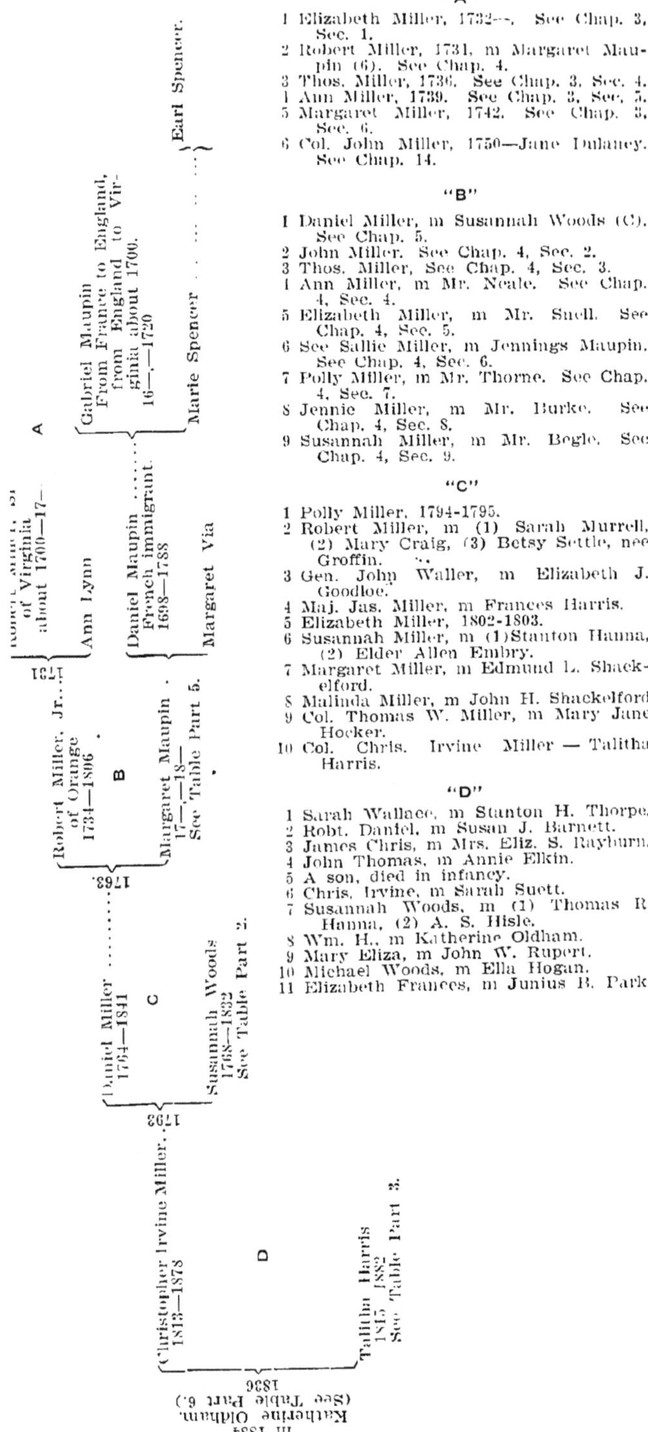

"A"

1 Elizabeth Miller, 1732—. See Chap. 3, Sec. 1.
2 Robert Miller, 1731, m Margaret Maupin (6). See Chap. 4.
3 Thos. Miller, 1736. See Chap. 3, Sec. 4.
4 Ann Miller, 1739. See Chap. 3, Sec. 5.
5 Margaret Miller, 1742. See Chap. 3, Sec. 6.
6 Col. John Miller, 1750—Jane Dulaney. See Chap. 14.

"B"

1 Daniel Miller, m Susannah Woods (C). See Chap. 5.
2 John Miller. See Chap. 4, Sec. 2.
3 Thos. Miller, See Chap. 4, Sec. 3.
4 Ann Miller, m Mr. Neale. See Chap. 4, Sec. 4.
5 Elizabeth Miller, m Mr. Snell. See Chap. 4, Sec. 5.
6 See Sallie Miller, m Jennings Maupin. See Chap. 4, Sec. 6.
7 Polly Miller, m Mr. Thorne. See Chap. 4, Sec. 7.
8 Jennie Miller, m Mr. Burke. See Chap. 4, Sec. 8.
9 Susannah Miller, m Mr. Begle. See Chap. 4, Sec. 9.

"C"

1 Polly Miller, 1794-1795.
2 Robert Miller, m (1) Sarah Murrell, (2) Mary Craig, (3) Betsy Settle, nee Groffin.
3 Gen. John Waller, m Elizabeth J. Goodloe.
4 Maj. Jas. Miller, m Frances Harris.
5 Elizabeth Miller, 1802-1803.
6 Susannah Miller, m (1)Stanton Hanna, (2) Elder Allen Embry.
7 Margaret Miller, m Edmund L. Shackelford.
8 Malinda Miller, m John H. Shackelford
9 Col. Thomas W. Miller, m Mary Jane Hocker.
10 Col. Chris. Irvine Miller — Talitha Harris.

"D"

1 Sarah Wallace, m Stanton H. Thorpe.
2 Robt. Daniel, m Susan J. Barnett.
3 James Chris, m Mrs. Eliz. S. Rayburn.
4 John Thomas, m Annie Elkin.
5 A son, died in infancy.
6 Chris. Irvine, m Sarah Suett.
7 Susannah Woods, m (1) Thomas R. Hanna, (2) A. S. Hisle.
8 Wm. H., m Katherine Oldham.
9 Mary Eliza, m John W. Rupert.
10 Michael Woods, m Ella Hogan.
11 Elizabeth Frances, m Junius B. Park.

Article 6—Early Marriages in Madison County, Kentucky, gleaned from the First Marriage Register of the County Court.

Miller, Margaret—Wm. Clark, Dec. 11, 1787.
Miller, Andrew—Margaret Graham, July 14, 1791.
Miller, Elizabeth—Robert Alcorn, January 30, 1791.
Miller, William—Charity King, October 20, 1795.
Miller, Elizabeth—George Shelton, November 21, 1795.
Miller, Ann—John Reid, April 18, 1796.
Miller, Isabella—Alex. Adams, July 27, 1797.
Miller, Nancy—James Shield, June 1, 1797.
Miller, George—Sally Eates, June 7, 1798.
Miller, Robert—Sally Estill, June 12, 1798.
Miller, Elizabeth—Wm. Kavanaugh, June 13, 1798.
Miller, Charity—James Hawkins, April 5, 1799.
Miller, Thomas—Sally Adams, March 25, 1802.
Miller, Polly—Ambrose Wallen, January 3, 1800.
Miller, Thomas—Anna Woods, July 29, 1806.
Miller, John—Polly Brown, February 9, 1804.
Miller, William—Hannah Lackey, June 19, 1804.
Miller, Michael—Polly Jones, October 20, 1807.
Miller, Dulaney—Statilda Goggin, May 8, 1810.
Miller, Anna—David Hopper, January 20, 1811.
Miller, John H.—Patsey I. Field, August 12, 1834.
Miller, Wm. G.—Julia Ann Miller, July 1, 1834.
Miller, Julia Ann—Wm. G. Miller, July 1, 1834.
Miller, Samuel—Sarah Ballard, October 14, 1835.
Miller, Stephen—Georgia Ann Watts, July 23, 1835.
Miller, Alzira—Richard Gentry, Jr., August 18, 1836.
Miller, Will B.—Minerva Barnes, September 4, 1837.
Miller, Thomas—Patience West, February 20, 1812.
Miller, Fannie—Wm. Watts, December 22, 1812.
Miller, Virginia—Thomas Land, February 14, 1814.
Miller, Jacob—Synthiana Turner, November 19, 1816.
Miller, Charity—Elias Gully, May 8, 1817.
Miller, William—Betsy Goin, November 30, 1820.
Miller, Susannah—Stanton Hume, October 30, 1821.
Miller, James—Frances M. Harris, July 24, 1823.
Miller, William—Malinda Jones, December 23, 1824.
Miller, Samuel—Susannah Jones, August 12, 1824.
Miller, James P.—Emily Rucker, July 13, 1826.
Miller, Margaret—Edmund L. Shackelford, February 9, 1826.
Miller, Wiley—Lucinda Todd, November 13, 1828.
Miller, John—Elizabeth Goodloe, April 22, 1830.
Miller, Malinda—John H. Shackelford, December 16, 1830.
Miller, Cynthiana—James Parges, September 20, 1832.
Miller, John G.—Elizabeth Watts, May 21, 1833.
Miller, Miriam—John Heathman, June 24, 1833.
Miller, Andrew K.—Elizabeth B. Holloway, October 18, 1832.
Miller, Sally Ann—Solon Harris, July 25, 1837.
Miller, Elizabeth—Obed D. Hale, September 2, 1839.
Miller, Wm. M.—Mary Jane Patterson, April 2, 1839.
Miller, Tdna—Wm. Hill, April 6, 1843.
Miller, Sarah Ann—Samuel C. Ware, February 29, 1839.
Miller, Amanda M.—Stephen Noland, September 24, 1839.
Miller, Mary A. E.—Sidney W. Harris, April 4, 1844.

Miller, Nancy Ann—William Stevens, Nov. 7, 1844.
Miller, Stephen B.— Elizabeth Stevenson, Aug. 15, 1846.
Miller, Ann M.—James R. Williams, Jan. 10, 1849.
Miller, Harriet—Killion Berry, July 13, 1848.
Miller James—Kaney Jett, Oct. 2, 1806.
Miller, John—Sallie Ann Philips, August 1, 1855.
Miller, Alfred—Minerva Jane Bibb, April 19, 1846.
Miller, Thos. W.—Mary Jane Hocker, June 1, 1841.
Miller, Chas. Irvine—Tolika Horris, September 1, 1836.
Miller, Caledonia—Ulm O. Chenault, May 1, 1856.
John D. Miller—Eliza Embry, October 23, 1828.

Article 7—Some Miscellaneous Marriages in Madison County, Connected with the families:

Arvine, Sallie—John Hill, November 3, 1853
Arvine, A. J.—Sallie Ann Richardson, September 6, 1849.
Arvine, John C.—Mary Richardson, October 23, 1852.
Arvine, Nathan—Melina Ricardson, December 31, 1837.
Arvine, Wm.—Sally Ann Oldham, February 13, 1845.
Arvine, Jamison—Sally Ann Holeman, October 4, 1842.

Ballard, John P.—Jany J. P. A. S. D. Karr, November 26, 1833.
Ballard, Michael Wallace—Elizabeth Hockersmith, March 12, 1835.
Ballard, John Powers—Jane Wallace Jarman, May 7, 1835.
Ballard, Palestine P.—Mary Ann Francis, April 16, 1840.
Ballard, Tiberius B.—Martha Jane Heatherly, June 18, 1840.
Barnes, Sidney—Lucinda Moberly, November 9, 1854.
Blythe, James—Jane Harris White, October 15, 1834.

Chenault, Nancy—Alex. Tribble, October 26, 1843.
Chenault, Nancy—John W. Huguely, Jr., August 30, 1843.
Chenault, David—Patsy Tribble, January 31, 1850.
Chenault, Wm. O.—Caledonia Miller, May 11, 1856.
Chenault, Emily C.—James F. Quisenberry, October 14, 1847.
Chenault, Mrs. Ann—Wm. R. Letcher, October 2, 1850.
Chenault, Elviru—Wm. Shearer, December 23, 1851.
Chenault, David A.—Sarah A. Smith, June 4, 1851.
Chenault, Elizabeth F.—Joseph Brinker, July 12, 1855.
Chenault, Susannah—David Oldham, February 8, 1837.
Chenault, Elizabeth—Samuel Bennett, December 11, 1834.
Chenault, Mattie—Talitha Harris, October 30, 1833.
Chenault, Josiah P.—Norcissa Oldham, October 29, 1833.
Chenault, Harvey—Anna Douglas, March 30, 1826.
Chenault, Nancy—Samuel B. Taylor, March 15, 1827.
Chenault, David—Louisa Quisenberry, October 25, 1827.
Chenault, Alaker—Lynia McRoberts, November 17, 1835.
Chenault, Anderson—Nancy Harris, August 3, 1837.
Chenault, Mary B.—Elias Burgin, December 5, 1839.

Cobb, James—Lucinda Hamilton, February 22, 1831.
Cobb, Matilda—John Owen, January 15, 1838.
Cobb, Samuel—Permilia Ann Park, February 14, 1838.
Cobb, Richard—Minerva Park, February 8, 1842.

Cobb, Jesse—Eliza Park, November 1, 1842.
Cobb, Jesse—Tabitha Park, Feb. 14, 1850.

Collins, Paulina—Richard Davis, March 16, 1826.
Collins, Elizabeth—Robert D. Kidd, October 8, 1832.
Collins, Mariam F.—Robert Yates, August 1, 1844.
Collins, Milly—Robert M. Watts, March 28, 1845.
Collins, Patsey—George W. Park, November 16, 1848.

Covington, Milton—Pauline Dillingham, January 22, 1833.
Covington, Milly—Benj. Simpson, November 3, 1836.
Covington, Jeptha—Sally Ann Crews, October 31, 1839.
Covington, Jeptha M.—Mary Scudder, May 26, 1842.
Covington, Robert—Amy Berk, May 15, 1843.

Dudley, Nancy—Allen Embry, October 22, 1844.
Dudley, Ambrose F.—Nancy Moberley, September 4, 1827.

Dulaney, Wm.—Permelia Yates, December 9, 1830.

Duncan, Sarah—Talton Embry, January 29, 1829.
Duncan, Emily—Harry Goodloe, November 29, 1831.
Duncan, Miranda—Frances Barnett, September 26, 1844.
Duncan, Geo. W.—Mary Ann White, February 18, 1847.
Duncan, Mary—Joseph C. Straughn, September 21, 1848.
Duncan, Geo. H.—Matilda Boyd, June 28, 1855.
Duncan, Caroline—Shelton Harris, April 19, 1849.

Embry, Lucilla—Francis M. Hampton, September 14, 1852.

Estill, John—Ann Sullinger, June 20, 1839.
Estill, Peter W.—Sallie Cochran, October 7, 1852.

Gilbert, Rhoda A.—Benj. N. Webster, November 17, 1846.

Goodloe, David S.—Sallie Ann Smith, December 3, 1835.
Goodloe, Arch'd W.—Maria Ann Estill, August 23, 1825.
Goodloe, Octavius—Olivia Duncan Duncan, June 1, 1837.
Goodloe, Harry—Emily Duncan, November 29, 1831.
Goodloe, Lucy Ann—David P. Hart, June 7, 1838.
Goodloe, Sallie—Curran C. Smith, July 5, 1854.
Goodloe, Olivia—Richard P. Gregory, November 9, 1854.

Gordon, Willis—Mary C. Broaddus, October 31, 1833.
Gordon, Jefferson—Elzira Harris, July 18, 1827.
Gordon, William—Parabee Woods, March 4, 1841.

Hocker, Elvira—George W. Broaddus, December 11, 1828.
Hocker, Joseph—Elzira Brassfield, January 5, 1832.
Hocker, Wm. K.—Virginia F. Brown, November 5, 1846.
Hocker, Maria—Josiah Lipscomb, October 7, 1853.

Holman, James M.—Fannie Newby, November 21, 1839.
Holman, Paulina—John Bowling, January 11, 1833.
Holman, Permelia—David Gordon, January 2, 1834.
Holman, Nancy—Greenberry Harvey, February 6, 1845.
Holman, Sally Ann—Jameson Arvine, October 4, 1842.

Holman, Nancy J.—Allen Tudor, March 8, 1849.
Holman, Minerva—Wm. Pullins, November 30, 1848.
Holman, Helen—Wm. S. Atkison, May 2, 1850.
Holman, Nancy—Haman Million, September 28, 1852.
Holman, Elizabeth—Wm. S. Million, October 18, 1853.

Hume, Susan E.—Zacheus Taylor, December 13, 1830.
Hume, Amanda Malvina—John Challis, May 24, 1838.
Hume, Martha—Frederick Hieatt, March 29, 1840.
Hume, Louisa F.—John Park, November 5, 1840.
Hume, Elizabeth—Wm. Duncan, December 22, 1840.
Hume, Susan Jane—John H. Embry, January 9, 1850.

Irvine, Sarah L.—Addison White, September 4, 1841.
Irvine, Wm. M.—Elizabeth S. Irvine, ovember 3, 1846 .
Irvine, Elizabeth S.—Wm. M. Irvine, November 3, 1846.
Irvine, Thomas H.—Mary Ann Williams, September 20, 1832.

Jarman, Edward—Lucinda Turner, March 11, 1839.
Jarman, Sarah—John Crutchfield, August 17, 1826.
Jarman, Sallie—Thomas Price, December 16, 1828.
Jarman, Eliza—Solomon Park, September 23, 1829.
Jarman, Mary Ann—Silas Cothran, October 21, 1830.
Jarman, Sallie W.—Martin G. Cornelison, January 7, 1832.
Jarman, Jane Wallace—John Powers Ballard, May 7, 1835.
Jarman, William—Amanda Clark, October 22, 1835.
Jarman, Lavinia Elizabeth—Fountain Maupin, Sept. 9, 1837.
Jarman, Mrs. Sarah—Thomas Goodman, October 12, 1837.
Jarman, Verona—Thomas Smith, December 14, 1837.
Jarman, John—Agnes Weatherhead, March 21, 1838.
Jarman, Polly P.—Greenville Hubbard, Sept. 29, 1836.
Jarman, Virginia M.—Wm. B. Kidd, May 21, 1846.
Jarman, Elizabeth—James Dowden, January 13, 1848.
Jarman, Sidney S.—Mary Smith, December 18, 1849.
Jarman, Eliza W.—Thomas C. Oder, May 24, 1853.
Jarman, Andrew W.—Amelia West, January 15, 1855.

Lacey, Samuel M.—Susan Watts, April 26, 1832.
Lackey, Samuel—Hannah White, March 12, 1835.
Lackey, Eliza Ann—Beverley Broaddus, Mary 31, 1838.
Lackey, Wm. M.—Martha Ann Hocker, December 8, 1837.
Lackey, Jane—Thomas W. Ballew, February 10, 1848.
Lackey, Dulaney M.—Eliza Goodloe, August 23, 1853.

McCreery, Ed. R.—Sabina Bennett, November 15, 1832.

McDowell, Samuel—Martha Hawkins, June 26, 1828.

Martin, Sarah—Athenasius Thomas, November 21, 1826.
Martin, Minnie—Thomas Cox, November 21, 1826.
Martin, Sarah—James Black, December 10, 1829.
Martin, Elizabeth—David Black, May 1, 1833.
Martin, Sallie—David Hendren, September 12, 1833.
Martin, Winfred Ann—James Black, March 29, 1836.
Martin, Aaron—Sallie Sims, April 25, 1839.
Martin, Liberty B.—Elizabeth Cox, April 30, 1840.
Martin, Richard G.—Susan Jones, September 15, 1840.

Martin, Mahala—Ezekiel Cox, March 29, 1833.
Martin, Sarah H.—Lamentation Bush, August 4, 1836.
Martin, Minerva—Albert A. Curtis, February 3, 1845.
Martin, Margaret—James W. Cochran, March 22, 1853.
Martin, Lucy—James A. Ballard, August 11, 1853.

Mize, Mrs. Mariam—Thomas H. Blakemore, March 27, 1851.

Moberley, Wm. J.—Dianna J. Field, December 21, 1830.
Moberley, Thos. S.—Nancy Lipscomb, March 5, 1844.

Park, Ann Eliza—Joseph O. Scrivner, December 21, 1848.
Park, Milly—James A. Wagers, November 1, 1855.

Richardson, Melina—Nathan Arvine, December 21, 1837.
Richardson, Robert—Lavinia Moberley, February 1, 1849.
Richardson, Sallie Ann—A. J. Arvine, September 6, 1849.
Richardson, Dudley—Ann Eliza Pearson, August 26, 1847.
Richardson, Mary—John C. Arvine, December 23, 1852.
Richardson, Samuel H.—Elizabeth Park, February 10, 1853.

Rodes, Eliza—Robert H. Stone, May 1, 1844.
Rodes, Sallie—John Watson, November 14, 1844.
Rodes, Isabella Amelia—John M. McDowell, Dec. 22, 1852.

Sims, Abram—Gracey Roberts, April 27, 1826.
Sims, Samuel—Patsey Burroughs, September 24, 1829.
Sims, Francis—Elizabeth Ellison, January 29, 1835.
Sims, Sallie—Aaron Martin, April 25, 1839.
Sims, Amanda—Jacob White, December 16, 1839.
Sims, Sallie Ann—Henson Cox, November 25, 1852.

Stone, Matilda R.—Arch'd W. Turner, November 29, 1827.
Stone, Thomas M.—Elizabeth McClannahan, Aug. 25, 1829.
Stone, Carlisle—Owen W. Walker, December 30, 1830.
Stone, Martha J.—Nathan W. Wilson, September 7, 1836.

Tevis, Nancy—Wm. E. Wilkerson, December 23, 1845.

Thorpe, Thomas—Elizabeth Baxter, November 24, 1818.
Thorpe, Eliza—Abraham Banta, December 27, 1825.
Thorpe, Bazil L.—Anna Bellomy, February 2, 1830.
Thorpe, Eleanor—James W. Smith, August 25, 1818.
Thorpe, Mahala—Wm. Banta, December 19, 1822.

Watts, Margaret—Austin Boulevare, January 16, 1838.
Watts, Willis—Frances W. Quinn, October 28, 1837.
Watts, John M.—Amelia Gibbs, June 28, 1839.
Watts, Robert M.—Milly Collins, March 28, 1845.
Watts, George—Jemima Morrison, January 21, 1846.
Watts, Wm. G.—Sallie G. Collins, February 13, 1850.
Watts, Susan—Samuel M. Lackey, April 26, 1832.
Watts, Georgia Ann—Stephen Miller, July 23, 1835.
Watts, Elizabeth Jane—John G. Miller, March 21, 1833.

Williams, Mary Ann—Thos. H. Irvine, September 20, 1832.
Williams, Elizabeth—John Woods Barclay, Feb. 12, 1846.

Article 8—Items Connecting the Miller Name with Events.

The histories of our country give many interesting accounts of the pioneer periods of Kentucky, and in many of the events of that period the Miller name was represented, and took active part, and the old archives of the State and Counties thereof show the part they played in the formation and development of our country, and the making of the laws and societies of same.

Here follows some little history with which the name, Miller, is connected, that will be interesting to many, and shows—to some extent—the important events in which the Millers took part.

(From Collins' and other histories and Court Records)

THE MILLER COMPANY.

Section 1. In the spring of 1775, William Miller, John Miller, and twelve other gentlemen came in canoes down the Ohio River, and up the Licking to the Lower Blue Licks, where they were joined by Hinkson's company. Each party sent out men who explored and examined the country, and reported at the Blue Licks. From whence they traveled the Main Buffalo Trace towards the point where the City of Lexington now is, till reaching a trace turning West, where the Hinkson Company departed. The Miller party camped on Miller's Run at the crossing of the Lower Limestone, or Ruddell's Road, and went over the country and selected lands for the improvement, and divided same by lot. (Collin's Ky. Hist.)

JOHN MILLER.

Section 2. In 1784, John Miller settled about one mile from Hinkson Creek, towards Blue Lick, and one mile North-east of what is now Millersburg—then known as Miller's Station. Millersburg was established in 1817, and named for this John Miller.

The Millersburg Seminary was established there in 1852, by Rev. John Miller, M. D. (Collins' Ky. Hist.)

COL. JOHN MILLER.

Section 3. In the fall of 1784 Col. John Miller left his home and friends in Albemarle and came to Kentucky, at that time a part of Virginia, and settled in the cane on the head waters of Otter Creek, in Madison county, the very spot where the city of Richmond is, and acquired property there, which he improved, building the first house at the place. He was among the first magistrates of the county by commission from His Excellency, Patrick Henry, Governor of Virginia. The town of Richmond was laid off "beginning at" John Miller's fodder house, and the Legislature authorizing the removal of the county seat from Milford to Richmond, directed the Court to adjourn to "John Miller's barn."

COL. NICHOLIS MILLER.

Section 4. In Hardin County, Col. Nicholis Miller, Dan Vertrees and others, went one day in pursuit of a maurading band of indians, came suddenly upon them when a desperate fight ensued. At the first shot Vertrees fell, another was siezed by a powerful savage, who wrenched the gun from his hands, and was in the act of tomyhawking him, when Miller quickly killed the indian, causing the other marauders to flee in confusion. (Collins' Ky. Hist.)

HENRY MILLER AND CHRISTOPHER MILLER

Section 5. History relates that in June, 1794, from his headquarters at Fort Greenville, Ohio, General Wayne (Mad Anthony) dispatched a company of his men, among whom was one Henry Miller, with orders to bring into camp an Indian as a prisoner to be questioned as to the enemy's intention. Henry Miller had been raised among the Indians, having been captured in his youth, with his younger brother, Christopher Miller, and adopted into their tribe—the younger brother still remained with the savages. Pressing on cautiously into the Indian country they finally found a camp on the Anglaize River of three Indians—situated on a high, open piece of ground—the only shelter near was a large newly fallen tree, the top thereof full of leaves—going round to the rear of the camp, they went on their all fours, sheltered by the tree top, to within about sixty yards of the camp. The Indians were busy cooking meat, making merry antics, and having a big time, unaware of danger. One of the white party, a perfect athlete, was to capture one Indian, while Miller and another comrade were to manage the other two. Two of the Indians being quickly slain, the other Indian fled down the river bank, turned suddenly and sprang off the bluff into the water to cross. The river bottom was of soft mud, and the Indian sank down half way up his body; before he could get out one of the men (McClellan) was upon him threatening to kill him unless he threw up his hands and surrendered, and he did surrender. After washing the mud and paint off of him he was found to be a white man. He refused to speak or give an account of himself. He was tied on a horse and the party, with their prisoner, set out for headquarters, Henry Miller riding along by his side, and in the Indian language tried to engage him in conversation. At length it flashed across Henry Miller's mind that he might be his long lost brother, and he called him by his brother's Indian name, which surprised the prisoner, and with an eager look he asked how he knew his name—the mystery was then and there solved—they were brothers. Providence had spared him, while his savage companions were slain. Arriving at the fort, the prisoner was put in the guard-house, refusing to give up his Indian habits—in taste and manners he was an Indian. Days went by before he quit his sulkiness and reserve and talked with any freedom. At last, on promise of release, he agreed to give up his savage life and join Wayne's army. He kept his faith, and became as trusty as his brother Henry in his new relation of life. (Collins Ky. His.)

CHRISTOPHER MILLER, OF HARDIN COUNTY.

Section 6. He was taken prisoner by the Indians in 1783, when about fifteen years of age, and remained a prisoner among them (an Indian by adoption and mode of life) for eleven years. In 1794, he was taken from them as narrated in Section 5, and immediately entered into the service under General Wayne, going into the environs of the Indian towns, taking prisoners from them and bringing them to his general. It became necessary to send another flag of peace to the enemy—several having been sent and none returned. The eyes of the officers were centered on Miller. He was approached by General Wayne and given the assurance that if he would undertake the task, and should succeed, he should receive from the government an independent fortune. The arrangement was made and Miller as ambassador set out on his perilous mission—anxious eyes followed him, but with scarcely a gleam of hope that he would ever return.

Two years before Col. Hardin and Maj. Truman had gone on a similar errand of peace, but never returned, their lives paying the forfeit of a misplaced confidence. But Miller performed his undertaking—effected the object of his mission and returned safely. Peace was concluded. Time went on, General Wayne died, and Miller was forgotten. Once he applied to Congress, but for want of sufficient proof of his extraordinary service Congress made him no allowance.

On January 13, 1819, a quarter of a century after the service had been rendered and when he (Miller) was the acting representative from Hardin County, the Legislature of Kentucky unanimously adopted a resolution setting forth the facts as herein related, as within the personal knowledge of several members of that body, and appealing to Congress to make a liberal provision for Christopher Miller, to whom they conceived the general government greatly indebted, not only upon the principle of rewarding real merit, but on the score of justice founded on a promise made by a man on the part of the United States on whose assurance Miller had a right to rely. (Collins.)

THE JOHN HINKSON AND THE JOHN MILLER COMPANIES.

Section 7. The first white men (according to history) known to have navigated the Licking River for any distance were The John Hinkson and The John Miller Companies, of fourteen men each, hereinbefore mentioned in Section 1, who passed in canoes to the Lower Blue Licks on Main Licking, and thence out into Bourbon and Hardin Counties, to build cabins, make improvements and pitch crops. (Collins.)

Section 8. Samuel Freeman Miller (1816-1890) an American jurist, born in Richmond, Madison county, Ky., in 1816, graduated at the Medical Department of Transylvania University in 1838, and removed to Barboursville to practice his profession and read law under Judge Ballinger and was a thorough emancipationist. He removed to Iowa in 1850, where he became conspicuous as a jurist, and was appointed Justice of the United States Supreme Court by President Lincoln; his decisions gave him a National reputation and he was especially noted for his opposition to the encroachments of railroad corporations. He became a great historical character—probably one of the ablest on the bench..

In 1877 he was a member of the Electoral Commission and in 1887 was the Orator of the Continental Constitution Celebration held at Philadelphia.

He was, during his whole life, deeply interested about the mountains of Kentucky. In his beginning as a lawyer, he, Richard H. Menefee, Silas F. Woodson (afterwards Governor of Missouri, 1872-4), Judge Ballinger (afterwards a Federal Judge of Texas), and many others, the most talented of the young men of the State, and we might say of any other state, were members of a County Debating Club, which convened weekly for the discussion of some select subject, in which could be heard abler debates than in the halls of Congress.

Section 9. Members of the General Assembly of Kentucky and Constitutional Convention bearing the name Miller:

IN THE SENATE.

Christopher Miller, from the County of Hardin, 1818-19; 1822-3.
Robert Miller, from the County of Madison, 1829, 1834-8.
Isaac P. Miller, from the County of Jefferson, 1851-5.

IN THE HOUSE OF REPRESENTATIVES.

John Miller, from the County of Madison, 1792-4.
John Miller, from the County of Harrison, 1801.
Nicholas Miller, from the County of Hardin, 1801, 1803, 1804.
Daniel Miller, from the County of Madigson, 1806, 1808, 1811.
Major William Miller, from the County of Madison, 1814.
Maurice L. Miller, from the County of Jefferson, 1820, 1821.
Clayton Miller, from the County of Adair, 1824.
James Miller, from the County of Simpson, 1825.
Robert Miller, from the County of Jefferson, 1831.
Warwick Miller, from the County of Jefferson, 1834-40.
Isaac P. Miller, from the County of Jefferson, 1842-3, 1847.
Robert Miller, from the County of Jefferson, 1848.
William D. Miller, from the County of Knox, 1849.
Gearge W. Miller, from the County of Laurel, 1852-5.
William Malcolm Miller, from the County of Madison, 1855-7.
Otho Miller, from the County of Clinton, 1861-3.
William H. Miller, from the County of Ohio, 1863-5.
Martin Miller, from the County of Cumberland, 1867-9.
Pearson Miller, from the County of Wayne, 1873-5.
Thomas Miller, from the County of Breckinridge, 1873-5.
Richard White Miller, from the County of Madison, 1904-5-6.

IN THE CONSTITUTIONAL CONVENTION, 1892-3.

William H. Miller, from the County of Lincoln.
William H. Miller, from the County of Ohio.

From the first settlement of Kentucky, whilst her territory was a part of Virginia, before and after she was admitted as a state of the Union—down through the years to this day the name has furnished a representative from some section in the law-making department, as well as in various important offices created to carry the laws into effect.

Section 10. Lieutenant William Miller.—But one instance is found recorded in the pioneer period of Kentucky where the Miller name has been reproached, and that in Estill's defeat at Little Mountain, in which Lieutenant William Miller has been charged by some writers or reporters with the cowardly act of ingloriously deserting with his few men, thereby losing the day.

Such an act is not characteristic of the family, and if true, deserved unreserved censure.

Miller and his men, six in all, under order had crossed the creek and came in combat with the Indians, and two of his men were killed and two others wounded before he retreated. Was this cowardice? The remaining force, under Col. Eskill retreated immediately after the death of Eskill and eight of his men.

One historian writes: "One-third on each side had fallen, and the fire was still vivid and deadly as at the opening of the combat.

Estill, determined to bring it to a close, ordered Lieutenant Miller to turn their flank with six men and attack them in the rear. While Miller was making a small detour to the right for the purpose, most probably of executing his orders in good faith (over unknown ground—for there are various constructions placed upon his conduct) the Indian commander became aware of the division of his adversary's force, and, with that rapid decision which so often flashed across Napoleon's battle fields, and whether exibited upon a great or small scale, mark the great commander—determined to frustrate the plan by crossing the creek with his whole force and overwhelming Estill, now weakened by the absence of Miller. This bold thought was executed with determined courage, and after a desperate struggle, Estill was totally overpowered and forced from the ground with slaughter; himself and nearly all his officers were killed, and it was but a poor consolation that an equal loss had been inflicted on the enemy. (Collins.).

The view of the matter as expressed in the above quotation seems to be the most reasonable and certainly the most charitable.

In executing such an order over unknown ground, it matters not with how great diligence the subaltern was trying to carry it out, under the strain and trying ordeals of the moment, a very short time would seem to the commander and those with him as a long while.

Had the Wyandotts been repulsed, under the circumstances as they were at that time, would Miller have been censured? Certainly not. Nothing succeeds like success.

In the recent bloody slaughter of the Russians and Japanese in which the great Russian leaders were out generaled in every engagement, although bringing to bear their best endeavors, they did not escape censure by the Russian Czar when they should have been extolled, the Russian authorities thrusting the blame on faithful under officers, who had exposed themselves and men to the storms of battle, contagious disease and hardships indescribable.

Section 11. John Miller. September 25, 1787, came into court and made oath that he had served nine days as Commissioner, and a certificate is ordered him accordingly.

January 28, 1787. On motion of John Miller, his ear mark, to-wit: A crop and two slits in the left ear, is ordered to be recorded.

October 4, 1791. John Miller produced his commission as Colonel of Militia.

Section 12. Ichabod B. Miller was a settler in Kenton County as early as 1788.

Section 13. Jacob Miller's name appears on the original roll and muster of scouts in the U. S. service ordered by Brig. General Charles Scott, of Kentucky, on the frontiers of Madison County from May 1, 1792 to August 22, 1792, with six other names on the roll.

Section 14. Major Anderson Miller, in 1805, made up a large lot of gun powder at his father's home in the Northern part of Jessamine County; hauled it by wagon to Louisville, bought a flat boat and shipped it to New Orleans, which was very profitable to him. (Collins).

Section 15. Madison Court House and County Seat—March 6, 1798 (B page 49). The commissioners appointed by law to ascertain the losses that the citizens of the town of Milford may sustain by the removal of the Seat of Justice therefrom made report thereof which was ordered to be recorded.

The Court having considered all circumstances agreeable to an act entitled "An act for moving the Seat of Justice, and for other purposes for the County of Madison," they are of opinion that it is expedient to move it to the centre of population.

Ordered that the ridge near John Miller's barn, and brick kiln, is appointed and fixed on for the permanent seat of justice for this county. Ordered that when the Court adjourns today they adjourn to meet tomorrow at 10 o'clock, at the permanent Seat of Justice as just fixed on this day, there to set in John Miller's barn, by adjournment from time to time till the court house is erected.

Ordered that the several officers of this court give due attendance agreeable to the above order.

March 7, 1798 (B. page 497). Colonel John Miller of Madison County, Kentucky and Colonel James Barby of Madison County, Virginia, being the only two persons setting up any claim to the land fixed on for the permanent seat of justice for this county and adjoining thereto, which have been made known to this court, they being present, "was" called on by this court to show cause why a town should not be established adjoining the Public Square to contain fifty acres of land, to be laid off in lots and streets, and to be be disposed of according to law, have consented that the same should be done. Ordered that John Miller, Robert Rodes, Green Clay, Robert Caldwell and John Patrick or any three of them be appointed as commissioners to let out and superintend at the place appointed for the permanent seat of justice the building of the Court House, Gaol, Whipping Post, Stocks and Stray Pen, either by private or public contract as they may think proper, and that the s'd buildings be erected on such plans as they may think proper, and that the said commissioners cause to be affixed at each corner of the Public Square a stone.

John Crooke, surveyor of this county, returned the following platt and certificate, which was ordered to be recorded:

Madison, Sct., March 7, 1798

Laid off in Miller's field 2 acres of land for the purpose of erecting the Public Buildings, etc. Beginning at a stake by the side of the fence, near the Fodder House, thence N. 66, W. 17 poles, 15 foot to a stake; thence N. 24, E. 17 poles 15 foot to a stake; thence S. 66, E. 17 poles 15 foot to a stake; thence S. 24, W. 17 poles 15 foot to the beginning.

John Crooke, S. M. C.

July 3, 1798 (B. page 517). On motion of John Miller, a town embracing fifty acres of land, was established on his land, and the said town was to be known and called by the name of Richmond. Lots No. 36, 37, 38 and 39 reserved to said John Miller and the said fifty acres vested in James French, John Patrick, William Irvine, Archibald Woods, Robert Rodes, William Kearley, William Goodloe, Christopher Irvine and Archibald Curle, as trustees, etc.

Note:—John Crooke was the first surveyor of the county; succeeded by his son, Kiah Crooke, and the latter's son, Benjamin F. Crooke, now living near the village of Crooksville, on Muddy Creek, in Madison county, Kentucky, is a surveyor and has repeatedly been elected to the office of County Surveyor.

Section 16. William Miller, 1782-1849, born in Massachusetts, served on the Canadian frontier in 1812. He proclaimed that the coming of Christ would occur in 1843, and founded the Sect of Adventists, sometimes called Millerites. (Appleton's Cyclo.)

Section 17. Cincinnatus H. (Joaquan) Miller, born in 1841. He was a western adventurer until 1866, when he became Judge of Grant county, Oregon, and served till 1870. He has published several poetical and prose works among them the "Songs of the Sierras." (Appleton's Cyclo).

Section 18. Warner Miller, born in 1838, was a member of the New York Legislature from 1874-8. Represented New York in the U. S. Congress (Republican) 1878-81, and in the Senate 1881-7. (Appleton's Cyclo).

Section 19. William H. H. Miller, born in 1841. He became a law partner with General Benjamine Harrison in 1874. Was Attorney General in Harrison's Cabinet 1889-93. Appleton's Cyclo).

Section 20. John Franklin Miller, an American soldier, born in Union County, Indiana, July, 1831, died in Washington, D. C. May 8, 1886. He was educated at the New York State Law School in 1852, with the degree of L. B., and began the practice of law at South Bend. The next year he went to California and there practiced three years, when he returned to Indiana and resumed the practice. He took an active part in the Freemont campaign in 1856. He was a member of the State Senate at the outbreak of the Civil War, and resigned to become Colonel on the staff of Governor Morton and was soon given the command of the 29th Indiana Volunteers. On reaching the field of action he was placed in command of a brigade, serving almost from the beginning of hostilities in the West, under Generals Sherman, Buell, Rosencrans and Thomas. At the battle of Stone River he distinguished himself by charging at the head of his brigade across the river and driving Breckinridge from his position, receiving a bullet in his neck during the charge. For his gallantry he was promoted to Brigadier General. In the battle of Liberty Gap he made another charge with his brigade, and at the moment of victory was stricken down by a second bullet which entered his left eye, and lodged in the bone of the forehead. Despite the constant pain he carried the bullet for twelve years, various surgeons declining to attempt its removal thorugh fear of destroying the other eye, or of impairing his brain, but it was subsequently extracted in 1875. He commanded the left division of 8000 men at the battle of Nashville, and was brevetted a Major General for conspicuous bravery. At the close of the war he was offered a commission of high rank in the army, but declined it, and returned to California to practice law. He was almost immediately appointed Collector of the Port of San Francisco. After serving four years declined a reappointment. He then abandoned his profession and engaged in other business pursuits and became President of the Alaska Commercial Company. He was a Republican candidate for Presidential Elector in 1872, 1876 and 1880. He was a member of the California Constitutional Convention in 1872. Was elected United States Senator January 12, 1881, and took his seat the following March 4. On the organization of the 47th Congress, he was appointed a member of the Committee on Foreign Relations, and on Naval Affairs, and in the 48th and 49th Congresses, was Chairman of the Committee on Foreign Relations and member of the Committee on Civil Service and Retrenchment.

Memorial addresses on the life and character of John Franklin Miller (a Senator from California) were delivered in the Senate and

House of Representatives in the first session of the forty-ninth Congress, May 28, and June 19, 1886, with funeral services at the City of Washington March 13, 1886, and at San Francisco, Cal., March 21, 1886.

Mr. Stanford, of California, in his address stated that "General Miller was descended from two of the most respected families of Virginia, and was of Swiss-Scotch extraction, his progenitor on his father's side having left Switzerland to find in America what was denied him in the land of his birth—the freedom to worship God in accordance with the dictates of his own conscience, while his paternal grand-mother's family were from Scotland.

In the first decade of the present (19th) century, his grandfather and father who were then located in Franklin County, Virginia, decided on leaving that State, and before doing so manumitted their slaves. It may be easily supposed that the strong appreciation of liberty and the rights of man posessed by John F. Miller came to him as a natural heritage from a father and grand-father whose sense of justice and liberty was so great as to impel them to make a voluntary sacrifice at a time when slavery was by many held to be lawful and right. Having started out from Virginia, the first halting place of the Miller family was at a point in Kentucky on the Ohio River, near Maysville, where after a short stay, they built flat-boats upon which they floated down the Ohio to the present site of Cincinnati. Subsequently the family home was chosen in Union County, Indiana, near Indian Creek, in the great Miami Valley. By a coincidence, the maternal branch of John F. Miller's family was of the same name as the paternal. His mother's father, John Miller, was a Colonel commanding volunteer forces in Indiana and Ohio, during the war of 1812, and won an extensive reputation for his successful warefare against the British and their Indian allies. His father was a man of great force of character, a natural leader, and exercised a wide and powerful influence in the state of his adoption. Here in Union County, Indiana, a few miles from Cincinnati, John F. Miller was born. A short time after his birth the family removed to South Bend, where his early days were passed.

Mr. Grosvenor, of Ohio, who became a subordinate to John F. Miller at a time when neither had received or witnessed the baptism of blood, spoke knowingly and eloquently of General Miller's war record, his unflinching discharge of duty and yet always considerate of the rights of men and that today his memory is green among the men who loved the Union in Nashville, and he is held in high regard among the people who at that time were the enemies of the Union. Mr. Grosvenor testified of his own personal regard for the memory of John F. Miller.

Mr. Stanford further said: "But Senator Miller manifested in various ways, official and personal, his fidelity and consistency in another sphere of life and duty. He adorned the doctrine of God our Saviour in all things, and was a good soldier of Christ, and when words were no more possible signified by gesture that his faith did not fail or falter. General Miller's life was a success. The work he undertook he did well, whether in camp, in commerce or in Congress.. He gained commendation on every side and in every path of duty in which he walked. Impartial history will delight to place his name as a private and public citizen, high among those who are worthy examples for their countrymen to admire and imitate."

General Miller married Miss Mary Chess, of Pennsylvania.

Two children were born of this marriage—a son and a daughter. The son died in SanFrancisco in 1878, at the age of seven years; the daughter survives. (From Memorial Addresses on the Life and Character of John Franklin Miller, in the U. S. Senate and House of Representatives, 1st session 49th Congress).

Section 21. James Miller, an American General, born in Petersborough, N. H., April 25, 1776, died in Temple, N. H., July 7, 1851. He was educated in the law, but in 1808 he entered the Army as Major. In May 1813, he participated in the capture of Fort George. As Colonel of the 21st Infantry he fought with gallantry at Chippewa and Lundy's Lane. The success of the Americans in the latter conflict was in the main due to the capture of a British battery by his command.

In reply to General Scott's inquiry if he could take the battery, he said, "I'll try, Sir." For these services he was brevetted Brigadier-General, and received from Congress a gold medal. He was Governor of Arkansas Territory 1819 to 1825, and Collector of Customs at Salem, Massachusetts from 1825 to 1849. (Appleton's Cyclo.)

Section 22. Benigne Emmanuel Clemant Miller, a French Philologist, born in Paris in 1812. (Id.)

Section 23. Edward Miller, an American physician, born in Dover, Delaware, May 9, 1760, died in New York, March 17, 1812. Attended medical lectures in the University of Pennsylvania; spent about a year in the Military Hospital at Baskingridge, N. J., and in 1782 went to France as the surgeon of an Armed ship. In 1783 entered on the practice of medicine in Maryland, and in 1788, graduated as M. D. in the University of Pennsylvania.. In 1796 he removed to New York and with Doctors Mitchell and Smith commenced the publication of the "Medical Repository" the first American Medical Journal. In 1803 he was appointed resident physician of the City of New York. He was a member of the American Philisophical Society. Professor of the Theory and Practice of Physics in the College of Physicians and Surgeons and one of the physicians of the New York Hospital. His "Report on the Yellow Fever of New York in 1805," is the source from which most later authors have drawn their arguments in support of the non-contageous nature of yellow fever. His writings with a biographical sketch were published by his brother, the Rev. Samuel Miller. (Id.)

Section 24. Hugh Miller, a British Geologist, born at Cromarty on the East coast of Scotland, October 10, 1802, died at Portabello, near Edinburg, December 26, 1856. He belonged to that half Scandanavian population inhabiting the shores of the German ocean from Fife to Caithness. On his father's side he was fourth in descent in a line of sailors from John Feddis, one of the last of the buchaneers on the Spanish Main, who returned to Cromarty to enjoy his money, and built "the long low house" in which his distinguished great grand son passed his youth. On his mother's side he was of Highland blood, and fifth in descent from Donald Roy of Ross-shire, famed for his piety and his second eye sight. His father was drowned in a tempest in 1807, a fate which had befallen several of his ancestors. (Id.)

Section 25. James Miller, a Scottish surgeon, born in 1812, died June 17, 1864. He was Professor of Surgery in the University of Edinburg for more than twenty years, and at the time of his death of Pictorial Anatomy to the Royal Academy and consulting surgeon to the Royal Infirmary of Edinburg and the Royal Hospital for sick children. He is especially noted for his Systematic Treatise on the "Principles and Practice of Surgery" (Edinburg, 1844), which passed through four editions and is highly esteemed. (Id.)

Section 26. Joseph Miller, an English actor, born probably in London in 1684, died there in 1738. He was popular on the stage, and performed with repute in several of Congreve's best comedies, particularly in "Love for Love" and "The Old Bachelor," to the success of which he is said to have materially contributed. In 1739 a book of jests passing under his name and supposed to be the compilation of John Motley, author of the "Life of Peter the Great," was published in London and has gained a celebrity which preserves the name of its assumed author. (Id.)

Section 27. Samuel Miller, an American clergyman, born near Dover, Delaware, October 31, 1769, died in Princeton, New Jersey, January 7, 1850. He graduated at the University of Pennsylvania in 1789, from which he received the degree of D. D. in 1804. He studied theology and was licensed to preach in 1791, and in June, 1793, was installed as colleague pastor with Doctors Rodgers and MacKnight of the First Presbyterian Chruch in New York City. He became very distinguished. (Id.)

Section 28. Thomas Miller, an English author, was born in Gainsborough, Lincolnshire, August 31, 1807; died in Loudon, October 25, 1874. He was at first a farmer's boy, devoted his leisure hours to study, and while following the trade of a basket-maker began to attract attention by his verses and occasional pieces in prose, chiefly describing rural life and scenery. He came under the notice of Moore, Campbell and Rogers, and the last named enabled him to set up as a book-seller, and thenceforth he became an industrious writer. Among his numerous novels are "Royston Gower," 1838; "Fair Rosamond," 1839; "Lady Jane Grey," 1840; "Gideon Giles, the Roper," 1841; and "Godfrey Malvern," 1842. The most popular of his writings are his country books, including, "A Day in the Woods," "Beauties of the Country," "Rural Sketches," "Pictures of Country Life," "Country Scenes," etc. He also wrote a "History of the Anglo-Saxons" and Lives of Turner, Beattie and Collins. His poetical works are "Common Wayside Flowers," 1841; "Poetical Language of Flowers," 1847; "Original Poems of My Children," 1850, and "Songs for British Riflemen," 1860. (Id.)

Section 29. William Allen Miller, an English chemist, born in Ipswick, December 17, 1817; died in Liverpool, September 30, 1870. At fifteen years of age he was apprenticed to his uncle, who was Surgeon to the General Hospital in Birmingham. At the expiration of five years he entered the Medical Department of King's College, London, where he studied chemistry under Dr. Daniell, whom he assisted in his laboratory. In 1840 he spent some time in the laboratory of Liebig in Giessen, became Demonstrator of Chemistry in King's College, and in 1845 Professor of Chemistry. With Dr. Daniell he had investigated the electrolysis of salts, conducting all the experiments. In 1851 he was appointed a commissioner on the water supply of London and an assayer of the mint. He was the author of an important treatice entitled, "Elements of Chemistry, Theoretical and Practical," London, 1869, and of many scientific papers. (Id.)

Section 30. Miller's Station, settled in 1784 by John Miller, about one mile from Hinkston Creek, towards Blue Licks, and one mile northeast of Millersburg, Ky.

Section 31. Miller's Bottom was on the Kentucky River, above the mouth of Station Camp Creek, some twenty-odd miles from Estill's Old Station in Madison County, Ky. The trace mostly traveled in 1780-1 between the two places led from Estill's Station by Mulberry Lick to Hoy's Lick on a branch of Station Camp about a half mile below where Harris Massie lived, thence down Hoy's Lick Branch a short distance, thence leaving Hoy's Lick Branch on the right, and what is now called Crooked Creek on the right, down into Station Camp Bottom, thence the bottom to a ford opposite the Little Picture Lick, thence up the Kenucky River to Miller's Bottom.

Section 32. John Harris Miller, born in Lincoln County, Ky., February 27, 1832, and died there in 1905, was American Consul to Falkland Islands under the second administration of President Cleveland (1896-1900). He was a humorous and spicy writer in the non de plume "Happy Jack." His productions were very amusing and much complimented by the readers.

Section 33. William Miller, made final settlement of his accounts as Sheriff of Madison County, Ky., in 1825.

Section 34. Joseph Miller, in 1824, was recommended and received from Governor Joseph Desha a commission as High Sheriff of Madison County, Ky., and qualified as such.

Section 35. List of counties, creeks, towns, etc., in the United States named in memory of some member of the Miller family, appearing on map:

State.	
Massachusetts—	Miller's Falls.
New York—	Miller Corners.
	Miller Place.
	Miller's.
	Miller's Mill.
	Miller's Port.
	Millerton.
	Miller's Lane.
Pennsylvania—	Miller (Cameron County).
	Miller (Northampton County).
	Miller Farm.
	Miller's (Lycoming County).
	Miller's (Lehigh County).
	Millersburg.
	Miller's Station.
	Millerstown.
	Millerstown Station.
	Millersville.
	Millerton.
Maryland—	Millers.
	Miller's Island.
	Millersville.
Virginia—	Millers.
	Miller's Tavern.
West Virginia—	Miller's Fork (creek).
	Miller (Marshall County).
	Miller (Morgan County).
	Millers.
	Miller's Camp Branch.
Georgia—	Miller County.

State.	
	Miller.
Florida—	Miller's Ferry.
	Millerton (14 miles west of Jacksonville).
	Millerton (Orange County).
Alabama—	Miller's Creek.
	Miller.
	Miller Ferry.
	Millerville.
Mississippi—	Miller.
Louisiana—	Millersville.
	Millerton.
Tennessee—	Millers (Washington County).
	Millersburg.
	Millers (10 miles southeast of Marysville).
Kentucky—	Miller's Creek.
	Millersburg.
	Millerstown.
Ohio—	Miller.
	Miller City.
	Millers (Fairfield County).
	Millers (Lorain County).
	Millers (Guernsey County).
	Millersburg.
	Millersport.
	Miller Station.
	Millerstown.
	Millersville.
Indiana—	Millers (Lake County).
	Millers (Gibson County).
	Millers (Spencer County).
	Millers (Bartholomew County).
	Millersburg (Lawrence County).
	Millersburg (Elkhart County).
Illinois—	Millersburg.
	Millersville.
Michigan—	Miller.
	Millersville.
Minnesota—	Miller.
	Millersburg.
	Millersville.
Iowa—	Miller.
	Millersburg.
Missouri—	Miller County.
	Miller.
	Millers.
	Millersburg.
	Millersville.
Arkansas—	Miller County.
Texas—	Miller.
	Miller Grove.
Oklahoma—	Miller.
Kansas—	Miller.
	Millerton.
Nebraska—	Miller.
	Millerboro.
	Millerton.

State.	
South Dakota—	Miller.
	Millers.
Wyoming—	Miller Creek.
Washington—	Miller Creek.
Colorado—	Miller Creek.
New Mexico—	Miller.
Arizona—	Miller's Peak (mountain).
California—	Miller (Mendocino County).
	Miller (Maria County).
	Millerton.
	Miller (Fresno County).
Oregon—	Miller's Creek.
	Millersburg.
Washington—	Millerton.
Alaska—	Miller Creek.

CHAPTER 2.

THE MILLER FAMILY.

Article 1—This Family is of Anglo-Scotch-Irish-Franco-German mixture, heavily charged with German. The German mode of spelling the name is Mueller, or Muller.

The several strains of blood had mixed in the Miller name and numerous branches had run into nearly if not every province of Europe. Keeping pace with the descendants would be just a little smaller undertaking than counting the curiosities thrown ashore by the mighty waves of the ocean, and to fathom the depths of the penetration of this blood into the strains of the nations would be more than the life work of an individual.

It must suffice that in a very, very limited measure does this volume deal somewhat traditionally with the beginning of this Miller family in America.

The unwritten or traditional record is that before the middle of the eighteenth century a number of the name (brothers, their wives and children and sisters) to secure to themselves liberty and that freedom to worship God as the dictates of their own consciences longed for, and for the betterment of their conditions in a material sense, came from Ireland to America. In the day of their immigration there was a great influx of people into the American colonies from the old world, and that Robert Miller and his wife and probably his children, or the older ones, set forth in Chapter 3, were immigrants and that they settled in the Colony of Virginia. Some of the immigrants of this family located probably in Pennsylvania and more northerly parts.

Miss Mary B. Miller, of Huntsville, Alabama, a great granddaughter of Colonel John Miller and his wife, Jane Dulaney (set forth in Sec. 7 of Chap. 3 and Chap. 14) has in her possession the old leather-covered Bible containing the family record, reaching as far back as 1732, which the immigrants aforesaid brought with them from Ireland (the exact date of the immigration we are unable to state).

The shades of time and the absence of records have obscured many facts and circumstances touching the early history of this family. A systematic, thorough search of the early court and other records of the old colonies would, it is believed, reveal a great deal of history that would be interesting to the present and coming generations of this family with the facts presented just as they were. That there were immigrations of the name anterior and posterior to the above mentioned is not questioned.

The writer has not the lucrative means to launch into the investigation of this interesting question as he would like and must be somewhat content with just the little that is in hand.

The numerous descendants of the immigrants have scattered and distributed themselves all over the continent—in the villages, towns and cities, on the farms and elsewhere, as farmers, preachers, lawyers, physicians, men of letters, men of commerce, stockmen, scientists, soldiers, politicians, fanatics, etc. Some have gained fame and are noted in history. And whilst all, by several rungs, have not reached the top of the ladder, but some to the contrary, notwithstanding, as a whole their record has not been surpassed by any other one name in our great nation.

The Miller name has been well represented in every great patriotic endeavor of our country—in the early colonial wars, in the Revolutionary war, in the war of 1812, in the Mexican war, in the various Indian wars, in the great Civil war of 1862, wherein father was arrayed against son and son against father, and brother against brother, etc., each contending for the right as he saw it, and in which many gave up their lives for the cause they espoused.

From 1780 to 1795 there were great streams of people flowing as a mighty tide from Virginia and other colonies or states to Kentucky—the Millers, the Woodes, the Harrises, the Wallaces, the Maupins, and the Kavanaughs from Virginia, and the Oldhams from the Dan and Yadkin Rivers of North Carolina (who had gone thither from Fauquier County, Virginia) were in the stream increasing in no small measure the tide of immigration into the Dark and Bloody Ground, traveling the only highways which had been blazed and trodden by the immortalized pioneer, Colonel Daniel Boone, and his compatriots, known as Boone's Trace, the Wilderness Road, and the Long Hunter's Path, etc. Many of these immigrants located in Madison County, and many in other parts of Kentucky. Many later on moving further west and some southward. A great many of them when they came to Kentucky were men of mature years, with families of their own; others finding help-meets after settling in their newly adopted home.

Other facts more especially pertaining to individuals will be set forth in the following chapters.

CHAPTER 3.

ROBERT MILLER, SENIOR

of Virginia.

(Mentioned in Chapter 2.)

Article 1.—Robert Miller, Senior, of Virginia, so styled because he had a son named Robert and because he made his permanent home in Virginia.

The place and date of his birth we are unable to state with certainty, but he was probably born in Ireland near the beginning of the eighteenth century, and was the father of our branch of the Virginia family. He had German blood in his veins, besides other strains mentioned in Chapter 2. About the year 1731 he was married to Miss Ann Lynn. They probably settled in Goochland, Orange, or Albemarle County, where they reared the family.

The formation of counties of Virginia, unless one be perfectly familiar with the dates of the formations and of the exact locality of the home, connected with close study and thought, makes it difficult at this day to state with exactness the county in which was located the home of a person one hundred and fifty to seventy-five years ago.

The subject was a man of high standing and fidelity to his country, to which he had affirmed allegiance. He gave his children good breeding, a good name and fair education—this family has ever since been one of integrity and above reproach—and aided a great deal not only in the development of Virginia, but in the settlement, development and growth of Kentucky and the west and the influence of same exercised in the nation. They had three daughters and three sons. It is probable that every one of his sons served in the war for independence; his son John was a lieutenant and his son Robert was a private in the Virginia line. Their children were:

Section 1. Elizabeth Miller, born November 15, 1732.

Section 2. Robert Miller, born May 5, 1734. He married about the year 1763 to Margaret Maupin, a daughter of Daniel Maupin and Margaret Via, his wife, of Albemarle County, Va., (see Part 5, Chap. 3, Sec. 10) of whom further history is given in Chapter 4, styled Robert Miller, Junior, of Orange, because he established his home in Orange County.

Section 3. Thomas Miller, born March 20, 1736. In the family register of the late Colonel Thomas W. Miller, of Stanford Ky., is the note that this subject was buried in Kentucky, but the date and place of his death and burial are not given. One Thomas Miller, in 1783, was an attorney at law of the Albemarle Bar, at Charlottesville, Va.

Section 4. Ann Miller, born November 15, 1739.

Section 5. Margaret Miller, born May 5, 1742.

Section 6. Colonel John Miller, born January 1, 1750. He married Jane Dulaney. They immigrated to Kentucky and settled in Madison County. Further details are given in Chapter 14.

CHAPTER 4.

ROBERT MILLER, JUNIOR

of Orange.

(Named in Chapter 3, Section 2.)

Article 1.—Robert Miller, Junior, of Orange, a son of Robert Miller, Senior, of Virginia, and Ann Lynn, his wife, was born May 5, 1734, probably in Ireland, and came to America, as stated in Chapter 2.

About the year 1763 he was married to Margaret Maupin, a daughter of Daniel Maupin, Senior, and Margaret Via, his wife, whose home was in Albemarle County, Virginia, and where the said Daniel Maupin died in 1788 (see Part 5, Chap. 3, Sec. 10). Robert Miller acquired lands in Orange County, Virginia, on which he settled and established his home, and where he died in 1806. After his death his widow, Margaret, qualified as administratrix of his estate. A copy of the inventory and appraisement of his personal estate is presented, to-wit:

"Pursuant to an order of the Worshipful Court of Orange County, to us directed, we have proceeded to appraise the estate of Robert Miller, dec'd., the schedule of which is hereto annexed. October 20, 1806.

	£	s.	d.
Mourning, a negro woman, appraised at	43	0	0
Jacob, a negro man, appraised at	78	0	0
Martin, a negro boy, appraised at	78	0	0
One bedstead and furniture, appraised at	10	0	0
One bedstead and furniture, appraised at	12	0	0
Two bedsteads and furniture, appraised at	16	0	0
One flax wheel and spools, appraised at		9	0
Two woman's saddles, appraised at	2	8	0
One desk, and one clock, and case, appraised at......	18	10	0
One cupboard, and walnut table, appraised at	6	6	0
One parcel of old books, and 1 dictionary, appraised at	2	6	0
Ten chairs and one looking glass, appraised at	1	14	0
One pair steelyards, appraised at	0	6	0
One pair fire dogs, pipe tongs and fire tongs, appraised at		16	0
One coffee can and one reel, appraised at	0	9	0
One case of bottles, appraised at	0	3	0
One safe, coffee mill and tea kettle, appraised at.....	0	18	0
Three pots, one oven, two pairs hooks, two pot racks, one skillet, appraised at	2	8	0
One bake plate and frying pan, appraised at	2	8	0
Five pewter basins, nine plates and three dishes, appraised at	2	8	0
One hackel, 1 cotton wheel and snuff box, appraised at	1	7	0
One piggin and one old trunk, appraised at..........	0	11	0
One parcel of old plows, hoes and hilling hoes, appraised at	1	5	0
One pair hames, chains and breeching, appraised at...		15	0
One roan horse, £16.10, and one gray ditto, £12......	28	10	0

One brindle cow and calf, £5, one black ditto and ditto, £4	9	0	0
One red ditto and ditto, £4.10, one brindle cow, £3.19	8	7	0
One red bull and one cow	4	4	0
One spire mortar and old saw	0	7	6
Seven slegs and two wedges	1	16	0
Total	£334	9	6

BENJ. STUBBLEFIELD,
JAMES BURTON,
GEORGE THORNTON,
THOS. LORRILLO.

At a court held for Orange County, at the Court House, on Monday, the twenty-sixth day of January, 1807, this inventory and appraisement of the estate of Robert Miller, deceased, was returned into court and ordered to be recorded.

Teste: REYNOLDS CHAPMAN, Clerk.

A Copy—Attest: C. W. WOOLFOLK, Clerk.

Robert Miller in his life time to-wit: On the 25th day of April, 1803, prepared a deed from himself and his wife, Margaret, to their son, Thomas Miller, which he, the said Robert, signed in the presence of John Plunkett, William Plunkett, and his son, John Miller, which was proven in Court, the 27th day of June 1803, however, his wife, Margaret, for some reason, did not sign and acknowledge the deed. The deed was recorded in Deed Book No. 23, page 31, Orange Circuit Court. A copy is in hand in these words:

"This indenture made this 25th day of April, one thousand eight hundred and three, between Robert Miller and Margaret, his wife, of the County of Orange, of the one part, and Thomas Miller, of the County aforesaid, of the other part, witnesseth: That the said Robert Miller, for the consideration of the sum of five hundred pounds in hand paid, hath granted, bargained and sold unto the said Thomas Miller, his heirs and assigns forever, a certain tract or parcel of land purchased of Jos. Eddins and Peter Thornton. To have and to hold the said tract or parcel of land with its appurtenances unto the said Thomas Miller, his heirs and assigns forever, to his and their own proper use. And the said Robert Miller, for himself, his heirs, executors and administrators, doth further covenant that he shall and will (warrant) the said land, with its appurtenances, unto the said Thomas Miller, his heirs and assigns forever, against the lawful claims and interruptions of any person or persons whatsoever.

In witness whereof, the parties have hereto set their hands and seals this day and year above written.

John Plunkett, Robert Miller [Seal]
William Plunkett.
John Miller. [Seal]

At a Court held for Orange County, at the Court House, on Monday, the 27th day of June, 1803, this indenture was proved by the oaths of John Plunkett, William Plunkett and John Miller, witnesses thereto, and ordered to be recorded.

Test. Reynolds Chapman, Clerk.

A copy from Deed Book No. 23, page 31.

Attest: C. M. Woolfolk, Clerk.

Robert Miller enlisted January 11, 1777, as a private soldier in Capt. Nathan Reed's company of 14th Virginia Regiment, commanded by Col. Charles Lewis, of Albemarle County. Col. Lewis died in 1779, whilst commander of the post at Charlottesville. In December, 1778, this company was designated as Captain Reid's company of the 10th Virginia Regiment, commanded by Colonel William Davies. In May, 1779, the 1st and the 10th Virginia Regiments were consolidated and the Company was called Captain Nathan Reid's and Lieutenant-Colonel Hopkins' Company, 10th Virginia Regiment, commanded by Colonel William Davies, and sometimes referred to as the 1st and 10th Virginia Regiment.

These facts are confirmed by the records and Pension Office, War Department, at Washington, D. C.

The 1st Virginia Regiment was engaged in the battles of Brandywine, Germantown, Guilford Court House, Camden, Ninety-Six and Eutaw Springs. The 14th Virginia Regiment was in the battles of Long Bridge, King's Mountain and Ninety-Six, and the 10th Virginia Regiment .n the battles of Guilford Court House, Eutaw Springs and Yorktown.

History shows that Captain Nathan Reed's company experienced hard service.

The canteen and flint lock pistols carried and used by Robert Miller, whilst a soldier in the Revolutionary Army, his son, Daniel Miller, brought with him when he emigrated from Virginia to Madison County, Kentucky, and which he safely kept till his death in 1841. After his death these war relics passed into the hands of his youngest son, Christopher Irvine Miller, which he in turn kept till his death. He used the canteen in his wood-shop as a receptacle for oil with which he mixed paints—the oil acting as a preserver of the canteen. After the death of C. I. Miller, the canteen went into the hands of his son, James C. Miller, now living on Muddy Creek, (postoffice, Moberley, Ky.), where his father lived and died, and he yet has the canteen well preserved. The flint-lock pistols and holsters, it is believed, were turned over to Mrs. Junius B. Park, daughter of C. I. Miller, and if same were not destroyed by fire at Irvine, Ky., a number of years ago, it is not known where they are. It would indeed be gratifying to know that they are intact, and to keep and preserve same as relics.

The oldest child, Daniel Miller, was born May 28, 1764: the dates of the birth of the other children are unknown, but their births were between the years 1764 and 1780.

Through the years intervening the descendants of Robert Miller and Margaret Maupin, his wife, have been distributed over Virginia, Kentucky, the West, and elsewhere. Many of them have held prominent positions in every walk and calling. His daughters all married and raised families, but of them very little data is at hand.

Their children were:

Section 1. Daniel Miller, born in the County of Albemarle, Colony of Virginia, May 28, 1764. Was nearly grown at the close of the Revolutionary War. In Nelson County, Virginia the 28th of November 1793, he married Susannah Woods. (See Part 2, chap. 19, section 8.)

A fuller account is given in chapter 5.

Section 2. John Miller. It is said that he remained in Virginia, married and raised a family. We have not traced his descendants or learned his history.

Section 3. Thomas Miller. Some say that he remained in Virginia, married and raised a family. To him his father conveyed his land in Orange county April 25, 1803. (Many years ago, these brothers, were visited in Virginia by their nephew, Colonel Thomas Woods Miller, at that time a resident of Madison county, Ky., afterwards a resident of Stanford, Ky., where he died).

Section 4. Anna Miller married Mr. Neale.

Section 5. Elizabeth Miller married Mr. Snell. "a"

Section 6. Sallie Miller married Jennings Maupin. (See Part 5, Chap. 4, Section 10).

Section 7. Polly Miller married Mr. Thorne.

Section 8. Jennie Miller married Mr. Burke.

Section 9. Susannah Miller married Mr. Begle.

"a" Mrs. Snell, visited her brother, Daniel Miller in Madison county, Ky., after the death of his wife and remained with him some time. It is regretted that a fuller account of Daniel Miller's brothers and sisters and their descendants is not here given, but we have not succeeded in obtaining any further data or knowledge of them.

CHAPTER 5.

DANIEL MILLER.

(Named in Section 1, Chap. 4, Part 1).

Article 1.—Daniel Miller, son of Robert Miller (Junior) of Orange and his wife, Margaret Maupin, was born in the County of Albemarle or Orange, Colony of Virginia, May 28, 1764, being nearly grown at the close of the Revolutionary War.

In Nelson County, Virginia the 28th of November, 1793, he was married to the daughter of Colonel John Woods and Susannah Anderson his wife, namely, Susannah Woods. The said Colonel John Woods, being a son of Michael Woods, senior (afterwards called Michael Woods of Blair Park) and his wife, Mary Campbell. The said Susannah Anderson being a daughter of Rev. James Anderson of Pennsylvania, who was a Presbyterian preacher.

Daniel Miller, April 21, 1779, in Albemarle County, Virginia, was one of the signers of a declaration of independence by the citizens of said county.

In the spring of 1795, about the month of May (we fix this date, for his oldest child, Polly, born in 1794, died May 24th, 1795, and was buried by the wayside on their journey from Virginia to Kentucky), Daniel Miller and his wife and babe, in company with his brothers-in-law, Reids, and his wife's sisters, and their families and others, left their old home, parents, relatives and friends in Virginia, and set out across the wilderness for Kentucky, traveling the wilderness road and Boone's trace and reached Madison County and settled on Hickory Lick, a branch of Muddy Creek, where he acquired property as follows, as appears from examinations of the County Court records, page 223, of Deed Book D., showing that on May 3, 1797, one David Trotter conveyed to him 103 acres of land on said creek, and page 389 of the same book, showing that on May 6, 1798, one Wm. Minix Williams conveyed to him 100 acres on the same creek, and page 130 of Deed Book H., showing that on March 6, 1798, one Henry Banta conveyed to him 98 acres on the same creek, and page 276 of Deed Book K., showing that on September 3, 1814, one W. W. Williams conveyed to him 100 acres on the same creek, and pages 136 and 149 of Deed Book N. showing that on April 15, 1818, the heirs of Foster Jones conveyed to him 100 acres on the same waters, (said land coming to said heirs from their grand-father, Christopher Harris, Senior, deceased) making in all 501 acres, acquired there by Daniel Miller. He put valuable improvements on same and occupied same as a home for a number of years for there is where his youngest child was born. He was, however ousted of the possession of the greater portion of the Hickory Lick lands by General Green Clay, who seems to have had prior claims—as was the case in many instances in those days—the matter being in litigation between them for sixteen or seventeen long years, from 1810 to 1817, the case going at least twice to the Court of Appeals of Kentucky. Finally a small part of said land was set apart to Daniel Miller, by way of remuneration for improvements he had put thereon, to which remnant as appears of record Green Clay made to said Daniel Miller a quit claim deed in 1817.

Daniel Miller, by and by parted with what little remained of his Hickory Lick purchases (Hickory Lick being a branch of Muddy Creek, and his lands being near the mouth of said branch) and bought lands on Drowning Creek only a very few miles distant and moved there and died there, the 23d of April, 1841, at the age of 76 years 10 months and 25 days. Here he established a blacksmith shop, where the work in this line of business was done for a large part of the surrounding country. He, also, constructed and put in operation a grist mill and made meal and flour for the people of the vicinage, and Daniel Miller's mill and shop were noted and known for miles and miles. A public road was opened to his mill, which is to this day called Daniel Miller's Mill Road, and the records show when this road was established, and many subsequent entries on the records speak of same and often call for the intersection and otherwise of the Daniel Miller Mill Road.

His home on Drowning Creek, as well as his former home on Hickory Lick, were on the direct route from Richmond to the county seat of Estill County and other mountain county seats, where the noted lawyers of his day practiced law, and Daniel Miller's house was their stopping place on their way to and fro.

He was very often commissioned by the court to take depositions, appraise estates, etc., and in 1799 he, Thomas Collins and Samuel Gilbert took the depositions of Joseph Proctor the old pioneer, Indian fighter and preacher, and others.

He must have moved from Hickory Lick to Drowning Creek, in about the year 1822, and lived there till his death in 1841—nine years of the time a widower, his wife having died in 1832, for page 193 of Deed Book P., shows that on June 22, 1822, one Robert Tevis conveyed to him 327 acres, one rood and 34 poles of land on Downing Creek and after his daughter Malinda had married John H. Shackelford, to-wit: on September 24, 1835, he bought their land on Drowning Creek. See Deed Book V., page 361.

Upon the Tevis land on Drowning Creek he put valuable and permanent improvements—the dwelling and other outhouses he built, are standing there yet, in a splendid state of preservation.

Before his death, to-wit: on the 31st of January, 1835, he conveyed his Drowning Creek lands to his two youngest sons Thomas W. Miller and Christopher Irvine Miller, reserving forever as a burial place for his family the plot of ground where his wife was interred, and where his remains were afterwards buried. See Deed Book Z., page 315.

After this date, 5th of November, 1836, he conveyed to Elijah Yates his 100 acres of land on Muddy Creek (the remainder of his Hickory Lick lands) by deed recorded in Deed Book W., page 396.

Here in the burial plot above named the mortal remains of Daniel Miller and his wife were buried, about two hundred yards more or less, somewhat northwest of the dwelling house, and stones were put to mark their graves with proper inscriptions. Since then the children had the remains removed and re-interred in a lot in the Richmond Cemetery where same now rest, with marble stones properly inscribed to identify them.

They raised to be grown and have families of their own four sons and three daughters. all highly respected and regarded--as good people as the country produces, mention of whom will be made in the sections immediately following.

It is said of Daniel Miller, that his daughter Malinda reputed to be very handsome, was his great favorite and married a gentleman of splendid breeding and family to whom no reasonable objection could have been raised, but he did not wish his daughter to marry and leave him, and after she did marry, and when about to say "good bye," and leave for distant parts, he remarked to her "good-bye Malinda, I now bury you, for I never expect to see you again," and it is told that he never after that time saw her.

Mr. Wm. L. Blanton, as successor to his father, Greenup D. Blanton, now owns and lives at the old Drowning Creek home, and a few years ago was making some repairs to the house, in the building of which nails made by Daniel Miller with his own hands were used, and Mr. Blanton secured a few of these old nails and gave them to us, which we now hold as souvenirs.

Daniel Miller was very exact and systematic in all that he did, and it is said of him that he, even when taking off his hat, or placing it on his head, would take hold of it every time in the same place and in the same way, and that he ever wore a stiff high-top or bee-gum hat.

We have in our possesion a buck-horn handle walking stick made of hickory wood and in imitation of real cane, which he used for a number of years and which has finger and thumb prints worn into the handle by being constantly taken hold of in the same way—said to have been worn in it by himself by long and constant use. The cane was handed down to us through his youngest child—our father—and we greatly appreciate it.

He represented Madison County in the General Assembly of Kentucky, in the years 1806, 1808 and 1811, and helped make many of the laws of the State in that time.

His first home on Muddy Creek, was near Debans Run near the cabin of Duree where in 1782 Peter Duree, John Bullock and his wife, who was the daughter of old man Duree, were massacred by the Indians, which event is related by Ambrose Coffee in deposition taken in 1799, by Daniel Miller, Thomas Collins and Samuel Gilbert, commissioners of the court.

He was a commissioned Major of Militia and was addressed as Major.

Many old people who were living just a few years ago and a few who are now living knew Daniel Miller well, and all would speak in high terms of him, and give him a good name and tell many interesting stories in regard to his peculiarities. Have seen several who have since left the shores of time who spoke of him as a teacher, having gone to school to him and they would invariably refer to his pains-taking and the peculiarity and regularity of his habits. It seems that he was a man of some education for his day and was not satisfied without imparting knowledge to the youth of the country.

At the time of his death he had several grand-children grown or nearly grown, who, in after years, had vivid recollections of him and who often talked of him besides others of an older generation. They all gave him reverence.

Susannah Woods, his wife, was born in Nelson County, Virginia. September 21, 1768 and died on Drowning Creek August 13, 1832, in the 64th year of her age. Mention of her death and burial has already been made. She was regarded as a fine woman in appearance as well as in what she did and it is said she was a great favorite of her father, Colonel John Woods of Albemarle. (See Part 22, Chap. 19, Section 8).

Their children are named in the coming sections:

Section 1. Polly Miller a daughter was born in Albemarle County, Virginia October19, 1794, and when her parents were moving the next spring to Kentucky, she was violently attacked with whooping cough which caused her death May 24, 1795, age 7 months and 5 days, and her remains were buried by the wayside under a large tree on the route they were traveling.

Section 2. Colonel Robert Miller, a son, was born in Madison County, Kentucky, June 22, 1796, the year after his parents' arrival in Kentucky. A further account of whom is given in Chapter 6, of Part I.

Section 3. General John Miller, a son, was born in Madison County, Kentucky, June 30, 1798, a narrative of whom will be found in Chapter 7, Part 1.

Section 4. Major James Miller, a son, was born in Madison County, Kentucky, August 3, 1800. A further account of whom is given in Chapter 8, Part 1.

Section 5. Elizabeth Miller, a daughter, was born in Madison County, Ky., March 28, 1802, and died August 27, 1803.

Section 6. Susannah Miller, a daughter, was born in Madison County, Ky., March 26, 1804. A further account of whom is given in Chapter 9, Part 1.

Section 7. Margaret Miller, a daughter, was born in Madison County, Kentucky, December 29, 1805. A further account of whom is given in Chapter 10, Part 1.

Section 8. Malinda Miller, a daughter, was born in Madison County, Kentucky, January 15, 1808. A further account of whom is given in Chapter 11, Part 1.

Section 9. Colonel Thomas Woods Miller, a son, was born in Madison County, Kentucky December 3, 1811. A further account of whom is given in Chapter 12, Part 1.

Section 10. Christopher Irvine Miller, a son, was born in Madison County, Kentucky, December 20, 1813. A narrative of whom will be found in Chapter 13, Part 1.

Accounts of the aforenamed progeny are set forth in the Chapters 6 to 13, following.

CHAPTER 6.

COLONEL ROBERT MILLER.

(Named in Section 2, Chapter 5, Part I.)

Article 1.—Colonel Robert Miller, son of Daniel Miller and Susannah Woods, his wife, was born in Madison County, Kentucky, June 22, 1796, the year after the arrival of his parents in Kentucky from Virginia.

COL. ROBERT MILLER

After coming to manhood he left the county of his birth and went to Lincoln County, Kentucky, and lived there a number of years, and moved with his family to Adair County and made his home in Columbia. Robert Miller had a good English education and was a beautiful scribe; he was of fine address and an elegant gentleman. He was thrice married, first to Sarah Murrell, the mother of his children; second, Mary Craig, and third, Mrs. Betsy Settle, nee Griffin. He died of cholera September 3, 1873, aged seventy-seven years, two months and eleven days. He was a colonel of militia in antebellum days. The children of his first marriage:

Section 1. Susannah Jane Miller, born May 3, 1823, married March 25, 1846, by Rev. F. Rout, to George Frank Lee, son of George Lee and Lucy Anderson Thomson, his wife. George F. Lee was born December 5, 1820, died August 22, 1896. Mrs. Lee died July 18, 1900. Mr. Lee represented his county in the Legislature in 1855-6. In 1851 he located on a farm in Boyle County. Was an elder in the Presbyterian Church almost fifty years. In 1874 was elected County Judge and served for sixteen years. He graduated at Centre College in the class of 1839. Their children:

1. Eugene Wallace Lee, born April 8, 1847, in Lincoln County, and died in Danville, Ky., February 27, 1905. He married Clara Warren, of Louisville, Ky. Their children:
   1. Allie M. Lee, born October 21, 1870, died July 1, 1889.
   2. Hortense Lee.
   3. Virginia Lee.
   4. Eugene W. Lee, Jr.
   5. George F. Lee.
   6. Robert Miller Lee, born Oct. 12, 1872, died Mar. 29, 1873.
   7. Susie Lee, born January 9, 1880, died July 17, 1880.
2. George Lee, born April 24, 1849, in Lincoln County, Ky.; married Louise Caldwell, of Taylor County, Ky. Their children:
   1. James Caldwell Lee.
   2. Susan J. Lee, died.
   3. Clara Lee.
   4. Robert M. Lee.
   5. David R. Lee.
   6. Louisa L. Lee.

George Lee is now farming in Boyle County, Ky.

3. Sarah Virginia Lee, born Novvember 26, 1851, in Boyle County. Single.

4. Lucy Ann Lee, born March 13, 1854, in Boyle County; married Rev. Dr. I. S. McElroy. Now living in Columbus, Georgia. Their children are:

1. Susie Lee McElroy.
2. Lottie Tate McElroy.
3. J. Proctor McElroy.
4. Stewart McElroy.

5. Lizzie Amelia Lee, born Oct. 6, 1857, in Boyle County; married David P. Rowland. (See Part 1, Chap. 10, Sec. 3.) Their children:

1. Sidney V. Rowland, Jr.
2. Susan Lee Rowland.
3. Frank Lee Rowland
4. Virginia Rowland, died February 22, 1905.

6. Robert Miller Lee, born Feb. 13, 1861, in Boyle County; died Aug. 8, 1873.

7. Frank Nelson Lee, born May 13, 1866, in Boyle County; unmarried. Was County Treasurer about eleven years; City Clerk thirteen years. Now Assistant Cashier of Farmers National Bank, Danville, Kentucky.

Section 2. Elizabeth Miller, born Oct. 9, 1825, died July 1, 1867. She married December 16, 1847, to Josiah Ellis Lee, by Rev. J. Bogle. Mr. Lee was born March 31, 1825, and was a son of George Lee and Lucy Anderson Thomson, his wife.* Their children:

1. Sallie Miller Lee, born Jan. 8, 1849, died March 5, 1854.

2. Lucy Lee, born Feb. 21, 1851; married Thomas H. Bell. Their children:

1. Lizzie Bell; married W. W. Johnson.
2. Joshua Fry Bell.
3. Mary M. Bell.
4. Frances Johnston Bell.
5. Lucy Lee Bell.
6. Miller L. Bell.
7. Josephine Bell.

3. George Miller Lee, born June 19, 1853; married Mollie A. Johnson, December 25, 1884. They now live on his father's old farm in Boyle County. Their children:

1. Elizabeth Miller Lee.
2. Madison Johnson Lee.
3. James A. Lee, Jr.

4. James Ambrose Lee, born Dec. 25, 1856; died unmarried.

5. Josiah Nelson Lee, born Dec. 3, 1859; lives on the old farm with his brother, G. Miller Lee, and is unmarried.

6. Edmund Shackelford Lee, born May 3, 1862; married Stella Collins, of Covington, Ky. They have eight children.

E. S. Lee is Cashier of the First National Bank, Covington, Ky.

Section 3. Margaret Miller, born Dec. 20, 1829; married Jan. 22, 1851, to Cary A. Griffin. Their children:

1. Robert Miller Griffin, born Nov. 21, 1851; married Minnie W. Miller. They live in Kansas City, Missouri.

---

*Josiah E. Lee married the second time Fannie Bell and had two children.

2. Mary Susan Griffin, born March 10, 1854; married Harry White. They now live in Canada.
3. George M. Griffin, born Oct. 5, 1856; married Maggie P. Gentry.
4. Sarah E. Griffin, born Jan. 22, 1859; married Rev. John McCarthy. They now live in Huntington, West Virginia.
5. Martha J. Griffin, born Dec. 16, 1861; married Rev. Charles H. Miller.
6. Margaret C. Griffin, born Nov. 29, 1864; married W. L. Moore. They now live in Kansas City, Missouri.
7. Harry W. Griffin, born Sept. 4, 1868; married a Kansas City lady.

Section 4. George Miller, born Dec. 23, 1834; died Aug. 31, 1852.

Section 5. Robert Miller, born Feb. 17, 1838; died Nov. 12, 1867.

CHAPTER 7.

GENERAL JOHN MILLER.

(Named in Chapter 5, Section 3.)

Article 1.—General John Miller, a son of Daniel Miller and Susannah Woods, his wife, was born on Muddy Creek, near the mouth of its tributary, Hickory Lick, in Madison County, Kentucky, June 30, 1798.

He was educated in the county schools of his day, receiving, by close application and industry, a good common English education, the best his schools could impart. He became thoroughly conversant with military tactics and military affairs; he was a beautiful and swift penman, an excellent business man; he was in every sense an accomplished gentleman, as gentle as a dove, as brave as a lion. He was one of the most public spirited men of Madison County, was foremost in forwarding the interest of the community—procuring fine schools for the education of the boys and girls; he numbered many distinguished men among his acquaintances, notably, Lieutenant General Winfield Scott, who showed him marked attention on a trip East that he made, accompanied by his affectionate wife. He was prominent in laying the corner stone of the Henry Clay monument, being one of the field marshals and in command of the military contingent

GEN. JOHN MILLER

from Madison, Estill, Garrard, and Lincoln. His first introduction into military life, for which he ever had a fondness, came about in this way: During his young manhood, whilst living in Richmond, the young blood of the town and surrounding country organized a volunteer military company and uniformed it, which organization was equipped with guns and munitions of war by the State. John Miller was elected captain of the company. In the military system of the State all the officers were commissioned by the Governor; it was always the custom for each company to select by vote its own captain, and while the Governor was not bound by law to respect such selection, yet he invariably commissioned the choice of the company. After receiving his commission as captain, John Miller rose by regular promotion to major, lieutenant-colonel, colonel, brigadier-general, and major-general—that is, to the highest rank in the military arrangement of the State. A major-general's command was that of eight regiments; his command then comprised the militia of the Counties of Madison, Estill, Garrard, and Lincoln. At his death General Miller held a commission to raise a Brigade of Federal troops to be composed of four regiments—that is, he was authorized by the Federal Government to recruit such a Brigade, of which he would be given the command, to fight for the preservation of the Union, but his death ended his endeavors in this direction.

ELIZABETH I GOCDLOE
Wife of Gen. John Miller

The battle of Richmond, Kentucky, was fought August 30, 1862, between the Federal and Confederate forces, in which engagement the Federals were utterly routed. General Miller took an active part in this battle—he went into the battle as aid to General Schaoff, (August 30, 1862) and whilst trying to rally a disordered column near Mount Zion Meeting House, on the Big Hill Road, fell mortally wounded; he was removed to the residence of Mr. Thomas Palmer near by, where he breathed his last September 6, 1862. His remains were buried in the Richmond Cemetery, the inscriptions on the monument, towit:

"Gen'l John Miller,
Born June 30, 1798.
Mortally wounded Aug. 30, 1862,
while gallantly rallying a disordered column of soldiers
bearing the banner of the Union.
Died Sept. 6, 1862.

"Brave, generous and affectionate, he commanded the admiration of the virtuous when living; and in death their unfeigned regret."

By the side of his tomb is that of his wife on which is inscribed:

"Elizabeth J.
wife of
Gen'l John Miller.
Daughter of Wm. and Susannah Goodloe.
Born November 23, 1809. Died October 31, 1876."
"Her children rise up and call her blessed."

will perpetuate the memory of General Miller, his gallantry, his patriotism, and the note of that event, and of his good wife so long as the monument stands.

A letter from the Treasury Department, Washington City, bearing date September 2, 1862, signed by the Commissioner of Internal Revenue was forwarded to General John Miller, Richmond, Ky., notifying him of his appointment by the President of the United States as Collector of Internal Revenus, under the act of Congress, approved July 1, 1862, entitled "An act to provide Internal Revenue to support the Government, and to pay interest on the public debt," for the 2nd Collection district of the State of Kentucky, comprising the Counties of Boyle, Cumberland, Clinton, Adair, Casey, Taylor, Green, Russell, Pulaski, Wayne, Lincoln, Madison, Garrard, Rockcastle, Laurel, Whitley, Knox, Harlan, Letcher, Pike, Floyd, Johnson, Perry, Owsley, Estill, Clay, Breathitt, Wolfe, Magoffin, and Jackson, and Wm. M. Spencer, Esq., of Greensburg, was appointed assessor for the same district.

Mr. Miller's commission as collector with a bond in the penal sum of $50,000, was the same day forwarded to Hon. Bland Ballard, Judge, U. S. District Court, Louisville, for execution by General Miller, who was directed to divide his district into such divisions as he might deem expedient, designate them by numbers and appoint Deputy Collectors, in each for whose official conduct he would be held responsible, etc., but four days after the date of this letter and commission, General Miller died.

In his young manhood, he acquired considerable reputation as a military officer and disciplinarian, and at almost all the military displays in his section, he was placed in command.

In 1840, the great celebration of the Settlement of Kentucky, was held at Boonsborough with a Military Encampment consisting of all the Volunteer and Amateur Military Companies of the State in attendance for a week or more. It was a state occasion and celebration and attended by large crowds, besides the military array and display. General Miller was made commandant of the encampment, considered quite a distinction, as there was much discussion as to who would be the proper man to conduct it. General Leslie Combs was one of his sub-altern officers. In his day an annual board of visitors, consisting of seven persons appointed by the President of the United States, two Senators by the President of the Senate, and three Representatives by the Speaker of the House, attended the annual examinations of the United States Military Academy at West Point and made annual report on the condition of the academy. General William Henry Harrison died within about one month after his inauguration the 4th of March, 1841, as President-elect of the United States, which event placed the Vice President, Mr. Tyler, in the high office of President. During this term General Miller was selected by the President as one of the seven distinguished gentlemen to attend in 1841 the annual examination of the academy. Colonel John Speed Smith, who up to the time of General Harrison's candidacy for the Presidency had been a Democrat, became an ardent supporter of General Harrison; he had been one of General Harrison's aids-de-camp during the Indian wars and was a warm personal as well as political friend of General Harrison, and Colonel Smith greatly interested himself in procuring the appointment for General Miller.

Mr. Owsley was elected Governor of the State of Kentucky in 1844; during his administration the trial and execution at Manchester, Clay County, Ky., of Dr. Abner Baker for the murder of his brother-in-law, Daniel Bates, occurred. There was very great excitement not only in Clay County, but also in the counties of Madison and Garrard, in which each of the parties had many relatives and friends; very strenuous efforts were made by the friends of Dr. Baker to have him pardoned, which efforts were as strenuously resisted by the friends of Mr. White; the Governor, however, declined to intercede. Fearing an effort at rescue, upon petition, the Governor, to prevent rescue and preserve the peace and dignity of the State, called out the militia of Madison County and placed General Miller in command thereof; and he marshalled his forces and they marched to the scene of the apprehended trouble; it was considered a very responsible and difficult position. He and his men were on duty several weeks at Manchester, remaining till after the execution.

General Miller was a prominent merchant of Richmond, Ky., from his early manhood until a very short time before his end. In his mercantile life he made many horseback trips from his native town to Baltimore, Philadelphia and other Eastern cities for merchandise. On one of these Eastern trips, in 1835, he arrived from Baltimore in Philadelphia on the evening of March 13, 1835, and stopped at the United States Hotel. A letter in his own hand, written by him at 10 o'clock p. m. the next day, at said hotel, to his wife Elizabeth, begins in this way: "Having an opportunity by the Hon. Davy Crockett, I drop you a line." Col. Crockett, the Representative from Tennessee, was figuring upon a large scale in the East, receiving great ovations of immense crowds and the night this letter was written General Miller attended the theater on Arch Street to witness a reception given Colonel Crockett, who when he (Crockett) took his seat in the box was cheered for several minutes heavily. "Go ahead," etc., etc., rang from side to side by an immense crowd, which General Miller writes was much the largest he had ever seen in the city, and he had the pleasure of an introduction to Colonel Crockett by Representative Mr. Low.

On more than one occasion General Miller visited his kinspeople in Virginia, making the trip on horseback.

He owned and occupied as his home, till just before his death, the handsome and desirable property on Lancaster Avenue, now owned and occupied by William W. Watts, Esquire: on the site of the old mansion Mr. Watts has erected a large palatial residence.

General John Miller, on the 23d day of April, 1830, was married, near Richmond, Ky., to Elizabeth Jones Goodloe. She was born November 23, 1809, and died October 31, 1876. (See obituary.) She was a daughter of William Goodloe and Susannah Woods, his wife. (See Part 2, Chap. 11.) Mrs. Miller was a most excellent Christian woman, wife and mother.

Obituary—Miller. (Died) At the residence of Gen. David S. Goodloe, in Lexington, on Tuesday, October 3, 1876, Mrs. Elizabeth J. Miller, aged 67 years, having been born November 23, 1809. This excellent lady was a daughter of William Goodloe, Sr., and a native of Madison County. In early womanhood she was married to Gen. John Miller, and thereafter lived in the town of Richmond until her husband's death, who, it will be remembered, lost his life in the ranks of the Union army in the battle near this place, August 30, 1862. Mrs. Miller subsequently removed to Paris, Ky., and continued to reside there until her death. Her acquaintance and relationship were wide and general throughout many of the counties of Central Kentucky and in other States, and it can be said with no exaggeration, but with perfect truth, that wherever and by whomsoever known she commanded the most affectionate and heartfelt love and respect. Her virtues and personal character and intelligence were of the highest order. She was a prudent, generous and affectionate wife, mother, sister and friend. Her life was of chequered experience. She had known affluence and poverty, joy and many sorrows. Death, in varied and the severest terms, had again, again and again knocked at the portal of her house, and had borne away from her—parents, brothers, sisters, husband and children: but with unshrinking fortitude she bowed submissively to these trials and bereavements and prayed for strength to watch over and nurture the orphans thrown upon her care, thus rounding off beautifully her life and supplanting sorrow by duty. Her final departure from earth was very sudden and was a crushing blow to her family. Down to the very morning of her death she seemed in robust and perfect health, and was enjoying the society of relatives in Fayette preparatory to a visit to the home of her childhood, youth and maturer years. But, alas! that visit was never to be paid: but on the day following her remains were borne hither in pall and shroud, and in the presence of sorrowing kindred and friends were consigned to that narrow house appointed for all the living. But they who knew and loved her do not doubt that, life's Christian duties all discharged, she has met the reward of eternal rest promised to the saints of God through the merits and sacrifices of the Redeemer, who had been her trust and stay. Mrs. Miller was a woman of rare dignity of character, of noble presence, intellectual and cultured; her sympathies were broad, she practiced the truest benevolence, a good friend, loyal wife and devoted mother. She finished her education at one of the best boarding schools of the day at Lexington. She was always fond of her husband's brothers and a good friend to them—appreciated them at their full worth. The half has not been told of her goodness and worth.

The children of General John Miller and Elizabeth J. Goodloe, his wife:

Section 1. Susannah Woods Miller, born at Richmond, Ky., February 13, 1831. She married, May 25, 1851, her cousin, Dr. Michael Woods Barclay, of Lexington, Virginia. (See Part 2, Chap. 28, Sec. 2.) She died at Paris, Ky., March 30, 1877. She was a lovely character, a charming Christian. The marriage occurred in Richmond, Ky. Dr. Barclay died October 23, 1858, as set forth in the obituary notice, towit:

(Died) "In this place, on Saturday, October 23, 1858, at eleven p. m., at the residence of Gen. John Miller, Dr. M. W. Barclay, of pulmonary consumption. The subject of this notice was born in Lexington, Rockbridge County, Va., December 2, 1824; graduated at Washington College, Va., in 1844; received the degree of Medicine from Jefferson College, Philadelphia, in 1847; removed to Kentucky in 1849; was married in 1851; practiced medicine in Bourbon County until 1854, when he removed to St. Francis County, Ark., and there, after enjoying a lucrative practice of his profession until 1857, he was attacked with consumption, which terminated in his decease at the age of thirty-three years, nine months and twenty-one days. It rarely becomes necessary to chronicle the death of so interesting a character as the one under notice. Endowed by nature with superior intellect, the life which under all circumstances would have been marked with interest, was especially so with the super-added advantages of a refined and scholastic education. Who can but lament that one so gifted should have been cut down in the meridian of manhood; that the tree which promised so abundant a harvest of usefulness should in a few moments lie low with earth?. Nevertheless, 'being dead, he yet speaketh,' and they who survive as mourners remember the whispers of that faith which bade them prepare to meet him in the skies. They remember the fruits of that religion which taking its abode in his soul in 1855, in a distant State, was his 'firm foundation' during the pangs of dissolution. As husband, brother, son and friend his life was worthy of emulation, but as a Christian—being a devoted member of the Methodist Church—survivors contemplate his character with the greatest delight. Truly 'the righteous hath hope in his death,' for while his faith pointed to a heart purified from sin, to a love which only the ransomed know, and to a victory over the world complete and triumphant, that hope still sheds its fragrance over the grave, warning all of his glorious resurrection and their mortality. May God sanctify to the afflicted their deepest distress and distill within them the dew of heaven for solace now, and for glory hereafter.

"Life's duty done, as sinks the clay,
Light from its load the spirit flies;
While heaven and earth combine to say,
How blest the righteous when he dies."

Their children were:

1. Hugh Barclay, born October 17, 1852, at Clintonville, Bourbon County, Ky.; died March 30, 1855, in St. Francis County, Arkansas.

2. Bettie M. Barclay, born in Richmond, Ky., September 30, 1854; died June 20, 1876, at Paris, Ky.

1. Mary M. Barclay, was born at Glenann, St. Francis County, Ark., March 4, 1857; died March 13, 1877.

Obituary—Barclay. Died in this city, Mar. 13, 1877, at the residence of her grandmother, the late Mrs. Elizabeth J. Miller, Miss Mary M. Barclay, of consumption. Again death has entered a stricken household. Less than a year ago the deceased was apparently in the enjoyment of health, but the places that knew her shall know her no more. Stealthily disease laid its hand upon her, preparing the way for the approach of death. But her kindred who knew her best do not doubt that death was made the occasion to her of a happy exchange and great gain. Four years ago, upon professing faith in Christ as the Savior of sinners, she was received into the Baptist Church of this city; as they believe, persevered in the faith with childlike confidence in Jesus' power to save unto the end. After the development of her disease she seems to have been resigned to it without complaint. A short time before her departure she sang these words of a favorite song: "I am waiting, worn and weary," etc. Her purity of character, gentle manners and kindness of heart have left her memory embalmed in the hearts of many who sigh and shed tears over her early death. In mercy to her, we trust God has granted her exemption from the trials of life and rests with loved ones who have preceded her in the home of the justified. No feeling person can regard the removal of this lovely girl from earth to the realm of spirits without awful contemplation of the mysteriousness of the divine appointment, or without sympathy for a mourning household, especially for an afflicted mother, who, herself on a bed of sickness, without parents, without husband, and childless, is left to mourn the wreck of departed hopes. May the God of Jacob be found her refuge and strength. —Western Citizen (Paris).

Section 2. Sarah Clinton Miller, born in Richmond, Ky., Aug. 10, 1832; she married her cousin, David Goodloe, of Tuscumbia, Alabama, December 29, 1852. She died in St. Francis County, Arkansas, September 6, 1857. Their children were:

1. William M. Goodloe, married Mary Stephens, of Marietta, O.
2. Margaret C. Goodloe, of Paris, Ky.

Section 3. Margaret Shackelford Miller, born in Richmond, Ky., Mar. 28, 1834; married Rev. Edmund H. Burnam, a minister of the Regular Baptist Church; a number of years editor of the Regular Baptist Magazine, published at Mexico, Mo. For a long period served the church in Richmond, Ky., administering ordinances and preaching. He is a highly educated gentleman, a son of Thompson Burnam, a staunch Primitive Baptist in his day. Mrs. Burnam died February 3, 186—. Elder Burnam married again Ann Williams. (See Part 2, Chap. 11, Sec. 2). The issue of the marriage of Margaret S. Miller and Elder E. H. Burnam:

1. Prof. John Miller Burnam (Ph. D.), now filling the chair of Latin in the Cincinnati University, was born at Irvine, Ky., April 9, 1864. In 1869 he came with his parents to Boone County, Mo., where he remained until 1876, when his family returned to Richmond, Ky. From January, 1877, to June, 1878, he was a student at Central University, Richmond, Ky. In the fall of 1878 he entered Smith Academy, St. Louis, Mo., and the next year became a member of the Freshman class of Washington University. In September, 1880, Dr. Burnam matriculated at Yale University, New Haven, Conn. His career at that institution was most brilliant. He won the Hulbunt Scholarship in May, 1881, and the Berkeley Premium in Latin Composition the same year. In June, 1884, he received his A. B. degree and the Larned Scholarship ($300 per year). For two years after graduation he pursued his studies at Yale as a graduate student in Sanskrit (under the celebrated Whiting) Latin and (chiefly) Romance languages, and was made a Doctor of Philosophy in 1886. During the next three years Dr. Burnam continued his researches abroad, studying in France, Germany and Spain. Since his home coming he has pursued his special studies in Latin and Roman Palaeography with great zeal and has prepared a series of original articles on Statues and Prudontius which appear as a part of the American School at Rome, in the American Journal of Archaeology. His collection of manuscripts is one of the best in the United States, perhaps the best, and most comprehensive owned by a private individual in this country, in spite of the fact that the greater portion of his library was destroyed by the burning of the old university building in 1892. He was elected to membership in the American Philological Association in June, 1899.

Section 4. Daniel Miller, born in Richmond, Ky., March 19, 1836; died March 29, 1836.

Section 5. William Goodloe Miller, born in Richmond, Ky., March 19, 1836; died of cholera at Richmond, August 12, 1849.

Section 6. Elizabeth Goodloe Miller, born in Richmond, Ky., May 9, 1838; married William M. Hinton, at Paris, Ky., April 7, 1868. Mr. Hinton is a leading substantial citizen of Bourbon County. Their children:

1. William M. Hinton, born July 1, 1872, in Paris, Ky.
2. C. Oakford Hinton, born August 19, 1874, in Paris, Ky.
3. Bertha G. Hinton, born July 4, 1876, in Paris, Ky.
4. Robert T. Hinton, born July 11, 1878, in Paris, Ky.

Section 7. Mary M. Miller, born March 18, 1840, in Richmond, Ky. She married Charles Stephens, at Paris, Ky., October 22, 1867. Mr. Stephens was born in Paris, Ky., December 21, 1840. He is a successful merchant and leading citizen of that place. Their children are:

1. Dr. William Barclay Stephens, born in Paris, Ky., January 4, 1869; graduated from Georgetown College in the class of 1890, with A. M. degree. In the fall of the same year he entered the College of Physicians and Surgeons, Medical Department of Columbia College, in the city of New York. After the required three years' preparation, practicing during the time in the Roosevelt Hospital and Vanderbilt Clinic, he received his diploma. Also one from Vanderbilt Clinic for the special course of the treatment of the eye. Immediately upon graduation he located in San Francisco as specialist for the eye, ear and throat, where he is engaged in a large and extensive practice. He resides across the bay in the city of Alameda, where he also has office. He ranks amongst the first as specialist and authority. His office was destroyed by fire after the earthquake. He was appointed official bacterialogist by the Board of Health. The Alameda (California) Argus prints the following in the August 5 issue concerning Dr. W. Barclay Stephens, son of Mr. Charles Stephens, of Paris:

"Dr. W. B. Stephens was given a surprise last evening when he appeared to attend the meeting of the Board of Health, of which he is a member. It was the first session the Doctor has attended since his illness. He has become a Benedict since his recovery, and the fact was duly noted by the members of the board and the employees of the Health Department. As a mark of the high esteem in which the Doctor is held by them they presented him with an elegant cut glass set. The presentation was made, on behalf of the board and the Health Department employees, by Dr. W. O. Smith, who spoke of the friendly relations that existed between the Doctor and his co-workers, of his valuable service to the city, and of the great interest he took in the affairs of the Health Board. Congratulations were also extended as a result of the Doctor's wedding. Dr. Stephens was taken completely by surprise and could hardly find words to express his deep sense of appreciation for the kindly sentiments of those with whom he has been associated for so long. He was married Wednesday, June 24, 1903, to Louise Bruce, at the home of the bride's father, Captain James H. Bruce, No. 1262 Jackson Street, San Francisco, by the Rev. Guthrie, of San Francisco. There were no attendants and the ceremony was witnessed only by a few relatives and immediate friends of the couple."

William Barclay Stephens, in his youth was a perfect genius; in his maturer years, turned his genius to the human body and is now one of the noted surgeons for the operation on the head and about the brain; he is well known in the medical world. They have one child:

1. Bruce Miller Stephens, born August 5, 1904.

2. Dr. Charles Joy Stephens, born in Paris, Ky., January 1, 1869; graduated from Georgetown College in the class of 1895 with A. M. degree. He joined his brother in California in August of same year, entered the College of Dentistry of the University of California, where, after the required term of study (three years), he took his diploma and began practice of his profession in San Francisco. He was very successful until the earthquake occurred in April, 1906, when his handsome office with all the modern appliances was destroyed by fire, which followed the earthquake. He at present is practicing in Paris, Ky., but expects to return and resume practice in San Francisco.

3. Elizabeth Goodloe Stephens, born in Paris, Ky., September 12, 1875.

4. John Miller Stephens, born in Paris, Ky., July 6, 1879.

Section 8. John Barclay Miller, born in Richmond, Ky., July 7, 1843; married Llewellyn B. Holloday, December 20, 1882, at Paris, Ky.

Section 9. Lucy Anne Miller, born in Richmond, Ky., in 1845; now residing in Paris, Ky.; unmarried.

Section 10. Octavia G. Miller, born in Richmond, Ky., April 14, 1847; died of cholera in 1849.

All the daughters of General John Miller were handsome, stylish, well educated, accomplished women; their superiors are not in this country. General Miller and his wife educated their children in the best schools and gave them proper training and entered them in the best society, and they grew up to be women of graceful and beautiful manners; they respected all entitled to respect and were respected by every one who came in contact with them. Through the trials and vicissitudes of life each has kept her fair name. Two of the married daughters, Mrs. Hinton and Mrs. Stephens, of Paris, Ky., and the single daughter Miss Lucy, with their brother, John B., survive, and all reside in the same city, Paris, Ky. As their days have demanded so has their strength been. The good times John had with the family of his uncle Irvine in his young days, when he and Ed. Shackelford and often Marion Green, and sometimes others, would come out from Richmond in the fall of the year in the quailing season and spend times hunting the girds, are well remembered. Uncle Irvine and Aunt Talitha's home was to them a great place of enjoyment, where they had perfect freedom in the field of sport and pleasure.

CHAPTER 8.

MAJOR JAMES MILLER.

(Named in Section 4, Chapter 5, Part 1.)

Article 1.—Major James Miller, a son of Daniel Miller and Susannah Woods, his wife, was born in Madison County, Kentucky, August 3, 1800.

He was married in said county July 24, 1823, to Frances M. Harris, a daughter of John Harris and Margaret Maupin, his wife. (See Part 3, Chap. 41.) She was born March 26, 1802, and died December 17, 1880. About the year 1826 or 1827 he moved his family to Lincoln County, Ky., and bought a farm near Milledgeville, and lived there a few years; sold his farm, bought another on Dick's River, about five miles from Stanford, to which he moved and there made his permanent home and engaged in farming and stock raising until his death, which occurred May 2, 1869. The remains of both were interred in the Richmond Cemetery. Maj. James Miller was, under the old regime, a Major of Militia. He was a solid, good man, honest, kind, generous, and brave; he had a fair common English education and was a good scribe. At his home elegant entertainments were given. Although he held no office other than that mentioned, he possessed the qualifications of a statesman, and was well versed in the affairs of government. Many distinguished persons were guests at his home. His wife was a noble Christian woman and saint of God, endowed with a strong mind, well balanced, kind, affectionate, true, loyal and devoted wife and mother, with many friends. Both were highly esteemed by their neighbors, acquaintances and relatives and all spoke in the highest terms and most reverently of Major Miller and his wife. Their children were:

MAJOR JAMES MILLER

Section 1. Christopher Miller, a son, born in Madison County; died in his youth (Nov. 25, 1824—Aug. 18, 1829).

Section 2. Daniel Miller, a son, born in Madison County, Sept. 10, 1826; was never married; died a bachelor, having prior to his death, upon a profession of faith in the Savior, united with the old Baptist Church. He served many years in the capacities of Deputy Sheriff and Constable of his county.

Section 3. Margaret Susan Miller, a daughter, born in Lincoln County, Oct. 4, 1828; married Dr. William Pettus, May 17, 1859. She survived her husband many years and died. The remains of both lie in the cemetery at Danville. Their only son:

1. James Miller Pettus, born June 28, 1860; married a kinswoman, Miss Jennie Pettus, of Lincoln County, and purchased a farm near Stanford, on which he now lives.

Section 4. Malinda Miller, a daughter, born July 26, 1830; married Mr. John Butler, Nov. 17, 1868, with whom she lived a number of years and he died, after which she became the wife of Leo Hayden, a prominent citizen of Lincoln County, Feb. 9, 1875, whom she also survived. She ventured for the third time into the holy state of matrimony by joining her fortunes with John T. Stone, of Edgerton, Missouri, May 22, 1879, in which State they now live at Edgerton, Platte County, Missouri. Since the above was written Mr. Stone has died, and Mrs. Stone now lives at Stanford, Kentucky.

Section 5. John Harris Miller, born in Lincoln County, Ky., Feb. 27, 1832. He married a widow, Mrs. Angeline Brown Harris, widow of Charles Lee Harris, Feb. 9, 1875. She was born Oct. 9, 1832; died Sept. 8, 1881. (See Part VIII, Chap. 14, Sec. 8, and Part III, Chap. 4.) She died without issue, the subject surviving; after which he was married to Miss Sallie Phillips, of Stanford, which proved to be an unhappy union and a separation took place.

Under the second administration of Grover Cleveland, President of the United States, John H. Miller was appointed Consul to Falkland Islands, off the extreme southern east coast of South America, in the Atlantic Ocean, whence he went and spent four years of his life. He returned home by way of London, England, and other noted places, having a long and very interesting voyage, and was received at his Lincoln County home with open hands and kind-soft hearts by the people, who met him at the depot in throngs, with the brass band and drum, which was too much for him and completely overcame him and filled him too full for utterance when called upon for an account of himself; his actions spoke louder than his words.

He enlisted as a soldier in the Civil War of 1862, and espoused the cause of the South and entered the army's active service, two of his brothers being enlisted in the same cause.

He was a humorous and spicy writer under "Happy Jack," his nom de plume. His productions were much complimented and were very amusing to the reader. A sample is here offered, not, however, of his humorous:

"Gen. Wolford.

"To every Kentucky survivor of The Lost Cause. To the Editor of the Interior Journal:

U. S. Consulate, Port Stanley, Falkland Islands,
January 10, 1896.

"Comrades:—When the war closed the Kentucky soldiers returned home draped in mournful glory. Many flowers from the ranks of her contending wings had been cut down. We who survived 'The Lost Cause' had been denied citizenship. No day during the war was so sad, so dark as that day. Gen. Wolford, without solicitation or delay, came to our defense. Others who were considered great, not great like Wolford, Kentucky has never had but one Wolford, he was as good a man as Gov. Blackburn and greater than Blackburn—cringed, trembled and faltered. Not so then, never so with Wolford. Braver than all men, more generous, if possible, than brave, he came quickly but quietly to our rescue. Opposition vanished like trash before the wind. There stood the old man in his noble bearing, almost alone, brave and dauntless, but cool and collected, not defiant, not dismayed, not disheartened. His rugged and benevolent face and brilliant eye fairly beamed and twinkled with smiles and love as he extended us his open hand of sincere friendship as a free-will offering. The eye of Kentucky turned in astonished gaze upon Wolford. These were times of peril, but Wolford was not afraid; he had Truth, Goodness, Love, and Duty as his bodyguard. His great, big heart, that it was impossible to enlarge, imparted much of its goodness to every contracted nature that dared listen to his charming theme. Hear him:

"The war is ended, my countrymen. We are all glad, too glad for resentment. This is not the day for Kentucky to bolt her doors against any class of her manhood. Her doors must be unbolted and thrown wide open to all alike. The Southern soldier has fought his last battle. He has surrendered; we have brought him home with us, not as a prisoner. Heaven forbid. We shake our heads at the thought. Kentucky cannot afford, will not dare, hold as prisoners or aliens this brave band of her own sons who dared bare their breasts to battle's storm for their honest conviction. Kentucky needs such men to-day. They have stood for four years, true as steel against those hundreds of thousands of native patriots who rushed to the front so promptly, as well as against all those whom our money could hire from abroad. These are the men we have brought home, but not as prisoners, not as aliens. They must put on the whole armor of citizenship."

Such was his plea for us. Thank God for Wolford. No wonder our dear old mothers, dead and gone long ago, sung "Home Again" so sweetly.

When convinced of his right, he never hesitated, but did it on the instant. He never weighed consequences, nor looked about for friends. "How many men like Wolford have you in Kentucky?" asked the great Lincoln of Senator Garret Davis when Wolford was carried to Washington under arrest. "He is the only one, Mr. President; you can shoot him every morning for his convictions, but he will never surrender one." Mr. Lincoln knew Wolford was a man: he was a man himself, never surrendering a conviction; this taught Wolford to highly regard sincere conviction of others. Daring to do all he thought right, he never counted cost or thought of reward. He was a jewel above price. This simple child of nature, so profusely endowed with the best and richest gift that heaven has yet bestowed on man—a love for his fellows that casts out all fear, is gone.

Col. T. P. Hill, of Stanford, Ky., proposes that the Confederates erect a monument to his memory.

We must not insult or wound the feeling of his "Old Regiment." Wolford's men never would bear crowding on, none of us can forget that, but with their permission to render this heart offering to our "best friend" in our darkest day, we can give Col. Hill substantial assurance that we cannot forget that ready, willing, able hand that rescued us in the day of our calamity. We have lost our bravest and most generous foe in war, our best friend in peace. "We shall not look upon his like again.' Allow me to suggest the inscription for the monument.

Erected by the
Kentucky Confederates.

General Frank Lane Wolford,
Ist Ky. Cav., U. S. A.
Born Sept. 29, 1817, in Adair Co., Ky.
Died August 2, 1895.

Our closest enemy in war.
Our closest friend in peace.
Kentucky moved the hand that restored the
South, and Wolford moved
Kentucky.

We will try to do our duty. Good-bye, comrades.
J. H. MILLER,
Co. B. 6th Ky. Cav., C. S. A.,
Duke's Brigade, Morgan's Command."

The foregoing is not one of his humorous pieces, and is not signed in his nom de plume, "Happy Jack," under which name he usually wrote; but we think it good and therefore have presented same here.

The subject was not blessed with issue of either marriage. He died in Lincoln County, Ky., about two years ago, at the age of about 70 years. He was an amusing conversationalist and known for his honesty and strong affection for his friends, whom he never for a moment forgot.

Section 6. Fannie Miller, a daughter, born in Lincoln County, April 18, 1836; died young. 1836—1837.

Section 7. James Miller, a son, born in Lincoln County, July 2, 1834. He enlisted in the service of the Southern Confederacy in the Civil War of 1862, under General Morgan; was captured on Morgan's famous raid into the States of Indiana and Ohio, and lay for a time as a prisoner of war in the Federal prison Camp Douglas, Chicago, Illinois. After his release from prison he returned to his home in Lincoln County, Ky., and on the 10th of January, 1870, he married Gertrude Pettus. His wife died, and on the 17th of March, 1872, he married his second wife, Miss Susan Chenault. They lived for a time in Lincoln County, Ky., and moved to Kansas some thirty years ago. Later they moved to Tishomingo, Chickasaw Nation, Indian Territory, where he died, April 16, 1905. Carrying out his request before his death, his body was expressed to Richmond, Ky., and laid in the grave by the side of that of his first wife, Gertrude, in the cemetery at that place. After his death Mrs. Miller moved to Ardmore, Indian Territory, in the Chickasaw Nation, where she now lives. Issue of the first marriage:

1. William Pettus Miller, born Nov. 30, 1870. He is, or was in 1905, book-keeper on the U. S. Battleship Bainsbridge, with the Asiatic Squadron; headquarters Philippine Islands.

Issue of the second marriage: (See Part 6, Chap. 14, Sec. 4.)

2. James Chenault Miller, born July 25,1873; died July 5,1874.
3. Mary Waller Miller, born Nov. 26, 1874; married Arlie Samuel Crouch. Living now at Ardmore, I. T., he having lately come from the Kansas and Oklahoma oil fields. Issue:
    1. James Miller Crouch, born 1903.
4. Helen Chenault Miller, born Feb. 22, 1878. She is with the Dawes Commission in Ardmore, I. T.
5. Francis James Miller, born Oct. 25, 1879. Living with and keeping house for her mother at Ardmore, who has been almost helpless for years, because of her great flesh.

Section 8. Elizabeth Duncan Miller, a daughter, was born in Lincoln County, Nov. 28, 1838. After her arrival at mature years she married Dudley Portwood, Dec. 15, 1868. He was born Nov. 29, 1822; a substantial farmer of Jessamine County, where they lived many years, where children were born to them. Some years since they moved to the State of Texas, and now (1905) live in the city of Ft. Worth; both old and infirm, Mr. Portwood being 84 years old, his wife many years younger. We visited them at Ft. Worth in 1904. Mr. Portwood died in 1906. Their children:

1. James Miller Portwood, born Aug. 2, 1870; married Pearl Holland, of Orange, Texas. Children:
    1. Nan Portwood.
    2. Catherine Portwood.
2. Fannie Harris Portwood, born Dec. 29, 1871; married Ben. O. Smith, of Ft. Wotrh, Texas. Child:
    1. Ben. O. Smith, Jr.
3. Dudley Portwood, born Dec. 12, 1873; married in Ft. Worth, Texas, Mary Tully, of Ft. Worth, Texas. Children:
    1. Howard Portwood.
    2. Alice Portwood.

Section 9. William Harris Miller, a son, and the youngest child, born in Lincoln County, June 17, 1842, named for his uncle William Harris; was educated in the common schools of the county and at Centre College, Danville, Ky. Before completing the course at college he abandoned his studies to champion the cause of the Southern Confederacy, and in 1862 enlisted in Company B, 6th Ky. Cav., the fortunes of which command he shared until captured at Chishire, Ohio, in 1863. In the following year he made his escape from the Federal prison at Chicago (Camp Douglas), Illinois, and rejoined General Morgan in Virginia, remaining until the fatal day that ended General Morgan's life at Greenville, Tennessee, at which time and place Mr. Miller was present and received a severe wound. He was discharged in 1865, and soon after returned to his Lincoln County home, and having decided upon the profession of law, entered the office of Squire Turner, of Richmond, Ky., under whom he did his preparatory reading. Was admitted to the bar in 1866, and located at Stanford for the practice of his profession. In 1868 was elected Clerk of the Lincoln Circuit Court, and during his encumbency edited, in connection with M. C. Saufley, the Central Dispatch. In 1873 was appointed Assistant Clerk of the House of Representatives. In 1874 was defeated for the office of Circuit Court Clerk. In politics he was a Democrat, and in 1876 was Presidential Elector for the Eighth Congressional District of Kentucky. In 1878 was elected County Attorney of Lincoln County, and served his constituents as such. He was the delegate from Lincoln County to the convention that framed the present Constitution of the State of Kentucky. In 1879 he was married to Miss Katherine Portman, daughter of M. C. Portman, of Stanford, Ky., Dec. 9, 1879. His wife was born Sept. 2, 1853. They were blessed with one child, a daughter, (1) Malinda Catherine Miller, born April 22, 1882. Wm. H. Miller died in Lincoln County, his wife and daughter surviving; now (1905) living at Stanford.

We here relate a coincidence:

This subject and the writer both bore the same name exactly, "William Harris Miller," the former a citizen of Lincoln, the latter of Madison County, sons of brothers, and the former's mother an aunt of the latter's mother, and both were great personal friends. During the space 1880-1893 the latter was Clerk of the Madison Circuit Court and had a close friend in the office as assistant (Col. R. X. White); one day he went to the postoffice and received a card from the blank book manufacturing establishment of John P. Morton & Co., Louisville, directed to W. H. Miller, Richmond, Ky., in substance: "Please acknowledge the receipt of 100 abstracts of title we sent you at Stanford, Ky."

On returning to the clerk's office the latter showed the card to his deputy, Col. White, and told him he had made no such order and would answer the card in a way that in the future there would be no such confusion and mixture of the mail matter, and did immediately answer thus: "Sirs:—Your card in regard to the abstracts of title received. I ordered none and received none. I have a cousin residing at Stanford, Ky. His name is W. H. Miller; my name is W. H. Miller. His father was a Miller; my father was a Miller. His mother was a Harris; my mother was a Harris. His wife is named Kate; my wife is named Kate. He used to be Circuit Court Clerk; I am now Circuit Court Clerk, and about the only difference between us is, he is a lawyer, and I am not; he is older and has more sense than I."

The reply was shown to Col. White, to whom we stated we could say further, if necessary: He had an Uncle Bob, I had an Uncle Bob; he had an Uncle John, so did I; he had an Uncle Tom, so did I; he had Aunts Susan, Malinda, and Margaret, so did I, and the Colonel, with an interjection, said: "It will be published in every paper of the State." It was pretty extensively published. The book concern never after got our orders mixed.

We have received letters from our cousin addressed to W. H. Miller and signed with the same name, as though one was writing to himself.

On one occasion we received a letter from him saying he had a dun from a jewelry establishment of Louisville, and as he did not owe the bill he wrote the firm giving the address of six W. H. Millers of his acquaintance, telling the firm to dun all of them and may be in the rounds they would strike the right one; and in same told them of the writer, but at the same time writing them that he had no idea it was the writer, as he had an idea that the writer had never seen in or knew anything of a jewelry store.

CHAPTER 9.

SUSANNAH MILLER.

(Named in Section 6, Chapter 5, Part I.)

Article 1.—Susannah Miller, a daughter of Daniel Miller and Susannah Anderson, his wife, was born in Madison County, Ky., March 26, 1804.

MRS SUSANNAH MILLER HUME-EMBRY

She was a very bright, sensible woman and of strong, fixed opinions of her own, a devout Christian, and member of the old Baptist Church from an early period in her life till her death. On October 30, 1821, she was joined in the holy state of matrimony with Stanton Hume (born Nov. 12, 1790), a substantial and well-to-do citizen of Madison County. They lived and raised a family of five children. Her husband died many years before she. After his death she was united in marriage to Elder Allen Embry, an old Baptist preacher, Sept. 27, 1858, whom she also survived, and died the 11th of November, 1871, well beloved by all who knew her.

Notes: The Hume Family, of Madison County, Ky.

The Humes came originally from Scotland to America.

1. George Hume, who settled in Madison County, Ky., in an early day, was born May 21, 1759. His wife, Susannah, was born January 3, 1762. They came from Virginia. He died October 24, 1816; his will bears date July 5, 1814, probated February 3, 1817. His wife died February 15, 1831. Their children:

1. Thomas Hume.

2. Larkin Hume, born March 20, 1788; married Nancy Moberley, a daughter of John Moberley and Miss Jenkins, his wife. (See Part 7, Chap. 18.) His wife was born February 25, 1794; died August 21, 1863. Larkin Hume died Nov. 29, 1835; his will bears date Sept. 5, 1833, probated Jan. 4, 1836. Their children.

1. Amanda M. Hume, married John Challis, of Madison Co., Ky., May 24, 1838, (both dead).

2. Louisa F. Hume, married John Park, of Irvine, Ky., Nov. 5, 1840, (both dead).

3. Thomas Richard Hume, married Susannah Woods Miller. (See Chap. 13, Sec. 7.)

4. William Hume; married.

5. John Moberley Hume; married; was a Confederate soldier.

3. Stanton Hume, married Susannah Miller, as set forth in the beginning of Chapter 9. His will bears date Sept. 3, 1849, probated April 4, 1853.

4. Elizabeth Hume, born January 3, 1794; died January 18, 1864. She (Dec. 22, 1840) was the second wife of William Duncan, who was born Nov. 24, 1799, and died Oct. 19, 1862, his first wife being her sister Catherine.

5. Martha Jane Hume, born June 23, 1795; died Aug. 4, 1842; married Frederick Hyatt, of St. Louis County, Mo., Mar. 29, 1840.

6. Frances Hume, born July 22, 1800; died March 31, 1838; will dated March 28, 1838, probated April 2, 1838.

7. Emma Hume, born Feb. 12, 1803; died July 10, 1851. Married Thomas Thorpe, who was born July 17, 1800; died April 17, 1885.

8. Susannah Hume, born April 6, 1806; died Jan. 14, 1828.

9. Catherine Hume, born March 7, 1798; died Feb. 17, 1840. She was the first wife of William Duncan (see 4).

10. Louisa Hume, married Mr. Finks, of Virginia. Two children.

1. Early Finks.
2. Louisa Finks.

2. William Hume, died about 1822 or 3, leaving a widow, Sarah Ann, who died about 1841. Their children:

1. Sarah Ann Hume; will bears date March 21, 1826, probated Oct. 2, 1826.
2. William Hume.
3. Mary Hume.
4. Simeon Hume, married Margaret F. Harris, daughter of Robert Harris and Jael Ellison, his wife. (See Part 3, Chap. 21.) The inventory and appraisement of his estate is dated Feb. 14, 1845.
5. Gabriel Hume; will dated April 7, 1829, probated Aug. 31, 1829..
6. Thomas Hume.
7. Jane Hume.
8. Nancy Hume.
9. Betsy Hume.
10. Eliza Hume.

3. Benjamin Hume's inventory, returned in 1822.

4. Reuben Hume, wife Ann.
Lewis Hume.
George Hume.
John Hume.
Joel Hume.

The above named five were evidently brothers. The first four named made deeds to Joel Hume.

5. Susan E. Hume: married Zacheus Taylor, Dec. 13, 1830.

The children of Susannah Miller and Stanton Hume are named in the coming sections:

Section 1. Julia Anderson Hume, a daughter, born in Madison County, Feb. 13, 1823; was an energetic, stirring, business woman, a splendid manager and beautiful housekeeper and much admired by the relatives and friends; was of a very amiable and lovely disposition and ever generous to the faults of others, and of a forgiving spirit. She was married to Thomas Stanhope Ellis (born 1819, died Dec. 26, 1905), a gentleman of splendid habits and business qualities. For a number of years his occupation was that of a farmer, but for a long while a merchant, doing business at different times in Elliston, Waco, Richmond, and Silver Creek, in said county.

They were both members of the old Baptist Church. Mrs. Ellis died in 1903, her husband surviving; now (1905) living in Richmond; since died, Dec. 26, 1905, born 1819. The children born to them were:

1. Susan Elizabeth Ellis, born April 7, 1844; married John A. Higgins, March 1, 1870, a merchant of Richmond, Ky., and a staunch Presbyterian. Issue:
   1. Julia Higgins, a spinster.
2. Sallie Gunnel Ellis, born Dec. 12, 1850. Teacher for a number of years in the Deaf and Dumb Institution at Danville.
3. Mary Stanton Ellis, born July 4, 1854; married Oct. 6, 1886, to Rev. H. T. Daniel. Her husband died several years ago. She has a position in the Deaf and Dumb Institution at Danville, Ky.
4. Helen Carter Ellis, born March 3, 1869; died 18—.

Section 2. Margaret Miller Hume, a daughter, born Aug. 27, 1825; died December 5, 1829, very young.

Section 3. Susan Jane Hume, a daughter, born July 6, 1828; died Jan. 4, 1890; married to John H. Embry Jan. 9, 1850; lived a while in Madison County, Ky., and moved to Missouri, where they lived a number of years, and returned to and settled in Madison County, where they spent the remainder of their days. Mr. Embry was a hightoned honorable gentleman and farmer. They raised a family of ten children:

1. Mary Embry, born Oct. 12, 1850; unmarried. She and her single sister Sue have a home in Elliston, Madison County, Ky.
2. Jos. Hume Embry, born Jan. 9, 1852; died a bachelor, 18—.
3. Nannie W. Embry, born April 3, 1853; married William T. Griggs. Issue:
   1. Paul Sparks Griggs.
   2. Joel Taylor Griggs.
   3. John Embry Griggs.
   4. William Hume Griggs. (3 and 4 are twins.)
4. William S. Embry, born Oct. 27, 1854; died a bachelor.
5. Sue E. Embry, born Sept. 11, 1856. She and her sister Mary live together in Elliston.
6. Lucy D. Embry, born July 8, 1858; married Joel Park. (See Part VI, Chap. 8, Sec. 9.)
7. John T. Embry, born March 28, 1860; married Bessie Broaddus, and his wife died, leaving one child. (See Part VII, Chap. 7, Sec. 3.)
8. George Webb Embry, born Oct. 10, 1861; died a bachelor.
9. Irvine Miller Embry, born April 6, 1865; died April 17, 1865.
10. Ed S. Embry, born April 6, 1867; died Feb. 3, 1889.
11. Frank S. Embry, born Oct. 17, 1869; died.

Mrs. Embry was a member of the old Baptist Church.

Section 4. William Stanton Hume, a son, born Sept. 4, 1832; died Sept. 12, 1885; was an active man; married Miss Eugenia Burnam, accumulated a considerable estate, and died; his widow survives. To them were born:

1. John M. Hume, born April 4, 1858; died April 19, 1858.
2. Thompson Burnam Hume, born March 31, 1859; died November 29, 1859.
3. Edmund B. Hume, born Nov. 21, 1860; married Oct. 2, 1888, to Nettie Stockton; residents of Richmond, Ky.
4. Stanton B. Hume, born Aug. 26, 1863; married Oct. 8, 1889, to Pattie Miller. His widow lives in Richmond, Ky.
5. Curtis B. Hume, born Aug. 6, 1869; married Rella Harber.

7. Mary Wilson Hume, born July 7, 1872; married Harvey Chenault, a prosperous farmer, living near Richmond, Ky. (See Part V, Chap. 13, Sec. 9.)

8. Eugene F. Hume, born Sept. 23, 1876.

9. Sue Miller Hume, born Nov. 29, 1880; married Lewis Herrington; live in Richmond, Ky.

Section 5. Mary Louise Hume, a daughter, born May 9, 1839; died March 8, 1879; married Thomas J. McRoberts, a substantial business man of Boyle County, a large landholder, farmer and capitalist; one of the wealthiest men of Boyle County, now deceased. Their children:

1. William Hume McRoberts, born June 26, 1863; died Feb. 7, 1867.

2. Mary Margaret McRoberts, born July 4, 1865; died 19—.

3. Thomas Eugene McRoberts, born March 10, 1868; died Aug. 8, 1868.

4. John Robert McRoberts, born Feb. 25, 1870.

5. George Andrew McRoberts, born Nov. 20, 1871.

6. Susan Elizabeth McRoberts, born June 11, 1874; married Lewis N. Neale, of Madison County, Ky. They bought a fine, rich farm near Richmond, on which they now live. To them has been born one child:

1. Lewis Newland Neale, Jr.

CHAPTER 10.

MARGARET MILLER.

(Named in Chapter 5, Section 7.)

Article 1.—Margaret Miller, a daughter of Daniel Miller and Susannah Woods, his wife, was born in Madison County Ky., December 29, 1805 (to January 15, 1873).

MARGARET MILLER
Wife of E. L. Shackleford

She was a good woman in every sense of the word; a consistent member of the Presbyterian Church. February 9, 1826, she was united in marriage to Edmund L. Shackelford (born March 26, 1802; died April 21, 1876), an elegant gentleman and man of affairs, who studied law and was admitted to the bar in his young manhood; he afterwards abandoned the practice. For a number of years was Cashier of the Richmond Branch of the Northern Bank of Kentucky. After the Civil War, in 1865, he moved to Danville, Kentucky, where they spent the rest of their days. Their remains lie in the Richmond Cemetery.

Edmund Lyne Shackelford was a native born Kentuckian; his parents, however, came from Virginia to the State: he was a very estimable citizen and gentleman of great integrity, wholly devoted to duty, to his church, to his family, to his friends, to his county, and to his business; he commanded the respect of every one with whom he came in contact. The bank of Richmond, of which he was so long cashier, had its building on the corner of Main and Third streets, now the restaurant of Joe Giunchigliani; when he left in 1865 the county lost one of its best citizens. He died in Danville April 21, 1876; his remains were brought to Richmond and buried in the cemetery there, his wife having died January 15, 1873; her remains had been also interred in the same place.

EDMUND L. SHACKLEFORD

In Memoriam: Died in Danville, Ky., January 15, 1873. Mrs. Margaret Shackelford, wife of Edmund L. Shackelford, Esq., in the 68th year of her age. Mrs. Shackelford was the daughter of Major Daniel Miller, and was born in Madison County, Ky., December 29, 1805, and there lived till the autumn of 1865, when her husband removed his family to Danville to assume the duties of Cashier of the First National Bank. She was married on the 6th day of February, 1826; so that she lived with her husband for the unusual period of almost forty-seven years. Though the mother of eight children, she was permitted to see but three of them grow up to manhood or womanhood. These, one son and two married daughters, together with their venerable father, now mourn the loss of her—a loss felt all the more, especially by the latter, because they had so long traveled life's journey in company. Her sickness was of only four days' duration. Pneumonia, that dire enemy of the feeble and the aged, often completes its work of death with startling rapidity. Owing to the nature of her disease, and the suffering it induced, she was able to commune but little with her family or friends these few last days. What counsels she might otherwise have given them, or what expression of her religious feelings she might have made, we cannot tell. But the evidence of her piety and of a good hope through grace of a blessed immortality were not left to depend upon the experiences of the last hour. A life of faith and charity such as hers, is a testimony to be valued above all others. "Not every one that saith unto me, Lord, Lord, shall enter into the kingdom of heaven, but he that doeth the will of my Father which is in heaven." Mrs. Shackelford made a public profession of faith in Christ and united with the Presbyterian Church at Richmond, in the spring of 1864, and her walk proved her a follower of "the Son of Man who came not to be ministered unto but to minister and to give his life a ransom for many." Of Jesus of Nazareth, whom God anointed with the Holy Ghost, it is said, as we may say of no other, "He went about doing good," Yet, in a real, though an inferior sense, we may safely predicate the same of His departed hand-maiden. And though she could not, like Him, "heal all manner of sickness and all manner of disease among the people," she had the mind of Christ to minister according to her ability. This distinguishing trait of her character was admirably presented by her pastor, the Rev. Dr. McKee, in a most appropriate funeral discourse from these words, "For David after he had served his own generation by the will of God fell on sleep." Acts 13:36. Verily she did serve her generation. She served her family, her kindred, and the community where she lived, with a self-denial and a continuance in well-doing rarely equaled and still more rarely surpassed. Quiet and unostentatious in all her ways, she abounded in those tender ministries of love which are the true glory of Christian women. The sick, the poor, the distressed of all classes shared in her kind and unremitting charities. The writer of this brief tribute to her worth hath abundant reason to cherish her memory, and to speak of her goodness. He can never forget her attentions to the sick and dying of his own household, while he yet had a household; how her gentle voice and hands ministered to the comfort of his most beloved; how she watched with him and his children during the weary hours of night, when the life of the patient sufferer seemed fast ebbing away. In like manner could many others bear witness to her modest goodness. But the end hath come—the end of her serving. She resteth from her labors and her works do follow her. "Well done, thou good and faithful servant, enter thou into the joy of the Lord." And in that august day when the Son of Man shall sit upon the throne of his glory, and all nations be gathered before him, who fitter than thou to stand among them on his right hand and to hear the King say: "Come, ye blessed of my Father, inherit the kingdom prepared for you from the foundation of the world: for I was an hungered and ye gave me meat;

was thirsty and ye gave me drink; I was a stranger and ye took me in; naked and ye clothed me; I was sick and ye visited me; I was in prison and ye came unto me?"

But though it be well with her, there is another desolate home on earth. Heavy sorrow weighs down the spirits of the bereaved, though they sorrow not as those who have no hope. The loss of a mother, of such a mother, is an irreparable loss. The loneliness of him, who for almost half a century had her by his side as a sweet companion and faithful helper, none can fully realize, but those of a like experience. The desire of his eyes, the wife of his youth, has been taken from him in his old age. It is a dreadful stroke. The God of all consolation comfort these mourning hearts and give them grace to follow her even as she followed Christ. S. G.

Edmund Lyne Shackelford, the husband of Margaret Miller, and John H. Shackelford, who married Malinda Miller (see Chap. 11), were sons of George Shackelford and Martha Hockaday, his wife, who emigrated from Virginia to Kentucky. George Shackelford was a son of Lyne Shackelford and Elizabeth Taliaferro, his wife. Lyne Shackelford was a son of John Shackelford and Miss Lyne, his wife, and John Shackelford was a son of James Shackelford. Martha Hockaday was a daughter of Edmund Hockaday and Martha Otey, his wife, and Edmund Hockaday was a son of Edmund Hockaday.

To Margaret Miller and Edmund Lyne Shackelford were born:

Section 1. Martha Hockaday Shackelford, born Dec. 20, 1827; died Sept. 12, 1829.

Section 2. Mary Juliett Shackelford, born May 18, 1831; died March 18, 1833.

Section 3. Susan Frances Shackelford, born July 24, 1834; married Sidney V. Rowland, an elegant man, Feb. 22, 1853. She being a lovely woman with a bright, cheerful disposition. Lived in Richmond a number of years and moved to Danville, where they spent the latter years of their life. To them were born:

1. Edmund Shackelford Rowland, born Dec. 1, 1853; died Jan. 20, 1854.
2. William Shackelford Rowland, born March 7, 1855; married, first, Mary Bowman: they had two children, Hugh and Mary. He married his second wife, Miss McDowell.
3. David Pitman Rowland, born June 27, 1857; married, April 12, 1882, to Lizzie Lee. (See Part I, Chap. 6, Sec. 1.)
4. Edmund Lyne Rowland, born Jan. 17, 1860; married, May 30, 1882, Miss Bryant.
5. Hugh Goddin Rowland, born July 4,1861; died Dec. 13,1874.
6. Margaret Shackelford Rowland, born Jan. 4, 1864; married, Feb. 18, 1885, to Stephen B. White. They are both dead; left two children.

Section 4. William Henry Shackelford, a son, died in infancy in 1840.

Section 5. A son, not named, died in infancy, June 8, 1840.

Section 6. Edmund Lyne Shackelford, a son, born March, 1842. died Sept. 1, 1880; was a merchant of Richmond a long while. He never married. When his parents moved to Danville he stayed there much of his time, but would never surrender his home at Richmond, always claiming it as his home, where he invariably cast his vote, and not elsewhere. He died in Danville, Sept. 1, 1880, at the age of thirty-eight years and six months, and his body buried in the

Richmond cemetery. He had many warm personal friends, was kind-hearted, liberal and true, and known for his strict honesty.

Section 7. Margaret Miller Shackelford, born May 6, 1844; died June 19, 1874; married Robert Hann, Feb. 18, 1868. Her remains were buried in the Richmond cemetery. She was, indeed, a lovely character. Their children:

1. Edmund Lyne Hann, born March 5, 1869.
2. Alexander Robertson Hann, born April 29, 1872.

Section 8. Juliette Malinda Shackelford, a daughter, died young, in 1849—32 months old.

CHAPTER 11.

MALINDA MILLER.

(Named in Chapter 5, Section 8.)

Article 1.—Malinda Miller, a daughter of Daniel Miller and Susannah Woods, his wife, was born in Madison County, Kentucky, January 15, 1808.

JOHN H. SHACKLEFORD

She was a charming woman, and, as it is told, a favorite of her father. December 16, 1830, she was joined in marriage to John H. Shackelford (a brother to Edmund L. Shackelford, who had married her sister Margaret). He was born August 29, 1803; died March 22, 1875. See Chap. 10. He was a gentleman of splendid breeding, to whom her father had no personal objection, only he did not wish for his daughter to marry any one. She died, her husband surviving, leaving two little sons, who were reared, in the main, by their Aunt Margaret, who became as a mother to them. Mrs. Malinda Shackelford was a very stylish, graceful and beautiful woman. Their children:

Section 1. George Daniel Shackelford, born September 22, 1831; died June 28, 1874; married Ruth Warfield, whom he survived, and then he married Elizabeth Sweeney, January 6, 1857. He was a Confederate soldier, served in General Price's army and was wounded in battle. After he retired from the army he came to Richmond, Ky., where he engaged in the dry goods business. In 1870 he was elected Clerk of the Madison County Court on the Democratic ticket, dying in office, June 28, 1874. His brother James, under appointment, filled his unexpired term of about two months, giving the emoluments to his widow. The writer was Deputy during his entire term, except one year. George D. Shackelford was big-hearted, brave and generous, and loved his friends, and his friends were fond of him. The children of the last marriage were:

1. Linda Shackelford, born Dec. 23, 1857; died May 28, 1860.
2. Sweeny Shackelford, born Dec. 13, 1859; died Jan. 28, 1863.
3. Edmund Lyne Shackelford, born Jan. 29, 1862; killed mysteriously in St. Louis, Mo., Sept. 17, 1885.

MALINDA MILLER

4. Laura Shackelford, born July 16, 1864; married L. Rutherford Blanton, now a large coal dealer of Richmond, Kentucky. Children:
   1. Lindsey Blanton.
   2. George Daniel Blanton.
5. A daughter, born Nov. 28, 1866; died the next day.
6. A daughter, born May 22, 1861; died the next day.

Section 2. James Thomas Shackelford, born June 2, 1834, a prominent citizen mainly of Madison County, but having spent part of his early life in other places; a merchant and farmer. He filled the unexpired term of his brother George as Clerk, turning the proceeds over to his brother's widow. He was clerk in the Revenue office under Chas. H. Rodes, Collector, and continued on under Mr. Rodes' successor, Mr. John W. Yerkes, whilst at Richmond and after the office was moved to Danville, some seven or eight years in the Revenue service, and made an honest and faithful officer. A short while before his death, having sold a farm high up on Silver Creek, he purchased another nice farm lower down on the same creek, and was making preparations to enter actively into the farming business when suddenly stricken with paralysis, from which he could never rally, and quickly passed away (1904), honored, respected and admired by his fellows. He was a large, portly man, true as steel to a friend, to whom he would stick closer than a brother. He first married, Jan. 22, 1862, Mary Bates, daughter of Daniel Bates, and second, Mary Clay Keene, Jan. 20, 1869. (See Part II, Chap. 5, Sec. 1.) Issue of the first marriage:

1. Daniel Bates Shackelford, born April 4, 1863. He is the leading hardware merchant of Richmond, Ky., successor to his father in the business. He married Callie Chenault. (See Chap. 14, Sec. 2, and Part III, Chap. 48, Sec. 8.) Issue:
   1. Mary Bates Shackelford.
   2. Callie Miller Shackelford.
   3. Elizabeth Shackelford.
2. James Thomas Shackelford, born March 8, 1865; died July 23, 1866.

Issue of the second marriage:

3. William Rodes Shackelford, born October 26, 1869. He is a prominent lawyer of the Richmond bar. He is to be married, Jan. 29, 1907, to Anne Louise Clay, daughter of Hon. Cassius M. Clay, of Bourbon County, Ky. The marriage occurred as appointed. They live in Richmond, Ky. Mr. Shackelford is a Democratic candidate for County Judge, with flattering prospects of success.
4. Clay Keene Shackelford, born October 8, 1871; a resident of Richmond, Ky.
5. John Hockaday Shackelford, born Dec. 2, 1873. He is a rising man in the railroad business. He is very energetic.
6. Sarah Keene Shackelford, born Sept. 16, 1875; living with her mother in Richmond, Ky.
7. George Daniel Shackelford, born July 26, 1878; died March 29, 1886.
8. James Thomas Shackelford, Jr., born Dec. 20, 1880.
9. Mary Keene Shackelford, born Dec. 19, 1882; married George W. Goodloe, son of Judge John D. Goodloe, of Madison County, Ky. After the birth of the first and only child she died, and her death was greatly lamented by many relatives and friends. The child survived a short while and died. These deaths occurred in 1906.
10. A daughter, born and died Nov. 19, 1885.

CHAPTER 12.

COLONEL THOMAS WOODS MILLER.

(Named in Chapter 5, Section 9.)

Article 1.—Colonel Thomas Woods Miller, a son of Daniel Miller and Susannah Woods, his wife, was born in Madison County, Ky., the 3d day of December 1811; died April 23, 1891.

THOS. WOODS MILLER

His appearance in the world made it none the worse. He was never very robust, upwards of six feet and slender, a man and a gentleman, of fine carriage, tall, erect, respected by all, admired by many: a stranger to fear, honest and faithful in every trust; public spirited, favorable to every needful public and private improvement; an affectionate and good husband, a kind and indulgent father; a friend and helper of those who needed help. He married in Madison County, Ky., June 1, 1841, to Mary Jane Hocker, a daughter of Colonel Nicholas Hocker and Nancy Ellison, his wife. (See Part VII, Chap. 7, Sec. 1-4.) She was born Feb. 21, 1825; died 1905. He lived till about the year 1864 in the eastern part of Madison County, on Muddy Creek, and there had erected two nice, commodious dwelling houses, and was an extensive farmer during the time, when he moved to Stanford, Lincoln County, and there engaged in merchandising, in which he was successful, and there he spent the remainder of his days, and was the last survivor of his father's children. He was no drawback to any community; aided much in the growth of his town, where he built several substantial business houses and residences. He died there in 1891, survived by his wife, who had been afflicted nearly all of their married life. She died in 1905. He was a Colonel of Kentucky Militia. Only one child was born to them:

MARY JANE HOCKER
Wife of Thos. Woods Miller

Section 1. Susan Malinda Miller, a charming Christian woman, whom every one knew only to love, was born May 27, 1742. Married, October 15, 1861, to John Samuel Owsley, a substantial farmer of Walnut Flat, Lincoln County, Ky., of a historic family, who was born Oct. 3, 1840. Mrs. Owsley died Oct. 15, 1888, leaving these children:

1. Mary Eliza Owsley, born Dec. 25, 1864; married Nov. 1, 1883, to William Rucker Manier, of Nashville, Tenn. Issue:

1. William R. Manier, Jr., born Jan. 3, 1885.
2. John Owsley Manier, born March 18, 1887.
3. Mary Malinda Manier, born March 31, 1891.
4. Thomas Miller Manier, born Jan. 15, 1897.

2. John Samuel Owsley, Jr., attorney-at-law of Stanford, Ky.; one time Commonwealth's Attorney; born Jan. 20, 1867; married April 26, 1894, Miss Ella McElwain, of Franklin, Ky. Issue:

1. James McElwain Owsley, born Feb. 7, 1895.

3. Mattie Woods Owsley, born June 13, 1869; married, June 18, 1895, to W. P. Walton, who came from Virginia, an editor. Now residents of Lexington, Ky. Issue:

1. W. P. Walton, Jr., born May 14, 1896.
2. Miller Owsley Walton, born April 3, 1898.
3. Mary Miller Walton, born June 7, 1902.

4. Margaret Susan Owsley, born July 10, 1871; married, Dec. 31, 1896, to J. S. Wells, a druggist merchant of Danville, Ky. Issue:

1. Mary Manier Wells, born June 15, 1898.
2. Margaret Owsley Wells, born Feb. 12, 1903.
3. John Samuel Wells, born Jan. 3, 1905.

5. Malinda Owsley, born Aug. 19, 1873.

6. Thomas Miller Owsley, born April 2, 1875; married Jan. 15, 1903, to Miss Katherine McGoodwin, of Bowling Green. Mr. Owsley is a prominent attorney-at-law at Bowling Green. Issue:

1. Virginia McGoodwin Owsley, born Oct. 18, 1903.

7. Emma McGehee Owsley, born Aug. 8, 1877.

8. Michael Owsley, born June 20, 1881.

CHAPTER 13.

COLONEL CHRISTOPHER IRVINE MILLER.

(Named in Chapter 5, Section 10.)

Article 1.—Colonel Christopher Irvine Miller, a son and youngest child of Daniel Miller and Susannah Woods, his wife, was born near the mouth of Hickory Lick, a branch of Muddy Creek, at his parents' home, December 20, 1813.

CHRISTOPHER I. MILLER

He was upwards of six feet and weighed two hundred pounds. He was joined in marriage, by Elder Allen Embry, an old Baptist preacher, September 1, 1836, to Talitha Harris, a daughter of Christopher Harris and Sallie Wallace, his wife (see Part III, Chap. 30), the marriage occurring at the home of the bride's parents. Of this union eleven children were born, ten of whom were raised to maturity. He was a Colonel of Kentucky Militia; often issued the three days' notices to the militia to attend the regimental and battalion drills.

Christopher Irvine Miller was very fond of company and greatly enjoyed the presence of friends. Until age crept upon him, he enjoyed the sports of hunting, such as deer, birds, etc., and fishing, and so long as deer remained plentiful in the Kentucky mountains, he would set apart a week or two of every fall which he would spend in this enjoyment—he was a crack shot with the rifle and shot gun. No one pitted against him would return in the evening with more game in the bag than he. Many a long winter night at home by a bright wood fire in the presence of the family and others have we listened without tiring or getting sleepy to his hunting stories, which, if printed as told by him, would be good reading. He was full of humor.

TALTHIA HARRIS
Wife of Christopher I. Miller

No one had a kinder heart or cherished his friends more than did he, and nearly every one were fond of Irvine Miller. His enemies were few and far between.

He was a farmer and upon his farm, near his dwelling, he built a blacksmith shop, which was provided with everything that was in that day considered necessary and convenient for the operation of a first class shop—including a goodly supply of the best of tools of every sort and size; his edged tools always found to be sharp and in splendid condition, and he knew how to use them; he was a first class mechanic and could make anything from a needle or fish-hook to a wagon or plow. He never half-way did anything; he went on the principle that if a thing was worth doing at all it was worth doing well. His customers, who were many, not only in his own, but in adjoining counties, had the utmost confidence in him, not only in his work, but in his word, for his word was his bond and his work was his reward. He was a hard and constant worker and the greatest recreation he enjoyed was when on his hunting trips and an occasional outing, fishing in Station Camp Creek, or attending his church meetings. He operated his shop actively until just a few years before his death, then being physically unable to do so. His shop was known not only over the county, but adjoining counties. His work had a high reputation. He shod mules by the hundreds for the Southern market which were in those days driven through to market. He manufactured plows, wagons and all sorts of farming utensils, did an immense amount of horse shoeing. His celebrated turning plow, known as the "Miller Plow," was at that time the best plow made, and on many occasions given the premium over all other competitors at the fairs, and had a famous reputation and ready sale fast as made.

For many years before his death he and his wife were consistent and beloved members of the old Baptist Church at Flatwoods.

He was beloved, honored and respected by all who knew him, and at his death, which occurred October 14, 1878, at his Muddy Creek home, many relatives and friends mourned and lamented. He was much missed by his neighborhood for years thereafter. His sufferings, trials and labors have ceased and he is at perfect rest in the presence of his Maker and Redeemer.

His remains were placed under the sod in the burying plot near and in front of the residence on the farm lately owned and occupied by the late Elder John M. Park, and stone properly inscribed marks the grave. His children will cherish his memory as long as they live.

His wife, Talitha Harris, was born at the home of her parents on Muddy Creek, in said county of Madison, March 17, 1815. She survived from the death of her husband until January 2, 1882, when she passed from time to eternity, this event occurring at the home of her daughter, Susannah Hume, on Muddy Creek. She had not been strong and well for several years, was very sick sometime before her death. She did not fear to meet death, had abiding faith and trust in her Savior. She and her husband became members of the Flatwood Church at the same time.

She possessed a strong mind, good judgment, open and free speech; what she had to say she said it, in plain words, without deceit. Was admired by all her acquaintances. What she said and did was in the open, unhidden. She was very industrious and no woman could accomplish more with her hands in the same time than she. She was beneficent and kind, big-hearted, a loving and true wife, a good mother. She is now asleep in Jesus. It seems hard to be separated from so good a mother, but the will of God be done. How consoling to know that her troubles are ended, with the comfortable hope that she enjoys the sweet rest of that heavenly home of which she so sweetly and calmly spoke just before her departure. Her remains lie under the sod by the side of her husband's.

Mrs. Charles (Mary Miller) Stephens, of Paris, Ky., a daughter of General John Miller, writes that her "father and his brothers were well educated," and speaks of their beautiful hand-writing, and says: "I remember dear Uncle Irvine, too, wrote a beautiful hand. I think he was one of the gentlest, loveliest men I ever knew. Really we love and honor the memories of all our uncles and aunts. They were a remarkable family, and we honor our wise grandparents. Aunt Talitha, I remember, was one of the most genial, hospitable persons I ever knew, and so kind and sympathetic with children. She took me home with her once when I was a little girl—rode behind her on horseback—and in the evening Uncle Irvine would take the violin from its box and play the jolliest dance music, and you boys and girls and ourselves would have a happy time—your mother sitting by and enjoying it all. I recall many happy pictures of my childhood."

In 1846 C. I. Miller qualified as Deputy Sheriff for Jacob S. White, Sheriff of Madison County, Ky.

Accounts of their children are given in the coming sections: Nos. 1 to 11 inclusive:

Section 1. Sarah Wallace Miller, a daughter and first born, was born at home on Drowning Creek, June 7, 1837; was joined in marriage, June 5, 1856, by Elder John M. Park, an old Baptist preacher, to Stanton Hume Thorpe, at the home of her parents on Muddy Creek. She died May 27, 1897, survived by her husband, who lived a few years and died. The fruits of this union were ten children:

1. Amelia Nash Thorpe, born May 4, 1857; married William Joseph Wagers, Jan. 11, 1877, a Muddy Creek farmer. To them was born one child:

   1. James Wagers, now a young man and Deputy Clerk of the Madison Circuit Court.

2. Thomas Miller Thorpe, born Jan. 30, 1859; married Bettie Bonney; died leaving a widow and these children:

   1. William Thorpe.
   2. Hume Thorpe.
   3. Nathan C. Thorpe.
   4. Sallie Thorpe.
   5. Eliza Miller Thorpe.

   Thomas Miller Thorpe died leaving his wife surviving.

3. George Hume Thorpe, born Jan. 31, 1861; married Mrs. Bettie Thorpe, nee Bonney, widow of his brother, Thomas Miller Thorpe. No issue.

4. Christopher Irvine Thorpe, born May 31, 1863; died Jan. 12, 1864.

5. Stanton Hume Thorpe, born Dec. 10, 1864; married Henrietta Rayburn. Served two years as Clerk of the Madison Circuit Court, defeating his uncle, Will Miller, for the nomination, and for whom he had been deputy. Issue:

   1. Cecil Thorpe.

6. Robert Daniel Thorpe, born April 29, 1866. Single.

7. Hugh Thorpe, born Feb. 20, 1868; died March 12, 1890.

8. John Harris Thorpe, born May 2, 1872; married Kate McCord. She died leaving her husband and two children:

   1. Hugh Miller Thorpe.
   2. John Harris Thorpe.

9. Woods Thorpe, born May 4, 1875; died Oct. 30, 1876.

10. Sallie Elizabeth Thorpe, born Nov. 16, 1877; married Richard Cobb, a livery man of Richmond, Ky. Their children:

   1. Tabitha Park Cobb.
   2. Jesse Cobb.

Section 2. Robert Daniel Miller, a son, second child, born at home on Drowning Creek, March 1, 1839. He espoused the cause of the South in the Civil War of 1862 and enlisted in the Confederate Army, Chenault's Regiment, under the command of Gen. John H. Morgan. In the summer or early fall of 1862 he, with two companies of Confederate soldiers, under the temporary command of Capt. Jesse, proceeded from Tennessee to Central Kentucky, and on Monday, September 8, 1862, they came in contact with about 1,000 Federal soldiers in ambush on the top of Pine Mountain. Volley after volley of the enemy's balls was poured into them, killing and wounding several of the company, and killing nearly all their horses, and completely routing the little band, running them pell-mell over the rugged cliffs and declivities of the mountain. In the skirmish Miller's horse was shot and killed from under him, but he, with Harris Thorpe, Scott Stivers, —— Stevens and two Owen County men, his comrades in arms, made temporarily their escape. But the topography of the country, strange to them, wild and mountainous, alive with Federal soldiers and buskwackers, and becoming very much fatigued, almost starved, and seeing no possible way of getting safely out, they very wisely concluded to, and did on the following Wednesday, surrender to the home guards, and were paroled. Miller then remained with, and as best he could, ministered to the wants and comforts of his uncle, John Harris, who had been fatally shot in the battle, until his death, which occurred in a few days. He then attended to and saw that his remains were buried in as decent a manner as possible under the existing circumstances. Thereupon, he returned home, where he remained about two weeks, when under exchange, he re-entered the Confederate service, under the gallant and intrepid Gen. John H. Morgan; was engaged in many daring and rapid raids, and several severe conflicts; was again captured in General Morgan's famous raid into the States of Indiana and Ohio, and carried as a prisoner of war to Camp Morton, near Indianapolis, Indiana. In his removal from there to the Federal Prison, Camp Douglas, at Chicago, he made good his escape by jumping from the train of cars on which the prisoners were aboard, and made his way under difficulties, back to Madison County, Kentucky, which at that time was in complete possession of the Federal forces. Arriving at home late one rainy night, thinly clad, food and raiment were furnished him by his good mother, when he immediately retired to a thicket on the place, not even daring to take shelter under the parental roof, for fear of being recaptured by the enemy and endangering the safety of the liberty or lives of his father and mother, and being himself disposed of as a spy. Remaining concealed on the place for about a week, he left and went, accompanied by a friend, through the country to Paris, Ky., and there boarded a train of cars and was carried by railroad speed to the State of Minnesota, and there engaged in work for a time, until the opportunity presented itself, when he joined a company or wagon train, backed by Federal troops and crossed the Western plains to the territory of Idaho, the Indians of the section through which they traveled then being on the war path, and causing much trouble to the government, having several fights with the Indians on the way. He remained in the territories of Idaho and Montana, engaged in prospecting and mining for gold, until the year 1867, when he returned to the home of his parents.

During his absence from home he had been exposed to many dangers and hardships; he remained at home something like a year, and then went and located at Goodland, Newton County, Ind., about the first of 1868. The next year, towards its close, he returned to Madison County, Kentucky, and on December 22, 1869, was married to Susan J. Barrett, a daughter of Francis Barnett and Miranda Duncan his wife (who were married Sept. 26, 1844), at the residence of Coleman Covington, on Muddy Creek, by Elder John M. Park, an old Baptist preacher. Then he and his bride left for their home at Goodland, where they lived until the year 1876, when they returned to near Earl Park, Benton County, Indiana, a distance less than half a days' horseback ride from the spot where he made his escape from the Federal soldiers. He lived at near Earl Park for a number of years and then went with his family to Denver, Colorado, where his wife died. His wife was born March 20, 1857, and was killed by an accident on an elevator in Denver, Colorado, a number of years since.

He now lives in Woodward County, Oklahoma, about eleven miles from a little place called Doris, where he has entered and staked a claim for 160 acres of land, upon which he has lived for four years, being required by the Government to occupy the same five years before perfecting his title to the land. Their children:

1. Laura Frances Miller, born Oct. 3, 1870; married J. W. Horstman, of Denver, Colorado.

2. Miranda Matilda Miller, born Nov. 27, 1871; married E. P. Worcester; they live in Des Moines, Iowa. Their children:

   1. Earl Worcester.
   2. Irene Worcester.
   3. Eugene Worcester.

3. Talitha Ann Eliza Miller, born Nov. 29, 1873; died ———.

4. Eddie Lyon Shackelford Miller, born Jan. 19, 1895; died Sept. 3, 1896.

5. Susan Robert Miller, born Jan. 9, 1877, married J. D. Wilmot, of Denver, Colorado.

6. A daughter, Susannah, born Aug. 23, 1879; died Sept. 6, 1879.

7. Christopher Irvine Miller, born April 6, 1882; a railroad man of Denver, Colorado.

8. Leah Miller, the youngest, now living in Denver, Colorado.

Section 3. James Christopher Miller, a son, was born at the John Blanton House, on Downing Creek, Sept. 3, 1841. He favored the cause of the South and joined the Confederate army, Chenault's Regiment, under the command of General John H. Morgan, in the late Civil War of 1862. In that noted raid of the daring Morgan into the States of Indiana and Ohio, in which his men were in the saddle twenty-odd days without sleep, only what they got on the backs of their horses; he was captured at Cheshire, O., and taken as a prisoner of war, first to the Federal prison in Camp Chase, and there in that filthy place confined for a time; from there removed to Camp Douglas, at Chicago, where he remained in prison for eighteen months. When all hope for the success of the Southern cause was exploded, by taking the oath of allegiance to the Federal Government, he was released from prison and came home. When the rights of suffrage, which was taken from the Confederates, as rebels, was finally restored, through the efforts of such men as Gen. Frank Wolford, his first attempt to vote was under the bayonet, and the officers of the election refused him a vote, which the courts upheld.

During his service in the army he was in many bold raids under his noted leader, engaged in several battles, and exposed to all the dangers and hardships incident to such service.

Having learned under his father before entering the war, the trade of a blacksmith when he came home he followed that as an occupation until his marriage. After that event he followed farming some years, when he moved to Northern Indiana, Newton, County, where he lived a time and then came back to Madison County, Ky., and engaged again in blacksmithing, following the same for several years. He tired of that and began farming once more. He now lives on the old farm where his father lived and died.

September 22, 1869, he was joined in marriage to Mrs. Elizabeth S. Rayburn, widow of John Rayburn, deceased, and daughter of Wilson C. N. Broaddas, by Elder John M. Park, at her late home on Upper Muddy Creek. She was a descendant of the old Virginia family set forth in the attached Notes of the Broaddus family. James C. Miller and his wife are both members of the Old Baptist Church. To them were born these children:

1. Elizabeth Susan Miller, born August 27, 1870; married William Edgar Blanton, proprietor of a large lumber mill and plant in Richmond, Ky. Their children:
    1. Elizabeth Blanton.
    2. Edgar Blanton.
    3. Emmet Blanton.
    4. Susan Shackelford Blanton.
    5. Camilla Blanton.
    6. James Edgar Blanton.
2. Talitha Harris Miller, born Dec. 5, 1891; died Aug. 5, 1873.
3. James Christopher Miller, born Dec. 19, 1873, married Anna Bluez. They live at Almira, State of Washington. He is a farmer. Their children:
    1. Nannie Caroline Miller, born Nov. 11, 1902.
    2. Jesse Bluez Miller, born Dec. 28, 1904.
    3. Elizabeth Miller.
4. Mary Eliza Miller, born Aug. 5, 1880; teacher in Caldwell High School, of Richmond, Ky., and musician; married, June, 1907, to William E. Gilkeson, a coal operator and promoter, located at Blanch, Belle County, Ky.; the marriage took place at the writer's residence in Richmond, Ky., and was solemnized by Elder Charles H. Waters, of Maryland.
5. Katie Wilson Miller, born May 28, 1885; holds a first-class certificate of qualification to teach the public schools of Kentucky.

Note: The Broaddus Family.

Edward Broaddus emigrated from Wales in the early part of the eighteenth century and settled on Gwynn's Island, in the Pianki-Tank River, near its junction with the Rappahannock. In 1715 he moved to Caroline County (then King and Queen), where he resided till his death. He was twice married. The name of his first wife has not been handed down; his second wife was Mary Shipley. His descendants are scattered over Virginia, Kentucky and elsewhere. The children of his first marriage were:

1. Thomas Broaddus, was a Revolutionary soldier: lived and died in Caroline County at the age of 70 years. He married Ann Redd, who lived to be 96 years old. Their children:
    1. Edward Oldham, married Miss Brown.
    2. Thomas Broaddus, died at 83 years of age. He married, first, Martha Jones, of Essex County, and second, Miss Watkins.

3. Shildrake Broaddus, married Mary Ann Pankey.
4. Mordecai Broaddus, married Martha Reynolds.
5. John Broaddus, married America Broaddus, a daughter of Robin Broaddus.
6. Richard Broaddus, married Mrs. Jeter.
7. Redd Broaddus.
8. Catherine Broaddus, married Edwin Mobley.
9. Elizabeth Broaddus, married Golden Puller.
10. Ann Broaddus, married Captain Robert Sale.
11. Sarah Broaddus.

2. Richard Broaddus; married ———; had a son:

1. Edward Broaddus; married ——; emigrated to Kentucky in 1801, and settled in Madison County; and in 1825 was married again to Margaret Ham, and on the 27th of July, 1826, he and his wife Margaret made a deed to his sons, Beverley and Thomas, to 160 acres of land in Madison County, where the said Edward then lived. The children of his first marriage:

1. James Broaddus, married Nancy ————, on the 3d of May, 1830. James Broaddus and his wife Nancy made a deed to Robert C. Patterson to 100 acres of land on Hay's Fork of Silver Creek, Dec. 28, 1830; his widow Nancy was allotted dower in his estate. Their children:

1. Martha Broaddus, married Thompson Thurman.
2. Nancy Waller Broaddus, married Robert C. Patterson. (See Part 1, Chap. 14, Sec. 2.)
3. Mary Jane Broaddus, married Christopher Rowland.
4. Mildred G. Broaddus, married Hiram Doolin.
5. Elizabeth Broaddus; married ———.
6. Susan R. Broaddus, married Mr. Wilkerson.
7. William Broaddus.

2. Richard Broaddus, born Sept. 3, 1774; married Polly Mahone, Feb. 15, 1798. She was born June 2, 1773, and died June 5, 1837. He married again, Oct. 19, 1838, Martha Gillespie. She died March 22, 1848, and Richard Broaddus died May 8, 1850. His will bears date April 4, 1848; probated June 3, 1850. Silas Newland and George W. Broaddus were executors of the will. The children of his first marriage:

1. Cynthia Broaddus, born March 15, 1799; died Aug. 8, 1804.

2. Hudson Broaddus, born October 3, 1800; married Jane Reid, Dec. 24, 1819. (See Part I, Chap. 14, Sec. 3, and Part II, Chap. 21, Sec. 2.)

3. Sallie Broaddus, born Nov. 5, 1801; married, Dec. 24, 1816, Daniel Estill.

4. Simeon Broaddus, born July 2, 1803; married, Dec. 21, 1825, China Crews. She was allotted dower in his estate, Dec. 22, 1847. Among their children were:

1. Dr. Richard Broaddus, of Blue Springs, Mo.; married Lucy McCord.

2. Marcellus Broaddus, M. D., married; went to Texas and died.

3. Temple Broaddus, married Lucy Alexander; lives in Missouri.

4. Benjamin Broaddus, went to Idaho; has not been heard of for a long time.

5. Lycurgus Broaddus, died a bachelor in S. Carolina.

6. Laura Broaddus, married Dr. Hugh W. Hogan. Children:

1. George Broaddus Hogan, born Feb. 29, 1859; died Sept. 13, 1860.

2. Alice B. Hogan, born Oct. 25, 1860; married Ambrose B. Wagers.

3. Thomas Simeon Hogan, born Nov. 11, 1862; died Aug. 6, 1863.

4. Mary Ellen Hogan, born Dec. 11, 1864; married Michael W. Miller. (See Part I, Chap. 13, Sec. 10.)

5. Lula Hogan, born Feb. 14, 1866; married, first, Wm. Tisdale; second, Mr. Davis.

6. Samuel Grant Hogan, born March 19, 1869; died Sept. 3, 1883.

7. Henry Harney Hogan, born May 14, 1872; died.

8. David M. Hogan, born Dec. 15, 1874; married Flora Atkins.

9. John W. Hogan, born Nov. 1878; married —— Atkins.

10. Hubert W. Hogan, born Nov. 13, 1880; died Nov. 21, 1880.

7. Mary Ann Broaddus, married Charles Ball.

5. George W. Broaddus, born Sept. 4, 1805; married, Dec. 11, 1828, Elvira Hocker (see Part VII, Chap. 7, Sec. 1), and second, Cynthia Hunt. He was a Baptist minister.

6. Jesse Broaddus, born Nov. 18, 1806; died Aug. 3, 1808.

7. Patsey Broaddus, born June 4, 1808; died April 23, 1809.

8. Emily Broaddus, born Feb. 1, 1810; married, Aug. 12, 1826, to Silas Newland. Kept a public inn, or tavern, on the State road near Big Hill, in Madison County, Ky., where they died. Mr. Newland was very generous, hospitable and kind and well-to-do farmer. Had several children.

9. Matilda Broaddus, born Nov. 27, 1811.

Beverley Broaddus, born July 27, 1813; married, May 31, 1838, to Eliza Ann Lackey. (See Part I, Chap. 14, Sec. 11). She was allotted dower in his estate April 7, 1849. His orphan children, for whom Andrew K. Lackey was guardian, were:

1. Mary Jane Broaddus, married Michael Elkin.
2. Emily A. Broaddus, married John Rout.
3. Samuel T. Broaddus.
4. Richard D. Broaddus.

11. Wilson Cary Nicholas Broaddus, born Oct. 15, 1815; married, Jan. 30, 1838, to Nancy Ballew. He was a beautiful scribe and prosperous farmer of Madison County, Ky. Their children.

1. Elizabeth Susan Broaddus, married, first, John Rayburn, and second, James C. Miller. (See Part I, Chap. 13, Sec. 3.) Children of the first marriage:

1. Nannie Rayburn, married Nathan C. Bonney.
2. Charles S. Rayburn.

Children of second marriage are set forth in Chap. 13, Sec. 2.

2. George S. Broaddus, married Mary Tyree.

3. Elizabeth Broaddus; married John Jarman. (See Part V, Chap. 4, Sec. 1, and Part V, Chap. 3, Sec. 5.)

4. Whitfield Broaddus; married Sallie Mahone, Jan. 15, 1807.

5. Beverley Broaddus; married Mrs. Frances Redmond. On the 18th of July, 1832, he and his wife Franky made a deed to Thompson Thurman and Martha, his wife; ChristopherRowland and Mary Jane, his wife; James Broaddus, William Broaddus, Mildred Y. Broaddus, Elizabeth Broaddus, and Susan R. Broaddus, Robert C. Patterson and Nancy W. his wife, heirs of James Broaddus, to lands on Muddy Creek.

6. Elijah Broaddus; married Mary Barnett.

7. John Broaddus; married Mary Broaddus. His will bears date Jan. 23, 1826; probated May 4, 1829, wife Mary. Their children:

1. Frances Broaddus.
2. John Broaddus.
3. Lucy Broaddus; married Mr. Grimes.
4. Nancy Broaddus; married Mr. Munday.
5. Andrew Broaddus.
6. Thomas Broaddus.
7. Patsey Broaddus
8. Catherine Broaddus; married Mr. Price.

Mrs. Mary Broaddus' will bears date Feb. 17, 1840, probated Oct. 5, 1840, in which she names her son, Thomas Broaddus, and her grandchildren, John L. Price, Andrew Price, John Brooks, Mary Jane Brooks, and Sally Ann Brooks.

8. Thomas Broaddus; married Elizabeth Newland in 1813. (One Thomas Broaddus married Elizabeth Ross in 1810.) "On the 4th of August 1832, one Thomas Broaddus and Elizabeth his wife, made a deed to Alexander Ross to 75 acres of land on Paint Lick Creek." Thomas Broaddus' will was probated Feb. 25, 1828, in which he names Silas Newland and Richard Broaddus as executors and his children, to-wit:

1. Amelia Broaddus; married William Broaddus, and on the 16th of October, 1832, William Broaddus, of Rockcastle County, made a deed to Beverley Broaddus, of Estill, and William Broaddus, of Todd, reciting that William and his wife Amelia had separated and happily come together, and the grantees were to hold certain property bought of Jeremiah Broaddus for William as long as he continued to live with his wife and treat her well, but in case of his failure they were to hold it for his wife.
2. Martha Broaddus.
3. Mary Broaddus.

9. Jeremiah Broaddus.

10. William Broaddus; married Jane E. Moore.

11. Polly Broaddus; married Thos. Frances. Their children:

1. Susan Frances; married James D. Ballard. The parents of Thomas James Ballard and others.
2. Mary Francis; married Capt. Palestine P. Ballard, a former Justice of the Peace and Sheriff of Madison County, Ky., and Federal officer in Revenue service.
3. Jane Francis; married Thomas Jeptha Cornelison.
4. Elizabeth Francis.
5. John B. Francis; married, first, Susan Francis, and, second, Eliza Rowland. Issue of the first marriage:

1. Pattie Francis; married Daniel Maupin Terrill.

Issue of the second marriage:

2. David R. Francis, of St. Louis, former Mayor of St. Louis, Governor of the State of Missouri, and President of the St. Louis Purchase Exposition, the greatest of world's fairs.

3. Thomas Francis.

4. Mary Francis.

5. Hallie Francis.

6. Thomas Francis; married Elizabeth Gibbs.

7. Louis E. Francis; married, first, Emma Bronston, and, second, Laura Estill.

8. Edward E. Francis.

9. Daniel G. Francis; married Miss Ballard.

10. William F. Francis; died a bachelor.

11. Edith Francis; married Dr. Pettus, of Crab Orchard, Ky.

12. Margaret Francis; married, first, William Mize, and, second, Mr. Sam. Curd.

13. Julia Francis; married Henry Pigg.

12. Andrew Broaddus; married Gracie Askin. In the time of the California gold fever, Andrew Broaddus went with a company, in which was Christopher Carson, the noted western pioneer frontiersman, scout and pilot, across the plains of the West, the Sante Fe route to the gold regions; on the way, in camp, a number of buffalo came near and Mr. Broaddus, desiring to shoot a bison, in pulling a gun out of the wagon from the rear, the same was accidently discharged, entering his arm, making an ugly wound, which was dressed as best they could, and the company continued on their way. In a few days, Broaddus' arm getting seriously worse, with a common knife and saw, Mr. Carson amputated his arm and heated a lynch pin and seared it; the bone afterwards protruding was broken off and the would healed; and Mr. Broaddus spent his remaining days with one arm, and died in Madison County, Ky., Dec. 24, 1872, and his wife died Aug. 14, 1876. Whilst a resident of Missouri, prior to 1827, she made a visit to her friends in Kentucky, making the trip both ways on horseback, and thought it nice and enjoyed it. Their children:

1. John E. Broaddus; married Ann M. Royston in 1843.

2. Green B. Broaddus; died in Kansas. He was First Lieutenant in Humphrey Marshall's Regiment of Mounted Rifles in the Mexican War, and Major of the 7th Kentucky Infantry on the Federal side in the Civil War. He was in the battles of Perryville and Stone River, and in the latter engagement commanded a regiment. He married Patsey Ellen McHenry. He was more than once elected Sheriff of Madison County, Ky.

3. Jeremiah Broaddus; married Juliet Oldham. (See Part VI, Chap. 11, Sec. 13.) He was a prominent farmer of Madison County, Ky.

4. Andrew W. Broaddus.

5. William F. Broaddus; married Winifred Thomas. (See Part III, Chap. 5, Sec. 4.)

6. Sidney C. Broaddus; married Miss Forbes.

7. Elbridge J. Broaddus; was admitted to the bar at Richmond, Ky., in March, 1858; removed to Chilicothe.

Mo., in 1867, where he now lives. In 1874, was elected Circuit Judge of the 17th Judicial District of Missouri for six years, and several times re-elected, and is now Judge of the highest State Court and a man of much distinction in Missouri. He married, first, Ann Chambers, second, ————, and, third, Miss Alexander.

8. Mary Broaddus; died single.

9. Margaret Broaddus; married Capt. Nathan Noland, a farmer of Madison County, Ky., who died several years since; a man of very strong intellect and well beloved by all who knew him. He left a good heritage to his children, a good name. His widow yet lives; a good woman, admired by all who know her. Their children:

1. John Noland; lives with his mother; unmarried.
2. Elbridge Noland; married Maggie Thorpe. (See Part III, Chap. 13, Sec. 1.)
3. Mary Noland; married Nathan Bird Deatherage.
4. James Noland; married, first, Miss Cox, second, Nannie Harris. (See Part III, Chap. 44, Sec. 1.)
5. Green B. Noland; married Miss Nannie Griggs.
6. A. Sidney Noland; married Mayme Baxter.
7. Jeremiah Noland; married Miss Turley.
8. George Noland; married Miss ————.

10. Elizabeth Broaddus; married Major Ferrill.

3. Dolly Broaddus.

Besides by his first marriage, Edward Broaddus from Wales had one or two other daughters.

By his second marriage, to Mary Shipley, Edward Broaddus from Wales had these children:

4. John Broaddus; married Frances Pryor.

5. William Broaddus; married Miss Gaines, and was the first of the name, so far as known, to settle in Culpeper County, Va. Their children :

1. William Broaddus; married, first, Mrs. Martha Jones, widow of Capt. Gabriel Jones, the Revolutionary soldier, and a daughter of Robert Slaughter, first church warden of St. Marks. His second wife was Martha Richardson. He was a Major in the Revolutionary army and was for many years Clerk of the Culpeper County Court. Late in life he moved to Harper's Ferry, where he was paymaster in the army, and where he died. The children of his first marriage:

1. Catherine Broaddus; married William Mills Thompson.
2. Wiggington Broaddus.
3. Juliet Broaddus; married Col. Henry Ward, and had:
   1. William H. Ward; married Jane Roberts, daughter of a Revolutionary soldier, John Roberts. No issue.
   2. Woodville Ward; moved to Mississippi; unmarried.
4. Patsey Broaddus; married Meriwether Thompson.
5. William Broaddus; succeeded his father as Clerk of the Culpeper County Court; married Ann Tutt; had two children:
   1. Juliet Ann Broaddus; married Edward Herndon; had one child:
      1. Mary Eleanor Herndon; married John Roberts.
   2. William A. Broaddus; unmarried.

The children of the second marriage of Major William Broaddus, to Martha Richardson:

6. Sarah Ann Broaddus.
7. Lavinia Broaddus.

8. Maria Broaddus.
9. Mary Broaddus; married Thomas Keys.

2. Thomas Broaddus; married Mrs. Susannah White. Their children:

1. Edmund Broaddus; married, first, Nancy Sims, and, second, Somerville Ward. No issue of his second marriage. The children of his first marriage were:

1. James M. Broaddus.
2. Martha A. Broaddus.
3. Caroline M. Broaddus.
4. John A. Broaddus, D. D. The most accomplished and scholarly man who ever bore the name Broaddus.

2. William F. Broaddus; so strong was his intellect, so industrious his habits, and so eager his desire to excel, that through his own unaided efforts, he not only acquired a good knowledge of books and their contents, but became a highly popular and successful school teacher and minister of the Gospel, both in Virginia and Kentucky. He joined the Baptist Church when quite young, and commenced preaching in Virginia; he had a school and church at Middleburg, and at other places he preached and taught at different times. He moved to Kentucky and taught and preached in Lexington and Shelbyville. He returned to Virginia and there resumed his calling till advanced in years. He married, first, Mrs. A. Farrow, and, second, Mrs. Lucy E. Fleet. The children of his first marriage:

1. Edmund S. Broaddus.
2. Amanda F. Broaddus.
3. William H. C. Broaddus.
4. Mary L. Broaddus.
5. Thomas E. Broaddus.
6. John F. Broaddus.

The issue of his second marriage:

7. Lucy Maria Broaddus.

3. Andrew Broaddus; was born in Caroline County, Va., and there lived and died. He established a reputation as an orator, notwithstanding his education was very limited, having attended school only nine months in his life. He united with the Baptist Church when very young. He had barely become of age when ordained a minister of the Gospel, and was one of the most popular pulpit orators of his day. He wrote a number of works. His "History of the Bible" was favorably received by the religious people. He lived to be old. He married Mrs. Belle Simms. (Some say he was married four times.) His children:

1. Mary Susan Broaddus.
2. Virginia Broaddus.
3. Andrew Broaddus; also became a Baptist minister of great ability and was an able writer as well as speaker. He, also, lived in Caroline County, Va., to quite an old age. The record is that three generations, W. F. Broaddus, his son Andrew, and grandson Andrew, covering a period of one hundred years, had successively and successfully occupied the same pulpit and preached to the same people and descendants of the same.
4. Lucy P. Broaddus.
5. Louisa W. Broaddus.

(Besides there were six other children.)

4. Lucy Broaddus; married William Ferguson.
5. Maria Broaddus; married John S. Wallace. Children:
   1. Sarah Wallace.
   2. Thomas O. Wallace.
   3. Mildred Wallace.
   4. Mary Russell Wallace.

3. James Broaddus, born Dec. 27, 1756. He was an Ensign in the Revolutionary army. He married Mary A. Ferguson. Their children:

1. Elizabeth Broaddus, born Sept. 15, 1782; died in 1862; unmarried.

2. Catherine Broaddus, born Jan. 26, 1787; married Thomas N. Butts.

3. William D. Broaddus, born May 16, 1789; died in Culpeper County in 1850.

4. Sarah W. Broaddus; married James Burdette.

5. James G. Broaddus; married Elizabeth Susan Gaines, February, 1824.

6. Susan C. Broaddus; married Frederick Burdette, June 17, 1839.

6. James Broaddus; married Miss Gaines. Issue:
   1. William Broaddus; married and had children.
7. Shipley Broaddus; married Miss Connally.
8. Robin Broaddus; married Sarah Harwood. Their children:
   1. Warner Broaddus.
   2. William Broaddus; married Elizabeth Motley. Children:
      1. Reuben Broaddus; married Martha L. Oliver.
      2. Edwin Broaddus; married Eliza Montague.
      3. Robert Broaddus.
      4. Warner Broaddus.
      5. William Broaddus.
      6. Mordecai Broaddus.
      7. Betsy Broaddus; married Mr. Robbins.
   3. Robert Broaddus.
   4. Mary Broaddus.
   5. Caroline Broaddus.
   6. America Broaddus; married John Broaddus.
9. Elizabeth Broaddus; married Richard Gaines.

(The Broaddus Family, by A. Broaddus, D. D.)

Section 4. John Thomas Miller, a son, was born at the home on Muddy Creek, August 19, 1844; married to Anice Elkin, daughter of Robert M. Elkin and his wife, Malinda Elkin, at the Dr. Thomas S. Moberley place, on said creek, by Rev. Charles Dobbs, a Missionary Baptist preacher, on the 11th day of February, 1869. Of this union these children are the issue:

1. William Francis Miller, born Dec. 28, 1869. When in his fourteenth year, Aug. 22, 1883, he and the horse he was riding were killed by a bolt of lightning.

2. Robert Elkin Miller, born Oct. 28, 1871. He married Pattie Tevis; she died, and on the 18th of October, 1905, he married the second time, Mattie Rupert, daughter of Laban Rupert and Elizabeth Tribble, his wife. They live in Huntsville, Mo. Children of the first marriage:

1. Maud Miller.
2. Rheba Miller.

Issue of second marriage:

3. Margaret Katherine Miller, born November, 1906.

3. Malinda Miller, born March 15, 1874; married William Pearson. They emigrated to Huntsville, Missouri, where they now live. Their children:
   1. Joseph Miller Pearson.
   2. William Elkin Pearson.
   3. Robert Pearson.

4. Thomas Irvine Miller, born July 30, 1879; married Patsey Park, of Madison County, Ky., daughter of Joel Park and Lucy D. Embry, his wife. (See Part I, Chap. 9, Sec. 3, and Part VI, Chap. 8, Sec. 9.) They emigrated to Huntsville, Missouri, where they now live. Their children:
   1. George Park Miller.
   2. Anice Elizabeth Miller.

5. Mary Miller. She and her sister Susan were twins, born — day of ———, 18—. She went with her parents to Huntsville, Missouri and there was married to Joseph Richardson. Issue:
   1. Miller Sandford Richardson.

6. Susan Miller. She and her sister Mary were twins, born ——— day of ———, 18—. She went with her parents to Huntsville, Missouri, and there was married to Nicholas Dysart Minor.

7. Elizabeth Miller, born in Madison County, Ky., the ——— day of ————, 18—. She now lives in Huntsville, Missouri, with her parents.

Section 5. A son, not named, born at the home on Muddy Creek, Oct. 20, 1846; died Nov. 5, 1846; the remains buried in the burial plot near the house.

Section 6. Christopher Irvine Miller, a son, born at the home on Muddy Creek, April 18, 1848. When just blooming into manhood he left home and went to Richmond, and was clerk for a number of years in the grocery store of Ellis & Clay, when the firm dissolved and continued under the different firm names, and finally became a partner in a hardware store, which operated some years and closed. He was inventor and patentee of a churn; also of a shot and powder canister. Was quite a genius. He left Richmond and went to Earl Park, Benton County, Indiana, and secured a partner, A. D. Raub, and they erected a shop for the manufacture of the shot and powder canister, from which there were no great returns. He married Sarah Suet; no children were born to them. He was made a Justice of the Peace of Benton County, which office he held at the time of his death, in June, 1887. His remains were buried in the beautiful cemetery at Lawrenceburg, Indiana. He was well thought of and had a good standing with the people where he lived. Robert L. Cox, Principal of the Public Schools, Richard Carroll, Clerk of the Court, and George W. Tinsman, Township Trustee, all of Earl Park, Indiana, said of the subject, that "he was universally honored and respected and was without an enemy in this country."

Section 7. Susannah Woods Miller, a daughter, was born at the home on Muddy Creek, Aug. 2, 1850; married to Thomas Richard Hume, at the residence of her parents on said creek, Oct. 9, 1873, by Elder John M. Park, an Old Baptist preacher. (See Chapter 9.) Note. Mr. Hume was a son of Larkin Hume and Nancy Moberley, his wife; was an energetic and successful farmer and business man and accumulated a good estate; was an excellent husband and a substantial citizen. His wife was no drawback to him, being industrious, true and affectionate and liked by all who knew her. To this union these children were born:

1. Thomas Richard Hume, born July 26, 1874; went in the year 18— on a visit to the Provine of Canada; was stricken and died ———, 18—, on his way from there home, which event was a severe shock to his mother, his father having died some years previous. His remains were forwarded to Richmond, Ky., and there buried in the cemetery.

2. Nancy Moberley Hume, born Feb. 6, 1876; married Christopher Fogg Chenault, son of Anderson Chenault and Elizabeth Fogg, his wife. Mr. Chenault is an extentive farmer, owns an interest in the Elliston Roller Mills, large interest at Conway, Ky., in several thousand acres of land and mills. Has recently purchased the Stone or Terrell farm in the eastern suburbs of Richmond. (See Part V, Chap. 13, Sec. 9.) Their children:

1. Elizabeth Susan Chenault.
2. Anderson Hume Chenault.
3. Mary Emily Chenault.
4. Nancy Woods Chenault, baby.

They live on the Richmond and Irvine Pike, one mile east of Richmond, on the farm of the late Anderson Chenault, known as the Miller or Goodloe place.

3. Irvine Miller Hume, born Jan. 18, 1878. He and his brother George own land and property in partnership and live about two miles northeast of Richmond and are engaged in farming and raising and trading in stock.

4. George Larkin Hume, born Jan. 24, 1880. He and his brother Irvine are partners in business and live together, as stated in above Section 3.

Their father, Thomas R. Hume died, leaving his wife and children surviving and in good circumstances, and his remains were buried in the Richmond Cemetery. His widow afterwards married Algin S. Hisle, and they lived on her dowry on Muddy Creek, the old Hume home, until the sudden death of Mr. Hisle, Oct. 29, 1906, in the 67th year of his age.

Mr. Hume was a splendid man, a good farmer, stock raiser, economical, kind, good-hearted; an indulgent, generous and affectionate husband and father; a splendid provider for his family, and when he died the whole community felt the loss of a good and useful citizen, neighbor, relative and friend. He was exceedingly fond of his wife and children, with whom he took great pleasure, fondling his little children on his knees and in his lap, and he was never too tired to enjoy their climbing and pulling over him.

Section 8. William Harris Miller, a son, was born at the home on Muddy Creek, Oct. 22, 1852. He was raised on the farm until eighteen years of age, when, on the 28th of December, 1870, his father secured him a position as Deputy Clerk of the Madison County Court, under his cousin, George D. Shackelford, in which capacity he served till the death of Mr. Shackelford, which occurred the latter days of May, 1874, about three months before his time of office expired, and his brother, James T. Shackelford, was appointed to fill the vacancy and the subject was retained as Deputy under the latter. There is, however, excepted from the above period of service under George D. Shackelford one year, from August, 1872, to August, 1873, in which time he was Deputy for Charles K. Oldham, Sheriff of Madison County.

In 1874, his cousin, George Shackelford, being in very poor

health, and unable to make another race for office, at the solicitation of his said cousin and others, W. H. Miller, who had just arrived at the age of twenty-one years, became a candidate for the Democratic nomination for the office of Clerk of the Madison County Court, but at the primary election, held in May of that year, in which there were four aspirants, he was defeated, Mr. James Tevis securing the nomination.

At the regular election in August of the same year, 1874, William M. Embry was elected Clerk of the Circuit Court, and offered W. H. Miller the Deputy Clerkship, which he accepted, and on the 17th of August, 1874, he left the County Court office and qualified and acted as Deputy Circuit Court Clerk until April 15, 1879. Embry having died in office on March 9, 1880, before the expiration of his term in August of that year, on the 11th of March, the Honorable Joseph D. Hunt, Judge of said court, of his own volition, issued to said Miller a certificate in this language, to-wit:

"I, J. D. Hunt, Circuit Judge of the Tenth Judicial District of Kentucky, of which the counties of Madison and Fayette compose a part, do hereby certify that William H. Miller has been examined by the Clerk of the Fayette Circuit Court, under my supervision, touching his qualifications for the office of Clerk of the Circuit Court, and that he is qualified for that office.

"And, whereas, the office of Clerk of the Madison Circuit Court has become vacant by the death of William M. Embry, late Clerk of said Court, I do hereby appoint the said William H. Miller, of Madison County, to be Clerk of the Madison Circuit Court during the remainder of the term for which said William M. Embry was elected.

"Witness my hand as Judge of the Tenth Judicial District of Kentucky, this eleventh day of March, 1880.

J.D.HUNT,
Judge 10th Dist. Ky."

Under which certificate said Miller qualified by taking the oath and executing the bond by law required, and served as Clerk for the remainder of Embry's term.

In a heated Democratic primary contest he received the nomination, and in August, 1880, under that nomination was elected Clerk of the Circuit Court for the term of six years, qualified and acted as such. Was elected again in 1886 for another term of six years, qualified and acted as such. Was defeated for the nomination for the same office at the primary held preceding the regular election in August, 1892, by his nephew, S. H. Thorpe, who had been his deputy and lived with him for a number of years; but under the provision of the new State Constitution recently before adopted, his term was continued from August, 1892, till the 1st of January, 1893, when his successor took possession of the office.

He worked as deputy three years in the County Court and five years in the Circuit Court Clerk's office, and was Chief Clerk of the Circuit Court nearly thirteen years, equaling twenty-one years of hard service in the two courts.

In March, 1894, after being out of the Clerk's office for a little over a year, he was appointed United States general storekeeper and guager in the revenue service and, later on promoted in said service to the office of Deputy Collector under Hon. Chas. H. Rodes, Collector of Internal Revenue, and served through the remainder of Mr. Rodes' term, who was succeeded by Hon. John W. Yerkes, and he continued as deputy under Mr. Yerkes till January 1, 1899, when he resigned.

During Mr. Rodes' incumbency the office was located at Richmond, Ky.; when Mr. Yerkes became Collector the office, which was comfortably quartered in a fine, substantial, well fixtured and furnished government building, built purposely for that, the U. S. Court and Postoffice was, by the political influence of the Collector, removed, with all the records, etc., to Danville, the home of Mr. Yerkes, in rented quarters, which removal for a time exercised the people of old Madisan.

On the 27th day of February, 1884, the subject here was married to Katherine Oldham, a daughter of William Kavanaugh Oldham and his wife, Jacintha Catherine Brown, at the residence of her said father on Otter Creek, near Richmond, Ky., by Rev. Seneca X. Hall, a Methodist preacher. (See Part VI, Chap. 21, and Part VIII, Chap. 14, Sec. 7.) Of this union there was no issue.

Section 9. Mary Eliza Miller, a daughter, born at the home on Muddy Creek, Jan. 29, 1855; lived with her mother till she broke up housekeeping in 18—, and then made her home with her sister Susan and brother William; was living with her said sister when she was married, the 8th day of May, 1890, to John W. Rupert, a son of Laban Rupert and Elizabeth Tribble, his wife. Mr. Rupert has, for the greater part of his life, been engaged at different places as salesman for merchants. They lived awhile at Elliston, where he sold goods, and at Rice's Station, doing the same, and then moved to Richmond, where he was employed as clerk in a store. Clerking a number of years in the dry goods house of E. V. Elder, which place he gave up in January, 1905, sold out his effects and went to Woodward County, Oklahoma, and there remained until October, 1905, and becoming dissatisfied with the country, sold out and moved back to Kentucky, now living in Conway, Rockcastle County, Ky. Since the above was written they have removed to Berea, where he is merchandizing in his own name. They have no children born of them.

Section 10. Michael Woods Miller, a son, born at the home on Muddy Creek, Feb. 13, 1857. His father died in October, 1878, mother surviving, with whom he remained until she broke up housekeeping in 1881, and lived with his sister Susannah until the —— day of ————, 18—, when he was married to Ella Hogan, daughter of Dr. Hugh W. Hogan and Laura Broaddus, his wife. (See Part I, Chap. 13, Sec. 3. Note.) After his marriage he located at Elliston, where he acquired a home and built a blacksmith shop, which he operated a number of years, and then abandoned to accept employment in the Elliston Mills, then owned by W. T. Griggs, afterwards succeeded by the Elliston Mill Company, wherein he is still employed. Recently he united by experience and baptism with the United Baptist Church at Waco, Ky. To them these children have been born:

1. Eugene Miller, born the 18th day of September, 1886.
2. Christopher Hogan Miller, born 6th day of December, 1888.

Section 11. Elizabeth Frances Miller, a daughter, and the youngest child, was born at the home on Muddy Creek, July 15, 1864. Sister Bettie as we all called her, was the baby girl, born when mother was nearly fifty years old, and all of the family were very fond of her; she had a sweet disposition, was generous and kind-hearted. In May, 1882, when in her eighteenth year, without previous notice, she eloped with and was married the 8th of the month to Junius Burnam Park, in the city of Jeffersonville, state of Indiana, by Rev. Terrill. Her husband died the —— day of ————, 18—, and she survived him only a short while, dying the —— day of ————, 18—, and their remains were buried in the Richmond Cemetery. They left one child, a son:

1. Earl Gardner Park, born the —— day of ————, 18—; now living in Jacksonville, Florida.

CHAPTER 11.

COLONEL JOHN MILLER.

(Named in Section 6, Chapter 3, Part I.)

Article 1.—Colonel John Miller, a son of Robert Miller and Ann Lynn, his wife, mentioned in Chapter 3, was born in Albemarle, Nelson or Orange County, Virginia, July 1, 1750.

He was married in Albemarle County, Virginia, March 20, 1774, to Jane Delaney, and he died September 8, 1806. His wife was born January 1, 1751, and died March 13, 1844, living to the age of 93 years past. Her mother was Miss Durrett.

In the fall of 1784 Colonel John Miller, with his wife and young children who had been born before that date, left home and friends in Albemarle and moved to Kentucky, which at that time formed a part of the Commonwealth of Virginia, and settled on the head waters of a prong of Otter Creek, where the city of Richmond now is, and acquired and owned a considerable body of land there, upon which he put valuable and lasting improvements—building the first house that was built there, and where he ever after made his home till his death in 1806. His house was built on the spot where the Northern Presbyterian Church stands, and his spring was just east, near the present Zaring Mill and Bicycle Shop.

He was commissioned by Patrick Henry, Esq., Governor of Virginia, as Justice of the Peace, and the first Order Book of the Madison County Court, page 48, date June 26, 1787, shows that "Robert Rodes and John Miller, gentlemen, named in the commission of the Peace for the County, came into court and took the oath of fidelity to the Commonwealth and the oath of Justice of the Peace and of Oyer and Terminer."

The first court of the County of Madison was held at the house of George Adams, on Tuesday, the 22d day of August, 1786, as appears from the first entry in the first Order Book of the county, commencing on page 1. A copy of which is here presented:

"At the house of George Adams, in the County of Madison, on Tuesday, the twenty-second day of August, in the year of our Lord One thousand seven hundred and eighty-six.

"A commission of the Peace, and of Oyer and Terminer from His Excellency, Patrick Henry, Esquire, Governor of the Commonwealth of Virginia, directed to George Adams, John Snoddy, Christopher Irvine, David Gass, Jas. Barnett, John Bowles (or Boyle), Jas. Thompson, Archibald Woods, Nicholas George, and Joseph Kennedy, Gentlemen, constituting them Justices of the Peace, and of Oyer and Terminer in and for the said County of Madison, was produced and read. Whereupon the said John Snoddy and Christopher Irvine administered the oath of fidelity to the Commonwealth, and the oath of a Justice of the Peace, and of Oyer and Terminer to George Adams, Gent, who then administered the said oaths to the said John Snoddy, Christopher Irvine, David Gass, James Barnett, John Bowles (or Boyle), Archibald Woods, Nicholas George, and Joseph Kennedy, Gent., and thereupon a court was held for the said County of Madison. Present." (Here naming the Justices aforesaid.)

Note—The words "Oyer and Terminer" meaning a hearing and determining.

At this date (August 22, 1786) this name, "John Bowles," appears in the record as one of the Justices of the Peace, and it so appears at every subsequent court held until Tuesday, Oct. 24, 1786, when the name is written for the first time in the record "John Boyles," and the letter "s" should have been omitted, for he signed his name to documents "John Boyle." A deposition given by him, Aug. 30, 1806, to which he signed his name "John Boyle," is in words and figures as follows:

DEPOSITION OF JOHN BOYLE.

"In pursuance of an order of the Worshipful Court of Madison County directing us to call upon witness to establish the calls of an entry made in the name of John Mounce, for four hundred acres lying on Hayes Fork of Silver Creek, agreeable to said order, we called upon John Boyle, Sen'r, and being on the ground, the said Deponent deposeth and saith by way of interrogatives:

Question by John Kincaid: How long was it since you made the improvement, and who was in company with you?

Answer: I think it was in the year 1779, and in the month of May, and Hugh Seper was in company with me.

Question by same: Did not John Mounce, Yelverton Peyton, David Miller and myself—that is John Kincaid—come with you to this place on our way to Boonesborough?

Answer: Yes, I think in the month of June following I was here in company with the above-mentioned persons.

Question by same: What did you do with this improvement? Did you give it to anyone?

Answer: Yes, I gave it to John Mounce.

Question by same: Did Mounce make any addition to the improvement, at the time you gave it to him, by marking other trees?

Answer: I think he did mark some trees or saplings.

Question: Are you certain that this is the same Improvement that you first made for Black, and afterwards gave it to Mounce?

Answer: Yes.

Question by same: How far is this Improvement from the mouth of the branch that we went up on our route to Boonesborough?

Answer: I think about 25 or 30 steps.

Question by same: Is there any appearance of the old Improvement visible at this day?

Answer: Yes. I think there is upon two trees.

Question by same: How far is this Improvement from the Improvement below, called Mounces, on what is called Mounce's Fork?

Answer: I suppose it is about a quarter, as near as I can guess, without measuring.

Question by same: How far is it from that to my own Improvement down the creek?

Answer: I reckon it is about a half mile, as near as I can guess, without measuring.

Question by same: Can you describe the ground where my Improvement stood, or was made?

Answer: I can. It was in a good smart bend in the creek, in a flat bottom near the creek.

Question by same: Was not the marks made on Mounce's Branch (towit), the two first letters of Mounce's, and my own name, made as marks of a conditional line, as well as an Improvement for Mounce to hold land?

Answer: The branch was the conditional line between them, and, as well as I recollect, they both marked the two first letters of their names there.

Question by same: Was not Mounce to run up the creek, and I down from that place for quantity?

Answer: Yes.

Question by same: Was you with Mounce when he laid in his claim before the Commissioners and obtained a certificate?

Answer: Yes, I was.

Question by same: Was not this the very land for which he obtained a certificate?

Answer: I think the land he intended to hold was from Mounce's Fork up the creek.

Question by same: Was not this place from the intersection of the two forks so remarkable that a man who was formerly acquainted with it might know it again?

Answer: Yes. I should think so.

Question by same: What branch was it that you alluded to that you said we went up on our way to Boonesborough?

Answer: The same that mouths in just above this Improvement and comes down through John Kincaid's Improvement or plantation.

And further this Deponent further saith not.

JOHN BOYLE.

(The deposition of Yelverton Peyton follows the above.)

Madison. Sct.

We do hereby certify that the foregoing depositions of John Boyle and Yelverton Peyton was this day subscribed and sworn to before us, William Miller and Richard Calloway, Commissioners appointed by the County Court of Madison, taken in the presence of Samuel Snoddy and William Baugh. Given under our hands and seals this 30th day of August, 1906.

WILLIAM MILLER, L. S.
RICHARD CALLOWAY, L. S.

At a court continued and held for Madison County on the 2d day of September, 1806, the foregoing depositions were returned and ordered to be recorded.

Attest: WILL IRVINE, C. M. C.

The first Court House of Madison County was at Milford, on Taylor's Fork of Silver Creek, now called "Old Town"—only ruins of which can be seen—established by the Virginia General Assembly in 1789. The act of the Kentucky General Assembly directing the removal of the county seat from Milford to the new town of Richmond, authorized the Madison County Court of Quarter Sessions to adjourn to John Miller's new stable in Richmond.

Colonel John Miller was a representative from Kentucky County in the Virginia General Assembly and represented Madison County in General Assembly in the years 1792-4. He was the first settler of Richmond, who, in the fall of 1784, came with his family from Albemarle County, Virginia, as before stated, and settled in the cane near Main Street, on Lot No. 4, and afterwards built the first hewed log-house in the place. He was proprietor of the first hotel, or tavern, in the place. He was a Captain in the Revolutionary army and was at the siege of Yorktown. Afterwards he held a commission with the rank of Colonel. He died September 8, 1806, leaving his last will and testament, bearing date February 14, 1806, probated December 5, 1806; recorded in Will Book A, page 452, in these words and figures:

JOHN MILLER'S WILL.

In the name of God, Amen, I, John Miller, of Madison County, and State of Kentucky, do make and ordain this my last will and testament, revoking all others by me heretofore made. In the first place, it is my will and desire that all my just debts be paid by my Executors hereafter named as soon as conveniently may be after my decease. I give to my beloved wife, Jane Miller, during her natural life, and no longer, the plantation and tract of land whereon I now live, including the tract which I purchased of my son, Robert Miller, and also the tract I purchased of Cornelius Maupin; also all my negroes, live stock, household and kitchen furniture, all my unmentioned estate, after satisfaction and payments of my just debts, bequeaths and devises, hereafter mentioned, for and during the said term of her natural life, to be in full satisfaction of and in lieu of dower in my real and personal estate.

I give to my son, Robert Miller, and his heirs forever, twenty acres of land to be in a square and to be taken off of the east corner of my tract of land on which the town of Richmond stands. Also, one negro.

I give to my son, William Miller, and to his heirs forever, and to my son, John Miller, Jun'r, and to his heirs forever, the tract of land on which the said town of Richmond stands, to be equally divided between them, by such division line as they may agree upon, but it is to be understood that the devise is not to include or extend to any property I may hold within the boundary of said town, nor to any part of said tract I may have sold by written or verbal contract, nor to the part before devised to my son Robert.

I devise to my son, Thomas Miller, and to his heirs forever, one tract of land lying in the said county near the said town of Richmond which I purchased from Elijah Gaddy, containing one hundred acres. Also, two negroes.

I devise to my son, Delaney Miller, and to his heirs forever, one hundred and forty acres of land, being part of the tract whereon I now live, which I purchased of my son, Robert Miller, and Cornelius Maupin, to be laid off of the south end of said tract, and not to come nearer to the dwelling house than three hundred and fifty yards, to extend up the line between me and John Patrick and the improvement for quantity. Also, two negroes.

I devise to my son, Garland Miller, and his heirs forever, the balance of the aforementioned tract of land whereon I now live, be the same, more or less, except the part already devised to my son Delaney Miller, to be laid off in the manner and form before mentioned, or any other way they may agree upon to suit themselves, to have and enjoy the same after the determination of the other therein before devised to his mother. I, also, give him two negroes.

I devise to my son, Joseph Miller, and his heirs forever, one tract of land lying on the waters of Paint Lick Creek, deeded to me by David Wells, containing two hundred acres, be the same (more) or less. Also two negroes.

I give to my daughter, Anna Reid, one negro.

I give to my daughter, Elizabeth Kavanaugh, one negro.

I give to my daughter, Jane Lackey, two negroes.

I give to my daughter, Frances Miller, three negroes.

I give to my sons Delaney and Garland each, and to my daughter Frances, one horse and saddle, and two cows and calves, and one bed and furniture, to be paid them at the time of their marriage, or attaining the age of twenty-one years, whichever shall first happen, to be allowed to them out of the estate in my beloved wife's hands, by my Executors, if she should be then living, and if she should not be then living, give them the value of said articles in cash, the value to be ascertained by neighbors—one chosen by my Executors, one by such child entitled thereto, and a third chosen by these two; it is to be fairly understood that if I should, in my life time, give to any of my children a negro, and other property herein devised or given, that it is to be considered satisfaction of the devise or bequest of such negro, all as far as it answers the description herein given. It is further to be understood that the negroes herein given and devised are not to be paid to my said children until after the death of my wife, unless she shall choose to part with them, in which case she may at any time pay to any one, or more, any, all, or more of said negroes, with the assent of my Executors, or the survivors of them.

Should any of my children die before me, the devise and bequest herein made to said children are to stand good and effectual to the heirs of such person—according to the laws of descent in the Commonwealth. JOHN MILLER, L. S.

Signed as the first part of my will.

Presence of us.

WM. GOODLOE.

his
WM. X KARR.
mark

Continuation of John Miller's Will:

"I constitute and appoint my friends, William Irvine, Robert Rodes, Executors of this my last will and testament. I empower them to make convey—for my lands which at the time of my death I may have sold, and unconveyed, either by written or verbal contract. I, also, empower them to divide my negroes according to the division of them herein made, as equal as may be. I do, also, empower them to sell and convey, as to them may seem best, all my lots in the town of Richmond, and to dispose of any part of my personal estate, if necessary, to raise money for the payment of my debts, and the residue, if any, from the sale of the lots, and collections of my debts, to pay the same to my wife. I declare my wife is not to give security for the keeping of the property left her, nor is she to be answerable for its depreciation in value, etc. And, whereas, I have at sundry times given to my children who have grown to years of maturity, a negro, or negroes, etc., I do now ratify and confirm to them all and every gift which I may before have made, and do declare that when I have delivered them any negro without an express stipulation to the contrary, that it is to be considered a gift.

All my estate left after the death of my wife, and not herein otherwise disposed of, I give to my daughters, Anna Reid, Elizabeth Kavanaugh, Jane Lackey, and Frances Miller, to be equally divided between them, and I wish it to be understood that whereas I have by deed given to my daughter, Elizabeth Kavanaugh, and her heirs, a part of a lot in the town of Richmond of the value of fifty pounds, now unless the said gift can be rescinded, and the said lot or the value thereof to be equally divided between the brothers and sisters, she is not to receive any part of my estate as last above mentioned devised to Anna Reid, Elizabeth Kavanaugh, Jane Lackey, and Frances Miller. Shall each of them have received the sum of fifty pounds, should there be any balance, it is then to be equally divided between them.

In testimony whereof, I have hereunto set my hand, and affixed my seal this 24th day of February, 1806.

Signed in the presence of JOHN MILLER, L. S.

WILLIAM GOODLOE.

his
WILLIAM X KARR.
mark

At a court held for Madison County on the 5th day of December, 1806, this will was proved to be the last will and testament of John Miller, dec'd, by the oath of William Karr, a witness thereto, as the law directs, and William Goodloe, another witness thereto, who swore he subscribed his name to said will in the presence of said deceased, which was ordered to be recorded.

Attest: WILL. IRVINE, C. M. C.

The children of Colonel John Miller and Jane Dulaney, his wife, are set forth in the order of their birth in the coming sections:

Section 1. Robert Miller, the first child, born March 1, 1775, in Albemarle County, Va. He came to Madison County, Ky., in 1784, and first settled at Milford or "Old Town." He served in the State Senate from Madison County in 1829, 1834-8. He moved to the new town of Richmond, where more than one hundred years ago he was proprietor of a tavern. He died on his farm about one mile east of Richmond, June 21, 1861, having passed his eighty-sixth birthday. On the 12th of June, 1798, he was married to Sallie Estill, a daughter of Captain James Estill and Rachael Wright, his wife, natives of Albemarle. Their children were:

1. James E. Miller; married Harriet F. Tevis, Aug. 28, 1824. Their children:
    1. Sallie Miller; married.
    2. Wade Hampton Miller; married.
    3. John Dulaney Miller.
    4. Matilda Miller; married Mr. Cary. Two years ago were living at their old home not far from Sedalia, Mo.
    5. Robert Tevis Miller, of Independence, Mo., is now nearly eighty years old.
2. John Dulaney Miller; married Eliza Embry, Oct. 23, 1828. Had one child:
    1. Sarah Miller; married Matt Embry, her cousin. She lived only about a year after the marriage; died without issue, and afterwards Matt Embry married Irene Miller, a daughter of Wm. Green Miller and Julia Miller, his wife. (See Sec. 1-3-3.)
3. William Green Miller; married, July 1, 1834, Julia Miller, a daughter of Dr. Alexander Miller. They settled in Bloomington, Illinois. (See Part I, Chap. 15, Sec. 3.) Their children:

1. Cyrus Miller; left home and never heard of afterwards.
2. Harrison Miller; unmarried; died a few years ago in Armourdale, Kansas.
3. Irene Miller; married Matt. Embry, a son of Thomas Embry. (Sec. 1-2-1.) They live in the state of Illinois, where they raised a family.
4. Sallie Miller; married Mr. Herr, who died, leaving her a widow with a son:
    1. Benjamin Herr; married Estelle Hunt, of Lexington, and died leaving one son.
5. Alexander Miller.

4. Rachael Jane Miller; married Napoleon Tevis. Children:
1. Robert Tevis; married Mattie Mayfield. They are both dead. Their children.
    1. Sophia Tevis (dead); married John Lovejoy. Their children.
        1. Edith Lovejoy.
        2. Mary Lovejoy.
        3. Robert Lovejoy.
    2. Frank Tevis; married (wife's name unknown). Had one son.
    3. Elizabeth Tevis; married Fred Behrman. Issue:
        1. Tevis Behrman.
        2. Gertrude Behrman.
    4. James Tevis; dead.
    5. Robert Tevis.
2. John Tevis; dead.
3. Sarah Tevis (dead); married G. A. Lackey. Issue:
    1. Samuel Lackey; married Bettie Van Arsdale. Their children:
        1. Rebecca Lackey.
        2. Stella Tevis Lackey.
    2. Mattie Lackey; married S. W. Givens. Their children:
        1. Sallie Givens.
        2. Mary Byrd Givens.
        3. Gabe Givens.
    3. Mary Lackey; married Wm. Field. Their children:
        1. Mary Field.
        2. Melvin Field.
        3. Gertrude Field.
    4. Lena Lackey; married E. D. Peyton.
    5. Napoleon Lackey.
4. Joseph Tevis; died unmarried.
5. Green Tevis; died unmarried.
6. Eugenia Tevis; died unmarried.
7. Cyrus Tevis; died unmarried.
8. Mary Tevis; died unmarried.
9. Harriet Tevis; died unmarried.
10. Lilly Tevis (dead); married George Cheves. Had one son:
    1. George Cheves, Jr.; married Margaret Stone. Their children:
        1. Rosnel Stone Cheves.
        2. Samuel Guy Cheves.
11. William Tevis; died unmarried.
12. Elizabeth Tevis; married G. A. Peyton. Their children:
    1. Lilly Tevis Peyton; married Samuel Fulkerson.
    2. Anna Miller Peyton.
    3. Rachael Gibbons Peyton; dead.

13. Napoleon Tevis; married first Nellie Mills. Had daughter:
1. Naomi Ruth Tevis.
He married secondly Isabel Cash.

5. Sallie Ann Miller; married Solon M. Harris, July 25, 1837. (See Part III, Chap. 48, Sec. 2.) Their children:

1. Emmet Harris; married Nannette Anderson, widow now living at Lexington, Ky.

2. Callie Harris; married Will Craig, of Stanford, Ky.

3. Edna Elizabeth Harris; married George Phelps. Their children:

1. Anna Phelps; married Claude Walton, Richmond, Ky.

2. Robert Phelps; died (unmarried) young.

3. Mary Phelps; married Samuel M. Phelps, son of M. A. Phelps, of Richmond, Ky.

4. Carlisle Phelps; married Arthur C. Burton, Butler, Mo.

6. Solon Miller; died unmarried at his brother Robert's home.

7. Robert Miller, born two miles east of Richmond, Nov. 7, 1823. He married, March 24, 1859, Elizabeth Miller, daughter of Harrison J. Miller and Patsey Irvine Fields, his wife. (See Part I, Chapter 15, Section 2.) Robert Miller and his wife were strict Presbyterians. In 1863 he located two miles east of Richmond, on four hundred acres of fine land, and gave much time to cattle and mules. A short while before his death he sold his farm and stock and moved to Richmond, where he soon after died; his wife surviving and now living in Richmond. Their children:

1. Sallie Estill Miller; unmarried.

2. Pattie Field Miller; married Stanton B. Hume. (See Chap. 9, Sec. 4).) Mr. Hume died, leaving his widow and two children:

1. Stanton Hume.

2. Elizabeth Hume.

3. Harry J. Miller; married Jas. S. Winn, of Winchester, Ky.

4. Bessie Miller.

8. Edna Elizabeth Miller; married William Hill, April 6, 1843. They located in Lincoln County, Ky., on the Hanging Fork of Dick's River. Mr. Hill died. Mrs. Hill is now living, eighty-three years old. Their children:

1. James Estill Hill.

2. Sarah Elizabeth Hill; married Walter Carter. Their children:

1. Edna Elizabeth Carter.

2. William Hill Carter.

3. James Nevin Carter; married Mary Beasley. One child:
1. Lucile Carter.

4. Mary Dutch Carter.

5. Estill Carter.

6. Laura Pearl Carter.

7. Peter Walter Carter.

8. Ernest Thayer Carter; married Myrtle Hughes. Have one child:
1. Earl Carter.

9. Claudie Carter.

10. Sarah Maude Carter.

3. Robert Miller Hill; married Harriet MacCormack. Their children:

1. Wm. Edgar Hill; married Ludie ——. Their children:
1. Valley Hill.
2. Gertrude Hill.

2. Valley Hill.
3. Gertrude Hill.
4. Pattie Hill.
5. Bessie Hill.

4. Thomas Jefferson Hill. He is now Sheriff of Lincoln County. He married Nellie Wilson Cosby. Their children:

1. Arthur Cosby Hill; married Nelle Mershon.
2. Thomas Jefferson Hill, attorney-at-law, Stanford, Ky.
3. Frank Lee Hill.
4. William Harrison Hill.
5. Stella Carter Hill; married Joseph H. Murphy. Child:
   1. Joseph H. Murphy, Jr., born 1906.
6. Elijah Miller Hill.
7. Margaret Hill.
8. John Miller Hill.
9. Joseph Wolfe Hill.
10. Nellie Wilson Hill.
11. Rachael Tevis Hill.

5. John Miller Hill; married Jennie Lee Johnston. Their children:

1. William Johnston Hill.
2. Robert Raymond Hill.

6. William Harrison Hill; married Emma Albert. Their children:

1. Edna Hill.
2. Rachael Hill.
3. Elizabeth Hill.

Section 2. William Miller. Known as "Old Town Billy,' because he first settled at Milford, or Old Town, on Taylor's Fork, in Madison County, Kentucky; the second child of Colonel John Miller and Jane Dulaney, his wife. Was born in Albemarle County, Virginia, June 19, 1776. He died in Madison County, Kentucky, June 30, 1841. He married, first, Hannah Lackey, daughter of Samuel Lackey, Sr., and Dorcas Alexander, his wife. Hannah Lackey was born September 15, 1783; died December 13, 1814. She was the mother of his children. He married the second time Dorcas Lackey, daughter of Andrew Lackey. She was born in 1787, and died March 27, 1821. He was often the Commissioner of the Court for various purposes. William Miller was a wealthy man for his day. He owned a large number of negro slaves, besides other personal property and lands. He distributed among his children and grandchildren eighty-odd slaves. In 1825 he made his final settlement as Sheriff of Madison County, Ky.

Note: Samuel Lackey, Sr., was born April 24, 1746, and died Tuesday, January 5, 1830. He married, about 1773, Dorcas Alexander, who was born March 12, 1750, and died Monday, August 24, 1818. Their children:

1. John Lackey, born Oct. 1, 1774.
2. Gabriel Lackey, born March 6, 1776.
3. Samuel Lackey, born Oct. 27, 1777; married Jane Miller. (See Sec. 11.)
4. Alexander Lackey, born Jan. 22, 1780; died Jan. 3, 1854.
5. Hannah Lackey, born Sept. 15, 1783, the wife of William Miller, as aforesaid. She died Dec. 13, 1814.

Andrew Lackey was the father of Dorcas Lackey, the second wife of William Miller, as aforesaid.

The children of William Miller and his first wife, Hannah Lackey, were:

1. Samuel Lackey Miller, born July 11, 1805; died May 23, 1838. He married Mary Ann Addison about 1835. His father gave him a number of negroes and his sister, Dorcas A. Miller, left him several slaves. Their children:

1. William Miller (known as Wagoner), born June 15, 1836. He married Susan Chenault, daughter of Waller Chenault and Talitha Harris, his wife. (See Part III, Chap. 48, Sec. 8.)

2. Caledonia Miller, born Sept. 28, 1838. She married William O. Chenault, son of Waller Chenault and Talitha Harris, his wafe, May 11, 1856. (See Part III, Chap. 48, Sec. 8.) Their children:

1. Callie Chenault; married Daniel Bates Shackelford, son of James T. Shackelford and Mary Bates, his first wife. (See Chap. 11, Sec. 2, and Part III, Chap. 48, Sec. 8.)

2. Mattie Chenault; married Clarence E. Woods, the present hustling Myaor of the city of Richmond, Ky. (See Part III, Chap. 48, Sec. 8. and Part II, Chap. 13, Sec. 3.) They had one child:

1. Mamie White Woods.

3. Lizzie Chenault; married Daniel Harber, son of Wm. Harber. (See Part III, Chap. 48, Sec. 8.)

4. Mary Chenault; married James Smith, son of a former Sheriff of Madison County, Presley Smith. (See Part III, Chap. 48, Sec. 8.)

After the death of Samuel L. Miller, his widow, Mary Ann, married Sidney W. Harris, April 4, 1844. (See Part III, Chap. 48, Sec. 4.)

2. John Locke Miller, born Nov. 29, 1806; died Sept. 21, 1840. He was given a number of negro slaves by his father. He was never married.

3. Alzira Miller, born Jan. 25, 1808; married, Aug. 18, 1836, to Richard Gentry, Jr., oldest son of Reuben Eustice Gentry and Elizabeth White, his wife. (See Part III, Chap. 46, Sec. 1.) She died June 2, 1856. After her death her husband, Richard Gentry, married Mrs. Jael Woods Hocker Gentry, widow of his brother, Joel W. Gentry, with about six children. (See Part VII, Chap. 7, Sec. 1-12.) Joel W. Gentry was born March 15, 1815, and was married to Jael Woods Hocker, of Madison County, Ky., June 19, 1848, and he died Oct. 4, 1851. Mrs. Jael Woods Hocker Gentry is still living and resides in Sedalia, Missouri, on East Broadway.

Alzira Miller Gentry was greatly beloved by her husband's family. The Hon. George Graham Vest, United States Senator, in speaking of her husband, Richard Gentry, said: "Few men have I met who were the equal of Richard Gentry, and none who were his superior," and they were close personal friends for many years.

The farm of Richard Gentry was one of the largest and best improved in Missouri, over six thousand acres under cultivation. He was the most extensive sheep raiser in that western country of his day. The family of Richard Gentry and that of his brother, Major William Gentry, were very intimate. Richard was a compact and well built man, but not tall like his brother, Major William, who was full six feet, and the statue and carriage of a Prince. Richard was a most energetic person, everything around him moved like clockwork, and showed the most untiring industry and order. He was exceedingly hospitable; in that early day before the Civil War, all strangers visiting the state were taken to his home to show what could be done in Missouri. The children of Alzira Miller and Richard Gentry were:

1. William Miller Gentry, born Sept. 19, 1837. He and his brother, Reuben J., had fine country places, and they kept bachelor's hall near each other about three miles northeast of Sedalia; his brother, Reuben, however, married and broke the monotony of a bachelor's life, and subsequently died. After his death, William Gentry and Mrs. Bettie Hughes Gentry (who had five children by Reuben Gentry) were married, Dec. 2, 1885, and then moved over and lived at his brother's place, and his widow and three sons live there now. William Miller Gentry died May 1, 1889.

2. Reuben Joel Gentry, born Jan. 2, 1839; married Bettie Hughes, daughter of Reese Hughes and Sarah Birch, his wife, April 5, 1871. He died Oct. 5, 1881, and his widow married his brother, William Miller Gentry, as stated above (1). The children of Reuben Joel Gentry and Bettie Hughes, his wife, were:

1. Ruby Gentry, born April 8, 1872; married Dr. Ferguson March 9, 1892; died June 16, 1900.

2. Sallie B. Gentry, born Aug. 12, 1873; married Thomas Sturgis, Feb. 7, 1894. They had one child:

1. Margaret Elizabeth Sturgis, born June 14, 1896.

3. William Henry Gentry, born March 15, 1876; lives near Sedalia, Mo.

4. Charles Richard Gentry, born Feb. 8, 1878; lives near Sedalia, Mo.

5. Reuben Joel Gentry, born Dec. 19, 1880; lives near Sedalia, Mo.

3. Henry Clay Gentry, born Feb. 28, 1844; died July 26, 1864, during vacation from Kempers College, Booneville, Mo., only twenty years old. He was a most promising young man and very much like his father. William Miller, Reuben J., and Henry Clay Gentry were all three educated at Kempers College, Boonville, Missouri.

4. Laura Dorcas Gentry, born Sept., 1846; died Mar., 1856.

4. William Malcom Miller, born February 6, 1810; died Friday, July 16, 1889. About the time of President Lincoln's Emancipation Proclamation he owned thirty-odd negro slaves. Moses was the only one that remained with him till the freedom of the negroes, the rest having left their master, and a number of them enlisted in the Federal service. His father gave him a considerable number and he bought a number at his father's sale, and a number were given him by his uncle, Alexander Lackey. He owned a fine body of land and other personal property. When General Scott's command was in Madison County, Ky., on the 28th of July, 1863, eight head of blooded horses and mares were taken from him. In July, 1864, a fine horse, "Snap," was stolen from his pasture. On March 3, 1865, an excellent bay horse, five years old, was clandestinely taken from his premises. William Malcolm Miller was an exceedingly prominent, popular, influential and useful citizen-farmer of Madison County, Kentucky. He represented the county in the lower house of the State General Assembly in 1855-7. He married, April 2, 1839, Mary Jane Patterson, the mother of his children. After her death he married the second time, Mrs. Ann Eliza Heatherly, widow of Mahlon B. Heatherly, and a daughter of Edward B. Jarman and Judith Waddy Maupin, his wife. (See Part V, Chap. 4, Sec. 1.)

WILLIAM M MILLER

MARY J. PATTERSON
Wife of Wm. M. Miller

Note: "Mary Jane Patterson, the first wife of William Malcolm Miller, was a daughter of Robert C. Patterson and Nancy Waller Broaddus, his wife. She was born Feb. 13, 1824: married William Malcolm Miller April 2, 1839, as aforesaid, and died April 19, 1876. Her father, Robert C. Patterson, was born Sept. 19, 1797, and died Jan. 11, 1871. Her mother, Nancy Waller Broaddus Patterson, was born July 6, 1805, and died June 26, 1876." (See Part I, Chap. 13, Sec. 3. Note.)

The children of William Malcolm Miller and Mary Jane Patterson, his wife:

1. Judge William C. Miller, one of the most popular men the County of Madison ever produced, possessed of a splendid intellect, good education, fine looks, a ready speaker, splendid conversationalist, and a ready mixer; very infatuating in his manner and address. Was a member of the Richmond bar. In 1870 he was elected County Attorney, which office he filled one term, if not two, with great credit to himself and satisfaction to his constituents. Afterwards he was elected Judge of

the County Court, and twice re-elected, and died in office. He was born Jan. 26, 1840; married Susan White, daughter of Col. Richard X. White, of Richmond, Ky., Nov. 27, 1867. He died Oct. 21, 1885, leaving many friends. Their children:

1. Mary Miller; married Clarence E. Woods, the present Mayor of Richmond. She died childless and Mr. Woods married again, Mattie Chenault. (See above Sec. 2, and Part II, Chap. 13, Sec. 3.)

2. Richard White Miller, a very popular man; member of the Richmond bar, and politician; highly educated, polished gentleman. He represented Madison County in the State Legislature in 1904-5; elected on the Democratic ticket, was re-elected, and was at his death her Representative. Was defeated for Speaker of the House, but was a formidable contestant for the position. He was a gifted man and made a most prominent member. He was one of the foremost orators of the state, and contended earnestly, eloquently and fearlessly for his conception of the right. Besides, he was Chairman of the Democratic Committee of Madison County; member of the State Central Committee of the party of the Eighth District of Kentucky; was the House delegate to the National Divorce Congress; was in a high degree honest in the discharge of duties. Many complimentary expressions of Richard White Miller appeared in the state press. He was the candidate from Madison County for a seat in the United States Congress as a Democrat from the Eighth District of Kentucky when he was stricken with creeping paralysis, after delivering a telling speech at Stanford, Lincoln County, Ky., on the 28th of June, 1906, from which he never rallied, and died the 29th of June, and was buried in the Richmond Cemetery Sunday evening, July 1, 1906, the services being conducted by the orders of Elks and Knights Templar, and Rev. J. Addison Smith, Presbyterian divine, from the residence of Mrs. William M. Irvine, on Lancaster Avenue. A large concourse of people, relatives and friends from Madison County and other sections of the state, and from other states, accompanied the remains to their last resting place. The loss of Richard White Miller was felt by the whole state. It seemed that a brilliant future was in front of him, when his career on earth was brought to a close by death. His wife was absent visiting friends and relatives in the Southland when Mr. Miller was stricken, and did not reach his bedside till two hours after life was extinct; he died with his hand in that of his pastor, the Rev. Smith, his talk to whom just before his dissolution was most beautiful; his faith in his Redeemer was manifested and he did not fear death. His wife was Miss Sue Patton (see Part II, Chap. 5, Sec. 1), a great-granddaughter of Colonel David Irvine, the second Clerk of the Madison County and Circuit Courts (successor to his father, William Irvine, the first Clerk). They have a child:

1. Richard White Miller.

3. Mattie Miller; married Mr. McGowan. They live in Washington City, D. C.

2. Virginia D. Miller, born Oct. 31, 1842; married Samuel E. Lackey, July 4, 1867. (See Part I, Chap. 14, Sec. 11.) She died Oct. 25, 1895. They had only one child:

1. William Miller Lackey.

3. Leslie Miller, born Sept. 28, 1844; died Oct. 31, 1878. He was never married.

4. Malcolm Mimminger Miller, born Oct. 20, 1849. He married Lida Lackey, Feb. 7, 1877. (See Part I. Chap. 14, Sec. 11.) He is a popular and prominent citizen and farmer of Madison county, Ky., now living in Richmond, the county seat. Their children:

1. William Malcolm Miller, born March 18, 1881.
2. Mary Strawn Miller.
3. Margaret Dillingham Miller.

Last two twin girls, born March 3, 1882.

5. John Calhoun Miller, born Aug. 7, 1852. He was appointed and commissioned Judge of the Madison County Court to fill out the unexpired term of his brother, Judge William C. Miller. He married Mary Bates, daughter of Dr. Stephen Bates. He died June 11, 1900, leaving one child:

1. Ellen Gibson Miller.

5. Dorcas A. Miller; died testate and unmarried.

Section 3. Anna Miller, the third child of Colonel John Miller and Jane Dulaney, his wife, was born Nov. 3, 1777. She married John Reid, April 18, 1796, in Madison County, Ky. (See Part II. Chap. 21, Sec. 2.) They were both members of the Viney Fork Baptist Church in said county. Their children, viz:

1. Jane Reid; married Hudson Broaddus, Dec. 21, 1819, in Madison County, Ky. (See Part I, Chap. 13, Sec. 3. Note.) They emigrated to Missouri and settled and lived near Middle Grove, in Monroe County, and were the parents of four boys, viz:

1. Elijah Broaddus; married, and lives on the old home place, and has children, we do not know how many.

2. Thomas Broaddus; married, and lived in Chillicothe, Mo., until his death a few years since, leaving three children, viz:

1. Anna Broaddus.
2. Mary Broaddus.
3. Henry Broaddus.

3. Jefferson Broaddus; still lives in Chilicothe; has several children, whose names we are not able to give.

4. Christopher Broaddus, who was a bachelor; lived in St. Louis, the last we knew of him.

2. John M. Reid; married Elizabeth Dinwiddie, in Madison County, Ky., Sept. 9, 1824.

3. Thomas Reid; married Nancy Harris, in Madison County, Ky., April 19, 1820.

4. Jefferson Reid; died a few years ago at or near Kingston, Caldwell County, Missouri, leaving two sons and one daughter:

1. Kit Reid.
2. Sylvanus Reid.
3. Mary Reid; married some years ago, to whom we do not know, and went to California.

5. Susan Reid; married George Estill, of Howard County, Mo., and died without issue.

6. Eliza M. Reid; married Talton Fox, in Madison County, Ky., July 29, 1828, and emigrated therefrom and lived in Quincy, Ill., years ago, and perhaps died there, leaving children; how many we do not know, but understand some are in business there now.

7. Lucinda Reid; married Overton Gentry, in Madison County,

Ky., Oct. 7, 1824. (See Part II, Chap. 21, Sec. 2, and Part III, Chap. 46, Sec. 10.) They emigrated to Missouri and years ago lived near St. Joseph. The last information obtained they had one daughter.

8. Joseph Reid; married and reared a family, the names or number of whom we are unable to give, but he and they lived in and near Middle Grove, Monroe County, Mo.

9. Christopher (Kit) Reid; wten to California many years ago, and when last heard of was living in San Francisco with his wife and five children; further than this we know nothing.

10. William Reid; lived for many years and died at Spickard, in Grundy County, Missouri, leaving five children, viz:

1. George Reid, who now lives at Spickard.
2. John Reid, living in Mercer County, Missouri.
3. Delilah Reid.
4. Corena Reid.
5. Mary Reid.

All lived in and near Spickard.

11. Polly Reid; married Levi Williams; nothing known of their children, if any.

12. Corena Reid; married Hardin Yates, in Madison County, Ky. They emigrated to Missouri. She died and was buried in Grundy County in 1858, leaving three children, viz:

1. Anna Stuart Yates; married James Tolson, sometime in the fifties; Tolson was killed during the Civil War. After his death his widow, Anna Stewart Yates, remarried David Owens. Two children were born of her first marriage, viz:

1. Andrew C. Tolson; married Amanda Owens, in the early seventies, of which three children were born, viz:

1. James Tolson; married Josephine Anderson, and have two small boys.

2. Hattie Tolson; married Edward Anderson; they have two daughters.

3. Orion Tolson; is still single.

The Tolsons still live at Loredo, Missouri.

2. Laura Tolson; married Joseph Warren, of which union seven children were born, viz:

1. Andrew H. Warren; married Samma Means. No children.

2. James Warren; married, first, China Anderson, who died leaving one child. He married, second, Bertha Marryman.

3. Roena Warren; married Elvin Rooks, of which marriage there are five boys.

4. Fountain Warren; married Pearl Hearn; two children.

5. Columbus Warren; married Pauline Jackson. Two children.

6. Annie Warren; married Paul Anderson; one child.

7. Sallie Warren; married Mr. Kilburn, and have three children.

Children of the second marriage of Mrs. Anna Stuart Yates Tolson to David Owens, viz:

3. William Owens; married Amanda Pence, and have three children.

4. Polly Owens; married George Merrifield; no children.

5. Arthur Owens; married Mr. Bowman; they have four children.

2. Susan Jane Yates; married Hardin Jones. Of this union there were five children, viz:

1. John Jones: married Frances Davis, and live at New Boston, Macon County, Mo. Three children were born of them, viz:

1. Susan Jones.
2. Harvey Jones.
3. Elmer Jones.

2. Christopher Jones: married, and is living near New Boston. One child.

3. Corena Jones; married Dr. Howard, and lives at Bucklin, Linn County, Missouri. One child:

1. Dora Vashti Howard.

4. Robert Jones; married, and is living at Roger, Missouri, Sullivan County. No children.

5. Moses Jones; married, and living at Gravity, Iowa. No children.

3. Roena Elizabeth Yates, was married to Christopher Columbus Woods, Feb. 13, 1862. Of this marriage there were born:

1. Larkin Vaughan Woods; married Catherine Cook, and they have two children, viz:

1. Ruth Woods.
2. Charles Woods.

2. Mary Frances Woods; married William Marryman. No children.

3. Virginia (or Jennie) Woods; married Oscar Williams, a lawyer; they now live in Trenton, Missouri. To them one child was born:

1. Cloyd Patton Williams.

4. Nina Elizabeth Woods; married Cory Lewis Fickel. No children.

5. Georgia C. Woods, who died in the ninteenth year of her age.

6. Cora C. Woods; married Drury C. Moberley. No children. They are living at Ault, Colorado.

7. Ethel Woods; married Elmer A. Parkhurst; living at Loredo, Missouri. No children.

Note—Miscellaneous:

Sylvester Reid; married Elizabeth Hubbard, Aug. 13, 1829. (See Part 1, Chap. 20, Sec. 5.)

Polly Reid; married James Reid, Feb. 27, 1816. (See Part II, Chap. 21, Sec. 3.)

Isaac Reid; married Rhoda Tate, Sept. 9, 1825.

Miriam Reid; married Alexander R. Oldham, Sept. 15, 1831. (See Part II, Chap. 20, Sec. 5.)

Sallie Reid; married Thomas Todd, Jan. 15, 1829.

Section 4. Thomas Miller, the fourth child of Colonel John Miller and Jane Dulaney, his wife, was born March 30, 1779. He was twice married; first, March 25, 1802, to Miss Sallie Adams, in Madison County, Ky., and second, July 29, 1806, in the same county, to Miss Anna Woods, daughter of Archibald Woods and Mourning Shelton, his wife. (See Part II, Chap. 8, Sec. 7.)

On the ground where the beautiful Richmond Cemetery is situated, in the year 1800, Thomas Miller killed a wolf. In about the year 1818 he and his brother John emigrated to Alabama and settled near New Market, in Madison County, where Thomas Miller established his home, and his home was called "Hickory Flat." One writer states that "he was Representative in the Legislature and State Senator for sixteen consecutive terms, and declined to make the race for the seventeenth."

Dr. W. G. Norris, a distinguished citizen of New Market, in his history of the town says: "Thomas Miller, a brother of John Miller, settled four miles north of New Market at an early day. The two brothers, although dissimilar in many respects, were both men of note and worth. Each of them reared large families, all of whom were highly intellectual and no taint or stain of dishonor ever attached to any of them. Both brothers were strong Democrats. Thomas Miller served in the Alabama Legislature from 1823 to 1827 inclusive. Nature seemed to have marked him as a favorite. He was tall and well poportioned, with a head and face which the ablest artist would pronounce a masterpiece. His mental powers were equal to his physical. He was not a lawyer, yet was always ready in thought and language—exhibiting a vigor of mind and a degree of culture that did him credit. He was one of the best of neighbors. If a near resident became sick, he invariably attended to his wants, and if needed, sent his horses, hands, plows and hoes and worked out the crop in a day. His wife, Anna Miller, was a famous house-wife and a good physician in ordinary cases. He was a life-long Democrat, and died when about 70 years of age, leaving a bright record behind him. His son, William G. Miller, was a member of the House in 1845, and was a worthy son of a noble sire. He went to Bastrop, Texas, to live."

Thomas Miller was not exceedingly large, but was of a stout and powerful build and very muscular, and a stranger to fear. The story is told that on one occasion, whilst living near New Market, a man unfriendly to Mr. Miller, placed himself behind the front door of a store in New Market, and as Miller entered struck him over the head with a club, but failed to stagger him; nearby was an open tub of tar, and Miller grabbed his assailant, and with miraculous strength, thrust him head foremost into the tub of tar. The men present lifted the man from the tub and washed the tar off of him, and he had no further desire to molest Thomas Miller.

The children of the first marriage of Thomas Miller and Sallie Adams were two, the name of one we cannot furnish:

1. John Adams Miller; married Edna Bridges.
2. Name unknown.

The children of his second marriage to Anna Woods were:

3. Woods S. Miller; married Nancy Jane Miller, daughter of Joseph Miller and Susan Kennedy, his wife. (See Sec. 8.)

4. Thomas Miller; married Caroline Douglas, of Sumner County, Tennessee. Their children:
    1. Anna Miller; married Mr. Bunton, of Texas.
    2. Mary Miller.

5. Garland Burleigh Miller, was born in 1816. He was educated in Richmond, Ky. He married Sarah R. Dismukes, of Sumner County, Tenn., of the fine old Revolutionary family. After his marriage he established his home in Fayetteville, Lincoln County, Tenn., where his children were born and reared. He died at his home in 1860, where his wife continued to live until her death in 1882. She was a first cousin to the wives of Rev. Good-

loe Woods and Wm. Woods, two brothers who married sisters. (See Part II, Chap. 10, Sec. 8 and 11.) Their children:

1. Sarah M. Miller, born in 1841. She married Rush Williamson, a son of Colonel Robert Williamson, of Sumner County, Tenn. Rush Williamson was a Confederate soldier under General N. B. Forrest, and served through the entire war, and received three severe wounds. Her postoffice is Pulaski, Tennessee. Their children:

1. Robert Garland Williamson; died without issue.
2. George Estill Williamson; died in infancy.
3. William M. Williamson; married Sadie Neville, of Trinity, Alabama. His home is in La Grange, Georgia, and is of the firm of C. D. Smith & Co., railroad contractors, who build roads both North and South. Issue, one son:
    1. Rayburn Williamson; died in infancy.

2. Thomas K. Miller, born in 1843. He enlisted in the Confederate army in the Civil War—the third enlistment in Lincoln County, Tennessee. He served in the First Tennessee Infantry with Colonel Peter Tanseyk, two years in Virginia, and was then transferred to the command of General Forest. He made a gallant soldier. He was captured in Tennessee in the fall of 1863, as one of General Forest's scouts, was tried by court martial and sentenced to be hanged, though he had on a full Confederate uniform and not a paper or plan on his person, still the court condemned him. His mother went immediately to Washington to try and exert some influence with President Lincoln in his behalf, but she failed, though she remained two weeks. His sister, Mrs. Sallie Miller Williamson, remained in Nashville with him, and by the assistance of some of her father's old friends she succeeded at the last hour in having him reprieved until further orders by General Thomas, the commanding general at Nashville. They offered him life and liberty if he would take the oath and pilot them through Lincoln County where he lived, but he firmly refused and said: "If I had forty lives, I would give every one before I would betray a friend or be a traitor to my country." At that moment, his sister, who loved him dearly, and he so helpless, seemingly, in the hands of the enemy, almost lost her patriotism. He still was left in close confinement.

After a few months his mother returned to Washington City, and with a mother's pleading and prayers President Lincoln relented, and the last document President Lincoln ever signed was a pardon for Thomas Miller, which he was to have handed to his mother at 9 o'clock the next morning; but that night President Lincoln was assassinated, and President Johnson would never let Mrs. Miller have the pardon for her son, though she remained in Washington City three weeks longer.

In the spring of 1865, Mrs. Williamson, sister to the condemned man, went to Nashville to see Governor Brownlow. After entreating with him as a sister could, under such circumstances, the Governor asked of the President the pardon of Thomas Miller without the oath of allegiance, and he gave it.

About the time of the surrender Thomas Miller was free from that long, close confinement, which had almost wrecked his life. In the fall of that year he went to Texas and settled near Bastrop, and married Miss Lou Bell, of Bastrop, and engaged in the mercantile business in Webberville, and there in his store, in 1867, he was assaulted with shotguns and pistols by two or three of his deadly enemies and was killed, though he fought for his life. He left no issue. Thomas Miller was absolutely fearless.

3. George D. Miller, born in 1845; died in 1852, in the seventh year of his age.

4. Garland Burleigh Miller, born in 1847; died in 1902. He enlisted in the Confederate army in the fall of 1863 with his brother Thomas, at the time of his enlistment being only fourteen years of age, and served under General Forest, and remained until the surrender, and made a gallant soldier. He married in Fayetteville, Lincoln County, Tenn., Mary (Mamie) Gardner, daughter of Dr. R. C. Gardner, formerly of the firm of Gardner Brothers, of Nashville, Tenn., and after the war of the firm of Evans, Gardner & Co., of New York. The Gardner family was one of the best of Tennessee. In the fall of 1865 Garland Burleigh Miller went with his brother Thomas to Texas. He settled in Galveston and entered a strong, reliable business house in Galveston, doing a general commission, forwarding and receiving business, as clerk, in which he continued for several years, until he rose to be a member of the firm, and before his death, which occurred in February, 1902, he had amassed quite a fortune. In the great Galveston storm his financial loss was heavy. They had six children:

1. Garland Burleigh Miller; unmarried; Treasurer of the Falfurrias Immigration Company, Home Office, Falfurrias, Texas.

2. Richard Gardner Miller; married Martha Terrill, of San Antonio, Texas, Oct. 25, 1905; she died recently. He is President of the Falfurrias State Bank. Has one child:

1. Richard Gardner Miller, born Aug. 20, 1906; the mother died in October following.

3. William Goodloe Miller; died in infancy.

4. Mary Gardner Miller; married, Oct. 29, 1902, E. C. Lasater, of Falfurrias, Texas, an enterprising young man and owner of a fine cattle ranch near Falfurrias, and is interested in the State Bank, Cotton, Gin and Ice Factory, and has planted an Orange Nursery, the first in the state of Texas. Mr. Ed C. Lasater, the founder of Falfurrias, Texas—once the hunting-ground of the Lepans, the most docile and peaceful of the Indian tribes in the state, until driven away by the more ferocious and warlike Apaches and Comanches, who in turn were driven out by the adventurous Spaniards, who came over from Mexico to settle the country, subdued the Indians, built missions, called the land and cattle their own, and embarked in pastoral and agricultural pursuits in a more or less haphazard manner, until in due course of evolution these lands were acquired by the more far-seeing and thrifty American stockmen, who transformed the open and boundless prairies into huge and limitless pastures and by scientific methods improved the Texas Longhorns by blooded breeds, making stock raising more profitable, and bred up the Texas ponies by thoroughbred horses, evolving a breed that retains the hardiness of the Texas bronco with all the qualities of standard bred horses. This section has been opened for settlement to the thrifty husbandman, and where only a few years ago, and even now, thousands of cattle are roaming at large, hundreds of families already have—and

thousands more will—within the next few years, come to establish prosperous and happy homes that will make this section flourish as but few others will be able to do. The owner of this vast domain, Mr. Ed C. Lasater, one of the cattle kings of Texas, and one of the most intelligent and successful breeders of cattle and horses, who knew the richness of the soil and the health-giving properties of the climate, long foresaw that this section was destined to become the garden spot of the United States. Their children:

1. Albert Lasater.
2. Mary Miller Lasater, born Dec. 11, 1904.
3. Garland Miller Lasater, born Jan. 5, 1907.

5. Robert G. Miller; unmarried. He is connected with the State Bank of Falfurrias.

6. Laurence Kleber Dismukes Miller; unmarried.

The sons of Garland Burleigh Miller and Mamie Gardner, his wife, are actively engaged in building up the town of Falfurrias and the surrounding country.

5. Woods S. Miller, born in 1849; died in 1851.

6. Anna Woods Miller, born in 1852; died in 1873. She married Thomas Ross, of Lincoln County, Tenn. He was a Confederate soldier under Gen. Forest. They had five children:

1. Robert Ross; unmarried; lives in Tennessee.
2. Garland Ross; lives in Florence, Alabama.
3. Mary Ann Ross; married Manly Askins, a merchant of Huntsville, Alabama. They have two children:
    1. Hershell Askins.
    2. Miller Askins.
4. Sallie Ross; unmarried; lives in Huntsville, Ala.

Thomas Ross; lives in Huntsville, Ala.

7. Mourning Shelton Miller, born in 1854; died in 1855.

8. William Goodloe Miller, born in 1857; died in 1880; unmarried; a young man of fine promise.

9. Pauline Dismukes Miller, born in 1860; married, first Ewing Forbes, of Galveston, Texas, and second, Dr. M. S. Walters, of Giles County, Tenn. No issue of the second marriage. Issue of the first marriage:

1. Ewing M. Forbes; unmarried; lives in Memphis, Tenn.; is an investment banker, 310-11 Tenn. Trust Building.

6. Kleber Miller; married Mary Franklin, of Sumner County, Tennesse; died without issue.

7. Williamson Goodloe Miller; married Cornelia Sanders (Kernelia Douglas), of Sumner County, Tenn., first, and she married second, Lizzie Morgan. He was a member of the Alabama Legislature in 1845. He went to Bastrop, Texas, to live. Children of the first marriage:

1. Woods S. Miller; married Margaret Hemphill; lives at Goldthwale, Texas.

2. Goodloe Miller; married Candice Moore; live at Brownwood, Texas.

Children of the second marriage—six children, only two living:

3. Garland B. Miller; married Ida Banard; lives at Hemphill Prairie, Bartrop County, Texas.

4. Dollie (or Mollie) Miller; married Glenn Jackson; lives at Elgin, Texas.

8. Mourning Shelton Miller; married her cousin, Robert Green Miller, son of Joseph Miller and Susan Kennedy, his wife (see Sec. 8), March 12, 1840. She was born March 4, 1823. Her husband died June 20, 1842, and she married the second time, Norval Douglas, November 26, 1844 (see Sec. 8). Mrs. Douglass died August, 1860.

9. Mary Miller; married Woods Moore, of Mississippi. They immigrated to Texas and settled in Bastrop County. She died many years ago and Mr. Moore married his sister-in-law, Mrs. Ann Trigg. Children of Mary Miller and Woods Moore:

1. Thomas Moore; married Olivia Grady.
2. Worth Moore; married Lou Luckett; now dead.
3. James Moore; married Lizur Burleson.
4. Abbie Moore; married Peter Gill.
5. B. Moore; married Leigh Burleson.

10. Anna Woods Miller; married Marshall Trigg, of Franklin County, Tennessee. They immigrated to Texas and settled in Bastrop County. Mr. Trigg died and his widow married her brother-in-law, Woods Moore. Children of Anna Woods Miller and Marshall Trigg:

1. Sue Trigg; married Rufus Green.
2. Jones Trigg; married Mollie Erhard.
3. Kleber Trigg; married Mary Hubbard.
4. Mary Trigg; married Chester Erhard.
   All live in Bastrop, Texas.
5. Woods Trigg; dead.
6. William Trigg; died in infancy.
7. Ella Trigg; died in infancy.

Addenda.

Data of the family and descendants of Thomas Miller, son of Col. John Miller and Jane Dulaney, his wife, who married, first, Sallie Adams, and, second, Anna Woods, and who was the grandfather of Mrs. Green and Mrs. Trigg, of Bastrop, Bastrop County, Texas, who furnished the data through the hands of their cousin, Mrs. Sallie Miller Williamson, of Pulaski, Tennessee; also a granddaughter of said Thomas Miller. Mrs. Green writes:

"Thomas Miller first married Sallie Adams, 1803; second, Anna Woods, 1806; was born 1779. Anna Woods Miller died August 1857. Thomas Miller died 1841. Children, 8; sons, (1) Woods, (2) Garland, (3) Khleber, (4) Thomas, (5) Goodloe; daughters, (6) Anna, (7) Mourning and (8) Mary.

1. Woods Miller; married Nancy Jane Miller. Children, don't know; suppose you have them from Ellen McClain.

2. Garland Miller; married Mrs. Sallie Dismukes. (I sent all this as they are my father and mother.)

3. Khleber Miller; married Miss Mary ——— (other name do not know.) He died without children, and do not know further.

4. Thomas Miller; married Miss Caroline Douglas. Children, 3:
   1. Anna; dead.
   2. Louiza; dead.
   3. Carrie Miller. (No sons.)

Uncle Tommy and Aunt Caroline died long ago; only one girl living, and far away from us; west of San Antonio; a large family of children. How I loved Uncle Tom and Aunt Caroline. Their second daughter, Lou, was a great companion of mine and married a promising man, who did not out-live her very long, leaving the oldest of two little baby girls—one dead: one Uncle and Aunt kept, and when they died, she was taken by a wealthy brother of her father and educated in a convent in New York; when grown she would not leave it, but took the veil, and last I knew she had gone to a large convent in San Francisco; and "such is life," we cannot tell how it may go: but thanks there is a home where we all can be together again.

5. Goodloe Miller; married Miss Cornelia Sanders (have forgotten other name, first: second time, Miss Lizzie Morgan, after coming to Texas. Children (4 now living): first marriage, two sons, Woods and Goodloe; second marriage, one son, Garland, and daughter, Dolly, living; several dying while very young. Uncle Goodloe died in 1888, leaving four children:

1. Garland; living here, and five children.
2. His daughter (Dolly) has none.
3. Goodloe, one of the older boys, none.
4. The other I do not know; he has his second wife.

6. Anna Miller; married Marshall Trigg, of Tennessee. (Children 7.) Anna Woods Miller, born Feb. 20, 1825, near Huntsville, Alabama; married Marshall W. Trigg, born in Tennessee, near Winchester, Nov. 25, 1822; they were married October, 1842. They lived in Tennessee for two or three years, then moved to Mississippi, where their first three children were born. Their children: (1) Susan A., (2) Thomas J., (3) Khleber M., (Woods, dead; William, dead; Kate, dead; and Mary E. Trigg). Afterwards moved to Texas, about 1850, where we have been raised.

1. Sue A., oldest girl and child, was born April 30, 1845; married Rufus A. Green, of Alabama, January, 1869. Two children only living, girls:

1. Hattie A.; married W. J. Hill, of Columbia, Tenn., and have two children.

2. Minnie K.; married W. B. Runsome, of Texas, and have three children; two boys and one girl.

2. Thomas J. Trigg, born 1847; married Miss M. Erhard, of Bastrop; have no children and living yet in this town.

3. Khleber Miller Trigg, born 1749 (one gives this date, another 1747); married Miss Mary Hubbard. Also living here and have three children; two boys and one girl:

Mrs. Trigg writes: "Sister Sue—failed to put the dates of all my family, and as I am so very anxious to get the history of the Miller family (I am only connected by marriage), yet I want a book and my part of the family's history recorded. "Kleber Miller Trigg, born Oct. 7, 1847; married Mary Willis Hubbard, June 16, 1880. She was born Sept. 16, 1856. Their eldest son:

1. Thomas Marshall Trigg, was born March 21, 1882, and was married to Miss Annie Gamble Hoggins, Sept. 27, 1904. She was born April 14, 1882. My second son:

2. Kleber Miller Trigg, was born Aug. 26, 1889; and my third, a daughter:

3. A daughter; was born Dec. 26, 1892.

This is our short history, and hope it is not too late to insert." Mrs. Green further writes: "Here I will mention something about the name "Khleber" (spelled sometimes "Khleber" and sometimes "Kleber"). "I remember mother told me (as

I have never heard the name except the three— mother's brother, Khleber; my brother, Khleber, and his son, Khleber). She said grandpa loved to read and named Uncle Khleber for a great general in Napoleon Bonaparte's army, who he admired very much. He was a German, educated at Munich, and joined Napolcon in Egypt." Next is my sister:

4. Mary E. Trigg, youngest child and daughter. She married Mr. Erhard, of this town, and is living here. He has been Cashier of our bank for many years. They only have one child, now about 27 years old, living in Palestine, having studied engineering, occupies a prominent position in the machine shop there.

My mother lost three children; two died while young, and one son at the age of 18 years.

5. Woods Trigg.

7. Mourning Miller; married, first, Joseph K. Miller, having one son, J. K. Miller; second time, Norval Douglas, having two daughters, Anna and Mary. Children 3 (you have data to here).

8. Mary Miller; married Woods Moore, of Mississippi. Children 5: (1) Thomas, (2) Worth, dead, (3) James, (4) Biddy A. (always called "B"), and (5) Abigail, dead.

1. Thomas, is living here and father of five children. He married Miss Olivia Grady, of this county. Children all married.

2. Worth, you remember, was a fine man; married Miss Lou Lucket, from Kentucky, they having three children:

1. Powel, their oldest, died many years ago.

2. Worth, their second son, is living in Ft. Worth, a young lawyer (I believe). And youngest is a daughter:

3. Luttie Moore, now a young lady. She and her mother spend most of their time in Staunton, Virginia—this winter spending in Galveston; do not know much of them, hear occasionally. Cousin Lou has not been here for many years, although she has a brother (a doctor) living here.

3. James: married Miss Lizur Burleson. They have only two children, son and daughter:

1. Worth Moore.

2. Mary Belle Moore.

She spends her time here and in Ft. Worth with her daughter, who is married to a prominent specialist (ear, throat and dentist) Dr. W. R. Thompson; they have two children and he is wealthy. Their son is not married—is a doctor and surgeon. Cousin Lizur is a very lovable woman and loves to be here with the kinfolk (left of us) and we love to have her. Cousin Jim, as I told you, is a traveling man and has toured the world, and did come home, but has gone again to Europe expecting to go over it again; is now or will be soon in London. I told him I would like his assistance, but his stay was so limited, and so many to see him, found no time to help me. Although like myself, can only go so far and no more.

4. (Biddy A.) Cousin B. married Mr. Lee Burleson, of Waco, a lawyer, and brother to Cousin Lizur, nephew to Rev. Rufus Burleson, and son of Richard Burleson, who were founders and lived and died with the great Baptist College of Waco, now so prominent and prosperous and far known. Cousin B. has three children, two sons, (1) Burrell and (2) Richard, and one daughter (3) Mary Lee.

1. Burrell; married Mary Longley, a young lady of San Sabba.

2. Richard is a student of West Point.

3. Mary Lee Burleson; married a young man of our town, Mr. P. Gill; had two girls, both married; their father is dead.

Aunt Mary died March, 1867.

Section 5. John Miller, the fifth child of Colonel John Miller and Jane Dulaney, his wife, was born Sept. 30, 1780. He was married in Madison County, Kentucky, Feb. 9, 1804, to Polly Brown. In about the year 1818 John Miller and his family, and his brother Thomas and his family, emigrated from Madison County, Ky., to Alabama and settled in or near New Market, Madison County, where John Miller established his home, and where he and his wife died. (See Sec. 4, also Note foot Sec. 5 and Part VIII, Chap. 2, A.) Their children:

1. Nancy H. Miller, born Oct. 13, 1816; died in Richmond, Ky., at the age of twenty-five or thirty years; unmarried.

2. James O. Miller, born Aug. 29, 1809; died at New Market, Ala., at the age of thirty to forty years; unmarried.

3. Elizabeth Miller, born Aug. 12, 1805; married Alexander Jeffries, of Union Township, Alabama, a wealthy planter. She died there at seventy-five years of age. One night in the act of retiring, her dress caught fire, and she was so seriously burned that she died within a few days, leaving three children, two boys and one girl, viz:

1. John Jeffries; married, had a son:

1. Lewis Jeffries, a lawyer in Selma, Alabama.

2. Tandy or "Jardy" Jeffries.

3. Frances Jeffries; married Henry Hudson Ware. Their children:

1. Lula H. Ware; married Rufus Preston McGoodwin, of the Danville Planing Mill Co., Danville, Ky. Issue:

1. Nellie Ware McGoodwin; married William Hickman Carter. Issue:

1. Rufus Preston Carter.

2. Bessie Ware; married Eugene McGoodwin (brother to Rufus Preston McGoodwin). Eugene McGoodwin is now deceased. Issue:

1. Lula McGoodwin.

2. Eugene McGoodwin.

4. William Brown Miller, a son, was born in Richmond, Ky., Aug. 24, 1807. When he was nine to eleven years old, his parents moved to Alabama, taking this son with them, where he grew to manhood, and there married his first wife, Elizabeth Waddy (who had in her veins a strain of Cherokee blood), about the year 1827. She only lived a few years and died in New Market, leaving one son. On the 14th of September, 1839, William Brown Miller married the second time, Minerva Barnes, of Madison County, Ky. She died Sept. 18, 1856, in Dallas, Texas, leaving seven children. On the 2d of August, 1860, William Brown Miller married the third time, Mrs. Emma Dewey Miller, widow of M. M. Miller, of Cadiz, Ohio; unto them were born three children. William Brown Miller, Senior, died Jan. 4, 1899. He was nearly ninety-two years old at the time of his death and his estate was worth more than one hundred thousand dollars. His

wife, Emma Dewey Miller, only survived him two and a half months. She died March 17, 1899. The last Mrs. Miller's paternal grandmother was a granddaughter of the famous Lord Chancellor Hyde.

William B. Miller, Senior, emigrated to Texas in 1846 and settled in the wilderness five miles south of the present city of Dallas, where he established a home, "Millermore," and a farm cleared—and acre after acre added, until a large domain was the proud possession of this pioneer of early Texas. He lived to the ripe old age of ninety-one years and six months and died surrounded by his family and in the arms of Uncle Arch Miller, a faithful ex-slave. He now lies sleeping his last sleep in the family burial ground of the old home.

He left behind him the greatest of all heritages to his sons and daughters—a stainless name and life. The Dallas Morning News of Thursday, Jan. 5, 1899, published in its columns the following:

"A pioneer passes away. Death at the "Old Homestead" yesterday of William B. Miller. A landmark of early times. He was born in Kentucky early in the century. A few leaves from the history of his life:

"Mr. William B. Miller, one of the pioneers of Dallas County, died yesterday at the "Old Homestead," south of Oak Cliff. He was one of the ancient landmarks of Dallas County, was known as "Uncle Billy Miller," and in the days before the war owned a large number of slaves and a large tract of land. In fact, was a large land owner at the time of his death. "Uncle Billy" Miller, James M. Patterson, and Judge Hord, of Oak Cliff, have been regarded of late years as the three surviving pioneers of the North Texas of other days. The triumvirate was shattered yesterday when Mr. Miller passed away. The following facts are gleaned from the "History of Dallas County," published in 1892:

"William B. Miller, a pioneer of Dallas County ,was born in Madison County, Kentucky, in 1807, the second of seven children born to John and Mary Brown Miller, natives of Kentucky. The father moved to Madison County, Alabama, in 1818, and opened up a farm, and his death occurred in that state in 1846. His wife survived him until after the war. William B. Miller was reared to farm life and educated in the public schools of Madison County, and also at the Academy of Huntsville, Alabama. He subsequently rented land and engaged in farming, but in the year 1834 began merchandising in New Market, Ala., which he followed two years, when, on account of the Henry Clay Bankrupt Law he failed in business. He then moved to Tennessee and again engaged in farming for ten years, after which, in 1847, * * he came to Dallas County, settling in Precinct No. 4. In 1856 he bought 562 acres of land, but later sold seventy acres for $30 an acre, and afterward bought two acres back, giving therefor $12,500. He was married in Madison County, Alabama, in 1833, to Elizabeth Waddy, a native of that state, whose ancestry on one side is traceable back to the Cherokee Indians, noblest specimen of their race. By this marriage there was one child, Chareiaus, who married and settled in the Cherokee Nation in the Indian Territory; he was a gallant Colonel in the Confederate army from Texas, and was known as Crill Miller. His mother died in Alabama in 1835, and in 1837, the subject of this sketch married Minerva Barnes. She died in 1856, after having five children, viz., Alonzo, who died in 1855; Martha, who married W. C. Leonard, of Kaufman County; Mary, who became the wife of Mr.

Guess; Elizabeth, who married John Edmonson, and Susan, who married Dr. Ewing, of this city. In 1850 Mr. Miller chose for his third wife Mrs. Madison M. Miller, of Dallas. Three children were the result of this marriage: Charles, J. H., and Minnie Miller, the latter the wife of State Senator Phil Barry Miller, of this city. For more than forty-five years deceased was engaged in farming in Dallas County, and was recognized as one of the leading and progressive citizens of the community. Of late years, owing to advanced age and feeble health, he led a quiet life, leaving the management of his farm to his children. In politics he was an uncompromising Democrat, and had began voting the ticket upward of seventy years ago. He was a Southerner of the old regime, and the hospitality of ante-bellum days was a feature of life at the "Old Homestead," which is located five miles south of Dallas. He lived to the ripe old age of 91 years, and died respected by all who knew him. The funeral will take place this afternoon from the "Old Homestead."

The issue of his first marriage to Elizabeth Waddy:

1. Charelaus Miller(commonly called "Crill"), was born Oct. 16, 1829. Young Charelaus lived with his grandmother Miller until his father's second marriage to Miss Minerva Barnes, Sept. 11, 1839. He was married to Mary E. Walker, of Searcy, Arkansas, about 1861, and they reared a large family. Charelaus Miller, Senior, getting a large grant of land for himself and children in the Indian Territory, on account of the Cherokee strain on his mother's side, sold his Texas interests and moved to the Territory in 1887, where he engaged in farming and cattle raising, and where he was residing at the time of his death, June 4, 1892. Each one of his children inherited five hundred acres of land in the Territory besides his own share. Mary E. Walker, his wife, died March, 1901. Charelaus Miller was a gallant soldier in the Confederate army during the Civil War, and was promoted to the rank of Lieutenant-Colonel for conspicuous bravery. Of his children the following are a part:

1. Waddy Miller.
2. Lena Miller.
3. Carl Miller.
4. Estha Eva Miller.
5. Mattie Miller.
6. William B. Miller III.
7. Charelaus Miller, Jr.
8. John Hickman Miller, Jr.

Children of the second marriage of William Brown Miller, Senior, to Minerva Barnes:

2. Alonzo Miller.

3. Mary Brown Miller, was born March 23, 1842. She married George W. Guess, a lawyer of Dallas, Texas, in 1856. She died Jan. 17, 1861, leaving one child:

1. George W. Guess, Jr.

4. Martha M. Miller, was born July 3, 1840. She married Frank Leonard, a young farmer of Dallas County, Texas, in 1860. He enlisted in the Confederate army of the Civil War, and died whilst serving as a soldier, leaving one child:

1. Infant; died.

In 1879 Mrs. Leonard married Washington Leonard, a brother to her first husband, whom she survives, and lives now on her farm three miles from Terrill, Texas.

5. Virginia H. Miller, was born March 11, 1844. She was married to C. D. Kennedy, a Northern man, then of Lancaster, Texas, a saddler, now living in Dallas, Texas. To them were born three children:

1. Alonzo Kennedy, lives in East Dallas.
2. Wallace Kennedy; married Mrs. Robert Cockerel; live in Dallas, Texas, and have five or six children.
3. R. E. Kennedy; lives in East Dallas.

6. Susan M. Miller, was born March 19, 1846. She married Frank Robberson, in January, 1866. He was a dealer in horses in Dallas; he died the same year, leaving no issue. On the 12th of July, 1874, she was married to Dr. J. A. Ewing, of Dallas, Texas. She died Oct. 21, 1892, leaving two children:

1. Lucy Ewing, of Dallas, Texas.
2. William Gordon Ewing, of Dallas, Texas.

7. Bettie Hickman Miller, was born Oct. 16, 1848. She was married to John W. Edmondson in January, 1866, and lived three miles from Dallas, Texas, where she died Sept. 5, 1872, her husband still lives in Dallas. She left one son:

1. J. F. Edmondson.

8. William Brown Miller, Jr., (known as "Little Will" to distinguish him from his father), died Feb. 21, 1873, at the age of sixteen years.

Children of the third marriage of William Brown Miller, Senior, and Mrs. Emma Dewey Miller:

9. Charles M. Miller, was born July 10, 1861. He was married to Bertha E. Cleaves, of Cherokee, Iowa. They have two children:

1. Royal Cleaves Miller, of Dallas, Texas.
2. Emma Miller, of Dallas, Texas.

Charles M. Miller, like his father, is a farmer and stock raiser.

10. John Hickman Miller, was born Oct. 14, 1862. He was married to Floribel Melone, of Shelbyville, Kentucky, Nov. 1, 1893. To them were born three children. His wife died March 15, 1903, and on November 1, 1904, he was again married, to Katherine Bonney Melone. He is of the firm of Fife & Miller, Dallas, Texas, the largest exclusive carriage house in the state. The children of his first marriage:

1. Lloyd M. Miller.
2. Katherine Miller.
3. John Hickman Miller, Jr.

11. Minnie H. Miller, was born Dec. 2, 1865. She was married to Hon. Philip Barry Miller, of Barnwell, South Carolina, Nov. 9, 1885. Barry Miller is a very successful criminal lawyer, of Dallas, Texas, and ex-State Senator, and late Mayor of the city. This family live at "Millermore," the old home, where William Brown Miller, Senior, settled when he went to Texas in 1846, five miles south of Dallas, and three miles from its suburb, Oak Cliff. Rural Free Delivery No. 1, Dallas, Dallas County, Texas. Their children:

1. Tom Barry Miller.

2. William Brown Miller IV.
3. Philip Russell Miller.
4. Evelyn Dewey Miller.

5. Mary Ann Miller, born Oct. 24, 1819, of New Market, Alabama, where she died at the age of forty years, and her remains were buried there.

6. Joseph H. Miller, born March 27, 1812, was one of nature's noblemen, and enough could not be said in his praise. His occupation was varied. He was a planter and stock raiser; when the "Yankees" (as the Southern people called them) took all of his horses, they said they were the finest they had seen in the South. He had 1000 acres of land and about 100 negroes; he was also a merchant, owned a lumber and grist mill, a blacksmith shop and wagon and woodwork shop. He married Henrietta Virginia Crutcher. They had seven children, viz:

1. Mary B. Miller, a maiden lady, now living in Huntsville, Alabama; highly respected and much beloved. She and her sister Lula live together and are the only survivors of their father's children.

2. Lula Miller, lives in Huntsville, Alabama, as above stated; a fine woman, highly regarded and respected.

3. Hickman Miller; died when quite young.

4. Robert Miller; died when quite young.

5. John Kleber Miller; married Miss Minnie Landman. They died in January, 1897, within four days of each other, leaving three children:

1. Joseph H. Miller; has just finished school at the State University; studied civil engineering, and is now in the L. and N. office in Birmingham.

2. Robert Miller; died when twelve years of age.

3. Clare Miller; is with her aunt, Miss Mary B. Miller, in Huntsville, Alabama.

6. Joseph H. Miller; married Miss Jessie Saxson. He died in March, 1901, without issue surviving.

7. Kate Virginia Miller; married Dr. P. M. Hall. They left one child:

1. Virginia Hall, who now owns the Old Homestead in New Market, where she resides, a most excellent Christian woman, much beloved by all in her community.

7. Hickman Miller, born May 3, 1814; started to Texas to buy land and to cast his fortunes with his brothers William B. and John W. Miller, but only reached Greenville, Texas, when he was taken ill and died, June 22, 1848, at the age of about forty years.

8. Virginia H. Miller, born July 1, 1822; married Tate Lowry, a wealthy planter of Huntsville, Alabama. They died, leaving one son:

1. Dr. Samuel H. Lowry, of Huntsville; married Miss Jemima Pulley. He died a few months ago, leaving three children, two daughters and one son.

9. John W. Miller, was born March 19, 1825. He emigrated to Texas at an early date, probably in the fifties, and engaged in business with his nephew, Charelaus Miller (commonly called "Crill") in farming and milling, and with whom he always made his home until the date of his death, Jan. 4, 1880, at the age of 55 years. For many years he was blind; had been partially

blind since he was quite a child. He spent much of his time hunting and running mule-eared rabbits—the country at that time was thinly settled and all open prairie land. William B., his brother, and Crill, his nephew, kept large packs of hounds for the purpose of hunting; they all loved the sport very much. Crill had a tree at a deer lick, from which he had killed one hundred and eighty deer; he made a notch in the tree each time he killed a deer there.

10. Susannah Miller, was born Dec. 27, 1829. She married in New Market, Alabama, in about 1847, to William Buchanan Smartt, of McMinnville, Warren County, Tennessee, always known as W. B. Smartt. They lived on his farm, two miles from town. Mrs. Smartt now lives at Bell Buckle, Tenn. She is quite deaf, but a very interesting and entertaining woman. They had seven children:

1. John Miller Smartt. He was a perfect machine genius. He died at the age of twenty-five years in Shreveport, Louisiana; his remains were conveyed to Dallas, Texas, and buried, where the family then lived. He was never married.

2. George Randolph Smartt; unmarried. His home is in Bell Buckle, Tennessee. He was born in about 1853, and is a druggist.

3. Marion Othelia Smartt; married John Ramsay, of McMinnville, Tennessee. They lived together as man and wife twelve years ,when they married she was twenty-one and he eight months younger. Mr. Ramsay, by excessive drink, neglected his wife and children, failing to provide for them, and she left him and obtained a divorce, and lived alone seven years and married the second time, T. E. Manning. They live in Roswell, New Mexico. Mrs. Manning is now (1906) fifty-one years old. Children of her first marriage to John Ramsay:

1. Maud May Ramsay; died at the age of three years and four months; if living now would be twenty-nine years old.

2. Effie Smartt Ramsay; married Mr. Jenett, of Chicago four years ago; they now live in Roswell, New Mexico, moving there on account of Mr. Jennett's health. He had been employed by the Santa Fe Railroad in office work. They have one child:

1. Marion Othelia Jenett; named for her grandmother. Age two years and eight months.

3. Frederic Frulton Ramsay, went to old Mexico at the age of eighteen years, worked on the harbor at Monzanillo, Mexico, two years, went from there to Vera Cruz, worked there two years for the Walter Pierce Oil Company. He is now in the old City of Mexico, working in the Mexico City Banking Company, as paying teller, and is now twenty two years old.

4. Oscar William Ramsay, now eighteen years old, at work in a drug store in Roswell, New Mexico.

4. Frederic William Smartt, married Oct. 18, 1905, Mabel Arnold of Wartrace, Tennessee, where they reside. Mr. Smartt is forty nine years old, they have no children. He is a druggist, and has drug stores at Bell Buckle, Norton, and Deckard. Tennessee.

5. Alline Smartt, married firstly, John Matthews, who died leaving one child. She married secondly, Dore C. Gaul in

Dallas, Texas, he was a New Yorker, his sisters still live in Newberge, New York. He was a book-keeper, and died in the City of Mexico about ten years ago, leaving one son.

Issue of her first marriage to John Matthews:

1. Willie May Matthews; married Edward D. Wather, a hotel man in San Antonio, Texas. Their children:
   1. Allen Matthews Wather.
   2. (Baby) Wather.

Issue of her second marriage to Dore C. Gaul:

3. Ashford Nicholas Gaul; living with his mother in the city of Mexico.

6. Ann Lou Smartt; married in Dallas, Texas, Edward J. Gaston, a commercial man, now living in Oak Park, Ill. Issue:
   1. Ralph Smartt Gaston; seventeen years old; now attending school in Oak Park.

7. Maggie Smartt; died in infancy thirty-five years ago.

Note—The children of John Miller and Mary Brown, his wife, are not set forth in the order of their births in the foregoing sections. They were born in the following order, viz:

1. Elizabeth Brown Miller; born Aug. 12, 1805.
2. William Brown Miller; born Aug. 24, 1807.
3. James O. Miller; born Aug. 29, 1809.
4. Joseph H. Miller; born March 27, 1812.
5. Hickman Miller; born May 3, 1814.
6. Nancy H. Miller; born Oct. 13, 1816.
7. Mary Ann Miller; born Oct. 24, 1819.
8. Virginia H. Miller; born July 1, 1822.
9. John W. Miller; born March 19, 1825.
10. Susannah Miller; born Dec. 27, 1829.

Polly Brown, the wife of John Miller, was the only daughter of William Brown and Elizabeth ————, his wife. The said William Brown died in Madison County, Ky., in 1816, near Richmond. He lived neighbor to William Goodloe, who was co-executor with his widow of William Brown's will. (See Part VIII, Chap. 2, A.)

Section 6. Elizabeth Miller, the sixth child of Colonel John Miller, and Jane Dalaney his wife was born March 20, 1782, and died August 22, 1833. She married, June 13, 1798, William Woods Kavanaugh, son of Philemon Kavanaugh and Elizabeth Woods, his wife. He was known as "Big Bill" Kavanaugh, and he died Dec. 14, 1814, and his widow, Elizabeth Miller Kavanaugh, married again Nov. 9, 1820, Thomas Kennedy, and she died Aug. 22, 1833. (See Part II, Chap. 6, Sec. 12, and Part VII, Chap. 5.)

Section 7. Dulaney Miller, the seventh child of Colonel John Miller and Jane Dulaney, his wife, was born Dec. 13, 1783. He married Statilda Goggin May 8, 1810. The following were among his children:

1. John G. Miller, married Elizabeth Watts, his cousin May 21, 1833. (see section 12.)
2. Stephen G. Miller; married his cousin, Georgia Ann Watts July 23, 1835 (see section 12). She died, and on Aug. 15 1846, married Betsy Stephenson.
3. William Miller
4. Jane Miller
5. Eliza Miller

Section 8. Joseph Miller, the eighth child of Colonel John Miller and Jane Dulaney his wife, was born May 15, 1785. He married Susan Kennedy, Sept. 17 1807, she was born Sept. 17 1783. They emigrated in about the year 1816, from Madison County, Ky., and settled near Gallatin in Sumner County, Tennessee. The old dwelling house of General Joseph Miller, in Gallatin was built of grey stone, it is even now a superb old stone structure though stripped of surrounding great, glorious forest, and cracked as it is by the Earthquake of 1812. The Federals cut all the trees during the war, and it looks so alone and superbly dreamy. All the out houses and cabins were of stone too. It is now occupied by Samuel E. Lackey and his wife, Susan Kennedy Alexander, and family.

Kleber Miller, now dead, had a hammer of General Joseph Miller one his father Colonel John Miller, had at the battle of Yorktown during the Revolutionary War. Another member of the family owned some silver spoons with the Dulaney Crest on them, that were brought from Ireland.

The children of General Joseph Miller and Susan Kennedy his wife were:

I. Andrew K. Miller; born Aug. 24, 1810; died Feb. 7, 1853. He married Elizabeth B. Halloway, Oct. 18, 1832. Mrs. Elizabeth B. Halloway Miller, only passed away a few years ago. She was simply adored by her family. Andrew K. Miller died when still a rather young man, leaving three children, viz:

1. Susan Kennedy Miller; born Sept. 2 1834, married Elbridge G. Seawell, of Lebanon, Tennessee. She is now seventy years of age, but is capable, so alert, so cheerful and gifted, that she is a delight to all who know her.

Mrs. Nannie S. Boyd, her daughter writes of this family:

"A long law suit about property rather separated us from many of our Miller relations, and different tastes seemed to widen the breach, but I am very fond of many of them. For some reason our branch of the family is rather strenuous. The days are never long enough, and neither are the nights. We are great workers, like books, music, art and good company. The Millers are more sober and quiet. I do not know a professional man in the family, almost all are farmers, and they are men and women of character and force, no matter where they are, but they all take life seriously."

Mr. Elbridge G. Seawell and Susan Kennedy Miller his wife had four children all girls viz:

1. Elizabeth H. Seawell; who was a very charming, cultured woman. She married Dr. A. F. Claywell, of Lebanon, Tennessee, she died some years ago without children.

2. Nannie Seawell; a charming and accomplished woman, was art teacher at Ward Seminary, Nashville, Tennessee. In 1886-87 while a student of art, Mrs. Nannie Seawell (now Mrs. Boyd) was in Europe, as a student and there met Mr. Burnam of Richmond, Ky. and had some correspondence with his daughter, Miss Sallie Burnam, now deceased. In 1892 she married Captain Isaac S. Boyd, of Atlanta, Georgia. Mr. Boyd died almost three years ago, and it was his dearest wish that his children should have the best education that was possible for them. Mrs. Boyd's home is in Atlanta, Georgia. She is now temporarily at

5549 Madison Avenue, Chicago, Illinois, whilst her children are attending school at Chicago University. They had two children viz:

1. Elizabeth Seawell Boyd; now (1906) twelve years of age, leading her class in the grand Chicago University Elementary school.

2. Elbridge Boyd, a dear little fellow of ten years, who is also in the same school.

3. Janie Seawell; married James Q. Moore, of Nashville, Tennessee. They have two children viz:
1. Elbridge Moore.
2. Elizabeth Moore.

4. Roberta Seawell; married A. G. Brandon, of Nashville, Tennessee. They have two children:
1. Seawell Brandon.
2. Robert Boyd Brandon.

2. Elizabeth Miller; died at thirteen years of age.

3. Robert Woods Miller; born Aug. 29 1846. He married Elenora Baber. Robert Woods Miller is book-keeper for Phillips & Bettoff of Nashville, Tennessee. He is a lovely man, but extreme deafness has handicapped him in a business way so that he had to abandon his old business. He was in the Bank for many years. He has had other misfortunes besides deafness. They have one child viz:
1. Lillian Miller; married Robert F. Bransford. They have three children viz:
1. Margaret Bransford.
2. Miller Bransford.
3. Benjamin Moss Bransford.

2. Nancy Jane Miller; born Sept. 8, 1812. She married for her first husband, Woods Shelton Miller, Aug. 19, 1830. (See Sec. 4), secondly, James Alexander. Children of her first marriage:
1. Joseph Miller; born Aug. 13, 1831; married 1 Anna Dodd; 2, Bettie Douglas.
Children of first marriage:
1. Mary Kleber Miller; born Dec. 1863, died 1876.
2. Nannie Miller; married Emory Sweeney.
3. Florence Miller; married Nathan Bullock, she is dead, issue:
1. Werta Bullock.
4. Anna Miller; born July 29, 1871, married William Stewart, issue.
1. Joseph M. Stewart.
2. Mildred Stewart.

5. Maud Miller; born May 1873, married Alfred Zennion, New York City.
6. Susie Miller; born Oct. 1895.
Children of second marriage of Joseph Miller to Bettie Douglas:
7. Woodie Miller.
8. Helen Miller.
9. Joseph Miller, Jr.

2. Thomas Miller; born Aug. 7, 1833, married Lizzie Dhutt, had three sons and three daughters:

1. Laura Miller; married James Anderson, had two children.
2. Henry Miller; married Ida ————.
3. Ida Miller; died in infancy.
4. Woods Shelton Miller; married Alice Stilz. Their children:
   1. Thomas Miller.
   2. Anna Miller.
5. Anna Miller.
6. James Miller; died with consumption.

3. Archibald Woods Miller; born Dec. 5, 1835,married first Martha Alexander, and second, Susie Miller; all dead.

4. Robert G. Miller; born May 7, 1838, married Etta Head. Their children:
   1. Woods Lee Miller.
   2. Robert Goodloe Miller; died single.
   3. John W. Miller; married Kate Anderson.

5. Anna W. Miller; born Aug. 27, 1840.

Children of the second marriage:
6. Susan Kennedy Alexander; married Samuel E. Lackey, (see section 11) Nov. 2, 1869. Their children:
   1. William Nicholas Lackey; born Sept. 27, 1875, married Bernetta Anderson Oct. 25, 1905.
   2. Samuel Eugene Lackey; born Jan. 26, 1877.
   3. Alma Lackey; born August 28, 1880.

7. Jennie Alexander; born Jan. 8, 1855, married John Branch Donelson, July, 1874, son of Gen. Donelson. Their children:
   1. Rebecca Donelson; born Oct. 14, 1881, married Joe Chew, Texas; issue:
      1. Virginia Chew.
   2. Alexander Donelson; born May 29, 1884.
   3. Emma Donelson; born Oct. 21, 1886.
   4. Eugene Lackey Donelson; born June 10, 1892.
   5. Susie K. Donelson; born May 29, 1894; died June, 1894.
   6. John Branch Donelson; born Oct. 1896.

3. John Woods Miller; born Aug. 26, 1814; married Mary Ann Woods, Aug. 28, 1835; he died Aug. 23, 1850. Their children:
   1. Joseph Miller; married Josephine Lash.
   2. Andrew Miller; married Nannie Solomon.
   3. Susie Miller; married Archibald Miller, (see 8-3 above); issue:
      1. John Miller.
   4. Woodie Miller; married Jack Chambers.
   5. Nancy Jane Miller; married Richard Palmer.

4. Robert Green Miller; born Nov. 8, 1816; married March 12, 1840, his cousin, Mourning Shelton Miller, a daughter of Thomas Miller and Annie Woods, his wife. (See Sec. 4.) He died June 20, 1842, had one son:

1. Joseph Kleber Miller; born Jan. 20, 1841, died Feb. 6, 1904. He married Ellen Clearland, of Forsythe, Georgia. He lived at Gallatin, Tenn. Second wife, Ann Laura Gass, of Kentucky; had no children. The children of first marriage:
   1. Early Clearland Miller; born May 17, 1868. He married Ethel Somers, Oct. 15, 1890. Their children:

1. Kleber Miller; born Aug. 26, 1891.
2. Minta Miller; born Aug. 20, 1895.
3. Lily Bell Miller; born Sept. 1, 1897.
4. Ellen Miller; born Feb. 20, 1900.

2. Ellen D'Laney Miller; born March 2, 1874; married Rufe Douglas McClain, Nov. 16, 1898. They live in Gallatin, Tennessee. They have one child:

1. Harrison Kleber McClain; born Oct. 1, 1905; died Feb. 22, 1906.

After the death of Robert Green Miller, his widow, Mourning Shelton Miller, married again, Nov. 26, 1844, Norvall Douglas. (See Sec. 4-8.) Their children:

2. Anna E. Douglas; married Thomas A. Gill, moved to California. Their children:

1. Joseph M. Gill.
2. Alma Gill.
3.
4.
5.
6.

3. Mary C. Douglas; married Mark H. Young. They lived in Bastrop, Texas. Their children:

1. Jessie Belle Young; born Feb. 11, 1870.
2. William James Young; born Nov. 11, 1873.
3. Hallie Young; born Aug. 15, 1876.
4. Joseph Kleber Young; born Jan. 22, 1879.
5. Mary S. Young; born Feb. 26, 1881.
6. Mark H. Young, Jr; born July 25, 1883.
7. Anna Douglas Young; born April, 21, 1886.
8. Ellen Norvall Young; born Feb. 7, 1889.

5. Joseph Kleber Miller; born Sept. 2, 1819; died Jan. 6, 1841.

Section 9. James Miller, the ninth child of Col. John Miller and Jane Dulaney, his wife, was born Dec. 24, 1787; died in infancy.

Section 10. Garland Burleigh Miller, the tenth child of Colonel John Miller and Jane Dulaney, his wife, was born April 1, 1790. He married Mourning Woods, a daughter of Archibald Woods, and Mourning Shelton, his wife, Jan. 18, 1810. (See Part 11, Chap. 8, Sec. 10.) she was born April 7, 1792. They emigrated from Madison County Ky. to Tennessee, and settled in Franklin County on Beans Creek, where they spent their remaining days. Garland B. Miller died Dec. 11, 1832, and his wife in 1852. Their children:

1. Jane S. Miller; born April 2, 1811; died Oct., 1824.

2. Appoline Shelton Miller, born Nov. 11, 1812, she married Feb. 18, 1832, Thomas H. Woods, son of William Woods, and Mary Harris, his wife. See Part II, Chap. 10, Sec. 6, and Part 11, Chap. 9, Sec. 6.) She died Dec. 29, 1856, and Mr. Woods died Nov. 19, 1880. Their children:

1. William B. Woods; born May 11, 1833, married Emily Horton, Feb. 10, 1869; he died Nov. 7, 1871, and his wife died May 3, 1890. Issue:

1. Susan Woods; married James M. Horton Dec. 28, 1892; she died Sept. 16, 1895.

2. Garland Miller Woods; born Nov. 5, 1835; married Lucy Bostick, Dec. 24, 1865. Their home is in Tullahoma, Tennessee. Their children:

1. Thomas Harris Woods; born July 27, 1870.
2. Lewis Kleber Woods; born July 15, 1872.
3. William Goodloe Woods; born May 19, 1875.
4. Mary Annie Laurie Woods; born April 21, 1878.

3. Polly Ann Woods; born Nov. 19, 1837.

4. James Higgins Woods; born April 4, 1840; died Nov. 23, 1892.

5. David Goodloe Woods; born April 11, 1842.

6. Josephine S. Woods; born Feb. 15, 1844; married Mr. Pain, May 14, 1885; she died Aug. 21, 1885.

7. Joseph Kleber Woods; born Nov. 10, 1845; married Mary Jane Bass, Nov. 24, 1870; she died April 4, 1897.

8. Susan Samira Woods; born Nov. 6, 1847.

9. Archibald Wright Woods; born Oct. 24, 1850; he lives in Deckard, Tennessee.

10. Mourning Miller Woods; born July 28, 1852.

11. Thomas Milton Woods; born July 3, 1853; married Tempie Floyd, March 1, 1888. He died Jan. 4, 1899. Their children:

1. Archibald Anthony Woods; born Jan. 24, 1892; died Sept. 28, 1892.
2. Hugh Edward Woods; born July 30, 1893.
3. James Henry Woods; born Nov. 19, 1894.
4. Thomas Miller Woods; born June 29, 1896.
5. Thomas Shepherd Woods; born March 2, 1899, a posthumous child.

Thomas Harris Woods, and Appoline Shelton Miller, his wife, died and raised their family in Tennessee, and their descendants still live in that State.

3. Sallie Ann Miller; born Oct. 29, 1814; she married Aug. 25, 1830, John C. Lipscomb. She died June 1840. Two children who lived were born to them. viz:

1. Nancy Jane Lipscomb; married Newton Mann. The children born to them who are living are:

1. John Mann; married Ella Mosley. He is a farmer at Beans Creek, Tenn.; they have six living children:

1. Herbert Mann; in Kentucky.
2. Thomas Mann; at home Beans Creek, Tennessee.
3. John Mann; died in young manhood.
4. Tullia Mann; living at Beans Creek, Tenn.

None of these children are married.

2. Matthew Mann; a teacher in the Deaf and Dumb School at Knoxville, Tennessee. He is a mute and married Fannie Fleming, a mute; they have three children all of whom can hear and talk; the oldest daughter married:

1. Louise Mann; married, and had two children, viz:

1. Elizabeth.
2. Frances.

3. Horace Mann; a merchant at Riverside, Tennessee; married Hattie Voreese, they have three children, viz:

1. Ester Mann.
2. Theodore Mann.
3. Wilmer Mann.

4. Turner Mann; works in a company store at Birming-

ham, Alabama; married Florence Williamson, and had one child,: viz

1. Robert Newton Mann.

5. Emma Mann; married Joe Bogle; they live at Centreville, Tennessee, and have eight children, viz:

1. Abury Bogle; married Miss ———.
2. Garland Bogle; married Miss ———.
3. Robert Bogle.
4. Anne Bogle.
5. Reece Bogle.
6. Frank Bogle.
7. Joe Bogle, Jr.
8. Elizabeth Bogle.

6. Sallie Mann, (twin to Mollie;) married Mr. D. L. Smith. They live at Artesia New Mexico, and have four children, two boys and two girls, the oldest about thirteen years old, viz:

1. Nannie Mann Smith.
2. Mollie Bogle Smith.
3. Jesse Turner Smith.
4. Newman Breeden Smith.

7. Mollie Mann, (a twin to Sallie).

Son and daughter died about the time they were grown.

2. Garland B. Lipscomb; married Miss ——— and moved to Marshall, Texas. He served in the Confederate army in the Civil War, and died at Marshall, leaving a wife and children; probably some of his descendants are there now.

4. Elizabeth Miller; was born July 20, 1816; and died Oct., 1817.

5. Mourning Woods Miller, was born March 15, 1818. She married Robert C. Smith, June 4, 1839, by Elder J. R. Patrick. Mr. Smith it seems was a minister of the Gospel, probably of the Primitive Baptist Order. During the Civil War a company of armed men, claiming to be Federal soldiers, went to their home, and in the presence of Mrs. Smith killed and murdered her husband, Robert C. Smith, whilst she was begging for his life. In the year 1887, the writer was in Lincoln County, Tennessee, and attended services at Buckeye Church, some three miles from Fayetteville, and after services, in the neighborhood of the church, met Mrs. Smith, then an old woman and a widow, living in the vicinity, who related to him the facts in regard to the murder. She died in April 1889. Their children:

1. Ann Miller L. Smith; married John Lipscomb, of Beans Creek, Tennessee. She died about fourteen years ago. Mr. Lipscomb was named for his uncle, John Lipscomb, who married Sallie Ann Miller, and his wife was named for her aunt, the wife of said uncle. John Lipscomb Jr. after the death of his wife Ann, married again, and is now living with his second wife. The children of Ann Miller L. Smith and John Lipscomb:

1. Dr. Robert Lipscomb; married Louise Newlun, of Bronsborough, Tennessee. They have four children all living at Beans Creek, Tennessee:

1. Sarah Newlun Lipscomb.
2. John Lipscomb.

3. Margaret Lipscomb.
4. Martha Washington Lipscomb.

2. Annie Woods Lipscomb; married Dr. Whitmore Anderson, a veterinary surgeon, living in Ardmore, Indian Territory. Have two sons:
   1. John Moultrie Anderson.
   2. Lipscomb Anderson.

3. Jennie Lipscomb; married James C. Breeden, a merchant of Beans Creek, Tennessee. They have no children:

4. Granville Lipscomb; has been married three times. He had no children by his first two wives, his last wife was Lou Marshall Redman. They had one child. They live in Huntsville, Alabama.

5. Susan Lipscomb; married Robert Yarbrough. She died four years ago childless.

6. Fannie Lipscomb; married W. Q. Porter, an engineer of the N. C. and St. L. R.R. They live in Nashville, Tennessee, and have one child:
   1. John Porter.

7. William Lipscomb; married Nettie Ruledge, of Huntland, Tennessee. He is a Curio merchant, 1513 17th Street, Denver Colorado. They have no children.

8. John Lipscomb; single, clerk for the Frisco R. R. Co. He lives in Denver Colorado.

9. Amanda Lipscomb; single; she at this time lives with her sister, Mrs. Porter, in Nashville, Tennessee.

10. Horace Lipscomb; died in infancy.

2. Susan Smith; married T. G. Rucker, a retired conductor of the N. C. and St. L. R.R., having served in that capacity for fifty years. They live near Nashville, Tennessee. Had one daughter:
   1. Bettie Rucker; married Walter Winsted. Their children:
      1. Margaret Winsted.
      2. Walter Winsted.

   They live on Russell street in Nashville, Tennesssee.

3. Josephine Smith; married Joseph William Pamer. They lived and died at New Market, Alabama, leaving one son, and three daughters.

4. John Presley Smith; married ————————————. They raised a family of eight children. Three in Nashville, Tennessee, and some of them in Mississippi. His wife died, and he is the only survivor of his mother's children.

5. William Smith; married Sallie ——— about 1870; lived near Beans Creek, Tennessee, for a few years after their marriage, and then moved to Texas. He died in Belchville, Texas, two year ago, leaving his wife and about seven children, all living at Belchville.
   1.
   2.
   3.
   4.
   5.
   6.
   7.

6. Josephine Miller; born March 15, 1820. She married William Staples, Oct. 6, 1842, Elder Henry Larkins solemnizing the rites of marriage. She died Aug. 5, 1843.

7. Archibald Woods Miller; born May 27, 1822; died with the measles, Oct. 17, 1846, whilst a soldier in the Mexican war.

8. Susan Goodloe Miller, born December 24, 1824, she married Dr. John W. Moore, of Aberdeen, Mississippi, Feb. 1, 1844, Elder R. C. Smith performed the ceremony. They had three or more children who lived in Mississippi before the war. She died July 28, 1849. Dr. Moore went back to Beans Creek, Tennessee, and married a second wife.

1.
2.
3.

9. John Hector Miller; born Dec. 29, 1825. He married Ellen Elizabeth Morris, Sept. 21, 1848, Elder R. C. Smith solemnizing the marriage rites. He was a Primitive Baptist preacher. He resided at Frost, Navarre County, Texas. His wife died near Bowie, Montague County, Texas, May 30, 1884. Their children:

1. John Morris Miller; born Jan. 12, 1850; died Jan. 13, 1850.

2. Thomas Garland Miller; born Feb. 17, 1851; married Jan. 19, 1873, Nancy Avalina Autry, near Sugar Loaf Coryell County, Texas, by Elder Jesse Graham. Their children:

1. Eunice Ida Miller; born Oct. 16, 1873, near Florence, Bell County, Texas.

2. Elbert Woods Miller; born Feb. 16, 1877, on Cuddo Creek, Stephens County, Texaas.

3. Susan Ellen Miller; born June 14, 1879, near Ranger, Stephens County, Texas.

4. William John Miller; born Feb. 4, 1882, on Cuddo Creek, Texas.

3. Archibald Woods Miller; born Oct. 12, 1853. He was married Nov 11, 1883, by Elder Willis Russell, to Loutitia Nancy Thompkins, on Cedar Creek, Stephens County, Texas. His wife was born April 18, 1865. He is a farmer. Their children:

1. Ellen Candice Miller; born March 3, 1885, on Cedar Creek, Stephens County Texaas.

2. George Hector Miller; born Oct. 29, 1887, on Cedar Creek, Texas.

3. Nancy Rebecca Miller; born 1889.

4. William Robert Miller; born 1891.

5. Grover Cleveland Miller; born 18—.

4. William Joseph Miller, born March 5, 1856. He, in partnership with his brother Robert S. Miller, are owners of and dealers in horses and cattle, and reside, or lately did reside, in Clayton, New Mexico.

5. Robert Smith Miller; born June 23, 1858.

6. Edward Rather Miller; born Aug. 19, 1861; died May 23, 1884, near Bowie, Montugue County, Texas.

7. John Simon Miller; born May 10, 1864; married Lucy Bennett, in Lebanon, Indian Territory, Dec. 15, 1890. Their children.

1. Ellen Alvin Miller; born Nov. 1891.

2. Herbert Hill Miller; born July, 1893.

8. Sallie Ida Miller; born Dec. 19, 1867; married Prof. P. B. Orme, at the residence of Dr. W. J. Miller, in McGregor, Texas, Sept. 5, 1888. Elder Sammons solemnized the marital rites. Mr. Orme was born Dec. 23, 1856. Their children:

1. Lizzie Orme; born at Orme's School, Navarro County, Texas, Aug. 13, 1889; died July 11, 1890.

2. John Elner Orme; born at same place, Nov. 8, 1890.

3. James Robert Orme; born at Italy, Texas, Nov. 1, 1892.

4. Clara Inez Orme; born at Barry, Ellis County, Texas, in 1894.

9. Bettie Mourning Miller; born April 30, 1870.

10. Thomas Garland Miller; born December 27, 1827. He married S. E. Bridges January 29, 1846. His second wife was Mary Jane Kavanaugh, daughter of John M. Kavanaugh, to whom he was married June 24, 1853, by Elder Robert C. Smith. (See Part VII, Chap. 5, Sec. 1.) Thomas Garland Miller enlisted with the first volunteers to go out from Franklin County, Tennessee, into the Confederate army, and was Captain of the company, and remained in the service till the fall of Atlanta, at which place he lost a leg, which was torn off by the fragment of a shell exploding near him, which, also, killed his horse from under him. He was promoted from time to time up to the Atlanta, Ga., fight, at that time holding the rank of Colonel. He was captured once during the service, was exchanged immediately, re-entered the service, and remained until disabled by the severe wound received at Atlanta.

A few years before the war he commenced the study of the law. After peace was declared he resumed the study of law, but soon abandoned same, and enlisted in the service of his Lord and Master as a Primitive Baptist preacher, and he continued in this calling as long as he lived. About the year 1875 he emigrated from near Mulberry, Lincoln County, Tennessee, to near Mansfield, Tarrant County, Texas, where he lived unti. the marriage of his two children; after which he and his wife moved to Alvarado, Johnson County, Texas, and lived with their daughter, Mrs. Capt. W. R. Bounds, at whose residence he died, Jan. 22, 1891. His wife, Mary Jane Kavanaugh, died at the same place, Nov. 11, 1891. Children by his first wife, S. E. Bridges:

1. Maggie Miller; born Dec. 16, 1846. She married Francis Marion Turner, near Winchester, Franklin County, Tennessee, Nov. 20, 1867. Mr. Turner was born Jan. 2, 1846. Maggie is dead; Mr. Turner lives in Tuscaloosa, Alabama. Issue:

1. Bettie Emma Turner; born Feb. 13, 1869; died young.

2. Charles Robinson Turner; born Nov. 12, 1870.

3. Ross Miller Turner; born April 23, 1873. His occupation is that of a photographer and painter. He lives in Tuscaloosa, Alabama.

2. John Walker Miller; born April 1, 1855.

3. Mourning Appoline Miller; born November, 1856.

4. Susan Goodloe Miller; born April 15, 1858. She married Capt. William Riley Bounds, in Alvarado, Johnson County, Texas, July 19, 1885. Captain Bounds was born in Mississippi, Sept. 15, 1842. He has followed the occupation of farming and stock raising since the Civil War. His residence is Cleburn, Johnson County, Texas. Their children:

1. Thomas Riley Bounds; born at Alvarado, Texas, Nov. 17, 1885.
2. Ben. Hill Bounds; born near Alvarado, Texas, June 25, 1888.
3. Elvis Bounds.
4. Atlas Bounds.

The last two children were twin boys, born at Alvarado, Texas, Sept. 4, 1890; Elvis died when quite young in years. Ben Hill and his mother are both dead, Mrs. Bounds having died about five years ago.

5. Robert Smith Miller; born Nevember, 1859.
6. Thomas Wiley Miller; born Dec. 14, 1860.
7. James Harvey Miller; born July 10, 1862.
8. Thomas Gregg Miller; born in Tennessee Oct. 19, 1866. He is the only one alive when last heard from a few months ago. He married Lillie Harris in Alvarado, Johnson County, Tex.

11. William Joseph Miller; born Dec. 26, 1829; married at Bean's Creek, Franklin County, Tennessee, May 1, 1851, Fannie Ann Collins. After her death he married Louise Catherine Southworth, Oct. 4, 1855, at Fayetteville, Lincoln County, Tenn.; Elder Joseph White solemnized the marriage rites. He graduated at the Nashville Medical College, Nashville, Tennessee, and received his diploma in 1852-3. A few years thereafter, he went back to the same college and took a post-graduate course in surgery. He followed his profession first near where he was born on Bean's Creek, in Franklin County, Tenn.; afterwards in Fayetteville. From the latter place he enlisted in a company of the first volunteers in the Confederate cause as a surgeon. He was captured at the fall of Ft. Donaldson and carried to Camp Chase, Ohio, and there confined and held as a prisoner of war for nearly two years, when he was exchanged, and resumed the practice of medicine at Fayetteville, Tennessee; was recaptured and held as a prisoner for nearly six months; again exchanged and again resumed the practice of his profession at Sloantown, from which point he moved to Boons Hill, Tenn., thence, in September, 1872, to Branchville, Coryell County, Texas; at this place he practiced medicine for seven years, then moved to near Ennis, Ellis County, Texas, where he followed his profession until about two years before his death, which occurred at McGregor, July 17, 1899. He was noted for his kindness, generosity and rigid honesty, and truthfulness in all things. He was a true Southerner in every sense of the word. He held to the principles of the Democratic party, and beileved in the tenets of the Primitive Baptist Society and aligned himself

WILLIAM JOSEPH MILLER

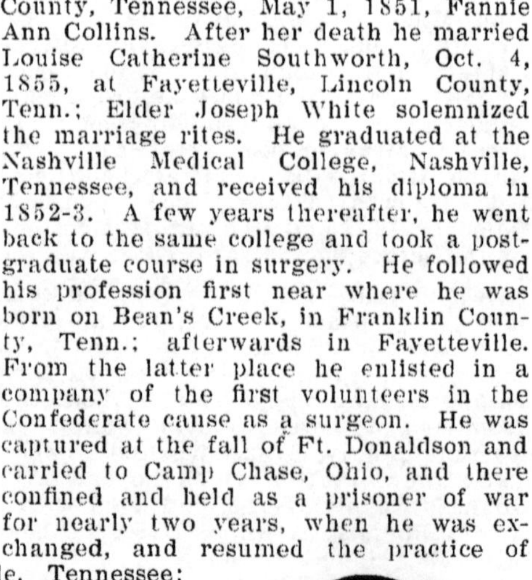

LOUISE C. SOUTHWORTH
Wife of Wm. Joseph Miller

his wife and two of his children, several years before he died, and died fully implanted in the faith.

Louise Catherine Southworth, his second wife, was born near Fayetteville, Tenn., March 29, 1835, and died at McGregor, Texas, in August, 1900.

He had one child by his first wife, Fannie Ann Collins:

1. Eliza Ann Miller; born in Franklin County, Tenn., Feb. 10, 1852. She married James Knox P. Moore, at Boons Hill, Lincoln County, Tenn., Dec. 13, 1871. She died April, 1904, at Wartrace, Tenn., their home. Their children:

   1. Garland Stephen Moore.
   2. Lena Moore; married Mr. ——— —.
   3. Fannie Lou Moore; married —— —.
   4. Tappie Hunt Moore.
   5. Birdie Moore.

Children of Dr. Wm. Jos. Miller and his second wife, Louise Catherine Southworth:

2. Thomas Southworth Miller; born in Giles County, Tenn., July 10, 1857. He married Ida Bruce Glass, in Coryell County, Texas, near the Grove, Oct. 5, 1881, at the residence of her father, W. F. Glass, by Rev. H. B. Ralls. The lineage of Ida Bruce Glass Miller can be traced back to Robert Bruce, of Scotland. She was born at High Hill, Texas, March 26, 1861. Thomas Southworth Miller is a farmer and stock-raiser, besides being a school teacher. He resides near Flat, Coryell County, Texas. Their children:

   1. Anita Louisa Miller; born Aug. 25,1882. School teacher.
   2. William Hill Miller (daughter); born June 12, 1884.
   3. Thomas Southworth Miller; born Aug. 18, 1886. Telegrapher.
   4. Eldridge Fletcher Miller; born June 11, 1890. Telegrapher.
   5. Ida Blackburn Miller; born May 9, 1896.
   6. Garland Burleigh Miller; born June 22, 1900.
   7. Kuroki Oyama Miller (daughter); born March 12, 1905.

3. William Hill Miller; born in Giles county, Tenn., June —, 1859; died in Laramie City, Wyoming, Sept. 9, 1885. He was a cowboy and cattleman and unmarried.

4. Ida Bada Miller; born in Fayetteville, Tenn., May 10, 1861. She married Joseph Euclid Wright, at McGregor, Texas, Nov. 6, 1889, Elder T. G. Miller solemnized the marriage. She died at McGregor April, 1896, childless.

5. Josephine Miller; born in Fayetteville, Tenn., Feb. 24, 1864. She married John M. Tyson, in McGregor, Texas, Feb. 26, 1884, Elder G. W. Norton solemnized the marriage. She died in Maysfield, Texas, Jan. 1, 1894. Mr. Tyson's address is Gorman, Texas. Their children:

   1. Herbert Greenwood Tyson; born March 24, 1885.
   2. Sue Edith Tyson; born Oct. 9, 1886.
   3. Mabel Miller Tyson; born June 15, 1889.
   4. Josie Cathline Tyson; born Feb. 3, 1891.

6. Lizzie Paschall Miller; born at Sloantown, Lincoln County, Tenn., Jan. 23, 1867. She died in McGregor, Texas, April, 1892. She was a school teacher, and unmarried.

7. Fannie May Miller; born at Sloantown, Tenn., Jan. 1, 1870.

She died Aug. 3, 1890, at McGregor, Texas. She was a school teacher, and unmarried.

8. Garland Burleigh Miller; born in Branchville, Texas, Nov. 6, 1873. He is Billing Clerk for the American Express Company, residing at Ft. Worth, Texas.

9. Woods (Woodie) Miller; born in Branchville, Texas, May 18, 1877. He married in McGregor, Texas, September, 1900, Alvah Southworth Millner. They reside in Dallas, Texas.

10. Gussie Louisa Miller; born near Ennis, Texas, April 16, 1881. She married Maurice Herschfield, in Waco, Texas, April 8, 1902. They reside at El Paso, Texas.

Section 11. Jane (Jennie) Miller, the eleventh child of Colonel John Miller and Jane Dulaney, his wife, was born April 18, 1792. She married Samuel Lackey. (See Sec. 2.) Their son, Dulaney Miller Lackey, now living at Lancaster, writes as follows: "My ancestors all came from Virginia. My father drove a wagon all the way to Kentucky with my grandfather; lived in a tent until they built a cabin in the cane-brake, and the old two-story log house still stands where we were all born—the deed signed to land by Patrick Henry, the first Governor of Virginia when Kentucky belonged to that state. The Lackey family are direct descendants of Oliver Cromwell. My wife was Mary Eliza Goodloe, daughter of Arch. Woods Goodloe; her mother was Maria Estill, daughter of James Estill, who lived where White's heirs have just sold to Col. J. W. Caperton, on Big Hill Pike. Uncle Robert Miller's wife was sister of her grandfather. I was married at your Uncle John Miller's where Buck Watts now lives."

Dulaney M. Lackey and his wife celebrated their Golden Wedding in 1903.

The children of Jane Miller and Samuel Lackey:

1. John Lackey; died a bachelor.

2. Eliza Ann Lackey; married, first, Beverley Broaddus, May 31, 1838, (See Part I, Chap. 13, Sec. 3. Note.) and, secondly, her cousin, Gabriel Lackey, of Missouri. Children of the first marriage to Beverley Broaddus:

1. Emily Broaddus; married John Rout, of Stanford, Ky.

2. Mary Jane Broaddus; married Michael Elkin, of Lancaster, Ky.

3. Samuel Thos. Broaddus; went to Missouri; married ———

4. Richard Broaddus; went to Missouri; married ———.

3. Samuel Miller Lackey; married, first, Susan Watts, April 26, 1832, and, second, Hannah White, March 12, 1835; he lived in Missouri. Their children:

1. Dr. Sidney Lackey; married, first, Sallie Didlake, of Missouri; his second wife's name we do not know. Children by his first wife:

1. Mitchell Lackey; killed at a barbecue at Lancaster, Ky.

2. Jane Arie Lackey; died at seventeen years of age.

4. Gabriel Lackey; married Rhoda Park. Their children:

1. Jennie Lackey; married Cam. Hayes, of Lincoln Co., Ky.

2. Samuel Lackey; married Virginia Miller. (See Sec. 2.)

3. Mollie Lackey; married John McRoberts, Cashier of a bank at Stanford, Ky.

4. Eliza Lackey; married Malcolm Memmings Miller, of Richmond, Ky. (See Sec. 2.)

5. Thomas Lackey; died young; unmarried.

6. William Miller Lackey; married Martha Hocker, Dec. 8, 1837. (See Part VII, Chap. 7, Sec. 1.) He lived and died in Stanford, Ky. Their children:

1. Samuel E. Lackey; married Susan Alexander. (See Sec. 8.) They live at Gallatin, Tennessee. He was a Confederate soldier, was one of the St. Albans' Raiders under the command of Lieutenant-Colonel Bennett H. Young, and afterwards was held as a prisoner at Montreal, Canada, and proceedings instituted against him and others in the Canadian Court for their extradition to the United States. His statement to the Court as then published is in this language:

"THE ST. ALBANS' RAIDERS.

S. E. Lackey's Statement.

Montreal, November 14, 1864.

"With the permission of your honor, I have only to say that I am a native of the Confederate States, to which Government I now owe allegiance. I have been thrown upon this Government, not designedly, but by the fortunes of war. I have violated no law of this country, or of Great Britain, unless it be unlawful for a Confederate soldier, driven by the hard fate of war, to ask the protection of the British flag. I am a soldier of the Confederate States army, having been recognized as such by the so-called United States Government, from the fact of having been held as prisoner of war. Our command now being held as prisoners of war at Camp Douglas, Illinois, from which place I made my escape, through the mercenary character of those gallant Yankees—a people who make war for plunder, and are bravest when they make war upon women and children. I have during the captivity of my command been detailed for special service inside the enemy's lines under the command of Lieutenant Bennett H. Young. I owe no allegiance to the "quasi" government of the United States. Whatever that I may have done, it has been done under the authority of Government and by the orders of its commissioned officers, prompted by a sense of duty which I owed to my country, my government, and my fellow-comrades."

2. Nicholas Lackey; died in 1886.

7. Andrew K. Lackey; married Nannie Bond, of near Nashville, Tennessee, and lived and died on Walnut Meadow, in Madison County, Ky., a highly respected citizen. Their children:

1. Jennie Lackey; married Jason Shumate. Their children:
   1. Nannie Shumate; married ————.
   2. Mattie Shumate, of Harrisonville, Missouri.
   3. Andrew Lackey Shumate.
2. Berthena Lackey; married Horace Woods, had one daughter:
   1. Susan Woods.

3. Thomas Morris Lackey; a speculator in real estate in Muscogee, Indian Territory.

4. Irene Lackey; married Richard Hockaday. Children:
   1. Nanie Bond Hockaday.

2. Lucy Hockaday.
3. Lillian Hockaday.
(2 and 3 twins.)

5. William Lackey; married Lizzie Stephenson. Children
1. Andrew K. Lackey.
2. Harry Lackey.
3. Lillian Hockaday.
4. Richard Lackey.

6. Diannah Lackey.
7. Florence Lackey; dead.
8. Andrew K. Lackey; now a merchant of Emma, Texas. He married Bettie Frances, a daughter of James B. Frances, and Mary Frances Wallace his wife (See Part 4, Chap. 4, Sec 1.) Have no children.
9. Samuel Lackey; married Allie Cochran, of Garrard County, now residents of Madison, County, Ky. Their children:
1. John Miller Lackey.
2. Margaret Lackey.
3. Andrew K. Lackey; killed by a stroke of lightning.
4. Alma Lackey (a daughter).
10. John Faris Lackey; married Pattie Cochran, of Madison County, Ky. Their children:
1. Mary Elizabeth Lackey.
2. James Lackey.
3. Andrew K. Lackey; dead.
4. John Bond Lackey.
5. Dianna Lackey.

8. Dulaney Miller Lackey; married Mary Eliza Goodloe, Aug. 23, 1853, (See Part 2, Chap. 11, Sec. 4.) They live in Lancaster, Ky. Their children:
1. Archibald Goodloe Lackey; married Vesta Cony. They live in Kansas City, Missouri. Their children:
1. Vesta Lackey; married Herbert Price, of Danville.
2. Mary Goodloe Lackey; died age 15 years.
3. Jenie Dulaney Lackey; single.
4. Maria Estill Lackey; died March, 1883.

9. Jane Lackey; married Thos. Woodson Ballew, Feb. 10, 1848. They settled in Garrard County, Ky. Their children:
1. Bettie Ballew; married her cousin, Charles Ballew.
2. Fannie Watts Ballew; married Joseph Burnside, of Garrard County, Ky. Their children:
1. Bessie Burnsides; married George McRoberts, of Stanford, Ky.
2. Jennie Burnsides; married John Farra, of Lancaster, Ky.
3. Woods Burnside; living now in Garrard County, Ky.

10. Robert Lackey; died a bachelor.
11. Malcolm Miller Lackey; married Belle Bogie, of Boyle County, Ky. Their children:
1. Nanie Lackey; died.
2. Jane Arie Lackey; married Robert L. Doty, of Madison County, Ky. (See Part 7, Chap. 7, Sec. 1.) Their children:
1. Robert Lackey Doty.
2. Hannah Arie Doty.
3. Emma Taylor Doty.
4. Elizabeth Kavanaugh Doty.

5. Malcolm Volney Doty.

3. Emma Lackey; dead; married Pleasant Tucker, of Parksville, Boyle County, Ky. Had one child:

1. Emma Cloyd Tucker; dead.

4. Charles Ballew Lackey.

5. Eliza Ann Lackey.

6 Mary Mack Lackey; married I. D. Goode, of Lincoln County, Ky. Have one child:

1. Irene Goode.

7. Irene Lackey; dead.

8. Candis Lackey; dead.

Section 12 Frances Miller, the twelfth child of Colonel John Miller and Jane Dulaney, his wife, was born June 18, 1894. She married William Watts, Dec. 22, 1812. They lived and died in Madison County, Ky. Mr. Watts died in 1837, and his wife in 1838. Their children:

1. John M Watts; married Amelia Gibbs, June 28, 1839.

2. Susan Watts; married Samuel M. Lackey, April 26, 1832 (See Sec. 11.)

3. Elizabeth Jane Watts; married John G. Miller, May 21, 1833. (See Sec. 7.)

4. Georgia Ann Watts; married Stephen G. Miller, July 23, 1835. (See Sec. 7.) She died and Stephen G. Miller, married the second time, Betsy Stephenson.

5. Margaret Watts; married Austin Bonlware, Jan. 16, 1838. They had:

1. Fannie Bonlware; married first Mr. Bently, and second Mr. Cord.

2. John Bonlware; married Miss Cord.

6. Robert M. Watts; married Milly Collins, March 28, 1845. (See Part 6, Chap. 9, Sec. 7.) Mr. Watts died. His widow now lives in the State of Texas. Their children:

1. William Watts; married ——; lives in Clark County, Ky.

2. Green Miller Watts; died when approaching manhood.

3. Robert M. (Doc) Watts; went to Texas.

4. Fannie Watts; married Joel Collins, went to Texas.

5. Tennis Watts; went to Texas.

7. Wiliam Green Watts; married first Sallie G. Collins. Feb. 13, 1850. (See Part VI, Chap. 8, Sec. 6.) They had no children. He married second Ann Elmore. They had:

1. William Watts; died in the fall of 1905.

8. Mary Watts; after the death of her parents her Uncle Robert Miller, was her guardian.

Note—Willis Watts married Frances W. Quinn, Oct. 28, 1837. George Watts—Jemina Morrison, Jan. 21, 1846.

Section 13. Infant child of Colonel John Miller and Jane Dulaney, his wife, born Oct. 16, 1798.

NOTE 1—JOSEPH DULANEY.

His will bears date July 13, 1813, probated Oct. 4, 1814. His wife was Frances. Children named in the will:

1. John Dulaney.

2. William Dulaney; married Delilah Maupin, May 10, 1804.

(See Part V, Chap. 12, Sec. 5, and Part V, Chap. 12, Sec. 19.) Issue:

1. Betsy Dulaney.
2. James Dulaney.
3. William Dulaney; married Parmilia Gates, Dec. 9, 1830.
4. Jane Dulaney.

Daniel Maupin was grandfather and guardian to the above four children of William Dulaney.

3. George Dulaney.

4. Joseph Dulaney; married Sallie Maupin, Feb. 8, 1812. (See Part V, Chap. 12, Sec. 7.)

5. Elizabeth Dulaney; married Weston Harris, Feb. 2, 1815.

6. Sallie Dulaney.

7. Frances Dulaney; married Patrick Woods, Feb. 1813. (See Part II, Chap. 7, Sec. 2.)

8. ——— Dulaney.

9. ——— Dulaney.

The last two daughters stated in the will as living with Elizabeth and Sallie, their sisters.

The Executors of the will were William Miller and William, George and Joseph Dulaney, three latter sons of the testator.

In a deed bearing date Sept. 19, 1819, from commissioner for Joseph Dulaney's heirs to George Dulaney in addition to the above names, appear these additional names:

1. Benjamin West and Elizabeth, his wife, late Elizabeth Barlow.
2. William Sutton and Lucinda his wife, late Lucinda Barlow.
3. Nancy Barlow.
4. Maria Barlow.
5. Odensa Barlow.
6. Henry A. Barlow.
7. America Barlow.

Heirs of Henry Barlow, deceased. (See Part 5, Chap 12, Sec. 5.)

Note 2:—LETTER FROM VIRGINIA.

Massie's Mill, Va., Jan. 26, 1906.

Mr. W. H. Miller, Richmond, Ky.

Dear Sir—My grandfather was named James Miller. My grandfather had two half-brothers, named Samuel and John; he also had two whole brothers named Robert and Fleming. They were all from Albermarle County. I don't know any of the Millers that you speak of, but have no doubt but what we are some of the same family. My father's name is James Miller. I had seven uncles, viz: David, Christopher, Vantrump, Napoleon, Daniel, George and Robert. My great uncles, Robert and Fleming, went to Missouri and settled in St. Charles County. My uncles David and Christopher, also went to Missouri and settled near St. Joseph; the rest of my uncles remained in Virginia, except uncle Vantrump, who moved to Tennesseee, about thirty years ago, and died there. There is a Mr. Robert Miller, who came from Augusta County and settled about two miles from Massie's Mill, Va. and I showed him your letter and asked him where his people came from, and he said his people came from Nelson and Albemarle Counties. I do not know whether I am related to this Mr. Robert Miller or not, but his features are very much like my grand-fathers, and his people and mine both came from Nelson and Albermarle, we think we must be of same family. Samuel Miller and John Miller, settled in Lynchburg, Va. and dealt largely in tobacco and railroad stocks, and both of them died there, John Miller died first and was worth about $100,000, Samuel Miller's wealth at the time of his death was said to be about $400,000.

Amherst and Nelson County Va. were both in one until the year 1808, and were called Amherst County, and it may be that you could find out about your people in clerk's office at Amherst Court House, Va. I have your letter to clerk of Circuit Court of Nelson County, and if you wish I will take pleasure in sending it to the clerk of Amherst, who may be able to give you the information desired. Anything I can do to aid you in finding out what you wish will be done with pleasure. I have a first cousin in this place who has the same initials as yourself, "W. H. Miller." Please let me know if you wish me to send your letter to the clerk of Amherst.

Very truly yours,
S. N. MILLER.

Note 3—From HISTORY OF ALBEMARLE, by Rev. E. Woods.

Mary Ann Miller; married first Robert Wood, son of Thomas Wood and Susannah Irvine, his wife. After the death of Mr. Wood she married Joseph Harper.

Louisa Miller; a sister to the first wife of President Tyler, married Charles J. Meriwether, a descendant of the emigrant from Wales, Nicholas Meriwether (who died in 1678) and Elizabeth Crawford, his wife. Their children were:

1. Mildred Meriwether; marrier George Macon.
2. Ann Meriwether; married Fred W. Page.
3. Eliza Meriwether; married N. H. Massie.
4. Charlotte Meriwether; the second wife of T. J. Randolph Jr.

Isaac Miller; married Mary, daughter of Nicholas Lewis.

CHAPTER 15.

DR. ALEXANDER MILLER,

of Madison County, Ky.

Mrs. Bessie Miller Oton, from Harriman, Tennessee, in a recent letter says: "The writer offers this modest account of her father's lineage, with regret that more is not obtainable, and the briefness of time allotted by publisher closes all avenues of investigation; for any error please attribute to head, not to heart."

B. M. O.

Mrs. Belle Miller Reynolds, of 324 Wabash Avenue, Kansas City, Missouri, also writes: "I have enclosed you some facts concerning my grandfather's life which may be of use to you. His biography, written some years before his death, has some quaint as well as true statements, and will be read in coming years with even more interest than by those of today. * * * Mrs. B. M. R."

"Dr. Alexander Miller was born in Rockingham County, Virginia, November 26, 1783, being one of ten children, eight boys and two girls—four of the boys being physicians.

DR. ALEXANDER MILLER

"His father, John Miller, served as an officer in the Revolutionary War; was born in Albemarle County, Virginia, 10th of January, 1749, his mother being Margaret Hicklin, of the same county, who was born February, 1760.

"His grandfather, Rev. Alexander Miller, a Presbyterian clergyman, was born in Autrim, Ireland, and a graduate of Edinborough University.

"The wife of Rev. Alexander Miller was Jane Evans, of Glascow Scotland.

"The father of Rev. Alexander Miller was the Duke of Autrim, Sir John Miller.

"Rev. Alexander Miller, who was an Orangeman, on account of religious persecution, fled to France, thence to America, and was an important factor in Presbyterianism in the early history of the church in Virginia."

A few lines from Dr. Alexander Miller's biography may be of interest to the readers of to-day:

"I was raised in Rockingham County and State of Virginia, in the Valley of Virginia, one of the best portions of the State, the residents were mostly descendants of Irish and Scottish parents attached to education, industry and morality. I never heard of a murder being perpetrated in the county before I left. Religious instruction was given principally by Presbyterians and Methodists.

"I studied medicine in Harrisonburgh under the care of Dr. P. Harrison an eminent physician, a pious and very worthy man. I left home for Kentucky April 3, 1806. I opened shop about the place where Owen Walker's store is located (Richmond, Ky.) May 15, 1806. I rented of John Burnam, and boarded with Major Robert Miller, and family. My large patronage from the citizens of Madison and surrounding counties was unprecedented.

"I was married to Miss Elizabeth Barnett, only child of Colonel James Barnett, in Oct. 1807, and moved to Silver Creek where I farmed, and practiced medicine for many years aided by one of the best of wives and children and neighbors. We left Richmond in the spring of 1811. In settling on Silver Creek, we had for our neighbors and with whom we spent much of our visits in sociability and kind interchanges, towit: Nicholas Hawkins, William Robertson, Major Mitchell, Colonel William Morrison, General Andrew Kennedy, John Moran, James Anderson, Captain Andrew Kennedy, Samuel Campbell, Moses Barker, Archibald Curl and all their families which was very numerous in nearly every family. These families were all in good circumstances, good livers, possessing great hospitality and high social qualities. The improvement in our farms and methods of farming has been very great, but it is to be regretted that our people are more attached to business than comforts with their happiness.

"I attribute much of my success in life to a kind over-ruling providence who has dealt very kindly with me. I have done a great amount of business, have never sued a man, prefering to settle difficulties with others in business out of courts, and have often suffered loss in preference to litigation, as the laws of our state are not much to be relied on, and litigation is sure to make enemies of our otherwise friends."

Dr. Miller made his home with his son, James B. Miller during the last years of his life, where he died at the ripe old age of ninety-five years. His five children were James B. Miller, Harrison Miller, Mrs. Green Miller, Cyrus Miller and Dr. Fayette Miller.

His father was prominent in the early development of Virginia, was regarded as an honorable man and devout christian, and reared his children under the puritan rules of Calvinistic doctrine.

Mrs. Oton has several way bills of miscellaneous merchandise dated Philadelphia, 1810, directed to Dr. Alexander Miller and Co., Richmond, Ky., also the original deed of seventy-five acres of land in Madison County, ceded Colonel James Barnett for official service (in the Revolution) signed by Lieutenant Governor John Pope, Secretary Gabriel Slaughter, dated at Richmond, Ky., January, 1819. The same package contains many written military orders at headquarters of General Washington, 1777, signed, G. W., C. C. C.

Dr Miller's mind was superior, his manner of quiet dignity and natural grace marked him indeed a Virginia gentleman He was of Scotch-Irish descent, referring proudly to his fore bear, the Duke of Autrim, a brilliant Scotch-Irish barrister, whose eloquence and ready wit turned many a dry cause into a successful brief. Dr. Miller to the last retained a clear intellect and deep interest in all the affairs of the day. He sank to rest in the home of his beloved son, and daughter (in-law) Mr. and Mrs. James B. Miller in Richmond, Ky. He passed out and beyond quietly "as the mist rises from the brook" with no stain of dishonor upon a long and well spent life, and his grand children revere his memory. He was a noted physician in his day and generation. On one occasion he was called to see a patient in the vicinity of Irvine, Ky. some thirty odd miles from his home, through the woods; on his way some hands were opening a road through a gap or cut in the hills and felling trees out of the way; a tree falling in a manner unexpected, caught a poor fellow under it, and so terribly crushed a leg that his life was despaired of. Dr. Miller happening along about the time of the sad occurrence was called to do what he could for the sufferer. He had the hands stretch the patient out, and with the instruments then in use by doctors he held the arteries and tied them and properly dressed and bound up the wound, and told them to wait on him dilligently, and do all they could to save the man's life, and to the utter astonishment of all the patient recovered.

Among Dr. Alexander Miller's brothers and sisters were:

A sister, Jane; died single.

A brother, Isaac Miller; was a farmer and died near Cadiz, in Trigg County, Ky.

A brother, Josiah Miller; was an able lawyer lived at Hopkinsville Ky.

A brother, William, Miller; was a farmer near Henderson, Ky

A brother, John Miller; was a lawyer of Hopkinsville, Ky.

A brother James Miller; was a farmer and politican, prominent and much admired, was close friend and helper of Lincoln. He lived near Bloomington, Illinois, and was Treasurer of the state for a number of years.

The children of Dr. Alexander Miller, and Elizabeth Barnett his wife, are described in the coming sections:

Section 1. James Barnett Miller, eldest child, was born at Silver Creek, Madison County, Ky. where he lived his venerable years almost out, respected and loved for his genial nature, coupled with a pungent humor, made him many friends. He was a successful planter and stock raiser, caring not for public office. He early married his cousin, Juliett McClellan Miller, of Bloomington, Illinois, a gem among women, and her home was a "House of Bethany" to all privileged to enter and abide there. Their five children were all to be proud of, viz:

1. Leslie Miller; the oldest son, lives in St. Louis, Mo.
2. James B. Miller; a skillful young surgeon, died five years ago in Kansas City, Mo.
3. Florence Miller; died in her youth.
4. Lula Miller; died in her youth.
5. Isabella McClellan Miller; the oldest daughter is the wife of Professor Charles Reynolds of Kansas City. Mrs. Reynolds has adorned her husband's high position, and drawn around her beautiful home, friends trusted and true. They have two handsome daughters and one son, viz:
    1. Florence Reynolds.
    2. Juliett Reynolds; married Alva Brissean.
    3. Charles Reynolds Jr.

Section 2. J. Harrison Miller, second son, born in Madison County, Ky. was a man whose christian character was held up as an example, lived on Silver Creek, owned large tract of land, beautifully improved. By intelligence and frugal management he accumulated an ample fortune. He married Patsy Irvine Field, whose home loving, energetic nature proved a valuable companion. They reared a large family of children, who have taken their rightful places in their adopted homes, among cultured christians, holding in sacred trust the lessons of integrity taught by their parents. Children:

1. Elizabeth Miller; the eldest daughter married Robert Miller, one of Nature's Noblemen. (See Chap. 14, Sec. 1.) They had four daughters, viz:
    1. Sallie Miller.
    2. Harry Miller; married James S. Winn. (See Part I, Chap. 14, Sec. 1.)
    3. Bessie Miller.

4. Pattie Miller; married Stanton B. Hume. (See Part I, Chap. 9, Sec. 4, and Part I, Chap. 14, Sec. 1.)

2. Martha Miller; the second daughter, married John Randolph Heth, of Virginia. They have two sons and one daughter, viz:

1. Stockton Heth; a successful business man of Omaha, Neb.
2 Harry Heth; also a successful business man of Omaha, Neb.
3. Minnie Ha Ha Heth; a beautiful daughter, married first William Vail and had one daughter, viz:
   1. Heth Vail.

She married, second, Charles Lawton, a mine inspector at Lawton, Michigan. No issue.

3. Julia Miller; died in the bloom of young womanhood.
4. Mary Belle Miller; has attained eminence in music, devoting her life to teaching and church service.
5. Lucy Miller; married William Wooten, of Texas. They had two sons, both died in infancy.
6. Margaret Miller; married Frank Henderson, of Houston, Texas.
7. Amelia Miller; married Captain Robert Bruce Terrill of Madison County, Ky. (See Part V, Chap. 12, Sec. 17.) Two daughters were born of this union:
   1. Mabel Terrill; married Vernon Riggs.
   2. Ethel Terrill; married Edwin Rugg.

8. Field Miller; married Lucy Shelby, of Fayette County, Ky. who died leaving one son.
9. James Harrison Miller; the oldest son, was unmarried.

Section 3. Julia Miller, only daughter, born in Madison County, Kentucky, married Green Miller, son of Robert Miller and Sallie Estill his wife. (See Chap. XIv. Sec. 1.) They had five children:

1. Alexander Miller; is unmarried.
2. Irene Miller; married Matt Embry. Left issue.
3. Sallie Estill Miller; married Benjamin Herr, of Monmonth, Ill.
4. Cyrus Miller; a successful physician; died years ago.
5. Harrison Miller; is unmarried; a successful business man in the West.

Section 4. Cyrus Miller; was reared in Madison County, Kentucky; lived to middle life unmarried, emigrated to Independence, Missouri, where he met and married Sarah Halloway. Four handsome children were sent to bless this union, viz:

1. Mary Belle Miller.
2. Julia Miller; married Irene McClannahan of Independence, Missouri.
3. Margaret Miller; married Philip Rugg, of Independence, Missouri. They have several attractive children.
4. Green Miller; married, and is living in California. (Cannot obtain names of his children.)

Section 5. Dr. Lafayette Morrison Miller, youngest child, born in Richmond, Ky. 1826, was a man of rare personality, handsome form and features. His wit and repartie won universal admiration and like the "Knights of the Round Table" he was a "Merrie fellow." He graduated with highest honors of the large class of 1847, at old Transylvania, Lexington, Ky. and was a special favorite of Dr. Ben Dudley, the surgeon. Dr. Miller went from Lexington to Philadelphia for a post graduate course at Blockly Hospital School. He was married March 3, 1846, by Rev. James C. Barnes, to Miss

Caroline Wilson Embry (whose father, Talton Embry, was with Co.onel Daniel and George Boone, in the early settlement of Kentucky) a beautiful, lovely woman, whose presence to her family and friends was like the passing of an exquisite strain of music.

Dr. Lafayette Miller, died in the prime of his manhood, loved by all classes in Jackson County, Missouri. Was surgeon in first company of volunteers commanded by Captain Edmund Halloway. He entered the Confederate service April, 1861; remained until a few weeks before his death 1862. Five children were born to this union, viz:

1. Elizabeth Barnett Miller: the eldest daughter, was married in Richmond, Ky., Oct. 3, 1867, by Rev. Burnett J. Pinkerton, in the presence of James B. Miller and Rev. Robert L. Breck, to Thomas Hill Oton, or Outon of Fayette County, Ky. Bessie Miller Oton is an Elocutionist of the highest merit, an artiste. As early as about 1890, she directed her talent in the line of public reading and by her own efforts has made herself a great name; her recitals are perfectly splendid and her listeners are completely charmed. She is also a writer of ability, many know her as "Gypsey" through the columns of the Sunny South. She is a thorough charming woman, small, beautiful and graceful, impulsive and warm hearted, and in her Southern tours was overwhelmed with attentions. The sketches from her pen for various papers and magazines were most kindly received, among them, sketches of literary work of "Laura C. Holloway" (author of "Ladies of White House" and other books.) "Leaves from the Life of a great surgeon" (Dr. Nathan Bowman of N. Y. formerly of Macon, Ga.) "Elocution a necessity for ministers" "Wayside Flowers" "Adrift" and "Memory Bells." She has been from time to time the New York correspondent for Kansas City Times, St. Louis Post-Dispatch, Sunny South, Lexington (Ky.) Press, and South Western Presbyterian, New Orleans, also Christmas Stories for children. Has, also, been a member of faculty of Plumer College, Wytheville, Va., Valley Seminary and Tishburn Military School, Waynesburg, Va., Fauquier Institute, Warrenton, Va. High School, and West End Academy, Atlanta, Ga. Isabell College, Talladega, Alabama, besides, she has numerious private pupils some of whom, have risen to eminence. She has been all over the union. Her native state Kentucky, should know her as does the South. She has had a hard, tough work, unaided, but has succeeded in spite of all, and there is not a blot on her life. Her present efforts are all for humane purposes, cruelty to animals specially.

Harry W. Grady's first criticism of her was "Mrs. Oton is a "ficile princepes" in her art, and as a woman so high bred and companionable she draws all hearts to her." Judge Hook, who was Supreme Judge of Georgia gave testimony beautiful and true, had met Mrs. Oton many times at Salt Springs, Chautauqua,Ga. In speaking of an entertainment she gave there he thus complimented her, "although suffering intensely, she held the rapt attention of her listeners, and with rapidity moved them from tears to laughter. Who would not be kind and appreciative of such a brave, noble and gifted little woman?"

Mrs. Oton is the daughter of two of the most talented and chivalrous families of Virginia and Kentucky, names old in history. She was reared in luxury, the ideal of proud parents, but when adversity's chilling blast swept over her young life, and she was forced to meet it, her true and noble nature faltered not, but by unceasing labor, aided by a brilliant genius she stands .today unchallenged in her art, while her universal kindness to all, and refined beauty has made her the people's idol, from New York to Mexico, where she is known, and Georgia will ever be ready to welcome Mrs. Bessie Miller Oton's return."

Mrs. Eugenia Dunlap Potts, in the Lexington Townscript said: "To say that she is a genius but feebly expresses her supreme versatility, her magnificent interpretation, her wondrous charm, when she recites, one loses sight of the imitative feature of her work. All that she does stands out as the emanation of her own brain. Viewed from an artist's stand-point it is an irreparable loss to the world, that this gifted woman is not on the dramatic stage. With the blood of the Blue Grass dashing in resistless current through her veins, the exceeding fineness of her nature, is the touch-stone to all that is best in her renditions. She is bewitching in every attitude, every line of her form breathes the poetry of motion. Every throb of her bewildering pulses gives out her perfect womanhood. The emotions whether grave or gay, majestic or grotesque, violent or pathetic emanate from her soul, through eye and lip, and voice and jesture with a fidelity that demands fullest sympathy from her hearers. Her voice alone with its varied cadences would give out the gamut of human passion were she motionless as a statue."

From the pen of "F" of Richmond, Virginia, in the Sunny South: "She has made many friends at the various summer resorts she has visited in Virginia, and added to her popularity as a conversationalist. We hope to secure her for a long time. Two of Mrs. Oton's scholars, whom she taught in Atlanta, Mrs. A. H. Alfriend, and her bright little twelve year son, Edward, also, if they are fair samples of her scholars, any city should be proud to be able to secure her services permanently. Little Edward Alfriend is a wonder, he bids fair in future years to deserve the sobriquet of 'The Southern Orator.' There are few, very few ladies in our country who have the gift of entertaining both with pen and tongue as Mrs. Oton has. Wherever she resides she will have as many friends and admirers as she has in her old home."

We here quote from the Illustrated Kentuckian, Lexington, Ky.: "The following eloquent tribute was paid to Mrs. Bessie Miller Oton on her second appearance at Seamen's Bethel in New Orleans on March 9, 1893, by Rev. Thomas R. Markham, D. D. pastor of Lafayette Presbyterian Church and Captain General of the United Confederate Veterans: 'A dowry lavished on this fair daughter of Kentucky, herself a scion of that Blue Grass stock who a week ago from this platform charmed our eye with the graces of manner and our ears with the 'concourse of sweet sounds.' In the interdependences of intellect, the masters of thought, and the monarchs of words are large debtors to the masters of expression. Who can measure Shakespeare's obligation for right interpretation and profound impression to Mrs. Siddon's Garrack and Booth? And we who here last Friday listened as the reader "lent to the rhyme of the poet the beauty of her voice" entered as through a newly opened door into the secret chambers of Longfellow's musings over hearts set in tune with his, as with her beside him we "Stood on the bridge at midnight." Roscius and Cicero, his pupil in elocution, held trials of skill to test whether the orator, or the gesticulator, could the more clearly and effectively render a thought, and Demosthenes, in defining eloquence, thrice repeated the word "action." So it is with us then, for while eye, ear and taste paid tribute to the modulated tones, it was the spirit with which these were uttered, and the "action suited to the word," the flash of the eye and the play of feature, the ease of movement and the grace of form, that completed the enchanter's spell, taking us captive at her will. But as words are powerless to paint the lily, and add a perfume to the violet, and as you are now to hear her for yourselves, and, too, lest I "lag superfluous on the stage," suffer in closing to say for myself that it has been a pleasure to know, and a privilege to hear, as it is an honor to introduce, one, who coming to us last week a stranger, is greeted by us tonight as a friend. I have the honor of presenting to this audience Mrs. Bessie Miller Oton." "The Bridge" is her most remarkable rendition. * * * This rendition has been given by Mrs. Oton before the author Longfellow himself, and with his great appreciation. In flowing rhythmic accents, intense with reverie and sad memory and the joyful resurrection of hope came the well known lines."

From the Southern Presbyterian, 1898: "Her naturalness of manner, showing in rare perfection the 'art concealing art,' her grace of movement, the modulated intonations of her cultivated voice; the versatile play of powers passing in easy transformation 'from grave to gay,' and drawing at will from the 'spring of laughter' or the 'fountain of tears'; her sympathetic impersonation of her author's thought, spirit and speech, 'the action suited to the word,' these varied and combined accomplishments and gifts held us with the spell of an enchantress, the assembly of intelligent and appreciative listeners that filled to overflowing the spacious room in which she achieved so signal a triumph. A pleasing episode of the evening, and a grateful surprise was the presentation to her of a laurel wreath, the victor's crown. This was made in well chosen words by Colonel Fred A. Ober, a veteran of the Army of Northern Virginia, who had had the pleasure of introducing to the veterans of the Soldier's Home this daughter of a veteran of the Confederacy, in which he made a pleasing and touching mention of her recitals there, and at the Seamen's Bethel, and the Memorial Church, under the care of Rev. Dr. E. Forman, the pastor of her childhood in Kentucky, her native state. Her reply given with marked emotion, her heart paying its tribute through tears, that moved ours, was a felicitous recognition of the attention and appreciation shown her in a city noted for its courtesy to strangers and its hospitality to visitors, to which she came two months since a stranger, knowing no one, and only asking to be heard; but now at parting leaving in it many friends, whose kindness had made her visit a pleasure that would live in her memory as a joy." (1898.)

A volume of testimony of the gifts and value of this remarkable woman from the Southern press, such as the Picayune (New Orleans), the Sunny South, the Southern Presbyterian, Atlanta (Ga.) Constitution, Lexington (Ky.) Transcript, Virginia papers, etc., Supt. M. A. Cassidy, Lexington, Ky., etc., but this must suffice.

To the union of Bessie Miller and Thomas Hill Oton were born two intelligent, admirable daughters, viz:

1. Caroline Embry Oton; now the wife of Richard Dunward McPhaul, prominent turpentine exporter of Bay Minette, Ala. They have one child, viz:
   1. Richard McPhaul, Jr.

2. Adelaide Davis Oton; married John Boon de Saussure, of Charleston, South Carolina, son of General Wilmot Gibbes de Saussure and Martha Gourdine de Saussure. Gen. de Saussure was the hero of Ft. Sumpter. His son is a refined gentleman and excellent business man.

Mrs. Oton's daughters attained enviable positions as teachers and scholars.

2. Talton Embry Miller, lives in St. Louis; married ——————
His children are:

1. James Miller; made a fine record in United States Navy; was accidentally drowned at Leage Island, Aug. 1, 1904, while anchoring the admiral's launch alongside the Minneapolis.
2. Leslie Miller.
3. Alexander Miller.
4. Helen Miller.
5. Charlotte Miller.

The mother of the above named children is dead.

3. Alexander Hood Miller; lives in St. Louis; has one daughter:

1. Carrie Anna Miller.

4. Lafayette Morrison Miller; died in Arkansas five years ago. His success in dentistry was that of a conscientious, finished workman, and the future full of promise. He was a Knight Templar and was buried with Masonic honors.

5. Alma Bartlett Miller; born in Jackson County, Missouri, to where Dr. Miller emigrated, in 1853; the youngest daughter married Rev. Russell Cecil, of Harrodsburg, Ky. They live in Richmond, Va., where Dr. Cecil is pastor of the historic Second Presbyterian Church. Mrs. Cecil is a model minister's wife, endearing herself to the people by her tact, gentleness and true piety. They have five handsome children, viz:

1. Russell Cecil, Jr.; practicing medicine at Johns Hopkins Hospital; is at this time cruising somewhere along the northern coast.
2. John Howe Cecil; commercial man of Richmond, Va.
3. Alma Cecil, a beautiful young maiden.
4. James McCosh Cecil; preparing for college.
5. Elizabeth Cecil, the baby.

PART II.

CHAPTER 1.

GENEALOGICAL TABLE OF THE WOODS FAMILY. 2. EARLY MARRIAGES IN MADISON COUNTY, KY., GLEANED FROM THE FIRST MARRIAGE REGISTER OF THE COUNTY COURT. 3. ITEMS CONNECTING THE WOODS NAME WITH EVENTS.

"A"

1. Elizabeth, m Peter Wallace (Part IV, Chap. 1).
2. Michael, m Mary Campbell ("B") (Chap. 4).
3. James (Chap. 3, Sec. 3).
4. William, m Elizabeth Wallace (Chap. 3, Sec. 4).
5. Andrew (Chap. 3, Sec. 5).

"B"

1. Magdalene, m 1 John McDowell, 2 Benj. Borden, 3 Col. John Bowyer (Chap. 5).
2. William, m Susannah Wallace (Chap. 6).
3. Michael, m Anne (Chap. 13).
4. Hannah, m Wm. Wallace (Part IV, Chap. 3).
5. Col. John, m Susannah Anderson (Chap. 19).
6. Margaret, m Andrew Wallace (Part IV, Chap. 6).
7. Richard, m Jennie ——— (Chap. 33).
8. Archibald, m Isabella ——— (Chap. 4).
9. Martha, m Peter Wallace, Jr. (Part IV, Chap. 15).
10. Andrew, m Martha Poage (Chap. 37).
11. Sarah, m Joseph Lapsley (Chap. 46).

"C"

1. James, m Mary Garland (Chap. 20). (
2. Mary, m John Reid (Chap. 21).
3. Michael, m Hettie Caruthers (Chap. 22).
4. Suity, m Samuel Reid (Chap. 29).
5. Sarah (Chap. 19, Sec. 5).
6. Anna, m Jonathan Reid (Chap. 48).
7. John, Jr., (Chap. 19, Sec. 7).
8. Susannah, m Daniel Miller (Part 1, Chap. 13).

Elizabeth Worsop. Born Nov. 15, 1656

- Thomas Worsop
- Elizabeth Parsons
  - Richard Parsons
    - William Parsons of Birr, or Parsontown.
  - Letitia Loftus
    - Sir Adam Loftus
      - Sir Dudley Loftus of County Dublin.
        - Adam Loftus Archbishop of Dublin and Lord Chancellor of Ireland; born in Yorkshire, Eng. 1534. Was Archbishop of Armagh at 27 years of age; ordained in 1559.
          - Rt. Rev. Edw. Loftus. of Levinhead.
        - Jane Purdon
          - T. Purdon
      - Anne Bagnall
        - Henry Bagnall of Newry.
    - Jane Vaughn
      - Walter Vaughn of Coldingrove.

married Katherine Oldham. See Genealogical Table, Part VI.

- Christopher Irvine Miller
  - Table to Part I.
  - Daniel Miller See Genealogical Table Part I.
    - Table to Part I.
  - Susannah Woods
    - "C"
    - Col. John Woods
      - "B"
      - Michael Woods of Albemarle, known as Michael of Blair Park.
        - "A"
        - John Woods
          - Son of an English Trooper in army of Oliver Cromwell 1649. Settled in County Meath, Ireland.
        - Elizabeth Worsop
          - (Continued to left.)
      - Mary Campbell
        - Of the Scottish Clan Campbell of Argylshire, Scotland.
    - Susannah Anderson
      - Rev. James Anderson. of Pennsylvania.
- Talitha Harris See Table to Part III.

Article 2.—Early Marriages in Madison County, Kentucky, Gleaned from the First Marriage Register of County Court.

Woods, Lucy—Caperton, Wm., Dec. 15, 1790.
Woods, Patrick—Cooper, Rachael, July 19, 1792.
Woods, Wm.—Kinkead, Ruth, Aug. 1, 1792.
Woods, Susannah—Goodloe, Wm., Feb. 23, 1796.
Woods, Margaret—Duncan, Chas. John, Dec. 17, 1795.
Woods, Hannah—Hutton, James, Jan. 11, 1790.
Woods, Susannah—Mellone, Richard, Oct. 3, 1797.
Woods, Margaret—Blake, Thos., Aug. 23, 1793.
Woods, Wm.—Harris, Polly, Jan. 5, 1802.
Woods, Adam—Hancock, Nancy, March 18, 1802.
Woods, Elizabeth—Taylor Talton, Feb. 4, 1802.
Woods, Judy—Taylor, John, March 11, 1802.
Woods, Wm.—Harris, Nancy, Sept. 25, 1802.
Woods, Syntha—Strong, John, Feb. 10, 1803.
Woods, Susannah—Williams, James, April 30, 1801.
Woods, Mary—Mullins, Wm., June 18, 1801.
Woods, Wm.—Clark, Susannah, Aug. 13, 1801.
Woods, Sally—Smith, Thos., Dec. 13, 1804.
Woods, Arch'd—Hill, Fanny, June 5, 1806.
Woods, Anna—Miller, Thos., July 29, 1806.
Woods, Adam—Kerley, Polly, March 24, 1807.
Woods, Abraham—Yates, Elizabeth, Nov. 29, 1806.
Woods, John—Duncan, Elizabeth, Dec. 28, 1809.
Woods, Wm.—Noland, Elizabeth, Jan. 10, 1808.
Woods, Polly—Heath, Benjamin, Jan. 10, 1805.
Woods, James—Embry, Betsy, Aug. 24, 1809.
Woods, Talton—Woods, Sally, March 28, 1810.
Woods, Arch'd—Shackelford, Elizabeth, Oct. 9, 1810.
Woods, Patrick—Dulaney, Fanny, Feb. 6, 1813.
Woods, Leannah—Land, Wm., Feb. 20, 1814.
Woods, Arch'd—Woods, Polly, Oct. 4, 1814.
Woods, Thursa—Yates, James, Oct. 20, 1814.
Woods, John—Thomas, Mary H., July 2, 1812.
Woods, Francis—Austin, Nancy, Dec. 11, 1815.
Woods, Elizabeth—Moberley, James, Sept. 28, 1816.
Woods, John S.—Mitchell, Polly, July 15, 1817.
Woods, Adam—Crigler, Betsy, Aug. 26, 1817.
Woods, Lucinda—Dantic, Paul, June 25, 1819.
Woods, John—Skinner, Phoebe, Dec. 20, 1820.
Woods, Hannah—Collins, Barbee, May 29, 1823.
Woods, Rusia—West, Hiram, Oct. 3, 1825.
Woods, Fanny—Cochran, Samuel, Dec. 19, 1826.
Woods, Thursa—Epperson, Green, Dec. 22, 1829.
Woods, Zach. W.—Lees, Ann, Jan. 7, 1830.
Woods, James—Oldham, Sophia, June 17, 1830.
Woods, Charlotte—Ballard, Thompson R., March 17, 1813.
Woods, Martha Ann—Estill, James M., Sept. 22, 1831.
Woods, Elizabeth—Boggs, Edward C., Sept. 19, 1833.
Woods, James—Caudle, Sallie, Nov. 13, 1832.
Woods, James—Hardin, Phoebe, Dec. 31, 1833.
Woods, Anderson W.—Sullivan, Lucy P., Oct. 30, 1836.
Woods, Parabee—Gordon, William, March 4, 1841.
Woods, Wm. G.—Gentry, Nancy Boone, Oct. 12, 1843.
Woods, Sophia—Harper, Perry, Feb. 29, 1836.

Article 3.—Items Connecting the Woods Name with Events.

(From History and Court Records.)

In the first settlement of Kentucky the Woodses were in the tide that flowed into the same, and took active part, not only in the settlement, but the development and growth thereof, as their fathers had also aided in the development of her mother, Virginia. And items of interest taken from record and history are here thrown in exhibiting some little events relative to the name Woods.

Section 1. John Woods was part of a company of fifteen men, known as Hinkson's Company, who, in March or April, 1775, came down the Ohio and up the Licking River in canoes in search of lands to improve. They landed at the mouth of Willow Creek, on the east side of Main Licking, four miles above the forks, where Falmouth now is, and took the route as told in Part I, Chap. 1, Sec. 1: The Miller Company narrative. (Collins.)

Section 2. In 1787, by an act of the Virginia General Assembly, Archibald Woods, of Madison County, was appointed one of ten trustees of the town of Boonesborough, established as a town by said Assembly in October, 1779. (Collins.)

Section 3. Archibald Woods was one of the first Justices of the Peace and of Oyer and Terminer, in the organization of the first court of Madison County, being commissioned by His Excellency Patrick Henry, Governor of Virginia, as such. (See Part I, Chap. 14)

Section 4. Woods Narrative (Col. His. p. 477): In the year 1781, or 2, near the Crab Orchard, in Lincoln County, a very singular adventure occurred at the house of Mr. (Michael) Woods. One morning he left his family, consisting of a wife, a daughter not yet grown, and a lame negro man, and rode off to the station nearby, not expecting to return till night. Mrs. Woods being a short distance from her cabin, was alarmed by discovering several Indians advancing towards it. She instantly screamed loudly in order to give the alarm, and ran with her utmost speed in the hope of reaching the house before the Indians. In this she succeeded, but before she could close the door the foremost Indian had forced his way into the house. He was instantly seized by the lame negro man, and after a short scuffle they both fell with violence, the negro underneath. Mrs. (Hannah) Woods was too busily engaged in keeping the door closed against the savages without to attend to the combatants, but the lame negro, holding the Indian tightly in his arms, called to the young girl to take the axe from under the bed and dispatch him by a blow on the head. She immediately attempted it, but the first effort was a failure; she repeated the blow and killed the marauder. The other savages were at the door endeavoring to force it open with their tomahawks; the negro arose and proposed to Mrs. Woods to let in another and they would soon dispose of the whole of them in the same way. The cabin was but a short distance from the station, the occupants of which having discovered the perilous situation of the family, fired on the Indians and killed another, when the remainder made their escape. (See Chap. 6, Sec. 2.) (Collins.)

Section 5. We here exhibit members of the Woods family who have represented sections of Kentucky in the General Assembly:

In the Senate—

Archibald Woods, from the County of Madison, 1826-9.

In the House of Representatives—
Archibald Woods, from the county of Madison, 1816-17, 1820-4.
Silas D. Woods, from the County of Pulaski, 1848.
Francis M. Woods, from the County of Lewis, 1855-7.
William Woods, from the County of Garrard, 1857-9.
John N. Woods, from the County of Crittenden, 1871-3.

McDOWELL, DESCENDANTS OF MAGDALINE WOODS.

Section 6. Judge Samuel McDowell, Senior. In 1783 Kentucky was established into a district, and a court of criminal as well as civil jurisdiction co-extensive with the district was established. The court held its first session in Harrodsburg in the spring of 1783, and was opened by John Floyd and Samuel McDowell, Judges; John May being the Clerk, and Walker Daniel, Prosecuting Attorney.

Judge Samuel McDowell was president of the nine conventions which met at Danville, Ky., between December 27, 1784, and July 26, 1790. Also of the convention that framed the first constitution of Kentucky. And he and William McDowell were two of the many subscribers to proposal Dec. 1, 1787, for establishing a society to be called the "Kentucky Society for Promoting Useful Knowledge."

Judge Samuel McDowell, Senior, was one among the Justices present at the first County Court held for Mercer County, on Tuesday, Aug. —, 1786; and he held the first Circuit Court in Estill County, June 20, 1808. He was a son of John McDowell and Magdalen Woods, his wife, a daughter of Michael Woods, of Blair Park, and Mary Campbell, his wife. The said John McDowell was killed in battle with Shawnee Indians at Balcony Falls, where the North River comes into the James River, in 1743.

Section 7. Dr. Ephraim McDowell, the greatest Kentucky surgeon, and renowned in History of Medical Science as the father of Ovariotomy.

Section 8. Joseph McDowell was in Captain James Brown's company of mounted Kentucky Volunteers against the Wiaw Indians in 1791.

Section 9. James McDowell, of Virginia, on the 14th of June, 1774, had surveyed for him, by James Douglas, 1,000 acres of land on a south fork of Licking Creek.

Section 10. Thomas McDowell was killed in Madison County, near the Louisa (Kentucky River), March 26, 1775, out of a company of sixteen men suddenly attacked by the same body of Indians who the day before had attacked Colonel Daniel Boone and Captain William Twetty's company, and killed Captain Twetty.

Section 11. John McDowell was a lot holder in Lexington, Ky., in 1783.

Section 12. Members of the Kentucky Legislature:

In the Senate—
William McDowell, from the County of Mercer, 1792-4, 1800, 1802.
William McDowell, from the County of Nelson, 1792-6.

In the House of Representatives—
John McDowell, from the County of Fayette, 1792, 1794-8.
John B. McDowell, from the County of Bullitt, 1865-7.

Section 13. Charles R. Woods, 1827-1885, commanded a regiment at Fort Donelson and Shiloh, a brigade at Corinth, and a regiment at Vicksburg. He led a division in Sherman's Georgia campaign. (a-c)

Section 14. William B. Woods, 1824-1887, was a member of the)hio Legislature, 1857-60. Speaker of the House in 1858. He was ommissioned Lieutenant-Colonel of Ohio Volunteers, and fought t Shiloh, Arkansas Post, Resaca, Dallas, Atlanta, Lovejoy Station, nd Bentonville. He led a division in Sherman's march to the sea. Ie was a United States Circuit Judge, 1869-80, when he became a ustice of the United States Supreme Court. (a-c)

Section 15. Historical facts concerning the arms and crest of he Irish branch of the ancient Woods family, taken from a copy urnished by John O'Hart, of No. 7 Belone Terrace, Dolly-.ount, Dublin, Ireland, author of "Irish Pedigrees," Landed Gentry n Ireland, at the time of the invasion of Oliver Cromwell, copied rom the manuscript of the 6th edition of "Irish Pedigrees," then eing prepared for the press, and were obtained from the archives f Trinity College, Dublin, and the office of the Ulster King at ırms, Dublin Castle, Dublin, Ireland.

Arms and Crest.

Arms—Sa, three garbs cor. crest—out of clouds a hand erect, olding a crown between two swords, in bend and bend sinister, oints upward.

The meaning of the Arms and Crest is: Out of gray clouds a esh color hand perpendicular, holding a gold crown and all between wo steel colored swords. Their significance—the sheaves of wheat n the arms indicate that the bearer came from a wheat-raising ountry—the crest implies a combat, a victory, and an unexpected eward—the two swords a combat, the result a gold crown from an .nexpected source—the hand out of a gray cloud.

Cucult, who (see page 689, Vol. 1, 6th edition of this work) is :o. 103 on the O'Nealles pedigree, was the ancestor of O'Coillte ;oill, Irish Wood, Coillte, Woods and O'Coillege, Anglicised, Reitty, iuizty, Galt, Woods and Woods.

Thus the O'Coillte were a branch of the Mac Morough family, /ho were the Kings of Lunster up to the period of the English in-asion of Ireland in the twelfth century, when the O'Coillte family eprived of their patrimony were scattered, some settling in Great 3ritain and others on the Continent.

Among the officers commonly called the Forty-niners, who in 649 fought for Charles I and Charles II, we find five who were ıamed Wood, and five who were named Woods: and the name Voods is among the names of the Cromwellian adventurers for land n Ireland in the Cromwellian period.

The name Woods appears among the French refugees (Hugue-ıots) who settled in England and Ireland before the reign of Louis XIV of France, while Henry Woods was one of the members of the rish Parliament of James II in 1697.

In Burke's "General Armory" are described the Armoriat Bear-ngs of 99 of the Wood family and six of the Woods family, but all of them are in England. The bearings described in the foregoing vere the ancient arms of the family in Ireland.

On page 136 of the MS, Volume F 225, in the library of Trinity College, Dublin, we find that John Woods of the County Meath narried Elizabeth, born 15th day and baptized 17th Nov., 1636, laughter of Thomas Worsop, of Dunshanlin, County Meath, by his vife Elizabeth, who was daughter of Richard, son of William Par-sons of Birr, or Parsontown by said Richard's wife Letitia, who was the daughter of Sir Adam Loftus, miles, who married Jane, daughter of Walter Vaughn, of Coldengrove, was son of Sir Dudley Loftus, miles, by his wife Anne, daughter of Henry Bagnall, of Newry, miles, and said Sir Dudley was the son of Adam Loftus, Lord Bishop of Dublin and Lord chancellor of Ireland, who married Jane, daughter of T. Purdon.

We further find that John Woods above mentioned, who married Elizabeth Worsop, had issue, sons and daughters. The sons and daughter were Michael, Andrew, William, and James, and Elizabeth, wife of Peter Wallace, all of whom emigrated to America in the beginning of the eighteenth century with the three sons of Michael—William, John, and Archibald.

From these Irish emigrants are descended the Wood, Woods families, now located in several of the United States, and all descended from Adam Loftus, Archbishop of Dublin, and Lord Chancellor of Ireland for Queen Elizabeth. From Adam Loftus the descent is, Adam Loftus married Jane Purdon, and among other children, Sir Dudley Loftus, miles, of Rathfranham, County Dublin, who married Anne, daughter of Henry Bagnall, of Newry, miles, and had among other children, Sir Adam Loftus, miles, who married Jane, daughter of Walter Vaughn, of Coldengrove, who had among other children Letitia Loftus, who married Richard Parsons, son of William Parsons, of Parsontown, and had among other children, Elizabeth Parsons, who married Thomas Worsop, of Dunshanlin, County Meath, who died May 27, 1686, and had among his children Elizabeth Worsop, born the 15th day and was baptized the 17th of Nov., 1656, who married John Woods, of the County Meath, and had with other children, Michael, Andrew, William, and James (and Elizabeth, wife of Peter Wallace). Michael Woods, eldest son of John Woods and Elizabeth Worsop, married Lady Mary Campbell, of the Clan Campbell Argylshire, Scotland, a near kinswoman of Archibald Duke of Argyle.

Adam Loftus, Archbishop of Dublin and Lord Chancellor of Ireland, was born at Levinhead, in Yorkshire, in 1534. He was the younger of the two sons of the Rt. Rev. Edward Loftus, of Levinhead, temp. Henry VIII, Robert being the elder and the ancestor of Viscount Loftus of Ely (extinct in 1725). The eldest son of Robert was Adam Loftus of Monasteraven, Queen County, who was appointed Lord Chancellor of Ireland in 1619, created a peer in 1622.

The graceful deportment of Archbishop Adam Loftus at the Cambridge examination attracted the attention of Queen Elizabeth, and after his ordination in 1559 he was appointed Chaplain to Dr. Craik, Bishop of Kildare. Loftus was advanced rapidly in the church; when he was but twenty-seven he was created and consecrated Archbishop of Armagh; six years later he exchanged Armagh for Dublin. With him a general system of education was a favorite project: by his influence an act was passed in 1570 directing that free schools should be established in the principal town of each diocese at the cost of the clergy. He was appointed Lord Chanellor of Ireland in 1573, and was foremost in supporting and carrying out Queen Elizabeth's foundation of the Trinity College, of which he was the first provost, on the site of suppressed Monastery of All Hallows. He expired at the Palace of St. Supulchres, Dublin, April 5, 1605, and was buried in the St. Patrick's Cathedral.

Section 16. List of places bearing name found on map:

State:		
	New Jersey—	Woodsville.
	Virginia—	Woods Cross Roads.
		Woods Lane.
		Woods Gap.

West Virginia—Woods.
Indiana— Woods.
Illinois— Woods.
Kansas— Woodsdale.
North Dakota—Woods.
Wyoming— Woods.
Oregon— Woods.

CHAPTER 2.

THE WOODS FAMILY.

of America.

Article 1.—The Woods Family are of Anglo-Scotch-Irish extraction. The American Family sprang from one John Woods, son of an English Trooper, who came to Ireland and was in the army of invasion of Oliver Cromwell, 1649.

The said John Woods was born in 1654 and married about 1681, to Elizabeth Worsop, a daughter of Thomas Worsop and Elizabeth Parsons, his wife. The said Elizabeth Parsons was a daughter of Richard Parsons and Letitia Loftus, his wife. The said Letitia Loftus was a daughter of Sir Adam Loftus and Jane Vaughn, his wife. The said Sir Adam Loftus was a son of Sir Dudley Loftus, of County Dublin, Ireland, and his wife, Anne Bagnall. The said Sir Dudley Loftus was a son of Adam Loftus and Jane Purdon, his wife. The said Adam Loftus was a son of the Right Rev. Edward Loftus, of Levinhead.

The last named Adam Loftus was born in Yorkshire, England, in 1534, and by the promotion of Queen Elizabeth was made, when only twenty-seven years old, Archbishop of Armagh, and subsequently Archbishop of Dublin and Lord Chancellor of Ireland. (See Chap. 1, Art. 3, Sec. 15.)

Five of the children of John Woods and Elizabeth Worsop, his wife—four brothers and one widowed sister and the wives of such as were married, and the children who had then been born to them in Ireland, near the close of the first quarter of the eighteenth century emigrated from the north of Ireland to America and settled in the Colony of Pennsylvania, some of them a little later on moving to the Colony of Virginia and locating themselves near the base of the Blue Ridge, as shown in Chapter 3, Part II.

These five children of John Woods and Elizabeth Worsop are the basis of the Woods and Wallace families of America noticed in this book.

The Woodses were very prolific, hardy, adventurous and resourceful, they not only aided in the settlement and development of Virginia, but in that of Kentucky and Missouri, and were conspicuous figures and took action in the great Revolutionary struggle for American independence—not only the Woods name, but the blood coursing in the veins of others wearing other names, in no small measure increased the strength of the Revolution.

In all the generations from long before the Declaration of Independence, down through the years to the present there have been patriots among them. In the war of 1812, in the Indian wars, in the Mexican War, in the Civil War that resulted in the freedom of the negro, and in the Spanish-American War, they performed some part.

We had data tracing the lineage of our immediate family back to John Woods, son of the English Trooper and Elizabeth Worsop, his wife, but of the numerous collateral branches forming since the immigration to America down to the present, much was wanting, and the Woods-McAfee Memorial, by Rev. Neander M. Woods has furnished much information that was lacking (made use of by his kind, generous and unlimited courtesy). The Rev. Neander M. Woods performed well a very hard and worthy task, for which he should be praised by the descendants of the Woods and Wallace emigrants from Ireland.

As the Miller, Woods, Harris, Wallace, Maupin, Kavanaugh, Oldham, and Brown families are connected by numerous inter-marriages, it is attempted in the coming chapters to give only a brief sketch of the descendants of John Woods and Elizabeth Worsop: not that it is expected at all to improve upon the work of the Rev. Neander M. Woods, for nothing of the kind is hoped for, as he has performed well his part, although in a work of the kind there will unavoidably occur some errors, but only this: as the families aforenamed have so intermarried as in a sense to form one family, an account of one is very incomplete without the other, and to simply have the records of these several families condensed into one connected volume for the benefit and pleasure of the family is the aim.

Perfection for this work is not claimed; it is only hoped that the imperfections shall not utterly destroy the object and the friends hereof should pardon all imperfections.

In spelling the name, some families have dropped the "s" and spell it "Wood."

CHAPTER 3.

JOHN WOODS OF IRELAND.

Son of English Trooper.

Article 1.—John Woods, of County Meath, Ireland, was born there in about 1654. He married Elizabeth Worsop, in about 1681. Elizabeth Worsop, his wife, was born Nov. 15, 1656. Of the children born to them were those named in the coming sections.

Section 1. Elizabeth Woods, a daughter, born in Ireland about 1682, or prior thereto. She was married to Peter Wallace, a Scottish Highlander, in Ireland about 1705. Peter Wallace died some time in the early part of the eighteenth century, and his widow after his death, about the close of the first quarter of said century, with her children, accompanied by her brothers, Michael, William, James and Andrew Woods, emigrated from the north of Ireland to America. She first stopped in Pennsylvania, where she remained some ten or fifteen years; then moved into Virginia and settled in Rockbridge County just across Blue Ridge from where her brother

Michael and two of her sons lived. A fuller account will be found in Part IV, Chapter 1.

Section 2. Michael Woods, a son, born in 1684, in the north of Ireland. He married Mary Campbell, of the Scottish Clan Campbell, of Argylshire, Scottland, about 1704 or 5. Died in 1762. Further notice of whom will be had in Chapter 4, Part II.

Section 3. James Woods, a son, born in Ireland; immigrated with his widowed sister, Elizabeth Wallace, and brothers, Michael, William and Andrew Woods, from there to America. For further particulars of him see Woods-McAfee Memorial by Rev. Neander M. Woods.

Section 4. William Woods, a son, born in Ireland and came along with his widowed sister, Elizabeth Wallace, and brothers, Michael, James and Andrew Woods, to America. For further particulars see Woods-McAfee Memorial by Rev. Neander M. Woods.

Section 5. Andrew Woods, a son, born in Ireland, and came with his widowed sister, Elizabeth Wallace, and brothers, Michael, James and William Woods, to America. For further particulars see Woods-McAfee Memorial by Rev. Neander M. Woods.

CHAPTER 4.

MICHAEL WOODS.

From Ireland to Albermarle County, Virginia, later called Michael Woods, of Blair Park.

(Named in Chapter 3, Section 2.)

Article 1.—Michael Woods, son of John Woods, and Elizabeth Worsop, his wife, after his death known as Michael Woods, of Blair Park, was born in the North of Ireland, in about 1675 to 1684.

In about the year 1704 or 5, he married Mary Campbell, of the Scottish Clan, Campbell of Argylshire, Scotland. He died in 1762. His wife died probably about 1742. His will bears the date Nov. 24, 1761, probated in the Albermarle, (Va.) County Court, at the June Term 1762.

Near the close of the first quarter of the Eighteenth century, he with his wife and children, and his widowed sister Elizabeth Wallace, and her children and his brothers, James, William and Andrew Woods, emigrated to America. Their first stop was probably in Pennsylvania, where he remanied a while and then moved with his family into Virginia, and settled at the Eastern base of the Blue Ridge, in what was then Goochland, now Albermarle County, just at the Gap in the mountain called "Woods Gap" and in after years "Jarman's Gap."

Michael Woods, senior, and his son-in-law, William Wallace, in 1737, secured grants for more than 1300 acres of land on Lickinghole, Mechum's River and Beaver Creek, embracing the present Mechum's depot, and Blair Park, (the old Woods homestead,) and at the same time Michael Woods, senior, purchased the 2000 acre patent of Charles Hudson on Ivy Creek. The first Presbyterian

Church, was Mountain Plains, bulit near the confluence of Lickinghole Creek, and Mechum's River, and named for and after Michael Woods 'plantation', and same still exists, having been converted in some way into a Baptist Church.

When these people came to America they landed on the banks of the Delaware, spent some years in Lancaster County, Pennsylvania, and thence ascended the valley of Virginia and crossed the Blue Ridge by Woods Gap, in 1734, and Michael Woods was, it is believed the first settler in Western Albermarle, and perhaps any where, along the East foot of the Blue Ridge in Virginia. His home was near the mouth of Woods Gap, for a long while has been known as Blair Park, but originally known as Mountain Plains. There he spent the rest of his life, which ended in 1762, his remains were buried about 100 yards from his dwelling. He is remembered now as Michael Woods of Blair Creek. He and his sons, and sons-in-law had as friends and neigbors, such noted persons as Colonel Peter Jefferson, surveyor and County or Lord Lieutenant of Albermarle County, his son, the statesman, Thomas Jefferson, author of the Declaration of Independence, and third President of the United States, Randolph Jefferson, General Lewis, James Munroe, fifth President of the United States, who bore witness to many legal documents for Michael Woods.

A land grant the 4th, June 1737, to Michael Woods is in these words and figures: "George the second, by the Grace of God, of Great Britain, France and Ireland, King Defender of the Faith, to all whom these presents shall come, greeting: Know ye, that for divers good causes, and considerations, but, more especially for and in consideration of the sum of five shillings of good and lawful money for our use paid to our Receiver General, of our Revenues in this our Colony and Dominion of Virginia we have given granted and confirmed, and by these presents for us our heirs and successors, do give, grant and comfirm unto Michael Woods, one certain grant, or patent of land containing four hundred acres, lying and being in the County of Goochland, on both sides of Lickinghole Creek, a branch of Mechum's River, and bounded as followeth to wit: Beginning at a black oak and running thence south eighty six degrees, east three hundred and twenty five poles, crossing the creek, to Pointers, south nine degrees, east two hundred and fifty five poles, crossing Lickinghole Creek, to Pointers north sixty eight degrees, west three hundred and ninety six poles, to a pine sapling, and north nine degrees, west one hundred and thirty five poles, to the first station, with all woods, under woods, swamps, marshes, low grounds meadows, floodings and his due share of all veins, mines and quarries as well discovered, as not discovered, within the bounds aforesaid, and being part of the said quantity of four hundred acres of land and the rivers, waters and water courses therein contained, together with the privileges of hunting, hawking, fishing, fowling and all other profits, commodities and hereditaments whatsoever, to the same, or any part thereof belonging, or in any wise appertaining to have and hold, possess and enjoy the said grant or parcel of land, and all other the before granted premises, and every part thereof, with their and every of their appurtenances unto the said Michael Woods, and his heirs and assigns forever. To the only use and benefit of him the said Michael Woods, his heirs and assigns forever. To be held of us, our heirs and successors, of our Mannor of East Greenwich in the County of Kent, in free and common soccage and not in capite, or by Knights service yielding and paying unto us, our heirs and successors for every fifty acres of land, and so proportionably for a lesser or greater quantity than fifty acres the fee rent of one shilling yearly to be paid upon the feast of Saint Michael, the Arch-Angel, and also cultivating and improving three acres part of every fifty acres the grant above mentioned within three years after the date of these presents. Provided always that if three years of the said fee rent shall at any time be in arrears and unpaid, or if the said Michael Woods his heirs or assigns do not within the space of three years next coming after the date of these presents(cultivate and improve three acres part of every fifty of the grant, above mentioned then the estate hereby granted shall cease and be utterly determined and thereafter it shall and may be lawful to and for us, our heirs and successors to grant the same lands and premises with the appurtances unto such other person or persons as we, our Heirs and Successors shall think fit.

In witness whereof, we have caused these our Letters Patent to be made; witness our trusty and beloved Wm. Gooch, Esquire, our Lieutenant Governor and Commander in chief of our said colony, and dominion at Williamsburg, under the seal of our said colony the 4th day of June, one thousand seven hundred and thirty seven, in the fourth year of our reign.

(Signed) WILLIAM GOOCH."

The children of Michael Woods, and Mary Campbell, his wife:

Section 1. Magdalene Woods, born 1706 died 1810, married John MacDowell, who was killed in 1743 in battle with the Shawanee Indians, at Balcony Falls, where the North comes into the James River. She married the second time Benjamin Borden, Jr. whom she survived, and married the third time Colonel John Bowyer. The subject of Chapter 5.

Section 2. William Woods, born at Castle Dunshanglin, Ireland, in 1705. He took an active part in the Colonial wars, holding the rank of Colonel. He married Susannah Wallace, a daughter of Peter Wallace, Sr. and Elizabeth Woods his wife. (See Part Iv. Chap. Vii. Sec. 11.) The subject also, of Chapter Vi.

Section 3. Michael Woods Jr., 1708-1777. He married Anne ————. The subject of Chapter XIII.

Section 4. Hannah Woods, 1710—, married Wm. Wallace, a son of Peter Wallace, Sr. and Elizabeth Woods, his wife. (See Part Iv. Chap. 11, Sec. 1, and Chap. III.)

Section 5. Colonel John Woods, born in Ireland, Feb. 19, 1712, old style, married Susannah Anderson, a daughter of Rev. James Anderson, of Pennsylvania, in about 1742. He died Oct. 14, 1791. The subject of Chapter Xix.

Section 6. Margaret Woods, 1714—, married Andrew Wallace, a son of Peter Wallace Sr., and Elizabeth Woods his wife. (See Part Iv. Chap. 11, Sec. Iv. and Chap. Vi.

Section 7. Richard Woods, 1715-1779, married Jennie ——. The subject of Chapter 33.

Section 8. Archibald Woods, 1716-1783, married Isabella ——— and raised a large family in Virginia. Fuller account in Chap. IV.

Section 9. Martha Woods, 1720-1790, married Peter Wallace Jr., son of Peter Wallace Sr., and Elizabeth Woods, his wife. (See Part Iv. Chap. XV.)

Section 10. Andrew Woods, 1722-1781, married Martha Poage. Fuller account in Chapter XXXVii.

Section 11. Sarah Woods, 1724-1792, married Joseph Lapsley. Fuller account in Chapter XXXXVi.

CHAPTER 5.

MAGDALENE WOODS.

(Named in Chap. 4, Sec. 1.)

Article 1.—Magdalene Woods, a daughter of Michael Woods, Senior, of Blair Park, and Mary Campbell, his wife, was born in 1706, and died in 1810.

She married first Captain John McDowell, who fell in battle with the Shawanee Indians at Balcony Falls, where North River comes into the James, in 1743, she married secondly, Benjamin Borden Jr., whom she survived, and married the third time Colonel John Bowyer.

From Waddell's annals of Auguta County, Virginia, page 37: "On the 28th of Feb. 1739, John McDowell, who settled in Borden's Grant, made oath at Orange Court 'that he imported himself, Magdaline, his wife, and Samuel McDowell, his son, and John Rutter, his servant, at his own charge from Great Britian in the year 1737, to dwell in this colony, and that this is the first time of proving their rights in order to obtain land pursuant to the royal instructions."

Waddell further says, "Captain John McDowell, was a prominent Captain of a military force of Auguta County, in 1742. Ephraim McDowell, then an old man, was a member of his son John's company. All grown men were enrolled without respect to age.

"Capt. John McDowell did not long enjoy the honor and perform the duties of his office. He and seven of his men were killed in a fight with Indians on Dec. 14, 1742, on North River near Balcony Falls, within the present County of Rock bridge. A letter from Judge Samuel McDowell, son of Capt. McDowell, written to Colonel Arthur Campbell in 1808, gives a somewhat detailed account of this first conflict of whites with Indians. Judge McDowell states that about the first of Dec. 1742, a party of thirty three Delaware Indians came into the settlement in Borden's Grant, saying they were on their way to assail the Catawba tribe, with which they were at war. They professed friendship for the whites, and were entertained for a day by Captain McDowell, who treated them with whiskey."

"From McDowell's they went down the south branch of North River and encamped seven or eight days. They hunted, went to the homes of white people, scaring women and children, taking what they wanted, and shot horses running at large. Complaint being made to Colonel Patton, the County Lieutenant, he ordered Captain McDowell to call out his company and conduct the Indians beyond the white settlement. The company consisted of thirty three or four men, and embraced all the settlers in what is now Rockbridge County. In the mean while the Indians moved their camp further south. The company of white men thirty three in number overtook the Indians and accompanied them beyond Peter Sallings, then the furthest white settlement. About one-half of the company were horseback, and the remainder on foot. One of the Indians was lame, and fell behind, all the whites passing him except one. The lame Indian left the path and went into the woods, and the white man who was in the rear fired his gun at him. Immediately the Indians raised the war-whoop and the fight began. As stated, the

Captain and seven of his men were killed. For a time the result was doubtful, but finally the Indians gave way, leaving seventeen of their men dead on the ground. The survivors took to the Blue Ridge, and pursued it till they reached the Potomac River. Several who were wounded died on the way and it was learned that only ten of them reached their home in Pennsylvania. The people of the settlement gathered on the field of slaughter and says Foote "took the men (eight) bloody corpses, on horse back and laid them side by side near McDowell's dwelling while they prepared their graves in overwhelming sorrow."

"John McDowell's grave may still be found in the family burying ground near Timber Ridge Church, marked by a rough stone."

Children of the first marriage of Magdalene Woods to Colonel John McDowell:

Section 1. Judge Samuel McDowell, (See Chap. 1, Sec. Vi.) married Mary McClung. Their children:

1. John McDowell; born in Virginia in 1757; was a Revolutionary soldier, and married his first cousin, Sarah McDowell (See Sec. 2): she died leaving issue, and he married the second time Lucy Le Grande, and moved to Fayette County, Kentucky, in 1784. He was a Major in the war of 1812. Children by first wife:

1. James McDowell; married Susan Shelby.
2. John McDowell; married Sarah McAlpin.
3. Samuel McDowell; married Betsy Chrisman.
4. Betsy McDowell; married William McPheeters.
5. Mary McDowell; married Major Thomas Hart Shelby.

Chldren by his second wife:

6. Joseph Nash McDowell; married Miss Drake.
7. Charles McDowell; married Miss Redd.
8. Betsy McDowell; married Henderson Bell.
9. Sallie McDowell; married James Allen.
10. Lucy McDowell; married David M. Woodson.

2. James McDowell, born in Rockbridge County, Virginia in 1760, was a Revolutionary soldier. He married Mary Paxton Lyle, daughter of John Lyle. In 1784, he moved to Fayette County, Ky. He was commissioned by Governor Shelby, Major in the war of 1812, and at the close of the war held the rank of Colonel. Their children:

1. Isabella McDowell; married Dr. John Poage Campbell.
2. Salie McDowell; married Oliver Keene, of Fayette County, Ky. He was a son of Francis Keene and Mary ——— -, his wife; of their children were:
   1. Sallie McDowell Keene; married Churchill Blackburn.
   2. Mary Keene; married George Boswell.
   3. Pauline Keene; married Judge Hickey.
   4, James McDowell; Keene.
   5. Christopher Greenup Keene.
   6. Oliver McDowell Keene; married Sallie Clay, granddaughter of General Green Clay. Their children:
      1. Mary Keene; married James T. Shackelford. (See Part I, Chap. 11, Sec. 2.)
      2. Sidney Clay Keene.

3. Samuel McDowell, was a Sergeant in Captain Trotters company in the war of 1812. He married Polly Chrisman of Jessamine County, Ky.

4. Juliet MacDowell; married Doctor Dorsey, of Fleming County, Ky.

5. Hettie MacDowell; married John Andrews.

6. Captain John Lyle McDowell, was a Captain in the war of 1812. He married Nancy Vance Scott. He died in Frankfort, Ky., in 1878.

3. Judge William MacDowell, was born in Rockbridge County, Va., March 9, 1762. He was of the Virginia Militia for a time during the Revolutionary War, though very young. He was an able lawyer. He came to Kentucky in 1784, and settled near Danville. In 1787 he represented Mercer County in the Virginia Legislature. Under President Madison he was made District Judge of Kentucky. He died at Bowling Green, Ky., full of honors. He married Margaret Madison, a daughter of John Madison, an uncle of the President. Their children:

1. Samuel I. McDowell; married Nancy Rochester, and left issue.

2. Lucinda McDowell; married Dennis Brashear.

3. Mary McDowell, was the first wife of Major George C. Thompson, of Mercer County, Ky.

4. William McDowell; married Miss Carthrae.

5. Agatha McDowell; married James G. Birney (1792-1857), a Kentucky lawyer of Mercer County, also a politican a graduate of Princeton. He was an enthusiastic advocate of the abolition of slavery, and Editor of the Philanthropist and secretary of the National Anti-Slavery Society, and in 1840 and 1844, was the candidate of the Abolition or Liberty Party for President of the United States. (Dic. Am. His. Jameson.) On May 9, 1810, John Patrick and wife, Elizabeth of Madison County, Ky., executed a deed of trust to William McDowell, and James Birney of Mercer County, Ky. and James Hagarty of Richmond, Va., to 200 acres of land near Richmond, Ky., which was released May 13, 1815.

6. Eliza McDowell; married Nathaniel Rochester, of Bowling Green, Ky.

4. Samuel McDowell was born in Rockbridge County, Virginia, March 8, 1764. He was a Revolutionary soldier and was in the closing campaign at Yorktown. In 1784 he moved to Kentucky and settled in Mercer County. He served in various expeditions against the Indians after coming to Kentucky. He was appointed by General Washington first U. S. Marshal for Kentucky, in 1792, which office he continued to hold under Presidents Washington, Adams and Jefferson. He married his kins woman, Anna Irvine. Their children:

1. John Adair McDowell; born March 26, 1789, married Lucy Todd Starling.

2. Abram Irvine McDowell; born April 24, 1793; married Eliza Seldon Lord.

3. William Adair McDowell; born March 21, 1795, married Marriah Hawkins Harvey, a kinswoman, of Fincastle Virginia. He was a soldier in the war of 1812. Their children:

1. Sarah Shelby McDowell; married Bland Ballard, the noted Louisville lawyer.

2. Harry Clay McDowell; married Annette Clay.

3. William Preston McDowell; married Kate Wright.

4. Edward Irvine McDowell, Captain 15th Ky. Federal fell in battle in the late Civil War.

4. Unknown.
5. Joseph McDowell; married Anne Bush.
6. Alexander Keith McDonald; married, first, Priscilla MacAfee, a daughter of General Robert B. MacAfee, and secondly, Anna Haupt.
7. Mary McDowell; married William Starling.
8. Sallie McDowell; married Jeremiah Minter.

5. Joseph McDowell, born Sept. 13, 1768. He came to Kentucky at sixteen years of age. He took part in the Indian campaigns. He was in Brown's company, with Scotts expedition in 1791, and in both expeditions of General Hopkins in 1812. He was a member of Governor Shelby's staff and was with him at the battle of the Thames in 1813. He died June 27, 1856. He married Sarah Irvine. Their children:

1. Samuel McDowell; married first, Amanda Ball, and secondly, Martha Hawkins, June 26, 1828; the second marriage occurred in Madison County, Ky.
2. Anna McDowell; married Abraham I. Caldwell.
3. Sarah McDowell; married Michael Sullivant of Columbus, Ohio.
4. Margaret Irvine McDowell; married Joseph Sullivant of Columbus. Ohio.
5. Magdaline McDowell; married Caleb Wallace, of Danville, Ky.

6. Dr. Ephraim McDowell, the famous surgeon, was born in what is now Rockbridge County, Virginia, Nov. 11, 1771. In 1784, when thirteen years old, he came with his parents to Kentucky and settled in Danville. He spent two years, 1793-4, at Edinburg, studying medicine. He was the first to successfully perform in surgery the removal of Ovarian Tumor. He married Sarah Shelby, daughter of Governor Isaac Shelby in 1802. Their Children:

1. Caleb Wallace McDowell; maried Miss Hall. He died in Missouri.
2. Mary McDowell; married Mr. Young.
3. Miss Adaline McDowell; married Mr. Deatrick, of Washington County, Tennessee.
4. Susan Hart McDowell; married Colonel David Irvine of Madison County, Ky. son of Colonel William Irvine, a pioneer of Madison County, Ky. William Irvine was the first clerk of the Madison County and Circuit Courts, and Court of Quarter sessions, holding said offices until his resignation just a while before his death. He was succeeded by his son David Irvine, who held same a long while.

The Irvine family is one of the most prominent families of Kentucky. Children of David Irvine and Susan Hart McDowell, his wife:

1. Sarah J. Irvine; married Colonel Addison White, Sept. 4, 1841, a native of Virginia. Issue:
    1. Newton K. White.
    2. Shelby Irvine White.
    3. A daughter Mrs. Patton, the mother of Sue Patton married Richard White Miller. (See Part I, Chap. 14, Sec. 2.)

    Col. Addison White was at one time U. S. Congressman.

2. Elizabeth S. Irvine; married her cousin, William M. Irvine, Nov. 3, 1846. (See Part III, Chap. 7, Sec. 3.)

3. Isaac Shelby Irvine; married Bettie Hood. Colonel Irvine was an elegant, substantial gentleman, and had an elegant residence on West Main street in Richmond. He died at Carthage, Tenn., Nov. 24, 1906. His wife preceded him.
4. David W. Irvine; a bachelor.

5. Miss McDowell; married Maj. Anderson, of Boyle County, Ky. and moved to Missouri.

7. Caleb Wallace McDowell, born April 17, 1774. He married his cousin, Elizabeth McDowell, daughter of Col. John McDowell, of North Carolina, and Margaret Moffett, his wife. Had only one child:

1. Miss McDowell; married Joseph Chrisman, Jr., of Jessamine County, Ky.

8. Sarah McDowell; twin to 9.
9. Magdaline McDowell; twin to 8.

(8) Sarah married Caleb Wallace, who became one of the three first Justices of the Kentucky Court of Appeals, being his first wife; she had no children.

(9) Magdaline married Andrew Reid, March 4, 1776, and remained in Virginia.

10. Martha McDowell, born June 20, 1766. She married Colonel Abraham Buford. He was at the battle of Point Pleasant, in Oct. 1774, and Lieutenant of milita in Buford County and Lieutenant Colonel in the Revolutionary Army. Their children:

1. Charles S. Buford; married first, Miss Adair, daughter of Governor John Adair, and secondly, Lucy Duke, daughter of Dr. Bazil Duke, and Charlotte Marshall, his wife.
2. William S. Buford; married Miss Robertson, daughter of Hon. George Robertson.
3. Mary Buford; married James K. Duke.

11. Mary McDowell, born in Rockbridge County, Virginia, Jan. 11, 1772. In 1784, she came with her parents to Kentucky. In Oct. 1774, she married Alexander Keith Marshall, son of Colonel Thomas Marshall, of Revolutionary fame, and nephew of Chief Justice Marshall. Their children:

1. Charles Thomas Marshall, born July 14, 1800, married Jane Duke.
2. James K. Marshall; married Catherine Calloway Hickman.
3. Mariah Marshall; married James Alexander Paxton.
4. Lucy Marshall; married her cousin John Marshall son of Captain Thomas Marshall.
5. Jane Marshall; married William Starling Sullivant, of Columbus, Ohio.

Section 2. James McDowell; married Elizabeth Cloyd. Their children:

1. Sarah McDowell; married her cousin, Major John McDowell, son of Judge Samuel McDowell. (See Sec. 1-1.)
2. Elizabeth McDowell; married David McGavack, and they moved to Nashville, Tennessee.
3. James McDowell, Colonel in the war of 1812, and he won honor and fame. He married Sarah Preston, daughter of Colonel William Preston, who was surveyor of Fincastle County, and had as assistants John Floyd, John Todd, — Douglas, Hancock Taylor, Hancock Lee and others, and who surveyed vast tracts of land in Kentucky from 1773 to 1785. Their children:

1. Susan McDowell; married Colonel William Taylor.
2. Elizabeth McDowell; married Hon. Thomas H. Benton, the great Missouri Statesman, and who was in the U. S. senate a long time. Their children:
   1. Miss Benton; married General John C. Fremont.
   2. Miss Benton; married Colonel Richard T. Jacob of Ky.
3. James McDowell, was a member of the U. S. House of Represenatives, and afterwards of the U. S. Senate, and then Chief Executive of Virginia. He was an eloquent orator. He married his first cousin Miss Preston, daughter of General Francis Preston, and Miss Campbell, his wife, daughter of Col. onel William Campbell, who commanded in the battle of King's Mountain.

Section 3. Sarah McDowell, married Colonel George Moffett. Their children:

1. Margaret Moffett; married her cousin, Colonel Joseph McDowell.
2. Mary Moffett; married her cousin, Major Joseph McDowell, son of Hunting John McDowell. Their children:
   1. Colonel James Moffett McDowell, of Yancey County.
   2. John Moffett McDowell, of Rutherford County.
   3. Miss McDowell; married her cousin, Captain Charles McDowell, of Burke County.
   4. Miss McDowell; married her cousin Caleb McDowell, son of Samuel McDowell and Mary Clung, his wife.

   Mary Moffett McDowell after the death of her husband, Major Joseph McDowell married again, Captain John Carson, the noted Indian fighter, by whom she had a number of children, among them:
   5. Hon. Samuel P. Carson, of Burke County, North Carolina.
3. Magdaline Moffett; married James Cochran.
4. Martha Moffett; married Saptain Robert Kirk, of U. S. army.
5. Elizabeth Moffett; married James Miller, owner of large Iron works, in Virginia.
6. George Moffett; married Miss Gilkeson. They moved to Ky.
7. James Moffett Jr; married Hannah Miller, sister to James Miller, husband of her sister Elizabeth.

Children of Magdaline Woods, and her second husband, Benjamin Borden, Jr:

Section 4. Martha Borden; married Benjamin Hawkins. Their children:

1. Miss Hawkins; married John Todd, who fell in the battle of the Blue Licks, in Kentucky.
2. Magdaline Hawkins; married Matthew Harvey. One child.
   1. Mariah Hawkins Harvey; married William A. McDowell.

After the death of Benjamin Hawkins, his widow Martha Borden Hawkins, married Robert Harvey, an older brother of her daughter's husband, Matthew Harvey.

Section 5. Hannah Borden, died young.

It is unknown whether Magdaline Woods, —— McDowell, —— Borden, —— Bowyer, and her third husband, Colonel John Bowyer, had any children or not. Benjamin Borden claimed under two patents, one for 500,000 acres of land in what is known as the Borden Grant, and the other for 100,000 acres among the forks of the James River.

CHAPTER 6.

WILLIAM WOODS.

(Named in Chap. 4, Sec. 11.)

Article 1.—William Woods, a son of Michael Woods, senior, of Blair Park and Mary Campbell his wife, was born at Castle Dunshanglin, Ireland, in 1705.

He emigrated to America with his father. He was a Lieutenant in the frontier Indian wars, in 1758, from Albermarle County, Va. and was active in the Colonial wars, holding the rank of Colonel. His home was in Fincastle County, Va., where he died ——, leaving his last will and testament, bearing date ——. At that time Fincastle County, embraced a very large territory. He married Susannah Wallace, a daughter of Peter Wallace, Sr. (who died in Ireland) and Elizabeth Woods, his wife (who when a widow emigrated to America, and died in Rockbridge County, Va.) (See Part Iv. Chap. 1.)

The children of William Woods, and Susannah Wallace, his wife:

Section 1. Adam Woods; married Anna Kavanaugh, according to some biographers. See Chapter 7 for further account, and Part Vii. Chap. 11, Sec. V.

Section 2. Michael Woods, born perhaps about 1746. He married Hannah Wallace, a daughter of Andrew Wallace, and Margaret Woods, his wife. See Part IV, Chap. 3, Sec. 6.) In about the year 1780, he emigrated with his family to Kentucky, and first stopped at Crab Orchard Station, where he was living in 1781-2, when the incident or adventure occured at his house as narrated in Collins History of Kentucky, (See Item 4, of Chap. 1) and also described by the Tattler further on in this chapter. He afterwards moved to Madison County, Kentucky, and entered, surveyed, and patented 1000 acres of land in Madison County, on Muddy Creek, adjoining of James Bridges settlement and pre-emption claim on the lower side. On the 25th of Jan. 1822, he and his wife, being both dead, his heirs, namely: William Woods, and Ruth his wife, James Hutton and Hannah his wife, late Hannah Woods, James Woods, David Chevis and Polly, his wife, late Polly Logan (late Polly Woods), Sallie Smith, late Sallie Woods, and her husband, Thomas Smith, John Woods and Polly his wife, Adam Woods and Nancy his wife, Andrew Wallace Woods and Margaret, his wife, united in a deed, conveying to William Black, assignee of William Tinchner, 300 acres, part of the 1000 acres survey and patent aforesaid, except 30 acres, theretofore conveyed to Samuel Tinchner. See statement of the Tattler under subdiv- 3-1, of this section. The children of Michael Woods, and Hannah Wallace, his wife:

1. William Woods; married Ruth Kinkead, Aug. 1, 1792.
2. Hannah Woods; married James Hutton, Jan. 11, 1790.
3. James Woods; married Betsy Embry Aug. 24, 1809.
4. Polly Woods; married first Samuel Logan, and second David Chevis.
5. Sallie Woods; married Thomas Smith, Dec. 13, 1804.
6. John Woods, was twice married, first to Mary H. (or Polly) Thomas, July 2, 1812, in Madison County, Ky., and second to

Susan March. There was no issue of the second marriage. His home was near Milford or old town, on land, owned in his life time by the late Major John D. Harris, where he lived until his death, May, 13, 1845, leaving a last will and testament, bearing date, March 9, 1844, probated June 2, 1845. The children of the first marriage:

1. Elizabeth Woods, born April 23, 1813, near Milford, or old town, in Madison County, Ky. She married Edward C. Boggs, Sept. 19, 1833. Their home was on the Big Hill Road, near the south eastern limits of the city of Richmond, Ky. where they died. The Tattler, of one of the Richmond papers produced the following: "Mrs. Elizabeth Woods Boggs, who was born April 23, 1813, about one mile from Milford, the first County seat of Madison County, is now living (since deceased) at the ripe age of seventy one, with her son, J. H. Boggs, about one mile east of Richmond. Mrs. Boggs' great uncle, Archibald Woods, among the first represenatives from this County in the Legislature, was sheriff in 1798, at the time of the County seat and Court House trouble, and removed the records from Milford to Richmond before the Anti-removal men arrived at the scene. Her grandfather, Michael Woods, and her grandmother, whose maiden name was Hannah Wallace, were natives of Ireland, but having moved to Scotland, about the middle of the last century, emigrated from there to Virginia in about 1775 and there her father, John Woods, was born, in 1777. (These dates are erroneous, Michael Woods, father came to America at a much earlier date. Michael was born in America, colony of Va.) He was next to the youngest of four sons, William and Adam older, and Andrew, younger than himself, besides the four boys there were five girls in the family of Michael Woods when he removed from Virginia to Kentucky, in about 1780, and settled at Crab Orchard Station, and lived there at the Fort with other settlers. He was in all the seiges and fights at Crab Orchard Station, and frequently took part in the scouts and pursuits of the Indians to recover stolen property. He afterwards moved to his place near Milford or Old Town, on land now owned by Major Jno. D. Harris where he died. John Woods bought out the other heirs and lived there until his death, May 13, 1845.

William Woods, is described as being stout, over six feet tall and with red hair. He was a bold and fearless man, and continually in fights with the Indians, but seems to have been discreet enough, and never fool-hardy. At one time he was returning on horse back, from a hunt, when suddenly he found that the Indians were all around him, except on the side towards a ravine, having a fleet horse he considered that discretion was the better part of valor, so he made him jump the ravine and thus escaped.

Polly Woods, one of the girls of this family married Sam Logan, who was the first tanner ever in Richmond. (One Sam Logan, on he 18th of Oct. 1799, married Peggy Briscoe, a daughter of Captain Wiliam Briscoe, and Elizabeth Wallace his wife of near Richmond, Ky. (See Part Iv, Chap 18, Sec. 1.) And Mrs. Boggs has many times heard her father tell the true story of an incident related in Collins History. One night, most likely in the spring of 1782, the Indians made a raid on the Station at Crab Orchard and stole all the horses. The next day all the men in and about the fort went in pursuit, leaving only a negro with a lame hand at Mr. Woods cabin and a white man sick in another cabin close by. The children had been going to and from the spring all morning and had noticed nothing suspicious, except their sagacious dog would walk slowly in the spring path and look towards the spring and growl, but never bark. Towards dinner time, Polly Woods, then seventeen years old, had gone with her little brother, John to a knoll, not far from the house to gather salad, and the negro man, was in the yard playing on a buffalo robe with little Betsy Woods, suddenly, Polly saw a huge Indian stealing up the spring path with his body bent, and on tiptoe leading a band of warriors, and she at once gave the alarm, at the top of her voice. The negro ran to the house in an instant to shut the door, but the Indian leader rushed in the door at the same time and there they clinched in a tremendous struggle, the negro being as good a wrestler as the Indian. During the scuffle at the door, little Betsy though only three years old, slipped in between them, in a minute or two they had gotten inside and Mrs. Woods, the mother of the family had secured the door. In one corner stood a rifle and the struggle was for the gun, the Indian forgetting to use his knife and tomahawk, which hung in his belt, but jabbering all the time to his companions out side who were trying to break down the door with their war clubs. Mrs. Woods ran for a knife near by, but seeing it was of no use seized the broad axe and hewed the Indian down, litterly cutting him to pieces before they could stop her. Meanwhile Polly had rushed with her little brother to the house of the sick neighbor, who though hardly able to move, seized his rifle and shot one of the indians out side. The savages then beat a hasty retreat, taking the dead body of their comrade with them. They had been concealed near the spring, and seized their opportunity to slaughter the family, but failed. By the continual practice the sagacity of the lower animals in the old days was almost perfectly developed. The intelligent dog mentioned above was a very valuable animal. On one occasion William Woods with his twelve-year-old brother John, had gone to the salt works on Goose Creek, for salt, accompanied by this dog, on their return they had stopped for the night and had lighted a fire when this old dog looked back in the direction they had come and growled, but knew better than to bark knowing that indians were about, William scattered the fire and came to the station, that night before stopping. A day or two after several men were killed in the same place by indians.

Mrs. Boggs had in her possession a box made of lignumvitae which belonged to her great grand father in Ireland, and was brought to America by her grand father when he came to Va. It is supposed to be two hundred years old. The children of Elizabeth Woods, and Edward C. Boggs:

1. James Howard Boggs, was born in Madison County, Ky. at his parents home. He was one of General John H. Morgan's raiders during the Civil War, Co. F. 7, afterwards the 11 Ky. Cavalry, (Col. D. Waller Chenault), was in the famous Ohio raid where he was captured, and made his escape from Camp Douglas. It was almost next to impossible to hold him a prisoner, his cunning and shrewd sagacity and determination worked to that end. He married Mary C. Pigg, a daughter of Johnson Pigg, and lived in Madison County, Ky. and after his father's death, owned and occu-

pied his fathers old home, until several years ago, he sold out and moved to near Nicholasville in Jessamine County, Ky. where he now owns a farm and is a breeder of Black Poll Cattle, South down sheep, and Angora goats.

2. Elizabeth J. Boggs; died at nine years of age.
3. Phoebe A. Boggs; married James M. Bowen.
4. Elizabeth Jane Boggs; married firstly, Mr. Adams, and secondly B. D. Miller.

2. Curtis J. Woods, died unmarried.
3. Sophia Woods; married Perry Harper, Feb. 29, 1836.
4. John C. Woods; married Miss Gillispie.
5. Jason Woods; married Susan Lipscomb.
6. Lavinia Woods: married Jacob Bronston, brother to Thomas S. Bronston, known as "Little Tom."

7. Adam Woods; married Nancy Hancock, March 18, 1802.
8. Andrew Wallace Woods; married Margaret ———.

9. Betsy Woods, mentioned by the Tattler, but who was probably dead in 1822, when Michael Woods heirs joined in the deed to William Black, assignee of William Tinchner, for her name is silent in the deed, or the latter was probably mistaken in the staement that the child was named Betsy. (One Elizabeth Woods married Talton Taylor, Feb. 4, 1802 and one Elizabeth Woods married James Moberly, Sept. 28, 1816.)

Section 3. Peter Woods,1762, came from Virginia to Madison County, Ky., with his wife, Jael Kavanaugh, a daughter of Charles Kavanaugh, senior, (who died in Madison County, Ky. in 1796) and An his wife, he was one of the executors of his father-in-law's will. He was a pioneer Baptist preacher, and lived for a number of years in Madison County, Ky. where he solemnized a great number of marriages and in about the year 1808, went to Tennessee, where he remained until about 1819, and removed to Cooper County, Missouri, where he died in 1825, leaving many descendants. On Aug. 23, 1786, one Peter Woods was recommended by the Madison County, Ky., Court, to the Governor, as a proper person to be commissioned Lieutenant of milita in Madison County. (See Part Vii. Chap. XIv.)

Section 4. John Woods, was a soldier in the Indian wars, and in the Revolutionary army. He married Abigail Estill, a daughter of Captain James Estill, and Mary Ann his wife. He came from Virginia to Madison County, Ky. in the early pioneer days, and in 1784, he in company with Samuel Estill, Azariah Martin, William Kavanaugh and others went in pursuit of Indians near the mouth of Station Camp Creek and the Little Picture Lick, described by Azariah Martin in his deposition. About the year 1808, he moved with his family to Tennessee, where he died in 1815. Mary Ann Estill's will mentions her children, Samuel, Wallace, William, Isaac, Abigail wife of John Woods, and the will is witnessed by Peter Woods and Susannah Shelton.

Section 5. Andrew Woods, born 1747, married Hannah Reid, of Virginia, but they had no children, so said. In the early pioneer days he came to Madison County, Ky., where he lived till about the year 1808, when he moved to Tennessee where he died in 1815. He was also a Baptist minister. Madison County Court Order:

"Oct. 28, 1788. On the motion of Andrew Woods, his ear mark, towit, a crop in the right ear, and a slit in the left ear, is ordered to be recorded.

Section 6. Archibald Woods, was born in Albermarle County,Va. Jan. 29, 1749. He married Mourning Shelton, a daughter of William Shelton, and Lucy Harris his wife, Aug. 15, 1773. (See Part 111, Chap. 3, Sec. Vi.) A fuller history is given in chapter Viii.

Section 7. William Woods, born Dec. 31, 1744, and known as Beaver Creek William Woods; married first, his cousin, Sarah Wallace, and second Mrs. Anna Reid, also his cousin. Further history of them will be found in chapter 12.

Section 8. Sarah Woods, 1761-1851, married Mr. Shirkey.

Section 9. Susan Woods.

Section 10. Mary Woods; married George Davidson.

Section 11. Hannah Woods; married William Kavanaugh, son of Charles Kavanaugh, senior (who died in Madison County, Ky. in 1796) and Ann his wife. (See Part Vii, Chap Viii.)

Section 12. Elizabeth Woods, married Philemon Kavanaugh, another son of the above named Charles Kavanaugh senior, and Ann his wife. (See Part Vii, Chap. IV.)

CHAPTER 7.

ADAM WOODS.

(Named in Chap. 6, Sec. 1.)

Article 1.—Adam Woods, a son of William Woods, and Susannah Wallace, his wife, according to sketch by Col. Charles A. R. Woods, married Anna Kavanaugh. See Part 11, Chap. 11, Section V.)

He came from Virginia to Madison County, Ky. in the early pioneer days, his wife died, and he went to Howard County, Missouri, where he died in 1826. He was a minister of the Baptist Chuch. On the 6th of March 1809, he and his wife Anna conveyed to their son Patrick Woods, land in said County, for the consideration of one dollar and love and affection for their son, and on the 5th of May, 1809, they conveyed to their son, Adam Woods, Jr lands on Tates Creek in said county. Their children:

Section 1. William Woods; married Susan B. Clark, a daughter of Benjamin Clark and Jane Mullins his wife. (See Part V, Chap. 13, Sec. 7.) A fuller history of him will be found in Chapter 49.

Section 2. Patrick Woods; married firstly, Rachel Cooper, in Madison County, Ky. July 19, 1892, and secondly, Frances Dulaney in the same county, Feb. 6, 1813. She was a daughter of Joseph Dulaney and Frances his wife. His name appears on the Madison County, Ky. Court records. He emigrated to the Louisiana Territory.

Section 3. Archibald Woods; married his cousin, Mary Wallace, a daughter of Michael Wallace and Jane Bratton, his wife. (See Part IV, Chap. 7, Sec. 4.) They emigrated to Missouri.

Section 4. Michael Woods, served in Colonel Slaughters regiment of Kentucky mounted men in the war of 1812. He was never married.

Section 5. Peter Woods, moved from Kentucky to Clay County, Missouri in 1815, and there reared a large family.

Section 6. John Woods, M. D. moved to California after the Mexican War.

Section 7. Hannah Woods, became the second wife of Colonel Barbee J. Collins. (See Part IV, Chap. XX, Sec. 1.)

Section 8. Anna Woods; married Mr. Brown in Ky. prior to 1815.

Section 9. Susan Woods; married Colonel Richard Mullens, and moved to California. (See Part V, Chap. X111, Sec. V.)

Section 10. Sallie Woods; married Judge Austin Walden, of Missouri.

Section 11. Adam Woods, Jr. On the 5th of May, 1809, Adam Woods, and his wife Anna conveyed to their son, Adam Woods, Jr. lands on Tates Creek in Missouri County, Ky.

On March 8, 1802, one Adam Woods, married Mary Hancock.

On March 24, 1807, one Adam Woods, married Polly Kerley.

Aug. 26, 1817, one Adam Woods married Betsy Crigler.

Madison County Court Order:

"Feb. 28, 1787. On the motion of Adam Woods, his ear mark, to wit: a half crop in the right ear, and a slit in the left, is ordered to be recorded."

CHAPTER 8.

ARCHIBALD WOODS.

(Named in Sec. 6, Chap. 6, Part II.)

Article 1.—Archibald Woods, a son of William Woods, and Susannah Wallace, his wife, was born in Albermarle County, Virginia, Jan. 29, 1749, he married Aug. 5, 1773, to Mourning Shelton, a daughter of William Shelton and Lucy Harris, his wife. She was born in 1756, and died Sept. 7, 1817. (See Part III, Chap. 3, Sec. 6-1.)

Extract from Hon. John D. Goodloe's Publication:

"The aforesaid Archibald Woods, son of William Woods, and Susannah Wallace Woods, was born in what is now Albermarle County, Va. on Jan. 29, 1749, and married Aug. 5, 1773, to Mourning Shelton, daughter of William Shelton, and Lucy Harris Shelton, she being a daughter of Major Robert Harris and Mourning Glenn Harris.

In 1774, Archibald Woods, moved to Monroe County, Va. from Montgomery County, Va. He entered the military service of the Colonial Government as Captain of Virginia militia, and at once set out from what is now Munroe County, Va., under Col. Russell, on a march of 200 miles to the relief of Fort Watauga. This expedition lasted about six weeks, and the return march was hastened by an express bringing the intelligence that the Shawnee Indians had commenced hostilities. On reaching home he found the people forted, and he was placed in command of the fort and local defenses, until spring. After this except, during intervals of inclement winter weather, he was almost constantly employed in the frontier defenses. first under Colonel Samuel Lewis, and then under Colonel

Andrew Donnelly, and lastly under Colonel James Henderson, until after the surrender of Cornwallis in 1781. He then surrendered his commission as Captain of Virginia militia to the Greenbriar County Court and never saw it afterwards. He first came to Kentucky in 1781. He returned to Virginia in Feb., 1782, and removed with his family to Estill Station, Madison County, Ky., in the fall of that year. The next year, 1783, he made his first Kentucky crop, on Pumpkin Run, where he had contracted with Col. Estill for 400 acres of land, including a spring represented to be ever lasting, but the spring going dry that year, the contract with Colonel Estill was canceled, and in Jan. 1784, he bought land on Dreaming Creek, a few miles north of the present site of Richmond, where he built Woods Fort, and there lived between 25 and 26 years. The first land he bought in Madison County, Ky. is described by him in a deposition as "1000 acres of as good land as any in the Estill Station survey," and "the price paid for it was a rifle gun."

The original commission of Patrick Henry, Governor of Virginia, appointing him with nine others "Gentlemen Justices of the Peace for Madison County, Ky., to take effect Aug. 1, 1785, the natal day of the County is still preserved, was in the possession of Judge William Chenault of Richmond, Ky. now deceased. The same document, also appoints the same persons, "Gentlemen Commissioners of Oyer and Terminer" with full jurisdiction to try and punish slaves for all penal and criminal offenses, including the infliction of capital punishment.

He was still a magistrate in 1798, and as such voted for the removal of the County seat from Old Town, (Milford) and presided at the Court that established and named the town of Richmond making it the County seat, and became one of its first trustees. He was appointed sheriff of Madison County May 4, 1801. After a long litigation and possession of a quarter of a century, he was finally evicted of his home and land on Dreaming Creek in a suit brought by one Patrick, and being disgusted with the land laws of Kentucky that in the afternoon of his life took from him his home and bulk of his estate on a mere technicality, he moved with his family, in the fall of 1809, to Williamson County, on Beans Creek, Middle Tennessee. In that state his wife, Mourning Woods, died Sept. 7, 1817, aged 61 years and 8 months.

On Jan. 30, 1818, he married Dorcas Henderson, and lived for a time in Franklin County, Tenn. This marriage proved to be a very unhappy one. and a separation having occured he returned to Madison County, Ky., in 1820.

In Jan 1833, being then a feeble old man of 84 years and well nigh stripped of his property, he filed an application at Washington for a pension for military services in the war of independence, and was promptly granted a pension of $480 per annum, to date from March 4, 1831. But for the affidavits of himself and witnesses then living in this application and the pension no proof could be had of his military service except the Virginia military land warrant.

He died Dec. 17, 1836, at the age of 89 years, 10 months and 17 days, at the residence of his son, Archibald, Fort Estill Madison County, Ky.; his will bears date March 17, 1836, probated June 2, 1837. The remains of himself and his first wife, Mourning Shelton, were interred in the family burying ground about two miles northeast of Richmond, not far from the residence on Otter Creek, now owned and occupied by Jeptha Chenault, but were subsequently many years ago removed and re-interred in the Richmond Cemetery, where they now rest.

Archibald Woods, senior, was a fine specimen of the old Virginia gentleman. He maintained his carriages, horses and driver up to his death. He was a man of marked intelligence, great personal pride and dignity, the hospitality of his home was proverbial, and his life, public and private, was pitched on the highest ideals of manhood and patriotism. The children born to Archibald Woods, senior, and Mourning Shelton, his wife, are set forth in the coming section:

Section 1. Lucy Woods, a daughter, born Oct. 25, 1774, married William Caperton, Dec. 15, 1790. Further account will be found in Chapter IX, Part 11.

Section 2. William Woods, a son, born March 22, 1776, married Mary Harris, Jan. 13, 1802. (See Part III, Chap. IX.) Further account will be found in Chapter X, Part 11.

Section 3. Susannah Woods, a daughter, born June 13, 1778, married William Goodloe, Feb. 23, 1796, died Oct. 2, 1851. Further account will be found in Chapter 11, Part 11.

Section 4. Mary Woods, a daughter, born July 31, 1780, married Colonel Barbe Collins June 25, 1795, died July 23, 1822. Besides other children not mentioned in Archibald Woods' will she had a son:

1. William Collins.

Section 5. Sarah Woods, a daughter, born Jan. 31, 1783. Died April 24, 1785.

Section 6. Archibald Woods, a son, born Feb. 19, 1785, married Elizabeth C. Shackelford, Oct. 10, 1810. Served in the House of Represenatives, Kentucky general assembly 1816-1817, 1820-4, and in the senate 1826-9.

Section 7. Anna Woods, a daughter, born Jan. 27, 1787, married Thomas Miller, July 29, 1806, moved to Tenn. (See Part 1, Chap XIv, Sec. 111.)

Section 8. Thomas Woods, a son, born May 5, 1789. Died Oct. 29, 1806.

Section 9. Ann Woods, a daughter, born May 15, 1791. Died May 15, 1791.

Section 10. Mourning Woods, a daughter, born April 2, 1792, married Garland B. Miller, Jan. 18, 1810. (See Part 1, Chap. XIv, Sec. V.)

CHAPTER 9.

LUCY WOODS.

(Named in Sec. 1, Chap. 8, Part II.)

Article 1.—Lucy Woods, a daughter of Archibald Woods, senior, and Mourning Shelton, his wife, was born Oct. 25, 1774, she married William Caperton, Dec. 13, 1790.

The persons named in the coming sections were the issues of the marriage:

Section 1. Archibald Caperton.

Section 2. Hugh Caperton.

Section 3. Thomas Shelton Caperton.

Section 4. William H. Caperton, born in Madison County, Ky.

in March, 1798, was under Gen. Jackson in the Creek campaign when only sixteen years of age. President Filmore appointed him U. S. District Attorney for the District of Kentucky. Among Kentucky's eminent lawyers none were more gifted. He was a born orator; his features were handsome, and form graceful, a great lawyer, a true and earnest advocate. He married Eliza Estill, a daughter of James Estill and his wife, Mary, a daughter of Judge Robert Rodes. The issues of this marriage were :

1. Woods Caperton; was murdered in Richmond, Ky., by the notorious Frank Searcy.
2. Mary P. Caperton, who married Leonidas B. Talbott.
3. Col. James W. Caperton, a successful and prominent lawyer of the Richmond Bar, one of the wealthiest residents of the county, who married Miss Katherine Cobb Phelps, in Oct. 1890. (See Part III, Chap. 3, Sec. 7, B. 1-1.)

Section 5. Green Caperton.

Section 6. John Caperton, a son of whom, A. C. Caperton, is a Baptist preacher, of Louisville, Ky.

Section 7. Andrew Caperton.

Section 8. Hulda Caperton; married her cousin Andrew Woods.

Section 9. Susan Caperton; married Wallace Wilson.

Section 10. Milton T. Caperton, a Baptist preacher of Austin, Texas; lived to be a very old man, having recently died.

CHAPTER 10.

WILLIAM WOODS.

(Named in Sec. 2, Chap. 8, Part II.)

Article 1—William Woods, a son of Archibald Woods, senior and Mourning Shelton, his wife, was born March 22, 1776, died July 8, 1840.

He on the 13th day of January 1802, was married to Mary Harris, a daughter of Robert Harris, and Nancy Grubbs his wife, she was born Jan. 2, 1780, died Jan. 17, 1838. (See Part III, Chap. 9.) He left Madison County, Ky., and went to Tennessee and located, and remained there until his death. In 1807 he and Nathan Lipscomb, as commissioners of the Court, took the deposition of Samuel Estill. The issues of the marriage are given in the coming sections:

Section 1. Nancy Woods, born Jan. 21, 1803, died Thursday Oct. 11, 1804.

Section 2. Archibald Woods, born Feb. 20, 1804; married Sallie G. Caperton, June 15, 1830.

Section 3. Samiramus Shelton Woods, born Sept. 1, 1805; married John M. Kavanaugh, a son of William Woods Kavanaugh, and Elizabeth Miller. (See Part VII. Chap. V, Sec. V, and Part 1 Chap. 14, Sec. 7.) she died the 16th of Sept. 1841.

Section 4. Lucy Woods, born Feb. 22, 1807.

Section 5. Mourning Woods, born Oct. 6, 1808.

Section 6. Thomas Harris Woods, born Aug. 31, 1810; married

Appoline Miller, Feb. 28, 1832. (See Part I, Chap. 14, Sec. 10, where their children are set forth.)

Section 7. Robert Harris Woods, born May 29, 1812; died May 7, 1821.

Section 8. William Crawford Woods, born April 1, 1814; married Sarah Ann Boyce, Dec. 14, 1843. A daughter, Susan Woods, married Matt M. Bearden, proprietor of the Elk River Mills, Fayetteville, Lincoln County, Tenn.

Section 9. John Christopher Woods, born Feb. 8, 1817, was deaf and dumb; died Aug. 27, 1838.

Section 10. Mary Ann Woods, born Feb. 20, 1819; married John M. Miller, Aug. 28, 1835.

Section 11. Elder James Gooodloe Woods,, born Feb. 2, 1823; married Susan Boyce, Nov. 30, 1843. He was living in May 1887, and several years thereafter, for we visited him at that time at Fayetteville, Lincoln County, Tenn. He died Oct. 19, 1895. He was an old Baptist preacher, and his membership was at Buckeye Church about three and a half miles from Fayetteville, it has a large membership, we attended serivces there May 15, 1887. His second wife was Lou ——, died July 9, 1905. The children of Rev. James Goodloe Woods and Susan Boyce, his wife, are:

1. James H. C. Woods, lives near Buckeye Church about three and a half miles of Fayetteville, Tenn.
2. William Ed. Woods.

WILLIAM ED. WOODS

3. ——— Woods.
4. Mattie Woods; married ——— Fleming.

The wives of Wm. Crawford Woods, and Elder James Goodloe Woods, viz: Sarah Ann Boyce and Susan Boyce, were first cousins to Sarah R. Dismukes, the wife of Garland B. Miller, of Part I, Chap. 14, Sec. IV.-V.

CHAPTER 11.

SUSANNAH WOODS.

(Named in Chap. 8, Sec. 3.)

Article 1.—Susannah Woods, a daughter of Archibald Woods, senior, and Mourning Shelton, his wife, was born June 13, 1778.

She married William Goodloe, Feb. 23, 1796; she died Oct. 2, 1851. She was a woman of strong mind, very domestic, and a splendid governess. Wm. Goodloe's mother was named Sarah, who died in Madison County, Ky. in 1814, and he had a sister, Elizabeth Jones, and one Elizabeth Jones died in the same County in 1815. Their children:

Section 1. John Goodloe, born Dec. 12, 1796; died Mch. 20, 1813.

Section 2. Sallie Short Goodloe, born 1798; married Howard Williams. They moved to Missouri in 1846. Their children:

1. David Williams, born Sept. 15, 1826; died Sept. 25, 1827.
2. William Goodloe Williams, a daughter, born Aug. 6, 1832; died Feb. 25, 1833.
3. Elizabeth Williams; married John Woods Barclay, Feb. 12, 1846.
4. John Williams; married Theresa George.
5. Archibald Woods Williams; married Kate Waddell.
6. Almira Williams; married Dr. Atchison, of Lexington, Mo.
7. Ann Wiliams, the second wife of Rev. Edmund H. Burnam.
8. George Williams.
9. Jefferson Williams.

Section 3. Mourning Goodloe, born —. She married Mitchell Royster, Mr. Royster was born Nov. 11, 1793. Children:

1. William Royster.
2. Woodson Royster.
3. David Royster, born March 15, 1823; died March 16, 1823

Mitchell Royster died, Sept. 28, 1823, and his widow, Mourning Goodloe Royster, married James W. Dudley. Their Children:

4. Susannah Dudley; married Thomas Wallace.
5. Mariah Dudley, married Joe McCann.
6. Sarah Dudley; married Noah Ferguson.
7. Ann Russell Dudley, born Oct. 21, 1832; died Sept. 4, 1833.
8. Caroline Dudley, born Feb. 6, 1835; died May 10, 1835.

Section 4. Archibald Woods Goodloe, born Nov. 9, 1803. He married Martha Maria Ann Estill, a daughter of James Estill. (See Part III, Chap. III, Sec. VII.) Aug. 23, 1825. Children:

1. Anna Goodloe.
2. Mary Eliza Goodloe; married Dulaney Lackey. (See Part I, Chap. 14, Sec. X, and Part III, Chap. III, Sec. VII.)
3. Archibald Woods Goodloe; married a beautiful and rich New Orleans girl.

Martha Estill Goodloe, died, and Archibald Woods Goodloe married the second time Catherine Sessions of Mississippi. Children:

4. Annie Goodloe.
5. Kate Goodloe.

Section 5. Judge William C. Goodloe, born in 1805, was an eminent lawyer, and jurist. He was judge of the Circuit Court of the district of which the County of Madison formed a part. He married Almira Owsley. Their Children:

1. Mariah Elizabeth Goodloe; married William Barrett. Their Children:

1. Mary Barrett; married Hon. John Speed Smith, a son of General John Speed Smith and Eliza Clay, daughter of General Green Clay, his wife. Mr. Smith was a very prominent and popular citizen of Madison County, Ky. He represented the county in the State Legislature at one time; was a Mason and Grand Master of the G. L. of Ky.

2. John Barrett, late Post master of Louisville, Ky. Attorney at law; died Nov., 1906, at Montrose, Col.

3. Will G. Barrett; married Miss Brooke Burke, of Owensboro, Ky.

4. Lizzie Barrett; married Fred Manier, of Harlan, Kansas.

2. Susannah Goodloe; maried R. H. Johnson. Their Children:

1. Almira Johnson; married John Osborne.
2. Will Johnson; married Ida Myers.
3. Mildred Johnson; married John Campbell.
4. Curran Johnson; (twin) married Miss Allie —.
5. Harvey Johnson, (twin).
6. Elizabeth Johnson; maried Ed. Moore.
7. Archibald Johnson; married Miss Julia —.

3. Amanda Goodloe; married John Craig, a substantial farmer and citizen of Boyle County, Ky. living near the city of Danville, on a fine rich farm. Their Children:

1. Almira Craig; married Alexander Irvine.
2. Lettie Craig; married Marshall Allen.
3. Elizabeth Craig.

4. Sallie Short Goodloe; married, July 5, 1854, Dr. Curran C. Smith, son of Colonel John Speed Smith, whose wife was a daughter of General Green Clay. Col. Smith had a national reputation; was aide-de-camp to General William Henry Harrison during the Indian wars, and was buried with military honors. Dr. Smith is now dead, but was a splendid physician in his day. His widow now lives in Richmond, and is a remarkably intelligent woman, but her hearing is almost gone. She is a kind, good woman, fond of literature, and strongly attached to her friends, and much admired for her qualities. Their children:

1. Mary Spencer Smith, the second wife of Dr. George W. Evans, they live on North street in Richmond, Ky. The mansion which they own and in which they live was built by Mrs. Evans' grandfather, the late Col. John Speed Smith.

2. Almira Smith; married Rev. Henry M. Rogers.

3. John Speed Smith, has been for a number of years, and is now holding a position in the service of the Federal Government, at Washington City.

4. Elizabeth Barrett Smith; married Judge James M. Benton, now Judge of Circuit Court of the Judicial District of Kentucky, of which the County of Madison forms a part. They live in Winchester, Ky. (See Part VII. Chap. 18.)

5. Curraline Smith, (twin) teacher in the Caldwell High school in Richmond Ky.

6. Willie Smith, daughter, (twin) deceased.

5. William Owsley Goodloe; married Victoria Payne. Children:
1. Mary Goodloe; married Will Wearren, of Louisville, Ky.
2. Elizabeth Goodloe.
3. Almira Goodloe; married Robert Hoskin. His wife, Victoria Payne Goodloe, died, and Rev. William Owsley Goodloe married again, Ida Rainey. Their children:
4. Annie Goodloe; married de Graffe Billings.

6. Caroline Boyle Goodloe; married William L. Neale. Their Children:
1. William Goodloe Neale, died.
2. Mary Neale; married Dr. N. L. Bosworth, of Lexington, Ky.

7. Archibald Woods Goodloe; married Fannie Edgar. No Children.

8. Mary Goodloe; married James Edgar. Their children:
1. Goodloe Edgar; married Mary McComis.

Section 6. Harry Goodloe, married Emily Duncan, Nov. 29, 1831. Their children:
1. Elizabeth Goodloe, born —, died —.
2. Lucy Duncan Goodloe, born —, died —; she married Hon. M R. Hardin, late Chief Justice of the Court of Appeals of Ky. issue:
1. Harry Goodloe Hardin, born —, died 1857.

3. Major William Goodloe, born —. He was a Major in the Federal Army during the Civil War; died —.

4. Emma Harris Goodloe, born —. She married George H. Simmons of Bardstown, Ky. they settled in Owensborough, Ky. Mr. Simmons was a tobacconist; he died —. His widow now lives in Owensborough, and owns a valuable farm near the city. Their children:
1. Harry Goodloe Simmos.
2. Emily Duncan Simmons.

5. John Duncan Goodloe, born —; married first, Jennie Faulkner White of Danville, Ky. (See Part VII, Chap V, Sec. V) and secondly, Nellie Gough of Lexington, Ky. Children of first marriage:
1. George W. Goodloe; married Mary Keene Shackelford. (See Part I, Chap. 11, Sec. 2.)
2. Paul Goodloe.
3. John Goodloe.
4. Jane Goodloe.

6. Harry Goodloe, born —; was a Confederate soldier and fell in battle at Green River Bridge, 186—.
7. David Short Goodloe, born —, died —.

Section 7. Elizabeth Goodloe; married General John Miller. (See Part 1. Chap. VII.)

Section 8. David Short Goodloe; married Sallie Ann Smith, daughter of Colonel John Speed Smith, Dec. 3, 1835. Children:
1. Speed Smith Goodloe; married Mary Shreve; born in 1837.
2. Casius Clay Goodloe, born in 1839, died in 1840.
3. William Goodloe, born in 1841, now deceased, married Mary Mann.
4. David Short Goodloe, born in 1843, unmarried.
5. Green Clay Goodloe, born in 1845; married Bettie Beck.
6. Percy Goodloe, born in 1848, died in 1849.

Section 9. Thomas Goodloe; married Mary Ware, an excellent woman, both died, leaving no children.

Section 10. Octavius Goodloe, born April 21, 1816. He died March 22, 1847. He married Olivia Duncan, June 1, 1837. Their Children:

1. Duncan Goodloe, born in 1837, died in 1903.
2. Emma Olivia Goodloe, born in 1839; married Mr. Richard Gregory. She is a widow, now living in Garrard County, Ky.
3. William Goodloe, a lawyer of Danville, Ky. He married Miss —. He died in 1899.

Mrs. Olivia Duncan Goodloe was a daughter of John Duncan and Lucy White his wife.

Section 11. Lucy Ann Goodloe; married David P. Hart, June 7, 1838. Had one daughter:

1. Susan Hart, born in 1839; at the age of twenty eight years, she married Edmund Shelby. They live in Lexington, Ky.

Section 12. George Goodloe, born March 28, 1819; died Oct. 13, 1836.

CHAPTER 12.

WILLIAM WOODS.

Known as Beaver Creek William Woods.

(Named in Chapter 6, Sec. 7.)

Article 1.—William Woods, a son of William Woods, and Susannah Wallace, his wife, and known as Beaver Creek William Woods, of Albermarle County, Va., was born in Pennsylvania, on the 31st, day of Dec. 1744.

His parents took him with them to Va. in the following March. In Albermarle County he died in 1837, aged 92 years. He was a man of fine sense and excellent character. He married first his cousin, Sarah Wallace, (See Part IV.) whom he survived, and married the second time, another cousin, Mrs. Ann Reid. (See Chap. 48) whom he also survived, and entered a third time into the holy bonds of matrimony with Mrs. Nancy Jones-nee Richardson.

He was in the Revolutionary army, a Commissioned Ensign, and afterwards a lieutenant in the Virginia line. He had only one son, but which wife was the mother of that son is the question that remains to be answered. Said son will be noticed in the coming section:

Section 1. William Woods, known as Beaver Creek William Woods, the second, died in 1829. He married Mary Jarman, a daughter of William Jarman, a brother of Thomas Jarman, late owner of lands at Jarman's Gap, formerly known as Woods Gap. (See Part V, Chap. IV, Sec. 1.) Their children are named in the following order:

1. James Woods; married Mildred-Ann Jones, of Bedford, on Beaver Creek, and died in 1868. They had several children of whom are: William Price Woods, married his cousin, Sarah Ellen Jones.

2. William Woods; married Nancy Jones, daughter of John Jones, lived near Crozet, and died in 1850.

3. Peter A. Woods, was a merchant in Charlottsville, and in Richmond, Va., married Twymonia Wayt, whom he survived, and afterwards married Mrs. Mary Poage Bourland, of Augusta, and died in 1870.

4. Thomas Dabney Woods; married Miss Hagan, and lived near Pedlar Mills, in Amherst County, and died in 1894.

5 Sarah J. Woods; married Jesse P. Key.

CHAPTER 13.

MICHAEL WOODS Junior.

(Named in Sec. 3, Chap. 4, Part II.)

Article 1.—Michael Woods, Junior, a son of Michael Woods, Senior, of Blair Park, emigrant from Ireland, and Mary Campbell, of the Scottish Clan Campbell, of Argylshire, Scotland, his wife, was born in Ireland in 1708, and came to America with his parents, and went with them from Pennsylvania to Va., and settled in Albermarle County, and lived southwest of Ivy Depot till 1773.

Later on he moved to and lived in Boutitourt County, on a plantation on the south side of James River, a few miles below Buchanan, about seven years, where he died in 1777. He had married Ann ——, and had born the children named in the coming sections:

Section 1. Jane Woods, married John Buster. Nothing further is known of them for certain.

Section 2. Susannah Woods; married Mr. Cowan. Have no further history of them.

Section 3. Samuel Woods, born 1738, died 1826. He married Margaret ———.

The children of Samuel Woods, and Margaret, his wife, were:

1. Samuel Woods, Jr.; married Mrs. Mary Woods, Nee McAfee, who was the widow with three children, of his uncle David Woods, who had one son, by a previous marriage. issue:

1. James Harvey Woods, 1792; married in 1781, Sarah who had one son by a previous marriage. Issue:

1. Samuel Dickson Woods.
2. Elizabeth Hannah Woods.
3. William Harvey Woods.
4. Thomas Clelland Woods, 1826-1868; married Mary Ann Jackson. Issue.

1. Child died young.
2. " " "
3. " " "
4. " " "

William C. Woods, 1853; married 1883, Annie Bogle Bond; issue:

1. Joseph Bond Woods, 1884.

2. William Clarence Woods, 1885.
3. Ellis Jackson Woods, 1889.

6. John D. Woods, dead.

7. Clarence E. Woods, present Mayor elect of Richmond, Ky.; married first, Mary Miller (see Part I, Chap. 14, Sec. 2), secondly, Mattie Chenault (see also Part 3, Chap. 48, Sec. 8.) Issue of second marriage:

1. Mamie White Woods.

5. Nathaniel Dedman Woods.
6. Mary McAfee Woods.
7. Butler Woods.
8. Alice Butler Woods.
9. Charles Walker Woods.
10. Edward Pason Woods.
11. Fannie Everett Woods.
12. Rev. Neander M. Woods; married first, Alice Birkhead, secondly, Sallie Henderson Behere, issue of first marriage:

1. Emma Birkhead Woods; married David Bell McGowan, now in St. Petersburg, Russia.

2. Florence Boone Woods; married Henry H. Wade, live in Memphis, Tenn.

3. Alice Dedman Woods; died at about four years of age.

4. Neander Montgomery Woods, Jr.; married Tallulah Gatchet, live in Memphis, Tenn.

Issue of second marriage:

5. Alice Behere Woods.
6. Annie Howe Woods; died in infancy.
7. Everett Dedman Woods.
8. Carrie Webb Woods.
9. James McAfee Woods.

Rev. Neander M. Woods, is a Presbyterian Minister of high standing, author of Woods-McAfee memorial.

2. Ann Woods, 1794; married George Bohon, issue:

1. James Bohon.
2. Abram Bohon.
3. Mary Bohon.
4. Catherine Bohon.
5. Clarke Bohon.
6. Nancy Bohon.
7. Joseph Bohon.
8. Isaac G. Bohon.
9. George Ann Bohon.

3. Sallie Woods, 1796.
4. Patsy Martha Woods; married Van Sheley, issue:

1. Woodford Woods Sheley, 1826.
2. Ann Mary Sheley, 1827.
3. John Jay Sheley, 1831; married C. America Morgan, issue:

1. Woodford Woods Sheley.
2. James Van Sheley.
3. Edmund Lee Sheley.
4. Ann Martha Sheley.
5. Charles Sheley; died.
6. Emma Virginia Sheley.

5. Woodford Woods; died young.

Section 4. David Woods, born in Albermarle County, Va., in 1740. He died in the fall of 1786. (See Chap. 14, where further account will be found.)

Section 5. Elizabeth Woods; married Dalertus Shepherd. Had a daughter, Magdalene Shepherd, married John Gilmore in 1791.

Section 6. William Woods, 1748, married Joanna Shepherd, of whom more will be found in Chapter 17.

Section 7. Sarah Woods, of whom there is no history.

Section 8. Martha Woods; married Thomas Moore, June 10, 1795. No further history.

Section 9. Magdalene Woods, born 1755; died in Lexington Va., in 1830, having married William Campbell. Left no issue.

Section 10. Anne Woods. No history of her.

Section 11. Margaret Woods; married David Gray, of Rockbridge County, Va., and moved to Ky. of whom more will be found in Chapter XVIII.

CHAPTER 14.

DAVID WOODS.

(Named in Sec. 4, Chap. 13, Part II.)

Article 1.—David Woods, a son of Michael Woods, Junior, and Anne, his wife, was born in Albermarle County, Va. in 1740, died in the fall of 1786.. He married (name unknown). .To whom were born:

Section 1. Anne Woods; married Jonathan Jennings.

Section 2. John Woods, of whom a further account is given in Chapter XV.

Article 2.—David Woods, survived his wife, Anne, afterward he married Mary McAfee, a daughter of James McAfee Junior.

In 1782-3, he moved from Virginia to Mercer County, Ky. and settled in the Cane Run neighborhood. The children of his last marriage were:

Section1. Nancy Woods. A further account of whom will be found in Chapter XVI.

Section 2. William Woods; married Catherine ———.

Section 3. Elizabeth Woods; married Benjamin Galey.

CHAPTER 15.

JOHN WOODS.

(Named in Art. 1, Sec. 11, Chap. 14, Part II.)

Article 1.—John Woods, a son of David Woods, and his first wife, was born in 1766.. Moved with his father to Cane Run, Mercer County, Ky. from Va.

He married Nancy Mosley. To whom were born:
Section 1. Sidney Woods.
Section 2. Rodes Woods.
Section 3. David Woods, moved to St. Louis, Missouri.
Section 4. Margaret Woods; married James M. Jones (whose second wife was Elizabeth Hannah Woods, a sister of Rev. Neander M. Woods author of Woods-McAfee memorial.) They had one child: John Sanford Jones, who died in Federal Military prison at Alton, Ill.
Section 5. Eliza Woods; married Mr. Bradley.
Section 6. Patsy Woods; married Mr. Porter, and had a son James Porter.
Section 7.Burch Woods; married; Mr. Marshall.
Section 8. Nannie Woods; married Willis Vivion.
Section 9. A daughter; married Mr. Garnet, and had a son, George Garnet.

CHAPTER 16.

NANCY WOODS.

(Named in Art. 2, Sec. 1, Chap. 14, Part II).

Article 1.—Nancy Woods, a daughter of David Woods, and his wife, Mary McAfee, was brought to Ky. by her parents, when a babe.

She married Harry Munday, of Mercer County, Ky. She died in Indiana in 1865, where all her children had gone. To them were born these chilren:
Section 1. Woodson Munday; married Mrs. Samuels, a widow.
Section 2. George Munday; married Lucy Gordon.
Section 3. Harry Munday; married Caroline Coghill.
Section 4. James Munday; married Almeda Thacker, of Anderson County, Ky.
Section 5. Katherine Munday; married John Hays.
Section 6. Elizabeth Munday; married Solomon Hays.
Section 7. Mary Munday; married Living Graves.
Section 8. Patty Munday; married James Smartt.

CHAPTER 17.

WILLIAM WOODS.

(Named in Sec. 6, Chap. 13, Part II.)

Article 1.—William Woods a son of Michael Woods, Junior, and his wife, Ann, was born in Albermarle County, Va. and known as Baptist Billy Woods, and was a Baptist Preacher, on which account he was known as Baptist Billy.

He married Joanna Shepherd, and his home was south of Ivy. In 1798 he was elected to the Virginia House of Delegates, and in 1809, was defeated for that office. In 1810 he moved to Livingston County, Ky. where he died in 1819. The children born to them were:

Section 1. Michael Woods, born in Albermarle County, Va. in 1776, was appointed a magistrate in 1816, and served as Sheriff in 1836. On the 13th of Ang. 1795, he married Lucy Walker. To them were born these children:

1. Martha Woods; married General John Wilson, and moved to California.
2. Mary Woods; married James Garth.
3. Elizabeth Woods; maried Captain John Humphreys, and settled in Indiana.
4. Henry Woods; died in youth.

Article 2.—Michael Woods survived his wife, Lucy Walker; afterwards married Mrs. Sarah Harris Davenport, nee Rodes, Sept. 22, 1808, and he died March 23, 1837.

By his second wife he had these children:

5. William S. Woods; died at Helena, Arkansas.
6. John Rodes Woods.
7. Robert Harris Woods.

Section 2. David Woods, died in Livingston County, Ky. in 1825, having married Sally Neal, to whom were born:

1. Tayner Woods.
2. Henry William Woods.
3. David Woods.
4. John N. Woods, was a member of the Kentucky Legislature, in 1871. He married Mary A. Marble, of Madison, Indiana, in 1848, and died Dec. 27, 1896.
5. Kitty Woods; married Richard Miles.
6. Mariah Woods; married Peyton Gray.

Section 3. John Woods, died having never married.
Section 4. Mary Woods; married Mr. Campbell.
Section 5. Susannah Woods; married Henry Williams.

CHAPTER 18.

MARGARET WOODS.

(Named in Sec. 11, Chap. 13, Part II.)

Article 1.—Margaret Woods, a daughter of Michael Woods, Junior, and Anne, his wife, married David Gray of Rockbridge County, Va., and moved to Kentucky.

To them were born these children:

Section 1. David Gray.

Section 2. William Gray; married Kitty Bird Winn, of Clark County, Ky., in 1812. They settled in Glasgow, and later moved to Greensburg, Ky. He was a practicing physician. Children were:

1. Versailles Gray.
2. John Courts Gray.
3. Theresa D. Gray; married first, Mr. — Vaughn, and second, Frank Hatcher.
4. Samuel Marshall Gray.
5. Elizabeth Catherine Ophelia Gray; married George K. Perkins, issue:
    1. Havana Perkins.
    2. China Perkins.
    3. John Perkins.
    4. Bertha Perkins.
    5. Campbell Perkins.
    6. Mollie Perkins.
    7. Fannie Perkins.

CHAPTER 19.

COLONEL JOHN WOODS.

of Albermarle.

(Named in Chapter 4, Section 5.)

Article 1.—Colonel John Woods, a son of the emigrant, Michael Woods senior (known as Michael Woods of Blair Park) and Mary Campbell, (of the Scottish Clan, Argylshire, Scotland) his wife, was born in Ireland, and came with his parents to America.

He was a very methodical man, and was a Captain in the Colonial army, and on Nov. 27, 1766, was commissioned a Major by Governor Fauquier, which rank he held for about four years, when on June 11, 1770, Lord Boutitourt, His Majesty's Lieutenant and Governor General, and Commander-in-Chief of the Colony and Dominion of Virginia, granted to him a commission as Lieutenant Colonel of the Militia of Albermarle, Thomas Jefferson being the Colonel of same. He held a like commission from Governor Nelson, bearing date Dec. 10, 1770. He made his last will and testament

Sept. 12, 1791, and died Oct. 14, 1791, at his home in Albermarle County, Va., in the 80th year of his age, having lived an honored and eventful life. The witnesses to his will were Menan Mills, William H. Shelton, and James Kinsolving. In his will he remembered his wife, Susannah, and his six living children. He appointed his sons, James and Michael executors. His body was buried in the old family burying ground at what is now known as Blair Park, reserved by his father Michael Woods senior, for that purose. The Inscription on his tomb stone towit: "Here lies the body of John Woods, son of Michael Woods, and Mary Campbell, who was born February, 18 1812, and departed this life Oct. 14, 1791." Colonel John Woods' military company was called the "Rangers."

He was not grown when he came from Ireland, he stopped a while with his parents in Pennsylvania, and they removed to Albermarle County, in the Valley of Virginia, but he went back to Pennsylvania and married Susannah Anderson, the beautiful and accomplished daughter of Rev. James Anderson, a Presbyterian Minister. He lived and died on Ivy Creek, a branch of Mechums River, in Albermarle. Having served in the Inter-Colonial wars, particularly in the French and Indian war, his commission as Lieutenant Colonel, signed by Norborne Baron de Bontetourt, Governor General of Virginia, is in the possession of J. Watson Woods.

Information furnished by the Virginia kin is that when Michael Woods reached America, he landed at a Northern port and came through Pennsylvania, crossed the Potomac river made his way up the valley of Virginia, crossed the Blue Ridge Mountains at Rock Fish Gap, and settled in what is now the Northern part of Albermarle County. On his way through Pennsylvania he stopped and was entertained at the house of Rev. Mr. James Anderson, a Presbyterian preacher, whose family had fled from Scotland (Mr. Woods native land) to Holland. and settled in Amsterdam, where he married a lady of rank, and emigrated to Pennsylvania, they had a beautiful daughter twelve years of age named Susannah. John Woods, then a boy four years her senior fell violently in love with the little Susannah, and vowed that he would come back and win her for his wife when he was a man; he kept his word, and in a few years returned and married.

In 1758 he served in the defense and protection of the frontier against the Indians. In 1745, as a messenger from Mountain Plains Church to the Presbytery of Donegal in Pennsylvania he delivered the call for the services of Rev. Hindman in the churches of Mountain Plains and Rockfish, to which churches his father-in-law, Rev. James Anderson often visited and preached to the congregations there gathered. His home was near the present Mechums River Depot. Their children were:

Section 1. James Woods, (1743-1823) married Mary Garland. The subject of Chapter 20.

Section 2. Mary Woods, born Dec. 2, 1746, died Oct. 19, 1828. She married John Reid, born Aug. 25, 1750; died June 29, 1816. The subject of Chapter 21.

Section 3. Michael Woods (1748-1826); married Hettie Caruthers. The subject of Chapter 22.

Section 4. Suity Woods, born 1752; married Samuel Reid. The subject of Chapter 29.

Section 5. Sarah Woods, born 1757;died 1770.

Section 6. Anna Woods, born 1760; married Jonathan Reid (See Chapter 29). The subject of Chapter 48.

Section 7. John Woods Jr., born 1763; died 1764.

Section 8. Susannah Woods, born Sept. 21, 1768; married Daniel Miller, Nov. 28, 1793. She died Aug. 13, 1832. (See Part 1, Chapter V.)

CHAPTER 20.

JAMES WOODS.

(Named in Chapter 9, Section 1.)

Article 1.—James Woods, a son of Colonel John Woods, of Albermarle County, Va. and Susannah Anderson his wife was born in Albermarle County, Va., Jan. 21, 1743.

He was one of the executors of his father's will. He followed in the foot steps of his father, and served in a Regiment of Va. Foot, as the Colonel during the Revolutionary war. His commission as Colonel was issued Nov. 12, 1776, and his Regiment was known successively as the 4th and 8th Va. He married Mary Garland daughter of James Garland, and Mary Rice his wife of North Garden, Albermarle County, Va., Feb. 25, 1779. His wife was born Oct. 13, 1760. They lived in Albermarle until 1795, when they emigrated to Ky. and settled on Paint Lick Creek, in Garrard County, where Colonel Woods died Sept. 11, 1822, and his wife Dec. 4, 1835, and they were buried near their home at what is known as the "Hanging Rock."

Several of their children moved to Missouri in the early part of the 19th century. Overton Harris and wife Mary Rice Woods to Boone County, Mo. in 1817, others in the same year and Anderson Woods, and wife Elizabeth Harris. Francis Woods and husband, William Slavin to the same county in 1823, and others settled in the counties of Munroe and Randolph. Colonel James Woods was a signer of the Albermarle Declaration of Independence, April 21, 1779.

Note.—Mary Rice the wife of James Garland, descended from the Anglo-Welshman. Thomas Rice who came to America in the early part of the 17th century and acquired lands in Gloucester County, Va., in 1779. (See Note Part VI, Chapter 13b.)

James Garland died in Albermarle County, Va. in 1812. He was the first of the name to settle in North Garden, coming there from Hanover County, and in 1761 bought land in the coves of the Mountains, south-west from the Cross Roads; his first purchase was from James and John Coffey, and afterwards from Robert Nelson. He owned more than 1000 acres. He purchased from Samuel and William Stockton upwards of 400 acres near the head of Mechums River, including the mill the Stockton's had built. He was a Justice of the Peace in 1783, Sheriff in 1791. Children:

1. Edward Garland; married Sarah Old, daughter of Colonel John Old. They lived on the south side of the North Fork of the Hardware, near the crossing of the old Lynchburg Road, was a Justice of the Peace in 1801, and 1808, and became commissioner of Revenue for St. Anna's, holding the office till his death in 1817.
2. Elizabeth Garland; married Thomas Garland.

3. Rice Garland. His farm was near Colonel John Woods. He was a Justice of the Peace in 1791, Legislator in 1808, Sheriff in 1811. He married Elizabeth Hamner and died in 1818.

4. Robert Garland, was an active lawyer and member of the Charlottesville Bar. He moved to Nelson County, Va., in about 1822.

5. Clifton Garland, was a magistrate in 1806, was defeated in 1813, by Jesse W. Garth for a seat in the Virginia House of Delegates, and died the same year, unmarried.

6. Mary Garland; married Colonel James Woods as above stated.

7. James Garland; married Ann Wingfield, daughter of John Wingfield and Mary Hudson, his wife. He lost his life at the Prison Barracks in 1793.

The children of Colonel James Woods, and Mary Rice Garland his wife, were:

Section 1. John Woods, born Feb. 25, 1780; married Jennie Brauk, issue:

1 Robert Woods.
2. James Woods.

Section 2. Mary Woods, born Jan. 6, 1782; died in infancy.

Section 3. James Garland Woods, born April 23, 1783; married Elizabeth Brank. He was an Elder in the Paint Lick Presbyterian church in 1820. Children:

1. Talitha Woods; married S. S. Barnett; emigrated to Texas and had a large family of children.
2. Arthusa Woods, never married.
3. Rice G. Woods, as early as 1855, was an Elder in the Paint Lick Presbyterian Church; married Martha Ann Givens. Children:
    1. Rachael Woods, died at 17 years of age.
    2. George Woods; died at 3 years of age.
    3. Elizabetm Woods; married Ed H. Walker. (See Part VII chap. V. Sec. V.) Children:
        1. Mary L. Walker.
        2. Margaret G. Walker; married Luther Gibbs. (See Part VII, Chap. V, Sec. V.) issue:
            1. Elizabeth Gibbs.
        3. R. Woods Walker; married Sallie May, issue:
            1. Edwin H. Walker.
            2. Mary May Walker.
            3. Elizabeth G. Walker.
        4. Jane M. Walker.
        5. Mattie G.. Walker.
        6. Edwin H. Walker; died at 21 years of age.
        7. John Walker; died in infancy.

    4. Sallie Woods; married J. C. Hays, had one child died at birth.
    5. Martha Ann Woods; married Richard A. Ogilvie, issue:
        1. R. Woods Ogilvie; married Jennie Lester; issue:
            1. Francis Ogilvie.
        2. Sue Akin Ogilvie; married Horace K. Herndon; no issue.

4. Solon Woods; married Mary Reid of Mo. had one child:
    1. Mary Solon Woods; married N. E. Walker in Mo. they had two sons.

5 Elizabeth Woods; married Jackson Givens, issue:

1. L. Brank Givens.
2. Solon Givens.
3. Delia Givens.
4. Mary Givens.
5. Margaret Givens.
6. Jackson Givens.
7. Ida Givens.

Section 4. William Woods, born May 9, 1784; married his cousin, Mary Reid, daughter of Samuel Reid and Suity Woods, his wife. (See Chap. XXIX, Sec. IV.) Their children:
1 William Woods.
2. Angeline Woods.
3. Rice Woods.
4. Mary Woods.
5. Cabel Woods; married ——— ——— issue in part:
   1. Ernest Woods.
   2. James Woods.

Section 5. Sarah Woods, born Jan. 1, 1786; married William Reid. (See Chap. XXI, Sec. IV.) Their children:
1. Anderson Reid.
2. Miriam Reid; married Alexander R. Oldham, Sept. 15, 1831. (See Part VI, Chap. IV, Sec. VI.)
3. Mary Reid.
4. Sylvester Reid; married Elizabeth Hubbard, Aug. 13, 1829.
5. Elizabeth Reid.

Section 6. Anderson Woods, born Jan. 18, 1788. He emigrated with his parents from Albermarle County, Va. to Ky. in 1795. He married in Madison County, Ky. May 4, 1809, Elizabeth Harris daughter of John Harris and Margaret Maupin, his wife. (See Part 111, Chap. XL.) Elder PeterWoods solemnized the rites. They emigrated to Boone County, Mo. in 1823. He died in Paris, Mo. Oct. 22, 1841, and his wife died Oct. 13 1868. Their children:
1. James H. Woods; married Martha J. Stone. (See Part 111, Chap. VII, Sec. IV, and Chap. XL, Sec. 1.) Children.
   1. James M. Woods.
   2. Ann E.Woods.
   3. William S. Woods.
   4. Minerva Woods.
   5. M. Fannie Woods.

2 Margaret Woods; married Clifton Maupin (See Part V, Chap. XI, Sec. 11.)
3. Polly Woods; married Caleb Stone. Chlidren:
   1. Carlsle Stone; died in Mississippi in 1879.
   2. James Stone; married Mamie Worthington. They live in Mississippi.
   3. Thomas M. Stone; died in Mississippi in 1874 unmarried.
   4. Bettie Garland Stone; married William Worthington. They live in Greenville, Mississippi.
   5. William A. Stone; married Mrs. Anita Martin. They live in Rosedale, Missippi.
   6. Caleb Stone; unmarried, lives in St. Louis, Mo.
   7. Cyrus T. Stone; unmarried, lives in Richmond, Ky.
   8. Samuel Stone; died in infancy.

4. Susan D. Woods; married Ashby Snell. Children:
   1. Mary Snell.
   2. Nora Snell.
   3. Amanda Snell.
   4. M. Fanna Snell.
   5. John W. Snell.
   6. Emma Snell.
   7. James Snell.
   8. Eliza Snell.
   9. John A. Snell.
   10. Overton Snell.

5. Rice Woods; married Mary C. Wilson. Children:
   1. John Woods.
   2. Anderson Woods.
   3. James Woods.

6. Harris Woods; married Eliza J. Curry. Children:
   1. Laura J. Woods.
   2. James Woods.
   3. Matilda Woods.
   4. Talitha Woods.
   5. Bettie Woods.
   6. John C. Woods.
   7. William H. Woods.
   8. Martha Woods.
   9. Daniel Woods.

7. Elizabeth H. Woods; unmarried.

8 Martha Woods: married. Willis Snell: Children:
   1. Elizabeth Snell.
   2. William H. Snell.
   3. Mary Snell.
   4. John C. Snell.
   5. Anderson Snell.
   6. Jennie Snell.
   7. Hampton Snell.
   8. Albina Snell.
   9. Emmerson Snell.

9. Talitha C. Woods; married first Martin Bodine,, and second William H. Dulaney. Children:
   1. Robert Bodine.
   2. Kate Bodine.
   3. May Bodine.
   4. William R. Bodine.
   5. Ashby Bodine.
   6. James H. Dulaney. (half brother to above.)

10. William Anderson Woods: unmarried.

11. Eliza M. Woods; married William F. Buckner, children:
   1. Bettie Buckner.
   2. Susan Buckner.
   3. Sallie Buckner.
   4. Charles Buckner.
   5. Anderson Buckner.
   6. Mary Buckner.
   7. Emma Buckner.
   8. Frances Buckner.

12. Matilda J. Woods; married D. O. Bean. Children:
   1. Bettie Bean.
   2. Carrie Bean.
   3. Wliliam A. Bean.
   4. Harris Bean.

Section 7. Susannah Woods, born Sept. 1, 1789; married Alexander Henderson.

Section 8. Rice Woods, born Nov. 6, 1790; died when just out of College at Lexington, Ky.

Section 9. Michael Woods, born Jan. 5, 1792; married Martha E. Denny. Children:

1. Caroline Woods; married Madison Stone.
2. James Woods; married Julia Wilhoite.
3. George Woods; died a young man.
4. Rice Woods; unmarried.
5. Michael Woods; married Lizzie Messerley.
6. Martha Woods; married John Samson, had nine children:
7. Fannie Woods; married William Rickman, had three children.
8. Margaret Woods; died young.
9. Sallie Woods; died young.

Section 10. Mary Rice Woods, born Sept. 24, 1795; married Overton Harris, son of John Harris, and Margaret Maupin, his wife. (See Part 111, Chap. XXXVII.) She died in Mo. Aug. 31, 1876.

Section 11. Elizabeth Woods, born June 7, 1798; married Garland Reid. Children:

1. Mary A. Reid; married John J. White, in Boone County, Mo., Jan. 1836, and had two children:
   1. Elizabeth White; dead.
   2. Sarah Jane White; dead.

2. Clifton G. Reid; died in Butler County, Mo., in the 24th year of his age.

3. Caroline E. Reid; married first, W. L. Brashear, and second Edward Holman. Children:
   1. Walter Q. Brashear.
   2. Lizzie D. Holman; married G. W. Amsbury; issue:
      1. Glenn H. Amsbury.
   3. Carrie B. Holman; married H. H. Skinner, issue:
      1. Edward H. Skinner.
      2. Carroll A. Skinner.
   4. Edward H. Holman; died at the age of four years.

4. Sarah W. Reid; married Dr. Martin Hickman 1843, issue:
   1. Nathaniel G. Hickman; died in 1881 unmarried.
   2. Carroll B. Hickman; married Mrs. Margaret Stall.

5. John B. Reid; married Nancy Hocker. Children:
   1. Clifton Reid.
   2. Elizabeth Reid.
   3. Sarah Reid.
   4. John Reid.
   5. Lula Reid.
   6. Arthur Reid.
   7. Luther Reid.

6. Susan J. Reid; married James Rumbold. Children:
   1. George O. Rumbold.
   2. Ellen J. Rumbold.

3. Lizzie Rumbold.
4. Mary Rumbold.

7. Dr. James A. Reid; married Annie Berry, 1862. Children:
   1. Clifton A. Reid.
   2. Annie L. Reid; married C. Cameron, issue:
      1. Reid A. Cameron.

8. Miriam G. Reid; married Eason S. Hickman. Children:
   1. Lizzie Hickman.
   2. Warren Hickman.
   3. Homer Hickman.
   4. Lee Hickman.

9. William N. Reid; married B. Jane Spiller. Children:
   1. Yulah Reid.
   2. Edward Reid. twin.
   3. Carrie Reid. twin.
   4. Charles Reid.
   5. Frank Reid.
   6. John Reid.
   7. George Reid.
   8. Ettie Reid.
   9. Nellie Reid.

10. Rachael W. Reid; married first, Captain Jefferson Taylor, and second Rev. W. Davenport. Children:
   1. John Taylor.
   2. Frank Taylor.
   3. Minnie Davenport.
   4. Burr Davenport.
   5. Sylvester Davenport.
   6. Ida Davenport.

11. Nathaniel G. Reid; married Nancy E. Goodall. Children:
   1. Martha Reid.
   2. Bessie Reid.
   3. Clifton Reid.

Section 12. Frances Woods; married William Slavin, emigrated and settled in Boone County, Mo. in 1823. Children:

1. Elizabeth Slavin; married William McClure. Children:
   1. Fannie McClure.
   2. Alexander McClure.
   3. Samuel McClure.
   4. Almira McClure.
   5. Clark McClure.

2. James Rice W. Slavin; died young.
3. Mary Jane Slavin; married Robert Nichols. Children:
   1. Overton Nichols.
   2. Isaac Nichols.
   3. Mary Nichols.

4. John Addison Slavin; married Emma Ruth Ross.
5. Sarah Margaret Slavin; married Thomas Wright, had eight children.
6. Martha Slavin.
7. Rachael Slavin; married Sidney Jackman, had eight children.
8. Elvira Frances Slavin; married William Tandy O'Rear; issue:
   1. William Alexander O'Rear; died in infancy.

2. Alice Frances O'Rear; married George B. McFarlane; issue:
   1. Elvira McFarlane; died in infancy.
   2. George Tandy McFarlane; died in infancy.
   3. Charles Roy McFarlane.
   4. George Locke McFarlane.
   5. William Lawrence McFarlane; died at the age of 16 years.

3. George O'Rear.
4. Charles Wayman O'Rear; died at the age of 29 years.
5. Louella O'Rear; married Charleston J. Trumbull. Children:
   1. Elvira E. Trumbull; married Robert B. Rogers.
   2. Sarah Trumbull.
   3. Ruth Trumbull.
   4. Hattie Trumbull.
   5. Mattie Trumbull.
   6. Newton Trumbull.

6. Woods Elavin O'Rear; married Flora Prewitt. Children:
   1. Clyde O'Rear.
   2. George McFarlane O'Rear.

7. Sallie Allie O'Rear; died at the age of 20 years.
8. Mattie O'Rear; married P. E. Locke. Children:
   1. Allie O'Rear Locke.
   2. Emma Lydia Locke.

9. Mary Varnia O'Rear; married H. M. Clark; issue:
   1. Miller Clark.
   2. Alice Clark.
   3. Elva Clark.
   4. Ruth Clark.

10. Robert O'Rear; died in infancy.
11. Anna O'Rear; died in infancy.

CHAPTER 21.

MARY WOODS.

(Named in Chapter 19, Section 2.)

Article 1—Mary Woods, a daughter of Colonel John Woods, of Albermarle, and Susannah Anderson his wife, was born in Albermarle County, Va. Dec. 2, 1746, and married John Reid of Nelson County, Va., formerly of Amherst. (See Chap. 48, and also Chap. 29, for brief history of the Reid family.)

John Reid was born Aug. 25, 1750. They emigrated to Madison County, Ky. in the period 1790-5, and settled and made their home on Otter Creek, a mile or two east of Richmond, where John Reid died June 29, 1816. His son, John Reid and his son-in-law, William Williams qualified as administrators of his estate. The subject, John Reid, before coming to Kentucky and whilst living in Albermarle, was a signer of the Declaration of Independence, April 21, 1779.

Mary Woods Reid his widow died at their Otter Creek home

Oct. 19, 1828, having first made and published her last will and testament, towit: "In the name of God, Amen. I, Polly Reid, widow and relict of John Reid, deceased, being weak in body but sound in mind, do make and ordain this my last will and testament, hereby revoking all others. First, my will and desire is that after my death my just debts, if any, and funeral expenses, be first paid out of the proceeds of my estate, consisting of the profits of my dowry in the lands and slaves of my said husband, John Reid, deceased. Second, my will and desire is that as my beloved son, Thomas Reid, by one misfortune or other has been reduced to almost penury and want, that he the said Thomas, have the balance of my estate, after paying as above, which estate consists in notes principally upon my son, James Reid, for the hire of my negroes and land, some of which are now in my possession, and one in the possession or my son, John Reid, in fine, I will and bequeath unto my said son, Thomas Reid all the estate of which I am seized and possessed, or entitled to as profits of my dowry estate, or otherwise, absolutely entitled to in my own right, reserving my original dowry estate, to be disposed of as the law directs. It being only my wish to will and bequeath such part of the profits of said estate, as may be left at my death, after paying for my support and maintenance out of the same, and such other estate as I may be entitled to in any way. Lastly, I appoint my son, Thomas Reid, executor of this my last will and testament. In witness whereof, I have hereunto set my hand and seal, this 17th day of October, 1828.

Signed. POLLY REID. [Seal]

Witnesses:—E. L. Shackelford, James Woods, Jacob Coulter.

Kentucky, Madison County Sct.

I, David Irvine, Clerk of the Court for the county aforesaid, do hereby certify that at a County Court held for Madison County on Monday the 2nd day of Feb. 1829, this instrument of writing was produced in open court, and proved to be the last will and testament of Polly Reid, deceased, by the oaths of James Woods and James Coulter, two subscribing witnesses thereto, and ordered to be recorded, and the same has been done accordingly.

Attest: DAVID IRVINE, C. M. C. C.

(See note to Part III, Chap. 45.)

The remains of Mary Woods, and John Reid her husband, were buried about two miles east of Richmond, Ky. in a plot of ground now an orchard, on the old William Goodloe farm, now owned and occupied by Christopher F. Chenault as a home. Marble stones, with inscriptions showing dates of their birth and death mark their graves, their brother-in-law, Daniel Miller and wife settled on Muddy Creek. Samuel Reid and his family settled on Paint Lick Creek. Their children were:

Section 1. Thomas Reid; married Susan Shelton, July 29, 1806, (See Part VII, Chap. IV, Sec. 1) and Nancy Harris April 19, 1820. (See Note to Part III, Chap. XLV.)

Section 2. John Reid; married Ann Miller, a daughter of Colonel John Miller, and Jane Dulaney his wife, April 18, 1796. (See Part 1, Chap. XIV, Sec. 111.) They had a number of children among them were:

1. Jane Reid; married Hudson Broaddus, Dec. 21, 1819. (See Part I, Chap. XIII, Sec. 3, Note.)
2. Lucinda Reid; married Overton Gentry, Oct. 7, 1824.

3. John M. Reid; married Elizabeth Dinwiddie, Sept. 9, 1824.
4. Corrinna Reid; married Hardin Yates, Aug. 18, 1829.
5. Elizabeth (or Elzira) M. Reid; married Talton Fox, July 29, 1828.
6. Jefferson Reid.
7. Susan Reid; married George Estill.
8. Joseph Reid.
9. Christopher Reid.
10. William Reid.
11. Polly Reid; married Levi Williams.
12. Thomas Reid. (See Part I, Chap. 14, Sec. 3.)

Section 3. James Reid; married Mary Reid, Feb. 27, 1816, and on the 1st of May 1834, he married Mrs. Sarah Robertson, a widow who had been married to William Robertson March 18, 1818, by Benjamin Lrvine, M. G., and her maiden name was Hooten. In Dec., 1835, James Reid was dead, and Anderson W. Reid, was administrator of his estate, and on the 27th, of April 1841, his widow, Sarah married Henry Evans, Mr. Evans and his said wife owned real estate in Richmond, Ky. which they conveyed to John P. Ballard Jan. 10, 1846, and lands on Muddy Creek adjoining Caleb Oldham and others, 100, 56½, and 22½ acres, which they conveyed to Elijah Yates, Dec. 20, 1854. Of his first marriage James Reid had these children:

1. Sarah W. Reid; married Jeptha Rice Gilbert, Feb. 22, 1836.
2. Sophia Reid; (her guardian was John Reid) married Mr. French.
3. Susan J. Reid, (her guardian was her step parents, Henry and Sarah M. Evans).

Section 4. William Reid; married Sarah Woods. (See Chap. 20, Sec. 5, for their children.)

Section 5. Anderson Woods Reid, was born in Va. April 27, 1783. He came with his parents to Madison County, Ky. On the 2nd of May 1809, he married Charlotte Embry, a daughter of Tarlton Embry. He acquired lands on Muddy Creek, on the upper Irvine Road, near Stephens shop, or the village now called Colyer, on which he built a substantial brick residence and made his permanent home. His wife died there June 21, 1835, and on the 11th of July, 1838, Mr. Reid married Barbara Ann Shrite, and he died Sept. 29, 1843. The remains of Mr. Reid and his first wife were interred some two hundred yards north of the dwelling, and tomb stones properly inscribed mark the graves. The farm is now owned and occupied by A. Sidney Noland as a home. Mr. Reid was a very substantial citizen and farmer. The children of his first marriage:

1. Nancy Embry Reid, born April 22, 1811, died May 15, 1834. She married Samuel Willis June 22, 1830. They had a daughter:
    1. Charlotte Elizabeth Willis; died April 6, 1834, age 6 months and 25 days.
2. William Loftus Reid; born March 5, 1813; died unmarried.
3. Mary Woods Reid; born Jan. 6, 1815; married Lucas C. Chrisman, Dec. 3, 1833. He was a tanner of leather. They had a daughter:
    1. Ann Chrisman.

4. John Reid, born in 1817; married July 15, 1841, Miriam Williams, a daughter of Nathaniel Williams and Celia Oldham, his wife.

(See Part VI, Chap. VII, Sec. 1.) Mr. Reid lived on Otter Creek, some six or seven miles northeast of Richmond, Ky., where he died some years since, his widow is now upwards of eighty years of age, with a bright, clear mind, and she knows much of the pedigree of her own people, and as to genealogy, is an encyclopedia of useful knowledge. Their children:

1. Charlotte Reid; married firstly Homer G. Baxter, and had children, then she married H. Clay Rice, of Estill County, Ky.
2. Celia Reid; married David Witt, of Station Camp, Estill County, Ky.
3. Martha Matilda Reid; died unmarried.
4. Annie Reid; married James Amerine, and had children. Mr. Amerine was killed in Irvine, Ky. by Hal Cockrill, several years ago.
5. Julia Reid: died in infancy.
6. Oliver G. Reid; married Mrs. Hickey of Illinois.
7. James Anderson Reid: married his cousin, Minnie Reid of Missouri.
8. Nathan Williams Reid; married Fannie Park, live in Mississippi.
9. Malcolm Miller Reid; married his second cousin, Rebecca Alexander.
10. Arthur Carrolton Reid; married Samira Reeves.

5. Martha Reid, born March 27, 1819; married Albert Comelison Sept. 22, 1836. They had a daughter:

1. Infant; born April 7, 1839: died May 11, 1839.

6. Elizabeth Reid, born April 19, 1822; married William Denham.
7. Talitha F. Reid, born Feb. 9, 1824; married Lindsay M. Thomas, Feb. 11, 1841, they went to Iowa.
8. Louisa Reid, born March 13, 1826; married Sidney Dozier Aug. 8, 1844. Issue:
   1. Ibsan Dozier.
9. Talton E. Reid, born March 3, 1828; died Aug. 6, 1829.
10. Josephus Reid, born Sept. 27, 1831; married firstly, Celia Williams Jan. 30, 1851, and secondly Miss Adams.

Section 6. Elizabeth Reid: married William Williams, Oct. 15, 1805. He enlisted in the war of 1812, as a private, and for conspicuous bravery was promoted Colonel. They had two sons:

1. James Williams.
2. William Williams.

These two sons lived and died near the Pond Meeting House, a few miles south west of Richmond, Ky.

CHAPTER 22.

MICHAEL WOODS.

(Named in Chapter 19, Section 3.)

Article 1.—Michael Woods a son of Colonel John Woods, of Albermarle, and Susannah Anderson, his wife, was born in Albermarle County, Va. near the middle of the eighteenth century, about the year 1748.

He married Hettie Caruthers of Rockbridge County, Va. and lived on his father's place on Mechums River till about 1801, and then moved to a farm in the southern part of the county, on the south side of Rockfish, recently occupied by Charles Harris, which was in 1807 cut off into Nelson County, which was then formed, where he lived the rest of his life. He was co-executor with his brother James of Colonel John Woods will. His own will bears date Feb. 22, 1825. He died in 1826. In his will is mentioned his children:

Section 1. James Michael Woods; married his cousin Margaret Caruthers, of Rockbridge. The subject of Chapter XXIII.

Section 2. John Caruthers Woods; married Miss Davis. The subject of Chapter XXIV.

Section 3. Samuel Caruthers Woods; married Sarah Rodes daughter of John Rodes and Francina Brown, his wife, of Nelson County. (See Part III, Chap. III, Sec. 7, and Part VIII, Chap. IV, Sec. IV.) The subject of Chapter XXV.

Section 4. William Moffett Woods; married Louisa Elizabeth Dabney, daughter of William S. Dabney, Sr., (see Part III, Chap. XV.) and secondly Martha J. Scott, daughter of Charles A. Scott.

Section 5. Michael Woods; died when about twenty one years of age.

Section 6. Susan Woods; married Nathaniel Massie. The subject of Chapter 27.

Section 7. Mary Woods; married Hugh Barclay. The subject of Chapter 28.

Section 8. Jane Woods; married William Hardy. They emigrated to Missouri.

CHAPTER 23.

JAMES MICHAEL WOODS.

(Named in Section 1, Chapter 22, Part II.)

Article 1.—James Michael Woods a son of Michael Woods, and Hettie (Esther) Caruthers his wife.

He married his cousin Margaret Caruthers of Rockbridge County, Va., emigrated to Marion County, Miss., and died about 1850-1. Leaving these children:

Section 1. Susan Elizabeth Woods; married James W. Clark.

Section 2. Michael James Woods, born 1839, served in the

Confederate Army, settled in Mississippi; married Miss Hibler, whom he survived. He afterwards married Miss Butts, and died in Mexico.

Section 3. John William Woods; went to Mississippi, where he was killed in a riot of the negroes in 1876.

CHAPTER 24.

JOHN CARUTHERS WOODS.

(Named in Section 2, Chapter 22, Part II.)

Article 1.—John Caruthers Woods a son of Michael Woods and Esther (Hettie) Caruthers.

He married Miss Davis, and moved to Marion Coutny, Mississippi in 1839. To them were born the following named children:

Section 1. William Woods of Kansas City, Missouri.

Section 2. A daughter married N. B. Langsford of Waxahatchie, Texas.

CHAPTER 25.

SAMUEL CARUTHERS WOODS.

(Named in Section 3, Chapter 22, Part II.)

Article 1.—Samuel Caruthers Woods, a son of Michael Woods and Esther (Hettie) Caruthers, his wife.

He married Sarah Rodes, daughter of John Rodes, of Nelson County, Va. emigrated to Missouri in 1839, where he died in 1866-7. (See Part III, Chap. III, Sec. 3, and Part VIII Chap. IV, Sec. 4.) To whom were born these children:

Section 1. M. Woods, lives at Eldora Springs, Missouri.

Section 2.

Section 3.

CHAPTER 26.

WILLIAM MOFFETT WOODS.

(Named in Section 4, Chapter 22, Part II.)

Article 1.—William Moffett Woods, a son of Michael Woods and Esther (Hettie) Caruthers his wife, was born March 27, 1808.

He married Louisa Elizabeth Dabney, daughter of Wm. S. Dabney, Sr. Oct. 4, 1837. She died Jan. 29, 1843. To them were born these children:'

Section 1. Senora Dabney Woods, born Aug. 2, 1838; died April 5, 1866.

Section 2. Julian Watson Woods, born May 15, 184 .

Article 2.—After the death of his wife, William Moffett Woods married Martha J. Scott, daughter of Chas. A. Scott; she was born April 20, 1814, and died March 7, 1872.. Of this marriage the following named children were the fruits:

Section 1. Mary Louise Woods, born Feb. 16, 1849; died Feb. 20, 1860.

Section 2. Daniel Scott Woods, born April 25, 1850; died April 5, 1860.

Section 3. Fanny Langhorn Woods, born Sept. 18, 1851; died June 30, 188 .

Section 4. Nannie Scott Woods, born Jan. 23, 1853; married C. L. Wagnor, Nov. 24, 1886.

Section 5. William Moffett Woods, born June 8, 1856; died Jan. 15, 1888.

Section 6. Susan Massie Woods born March 16, 1859; died Aug. 16, 1892.

The subject of this chapter died in Buckingham County, Va. in 1862, aged 54 years.

CHAPTER 27.

SUSAN WOODS.

(Named in Sec. 6, Chapter 22, Part II.)

Article 1.—Susan Woods a daughter of Michael Woods and Esther (Hettie) Caruthers, his wife; married Nathaniel Massie of Nelson County, Virginia.

Nathaniel Massie was for a considerable period of his life a successful merchant of Waynesborough, but as old age begun to creep on him he moved back to the old homestead on the border of Nelson County, where he died in 1871. His grand-father Charles Massie, an emigrant to America came from New Kent, and established his home in the southwestern part of Albermarle County, Va. on the waters of Lynch Creek, on what was known as the Wakefield Entry. His plantation was named Spring Valley and became noted from the perfection of its Albermarle pippins: though passed into other hands it is still designated by the name Mr. Massie gave it. Charles Massie purchased the place about 1768, he died in 1817. His son Charles Massie and wife Nancy, the father of Nathaniel Massie succeeded to the place in 1830. The children of Nathaniel Massie and Susan Woods his wife were:

Section 1. James Massie, was professor in the Virginia Military Institute.

Section 2. Nathaniel Hardin Massie, born about 1826, became prominent attorney at law of Charlottesville.

Section 3. Susan Massie; married Robert B. Moon.

Section 4. Hettie Massie; married William Patrick.

Nathaniel Massie's second wife was Elizabeth Rodes daughter of Matthew Rodes, and their children were:

Section 5. Rodes Massie.

Section 6. Edwin Massie.

CHAPTER 28.

MARY WOODS.

(Named in Section 7, Chapter 22, Part II.)

Article 1.—Mary Woods a daughter of Michael Woods and Ettie (Hettie) Caruthers his wife, married Hugh Barclay of Lexington, Virginia. To whom were born the following named children:

Section 1. John Woods Barclay of Lexington Va.

Section 2. Dr. Michael Woods Barclay moved to Kentucky. He married his cousin Susannah Goodloe Miller, a daughter of General John Miller and Elizabeth Goodloe his wife and died in 1858, leaving these children:

1. Hugh Barclay. 2. Bettie Barclay. 3 Mary Barclay. All of whom died young. (See Part 1, Chap. VII, Sec. 1.)

CHAPTER 29.

SUITY WOODS.

(Named in Section 4, Chapter 19, Part II.)

Division 1.

Article 1.—Suity Woods, a daughter of Colonel John Woods, of Albermarle, and Susannah Anderson his wife, was married at their home in Albermarle County, Va., to Samuel Reid, of Nelson County, Va.

They emigrated to Ky. and settled on the waters of Paint Lick Creek, in Garrard County, in 1782, and lived and died on the same farm near old Paint Lick church. Their children:

Section 1. Dr. James Reid. He married Betsy Murrell, of Barren County, Ky., and owned and occupied his father's old homestead, where he practiced medicine for many years. Children were:

1. Susan Reid.
2. Mary Reid.
3. George Reid.
4. James Reid.
5. Belle Reid.

Section 2. John W. Reid; married Jennie Murrell. They lived and died near Hustonville, Lincoln County, Ky. A fuller account of whom will be found in Chapter 20.

Section 3. Alexander Reid; married Polly Morrison Blain, daughter of John and Jane Blain. They lived and died in Garrard County, Ky. near Paint Lick. Their children were:

1. Almira Reid.
2. Jane Reid.

3. Nelson Reid.
4. Sallie Ann Reid.
5. Mariah Reid.

All of whom are dead.

Section 4. Mary Reid; married her cousin William Woods of Garrard County, Ky., son of James Woods and Mary Garland. (See Chap. XIX, Sec. IV.) William Woods was a very prominent man, and represented Garrard County in the Legislature in 1857-9. They died leaving the children mentioned in chapter XX, section IV.

The Reid Family.

In the first part of the seventeenth century, Samuel Reid came from Scotland to America and settled in Pennsylvania. He enlisted as a soldier in the Revolutionary Army, in which he faithfully served until peace was declared, and America was freed from the yoke of England. After the war he settled in the Valley of Virginia, in probably Nelson County. Many of his descendants now live in Virginia, Kentucky, Georgia, and other states of the Union.

In the Revolutionary Army Nathan Reid was Captain of a Company of the 14th Va. Regiment, commanded by Colonel Charles Lewis of Albermarle. In 1778 this company was designated as Captain Nathan Reid's company of the 10th Va. Regiment commanded by Colonel William Davies. In May, 1779, the 1st and 10th Va. Regiments were consolidated and this company was called Captain Nathan Reid's and Lieutenant Colonel Hopkins' Company, 10th Va. Regiment commanded by Colonel William Davies and some times referred to as the 1st and 10th.

John Reid; married Mary Woods as set forth in Chapter 21.

Samuel Reid; married Suity Woods, as set forth in the beginning of this chapter XXIX. and Jonathan (or Jno. N.) Reid married Anna Woods, as set forth in chapter XLVIII.

Notes:—The prevailing impression in our mind has been that Captain Nathan Reid, John Reid, Samuel Reid, and Jonathan Reid were brothers, having been so told years ago by one who professed to know, but who is long since dead (the venerable Robert Harris, of Drowning Creek, Madison County, Ky., who lived to be 96 years old). There were probably other brothers and sisters. They probably had a brother Alexander Reid. Andrew Reid died in Albermarle in 1751, and James Reid died in 1790.

Madison County, Ky. Record of the Family.

Early marriages in the County:

Reid, James—Ann Hall, Feb. 12, 1790.
Reid, John—Mary Mackey, April 2, 1793.
Reid, Mary—John Cloyd, Jan. 15, 1795.
Reid, Patsy—George Creath, Jan. 21, 1796.
Reid, John—Ann Miller, April 18, 1796.
Reid, Jenny—John McCord, March 23, 1797.
Reid, Fanny—Joseph Moore, March 21, 1799.
Reid, George—Mary Arnold, Jan. 6, 1803.
Reid, Patsy—Richard Oldham, Jan. 26, 1803.
Reid, Sallie—Joseph Leak, Dec. 18, 1803.
Reid, Betsy—William Williams, Oct. 15, 1805.
Reid, Thomas—Susannah Shelton, July 29, 1806.
Reid, Susannah—Benjamin Moberly, Oct. 4, 1808.
Reid, John—Betsy Lancaster, Jan. 7, 1812.

Reid, Jane—Andrew Wallace, Oct. 5, 1813.
Reid, Martha—Albert Comelison, Sept. 22, 1836.
Reid, Frances B.—Jeremiah Collins, Aug. 1, 1839.
Reid, John—Minerva Williams, July 15, 1841.
Reid, Alexander—Elizabeth Duff, Jan. 5, 1841.
Reid, Louisa—Sidney Dozier, Aug. 8, 1844.
Reid, Margaret—JohnMoore, Oct. 10, 1847.
Reid, Polly—Levi Williams, Dec. 27, 1814.
Reid, James—Polly Reid, Feb. 27, 1816.
Reid, Polly—James Reid, Feb. 27, 1816.
Reid, Jane—Hudson Breaddus, Dec. 21, 1819.
Reid, Thomas—Nancy Harris, April 19, 1821.
Reid, Lucinda—Overton Gentry, Oct. 7, 1824.
Reid, John Miller—Elizabeth Dinwiddie, Sept. 9 1824.
Reid, Isaac—Rhoda Tate, Sept. 9, 1825.
Reid, Elizabeth M.—Talton Fox, July 29, 1828.
Reid, Sylvester—Elizabeth Hubbard, Aug. 13, 1829.
Reid, Sallie—Thomas Todd, Jan. 15, 1829.
Reid, Nancy—Samuel Willis, June 22, 1830.
Reid, Corrinna—Hardin Yates, Aug. 18, 1829.
Reid, Miriam—Alexander R. Oldham, Sept. 15, 1831.
Reid, Mary W.—Lucius C. Chrisman, Dec. 3, 1833.
Reid, James—Mrs. Sarah Robertson, May 1, 1834.
Reid, Sarah W.—Jeptha Rice Gilbert, Feb. 22, 1836.
Reid, Talitha—Lindsay M. Thomas, Feb. 11, 1841.
Reid, James—Lydia Townsend, Dec. 23, 1842.
Reid, Sarah M.—Henry Evans, Apr. 27, 1841.
Reid, Sausen—Mary Jane Anderson, May 13, 1845.
Reid, Josephus—Celia Wiliams, Jan. 30, 1851.

John Reid Sr., settled at an early date in Madison County, Ky. On the 18th of March, 1818, his widow, Elizabeth, was allotted dower in his estate. Their children:

1. John Reid Jr.: one John Reid, married Mary Mackey, April 2, 1793. His children:
   1. Alexander Reid. (In 1799, one Alexander Reid's wife was Rebekah. In 1810, one Alexander Reid's wife was Mary.)
   2. Sallie Reid; married Joseph Leake, Dec. 18, 1803.
   3. John Reid. (One John Reid, married Betsy Lancaster, Jan. 7, 1812. In 1826, one John Reid's wife was Susannah.
   4. Betsy Reid; married Mr. John Reid Rogers.

2. Margaret Reid; married Joseph Hieatt.
3. James Reid, (one James Reid married Ann Hall Feb. 12,1790).
4. Polly Reid; married John Cloyd, Jan. 15, 1795.
5. Jane Reid, the wife of William Young.
6. Robert Reid.
7. William Reid, was in Cooper County, Mo. in 1821.
8. Sallie Reid, the wife of Joseph Wolfscale.
9. Elizabeth Reid, the wife of Mr. Creath. (One Patsy Reid, married George Creath, Jan. 21, 1796.

In 1779 an Alexander Reid, and his wife Rebekah lived in the County.

In 1801, an Alexander Reid, and his wife Mary, lived in the County.

Alexander Reid's deposition, taken in 1801, recorded in Deed Book E. page 248.

Alexander Reid of Garrard County in 1808.

The following named John Reid's appear on the records.
John Reid, of Caswell County, N. C., in 1810.
John Reid, of Lincoln County, in 1795.
John Reid, of Nelson County, Va. to Arichibald Woods and William Kavanaugh, land and mill on Main Muddy Creek in 1799.
John Reid, senior in 1814, died in 1816. (wife Mary Woods.)

See Chapters 21, 29, 30, 31, 32 and 48 for additional facts.

In an old Bible found in the Madison Circuit Court Clerk's office is a family record, from which the following was copied:

"Ellen Leake the daughter of Walter Leake, and Susannah his wife was born Sept. 15, 1813, and died the 22 of April 1814, at or about 11 o'clock with the plague or epidemic fever raging among us in the Western Hemisphere.

"Isaac Shelby Reid the son of John Reid, and Judith his wife, was born Sept. 28, 1813.

"Susan Reid was born ye Aug. 2, 1815; she is the daughter of John Reid, and Judith his wife.

"Mary Leake, the daughter of Walter Leake, and Susannah his wife was born the 14th of Oct. 1815.

"Josiah Leake, was born Sept. 23, 1811, the son of Walter Leake, and Susannah Leake.

"Oct. 29, 1828; Mary Samuel Leake Marshall was born, the daughter of Isham Marshall and Judith, his wife.

"Hannah Walters, born 1833, Dec. 29. Sarah was born July 9, 1836; these are children of Caroline and Pleasant her husband.

"April 8, 1809: John Newman and wife Nancy, late Nancy Reid of the one part conveyed to the heirs of Alexander Reid, ⅛ of all land of said heirs, except 300 acres, tract on Cumberland river in Knox County, called the Flat Lick tract, which Newman and wife agree to take for their third. Two of the heirs namely, Richard Oldham and Goodman Oldham, agree, etc. (Signed)

JOHN P. NEWMAN,
NANCY NEWMAN,
RICHARD OLDHAM,
For himself and John Reid, one of the heirs.
GOODMAN OLDHAM,
JOHN P. NEWMAN,
Gdn. for Polly and Hannah Reid.

Teste:—Overton Harris, John Oldham, James Smith.

CHAPTER 30.

JOHN W. REID.

(Named in Chapter 29, Section 2.)

Article 1.—John W. Reid, a son of Samuel Reid and Snity Woods, his wife, was born in Virginia in 1784, and came with his parents to Paint Lick, Garrard County, Ky., in 1795.

He married Jensie (Jennie) Murrell (who died in 1852). They lived for over forty years on the Old Paint Lick farm and died there. Their children were:

Section 1. Amanda Reid, born 1811; she married Mr. Lewis

McMurtry. In 1905 she was alive and then 94 years old; she died recently. Their son:

1. Dr. Lewis McMurtry; his wife died in child-birth. Dr. McMurtry has an infirmary on James Court, Louisville, Ky., and is one of the finest surgeons in the United States, specially treating diseases of women.

Section 2. James M. Reid: married Mary G. Hays. A fuller history of them is set forth in Chapter 31.

Section 3. John M. Reid; married Bettie A. Hays. A fuller history of whom is set forth in Chapter 32.

Section 4. Sallie Reid; married Dr. F. S. Reid.

Section 5. Eliza Reid; married Mr. Lee; she is dead.

Section 6. Susannah Reid.

Section 7. William Reid.

CHAPTER 31.

JAMES M. REID.

(Named in Chapter 30, Section 2.)

Article 1.—James M. Reid, a son of John W. Reid, and Jensey Murrell, his wife, was born in 1812.. He died in 1878.

He married Mary Y. Hays, a daughter of Hugh Hays and Elizabeth Blaine, his wife. She was born in 1820, and died in 1884. Their home was in Lincoln County, Ky. Their children:

Section 1. Forrestus Reid, was born on the old Reid farm on Paint Lick Creek, in Garrard County, Ky., was a number of years a resident of Lincoln County, and a prosperous farmer. Some years since he moved to Danville, Ky. where he now lives. He married Katherine Withers, a daughter of Horace Withers of Lincoln County, Ky. To them were born seven children, two of whom are dead.

Section 2. Sallie E. Reid; married Dr. Wiett Letcher, a prominent physician of Danville, Ky. To whom three children have been born.

CHAPTER 32.

JOHN M. REID.

(Named in Chapter 30, Section 3.)

Article 1.—John M. Reid, a son of John W. Reid and Jensey Murrell his wife, was born at the old home in Garrard County, Ky., in 1823. He died in 1878.

He married Bettie A. Hays, a daughter of Hugh Hays and Elizabeth Blaine, his wife, in 1854. She died in 1881. Their children:

Section 1. Dr. Hugh Reid, of Stanford, Ky. born in 1856.

Section 2. Fanny M. Reid; married Mr. Jones.

Section 3. James C. Reid.

Section 4. Mary Reid; married Mr. Foster.

Section 5. Bessie Reid.

CHAPTER 33.

RICHARD WOODS.

(Named in Section 7, Chapter 4.)

Article 1.—Richard Woods, a son of Michael Woods, senior, of Blair Park, and Mary Campbell his wife, was born about 1715.

He married Jean ——. He lived in a region of country that Boutetourt County, created in 1769, covered. He died in 1779, leaving these children:

Section 1. Samuel Woods.
Section 2. Benjamin Woods.

CHAPTER 34.

ARCHIBALD WOODS.

(Named in Section 8, Chapter 4.)

Article 1.—Archibald Woods, a son of Michael Woods senior of Blair Park and Mary Campbell, his wife, was born in Ireland about 1716.

He came with his parents to America, and finally settled in Virginia, living for a time in Albermarle County; afterwards on Catawaba Creek in what is now Roanoke County, Va., known as Indian Camp, where he lived till his death in 1783. He married Isabella—, To whom were born:

Section 1. William Woods, 1744.
Section 2. A daughter, born 1745; married Mr. Brazeal.
Section 3. Isabella Woods, 1747.
Section 4. John Woods, 1748. A further account of whom will be found in Chapter 35.
Section 5. A daughter 1750; married Mr. Cowan.
Section 6. A daughter 1752; married Mr. Trimble.
Section 7. James Woods 1755, of whom a further account is rendered in Chapter 36.
Section 8. Archibald Woods 1757.
Section 9. Andrew Woods, 1760; moved to Kentucky.
Section 10. Joseph Woods, 1763. Lived on Indian Camp homestead and died in 1832.

CHAPTER 35.

JOHN WOODS.

(Named in Section 4, Chapter 34.)

Article 1.—John Woods, a son of Archibald Woods, and Isabella — his wife, married Elizabeth Smith, and died at Indian Camp in 1840.

To them were born the children named in the coming sections:

Section 1. James Woods. He died Nov. 5, 1856. His wife's name is unknown. He left these children:

1. John Woods, went to Illinois and left three children: Mary Woods Hatfield, Addie Woods Boston and William Woods.
2. George Washington Woods; went to Illinois and then to Nevada, and left one daughter: Virginia Lee Woods, of Los Angeles, California.
3. Gabriel Woods, went to Missouri.
4. Joseph Woods.

Section 2. Absalom Woods, born in 1801; died in 1871. He never married.

Section 3. Archibald Woods; died in Craig County, Va. in 1875, leaving four children, viz: 1. John T. Woods, 2. Absalom Woods, 3. Oliver D. Woods, 4. Alice Woods married Mr. Beard.

Section 4. Sarah S. Woods; married William Doosing. They died leaving the following issue:

1. Eliza Doosing; married Mr. Hoffman, of Catawaba Valley.
2. John W. Doosing, of Catawaba Valley.
3. A daughter; married Charles Thomas, of Portland, Oregon.
4. Martha Doosing, of Catawba Valley.
5. Ann Doosing, of Catawba Valley.
6. Adaline Doosing, of Catawba Valley.

Section 5. Joseph Woods.

Section 6. William Woods, 1817-1882. Home at old Indian Camp, on the Catawba. He first married Harriet Pander, by whom he had these children:

1. Mary Woods; married John W. Thomas, and went to Oregon.
2. Sarah Woods; married George W. Lewis, of Catawba.
3. Archibald Woods, of Vine Grove, Ky.
4. Caroline Woods; married Major M. P. Spessard, of Craig County, Virginia.
5. Susan C. Woods; married G. W. Wallace, of Catawba, Valley.
6. John Woods; died in infancy.

The said Wiliam Woods, survived his wife, Harriet Pander, and afterwards married Sarah Jane Edington, by whom he had these children:

1. John W. Woods, of Roanoke, Va.
2. Annie E. Woods; died in 1884.
3. Joseph R. Woods, on old Indian Camp homestead.
4. Anna S. Woods, of Catawba Valley.
5. James Pleasant Woods, of Roanoke, County.
6. Oscar W. Woods, was surgeon in U. S. Army, and is now in the Philliphine Islands.

CHAPTER 36.

JAMES WOODS.

(Named in Section 7, Chapter 34.)

Article 1.—James Woods, a son of Archibald Woods, and Isabella ———, his wife, was born in Albermarle County, Va.

He first married Jane ——, moved to Kentucky, and died in Mercer or Fayette County about 1797. To him and his wife were born these children:

Section 1. Peggy Woods.
Section 2. Joseph Woods.
Section 3. Archibald Woods; married Ann Adams.

CHAPTER 37.

ANDREW WOODS.

(Named in Section 10, Chapter 4.)

Article 1.—Andrew Woods, a son of Michael Woods senior of Blair Park and Mary Campbell his wife, married Martha Poage a daughter of Robert Poage of Augusta County, Va.

His plantation was in Albermarle near his father. After his father's death he moved to Boutetourt County, near Mill Creek church, and was one of the first Justices of the Peace of that County. He died in 1781. He left the following named children:

Section 1. James Woods. An account of whom will be found in chapter XXXVIII.

Section 2. Elizabeth Woods. An account of whom will be found in chapter XXXIX.

Section 3. Rebecca Woods. An account of whom will be found in chapter XL.

Section 4. Robert Woods. See account in chapter XLI.

Section 5. Andrew Woods. An account of whom is rendered in chapter XLII.

Section 6. Archibald Woods. An account of whom will be found in chapter XLIII.

Section 7. Mary Woods. An account of whom will be found in chapter XLIIII.

Section 8. Martha Woods. An account of whom will be found in chapter XLV.

CHAPTER 38.

JAMES WOODS.

(Named in Section 1, Chapter 37.)

Article 1.—James Woods, a son of Andrew Woods, and Martha Poage, his wife, married Nancy Rayburn, Dec. 26, 1776, and lived in Montgomery County, Va. where he died Jan. 27, 1817.

To them were born the children named in the coming sections:

Section 1. Andrew Woods, of St. Charles, Mo.; married —— —— and had these children:

1. Andrew Woods, of Louisana; married Elizabeth ——.
2. Adaline Woods; married —— Courtney.
3. Robert Woods.
4. Emily Woods; married —— Whitman.

Section 2. Joseph Woods, born June 22, 1779, died April 20, 1859, at Nashville Tenn.

Section 3. Margaret Woods, born Sept. 12, 1781; married John Moore Walker, of Lyon County, Ky. left issue towit:

1. James Walker.
2. Catherine Rutherford Walker; married Rev. Robert A. Lapsley.
3. Agnes Walker; married Joseph Norvell.
4. Mary Jane Walker; married Dr. John D. Kelley.
5. Jeseph W. Walker.
6. Robert W. Walker; married Lelia Taylor.
7. John M. Walker.
8. Elsie Walker; married Reuben Kay.

Section 4. Robert Woods, born Dec. 25, 1786, of Nashville, Tenn., married Sarah West, to whom were born:

1. James Woods; married Elizabeth Campbell.
2. Josephine Woods; married John Branch.
3. Robert F. Woods; married Mariah Cheatham.
4. Joseph Woods; married Frances Foster.
5. Theodora Woods; married —— Handy.
6. Robina Woods; married William Armistead, of Nashville,Tenn.
7. Julia Woods; married R. C| Foster, of Memphis, Tenn.

Section 5. Martha Woods, born Oct. 4, 1790; married Alexander H. Robertson of Montgomery County, Va. To whom were born the following named children:

1. James W. Robertson; married Miss Graham, of Dover, Tenn.
2. Robert Robertson.
3. Joseph Robertson.
4. Alexander H. Robertson, Jr.

Section 6. James Woods, born Dec. 10, 1793; married Elizabeth A. Kay, and lived in Nashville, Tenn. To whom were born the following named children:

1. Robert K. Woods; married Susan Berry and lived in St. Louis, and had three children: 1. Susan Woods; married Givens Campbell, 2. Margaret Woods; married Greenleaf, 3. Anne Lee Woods; married Mr. Bliss, 4. Robert K. Woods, Jr.

2. Margaret Woods; married Mr. Handy.
3. Anna Woods; married R. B. Castleman of Nashville, Tenn. To whom were born: 1. Elizabeth Castleman, 2. James Woods Castleman.
4. Joseph Woods.
5. James Woods; married Adeline Milam, and left one son; Mark Milam Woods.
6. Andrew Woods; married Love Washington, and lived in Nashville, Tenn. To whom were born these children: 1. James Woods, 2. Mary Woods.
7. Elizabeth Woods; married Samuel Kirkman, and lived in Nashville, Tenn. To whom were born: 1. Elizabeth Kirkman. 2 Susan Kirkman.
8. Susan Woods; married G. G. O'Bryan, of Nashville, Tenn. To whom were born: 1. Susan O'Bryan, 2. Barsha O'Bryan.

Section 7. Elsie Woods, born May 10, 1795, and lived in Nashville, Tenn.

Section 8. Archibald Woods, born May 29, 1787, and lived in Nashville, Tenn.

Section 9. Agnes Green Woods, married Charles C. Trabue, and lived in Ralls County, Mo. To whom were born:

1. Joseph Trabue.
2. Robert Trabue; married Mary Bibb.
3. Anthony Trabue; married Christina Manley, and lived at Hanibal, Missouri.
4. Charles C. Trabue.
5. Sarah Trabue; married first John B. Stevens, secondly William Shivers.
6. George Trabue; married Ellen Dunn.
7. Jane Trabue; married J. H. Reynolds.
8. Martha Trabue, married George Thompson of Nashville, Tenn. To whom were born: 1. Agnes Thompson, married G. G. O'Bryan, of Nashville, Tenn. To whom were born a daughter, Agnes O'Bryan, 2. Elizabeth Thompson, married John P. W. Brown, 3. Charles Thompson, married Elizabeth Weeks. 4. Martha Thompson. 5. Frances Thompson. 6. John Hill Thompson, married Agnes Rickets. 7. Jane Thompson, married Alfred Howell. 8. Catherine Thompson, married Joseph L. Weakley.

CHAPTER 39.

ELIZABETH WOODS.

(Named in Sec. 2, Chap. 37.)

Article 1.—Elizabeth Woods, a daughter of Andrew Woods, and Martha Poage, his wife, lived in Rockbridge County, Va. and died in Jan. 1797.

She married David Cloyd. To whom were born the following named children:

Section 1. Martha Cloyd; married Matthew Houston, and lived at Natural Bridge, Va. To whom were born:
1. Sophia Huston. 2. Emily Houston. 3. Andrew Houston. 4. David Houston. 5. Matthew Hale Houston. 6. Cynthia Houston.

Section 2. David Cloyd, Junior.

Section 3. Margaret Cloyd; married Matthew Houston and lived at Lebanon Ohio. To whom were born: 1. Andrew C. Houston. 2. Romaine F. Houston.

Section 4. Mary Cloyd; married Mr. McClung.

Section 5. Andrew Cloyd.

Section 6. James Cloyd.

Section 7. Elizabeth Cloyd.

Section 8. Joseph Cloyd.

Section 9. Cynthia Cloyd.

CHAPTER 40.

REBECCA WOODS.

(Named in Sec. 3, Chap. 37.)

Article 1.—Rebecca Woods, a daughter of Andrew Woods and Martha Poage his wife; married Isaac Kelley, and lived in Ohio County, now West Virginia.

To whom were born the children named in the coming sections:

Section 1. Isaac Kelley junior; married Miss Gad. To whom were born: 1. Hamilton Kelley. 2. Simeon Kelley. 3. Wesley Kelley. 4. Benjamin Kelley.

Section 2. John Kelley, born 1784, died 1820. He married Elizabeth Wilson and lived in Ohio County, West Va. To whom were born these children:

1. Jane Kelley; married William Miller.
2. Isaac Kelley.
3. A. Wilson Kelley.
4. Aaron Kelley.
5. Sarah Kelley.
6. Rebecca Kelley.
7. Rev. John Kelley.

Section 3. James Kelley; married first Jane Robinson, and secondly, Eliza Gooding. He left the following children:

1. Isaac Kelley.
2. Samuel Kelley.
3. Joseph Kelley.
4. David Kelley.
5. Alexander Kelley.
6. Otis Kelley.
7. Eliza Kelley.

Section 4. Benjamin Kelley; married Charlotte Cross, to whom were born: 1. Isaac Kelley. 2. Eliza J. Kelley.

Section 5. Nancy Kelley; married Robert Poage. To whom were born: 1. Rebecca Poage. 2. Isaac K. Poage. 3. Gabriel Poage. 4. Elijah Poage.

Section 6. Martha Kelley; married Alexander Mitchell. To whom were born: 1 Nancy Mitchell. 2. Samuel Mitchell. 3. Isaac Mitchell. 4. Jane Mitchell. 5. Elizabeth Mitchell. 6. Zachariah Mitchell.

Section 7. Rebecca Kelley; married John Mays, and lived at West Alexander, Pennsylvania.
Section 8. Simeon Kelley.
Section 9. Narcissa Kelley; married Jonathan McCullock.

CHAPTER 41.

ROBERT WOODS.

(Named in Sec. 4, Chap. 37.)

Article 1.—Robert Woods, a son of Andrew Woods and Martha Poage his wife, lived in Ohio County, West Va.

He married first Lovely Caldwell, secondly Elizabeth Eoff. To whom were born the children named in the coming sections, but it is not known by which wife:
Section 1. Robert C. Woods; married Margaret A. Quarrier, and lived in Wheeling, West Va. To whom were born:
1. Emily Woods; married Thomas G. Black.
2. Mary Woods; married Alexander Q. Whittaker.
3. Harriett Woods; married Beverly M. Eoff.
4. Helen Woods; married William Tallant.
5. Margaret Woods; married Robert A. McCabe.
6. Alexander Woods; married Josephine McCabe.

Section 2. Andrew P. Woods.
Section 3. Eliza Jane Woods.

CHAPTER 42.

ANDREW WOODS.

(Named in Sec. 5, Chap. 37.)

Article 1.—Andrew Woods, a son of Andrew Woods, and Martha Poage, his wife, was born 1759, died Feb. 19, 1837; married Mary Mitchell McCullock.

Their home was at Wheeling, West Va. To them were born these children:
Section 1. Jane Woods; married Rev. James Hoge of Columbus, Ohio. To them were born:
1. Elizabeth Hoge; married Rev. Robert Nall of Tuskegee, Ala.
2. Mary M. Hoge; married Robert Neil of Columbus, Ohio.
3. Susannah P. Hoge; married Rev. M. A. Sackett, of Cleveland,O.
4. Rev. Moses A. Hoge; married first Mary B. Miller, secondly, Eliza Wells.
5. John J. Hoge; married first, Ann L. Wilson secondly, Mary Calhoun.
6. Margaret J. Hoge; married J. William Baldwin.
7. Martha A. Hoge; married Alfred Thomas.

Section 2. Andrew Woods; married Rebecca Brison. To whom were born:

1. James Woods of New Orleans, Louisana.
2. Oliver B. Woods; married Ann M. Anderson.
3. Luther T. Woods; married first, Mary E. Neil, secondly, Mary Hopkins.
4. John Woods; married Marilla Hale.
5. Archibald Woods; married Mary Matthews.
6. Alfred Woods; married Jane Railey.
7. Rev. Henry Woods; married Mary Ewing.
8. Rev. Francis M. Woods; married Julia Jenkins. To whom were born: 1. Rev. David J. Woods of Blacksburg, Va. 2. Mitchell Woods. 3. Andrew H. Woods. 4. Janet Woods. 5. Mary Woods. 6. Rebecca Woods.

Section 3. Samuel Woods of Woodbridge, California; married Elizabeth Leffler. To whom were born these children:

1. Andrew Woods; married E. Liffler.
2. Mary Jane Woods; married William L. Manley.
3. Margaret T. Woods; married J. Henderson of Stockton, California.
4. Jacob Woods; married Elizabeth V. Ward.
5. Hugh M. Woods.
6. Rebecca Woods.
7. Samuel Woods; married Anona Ellis.
8. Susan E. Woods; married Lafayette Creech.

Section 4. Robert M. Woods; married Rebecca Vance; lived at Urbana, Ohio. To whom were born the following named children:

1. Rachael Woods.
2. Alfred A. Woods.
3. Mary M. Woods; married J. W. Ogden, and had one child: Anne W. Ogden.
4. William N. Woods; married Ann McPherson.
5. Jane H. Woods; married Griffith Ellis.
6. Robert T. Woods.

Section 5. Margaret Woods; married Martin L. Todd, lived at Bellaire, Ohio, and had one child, Jane Todd.

Section 6. Mary Ann Woods; married Archibald Todd.

Section 7. Alfred Woods; married Elizabeth Sims; lived at Bellaire, Ohio. To them were born the following named children:

1. Margaret T. Woods; married Joseph S. Miller.
2. Louisa Woods; married S. Colin Baker of St. Louis, Mo.
3. Isabel Woods.
4. T. Sims Woods; married Mary Pancoast.
5. Robert Woods.
6. William A. Woods; married Emma Zinn.
7. Launcelot Woods; married Charlotte Teagarten.
8. Elizabeth Woods; married John W. Carroll.
9. Mary Ann Woods; married Henry Basel of St. Louis, Mo.
10. Martha N. Woods; married Richard Ritey.
11. Alfred Woods; married Esther Vogel.
12. Edgar Woods; married Louisa James.

CHAPTER 43.

ARCHIBALD WOODS.

(Named in Sec. 6, Chap. 37.)

Article 1.—Archibald Woods, a son of Andrew Woods, and Martha Poage, his wife, born Nov. 14, 1764, died Oct. 26, 1846.

He lived in Ohio County, West Va., and marraed Ann Poage. To them were born the chilren named in the coming sections:

Section 1. Elizabeth Woods; married George Paull of St. Clairsville, Ohio. To them were born:

1. Rev. Alfred Paull; married Mary Weed.

Section 2. Thomas Woods; married Mary Brison and lived in Wheeling, West Virginia. To them were born these children:

1. Ann Eliza Woods; married James S. Polhemus.
2. Sarah M. Woods.
3. Theodore Woods.
4. Archibald Woods.
5 Rev. Edgar Woods of Charlottsville, Va.; married Mariah C. Baker.
6. Lydia Woods.
7. John Henry McKee Woods.

Section 3. Martha Woods; married Charles D. Knox of Wheeling, West, Va. To whom were born the following named children:

1. Franklin Woods Knox; married Ruth Stewart.
2. Stewart Knox.
3. Robert Knox.

Section 4. Franklin Woods.
Section 5. Nancy Woods.
Section 6. Mary Woods.
Section 7. George W. Woods; married Cresah Smith.
Section 8. William Woods; died in infancy.
Section 9. John Woods; married Ruth Jacob. To whom were born:

1. Archibald Woods.
2. Joseph Woods.
3. George W. Woods.
4. Hamilton Woods.
5. Anne M. Woods.
6. Martha V. Woods.

Section 10. Emily Woods, of whom we have no history.
Section 11. William Woods (second of name in this family).
Section 12. Hamilton Woods.

CHAPTER 44.

MARY WOODS.

(Named in Sec. 7, Chap. 37.)

Article 1.—Mary Woods, a daughter of Andrew Woods, and Martha Poage his wife, was born Feb. 19, 1766, died May 25, 1830.

She married James Poage, and lived at Ripley, Ohio. To them were born the children named in the coming sections:

Section 1. Martha Poage; married George Poage.

Section 2. John C. Poage.

Section 3. Rev. Andrew W. Poage, lived at Yellow Springs, Ohio, and married Jane Gray, to whom were born:

1. Nancy M. Poage; married Thomas H. Reynolds.
2. James Poage.
3. John G. Poage; married Sarah J. Jones.
4. Andrew Poage, lived at Pamona, California, and married Mary B. Kline.
5. Mary Jane Poage.
6. Margaretta E. Poage.

Section 4. Mary Poage.

Section 5. James Poage Junior.

Section 6. Robert Poage, lived at Ripley, Ohio, married Sarah Kirker. To whom were born these children:

1. Rev. James S. Poage; married first Ann Voris, secondly, Susan L. Evans.
2. Thomas K. Poage; married first Sarah J. Henry, secondly, Jane Brickell.
3. John N. Poage; married Eliza Ann McMillan, to whom were born: 1. Alice E. Poage.
4. Sarah E. Poage.
5. Alfred B. Poage; married Esther A. Work.
6. William C. Poage.
7. Joseph C. Poage.
8. Mary Jane Poage.
9. Ann E. Poage; married first, William W. Wafer, second, Andrew Hunter.

Section 7. Elizabeth Poage, lived at Ripley, Ohio; married Rev. Isaac Shepherd, to whom were born:

1. James Hoge Shepherd.

Section 8. Ann Poage, lived at Ripley, Ohio; married Alexander Mooney. To whom were born:

1. John Mooney.
2. James Money.
3. Elizabeth Mooney.
4. Sophia Mooney.
5. Thomas Mooney.
6. Sarah Ann Mooney.

Section 9. Rebecca Poage; married John B. Knox, and lived at Yellow Springs, Ohio.

Section 10. Margaret Poage; married Rev. Thomas S. Williamson, and lived at St. Peter, Minnesota. To whom were born:
1. William B. Williamson.
2. Mary P. Williamson.
3. James G. Williamson.
4. Elizabeth P. Williamson; married Andrew Hunter, to whom were born: 1. Elizabeth Hunter; married Rev. E. J. Lindsay. 2. John K. Hunter.
5. Rev. John P. Williamson; married Sarah A. Vannice.
6. Prof. Andrew W. Williamson, of Rock Island, Illinois.
7. Nancy J. Williamson.
8. Smith B. Williamson.
9. Martha Williamson; married William Stout of Great Falls, Montana. To whom were born:
 1. Thomas Stout. 2. Alfred Stout.
10. Henry M. Williamson; married Helen M. Ely. To whom were born:
 1. Sumner Williamson. 2. William Williamson.

Section 11. Sarah Poage; married Rev. Gideon Pond. To whom were born:
1. Ruth Pond. 2. Edward Pond. 3. Sarah Pond. 4. George Pond. 5. Mary Pond. 6. Elizabeth Pond. 7. Ellen Pond.

Section 12. Thomas H. Poage.
Section 13. Rev. George C. Poage; married Jane Riggs, to whom were born the following named children:
1. James Poage.
2. Stephen Woods Poage.
3. Mary Ann Poage.
4. George Poage.
5. Arabella Poage.

CHAPTER 45.

MARTHA WOODS.

(Named in Sec. 8, Chap. 37.)

Article 1.—Martha Woods, a daughter of Andrew Woods, and Martha Poage his wife, died Dec. 14, 1834.

She lived in Boutetourt County, Va. and married Henry Walker. To whom were born the children named in the coming sections:
Section 1. Andrew W. Walker of Patts Creek, Va.; married Elizabeth Handly, to whom were born:
1. Henry Walker; married Maria Shawver.
2. John Walker; married Miss Nutten.
3. Archibald Walker.
4. Margaret Walker; married Thomas Harvey.
5. Martha Walker; married Joseph Harvey.
6. Emily Walker; married Israel Morris.
7. Mary Walker; married George Dondermilk.
8. Elizabeth Walker; married Andrew Elmore.
9. Jane Walker; married John Ferrier.
10 Malvina Walker; married James Richardson.
11. Andrew Walker.

12. Floyd Walker.
13. Newton Walker; married Julia Rapp, to whom were born:
    1. Euphemia Walker.
    2. Beirne Walker.
    3. Morris Walker.
    4. Samuel Walker.

14. Cynthia Walker.

Section 2. William Walker, of Warren County, Ky.; married first, Eleanor Moore, secondly, Sarah Lapsley. He left these children:

1. Robert Walker.
2. Henry Walker.
3. Martha Walker.
4. John L. Walker.
5. Catherine Walker.
6. Adeline Walker; married W. J. Landrum.

Section 3. Robert Walker, of Gap Mills, West Virginia; married Jane Allen. To whom were born:

1. Ann Eliza Walker.
2. Henry Walker; married Agnes Johnson.
3. Robert Walker; married Miss Robertson.
4. Martha Walker; married Jackson Clarke.
5. Lydia Walker.

Section 4. James Walker, of McDonough County, Illinois; married Margaret Bailey, to whom were born:

1. William S. B. Walker; married Elizabeth Head.
2. Martha Walker; married James M. Wilson.
3. Henry M. Walker; married Isabel Head.
4. James W. Walker; married Julia Head.

Section 5. Henry Walker, of Mercer County, West Va.; married Mary Snidow, to whom were born:

1. Martha Walker; married George Snidow.
2. William H. Walker.
3. Christian Walker.
4. Mary Walker.
5. James Walker.
6. Eliza Walker.
7. Lewis Walker; married Jane Carr.
8. Sarah Walker.
9. Elvira Walker.

Section 6. Archibald Walker.

Section 7. Joseph Walker, of Braxton County, West Va.; married Maria Gray, to whom were born:

1. Lucretia Walker.
2. Martha Walker.
3. Robert Walker.
4. Henry Walker.

Section 8. George Walker, of Giles County, Va.; married Susan Eakin, to whom were born:

1. Edwin Walker.
2. Leander Walker.
3. John A. Walker.
4. Avininta Walker.

Section 9. Mary Walker; married Tilghman Snodgrass, to whom were born:

1. Robert L. Snodgrass.
2. Henry W. Snodgrass.
3. Newton Snodgrass.
4. James Woods Snodgrass.
5. Cyrus Snodgrass.
6. Charles E. Snodgrass.
7. Thomas Snodgrass.
8. Lewis A. Snodgrass.
9. Jane Snodgrass.
10. Mary M. Snodgrass.

CHAPTER 46.

SARAH WOODS.

(Named in Sec. 2, Chap. 4.)

Article 1.—Sarah Woods, a daughter of Michael Woods, senior of Blair Park, and Mary Campbell his wife, married Joseph Lapsley, of Virginia.

To whom were born the children named in the coming sections:

Section 1. Joseph Lapsley, junior, born 1743; died 1792, was a Revolutionary soldier, made his will Dec. 23, 1791.

Section 2. Jean Lapsley, 1748; married James Cloyd, and moved to Lincoln County, Ky.

Section 3. Mary Lapsley, 1750; married John Hall, and moved to Lincoln County, Ky.

Section 4. John Lapsley, 1753. Of whom an account will be given in chapter XLVII.

Section 5. Martha Lapsley, 1756; married John Tomlin of Lincoln County, Ky.

Section 6. James Lapsley, 1760; of whom we have no further definite account.

CHAPTER 47.

JOHN LAPSLEY.

(Named in Sec. 4, Chap. 46.)

Article 1.—John Lapsley, a son of Joseph Lapsley, and Sarah Woods, his wife, was born Dec. 29, 1753, enlisted in the Revolutionary Army of Morgan's mounted men, was in the battle of Brandywine, Sept. 11, 1777, where he was wounded while carrying orders across the battlefield.

Dec. 22, 1778, he was married to Mary Armstrong. In 1795, he emigrated to Kentucky, and settled in Lincoln County. Of the union with Miss Armstrong the following named children were the fruits:

Section 1. Joseph B. Lapsley, born Oct. 5, 1779, was a Presbyterian preacher. His field of labor was in Kentucky and Tennessee. He was twice married, first to Rebecca Aylett, Sept. 27, 1804, secondly to his cousin, Sallie Lapsley. By his first wife, Rebecca Aylett he begot the children named:

1. John W. Lapsley, a lawyer of Selma, Alabama, died in 1889.
2. William Fairfax Lapsley; lived in Alabama.
3. Joseph M. Lapsley; died in Selma, Alabama, left two children:
   1. George H. Lapsley.
   2. Emma Baker. They live in Kansas City, Mo.

Section 2. Priscilla Catherine Lapsley, born June 23, 1781; married Colonel John Yantis, of Garrard County, Ky. Colonel John Yantis was of German birth, was a Revolutionary soldier. He also commanded a regiment in the war of 1812. For many years he represented Garrard County in the Kentucky Legislature. He was a son of Jacob Yantis. He lived near Lancaster until 1832, when he moved to Lafayette County, Mo., and died there in 1837.

Section 3. John A. Lapsley born Sept. 5, 1783; married Aug. 10, 1805, Mary Wear McKee, who was born Nov. 20, 1783, she was a daughter of William McKee, a commissioned officer in the Revolutionary Army. He emigrated to America from Ireland in 1725, went to Virginia in 1745, and to Kentucky in 1793, where he died Oct. 8, 1816, at the age of 92 years. His wife was Miriam Wear. To them were born:

1. Mary Jane Lapsley.
2. Amanda Lapsley; married Robert A. McKee.
3. Miriam Lapsley; married Warner Wallace.
4. Priscilla Lapsley; married Robert Robertson.
5. Joseph Lapsley.

6. William M. Lapsley; married Miss Baron of Perry County, Alabama, and left one child, Mary Lapsley.
7. John Lapsley.
8. Samuel Lapsley.
9. Robert Lapsley, went to Australia.
10. James Lapsley.
11. David Nelson Lapsley, born April 16, 1830; married Margaret Jane Jenkins, father of Dr. Robert McKee Lapsley, of Keokuk, Iowa.

Section 4. James F. Lapsley, born Jan. 7, 1786; married Charlotte Cleland, to whom were born:

1. Eliza Lapsley; married Lanta Armstrong.
2. Sarah Lapsley; married Mr. Robertson.
3. John P. Lapsley; married first, Eliza Johnston, secondly, Jennie ——.

4. James T. Lapsley; married first, Fannie Ewing and secondly, Elizabeth Bosemond.

Section 5. Samuel Lapsley, born Sept. 22, 1789; married Sallie Stevens.

Section 6. Sarah W. Lapsley, born Feb. 1, 1791; married William Walker, to whom were born:

1. Catherine Walker.
2. Adeline Walker; married General W. J. Landrum, a Brigadier General in the Federal Army, lived at Lancaster, Ky, and was at one time Collector of Internal Revenue.

Section 7. William Lapsley, born Sept. 28, 1793, lived in Tennessee.

Section 8. Mary C. Lapsley, born Feb. 26, 1796; married James McKee, to whom were born:

1. Miriam McKee; married Mr. Kelsey, and went to Denver, Colorado.
2. Mary Charlotte McKee; married William Dodd, of Koskiusko, Mississippi, and had besides others these children:
   1. John L. Dodd.
   2. Joseph C. Dodd. Both were prominent lawyers of Louisville, Ky.
3. Margaret McKee; married Mr. Henning.
4. John L. McKee; married Sarah Speake.
5. Samuel McKee; married Sallie Campbell. Samuel McKee was Colonel of 1st Ky. Regiment in the Federal Army, and was killed in battle at Murfreesborough, Tenn.
6. James Finley McKee; married Margaret Speake.

Section 9. Robert Armstrong Lapsley, born Jan. 11, 1798; married Catherine Rutherford Walker, a daughter of John Moore Walker who married Margaret Woods, a daughter of James Woods, and Nancy Rayburn, his wife. (See Chap. 38, Sec. 3.) To whom were born:

1. Joseph W. Lapsley; died unmarried.
2. John D. Lapsley; died unmarried.
3. Norvall A. Lapsley; died unmarried.
4. Robert Lapsley, born Feb. 10, 1833; married first, Alberti Pratt, and secondly, Mary Willie Pettus, by whom he had:
   1. Robert K. Lapsley.
   2. John Pettus Lapsley.
   3. Edmund Winston Lapsley.
   4. William Weeden Lapsley.
5. James Woods Lapsley.
6. Margaret Lapsley, born June 4, 1838; married first, Dr. James W. Moore, and secondly, James H. Franklin.
7. Samuel Rutherford Lapsley, born June 25, 1842, was a confederate soldier and received a fatal wound at the battle of Shiloh in 1862, while bearing the colors of his regiment.
8. Samuel McKee Lapsley, was a soldier in the Federal Army, died in 1862.

After the death of his first wife, Robert Armstrong Lapsley, married Mrs. Alither Allen, whom he also survived, and afterwards married Mrs. Mary Richardson, who out lived him. He died in 1872.

Section 10. Harvey Lapsley, born April 1, 1800. He died unmarried.

Section 11. Margaret Lapsley, born Feb. 17, 1802; married Moses Jarvis, to whom were born the following named children:

1. Mary Jane Jarvis; married Mr. Sharpe, no issue.
2. John L. Jarvis; married Miss Sharpe, left five children.

CHAPTER 48.

ANNA WOODS.

(Named in Chap. 19, Sec. 6.)

Article 1.—Anna Woods, a daughter of Colonel John Woods of Albemarle and Susannah Anderson his wife, was born in Albemarle County, Va., where she was married to John N. (or Jonathan) Reid, of Nelson County, Va., about the year 1788. (See Chap. 19, Sec. 6, and Chap. 29, Sec. 3.)

It is set forth in the Woods—McAfee memorial that she survived her husband, and married her cousin, William Woods. (See Chap. 12.) It is believed she came to Madison County, Ky., where she died Aug. 9, 1805.

One John Reid and his wife, Anna Reid were members of the Viney Fork church, which was organized in 1797, but they were another couple. It is known that some of her children lived in and were married in Madison County, Ky., as shown below.

There is a record in the Clerk's office of the Madison County Court, of a power of Attorney, bearing date Mch. 2, 1819 from Alexander Reid and James Reid of the city of Richmond, Va., appointing Andrew Wallace of Richmond, Ky., their attorney in fact to investigate, sue out, or compromise, or do any other lawful act, in ascertaining their rights and title to all lands in the state of Kentucky to which they are, or may be entitled as heirs of "John N. Reid" for Jonathan Reid, deceased, both being of the County of Nelson, (formerly Amherst) and state of Virginia conjointly with the other heirs of said descendents. It seems that Anna Woods husband, John N. Reid, was a native of Nelson County, formerly Amherst County, Va., and an heir of Alexander Reid deceased, but the relation is not very explicitly stated in the power of Attorney. The name was written "John N." for "Jonathan." The children of Anna Woods, and John N. Reid, or Jonathan Reid, were:

Section 1. Alexander Reid, who it seems was in the year 1819, a resident of the city of Richmond, Va., and joined with his brother James in the power of Attorney to his brother-in-law, Andrew Wallace of Richmond, Ky. above named. He was born Jan. 22 1789.

Section 2. Susannah Anderson Reid, born Dec. 27, 1787, she married in Madison County, Ky., Benjamin Moberly, Oct. 4, 1808, whom she survived, and on the 30th day of Oct. 1826, she married again in Madison County, Ky., William Oldham, son of Richard Oldham of Estill County, Ky., and Ann Pepper his wife. (See Part VI, Chap. 11.) Said William Oldham was born April 23, 1777, and died Sept. 26, 1849, she was his second wife, and he was her second husband. She died May 13, 1851. Children of her first marriage:

1. Susannah Moberley.
2. Polly Moberley.
3. Jane Reid Moberley; married John R. Oldham. (See Part VI, Chap. 37.)
4. Thomas Jenkins Moberley, went to Missouri and settled in Jackson County.
5. John Reid Moberley. (the eldest) He went to Missouri, and

settled in Jackson County, where he married ——— — - and had two sons:

1. John Moberley.
2. ——— Moberley.

6. Ann Moberley; married Adam Hill in Madison County, Ky., Aug. 14, 1828, they afterwards emigrated to Missouri, and in Missouri, one of her daughters Roena Hill, married a man by the name of Ralston, and a daughter of Mr. and Mrs. Ralston, towit: Annie Ralston, married Frank James the famous Missouri bandit, and whose son is a lawyer of Kansas City.

For children of the second marriage of Susannah Anderson Reid Moberley and William Oldham, see Part VI, Chap. 11.

Section 3. John Woods Reid, born June 10, 1793; died Oct. 11, 1799.

Section 4. Jane Reid, born Dec. 9, 1794; she married Andrew Wallace in Madison County, Ky. Oct. 5, 1813. She died April 14, 1863. (See Part IV, Chap. 7, Sec. 6, and Chap. 8.)

Section 5. James Reid, born Oct. 29, 1796. It seems that in the year 1819, he was a resident of the city of Richmond, Va., and joined with his brother Alexander Reid in the power of attorney to his brother-in-law, Andrew Wallace, of Richmond, Ky., above mentioned. He died in the South Oct. 9, 1837.

Section 6. Anna Woods Reid, born Sept. 12, 1799, died —.

CHAPTER 49.

WILLIAM WOODS.

(Named in Chap. 7, Sec. 1.)

Article 1.—William Woods, a son of Adam Woods, and Anna Kavanaugh, his wife, (1772-1846) married Susan B. Clark a daughter of Benjamin Clark, and Jane Mullins, his wife. (See Part V, Chap. 13, Sec. 7.) Their children:

Section 1. David Woods, (1800-1882) married Margaret Maupin, a daughter of Cornelius Maupin and Ann Bratton his wife. Their children:

1. Samira Woods; (1826-1901) married James Veal.
2. Angelina Woods; (1828———) married Aaron Dysart.
3. Overton Woods. (1830-1887.)
4. David Woods; (1832-1900) married Mattie A. Robinson of Bourbon, County, Ky. Their children:
    1. Colonel Charles A. R. Woods; (1865———) married firstly, Dora Lee Snoddy, secondly, Martha W. Clark, of Covington, Ky. Colonel Charles A. R. Woods is some what of a genealogist, and takes much interest in pedigrees. He made us a visit a few years since, and we visited several old grave yards and copied inscriptions from the tombs. Children of his first marriage:
        1. Gladys A. Woods, 1887.
        2. Archibald Douglas Woods, 1890.
    2. Harry E. Woods; (1866———) married Mary Ellen Crumpacker. They live in Norborne, Mo.
    3. Leon E. Woods, 1872.
5. Cornelius Maupin Woods, (1834———)

PART III.

CHAPTER 1.

GENEALOGICAL TABLE OF THE HARRIS FAMILY. 2. EARLY MARRIAGES IN MADISON COUNTY, KENTUCKY, OF THE HARRIS NAME, GLEANED FROM THE FIRST MARRIAGE REGISTER OF THE COUNTY COURT. 3. ITEMS CONNECTING THE HARRIS NAME WITH EVENTS.

Article 1.—Genealogical Table.

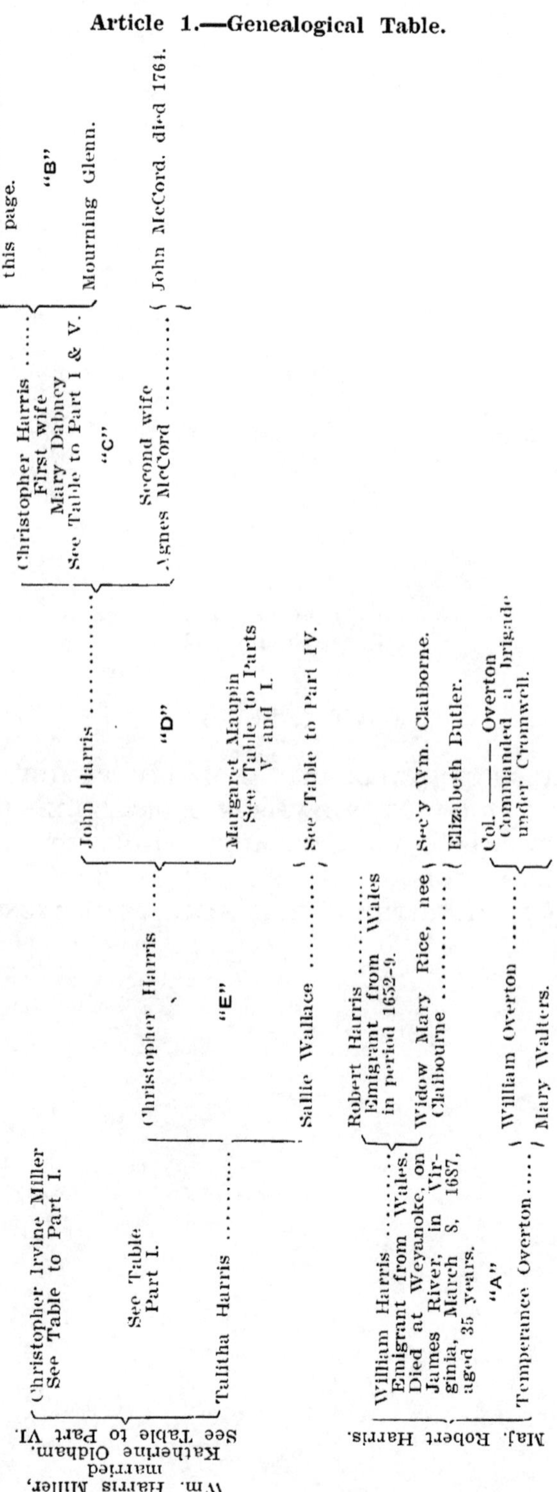

"A"

1. Christopher. Chap. 2, Sec. 1.
2. Robert, m Mourning Glenn. (Chap. 3.)

"B"

1. Christopher, m (1) Mary Dabney, (2) Agnes McCord. "C". (Chap. 4.)
2. Robert, m Lucretia Brown. (Chap. 3, Sec. 2.)
3. Tyre. (Chap. 3, Sec. 3.)
4. James, m Mary Harris. (Chap. 3, Sec. 4.)
5. William, m Hannah Jameson. (Chap. 3, Sec. 5.)
6. Lucy, m William Shelton. (Chap. 3, Sec. 6.)
7. Sarah, m John Rodes. (Chap. 3, Sec. 7.)
8. Miss ———, m William Dalton. (Chap. 3, Sec. 8.)
9. Mourning, m John Jouett. Chap. 3, Sec. 9.)
10. Elizabeth, m William Crawford. (Chap. 3, Sec. 10.)
11. Nancy, m Joel Crawford. (Chap. 3, Sec. 11.)
12. Anna, m John Dabney. (Chap. 3, Sec. 12.)

"C"

1. Dabney. (Chap. 4, Sec. 1.)
2. Sarah, m James Martin. (Chap. 5.)
3. Robert, m Nancy Grubbs. (Chap. 6.)
4. Mourning, m Foster Jones. (Chap. 11.)
5. Christopher, m Elizabeth Grubbs. (Chap. 12.)
6. Mary, m George Jones. (Chap. 4, Sec. 6.)
7. Tyre. (Chap. 4, Sec. 7.)
8. John, m Margaret Maupin. "D". (Chap. 16.)
9. Benjamin, m (1) Miss Jones, (2) Nancy Burgin. (Chap. 43.)
10. William, m Anna Oldham. (Chap. 44.)
11. Barnabas, m Elizabeth Oldham. (Chap. 45.)
12. James, m Susannah Gass. (Chap. 4, Sec. 12.)
13. Samuel, m Nancy Wilkerson. (Chap. 4, Sec. 13.)
14. Jane, m Richard Gentry. (Chap. 46.)
15. Margaret. (Chap. 4, Sec. 15.)
16. Isabella, m John Bennett. (Chap. 47.)
17. Overton, m Nancy Oldham. (Chap. 48.)

"D"

1. Robert, m Jael Ellison. (Chap. 17.)
2. Christopher, m Sallie Wallace. "E". (Chap. 28.)
3. Overton, m Mary Rice Woods. (Chap. 37.)
4. James, m Mourning Bennett. (Chap. 38.)
5. John. (Chap. 16, Sec. 5.)
6. William, m Malinda Duncan (Chap. 39.)
7. Elizabeth, m Anderson Woods. (Chap. 40.)
8. Frances, m James Miller. (Chap. 41.)
9. Susan, m Dr. Wm. H. Duncan. Chap. 42.)

"E"

1. Ann Eliza, m Robert Covington. (Chap. 29.)
2. Talitha, m Chris. Irvine Miller. (Chap.30 & Part I, Chap.13.)
3. James Anderson, m Susan Taylor. (Chap. 31.)
4. Christopher. (Chap. 32.)
5. John Miller Wallace. (Chap. 33.)
6. Polly, m Elder John M. Park. (Chap. 34.)
7. Margaret Frances, m Joseph Warren Moore. (Chap. 35.)
8. Sarah Overton, m Thomas M. Oldham. (Chap. 36.)

Article 2.—Early marriages in Madison County, Ky. gleaned from first Marriage Register of County Court.

Harris, James—Susannah, Gass, Dec. 2, 1790.
Harris, Lucy—Jones, Wm., Feb. 2, 1790.
Harris, Wm.—Oldham, Anna, Feb. 4, 1790.
Harris, Mary—Walker, John, Dec. 25, 1792.
Harris, Rebecca—Province, Andrew, Aug. 9, 1792.
Harris, Benjamin—Burgin, Nancy, June 14, 1792.
Harris, Isabel—Bennett, John, Oct. 2, 1794.
Harris, Parmarla—McCord, Robert, Dec. 31, 1795.
Harris, Samuel—Province, Sarah, Sept. 2, 1795.
Harris, Thomas—Barnes, Rachael, Dec. 7, 1796.
Harris, Thursa—Holland Allen March 8, 1796.
Harris, Nancy, Mrs.—Tevis, Nathaniel Aug. 8, 1797.
Harris, Foster—Manning, Sally, Oct, 19, 1797.
Harris, Anna—Leburn, Jacob, Feb. 28, 1799.
Harris, Mourning—Thorpe, Zacheriah, Oct. 17 1799.
Harris, Nancy—Thorpe, Josiah, Oct. 17, 1799.
Harris, Lucy—Wilkerson, Wm., Feb. 26, 1801.
Harris, Nancy—Woods, Wm., Sept. 25, 1802.
Harris, Higgason—Garland, Mary, Dec. 16, 1800.
Harris, Polly—Woods, Wm., June 5, 1802.
Harris, William Elliot,—Maunion, Mary, March 17, 1802.
Harris Tyre—Garland, Sally, June 2, 1803.
Harris, Barnabus—Oldham, Elizabeth, 19, 1803.
Harris, Nancy—Stone, Wm., Oct. 22, 1805.
Harris David—Cooksey, Nancy, May 30, 1805.
Harris, John—Warren, Jenny, March 21, 1805.
Harris, Samuel—Kennedy, Elizabeth, April 13, 1807.
Harris Tabitha—Joel, Bermam, March 16, 1809.
Harris, David—Maxwell, Nancy, Nov. 1, 1811.
Harris, Sally—David, Joseph, July 20, 1812.
Harris, Elizabeth—Rynot, James, Feb. 28, 1811.
Harris, Elizabeth—Davis Uriah, Nov. 29, 1813.
Harris, Jesse—Fowler, Jennina, Aug. 10 1813.
Harris, Robert—Taylor, Polly, July 7, 1814.
Harris, Becky—Dent, Bailey, April 13, 1815.
Harris, Weston—Delaney, Elizabeth, Feb. 2 1815.
Harris, Lavina—King, Henry, Nov. 11, 1815.
Harris, Robert—Lancaster, Elizabeth, July 3, 1815.
Harris, Nancy—Pasley, Henry, May 18, 1815.
Harris Wm.,—Smith, Anna, Dec. 5, 1816.
Harris, Polly—Richardson, Thomas, Dec. 25, 1816.
Harris, Milly—Sale Samuel, Nov. 21, 1820.
Harris, Elizabeth—Staguer, Richmond, June 21, 1821.
Harris, Nancy—Reed, Thomas, April 19, 1821.
Harris Leander—Clancker, Howard, Dec. 5, 1821.
Harris, Frances, M.,—Miller, James, July 24, 1823.
Harris, Margaret—Wright, Thomas, Jan. 1, 1824.
Harris, Paulina—Lancaster, Jeremiah, March 15, 1825.
Harris, Kettura,—Easter, Wm., Nov. 8 1827.
Harris, Elzira—Gordon, Jefferson, June 18, 1827.
Harris, John—Vaughn, Sally, Oct. 15, 1828.
Harris, Sherwood—Brumback, Theodosia, Oct. 22, 1829
Harris, John, C.,—Floyd, Sally, Nov. 11, 1830.
Harris, Agnes, M.,—Oldham, Milton, Feb. 3, 1831.
Harris, Mary—Wheeler, Wm., Feb. 4, 1830.

Harris Eliza—Stephen, B., Eubank, March 12, 1835.
Harris, Anderson—Araminta, Jane, Atkinson, Sept. 23, 1835.
Harris, Elizabeth—George Roberts, June 29, 1836.
Harris, Lemmy—Richard Tomlin, Oct. 3, 1836.
Harris, Thomas—Thursa Madison, Nov. 7, 1836.
Harris, Solon—Sallie Ann Miller, July 25, 1837.
Harris, Nancy—Anderson Chenault, Aug. 3, 1837.
Harris, Mary, Ann, E.—James Cooper, Aug. 10, 1837.
Harris, Sallie—Willis Tomlin, Sept. 6, 1836.
Harris, Hawkins—Didama Cradleburgh, Nov. 13, 1835.
Harris, Margaret—James Roberts, Jan. 24, 1840.
Harris, David—Elizabeth Moore, May 30, 1838.
Harris, Jael Kavanaugh—Martin B. Garvin, Oct. 17, 1841.
Harris, Gabriella—John Crigler, Oct. 20, 1840.
Harris, Lucien, J.—Sallie F. Bush, Dec. 8, 1832.
Harris, Talitha—Waller Chenault, Oct. 30, 1833.
Harris, Margaret—Simeon Hume, Dec. 6, 1838.
Harris, Sidney, W.—Mary A. E. Miller, Apr. 4, 1844.
Harris, Caroline—Michael L. Stoner, May 4, 1843.
Harris, Elizabeth—Joseph Pearson, July 21, 1847.
Harris, John, D.—Nancy Jane White, Sept. 20, 1849.
Harris, Malinda—Anderson Yates, Aug. 2, 1849.
Harris, Sarah—Thomas Oldham, Aug. 14, 1849.
Harris, Sallie W.—John E. Elmore, Nov. 24, 1853.
Harris, John K.—Mrs. Elizabeth K. Harris, Dec. 29, 1853.
Harris, Mrs. Elizabeth K.—John K. Harris, Dec. 29, 1853.
Harris, Christopher, C.—Frances J. Atkins, July 26, 1853.
Harris, Overton—Navmi Fielding, Feb. 3, 1842.
Harris, Christopher—Elizabeth Berry, Oct. 3, 1839.
Harris, James, A.—Susan A. Taylor, Jan. 1, 1845.
Harris, Nancy—Samuel Best, Aug. 15, 1846.
Harris, Frances—David A. Singleton, July 20, 1848.
Harris, Margaret—Joseph W. Moore, Feb. 9, 1848.
Harris, Shelton—Caroline Duncan, April 19, 1849.
Harris, Fannie—Thomas Coyle, Feb. 3, 1853.
Harris, Susan, M.—Benjamin F. Crooke, Dec. 22, 1853.
Harris, Mary W.—John M. Park, Jan. 15, 1852.
Harris, Talitha—Chris. Irvine Miller, Sept. 1, 1836.

Article 3.—Items connecting the Harris name with events, from History and Court records.

Section 1. The Muster Roll of Captain James Brown's Company of Mounted Ky., Volunteers in the United States service against the Wiaw Indians, commanded by Brigadier General Charles Scott, mustered in at the Rapids of the Ohio, June 15, 1791, by Captain B. Smith, 1st U. S. Regiment, shows therein the name Randolph Harris.

Section 2. Cynthiana, the County seat of Harrison County, was named for Cynthia and Anna, two daughters of the original proprietor, Robert Harris established Dec. 10, 1793, incorporated as a town in 1802, and was a city in 1860.

Section 3. Christopher Harris, (our ancestor) prior to 1790, located and entered claim to lands on the waters of Licking river, referred to in his will published in Chapter IV, as well as lands in Madison County, where he finally settled.

Section 4. Christopher Harris, junior, (son of the Christopher named in Article 3) was a pioneer Baptist preacher of Madison County, Ky.

Section 5. William B. Harris, was one of the Deputy Surveyors for James Thompson, the first surveyor of Lincoln County, appointed in Jan. 1781.

Section 6. Members of the Kentucky General Assembly.

In the Senate:

David K. Harris, from the County of Floyd, 1827-1834.
Henry C. Harris, from the County of Floyd, 1843-7.
Sylvester Harris, from the County of Meade, 1853-7.
John D. Harris, from the County of Madison, 1885-9.

In the House of Representatives:

William G. Harris, from the County of Simpson, 1826.
H. G. Harris, from the County of Simpson 1865-7.
Horatic T. Harris, from the County of Campbell, 1832.
John Harris, from the County of Madison, 1799.
Robert Harris, from the County of Madison, 1826-8.
Robert R. Harris, from the County of Madison, 1844.
William Harris, from the County of Madison, 1851-2.
Sylvester Harris, from the County of Meade, 1847.
Tyre Harris, from the County of Garrard, 1829-30.
John B. Harris, from the County of Johnson, 1848.

Section 7. June 24, 1788. "On motion of Christopher Harris; his ear mark towit: A crop, slit and under keel in the right ear, and slit and under keel in the left is ordered to be recorded."

August 26, 1788. "Ordered that Christopher Harris be exempt from paying a County levy for one black tythe more than he has."

Oct. 28, 1788. "Ordered that Alexander McKey, Christopher Harris and John Manion be appointed and authorized to celebrate the Rites of marriage in this County." And on the 23rd of Dec. following, Christopher Harris took the oath of fidelity, and gave bond.

Oct. 2, 1792, Christopher Harris, authorized to celebrate the Rites of marriage.

From these orders of the Court it seems that two Christopher Harrises, were ministers of the Gospel, and were authorized to solemnize the Rites of marriage, one in 1788, the other in 1792, probably father and son.

Section 8. March 5, 1789. "On motion of Thomas Harris, a Ferry is established in his name across the Kentucky river at the mouth of Sugar Creek, on the upper side thereof, and the rates of Ferriage to be as follows: For a man three pence, for a horse the same, and proportion for other things."

Section 9. March 6, 1798. "On the motion of Samuel Harris, his ear mark towit: A smooth crop in each ear, and a slit in the right was ordered to be recorded."

Section 10. Dec. 3, 1799. "Ordered that the following bounds be alloted to Robert Harris and David Thorpe, as Constables in the County, towit: Beginning at the mouth of Otter Creek, thence up the Otter Creek road to Archibald Woods, from thence with the Tates Creek road to the mouth of said Creek, thence up the Kentucky river to the beginning."

Section 11. The first station in what is now Shelby County, Ky., was established in 1779, and was Squire Boones station at the Painted Stone, and among the dwellers there at that time was Jeremiah Harris, (Collins.)

Section 12. David Harris was one of the seven first Justices of the Peace who organized the Allen County Court, April 10, 1815. (C)

Section 13. Isham G. Harris, born in Tennessee, in 1818 admitted to the bar in 1841, Tennessee Legislator 1849-53, Governor of the state from 1857 until its occupation by the Federal Army. He was Aide on General Johnston's staff, and served in the west throughout the war. He was U. S. Senator from 1877 until his death, July 18, 1897. (Amer. Cy.)

Section 14. Joel Chandler Harris, born in Georgia in 1848. He was admitted to the bar. Editor of the Atlanta, Georgia, Constitution, and author of "Uncle Remus, His Songs and Sayings," and other stories of Southern life.

Section 15. James Harris, an English philologist, born in Salisburg July 20, 1709, died Dec. 22, 1780. He was educated at Oxford, as gentleman Commoner, and thence passed as a student of law to Lincoln's Inn. His father died when he was twenty four years of age, leaving him a fortune, so that he abandoned the law, retired to his native town, and devoted himself to more congenial pursuits. He was elected to parliament for the borough of Christ Chuch 1761, and filled that seat during the rest of his life. In 1762, he was appointed one of the Lords of the Admiralty, and in the following year a Lord of the Treasury, but went out of office with the change of Administration in 1765. In 1774 he was appointed Secretary and Comptroller to the Queen. In 1744, he published "Three Treatises: I. Art. II. Music, Painting, and Poetry, III, Happiness, and in 1751, his famous work, "Hernies, or a Philisophical Inquiry concerning Universal Grammar," which has been considered a model of ingenious analysis and clear exposition. Lowth claiming for it, that it is the best specimen of analysis since the time of Aristotle. In 1775, he published "Philisophical Arrangements" as a part of a projected work, upon the "Logic" of Aristotle. His "Philisophical Inquiries" was published after his death in 1781. His collected works were published in 1792. A fine edition with a biography was published by his son in 1801. (Amer-Cyclo)

Section 16. John Harris an English Clergyman, born at Ugborough Devonshire in 1804, died in London Dec. 21, 1856. He studied Divinity, in Haxton Independent College, and became pastor of the Independent church in Epsom. When in 1850, it was determined to consolidate the various independent colleges in and about the Metropolis into one, he was chosen principal of the new institution called New College in which he was also professor of theology. While at Epsom he wrote his prize Essay against covetousness, under the title of "Mammon, in 1836." Other works written for prizes were "Britannia" 1837, an appeal in aid of the objects of the British and foreign sailors society, and "The Great Commission" 1842, an essay on Christian Missions. His most important works are "The Pre-Adamite Earth" 1847, "Man Primeval" 1849, and "Patriarchy, or the Family, its Constitution and Probation," 1855. (Amer-Cy.)

Section 17. Thadeus William Harris, an American Naturalist, born in Dorchester, Mass. Nov. 12, 1795, died in Cambridge, Jan. 16, 1856. He graduated at Harvard College. In 1815, studied Medicine, and practiced his profession at Milton Hill till 1831, when he was appointed Librarian of Harvard College. For several years he gave instructions in botany and general Natural History, in the College, and he originated the Howard Natural History Society for the students. He was chiefly distinguished as an entomologist. In 1837 he was appointed one of the Commissioners for a Zoological and botanical survey of Massachusetts, the result of which was his systematic catalogue of the insects of Massachusetts, appended to Prof. Hitchcock's report. In 1841, appeared his "Report on insects injurious to Vegatation" published by the Legislature It was repeated in 1852, some what enlarged and a new and enlarged edition by Charles L. Flint with engravings drawn under the supervision of Prof. Agassiz, by direction of the Legislature appeared in 1862. (Amer-Cy)

Section 18. Thomas Lake Harris an American Reformer born at Finny Stratford, England, May 15, 1823. He was brought to America when four years old by his father who engaged in Mercantile pursuits in Utica, N. Y. By his mother's death and financial reverses he was thrown from boyhood on his own efforts for education and support. He from a very early age, had strong religious tendencies, became a great reformer, and organized the society "Brotherhood of the New Life."

Section 19. William Harris, an American Clergyman, born in Springfield, Mass., April 29, 1765, died Oct. 18, 1829. He graduated at Harvard College in 1786, was ordained priest in the Episcopal Church in 1792, and took charge at once of the Church and Academy in Marblehead, Mass. In 1802 he became Rector of St. Marks Church, in N. Y. where he established a classical school. He was chosen in 1811 to succeed Bishop Moore, as president of Columbia College, and for six years retained his rectorship in connection with this office. He was assisted in the duties of the presidency by Dr. J. M. Mason, under the title of provost, an office which was established in 1816, from which time until his death, Dr. Harris devoted himsely entirely to the college. (A-C)

Section 20. William Torrey Harris, an American philosopher, born in Killingly, Conn., Sept. 10, 1835. He entered Yale College in 1854, but did not graduate. The degree of A. M. was conferred upon him by the College in 1869. In 1857 he went to St. Louis, and in the following year became a teacher in one of the public schools. Ten years later he was made Superintendent of Schools, a post which he was holding in 1874. He was one of the founders of the philosophical society of St. Louis in 1866, and in 1867, established the Journal of Speculative Philosophy, a quarterly magazine, and to which he contributed many philosophical articles of his own, besides translations of the principal works of Hegel. The Journal has also published translations from Liebnitz, Descartes, Kent, Fichte and Schilling, and from recent German and Italian philosophers, and many remarkable papers on art. In 1874, Mr. Harris was elected President of the ational Teacher's Association. (A-C.)

Section 21. The first permanent settlement on the site of Harrisburg, Pennsylvania, was made about 1726, by an Englishman, named John Harris, who in Dec. 1733, obtained from the proprietaries of Pennsylvania a grant of 300 acres of land, near his residence, and purchased of others 300 acres adjoining. He carried on a considerable trade with the indians of the vicinity. In 1752, the Penns granted to his son, John Harris junior, the right to establish a ferry over the Susquehanna, and the place was long known as Harris Ferry. It became the Capital of the state in 1812, and received a city charter in 1860. (A-C.)

Section 22. Samuel Harris of Virginia known as "Father Harris" and sometimes addressed as "Colonel," was a Baptist minister and often moderator of the meetings and associations of the Virginia Baptists, who opposed the unholy union of church and state taxation to support the established church, and her clergy and the glebes, and presented many petitions and memorials to the law making power, in their valiant fight for religious liberty.

One of his meetings in Culpeper was invaded by a band of opposers, headed by Captain Ball, to prevent his preaching bringing on a scuffle and tumult, closing the meeting in confusion. On another occasion while preaching at Ft. Mayo, he was summarily interrupted and outrageously accosted. These were turbulent times in old Virginia for Baptist preachers, who were struggling for a better day to come. He and his co-workers, and contemporaries, such as Elders, John Burrus, John Young, Ed Herndon, James Goodrich, Bartholomew Choning, John Waller, William Webber, James Greenwood, Robert Ware, Jeremiah Moore, David Barrow, Lewis Craig, Elijah Craig, John Dulaney, James Childs, Nathaniel Saunders, William M. Clannahan, John Corbley, Thomas Ammon, Anthony Moffett, John Pickett, Adam Banks, Thomas Maxfield, Jeremiah Walker, John Weatherford, David Tinsley, John Shackelford, Ivison Lewis, John Tannor, David Thomas, Augustine Eastin and others, and the Baptist societies they represented were in derision called and referred to in such reproachful names as "disturbers of the peace," "ignorant and illiterate set," "poor and contemptible class," "schismatics" "false prophets," "wolves in sheeps clothing," "perverters of good order" "callers of unlawful assamblics," for the purpose of casting odium upon them, but they patiently endured all, and stood firm in the Lord, suffering persecutions, imprisonments, and fines for conscience sake, and trusting in the salvation of the Lord, fought, bravely for civil, as well as religious liberty, contesting every step of ground, which was most gloriously won. No other religious society stood so firm and unrelenting, in the struggle as did the Baptists, conspicious among whom was Samuel Harris, the subject of this sketch.

Section 23. List of towns, creeks, etc., named for Harris found on Map:

State	
New Hampshire—	Harrisville.
	Harrisville Lake.
New York—	Harrisburg.
	Harris Hill.
	Harrison.
	Harrisville.
Maryland—	Harris Creeek.
	Harris Lot.
Virginia—	Harris.
	Harris Creek.
	Harriston.
	Harrisville.
South Carolina—	Harris Springs.
Georgia—	Harris.
	Harrisburg.
	Harris City.
Mississippi—	Harris Bayou.
	Harriston.
	Harrisville.
Kentucky—	Harris.
	Harrisburg.
	Harris Grove.

Indiana—	Harris.
	Harrisburg.
	Harriston.
	Harristown.
	Harrisville.
Wisconsin—	Harrisville.
Minnesota—	Harris.
Iowa—	Harris.
Arkansas—	Harris.
	Harrisburg.
Texas—	Harris County.
	Harris.
	Harrisburg.
	Harris Creek.
	Harris Ferry.
Colorado—	Harris.
	Harrisburg.
California—	Harris. C-6.
	Harris. J-17.
Washington—	Harriston.
Massachusetts—	Harris.
Rhode Island.	Harrisville.
New Jersey—	Harris.
	Harrisia.
Pennsylvania—	Harris. I-21.
	Harris. K-22.
	Harrisburg.
	Harrisville.
	Harrisville Station.
West Virginia—	Harris Ferry.
	Harrisville.
North Carolina—	Harris Mines.
	Harrisville.
	Harris.
Alabama—	Harris. B-6.
	Harris. I-11.
	Harrisburg.
Tennessee—	Harris.
	Harrisburg.
Ohio—	Harris.
	Harrisburg. C-18.
	Harrisburg. J-18.
	Harris Station.
Illinois—	Harris.
	Harrisburg.
	Harristown.
Michigan—	Harris.
	Harrisburg.
	Harrisville.
Missouri—	Harris.
	Harrisburg.
	Harriston.
Indian Territory	Harris.
Kansas—	Harris.
Nebraska—	Harrisburg.
South Dakota—	Harrisburg.
Montana—	Harris.
Utah—	Harrisville.

Arizona—	Harrisburg.
Oregon- -	Harris.
	Harrisburg.
Florida-	Harris Lake.

CHAPTER 2.

THE HARRIS FAMILY.

Article 1.—The ancestor of this family came to America from Wales, probably near the middle of the seventeenth century, and settled in the Colony of Virginia. The stock being Anglo-Welsh.

In the period 1780-1790, there was a great migratory movement from Virginia and other states to the new and fertile regions of Kentucky, "The Dark and Bloody Ground." Among the emigrants from Albemarle and adjacent counties of Virginia, were Christopher Harris, senior, his second wife, Agnes McCord, besides a greater number of his sons and daughters, in two sets, numbering in all seventeen and a host of grand children, who composed an amazing throng for one family to swell the population of the new country, some of whom were in Kentucky as early as 1783, many at later dates moved to the Territory of Missouri. Christopher Harris, Sr. travelled a great deal over the Kentucky wilds and entered lands on the waters of the Licking river, but settled and established his home in Madison County, Kentucky, where he owned lands on Silver, Muddy and Downing Creeks, in addition to a large body of land in Albemarle, and he owned a number of negro slaves, which he had brought to Kentucky.

Schedule of his family who came besides collateral branches of the Harris family.

Robert Harris, (wife Nancy Grubbs) Elder Christopher Harris, (wife Elizabeth Grubbs) John Harris, (wife Margaret Maupin) Benjamin Harris, (first wife, Miss Jones, second wife, Nancy Burgin) William Harris; (wife Anna Oldham) Barnabas Harris; (wife Elizabeth Oldham) James Harris; (wife Susannah Gass) Samuel Harris; (wife Nancy Wilkerson) Overton Harris; (wife Nancy Oldham) Mournin Harris, husband, Foster Jones, and her children, Tyre Harris Jones, Mosias Jones, Nancy Jones, Christopher Jones, Elizabeth Jones, Lucy Jones. Tyre Harris; (wife Sallie Garland) Higgason Harris; (wife Nancy Garland(Sarah Harris, and husband, James Martin, and children, Tyre Martin, Robert Martin; (wife Polly Noland) Nathan Martin, Mary Martin and husband, J. Pleasant Profit, young David Martin, son of James Martin deceased. Thomas Harris; (wife Mary Ann Booten) Robert Harris; (wife Mary Taylor) Robert Harris; (wife Jael Ellison) Christopher Harris (wife Sallie Wallace) Mary Harris, and husband, George Jones, Jane Harris and husband, Richard Gentry, all children, and children in law, and grand children of Christopher Harris, senior, besides a number of his negro slaves, and collateral branches, viz:

Randolph Harris, of Captain Brown's company against the Wiaw Indians, in 1791. Sherwood Harris, James Harris, Sterling Harris, (wife Silva) and son, Solomon Harris, and brother, Benjamin Harris, William Harris, Thomas Harris, (wife Rachael) Weston Harris, (wife Elizabeth Dulaney) Samuel Harris, William Harris, (wife Mary Manion) David Harris, (wife Nancy Cooksey) John Harris;

(wife Jennie Warren) and Foster Harris, (wife Sallie Manning) and others. (See notes.) All came to Kentucky prior to 1790 (some of whom were here several years before said date) from their old Virginia homes, and travelled the wilderness road. Some of them married in Kentucky; one married in Madison County, Ky.

Note—Since the above was written we are indebted to Mrs. Cassius M. Clay, of Paris, Ky., for the following additional facst:

"Major Robert Harris was a member of the Virginia House of Burgesses from Hanover County, 1736-1738, 1740-1742, and Justice of the Peace of Louisa County in 1742, and Surveyor in 1744.

"His wife, Mary Rice nee Claiborne, was a daughter of Secretary William Claiborne who came to Virginia with George Wyant in 1621. William Claiborne was born in 1587, and died in 1676, he married Elizabeth Butler. He was secretary of state in Virginia in 1625-1635, 1652-1660, treasurer in 1642-1660. Surveyor Gentry in 1621-1625. He was a Justice of the Peace of York and Northumberland in 1653. Member of the Council in 1623. In 1629 he commanded an expedition against the indians; again in 1644, he did the same. In the Northampton records, April 1653, is an order referring to the worshipful Colonel William Claiborne Esq. Deputy Governor. "Temperance Overton, (the wife of William Harris) came to this country with three brothers and settled in Virginia. She was a daughter of William Overton, and Mary Waters, William Overton was a Colonel under Oliver Cromwell, and commanded one wing of the army at the battle of Dunbar; for some cause he was cast into the Tower of London by Cromwell, and died there."

Article 2.—One Robert Harris of Wales, (1630-1700) about 1650, married Mrs. Rice, whose maiden name was Claibourne, daughter of Secretary William Claiborne, to whom was born, in 1752, a son, William Harris.

They came to America, and settled in the Colony of Virginia, on the James River, near Weyanoke. The said William Harris, married Temperance Overton, a daughter of a wealthy tobacco grower, William Overton, and Mary Walters, his wife. The said William Overton, was a son of Colonel —— Overton, who commanded a Brigade of Iron sides under Oliver Cromwell.

William Harris became also a tobacconist, raising and dealing in that weed, which was at that time a medium of exchange, and became fairly well off in this world's goods, but he died before he reached old age, and a bronze tablet and stone, marked the resting place of his mortal remains. From this emigrant, sprang our American family, the blood courses, in the veins of hundreds and hundreds of families and persons of other names, scattered all over America and elsewhere. The family as such is noted for courage, brain, strength, and industry, endurance, honesty, and influence; many have held, and many yet hold high positions or trust, in political, in economical, in agriculturaal and in commercial industry, in the ministry fearless, but God-fearing servants, in the various branches of learning, in the army, in the navy, and in every calling and profession, some noted lawyers, some famous as physicians, some humorous and learned writers.

William Harris, died March 8, 1687, at the age of thirty five years. His remains were buried in an old Colonial church at Weyanoke on the James river, and a bronze tablet, commemorating his death and age marked his burial place. The old church long since going to ruins, on the first of July 1875 the tablet was removed to Norfolk, Va., and placed in the walls of St. Pauls old church. Engraved on the tablet is the following.

"Here lyeth ye body of

William Harris

who departed this life ye 8th day of March, 1687

Aged 35 years.

On the 1st day of July, 1875, this stone and tablet was brought from Weyanoke, on the James River. It was found among ruins of an old Colonial Church."

Proof is sufficient for stating that said tablet marked the grave of our ancestor.

To William Harris, and his wife, Temperance Overton, were born three sons:

Section 1. Christopher Harris.

Section 2. Major Robert Harris. He married Mourning Glenn. He died in Brown's Cove, Albemarle County, Va., in 1765. A fuller history of whom is given in Chapter 3.

Section 3. Overton Harris; married Anne Nelson. The subject of Chapter 49.

Notes from Madison County Court Records:

July 6, 1795, Benjamin Harris and wife Nancy (nee Burgin) conveyed to Evan Watson, 72 acres of land on Muddy Creek, about two miles form Mulberry Lick. The deed was not acknowledged by the wife till 1809.

Oct. 1, 1814. Their daughter Polly Harris conveyed her one third interest in 34 acres, Sept. 25, 1815, to Overton Harris. Their other children, Tyre Harris, and Nancy Harris and her husband, Henry Pasley, conveyed to Overton Harris their two thirds as heirs of Benjamin Harris' deed, in lands on Otter Creek.

Feb. 1, 1808, Barnabas Harris, and wife Elizabeth (nee Oldham) conveyed to Evan Watson 135 acres on Muddy Creek, deed not acknowledged by wife till March 21, 1809. The first date they also conveyed to John Harris, 50 acres on Muddy Creek, adjoining Evan Watson, John Harris and William Harris.

Sept. 6, 1809. Barnabas Harris executed a power of attorney to Overton Harris, (his brother) to settle his business, and convey to Samuel McMullens, his interest of one half of 800 acres entered in the name of his father (Christopher Harris) on Hinkston's Fork of Licking in Bourbon, County, Ky.

Sept. 1, 1809. Samuel Harris and wife, (Nancy nee Wilkerson,) conveyed to James Jones, 150 acres on Paint Lick Creek, part of William Van Cleaves patent of 720 acres. Aug. 4, 1830. They conveyed to Richard Fowler, land in Madison County, Ky. Sept. 21, 1831. They conveyed to Edwin Phelps, the farm upon which they were living on Calloways Creek.

Dec. 2, 1809. Richard Gentry, and wife Jane (nee Harris), Christopher Harris, John Harris, Thomas Burgin, guardian of Polly Harris, infant (child) of Benjamin Harris deceased, William Harris, Margaret Harris, John Bennett and wife, Isabella (nee Harris) Samuel Harris, Barnabas Harris and Overton Harris, heirs and devises of Christopher Harris, deceased, conveyed to Samuel McMullens, and James Guthrie, 600 out of 1200 acres on Hinkston's Fork of Licking in Bourbon County, Ky.

Sept. 5, 1816. William Harris and wife Anna (nee Oldham) conveyed to John Speed Smith 42 acres on Muddy Creek.

Jan. 1, 1799. Inventory and appraisement of the estate of James Harris, who died in 1797-8, was made by Colonel John Miller and Robert Rodes, and returned to the Court.

Aug. 4,, 1814. Christopher Harris and wife Sallie (nee Wallace) conveyed to James Reid 24 acres, 2 roods, and 14 poles, on Mud Branch of Otter Creek, which Michael Wallace lived and died possessed of (near Richmond).

May 5, 1816. Robert Harris and wife (nee Grubbs) conveyed to Frances Stone 85 acres, 2 roods, and 28 poles, on Tates Creek.

1799. Christopher Harris, and wife, Elizabeth (nee Grubbs) conveyed to William Shackelford 100 acres, on Muddy Creek.

April 3, 1815. They conveyed to Zachariah Thorpe, (their son-in-law) 25 acres, including the Mill and Mill seat of said Thorpe on Muddy Creek.

Aug. 29, 1797. James Harris conveyed to John Mullens, Jr. the land conveyed to grantor by Green Clay, adjoining James Berry and others.

Dec. 2, 1790. James Harris married Susannah Gass, (daughter of David Gass, and Sarah, his wife.) In 1796 James Harris was riding along the road between Silver Creek and the residence of David Gass in company with Squire Boone (brother to Colonel Daniel Boone) conversing about old times and the old mill seat of Squire Boone at St. Asaph's, and Gerusha's Grove, on Silver Creek, and he told Boone of the black walnut tree upon which Boone had cut his letters S. B. in 1775, which circumstance Boone had not forgotten. Shortly after this conversation, towit: April 29, 1796, Squire Boone gave his deposition at St. Asaphs, and Gerusha's Grove in regard to the land, and the letters and date on the trees.

David Gass died in 1806, and in his will he mentions his children towit: John Gass, William Gass, James Gass, David Gass, Mary Black, (and her children, Amy, Eleanor, James and David) Margaret Gass wife of John Mitchell, (and her son James) Thomas Gass, Susannah Harris and Sarah Black.

Sept. 25, 1807. James Harris, John Mitchell and David Gass, executed a power of attorney to John Gass, of Bourbon County, Ky. to prosecute suits etc. in their name etc.

Oct. 5, 1807. James Harris and wife Susannah, executed a quit claim deed to David Gass, as heir of David Gass, sr., deceased to land on Silver Creek.

Oct. 16, 1807. They conveyed to James White 60 acres on the east side of Muddy Creek.

Aug. 20, 1798. Edward Harris of Newburn, North Carolina, conveyed to James Harris 750 acres on both sides of Muddy Creek, witnesses, James Harris, Archibald Harris and Andrew Province.

Sept. 12, 1795. Samuel Harris; married Sarah Province.

Dec. 1, 1800. James Harris conveyed to Higgason Grubbs, all his right to land on west side of Muddy Creek, granted to Edward Harris and conveyed by Edward Harris to James Harris.

Dec. 14, 1809. James Harris of Albemarle conveyed to Jesse Noland 50 acres on Tates Creek. Dec. 28, 1809. he conveyed to

William Boone 17 acres, and to Jesse Noland 20 acres on the same waters. (See Chap. 3, Sec. 4.)

Aug. 17, 1809. Andrew Harris and wife Ede, by Joseph Kennedy agent in fact of Williamson County, Tenn. conveyed to Thomas C. Ballard 77 acres on Paint Lick Creek.

July 3, 1792. Sherwood Harris, wife Henrietta Harris, acknowledged deed to Barney Stagner per certificate of John Harris and Asa Searcy.

Dec. 6, 1798. Joel Harris, of Albemarle County, Va., executed a power of attorney to John Harris, Daniel Maupin and James Berry to act for him and convey lands etc. Nov. 17, 1807, the said Joel Harris conveyed to Daniel Maupin an undivided moiety of 1000 acres on waters of Cow Creek and Indian Creek, emptying into the Salt Spring Fork of Licking granted to Joel Harris June 26, 1799, witnesses, John Patrick, John Harris and William Dulaney,and other conveyances as follows: 200 acres to Joseph Holdman, 200 acres to Richard Johnson in the forks of Tates Creek, and 200 acres to John Denham, adjoining above. April 10, 1817, Daniel Maupin attorney in fact for Joel Harris of Albermarle conveyed to Samuel Robinson 288½ acres on Muddy Creek. (See Chap. 111, Sec. IV.)

Dec. 7, 1796. Thomas Harris; married Rebecca Barnes.

Aug. 28, 1804. Thomas Harris conveyed to William Titus 40 acres on Silver Creek.

April 1, 1805. Henry Harris for love and affection conveyed to Elizabeth Eastes 91 acres on Downing Creek.

Feb. 21, 1815. Henry Harris and wife Anna for love and affection conveyed to Bettie Jameson 114 acres on Downing Creek.

Sept. 4, 1806. Thompson Harris executed an obligation in trust for his wife, Fannie (probably Fannie Jones) Children:

1. Wiley Rodes Harris.
2. Tempe Barnes Harris.

Oct. 2, 1809. Thompson Harris and wife Fannie conveyed to George Hubbard, 135 acres in the forks of lower Woods Fork of Muddy Creek.

Oct. 17, 1817. They conveyed to Archibald Woods, 150 acres (excepting 50) on Woods Fork of Muddy Creek, the same land conveyed by the latter to John Wilburn and by the latter to Thompson Harris.

Sept. 29, 1813. William Harris and wife Jane of Jessamine County, Ky., conveyed to Reason Nichols 55 acres on the Kentucky river.

June 19, 1818. John Harris and wife, Polly conveyed to Gideon Gooch, 60 acres on Baughs Branch of Silver Creek.

May 30, 1805. David Harris; married Nancy Cooksey.

Nov. 1, 1811. David Harris; married Nancy Maxwell.

Oct. 28, 1819. David B. Harris, and wife Nancy conveyed to Tandy C. Page 140 acres on Silver Creek.

Oct. 1, 1796. Mosias Jones executed a power of attorney to his son, Thomas Jones of Greenbrier County, Va. to convey 130 acres to James Kincaid.

Jan. 8 1808, Mosias Jones' will probated, May 2, 1808, children: William Jones given land on Otter Creek, adjoining Isaac Newland, Lucy Maupin, Mosias Jones, Foster Jones, Frances Harris, Elizabeth Daverson, George Jones, Ann Gamison, Thomas Jones, Roger Jones, Sarah Curroum, and John Jones, witnesses, Martin Gentry, Moses Bennett and John Maupin.

April 13, 1816. Inventory of estate of William Jones, deceased made.

Nov. 15, and 27, 1814. Foster Jones (wife Peggy;) Inventories of his estate made, by John Brown, Thomas Collins, Samuel Gilbert and William Douglas, widow, Peggy, alloted dower of negroes.

Dec. 3, 1796. Foster Jones and wife, Mourning (nee Harris) conveyed to Margaret Black, of Woodford County, 37¾ acres on Otter Creek.

Nov. 16, 1797. Thomas Jones of Franklin County, Va. conveyed to representatives of Jesse and Hosea Cook, of Franklin County, Ky. 400 acres on Silver Creek in Madison County, Ky.

Feb. 25, 1814. Robert Jones deceased, inventory made.

June 3, 1815. Elizabeth Jones, deceased, inventory made.

July 21, 1815. James Jones will probated Feb. 5, 1816, brothers, Humphrey and William, besides other brothers and sisters not named.

June 1, 1826. Irvine Jones, deceased, inventory made, wife Rachael alloted dower, Nov. 6, 1826.

CHAPTER 3.

MAJOR ROBERT HARRIS.

(Named in Chap. 2, Sec. 2.)

Article 1.—Major Robert Harris, a son of William Harris, the emigrant, who came from Wales, and Temperance Overton, his wife, was born about the year 168-, and his home was in Virginia, Brown's Cove, Albemarle County.

He married Mourning Glenn. She was a remarkable woman, kind, generous, charitable, a devout christian, and much beloved by her acquaintances and offspring. Her children and descendants down through the generations gave a daughter her name "Mourning, showing their high estimation of Mourning Glenn Harris.

Note—Glenn.

1. David Glenn and Thomas Glenn were of Captain James Harrod's Company, of thirty one men, who in May 1774, came down the Monongahela and Ohio rivers in canoes to the mouth of the Kentucky river, and up it to the mouth of Landing Run, (Oregon) in Mercer County, east of where Salvisa is, thence across to Salt River near McAffe's station, and up it to Fountain Blue, and on to where Harrodsburg is. (Harrods Station.)

2. David Glenn was one of Captain James Harrod's Company, of thirty men, who on Jan. 2, 1777, went from Harrodsburg by McClellon's Fort, (Georgetown) the Lower Blue Licks, and Mayslick, and struck the Ohio river near the mouth of Cabin Creek, for gun powder, which they obtained and returned with to Harrodsburg.

3. David Glenn, was a resident of Harrods Fort, 1777-8.

4. Moses F. Glenn, legislator from Nicholas County, Ky. 1837-9.

5. Robert E. Glenn, state senator from Todd County, Ky. 1859-1863.

6. Robert E. Glenn, legislator from Todd County, 1843-6.

7. William Glenn, representative from Daviess County, Ky. 1817.

8. William Glenn of the Flemingsburg Messenger 1849-51, and the Pittsburg, (Illinois) Bugle, 1851-56.

9. Glennsfork, a town in Adair County.

Major Robert Harris, took up land in Brown's Cove, in Albemarle County in 1750, he was one of the early settlers on Doyle's River. He obtained patent for more than 3000 acres in that vicinity. He died in 1765. His will bears date June 18, 1765, probated Aug. 8, 1765, in words and figures as follows towit:

"In the name of God, Amen. I Robert Harris of the County of Albemarle, being of perfect mind, and memory, do make and ordain this my last will and testament, in manner and form following: first and principally I recommend my soul to God, who gave it me, not doubting but through the merits of my blessed saviour to have full pardon and remission of my sins, and my body, I recommend to the earth from whence it came, to be buried in such manner, as my executors hereafter named shall see fit. And as touching such temporal estate as it hath pleased God to bestow on me, I give and dispose of in manner and form following. Imprimis: I give and bequeath to my son, Christopher Harris forty acres of woodland, ground lying and being in the County of Albemarle, on a large spur of the Blue Ridge of Mountains near to a place commonly called and known by the name of the "Bear cornfield," to him and his heirs and assigns forever.

Item: I give and bequeath to my son, William Harris, after the decease of my loving wife, Morning (Mourning) Harris, all the land which I hold in the County of Albemarle to him and his heirs forever.

Item: I leave to my loving wife Mourning Harris, the sole use and benefit of all the lands and plantations during her natural life, which is above given to my son, William Harris after her decease.

Item: I leave to the said loving wife, the sole use and benefit during her natural life, six slaves, that is to say, Harry, Peter Dick and Aaron, men, Patta and Nanny, women.

Item: My will and desire is, after the decease of my wife, that if my negro man, Harry should be then living, in that case I give and bequeath the said Harry, to my son, Robert Harris, junior, to him and his heirs.

Item: My will and desire is, after the decease of my wife, that if my negro man, Peter, should be then living, in that case I give and bequeath the said Peter to my son, Tyre Harris, to him and his heirs.

Ietm: My will and desire is, after the decease of my wife, that if my other four negroes, Dick and Aaron, men, and Patta and Nanny, women, be then living, I give and bequeath them and their increase to my son, William Harris, to him and his heirs.

Item: My will and desire is, that if my son, William Harris should die before he attains the lawful age, or without issue, that in that case, he the said William Harris should be further educated, the charges thereof shall be paid out of the estate given him, after the whole being sold, by my executors herein after named, and the remainder of the money arising from such sale be equally divided amongst all my children, or their legal representatives.

Item: My will and desire is, that my son William Harris to be under the tuition, direction and government of my son-in-law, John Rodes, until he shall attain to lawful age.

Item: I give and bequeath to my loving wife, when all my lawful debts, and funeral expenses is paid all the residue of my estate, be it of whatever nature or quality soever, to her and her heirs forever. I do constitute and nominate and appoint my sons-in-law, John Rodes and William Shelton, to be my executors of this my last will and testament. As witness my hand and seal this eighteenth day of June in the year of Our Lord, one thousand seven hundred and sixty five.

(Signed) Robert Harris. (L. S.)

Signed, sealed, etc., in the presence of Daniel Maupin, John Mullins, James William Maupin, Courtley Mullins.

At a Court held for Albemarle County, the 8th day of Aug. 1765, this will presented in Court, proved by the oath of Daniel Maupin and William Maupin witnesses thereto, and ordered to be recorded, and on the motion of John Rodes and William Shelton, the executors therein named, certificate is granted them for obtaining a probate thereof, in due form on giving security. Whereupon they with David Rodes and Christopher Harris their securites entered into and acknowledged their bond according to law.

Teste, Henry Frye, C.

A copy, Teste, W. L. Maupin, Clerk.

Major Robert Harris, and his wife Mourning Glenn, had ten children, towit:

Section 1. Christopher Harris: married first Mary Dabney, and second, Agnes McCord. For further particulars see Chapter 4.

Section 2. Robert Harris, was a Captain of Virginia state milita in the Revolutionary war. He married Lucretia Brown, a daughter of Benjamin Brown senior, and Sarah Dabney his wife of Albemarle (See Part VIII, Chap. 11, Sec. 7.) He emigrated to Surry County, North Carolina, where he died in 1796.

Section 3. Tyre Harris, emigrated to Caswell County, North Carolina, where in 1783 he was deeded real estate by Jesse Oldham and wife, Elizabeth. (See Part VI, Chap. 11.)

Section 4. James Harris; married Mary Harris of Albemarle. He died in 1792. They had ten children, viz:

1. Thomas Harris: married Susan Dabney. (See Chap. XV, Sec. 11.)

2. Joel Harris, of Albemarle, was appointed a Justice of the Peace in 1801, was commissioner of Revenue of said County, from about 1811, till his death in 1826. He patented and owned 1000 acres of land on the waters of Cow Creek and Indian Creek, emptying into Salt Spring Fork of Licking, Ky., granted to him June 26, 1799, besides large tracts in Madison County, Ky., on the waters of Muddy Creek, and Tates Creek. On Dec. 6, 1798, said Joel Harris of Albemarle County, Va., executed a power of attorney to John Harris, Daniel Maupin and James Berry, of Madison County, Ky., creating them his attorney in fact etc.

Nov. 17, 1807, he conveyed to Daniel Maupin the undivided moiety of the 1000 acres on Cow and Indian Creeks branches of the Licking river, (the deed witnessed by John Patrick, John Harris and William Dulaney) and on the same date he made the following conveyances: 200 acres to Joseph Holdman in Madison County, and 200 acres to Richard Johnson in the forks of Tates Creek in Madison County, Ky., and 200 acres to John Denham adjoining above. April 10, 1817, Daniel Maupin attorney in fact for Joel Harris of Albemarle, conveyed to Samuel Robinson 288½ acres on Muddy Creek, in Madison County, Ky. (See notes

Chap. 11) Joel Harris, married Anna ——. They had four children, three sons, and a daughter, viz:

1. Ira Harris; married Sarah Lewis, daughter of Howell Lewis of Albemarle. He died in 1863. Issue of marriage:

1. Charles Warren Harris, born Feb. 15, 1822; married Angeline Mildred Brown, May 16, 1853. (See Part VIII, Chap. 14, Section 8.) He died April 23, 1850, and afterwards his widow married John Harris Miller, of Lincoln County, Ky. (See Part 1, Chap. VIII, Sec. V.) The children of Charles W. Harris and Angeline M. Brown were:

1. Mary Howell Harris; born Sept. 15, 1854; died Jan. 12, 1857.

2. Charles Lee Harris; born July 24, 1857; when grown purchased a farm near Stanford in Lincoln County, Ky., where he died several years ago.

2. Benjamin Harris; died unmarried.
3. Lewis Harris; died unmarried.
4. Waller Harris; married Mary Frances Brown, daughter of Bezaleel Brown, (See Part VIII, Chap. XI, Sec. VII.)
5. Mary Ann Harris; married Burlington Dabney Brown. (See Part VIII, Chap. XIV, Sec. 11.)

2. Joel Harris.
3. Clifton Nathan Harris; married Mary Lewis daughter of Howell Lewis of Albemarle, moved to Lexington, Va., where he made his home till his death.

3. Nathan Harris; married —— ——. Of their children were:
1. Hon. John T. Harris.
2. Rev. William A. Harris, for many years principal of the Female Seminary at Staunton, Virginia.

4. James Harris; married Mary McCullock, daughter of John McCullock, and Mary —— his wife. He was appointed a Justice of the Peace of Albemarle County in 1807. In 1822 he sold his property and moved to another part of the Country. (See notes Chap. 11.)

5. Lucy Harris; married Thomas Grubbs, who in 1758, was in actual service against the Indians on the Virginia frontier.

6. Mourning Harris; married Cornelius Maupin. (See Part V, Chap. IV, Sec. 111.)

7. Sarah Harris; married James Harrison, son of Richard Harrison and his wife, Mary, daughter of Peter Clarkson.

8. Susan Harris; married Nicholas Burnley. They had three children, viz:
1. James Harris Burnley, moved to Pickaway County, Ohio.
2. Joel Burnley; moved to Pickaway County, Ohio.
3. Mary Burnley; married John T. Wood.

9. Ann Harris; married Mr. Hayden.
10. Jane Harris; married Cornelius Dabney. (See Chap. 15.)

Section 5. William Harris; married Hannah Jameson. He died in 1776, and his widow married Daniel Maupin, being his third wife. (See Part V, Chap. IV, Sec. 11.)

Section 6. Lucy Harris; maried William Shelton, who was an executor of Robert Harris will probated in 1765. He survived his wife and married secondly Sarah ——. William Shelton was a signer of the Albemarle Declaration of Independence of April 21, 1779.

He died in 1803. The children of Lucy Harris and William Shelton:

1. William Harris Shelton, emigrated from Albemarle to Kentucky.

2. Mourning Shelton; married Archibald Woods (See Part 11, Chap. 8.) They emigrated from Albemarle to Madison County, Kentucky.

3. Dabney Shelton, sold out in 1817 to Francis McGee, in which year he was living in Augusta County, Va.

4. Sarah Shelton; died.

5. Lucy Shelton; married Elliott Brown.

6. Agnes Shelton; died.

7. Weatherston Shelton; married Elizabeth Harrison and moved to Mason County, Va.

8. Thomas Shelton, sold out in 1817, to Francis McGee, at the time was living in Augusta County.

Note--Rev. Edgar Woods, in his History of Albemarle mentions as a daughter of Lucy Harris and William Shelton: Elizabeth Shelton, married Richard Moberly, who emigrated to Madison County, Ky. In Part VIII, Chap. IV, Sec. 11, Elizabeth Shelton who married Richard Moberly is set forth as a daughter of Thomas Shelton and Elizabeth Kavanaugh, nee Woods, his wife, which we believe to be correct, their marriage occured in Madison County, Ky. March, 3, 1802, and their son was named Thomas Shelton Moberley.

Section 7. Sarah Harris; married John Rodes, who was born in Albermarle Nov. 16, 1729, their marriage occured May 24, 1756. John Rodes was a son of John Rodes, and Miss —— Crawford his wife, who were married in 1723.

(See "The Rodes Family" note at the foot of this Chapter.) He was an executor of the will of his father-in-law, Maj. Robert Harris, probated in 1765. The children of Sarah Harris and John Rodes:

1. Mary E. Rodes; born Feb. 14, 1757.

2. Robert Rodes, born in Albemarle May 11, 1759. He was a Captain in the Revolutionary army, and was taken captive at Charleston, S. C. He married Elizabeth Dulaney, sister to the wife of Colonel John Miller and in 1783, they emigrated from Albemarle to Madison County, Ky. Robert Rodes was one of the noblest of Kentucky pioneers. They settled on Shallow Ford Creek and lived there in 1780. He was one of the first Justices of the Court of Quarter Sessions of the County. In 1787 he was made one of the Trustees of the town of Boonsborough. In 1774 Hancock Taylor, an uncle of President Zachary Taylor came to Kentucky as a surveyor, was killed by Indians and buried on Taylor's Fork of Silver Creek, in Madison County, the Fork taking its name from said event, and in 1803, Colonel Richard Taylor, a brother of Hancock Taylor came to the County hunting the grave of his brother, and Captain Robert Rodes and his son, William went with Colonel Taylor, and showed him the grave. The children of Robert Rodes and Elizabeth Dulaney his wife, were, viz:

1. Mary Eddings Rodes, born June 27, 1782; married James Estill, June 10, 1800. Their home was "Castle Wood" Madison County, Ky. Their children were:

1. Eliza Estill; married William Harris Caperton. (See Part 11, Chap IX, Sec. IV.) Their children, viz:

1. Woods Caperton.

2. Mary Pauline Caperton; married Leonidas B. Talbott of Boyle County, Ky. issue:

1. William C. Talbott; married Annie French, issue:
1. Clyde Talbott; married Samuel Phelps Todd of Madison County, Ky.

3. Colonel James W. Caperton, a prominent and well known lawyer, banker, captalist and land owner of Madison County, Ky. residence West Main street, Richmond, "Blair Park" named in honor of his ancient ancestor, Micheel Woods of Blair Park, Albemarle County, Va. He married Catherine Cobb Phelps. (See Part 11, Chap. IX, Sec. 4.) issue, viz:
1. Mary James Caperton.
2. Catherine Phelps Caperton.

2. Maria Estill; married Archibald Woods Goodloe. (See Part 11, Chap. XI, Sec. IV.) issue, viz:
1. Anna Goodloe.
2. Archibald Goodloe; married —— —— of New Orleans, issue:
1. Mary Goodloe; married —— ——. Living in New York City.
3. Mary Eliza Goodloe; married Dulaney M. Lackey, living in Lancaster, Ky. (See Part 1, Chap. XIV, Sec. X.)

3. James M. Estill; married Martha Ann Woods, Sept. 22, 1831, issue, viz:
1. Elizabeth Estill; married William R. Garrison, live in New York City, issue:
1. Minnie Garrison; married Easton de Chandon, Nice, Ky.
2. Estille Garrison; married Charles Ramsay, uncle to the present Earl of Dalhmire, Scotland.
3. William Garrison, Jr.; married Cathline Conduit daughter of Frederick R. Conduit eminent lawyer of New York City.
2. Josephine Estill.
3. Martha Estill; married W. W. Craig.
4. Maud Estill.
5. Robert Estill.

4. Rodes Estill; married Eliza Payne of Fayette County, Ky., had no children, but an elegant home, "Estill Hurst" Georgetown, Ky. now owned by his niece Mrs. Lizzie Holmes Lewis.

5. Mary Estill; married William E. Holmes, of Natches, Miss., lived in Carroll Parish, Louisiana, issue:
1. Lizzie Rodes Holmes; married Dr. — Lewis of Va. issue:
1. Estill Lewis; married Dr. — Yager of Georgetown, Ky. issue:
1. Rodes Estill Yager.
2. Dianna Lewis Yager.
3. Arthur Holmes Yager.
4. Elizabeth Dunbar Yager.

2. Sallie Harris Rodes; married Dr. Anthony W. Rollins, July 18, 1809, in Richmond, Ky., afterwards moved to Boone County, Missouri, where both died and were buried. Their children:
1. James Sidney Rollins; born 1812.

2. Robert Rodes Rollins.

3. Eliza Rollins; married Dr. James Bennett. (See Chap. XLVIII.)

4. John C. Rollins; married Nancy Stephens.

5. Clifton C. Rollins; died unmarried.

6. Sarah H. Rollins; married Hon. Curtis F. Burnam, distinguished and learned lawyer, and member of the Richmond bar, born in Richmond, Ky. March 24, 1820, graduated at Yale College in 1840, and in the Law Department of Transylvania University in 1842, since he has enjoyed the fruits of a lucrative practice of the law. He represented Madison County, in the State Legislature 1851-3, and 1859-63, serving on important committees. Was Presidential Elector for Scott and Graham in 1852. A strong supporter of the Union during the Civil War. Had the support of the Republican party for the U. S. Senatorship in 1863, republican elector for the state at large in 1864. In 1875 Mr. Grant gave him the appointment as first assistant secretary of the Treasury, which position he resigned the next year. In 1846, he had conferred on him the degree of A. M. by Yale College and that of L. L. D. by Centre College afterwards. In 1883, he visited the principal places of Europe and the Holy Land, was President of the Kentucky Bar Association in 1884, Delegate elect from Madison County to the Convention which framed the present State Constitution in 1792. He has been an important factor in State and National politics. Is now, and has been, for a term or more, State Senator from Madison County. He is an honest and just man, and highly esteemed by his constituents. Has been for a long time the stay of the Regular Baptist Church of Richmond, Ky. He has passed eighty seven winters. The children of Sarah H. Rollins and Hon. Curtis F. Burnam, viz:

1. Judge Anthony Rollins Burnam. An eminent lawyer and jurist of Richmond, Ky. Late Judge, and Chief Justice of the Court of Appeals of Kentucky, one of the first lawyers of the State, and of the Richmond bar, for a long time partner of his father in the practice of the law, under the firm name of C. F. & A. R. Burnam. In July 1906, he was for the second time selected as a member of the State Board of Election Commissioners by the Republican State Central Committee. He married Miss Margaret Summers, an elegant christian lady.

2. Thompson S. Burnam, born 1852, one of the foremost farmers of the County of Madison; married first, Miss Bettie Moran, and second, Miss Logan.

3. Miss Sallie Burnam.

4. Miss Lucy Burnam.

5. Judge James R. Burnam, at one time represented Madison County in the Ky. Legislature, also, Judge of the Madison County Court, one term of four years; married Miss —— Gay. His widow now resides in Richmond, Ky.

6. Robert Rodes Burnam, a popular banker, of the Madison National Bank, of Richmond, Ky., married Miss Cynthia Smith of Richmond.

7. Edmund Tutt Burnam, an attorney at law, of the Richmond bar, once represented Madison County in the Kentucky Legislature. He married Miss Jessie Kennedy, of Covington, Ky., their home is Richmond, Ky.

8. Miss Mary Burnam; married Waller Bennett, a popular, wealthy, and influential citizen of Richmond, Ky. (See Chap. XLVII.)

3. Elizabeth Rodes; married Wallace Estill. Their children:

1. William Estill, of Fayette County, Ky., married Miss Ferguson.

2. Robert Rodes Estill of Missouri: married Miss — Turner.

3. John H. Estill: married Miss Ann Sullinger June 20, 1839.

4. Jonathan T. Estill, late of Madison County, Ky.; married Louisa Oldham July 24, 1849. (See Part VI, Chap. XIV, Sec. V.)

5. Clifton Rodes Estill; died in Madison County, Ky. unmarried..

6. Miss —— Estill; married first, Mr. — Curle, second, Mr. — Wright. Their grand daughter Eliza J. Curle, married Thomas Varnon, of Stanford, Ky.

4. Nancy Rodes; married Samuel Stone, of their children were:

1. Robert R. Stone; married Elizabeth Walker. Their home was in Lexington, Ky.

2. James C. Stone, was Colonel of a Ky. Regiment in the Mexican War; married Matilda Hanson. Of their children:

1. Samuel Hanson Stone; married Patter Harris daughter of John D. Harris and Nancy J. White his wife. (See Chap. XXXIX.)

2. James Stone.

5. John Rodes; died unmarried.

6. William Rodes, (called Colonel Wm. Rodes) was an elegant and refined gentleman, was for a number of years, master Commissioner of the Madison Circuit Court, and was County School Commissioner and held other positions of trust, and lived to an old age. He married Miss Pauline G. Clay. Children:

1. Eliza Rodes; married Robert H. Stone May 1, 1844. (See Chap. VIII, Sec. V.)

2. Sallie Rodes; married John Watson Nov. 14, 1844.

3. Belle Amelia Rodes; married Colonel John H. McDowell December 22, 1852.

5. Green Clay Rodes; died unmarried.

6. William Cassius Rodes; died at the age of ten years.

7. Clifton Rodes; married Amanda Owsley. Their children:

1. Hon. Charles H. Rodes, a prominent citizen, lawyer and capitalist of Danville Ky. was collector of Internal Revenue for the Eighth District of Kentucky, under President Grover Cleveland's second administration. He married Miss Mary Davis.

2. John S. Rodes; died unmarried.

3. Sallie E. Rodes; married Thomas E. Tutt.

4. Myra S. Rodes; died unmarried.

5. Boyle O. Rodes, a popular clever gentleman of Danville, Ky., married Miss Susan C. Cromwell, died 190-.

6. William Rodes; died unmarried.

7. Clifton Rodes; died unmarried.

8. Ann E. Rodes; married John G. Barrett.

9. Amanda Rodes; married first, William C. Anderson, and

second, Stephen L. Yerkes.

10. Elizabeth Rodes; married Joseph Helm.

11. Robert Rodes; married Mary Grider.

3. Henrietta Rodes, born May 25, 1761; married Rev. Bernis Brown. (See Part VIII, Chap. 11, Sec. IV.)

4. Ann Rodes, born July 22, 1763; married John Garth.

5. Captain John (Jack) Rodes, born June 2, 1766, died 1839. He married Francina Brown. (See Part VIII, Chap. IV.) He lived on his fathers estate, south of Moorman's river, in Albemarle; was appointed a Magistrate in 1808, was sheriff in 1832 and died in 1839. Their children were:

1. William Rodes; married Clarissa Yancey.
2. Sydney Rodes; married Powhatan Jones.
3. Sarah Rodes; married Samuel Woods, of Nelson County, Va., (See Part II, Chap. 15.)
4. Lucy Rodes; married Mr. Newlands, emigrated west.
5. Frances Rodes; married Garland Brown.
6. Tyre Rodes.
7. Ryland Rodes; married Miss Virginia Woods.
8. John Rodes; married Mrs. Ann Morris, no issue.
9. Cynthia Rodes; married Jack M. Smith.
10. Virginia Rodes; married Wilson C. Smith.

6. Clifton Rodes, born Aug. 8, 1768, was Captain of Co. 2, 2 Bat. 47th, Albemarle County, Va., Reg. 1794-1802, acting Magistrate in 1807. He lived near Ivy Depot on a farm given him by his father, which he sold in 1810. He married Elizabeth daughter of John Jouett, and was administrator of Jouett's estate. He afterwards emigrated from Albemarle to Kentucky.

7. Tyre Rodes, born Dec. 24, 1770, emigrated from Albemarle to Giles County, Tenn.

8. Charles Rodes, born Feb. 22, 1774.

9. Sarah Harris Rodes, born July 3, 1777; married first, Mr. William Davenport, and second, Micajah Woods.

10. Mary Rodes.

Section 8. Miss — Harris; married William Dalton.

Section 9. Mourning Harris; married John Jouett in Albemarle. He was a Captain of Virginia State Militia in the Revolution, also, he was a signer of the Albermarle Declaration of Independence April 21, 1779, as was his son John. He died in 1802. Children:

1. Matthew Jouett, was a Captain in the Revolution and fell in the battle of Brandywine.

2. John Jouett, was Captain of Va. State Milita in the Revolution. He married Sarah Robards, sister of the first husband of President Jackson's wife. They emigrated from Albemarle to Ky. and settled in Mercer or Woodford, in 1784-5. He was a very phominent man in the formation of the state, represented Mercer in the Ky. Legislature in 1792, and Woodford in 1795-7. Was one of the many subscribers to the "Proposals for establishing a Society to be called "The Kentucky Society, for promoting useful knowledge" Dec. 1, 1787, was among the prominent men of the state whose names were presented, from which were selected the five commissioners under the act of 1792, to fix on the place for the permanent seat of State Government. John Jouett Jr. was a signer of the Albermarle Declaration of Independence, April 21, 1779. His son:

1. Matthew Harris Jouett, was born in Mercer County, Ky. April 23, 1788, and died in Fayette County, Ky. Aug. 10, 1827, at the age of thirty one years. He was a very celebrated artist, although he died young, he had brought himself into public notice by his productions of elegant portraits of many distinguished Kentuckains, which gave him fame. In many of the old Ky. homes suspend priceless pictures of noble, grand ancestors, the work of his hands, which testify of his talent.

3. Robert Jouett, was a Captain in the Revolution and afterwards a member of the Albemarle bar, at Charlottesville. He died in 1796. He was also Colonel of Artillery 7th Va. 2nd. div. in the Revolution. His daughter married James W. Boulden of Charlotte County.

4. Margaret Jouett; married Nathan Crawford.
5. Mary Jouett; married Thomas Allen.
6. Frances Jouett; married Menan Mills.
7. Elizabeth Jouett; married Clifton Rodes.
8. Charles Jouett was a Captain in the 47th Regiment 2nd. division Albemarle troops 1794-1802. He emigrated westward and in the latter part of 1804, was in Detroit.
9. Susan Jouett; married Thomas C. Fletcher.

Section 10. Elizabeth Harris; married William Crawford. Of their children, was:

1. William Harris Crawford U. S. Senator, from Georgia, Minister to France, Secretary U. S. Treasury under President Monroe, and a prominent candidate for the Presidency, in 1824.

Section 11. Nancy Harris; married Joel Crawford.

Section 12. Anna Harris; married John Dabney. (See Chap. XV, Section 11.)

Note—The Rodes Family of Albemarle.

The first of the name to settle in Albemarle, was John Rodes, born in 1697, he came to Albemarle in 1749, and in that year bought from James Armor, 400 acres of land on the North Fork of Rockfish, and in the conveyance was described as of St. Martin's parish, Louisa. He also, purchased land on Moorman's River, and died in 1775. His wife was Mary Crawford. He left five daughters and four sons:

1. David Rodes, came to Albermarle in 1756, and lived on the north side of Moormans River. Managed his plantation and conducted a store, was appointed Magistrate, and served as sheriff probably in 1776-7. He was twice married, first it is believed to Mary, daughter of Matthew Mills, secondly, to Susan, daughter of Nelson Anderson. He died in 1794. Children of the first marriage:
   1. John Rodes; died in 1823, unmarried.
   2. Matthew Rodes; married Nancy Blackwell.
   3. Charles Rodes.
   4. Mary Rodes; married Robert Douglas.
   5. Elizabethh Rodes; married Horsley Goodman.
   6. Nancy Rodes; married William Dulaney.
   7. Ann Rodes; married James Ballard. (see Part V, Chap. X111.)
   8. Lucy Rodes; married Joseph Twyman.
   9. Martha Rodes; married Joel Yancey. (See Part V, Chap. X111, Section VI.)
   10. Mildred Rodes; married William Waldin.

2. John Rodes; married Sarah Harris (See Sec. VII preceding.)
3. Clifton Rodes, first lived at the foot of Buck's Elbow, on a place he bought in 1769, from Matthew Mullins, and afterwards sold to Cornelius Maupin. In 1773 he purchased from William Lewis a plantation near Ivy Depot, where he lived till 1788, when he sold it and soon thereafter removed to Kentucky. He was a magistrate and served as sheriff in 1783. He married Sarah Waller after coming to Kentucky he settled in Fayette County, about 1789. His son:
1. John Rodes; married Jane Stapleton Burch.

4. Charles Rodes, lived where his father first bought, on the waters of Rockfish. The land now lies in Nelson County. He died in 1798. His daughters names are not given.

CHAPTER 4.

CHRISTOPHER HARRIS.
(Named in Chap. 3, Sec. 8.)

Article 1.—Christopher Harris, a son of Major Robert Harris, and Mourning Glenn, his wife, the emigrant from Virginia to Madison County, Ky. related in Chap. 2, first settled in Albemarle County, Va. in 1750, and patented three thousand acres of land on Doyles River.

Afterwards he emigrated to Kentucky, and acquired lands in the County of Madison, also on the waters of Lickin River, besides the lands he owned in Albemarle County, Va., and was the owner of a number of slaves. He made many visits to Colonel Daniel Boone's old Fort at Boonsborough, and was often sheltered there, and sat around the cabin fires and enjoyed the company of the old pioneers, he being one himself. Two of his sons married daughters of the old pioneer, Higgason Grubbs. (See Chap. 1, Sec. 7.)

He first married Mary Dabney, a daughter of Cornelius Dabney, senior, and Sarah Jennings, his wife. (See Chap. XV, Sec. IV.) A brief history of the Dabneys and Jennings is given in Chap. XV. He survived his wife, Mary Dabney, and married secondly, Agnes McCord, evidently a daughter of John McCord whose will was probated March 8, 1764, in the Albemarle Court, and a copy certified to by the clerk, is in the following words and figures:

"John McCord's Will.

"In the name of God, Amen. The last will and testament of John McCord, senior, of Moorman's River is as followeth: I being sound in judgment, do commit my soul to Jesus Christ and my body to be buried at the direction of my executors, within my own plantation or elsewhere as they may think proper. I do order my sons, John and Benjamin McCord, my executors. I do further will and bequeath this plantation that I am now dwelling on, on Moorman's River, to my said son John, only he is to pay unto Christopher Harris the sum of two pounds, and I do order that my dear wife shall have her bed and one cow, and mare or horse, and my Bible during her life, which Bible is to be returned to John, and I do further bequeath to my son Benjamin McCord, that plantation at Ivy Creek, the little horse and the gray colt, and that what iron tools for working the plantation be equally divided between Benjamin and John McCord, and whatever stock or plennishing is, may be disposed of at my wife's direction, between John and Benjamin McCord. I do order what debts or funeral charges be paid out of the whole all which I conclude as my last will this second day of March, one thousand seven hundred and sixty four. I do order my son William Duram on the commands, and Mr. Thompson's chatecise. As witness my hand.

John McCord. (L. S.)

Delivered in presence of Gabriel Maupin, James Little.

At a Court held for Albermarle County, the 8th day of March 1764, this last will and testament was presented in Court and proved by the oath of Gabriel Maupin a witness thereto, and the dentity of the testators hand through the whole will was proved by the oaths of Samuel Black and John Price, and ordered to be recorded, and on motion of John and Benjamin McCord, the executors therein named who made oath according to law, certificate is granted them for obtaining a probate thereof in due form, giving security, whereupon they with William Woods and William Owens their security entered into and acknowledged their bond according to law.

Teste, HENRY FRY, Clerk.

A copy Testo, W. L. Maupin, Clerk.

Christopher Harris died in Madison County, Ky. in 1794, and his will bearing date Feb. 20, 1794, was probated March 4, 1794, and recorded, same is in the following words and figures:

"Christopher Harris' Will."

"In the name of God, Amen. I Christopher Harris being through the abundant mercy and goodness of God, tho weak in body, yet of perfect understanding and memory, do constitute this my last will and testament, and desire it should be received by all as such. Imprimis: That I will and desire that my first children, viz: Dabney Harris, Sarah Martin, Robert Harris, Mourning Jones, Christopher Harris and Mary Jones should have the following negroes, (excepting thirty pounds out of my son, Dabney's legacy, which is to be paid by the executors of this part of my will for the use and benefit of my wife, and other children) viz: Ritter and her children, Pomp, Moses, Alice, George, Betty, Lucy and Deephy, the above negroes, to be divided agreeable to Cornelius Dabney, Sr. I will and I do appoint Foster Jones and Christopher Harris as executors of the above part of this will, and as to the balance of my estate, I direct that just my debts shall be paid out of what money I have by, or is owing to me.

The house where I live I direct shall be furnished, which, together with the tract of land whereon I live I leave to my dear and loving wife during her life and at her death to my son Overton Harris.

As to the balance of my negroes, David, Cato, Fanny, Stephen and Eady, together with my house hold furniture, stock of every kind and plantation utensils I desire that my wife may have the whole benefit of them during her life or widow-hood, and if she should marry the whole to be sold, and equally divided amongst her, and her children. As to my lands on Muddy Creek, I will and bequeath them as follows: The Drowning Creek tract of land I will and bequeath to my son, John Harris. The Sycamore Spring tract to my son, Benjamin Harris. The tract on which my son William has built to my son, William Harris, and the tract called the Holly Tract, to my son, Barnabas Harris. And my lands in Albermarle County, together with the stock that is thereon, I direct shall be sold, and that my sons, James and Samuel Harris, shall receive of the money as much as Colonel John Miller and Robert Rodes shall judge the land to be worth that I willed to my other sons, viz: to be made equal to them.

As to my three daughters, viz: Jane Gentry, Margaret Harris and Isabel Harris, my will and desire is that Jean Gentry should receive ten pounds, and Margaret and Isabel Harris to have fifty pounds apiece out of the balance of what my Albemarle land, and the profits arising from that place, and if that should not be sufficient that it shall be made up to them out of any personal estate that my wife and executors after mentioned shall think best.

As to my lands on Licking waters my will is that if they are obtained it should be sold and equally divided amongst my last set of children.

And I do appoint my dear and loving wife, with John Sappington, and John Harris to execute that part of my will that respects my wife and her children. As witness my hand and seal this twentieth day of February, one thousand and seven hundred and ninety four. Christopher Harris. (Seal)

Witness: Hartly Sappington, Richard Sappington, Joseph Wells.

At a Court held for Madison County on Tuesday, the 4th day of March 1794, this will was proved to be the last will and testament of Christopher Harris, by the oath of Joseph Wells, Hartly and Richard Sappington, witnesses thereto, and ordered to be recorded.

Teste, Will Irvine.

Tuesday March 4, 1794.

On motion of Foster Jones, Christopher Harris Jr., Agnes Harris John Sappington and John Harris the executors therein named, a certificate is granted them for obtaining a probate thereof in due form, they having first made oath, and together with John Miller, James Berry, William Jones, William Irvine and Joseph Pelpithier securities, entered into and acknowledged their bond in the penalty of two thousand pounds, conditioned as the law directs."

In the will which speaks for itself he styles the children by his first wife, his "first children," and those by his last wife his "last set of children," and refers to the will of Cornelius Dabney, Sr. (father of his first wife.) He appoints Foster Jones and Christopher Harris (his son-in-law, and son) executors of the first part of his will applying to his first children and his wife (Agnes) and John Sappington and John Harris (his son) executors of the part applying to his last wife and her children.

Article 3.—By his first wife, Mary Dabney, Christopher Harris had the children named in the emoing sections.:

Section 1. Dabney Harris, who was a resident of Surry County, North Carolina on May 5th 1795, and whose son Christopher Harris at that time being a man of maturity, came to Madison County, Ky., from North Carolina, with a power of attorney from his father (Dabney Harris) authorizing his said son to receipt for his (Dabney Harris) part of his fathers estate, and from this it is known that Dabney Harris had one child but as to any other children, no history is at hand:

1. Christopher Harris, of North Carolina, Surry County. He doubtles had several other children.

Section 2. Sarah Harris; married James Martin whom she survived. To whom Chapter V, will be devoted.

Section 3. Robert Harris, who married Nancy Grubbs, will be the subject of Chapter VI.

Section 4. Mourning Harris, who married Foster Jones, the subject of Chapter 11.

Section 5. Christopher Harris; married Elizabeth Grubbs, the subject of Chapter. XII.

Section 6. Mary Harris; married George Jones, son of Mosias Jones, of whom no further history is at hand.

Section 7. Tyre Harris.

By his second wife, Agnes McCord, Christophher Harris had the children mentioned in the following sections:

Section 8. John Harris; married Margaret Maupin, a daughter of John Maupin and Frances Dabney, his wife, the subject of Chapter XVI.

Section 9. Benjamin Harris; married firstly, Miss — Jones, and secondly, Nancy Burgin, the subject of Chapter XLIII.

Section 10. William Harris; married Anna Oldham, a daughter of Jesse Oldham and Elizabeth Simpson his wife, Feb. 4, 1790, the subject of Chapter 44.

Section 11. Barnabas Harris; married Elizabeth Oldham, a daughter of Ready Money Richard Oldham and Ursley Williams, his wife in 1803. The subject of chapter 5.

Section 12. James Harris, was a devisee of his fathers will, but died about 1797-8. An inventory and appraisement of his estate made Jan. 1, 1799, by Colonel John Miller and Robert Rodes was returned to the Court, and he was not living to join in the deed made Dec. 2, 1809 by the heirs of Christopher Harris deceased, and his second wife, Agnes McCord, to Samuel Williams and James Guthrie to 600 acres on Hinkston's Fork of Licking in Bourbon County, Kentucky. His wife was Susannah Gass, daughter of David and Sarah Gass, see Chap. 2, notes.

Section 13. Samuel Harris, was a devisee of his father's will. He married Nancy Wilkerson. It appears from the Court records that Samuel Harris entered as one of the sureties on the bond of his brother, Overton, and brother-in-law, John Bennett as executors of the will of his sister, Margaret Harris, who died testate and unmarried in the year 1814. On Aug. 4, 1830, Samuel Harris and his wife, Nancy, conveyed to Richard Fowler land in Madison County and on the 21st of Sept. 1831, they were living on their farm, on Calloway's Creek in Madison County, Ky. which on that date they conveyed to Edwin Phelps and they emigrated westward, probably to Missouri. (See Chap. 1, Sec. IX, and also note at the foot of Chapter XLV.)

Section 14. Jane Harris; married Richard Gentry, the subject of Chapter XLVI.

Section 15. Margaret Harris; died testate and unmarried and in her will gave her property to her sisters, Jane Gentry and Isabella Bennett, and appointed her brother, Overton, and her brother-in-law, John Bennett, executors thereof.

Section 16. Isabella Harris; married John Bennett, Oct. 2, 1794, the subject of Chapter XLVII.

Section 17. Overton Harris; married Nancy Oldham a daughter of Ready Money Richard Oldham, and Ursley Williams his wife, the subject of Chapter XLVIII.

Seventeen children were born to Christopher Harris, the fruits of his marriages to Mary Dabney and Agnes McCord, all of whom lived to maturity, and all raised families of their own, except his daughter Margaret. Such a record is hard to surpass.

CHAPTER 5.

SARAH HARRIS.

(Named in Chap. 4, Sec. 2.)

Article 1.—Sarah Harris a daughter of Christopher Harris, the old Kentucky pioneer, and Mary Dabney his first wife, was born in Albemarle County, Va., and was married there to James Martin.

They came with their children to Madison County, Ky. in the immigration named in Chapter 2. James Martin died in Madison County, Ky. about the first of the year 1799, having first made and published his last will and testament, which bears date July 5, 1796, probated March 5, 1799, and his wife Sarah and sons, William, Tyre and Robert Martin were appointed executrix and executors. (Will book A. page 192) when this will was written they had a grand-son, David Martin, son of his deceased son, James Martin. Their children:

Section 1. Azariah Martin, was born in Albemarle County, Va. and came to Madison County, Ky. prior to 1784. His wife's name we haven't found out. He was well acquainted with Estill's old Station, and other noted places. He was a scout, Indian spy, hunter and skilled woodsman, and went into what was then a wild, unsettled country, and made his home, on Station Camp Creek, about two miles from the Little Picture Lick, or Blue Banks, where the Indians blazed the trees with their tomahawks, and painted figures and pictures on the blazes with red and black paint, directly on the War Path, which Lick was noted, and often mentioned and it also was directly on the War Road, and on the trace leading from Estill's Station by the Mulberry Lick, Hoys Lick, Station Camp Ford, opposite the Little Picture Lick to Miller's Bottom on the Kentucky river, and the mouth of Millers Creek, and so on. He seemed to be well acquainted with the woods, the licks, traces, etc., in that whole section as well as with Estill Station settlements. In April 1784, he in company with Samuel Estill, Harris Massie, John Woods, William McCreery and several others, among the others being Humphrey, Baker, Colonel Estill, Alex Reid, Benjamin Estill, Benjamin Cooper, Braxton Cooper, Sharswell Cooper, Patrick Woods, Charles Shurley, Higgason Harris, Daniel Hancock and Jesse Noland, went in pursuit of an Indian Camp, near the mouth of Station Camp Creek, and pursued the indian trail up said creek, across the Red Lick Fork, for some distance. Shortly after this scout, he and William Cradlebough, a noted scout, woodsman and indian fighter went the same route, Cradlebough was an unusually hardy, brave and adventurous spirit and well acquainted from Boonsborough to the Middle Fork of the Kentucky, and up the latter deep into the country seldom trodden by white men, and was one of the earliest pioneers, and who with Brooks and Calloway, (Thomas Brooks and John Calloway) in 1780 had hunted and encafped for days and days, up the Middle Fork, and made and named Rock Back Encampment, Williams Creek, Cabin Creek were named by them, and Martin got much information from Cradlebough of the woods, the Little Picture Lick, and other Licks, the War Road and other traces, and of indian habits.

In Nov. or Dec. 1780, Cradlebough, Thomas Brooks and John Calloway, hunted and spied into the wilds of the Middle Fork and camped several days at a place on the south side of said fork, nearly opposite where one McWillard was living in 1805, and at this place they made a canoe in which they paddled up and down the river, and they cut on a beech tree the first or initial letters of their names: W. C. 1780, and J. C. and which they named Rock Back Encampment, and then about four miles above on the south side of the river at a Buffalo Lick on a branch near the mouth they marked "Brooks 1780," and F. C." they camped in a botom about four miles above the mouth of the creek, that they named Williams Creek because William Cradlebough whilst out hunting first found it, and here they encamped and cut down several trees, and cut on a tree the letters W. C. B. (but in 1805 this was called upper Twins) and on a creek they built a cabin and called the creek Cabin Creek. (which in 1805 was called Lower Twins.) At this place in an oak and beech they cut out cutlets, and their initial letters, which marks were there in 1805, the place is about three quarters of a mile up from the mouth of the creek. When this party of three left Estill Station on this hunt they no doubt went the trace that led by Azariah Martins place, and the Litle Picture Lick.

In 1805 James McCormick and William Bryant were commissioned by the Court to take depositions to perpetuate testimony and with William Cradlebough went to Rock Back Encampment, and there commenced the taking of the deposition of Cradlebough, and adjournment from one to another of the Encampments of Cradlebough, Brooks and Calloway of 1780 made twenty five years prior thereto, and found the facts as Cradlebough had described to them two years previous, which their depositions and statements prove. James McCormick then being on the Middle Fork, made this statement in writing:

In the fall of 1798 James Trabue applied to him to survey for him on the Middle Fork of the Kentucky, and furnished him with several entries, one calling for a Buffalo Lick at the mouth of a small creek on the north side with a tree marked thus "Brooks 1780" which tree and lick he saw the same fall and the marks that were on the tree appeared to be very old or old enough to have been marked at the same date. There were several entries that called for another encampment, called the Rock Back Encampment which by the direction of William Cradlebough he found at the same time with W. C. 1780, and J. C. 1780, cut on a small beech tree, which mark also appeared old enough for that date which Rock and Tree William Cradlebough this day swore to in his presence, also the bottom he surveyed for Daniel Trabue, with the trees fell down, was so well described by William Cradlebough, and the course of the river that he verily believed it to be the same bottom, notwithstanding the trees were rotted and gone, and being present with him in search of the bottom Aug. 12, 1805. James McCormick."

It seems that the old scout and indian fighter, Joseph Proctor, who was 47 years old in 1805, and who had been in Kentucky ever since before the big battle at Boonsborough, was perfectly familiar with the geography and topography of the country from personal observation and experience and knew all the stations, traces, licks, water courses and all places of note and was a mighty hunter. According to Proctor, the indians who travelled the south fork of Station Camp generally crossed the river about the mouth of said creek, and came through the Little Picture Lick up the creek opposite where Azariah Martin lived in 1801, on the east side of the creek through a large caney bottom, to the South Fork of Station Camp. He describes the War Road and says, "what I mean by the War Road, is that, that runs up the South Fork of Station Camp from the Indian Picture Lick out at the head of the War Fork, and on out to the Wilderness Road. Speaking of the place called Blue Banks to which the Little Picture Lick is near he says, on a high ridge the banks on the south side are naked to the blue, where the buffaloes used to wallow. The same remains as he said in 1805 to this good day 1907, one hundred and two years after he gave his deposition. He located all the licks and traces in that whole section, and mentions a bark camp, nearly thirty yards long, (Indian Camp) on the War Road. In 1780 or 1781 he and Samuel Estill were pilots for Colonel George Adams and his company of scouts, in pursuit of, and on the trail of indians, and night came on them when they had reached a point above where Azariah Martin lived and above the Forks of Station Camp Creek, and they lost the trail of the indians, but the next morning they found the indian trail where they crossed the Red Lick Fork. During the pursuit a free negro by the name of Hines, and another man, by the name of John Dumford came to Hines Lick and there Hines was killed by the indians at the Lick, from which occurence said lick took its name.

He and Peter Hackett speak of Shelby and Logan's campaign up the Kentucky river. Hackett was on Station Camp in the fall of 1780, the fall after James Estill was killed and with the Shelby Campaign in pursuit of indians since then, when he passed up on Station Camp by the Little Picture Lick. Azariah Martin had besides other children, sons:

1. Littleberry Martin.
2. Liberty Martin; married Elizabeth Coz, April 30, 1840.

Section 2. Christopher Martin; married Anna Turner July 28, 1790.

Section 3. David Martin; married Sallie Turner.

Section 4. William Martin; married Winifred Gentry, this wedding occured most probable in Albemarle County, Va. but they came to Madison County, Ky. where William Martin died in the early part of the year 1841, having made and published his last will and testament which bears date April 13, 1839, probated May 31, 1841. (Will Book G. page 418.) In which he names his children:

1. Richard Gentry Martin; married Susannah Jones, Sept. 15, 1840. Their children.
    1. William Martin; married Mollie O'Bannon.
    2. Humphrey Martin; married Jennie Yantis.
    3. Winifred Martin; married John Black, her cousin (See Section 12.)

4. Richard G. Martin; died unmarried.
5. Nannie Martin; married James Bratton.
6. Robert Martin; married Pattie Jones.

2. John Martin; married Mary Barnett April 5, 1821, Children:
1. William Martin; married his cousin, Mary Thomas. (See Section X.)
2. Margaret Martin; married William Cochran.
3. Mary Martin; married Solon Moran.
4. Nathan Martin, when a bachelor emigrated to Missouri.

3. James Martin, emigrated to Missouri and there married and raised a large family and had a son:
1. William Martin.
4. Lucy Martin; married Austin Ballard, no issue.
5. Tyre Martin, emigrated to Missouri, where he married.
6. Elizabeth Martin; married Elias Sims, besides other children she had a son:
1. William Sims, known as Buffalo Bill, who was a Banker in Mexico, Missouri.

7. David Martin; married Samiramus Brassfield, was a farmer and a very prominent and useful and beloved citizen of Madison County, Ky., and represented the County in the Legislature. He married Samiramus Brassfield, a daughter of James Brassfield and Polly Moberley his wife. Their children:
1. William Martin; married Martha Wagle issue:
   1. Peyton Martin.
   2. Samiramus Martin. (
   3. William Martin.

2. Minerva Martin; married Albert A. Curtis, Feb. 3, 1845. Mr. Curtis was at one time a prosperous merchant in Irvine, Ky. popular and influential and elected to the State Legislature. Their children:
   1. William P. Curtis.
   2. Ann Curtis.
   3. David Curtis.
   4. Mary Curtis.
   5. Albert A. Curtis.
   6. Ed Curtis.
   7. Thomas Curtis.
   8. Bessie Curtis.

3. James Martin; married Henrietta Lipscomb. They emigrated to Texas, where Mr. Martin died a few years ago. Their Children:
   1. Duke Martin.
   2. John Martin.
   3. David Martin.
   4. William Martin.
   5. Walter Martin.
   6. Frank Martin.
   7. Clinton Martin.
   8. James Martin.
   9. Samiramus Martin.
   10. Ida Martin.

4. Bettie Martin; died in Madison County, Ky. unmarried.
5. David Gentry Martin; married firstly, Sallie Oldham, the

only daughter of Thomas M. Oldham, and Sarah Overton Harris his wife. (See Part VI, Chap. 38, Section 1.) She died without living issue, and Mr. Martin married secondly, Temperance C. Oldham a daughter of Othniel R. Oldham and Sydonia Noland his wife. (See Part VI, Chap. XVII, Section VI.)

8. Mary Martin; married Garland Maupin. (See Part V, Chap. XII, Section 1.)

9. Nancy Martin; married John Holman. Their children:

1. Sallie Ann Holman; married Jamison Arvine, Oct. 4, 1842.
2. Nancy J. Holman; married Allen Tudor, Mch. 8, 1849.
3. Minerva Holman; married William Pullins, Nov. 30, 1848.
4. Helen Holman; married William S. Atkinson, May 2, 1850.
5. Nancy Holman; married Haman Million, Sept. 28, 1852.
6. Elizabeth Holman; married Wm. S. Million, Oct. 18, 1853.
7. James M. Holman; married Fannie Newby, Nov. 21, 1839.

10. Sarah Martin; married Athenasius Thomas, Nov. 21, 1826. Their children:

1. William M. Thomas; married first Lucy Hensley, second, Nancy Pigg.
2. Tyre Thomas; died in Texas, unmarried.
3. Mary Elizabeth Thomas; married her cousin, William Martin. (See Section IV-11.)
4. Winifred Thomas; married William F. Broaddus.

11. Minerva Martin; married first Thomas Cox, no issue, and second, Mr. Ferrill, and they emigrated to Missouri, and raised children. She was living in 1905.

12. Winifred Martin; married James Black, March 29, 1836, issue:

1. Sarah Black; married Jacob S. Bronston. (See Part V, Chap. 13, Sec. 7.)
2. Almira Black; married George Smith.
3. John Black; married his cousin Winifred Martin. (See 1-3 of Section 4 above.)

Section 5. Tyre Martin; married his cousin, Mourning Jones. Sept. 22, 1798. They emigrated to St. Louis, Territory of Missouri. (See Chap. 11, Sec. 6, Part 1, Chap. 13, Sec. 3, note.)

Section 6. Robert Martin; married Polly Noland Jan. 17, 1799. Their children:

1. Jack Martin; married - —— ——
2. William Martin; married —— —— ———
3. Nancy Martin; married Noah D. Creed.
4. Miss —— Martin; married David Black.
5. Miss —— Martin Cleve Black.
6. Miss —— Martin; married Ril Keys.

Section 7. Hudson Martin, a second Lieutenant in the 9th Virginia, during the Revolution. For a number of years he was Deputy Clerk of the County Court, and later on a Justice of the Peace. He married Jane Lewis the eldest daughter of Nicholas Lewis. About 1800 he moved to Amherst in the vicinity of Fabers Mills, where his descendants now live. In 1834 Captain John Thomas testified before the County Court on behalf of his heirs, that Hudson Martin served in the Revolutionary Army. He was Lieutenant of the 9th Va. Of his children were:

1. John M. Martin, he became a member of the Albemarle Bar in 1809.
2. Hudson Martin; married Mildred Minor a daughter of Dabney Minor. He at one time lived in Arkansas.

Section 8. Nathan Martin.

Section 9. James Martin; married in Virginia, where he died leaving a son, named and called by his father in his will, his grand son:
1. David Martin.

Section 10. MaryMartin; married Julian Pleasant Profit as shown in her fathers will. Pleasant Profit died in Madison County, Ky., in 1818, calls his wife Polly in his will but fails to call the names of his children:
1. Sallie Profit; married Smallwood V. Noland, July 3, 1823.

Sarah Martin survived her husband, James Martin, and afterwards married George Jones. Her children (except James who died and Hudson who remained in Virginia) came with them to Madison County, Ky. At the time the most of them were grown and some of them brought wives with them, and had families of their own.

The Martin family of Albemarle.

The year Albemarle County was organized, 1745, Captain Joseph Martin as he was called in the patents, obtained grants for more than 1400 acres of land on Priddy's Creek, and 800 acres on Piney Run. His will disposing of lands in Essex County leads to the thought that he came from that part of the Colony to Albemarle. He and his wife, Ann, had eleven children:
1. Brice Martin.
2. William Martin.
3. Joseph Martin.
4. John Martin.
5. George Martin.
6. Sarah Martin; married John Burrus.
7. Mary Martin; married Mr. Hammock.
8. Susan Martin.
9. Martha Martin.
10. Ann Martin.
11. Olive Martin; married probably Ambrose Edwards.

Captain Joseph Martin, died in 1761.

James Martin owned at an early date a considerable tract of land that now belongs to the Grayson family near the present site of the Miller School. In 1759 he gave 200 acres to each of his six sons, viz:
1. Stephen Martin.
2. John Martin.
3. Obediah Martin.
4. James Martin.
5. William Martin.
6. David Martin.

Most of these sons emigrated from Albemarle to Kentucky, and some it is believed to North Carolina, about the time of the Revolution or about its close.

One John Martin lived in the western part of North Garden. His place was formerly known as the Pocket Plantation. He was prosperous, and became the owner of more than 1500 acres. He died in 1812. His wife was Elizabeth, believed to have been Elizabeth Wheeler. Their children were:

1. Benjamin Martin.
2. Sarah Martin; married John Watson.
3. Mary Martin; married William Wood.
4. Susan Martin; married Hickerson Jacob.
5. Clarisa Martin.

One John Martin in 1762, purchased from Joseph Thomas upwards of 600 acres of land in the Southern part of the County on Ballingers Creek. He died in 1810. He married Ann Tooley daughter of James Tooley. Their children were:

1. Sarah Martin; married James Wood.
2. Ann Martin; married John Dawson.
3. Dabney Martin.
4. James Martin.
5. Celia Martin.
6. Alice Martin.
7. Simeon Martin.
8. Massie Martin.
9. Lindsay Martin.

Thomas Martin was already settled on the South Fork of the Hardware in 1764. where his descendants have been residents ever since. He died in 1792. He and his wife, Mary had ten children:

1. Abraham Martin.
2. George Martin; married Barbara Woods, and died in 1799.
3. Thomas Martin.
4. Charles Martin and his wife, Pattie probably went to Halifax County.
5. John Martin, was a Captain in the Revolutionary Army. He married Elizabeth Lewis, and emigrated to Fayette County, Ky.
6. Pleasant Martin, moved to Amherst County.
7. Letitia Martin; married Richard Moore.
8. Mildred Martin; married Oglesby.
9. Ann Martin; married Mr. Blain.
10. Mary Martin; married Benjamin Dawson.

Hudson Martin was a second Lieutenant in the 9th Va. during the Revolution and for a number of years Deputy Clerk of the Albemarle Court, and subsequently a Magistrate. He married Jane Lewis about 1800, he moved to Amherst, in the vicinity of Fabers Mills. (See Section 7.)

Early in the last century, a Thomas Martin, married Mary Ann White, daughter of Daniel White. His home was west of Batesville, north of the place now occupied by William H. Turner, Jr. He died in 1821, his children were:

1. Ann Martin; married John L. White.
2. Azariah Martin.
3. Dianna Martin; married James Lobban.
4. Thomas Martin.
5. Mary Martin; married William Stone.
6. Charles Martin.
7. Elizabeth Martin.
8. David Martin.
9. Henry Martin.
10. Barbara Martin; married John Lobban.
11. Lucy Martin; married William H. Garland.

CHAPTER 6.

ROBERT HARRIS.

(Named in Sec. 3, Art. 3, Chap. 1, See Item 10, Chap. 1.)

Article 1.—Robert Harris, a son of Christopher Harris, the old Kentucky pioneer, and Mary Dabney his wife, was born in Virginia, where he married Nancy Grubbs, daughter of Higgason Grubbs, an old Madison County pioneer, and one of the early holders of the Fort at Boonsborough.

In the migration named in Chapter 2, Robert Harris, and his wife Nancy Grubbs came from Virginia, and settled in Madison County, and often visited their father and father-in-law, aforenamed at Boonsborough and Grubbs Fort, where they enjoyed the company of old holders of the fort, and were all acquainted with the old pioneers Daniel Boone, Simon Kenton and others. They spent their remaining days in Madison County. The children born to them are named in the coming sections:

Section 1. Nancy Harris; married William Stone, Oct. 22, 1805, the subject of Chapter 7.

Section 2. Kate Harris: married James Stone, the subject of Chapter 8.

Section 3. Mary Harris; married William Woods, Jan. 13, 1802, (See Part II, Chap. 10.) the subject of Chapter 9.

Section 4. Tyre Harris; married Sally Garland, June 2, 1803, the subject of Chapter 10.

Section 5. Higgason Harris; married Nancy Garland, Dec. 16, 1800. He was a member of the Viney Fork Baptist Church.

CHAPTER 7.

NANCY HARRIS.

(Named in Section 1, Chapter 6.)

Article 1.—Nancy Harris, a daughter of Robert Harris and Nancy Grubbs his wife, was born in Albemarle County, Va., and came to Madison County, Ky. with her parents, in the immigration named in Chapter 2, and on Oct. 22, 1805 she was united in marriage to William Stone.

The fruits of this union were the children named in the coming sections:

Section 1. Matilda Stone; married Arichibald W. Turner, Nov. 29, 1827, to whom were born:

1. William Stone Turner; married Miss Marney, dead.
2. Squire Turner; married Miss Stone, a daughter of William Stone.
3. Minerva Kate Turner; married Mr. Garth of Columbia, Mo.

Section 2. Mary Ann Stone; married Arichibald Turner, the same man that her sister, Matilda married.

Section 3. Minerva Stone; married Adam Irvine to whom were born:

1. William M. Irvine, a graduate in law, and licensed to practice but abondoned same, an influential, prominent and wealthy citizen of Richmond, Ky. until his death a few years since, who married his cousin Elizabeth Irvine, a daughter of David Irvine, second clerk of the Madison County Courts, succeeding the first clerk, his father, William Irvine.

The subject of this chapter survived her husband, Adam Irvine, and afterwards married her cousin, Caleb Harris; a daughter of Tyre Harris and Sally Garland his wife, to whom were born: (See Chap.10, Section 3.)

1. J. Stone Harris, a very prominent man of Fulton, Missouri.

Section 4. Martha J. Stone; married James Woods a son of Anderson Woods and Elizabeth Harris his wife. (See Chap 40, Section 1, of this part, and Part II, Chapter 20, Section 6.) To them were born:

1. Ann Woods; married Dr. —— ——— of Rocheport, Mo.
2. Minerva Woods.
3. James Woods a prosperous man of Nebraska City.
4. William Stone Woods a banker of Kansas City, Mo.

Section 5. Mattie Stone; married Michael Woods.
Section 6. Milton Stone; died in Mexico.
Section 7. John Francis Stone; married Arthusa Hardin.
Section 8. William Stone; married first, Mary Hicks, secondly, Mary Dickey.
Section 9. Thomas Stone; died young.
Section 10. Nancy Stone; died young.

CHAPTER 8.

KATE HARRIS.

(Named in Sec. 1, Chap. 6.)

Article 1.—Kate (Catherine) Harris a daughter of Robert Harris and Nancy Grubbs his wife, was born in Albemarle County, Va., and came with her parents in the migration named in Chapter 2, to Madison County, Ky. where she was united in marriage to James Stone.

The fruits of this union were the children named in the coming sections

Section 1. Sally Ann Stone; married William Jason Walker late a wealthy merchant, banker and farmer of Richmond, Ky. to whom were born:

1. Annie Walker; married Richard J. White.
2. Sallie Walker; married Burnet J. Pinkerton.
3. Mary Jane Walker; married Dr. William H. Mullins.
4. Kate Walker.
5. Charles J. Walker, a Colonel in the Federal Army in the war of 1862, long since dead.

6. Dr. James S. Walker, went South.
7. William Walker, long since dead.
8. Joel Walker, went North, probably to Maine.
9. Robert S. Walker, went to Florida, and died.
10. Percy Walker; died in young manhood.

Section 2. Carolie Stone; married Owen Walker, Dec. 30, 1830, late a capitalist, wealthy and influential citizen of Richmond, Ky. to whom were born:

1. Sallie E. Walker.
2. Kate Stone Walker.
3. Coralie Walker.
4. Owen Walker, long since dead.
5. Caleb S. Walker, long since dead.
6. J. Stone Walker; married first, —— Moss, secondly, —— Boone.
7. June Walker, long since dead.
8. John B. Walker; deceased.
9. Eugene W. Walker, of Richmond, Ky., married —— — -

Section 3. Mary Jane Stone; married Nathaniel Wilson, Sept. 7, 1836, deceased.

Section 4. Caleb Stone; married Miss Wilson, a sister to Nathaniel Wilson.

Section 5. Robert H. Stone; married Eliza Rodes. (See Chap. 3, Section 7.)

CHAPTER 9.

MARY HARRIS.

(Named in Chap. 6, Sec. 3.)

Article 1.—Mary Harris a daughbter of Robert Harris and Nancy Grubbs his wife, was born in Albemarle County, Va., and came with her parents to Madison County, Ky. in the immigration related in Chapter 2, in which county on the 13th day of Jan. 1802 she was married to William Woods, a son of Archibald Woods, and Mourning Shelton his wife. (See Part II, Chap. 10)

Their children:

Section 1. Nancy Woods, born Jan. 21, 1803.

Section 2. Archibald Woods, born Feb. 20, 1804; married Sallie G. Caperton, June 15, 1830.

Section 3. Samiramus Shelton Woods, born Sept. 1, 1805; married John M. Kavanaugh a son of William Woods (big Bill) Kavanaugh and Elizabeth Miller his wife. (See Part VII, Chap. 5, Sec.1) Dec. 10, 1822. Their home was in Franklin County, Tenn. Their children:

1. Elizabeth Kavanaugh; married Mr. —— Turner. Children:
   1. James Henry Turner.
   2. Sue Lou Turner.
   3. —— Turner, a son.
2. William Kavanaugh.
3. Robert Kavanaugh.

4. Thomas Kavanaugh.
5. Mourning Kavanaugh.
6. Margaret Kavanaugh.
7. Mary Jane Kavanaugh, the second wife of Major Thomas G. Miller. (See Part I, Chap. 14, Sec. 10.)

Section 4. Lucy Woods, born Feb. 22, 1807.

Section 5. Mourning Woods, born Oct. 6, 1808.

Section 6. Thomas Harris Woods, born Aug. 31, 1810; married Appoline Miller, Feb. 28, 1832. (See PartI, Chap. 14, Sec. 10.)

Section 7. Fobert Harris Woods, born May 29, 1812.

Section 8. William Crawford Woods, born April 1, 1814; married Sarah Ann Boyce, Dec. 14, 1843, issue:
1. Mattie Ann Woods; married Mr. Miles.
2. Mrs. Ellis Blake.
3. Mary Harris Woods.

Section 9. John Christopher Woods, born Feb. 8, 1817.

Section 10. Mary Ann Woods, born Feb. 20, 1819; married John M. Miller, Aug. 28, 1835. (See Part I, Chap. 14, Sec. 8, and Part II, Chap. 10, Sec. 10.) a son of Joseph Miller and Susan Kennedy his wife.

Section 11. James Goodloe Woods, born Feb. 2, 1823. He married Susan Jane Boyce, Nov. 30th, 1843. He was a primitive Baptist preacher. He died Oct. 19, 1895. (See Part II, Chap. 10, Sec. 11) Their children:
1. James H. C. Woods.
2. William Ed Woods.
3. Mattie Woods; married Mr. —— Fleming.
4. —— Woods, a son.

CHAPTER 10.

TYRE HARRIS.

(Named in Chap. 6, Sec. 4.)

Article 1.—Tyre Harris a son of Robert Harris and Nancy Grubbs his wife was born in AlbemarleCounty, Va., and came with his parents to Madison County, Ky. in the immigration related in Chapter 2, where on June 2, 1803, he was married to Sallie Garland.

TYRE HARRIS

They emigrated from Madison County, Ky., to Missouri and settled in Boone County in 1816. Tyre Harris spent a long and useful life in his adopted County, was one of the pioneers. He was a successful farmer, and thoroughly identified with the interests of his county in all public enterprises. He was strong in character and intellect, very firm in his convictions and a power in his county, and held many positions of public trust. He served as County Judge 1826-1828, and 1830-1832, Represenative in the State General Assembly 1826-1828, 1868-1870, State Senator 1842-1846. Their children:

Section 1. Overton Harris; (deceased) married Mary Ellington. They have a grand-son:

1. Walter Harris, living in Sturgeon, Missouri.

Section 2. Malinda Harris (deceased) married Samuel Jameson. Their children are in several states:

1. Miss —— Jameson; married Joseph Boyd, Mexico, Mo.
2. Miss —— Jameson; married John Ferrill, Fulton, Mo.
3. Miss —— Jameson; married Mr. —— Harrison, issue.
   1. William Harrison, Duluth, Minnesota.
   2. Samuel T. Harrison, Duluth, Minnesota.
4. Miss —— Jameson; married Dr. Baskett, Mexico, Mo.
   1. Miss Jael Yates, Fulton, Mo., a great grand daughter.
   2. Martin Yates Jr. Fulton, Mo., a great grand son.

1. Mrs. Dr. Westmoreland, Columbus, Miss., a great grand daughter.
2. Henrietta Pierson, Sedalia, Mo. a grand daughter.

Section 3. Caleb Rice Harris; (deceased) married Mrs. Minerva Irvine widow of Adam Irvine, deceased, and daughter of Nancy Harris and William Stone, (See Chap. 7, Sec. 3) issue:

1. John Stone Harris, home, Fulton, Mo.

Section 4. Paulina Harris; married Joseph Frakes, issue:

1. Kate Frakes; married Mr. —— Richards, home, Centralia, Missouri.

Section 5. William Hayden Harris, deceased; married Amelia Ellington, issue:

1. Joseph Harris, Post Master, Kansas City, Mo.

Section 6. Susan Harris; married John Jameson of Fulton, Mo. issue:

1. Clare O. Jameson; married Mr. Atkinson of Fulton, Mo.

2. Mr. —— Jameson a son, married —— —— issue:
    1. Anna Belle Jameson, Fulton, Missouri.
    2. William E. Jameson, Fulton, Missouri.
    3. John T. Jameson, Fulton, Missouri.

Section 7. Thomas Berry Harris, died in Fulton Mo. in 1892. He married a kinswoman, Mary Frances Harris daughter of Overton Harris and Mary Rice Woods his wife, who settled in Boone County, Missouri from Madison County, Ky. The marriage occured July 25, 1852. (See Chap. 37, Sec. 6.) for issue and etc.

THOMAS BERRY HARRIS

Thomas Berry Harris was born in Madison County, Ky. in 1815, and went with his parents (or rather was carried by them) in 1816, to Boone County, Mo. About the year 1836, Mr. Harris moved to Calloway County, and engaged in farming until about 1849, when he removed to Fulton, and in partnership with D. M. & J. H. Tucker, built up the flourishing and best known merchantile establishment in Central Missouri. Having married he left Fulton and reengaged in farming. Up to the time of his death he was a very prominent and useful citizen. In 1852 he was elected County Clerk, served on the Board of Managers of the Insane Asylum, which under the long superintendency of Dr. T. R. H. Smith did a grand work, and was free from the scandals of its later years. He efficiently aided in organizing the present school system of Fulton, being a member of the first board of education and by his wise and progressive views gave direction to the incipient organization and assisted in drawing up the first Code of Rules and Regulations for the public schools of Fulton. His most important work was as a member of the Constitutional Convention of 1865. He was a christian in the broadest and best sense. Unostentatious and tolerant, bigotry and hypocrisy had no part in his nature. He was not a "barren fig tree." His remains lie in the new cemetery at Fulton. His widow Mrs. Mary Frances Harris entered into rest Wednesday evening, Feb. 28, 1906, at the residence of her son, William Christopher Harris, 815 Court street, Fulton, Mo., she was born in Boone County, Mo. Nov. 10, 1827. She had more than completed the period alloted by the Psalmist as the limit to human life, when quietly and peacefully she fell asleep in Jesus. At the age of thirteen she was converted and united with the Baptist church, being baptized by Rev. Robert Thomas and ever afterwards was a devoted, earnest and consecrated christian. She was educated at Bonne Femme Academy, a most excellent school, and Columbia College. After her marriage the remainder of her life was spent in Calloway County, the last thirty nine years at the family resi-

MARY FRANCES HARRIS
Wife of Thomas Berry Harris

dence on Court Street in the city of Fulton. Mrs. Harris Possessed a strong personality, she belonged to that class of women whose voices still speak to us from the past. Erect and graceful, even in her declining years she retained in large part that refined beauty of form and face that had marked her early and matured womanhood. Of her a former pastor and friend said: "she had a clear mind, a good judgment, unflinching devotion to duty, a laudable ambition, unselfishness and a faith that towered in majesty and beauty. A grander character I have never known, and her influence can never die. She approached as nearly to perfection in the art of motherhood as is attainable in a sinful world. Her love for and pride in her children was beautiful and in her old age she felt that she was amply repaid for all her toils and anxieties." Another pastor and friend said: "softened by sorrow, and refined by affection, her life was a benediction to all who came in contact with her, she left to her children the richest legacy, one can leave to posterity, the fragrance of a pure, beautiful and useful life." On Friday March 2, 1906, after simple services at the family residence conducted by her pastor, in the family lot, in the cemetery at Fulton while the last rays of the setting sun gave promise of another day her sacred dust was committed to mother earth, there to rest until the resurrection morn.

"And is she dead whose glorious mind and soul lifts them on high?
To live in the hearts we leave behind is not to die."

Their children are set forth in Chapter 37.

REV. ROBERT HARRIS

Section 8. Rev. Robert Harris, son of Hon. Tyre Harris and Sallie Garland, his wife, was eighty-nine years of age the 22nd day of February, 1907, and a noted and distinguished Baptist minister, a Godly man, a native Missourian, highly esteemed not only by the family and his religious associates, but by all his extensive acquaintances, made during a long life of pious walk and Godly conversation. He preached a sermon on his eighty-ninth birthday in California, Mo., to a large congregation. His picture is herewith reproduced. He married Frances Copher in Boone County, Mo. Their children:

1. Tyre Harris, Windsor, Mo.
2. Susan Harris; married Mr. —— Hill, California, Mo.

Section 9. James Berry Harris, born in Boone County, Mo., married Lucy Cockerel of Cooper County, Mo., in 1905, died in Fulton County, Mo., at the residence of Judge Samuel F. Moore, aged 84 years, issue:

1. William Thomas Harris.
2. Miss —— Harris; married Howard Sutherland, Elkin, West Virginia.
3. John T. Harris, Labor Department, Washington, D. C.
4. James W Harris, of Harris, Polk Hat Company, St. Louis, Mo.
5. Martha Virginia Harris; married Mr. Henderson Hancock, Maryland.

Section 10. Tyre Crawford Harris, minister of the Baptist

church of Boone County, Mo. and President of the Baptist Female College in Columbia, Mo.; married Lavinia Hughes of Howard County, Mo. He died in 1854 leaving three children:

1. William L. Harris; married. His wife and children live in Fayette, Missouri.
2. Mary Cameron Harris; married Mr. —— Vorries, deceased.
3. Miss —— Harris; married William McCracken, Fulton, Mo.

Section 11. Benjamin F. Harris, 815 Court street, Fulton, Mo.; married Lucy Hensley, daughter of Samuel Hensley. Have five children:

1. Mary Susan Harris; married Mr. Vivion of Fulton, Mo.
2. Alnett Harris; married Mr. Vivion, Butte City, Montana. (St. R. R. Co.)
3. William T. Harris, Butte City, Montana.
4. Benjamin W. Harris, Fulton, Missouri.
5. Samuel H. Harris, Butte City, Montana.

Section 12. Sallie Ann Harris born in Boone County, Mo. married Dr. Archibald Dinwiddie of Boone County, Mo., left two children:

1. Dora Dinwiddie; married Mr. Mayer of Sturgeon, Mo.
2. Dr. Tyre Dinwiddie, Higbe, Missouri.

Section 13. Mary Catherine Harris; married George Burroughs of Howard County, Mo. died in Fulton, Mo. in 1904. Had four children:

1. James Burroughs; dead.
2. Augustus Burroughs, died in Oregon.
3. Laura Burroughs; dead.
4. Thomas H. Burroughs; dead.

Note—Only two of the children of Tyre Harris and Sallie Gar land are living, viz:

B. F. Harris, 609 Nicholas street, Fulton, Mo.
Rev. Robert H. Harris, Walker, Missouri.

CHAPTER 11.

MOURNING HARRIS.

(Named in Chap. 4, Sec. 4.)

Article 1.—Mourning Harris a daughter of Christopher Harris and his first wife Mary Dabney, was born in Albemarle County, Va., and was there married to Foster Jones.

They emigrated to Madison County, Ky. as related in Chapter 2, and settled on lands they acquired on Muddy Creek near to the mouth of Hickory Lick, where Foster Jones died in 1814. Children:

Section 1. Tyre Harris Jones, prior to 1817, emigrated from Madison County, Ky. and settled in St. Louis, Territory of Missouri; married Sarah Maupin, daughter of Mosias Maupin and Leah his wife. (See Part V, Chap. 4, Sec. 10.)

Section 2. Mosias Jones, prior to 1817, emigrated from Madison County, Ky. and settled in St. Louis, Territory of Missouri.

Section 3. Nancy Jones; married Mr. Sappington. They prior to 1817, emigrated from Madison County, Ky. and settled in St. Louis, Territory of Missouri.

Section 4. Christopher Harris Jones, prior to 1817, emigrated from Madison County, Ky. and settled in St. Louis, Territory of Mo.

Section 5. Elizabeth Jones; married Green B. Baxter. They prior to 1817, emigrated from Madison County, Ky., and settled in St. Louis, Territory of Missouri.

Section 6. Mourning Jones; married Tyre Martin, Sept. 22, 1798. (See Chap. 5, Sec. 5.) They prior to 1817 emigrated from Madison County, Ky. and settled in St. Louis, Territory of Missouri.

Section 7. Lucy Jones, prior to 1817, emigrated from Madison County, Ky. to St. Louis, Territory of Missouri.

Note—The 6th of Nov. 1817, and April 15, 1818, all of the above named children of Foster Jones and Mourning Harris his wife, then in St. Louis, Territory of Mo. united as grantors in deeds conveying to Daniel Miller of Madison County, Ky. certain lands on Muddy Creek in Madison County, Ky., which deeds were properly acknowledged before officers in St. Louis and forwarded to Richmond, Ky., and recorded.

Mosias Jones, Sr. father of Foster Jones, died in Madison County, Ky., in 1808; in his will he mentions his children: William, Lucy Maupin, (wife of W. B. Maupin) (See Part V, Chap. 4, Sec.) Mosias Foster, Frances Harris, Elizabeth Daverson, George Jones, Ann Garrison, Thomas, Roger, Sarah Carroum and John, and the will is witnessed by Martin Gentry, Moses Bennett and John Maupin. (See notes Chap. 2.)

CHAPTER 12.

CHRISTOPHER HARRIS.

(Named in Chap. 4, Sec. 5.)
See Chap. 1, Sec. 4, and 7.

Article 1.—Christopher Harris, a son of the Old Kentucky pioneer Christopher Harris and his first wife, Mary Dabney, was born in Virginia and in Albemarle County married Elizabeth Grubbs a daughter of Higgason Grubbs, a Madsion County, Ky., pioneer.

They emigrated to Madison County, Ky., as related in Chapter 2, and often visited their father, Higgason Grubbs, at the old Fort at Boonsborough as well as at Grubbs Fort, and enjoyed the society of the old Forters, and were acquainted with many of the early comers. Christopher Harris was a regularly ordained minister of the Primitive Baptist church. The following entry appears on the County Court records:

"Oct. 2, 1792. Ordered that Rev. John Manion Fedrigill Adams, Thomas Shelton, Christopher Harris, Andrew Tribble, Charles Kavanaugh, Thomas Chilton and Alexander McKay, be authorized to celebrate the rites of marriage."

It appears from the record that Christopher Harris solemnized maritàl rites in Madison County, Ky.

Excerpt from A. C. Quisenberry's History:

"Whilst on the move from Virginia to Kentucky, in Dec. 1780, at Holston, Virginia in the re-organization there of the old Providence Church of Primitive Baptists (Separatists) Mary Harris was one of the re-organizers, and then and there Elder Robert Elkin was chosen pastor of the flock. (The Mary Harris named, was not the wife of Rev. Christopher's father, for his first wife had been dead a long while). She is perhaps the Mary Harris who became the wife of William Woods..

On account of intelligence of various Indian incursions and molestations of the infant settlements of the interior of Kentucky and especially of Boonsborough, the destination of most of the company, this organization rested at Holston until 1783, where they in the time raised three crops of corn, then in a body moved on to Craig's Station on Gilbert's Creek, in Lincoln County, Ky. where they remained until Nov. 12, 1785, when a minor part of the church departed for South Western Kentucky, and the Major portion moved on to the waters of Lower Howard's Creek, in what is Clark County, Ky. not very far from Boonsborough, where new church officers were elected and the organization named Howard's Creek Church, afterwards Providence. In 1787, they constructed of logs a house of worship, probably the first house of worship built by white settlers on Kentucky soil.

Shortly after the arrival at Lower Howard's Creek, a great spiritual revival in the church commenced, lasting something like two years, and many were baptized into the fellowship of the saints. including the names, Christopher Harris, Squire Boone, Junior, (Nephew of the great pioneer Colonel Daniel Boone.) The preaching brethern were Elders James Quisenberry, Andrew Tribble, Robert Elkin etc."

Christopher Harris placed his membership in Dreaming Creek Church, (Mt. Nebo) located in Madison County, about one or two miles North east of the city of Richmond, on the farm now owned by Irvine Miller Hume, and George Larkin Hume, on Dreaming Creek, prong of Otter Creek.

The Primitive Baptist Church, at Viney Fork, in Madison County, Ky. was organized March 25, 1797, the first preliminary steps were taken Jan. 22, preceding, with the help of Elders Peter Woods and Christopher Harris from Dreaming Creek, and Andrew Tribble and Isaac Newland from Tates Creek, and on the second Saturday of Aug. 1797, Elder Christopher Harris was called as pastor, which call he accepted and faithfully ministered to the flock, until the second Saturday of Nov. 1813.

Further Excerpt from History:

"In May 1796, Christopher Harris was chosen moderator of the Tates Creek Association serving for ten years as such, when, about 1816, he moved to the Green River Country, and united with Mt. Zion Church, in Warren County, and the next year was elected moderator of Gasper River association, and was continued as such until 1820, when he and his churches entered into the constitution of Drakes Creek association, of which he was chosen Moderator for five successive years, his career being closed by a call to appear before the Courts above, in about the year 1726, thus ending his labor below. The children of Christopher Harris and Elizabeth Grubbs his wife:

Section 1. Tyre Harris born in Virginia, Albemarle County, Feb. 21, 1778. He went to Simpson County, Ky.

Section 2. Thomas Harris, born in Albemarle County, Va. Jan.

18, 1780; married to Mary Annie Booten, a daughter of Favis Booten and Ruth Estill, his wife. Favis Booten died in 1806, Ruth his wife was a daughter of Samuel Estill and after the death of Favis Booten, the said Ruth married William Kavanaugh. (See Part VII, Chap 8.) After the death of Thomas Harris, his widow Mary Ann married Joel Embry, to whom children were born, one of her Embry sons she named Thomas Harris Embry, in honor of her first husband. Thomas Harris when he died was a member of the Viney Fork Primitive Baptist Church. His will bears date March 15, probated April 7, 1806.

Section 3. Nancy Harris born in Albemarle County, Va. Feb. 2, 1782. She came with her parents to Madison County, Ky. as related in Chapter 2, on the 17th of Oct. 1799, she married Josiah Thorpe. (See "Thorpe" under Sec. 4.) They were both members of the Viney Fork Primitive Baptist Church.

Section 4. Mourning Harris, born in Albemarle County, Va. Oct. 31, 1783, died July 4, 1865; married Zacariah Thorpe, Oct. 17, 1799, in Madison County, Ky. (See note "Thorpe" below) Mourning Thorpe and her husband were members of Viney Fork Primitive Baptist Church. A further account is given in Chapter 13.

Note—"Thorpe."

Thomas Thorpe; married Eleanor Holliday, a daughter of William Holliday. He came from Albemarle County, Va. to Madison County, Ky. prior to 1794. In July 1794, Robert Moore and Mary his wife conveyed to him land on the waters of Otter Creek. In 1803, Elijah Bennett and Patsey his wife conveyed to him land on Muddy Creek. May, 18, 1812, John Moore, Senior, conveyed to him 100 acres on Muddy Creek. He died in 1818, his will dated March 18, probated July 6, 1818. His wife Eleanor was sole devisee and executrix of the will (she afterwards on Aug. 25, 1818, married James W. Smith.) His negro man, Ben, after testators death was to be emancipated. The children were:

1. Jeremiah Thorpe.
2. Zachariah Thorpe; married Mourning Harris aforesaid. In April 1815, Christopher Harris and his wife Elizabeth conveyed to Zachariah Thorpe 25 acres of land on Muddy Creek including said Thorpe's mill, which property was where the village of Elliston is.
3. Josiah Thorpe; married Nancy Harris, as aforesaid.
4. William Thorpe.
5. James Thorpe.
6. Susannah Thorpe, the wife of John Morris, married March 4, 1806.
7. Dodson Thorpe.

On Aug. 1, 1808, the above named Jeremiah, Zachariah, Josiah, William, James and John Morris and Susannah his wife, as heirs of William Holliday, conveyed to the said Dodson Thorpe, lands in Garrard County, Ky.

Section 5. Robert Harris; married Mary Taylor. A fuller history of whom is given in chapter 14.

Section 6. Tabitha Harris, born Sept. 16, 1791; maried March 16, 1809 Joel Burnam of Madison County, Ky.

Section 7. Fannie Harris, born Sept. 10, 1793; married first Mr. Black, secondly, Thomas Ernest, and thirdly Samuel Hayden.

Section 8. Christopher Harris, born Nov. 29, 1795; married Miss —— Vivion.

Section 9. Susannah Harris, born Feb. 13, 1798; married Thomas Bluett.

Section 10. Elizabeth Harris, born Jan. 24, 1800; married Richard Hudson.

Section 11. James Harris, born Feb. 18, 1802; married Miss Watts. He was a member of the Viney Fork Primitive Baptist Church.

Section 12. Hensley Harris, born Nov. 26, 1804; married Malinda Vineyard, and went to South Western Kentucky.

CHAPTER 13.

MOURNING HARRIS.

(Named in Chapter 12, Sec. 4.)

Article 1.—Mourning Harris, a daughter of Christopher Harris and Elizabeth Grubbs his wife, was born in Albemarle County, Va. Oct. 31, 1783.

She came with her parents to Madison County, Ky. as related in Chapter 2, and on Oct. 17, 1799, married Zachariah Thorpe. They were members of the Viney Fork Primitive Baptist Church. Their children:

Section 1. Thomas Thorpe, born in Madison County, Ky. July 17, 1800; died April 11, 1885; he married Emma Hume, she was born Feb. 12, 1803; died July 10, 1851. (See Part I, Chap. 9, Note.) Their children:

1. Martha Thorpe, born Aug. 4, 1824, died March 20, 1890, she was the second wife of her first cousin, Shelton Harris, (See Chap. 14, Sec. 1.) issue:

 1. Robert Harris; married Theresa Anderson, went to Missouri.
 2. Mary Emma Harris, went to Missouri.

2. George Hume Thorpe, born Dec. 6, 1826; died April 7, 1859; married Elizabeth Yates. Their children:

 1. Emma Thorpe; married Rev. George T. Strausberry.
 2. Muggy Thorpe; married Elbridge Noland. (See Part I, Chap. 13, Sec. 3, Note.)
 3. Georgia Thorpe; married Elbridge Broaddus. (See Part VI, Chap. 11, Section 13.)
 4. Elizaabeth F. Thorpe, born Nov. 25, 1855; died May 10, 1858.

3. Harris Thorpe, was a soldier in Captain Thomas B. Collins Company F. 7th, afterwards 11th Kentucky Confederate Cavalry, Colonel D. Waller Chenault, General, John H. Morgan's command died unmarried.

4. Stanton Hume Thorpe; married Sarah Wallace Miller (See Part I, Chap. 13, Sec. 1.)

5. Thomas Thorpe, was a confederate soldier, in the early part of the war, was two terms County Assessor, and two terms County Court Clerk; married Florence Shearer.

6. Mourning Thorpe; married William Reid Wallace. (See Part IV, Chap. 11.)

7. Louisa Thorpe, born Oct. 15, 1841, died Nov. 28, 1892; married Robert Christopher Harris Covington; born April 18, 1835; died March 22, 1863, at Monticello, Ky., where he was buried, at the time of his death was a member of Captain Thomas B. Collin's Company, F. 7th, afterwards 11th Kentucky Confederate Cavalry, Colonel D. Waller Chenault, command of the daring raider, General John H. Morgan.

8. Susannah Thorpe; married John Harris Covington. (See Chap. 29, Sec. 2.)

Section 2. Tyre Thorpe, emigrated to Missouri in 1818.

Section 3. James Thorpe, emigrated to Missouri in 1818.

Section 4. Harris Thorpe; married Miss -- Burnam, emigrated to Missouri in 1818.

Section 5. Nancy Thorpe; married Mr. Owens.

Section 6. Elizabeth Thorpe; married Mr. Abraham Banta, Dec. 27, 1825; died in Fremont County, Cal. in about 1878.

Section 7. Sarah Thorpe; married Henry Burnam, were members of Viney Fork Church.

3. Georgia Thorpe; married Elbridge Broaddus. (See Part VI,

Section 8. Mahala Thorpe; married William Banta, Dec. 19, 1822.

CHAPTER 14.

ROBERT HARRIS.

(Named in Chap. 12, Sec. 5.)

Article 1.—Robert Harris, a son of Christopher Harris and Elizabeth Grubbs his wife, was born in Albemarle County, Va., March 6, 1787.

He came to Madison County, Ky. with his parents, when a tender child, as related in Chapter 2; in the latter County he was married to Mary Taylor, July 7, 1814. He died on Drowning Creek, after living nearly one hundred years. When a man something like thirty years of age, he went to Missouri, then a territory, and whilst there put up with the old pioneer, and woodsman, and hunter, Colonel Daniel Boone, and helped Colonel Boone make salt, at Boone's Lick in said Territory, his horse ran in Colonel Boone's cornfield. He was intimately acquainted with Colonel Boone and two of his sons of whom he very often talked, he had very high regard for the whole family and esteemed Nathan Boone, and gave him the name of being an exceedingly clever man, and said that the settlers would come from a distance to the Boone home, for corn, and such like, and Boone would send them to his crib to help themselves without charge, not knowing what they got.

Robert Harris served as a soldier in the war of 1812, and at the date of, and many years before his death, received a pension for his service in the said war. To him and his wife, a great number of children were born, but only about six lived to maturity, towit:

Section 1. Shelton Harris, was born Sept. 20, 1820, and died May 9, 1896. He first married Caroline Duncan, whom he survived afterwards, he married his first cousin, Martha Thorpe. (See Chap. 13, Sec. 1, and Part VII, Chap. 9, Sec. 3.) Children of the last marriage:

1. Mary Emma Harris, went to Missouri, and married in that state.

2. Robert Harris; married Miss Theresa Anderson, daughter of Rev. Abijah Anderson. He emigrated to Missouri.

Section 2. Fannie Harris, was married to Thomas Coyle, Feb. 3, 1853. Their children:

1. Algernon S. Coyle; married Kate Amerine. He died in Richmond, Ky. leaving children:

1. Bessie Coyle; married James Hamilton.

2. Mary Coyle.

3. Ed C. Coyle; married Crickett Terrill. They live in Richmond, Ky. Mr. Coyle is an extensive coal dealer.

4. Frank E. Coyle.

2. Mary Ethel Coyle; married John W. Butler.

3. Fannie Coyle; married Samuel Friend.

Section 3. Elizabeth Harris; married Joseph Pearson, July 21, 1847, they lived just across Drowning Creek in Estill County, Ky. where they died. Besides other children, they had a son:

1. Robert H. Pearson; married Miss —— Moss.

Section 4. James Harris; married Mary Searcy. Their home was in Speedwell, Madison County, Ky. until many years after Mrs. Harris' death. Mr. Harris died near that village, leaving these children:

1.Caroline Harris, who became the second wife of Jeremiah Broaddus. She is now a widow.

2. Fannie Harris; unmarried.

3. Mattie Harris, died young.

4. Joseph Harris; married Callie Gaines. He is an efficient rail road man, has been promoted from time to time, and is now conductor on the L. and A. R. R.

5. Robert Harris; married Leslie Hurley. He is also a very popular and efficient officer in the Railroad service, having been promoted from one position to another, and is now a conductor on the L. and A. R.R.

Section 5. Mary Harris; married a Mr. —— Bolin, and emigrated from the state of Kentucky, where abouts unknown.

Section 6. Hensley Harris; married Emma Benton; he died in Madison County, Ky. many years ago, leaving children:

1. Minnie Harris.

2. Hattie Harris.

3. Amanda Harris.

CHAPTER 15.

——— JENNINGS — —

Article 1.—Sir Humphrey Jennings of County Middlesex, England. Had a son, (and probably other children) towit:

1. Robert Jennings, had sons:

1. William Jennings, of Acton Place, London, who accumulated an immense fortune, of many million dollars. He died a bachelor and had no children.

2. Charles Jennings, had only one child, towit:

1. Sarah Jennings, became acquainted with Mrs. Cornelius Dabney, whilst they lived in England, and was her warm personal friend. Mrs. Dabney was an invalid, and Sarah Jennings remained with her, and when the Dabney family emigrated to America, Sarah Jennings came with them, and settled in Hanover County, and in April 1721, she became the second wife of the said Cornelius Dabney, senior. (See Art. 2.)

DABNEY.

Article 2.—The name was originally spelled "de Aubigne" or "D" Aubigne, since Americanized to "Dabney."

After the revocation of the Edict of Nantes, three brothers, John Dabney, (the eldest) Cornelius Dabney, and George Dabney, left France, and went to Wales. Early in the Eighteenth Century, when well advanced in years, these brothers, (John and Cornelius then having grown children) left France or England and emigrated to America, with their wives and children. George Dabney settled in Massachusetts, and John Dabney and Cornelius Dabney settled near Piping Tree Ferry, on York River in Hanover County, Va. Cornelius Dabney had a son, George Dabney, who came with them to America. The Dabneys were French Huguenots and to escape persecution came to America.

Mrs. Cornelius Dabney, lived only a short while after arriving in America, and after her death in April 1721, said Cornelius Dabney, (afterwards designated as Cornelius Dabney, senior) married Miss Sarah Jennings. (See Art. 1.) Charles Winston Dabney, of Dalton Junction, Hanover County, Va. had seen the Court Record at Hanover Court House, of the marriage which occured in April 1721, this record was destroyed by fire in 1865.

Cornelius Dabney, senior, died in 1764-5, leaving his last will and testament, which was probated in 1765, in the Hanover County Court in which mention is made of Sarah, his wife, and the names of most of his children. Mr. William Winston Dabney of Enfield, King William County, Va. has a copy of the will. The children of Cornelius Dabney, senior and Sarah Jennings, his wife.

Section 1. Cornelius Dabney, Junior; married Lucy Winston.

Section 2. John Dabney, known as John Dabney of Albemarle, married first Anna Harris, (See Chap. 3, Sec. 12) and secondly, Margaret Smith. The children of the first marriage:

1. Sarah Dabney; married Thomas Waller.
2. Mary Dabney; married Thomas Minor.
3. William Dabney; married Miss —— Quarles.

4. John Dabney; married Anna Harris. (See Chap. 3, Sec. 7.)
5. Anna Dabney; married Henry Terrill.
6. Elizabeth Dabney; married Bernard Brown. (See Part VIII, Chap. 2, and 3.)
7. Susan Dabney; married Thomas Harris. (See Chap. 3, Sec. 9, and Chap. 1, Item 8.)
8. Lucy Dabney; married Thomas McKeynolds.
9. Rebecca Dabney; married Thomas Warren. (or Warner.)
10. Cornelius Dabney; married Jane Harris. (See Chap. 3, Sec.4)
11. Nancy Dabney; married John Hunter.

Section 3. William Dabney; married Philadelphia Gwathney.

Section 4. Mary Dabney; married Christopher Harris, and after her death, Christopher Harris, married again Agnes McCord. (See Chapter 4.)

Section 5. Elizabeth Dabney; married Daniel Maupin, son of Daniel Maupin and Margaret Via his wife. (See Part V, Chap. 3, Sec. 4, and Chap. 11.)

Section 6. Frances Dabney; married John Maupin, son of Daniel Maupin and Margaret Via his wife. (See Part V, Chap. 3, Sec. 3, and Chap. 4)

Section 7. Ann Dabney; married Mr. —— Thompson.

Section 8. Miss —— Dabney; married Matthew Brown.

Section 9. Miss —— Dabney married William Johnson.

Cornelius Dabney, senior, was ninety years old, and probably older, when he died. He was born 1670-5.

Notes—In 1759, John Dabney, of Hanover, bought in Albemarle County from Joel Terrill and David Lewis, 400 acres of land, and from Joel Terrill, 400 acres more, which included the present Bird wood plantation, and the oldest tavern perhaps in all the sections, called at the time "Terrill's Ordinary." John Dabney soon returned to Hanover, where he died. In 1773, trustees sold his place of 600 acres to James Kerr, and the remainder to Robert Anderson.

In 1764, William Dabney a brother to John Dabney, purchased from Archibald Woods 400 acres on Mechum's River, above the present depot of that name. He sold his place in 1768, to William Shelton.

In 1803, William S. Dabney came to the County and bought from William C. Nicholas, nearly 900 acres on the head waters of Ballingers and Green Creeks, now in the possession of Edward Coles. He died in 1813. His wife was Sarah Watson, of Green Spring, Louisa County. Their children:

1. Maria Dabney; married Colonel Samuel Carr.
2. James Dabney.
3. William S. Dabney, succeeded his father to the farm. He was very efficient, and successful in private business, as well as in public concerns. He was appointed Magistrate in 1835. In 1856, his plans for improvements to the Court House were formulated and accepted. He married Susan Gordon, and died in 1865. He had two sons:
   1. William C. Dabney, was a leading professor of the Medical Faculty in the University of Virginia.
   2. Walter Dabney, was the leading professor of the Law Faculty, in the University of Virginia.

4. Mary Senora Dabney; married Benjamin M. Perkins.

5. Louisa Dabney; married William M. Woods. (See Part II, Chap. 26.)

6. Walter Dabney, emigrated to Arkansas.

Mildred Dabney, daughter of Samuel Dabney and Jane Meriwither his wife, married Dr. Reuben Lewis, brother to the celebrated Explorer, Meriwither Lewis. She died at her home near Ivy Depot in 1851. Dr. Lewis was a son of William Lewis and Lucy Meriwither his wife, the said Lucy was a daughter of Thomas Meriwither.

Mary Dabney; married John Carr, of Bear Castle, Louisa County a son of Major Thomas Carr, of King William, John Carr died in 1769.

Colonel Samuel Dabney; married Ellen Carr.

The immense fortune amassed by the bachelor, William Jennings, of Acton Place, London, England, mentioned in Art. 1 was claimed through his niece, Sarah Jennings the second wife of Cornelius Dabney, senior, and the only child and daughter of Charles Jennings brother to William, of Acton Place; many heroic efforts have been made by the American descendants of said Sarah to recover the fortune from England but all have been abortive. As late as 1875, Sis and McCliesh of the agency for prosecution and recovery of claims in the United States, Great Britian, its Colonies and foreign states (of Georgetown, D. C.) represented heirs in America, and were in correspondence with many, and one with whom they corresponded was the late Hon. Thomas C. Maupin, then living in Vacaville, Salano County, California. (who died in 1885 in his 89th year) The agents were urging him to give his deposition so as to perpetuate his evidence. They enclosed to Mr. Maupin notes of statements which they said the late Dr. Charles Brown (of Albemarle) had made.

CHAPTER 16.

JOHN HARRIS.

1765-1810.
(Named in Sec. 1, Art. 4, Chap. 4.)

Article 1.—John Harris a son of the old Kentucky pioneer Christopher Harris and Agnes McCord, his second wife, was also a pioneer, Kentuckian coming from Albemarle County, Va. in the Harris immigration, named in Chapter 2.

MARGARET MAUPIN
Wife of John Harris

Having married in the state of Virginia, Margaret Maupin, born 1767, died 1858, a daughter of John Maupin and Frances Dabney his wife, named in Section 4, Chapter 15. (See also, Part V, Chap. 4, Sec. 13.) John Harris was one of the executors of the will of his father described in Chapter 4. He was often commissioned by the Court to take depositions and to render other service. In 1802 he and John Kincaid met on Silver Creek at Squire Boone's mill seat and took the deposition of Squire Boone. He represented Madison County in the Kentucky Legislature in 1799. He and his wife were members of the Viney Fork Baptist Church. He was a signer of the Albemarle Declaration of Independence April 21, 1779.

About the year 1809, he in company with his son Overton, went in a Flat Boat down the Ohio River to the Mississippi and down the latter to New Orleans, on a business trip. On their return towards home, John Harris died very suddenly and his flesh and bones were buried in the Mississippi swamps, with nothing to mark the place of his interment, and his grave has never since been found. His son, Overton, with a sad heart came on back home, and related the terrible news to his mother and the rest of the family, which was indeed shocking and sorrowful news. His wife was left a grief stricken widow. However, a kind providence had left her with a number of excellent sons and daughters to minister to her wants and comfort, and protect her, and by whom she was tenderly and kindly cared for her remaining days. She lived something like fifty years after this occurence, and died at the ripe age of upwards of ninety years, staying with her children, but most of the time at her son Christopher's where she had a house built purposely for her, in the yard near the main house called Grand-ma's house, and which she always occupied when not away at some one of her children's home.

After her husbands death, her son James, had gone into the Black Hawk War and in Canada was captured by the Indians by whom he was held in captivity for two years . She and her son Christopher were the administrators and wound up the estate of her deceased husband, to the entire satisfaction of all concerned. Will Woods, John Brown, Thomas Collins and John Moberley were the appraisers of the estate. She brought with her from Virginia an old fashioned gracefully formed tea kettle, now in the possession of the writer, which he received from his Aunt Sarah Oldham, a granddaughter of Margaret Maupin Harris, which is very ancient.

The obituary notice of Mrs. Margaret Harris published in the town paper, after her death, reads as follows:

"Obituary"

"Died on the fifth inst. at the residence of her son-in-law, Colonel James Miller, in Lincoln County, Ky. Mrs. Margaret Harris, aged 88 years, 9 months and 24 days. The deceased was born in Albemarle County, Va. on the first day of Feb. 1767, and was the widow of John Harris,one of the Judges of the Madison Circuit Court, (Court of Quarter Sessions) under the old Constitution of Kentucky to whom she was married in 1785, and whom she accompanied to Kentucky in the fall of 1795. In 1800, she became a member of the old Regular Baptist Church at Viney Fork, in Madison County, Ky. under ministration of the Rev. Christopher Harris, by whom she was baptized, and remained a most exemplary and consistent member of that church in full faith and fellowship until the day of her death. She was a woman of extraordinary good sense and energy of character, and of unswerving devotion in the dischage of every duty, which she owed to religion, to humanity, and to her family, friends, and neighbors, by whom she was universally beloved and respected, and indeed by all who knew her. It is the lot of few to live to so great an age, so uniformly in the enjoyment of all their faculties so that during her long widow-hood she was equal to all the cares and responsibilities of her situation. She was an object of love and veneration to her numerous descendants, of whom she left six living children and three or four great, great, grand children. May those who survive her learn from her example not only to live the life of a christian, but to die the death of one. The Savior said of young children "of such is the Kingdom of Heaven" but when one has lived almost a century as blameless as "one of those little ones" and at last meets death willingly and composed and in the full hope of Heaven, surely to such it will be said "well done thou good and faithful servant, enter into the joys of thy Lord, thy dwelling is the secret place of the Most High, abide under the shadow of the Almighty forever." Her remains were interred on the 7th inst. on the farm of her son, Major William Harris of this County.

John Haris settled on the head waters of Hickory Lick in Madison County, Ky., as early as 1790, as appears from the Court records.

To the said John Harris and Margaret Maupin his wife, were born the children named in the coming sections:

Section 1. Robert Harris; married Jael Ellison, the subject of Chapter 17.

Section 2. Christopher Harris; married Sally Wallace, the subject of Chapter 28.

Section 3. Overton Harris; married Mary Rice Woods, the subject of Chapter 37.

Section 4. James Harris; married Mourning Bennett, the subject of Chapter 38.

Section 5. John Harris, born Dec. 30, 1795, went to Missouri, where he died.

Section 6. William Harris; married Malinda Duncan, the subject of Chapter 39.

(20)

Section 7. Elizabeth Harris; married Anderson Woods, the subject of Chapter 40.

Section 8. Frances M. Harris; married James Miller, the subject of Chapter 41.

Section 9. Susan Harris; married Dr. William L. Duncan, the subject of Chapter 42.

CHAPTER 17.

ROBERT HARRIS.

(Named in Sec. 1, Chap. 16.)

Article 1.—Robert Harris, a son of John Harris and Margaret Maupin, his wife, was born in Albemarle County, Va. about day break Oct. 27, 1786, and in the immigration movement named in Chapter 2, came with his parents to Madison County, Ky. at the time a mere lad.

ROBERT HARRIS

He married Jael Ellison April 23, 1812, she was a daughter of Joseph Ellison and Mary Kavanaugh, his wife. (See Part VII, Chap. 7, Sec. 2.)

The will of the said Joseph Ellison bears date Dec. 4, 1814, which was witnessed by Christopher Harris and Harvey Beatty, wherein "After my debts being paid." He gave to his wife Mary Ellison all his personal property, and his negroes Barney, Ritter, Hanibal, Selah, Stephen, Asia and Mariah, to dispose of according to her own will and he gave unto Nicholas Hocker and his wife, Nancy about 60 acres of land on Muddy Creek, also ten acres on said creek, and he gave unto Robert Harris, and his wife Jael, all his remaining tract of land, except one third including Mansion house for his wife Mary, as long as she shall live, then after her death to Robert Harris, and he appointed Robert Harris, Nicholas Hocker, and Thomas Ballew, executors.

JAEL ELLISON
Wife of Robert Harris

Mary Ellison was a daughter of Charles Kavanaugh, Senior, a Methodist preacher, and a full sister to the William Kavanaugh who married Hannah Woods, and Jael Kavanaugh, who married Peter Woods, a Baptist preacher, and Philemon Kavanaugh, whose widow, Elizabeth Woods, after his death married Thomas Shelton, also a Baptist preacher, and who was killed by the Indians on the Wilderness road between Virginia and Kentucky, and Sarah Ann Kavanaugh, who married James Moore.

Robert Harris represented Madison County in the Kentucky Legislature in 1826-8. To the said Robert Harris and Jael Ellison, his wife, were born the children named in the coming sections, towit:

Section 1. John McCord Harris, the subject of Chapter 18.

Section 2. Mary Ann Elizabeth Harris, the subject of Chapter 19.

Section 3. Robert Rodes Harris, the subject of Chapter 20.

Section 4. Margaret Frances Harris, the subject of Chapter 21.

Section 5. Joseph Ellison Harris, the subject of Chapter 22.

Section 6. Malinda Miller Harris, the subject of Chapter 23.

Section 7. Jael Kavanaugh Harris, the subject of Chapter 24.

Section 8. Pauline Rodes Harris, was born Nov. 17, 1826, she and her sister Sallie, who have ever remained single, own and live at their fathers old homestead and they have not lived elsewhere since their father's death. Cousin Pauline is 79 years of age, but her mind is bright as a new dollar, and she enjoys the company of friends. She occasionaly goes to town to see her niece, and transact necessary business.

Section 9. James Overton Harris, the subject of Chapter 25.

Section 10. Nancy Hocker Harris was born April 28, 1831, she died at the old homestead, which she and her two sisters Pauline and Sally, then owned and where they were living. She was an exceedingly bright, clever woman, and her friends missed her when she departed.

Section 11. Susan Miller Harris, the subject of Chapter 26.

Section 12. Sarah Wallace Harris, the youngest daughter was born Dec. 26, 1835, and the same can be said of her as of her sister Pauline, who live together at the old homestead which is theirs.

Section 13. Villiam Christopher Harris, the subject of Chapter 27.

CHAPTER 18.

DR. JOHN McCORD HARRIS.

(Named in Sec. 1, Chap. 17.)

Article 1.—John McCord Harris, a son of Robert Harris and Jael Ellison his wife, was born in Madison County, Ky. March 4, 1813.

DR. JOHN McCORD HARRIS

ELLEN ANDER ON
Wife of Dr. John McCcrd Harris

He was a noted physician of Richmond, where he made his home, and had a large practice over the entire County, and out of it, and accumulated a comfortable fortune. He married Miss Ellen Anderson, she survived him. The fruits of this union are named in the coming sections:

Section 1. Robert Harris, a very promising, bright and popular young man, when he was shot down on the streets of Richmond and instantly killed by William Willis, who had married his only sister.

Section 2. Nannette Harris; married William Willis, afterwards the slayer of her brother, from whom she later separated, and became the wife of Mr. Garrison, who practices law in Louisville.

CHAPTER 19.

MARY ANN ELIZABETH HARRIS.

(Named in Sec. 2, Chap. 17.)

Article 1.—Mary Ann Elizabeth Harris, a daughter of Robert Harris and Jael Ellison his wife, was born in Madison County, Ky. Sept. 4, 1814.

She married Dr. James Cooper, Aug. 10, 1837, and emigrated to Missouri. The fruits of this union were the children named in the coming section:

Section 1. Ann Elizabeth Cooper; married Robert Coyler.

Section 2. Eberly Bascom Cooper; married Ellen Lowen, issue of this union:

1. Nannette Jael Cooper; married William March.

CHAPTER 20.

ROBERT RODES HARRIS.

(Named in Sec. 3, Chap. 17.)

Article 1.—Robert Rodes Harris, a son of Robert Harris and Jael Ellison his wife, was born in Madison County, Ky. Nov. 17, 1816.

By profession he was a lawyer, and in 1844, represented Madison County, in the Kentucky Legislature. He married —— Turner, to them were born:

Section 1. Robert Rodes Harris.

CHAPTER 21.

MARGARET FRANCES HARRIS.

(Named in Sec. 4, Chap. 17.)

Article 1.—Margaret Frances Harris, a daughter of Robert Harris and Jael Ellison his wife, was born in Madison County, Ky. May 27, 1819.

She married Dec. 6, 1838, Simeon Hume. (See Part I, Chap. 9)

Simeon Hume's brothers and sisters were: Sarah Ann Hume, William Hume, Garland Hume, Thomas Hume, Jane Hume, Nancy Hume, Betsy Hume, Eliza Hume, Mary Hume, their mother was named Sarah Ann.

To them were born the children named in the coming sections:

Section 1. William Allen Hume, went to Missouri; married Lydia Turner.

Section 2. Sallie Ann Hume; married Samuel Worthley whom she survived. To them were born:

1. Maud Worthley; married Mr. —— ——.

Sally Ann Worthley, afterwards married Hardin Jones, and they live in Missouri.

Section 3. Robert Harris Hume; married Miss —— Stumbo, he was a confederate soldier. His home is Trenton, Mo.

Section 4. Jael Frances Hume; married John Presley Oldham, (See Part VI, Sec. 3, Sec. 10.) issue:
1. Margaret Oldham; died.
2. Mary Oldham; married Meridith Hayden.
3. Sally Oldham.

CHAPTER 22.

DR. JOSEPH ELLISON HARRIS.

(Named in Sec. 5, Chap. 17.)

Article 1.—Joseph Ellison Harris, a son of Robert Harris, and Jael Ellison his wife, was born in Madison County, Ky. Jan. 13, 1821. He was educated in medicine and was a practicing physician.

He emigrated to Missouri, and married Jennie McDonald. His wife died and afterwards he married Mrs. Eva. Bishop, (See Part V, Chap. 12, Sec. 1-5-1) to them were born the children named in the coming sections:

Section 1. Robert M. Harris; married Anna Payne.

Section 2. Mary Ann Harris; married Charles Bowling.

Section 3. Malinda Harris; married Fred Rettish.

Section 4. Ada Harris; married William Muff, issue:
1. Harris Muff.

Section 5. Pearl Harris; married George Walker, no children.

Section 6. May Harris; died single.

CHAPTER 23.

MALINDA MILLER HARRIS.

(Named in Sec. 6, Chap. 17.)

Article 1.—Malinda Miller Harris, a daughter of Robert Harris and Jael Ellison his wife, was born in Madison County, Ky. Sept. 20, 1822.

Her home for a number of years has been in the state of Missouri, (Trenton.) She is at this time (1905) on a visit in Madison County, Ky., to her sisters and other relatives, and is 83 years old past, but her mind is bright and clear, and she is a good encyclopedia of useful knowledge, and correct information as to the names and history of the family. She was united in marriage to Anderson Yates, Aug. 2, 1849, and they lived in Madison County, Ky. till late in life, and some of their daughters had married and gone to Missouri, whence they went, and out there Mr. Yates died, and Missouri has remained her home ever since. To them were born the children named in the coming sections:

Section 1. Malinda Yates; married Robert Ballew. They emigrated to Missouri, now living near Still Water, Payne County, Oklahoma.

Section 2. Nannie Yates; married Walter Ballard. Their home is in Richmond, Kentucky.

Section 3. Sally Yates, her home is in Trenton, Missouri, she is a teacher, principal in a High School.

Section 4. Pattie Yates; married Edwin Howe Perry, and their home is in Misouri. She is now in ill health. Mr. Perry is an attorney at law, and apointed by the U. S. Government to do some sort of legal service in Cuba, and is at present located in the ci y of Havana, Cuba, No. 1 Tacon Street.

CHAPTER 24.

JAEL KAVANAUGH HARRIS.

(Named in Sec. 7, Chap. 17.)

Article 1.—Jael Kavanaugh Harris, a daughter of Robert Harris and Jael Ellison his wife, was born in Madison County, Ky. Sept. 30, 1824.

She married Martin B. Garvin, Oct. 17, 1841, and lived a time in said County, and migrated to Missouri. The fruits of this union were the children named in the coming sections:

Section 1. Malinda Garvin; married Pem Winn, late husband of her deceased sister Mary Ann Garvin.

Section 2. Mary Ann Garvin; married Pem Winn, and died, and Winn afterwards married her sister Malinda Garvin of section 1.

Section 3. Pauline Garvin; married Samuel Peery.

Section 4. William Overton Garvin; married Vada Riggs.

Section 5. Jael Woods Garvin; married Dr. —— Whitley.

Section 6. John Harris Garvin; married —— Woltz.

CHAPTER 25.

JAMES OVERTON HARRIS.

(Named in Sec. 9, Chap. 17.)

Article 1.—James Overton Harris, a son of Robert Harris and Jael Ellison his wife, was born in Madison County, Ky. April 22, 1829.

He migrated to Missouri and married Abigail Chamberlain, to whom were born:

Section 1. Annie Pauline Harris; married —— . . .

Section 2. William Harris.

Section 3. John Harris.

CHAPTER 26.

SUSANNAH MILLER HARRIS.

(Named in Sec. 11, Chap. 17.)

Article 1.—Susannah Miller Harris, a daughter of Robert Harris and Jael Ellison his wife, was born in Madison County, Ky. June 8, 1833.

She married Benjamin Franklin Crooke of said County, Dec. 22, 1853, and after a while they migrated to Missouri where they lived for a time, and then removed to Madison County, Ky., where they continued to make their home, and where she died, afterwards Mr. Crooke married Minerva Gentry. Mr. Crook's grand father, John Crooke was the first surveyor of Madison County, Ky., whose son the father of the subject, was the second County Surveyor, and his son the subject, succeeded his father, and has been elected a number of times to the office, and is now an active surveyor, although getting along in years and is an honorable high toned gentleman, and Christian and member of the Mehodist Church. and an excellent surveyor. The children born to Susannah Miller Harris and her said husband are named in the coming sections:

Section 1. Robert Harris Crooke, a lawyer of Richmond, Ky., was a formidable candidate on the Democratic ticket for delegate to the Constitutional Convention that framed the present State Constitution, but was defeated by the Honorable Curtis Field Burnam. At the November Election 1905, as the Democratic Nominee was elected County Attorney, of said County of Madison.

Section 2. Joseph Crooke.

Section 3. William Crooke; died when a young man.

Section 4. John Crooke.

Section 5. Nannie Crooke; married Collins Yates. (See Part VI, Chap. 8, Sec. 6-7.)

Section 6. Cassius Crooke; married Martha ——.

Section 7. Margaret Crooke, lives with her father and step mother at their old home.

CHAPTER 27.

WILLIAM CHRISTOPHER HARRIS.

(Named in Sec. 13, Chap. 17.)

Article 1.—William Christopher Harris, a son, and the youngest child of Robert Harris, and Jael Ellison his wife, was born in Madison County, Ky. May 28, 1838, where he spent his life, on and adjacent to the homestead of his father.

He married Lyda Francis a daughter of Thomas Francis. The fruits of this union were the children named in the coming section:

Section 1. Overton Woods Harris.

Section 2. Thomas Francis Harris, living with his mother.

Section 3. Robert Rodes Harris; dead.

Section 4. Mary Bohanan Harris, living with her mother.

Section 5. Eliza Christopher Harris, living with her mother.

CHAPTER 28.

JUDGE CHRISTOPHER HARRIS.

(Named in Sec. 2, Chap. 16.)

Article 1.—Judge Christopher Harris, a son of John Harris and Margaret Maupin, his wife, was born in Albemarle County, Va. April 1, 1788.

JUDGE CHRISTOPHER HARRIS

When a mere urchin he was brought by his parents, in the migration named in Chapter 2, to Madison County, Ky. On the 20th day of Feb. 1812, he was united in marriage to Sally Wallace a daughter of Michael Wallace, and Jane Bratton his wife, said Sally Wallace was born Sept. 1787, and died Oct. 26, 1836. (See Part IV, Sec. 3, Chap. 7.) To them were born the children named in the coming sections:

Section 1. Ann Eliza Harris; married Robert Covington, the subject of Chapter 29.

Section 2. Talitha Harris; married Christopher Irvine Miller, the subject of Chapter 30.

Section 3. James Anderson Harris; married Susan Taylor, the subject of Chapter 31.

Section 4. Christopher Harris, the subject of Chapter 32.

Section 5. John Miller Wallace Harris, the subject of Chapter 33.

Section 6. Polly (Mary) Woods Harris married Elder John M. Park, the subject of Chapter 34.

Section 7. Margaret Frances Harris; married Joseph Warren Moore, the subject of Chapter 35.

Section 8. Sarah Overton Harris; married Thomas M. Oldham, the subject of Chapter 36.

ELIZABETH BERRY
Second wife of Judge Christopher Harris

Judge Christopher Harris, the father of said children after the death of his wife, Sally Wallace, towit: on the 31st, of Oct. 1839, married Elizabeth Berry, 1800-1884, who was born Feb. 5, 1800, but there was no issue of this union, she survived several years after the death of her husband, April 14, 1871, he having passed his 83rd, birthday.

Judge Christopher Harris, was sixty or seventy years ago, a Justice of the Peace of Madison County, and was the first Judge elect, of the Madison County Court under the Constitution of the State, adopted about the year 1850. He was elected as the Democratic Nominee by a large majority at a time when his party was much in the minority, showing his wonderful popularity with the people of his County. He was a man of strong mind, and fine judgment, kind heart, strict honesty, plain speech, and well known, and had hosts of friends. He was generous and charitable, a good neighbor, and a comfort to the poor and needy. He and his mother were the administrators of his father's estate, and they settled those matters to the entire satisfaction of all the parties interested. He was a great comfort, and pleasure to his mother, during her widowhood and in her declining years.

His second wife, was a good woman, and made a splendid wife, an excellent step-mother and grand step-mother, her step-children and step-grand-children, all loved her as a mother, her life was beautiful. Her father James Berry, was in the battle with the Wyandotte Indians, at Little Mountain, led by Colonel Estill, and was wounded in that battle. He died in 1822. In his will he names his children: Nancy Berry, Anna Turner, Susannah Parrish, Elizabeth Berry, William Berry and James H. Berry, and testators sister Martha Berry.

CHAPTER 29.

ANN ELIZA HARRIS.

(Named in Sec. 1, Chap. 28.)

Article 1.—Ann Eliza Harris, a daughter of Judge Christopher Harris, and Sally Wallace his wife, was born in Madison County, Ky., June 18, 1813, and before she was sixteen years of age, towit:

On the fifth day of March 1829, she was married to Robert Covington, (See Part VII, Chap. 18, Sec. 1) and they lived till years were creeping on them in said County, when they following up their children went to Newton County, Indiana, where they spent the remnant of their days, which was brief. Their children are named in the coming section:

ANN ELIZA HARRIS
Wife of Robert Covington

Section 1. Robert Christopher Harris Covington, was born in Madison County, Ky. April 18, 1835, and died March 22, 1863. He maried Louisa Thorpe a relative and daughter of Thomas Thorpe and Emma Hume his wife. (See Chap. 3, Sec. 1-7) After his marriage in the year 1862, he enlisted in Chenault's Company, Duke's Brigade, Morgan's command of the Confederate Army, and died in the service of brain fever, at Monticello, Ky. March 22, 1863, where his remains were buried. His wife, Louisa Thorpe, was born Oct. 15, 1841, and died Nov. 28, 1892, living nearly 29 years a widow, to them were born:

1. Thomas Thorpe Covington, a merchant, at one time Mayor

of Richmond, now a councilman. He married Kate Spears.

2. Robert Christopher Harris Covington, a merchant of Richmond Ky., married Mary Morrow.

Section 2. John Harris Covington, born in Madison County, Ky., married a relative, Susan Thorpe, a sister to the wife of his brother, named in Sec. 1. (See Chap. 13, Sec. 1-8.) They lived a number of years in Madison County, and emigrated to Indiana and settled near Goodland, in Newton County, where he died leaving his widow, now living in Chicago, and these children:

1. Annie Covington; married Frank Clark, Chicago police force.
2. Harris Covington; married Anna Wallace, live in Chicago.
3. Robert H. Covington; married ——— ———, live in Chicago.
4. Thomas Covington lives in Chicago.
5. Lulu Covington; married Mr. Cady. Live in Chicago.
6. Florence Covington, lives in Chicago.
7. John Covington, lives in Chicago.
8. Willie Covington, lives in Chicago.
9. Susan Elizabeth Covington, lives in Chicago.
10. Son; died in infancy, twin.
11. Son; died in infancy, twin.

Section 3. Mary Frances Covington, was born in Madison County, Ky., she married Dr. John W. Christopher, to whom were born:

1. Laura B. Christopher, born Nov. 5, 1858, died April 15, 1863.
2. Bobbie D. Christopher, born March 18, 1861; died May 16, 1863.
3. Horace Christopher; dead.
4. Florence Christopher; married ——— ———

Section 4. Sarah Elizabeth Covington; died young.

Section 5. Talitha Covington, born in Madison County, Ky. went with her parents to Goodland, Ind., and there married Lewis K. Cole, they went to Chicago where they live. They had one son, Dean Cole, who died in young manhood, and a son Robert Cole, died at two years of age.

CHAPTER 30.

TALITHA HARRIS.

(Named in Sec. 2, Chap. 28.)

Article 1.—Talitha Harris, a daughter of Judge Christopher Harris, and Sallie Wallace his wife, was born in Madison County, Ky., March 17, 1815, and died Jan. 2, 1882.

On the 1st day of Sept. 1836, she was married to Christopher Irvine Miller, a son of Daniel Miller and Susannah Woods his wife. She was for a number of years, an esteemed member of the Old Flatwoods Predestinarian Baptist Church, and an excellent woman.

Of her and her husband and their children, a fuller account will be found in Part 1, Chapter 13, which is referred to and made a part hereof.

CHAPTER 31.

JAMES ANDERSON HARRIS.

(Named in Sec. 3, Chap. 28.)

Article 1.—James Anderson Harris, a son of Judge Christopher Harris, and Sally Wallace his wife, was born in Madison County, Ky. in which County he was married to Susan Taylor a daughter of Samuel B. Taylor and Nancy Chenault, Jan. 1, 1845. (See Part V, Chap. 13, Sec. 9.)

When a young man he was Constable of the County, and had, also, considerable experience as salesman and clerk, in one of the largest general stores of merchandise in Richmond, which proved to be worth much to him in his business in after years.

JAMES ANDERSON HARRIS

Subsequent to his marriage he settled in Lincoln County, and bought and owned a rich farm about two miles from the County seat, Stanford, and westward from the town on the Hanging Fork branch of Dick's River, and was a farmer and cattle raiser and cattle feeder, and handler of good horses, on a rather large scale, and in which he was very successful.

At his home the latch string hung on the outside and friends and relatives were ever welcome. He raised a family of two sons and six daughters, all agreeable and kind to one another and a pleasure to other people.

He died at his home leaving his widow and children in good circumstances. His widow, Aunt Susan Harris now (1906) lives at the old homestead with her only surviving son Samuel Harris. Their children are named in the coming sections.

Section 1. Sally Wallace Harris; married Samuel Baughman, a substantial farmer of Lincoln County. They now live at Stanford. Mr. Baughman is a good business man, and has handled with success and much pleasure to himself, many fine blooded horses, and has been more than once elected sheriff of his County, which office he executed with credit. Sally his wife, for many years had not been in good health, but recently has greatly improved, and is about with her family and friends. To them were born the following children:

SUSAN TAYLOR
Wife of James Anderson Harris

1. James Harris Baughman; married Laura Logan Carter, no issue.
2. Kittie Ann Baughman; died when only nine weeks old.
3. Nancy Chenault Baughman; married Walker B. McKinney, issue:

1. Nancy Catherine McKinney.

4. Katherine Baughman; married William H. Wearren, issue:
   1. Annette James Wearren.
   2. Sallie Harris Wearren.

5. Susan Taylor Baughman; married William N. Craig, issue:
   1. Sallie Mills Craig.
   2. Annie Vanarsdal Craig.
   3. Samuel Baughman Craig.
   4. Elizabeth Warren Craig.

6. John Samuel Baughman; married Lena Bruce, issue:
   1. Eddie Bruce Baughman.

7. Chloe Smith Baughman; married Shelton M. Saufley.

Section 2. Nannie Harris; married George P. Bright of Lincoln County. They lived on a farm near Hubble a number of years, moved to Danville, in Boyle County, where they remained a time, and then removed to Stanford, of which town they are now residents. Nannie Bright has been an invalid for years, but she is a sweet good woman, a beautiful house-keeper, unselfish, kind and generous to every one, and respects the feelings af all, ever ready to minister to the wants of others, and it is a pleasure to be with her, and her husband George P. Bright always receives you with a kind welcome greeting. He enlisted in the cause of the south in the rebellion of 1862, and served faithfully in that struggle for what he considered the right. Their children are here named:

1. Greenberry Bright; married Miss Alice Holmes, his wife has recently departed this life, leaving children:
   1. Lottie Chenault Bright.
   2. George P. Bright.
   3. Alice Edith Bright.

   Mr. Bright lives in Phoenix, Arizona, where he married again.

2. Sue Bright; married Churchill Yeager, an industrious kind hearted, energetic man, who has since died, leaving his widow and a very bright intelligent daughter:
   1. Nancy Yeager, a bright child and pleasure to her mother.

3. Anna Evans Bright; married Joseph Johnston, Mr. Johnston, was educated in the law, and licensed to practice, but is now a travelling salesman, residing at this time in New Orleans, Louisana.

Section 3. Reuben Harris, who was a splendid horseman, brave, generous, and kind, and warm attachment to his friends who were many, when mounted on a fine horse, charming as a rider, and knew how to handle and train a horse, wearing the blue ribbon from many exhibitions. He married Eliza Engleman, a sister to the husband of his sisters, Susan and Annie. He died leaving his widow with these children:

1. Lavisa Harris.
2. Samuel Harris.
3. James Harris.

Section 4. Samuel Harris, who has not as yet, taken unto himself a wife, although he has passed the half century mark, but as long as there is life, there is hope. Some nice girl would do well to get him, for he could and would provide for all her wants, real and imaginary and make a good husband. He is a farmer and deals largely in cattle and has been successful in his business, to which he pays close attention. He is a large stock holder and officer in the

Stanford Bank. He lives with his aged mother at his father's old homestead, and his home is like it was in his father's lifetime, as you enter you feel welcome and at home, welcome while you remain and depart with good feeling.

Section 5. Susan Harris, was a most estimable, industrious kind girl and woman, fond of her realatives and friends, and other company, who were ever welcomed at her home, ready at all times to attend the sick and distressed, and when she passed away never to return, her presence was missed. She married George R. Engleman, a jovial good fellow. The writer boarded with them for something like a year, and their attention and kindness to him was more than deserving. Their children are here named.

1. Anna Bronaugh Engleman: married Rowan Saufley, a son of Judge M. C. Saufley.

2. Bessie Taylor Engleman, who unfortunately lost her hearing shortly after her birth, and is deaf and dumb, was educated at the Deaf and Dumb Institution at Danville, and is a beautiful, lovely girl, now grown to womanhood.

3. Eliza (Midget) Engleman, the youngest child, a handsome fine girl, now a grown young lady.

Section 6. Elizabeth (Bettie) Harris, when you go to speak of her, words are wanting to give the proper definition of her character, which is lovely, there being but few women in any sense her superior; she is a domestic adornment. When quite a maiden, she married Mr. Harry Bush, (becoming his seceond wife) a good man of high standing, a citizen of Lincoln County. Her married life was brief, Mr. Bush only lived a very few years, she is now a widow and makes her home principally with her sister and brother-in-law, Mr. and Mrs. Ephraim Woods. (See Part VI, Chap. 10, Sec. 12-4-a,)

Section 7. Margaret Miller Harris, like all her sisters who all had the best of training, is a good woman, beloved by all who know her. She married Ephraim Woods a substantial farmer of Lincoln County, who trades extensively in live stock, buying and selling, and has made the business a profit to himself; when one leaves their house a feeling possesses him that he was welcome. Their children are here named:

1. Susan Fisher Woods.
2. Bessie Harris Woods; married Sanford Miller Allen, issue:
   1. Margaret Woods Allen.
   2. Julian Grosjean Allen, Jr.
   3. Elizabeth Bush Allen.
3. Annie Belle Woods; married Samuel Jackson Embry, issue:
   1. Pearl Burnside Embry.
   2. Robert Woods Embry.
4. Robert Benton Woods, Jr.
5. James Harris Woods; married Sophia Timothy McCormack, issue:
   1. Mary Louise Woods.
6. Sallie Taylor Woods.
7. Ephriam P. Woods, Jr., lived only about seven months and a half.

Section 8. Annie Montgomery Harris, kind hearted, devoid of selfishness, and good, ready at all times to nurse and care for the sick and comfort the distressed. She has lived a widow with three little daughters to raise and educate which work she has performed vell, and her daughters are now young accomplished ladies. Her ıusband was Frank Engleman, a brother to the husband of her ister Susan and the wife of her brother Reuben, and to them were orn:

1. Sue Taylor Engleman.
2. Nancy Engleman.
3. Bessie Kay Engleman, she met with a horrible death, on the 18th day of May 1906, at the point in front of Ephriam D. Woods residence where the dirt road crosses the L. & N. Railroad, in Lincoln County, Ky. when a fast train ran into her buggy and killed her instantly, fearfully mangling her body, the same place where her mother and cousin, Sue Woods, were badly hurt a few years since.

CHAPTER 32.

CHRISTOPHER HARRIS.
(Named in Sec. 4, Chap. 28.)

Article 1.—Christopher Harris, a son of Judge Christopher Harris and Sally Wallace his wife, was born in Madison County, Ky. April 20, 1819, was never married.

He was the very essence of courage, though kind and a true riend to those of whom he was a friend, a perfect stranger to fear ıe knew no fear, except the fear of God. Was a strong muscular nan, and greatly admired for many excellent qualities, as a man. Ie left Madison County and went to Lincoln or Garrard. One day, he 16th of July 1860, in a thicket in Garrard County his body was 'ound, but the living principle which once occupied it was gone, tripped of his money and other valuables. The cause thereof was ıever known. He might have died of heart disease of which it is aid he was affected, or he might have been murdered and robbed. lis death is likely to remain a mystery in time to all save the omnipotent, omniscient and omnipresent God.

CHAPTER 33.

JOHN MILLER WALLACE HARRIS.

(Named in Sec. 5, Chap. 28.)

Article 1.—John Miller Wallace Harris, a son of Judge Christopher Harris and Sally Wallace, his wife, was born in Madison County, Ky., May 30, 1821. He was never married.

JOHN MILLER WALLACE HARRIS

When the Civil War came on and the North and South were arrayed one against the other, in a great struggle for States rights embracing the question of negro slavery, he embraced the cause of the South, and enlisted in the confederate army. However it was not his fate to live to see the downfall of the cause he had espoused. On Monday, the 8th day of Sept. 1862, in the ranks of two companies of Confederates, under the command of Captain Jesse, on the way from Tennessee to central Kentucky, as they topped the Pine Mountain the most lofty of the Kentucky Ranges, came in contact with an ambuscade of a greatly superior force of Federals, who poured into Captain Jesse's men, hot heavy and vivid discharges from their guns, completely routing them, killing several of the men on the spot, in which engagement, John Miller Wallace Harris received a deadly wound, from which he lingered about one week and expired. His remains were buried near the spot where he breathed his last, and have never been removed by any of the family.

Here let it be noticed that in the battle of Richmond, Ky., Aug. 30 1862, occuring something like nine days in advance of the one at Pine Mountain, General John Miller, a relative of this subject and a brother to the husband of his sister, Talitha, and for whom the subject was in part named, while trying to rally a disordered column of Federal soldiers, received his death wound, and lived only about a week, the General on the one side, and the subject on the other of the great questions of which the country was at war. (See Part I, Chapter 7.)

CHAPTER 34.

POLLY (MARY) WOODS HARRIS.

(Named in Sec. 6, Chap. 28.)

Article 1.—Polly (Mary) Woods Harris, a daughter of Judge Christopher Harris and Sally Wallace his wife, was born in Madison County, Ky., Sept. 25, 1823.

She was quiet in her disposition, kind and well beloved by her kin, without exception, her friends and her neighbors loved her, she died just a few years since, at the age of about 80 years, Aug. 1, 1901. On the 15th day of Jan. 1852, she became the second wife of Elder John M. Park, an old Baptist preacher, of high standing in that religious society. To them were born the children named in the coming sections: (See Part VI, Chap. 31, Sec. 1.)

Section 1. Margaret Susan Park, who married William Francis Elkin, a son of Robert M. Elkin and Malinda Edmonson his wife, no issue of this union. She survived her husband but a few years, and was a great sufferer a long time before her death May 1, 1901, though of a cheerful bright and happy disposition.

Section 2. Christopher Harris Park, named for his maternal grand-father; married Ella Broaddus a daughter of H. Clay Broaddus and Bettie Bush, his wife, and now (1906) the proprietor of a Hotel in Irvine, Ky. To them were born:

1. John Clay Park.
2. Christopher Harris Park.
3. Pleasant Broaddus Park.

Section 3. A son not named, died in a few days after birth. (See Part VII, Sec. 1-2-2.)

CHAPTER 35.

MARGARET FRANCES HARRIS.

(Named in Sec. 7, Chap. 28.)

Article 1.—Margaret Frances Harris, a daughter of Judge Christopher Harris and Sally Wallace his wife, was born in Madison County, Ky. April 8, 1826, was married to Joseph Warren Moore, Feb. 9, 1848.

MARGARET FRANCIS HARRIS
Wife of Joseph Warren Moore

JOSEPH WARREN MOORE

They lived in Madison County till after their children were born, and then emigrated and settled near Emerson, Marion County,

Mo., where she died Aug. 13, 1900, her husband yet (1905) surviving, an old man. Their children are named in the coming sections:

Section 1. Rueben Moore, went to Missouri with his parents, anl there married; since he has died.

Section 2. Christopher Harris Moore, went to Missouri with his parents and there married.

Section 3. Sally Elizabeth Moore, went to Missouri with her parents and there married, and whom her husband survived.

Section 4. Mary Buchanan Moore, went to Missouri with her parents and there married, and are now (1906) residents of that state.

Section 5. Annie Moore, went to Missouri, with her parents, where she now lives.

Section 6. Margaret Moore, went to Missouri with her parents, and she died there.

Section 7. Jenny Moore, went to Missouri with her parents and there married, and yet lives. Some time in 1870, this whole family left Madison County, Ky., and went to Missouri.

CHAPTER 36.

SARAH OVERTON HARRIS.

(Named in Sec. 8. Chap. 28.)

Article 1.—Sarah Overton Harris a daughter and youngest child of Judge Christopher Harris and Sally Wallace, his wife, was born in Madison County, Ky. July 10, 1828.

On the 14th day of Aug. 1843, she married Thomas Moberley Oldham a son of Caleb Oldham, and Abigail Moberley his wife. (See Part VII, Sec. 32.) She died, her husband surviving, living at the old original grand-father, John Harris homestead on the head of Hickory Lick, branch of Muddy Creek, and where their son Joe and his wife now live (with his father, since deceased.) Aunt Sarah was an excellent woman, she never forgot her relatives and friends, and always made it a point to visit them, and wanted them to visit her, and she was indeed fond of them, and had lots of friends, she was ever ready and would go at any time of night or day to the bed of the sick, and to those in distress.

We have in our possession, and which we highly prize, an old fashioned, gracefully formed, copper tea-kettle, which she gave us, that belonged to her grand-mother, Margaret Maupin Harris, and who brought it from Virginia with her in the migration named in Chapter 2, and the Lord only knows its age. To them were born the children named in the coming sections:

Section 1. Sallie Elizabeth Oldham, born in Madison County, Kentucky; married David G. Martin, Jan. 9, 1892, in the 40th year of her age. David Gentry Martin was a son of David Gentry Martin, and Samiramus Brassfield his wife. (See Chap. 5, Sec. 4, and Part VI, Chap. 31, Sec. 1.) Her husband survived her and afterwards married Temperance Chambers Oldham, a daughter of Othniel R. Oldham and Sydonia Noland his wife. (See Part VI, Chap. 17, Sec. 6.) Mr. Martin owns a 600 acre farm near Boone in Rockcastle County, Ky., located on Boone's trace, the pioneer and in which he lives. No living issue of either marriage.

Section 2. Joseph Christopher Oldham, born in Madison County, Ky., married Mattie Williams, a daughter of W. Thomas B. Williams, late a leading citizen, farmer, banker, financier and capitalist of Irvine, Estill County, Ky. They own and occupy, the old homestead of their great grand-father, John Harris, on Hickory Lick, branch of Muddy Creek in Madison County, Ky Joseph C. Oldham deals extensively in cattle and hogs.

CHAPTER 37.

JUDGE OVERTON HARRIS.

(Named in Chap. 16, Sec. 3.)

Article 1.—Judge Overton Harris, a son of John Harris and Margaret Maupin his wife, was born Nov. 24, 1789, in Madison County, Kentucky.

He it was who accompjanied his father in a Flat Boat, down the Kentucky, Ohio and Mississippi Rivers, to New Orlenas, in 1810, on the occasion of his father's death, as related in Chapter 16. He married in Garrard County, Ky., Mary Rice Woods, a daughter of James Woods and Mary Garland his wife, Dec. 1, 1814. She was born Sept. 24, 1795. (See Part II, Chap. 20, Sec. 10.) In the fall of 1817 they emigrated and settled in Boone County, Mo. Mr. Harris died in 1844, and Mrs. Harris died Aug. 31, 1876.

MARY RICE WOODS
Wife of Judge Overton Harris

Mr. Harris was the first sheriff of Boone County in 1821, which office he held till appointed assessor and collector by the Governor in 1822. He was Major of the 3rd division, mounted militia in the Black Hawk war, and was in the war of 1812; County Judge of Boone County a number of years. He possessed a strong mind, was very religious, of a cheerful nature and had the confidence of the people. Their children:

Section 1. John Woods Harris, born Aug. 31, 1816, in Madison County, Ky., married Ann Mary McClure. Their children:

1. Martha Maupin Harris; married General William Jackson Hendricks, lawyer of New York. Their children:
   1. Annie Hendricks; married Robert Burns Wilson; poet and artist, Frankfort, Ky. Their children:
      1. Annie Elizabeth Wilson.
   2. Sophia Kemper Hendricks; married Dr. Frederic Smith Pickett, Cleveland, Ohio.

3. Jane Carlyle Hendricks.
4. John Harris Hendricks.
5. Jacqueline Hendricks.

2. Frances Bond Harris; died when a child.

3. Jane Woods Harris; married John Johnson Rogers, she is now a widow living in Lexington, Ky. Their children.
1. Martha Hendricks Rogers.
2. Mary Evelyn Rogers; died when an infant.
3. Virgil Johnson Rogers.

4. Virgil McClure Harris, of the merchantile Fruit Co., St. Louis, Mo., married Isabel McKinley, of St. Louis, no issue.

5. John Woods Harris, banker and capitalist; married Susan Oldham, daughter of Rev. William Abner Oldham, and Talitha Evans, his wife. (Seee Part VI, Chap. 14, Sec. 2.) Their children:
1. John Woods Harris, Junior.
2. Mary Harris.

Section 2. James Harris, born May 17, 1818; married Sabra Jackson. Their children:

1. Miss —— Harris; married H. C. Pierce; died in Columbia, Missouri.
2. Sallie Harris; married Mr. —— Bradley, East 9th, Street, Fulton, Mo.
3. John S. Harris, banker, Ashland, Missouri..
4. Overton Harris, merchant, Denison, Texas.
5. Wade J. Harris, merchant, Fulton, Mo.
6. Julia Harris; married Mr. Johnston, East 9th, Street, Fulton, Missouri.
7. Miss Harris; married Samuel Baker; dead.
8. Miss Harris; married John Trimble, McCredie, Mo.
9. David H. Harris, lawyer, Fulton, Mo.
10. Louise Harris; married Mr. Holland, St. Louis, Mo.
11. Miss Harris; married Stockton Dorry, Columbia, Mo.
12. W. B. Harris, farmer and stockman, McCredie, Mo.
13. James H. Harris, farmer and stockman, McCredie, Mo.

Section 3. Martha Ryland Harris, born Jan. 15, 1821; married John Mills Maupin. (See Part V, Chap. 11, Sec. 2.) She died leaving one son:

1. John Overton Maupin, living near Columbia, Mo.

Section 4. William Anderson Harris, born March 25, 1823; married Elizabeth Robnett. Their children:

1. James Harris; died young.
2. Pleasant Robnett Harris, Schell City, Vernon County, Mo.
3. Mary Catherine Bingham; dead.

Section 5. Sarah Elizabeth Harris, born July 22, 1824; married George Hunt; both dead, issue:

1 A child; died in infancy.

Section 6. Mary Frances Harris, born Nov. 10, 1827, in Boone County, Mo., married her cousin Thomas Berry Harris, son of Tyre Harris and Sallie Garland his wife, the marriage ceremony was solemnized by Elder Noah Flood, minister of the missionary Baptist Church, July 13, 1852, at the residence of her father in Boone County, Mo. (See Chap. 10, Sec. 7.) Their children:

1. Martha Overton Harris, of Fulton, Missouri.
2. Sallie Tyre Harris; married Judge A. M. Wathall, 1405 Myrtle Chpt El Paso, Texas. Their children:

1. Henry Vaughn Wathall, lawyer, El Paso, Texas
2. William Maupin Wathall; deceased.
3. Mary Miller Wathall.
4. Sallie Tom Wathall.

3. Susan Harris, of Fulton, Missouri.
4. William Christopher Harris, president of the Calloway Bank, Fulton, Mo.
5. Mary Elizabeth Harris; married Dr. J. A. Vansant, of Mt. terling, Ky. Their children.
    1. Thomas Harris Vansant.
    2. James Albert Vansant, Junior.
    3. Mary Frances Vansant.

6. Overton Thomas Harris, wholesale dry goods merchant, of Rile-Stix, St. Louis, Mo.
7. Tyre Crawford Harris, of wholesale Polk Hat Co., St. Louis, Mo.
8. Isabel Harris, 815 Court street, Fulton, Mo.

Section 7. Overton Michael Harris, Judge; married Amanda 'ood. Their children:

1. Clifton Woods Harris.
2. James Harris, Kansas City, Mo.
3. William Overton Harris, Sedalia, Missouri.
4. Lilly F. Harris, Sedalia, Mo.
5. Beulah Harris; married E. C. Yancey, Sedalia, Mo.
6. Mary Harris, Sedalia, Mo.
7. J. Brown Harris, attorney at law, Dallas, Texas.
8. Emmet Harris, Dallas, Texas.
9. Nellie Harris, Sedalia, Mo.

Table of Genealogy

- Mary Frances Harris, [illegible]
  - Overton Harris
    - John Harris
      - Christopher Harris
        - Robert Harris
          - William Harris
            - Robert Harris
            - Mrs. Mary Rice, nee Clairborne
          - Temperance Overton
        - Mourning Glenn
      - Agnes McCord
    - Margaret Maupin
      - John Maupin
        - Daniel Maupin
          - Gabriel Maupin
            - Earl Spencer
          - Marie Spencer
        - Margaret Via
      - Frances Dabney
        - Cornelius Dabney
        - Sarah Jennings
          - Charles Jennings
            - Sir Humphrey Jennings
  - Mary Rice Woods
    - James Woods
    - Mary Garland
      - John Garland
      - Mary Rice

CHAPTER 38.

JAMES HARRIS.

(Named in Chap. 16, Sec. 4.)

Article 1.—Jame Harris, a son of John Harris and Margaret Maupin his wife, was born in Madison County, Ky., May 7, 1794, was a soldier in the Black Hawk war, against the Indians, and was captured in Canada by the Indians, and made run the gauntlet, while some of his fellow prisoners were slain; the Indians greatly admired him for his sagacity and bravery, and adopted him into their tribe, in which relation he was held by them, for something like two years, and from the Indians through the French, he was finally ransomed by his people, the ransom price being a red blanket. .He served in the war of 1812.

He married Mourning Bennett, a daughter of John Bennett and Isabella Harris his wife, and they made their home in Boone County, Mo., the said Isabella, was a daughter of Christopher Harris, and his second wife, Agnes McCord. (See Chap. 47, and Chap. 4, Sec. 9.) The children of James Harris and Mourning Bennett, his wife:

Section 1. John Harris; married ——— ——— children:

1. Anna Harris; married Mr. Morrrison, Denver, Colorado.
2. Mark Harris; married first, Miss McBain, secondly, Miss McKine.
3. Georgia Harris; married Dr. ——— Head.
4. Ed Harris; married ——— ———.

Section 2. Robert Harris.

Section 3. James Harris.

Section 4. Anderson Woods Harris, born near Columbia, Mo., died in 1901. He married Gabrilla Nelson, of South Carolina. Their children:

1. James Harris; married Julia Woods; both dead.
2. Minerva Harris; married J. F. Johnson, a farmer, of Harris, Missouri.

OVERTON HARRIS

SUSAN JONES
Wife of Overton Harris.

3. Jerusha Harris; married T. N. Wood, a farmer of Harris, Missouri.

4. Ann Taylor Harris: married J. H. Harryman, a farmer of Harris Mo.

5. Overton Harris, the model farmer, and owner of Model Herefords, of Harris Sullivan County, Mo., who was awarded the Premier Champion-ship honor as the most successful exhibitor at the Universal Exposition of Hereford cattle, at St. Louis, Mo., presented to him Friday afternoon Sept. 23, 1904, at three oclock in the Live Stock Forum. The award was determined by the largest aggregate amount awarded to animals exhibited on certain special sections by any one exhibitor of said breed, at the Universal Exposition $4,555 was his aggregate award. Overton Harris with his Herefords led all breeders at the World's Fair, capturing thousands of dollars in prizes. He married, first Miss Susan Jones; she died in 1903. Their children:

1. Clifford Burdette Harris, now (1906) twenty years of age, an eminently prominent young man, of the Harris Banking Company, of Harris, Mo. He married Miss Clara Moore, a daughter of A. B. Moore, of Bowling Green, Ky.

2. Alma Estille Harris; married O. H. Moberley, who is engaged in the General Merchandise business in Pontiac, Livingston, County. Ill.

3. Clara Blanche Harris; married A. T. Leach, secretary and treasurer of the Kenfield Publishing Company, Chicago, Ill.

4. Elizabeth Amber Harris, now attending the Loring School in Chicago, Ill.

5. Anderson Woods Harris, attending the Culver Military Academy, in Culver, Ind.

6. Augustus Overton Harris, attending the Culver Military Academy, in Culver, Ind.

Section 5. Woodson Harris.

Section 6. Margaret Harris.

Section 7. Mourning Harris.

Section 8. Sarah Harris.

Section 9 Nancy E. Harris.

Section 10. Warren Harris.

Section 11. —— Harris.

Section 12. —— Harris.

Section 13. - — Harris.

CHAPTER 39.

MAJOR WILLIAM HARRIS.

(Named in Chap. 16, Sec. 6.)

Article 1.—Major William Harris, a son of John Harris and Margaret Maupin his wife, was born on Muddy Creek, in Madison County, Ky., May 16, 1805; died October 25, 1872.

Major WILLIAM HARRIS.

He represented Madison County in the Kentucky Legislature, in 1851-3; was Common School Commissioner of said County, for twenty years. He took great interest in County affairs, and worked for the welfare and betterment of the pubilc. He was a wealthy farmer, enterprising, progresive, and a public spirited man. He maried Malinda Duncan, a daughter of John Duncan, and Lucy White his wife, she was born in 1808, and died in 1873. They had only one child a son:

Section 1. Hon. John Duncan Harris, born Dec. 29, 1829, three miles south of Richmond, Ky. He graduated from Bethany College, Va., in 1847; read law under Judge William C. Goodloe, but never practiced, preferring the occupation of a farmer. Sept. 20, 1849, he married Nancy White, a daughter of Valentine M. White, and Jane Gentry his wife. (See Chap. 45.) He owned about 2500 acres of well improved blue grass land, including his father's old homestead, and that of his wife's father. He was many years the President of the Madison Female Institute, a school of learning for girls. He was elected to the State Senate in 1885, made an active energetic member. He was defeated in his candidacy for Governor of the State in 1887. He died in 1905, his wife having preceded him to the grave. Their children:

MALINDA DUNCAN,
Wife of Major William Harris.

1. William Valentine White Harris, born in 1858; died in 1864.

2. Pattie Harris; married Samuel H. Stone, now residents of Louisville, Ky. Mr. Stone held the office of Auditor of Pubilic Accounts, of Kentucky and a competent official. To them were born: (See Chap. 3, Sec. 7, B-4-b, 1.)

1. Nannie Rodes Stone, born Dec. 15, 1873; died Aug. 8, 1874.

2. William Harris Stone, born April 19, 1875; died June 4, 1901.

3. James Clifton Stone.

4. John Harris Stone, born July 10, 1886; died Sept. 18, 1900.

5. Samuel Hanson Stone, Jr.

3. John Duncan Harris, 1865-1883, a bright and promising young man who died at the age of seventeen.

4. Mary Harris; married Cassius M. Clay, a wealthy farmer of Bourbon County, and who represented Bourbon County in the House of Representatives of the Kentucky Legislature, in 1871-5. To them were born:

1. Cassius M. Clay, Jr.
2. John Harris Clay.

Section 5. William V. Harris, 1854-1864.

Hon. JOHN D. HARRIS.

NANCY J. WHITE,
Wife of Hon. John D. Harris.

CHAPTER 10.

ELIZABETH HARRIS.

(Named in Sec. 7, Chap. 16.)

Article 1.—Elizabeth Harris, a daughter of John Harris, and Margaret Maupin, his wife, was born in Madison County, Ky., Sept. 30, 1791.

ELIZABETH HARRIS.
Wife of Anderson Woods,

She married May 4, 1809, Anderson Woods, a son of James Woods and Mary Garland his wife, of Paint Lick, Garrard County, Ky. (See Chap. 20, Sec. 6, Part II.) They were members of the Viney Fork Baptist Church, and were granted letters of dimission when they moved to Boone County, Mo., in 1823. He was a pioneer Baptist preacher of Boone County. The fruits of this marriage were the children named in the coming sections:

Section 1. James Woods; married Martha Stone. (See Chap. 7, Sec. 4, and Part II, Chap. 20, Sec. 6.)

Section 2. Margaret Woods; married Clifton Maupin. (See Part V, Chap. 11, Sec. 2.) She lives in Centralia, Mo.

Section 3. Polly Garland Woods; married Caleb Stone, to whom were born these children:

1. Carlisle Stone; died in Mississippi in 1879, a femme sole.
2. James Stone; married Mamie Worthington, residents of Mississippi.
3. Thomas M. Stone; died in Mississippi in 1879, was never married.

Bettie Garland Stone; married William Worthington, residents of Greenville, Miss.

5. William A. Stone; married Mrs. Anita Martin, residents of Rosedale, Miss.
6. Caleb Stone, resident of St. Louis, Mo.
7. Cyrus Turner Stone, resident of Richmond, Ky.
8. Samuel Stone; died in infancy.

Section 4. Susannah Woods; married Ashby Snell. (See Part II, Chapter 20, Section 6.)

Section 5. Rice Woods; married Eliza C. Wilson. (See Part II, Chapter 20, Section 6.)

Section 6. Harris Woods; married Eliza Curry. (See Part II, Chapter 20, Section 6.)

Section 7. William Garland Woods. (See Part II, Chapter 20, Section 6.)

Section 8. Martha Woods; married Willis Snell. (See Part II, Chapter 20, Section 6.)

Section 9. Talith Woods; married first, Martin Bordine, secondly, W. H. Dulaney. (See Part II, Chapter 20, Section 6.)

Section 10. Eliza Woods; married W. F. Buckner, Paris, Mo. (See Part II, Chapter 20, Section 6.)

Section 11. Matilda Woods; married D. O. Bean. (See Part II, Chapter 20, Section 6.)

CHAPTER 41.

FRANCES HARRIS.

(Named in Sec. 8, Chap. 16.)

Article 1.—Frances Harris, a daughter of John Harris and Margaret Maupin, his wife, was born in Madison County, Ky., March 26, 1802, married in said County, July 24, 1823, James Miller a son of Daniel Miller, and Susannah Woods his wife.

A fuller account will be found in Part I, Chapter 8, to which the reader is referred.

CHAPTER 42.

SUSAN HARRIS.

(Named in Sec. 9, Chap. 16.)

Article 1.—Susan Harris, a daughter of John Harris and Margaret Maupin his wife, was born in Madison County, Ky., May 10, 1808.

She married Dr. William H. Duncan, and made their home in Missouri. To whom were born the children named in the coming sections:

SUSAN HARRIS,
Wife of Dr. William H. Duncan.

Section 1. Margaret F. Duncan; married T. T. Allen.

Section 2. Sarah E. Duncan; died young.

Section 3. Sarah C. Duncan; died young.

Section 4. John W. Duncan; died young.

Section 5. James S. Duncan.

Section 6. Martha W. Duncan; married G. W. Trimble.

Section 7. William O. Duncan; married first, Simpson, second, Beattie.

Section 8. Ann Eliza Duncan; died young.

Section 9. John Harris Duncan, a popular and prominent physician, of St. Louis, Mo., and to whom the writer is much indebted for a great deal of the data of Harris genealogy, and to whom his thanks are tendered. He married S. Belle Dulaney.

CHAPTER 43.

BENJAMIN HARRIS.

(Named in Sec. 2, Art. 4, Chap. 1.)

Article 1.—Benjamin Harris, a son of the old Kentucky pioneer, Christopher Harris and Agnes McCord his second wife, was born in Albemarle County, Va., and came to Madison County, Ky., in the migratory movement, named in Chap. 2.

His first wife was Miss Frances Jones. (See Note at foot of Chap. 45.) He married his second wife in Madison County, Ky., June 4, 1792, Nancy Burgin, she survived him, and on Aug. 8, 1797, the said Nancy Harris, married Nathaniel Tevis. He was Captain of Virginia State Militia in the Revolution. John and Hartleg Sappington were appraisers of his estate. He was a signer of the Albemarle Declaration of Independence, April 21, 1778. To Benjamin Harris, and Nancy Burgin his wife, the children named in the coming sections were born:

Section 1. Polly Harris; married Thomas Richardson, Dec. 15, 1816, to whom were born:

1. Elliot Richardson; married Susan Peyton.
2. James Richardson; married —— Simpson. He represented Lincoln County in the Kentucky Legislature, in 1853-5.
3. Aaron Burr Richardson, enlisted in Captain James Stone's Company, in the Mexican War, and died in the service in 1845.
4. Thomas Jefferson Richardson, enlisted in Captain James Stones Company in the Mexican War, and died in the service in 1845.
5. Robert Richardson; married Lavinia Moberley, Feb. 1, 1849.
6. Samuel H. Richardson; married Elizabeth Park, Feb. 10, 1845.
7. Benjamin (Bud) Richardson; married Margaret Peyton. He was killed by the Federal soldiers. His widow married Benjamin Price, Mr. Price died, and she married Galen J. White, and she died, Mr. White surviving.
8. Sallie Ann Richardson; married A. J. Arvine, Sept. 6, 1849, issue of marriage:
    1. John Arvine.
9. Mary Richardson; married John Christopher Arvine, Dec. 23, 1852. Children:
    1. John Arvine; married Ida ——.
    2. Nannie Arvine; married Mr. Shane.
    3. Shelby Arvine.
    4. Christopher Arvine.
    5. Bettie Arvine; married Mr. Brown. They live in Missouri.
    6. Bettie Arvine.
    7. Richard Arvine.
10. Melina Richardson; married Nathan Arvine, Dec. 21, 1857. Children:
    1. Thomas D. Arvine; died unmarried.
    2. Sallie Arvine; married Durrett White, Mr. White enlisted in the Confederate Army, in Captain Thomas B. Collins Company F, 7th, (afterwards the 11th) Kentucky Cavalry, General John H. Morgan's command, and was captured on the Ohio raid and imprisoned in Camp Douglas. Mr. White some time

after the war emigrated with his family to Missouri, and died in that State.

3. Mary Etta (Duck) Arvine; married William F. White. They moved to Lexington, Ky., and Mr. White there engaged in the livery business in partnership with J. Tevis Wilkerson. and died in that city.

Section 2. Tyre Harris.

Nancy Burgin the second wife of Benjamin Harris, was a daughter of Isaac Burgin and Mary his wife, who died in 1794, he had other children, but Nancy is the only one of them called by name in his will.

CHAPTER 14.

WILLIAM HARRIS.

(Named in Sec. 3, Art. 4, Chap. 4.)

Article 1.—William Harris, a son of the old Kentucky pioneer, Christopher Harris and Agnes McCord his second wife, was born in Albemarle County, Va., and came to Madison County, Ky., in the migratory movement named in Chapter 2.

He was a private in the Virginia State Militia in the Revolutionary war. He married in Madison County, Ky., Feb. 4, 1790, Anna Oldham a daughter of the old pioneer, Jesse Oldham, Sr., and Elizabeth Simpson, his wife. (See Part VI, Chap. 3, Sec. 5.) He owned and lived on land on the Hickory Lick Branch of Muddy Creek, until 1817, on the 6th of Sept. 1817, he conveyed this land to Colonel John Speed Smith, and moved to another part of the County, in a more northerly part, and on the 10th of March, 1818, made another deed of conveyance to Colonel Smith. We have been unable to satisfactorily name and trace all his children, but the following are some of them:

Section 1. Jesse Harris; married Jemima Fowler, Aug. 4, 1813, and he lived and died in Madison County, Ky. Their children were:

1. Richard Fowler Harris, he was a blacksmith by occupation. He married Nancy Berkley. He also traded considerably in live stock, buying in Kentucky, and selling in the southern market. Their children:

1. Eliza Catherine Harris; married firstly, Pleasant Berry, secondly, William C. Ogg, and thirdly, Ira N. Scudder. No issue of the last two marriages. Children of the first marriage:

1. Everet M. Berry; married Ann Shillings.
2. Mollie Berry; died unmarried.
3. Ira Berry; married Mary Shearer.

2. Dr. John William Harris; married firstly. Eliza Green, and secondly, Mrs. Sarah Shearer, nee Green, sister to his first wife. Children of the first marriage:

1. Nannie Harris; married James Noland.
2. Mary Harris; married Raines Green.

3. Lou Ann Harris; married Milton Reynold. Children:
   1. Lee Reynold.
   2. Harris Reynold.
   3. Jesse Reynold.
   4. Claudus Reynold.
   5. Otis Reynold.
   6. Grace Reynold.
   7. Andra Reynold.
   8. Oscar Reynold.

4. Jesse Berkley Harris; married Bettie Powell. He is a professional school teacher, and was at one time professor of the Caldwell High School in Richmond, Ky., and did much to build up that institution. His home is in said city. Their children:

1. Lela Jane Harris, a school mistress; a teacher in Caldwell High School.

2. John B. Harris; married Miss Burrus; works in printing office in Washington City.

3. Bessie Harris, a school mistress. Held position in Caldwell High School.

2. Colonel William Harris, born, lived and died in Madison County, Ky., a bachelor.

3. Nancy Harris; married Samuel Best, Aug. 15, 1846. Children:
   1. Mary Best; married John Burnam.
   2. Ann Eliza Best; married B. F. (Doc) Vaughn.

4. Eliza Harris; married Stephen B. Eubank, March 12, 1835 Children:
   1. Nancy Catherine Eubank; married Irvine Benton.
   2. Richard Claibourne Eubank; died single.

Section 2. Agnes M. Harris; married Milton Oldham. (See Part V, Chap. 4, Sec. 8.)

Section 3. Richard M. Harris; married Louisa Oldham. (See Part V, Chap. 4, Sec. 10.)

See note at the foot of Chapter 45.

CHAPTER 45.

BARNABAS HARRIS.

(Named in Sec. 4, Art. 4, Chap. 4.)

Article 1.—Barnabas Harris, a son of the old Kentucky pioneer, Christopher Harris, and Agnes McCord, his second wife, was born in Albemarle County, Va., and came to Madison County, Ky., in the migratory movement named in Chapter 2.

He married in Madison County, Ky., 17—1803, to Elizabeth Oldham, a daughter of Ready Money Richard Oldham, and Ursley Williams his wife. His wife, Elizabeth survived him, and afterwards she married Mr. Clark. (See Part VI, Chap. 4, Sec. 1.)

Note: -The names of all the children of Benjamin Harris and his first wife, Miss ——— Jones, to whom he was married in Virginia, the subject of Chapter 43. Samuel Harris and his wife, Nancy Wilkerson, who were probably married in Virginia, the subject of Chapter 4, Sec. 6. William Harris and his wife, Anna Oldham, who were married in Madison County, Ky., Feb. 4, 1790, the subject of Chapter 44. Barnabas Harris and his wife, Elizabeth Oldham, who were married in Madison County, Ky., in 1803, the subject of Chapter 45, being unknown to the writer, the following list is presented, that persons who know may recognize some of the children of the above named couples, viz:

Permilia Harris, married Robert McCord, Dec. 31, 1795.
Samuel Haris—Sarah, Province, Sept. 2, 1795.
Thomas Harris—Rachael Barnes, Dec. 7, 1796.
Thursa Harris—Allen Holland, May 8, 1796.
Foster Harris—Sallie Manning, Oct. 19. 1797.
Anna Harris—Jacob Leburn, Feb. 28, 1799.
Lucy Harris—William Wilkerson, Feb. 26, 1801.
Nancy Harris—William Woods, Sept. 25, 1802.
William Elliot Harris—Mary Manning, March 17, 1802.
David Harris—Nancy Cooksey, May 30, 1805.
Samuel Harris—Elizabeth Kennedy, April 3, 1807.
David Harris—Nancy Maxwell, Nov. 1, 1811.
Sallie Harris—Joseph Davis, July 20, 1812.
Elizabeth Harris—James Rynot, Feb. 28, 1811.
Elizabeth Harris—Ariah Davis, Nov. 29, 1813.
Western Harris—Elizabeth Dulaney, Feb. 2, 1815.
Lavinia Harris—Henry King, Nov. 11, 1815.
Robert Harris—Elizabeth Lancaster, July 3, 1815.
William Harris—Anna Smith, Dec. 5, 1816.
Milly Harris—Samuel Sale, Nov. 21, 1820.
Elizabeth Harris—Richmond Stagner, June 21, 1821.
Nancy Harris—Thomas Reid, April 19, 1821.
Launder Harris—Howard Clanker, Dec. 5, 1821.
Margaret Harris—Thomas Wright, Jan. 1, 1824.
Pauline Harris—Jeremiah Lancaster, March 15, 1825.
John Harris—Sallie Vaughn, Oct. 15, 1828.
Sherod Harris—Theodocia Brumback, Oct. 22, 1829.
John C. Harris—Sallie Floyd, Nov. 11, 1830.
Mary Harris—William Wheeler, Feb. 4, 1830.

CHAPTER 16.

JANE HARRIS.

(Named in Sec. 7, Art. 4, Chap. 4.)

Article 1.—Jane Harris, a daughter of the old Kentucky pioneer, Christopher Harris, and Agnes McCord his second wife, was born in Albemarle County, Va., and was there married, April 1, 1784, to Richard Gentry, 1763-1793, and they in the migratory movement named in Chapter 2, came to Madison County, Kentucky, in 1786, where they settled and spent their remaining days.

To them were born the twelve children named in the coming sections: she died in about 1820, and Richard Gentry married Nancy Guthrie, and raised some more children. He was a Captain in the Revolutionary War, enlisted in Albemarle County. Children of Jane Harris and Richard Gentry:

Section 1. Reuben Eastus Gentry, born June 6, 1785; died in 1839. He married Elizabeth White, a daughter of Joel White of Madison County, Ky., and moved to Missouri in 1809; she died in 1818. They were the ancestors of the prominent family of Gentry, of Pettus County, Missouri. Their children:

1. Richard Gentry; married Alzira Miller. (See Part 1, Chap. 14, Sec. 2) and secondly, Mrs. Jael Woods Hocker Gentry, widow of his brother. (See Section 2.)
2. Joel W. Gentry, born March 15, 1815; married Jael Woods Hocker, June 19, 1848, and died Oct. 4, 1851. (See Part VII, Chap. 7, Section 1.) His widow married her brother-in-law, Richard Gentry. (See Sec. 1, and Part VII, Chap. 7, Sec. 1.)
3. Reuben E. Gentry.
4. Major William Gentry; married —— ——. The parents of Jane Redd Gentry Shelton, of 4467 Lindell Boulevard, St. Louis, Missouri.
5. Jane Harris Gentry.

Section 2. David Gentry, born April 11, 1787; married Susannah Maupin of Madison County, Ky., July 28, 1804, and moved to Missouri, they raised a large family, mostly girls. (See Part V, Chap. 12, Sec. 4.)

Section 3. General Richard Gentry, born Aug. 25, 1788; married Ann Hawkins of Madison County, Ky., daughter of Nicholas Hawkins, and moved to Missouri in 1816. He was a Major General of Missouri troops, in the Black Hawk Indian War, and in 1837, accepted a commission from the Secretary of war as Colonel of Volunteers for the Seminole indian war, and took his regiment of Missourians to Florida. On Christmas Day he was killed in battle at Ochochobee Lake. His children were:

1. Ann Eliza Gentry; married John Boyart.
2. Richard Harrison Gentry; married Mary Wyott, the parents of Richard Gentry, Esq., a very prominent man of Kensas City, Missouri.
3. Oliver Perry Gentry; married Eliza Bowers.
4. Jane Gentry; married John Hudnan.
5. Dorothy Ann Gentry; married Henry Crumbough.

6. Mary Gentry; married first, Robert Clark, second, Boyle Gordon.
7. Thomas Burton Gentry; married Mary Todd.
8. Nicholas Hawkins Gentry; unmarried, a southern patriot, killed in Civil War.

Section 4. Christy Gentry, born Oct. 14, 1780; married Lucy Christy, of Clark County, Ky. He moved to Missouri, and became a very prominent missionary Baptist minister and raised a large family in Marion County, Mo.

Section 5. James Gentry, born June 1, 1792; married Ann Campbell of Madison County, Ky. He died in Galena, Ill., and his family moved to California in 1849.

Section 6. Joseph McCord Gentry, born March 21, 1794; died in infancy.

Section 7. Nancy Gentry, born Oct. 3, 1795; married Jeremiah Bush of Clark County, Ky., she was a woman of rare intelligence, and strength of character and raised a large family. Some of her children were:

1. Judge James Bush.
2. Ambrose Bush.
3. Richard Bush.
4. Volentine Bush.

Several live in Missouri and Texas.

Section 8. Joshua Gentry, born June 6, 1797; married Miss Henry of Missouri and settled in Marion County, Mo., where he raised a large family. He was a very prominent man, built the Hanibal and St. Joseph Railroad, of which he was President in 1864, when he died.

Section 9. Joseph Gentry, born Aug. 29, 1799; married Elizabeth Tribble, lived in Madison, and afterwards in Lincoln County, Ky. His children were:

1. Jane Gentry.
2. Peter Tribble Gentry.
3. Mary Frances Gentry.
4. Nancy Boone Gentry.
5. Joseph Gentry.
6. Richard Gentry.
7. Alexander Gentry.
8. Maria Gentry.
9. Overton Harris Gentry.
10. William Harrison Gentry.

Section 10. Overton Gentry, born June 10, 1802; married Lucinda Reed of Madison County, Ky. (See Part 1, Chap. 14, Sec.3.) He lived in Lincoln County, Ky. They raised seven sons and four daughters:

Section 11. Rhodes Gentry, born Aug. 5, 1804; married Ollie Moore and moved to Rolls County, Mo., where he died. His descendents are mostly in Oregon and California.

Section 12. Jane Gentry, born March 28, 1806; married firstly, Volentine White, secondly, James Blythe, Oct. 15, 1834. Children of the first marriage:

1. William Henry White; married Margaret Faulkner. (See Part VII, Chap. 5, Sec. 5.)
2. Richard J. White; married Lucy Taylor.

3. Durrett White, murdered by Federal soldiers during the Civil War.

4. Nancy Jane White; married John D. Harris. (See Chap. 39.)

Children of the second marriage:

5. Lucy Blythe; married Captain William E. Simms, of Paris, Kentucky.

6. Dovy Blythe; married Joseph C. Anderson; she is a widow, living in Lexington, Ky. Has a son, James Blythe Anderson.

7. Melissa Blythe; died unmarried.

Note: The Gentry Family of Albemarle County, Va.

Nicholas Gentry first wife, Mary —— and second wife Jean —— died in 1779, leaving eleven children, viz:

1. Moses Gentry, bought land in 1778, from Samuel Gay, on the old Lynchburg Road, north of Garland's store. He was a ruling elder in the Cove Church. He died in 1810. He married —— —— Their children were:

 1. Claiborne Gentry; married Jane Maxwell, daughter of Bazaleel Maxwell.
 2. Nicholas Gentry; married Mary Maxwell, daughter of Bazaleel Maxwell.
 3. Frances Gentry; married Thomas Fitzpatrick.
 4. Joanna Gentry; married Joseph Walters.

2. David Gentry; married first —— —— and secondly, Mary Eustace, daughter of Reuben Eustace. He and his brother, Martin, were owners of land on Doyle's River, prior to 1778, which they afterwards sold to Benajah Brown. Some of his children:

 1. Winifred Gentry; married William Martin, son of James Martin and Sarah Harris, his wife. (See Part III, Chap. 5.)
 2. Richard Gentry; married Jane Harris, daughter of Christopher Harris and Agnes McCord, his wife. (See Part III, Chap. 46.)

3. George Gentry, who died in 1818, was a son of this David Gentry, or his brother, Martin Gentry, and his home was not far from Free Union. His wife's name was Elizabeth. Their children were:

 1. James Gentry, who was a private in the state militia in the Revolutionary service.
 2. George Gentry, was a private in the state militia in the Revolutionary service.
 3. William Gentry.
 4. Frances Gentry; married Nathaniel Tate.
 5. Austin Gentry, emigrated to Madison County, Ky.
 6. Aaron Gentry, emigrated to Knox County, Tenn.
 7. Christopher Gentry; married Sarah —— —— and died in 1822. Their children were:
  1. Martha Gentry; married Joel Maupin.
  2. Mary Gentry; married Henry Via.
  3. Frances Gentry; married Thomas Gibson.
  4. Elizabeth Gentry; married James Dunn.
  5. Paschal Gentry.
  6. Henry Gentry.
  7. Dicey Gentry; married Garrett White.
 8. Martha Gentry; married John Walton.
 9. Elizabeth Gentry; married Edward Ballard, son of John Ballard and Elizabeth Thompson his wife. They emigrated to Madison County, Ky. (See Part V, Chap. 13.)
 10. Nancy Gentry; married Edward Walton.

3. Nicholas Gentry, son of Nicholas and Mary Gentry; married ——— ——— His son:

1. Addison Gentry; married Lucy Leake, a sister to Shelton F. Leake.

4. Mary Gentry; married Mr. Hinson.

5. Robert Gentry, believed to be the same Robert Gentry who bought in 1776, from Martha, widow of Samuel Arnold, a place on the head-waters of Ivy Creek, which he and his wife Judith sold in 1776, to John Woodson.

Philip Joyner, whose daughter was the wife of one Robert Gentry, who once owned the land the university stands on, devised the land to his two grand-sons, Charles and Jesse Gentry, one of whom sold in 1775, and the other in 1783. It seems that these two grand-sons emigrated to North Carolina. Whether Robert, son of Nicholas Gentry, was the son-in-law of Philip Joyner is not known.

6. Benajah Gentry, lived on Biscuit Run, where he commenced to purchase land in 1764. In 1817, he transferred his property to his son, Robert Gentry, but he did not die till 1830. He married ——— ——— His children were:

1. Martha Gentry; married Elijah Dawson, son of Rev. Martin Dawson who emigrated to Calloway County, Mo.

2. Elizabeth Gentry; married William Goodman.

3. Robert Gentry; married Mary Wingfield, daughter of Francis Wingfield, and were the parents of:

1. Albert Gentry.

7. Nathan Gentry.

8. Martin Gentry, born Sept. 4, 1747, died April 23, 1827; married January 23, 1766, Mary Timberlake, daughter of Philip Timberlake, and Mary his wife, who was born Aug. 12, 1784, and died Nov. 19 1827. Some of their children were:

1. Bettie Gentry, born Dec. 27, 1766; married Daniel Maupin son of Daniel Maupin and Elizabeth Dabney his wife. She died in Madison County, Ky., June 10, 1804. (See Part V, Chap. 12.)

2. Josiah Gentry, born June 6, 1768; married Miss Nancy Mullins. They emigrated to Madison County, Ky., where he died near the town of Richmond. (See Part VIII, Chap. 14.)

3. Bartlett Gentry; born March 16, 1770.

4. Patsey Gentry, born May 22, 1772.

5. Nancy Gentry, born July 15, 1783.

There probably were other children.

9. Elizabeth Gentry; married Mr. Haggard.

10. Jane Gentry; married Mr. Timberlake.

11. Ann Gentry; married Mr. Jenkins.

CHAPTER 17.

ISABEL HARRIS.

(Named in Sec. 9, Art. 4, Chap. 4.)

Article 1.—Isabel Harris a daughter of the old Kentucky pioneer, Christopher Harris and Agnes McCord his wife, was born in Albemarle County, Va., and was in the migratory movement named in Chapter 2, and was married in Madison County, Ky., Oct. 2, 1794, to John Bennett.. (See Part VI, Chap. 2, Note.)

Said John Bennett and his brother-in-law, Overton Harris were executors of the will of his wife's sister Margaret Harris. To them were born the children named in the coming sections:

Section 1. Samuel Bennett; married Elizabeth Chenault, Dec. 11, 1834. (See Part V, Chap. 13, Sec. 9). He was a prosperous farmer of Madison County, Ky. To them were born these children:

1. William Bennett, a farmer and popular and prosperous man, who resided and recently died in Madison County. He married Annie Neale, a daughter of Col. William L. Neale.

2. John Bennett, was a lawyer of Richmond and had a large practice; conscientious and true to his clients, popular with the people. Represented Madison County in the State Senate in the years 18——, having been elected on the Republican ticket, when the Democratic party was in the majority, and had control of State affairs, but Bennett was ever faithful to his constituents, and admired by those politically opposed to him. He died a bachelor.

3. James Bennett, a substantial citizen and farmer of Madison County, residing now (1905) in Richmond. He married Sally L. Clay, a daughter of General Cassius Marcellus Clay, Kentucky Statesman.

4. Dr. David Bennett, a prominent physician of Lexington, Ky.

5. Sue A. Bennett; died a femme sole.

6. Belle Harris Bennett, very religious woman, and church worker.

7. Walter Bennett, a popular and influential citizen of Richmond, Ky., banker and financier. He married Mary Burnam, a daughter of Hon. Curtis F. Burnam and Sarah Rollins his wife (See Chap. 3, Sec. 7, B-2-8-7.)

8. Samuel Bennett, the youngest child was at one time a dry good merchant of Richmond. He married Mary Warfield, they now live in Lexington, Ky.

Section 2. James Bennett; married Mrs. Eliza Rollins. (See Chap. 3, Sec. 7, B-2-C.)

Section 3. Benjamin Bennett; died young.

Section 4. Mourning Bennett; married James Harris. (See Chap. 38.)

CHAPTER 48.

OVERTON HARRIS.

(Named in Chap. 4, Sec. 10.)

Article 1.—Overton Harris, a son and youngest child of the old Kentucky pioneer, Christopher Harris and Agnes McCord his second wife, was born in Albemarle County, Va., and in the migratory movement named in Chapter 2, he came to Madison County, Ky.

He chose and won for a wife, Nancy Oldham, a daughter of Ready Money Richard Oldham, and Ursley Williams his first wife. (See Part VI, Chap. 4, Sec. 3.) He died in 1827, leaving his last will and testament, probated Nov. 6, 1827. After his death his widow, Nancy Oldham Harris, married Anderson Chenault, Senior, (See Part V, Chap. 13, Sec. 9.) Aug. 3, 1837. Children of Overton Harris and Nancy Oldham his wife:

Section 1. Franklin Harris, a physician, died without issue, was a soldier in the Mexican War.

Section 2. Solon Harris, he and his brother, Lucien, were twins. He married Sallie Ann Miller, daughter of Robert Miller and Sallie Estill his wife, (See Part I, Chap. 14, Sec. 1) July 25, 1837. Their children:

1. Emmet Harris; married Nannette Anderson. She is a widow now, living in Lexington, Ky.
2. Carlisle Harris; married Will Craig of Stanford, Ky.
3. Edna Harris; married George Phelps. (See Part I, Chap. 14, Section 4.)

Section 3. Lucien Harris, he and his brother, Solon, were twins. He married Sallie F. Bush, Dec. 8, 1832.

Section 4. Sidney Harris, was twice married, firstly to Mrs. Elizabeth Brookin, and secondly to Mrs. Mary Jane Miller, nee Addison, widow of Samuel Miller. (See Part I, Chap. 14, Sec. 2.) This second marriage occured April 4, 1844. Children of the first marriage:

1. Overton Harris; married Rowenna Lacoste.

Children of the second wife:

2. Sidney Harris; married Mary Mallard.
3. Joe Addison Harris; married Rosa Douglas. They live in Kimbell County, Texas, Post Office, Beredon.
4. J. Franklin Harris; married firstly, Emma Caufield and secondly, Minnie Armstrong. Child of the first marriage:
    1. Emma Caufield Harris.

    Children of the second marriage:

    2. Mary Harris.
    3. J. Franklin Harris, Jr.

    J. Franklin Harris has lived in Sutton County, Texas, for the last thirty years, and was at the Kentucky and Madison County Home Coming in June 1906.
5. Talitha Harris; married firstly James B. Letcher, and secondly William Arbuckle. Issue of the first marriage:
    1. William R. Letcher, member of the Richmond bar; married Annie Pearson of Montgomery, Alabama, now live in Richmond, Kentucky.

    Children of the second marriage:

    2. Millard Filmore Arbuckle.

3. Matthew Arbuckle.
4. Harriet Arbuckle.
5. Charles Arbuckle.
6. Robert Arbuckle.

Section 5. Christopher C. Harris; married Frances J. Adkins, July 26, 1853, rather late in life they moved to Missouri. Their children:

1. Ravenna Atkins Harris; married firstly Sallie Jones, and secondly Mrs. Margaret Anderson nee McGuire, there has been no issue of the second marriage. The children of the first marriage were:

1. Nancy J. Harris; married Lee Baker, they live in Lexington, Kentucky.
2. George C. Harris.
3. William M. Harris.

Ravenna A. Harris, lived in the west for a time, but returned and is now a citizen of Madison County, Ky.

2. Nannie Harris; married Theodore K. Lisle. They live in Butler, Bates County, Missouri. Their children:

1. Ida Lisle; dead.
2. Harris Lisle; unmarried.
3. Frankie Lisle.
4. Richard Lisle.

3. Overton Harris; married Emma Etzler. They live in Lawton, Oklahoma. Their children:

1. Frankie Harris.
2. Lizzie Harris.
3. Ruth Harris.

4. John B. Harris; married Ella Clark. They live in Lawton, Oklahoma. Their children:

1. Francisco Harris.
2. Clark Harris.
3. Caroline Harris.

5. Malboy Harris; married George W. Clardy. They live in Kansas City, Mo. Their children:

1. Christopher Harris, and four others names unknown to writer.

6. Lizzie Karr Harris; married Joseph Clark. They live in Kansas City, Mo. Their children names are not furnished.

Section 6. Overton Harris, Junior, died unmarried. One Overton Harris, married Nannie Fielding Feb. 3, 1842.

Section 7. Elizabeth Harris; married Joseph Tevis. Their children:

1. Nancy Tevis; married William E. Wilkerson, Dec. 23, 1845. Their children:

1. Joseph Tevis Wilkerson; married Ellen Russel.
2. William B. Wilkerson; married first Lula Pigg, and secondly Mattie Pigg.
3. Elizabeth Wilkerson; married Benson Cobb.
4. James Wilkerson; married Ethel Mann.
5. Mary Wilkerson; married Charles Tipton.
6. Christopher Harris Wilkerson; married Mrs. Jennie Mulhollen.
7. Dudley Tribble Wilkerson.
8. Lucy Wilkerson; married A. L. Darnaby, of Lexington, Ky.

2. James Tevis, was a confederate soldier in Captain Thomas B. Collins, Company, F., 7th, afterwards the 11th, Kentucky

Cavalry, Colonel D. Waller Chenault, under the command of General John H. Morgan, and was on the noted raid into the states of Indiana and Ohio. In 1874, he was elected clerk of the Madison County Court, which office he held two terms, of four years each. Afterwards he was elected Judge of the Richmond Police Court. He has been dead several years. Their children:

1. Sallie Tevis; dead.
2. Russell Tevis; dead.
3. William Wilkerson Tevis.
4. David Russel Tevis; married Elizabeth Lewis Smith. He was lately Mayor of the City of Richmond, since moved to Seattle, Washington.
5. Hugh Russel Tevis.
6. Daisey Tevis; dead.
7. Joseph H. Tevis.
8. Anna Hogue Tevis.

Two children died in infancy unmarried.

3. —— Tevis; died.

Section 8. Talitha Harris; married Waller Chenault, Oct. 30, 1833. (See Part V, Chap. 13, Sec. 9.) Their children:

1. William O. Chenault, was twice married, first to Caledonia Miller, daughter of Samuel Miller and Mary Ann Addison his wife, (See Part I, Chap. 14, Sec. 2) and secondly, Lucy Glibert. Children of the first marriage:

1. Callie Chenault; married D. B. Shackelford. (See Part I, Chap. 11, Sec. 2, and Chap. 14, Sec. 2.)

2. Lizzie Chenault; married Daniel Harber. Their children:
   1. Nicholas Harber.
   2. Overton Harber.

3. Mattie Chenault; married Clarence E. Woods. (See Part I, Chap. 14, Sec. 2, and Part II, Chap. 13, Sec. 3.) Had one daughter:
   1. Mary Woods.

4. Mary Chenault; married James M. Smith. Their children:
   1. Kate Smith; married Julian Proctor Van Winkle.
   2. Mattie Smith; married Isaac Newton Combs.
   3. Preston Smith.
   4. William Smith.
   5. Harvey C. Smith.

2. Elizabeth Chenault; married Joseph Brinker.

3. Captain Joseph Chenault, fell in the battle of Horse Shoe Bend in 1863, whilst in the service of the Confederate Army.

4. Susannah Chenault; married William (Wagoner) Miller, son of Samuel Miller and Mary Ann Addison his wife. (See Part I, Chap. 14, Sec. 2.)

5. Carlisle Chenault; married Thomas D. Chenault. (See Part 5, Chap. 13, Sec. 9.) Their children:

1. Lila Chenault; married Nelson Gay.
2. John B. Chenault; married first Lena Jennings, and secondly Miss —— ———.
3. Ann Chenault; married Mr. —— McCown.
4. Thomas D. Chenault, Jr., married Laura Walker, daughter of J. Stone Walker.
5. Carlisle Chenault.
6. Eleanor Chenault.

6. Christopher D. Chenault, was twice married, first to Florence Dillingham, daughter of Henry B. Dillingham and Margaret Yates

his wife, and secondly, to Sallie D. Humphreys. Children of the first marriage:

1. Margaret Chenault; married James Crutcher.
2. Florence Chenault.
3. Joseph Chenault; married Bessie Spears.
4. Miss Kit Chenault; married Harrison Simrall of Lexington, Kentucky.

7. Dr. Waller Chenault; married Sallie Webb of New Castle, Ky., had one son:

1. Waller Chenault, a resident of Madison County, Ky., unmarried.

8. Nancy Chenault; married Dr. George W. Exans, he served in the Federal Army. She died and afterwards Dr. Evans married Mary Spencer Smith. (See Part 2, Chap. 11, Sec. 5.) Children of Nancy Chenault and Dr. G. W. Evans:

1. George W. Evans; married Minna Crutcher.
2. Leslie Evans; married Laura Lyn. (See Section 9.)
3. Joe Evans, expert handling steam scraper in work on Panama Canal.
4. Mary Evans; married Thomas Pickles, editor "Kentucky Register," published in Richmond, Ky.
5. Overton Evans.
6. William Evans, twin.
7. —— Evans, twin; dead.

9. Overton Harris Chenault; married Lila McCann. He is a wealthy farmer and stockman of Fayette County, Ky. Handles blooded horses.

10. Laura Chenault; married P. H. Eastin, issue:

1. David Eastern.

11. Ella Chenault; married William D. Watts. Their children:

1. Alline Watts.
2. Lillian Watts; married Mr. —— Smith of Lexington, Ky.
3. Ethel Watts; married Dr. Harry Blanton, of Richmond, Ky.

12. David Chenault; married Bettie Bronston.

Section 9. Caroline Harris; married Michael L. Stoner, May 4, 1843. His grand-father Michael Stoner, was one of the bold and daring spirits in the very earliest pioneer days of Kentucky. In 1767, he was on Cumberland River, at the mouth of Stone River, below the mouth of the Rockcastle, with Harrod on a hunting expedition, where they met a party from South Carolina, composed of Isaac Lindsey and four other hardy adventurers. In 1774, in company with Daniel Boone, he made the extraordinary trip from Virginia to the Falls of the Ohio, by order of Governor Dunmore, to conduct a party of surveyors into the settlements. In 1776, he built a cabin on Stoner Fork of Licking River, now called Stoner Creek.

He and Simon Kenton, were in Fayette County together in the latter part of the year 1775, Stoner having come with Boone to Kentucky in 1774, met with Kenton at the Blue Lick, in 1775, and Kenton left his camp and accompanied Stoner to the interior settlements, where Kenton spent the winter of 1775-6. Michael Stoner was a scout and indian spy, and hunter for the Boonsborough Fort.

He raised corn in what is Bourbon County, in 1776, on the place where Samuel Clay lived for many years. (Collins) The old adventurous pioneer, Michael Stoner married Miss Franky Tribble, daughter of the pioneer preacher, Andrew Tribble and they had a son:

1. George Washington Stoner, who married Nancy Tribble, daughter of Peter Tribble (son of Andrew) and Mary Boone his wife, the latter a daughter of George Boone, a brother to Daniel Boone. Of their children were:

1. Michael L. Stoner; married Caroline Harris, as aforesaid.

2. Minerva T. Stoner; married first John Grubbs, a son of Jesse Grubbs and Nancy Oldham his wife. (See Part VI, Chap. 36, Sec. 3) and a grand-son of Higgason Grubbs another noted old Kentucky pioneer. She survived her husband, and married the second time General Richard Williams of Montgomery County, Ky., a brother to the late General John S. (Cerro Gordo) Williams. She now lives at Mt. Sterling, Ky. (Since this writing she has died.) Children of Caroline Harris and Michael Stoner:

1. Nannie Harris Stoner; married J. S. Crawford.
2. George Overton Stoner; married Zilpa Rose.
3. Talitha Chenault Stoner; married G. L. Whitney.
4. Peter Tribble Stoner; married Mary Donelson.
5. Maria Stoner; married J. R. Lyn. She is now a widow living with her son-in-law, Leslie P. Evans, two miles east of Richmond, Ky. Their children:

1. Laura Lyn; married Leslie Evans. (See Sec. 8.) Their children:

1. Nannie Evans.
2. Leslie Peter Evans.

6. William Little Stoner; married Annie Sutherland.
7. Lillie Stoner; married William Hunt.
8. William H. Stoner.
9. David Stoner; married Luetta Donalson.

Section 10. Nancy Harris; died while attending school at Georgetown, Ky.

Note:—The Reverend Andrew Tribble was born March 22, 1741, and was married in 1768, to Sally Burrass. She was born Sept. 30, 1753. The former died Dec. 30, 1822, and the latter Dec. 15, 1830. Their children were born in the following order:

1. Frances T. Tribble, born Sept. 3, 1769; married Michael Stoner, he was born Sept. 30, 1753, and he died Sept. 3, 1814. (A)

2. Samuel Tribble, born Dec. 30, 1771.

3. Peter Tribble, born Oct. 8, 1773, married Oct. 8, 1793, Polly Boone, she died Sept. 14, 1831. (B)

4. Thomas Tribble, born June 13, 1776.

5. Nancy Tribble, born Nov. 6, 1778; married April 3, 1794, David Chenault. (See Part V, Chap. 13, Sec. 9.)

6. Sally B. Tribble, born Feb. 9, 1781; married March 7, 1799, David Crews. (See Part V, Chap. 12, Sec. 1-2.) She died Feb. 2, 1810, and David Crews married again.

7. Silas Tribble, born June 3, 1783; married Oct. 30, 1809, Jerusha White. He died Nov. 18, 1842.

8. Andrew Tribble, born Dec. 2, 1785; married June 24, 1810, Lucy Boone.

9. Mary Tribble, born March 29, 1788; married Dec. 23, 1806, to Joseph Stephenson. Their son:

1. James M. Stephenson; died Sept. 28, 1809.

10. John Tribble (General), born Aug. 15, 1790; married first Sept. 18, 1834, Martha A. White, (daughter of Galen White and Mildred his wife. Galen White died Nov. 4, 1833, and Mildred his wife, died May 17, 1819, of their children, Henry White, died Oct. 13, 1813, Franky White, died Nov. 1812, James White, died Dec. 20, 1827, Jefferson White, died June 10, 1829.) Martha A. the wife of General John Tribble, died June 20, 1850, at four o'clock, P. M., and May 6, 1852, Gen. Tribble, married Sally Coffey, the latter died 10-15 A. M., Jan. 3, 1865. General Tribble

and his firist wife Martha A. White, were the parents of Rev. Andrew Jefferson Tribble, a Baptist minister who lives near Richmond, Madison County, Ky. The late John Tribble, and the Hon. Durrett W. Tribble who at one time represented Madison County in the Kentucky Legislature, and others.

11. Patsey Tribble, born March 7, 1794; married Oct. 5, 1812, Jacob White.

12. Dudley Tribble, born May 1, 1797; married Jan. 21, 1819, Matilda H. Tevis, and were the parents of the late James P. Tribble. Dudley Tribble now a citizen of Richmond, Ky. Robert G. Tribble, who removed to Missouri and others.

(A) Leonard G. Stoner, son of Michael Stoner; died May 20, 1812.

(B) Samuel Tribble; died May 3, 1831.
William Tribble; died 1831.
Peter Tribble; died Oct. 21, 1836.
Sally Simpson; died Aug. 4, 1824.
(A) Sally Ann Stoner; died April 23, 1831.

CHAPTER 49.

OVERTON HARRIS.

(Named in Chap. 2, Sec. 3.)

Article 1.—Overton Harris, (data furnished by Hon. Willis Overton Harris, a son of William Harris and Temperance Overton his wife, and a younger brother of Major Robert Harris of Albemarle; married Anne Nelson, and of the issue of the marriage was a son.

Section 1. Nelson Harris; married Mary Prior, and they lived at Buck Hill, in Louisa County, Va., and among their children was a son:

1. Hilary Harris; married Phoebe Ann Hobson, and they made their home in Powhatan County, Va. The children born to them were:

1. Maria Harris, now living unmarried.
2. Joseph Hobson Harris, killed in Tenn., in 1858.
3. John Nelson Harris.
4. Lavinia Harris; married Daniel Hatcher.
5. Christiana Harris, now living unmarried.
6. Hilary V. Harris, was a Captain in the Confederate States Army, and was killed at Sailors Creek in 1865.
7. Sarah Octavia Harris; died unmarried.
8. Abner Harris; married Flora Harris, daughter of Nathan W. Harris, of Frederickshall, Va.
9. Willis Overton Harris; married Caroline Adams, daughter of Benjamin Adams of Louisville, Ky. W. O. Adams saw service in the Civil War as member of the Corps of Cadets of the Virginia Military Institute. Since 1868, he has practiced law in Louisville, Ky., and served an unexpired term on the Circuit Court bench, from 1887 to 1888. He was the special judge who rendered the decision in the Clark Circuit Court in the proceedings against the Hon. William Morgan Beckner, by which that talented and distinguished lawyer was suspended from the practice for two years, which judgment was reversed by the Court of Appeals of Kentucky.

PART IV.

CHAPTER 1.

1. GENEALOGICAL TABLE OF THE WALLACE FAMILY. 2. EARLY MARRIAGES IN MADISON COUNTY, KENTUCKY, OF THE WALLACE NAME GLEANED FROM THE FIRST MARRIAGE REGISTER OF THE COUNTY COURT. 3. ITEMS CONNECTING THE WALLACE NAME WITH EVENTS.

Article 1.—Genealogical Table.

Wm. Harris Miller married Katherine Oldham. See Table to Part VI.
- Christopher Irvine Miller. See Table to Part I.
- Talitha Harris. See Table to Part III. ....
  - Christopher Harris. See Table to Part III.
  - Sallie Wallace ....
    - Michael Wallace. Emigrant from Virginia to Kentucky. C ....
      - Andrew Wallace. Emigrant from Ireland to America. ....
        - Peter Wallace. Died in Ireland.
        - A
        - Elizabeth Woods. See Table to Part II. Left a widow. Emigrant from Ireland to America; daughter of John Woods and Elizabeth Worsop, his wife.
      - B
      - Margaret Woods. See Table to Part II.
    - Jane Bratton

"A"

. William, m Hannah Woods. Chap. 3.
. Susannah, m William Woods. Part II, Chap. 3. (Chap. 2, Sec. 2).
. Samuel, m Esther Baker. Chap. 5.
. Andrew, m Margaret Woods. "B" Chap. 6.
. Adam. Chap. 14.
. Peter, Jr., m Martha Woods. Chap. 15.
5. Hannah, m Josiah Wallace. Chap. 6. Sec. 5.
6. Mary, m Thomas Collins. Chap. 20.
7. Margaret, m William Ramsay. Chap. 21.
8. Jean, m Mr. Wilson. Chap. 6, Sec. 8.
9. John. Chap. 6, Sec. 9.

"B"

. Michael, m Jane Bratton. "C" Chap. 7.
. Samuel, m Ann J. Anderson. Chap. 6. Sec. 2.
. Elizabeth, m Capt. William Briscoe. Chap. 18.
. Sarah, m Alexander Henderson. Chap. 19.

"C"

1. Ella, m 1, John P. Ballard; 2, Robert Cox. Chap. 7, Sec. 1.
2. Jane, m 1, Nicholas Kavanaugh; 2, Mr. Canole. Chap. 7, Sec. 2.
3. Sallie, m Christopher Harris. Chap. 7, Sec. 3. Part 3, Chap. 28.
4. Polly, m Archibald Woods. Chap. 7, Sec. 4. Part II, Chap. 7, Sec. 3.
5. Annie R., m Thomas C. Maupin. (Chap. 7, Sec. 5, Chap. 20, Sec. 5). Part V, Chap. 11, Sec. 2.
6. Andrew, m Jane Reid. Chap. 8.
7. Peggy, m William Jarman. Chap. 13.

Article 2.—Early Marriages in Madison County, Ky., gleaned from the first Marriage Register of County Court.

Wallace, Hannah—Okley, Abner, April 7, 1805.
Wallace, Mary—Warmsley, Wm., Jan. 27, 1807.
Wallace, John—Walker, Elizabeth, May 1, 1809.
Wallace, Eleanor—Ballard, John, Dec. 26, 1809.
Wallace, Andrew—Reid, Jane, Oct. 5, 1813.
Wallace, Polly—Woods, Archibald, Oct. 4, 1814.
Wallace, John—Wallace, Isabella, Dec. 9, 1815.
Wallace, Elizabeth, E.—James O. Boatman, Aug. 27, 1837.
Wallace, Martha, Frances—Robert W. Langley, Feb. 19, 1846.
Wallace, Rachael, Ann—Wm. F. Bates, Oct. 16, 1851.
Wallace, Sarah—Wm. Johnson, Nov. 30, 1854.
Wallace, Isabella—Wallace, John, Dec. 9, 1815.
Wallace, Jane—Kavanaugh, Nicholas, Jan. 12, 1817.
Wallace, Elizabeth—Yates, John, Aug. 26, 1819.
Wallace, Patsy—Kerfoot James, Dec. 4, 1822.
Wallace, Ella, (Ballard)—Cov, Robert, Jan. 31, 1826.
Wallace, Nancy—Cergacy, Rev., Jefferson, Oct. 29, 1833.
Wallace, Sarah, M.—Irvine W. Anderson, Oct. 26, 1843.
Wallace, Ann M.—Brown Lee Yates, Feb. 19, 1846.
Wallace, Margaret, Jane—James Baldock, Oct. 19, 1852.
Wallace, Bettie S.—William A. Anderson, Nov. 8, 1856.
Wallace, Allen—Ann S. Dinwiddie, May 12, 1835.

Items Connecting the Wallace Name with Events from History and Court Records.

Section 1. John S. Wallace, was one of three settlers in Losantiville (now Cincinnati) when in the fall of 1789, seventy soldiers stationed at Fort Washington, at said place for the defense of the settlers, were about to abandon their post for want of supplies, who went down in canoes from six to ten miles into what are now Kenton and Boone Counties in Kentucky, secreted their canoes in the mouth of a small branch, and by their faithfulness killed buffalo, deer and bear enough to provide the soldiers for six weeks, until supplies came from Pittsburg. (C)

Section 2. Caleb Wallace, was one of the three first Judges of the Kentucky Court of Appeals. Also one of the many subscribers to the proposals for establishing a society to be called "The Kentucky Society for Promoting Useful Knowledge," Dec. 1, 1787. (C)

Section 3. William Wallace. The first Court of Quarter Sessions of Logan County was held in 1801. The first Circuit Court thereof in 1803, by Nineva Edwards, Judge, and two associate Justices. The next Judge was William Wallace. (C)

Section 4. A Mr. Wallace, a scotchman, in 1791-2, was successor to a scotchman named McQuilty, who taught the first school in Mayslick in Mason County, Kentucky in 1789-90. (C)

Section 5. The names who served in the Kentucky Legislature:

In the Senate—

Caleb B. Wallace, from the County of Boyle, 1850-1.

In the House of Representatives—

William Wallace, from the County of Crittenden, 1848.
Samuel Wallace, from the County of Woodford, 1835.
Salem Wallace, from the County of Madison, 1845.

John Wallace, from the County of Boone, 1836, 1838-1842, and 1842-6 (C)

Section 6. William A. Wallace, born in 1827. He was a member of the Pennsylvania Senate in 1862-7, and represented that state in the U. S. Senate as a Democrat in 1875-1881. (A-c)

Section 7. William H. L. Wallace, 1821-1862. Served during the Mexican War. He commanded a brigade at Fort Donelson, and at Shiloh in the Civil War, was mortalyy wounded at Shiloh after a gallant stand against the enemy. (A-c)

Section 8. John W. Wallace, was the reporter of cases in the U. S. Supreme Court 1863-1875. (23 volumes) A-c)

Section 9. Llew Wallace, born in 1827, was a lawyer of Indiana, politican, soldier and man of letters. He volunteered in the Civil War, and commanded a division at the battle of Fort Donelson, and was made Major-General of Volunteers. Previous to the battle of Shiloh his division was stationed at Crump's Landing, near the main Army and could not reach the field for the first days fighting, but took part in same the second day. He commanded the defense of Cincinnati in anticipation of General E. Kirby Smith's attack in July 1864; in the battle of the Monococy Wallace though defeated by General Early gained time to save the Capital. He was Governor of Utah in 1878-1881. Minister to Turkey in 1881-5. He wrote the "Life of President Harrison," and the novels, "A Fair God," "Ben Hur," and the 'P'rince of India." (A-c)

Section 10. Alfred Russel Wallace, an English Naturalist, born at Usk Monmouthshire, Jan. 8, 1822. He was employed for several years in the architectural office of his brother, and then devoted himself to natural history. In 1848, he accompanied Mr. H. W. Bates in a scientific expedition to Brazil, where after a protracted sojourn in Para, he explored the primeval forests of the Amazon and Rio Negro, returning to England in 1852. His valuable collections especially rich in the departments of Ornithology and botany, were in great part destroyed by shipwreck. In 1853, he published "Travels of the Amazon and Rio Negro," and "Palm Trees of the Amazon and their Uses," and in 1854 undertook a journey to the East Indies, where for a period of nearly eight years he explored the greater part of the islands constituting the Malay Archipelago, and portions of Paupa. While pursuing his researches relative to the fauna and flora of these regions, Mr. Wallace, unaware of Darvin's previous labors, in the same direction, attempted the solution of the problem of the origin of species, and arrived at almost the same general conclusions which were simultaneously reached by that naturalist. His paper 'On the tendency of varieties to depart indefinately from the original Type," transmitted through Sir Charles Lyell to the Linnoean Society, was read before that body on July 1, 1858, coincidently with the reading of Mr. Darvin's paper, "On the tendency of species to form varieties, and on the pérpetuation of species and varieties by means of natural selection." Though recognizing the efficacy of Natural selection in producing most of the changes attributed to its action, by Mr. Darvin he denies its competence to effect without the joint agency of some higher cause, the transition to man from the Authropoid Apes. In 1862, Mr. Wallace returned to England, where for several years he was mainly engaged in the classification of his collection which embraced upwards of 100,000 entomological specimens, and more than 8,000 birds. The result of his Eastern explorations were partially embodied in "The Malay Archipelago, the Land of the Orang-Utan, and the Bird of Paradise," (1869). Mr. Wallace has of late been prominently associated with the believers in the so-called spiritualistic phenomena, to the examination of which he has devoted special attention. His observations were published in a series of essays in the "Fortnightly Review" for 1874 reprinted as "Miracles and Modern Spiritualism." (1875) In 1868, he received the royal medal from the Royal Society, and in 1870 the gold medal from the Geographical Society of Paris. In 1870, he published "Contributions to the Theory of Natural Selections." His elaborate work, "On the Geographical Distribution of Animals," appeared in 1876, in English, French and German. (A-c)

Section 11. Horace Binney Wallace, an American Author, born in Philadephia Feb. 26, 1817; died in Paris Dec. 16, 1852. He graduated at Princeton College and studied law, but never practiced. In connection with Judge Hare he edited and annotated "American Leading Cases," "Smith's Leading Cases" and "White and Tudor's Leading Cases in Equity," which have passed through numerous editions. He published anonomously "Stanley, or the Recollections of a Man of the World," a novel, (Philadelphia 1838) and after his death were published "Art and Scenery in Europe, with Other Papers," and "Literary Criticisms" and other papers. (1856.) (A-c)

Section 12. Sir William Wallace, a Scottish patriot, born about 1270, executed at Smithfield Aug. 23, 1305. He was of Anglo-Norman decent, the younger son of Sir Malcolm Wallace, knight of Ellerslie. While at the high school in Dundee, in an altercation he stabbed the son of the English Governor of Dundee Castle and fled. For sometime he was an outlaw, in the fastnesses of the Southern Higlands, and his accomplishments, personal prowess, and bravery drew around him a considerable number of followers, including several men of note. After the insurrection broke out in 1297, he attacked the English Justiciary holding Court at Scone, took many prisoners, and killed many more. At the same time Sir William Douglas, and others of his adherents surprised and compelled the surrender of the English garrisons in the castles of Durisdeer and Sanquhar. Edward I, sent into Scotland an army of 40,000 men with a small cavalry troop, under Sir Henry Percy and Sir Robert Clifford. The Scottish force had assembled at Loçhmaben, and on the approach of the English a night attack was made by Wallace, who was forced to fall back toward Irvine in Ayrshire. Dissensions arose among the Chiefs in the Scottish army and a treaty was agreed upon. Wallace and Murray of Bothwell, alone of the leaders protested and retired into the Northern Counties where they speedily recruited a powerful force, and surprised and captured the English garrisons at Aberdeen, Dunnoltar, Forfar, and Montrose. Wallace had begun the seige of Dundee, when he heard of the advance of a powerful English army toward the River Forth, in the direction of Stirling. He at once abandoned the siege and recruiting as he went reached Stirling with 40,000 foot, and 180 horse. The English 50,000 foot and 1,000 horse, were under the command of the earl of Surrey. Several titled deserters from the Scottish army, who were with Surrey, were deputed to persuade Wallace to capitulate, a free pardon being offered unconditionally in the name of the English King. The terms were rejected and a large portion of Surrey's force crossed the river, and fought the great battle of Cambus Kenneth, or Strotingbridge, Sept. 10, 1297. From their advantageous position Wallace's men drove them back, and pursued them to the border town of Berwick. King Edward's forces were almost completely cut to pieces and Wallace by general consent, in the absence of the lawful Monarch (John then in the tower of London) was declared guardian of the Kingdom of Scotland. A severe famine following suggested the invasion of the Northern Counties of England, Wallace laid waste the country, from the borders to New Castle and returned with his spoils to attempt an organization of Scotland.

Meanwhile Edward had raised an army of 80,000 infantry and 7,000 horse, a portion of this force, landed by sea, on the North East coast and suffered a partial reverse, but the main body advanced Northward from the border and on July 22, 1289, came up with the Scottish forces near Falkirk, where a decisive engagement was fought, in which the army of Wallace was defeated with a loss according to various historians of 15,000. For several years after this Wallace carried on a guerilla warfare, and he also went to Paris, to secure French intervention. In Feb. 1304, he was declared an outlaw. Large rewards were offered by Edward for his arrest, and he was ultimately betrayed by Sir John Moutieth. The day after his arrival in London, the form of a trial was gone through in Westminster Hall, the prisoner in derision of his pretensions to the throne of Scotland being decorated with a crown of laurel. He was condemned to death, and the same day dragged at the tail of a horse to West Smithfield and then hung, drawn and quartered. His hand was set upon London bridge and his limbs were exposed at New Castle, Berwick, Perth and Sterling. (A-c)

Section 13. William Vincent Wallace, an Irish composer in Waterford in 1815, died at the Chateau de Bayen Haute, Garoune, France, Oct. 12, 1865. He received his earliest musical instruction from his father, a military band master, and at the age of 15 could play on every instrument of the orchestra and had written numerous compositions for military bands, as a performer on the piano, forte and violin, he showed great excellence. At the age of 18, on account of failing health he went to New South Wales, and was long engaged in agricultural pusuits. He gave his first concert at Sydney with great success, and thenceforth travelled extensively over the Southern Hemisphere deriving large emoluments in the Spanish American cities from his performances on the violin and piano forte After a professional tour in the United States he returned in 1845, to England, where his first opera "Montana" was produced with great success . He then produced in rapid succession "Matilda of Hungary" "The Maid of Zurich," "Gulnare" and "Olga," several of which were performed in Germany, and elsewhere in Continental Europe. In 1849, he was commissioned to write an opera for the grand opera of Paris, but had scarcely begun the work when he became blind. For the purpose of recovering his eyesight, he made a voyage to Rio de Janerio, whence he in 1850 came to the United States. Several years later he returned to England where in 1854, his "Lurline" and in 1861, his "Amberwick," were brought out. In 1862, he produced "Loves Triumph" and in 1863, "The Desert Flower." (A-c)

From Madison County Kentucky Court Orders:

Section 14. Michael Wallace. March 7, 1797. On the motion of Michael Wallace, his ear mark, towit: A crop and over keel, and under keel in the left ear, was ordered to be recorded.

November 5, 1799. Hands allotted to work under Michael Wallace, as surveyor of the state road. His own hands, William Kerr, Cornelius Maupin. John Reids hands, James Coulter's hands, William Kavanaugh, James Coulter, Jr., Captain William Briscoe's hands.

In Culpeper County, Virginia.
From Notes by Dr. Slaughter. (Sec. 15 to 31.)

Section 15. Michael Wallace, born 1738; married Mary Kelton Glassell, daughter of Andrew Glassell and Elizabeth Taylor his wife. Andrew was a son of Robert Glassel and Mary Kelton, and Robert was a son of John Glassel of Runkan, Scotland, and Mary Coalter his wife.

Section 16. Dr. Michael Wallace, was born in Scotland, in 1755, and in his youth was apprenticed at Glascow, to Dr. Gustavus Brown of Port Tobacó, Maryland, to learn medicine, the indenture of apprenticeship, is now in the possession of one of his descendants in Kentucky. This shows the way doctors were made in those days. Dr. Michael Wallace presented an account to the vestry for 800 pounds of tobacco, for successfully treating Eliza Maddox. He is an ancestor of the Winston families now living in Culpeper, and the Wallace families of Fredericksburg and Stafford County, Va. Their children were:

1. Ellen Wallace; married Mr. Somerville.
2. Gustavus Wallace.
3. H. Nelson Wallace.
4. Elizabeth Wallace; married Mr. —— Wallace.
5. Louisa Wallace; married Mr. —— Goodwin.
6. James Wallace.
7. Marianna Wallace; married Mr. —— Conway.

Section 17. Dr. James B. Wallace; married Sarah Ann Clayton.

Section 18. G. M. Wallace, of Stafford County, Va., married Dora Green, daughter of George Green and Bettie Ashby his wife.

Section 19. Mary Wallace; married William A. Winston, and had:

1. Walker Winston; died unmarried.
2. Martha Winston; married Dr. Payne, issue:
   1. William Henry Payne.
3. Mary Winston; married Daniel F. Slaughter, issue:
   1. Mary Slaughter.
   2. Ellen Slaughter.
   3. Caroline Slaughter.
   4. John Slaughter.
   5. Daniel Slaughter.
4. James Winston, went to California.
5. Wallace Winston.
6. Isaac Winston.
7. Caroline Winston; married John S. Hamilton, issue:
   1. Hugh Hamilton.
   2. Mary Hamilton.
8. Arthur Winston.
9. Lucien Winston.

Section 20. Mary Wallace, of Augusta, Ga., married John St. Pierre Gibson, issue:

1. Dr. Edwin Lacey Gibson; married Mary Miller of Raleigh, North Carolina.
2. Elizabeth Pendleton Gibson.

Section 21. A. Henderson Wallace, enlisted Oct. 1864, in Company C. 30th Virginia Infantry, Corse's Brigade, Pickett's Division of the Confederate Army.

Section 22. Thomas Wallace's will bears date June 1814, probated Sept. 21, 1818. He owned land in Madison County, Ky., and in Ohio. His children named:

1. James Wallace.
2. Caroline Wallace, and others.

He had a brother John Wallace, and a nephew, G. B. Wallace.

Section 23. Mr. ——. Wallace; married Martha Hill, daughter of Russel Hill and Peggy Baptist hi swife.

Section 24. Elizabeth Wallace, of King George County; married Philip P. Nalle, warden of St. Paul's Church, and a son of Martin Nalle and Nellie M. Barbour his wife.

Section 25. Prof. Clarence B. Wallace of Nashville, Tenn., married Mary B. Barbour, daughter of John S. Barbour and Elizabeth Byrne his wife, of Pittsburg.

Section 26. Cecilia Wallace and Mary Ann Wallace, were members of the Presbyterian Church of Culpeper, which in 1837, comprised the Counties of Culpeper, Madison, Orange, Spottsylvania and Rappahannock, which church was organized in 1813.

Section 27. Malinda Wallace; married Thomas Marshall in 1806.

Section 28. Susannah Wallace; married James B .Rice, in 1800.

Section 29. William Wallace; married Mildred Walker, in 1791.

Section 30. William Wallace; married Eliza Yates, in 1806.

Section 31. Oliver Wallace; married Anna Wright, in 1795.

Section 32. Malcolm Wallace, son of Peter Wallace, Jr., and Martha Woods, was in the army under General Morgan at Boston, and died there in the service in 1775. (See Chap. 15, Sec. 1.) (N M W)

Section 33. Samuel Wallace, son of Peter Wallace, Jr., and Martha Woods, was an officer in the Revolutionary Army, and commanded at Fort George, on the Virginia frontier, during the French and Indian War. (See Chap. 15, Sec. 2.) (N M W)

Section 34. James Wallace, son of Peter Wallace, Jr., and Martha Woods, was an Ensign in the third Virginia Regiment of the Revolution, and died of small-pox in Philadelphia in 1776.(N M W) (See Chapter 15, Section 3.)

Section 35. Captain Adam Wallace of Rockbridge County, Va., son of Peter Wallace, Jr., and Martha Woods, was Captain of a company of the tenth Virginia Regiment, and was with Buford at the terrible massacre on the Waxhaw, in South Carolina, May 29, 1780. After killing many of the enemy with his espontoon (a kind of pike), he died bravely fighting. Another brother, Captain Hugh Wallace in the regular army, died in Philadelphia of small-pox. See Chap. 15, Section 4. (N M W and Augusta County annals by Waddell.)

Section 36. Andrew Wallace, son of Peter Wallace, Jr., and Martha Woods, was Captain of a company of the 8th Virginia Regiment, and was killed at Guilford Court House, South Carolina, in 1781. (See Chap. 15, Sec. 5.) (N M W)

Section 37. "Big Foot" (William) Wallace, was born in Rockbridge County, Va., in 1816, the County in which the widow Elizabeth Woods Wallace and her sons, had settled some eighty years previous as related in the next Chapter, and Big Foot Wallace was a descendant of Peter Wallace, Senior and his widow Elizabeth. This subject emigrated to Texas in about 1835, and played such a prominent part in the affairs of Texas, and in the encounters with the predatory bands of Indians and Mexicans, that his name was made famous. He was a comrade in arms of Captain David McFadden, a veteran of three wars, and still an active farmer, and stock raiser of McLennon County, Texas, where he settled in 1851, two miles beyond the danger line, being what was called the out side settler, and was constantly on the alert, with his rifle against the plundering blood-thirsty commanches, and who still rides his broncho, and looks personally after his farms and ranches.

Big Foot Wallace was of the band of Texans who chased General Woll, at the head of a Mexican Army across the Rio Grande, into Mexico, as related in Part VI, Chapter 13a, Section 1, and was one of the prisoners of Mier, captured the day after Christmas Day 1842, and placed in the Lottery of Death, and the brave Texan who exclaimed "Another Alimo" and said "Don't talk to me of Mexican magnanimity; it means fill us with beans one day, and bullets the next." And who in 1844 led the last remnant of the nearly starved and naked prisoners of Mier back across the Rio Grande, and upon reaching the Lone Star got down on their knees and kissed her soil, they had helped to buy with blood and tears. He died at his ranch in Freeo County, south of San Antonio, Texas, in 1904, and was buried in the state cemetery at Austin. (See Chap. 3, Sec. 4-8-3.)

Section 38. List of towns, lakes, etc., named for Wallace, found on map:

New York— Wallace.
Pennsylvania— Wallace.
Wallace Junction.
Wallaceton.
Walleceville.
North Carolina—Wallace.
Georgia— Wallace.
Wallaceville.
Kentucky— Wallace Station.
Wallaceton.
Ohio— Wallace Mills.
Michigan— Wallace.
Wallaceville.
Missouri— Wallace.
Arkansas— Walleceburg.
Texas— Wallis Station.
Wallaceville.
North Dakota— Wallace.
California— Wallace.
Oregon— Wallace.
Virginia— Wallace.
Wallace's Mills.
Wallace Switch.
Wallaceton.
West Virginia— Wallace.
South Carolina—Wallaceville.
Alabama— Wallace.
Mississippi— Wallace.
Louisana— Wallace Lake.
Wallace.
Indiana— Wallace.
Illinois— Wallace.
Wisconsin— Wallace.
Minnesota— Wallace R-32.
Wallace T-15.

Kansas-	Wallace County.
	Wallace.
Nebraska	Wallace.
Idaho	Wallace.
Washington- -	Wallace.

CHAPTER 2.

THE WALLACE FAMILY.

Article 1.—This family is of Anglo-Norman-Scotch-Irish blood, and by many of the name, believed that their lineage runs back to Sir Malcolm Wallace, Knight of Ellerslie, of the thirteenth century, father of the noble Highlander, Sir William Wallace, Scottish Chieftain, patriot and martyr.

The family in all its branches, and generations have been noted for courage, gallantry and patriotism, many have sacrificed their lives for their country. A braver, and more gallant soldier than a Wallace, never enlisted in an army.

The father of our family, Peter Wallace, a Scottish Highlander, born in about 1680, who spent the latter part of his life in North Ireland, and died there a short time before the closing of the first quarter of the Eighteenth Century, married Elizabeth Woods, a daughter of John Woods and Elizabeth Worsop his wife. The said John Woods was the son of an English Trooper, who came to Ireland, and was in the army of invasion of Oliver Cromwell, 1649. A fuller history of John Woods and Elizabeth Worsop his wife is given in Part II, Chapters 2 and 3. Of the issues of the marriage of Peter Wallace and Elizabeth Woods, (who was born and married in Ireland) was at least six children. After the death of her husband. Peter Wallace, Elizabeth, then a widow, and her six children, and may be more, with her brothers, Michael Woods, James Woods, William Woods and Andrew Woods, in about the closing days of the first quarter of the Eighteenth Century, bid adieu to the country of their nativity, and their clans, and emigrated, sailing across the mighty Atlantic, to a port in the New World, America, touching first the Colony of Pennsylvania, where Elizabeth rested for several years. Her sons William, Andrew, etc., and her brother Michael Woods, having moved into the valley of Virginia and settled in Goochland, now Albemarle and Rockbridge Counties. on each side of the Blue Ridge Mountains; she in a few years followed, went to Rockbridge County, and selected a home just across the Blue Ridge mountains from the home of her brother. Three of her sons and one of her daughters had married their first cousins, children of their Uncle Michael Woods, and Mary Campbell his wife, of whom more will be told in the Chapters following. Her children who came over with her from Ireland were:

Section 1. William Wallace; married Hannah Woods. (See Part II, Chap. 4, Sec. 4.) The subject of Chapter 3.

Section 2. Susannah Wallace; married William Woods. (See Part II, Chap. 4, Sec. 2, and Part II, Chap. 6.)

Section 3. Samuel Wallace; married Esther Baker. The subject of Chapter 5.

Section 4. Andrew Wallace; married Margaret Woods. (See Part 2, Chap. 4, Sec. 6.) The subject of Chapter 6.

Section 5. Adam Wallace. The subject of Chapter 14.

Section 6. Peter Wallace, Junior; married Martha Woods. (See Part 11, Chap. 4, Sec. 9.) The subject of Chapter 15.

CHAPTER 3.

WILLIAM WALLACE.

(Named in Chap. 2, Sec. 1.)

Article 1.—William Wallace, a son of Peter Wallace, senior, the Scottish Highlander, who died in Ireland and Elizabeth Woods the widow emigrant from Ireland, to America, was born in Ireland, and was also an emigrant from Ireland; married Hannah Woods, a daughter of his uncle Michael Woods and Mary Campbell his wife. (See Part II, Chap. 4.)

As early as March 29, 1747, he was one of the inhabitants of Ivy Creek and Mountain Plains congregations, who joined with Rockfish in signing a call to Rev. Samuel Black, to serve them as pastor. He with his brothers, and father-in-law, moved from Pennsylvania to Virginia and settled not far apart, in Albemarle just East, and Rockbridge, just West of the Blue Ridge Mountains, and near the foot, and the Gap in the Ridge, then named Woods Gap, at a later date called Jarman's Gap, near the present Greenwood station. Their children were:

Section 1. Michael Wallace; married Ann Allen. The subject of Chpater 4.

Section 2. John Wallace; married —— —— and in 1780 sold his lands in Virginia, and moved to Washington County, that state and subsequently emigrated to Kentucky.

Section 3. Jane Wallace; married Robert Poage, son of Robert Poage, Senior, and Elizabeth his wife. Robert Poage, Senior, appeared in Orange Court May 22, 1740, to prove his importation with the view of taking up public lands. He, his wife Elizabeth, and nine children came from Ireland to Philadelphia, and thence to the colony of Virginia at his own expense. He settled three miles north of Staunton, on a plantation he purchased from William Beverley, as the land was in Beverley's manor, 772 acres originally. He acquired other lands directly from the Government in the County of Orange, on the west side of the Blue Ridge. His will dated Oct. 20, 1773, was probated March 6, 1774. His son John and William Lewis were executors. He had sons, John, Thomas, Robert, George and William, and daughters, Martha Woods, Elizabeth Crawford, Margaret Robertson, Mary and Sarah, one of the two latter was the first wife of Major Robert Breckenridge, who died leaving two sons, Robert and Alexander Breckenridge, who became prominent citizens of Kentucky.

James Poage, son of said John Poage, married his cousin Mary Woods, daughter of Martha Poage Woods above mentioned.

Section 4. William Wallace; married Mary Pilson, and lived at the old homestead of his father, near Greenwood, where he died in 1809. Their children were:

1. William Wallace, was connected with the Merchantile business of John Pilson, until his death in 1812, unmarried.
2. Richard Wallace, continued his brother William's business, and died in 1832, unmarried.
3. Hannah Wallace; married John Lobban.
4. Samuel Wallace.

One Samuel Wallace emigrated to Madison County, Ky., and was in Madison County, Ky., in 1801, and in that year was a witness to the taking of depositions of John Cochran, and John Bezaleel and David Maxwell. Samuel Wallace of Madison County, Ky., married Ann J. Anderson. His will bears date Feb. 27, 1840, probated Jan. 3, 1842. He states in his will that he had brothers, Michael and John, the latter was dead. The following were devisees of his will, viz:

"Elizabeth Duff."
"Mary A. Anderson, sister to his wife."
"Allen Anderson, brother, to his wife."
"Elizabeth A. Moran, sister, to his wife."
"Michael Wallace, his brother."
"John Wallace, his brother, deceased."

5. Mary Wallace.
6. Elizabeth Wallace.
7. John Wallace.
8. Michael Wallace, lived at the old homestead; married Lavinia Lobban, and was a ruling Elder in the Mountain Plains Presbyterian Church, until his death in 1845. Their children were:

1. Samuel Wallace, emigrated to Texas, and was perhaps in the Fannin Massacre at Goliad, as William Wallace who died two years ago in Texas, known as Big Foot Wallace, had a brother whose life was taken in that awful war.
2. Mary Wallace.
3. William Wallace, born in 1816, emigrated to Texas, and the same person known in Texas as Big Foot Wallace. (See Chap. 1, Sec. 37.) A sketch of whose life dictated by Captain David McFadden, a veteran of three wars, and a personal friend chum, and comrade of Wallace, now living at Waco, Texas, is here given, towit:

"Sketch of the Life of William Wallace."

"I became acquainted with Big Foot Wallace in 1849. I think his real name was William, but am not certain as to that. He was from Virginia to Texas, in the year about 1835. He had a brother and cousin who were in Fannin's massacre at Goliad* and he came to Texas to avenge their death. He spent his life on the frontiers of Texas, killing indians whenever he had a chance. Did not like domestic life, preferred camp life. He called his rifle (which I have seen many times) "Sweet Lips." I think he was the best scout and indian fighter, I was ever with, understanding their mode of fighting best. He was one of the Maier prisoners of Mexico, while in prison he drew a white bean,

Mexican's shot their prisoners in those days, except those drawing white beans. Every tenth bean was white (black) and every one who drew a white one was spared. He being one of the lucky ones. He served through the Mexican War, belonging to Ben McCulloch's Company and Jack Hay's Regiment of Texas Rangers. I understand he was a descendant of the Wallaces of Scotland. He was about six feet, two inches tall, weighed about 200 lbs., raw bone, and a powerful man. My first association with him was at Austin, Texas, our Capital where he was camped under a big Live Oak Tree. He was fond of hunting and there being plenty of game he kept himself in amunition in this way, and was always ready to go for the Indians. While in camp at Austin, he fell in love with a girl, he made up his mind the next time he called on her, he would propose to her, but he was called out, and before he got back he took fever and all his hair came out, so he decided not to go back until his hair grew out again, as he was a hard looking customer any way. He went up on the Colorado river to a cave in which he had stayed often, this cave being on an indian trail. Then he greased his head with bear's oil, thinking that would grow hair, but it failed to do the work, and while he was in this cave, they made up a scout in Austin and he went with them upon the Llano river about 150 miles above Austin, Texas. They wanted him with them because he was a good scout and Indian trailer. When they reached the Llano river the indians began to shoot up smokes, which could be seen for miles around, these smokes were signals used by the indians as their knowledge of the enemy being in the country. So Wallace and his men struck camps for the night. Wallace told the Captain of the scout that he wanted to get up the following morning about two hours before day, prospecting and looking for signs of indians, as he knew there were plenty of them in the surroundings. The Llano river is a tributary of the Colorado river, which is surrounded by a very rough and mountainous country and exceedingly deep gulches. On the morning he was awakened and started for a trail and while he was rounding the bend in one of these gulches which made a very short and narrow bend, he found himself face to face with a very large indian, being too close to each other to use their fire arms, and also, being somewhat surprised, they each stood eyeing the other for a minute and then they made a dash at each other and clinched. Wallace stated that he could throw his enemy very easily, but on account of the indian being naked and greased with bear's oil, which made him so very slick that he could not hold him on the ground. After throwing him several times repeatedly and finding that he was not accomplishing much, he decided he must try some other means of conquering his enemy, or else he would never peruse the smiling countenance of his lovely maiden in Austin, Texas, again; after clinching once more his breath coming short, he made a desperate effort to throw the indian as hard as possible, and in this he succeeded, throwing him very hard with his head upon a rock, which rendered him unconscious, this affording Wallace an opportunity to get his knife, he did so, and stabbed the indian a death blow, but the indian revived for a little, and stood throwing himself upon Wallace once more, he drew his knife, but being too weak by this time, he fell dead with the knife in hand which planted its point in the earth.

Wallace stated that he buried him to the best of his ability with chunks and rocks, and then returned to camp with a report of his mornings adventures. The scouting party remained in this camp for about one week, but accomplished very little, as the indians had discovered them and fled. Wallace said afterwards that on account of his hair being so slow in growing out that he lost the pride of his heart, as some other man had captured her during his absence. He afterwards was captured by the indians who were very much afraid of him, and at their Chief's command he was tied to a stake to be burned alive. The indians then begun to bring their wood and fuel, piling it around him when an old indian squaw interferred by begging for his life, pleading with the chief not to kill him, but turn him over to her. She succeeded in her pleadings and Wallace remained with her and chumned with one of her sons who was near his own age for about six months, but all the time he was watching his chances of escape, so finding an opportunity he left them and returned to his own Texas settlements.

Wallace died in Freeo County, Texas, south west of San Antonio, Texas, on his ranch last February two years ago, 1904, having reached the age of eighty years and never was married, but lived the lonesome life of a bachelor. Wallace was a fearless, but kind hearted man, spending the earliest and best days of his life on the frontiers of Texas, protecting the many helpless settlers therein.

I have given you the history of Wallace to the best of my remembrance from first acquaintance with him, but I am sorry to say that most of the dates I have forgotten. The other parties you refer to I have either forgotten, or else was never associated with them. I forgot to state that on one of his scouting trips with a company he killed a very large indian who had an enormous foot, hence his name Big Foot Wallace.

Yours Truly,

January 11, 1907. D. McFadden.

Captain McFadden, the veteran of three wars, was a comrade, associate, and chum of Wallace, and he himself had had many thrilling experiences on the Texas frontiers, and had many engagements with the Comanches and Mexicans, and was no mean scout. He is now resting at his home in McLennon County, enjoying the comforts of home, peace and happiness, the reward of the services of such men as himself and Wallace.

Additional sketch, furnished by Mrs. Rebecca J. Fisher, President of the William B. Travis Chapter, Daughters of the Republic of Texas, Austin, Texas, Capital "State Librarian."

"William A. "Big Foot" Wallace."

William A. Wallace was born in Lexington, Rockbridge County, Va., in the year 1816. He went to Texas in 1836, a few months after the battle of San Jacinto, for the purpose, he says, of taking pay out of the Mexicans for the murder of his brother, and his cousin, Major Wallace, both of whom fell at "Fannin's Massacre." He landed first at Galveston, from Galveston, Wallace went to La Grange, then a frontier village, where he resided until the spring of 1839, when he moved to Austin, just before the seat of Government was established at that place. He remained at Austin until the spring of 1840, when finding that the country was settling up around him too fast to suit his notions, he went over to San Antonio, where he resided until he entered the serivce. He was in the battle of

Salado, in the fall of 1842. In the fall of 1842, he volunteered in the "Mier Expedition." After his return from Mexico, he joined Colonel Jack Hays's Ranging Company, and was with it in many of those desperate encounters with the Comanches and other Indians, in which Hays, Walker, McCulloch and Chevalier gained their reputation as successful indian fighters. When the Mexican War broke out in 1846, Wallace joined Colonel Hay's regiment of mounted volunteers, and was with it at the storming of Monterey, where he says he took full toll out of the Mexicans for killing his brother and cousin at Goliad in 1836.

After the Mexican War ended, he had command of a ranging company for some time, and did good service in protecting the frontiers of the state from the incursions of the savages. Subsequently he had charge of the mail from San Antonio to El Paso, and though often waylaid and attacked by indians, he always brought it through in safety. He is now (1870) living upon his little ranch, thirty miles west of San Antonio.

Sketch of Wallace's life in "The Adventures of Big Foot Wallace, The Texas Ranger and Hunter, by John C. Duval."

Wallace paid a visit to his old stamping ground, Austin, in 1889.

For a longer sketch see "Early settlers and Indian Fighters of South west Texas. By A. J. Sowell" pp. 53-88.

4. Martha Wallace; married Peter Le Neve.
5. Michael Woods Wallace.
6. Lavinia Wallace; married Dr. A. Hamilton Rogers.
7. J. Harvey Wallace.
8. Sarah Wallace; married Thomas L. Courtney.
9. John R. Wallace; married Elizabeth Smith, daughter of Joe Smith. Their children were:
    1. Jesse Wallace.
    2. Samuel Wallace.
    3. William H. Wallace; died in 1854.
    4. Mary Wallace; married William Smith.
    5. John Pilson Wallace.
10. Charles Wallace.

Section 5. Sarah Wallace; married "Beaver Creek," William Woods. (See Part II, Chap. 12.)

Section 6. Hannah Wallace.

One Hannah Wallace, married Abner Oakley April 7, 1805, in Madison County, Ky., probably the subject.

Section 7. Josiah Wallace; married Hannah or Susan Wallace. In 1796 he sold his plantation in Albemarle County, Va., to Edward Broaddus, and emigrated to Kentucky.

*In 1836, James W. Fannin, of Texas, commanded a force at Coleta River against General Urria, who surrendered to the Mexicans. After his surrender 357 of his men, including General Fannin himself were shot to death by the Mexicans. Of the victims were a brother and a cousin of Big Foot Wallace, and he went to Texas just after the news of this event reached him.

CHAPTER 1.

MICHAEL WALLACE.

(Named in Chap. 3, Sec. 1.)

Article 1.—Michael Wallace, a son of William Wallace and Hannah Woods his wife, commanded a military company in the Revolutionary Army.

He married Ann Allen. In the year 1786, he sold out his lands in Virginia and moved to Kentucky, and settled on Paint Lick Creek some twelve to fifteen miles from where the city of Richmond stands, and in 1790, acquired something like four hundred acres of land there, on the waters of said creek, the creek being the line now, between Madison and Garrard Counties, by deeds from Stephen Merrit, Robert Henderson and William Miller. (See Deed Book, A. pages 172 and 241, and B page 140.) Afterwards in 1797, he conveyed 170 acres of said land to his son, William Wallace and 137 acres, to his son, Michael Wallace, Junior, (See Deed Book D. pages 226, and 228), his wife Ann joining in these deeds.

In 1807, his son, John Wallace executed to his father, Michael Wallace, senior, and Michael Wallace, junior, a paper having the purport of a mortgage, on certain property to protect them as his securities on a certain obligation. (See Deed Book, F. page 520.)

Descendents of this Michael Wallace, to this day live on the waters of Paint Lick, and own and occupy some, if not all of the original tracts of said ancestor.

It appears from the Chart of Hon. O. T. Wallace of Point Leavell, Kentucky, that Michael Wallace and Ann Allen his wife, had nine children, towit:

Section 1. William Wallace; married Sally Shannon, and had these children, viz:

1. Salem Wallace; (1795-1868) married Elizabeth Shannon, (1800-1823) and he married secondly, Eliza Jane Turpin (1813-19—), children of the first marriage:

1. Sarah Martha Wallace; 1822—— married Irvine W. Anderson, Oct. 26, 1843.
2. Nancy Jane Wallace, 1834-5.
3. William Wallace, 1836; married Mary Susan Higgins.
4. Elizabeth Shannon Wallace, 1838; married William Allen Anderson, Nov. 8, 1856.
5. Ann Wallace, 1840; married Joseph S. Robinson.
6. Mary Frances Wallace, 1842; married James B. Francis.
7. Oliver Terrill Wallace, 1845, surveyor, and author of Wallace's Chart; married Nancy Emily Shearer, (See Part V, Chap. 13, Sec. 9.) children:
    1. William A. Wallace, 1871.
    2. Ann C. Wallace, 1873.
    3. Elvira Wallace, 1875.
    4. Jennie Wallace, 1877.
    5. Oliver T. Wallace, Jr., 1883.
    6. Shannon Wallace, 1892.
8. Margaret Wallace, 1847-1886; married John B. Parkes.
9. Salem Wallace, 1850.
10. Henry Lee Wallace, 1855; married Ann C. Higgins.

Salem Wallace, Senior, represented Madison County in the Kentucky Legislature in 1845, and he owned and occupied as a home on Paint Lick Creek, the land or a part of it, that his father settled on when he came to Madison County, Ky., and same is still in the family.

2. Rankin Wallace, 1797-1848; married Mary Ann Wallace.
3. Shannon Wallace, 1799-1858; married Betsy Reid.
4. Cylon Wallace, 1801-26.
5. Jane Wallace, 1803-7.
6. Betsy Wallace, 1805-54; married Mason Wallace.
7. William Wallace, 1807-46; married Lucy Wallace.
8. Jason Wallace, 1809-65; married Isabella Wallace.
9. Arnon Wallace, 1811-50; married Martha Agnes Roberts.
10 Sarah Ann Wallace, 1816-75; married —— Griffith.

Section 2. John Wallace; married —— Mackey.
Section 3. Allen Wallace; married Nancy Terrill.
Section 4. Michael Wallace; married Nancy Shannon.
Section 5. Josiah Wallace; married Polly Mason.
Section 6. Polly Wallace; married —— Giles.
Section 7. Hannah Wallace; married James Anderson.
Section 8 Betsy Wallace; married William Shannon.
Section 9. Sallie Wallace; married William Duff.

CHAPTER 5.

SAMUEL WALLACE.

(Named in Sec. 3, Chap. 2.)

Article 1.—Samuel Wallace, a son of Peter Wallace, senior, the Scottish Highlander, who died in Ireland, and Elizabeth Woods, the widow emigrant from Ireland to America, his wife, was born in Ireland, and was one of the emigrants to America, as related in Chapter 2.

He moved with his mother from Pennsylvania to Rockbridge County, Va., and there remained a short while. He married Esther Baker of Cab Creek, settlement, in what is now Charlotte County, Va., in 1741, where he made his home till 1782, when he removed to Kentucky, where he died about 1800, past 90 years of age. Four children were born to him and his wife Esther, named in the coming sections:

Section 1. Judge Caleb Wallace, born in 1742, emigrated to Kentucky in 1782. Was a ruling Elder of the Presbyterian Church and a honored and distinguished lawyer. Was one of the three first judges of the Court of Appeals of Kentucky, at its organization in 1792, and was a subscriber to the proposal for establishing a society to be called "The Kentucky Society for Promoting Useful Knowledge" Dec. 1, 1787. He was one of the ablest and most honored Jurists of his times. He married Sarah McDowell. (See Part II, Chap. 5, Sec. 1-8.) He died in 1814. Of his children, was a son:

1 Samuel Wallace, who married ——— ——— and had a son:
1. Caleb Wallace; married ——— ——— and had a son:
1. Caleb Manor Wallace; married Ann Oldham, the only daughter of David D. Oldham, and Susan Chenault his wife. (See Part VI, Chap. 14, Sec. 1.)

Section 2. Elizabeth Wallace, born 1745; married Colonel Henry Pawling, who died in 1814.

Section 3. Andrew Wallace, born 1748; married Catherine Parkes, emigrated to Kentucky, and died in 1829.

Section 4. Samuel Wallace, in his young man-hood started on a trip to Scotland, and was never heard of by his people afterwards.

CHAPTER 6.

ANDREW WALLACE.

(Named in Chap. 2, Sec. 4.)

Article 1.—Andrew Wallace, a son of Peter Wallace, senior, the Scottish Highlander, who died in Ireland, and Elizabeth Woods, his wife, an emigrant toAmerica; was born in Ireland, and was himself an emigrant to America.

About the year 1748, or a little before, he married Margaret Woods, daughter of his Uncle Michael Woods and Mary Campbell of the Scottish Clan, from Argylshire, Scotland, his wife. (See Part 2, Chap. 4.) In 1748, Michael Woods conveyed to Andrew Wallace 400 acres of land, 200 acres of which was in the way of dowry with his daughter, evidently for the purpose of making his recently married daughter and her husband a home. Andrew Wallace was surveyor to open the road from D. S. to Mechum river ford in Albemarle, and his brothers-in-law, Archibald Woods and Michael Woods Jr., assisted the surveyor in clearing it.

Andrew Wallace with his brothers and Uncle Michael Woods moved from Pennsylvania to the valley of Virginia, and Andrew settled in what is now Albemarle County, at the present Ivy Creek Depot, on part of the Charles Hudson entry, where he lived till his death in 1785, and was a member of the Ivy Creek congregation of Presbyterians, the inhabitants of which on March 29, 1747, joined with Mountain Plains and Rockfish, and signed a call of the Rev. Samuel Black to the pastorate of said churches. His wife preceded him to the grave several years. Their children were:

Section 1. Michael Wallace, born in 1752, in Albemarle County, Va., where he married Jane Bratton. He emigrated to Madison County, Ky., as early as 1790, of whom further details are given in Chapter 7.

Section 2. Samuel Wallace. (See Chap. 3, Section 4-4.)

Section 3. Elizabeth Wallace; married Captain William Briscoe. The subject of Chapter 18.

Section 4. Sarah Wallace; married Alexander Henderson. The subject of Chapter 19.

Section 5. Hannah Wallace; married Michael Woods. (See Part II, Chapter 6, Sec. 2.)

Note:—One Hannah Wallace; married Josiah Wallace, and one Hannah Wallace; married Abner Oakley April 7, 1805.

Section 6. Mary Wallace; married Thomas Collins in Virginia, they emigrated to Madison County, Ky., about 1790. The subject of Chapter 20.

Section 7. Margaret Wallace; married William Ramsey. They remained in Albemarle County, Va., where Mr. Ramsey died in 1825. The subject of Chapter 21.

Section 8. Jean Wallace; married Mr. —— Wilson.

Section 9. John Wallace.

Notes:

"A" James Wallace, owned land in Fayette County, Ky., which was divided among his heirs, Dec. 10, 1813, viz:

1. Thomas R. Wallace.
2. James Wallace.
3. Alexander Wallace.
4. William Wallace.

"B" John Wallace of Fayette County, Ky. His will bears date June 2, 1813, probated April term 1814, wife Jane. Children:

1. John Wallace.
2. James F. Wallace.
3. Abraham Hill Wallace.
4. Andrew S. Wallace.
5. Jane Wallace.
6. Margaret Wallace.
7. Martha Wallace.

"C" William Wallace, of Fayette County, Ky. Report of allotment of his portion of the slaves of his father, Cornelius Wallace, dated June 23, 1821, approved July 1821.

"D" John Wallace, of Fayette County, Ky. Will bears date July 4, 1849, probated July 16, 1870, wife Lucy, children:

1. Margaret Wallace, wife of Mr. Patton. She was dead when the will was probated.
2. Susan Wallace, wife of Mr. —— Burnsides. She was dead when the will was probated.
3. Lucy Ann Wallace, wife of Mr. —— McClellon.
4. John B. Wallace.
   1. Emily Jane Wallace, grand-daughter of testator.

CHAPTER 7.

MICHAEL WALLACE.

(Named in Chapter 6, Sec. 1.)

Article 1.—Michael Wallace, a son of Andrew Wallace and Margaret Woods his wife, was born in Albemarle County, Va., in 1752, and died Aug. 2, 1809, as hereafter proven.

He married Jane Bratton in Virginia and about or prior to 1790, emigrated from Albemarle to Madison County, Kentucky, and settled on the head waters of a prong of Otter Creek, where the City of Richmond was built. On the 2nd of July, 1793, he acquired for 1000 pounds current money, 300 acres of land from Colonel John Miller, (the founder of Richmond) and his wife Jenny, on the waters of Otter Creek, adjoining David Trotter's land, and Hoy's pre-emption. (The Dillingham addition to the city of Richmond, now covering a portion of said land.) and upon which land, Michael Wallace and his wife, Jane Bratton lived and died and upon which their remains were buried, just back of the old Edmund L. Shackelford house, some 100 or more yards from the Irvine pike. The stones marking their graves still remain, although the stone to his wife's grave is broken, and they show, that Michael Wallace died Aug. 2, 1809, in the 57th year of his age, proof that he was born in 1752. The date of his birth was about four years subsequent to the date of the deed to his father and mother from Michael Woods to 400 acres of land in Albemarle County, Va., mentioned in Chapter 6.

(Rev. Neander M. Woods, in his Woods—McAfee memorial, to which we are much indebted for valuable data: supposes that this Michael Wallace went from Virginia to Pennsylvania and was the father of Andrew, of Carlisle, ancestor of General Llew Wallace, author, man of letters and soldier, but gives no account of his wife, which supposition is error, because this Michael Wallace came and settled in Madison County, Ky., as above stated.)

The stone shows that Jane Wallace his wife died Feb. 12, 1836, in the 75th year of her age, proving her birth in 1761. She survived her husband 27 years. Michael Wallace was at an early day appointed and acted as surveyor of the state or Great Road, in Madison County, Ky., and was allotted the hands on his own lands, and the lands of William Kerr, Cornelius Maupin, John Reid, James Coulter, William Kavanaugh, James Coulter, Jr,. and Captain William Briscoe. (See Chap. 1, Sec. 14.) James Coulter's will, probated in 1806, was witnessed by James Bratton. Coulter and his wife were buried in the same grave yard that Wallace and his wife were buried in. John Bratton, married Susannah Burton, Jan. 7, 1810. When Michael Wallace died, administration on his estate was granted to his widow, Jane Wallace, Jan, 1, 1810. His home at Richmond, was twelve to fifteen miles from the home of his double-first cousin Michael Wallace, (son of William Wallace and Hannah Woods), who married Ann Allen, on Paint Lick Creek, as stated in Chapter 4. Michael Wallace, the subject, was one of the signers of the Albemarle Declaration of Independence April 21, 1779. The children of Michael Wallace and Jane Bratton his wife were:

Section 1. Ella Wallace; married John P. Ballard, Dec. 26, 1809, her husband died, and on the 31st of Jan. 1826, she married Robert Cox. Her home was on the State Road in Madison County, Ky., ten miles south of Richmond, at Bobtown. The children of her first marriage were:

1 Michael Wallace Ballard; married Elizabeth Hockersmith, March 12, 1835, and went West.

2. John Powers Ballard; married Jane Wallace Jarman, his cousin, May 7, 1835, (See Chap. 13, Sec. 5,) and went West.

No issue of second marriage to Robert Cox. Ella Cox died, and Robert Cox married again.

Section 2. Jane Wallace; married Nicholas Kavanaugh, son of William Kavanaugh and Hannah Woods his wife, Jan. 12, 1817. (See Part VII, Chap. 12.) Kavanaugh died, and she married the second time Canole. Their home was made in Missouri, in Lone Jack.

Section 3. Sallie Wallace, born September — 1787; married Christopher Harris, Feb. 20, 1812, she died Oct. 26, 1836. (See Part 3, Chap. 28.)

Section 4. Polly Wallace; married her cousin, Archibald Woods, Oct. 4, 1814. He was a son of Adam Woods and Ann Kavanaugh his wife. (See Part 2, Chap. 7, Sec. 3.)

Section 5. Annie R. Wallace, was a beautiful and noble woman. She married Thomas C. Maupin, son of John Maupin and Nancy Collins his wife, Sept. 2, 1819, and they emigrated from Madison County, Ky., to Missouri. (See Chap. 20 Sec. 3.) Further history of this couple is given in Part V, Chap. 11, Sec. 2.

Section 6. Andrew Wallace; married Jane Reid in Madison County, Ky., Oct. 5, 1813. A fuller account of them is given in Chapter 8.

Section 7. Peggy Wallace; married William Jarman. A further history will be found in Chapter 13.

CHAPTER 8.

ANDREW WALLACE.

(Named in Chap. 7, Sec. 6.)

Article 1—Andrew Wallace, a son of Michael Wallace and Jane Bratton his wife, was born in Madison County, Ky., July 5, 1792.

He married Oct. 5. 1813, Jane Reid a daughter of Jonathan Reid and Anna Woods his wife. She was born Dec. 9, 1794. (See Part II, Chap. 48, Sec. 4.) He lived at or near Richmond, Madison County, Ky., a number of years, and about 1836, he moved with his family to Irvine in Estill County, Ky., where he died, Oct. 10, 1842, and his wife, April 14, 1863. The children born to them were:

Section 1. James Wallace, born Aug. 24, 1814; died July 1, 1816.

Section 2. Susan Ann Wallace, born March 17, 1816; married Napoleon Bonaparte Busby, and died at her home in Irvine, Ky., Nov. 10, 1886. Further account given in Chapter 9.

Section 3. Mitchell Wallace, born Oct. 19, 1817; died July 1, 1818.

Section 4. Archibald Wallace, born July 23, 1819; died Dec. 4, 1833.

Section 5. John M. Wallace, born March 7, 1822; married Elizabeth Jane McKinney. The subject of Chapter 10.

Section 6. Jane E. Wallace, born Nov. 17, 1824; died April 19, 1826.

Section 7. Mary E. Wallace, born Aug. 18, 1826; died Aug. 1, 1835.

Section 8. William Reid Wallace, born Dec. 13, 1828; married Mourning Thorpe. The subject of Chapter 11.

Section 9. Thomas K. Wallace, born Aug. 20, 1830; married Margaret Bryson. The subject of Chapter 16.

Section 10. Sarah Harris Wallace, born Aug. 16, 1834; married Edward B. Conroy. The subject of Chapter 17.

Section 11. Andrew Wallace, born Sept. 17, 1836; married Clara Ellen Tracey, May 9, 1861. The subject of Chapter 12.

CHAPTER 9.

SUSAN ANN WALLACE.

(Named in Chap. 8, Sec. 2.)

Article 1.—Susan Ann Wallace, a daughter of Andrew Wallace and Jane Reid his wife, was born in Madison County, Ky., at Richmond, and went with her parents to Irvine, Estill County, Ky., and there married Napoleon Bonaparte Busby, and established a home at Irvine, where she died leaving these children:

Section 1. James Busby, was at one time a successful young merchant of Irivine. He married Miss —— Cockrill, and moved to Richmond and engaged in the business of a grocer, and restaurateur and failed and removed to Irvine where he died, leaving a son:

1. Eugene Busby.

Section 2. Eugene Busby, was associated with his brother in business. He married Mattie Salter, and died without living issue.

CHAPTER 10.

JOHN M. WALLACE.

(Named in Chap. 9, Sec. 5.)

Article 1.—John M. Wallace, a son of Andrew Wallace and Jane Reid his wife, was born March 7, 1822, at Richmond in Madison County, Kentucky.

He went with his parents to Irvine, Estill County, Ky., and there was married to Elizabeth Jane McKinney, who was born Feb. 6, 1827, on Hardwicks Creek, on which creek they lived for a number of years and then moved to Irvine, Ky., where Mr. Wallace died Dec. 2, 1893, an esteemed and highly respected citizen. His widow is now living in Irivine. Their children, viz:

Section 1. Thomas Eldora Wallace, a daughter, born Feb. 13, 1856; died Aug. 13, 1856.

Section 2. David Andrew Wallace, born July 11, 1857; married Lena White, daughter of Hon. Bamford White, an honored citizen and lawyer and politician of Irvine, Ky. Mr. Wallace is a leading merchant of Irvine, and popular with the people of his town and county.

Section 3. Silas Elbridge Wallace, born July 10, 1859. He lives at Irvine, Ky., and a dealer in live stock, and a bachelor.

Section 4. Jennie Elizabeth Wallace, born Oct. 22, 1861; married Maxwell Gaddis Whiteman, May 29, 1883. Their home is in Irvine, Ky. Their children are:

1. Villa E. Whiteman.
2. Miller Franklin Whiteman.
3. Lou Lilly Whiteman.
4. Sallie Conroy Whiteman.
5. Gaddis Whiteman.
6. Edna Whiteman.
7. John Wesley Whiteman.
8. Emuriel Whiteman.
9. (unnamed) Whiteman.

Section 5. John A. Wallace, born Aug. 23, 1780. Salesman in the store of his brother David Andrew Wallace, unmarried.

Section 6. Lou Annie Wallace, born Oct. 29, 1867, unmarried and lives with her mother in Irvine, Ky.

CHAPTER 11.

WILLIAM REID WALLACE.

(Named in Chap. 9, Sec. 8.)

Article 1.—William Reid Wallace, son of Andrew Wallace and Jane Reid his wife, was born in Madison County, Ky., and went to Irvine, Estill County, Ky., with his parents.

He returned to Madison County, Ky., to select his wife, and married Mourning Thorpe, daughter of Thomas Thorpe and Emma Hume his wife. (See Part III, Chap. 13, Sec. 4.) Mr. Wallace was born Dec. 13, 1828. After his marriage he located and kept his own house in the village of Elliston, Madison County, Ky., and while living there on the 18th day of June 1861, he was murdered in cold blood and unprovoked, by one Burgess, on account of his political convictions, being a southern sympathiser. The great Civil War had commenced, and justice was loosely dealt out by the courts of the land, and Wallace's slayer went free, without punishment, but for a quarter of a century was afraid to remain near, where he committed the murder, and stayed away, but he had Wallace's blood on him, whose spirit haunted him the balance of his days, and he had no peace of mind for his outrageous and heinous crime. Mr. Wallace's widow is still living. Their children, viz:

Section 1. Emma Wallace; married Irvine M. Scrivner. (See Part VI, Chap. 31, Sec. 1.) Their children:

1. William Joe Scrivner.
2. Harris Scrivner.
3. Mary Scrivner.
4. Florence Scrivner.
5. Louise Scrivner.
6. Jonah Scrivner.
7. Sarah Elizabeth Scrivner.

Section 2. Mary Willie Wallace, a posthumous child, born Oct. 14, 1861; died Sept. 10, 1878.

CHAPTER 12.

ANDREW WALLACE.

(Named in Chap. 8, Sec. 11.)

Article 1.—Andrew Wallace, a son of Andrew Wallace, and Jane Reid his wife, was born in Madison County, Ky., Sept. 17, 1836.

He went to Irvine, Estill County, Ky., where he married Clara Ellen Tracey, who was born Feb. 28, 1844, daughter of Augustine Tracey and Sallie Curry, his wife, and they made their home in Irvine. Mr. Wallace was a mechanic, and did the work of a carpenter, and kept a shop, where he did work, and also conducted farming and wagoning. When the Civil War broke out he enlisted in the Federal Army. After the war he was elected Jailer of Estill County, which office he held from 1866 to 1870. He died at his home, Sept. 29, 1903, his widow now lives in Irvine. The children born to them, viz:

ANDREW WALLACE.

Section 1. Edward Brooks Wallace born Oct. 19, 1862. He is a splendid mechanic, now living in the city of Cincinnati, Ohio. He married first, Maud Maupin, daughter of Calumn Maupin and Mary Turner Park his wife, Dec. 23, 1886. (See Part 5, Chap. 6, Sec. 3,) she died Nov. 23, 1897, and on the 15th of Dec. 1901, he married Maria Dourel. The children of the first marriage:

CLARA ELLEN TRACEY.
Wife of Andrew Wallace.

1. Edgar Wallace.
2. Park Wallace.

Section 2. Coleman Covington Wallace, was born in Irvine, 1864. He located in Richmond, Ky., and conducted successfully for a time a store, and was chairman of the Republican County Committee, and was a strong candidate for sheriff of Madison County, and many claim that he was elected, but counted out by fraud. He is the present Post Master of Richmond, Ky. He married Mary Luxon, daughter of William E. Luxon and Mary Ballard, his wife, issue:

1. William Luxon Wallace.

Section 3. William Andrew Wallace, born Feb. 26, 1866, died Dec. 18, 1867.

Section 4. James Austin Wallace, born Aug. 5, 1867; married Mrs. Hattie B. Clay, May 2, 1901, she died May, 8, 1902, no issue:
James Wallace was clerk of the Estill Circuit Court, two terms, 1893 to 1904, resides at Irvine, Ky., and is a cattle dealer.

Section 5. Henry Gardner Wallace, born Feb. 24, 1869. He left Irvine and settled in Madison County, Ky., where he married Lilly Anderson Nov. 24, 1891

Section 6. Sarah J. Wallace, born June 1, 1872; died Nov. 24, 1888.

Section 7. Andrew Wallace, born Feb. 2, 1873; died July 2, 1873.

Section 8. Charles Wallace, born April 1, 1874; died Aug. 28, 1875.

Section 9. Thomas Quirk Wallace, born Sept. 12, 1875; married Carrie J. Congleton Sept. 16, 1896. Has been Post Master at Irvine, Ky., a number of years and was U. S. Store-keeper-Gauger during Internal Revenue Collector, John W. Yerkes, incumbency, issue of marriage:

1. Ethel Payne Wallace.
2. Lilly Wallace.
3. Thomas Wallace.

Section 10. Kate May Wallace, born May 12, 1878; married Estill Payne, Aug. 16, 1894, issue:

1. Eva Payne.
2. Estill Payne.

Section 11. Tracey Wallace, born Sept. 5, 1879. He is preparing himself for a physician and is teaching school.

Section 12. Albert Rice Wallace, born April 6, 1882; died Dec. 7, 1882.

Section 13. Daniel F. Wallace, born March 4, 1885. Has a position under his brother Coleman in the Richmond, Post Office. He married recently Anna Engle, daughter of Robert Engle.

Section 14 (unmarried) Wallace; died in infancy.

Section 15. (unmarried) Wallace; died in infancy.

Section 16. (unmarried) Wallace; died in infancy.

CHAPTER 13.

PEGGY WALLACE.

(Named in Chap. 7, Sec. 7.)

Article 1.—Peggy Wallace, a daughter of Michael Wallace and Jane Bratton his wife; married William Jarman.

They lived and died in Madison County, Ky. Their children and descendants were:

Section 1. William Jarman; married Amanda Clark, Oct. 22, 1835. Their children:
1. William Jarman.
2. James Jarman.
3. Amanda Jarman.
4. Sarah Jarman.
5. Margaret Jane Jarman.
6. Susan Jarman.

Section 2. Michael Wallace Jarman lived the life of a bachelor, and died at his brother Andrew's home in Madison County, Ky.

Section 3. Andrew Wallace Jarman, born Aug. 12, 1827, in Madison County, Ky., married Pamelia West, Jan. 15, 1855, she was born May 7, 1823. They made their home in the southern part of the County, near Berea, where they both died. Mrs. Wallace survived her husband, and died June 2, 1902. Their children:
1. Palestine Jarman; married —— —— and went to Missouri.
2. James W. Jarman.
3. Sallie Jarman; married William Adams.
4. Kizziah Jarman; married James L. Cornelison.
5. Mary Eliza Jarman; married Ballard Million.

Section 4. Polly P. Jarman; married Greenville Hubbard, in Madison County, Ky., Sept. 29, 1836. They made their home at Speedwell, where they died. Their children:

1. John Hubbard; married Miss —— Parker, and died in Rockcastle County, Ky.

2. James Hubard; married first, Julia A. Gentry; she was born May 23, 1857, and died Nov. 23, 1897. Mr. Hubbard married again, Mrs. Mollie Rhodus, nee Harris, daughter of Jack Harris and Kitty Ballard his wife.

3. Michael Hubbard, was born in Madison County, Ky. He went to Illinois; married —— —— and died in said state.

4. Margaret Hubbard, was born at Speedwell; married Dock Todd. They live near Speedwell.

5. Mollie Hubbard, was born near Speedwell, has never married. She makes her home principally with her sister Margaret.

Section 5. Jane Wallace Jarman; married John Powers Ballard, May 7, 1835. (See Chap. 7, Sec. 1.) They emigrated to Missouri and died childless.

Section 6. Margaret Ramsey Jarman; (twin to Elizabeth) married first, James Rhodus, second, Richard Cornelison, and third, Wilson Davis, the latter marriage occuring in Madison County, Ky., Nov. 30, 1834. There were no issues of the two last marriages. Issue of the first:

1. William Rhodus, drowned in his youth in Silver Creek.

2. Elizabeth Jane Rhodus; married William B. Johnson, the present Jailer of Madison County, Ky., elected on the democratic ticket. He has ever been a staunch democrat.
3. Agnes Rhodus; married William Reynolds.
4. Samuel Rhodus; thrown from a horse and killed.
5. James Rhodus; married Mollie Harris, daughter of Jack Harris and Kitty Ballard, his wife. Mr. Rhodus died, and his widow married James Hubbard.

Section 7. Elizabeth Houston Jarman; (twin to Margaret) married James Dowden, Jan. 13, 1848, in Madison County, Ky., and they lived and died near Berea, in said County. Their children:

1. Melissa Dowden; married George F. Ames. They went to Springfield, Mo.
2. Margaret Ann Dowden; (called "Judith") married Martin Baker. They occupy the old home on Silver Creek, near Berea.
3. Sarah Elizabeth Dowden, (called "Sweet"); married John Davis. They live on Silver Creek, near Berea, no issue.
4. Michael Dowden; married Amanda Richardson and died. Their children :
    1. James Dowden.
    2. Ernst Dowden.
    3. Forest Dowden.
    4. Sarah Elizabeth Dowden; clerk in one of the Berea banks.
    5. Fannie Dowden.

Section 8. Fannie Jarman; married Richard Comelison, had two children, both died in infancy.

Section 9. Sallie W. Jarman; married Martin Gentry Cornelison in Madison County, Ky., June 7, 1832. Mr. Cornelison died, and on the 29th of Sept., 1842, she married Henry Bascombe Rhodus. Children of the first mariage:

1. Mary Susan Cornelison; died at nine or ten years of age.
2. Margaret Jane Cornelison; married William Bush.
3. Richard Cornelison; married Sallie Cole.
4. John Cornelison; married Lurindy Terrill.
5. Dorendy Cornelison; married Malon B. Duncan.
6. Dosha P. Cornelison; married Frank Cole.

William Jarman, senior, and Peggy Wallace his wife the 16th of Nov. 1813, conveyed to David Gordon, 22 acres, 3 roods and 13 poles of land adjacent to Richmond that was alloted to the said Peggy, out of the estate of her father, Michael Wallace, deceased, and June 28, 1813, Wiliam Jarman sold Robert Rodes two negro slaves, Pompy and Mourning, and April 7, 1835, he conveyed to his brother-in-law, Andrew Wallace an interest in the estate of Michael Wallace, deceased.

CHAPTER 14.

ADAM WALLACE.

(Named in Sec. 5, Chap. 2.)

Article 1.—Adam Walace, a son of Peter Wallace, senior, the Scottish Highlander who died in Ireland, and Elizabeth Woods, the widow emigrant from Ireland to America, his wife.

He was born in Ireland, and was himself an emigrant from Ireland. to America, as related in Chapter 2. No further trace of him has been obtained.

CHAPTER 15.

PETER WALLACE, JUNIOR.

(Named in Sec. 6, Chap 2.)

Article 1.—Peter Wallace, Junior, a son of Peter Wallace, Senior, the Scottish Highlander who died in Ireland, and Elizabeth Woods the widow emigrant from Ireland to America, his wife, was born in Ireland in 1719, and died in 1784.

He was an emigrant from Ireland to America, as related in Chapter 2. He married Martha Woods, daughter of his uncle Michael Woods, after his death called Michael Woods of Blair Park, and Mary Campbell of the Scottish Clan Campbell, from Argylshire, Scotland, his wife, See Part II, Chap. 4, Sec. 9. The said Martha was born in 1720, and died in 1790. He moved with his mother from Pennsylvania to Rockbridge County, Va. Of the marriage nine children were the fruits, accounts of whom are given in the coming sections:

Section 1. Malcom Wallace. He was in the army under General Morgan at Boston, and died there in the service of his country in 1775.

Section 2. Samuel Wallace, born in 1745. He married Rebeka Anderson, who died in 1786. He was an officer in the Revolutionary Army, and commanded at Fort Young on the Virginia Frontier, during the French and Indian War.

Section 3. James (or Hugh) Wallace was an ensign in the Third Virginia Regiment, and died of smallpox in Philadelphia in 1776.

Section 4. Adam Wallace. The captain of a Rockbridge Company in the tenth Virginia, and was killed by Tarleton's Troops, while bravely fighting against fearful odds, at the Waxhaw, South Carolina, May 29, 1780.

His sword, or espontoon, used on that bloody day was in the possession of John A. R. Varner, of Lexington, Va., a descendant of his brother, Samuel, a few years ago. Wallace's company was composed of fifty Rockbridge men. Colonel Buford's Regiment had been detached from the Northern Army and ordered to go to the relief of the beleaguered garrison at Charleston, South Carolina. On their way they learned that General Lincoln had capitulated, and Colonel Buford was ordered to fall back again toward the North. Cornwallis hearing of Buford's retreat, sent his dashing unscrupulous cavalry officer, Colonel Tarlton, with three hundred picked men in pursuit, and after a forced march of one hundred miles he overtook Buford at Waxhaw, South Carolina. Before Buford and his Virginians could prepare for the attack the British cavalry was upon them from front and rear, and both flanks. The Virginians delivered their fire, but before they could reload Tarlton's cavalry men were on them with their pistols and swords. Out of four hundred men of Buford's command, three hundred were killed or wounded. The wounded were hacked to pieces in the most inhuman manner.

It was in this terrible encounter that Captain Adam Wallace fell. He was a young man of twenty-five years, and stood six feet two inches in his stockings,—the very picture of vigorous manhood.

Colonel Buford seeing his men in confusion, fled early in the fight, but young Wallace disdained to flee, and standing his ground met steel with steel. His trusty sword was wielded with tremendous vigor, and he managed to kill a number of Tarlton's dragoons before he received the fatal blow which ended his noble young life

Four brothers of young Andrew, towit: Malcolm, Samuel, Andrew and James (or Hugh), sons of Peter Wallace, Jr., and Martha Woods, his wife, sacrificed their lives for the independence of their country.

In a speech delivered in the Virginia House of Delegates by late Governor James MacDowell, occurs this sentence concerning the brave young soldier who owned that sword.

"That dark and dismal page in the history of the Revolution, that carnival of cruel and unjustifiable slaughter, stamped with the name of Waxhaw, is illuminated only by the splendid heroism of a soldier from the valley of Virginia, whom I am proud to claim as a kinsman, Captain Adam Wallace, of Rockbridge."

Of all the members of the Wallace-Woods Clans, none had a nobler record, in the great struggle for freedom from the British Yoke, than did Peter Wallace, Junior, and his wife Martha Woods, who gave five brave sons to that sacred cause: Samuel, Malcolm, Andrew, James (or Hugh), and Adam. (Woods-McAfee Memorial, by Rev. N. M. W.)

Section 5. Andrew Wallace, was Captain of a company in the eighth Virginia Regiment, and was killed at Guilford Court House in 1781. It seems that he was never married, and was young when

Section 6. John Wallace. (See Chapter 1, Sec. 1, and Note in Chap. 4) wife Jane.

Section 7. Elizabeth Wallace: married Colonel John Gilmore of Rockbridge County, Va.

Section 8. Janet Wallace.

Section 9. Susannah Wallace.

CHAPTER 16.

THOMAS K. WALLACE.

(Named in Chap. 8, Sec. 9.)

Article 1.—Thomas K. Wallace, a son of Andrew Wallace and Jane Reid his wife, was born in Madison County, Ky., Aug. 20, 1831.

He left the County when about five years of age, in 1836, with his parents, and went to Irvine, Estill County, Ky., and when he was about eleven years of age his father died the 10th day of Oct. 1842; he was educated principally in Irvine, going to school in the winter and working in the fall and winter until about twenty-four years of age; in Jan. 1855, hoping to improve his opportunities he emigrated to Missouri and stopped on the Grand Prarie, in the Northern part of Boone County, where he engaged in farming until the Civil War broke out; in 1862, he went with the South and enlisted in the Confederate Army, he remained in the army to the end of the struggle, when he returned to Boone County. Before the war, on the 28th of Feb. 1858, he was married to Margaret Bryson, she was born in Howard County, Mo., the 8th day of June 1833, she was a daughter of Solomon Bryson. Her parents were born and reared in Madison County, Ky. Solomon Bryson's parents died when he was very young,

he fell in battle.
and he was raised an orphan and knew but little of his people. His wife was a Miss Hendren, related to the old Madison County family of that name. Mr. Bryson and his wife left Madison County, Ky., about 1831, and she heard after that but little from her people, and lost trace of her genealogy.

Thomas K. Wallace was trying to make a start in the world, and provide for his wife and little children, and was not at all inclined to join the army, but the circumstances and conditions were such that it seemed impossible for a southern-rights man, (he being one) to remain at home in peace and safety. The radical party had become oppressive, the guerrillas were scouring the country, breaking into and pillaging houses, taking any and every thing they wanted, and many things they didn't want, and mistreating the people opposed to their methods. That did not suit young Wallace, therefore, taking his gun and best horse he joined in with others, who bethought themselves to make the pillagers afraid to leave the station on the Pacific Railroad, near which was Mr. Wallace's home, but the pillagers were soon re-enforced and there remained in the summer of 1862, the only alternative for Wallace to enlist in the southern army. So, in the fall he joined a company that was being made up to go South, this company started out travelling at night to keep from being seen as much as possible, and succeeded in crossing the river, but after the first night the enemy got on their trail, and sent runners to stations ahead, and they had to fight night and day. In an engagement in the evening of the third day, Mr. Wallace was wounded in the right arm, captured and carried to a station and held there as a prisoner about two weeks, when a start was made with the prisoners for Jefferson City. On the way late in the evening when the sun was sinking beneath the Western horizon, and all were weary, and the bushes by the way were thick, the guards riding and the prisoners afoot, Wallace watching and waiting his chance, sprang out into the thicket and made his escape, by concealing himself in a gully and as it was growing dark, the search for him was soon ended, and he winded his way in a south easterly direction for several miles, and finally came to a house, around which he spied until he discovered the absence of men, then he ventured up and revealed his condition and his wants, and luckily they were true southern sympathizers; in a short while horses were made ready and one of the ladies of the house went with him about five miles to the home of a widow lady, whose son piloted Wallace about twenty miles further into the Glasconade Hills, near Rolla, where he found a Confederate Recruiting Officer with whom Mr. Wallace remained until the latter part of the winter, from which point he was piloted to the Missouri Cavalry forces in Arkansas, where Wallace got with his company again.

His arm had not gotten well from the wound, shivered pieces of bone were working out, and whilst he was unable to do certain active service, he was detailed on the courier lines and to taking the wounded and the dying from the fields of battle, which services he faithfully and gallantly rendered.

He was under General Steel when that officer attempted to go through to Shreveport, and was in the battles of Old River Lake, Poison Springs and Saline River. Gen. Steele, however, was driven back; he was with General Price's army on his raid into Missouri, when he went to the river and drove everything before him. He belonged to the fourth Missouri Cavalry, General Marmaduke's Brigade, division commanded by General John Q. Burbridge, who surrendered at Shreveport.

After the restoration of peace, Mr. Wallace on account of his crippled arm, unable to wield an axe, or do much manual labor, everything looked dark to him, but he found friends who backed him until he could walk alone, and the prospects brightened.

From the years 1855 to 1882, Thomas K. Wallace lived in Boone and Audraine Counties, Missouri; in the latter year he sold out and went to Bourbon County, Kansas, and lived there for five years, and then went to Oklahoma, built a store house and stocked it with drugs for his son, Napoleon E. Wallace, and Mr. Wallace remained there for a year and a half, until the opening of the '"Strip" to where he went and obtained a claim and remained on it six years, and then sold out and moved to Guthrie, Oklahoma, where he is now permanently located, 606, East Mansur Ave., and there hopes to live out the balance of his days, where he has a beautiful home. When he left his farm in Missouri, he thought his days here on earth were few, he yet survives, 75 years old. Their children:

Section 1. James Andrew Wallace, born April 8, 1859; died April 25, 1859.

Section 2. John Nathan Wallace, born Nov. 11, 1860. He married firstly, Nora Keene, of Boone County, Mo., a daughter of Alexander Keene, an early settler and pioneer of Boone County, near Columbia. He married secondly, Ella Henton, who came with her parents from Illinois to Kansas. John Nathan Wallace's home is Guthrie, Oklahoma, and he is the pioneer drug man of the place, his place of business is at the corner of First and Oklahoma Avenues. He went to Guthrie when the Country was first opened, and was far-sighted enough to see a future for Guthrie and immediately embarked in business and has been an active factor in the Commercial Circles of Guthrie ever since.

His store is neatly arranged and equipped, and contains a large and well selected stock of drugs, medicines, chemicals, herbs, patent medicines, extracts, toilet articles, etc. The prescription department is given special attention, and has gained quite a reputation among physicians for skill and care. A first class line of jewelry is also carried in stock, and quoted at the lowest prevailing prices. Everything in the way of diamonds, watches, clocks, cut glass, gold, and silver ware etc., is carried, and from the assortment, one can make a satisfactory selection. Besides being active himself, Mr. Wallace gives employment to a number of competent hands, but he is personally on hand to look after details. The issue of his marriage:

1. Leonard Buford Wallace, born May 5, 1885.

The issue of the second mariage:

2. Evan Oswold Wallace, born Dec. 22, 1891.

Section 3. Thomas P. Wallace, born Aug. 18, 1862; died Oct. 9, 1887.

Section 4. Napoleon E. Wallace, born May 28, 1866. He married Naoma France, a daughter of James France, of Illinois; her parents live now in Guthrie, Oklahoma. Napoleon E. Wallace, and his family live in Apacha, Oklahoma, about one hundred and twenty-five miles from Guthrie. They had one child:

1. Iona Mercy Wallace, born Feb. 16, 1899.

Section 5. Sarah Frances Wallace, born Jan. 7, 1869; unmaried and now lives with her parents in Guthrie, Oklahoma.

Section 6. Benjamin A. Wallace, born Jan. 1, 1873; died Jan. 4, 1882.

Section 7. Josephine A. Wallace, born May 2, 1876; died March 24, 1882.

CHAPTER 17.

SALLY HARRIS WALACE.

(Named in Sec. 10, Chap. 8.)

Article 1.—Sally Harris Wallace, a daughter of Andrew Wallace and Jane Reid his wife, was born in Madison County, Ky., Aug. 16, 1834.

SARAH HARRIS WALLACE,
Wife of Edward Conroy.

When her father moved to Irvine, Ky., he took this daughter with him, but he died there in 1842, when she was about eight years of age. Much of her time after she grew up, was spent with relatives in Madison County. Late in life she was married to Mr. Edward B. Conroy, one of the most prominent and one of the best financiers and business men of Estill County, one of the Trustees and Treasurer of the town, which position he has held a number of years, and was County Trustee of the Estill County Rail Road bonds, of the Richmond, Nicholasville, Irvine and Beattyville Railroad Company, and is a man of the highest repute, and in good financial condition, quiet and unassuming, and he and his wife are much beloved by the people of their County and especially by the poor people, to whom they have granted many charities. The Lord has given them no children of their body.

CHAPTER 18.

ELIZABETH WALLACE.

(Named in Chap. 6, Sec. 3.)

Article 1.—Elizabeth Wallace, a daughter of Andrew Wallace and Margaret Woods his wife.

She married Captain William Briscoe, who came from Virginia, and settled in Madison County, Ky., on the waters of Otter Creek, near where the town of Richmond was afterwards established, acquiring a homestead adjoining that of his wife's cousin John Reid, whose wife was Mary Woods, a daughter of Colonel John Woods, and Susannah Anderson his wife, of Albemarle County, Va.

He and his brother-in-law, Michael Wallace occupying homes near each other, if not adjoining. He acquired deed to his lands, July 24, 1787 from one Peter Taylor and his wife. On the 24th of July 1803, he and John Reid had an exchange of small pieces of land, when he and his wife Elizabeth made a deed to John Reid to fourteen acres of land and John Reid and Mary his wife made to him a deed to fourteen acres.

Oct. 7, 1794, County Court Order, towit: "Ordered that William Briscoe extend his road from the widow Blacks to Otter Creek."

He held the title of Captain. The order in alloting hands to Michael Wallace, surveyor of the State Road, includes Captain Briscoe's hands. He was a Captain in the Revolutionary Army. He died between the 9th day of Dec. 1830, and the 3rd day of Jan. 1831, for his will bearing date Dec. 9, 1830, was probated Jan. 3, 1831, and recorded in the Clerk's office of the Madison County Court; in his will he appointed his son-in-law, Samuel Logan, and his friend William Goodloe, executors. The will is in the following words and figures:

" William Briscoe's Will."

"In the name of God, amen. I, William Briscoe, of the County of Madison and state of Kentucky, being weak in body, but of sound mind and memory make, ordain and constitute this my last will and testament, hereby revoking and rendering null and void all former wills.

First—I resign my soul to God, who gave it, and my body to be buried by my executors in a decent manner, in humble hope of a glorious resurrection. And for the worldly goods with which it has pleased God to bless me, I give and devise them, (after paying all my just debts and burial expenses) in the manner following, viz:

First—I give and bequeath to my daughter, Peggy Logan, one note on Samuel Logan for sixty dollars, due Oct. 4, 1825, and one other note on Samuel Logan for forty-five dollars, due July 27, 1817, and one other note on William Logan, for one hundred dollars, due Oct. 6th, 1828. And whereas, I did in, or about, the month of Sept. 1818, lend unto my son-in-law, Samuel Logan, five hundred dollars, I also give and bequeath the said five hundred dollars to my said daughter, Peggy Logan, and her heirs forever. I also give and bequeath to my said daughter, Peggy Logan, five hundred and ninety-five dollars.

And it is further my will and desire that my son, Parmenus Briscoe, be charged with one hundred and twenty three dollars, and twenty-five cents, which I advanced to little John Briscoe, for him.

And it is further my will and desire that each of my sons, be charged with each and every advance I have made them, and the amount ascertained. And the residue of my estate be so devised among them, as to make each equal, (viz:) Andrew Briscoe, William Briscoe, Parmenus Briscoe, Philip Briscoe, and John Briscoe.

Also I give and bequeath to my grand-son, Andrew B. Logan, my bed, bed stead and furniture forever.

I do hereby constitute and appoint my son-in-law, Samuel Logan, and my friend, William Goodloe, executors of this my last will and testament. Witness my hand and seal, this 7th day of Oct. 1829.

WILLIAM X. BRISCOE. (Seal)

Done in the presence of:
Thompson Burnam.
Howard Williams.
Will J. Moberley.

"State of Kentucky, Madison County, Sct.

I David Irvine, Clerk of the Court for the County aforesaid, hereby certify that at a County Court held for Madison County, on Monday, the 3rd day of Jan. 1831, this instrument of writing was produced in open Court, and proven to be the last will and testament of William Briscoe, deceased, by the oaths of Thompson Burnam, Howard Williams and William J. Moberley, witnesses thereto, and ordered to be entered of record, and the same has been done accordingly. Attest: DAVID IRVINE, Clerk."

William Briscoe was one of the signers of the Albemarle Declaration of Independence, April 21 1779, being at that time a resident there. The children:

Section 1. Peggy Briscoe; married Samuel Logan in Madison County, Ky., Oct. 18, 1799. They had a son:

1. Andrew B. Logan, devisee of his grand-father's will.

Section 2. Andrew Briscoe; married in Madison County, Ky., Feb. 25, 1796, Ann Kavanaugh, a daughter of William Kavanaugh, and Hannah Woods his wife. (See Part VII, Chap. 10.)

Section 3. William Briscoe, devisee of his father's will.

Section 4. Parmenus Briscoe, devisee of his father's will. He was the guardian of the children of his brother, Philip Briscoe, who was dead the 6th day of July 1831, the date of a receipt for his wards' share in the estate of their grand-father, Captain Wililam Briscoe, of record in the Madison County Court Clerks office.

The town of Versailles, Woodford County, Ky., was established, June 12, 1792, on the lands of Hezekiah Briscoe and Parmenus Briscoe, was one of the seven trustees to lay off the same into lots and streets, and to dispose of the lots, execute deeds, and adopt rules and regulations etc.

Notes: Mr. Briscoe represented Mercer County in the Kentucky Legislature in 1799.

Jeremiah Briscoe was senator from the same county in 1820.

On the 9th of Nov. 1807, Cornelius Maupin and Ann his wife of Madison County, Ky., executed a deed, conveying to Parmenas Briscoe, land on Pitmans, or Sinking Creek, a branch of Green River.

Section 5. Philip Briscoe; married —— —— raised a family of children, and was dead when his father's will was probated. He was a devisee. In 1829, Parmenas Briscoe qualified as guardian for Philip Briscoe's infant children, and as such, on the 6th of July 1831, signed a receipt for their share of the estate of Captain William Briscoe, deceased, their grand-father. The children of Philip Briscoe, viz:

1. Elizabeth Wallace Briscoe.
2. Margaret Briscoe.
3. Emily E. Briscoe.
4. Martha Briscoe.
5. Mary Briscoe.

Section 6. John Briscoe, was an attorney at law. In 1827, he was granted by the Madison County Court, a certificate of honesty, probity and good demeanor. A receipt by him for his portion of the estate of his deceased father Captain William Briscoe, is of record in the clerks office of the Madison County Court.

CHAPTER 19.

SARAH WALLACE.

(Named in Chap. 6, Sec. 4.)

Article 1.—Sarah Wallace, a daughter of Andrew Wallace and Margaret Woods his wife; married in Virginia, Alexander Henderson, and they about the year 1787, emigrated therefrom to Madison County, Ky., and settled and established their home on Paint Lick Creek.

On May 3, 1794, Alexander Henderson and his wife Sarah, (See page 139) executed and acknowledged a deed, conveying to Robert Henderson, certain lands in said county, on said creek.

On the 3rd day of Nov. 1795, John Reid, of Lincoln County, Ky., executed a deed conveying to Alexander Henderson certain lands on Paint Lick Creek. His life and progeny we have traced no further. No doubt his descendents are scattered through Garrard and Madison Counties.

CHAPTER 20.

MARY WALACE.

(Named in Chap. 6, Sec. 6.)

Article 1.—Mary Wallace, a daughter of Andrew Wallace and Margaret Woods his wife; married Thomas Collins and they settled at an early date, probably prior to 1787 on Muddy Creek in Madison County, Ky., acquiring lands where the late Christopher Irvine Miller lived, and adjacent lands.

They came from Albemarle County, Va.,

He died about 1820, and his son-in-law, John Williams and Richard Moberley qualified as administrators of his estate, and Robert Covington, Stanton Hume and Larkin Hume appraisers.

Thomas Collins was often commissioned by the Court to take depositions and other official work of the Court. For love and affection in 1807, and 1812, he deeded lands on Muddy Creek to his sons, Barbee Collins and Garland Collins, a part of which was afterwards purchased and occupied as a home by Christopher Irvine Miller, who died in 1878, and now owned by Irvine Miller Hume and George L. Hume. Thomas Collins and his wife Polly on March 10, 1818, conveyed to Larkin Hume, two hundred acres of land in the same neighborhood and adjoining the above The History of Albemarle County, Va., notes Thomas Collins as an emigrant therefrom to Madison County, Ky. And he was a signer of the Albemarle Declaration of Independence April 21, 1779. His children are named in the coming sections:

Section 1. Colonel Barbe Collins; married Mary Woods, a daughter of Archibald Woods and Mourning Shelton his wife, June 25, 1795. His wife died July 23, 1822. (See Part II, Chap. 8, Sec. 4.) On the 27th of May 1823, Colonel Barbe Collins, married (a cousin to his first wife) Hannah Woods, a daughter of Adam Woods and Ann Kavanaugh his wife. (See Part II, Chap. 7, Sec. 7.) His life and progeny we have traced no further. He conveyed his Muddy Creek lands to Caleb Oldham. He had a son by his first wife:

1. William Collins.'

Section 2. Garland Collins; married Betsy Moberley, in Madison County, Ky., Nov. 1, 1798. They conveyed their Muddy Creek land to Caleb Oldham. Garland Collins was one of the constitutors of the Viney Fork Baptist Church.

Section 3. Nancy Collins; married Oct. 29, 1795, in Madison County, Ky., John Maupin, a son of Daniel Maupin, senior, and Elizabeth Dabney his wife. (See Part V, Chap. 11, Sec. 2.)

John Maupin and his wife moved to Boone County, Mo. There on the 10th of May 1822 John Maupin and Nancy his wife, acknowledged before Silas Riggs and Tyre Martin, Justices of the Peace of Boone County, Mo., a deed to John Williams an heir of Thomas Collins, which deed is of record in the clerks office of the Madison County Court. (See Part V, Chap. 11, Sec. 2.) The said John Maupin and Nancy Collins his wife, were the parents of Thomas C. Maupin who on the 2nd of Sept. 1819, in Madison County, Ky., married Ann R. Wallace, a daughter of Michael Wallace and Jane Bratton, his wife, (see Chap. 7, Sec. 5), and who moved to Howard County, Mo., and afterwards Boone County, Mo.; there on Nov. 8, 1820, Thomas C. Maupin and Ann R. Wallace, his wife, of Howard County, Mo., constituted David Gordon of Madison County, Ky., their attorney in fact to sell the land Mrs. Maupin inherited from the estate of her father, Michael Wallace, deceased. And on the 1st day of May 1822, the said Thomas C. Maupin and Ann R. his wife, then of Boone County, Mo., made a deed to William Rodes of Madison County, Ky., to the land Gordon was empowered to sell, and John Maupin and his first wife Nancy, were also living in Boone County, Mo. (See Part V, Chap. 11, Sec. 2.)

Section 4. Thomas Collins.

Section 5. Peggy Collins; married Sylvanus Massie, June 13, 1813. They united in deed with John Williams and Elizabeth his wife, to Caleb Oldham. Sylvanus Massie (son of Sylvanus Massie, who died in 1808, and Mary his wife) had a brother, Thomas.

Section 6. Sallie Collins; married William Duncan, Feb. 21, 1805. (See Part VII, Chap. 9.) Sallie Collins was a member of the Baptist Church at Viney Fork.

Section 7. Betsy Collins; married John Williams, Jan. 29, 1793. They joined in deed with Sylvanus Massie and wife, to Caleb Oldham. She, Betsy Collins was a member of the Viney Fork Baptist Church.

Section 8. William Collins, was a member of the Viney Fork Baptist Church.

CHAPTER 21.

MARGARET WALLACE.

(Named in Chap. 6, Sec. 7.)

Article 1.—Margaret Wallace, a daughter of Andrew Wallace and Margaret Woods his wife; married William Ramsay, who settled in Albemarle County, Va. in 1774.. He died in 1825.

William Ramsay was a signer of the Albemarle Declaration of Independence, April 21, 1779. To them these children were born:

Section 1. Andrew Ramsay; married —— —— and in 1814, were living on a farm on the Staunton Road. His children:

1. Thomas Ramsay.
2. Higginbotham Ramsay.
4. William Albert Ramsay.
5. Mary J. Ramsay.
6. Andrew Wallace Ramsay.

Section 2. John Ramsay; married Mary Black, a daughter of Samuel Black and Mary his wife. He died in 1815. Issue:

1. William Ramsay.
2. Jane Ramsay; married John G. Lobban.
3. Catherine Ramsay.
4. Joseph T. Ramsay.
5. Mary Ramsay; married James C. Rothwell.
6. Dorcas Ramsay.

Section 3. William Ramsay; died in 1832; married —— —— issue:

1. Jane Ramsay; married Jarrett Harris.
2. William S. Ramsay.
3. Margaret Ramsay; married Meredith Martin.
4. Mary Ramsay; married Jeremiah Wayland.

The Ramsay family of Albemarle.

Rev. John Ramsay, was the Rector of St. Anne's parish, lived in the southern part of the county; died in 1770.

In 1772, John Ramsay of Augusta, purchased from Archibald Woods, nearly four hundred acres of land on Stockton's Creek, and five years later sold same to Alexander Ramsay, probably his brother.

John Ramsay, married Mary Black, a daughter of Samuel Black and Mary his wife.

In 1774, William Ramsay, supposed to be another brother, bought from Adam Dean in the same vicinity, more than four hundred acres, and ten years later from Alexander Ramsay all that belonged to him.

William Ramsay; maried Margaret Wallace, a daughter of Andrew Wallace and Margaret his wife, and a grand-daughter of Michael Woods senior. His home was on the place where James M. Bowen resided. He first built the mill on the place which in early times went by the name of Ramsay's mill. The old dwelling still stands near the head of the mill pond. He died in 1825.

PART V.

CHAPTER 1.

GENEALOGICAL TABLE OF THE MAUPIN FAMILY. 2. EARLY MARRIAGES IN MADISON COUNTY, KENTUCKY, OF THE MAUPIN NAME GLEANED FROM THE FIRST MARRIAGE REGISTER OF THE COUNTY COURT. 3. ITEMS TOUCHING THE MAUPIN NAME.

Article 1.—Genealogical Table.

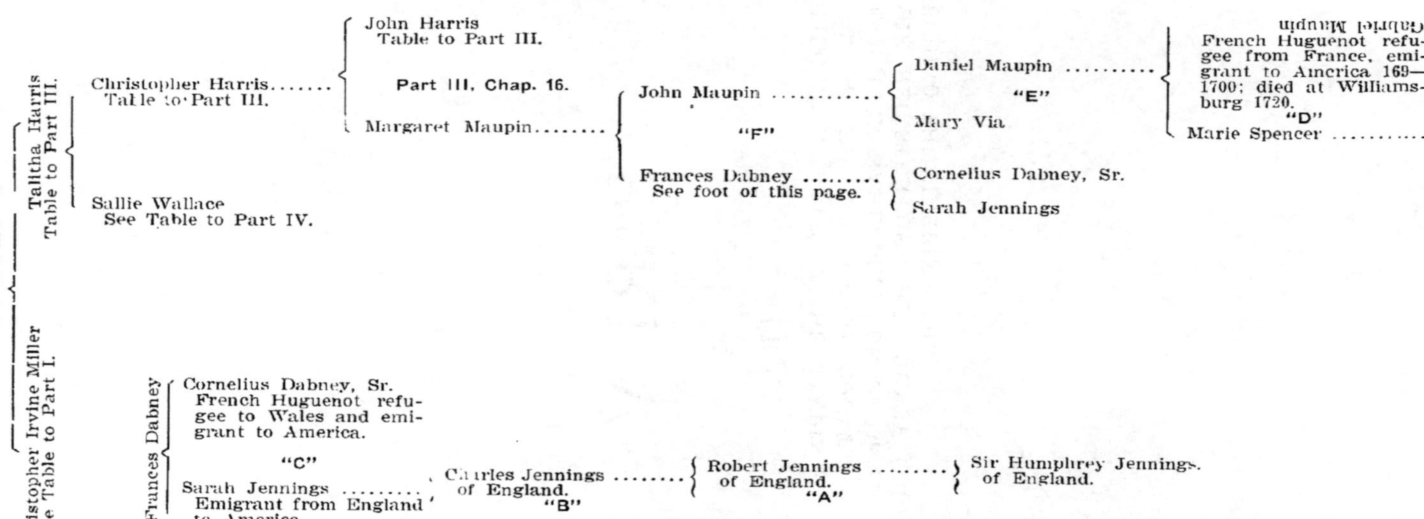

See Table to Part VI.
Talitha Harris
Table to Part III.
Christopher Irvine Miller
See Table to Part I.
Christopher Harris
Table to Part III.
Sallie Wallace
See Table to Part IV.
John Harris
Table to Part III.
Part III, Chap. 16.
Margaret Maupin
John Maupin
"F"
Frances Dabney
See foot of this page.
Daniel Maupin
"E"
Mary Via
Cornelius Dabney, Sr.
Sarah Jennings
Gabriel Maupin
French Huguenot refugee from France, emigrant to America 169—1700; died at Williamsburg 1720.
"D"
Marie Spencer
Earl Spencer.
Frances Dabney
Cornelius Dabney, Sr.
French Huguenot refugee to Wales and emigrant to America.
"C"
Sarah Jennings
Emigrant from England to America.
Charles Jennings
of England.
"B"
Robert Jennings
of England.
"A"
Sir Humphrey Jennings.
of England.

"A"

1. William Jennings, of Acton Place, London. Part III, Chap. 15.
2. Charles Jennings. "B" Part III, Chap. 15.

"B"

1. Sarah Jennings, married Cornelius Dabney, Sr. "C" Part III, Chap. 15.

"C"

1. Cornelius, Jr., m Lucy Winston. Part III., Chap. 15, Sec. 1.
2. John, m Anna Harris. Part III, Chap. 15, Sec. 2.
3. William, m Philadelphia Gwathney. Part III, Chap. 15, Sec. 3.
4. Mary, m Christopher Harris. Part III, Chap. 15, Sec. 4.
5. Elizabeth, m Daniel Maupin. Part III, Chap. 15, Sec. 5.
6. Frances, m John Maupin. Part III, Chap. 15, Sec. 6.
7. Ann, m Mr. Thompson. Part III, Chap. 15, Sec. 7.
8. Miss, m Matthew Brown. Part III, Chap. 15, Sec. 8.
9. Miss, m Wm. Johnson. Part III, Chap. 15, Sec. 9.

"D"

1. Daniel Maupin, m Margaret Via. "E" Chap. 3.
2. Gabriel, m Ann Ballard. Chap. 2.
3. Mary. Chap. 2.

"E"

1. Gabriel. Chap. 3, Sec. 1.
2. Thomas. Chap. 3, Sec. 2.
3. John, m Frances Dabney. "F" Chap. 4.
4. Daniel, m Elizabeth Dabney. Chap. 11.
5. William. Chap. 3, Sec. 5.
6. Zacharias, m Elizabeth Jarman. Chap. 3, Sec. 6.
7. Jesse. Chap. 3, Sec. 7.
8. Mary, m Matthew Mullins. Chap. 13.
9. Jean, m Samuel Rea. Chap. 3, Sec. 9.
10. Margaret, m Robert Muller. Chap. 3, Sec. 10. Part I, Chap. 4.

"F"

1. Sarah, m Wm. Jarman. Chap. 4, Sec. 1.
2. Daniel, m 1, Hannah Harris; 2, Patsey Gentry; 3, Martha Jarman.
3. Cornelius, m 1, Harris; 2, Tomlin; 3,Paul. Chap. 4, Sec. 3.
4. William, m Jane Jameson. Chap. 4, Sec. 4.
5. Thomas, m 1, Cobb; 2, Maupin. Chap. 4, Sec. 5.
6. John, m Craig. Chap. 4, Sec. 6.
7. Fannie, m Wm. Shelton. Chap. 4, Sec. 7.
8. Gabriel, m Bailey. Chap. 5.
9. Robert, m McGehee. Chap. 4, Sec. 9.
10. Jennings, m Sallie Miller. Chap. 4, Sec. 10.
11. Carr, m Burch. Chap. 4, Sec. 11.
12. Dabney. Chap. 4, Sec. 12.
13. Margaret, m John Harris. Chap. 4, Sec. 13. Part III, Chap. 16.

Article 2.—Early Marriages in Madison County, Ky., gleaned from the First Marriage Register of the County Court.

Maupin, Fanny—Lynch, David, Feb. 12, 1793.
Maupin, Polly—Golden, William, April 9, 1795.
Maupin, Sarah—Stevens, James, Jan. 27, 1799.
Maupin, Elizabeth—Watson, David, Jan. 22, 1801.
Maupin, Patsey———Dinwiddie, Jan. 30, 1800.
Maupin, John—Collins, Nancy, Oct. 29, 1795.
Maupin, Delia—Delaney, William, May 10, 1804.
Maupin, Susannah—Gentry, David, July 28, 1804.
Maupin, John—Richardson, Elizabeth, April 12, 1804.
Maupin, Daniel—McWilliams, Peggy, June 16, 1805.
Maupin, Polly—Cornelison, Richard, Sept. 11, 1810.
Maupin, Mariah—Goodman, James, Sept. 18, 1810.
Maupin, Sally—Delaney, Joseph, Feb. 8, 1812.
Maupin, Polly—Nall, Jesse, March 25, 1813.
Maupin, Nancy—Bowlin, James, May 24, 1814.
Maupin, Margaret, H.—Shefflitt, Joshua, June 30, 1814.
Maupin, Dabney—Shlffiett, Polly, April 17, 1817.
Maupin, Leland, D.—Elizabeth J. Moore, June 15, 1837.
Maupin, James—Eleanor McBane, Jan. 14, 1839.
Maupin, Polly—Joseph Fowler, Aug. 23, 1837.
Maupin, Nancy—James Roberts, Aug. 30, 1842.
Maupin, George, W.—Susan E. Haley, June 17, 1845.
Maupin, James—Banta, Elizabeth, Feb. 24, 1820.
Maupin, Thomas C.—Wallace, Ann, Sept. 14, 1819.
Maupin, Peachy—Canole, Henry, Jan. 25, 1821.
Maupin, Sally C.—Emarine, Abraham, Jan. 10, 1822.
Maupin, Wilson, R.—White, Rebecca, Sept. 17, 1823.
Maupin, Susannah—Pinkston, Bazil, June 21, 1825.
Maupin, Polly—Gilbert, Will P., July 19, 1826.
Maupin, Frances, D.—Wright, John, R., July 4, 1826.
Maupin, Franky—Champ, William, Nov. 13, 1826.
Maupin, Talitha—Gates, Jefferson, Jan. 2, 1826.
Maupin, Cynthia—Gates, Thos. E, May 10, 1827.
Maupin, Washington—Walker, Mary, Aug. 19, 1828.
Maupin, Daniel, C.—Walker, Nancy J. Jan. 6, 1831.
Maupin, Eliza—Gooch, Chisel, Feb. 18, 1830.
Maupin, Overton—Cooper, Susannah, Oct. 6, 1831.
Maupin, Cynthia—Cooper, Covington, Oct. 27, 1831.
Maupin, Patrick—Moberley, Margaret, Feb. 6, 1834.
Maupin, Fountain—Levin, Elizabeth, Jarman, Sept. 9, 1837.
Maupin, Sallie Ann—Russel, Smallwood, Feb. 13, 1840.
Maupin, Thomas H.—Elizabeth Jane Maupin, April 27, 1843.
Maupin, John D.—Mary R. Walton, June 12, 1849.

Article 3.—Items Touching the Name Maupin.

Section 1.—Exhibit of names of the family appearing on the early Madison County Court records:

1790. Cornelius Maupin and wife Ann, settled on Otter Creek, near where the town of Richmond is.

1790. Daniel Maupin, senior, settled on Muddy Creek, died in 1803, leaving a last will and testament. He survived his wife, Elizabeth Dabney.

1790. Daniel Maupin, junior, and wife Betsy, (the latter died in 1804, and on the 16th day of June 1805 he married Peggy McWilliams) settled on Little Muddy Creek, where he acquired lands also, on Otter Creek, Silver Creek, and in Montgomery County, and died in 1832, leaving a last will and testament.

1790. Daniel Maupin and wife Susannah, owned land on Tates Creek and Paint Lick Creek, and was living on Paint Lick in 1832, when he sold his home to Samuel W. Ross, and moved to Clark County, Ky.

1790. Thomas Maupin and wife Margaret, settled on and owned land and a mill on Silver Creek where he died in 1855, leaving a last will and testament.

1790. Jesse Maupin and wife, Sarah, settled and owned land near Milford or Old Town on Taylor's Fork of Silver Creek, where he died in 1827, leaving a last will and testament.

1804. Billainy Maupin, improved and settled on 400 acres of land on Goose Creek, waters of the Kentucky.

1804. John Maupin, improved and settled on 400 acres of land on Buzzard Branch of Goose Creek, waters of the Kentucky.

1795. Thomas C. Maupin; married Ann Wallace, Sept. 14, 1819.

Mosias Maupin and wife Leah, on Drowning Creek.

1795. John Maupin; married Nancy Collins, Oct. 29, 1795, and owned land on Otter Creek near Richmond, and his wife inherited land of her father, Thomas Collins, on Muddy Creek and in 1822, they were living in Boone County, Mo.

1803. Chapman Maupin of Albemarle County, Va.

1803. Daniel Maupin, saddler, of Albemarle County, Va. (See list of early marriages for others.)

Section 2. In the Madison County Court: 1790, March 2, "On the motion of Cornelius Maupin his ear mark a crop and slit in the right ear and a hole in the left is ordered to be recorded."

Section 3. Aug. 7, 1804.

Order showing that John Maupin is entitled to 400 acres of land on a creek known by the name of Buzzard, a branch of Goose Creek, waters of the Kentucky.

Section 4. May 7, 1804.

Order that Bellamy Maupin is entitled to 400 acres of land by virtue of an actual settlement thereon on Collins Fork of Goose Creek.

Section 5. Exhibit of members of the Kentucky Legislature:

In the Senate—

Robert D. Maupin, from the County of Barren, 1827-32.

In the House of Representatives—

Robert D. Maupin, from the County of Barren, 1824-6, 1843.
Washington Maupin, elected from the County of Madison, resigned.
Leland D. Maupin, from the County of Madison, 1849.

Section 6. A highly respected citizen of Charlottesville, Albemarle County, Va., who was raised in that County and well acquainted with the family there, (W. N. Parrott, Esquire, a veteran of the Civil War) writes of them:

"They are mostly Methodists in religion; many of them have held positions of responsibility and trust; they are church going, law abiding, brave, heroic, and patriotic. I know of no name in the County that sent more sons to the confederate army, or who made better soldiers. No man need ever blush with shame for any act done, either on the battle field, or in camp, by any of them."

"C. B. Maupin, a member of the same company as myself, lost his life in Pickett's celebrated charge at Gettysburg.

"You may justly feel proud of their military record.

"There were three in the Revolutionary Army, Cornelius, Daniel and William.

William Maupin, married a Jameson, their children were:

1. Tilman J. Maupin; married Pyrenia Brown, a daughter of Bernard Brown.

2. Albert Maupin; married Patsy Jarman, a daughter of Dabney Jarman.

3. Logan Maupin; married a Simms, his son, W. L. Maupin is clerk of our Circuit Court, he also, had a son killed in the confederate army, named Isaac, and W. C. Maupin another son of William Maupin, went to Missouri and went from there to Congress.

Jennings Maupin; married Sallie Miller, their children: Tyre, James and Fannie. Fannie, married Colonel Henry Lindsey, left a family. Tyre Maupin at the beginning of the war, was an ardent whig, and had the name of being the best posted man in Virginia on political matters.

Dr. Socrates Maupin, was first professor of chemistry in Hampden-Sidney College, Virginia, then at the University of Virginia, died in 1871, from injuries received in a runaway accident in Lynchburg, and was a son of Chapman Maupin, and Chapman Maupin was the third in descent of Gabriel's line; he died in 1861.

"Zacharias Maupin; married Elizabeth Jarman.

Sarah Maupin, daughter of one John Maupin, married William Jarman. He died in 1813.

"Daniel Maupin was married three times, his third wife was a Jameson, their children: Merret, when grown weighed 126, but at his death weighed 360 pounds, he has two children living, namely: Cornelia, married W. B. Railey of Moorman's River and William Maupin, who lives on his father's old place.

John, sadler, died single. Sarah married Dr. Peary, of Missouri; has a large family.

Captain H. C. Michie of Charlottesville, Va., as Captain of Company H. 56th Regiment, Virginia Infantry, Confederate Army with his company crossed the stone wall on Cemetery Ridge at Gettysburg. He is a manly man of the highest courage, of large means, and influence, an ardent lover of the Confederate soldier, and their true friend, and ever ready to contribute to their needs; feeling justly proud of the record he and his company made, testifies as follows:

Charlottesville, Va., March 28, 1906.

To all whom it may concern:

It was my good fortune to have seven of the Maupin family in my company during the Civil War. Whether in camp, on the march, or in battle, they were always ready for any duty, and no soldier carried his bayonet farther in battle. Two of these gallant fellows, Corporal, David Maupin, and Private, Carson Maupin, were killed at the High Water Mark of the Rebellion, (so called by the Yankees) in the charge of Pickett's division at Gettysburg, and Sergeant, James R. Maupin now of Albemarle County, Va., was wounded and captured at the same battle. Some of these gallant fellows left their blood on nearly every battle ground fought on Virginia and Maryland soil, and one of them rose to the rank of Lieutenant of the company, a company which left thirteen dead at Gettysburg. There were many of the name in other companies of the army of Northern Virginia, and I have never heard that there was a drone among them.

H. C. Michie.

Late Captain Company H. 56th Regiment, Virginia Infantry.

Since the war Captain Michie has been Brigadier-General of Confederate Veterans.

Many of the Maupin family emigrated from Virginia to Kentucky in the first settling of the latter, and located in different parts thereof; many of them settling in Madison County, later on a number of them went from Kentucky to Missouri. It can be truthfully said of this family, generally they are full of life, high spirited, lovers of freedom, and sport, true to their friends, generous to a fault, and whatever their imperfections and faults may be, and their faults do not exceed the faults of other good families, no one, rich or poor, high or low, peaceably inclined ever entered their portals without being received with hospitality, and made easy and welcome. The latch string hangs on the outside at their home. They are not lacking in patriotism, are ever ready to enlist in the cause of their Country. In the Civil War this family furnished its quoto of soldiers. A true Maupin will not turn a hungry one from his door without feeding him, and if he is cold and naked he will clothe him.

Section 7. Maupin, name of a town in Kentucky, Clinton County.

Maupin, name of a town in Missouri, Franklin County.

CHAPTER 2.

THE MAUPIN FAMILY.

Article 1.—The name Maupin, is of French origin, and is pronounced as though is was spelled "Maupan."

The family tradition is that one Gabriel Maupin, a French Huguenot, and a General in the French Army, whose wife was Marie Spencer, daughter of Earl Spencer, an English Nobleman, to avoid persecutions which were being heaped upon the Huguenots, left France near the beginning of the eighteenth century, and went to England. He was probably a resident of France at the time of his marriage, as some claim. However he did not remain in England very long, but soon sailed for America with his wife, and at least two children, Daniel and Gabriel, one of whom was born in France, and the other in England. His emigration from England occured very early in the century. He settled with his family in Virginia. It has been stated, probably correctly, that he died in Virginia in 1720, after making and publishing his last will and testament, bearing date, Dec. 2, 1719, probated April 20, 1720, and recorded at Williamsburg, leaving sons, Daniel Maupin and Gabriel Maupin, and a daughter, Mary Maupin (and perhaps other children.)

Communication has been had with the Clerk of the Court at Williamsburg, in an effort to secure a copy of the will, resulting in intelligence from the clerk, that the records of the Court were destroyed by fire during the Civil War, which misfortune wiped out much valuable early and interesting history of the family.

Daniel Maupin married Margaret Via, and died in Albemarle County, Va., in 1788, leaving his last will and testament, which is of record at Charlottesville, a copy of which is exhibited in Chapter

3, in connection with the further history of Daniel Maupin, designated as Daniel Maupin, Senior.

Reverend Edgar Woods, in his History of Albemarle, published in 1901, states that "Two brothers, Daniel and Gabriel Maupin, came to the County just before the middle of the last century.

Daniel entered more than fifteen hundred acres in the Whitehall neighborhood. He died in 1788. He and his wife, Margaret had seven sons, and three daughters: Thomas, Gabriel, Daniel, John, Margaret, the wife of Robert Miller, William, Zachariah, Jesse, Jane, the wife of Samuel Rea, and Mary the wife of Matthew Mullens.

Reverend Edgar Woods, further says: "Gabriel died in 1794. He seems to have lived in the vicinity of Free Union, and Thomas, Bland, Daniel and Gabriel were the names of his sons," and further says: "The truth is, the families of this stock were generally so numerous, containing hardly ever less than ten, and sometimes thirteen children, and the same names were so often repeated in the different households, that it would be well nigh impossible at this date to make out an accurate statement of their lines of descent. They frequently inter-married among themselves, and with the Harrises, Jarmans, and Via's and their descendants are widely scattered over the West, particularly in Kentucky and Missouri. They seem to have been in their generations an industrious, quiet and home people."

Gabriel Maupin of Free Union, married Ann Ballard, daughter of Thomas Ballard a son of Thomas Ballard, who (the latter) settled on 320 acres of land near the foot of Piney Mountain, as early as 1738. (One Gabriel Maupin died in Albemarle County, Va., in 1794.) Their children:

1. Thomas Maupin; married Annie Spencer, sister to the wife of his brother Daniel. Their children:

1. John Maupin; married Rosa Maupin, daughter of Daniel Maupin.

2. Clifton Maupin; married Betsy Maupin, daughter of Daniel Maupin.

3. Arthur Maupin.

4. Joel Maupin.

2. Bland Maupin, emigrated to Bedford County, Tennessee.

3. Daniel Maupin; married Sallie Spencer, sister to the wife of his brother, Thomas. Their children:

1. Pleasant Maupin; married Lucy Wood.

2. David Maupin; married Jerusha Snow; died in Albemarle, in 1821.

3. Rice Maupin; married Miss Carr.

4. Gabriel Maupin; married Miss Mallory.

5. Thomas Maupin; married Miss Gibson.

6. Nicholas Maupin, emigrated to the West.

7. Susan Maupin; married Daniel Via.

8. Sallie Maupin; married William Via.

9. Rosa Maupin; married John Maupin, a son of Thomas Maupin.

10. Polly Maupin; married Henry Gibson.

11. Betsy Maupin; married Clifton Maupin, son of Thomas Maupin.

12. Patsey Maupin; married Turner Woods.

4. Gabriel Maupin, (one Gabriel Maupin, died in Albemarle County, Va., in 1858.)

5. Ann Maupin; married George Turner, son of Charles Turner, in 1791.

It has often been related in the family that the emigrant, Gabriel Maupin, senior, was a very devout religious man, and that when coming over the sea the ship sprang a leak, and the passengers became alarmed, and thought they would go down and be lost, and Mr. Maupin was called upon to pray. Whereupon he offered up a fervent and effectual prayer to the Most High, and the leak stopped, and when the vessel arrived at the American port, an examination of same was made, when it was discovered that the stoppage of the leak was caused by a large fish in some miraculous and mysterious way becoming tightly wedged in the crack.

The Albemarle family of Maupin have usually been attached to the Methodist church.

Daniel Maupin was an original trustee of Austin's or Bingham's meeting house.

Daniel Maupin, known as "Saddler Daniel," (son of John Maupin and Frances Dabney his wife) and his wife, Hannah Harris, nee Jameson, in 1834, gave the ground for Mount Moriah Meeting House, near Whitehall in Albemarle, which for many years went by the name of Maupin's Meeting House.

The names "Daniel" and "Gabriel" given so often in the families makes it somewhat difficult at this date to trace the lineage correctly. The Daniels for identification bore such prefixes to the name as "Cuff," "Rough," "Tough," "Saddler," "Soldier," etc.

After the letters A B C D E F and G following appear the names and brief history of certain ones of the family, all of whom except possibly George W. Maupin and Charles W. Maupin emigrated from Albemarle County, Va., to Madison County, Ky., whose lineage is not traced back in this record, they were however sons of Daniel Maupin and Margaret Via, described in Chapter 3, and the little history gathered of them is set forth after said letters, that any one desiring to do so, may more readily trace their lines back.

"A." Mosias Maupin and his wife Leah —— emigrated from Albemarle County, Va., to Madison County, Ky., and acquired lands and settled on the waters of Drowning Creek, which he sold, and on the 6th of Sept. 1804, he and his wife Leah, conveyed same to Joshua Dillingham, and Mosias Maupin emigrated from Madison County, Ky., to Missouri, and settled in Calloway County, where he died, Oct. 29, 1816. He had these children by his wife Leah.

1. William Maupin, born Feb. 14, 1787.
2. Lewis Maupin, born March 12, 1790.
3. James Maupin, born Feb. 25, 1792.
4. Lucy Maupin, born July 8, 1794; married E. Greensheet in 1812.
5. Sarah Maupin, born Aug. 22, 1795; married Tyre Jones, Dec. 25, 1804; she died July 13, 1821. (See Part III, Chap. 11, Section 1.)
6. George Maupin, born Nov. 30, 1796, in Madison County, Ky. He emigrated to Missouri, and settled in Calloway County, where he died Nov. 2, 1861. He married in Calloway County, Nancy Miller, Oct. 17, 1820. Nancy Miller was born Nov. 11, 1803, in said County, and died there Sept. 26, 1849. Her father and two of his brothers, Abraham Miller and Samuel Miller, were born in Pennsylvania, and when young men removed to Missouri, and their home in Missouri was some distance from that of George Maupin in Calloway County. George Maupin represented Calloway County in the State Legislature before the Civil War. The children of George Maupin and Nancy Miller were:

1. Sarah N. Maupin, born Dec. 7, 1821; married Theodore Bearin, April 22, 1854. Had one child:

 1. George Bearin.

2. Lucy A. Maupin, born Feb. 8, 1823; married William Ewing, March 6, 1845. They had five children:

 1. Nancy Jane Ewing.
 2. Jacob Ewing.
 3. Henry L. Ewing.
 4. Sarah Ewing.
 5. George Ewing.

3. Marilda M. Maupin, born June 22, 1824; married Woodson B. Haley, Nov. 25, 1854.

4. Nancy R. Maupin, born Aug. 20, 1825; married Warren Jameson, Dec. 6, 1849; died —— ——

5. Addison B. Maupin, born Oct. 27, 1827; married Ann E. Denham, Dec. 19, 1856. They live now at Jamestown, Mo.

6. Benjamin F. Maupin, born Jan. 4, 1829; married Catherine W. D. Bennett, March 2, 1848. He left Missouri at the age of eighteen years, and now lives in Eureka, Ill. They have two children living:

 1. William J. Maupin, born 1856.
 2. B. F. Maupin, born 1880.

7. William Taylor Maupin, born in Calloway County, Mo., Aug. 30, 1831, now living in Hennesey, Oklahoma. He married Dec. 17, 1855, in Audrian County, Mo., Sarah Miller, who was born in Calloway County, Mo., she died in 1894, and William Taylor Maupin has his second wife.

He was a Justice of the Peace of Mexico, Mo., at the outbreak of the Civil War. He is a minister of the Disciples Church. To him and his first wife Sarah Miller, twelve children were born, only three living, eight of them having died prior to 1863, the living ones, towit:

1. William M. Maupin, born in Taylorsville, Illinois, Aug. 31, 1863. He learned the printer's trade and toured the country, and now lives in Lincoln, Nebraska, and is associate editor of the Commoner, of which paper and plant, the distinguished and honorable William Jennings Bryan is the proprietor. William M. Maupin remembers hearing his father tell about the family coming originally from Virginia and locating in Kentucky afterwards pushing further on to Missouri, but he left home at an early and tender age, and never seized an opportunity to compile the family history; his mother's death scattered the few family records they had. He married twice, first Jennie Hammond, in 1887, his wife died in 1892, and in 1894, he married his second wife, Lottice Armisted. Of the first marriage two children were born, viz:

 1. Louise Blaine Maupin.
 2. Sarah Louise Maupin; died at the age of two years.

Of the second marriage four children were born, three of them living, viz:

 3. William Armisted Maupin; died at the age of two years.
 4. Lorena Elizabeth Maupin.
 5. Lorothy Catherine Maupin.
 6. Richard Metcalf Maupin, born in 1906.

2. Kitty Maupin, born in Harristown, Illinois, Oct. 6, 1867; married George L. Burkhalter in 1883, when not quite sixteen years years old. They live in Needles, Cali-

fornia, and Mr. Burkhalter is a conductor on the Santa Fe Railroad. They have three living children:

1. Gertrude Burkhalter.
2. William Taylor Burkhalter.
3. Jennie Burkhalter.

3. T. Whitmer Maupin, was born in Cuba, Illinois, in 1872. He married Miss Clara Jones. They have no children. They live in Oregon, Mo. Whitmer Maupin is a painter.

8. Mary E. Maupin, born July 31, 1835; married Peter Moore. She is a widow now living in Peoria, Illinois. She had a son living in Peoria.

7. Thomas Maupin, born Feb. 25, 1798.—

8. Daniel Maupin, born May 25, 1804.

"B." Thomas Maupin, a son of —— —— Maupin and his wife, and a grand-son of Daniel Maupin, senior, and Magaret Via his wife, was born in Albemarle County, Va., about the year 1758. He was a soldier under General Washington, in the Revolutionary War. He marched from Albemarle County, Va., in 1780, as a private in Captain John Miller's Company. Afterwards Captain John Martin's company under Colonel Lindsay in the Virginia line, serving as a substitute for his father. He was wounded in battle. Thomas Maupin was a private in a company of the second Virginia Regiment, which for a time formed a part of a battalion commanded by Lieutenant Colonel Thomas Posey, composed of parts of different regiments of the Virginia line. His name first appears on a muster roll, dated April 15, 1782, and last on one dated Sept. 9, 1782, which latter roll shows him an orderly in hospital. He married in Albemarle County, Elizabeth Michie, a daughter of Patrick Michie and Frances his wife. (and her sister Mary Michie, married John Maupin). They emigrated to Kentucky after the war, and located twelve miles south of Richmond, in Madison County, on Silver Creek, where he acquired lands and owned a grist mill, and mill seat. On Aug. 11, 1806, Joseph Montgomery of Albemarle County, Va., conveyed to him, one hundred and twenty acres of land on said creek, adjoining the lands of Thomas Faris, John Burnsides, Andrew Hamilton, Durrett White, and John Cochran. His wife Elizabeth Michie, died and July 10, 1825, he married again Margaret Burnsides of Madison County, Ky., daughter of Robert Burnsides and his wife who was the widow of Thomas Faris, at the time she married Robert Burnsides, and Thomas Faris was her second husband, her first husband, Mr. Noakes, having been massacred by the Indians, she making her escape.

Nov. 2, 1830, Thomas Maupin and his second wife, Margaret, conveyed to Volentine White lands on Silver Creek. The 13th day of Aug., 1832, Thomas Maupin, a resident of Madison County, Ky., made application for a pension for service in the Revolutionary War, in the Virginia line, which was allowed. He continued to live at his Silver Creek home until his death, which occured Feb. 25, 1855, age 97 years; leaving his last will and testament, bearing date Nov. 20, 1844, probated March 5, 1855. His second wife, Margaret was then living, and was allowed the pension for her husband's service in the Revolutionary War, as appears from a record on the order book of the County Court, towit:

"May 5, 1856."

"Satisfactory evidence was this day exhibited to the Court that Thomas Maupin, deceased, was a Revolutionary Pensioner of the United States at the rate of $30 per annum, and was a resident of the County of Madison and State of Kentucky, and died in the said County and state the 25th day of Feb. 1855, leaving Margaret Maupin his widow, who has not intermarried since his death."

Thomas Maupin and his first wife, Elizabeth Michie, had born to them four sons and five daughters, whose names are below given as they came in the family, viz:

1. Frances Maupin, born in 17—; married Jan. 20, 1814, Asa Smith who was born near Richmond, Madison County, Ky., Jan. 10, 1792. Mr. Smith survived his wife, and married the second time Annie Phelps, who died in 1860; and Asa Smith, died near Denver, Colorado, July 13, 1874. He had ten children of his first marriage, and none of the second. Asa Smith entered and served as a private in Captain David Brown's Company fifth (Rennick's) mounted regiment, Kentucky volunteers, in the war of 1812, from Aug. 24, 1813, to Nov. 9, 1813, and as a private in Captain Robert Patterson's Company of Infantry, 14th (Mitchisson's) Regiment, Kentucky Militia, in the same war from Nov. 20, 1814, to April 15, 1815. Asa Smith was an unusually bright and polished gentleman. His father was a sergeant in the Revolutionary War. Asa Smith had a brother, William, who died intestate in Alabama; Frances Maupin his wife, died at an early age. The children born to them were, viz:

1. Merrill Smith, born in Madison County, Ky., June 15, 1815; married Mattie Reid July -- 1859. He died at Leavenworth, Kansas, in 1870, where his widow now resides. They had two children, only one of them living, towit:

1. Miss —— Smith; married Dr. Lindsay. They live in Topeka, Kansas.

2. Elizabeth (Bettie) Smith, born in Madison County, Ky., —— 1817; married Samuel Fernandis in 1837. Mr. Fernandis was born at Pittsburg, Mississippi, in 1809. He died at Leavenworth, Kansas, Feb. — 1856, and his wife, died there July 11, 1870. The children born to them, were:

1. Henry F. Fernandis, born 1838; died at Leavenworth, Kansas, in 1857.

2. Wiliam F. Fernandis, born 1840, called "Pussy." He came home from college to spend vacation and whilst out hunting with some companions was accidently shot, and died almost instantly.

3. Anna Louise Mary Josephine Isabella Fernandis, born 1841; died at seven years of age. (1748)

4. A son— Fernandis; died in 1848, at the age of two years.

5. Fannie Inez Fernandis, born March 5, 1849, near the old bridge home, not far from Leavenworth, Kansas. She married John M. Cole, March 5, 1870. Mr. Cole was born in Ireland, Dec. 2, 1846. He served through the Civil War in the —— —— Army, having two honorable discharges. His wife died at El Paso, Texas, May 14, 1900. The children born to them viz:

1. Bessie Cole, born Oct. 31, 1871; she married Horace Broaddus, Feb. 11, 1892. They live in El Paso, Texas. The children born to them, viz:

1. Horace Broaddus, born Jan. 5, 1894.

2. Frances Cole Broaddus, born March 14, 1899.

3. John Morgan Broaddus, born July 21, 1901.

2. Lillian Cole, born July 12, 1874; unmarried.

3. Herbert Cole, born July 8, 1878; unmarried.

4. Mary Louise Cole, born July 6, 1881: she is called "Mazie" and is unmarried.

6. Samuel Fernandis, born 1852; married — — — — . He is still living. Only two of his three children are living, towit:

1. Bessie Fernandis; married Arthur Lapskey.
2. Minnie Fernandis; married William Herbert.

7. Joseph Fernandis, born 1854; married —— —— had two children, one living, towit:

1. Samuel C. Fernandis; married first, Miss —— Graves and second, —— —— No issue. He is still living.

3. James Thomas Smith, born 1819. His death occured Aug. 14, 1826, momentarily by falling into the Black Warrior River at Tuscaloosa, Alabama, drowning before assistance could reach him. (As written by Asa Smith in his family Bible.)

4. Fountain Maupin Smith, born at Tuscaloosa, Ala., Oct. 24, 1823. He married Emily Frances George, Feb. 5, 1856; she was born April 2, 1837. Fountain M. Smith is now living at Tonganoxie, Kansas, in his eighty fourth year. The children born to them, towit:

1. Asa C. Smith, born Nov. 15, 1856; died Aug. 30, 1857.

2. Willie Frank Smith, born June 26, 1858; married Jan. 10, 1905, to Naomi Hayden, of Kansas City, Mo.

3. Budd Smith, born May 23, 18860; married to Catherine Gausz, May 28, 1897. Their children, viz:

1. Mary Frances Smith, born May 3, 1898.

4. Fountain Maupin Smith, born Nov. 10, 1861; married Sept. 19, 1905, to Annie Capleise, issue, viz:

1. Fountain Chester Smith, born Sept. 29, 1906.

5. Andrew Jackson Smith, born Aug. 17, 1863; married Jennie Bricker July 25, 1906.

6. Emily Frances Smith, born Feb. 9, 1868.

7. Henry Edgar Smith, born Feb. 17, 1872; died Oct. 19, 1875.

8. Dollie Lee Smith, born Oct. 2, 1874; married to William Leslie Lutz, May 27, 1903, issue, viz:

1. William Fountain Lutz, born April 7, 1904.

5. James Smith, born 1826, in Alabama; died in Arkansas in 1902.

6. William Smith, born 1829; married Mary Davis in 1866, lives in Paris, Texas.

7. Emily Smith, born 1828, in Howard County, Mo., married S. B. Snow in 1848. They did live at Mangrove, Oklahoma. The names of their children not furnished.

8. John Smith, bern in 1831, or 2, in Howard County, Mo., married Mary Roberts. He died at Beaver Creek, Colorado, November — 1891.

9. Mary Smith, born June 1835, in Howard County, Mo., married William Renick in 1859. They live at 6th North 20th Street, Joplin, Mo. They had six children, only two living.

10. Asa Smith; unmarried.

2. Mariah Maupin; married James Goodman, Sept. 18, 1810, in Madison County, Ky. They removed to Platte County, Mo., where they died. Their children:

1. Tine Goodman.
2. Charles Goodman.
3. Michie Goodman.
4. Thomas Goodman.
5. Joseph Goodman.

6. Margaret Goodman; married Joshua Pumphrey, issue:
1. Elijah Pumphrey; dead.
2. Thomas Pumphrey; dead.
3. Joseph Pumphrey, lives in St. Joseph, Mo.
4. James Pumphrey, lives in St. Joseph, Mo.
5. John Pumphrey, lives in St. Joseph, Mo.
6. Alice Pumphrey; married Frank Affhalter, live in Kansas.
7. Lucie Pumphrey; married Lee Overstreet.
8. Anna Pumphrey; married John Betts, live near Edgerton, Mo.
9. Von Pumphrey; died when quite small.

3. Michie Maupin, born in 1779; married first, Elizabeth Gentry, and second, Mrs. Verona America Taylor, widow of Dr. Taylor. Michie Maupin died Aug. 9, 1876, aged 97 years. Children of the first marriage:

1. James Harrison Maupin; married, first, Elizabeth Ann Smith, daughter of Thomas Smith and wife, who was a Miss Jarman, a Kentuckian. He married second, Estille Euphomia Maxley from Fauquier County, Va., Feb. 3, 1885. Mr. Maupin's occupation is that of a farmer, and his home is Edgerton, Platte County, Mo. There were no children of the second marriage. The children of the first marriage, towit:

1. Verona Maupin; married Charles Stout. They lived in Platte County, Mo. After the death of Mr. Stout, she married again John William Jordon, of Cambridge, Saline County, Mo. Issue of the first marriage:
1. Harry Stout, lives in Platte County, Mo.
2. Frank Stout, lives in Platte County, Mo.

Issue of the second marriage:
3. Julia Jordon, born 1893.
4. James William Jordon, born 1896.

2. William Maupin; married first Myranda Seales, and second, Mrs. Dudy a widow. Issue of the first marriage:
1. Nannie Stella Maupin; married Levi Judah, of Dekalb, Missouri.

Issue of the second marriage:
2. John William Maupin.

3. James Thomas Maupin, the youngest son, is an old bachelor.

2. David Maupin; married Mary Hering. He is a farmer.

3. Richard Maupin; married Kate Medows. His occupation was that of a farmer.

4. Patrick (Patty) Maupin; married Lucy Bradley, of Camden Point, Mo. Since 1843, they had lived in Texas, till his death. He was a tiller of the soil.

5. Michie Maupin; married Sue Stone(daughter of the late John T. Stone of Edgerton, Platte County, Mo., whose second wife was Mrs. Malinda Miller Hayden, daughter of Major James Miller and Frances Harris his wife, who lived and died on Decks River, Lincoln County, Ky.) of Dearborn, Mo.

6. William Maupin; died at the age of about twenty-two years.

7. Elizabeth Maupin; married Joe Cox. They live in Dearborn, Missouri.

8. Susan Jane Maupin; died in infancy.

9. Nancy Maupin; died at the age of nine years.

10. Mollie Maupin; married Samuel Hamilton a native of Kentucky. They lived in Platte County, Mo., for many years,

but for the last thirty years have lived in Texas.

Issue of the second marriage of Michie Maupin and Mrs. Taylor:

11. Lucy Maupin of Springfield, Mo. married Mortimer Park of Platte County, Mo., where they live.

4. Emily Maupin; married Larkin Stamper. Their children:

1. Elizabeth Stamper, born March 13, 1826; died May 18, 1864; married Levi Preston Cox; born Jan. 7, 1817; died Jan. 1886. Their children :

1. Larkin Jabes Cox, born Aug. 12, 1843, was a confederate soldier, wounded in battle and died Nov. 1, 1862; unmarried.

2. Lucy M. Cox, born Sept. 6, 1844; married Rufus Ketron, issue:

1. Nannie Ketron; married Delbert Sanders, issue:

1. Della May Sanders.

2. Jessie Sanders.

3. Mattie Sanders.

3. Emma Cox, born Nov. 22, 1845; married Frank Mennick, no issue.

4. Nathan Thomas Cox, born Nov. 12, 1847; married Susannah Mennick, issue:

1. John D. Cox; married Lola Thomas.

2. Levi Jabes Cox; married Eula Thomas, issue:

1. Nanna Cox.

3. Dora Emma Cox; unmarried.

4. Nathan Thomas Cox, Jr.; died in infancy.

5. Mariah A. Cox, born April 11, 1851; died Sept. 24, 1864; unmarried.

6. Joseph Michie Cox, born Feb. 26, 1853; married Martha Tye, issue:

1. Charles Cox, born Aug. 1877; married Elizabeth Sterling, had issue.

2. Joshua Cox; unmarried.

3. Effie E. Cox, born Dec. 1882; married Fred B. Hurd, no issue:

4. Levi Preston Cox; died in infancy.

5. Ernest J. Cox; unmarried.

6. Manona Cox.

7. John Randolph Cox.

8. Fannie Mabel Cox.

7. Levi Preston Cox, born Dec. 23, 1857; married first, Sarah Frances Mauzy, born June 13, 1862; died June 22, 1894, and he married second, Mary Bell Woods, born Sept. 4, 1857. Issue of the first marriage:

1. Mary Elizabeth Cox, born Sept. 27, 1880; married Grant B. Grumbine, M. S. born Aug. 24, 1879. He is principal of Woodson Institute, Richmond, Mo.

2. Lucinda Jane Cox, born Sept. 3, 1882; married Rev. Francis N. Campbell.

3. Minnie May Cox, born Nov. 15, 1884; married Fred L. Runkle, issue:

1. Frances Lucile Runkle, born Oct. 20, 1901.

2. Levi Preston Runkle, born Aug. 26, 1904.

4. Martha Lee Cox, born Aug. 27, 1888; unmarried, twin.

5. Clarissa Dee Cox, born Aug. 27, 1888; unmarried, twin.

Issue of the second marriage:

6. Levi Preston Cox, born March 21, 1898; died Nov. 23, 1898.

7. Vivian I. Cox, born Aug. 5, 1899.

8. Jessie Cox, born and died April 6, 1860.

9. John S. Cox, born May 13, 1861; died March 22, 1905; married Isabella Seals; issue:

1. Ethel S. Cox, born Feb. 1, 1885; unmarried.

2. Madonna E. Cox, born Dec. 24, 1892.

2. Mariah Stamper: married General Elijah Gates. (see below 8.)

3. Joel Stamper; married Kate Weldon, issue:

1. Phoebe Stamper, no issue:

4. Michie Stamper: unmarried.

5. Susan Stamper: married Colonel John Hudgins of Breckinridge, Mo.

1. Inez Hudgins, born Jan. 29, 1854; married James Fahey, issue:

1. Henry Fahey: unmarried.

2. Fred Fahey: unmarried.

3. Iris Fahey.

4. John Fahey: unmarried.

2. Henry Hudgins, born Jan. 28, 1856; married Georgia Parker, issue:

1. Mary Hudgins.

2. John Hudgins.

3. Edith Hudgins.

4. Henry Hudgins.

5. Julia Hudgins.

3. Dora Hudgins, born May 28, 1858; married A. D. Hoover, issue:

1. Fannie Hoover; unmarried.

2. Larkin Hoover; unmarried.

3. John Hoover: unmarried.

4. Emma Hudgins, born April 13, 1860; married Harvey W. McClintock, issue.

1. John McClintock: unmarried.

2. Warren McClintock; unmarried.

5. Jael Hudgins, born March 3, 1862; married David S. Long, no issue:

6. Larkin Hudgins, born Jan. 28, 1864; married first, ——— ——— and second Myrtle Gray. Issue of second marriage:

1. Alice Hudgins; unmarried.

2. Helen Hudgins; unmarried.

3. Agnes Hudgins; unmarried.

7. Erin Hudgins, born April 5, 1866; unmarried.

8. Warren T. Hudgins, born April 12, 1868; unmarried.

9. Agnes Hudgins, born June 13, 1870; married Oliver Spears, issue:

1. Maurice Spears.

2. Susan Spears.

10. Lucy Hudgins, born Oct. — 1872; married Charles Vadnias, issue:

1. Raymond Vadnias.

2. Charles Vadnias.

11. Charles Hudgins.

6. Ann E. Stamper: married Dr. Frank Starks, issue.

1. Price Starks: unmarried.

2. Charles Starks: married ——— ———: no issue.

3. Josephine Starks; married William Woodson, had issue.
7. John S. Stamper; married Amelia Meadows, issue:
1. Larkin Stamper; married Bertha Gibson, had issue.
2. Emma Stamper; married George Gwinn, had issue.
3. Austin Stamper; married Anna Wingate, had issue.
4. Anna Stamper; married John Ray, had issue.

5. Nancy Maupin; married Thomas Stagner of Madison County, Ky., son of Barney Stagner, who was a brother to Anna Stagner married Robert James, Sarah Stagner of Howard County, Mo., Jesse Stagner, (wife Polly) John Stagner (wife Polly). Richmond Stagner married Elizabeth Harris. Nelly Stagner, married Charles C. Moorman. Thomas Stagner and his wife, lived and died two and a half miles east of Richmond, Ky., their old home now owned by Mrs. Christopher F. Chenault. Thomas Stagner's will bears date 1856, probated 1860. Their children were:

1. Rosanna Stagner; married John B. Arnold, Jan. 12, 1841.
2. Barney C. Stagner.
3. Lytle R. Stagner.
4. Jasper N. Stagner.
5. John Speed Stagner.
6. Andrew J. Stagner.
7. Henry C. Stagner.
8. Richard Stagner.
9. Michie Maupin Stagner.
10. Patrick Stagner.
11. James Stagner.

6. James Maupin; married Eleanor McBane in Madison County, Ky., Jan. 14, 1839. They lived and died in the south-western section of the county, near Berea.

7. Fountain Maupin; married Levin Elizabeth Jarman, in Madison County, Ky., Sept. 9, 1837. Her mother's given name was Elizabeth. They emigrated to Buchanan County, Mo., and raised four children, and both died in St. Joseph, Mo. Their children:

1. Thomas Maupin; married Liddy Brooks. They have a son:
1. Thomas Maupin.
2. Patrick (Patty) Maupin; married —— ——
3. Puss Maupin; married Captain Daniel Meadows, issue:
1. James Meadows.
2. Fountain Meadows.
3. William Meadows.
4. John Meadows.
5. Elijah Meadows.
6. Fannie Meadows.
7. Annie Meadows.
8. Josie Meadows.

4. Myrah Maupin; married first, Mr. —— Shoots, and second, Harry Eades, issue of the first marriage:
1. James Shoots.
2. Liddy Shoots.
3. Vin Shoots.
4. [illegible] Shoots.

There were also, issue of the second marriage.

8. Mary Maupin; married John Gates. They settled on Dicks River, in Lincoln County, Ky., their home was near to Major James Miller. Mr. Gates died and Mary Maupin Gates, married again, James W. Pullins, who both died in Lincoln County, Ky.

Issues of the first marriage:

1. General Elijah Gates, served in Price's army in the Civil War, and was a gallant Confederate soldier, one of his legs was shot off in battle. He was at one time Treasurer of the State of Missouri. He married his cousin Mariah Stamper, daughter of Larkin Stamper and Emily Maupin his wife. Their home was in St. Joseph, Mo. Their children:

1. Elmina Gates; married Horace Lions. P. O. Address Kansas City, Mo., issue:

1. Nelly Lions; married David Howe.

2. Vice Lions; married Richard Waite, issue.

1. David Waite.

3. Horace Lions; unmarried.

4. Joel Lions; unmarried.

5. Edwin Lions; unmarried.

2. John E. Gates; unmarried.

3. Luella Gates; married John McCarty of St. Joseph, Mo., issue:

1. Burr McCarty.

4. Joel E. Gates; married Vicie Buford. They live in St. Joseph, Mo., and Mr. Gates is Clerk of the City Court.

5. Elijah Gates, Jr., unmarried, a resident of Kansas City, Missouri.

6. Charles Gates; unmarried, resident of St. Joseph Mo.

7. Benjamin Gates; married Sarah Shonan. Their home is in St. Joseph, Mo., no issue.

8. Margaret E. Gates; married W. R. Robinson, of St. Joseph, Mo.

9. Georgia Gates; married George Woods, issue:

1. Margaret Woods.

9. Patrick Maupin; married in Madison Count, Ky., Feb. 6, 1834, Margaret Moberley. They went to Missouri. They had but one child, when Patrick Maupin died, and his widow afterwards married Jeremiah Barnes, issue:

1. William Maupin, was Captain of a company in the Confederate Army, and lost his life in the war.

Children of the second marriage of Thomas Maupin to Margaret Burnsides, viz:

10. Elizabeth J. Maupin; married in Madison County, Ky., April 27, 1843, to Thomas Howard Maupin, son of Daniel Maupin and Margaret McWilliams. (See Chap. 12, Sec. 22.)

11. Jesse R. Maupin, was willed the mill property on Silver Creek. He lived and died in Madison County, Ky.

Thomas Maupin, who married first Elizabeth Michie and second Margaret Burnsides, was a first cousin to Daniel Maupin, who married Betsy Gentry first, and Margaret McWilliams second, (See Part V, Chap. 12,) also a first cousin to Fannie Jarman the wife of James Bell Ballard, also a first cousin to Margaret Maupin the wife of John Harris. (See Part V, Chap. 4, Sec. 13, and Part III, Chap. 16.) And the said Thomas Maupin was a grand-son of Daniel Maupin and Margaret Via his wife. (See Part V, Chap. 2.)

The following is a copy of a record or memorandum of W. Elbridge Harris, of Madison County, Ky:

"My grandmother, Fannie Ballard, was a double first cousin to Daniel Maupin (who died in Madison County, Ky.), and a first cousin to old Thomas Maupin (who died in Madison County, Ky.)

The said Daniel Maupin's first wife was a daughter of Josiah Gentry and second wife a McWilliams. Thomas Maupin's first wife was a Michie.

My ancestors on my mother's side:

"My mother was a daughter of James Bell Ballard, and Fannie Ballard nee Jarman. My great grand-father was John P. Ballard, his wife was Mollie Powers whose mother's maiden name was Bell.

My great-grand mother's maiden name was Sally (1) Maupin, whose mother's name was Dabney, her mother was a Jennings, who emigrated from England to Virginia, Albemare County.

(1) Frances.

"C" Daniel Maupin, native of Albemarle County, Va., probably a son of Zacharias Maupin and Elizabeth Jarman his wife, (See Chap. 3, Sec. 6) married in Virginia Susannah —— —— They emigrated to Madison County, Ky., prior to the beginning of the nineteenth century. He acquired lands on Tates Creek, Silver Creek and Paint Lick Creek.

Sept. 22, 18825, Daniel Maupin and his wife Susannah, conveyed to James Levell, 139 acres of land on Tates Creek. They were living on their farm of 103¾ acres on Paint Lick Creek, when on Oct. 29, 1832, they sold and conveyed same to Samuel W. Ross, and moved to Clark County, Ky., and in the early part of the year 1832, John White and wife, conveyed to said Daniel Maupin 235 acres of land in Clark county, where they made their home, and where Daniel Maupin died in 1834, leaving his last will and testament, bearing date April 25, 1833, probated at the January term of Court 1835, devising his property to his wife Susannah.

In 1836, the widow Susannah Maupin, made conveyance of the land to her son Wilson R. Maupin.

The will does not mention the names of their children, but they had, viz:

1. Wilson R. Maupin; married in Madison County, Ky., Sept. 17, 1823, Rebecca White. He probably married the second time Polly —— He finally settled in Montgomery County, Ky., where he died in 1879, leaving his last will and testament, bearing date, Aug. 22, 1877, probated May 19, 1879, devising property to his wife, Polly, and his children and grand-children. The children mentioned in the will are:

   1. Daniel Maupin, who was blind, and so stated in Wilson R. Maupin's will . Nevertheless, he was appointed and qualified as executor. His home was in Montgomery, County, Ky., where he died in 1891, leaving also his last will and testament bearing date, Sept. 27, 1891, probated Dec. 21, 1891. His wife was named Cordelia—— He had a daughter:

      1. Della Crab. Besides other children whose names he fails to mention in the will.

   2. Spencer Maupin; married —— —— Their children:

      1. Daniel Maupin.
      2. Mary Maupin.
      3. John Maupin.
      4. James Roger Maupin.

   3. John Maupin.

Daniel Maupin and his wife Susannah, had other children besides Wilson R. Maupin, and probably the marriages set forth in Chapter 1 embraces a number of their children.

"D." George W. Maupin; wife Ann —— died in Portsmouth, Va., in 1825, leaving his last will and testament appointing his wife, Ann, sole executrix and guardian of his children. He failed to mention the number and names of his children, probably a son of William Maupin of Chapter 3, Section 5.

"E." Billainy Maupin, emigrated from Virginia and made an

actual settlement on four hundred acres of land on Collins Fork of Goose Creek, in what was then Madison, now Clay County, Ky., which appears from an order of the Madison County Court, of May 7, 1804. Probably a son of Zacharias Maupin and Elizabeth Jarman of Chapter 3, Section 6.

"F." John Maupin, emigrated from Virginia, and entered four hundred acres of land on a creek, known by the name of Buzzard, a branch of Goose Creek, waters of the Kentucky, which appears from a Madison County Court order, of Aug. 7, 1804. Probably a son of Zacharias Maupin and Elizabeth Jarman of Chap. 3, Section 6.

"G." Charles W. Maupin of Albemarle County, Va., married Mary Harrison, a daughter of Richard Harrison, emigrated to St. Louis, Mo., where he died in 1867. Probably a son of William Maupin of Chap. 3, Sec. 5.

CHAPTER. 3.

DANIEL MAUPIN, SENIOR.

(Named in Chapter 2.)

Article 1.—Daniel Maupin, designated as Daniel Maupin, Senior, son of the emigrant Gabriel Maupin and Marie Spencer his wife, was born perhaps in France about 1699-1700, and was brought with his parents to Virginia. He settled on Morman's River in 1748.

He entered more than fifteen hundred acres of land in the Whitehall neighborhood, and made his home there. He married Margaret Via, and they raised a family of ten children; seven sons, and three daughters. He died in 1788, having made and published his last will and testament, which bears date Aug. 26, 1788, probated Oct. 9, 1788, and recorded at Charlottesville, Va. A copy of which is in these words and figures:

"Daniel Maupin's Senior, Will."

"In the name of God, amen. I, Daniel Maupin, senior, of Albemarle County, being in a low state of health, but of perfect mind and memory, I leave this my last will and testament: I give and bequeath to my good and lawful wife, Margaret, all my estate, real and personal, during her widowhood. And I give to my son, Gabriel Maupin, an equal part of my estate, and I give to my son, Thomas Maupin, an equal part of my estate, and I give to my son, John Maupin, an equal part of my estate, and I give to my son, Daniel Maupin, an equal part of my estate. I give to my son, William Maupin, an equal part of my estate, and I give to my son, Zacharias Maupin, an equal part of my estate, and to my son, Zacharias I give five pounds extraordinary more than the rest of my children, and I give to my son, Jesse Maupin, an equal part of my estate, and I give to my daughter Mary Mullens, an equal part of my estate, and I give to my daughter Jean R a, an equal part of my estate, and I give to my daughter Margaret Miller, an equal part of my estate. And my desire and will is, if there cannot be an equal division of my estate, among my sons and daughters, that my estate may be sold at public auction, and the money equally divided amongst my sons and daughters, and this being my last will, I hereby appoint my son, John Maupin, his son, Daniel Maupin, and Maxey Ewell, executors of this my last will.

In witness whereof, I have hereunto set my hand this 26th, day of Aug. 1788. DANIEL (X) MAUPIN.

William Jarman.
Lewis Davis, Jr.
James Cone.

At a Court held for Albemarle County, Oct. 9, 1788, this last will and testament of Daniel Maupin, senior, deceased, was produced into Court, and proved by the oaths of William Jarman, and Lewis Davis, Jr, two of the witnesses thereto, and ordered to be recorded, and a probate of the same was granted John Maupin, Daniel Maupin and Maxey Ewell, therein named who gave bond and security, according to law.

Teste, JOHN NICHOLAS, C. C.

A copy—Teste, W. L. MAUPIN, Clerk.

Margaret Via Maupin, the wife of said Daniel Maupin, was living at the date of the probate of the will. Their children:

Section 1. Gabriel Maupin. He was a witness to the will of John McCord, probated in Albemarle County, Va., March 8, 1764. One Gabriel Maupin died in Albemarle County, Va., in 1794. The children of one Gabriel Maupin and wife Ann Ballard, are set forth in Chapter 2, probably the same person as the subject of this section.

Section 2. Thomas Maupin. Probably the father of Thomas Maupin, described in Chapter 2, Section B.

Section 3. John Maupin; married Frances Dabney, daughter of Cornelius Dabney, senior, and Sarah Jennings his second wife. (See Part III, Chapter 15.) A further history of whom is given in Chapter 4.

Section 4. Daniel Maupin; ("Cuff Daniel") married Elizabeth Dabney, daughter of Cornelius Dabney, senior and Sarah Jennings his second wife. (See Part III, Chapter 15.) A fuller history of whom is given in Chapter 11.

Section 5. William Maupin. He was a member of a company of men raised in Albemarle County, Va., in 1758, to defend and protect the frontier against Indians. He was a witness to the will of Robert Harris, senior, probated in Albemarle County, Va., Aug. 8, 1765. His wife was probably a daughter of Chapman White. He died in 1814. Among his children were the following, viz:

1. Chapman W. Maupin. He married —— —— and died in Albemarle County, Va., in 1861. Their children in part were:

1. Dr. Socrates Maupin. He was first professor of Chemistry at Hampden-Sidney College, Virginia, and then of the University of Virginia. He died in 1871, from injuries received in a runaway accident in Lynchburg, Va.

2. Addison Maupin. He lived before the Civil War on Carr's Hill adjoining the university. He married —— —— and of his children was a son:

1. J. Addison Maupin of Richmond, Va. Author of the Maupin Bill of recent notoriety.

2. John Maupin; married first Mary Michie, daughter of Patrick Michie and Frances —— his wife, and second Mrs. Nancy Cobbs nee Nancy Waddy. Issue of the first marriage:

1. Polly Maupin; married her cousin George Maupin.

Children of the second marriage:

2. Ira Maupin; married twice, first —— and second Virginia Price. He died in Albemarle County, Va., in 1873.

3. Chapman C. Maupin; married Mildred Jarman, sister to the wife of his brother John Maupin. He died in Albemarle County, Va., in 1862. Of their children was a daughter, viz:

1. Sallie Maupin; married Joseph Perkins. They live on the old family lands on Moorman's River. Her only brother —— Maupin, enlisted in the Confederate Army and took sick and died in the service.

4. John Maupin; married Eliza Jarman, sister to the wife of his brother, Chapman C. Maupin.

5. Thompson Maupin; married his first cousin, Mildred Keblinger.

6. Asa Maupin; died unmarried.

7. Judith Waddy Maupin. She was attending school in Charlottesville, Albemarle County, Va., she quit school and married Edward B. Jarman, son of John Jarman and Betsy Broaddus, his wife. They settled in Madison County, Ky., where they spent the rest of their lives, honored and respected. In 1858, Mrs. Judith W. Jarman, visited her uncle Chapman Maupin in Albemarle County, Va. (See Chap. 4, Sec. 1, for issue. See also Part I, Chap. 13, Sec. 3, note.)

3. Miss —— Maupin; married Mr. Keblinger. They had, besides other children, a daughter:

1. Mildred Keblinger; married her first cousin Thompson Maupin.

4. Amos Maupin.

Section 6. Zacharias Maupin; married Elizabeth Jarman, daughter of Thomas Jarman of Moorman's River, Albemarle County, Virginia.

Section 7. Jesse Maupin, was probably twice married.

Jesse Maupin emigrated from Albemarle County, Va., to Madison County, Ky., and acquired property on Taylor's Fork of Silver Creek, near Milford or Old Town. May 10, 1818, Jesse Maupin and his wife Sarah, conveyed to Christopher Clark, land on Taylor's Fork, near Old Town. May 1, 1820, they conveyed to Elkaney Bush 119 acres of land. March 8, 1821, they conveyed to Philip Gillispie 67½ acres of land on Taylor's Fork, and to Lewis H. Gillispie 67½ acres of land on the same water course. Dec. 30, 1822, Richard Muir and wife conveyed to Jesse Maupin fifty acres of land in Fayette County, Ky.

His said wife was Sarah, formerly the wife of one Sweeny, but by whom Jesse Maupin had no children. He died in 1827, leaving his last will and testament, bearing date Feb. 25, 1827, probated Oct. 1, 1827, wherein he mentions his wife Sarah, and shows that she was the widow Sweeney before his marriage to her, and he devised to her Sweeney children certain property, and names his own heirs thus:

Thomas Maupin's youngest.
Ambrose Maupin's youngest.
William Maupin's youngest.

Section 8. Mary Maupin; married Matthew Mullens in Albemarle County, Va. Matthew Mullens was a member of a company raised in Albemarle County, in 1758, to defend and protect the frontier against the Indians. A fuller account of whom is given in Chapter 13.

Section 9. Jean Maupin; married Samuel Rea in Albemarle County, Va. He had a place near Rea's Ford and in 1788, bought a farm on Beaver Creek, between Crozet and Whitehall in Albemarle County. Samuel Rea was a signer of the Albemarle Declaration of Independence April 21, 1799. Their children:

1. Daniel Rea.
2. Andrew Rea.
3. Thomas Rea; married Ann Ballard, daughter of Bland Ballard, and they lived beneath Bucks Elbow. He died in 1850. Their children:
    1. Daniel Rea.
    2. Jean Rea; married Garland Maury.
    3. Bland Rea; married first Sarah Alexander, and secondly Elizabeth Jones, daughter of Colonel John Jones. In his youth he was associated with Benjamin Ficklin in the manufacture of tobacco. Afterwards settled as a farmer, near the old homestead, where he died in 1868. Their children:
        1. John A. Rea.
        2. Joseph Rea.
        3. William Rea.
        4. James Rea.
        5. Mary Rea; married Bernard Tilman.
        6. Maria Rea; married Oscar Lipscomb.
    4. Jeminia Rea; married Richard Beckett.
    5. Ann Rea; married John Bales.
    6. Samuel Rea.
    7. Margaret Rea; married George Wolfe.
4. Robert Rea; married Elizabeth Maupin, daughter of Daniel Maupin and Elizabeth Dabney his wife. (See Chap. 11.) They lived in the Beaver Creek neighborhood, in Albemarle County, Va. He died in 1831.
5. Margaret Rea; married Ezekiel McCauley.

Samuel Rea was a signer of a Declaration of Independence by the citizens of Albemarle April 21, 1799.

Section 10. Margaret Maupin; married Robert Miller, and they were living in Orange County, Va., at the time of his death in 1806. A history of whom is given in Part 1, Chapter 4.

The Rea Family of Albemarle.

Note—At the formation of Albemarle, the name Rea is found on the records.

In 1747 Fergus Rea bought a portion of the Chiswell patent, on the Rochfish.

About the same time John Rea, was the owner of land on the Rivanna, near Martin King's Ford, the present Union Mills.

Andrew, Thomas and Samuel Rea, were considerably interested in real estate during the period 1744-1788. In 1744, Andrew Rea entered a small tract on the south side of the Rivanna, a short distance above the mouth of Ivy Creek, and at the time was the owner of land adjoining. He gave the name to the Ford called Rea's Ford. In the patent the name is written, Reay, should be Rea, and not Reay, nor Ray, as often spelled.

Thomas Rea owned land on the head waters of Mechum's, near Round Mountain and subsequently purchased near Rea's Ford, and on Meadow Creek, not far from the old poor house.

Samuel Rea, also had a place near Rea's Ford, and in 1788, bought on Beaver Creek, between Crozet and Whitehall.

Andrew Rea's wife, was named Mary.

Thomas Rea's wife, Ursula Smith, daughter of Thomas Smith.

Samuel Rea's wife, was Jean Maupin, daughter of Daniel Maupin and Margaret Via his wife, as aforesaid.

CHAPTER 4.

JOHN MAUPIN.

(Named in Chapter 3, Section 3.)

Article 1.—John Maupin, a son of Daniel Maupin, senior, and Margaret Via his wife, was a member of a company of men raised in Albemarle County, Va., in 1758, to defend and protect the frontier against the Indians.

He was born about 1725, and died in 1806. He married Frances Dabney, a daughter of Cornelius Dabney, senior and Sarah Jennings his wife, of the same County. (See Part III, Chap. 15.) He was co-executor with his son Daniel and Maxey Ewell, of his father's will probated in 1788. Their children:

Section 1. Sarah Maupin; married William Jarman, son of Thomas Jarman of Moorman's River, who settled there in 1762. William Jarman established himself in 1790, near the present Mechums Depot. He soon after built the mill at that place, which was for many years known by his name, and on the site of which one has existed ever since. In 1805, he and Brightberry Brown, undertook the construction of Brown's Turnpiks, beginning at a place called Camping Rock, crossing the ridge at Brown's Gap, descending through Brown's Cove, and terminating at the present Mechums Depot, which was formerly accepted the next year by commissioners appointed from both sides of the Mountain. They had five sons, and six daughters, towit:

1. James Jarman, who in 1819, sold his half of the turnpike to Ira Harris for $100. (See "The Jarman Family.")

2. Thomas Jarman, bought the land on the summit of the ridge at the old Woods Gap, and since his purchase, the Gap has generally gone by his name.

3. Mary Jarman; married Beaver Creek William Woods, Jr. (See Part II, Chap. 12, Sec. 1.)

4. John Jarman; married Betsy Broaddus, a sister to the late Richard Broaddus of Madison County, Ky. (See Part VI, Chap. 13, Sec. 3, note.) Their children:

1. Edward B. Jarman; married Judith Waddy Maupin of Albemarle County, Va., a daughter of John Maupin and his

second wife, Mrs. Nancy Cobbs nee Waddy. After the marriage they settled in Madison County, Ky., where they spent their remaining days, both highly respected by the people who knew them. (See Chapter 3, Sec. 5.) Their children:

1. Mary Eliza Jarman; married Thomas H. Grubbs of Mt. Sterling, Ky., where Mr. Grubbs now lives. (See Part VI Chap. 36, Section 4.)

2. Ann Elizabeth Jarman; married first Mahlon B. Heatherly, and secondly William Malcom Miller. (See Part I, Chapter 14, Section 2.)

3. John B. Jarman; died young.

4. James Ira Jarman; died young.

5. Sallie Chapman Jarman; marrined William J. Hanna. Their home is in Harrodsburg, Ky. Their children:

1. Mary Vaughn Hanna.
2. Margaret Chapman Hanna.
3. William J. Hanna.
4. Edward Price Hanna.
5. Ira Virginia Hanna.
6. Edward Barbour Jarman; died.
7. Judith Waddy Jarman; married Richard Pettus.
8. William F. Jarman; unmarried. Lives at Kingston, Madison County, Ky.

2. James Jarman; married his first cousin Sallie Jarman.

3. John B. Jarman; married Salinda Hayes.

4. Mary Jarman; married Richard Apperson.

5. Sallie Jarman; married Thomas Price, Dec. 6, 1828. Their Children:

1. John Morton Price; married Mary Eliza Park, and lived a few years in Atchison, Kansas. He was a shrewd business man, and at one or more times of his life was very wealthy, and had a beautiful home in Atchison. From some cause in his later life he lost heavily.

2. Mary Price; married her first cousin, Thomas Jarman.

6. Waller Jarman.

7. Beverly Jarman.

5. Fannie Jarman; married James Bell Ballard, son of John Ballard and Elizabeth Thompson, daughter of Roger Thompson his wife.

6. Pleasant Jarman; married Elizabeth Ballard, daughter of John Ballard and Elizabeth Thompson his wife, and were the parents of:

1. William Jarman, who was formerly the leading tailor of Richmond, Ky.

7. William Jarman; married Peggy Wallace, daughter of Michael Wallace and Jane Bratton his wife. (See Part IV, Chap. 13.)

8. Miss Jarman; married William Ballard.

9. Miss Jarman.

10. Miss Jarman.

11. Miss Jarman.

Note:—The Jarman Family of Albemarle County, Virginia

Thomas Jarman, the first of the name to settle in Albemarle, obtained a grant for lands on Moorman's River in 1762. He married ——— ——— Of their children:

1. Elizabeth Jarman; married Zacharias Maupin. (See Chap. 3, Section 6.)

2. Mary Jarman; married Benajah Brown. (See Part VIII, Chap. 2, Section 5.)

3. William Jarman; married Sarah Maupin. (See Chap. 4, Section 1.)

4. Martha Jarman; married Daniel Maupin. (See Chap. 4, Section 2.)

5. Frances Jarman; married John A. Michie.

6. James Jarman, lived on the east side of the road in Brown's Cove, about one mile south of Doylesville. He married Bettie Brown, daughter of Bernard Brown. He was appointed a magistrate in 1819, and was frequently employed in the county business, and died in 1847. Of his children there were:

1. Mary Ann Jarman; married Colonel William T. Brown. (See Part VII, Chap. 2, Section 2-1.)

2. Miletus Jarman, succeeded his father in the occupation of the old homestead. He died in 1874. He married Miss Hansberger. Their children:

1. Robert Jarman; died single.
2. Henry Jarman; died single.
3. Clotilda Jarman; married J. W. Rodes.
4. Etta Jarman; married Mr. Bethune.
5. Mary Kitty Jarman; married Marion Bowen. Their children:

1. Sarah Bowen; married Dr. Thompkins. Children:
1. Mattie Thompkins.
2. Kate Thompkins.
3. Robert Thompkins.
4. Samuel Thompkins.

Section 2. Daniel Maupin, known as "Saddler Daniel," was co-executor with his father John Maupin and Maxey Ewell of the will of his grand-father, Daniel Maupin, senior, probated in 1788. He married three times, first Martha Jarman, (See Sec. 1, above) second Patsey Gentry and third Mrs. Hannah Harris nee Jameson, widow of William Harris, deceased. (See Part III, Chap. 3, Sec. 5) In 1834 he and his wife Hannah deeded the ground for Mount Moriah Meeting House, near Whitehall in Albemarle, which for many years went by the name of "Maupin Meeting House," and was a favorite place for holding camp meetings. In 1795, Henry Austin, conveyed to Daniel Maupin and others the title to a parcel of land for a church, then called "Austin Meeting House," afterwards "Bingham's Church." Children of the first marriage:

1. Miriam Maupin; married Bernard M. Brown, son of Bernard Brown, senior and Elizabeth Dabney his wife. (See Part VIII, Chapter 8.)

2. Kate Maupin; married William Harris. No children.

Children of the second marriage:

3. Joel Maupin; married Martha Gentry, daughter of Christopher Gentry and emigrated to the West.

4. James Maupin; married Derindy Hauger. Their children:

1. Mary Maupin; married Mr. Hauger, no issue.
2. Tabitha Maupin; married Mr. Kenly, no issue.
3. John H. Maupin; married Bettie Harris, daughter of Thomas W. Harris and Betsy Maupin his wife.

5. Nimrod Maupin; married Miss Harris. Their children:

1. Lilburn Maupin, emigrated West.
2. James Maupin, emigrated West.

6. Lilburn Maupin; married Miss Kent, they had one child:

1. Sallie Maupin; married Mr. Bowles.

7. Martin Maupin; died a bachelor.

8. Frances Maupin; married Dabney M. Jarman. Children:

1. W. D. Jarman; married Catherine Lindsey, daughter of

Colonel Harry Lindsey and Fannie Maupin (daughter of Jennings Maupin and Sallie Miller his wife. See Sec. 10-5.)

2. John L. Jarmman; married Mary Fry . Children:
   1. Minnie Jarman; single.
   2. Lizzie Jarman; single.
   3. Jennie Jarman; single.
   4. Matthew F. Jarman; married first Mary Fairfos, no children, and second Miss Fretwell. Their children:
      1. Martha Jarman.
      2. Eren Jarman.
      3. John Jarman.
      4. Thomas Jarman.
      5. Matthew Jarman.
      6. Elizabeth Jarman.
3. Mary Jarman; married W. J. Keblinger. Their children:
   1. Wilbur Keblinger; never married.
   2. Lutie Keblinger; married G. W. Gulley. Children:
      1. Atress Gulley; single.
      2. Thomas Gulley; married a Baltimore lady, no children.
   3. Mollie Keblinger; married, first, Dr. R. K. George, no children, and second, Andrew Cronen, have about eight children; only know the names of:
      1. William Cronen; married up north.
      2. Harriet Cronen; single.
   4. Cadis Keblinger; married Annett Jackson. Children:
      1. Lula Keblinger; married —— Woodward.
      2. Mary Keblinger; married —— Nalle.
      3. Willie Keblinger; married —— ——
4. James D. Jarman.
5. Elizabeth Jarman; married Burlington Fretwell. Children:
   1. Dabney Fretwell; married Bettie Woodson.
   2. James Fretwell.
   3. Minnie Fretwell.
   4. Harry Fretwell.
   5. Annie Fretwell.
   6. Snoole Fretwell.

9. Mary Maupin; married John Hayden. Children:
   1. Asa Hayden.
   2. William Hayden.
   3. John Hayden, killed in the Civil War.
   4. James Hayden; married Miss Bledsoe. Children:
      1. John Hayden, and two other boys.
   5. Elizabeth Hayden; married —— Maxwell.
   6. Fannie Hayden; married —— Ewing.
   7. Margaret Hayden; married —— ——.

10. Betsy Maupin; married Thomas W. Harris. Children:
   1. James Harris.
   2. Sallie Harris; married Rice Woods, no children.
   3. Bettie Harris; married J. H. Maupin of Missouri, son of James Maupin. No children.
   4. William Harris; married Jennie Maupin, daughter of T. J. Maupin.
   5. Oswin Harris; married Mollie Maupin, daughter of T. J. Maupin.
   6. George Harris; married Eliza Foster. Children:
      1. Helton Harris; married —— Marshall.
      2. Ida Harris; died single.

3. Edgar Harris; married —— ——
4. Stuart Harris; married Miss Hildebrand.
5. Cordelia Harris; married W. G. Gillispie. Children:
    1. Eva Gillispie; single.
    2. Mable Gillispie; single.
    3. Morris Gillispie; single.
    4. Charles Gillispie; single.
    5. Randolph Gillispie; single.

Children of third marriage of Daniel ("Saddler") Maupin and Mrs. Hannah Harris:

11. Merrett R. Maupin; married Polly Maupin, daughter of "Mountain" William Maupin and Jane Jameson, his wife. (See Section 4.) When just grown he weighed one hundred and twenty six pounds, and at his death, three hundred and sixty pounds. Their children:

1. William D. Maupin; married first Ella Childress. Five children:
    1. The oldest, married Jarman Brown.

Dont know the names of the others.

William D. Maupin's second wife was Miss Fisher; had issue. He lives at his father's old place in Albemarle.

2. Cornelia Maupin; married W. B. Railey. They live at Moorman's River, Virginia. Their children:
    1. Linwood Railey; single.
    2. Merritt Railey; single.
    3. Emma Railey; single.
    4. Janie Railey; single.
    5. Bettie Railey; married Arthur Stevens, no issue.
    6. Lula Railey; married Luther Sandridge, no issue.
    7. Virgie Railey; married Grayson Wood, have some small children, can't give their names.

12. John W. Maupin, was a saddler by trade and died a bachelor.

13. Sarah Maupin; married Dr. Peery. They emigrated to Missouri at the time having several children; names not known.

JOHN W. MAUPIN.

Section 3. Cornelius Maupin, was a soldier in the Revolutionary Army, and was with the continental troops, at the seige of Yorktown and the surrender of Cornwallis, and his name was on the pension list for the service. He married four times, don't know his wives given names. His first wife was Miss Harris, second Miss Tomlin, third Miss Paul and fourth Miss Ellis.

Note:—One Cornelius Maupin, after the Revolutionary War emigrated from Albemarle County, Va., to Kentucky, and settled in Madison County, on the waters of Otter Creek, near the present city of Richmond, where he acquired lands. He also owned lands on the waters of Green River. March 5, 1793, Peter Taylor and wife Nancy, conveyed to him 56 acres on a branch of Otter Creek, adjoining Richard Calloway, James Estill deceased,, Hoy, Briscoe, etc. Nov. 9, 1807, Cornelius Maupin and his wife Ann, conveyed to Parmenas Briscoe, land on Pitman or Sinking Creek, a branch of Green River, witnessed by Peter Woods, John

Grudgett and Jer. Shropshire. Dec. 13, 1802, he and his wife Ann, conveyed to Dulaney Miller, land on Otter Creek. March 2, 1790, "on motion of Cornelius Maupin, his ear mark a crop and slit in the right ear, and a hole in the left is ordered to be recorded." He perhaps went to Missouri. Don't know of but one son of Cornelius Maupin. (Son of John Maupin.)

1. Bernard Maupin, called "Barnie," married —— —— he had two sons:

1. Charles Maupin, was single when he went to Missouri in 1852.

2. Silas Maupin; married Miss —— Norris, when living in Virginia was famous for attending camp meetings. He went to Missouri in 1852, and the last heard of, had gone to Mexico. Had no children when he left Virginia.

2. Margaret Maupin; married David Woods. (See Part II, Chap. 49, Section 1, and Chap. 11, Section 8.)

Section 4. William Maupin, known as "Mountain Billy Maupin," was a soldier in the Revolutionary Army, and was with the Colonial Troops, at the seige of Yorktown, and surrender of Cornwallis. His name appears on the pension list for services in that war. The canteen he used in the army is yet preserved, and in the hands of the family in Albemarle. He married Jane Jameson, a daughter of Samuel Jameson, who purchased in 1765, the land in the old Woods Gap from Archibald Woods, who had entered it in 1756. Their children were:

1. Tilman J. Maupin; married Pyrenia Brown, daughter of Bernard Brown, Jr., and Miriam Maupin, his wife. (See Part VIII, Chap. 8.) He died in 1881, in Albemarle. Their children:

1. Samantha Maupin; married Captain James Wiant. Mr. Wiant died of wounds received in Pickets charge at Gettysburg. Their children:

1. Nannie Wiant; married —— Clark. Do not know the names of their children. They live in Richmond, Va.

2. Thomas Wiant; single.

2. Georgia Maupin; married Robert Woods. Children:

1. Emma Woods; married T. R. Chapman. They had only one child:

1. Georgia Chapman; married Enos Todd, son of Ex-Admiral Andrew Todd, of the United States Navy. Her husband is dead, she has one little boy.

2. Nannie Woods; married W. G. Barksdale; no issue:

3. Avis Woods; married —— ——

4. Norman Woods; married —— —— Has one little girl.

5. Mande Woods; married Curtis Lipscomb. Have two small girls.

3. Virginia Maupin; married William Harris, son of Thomas W. Harris and Betsy Maupin his wife. She married second Asbury Lindsey. No issue of the second marriage, she had one son, viz:

1. William Harris, never married, died of wounds received at Sharpsburg, Maryland, Sept. 17, 1862.

4. Mary (Mollie) Maupin; married Oswin Harris.

5. W. B. Maupin; married Lucy Jones, daughter of Mosias Jones, senior. (See Part III, Chap. 11, note.) Children:

1. Moses Maupin; married Miss Fry. Have three small children.

2. Chapman Maupin; married —— Have one child.

3. Belle Maupin; married C. C. Tilman. Have a child.

4. Lois Maupin; married —— —— no issue.

5. Tandy Maupin; single.
6. Tilman Maupin; single.

2. Logan Maupin; married Eliza Sims, daughter of Isaac Sims. Their children:

1. Julia Maupin; single.
2. Isaac Maupin, killed in Confederate Army, whilst in battle.
3. William L. Maupin, now clerk of the Albemarle County and Circuit Courts; married Eliza Garland. Had six children:
    1. —— Maupin; married Woods Garth, no children.
    2. —— Maupin; married Woods Garth, no children.
    3. Julia Maupin; single.
    4. Bessie Maupin; single.
    5. Sarah Maupin; single.
    6. Willie Maupin; single.

3. Albert A. Maupin; married Patsey Jarman, daughter of Dabney M. Jarman, and Fannie Maupin his wife. Their children:

1. Oscar Maupin; married Mollie Flarn.
2. Mattie Maupin; single.
3. Emily Maupin; single.
4. Frank Maupin.
5. Mary Maupin.
6. Frances Maupin; married James H. ——
7. Ella Maupin; married William Lewis, no issue.

4. Waller Maupin; married —— —— and left a family. Has a son who is a member of the Methodist Conference in Missouri.

5. William O. Maupin, emigrated to Missouri and got to be judge of one of the courts, and was elected from that state to the United States Congress. Before he left Virginia in 1835, he was an attorney of the Albemarle bar at Charlottesville.

6. Frances Maupin; married Pascal Maupin, son of Jennings Maupin and Sallie Miller his wife. (See Section 10.) No children.

7. Polly Maupin; married Merrett R. Maupin, son of saddler Daniel Maupin and Mrs. Hannah Harris nee Jameson. (See Sec. 2, for children.)

Note:—The Jameson Family of Albemarle.

Jamesons settled in an early day on Morman's River in Albemarle County, Va., both above and below Whitehall.

John Jameson took out a patent for land on the south side of that river in 1741, and Samuel Jameson on the branches of Spring Creek in 1747, and in 1765. Samuel Jameson purchased the land in the old Woods Gap, from Archibald Woods, who had entered it in 1756, and Samuel Jameson died in 1788. His wife was named Jean —— They had nine children, the names of four of them are here given:

1. Alexander Jameson.
2. Thomas Jameson.*
3. John Jameson.*
4. Samuel Jameson; died in about 1805. His wife was named Margaret. Their children were:
    1. Hannah Jameson; married first William Harris and second Saddler Daniel Maupin, as set forth in Section 2.
    2. Jane Jameson; married William Maupin (as set forth in Section 4, above.)
    3. Elizabeth Jameson; married James Harris, lived near Free Union.
    4. Catherine Jameson; married Nathan Mills.
    5. Mary Jameson; married Nehemiah Birkhead.

6. William Jameson.
7. Samuel Jameson.

The Madison County Court records of 1826 and 1830 show additional children of Samuel Jameson, deceased, and his wife Margaret, who survived, to-wit:

8. David K. Jameson of Franklin County, Ala., in 1826.
9. Martha Jameson of Franklin County, Ala., in 1826.
10. Harvey Jameson of Lawrence County, Ala., in 1830.
11. Joseph Jameson.
12. Jane Jameson.

*Dr. Thomas Jameson practiced medicine in Charlottesville in the early part of the nineteenth century and was probably of this family.

A number emigrated to Kentucky, and the following names of the family appear on the early Court records of Madison County, Kentucky.

Joseph Jameson.

Samuel Jameson and his wife Margaret —— who survived him.

Robert Jameson, Margaret Jameson, Joseph Jameson and Jane Jameson. Martin Jameson and wife Barbary, David K. Jameson and wife Martha, Harvey Jameson.

**John Jameson and Betsy his wife. He died and John and William Harris and John Brown, were appraisers of his estate, and Daniel Miller and William Harris were the Courts commissioners to make settlement of the accounts of the administrator.

Nancy, wife of William (1818) and niece of Betsy Woodson.

Section 5. Thomas Maupin; married Miss Cobbs and second —— Maupin.

Section 6. John Maupin; married Miss —— Craig.

Section 7. Fannie Maupin; married William Shelton.

Section 8. Gabriel Maupin; married Miss Susannah Bailey. See Chapter 5.

Section 9. Robert Maupin; married Miss —— McGehee, (or McGee.)

One Robert Maupin settled in Barren County, Ky., and was State Senator from 1827 to 1832, and in the lower House from 1824 to 1826, and in 1843. Perhaps the same man as the subject.

Section 10. Jennings Maupin; married Sallie Miller, daughter of Robert Miller and Margaret Maupin his wife. (See Part I, Chap. 6.) They remained in Virginia. Their children were:

1. Jink Maupin; married Miss —— Winslow. Had children, and they went West, and at one time he was sheriff of Green County.

2. Paschal Maupin; married Frances Maupin, daughter of William Maupin and Jane Jameson his wife. (See Sec. 4.) No issue.

3. John M. Maupin, was a very distinguished criminal lawyer of Williamsburg, Va. He married Miss —— Armisted. Their children:

   1. Sallie Miller Maupin; married Mr. Bedgood. They had one son and two daughters.

   2. Kate Maupin; married Mr. Cook of Baltimore, Maryland.

4. Logan Maupin. He visited his uncle Daniel Miller, in Madison County, Ky., in about 1840, and subsequently made a second visit to said County to see relatives. He married a Northern lady. They had no children. They separated and he returned to Vir-

ginia, and went down about Norfolk or Williamsburg, where he died.

5. Fannie Maupin; married Colonel Henry Lindsey. Their children:

1. Littleton Lindsey; married Miss —— Brown. Had eight children. He emigrated to Missouri. He is dead.

2. Asbury Lindsey; married Mrs. Virginia Harris, widow of William Harris, and daughter of Tilman J. Maupin. (See Section 4-1-3.) No issue.

3. Catherine Lindsey; married W. D. Jarman, son of Dabney M. Jarman and Fannie Maupin his wife. (See Sec. 2-8.) Their children:

1. Henry D. Jarman; married Laura Dull. Their children:

1. Homer B. Jarman.

2. Mae Jarman.

3. Dice Jarman; married Harry Price of Maryland, they had a daughter, viz:

1. Dorothy Reid Price; died single.

4. Bledsoe Jarman; married Miss —— Sloan, no children.

5. John Jarman; single.

6. Judson Jarman; single, twin.

7. Frank Jarman; single, twin.

8. Catherine Jarman; single.

9. Hope Jarman; single.

10. Joseph Jarman; single.

11. Howell Jarman; single.

12. Louisa Jarman; single.

2. James E. Jarman; married Mary Jones. Children:

1. Benjamin Jarman; married Anna Young, have one baby daughter.

2. Zacharias Jarman; single.

3. Bernard Jarman; single.

4. Anna Jarman; single.

5. Mary Jarman; single.

3. Lutie Jarman; married Henry M. Tilman, have two small boys.

4. Joseph I. Jarman; married Mary Ellen Wiley, daughter of Dr. Wiley, President of Emory and Henry College. Joseph J. Jarman is now President of the State Female Normal School at Farmville, Va. They have four small children.

5. Robert Jarman; married Irene Smith. They have four small children.

6. Ed. Jarman; married Miss Webb. They have a small boy.

4. Mary Lindsey; married R. M. Cleveland. Their children:

1. Bessie Cleveland; dead.

2. Jerry Cleveland; single.

3. Charles Cleveland; single.

5. Mag Lindsey; married Thomas Dunn. Their children:

1. John Dunn; married ——— ——— no issue.

2. Annie Dunn; married G. W. Walker, have three small children.

3. Cornelia Dunn; married Mr. —— Haycock, have one small child.

4. Littleton Dunn; single.

5. William Dunn; single.

6. Ellen Lindsey; married James Gillum; no children.

6. Tyre Maupin was a distinguished editor and politician. At

the beginning of the Civil War he was an ardent whig, and he is said to have been at one time the best posted man on politics in Virginia. He married Miss —— Shelton. Their children:

1. Deale Maupin, have no history of him.

2. Junuis Maupin was a union man during the war, and a republican in politics since. He spent most of his time in the public printing office in Washington, D. C. He married Ann Houseworth. Their children:

1. John Maupin.
2. Miss Maupin; married Mr. McChung.
3. Miss Maupin; married Mr. —— Betts.
4. Ella Maupin; married T. M. Shelton. Their children:
   1. Fred Shelton; single.
   2. Harry Shelton; single.
   3. Luculius Shelton; single.
   4. Anna Shelton; single.
   5. Lydia Shelton; single.

3. Algernon Maupin, was also a union man during the Civil War, and a republican since, and spent the greater portion of his life in the public printing office, at Washington, D. C. He married —— —— and had two sons:

1. Algernon Maupin.
2. ——. Maupin.

4. John Maupin; died single.

5. Miss Maupin; married John Walker McMullen. Children:

1. John McMullen, lives in the West.
2. Mary McMullen; married W. B. Sims. Their children:
   1. Bernard Sims; married Bessie Strother; have four children.
   2. Walker Sims; married Mary Gibbs; have two children.
   3. Cordelia Sims; married James Weaver; have four or five children.
   4. Caddie Sims; married Eugene Jarrett lately; no issue.
3. Matilda McMullen; married Frank Sims, he is dead. Their children:
   1. Minnie Sims; married J. F. Hughes, no children.
   2. Tyetta Sims; married Mike Williams, have two children.
   3. Tyre Sims; married Miss Bruden, no children.
   4. Frank Sims; married Sallie B. Williams, no issue.
4. Henrietta McMullen; married K. W. Shelton. Their children:
   1. Stella Shelton; single.
   2. William Shelton; single.
   3. Alma Shelton; single.
   4. Henrietta Shelton; married Russel Melone, have two children.

Section 11. Carr Maupin; married Miss Nancy Burch.

One Carr Maupin, perhaps this man, settled in Montgomery County, Ky., and died there in the fall of 1845, leaving a will bearing date Aug. 14, 1845, probated at November term of Court 1845; his wife then was named Nancy, and a son and a daughter, towit:

1. Caleb Maupin.
2. Sinthy Maupin; married —— Adams.

His son Caleb was executor of the will. He divided his estate equally among his children. He had other children besides the above mentioned, but the number and names are not set forth in the will.

3. James Maupin, was living in Montgomery County, Ky., in 1810.

Section 12. Dabney Maupin; died young, unmarried.

Section 13. Margaret Maupin, was born in Albemarle County, Va., in 1767. She married John Harris, son of Christopher Harris and Agnes McCord his wife. (See Part III, Chap. 16.) They emigrated from Albemarle to Madison County, Ky., and settled on the waters of Muddy Creek, near the present village and railroad station of Brassfield. Margaret Maupin Harris, died in 1855. Her husband John Harris died in 1810.

Note:—Descendants of John Maupin and Francis Dabney his wife who enlisted and went out from Albemarle in the Civil War, and served in the confederate army:

Tazewell Brown, Bernard Brown, William B. Maupin, James D. Brown, Ira Harris, William D. Jarman, Allen Henry Brown, William Harris, John L. Jarman, William A. Brown, Isaac Maupin, William H. Terrill.

CHAPTER 5.

GABRIEL MAUPIN.

(Named in Chapter 4, Section 8.)

Article 1.—Gabriel Maupin, a son of John Maupin and Frances Dabney his wife, was born in Albemarle County, Va.

He married Susannah Bailey. They emigrated to Madison County, Ky., and settled on Drowning Creek, where Gabriel Maupin died about or prior to 1825. On the 21st of June 1825, his widow Susannah married Bazil Pinkston, and in 1826, Gabriel Maupin's sons, John and Callum, then over fourteen years of age chose Bazil Pinkston as their guardian, and he qualified as such. The children of Gabriel Maupin and Susannah Bailey, his wife, viz:

Section 1. William Overton Maupin, was born in Madison County, Ky., in 18 – on the 6th day of Oct. 1831, he was married to Susannah Cooper. He owned a farm near the old Drowning Creek Church, now Panola, where they both died. The subject of Chapter 6.

Section 2. John Maupin; married first Miss – – Thompson, and second Rachael Green. The subject of Chapter 7.

Section 3. Callum Maupin, never married; died at Little Rock, Arkansas.

Section 4. Dabney Maupin; married Polly Shifflett, April 17, 1817.

Section 5. Jennings Maupin; died single.

Section 6. Polly Maupin; married first Will P. Gilbert, July 19, 1826, and second Miss Hall. The subject of Chapter 8.

Section 7. Frances Dabney Maupin; married John R. Wright, July 4, 1826.

Section 8. Betsy Maupin; died single.

Section 9. Margaret Harris Maupin; married Joshua Shifflett, June 30, 1814. The subject of Chapter 9.

Section 10. Cynthia Maupin; married Covington Cooper, Oct. 27, 1831.

Section 11. Susan Maupin; married Mr. —— Stifner. The subject of Chapter 10.

Section 12. Sallie C. Maupin; married Abraham Emarine, July 10, 1822.

CHAPTER 6.

WILLIAM OVERTON MAUPIN.

(Named in Chapter 5, Section 1.)

Article 1.—William Overton Maupin, a son of Gabriel Maupin and Miss Susannah Bailey, his wife, was born in Madison County, Ky., at his father's home, in 18—.

On the 6th day of Oct. 1831, he was married to Susannah Cooper. He owned a farm on Drowning Creek, near where Panola now is, where his wife died. He died at the home of his daughter, Mary. To them were born these children:

Section 1. Robert Harris Maupin, who went to Missouri and married first Mary Viola Pearson, and second Phoebe Junk Benight. He has two children, viz:

1. Viola Maupin; married James Andrew Ford, a well to do citizen of Marysville, Missouri.
2. Howard Maupin; married at Marysville, Mo., and is doing well.

Section 2. Mary Maupin; married John Woolery, issue:

1. Nannie, married James Dalton.
2. Johnnie, (a daughter) married George Jones.
3. Sue Mag; married John Dalton.
4. William; married Malinda Garrett.

Section 3. Callum Maupin, now a merchant of Richmond, Ky., married Mary Turner Park. Callum Maupin made his home for a number of years, as one of the family of Christopher Irvine Miller, where he worked in his shop and learned the blacksmith business. When the Civil War came on he enlisted in the confederate army, and after the war returned home, and subsequently married as above stated, and was a merchant a number of years at Elliston and Waco, and then moved to Richmond, Ky., and is now a groceryman. He was City Councilman two terms 1898-1902. Issue:

1. Maud Maupin; married Edward B. (Bush) Wallace. (See Part IV, Chap. 12, Sec. 1.) Issue:
    1. Edgar Wallace.
    2. Park Wallace.
2. Fannie Maupin; married J. B. Wortham, issue:
    1. Jesse Wortham.
3. Winnie Maupin; married E. J. Clark, issue:
    1. Morris Clark.
    2. Mary Elizabeth Clark.
4. Malcom Miller Maupin; married Lizzie Edwards, issue:
    1. Grace Estille Maupin.
5. Sudie Maupin; married D. R. Riddell, issue:
    1. Malcom Riddell.
    2. Bertram Riddell.
6. John G. Carlise Maupin; single.

Section 4. Susan Frances Maupin; married William Christopher Todd, no issue.

Section 5. Christopher Harris Maupin, a farmer of Madison County, Ky., married Mary Eliza Wilson. He owns a good farm on the waters of Mudy Creek. Their children:

1. Lenora Maupin; married first Henry Shifflett, and second Seth W. Tudor.
2. Percy Maupin.
3. John Overton Maupin.
4. Sada Susan Maupin.
5. Julian Maupin.
6. Mary Maupin.
7. Amanda Belle Maupin.

Section 6. Cassius C. Maupin; married Sallie Edmonson, issue:

1. Eva Maupin; married James Wilcox, issue:
    1. Warren Wilcox.
2. Robert Maupin; married Anna Todd.
3. William Maupin; married Nancy Johnson nee Brown.
4. Kate Maupin.

Section 7. William Martin Maupin; married Sallie Ellison, issue:

1. Robert Maupin; dead.
2. William Maupin.
3. Annie Maupin.

CHAPTER 7.

JOHN MAUPIN.

(Named in Chapter 5, Section 2.)

Article 1.—John Maupin, a son of Gabriel Maupin and Miss Susannah Bailey his wife, was born in Madison County, Ky.

He went to Fayette County, Ky., and married first Miss Thompson, and second Rachael Thompson. Their children:

Section 1. John Maupin, went to the Indian Territory, and there married Helen —— and died in that country.

Section 2. James Maupin, went to the Indian Territory, and died, was never married.

Section 3. Robert Maupin, enlisted in the Confederate Army, and was killed in battle.

Section 4. —— Maupin, enlisted in the Confederate Army, and was killed in battle.

Section 5. Margaret Maupin; married Robert Trumbo, who owned a splendid farm within three miles of Frankfort, Ky., whereon they lived when Mr. Trumbo died, issue:

1. Andrew Trumbo.
2. Robert Trumbo.

Section 6. Annie Maupin; married Dr. Beshoar, an influential and popular man, and leading citizen of Trinidad, Colorado.

Section 7. Susan Maupin; married William Burns.

Section 8. Frances Maupin; married first Mr. —— Sayers, and they had twelve children. He died and she married, second, Mr. —— Lewis, of New York City. They now live at Raton, New Mexico.

Section 9. Robert Maupin; married Pickett Woodson.

CHAPTER 8.

POLLY MAUPIN

(Named in Chapter 5, Section 6.)

Article 1.—Polly Maupin, a daughter of Gabriel Maupin and Miss Susannah Bailey his wife, was born in Madison County, Ky.

On the 19th day of July 1826, she married Will P. Gilbert, after his death she married second, Mr. —— Hall. Children by her first husband:

Section 1. Sarah Gilbert; married Judge John W. Bourne, at one time Judge of the Madison County Court, no issue.

Section 2. Susan Gilbert; married Mr. —— Bailey.

Section 3. Rhoda A. Gilbert; (a daughter) married Ben N. Webster, Nov. 17, 1846. (See Chap. 13, Sec. 7-10.) Issue:

1. Ben Webster.
2. Kate Webster; married Willie ——.
3. Mary Webster; married Walter C. Scott, of Lexington, Ky.

Child by second husband:

4. Hall (a daughter.)

CHAPTER 9.

MARGARET HARRIS MAUPIN.

(Named in Chapter 5, Section 9.)

Article 1.—Margaret Harris Maupin, a daughter of Gabriel Maupin and Miss Susannah Bailey his wife, was born in Madison County, Kentucky.

On the 30th of June 1814, she married Joshua Shifflett. Their children:

Section 1. Allen Shifflett; married Nancy Cooper.

Section 2. Sidney Shifflett; married —— Dillon.

Section 3. John Shifflett.

Section 4. Margaret Shifflett; married Jacob Hughes, a tanner.

Section 5. Mary Shifflett; married William Rubles.

Section 6. Susan Shifflett; married William H. Smith, issue:
1. Claude Smith; married —— ——
2. William H. Smith, Jr., married —— ——

CHAPTER 10.

SUSAN MAUPIN.

(Named in Chapter 5, Section 11.)

Article 1.—Susan Maupin, a daughter of Gabriel Maupin and Miss Susannah Bailey, his wife, was born in Madison County, Ky.

She married Mr. —— Stifner, of Fayette County, Ky. Mr. Stifner was the first engineer to conduct the first train of cars over the first railroad, between Frankfort and Lexington, and probably the first railroad built in the state, and was the engineer on that road for a long term of years. They are both dead now, but Mrs. Stifner died only a year or so ago, at Ludlow, Kentucky. Children:

Section 1. John Stifner, machinist for the Louisville and Nashville Railroad at Covington, Ky., and a very useful man, who stands high in his profession.

Section 2. Harry Stifner.

Section 3. Fanny Stifner; married Mr. —— Lockwood, of Ludlow, Kentucky.

CHAPTER 11.

DANIEL MAUPIN.

(Named in Chapter 3, Section 4.)

Article 1.—Daniel Maupin, a son of Daniel Maupin, senior, of Albemarle County, Va., and Margaret Via his wife, and named in his father's will which was probated in 1788, was born in said County of Albemarle about 1727-9.

He married Elizabeth Dabney, a daughter of Cornelius Dabney, senior, and Sarah Jennings his wife. (See Part III, Chap. 15, Article 2, Sec. 5.) And known as "Cuff" Daniel Maupin, and he came from Albemarle County, Va., to Madison County, Ky., as early as 1785. He was a member of a company raised in Albemarle County, Va., in 1758, to guard and defend the frontier against the Indians. He was a witness to the will of Robert Harris, senior, probated in Albemarle County, Va., Aug. 8, 1765.

The said Daniel Maupin, prior to 1798, came from Albemarle County, Va., to Madison County, Ky., and settled on the waters of Muddy Creek, where he acquired land, and where he lived till his death in 1803. On March 5, 1798, (D. page 381) Green Clay conveyed to him 50 acres of land on said creek, adjoining Moseley's survey.

He was styled on the record, as "Daniel Maupin, senior," of Madison County, Ky., and another Daniel Maupin whose wife was Betsy, was styled on the record as "Daniel Maupin, junior," until the death of Daniel Maupin, senior, after which occurence, the word 'junior" did not follow his name on the record. There was still another Daniel Maupin, who at one time lived on Paint Lick Creek, whose wife was named Susannah.

The name of the wife of said Daniel Maupin, senior, of Madison County, Ky., nowhere appears on the Court records of said County, at least a thorough search has been made without avail. She evidently was dead before he made his will, but she died in Madison County, Ky. He not only had children, but at least one grand-child as shown in his will.

On Oct. 4, 1801, (E. page 260) the said Daniel Maupin, senior, of Madison County, Ky., by deed gave to his son John Maupin, fifty pounds he collected for him that was in the hands of Bernard Brown of Albemarle County, Va., who was his acting attorney at law, and other personal property. He died in 1803, as aforesaid, having first made and published his last will and testament, bearing date Oct. 11, 1802, probated Dec. 5, 1803, and recorded in Will Book A, page 277, by which he appoints his friend John Harris executor. The will is in the following words and figures:

"Daniel Maupin's Will."

"I Daniel Maupin, of Madison County, Ky., being of sound mind, though weak in body, considering the certainty of death, and the uncertainty of when it may happen, have thought fit to make this my last will and testament, in the following manner, that is to say: I give and bequeath unto Margaret Burnett, the fifty acres of land that I live on, as long as she lives and is single, and at her death or marriage I bequeath it to her daughter, Lucy Burnett to her sole use and bequest, and my will further is, that all and every part of my personal estate should be sold and equally divided amongst my five daughters or their heirs, viz: Sarah Stephenson, Margaret Burnett,

Elizabeth Ray's children, Mary Goulding and Fanny Lynch. After my debts are paid, which is to be paid out of my personal estate, and the sum of twelve pounds due from me to Lucy Burnett, is to be paid her out of the same, with my funeral expense by my executor hereafter named. And that no misunderstanding may take place in the construction of this will, it is to be understood that Elizabeth Ray's two children are to stand as one legatee in the above distribution, and finally I resign my soul to God trusting through the mediation of His Son to enjoy eternal life, and I hereby appoint my friend John Harris to be my executor on this will.

In testimony of which I have hereunto set my hand and affixed my seal this eleventh day of October, one thousand eight hundred and two. DANIEL MAUPIN (L S.)

Attest:
Anna Harris.
William Harris.
James X Oldham.

Codical made to the above will this 9th day of Feb. one thousand eight hundred and three, hereby altering the above bequest respecting my land, and do hereby will it to my daughter Margaret Curby, as long as she lives, and then as above directed to the sole use and bequest of her daughter Lucy Burnett.

As witness my hand and seal this ninth day of Feb. eighteen hundred and three. DANIEL MAUPIN. (L S.)

Test:
Charles Neal.
Anna Neal.

At a Court held for Madison County, on Monday the 5th day of December 1803, this will was proved to be the last will and testament of Daniel Maupin, deceased, by the oaths of Anna Harris, William Harris and James Oldham, witnesses thereto, and also the amendment to said will was proved to be act and deed of the said Daniel Maupin, deceased, by the oath of Charles Neale and Anna Neal, witnesses thereto, and ordered to be recorded.

Attest: WILL IRVINE, Clerk."

The fifty acres of land deeded to him by General Green Clay, was near the present village of Crooksville, where he made his home, and where he died. In the following sections are set forth the children of Daniel Maupin and Elizabeth Dabney his wife, towit:

Section 1. Daniel Maupin, was born in Albemarle County, Va., Dec. 6, 1760. where he was married to Elizabeth Gentry. She died in Madison County, Ky., June 10, 1804, having been born Dec. 27, 1766, and June 16, 1805, Daniel Maupin married his second wife Margaret McWilliams in Madison County, Ky. See fuller history of Daniel Maupin in Chapter 12.

Section 2. John Maupin, born in Albemarle County, Va. In Madison County, Ky., Oct. 4, 1801, his father Daniel Maupin senior, gave him fifty pounds, and other personal property. (See Chap. 1, Article 3, Sections 1-2.) He came from Albemarle Virginia to Madison County, Ky., in an early day as early as 1790, and on Oct. 20, 1795, married in Madison County, Nancy Collins, daughter of Thomas Collins and Mary Wallace his wife. (See Part IV, Chap. 20, Section 3.) Thomas Collins also had come from Albemarle and settled on Muddy Creek in Madison, where he lived and died, owning a large tract of land, (embracing the farm lately owned by Christopher Irvine Miller, and now by his grand-sons, Irvine and George Hume) on which Thomas Collins lived. John Maupin and wife

Nancy Collins first settled on a farm on Otter Creek, a few miles north east of Richmond, where they lived till about 1819, when they with their son Thomas Collins and wife Annie (R. Wallace) moved first to Howard thence to Boone County, Mo. March 1, 1809, Samuel Mitchell of Rutherford County, Tenn., by his attorney in fact, Stephen B. White, conveyed to John Maupin 181 acres of land on Otter Creek, adjoining Captain Irvine and others. Sept. 7, 1819, John Maupin and Nancy his wife, conveyed to Mose Bennett 142 acres on Otter Creek, adjoining Hardin Golden, and on Sept. 13, 1819, they conveyed to Hardin Golden 143 acres on same waters on the great road, leading from Richmond to the mouth of Muddy Creek, these conveyances made just before their emigration to Missouri. The Mose Bennett land now owned and occupied as a home by James Noland. In Boone County, Mo., May 10, 1822, John Maupin and Nancy his wife acknowledged a deed conveying to John Williams an heir of Thomas Collins, lands on Muddy Creek, in Madison County, Ky. John Maupin was a witness to the will of Mosias Jones, probated in the Madison County Kentucky Court in 1808. The children of John Maupin and Nancy Collins his wife were:

1. Thomas Collins Maupin, was born in Madison County, Ky., Sept. 2, 1796. He married Sept. 2, 1819, Annie Reid Wallace, a daughter of Michael Wallace, and Jane Bratton his wife. (See Part IV, Chap. 7, Sec. 5.) They emigrated with their parent's family in about 1819, to Missouri, first to Howard and then to Boone County. In Boone County, on the 1st day of May 1822, they made and acknowledged a deed conveying to William Rodes, the said Annie's share in the lands of her deceased father, Michael Wallace, lying adjacent to the town of Richmond, Ky. Thomas C. Maupin died at the residence of his son-in-law, Colonel G. B. Stevenson, in Ysleta, El Paso County, Texas, July 30, 1885, at the age of nearly 89 years. The obituary notice of his death by W. F. Switzer of Washington, D. C., and published Friday, Sept. 5, 1885, in the Missouri Statesman, is in this language:

THOMAS COLLINS MAUPIN.

Obituary—Thomas C. Maupin.

Our older residents will well recollect Thomas C. Maupin, who for many years before his removal to California, and subsequently to Texas, was one of the best known and most popular citizens of Boone County, for during his long residence here, he filled many important public trusts. He was born in Madison County, Ky., Sept. 2, 1796, and died July 30, 1885, at the residence of his son-in-law, Colonel G. B. Stevenson, in Ysleta, El Paso County, Texes, and aged nearly eighty-nine years. Mr. Maupin was happily married in early life in Richmond, Ky., to Miss Annie Reid Wallace, a noble woman, who died Jan. 26, 1880, in

ANNIE REID WALLACE,
Wife of Thomas Collins Maupin.

Vacaville, California, and was buried in the Odd Fellows Cemetery of that place, where the remains of Mr. Maupin will be interred as soon as practicable. Eleven children were born to Mr. Maupin, only one of whom survives, Mrs. G. B. Stevenson, whose faithful offices to the aged patriarch were so tender and constant, that they attracted the admiration and praise of all. When quite young, Mr. Maupin united with the Baptist Church, and his life may be said to have been a Psalm. For sixty three years he believed in the doctrines of the church of his choice, and died ardent in his faith. He was a most charitable man, and his hand was always open to the needy and helpless. His fine social qualities made him popular with all classes, and his strong common sense, aided by a good education, and backed by a moral character, that sustained no blemish, gave him great influence with the people. He occupied different stations of honor while a citizen of Boone County. He was elected Sheriff in 1830, 1844 and 1846, the last time without opposjtion. During his first term and on Dec. 13, 1831, the first legal execution which ever occured in the county, took place, the hanging of Samuel Earls, alias Samuel Samuels, who was taken to the gallows north of Columbia in a cart drawn by a yoke of oxen and driven by Adam, a colored man; the cart, oxen and Adam the property of Mr. Maupin, who superintended the execution. In 1839, he was one of the trustees of Bonne Femme Academy and took great interest in the location of the state university in Columbia, subscribing $200 to secure it. In 1834 and 1836, he was elected to the House of Representatives, and in 1838, to the Senate of the General Assembly, which latter position he resigned in 1840. The El Paso, (Texas) Lone Star, says, that on the day of his funeral and burial a great many friends met at the last home he knew to look for the last time on the grand old man and pay their tribute of respect and love to one who was to them all, an example in love, purity, cheerfulness, integrity and christian faithfulness.

W. F. S.

Mr. Maupin gave $3,000 to Bonne Femme Academy, and it was through his influence that the State University was located at Columbia, Boone County, Mo., where his sons were educated. He was a warm personal friend of Judah P. Benjamin, once at the head of the Louisiana Bar, and was of President Davis' Cabinet. He and his noble wife, in 1850, with their thirteen year old daughter, Annie, emigrated from Boone County, Mo., and went across the plains, with a wagon train to California and settled and made their home in Vacaville, Solana County, where Mrs. Maupin died as stated in the obituary.

Thomas Colins Maupin was the first born of John Maupin and Nancy Collins, and to him and his lovely wife, Annie Reid Wallace, eleven children were born, five of whom died very young. The six who lived to any age, brief accounts are given as follows:

1. Sidney Maupin.

He married Zerilda H. McKinney of Howard County, Mo., in 1849. They lived in Columbia, Mo., until 1850, when they went across the plains to California and settled in Solano County, and afterwards moved to Contra Costa County, where he and three of his children were burned to death by the house in which they were living, and at the time asleep, taking fire in the night, the lower part being consumed almost before waking, wife and one child (a son) were rescued. Several years afterwards the son was run over by a railroad train and killed.

Sidney Maupin was once a merchant of Columbia, Mo. He

was educated for a physician, but never liked the profession. When he lost his life in the fire, he had just finished a very nice house for his family near Mount Diablo, California. He was a highly educated man, quite talented, and a high mason. His mother said of him "he was a true Wallace."

2. Amanda Maupin, born near Columbia, Boone County, Mo., married M. J. Lamme of Warren County, Mo., who was born March 20, 1815, a man of fine business qualifications. He was a large owner in a line of steam boats on the Missouri River, and also in merchantile interests. They went across the plains to California in 1850. His wife Amanda, died of cholera on the plains. Their children were two girls:

1. Laura L. Lamme, born in Nashville, Boone County, Mo., Dec. 22, 1843, was educated in the Mary Atkins Seminary, Benecia, Solano County, California. She married W. B. White, of St. Louis, Mo., March 20, 1871, in St. Louis.

2. Alcis T. Lamme, born in Boone County, Mo., July 16, 1847, was educated in the Mary Atkins Seminary, Benecia, Solano County, California. She married Howard Cunningham of San Francisco, California, Dec. 27, 1874, issue:

1. Emma Cunningham, born and educated in San Francisco.

This whole family were in San Francisco during the terrible earthquake and fire in 1906.

3. Thomas Milton Maupin, born 1831. In 1857, when twenty six years old, he went as an invited guest by General Crab of California to visit Sonoro. There was quite a large party. General Crab had been solicited by his father-in-law, who was at the time Governor of Sonoro, to bring a party of friends gentlemen of good standing to help Americanize the country. Betwen the time of the invitation and the arrival of this party of friends, the Governor aforesaid had been deposed and another placed in power. On the arrival a company of 500 soldiers was sent to meet them and thinking they were being

COL. CEO. B. STEVENSON.

ANNIE MAUPIN,
Wife of Col. Geo. B. Stevenson.

met by a guard of honor, they laid down their arms, and this done, they were driven like convicts into an old church in Corboco, and there allowed to remain three days, then all were taken out and shot.

4. John Christopher Maupin; died when young in Vacaville, Solano County, California, unmarried.

5. Michael Wallace Maupin; died when quite young in Vacaville, Solano County, California, unmarried.

6. Annie Maupin, born near Columbia, Boone County, Mo., Oct. 23, 1837. In 1850 she went with her parents across the plains to California. She was educated in the Mary Atkins Seminary, Benecia, Solano County, California. On the 26th day of November, 1856, she was married to Colonel George B. Stevenson, of Versailles, Woodford County, Ky. He was born Aug. 10, 1830, and died in El Paso, Texas, June 23, 1897. Their home was Ysleta, El Paso County, Texas.

Mrs. Stevenson was living in Velardina Esta de Durango, Mexico, until recently she left on account of the peons, and went to El Paso, Texas. Their children:

1. William Thomas Stevenson, born in Solano County, California, Aug. 30, 1857. He was educated at the Pacific Methodist College, Vacaville, and St. Marys' Military School, Benecia, Solano County, California. He is interested in mines and mining, also an assayor. His residence is in Torrcon, Esta de Durango, Mexico; recent disturbances in Mexico will perhaps cause the removal of his home. On the 3rd day of October, 1879, he was married to Miss Ella Dalton, of Vacaville, Solano County, California. They had three children, viz:

1. Ethel Dalton Stevenson, born in Ysleta, El Paso County, Texas, Nov. 10, 1881, and died there Aug. 30, 1883.

2. Norma D. Stevenson, born in Ysleta, El Paso County, Texas, Oct. 25, 1887.

3. Eva Stevenson, born in San Francisco, California, Oct. 24, 1900.

2. Andy Vincent Stevenson, born in Selveyville, Solano County, California, Dec. 27, 1858. He was educated at the Pacific Methodist College, Vacaville, Solano County, California. He is strictly a rail road man. Agent of the freight department of the Union Pacific Oregon, short line, and the Oregon Railroad and Navigation Company. His residence is Oakland, Califfornia. On the first day of Jan. 1884, he was married to Miss Lola Derby Cross of Oakland, California, June 1, 1884, at Vacaville, Solano County, California. Mr. and Mrs. Stevenson were living in Oakland, California, at the time of the fearful earthquake in 1906, causing an almost complete collapse of the hotel in which they had been boarding for several years in Oakland, from which they rushed, seeking safer quarters. The shock so prostrated Mrs. Stevenson that they fearing on her account to remove into a larger house, yet remain in the quarters they entered when they left the hotel. They had four children:

1. Bush C. Stevenson, born Nov. 6, 1885, in Vacaville; died when five months old, April 3, 1886, in Vacaville.

2. Earle Vincent Stevenson, born in Vacaville, Solano County, California, May 18, 1887.

3. Lola Neville Stevenson, born in El Paso, Texas, Jan. 4, 1893.

4. Frank Ira Stevenson, born in El Paso, Texas, April 10, 1896.

3. George Maupin Stevenson, born in Solano County, California, April 7, 1861. He was educated at the Pacific Meth-

odist College, in Vacaville, Solano County, California. He is owner of brick and cement properties near El Paso, Texas. His vocation is that of a telegrapher, and Wells-Fargo agent. He was in the signal service during the Spanish-American War. He is unmarried.

4. Charles Albert Stevenson, born in Selveyville, Solano County, California, Nov. 8, 1862. He was educated at the Pacific Methodist College in Vacaville, Solano County, California. He is a member of Vacaville Lodge, No. 134 F. & A. M., Vacaville Chapter No. 81. R. A. M. and the Vacaville Commandery No. 38. K. T. and Division No. 195. O. R. T. On the first day of June 1884, he was married to Miss Nora Naomi Long, of Vacaville, Solano County, California. He is a land owner and orchardist in Solano County. His residence is in Vacaville. They had two children:

1. Richard Stevenson, born in Vacaville, Solano County, California, Jan. 1, 1886.

2. Gerster Naomi Stevenson, born in Vacaville, Solano County, California, Nov. 19, 1887.

5. Clara Estelle Stevenson, born in Solano County, California, Sept. 26, 1865, died Jan. 23, 1867.

6. Herbert Elmer Stevenson, born in Vacaville, Solano County, California, July 3, 1871. He was educated in El Paso, Texas, and graduated from Rush Medical College, Illinois, in 1899, and returned and located in El Paso, Texas, where he still lives. He is a surgeon and a physician and was a surgeon in the Spanish-American War. His residence is El Paso, Texas. On the first day of June 1896, he was married to Miss Florence G. Vilas of El Paso, Texas. They had two children:

1. Herbert Vilas Stevenson, born in El Paso, Texas, Dec. 20, 1901; died May 3, 1903.

2. Walter Herbert Stevenson, born Feb. 11, 1904.

7. Fred Elton Stevenson, born in Vacaville, Solano County, California, July 10, 1875. He was educated in El Paso, Texas. He is a stenographer and translator. His present residence is Torreon, Esta de Durango, Mexico. On account of recent disturbances there, he will probably not make his permanent home in Mexico. On the 25 day of Sept. 1901, he was married to Miss Mittie C. Browning, of Armarilla Potter, Texas. They had two children:

1. George Browning Stevenson, born in Armarilla, Texas, July 30, 1903, died in Velardino Esta de Durango, Mexico, July 25, 1905.

2. Florence Stevenson, born in El Paso, Texas, Sept. 22, 1903.

2. Clifton Maupin; married Margaret Woods, a daughter of Anderson Woods and Elizabeth Harris, his wife. (See Part III, Chap. 40, Sec. 2.) Anderson Woods was a pioneer Baptist minister of Boone County, Mo. Their children:

1. Elizabeth Maupin; married William Maupin. They had eight children:

2. Nancy Garland Maupin; married Thomas Western. They had three children, two living and one dead:

3. Amanda M. Maupin; married William Gibson, and he died, and she married secondly, William Jacoby. She had four children, two living and two dead:

4. Susan T. Maupin; died in infancy.

5. Anna Maupin; married firstly Stafford Graham and secondly James Faris. Mr. Faris is in his eighty fourth year, and

still managing his own business. They have a home near Santa Cruz. They have children:

1. Dr. —— Faris. Has been practicing medicine the last year in John Hopkins Hospital having ranked eighth in his graduating class, all under twelve were permitted to remain and practice. He expects to attend the medical convention in Boston. The most prominent physician is greatly interested in him. He is very fond of his chosen profession.

2. Margaret Faris, at home a great comfort to the old folks.

6. Rice Clifton Maupin; died during the war unmarried.

7. Natt W. Maupin; married Fannie Hawkins. They had four children, two living and two dead:

8. James H. Maupin; married Jennie Gose. Had no children.

9. Margaret E. Maupin; married James S. Elzea, issue:

1. Bessie Elzea, a very bright and attractive girl.

3. Sallie Maupin; married Isaac Black. They lived in Howard County, Missouri.

4. Polly Ann Maupin; married Milton G. Maupin, they lived in Howard County, Mo. (See Chapter 12, Sec. 1.)

5. Elizabeth Maupin; married George Gordon of Columbia. Their children:

1. William Gordon.
2. Jane Gordon.
3. John Gordon.
4. Sarah Ann Gordon.
5. Emily Gordon.
6. David Gordon.
7. Jefferson Gordon.
8. Caroline Gordon.

6. John Mills Maupin; married Martha Ryland Harris, daughter of Overton Harris and Mary Rice Woods his wife. (See Part III, Chap. 37, Sec. 3.) Issue:

1. John Overton Maupin, resident of Columbia Boone County, Missouri.

NOTES——GORDON.

Marriages.

Robert Gordon, married Mary Kennedy, June 1, 1791.
Robert Gordon, married Sarah Robertson, April 18, 1805.
Samuel Gordon, married Rachael Herring, Nov. 10, 1790.
James Gordon, married Elizabeth Strocksted, March 8, 1807.
David Gordon, married Jency Boyle, March 2, 1797.
John Gordon, married Viney Duncan, Feb. 12, 1818.

Thomas J. Gordon, married Elzira Harris, Jan. 18, 1827, a daughter of John Harris and Jennie Warren his wife. Elzira died in 1882, and willed her property to Gordon Vivion and Jennie Vivion.

Willis Gordon, married Mary C. Broaddus, Oct. 31, 1833.
William Gordon, maried Parabee Woods, March 4, 1841.

In 1795 Samuel Gordon, senior, conveyed to A. Province 50 acres of land on Paint Lick Creek, and July 6, 1795, he conveyed land on the left hand fork of Maxwells Creek, a branch of Paint Lick to Samuel Gordon, Jr.

In 1813 David Gordon bought of William and Peggy Jarman, 22 acres near Richmond, the same which was alloted to Peggy Jarman of the estate of her father Michael Wallace, deceased. In 1814, he bought of T. T. Lewis land on the Pumpkin Run, branch of Otter Creek and in 1817, A. Lewis' heirs deeded him 100 acres of land on west end of Bond Estill's patent. He was attorney in fact for Thomas C. Maupin (and his wife Annie Reid Wallace) who had moved to Boone County, Mo., in 1819. In 1826, David Gordon and Jane, his wife (nee Jency Boyle), conveyed to A. W. Goodloe, 190 acres of land on Pumpkin Run.

Another David Gordon, died in Madison County, Ky., in 1816; his will of July 2, 1814, was probated July 2, 1816, wife Siler, sons, Jesse Gordon and Allen Gordon.

In 1826, Robert Gordon and wife Sarah, executed a power of attorney to John Harris.

In 1834 Willis Gordon deeded personal property to Thomas J. Gordon.

In 183-- Thomas J. Gordon bought land at a commissioners sale, which he in 1834, conveyed to James E. Miller.

In 1840 John B. Gordon bought 30 acres of land near Richmond on the Richmond and Big Hill Road of Andrew Wallace, and Jane Reid his wife, being the home place of Mr. and Mrs. Wallace, and in 1843 he bought 5¾ acres, conveyed to him by commissioner for Andrew Wallace.

Section 3. Sarah Maupin, she married James Stephenson in Madison County, Ky., Jan. 27, 1792, and was a devisee of her father's will probated in 1803.

Section 4. Margaret Maupin; married first in Albemarle County, Va., Mr. Burnett. They had one child:

1. Lucy Burnett, mentioned in the will of her grand-father, Daniel Maupin, senior, of Madison County, Ky.

Mr. Burnett having died, the said Margaret married the second time in Madison County, Ky., George Kirby (spelled in the will Curby.) On the 13, day of Sept. 1815, the said George Kirby and Peggy his wife, and the said Lucy Burnett, by an instrument of writing of record, empowered Henry Banta to transact their business, and more especially and particularly to attend to their claim in and to the tract of fifty acres of land on Muddy Creek, deeded to Daniel Maupin by Green Clay and which was Daniel Maupin's home when he died in 1803. (located near the present village of Crooksville.)

On the 31st day of August, 1821, Henry Banta and his wife Wilmoth conveyed this same land, Daniel Maupin's old homestead to Nicholas Hocker. The boundary recited in the deed as, "beginning at the north east corner of Robert Moseley's survey, etc."

Section 5. Elizabeth Maupin; married in Albemarle County, Va., Robert Rea, a son of Samuel Rea and Jean Maupin his wife. (See Chap. 3, Sec. 9.) They lived in the Beaver Creek neighborhood in Albemarle, where Mr. Rea died in 1831. The said Elizabeth was a devisee under the will of her father, Daniel Maupin, probated in Madison County, Ky., in 1803.

Section 6. Mary Maupin; married William Goulding in Madison County, Ky., April 9, 1795. She died and Mr. Goulding married again and he lived till near the beginning of the Civil War, and died at the advanced age of one hundred and eight years. He built, tradition says, at the old town Milford, the first court house that was ever erected in Madison County, Ky. Mary Goulding was a devisee of the will of her father, Daniel Maupin, probated in Madison County, Ky., in 1803.

Section 7. Fannie Maupin; married David Lynch in Madison County, Ky., Feb. 12, 1793. She was a devisee of the will of her father Daniel Maupin, probated in Madison County, Ky., in 1803.

Section 8. Cornelius Maupin. A letter from J. L. Bishop esq, attorney at law, of Selma, Alabama states that he married Ann Bratton. One Cornelius Maupin, acquired lands and settled in Madison County, Ky., on the waters of Otter Creek, near the present city of Richmond, he also owned lands on the waters of Green River. On March 5, 1793, Peter Taylor and Nancy his wife, conveyed to him 56 acres of land on a branch of Otter Creek, adjoining the lands of Richard Calloway, James Estill, deceased, Hoy, Briscoe, etc. Nov. 9, 1807, Cornelius Maupin and his wife, Ann conveyed to Parmenas Briscoe land on Pitman or Sinking Creek, a branch of Green River witnessed by Peter Woods, John Grudgett and Jer. Shropshire. Dec. 13, 1802, he and his wife Ann, conveyed to Delaney Miller, land on Otter Creek. March 2, 1790, on the motion of Cornelius Maupin his ear mark, a crop and slit in the right ear, and a hole in the left, is ordered to be recorded. Whether the party to these transactions, Cornelius Maupin was the subject of this section, or the subject of section three of Chapter four, the writer is not advised. According to Col. Charles A. R. Woods, a daughter, viz:

1. Margaret Maupin; married David Woods. (See Part II, Chap. 2, Chap. 49, Sec. 1 and Chap. 4, Sec. 3, of this part.)

Section 9. Thomas Maupin; married first Elizabeth Michie, and second Margaret Burnsides. History of whom will be found in Chap. 2, B.

Note:—Descendants of Daniel Maupin and Margaret Via his wife, who enlisted in Albemarle County, Va., and served in the Confederate Army, in the Civil War:

1. Carson Maupin.
2. Rice Maupin.
3. Gabriel Maupin.
4. J. R. Maupin.
5. John Rice Maupin.
6. David Maupin.
7. C. P. Maupin.
8. James H. Maupin.
9. Gabriel O. Maupin.
10. B. T. Maupin.
11. John D. Maupin.
12. G. N. Maupin.
13. Thomas R. Maupin.
14. B. P. Maupin.
15. Horace Maupin.
16. John W. Via.
17. C. E. Via.
18. M. P. Via.
19. John Wood.
20. Thomas Wood.
21. T. J. Maupin.
22. T. Snow.
23. P. Snow.
24. Skidmore Wood.
25. Clifton Wood.
26. N. J. Maupin.

Descendants of John Maupin (and Frances Dabney), a son of Daniel Maupin and Margaret Via, who were Confederate soldiers:

1. Tazewell Brown.
2. James D. Brown.

3. Allen Henry Brown.
4. William A. Brown.
5. Bernard Brown.
6. Ira Harris.
7. William Harris.
8. Isaac Maupin.
9. William B. Maupin.
10. William D. Jarman.
11. John L. Jarman.
12. William H. Terrill.

CHAPTER 12.

DANIEL MAUPIN.

(Named in Chapter 11, Section 1.)

Article 1.—Daniel Maupin, a son of Daniel Maupin and Elizabeth Dabney his wife, was born in Albemarle County, Va., Dec. 6, 1760, he died in Madison County, Ky., Aug. 29, 1832, and was known as "Tough" Daniel Maupin.

He first married in Virginia Elizabeth (Betsy) Gentry, who was born in Albemarle County, Va., Dec. 27, 1766, and she died in Madison County, Ky., June 10, 1804, and on the 16th day of June 1805, said Daniel Maupin married the second time, Margaret McWilliams, this marriage occurring in Madison County, Ky. She was born in Virginia Feb. 28, 1781, and died in Madison County, Ky., May — 1865.

Daniel Maupin was a soldier in the Revolutionary Army, and was with General Washington during that dreadful winter of 1778 at Valley Forge, then being in his eighteenth year, and was with him at the surrender of Lord Cornwallis at Yorktown in 1781, his name was on the pension list for Revolutionary service. The following is a copy from the Madison County Court Order Book:

"August 13, 1853. The Declaration of Margaret Maupin, widow of Daniel Maupin, deceased. Revolutionary Pensioner of the United States, made for the purpose of obtaining the benefit of the act of Congress passed and approved the 3rd of Feb. 1853, and any other act of Congress was produced, sworn to, and subscribed, in open Court, by said Margaret Maupin, and ordered to be certified."

"It is hereby ordered to be certified that satisfactory evidence has this day been presented to the Court by the oaths of Leland D. Maupin and William R. Letcher, two credible and disinterested persons that Daniel Maupin, deceased, of said county, a Revolutionary pensioner and for whose service in the Revolutionary War his widow Margaret Maupin drew what was due her at the time of his death some time after he died. That the said Daniel Maupin died in the County of Madison and State of Kentucky, on the twenty ninth day of August in the year eighteen hundred and thirty two, leaving the applicant, the said Margaret Maupin, his widow, who still remains his widow having never married again."

After the war, he with his wife Betsy and children then born, left Albemarle County, Va., as early as 1785, and emigrated to Madison County, Ky., where he settled and lived only a few miles from Richmond, on what is now the Big Hill pike, near the present residence of Thomas D. Chenault, senior, and near same he and his first wife Betsy, and second wife Margaret, were buried. He acquired considerable property in said county on Muddy Creek, Little Muddy Creek, Otter Creek, Silver Creek, and Harts Fork.

On Aug. 12, 1803, (E page 520) Daniel Maupin, Junior, of Madison County, Ky., made to Daniel Maupin of Albemarle County, Va., "saddler," a power of attorney to deed to Chapman Maupin land claimed by Daniel Maupin (Junior) as assignee of Samuel Rea, by patent dated Sept. 27, 1793, in Albemarle County, Va., 148 acres, and a small slip of land in said county, between Robert Brown, Junior, and Humphrey Becket, and to receive from Chapman Maupin an assignment on a bond the said Chapman Maupin had on Chapman White for $500.

May 7, 1804, (E page 700) Samuel Estill conveyed to him 120 acres of land on Muddy Creek, close to old Estill Station. Aug. 20, 1807, (F page 454) George Campbell and wife Ann of Williamson County, Tenn., conveyed to him 150 acres of land on Silver Creek adjoining Lindsey Carson, David Moore etc. March 15, 1810, (H page 5) Deed between him and Higgason Grubbs, making division of a 1000 acres of land in Montgomery County, on Cow and Gudgeon Creeks, emptying into the Salt Spring Fork of Licking on the south side above the upper Salt Spring, which they held in equal moiety by deeds from Joel Harris of Albemarle County, Va., having a patent for said 1000 acres May 17, 1809, divided by mutual consent, witnessed by John McWilliams, John C. McWilliams and Garland Maupin. March 10, 1812, (H page 413) Deed to him from Wm. Anderson and Betsy his wife to 150 acres of land on Harts Fork of Silver Creek, being part of a preemption of 1000 acres granted to Daniel Boone etc.

Feb. 6, 1796, (G page 261) Samuel Estill and Jane his wife, conveyed to him 124 acres of land, including plantation on which said Daniel Maupin now (then) lives, on Muddy Creek adjoining Hubbard. Oct. 6, 1814, (K page 386) he and his wife Peggy, conveyed to Wm. Bentley and Anthony W. Rollins four acres of land on Little Muddy Creek including Tan Yard. March 20, 1816, (L page 336) they conveyed to Garland Maupin a part of a 1000 acres of Daniel Boone, assignee of Joseph Hughes on Harts Fork. March 21, 1817, (L page 451) for $1 and love and affection they conveyed to David Crews, 80 acres of land on Silver Creek. Jan. 7, 1817, (M, page 71) as attorney in fact for Joel Harris of Albemarle, deeded to V. Tudor, lands on Otter and Muddy Creeks. Sept. 18, 1819, (O, page 38) made deed to Garland Maupin to 72 acres of land on Harts Fork. March 19, 1823, deed for love, etc., to his son, James Maupin to land on Otter Creek. Jan. 9, 1830. (T, page 139) Deed to James Estill. (X, page 592) Deed to William Bently including Tan Yard.

Aug. 28, 1826. (R page 198.) Agreement between James Dulaney, son of Wiliam Dulaney, and his grand-father Daniel Maupin, as to guardianship.

His will bears date April 3, 1829, was probated Oct. 1, 1832, nd recorded in Will Book E, page 508, in these words and figures:

"Daniel Maupin's Will:"

"In the name of God, amen. I, Daniel Maupin, of the County of Iadison, and State of Kentucky, being aged and infirm in health, but ound in mind and memory, and knowing that my dissolution can e at no great distance of time, do ordain this my last will and tesament: My will and desire is, that my just debts be all paid, which lone, and my funeral expenses also paid, my desire is that my resent beloved wife, Peggy Maupin, have and enjoy the residue of ny estate during her widow-hood, under the limitations or restrictons hereinafter named. If my wife should again marry from that ime, she is to have one third only of my estate during the residue of her life, and after her death, whether she shall marry or not, the vhole of my estate not before divided among my children by my said last wife. If any of my children by my last wife shall marry or leave their mother during her life time my will and desire is hat such child or children, shall have advanced to him or them, what my executors shall think reasonable, considering the extent of ny estate, and doing equal justice among my children, and their mother. The part so advanced to be taken into consideration in he final division. In case I make any advancements to any of my children by my last wife, before my death, the same is to be considered, and as also, I have already advanced unto my sons, Washington Maupin, twelve hundred dollars, and to my daughter, Cynthia, intermarried with Thomas Gates, six hundred dollars, which is also to be considered by my executors as so much in the division as part of their part of the distribution of my estate, among the children of my said last wife.

The children which I had by my first wife, Betsy Maupin, I have done for them what I considered as much as I am able to do, for my last sets. It is my wish therefore, that they have no farther share or portion of my estate.

It is my desire that my estate of every description, be under the direction and superintendence of my executors, and that my beloved wife pursue their advice in its management and keeping it from waste and destruction. I hereby revoke all former wills and do declare this my only last will and testament, and I do hereby constitute and appoint my son, Washington Maupin, my son Leland Maupin, when he arrives at age of twenty one years, and my friend Archibald Woods, Jr., exceutors of this my last will and testament.

In testimony whereof I have hereunto set my hand and seal this third day of April 1829. DANIEL MAUPIN. (Seal.)

Signed, sealed and acknowledged in our presence and we witnessed it, in the presence of the testator, the day it bears date.

Archibald Woods.
W. R. Letcher.
Joseph Barnett, senior.

Kentucky, Madison County, Sct.

I, David Irvine, clerk of the Court aforesaid, do hereby certify that at a County Court held for Madison County on Monday the first day of Oct. 1832, this instrument of writing was produced in open Court, and proved to be the last will and testament of Daniel Maupin, deceased, by the oaths of Archibald Woods, Jr., and William R. Letcher, witnesses thereto, and ordered to be recorded, and the same has been done accordingly.

(Copy) Attest: DAVID IRVINE, Clerk.

The children of Daniel Maupin and Betsy Gentry his first wife, are named in the coming sections:

Section 1. Garland Maupin, was married to Mary Martin, a daughter of William Martin and Winefred Gentry, his wife. (See Part III, Chap. 5, Sec. 4-8.) Children:

GARLAND MAUPIN

1. Milton G. Maupin; married Polly Ann Maupin, a daughter of John Maupin, and Nancy Collins his wife, (See Chap. 11, Sec. 2,) they had no children, but adopted a son, known by the name of George Maupin, who lived in Howard County, Mo. (See Chap. 4, Sec. 6.)

2. James G. Maupin; married first Lucy Ann Simms, a daughter of Elias Simms and Elizabeth Martin his wife. He married a second time Fannie Wilhoit.

Chidren by his first wife:

1. Milton A. Maupin, born in 1844; married Emma Taylor, children:

1. James T. Maupin.
2. Edward H. Maupin.
3. Joseph P. Maupin.
4. John W. Maupin.
5. Milton A. Maupin.
6. Minne L. Maupin.

All of whom reside at Corpus Christie, Texas, with their father, or did several years ago.

7. John H. Maupin; married Abba Turner, have a little son.

8. James Thomas Maupin; married Miss Osborne, no children.

2. Mary E. Maupin, born in 1846; married B. P. Jackson, and did live at Glasgow, Mo.

3. William T. Maupin, born in 1848; married Gabrella Yates, children:

1. Wade Maupin.
2. Nannie Maupin.
3. Lou Maupin.
4. Samuel Maupin.
5. Ralph Maupin.
6. Dale Maupin.

4. John E. Maupin, born in 1850; married Mary Allen, and lived at Middle Grove, Mo.

Children of James G. Maupin and second wife Fannie Wilhoit:

5. Edward G. Maupin; married ——— ——— and lived at Yates, Missouri, issue:

1. James Edward Maupin.

6. Kate Maupin; married Cash Marshall, issue:

1. Lucile Marshall.

3. Garland Maupin; married Sarah Jane Woods. Their children:

1. Addison Maupin.
2. Columbus Maupin.

4. Malinda Maupin; died in Howard County, Mo., Nov. 26, 1849. She married her cousin Daniel Crews, son of David Crews and Elizabeth Maupin his wife, (See Sec. 2) she had eight children (five of whom died in childhood), viz:

1. William H. Crews, was a confederate soldier, and married Mary Elizabeth Maupin his cousin. (See Sec. 19-1.) William H. Crews was a son of Daniel Crews, and Malinda Maupin his wife. He enlisted in the Confederate Army, and served through the Civil War. Their children:

1. William M. Crews; married Florence A. Deatherage. Their children:
   1. Elender Crews.
   2. Evalyn Crews.
2. Robert D. Crews; died single.
3. Joseph B. Crews; married Sarah A. Skinner. Their children:
   1. Margaret Crews; married Arthur Daugherty.
   2. Mary Crews; died single.
   3. Harry M. Crews.
   4. Joseph E. Crews.
   5. Robert L. Crews.
   6. Ida A. Crews.
4. Mary Crews; married H. M. Hackley, no children.
5. Edna Crews; married L. C. Thurman. They left five orphans:
   1. William Thurman.
   2. Edna May Thurman.
   3. Archie Thurman.
   4. Rowland Thurman.
   5. Wayne Thurman.
6. Margaret Crews; married Lynch Thurman. Their children:
   1. Emmetta Thurman.
   2. Mary Lillian Thurman.
   3. Farris Thurman.

2. Evelyn A. Crews, born June 24, 1842, married James Lewallan Bishop Aug. 24, 1863. He was a Federal soldier, and was killed in the streets of Memphis, Tenn., June 24, 1864, by a negro soldier. Their children:

1. James Lewallan Bishop, born Oct. 3, 1864, at the home of Milton Maupin, in Howard County, Mo., and was married Oct. 30, 1889, at Selma, Alabama, to Agnes Wakefield Ware. He is a prominent attorney of that place. Their children:
   1. Jennie Hooper Bishop; dead.
   2. James Lewallan Bishop; dead.
   3. Mary Hooper Bishop.
   4. Evelyn Penn Bishop.

After the death of her husband, Mrs. Evelyn A. Crews Bishop, married Joseph Ellison Harris, son of Major Robert Harris and Jael Ellison his wife, late of Madison County, Ky. (See Part III, Chapter 22.)

3. Mary Ann Crews, born at Trenton, Mo., married Charles W. Bowline, and had several children. They live at Trenton.

4. Malinda Jael (Lillie) Crews; married Frederick L. Reitter. They live at Trenton, Mo., and have children.

5. Mary Crews; died unmarried.

6. Pearl Crews; married Mr. —— Duff. They live at Trenton, Mo., and have children.

7. Joseph Crews; died in infancy.

8. John D. Crews; married Mary Elizabeth Eubanks, and had a son:

1. James D. Crews, junior, lives at Sturgeon, Mo., married Lena Massingale. Their children:

1. Willard Crews.
2. Roger Crews.
3. Carroll Crews.

5. Martha Maupin; married Rev. James Vincent, and died in Boone County, Mo., Aug. 14, 1899. Their children:

1. Garland Vincent; married Mollie Gulley, of Grundy County, Mo. He was killed at Waynewood, Indian Territory. Children:

1. Charles Vincent; married —— —— and they live at Waynewood, Indian Territory.
2. —— Vincent.

2. Grant G. Vincent; married ——— ——— and live in Arkansas. They have children.

3. Belle Vincent; married Mr. —— Davis. Her husband died, leaving her with three children, and they live with her brother, Grant Vincent, in Arkansas.

6. Mary Maupin; married her cousin, James Crews, son of David Crews and Elizabeth Maupin his wife, (See Sec. 2,) and live at Clark, Missouri. They had six children:

1. Lindon Crews.
2. Cas Crews.
3. Jid Crews.
4. —— Crews.
5. —— Crews.
6. —— Crews.

Section 2. Elizabeth Maupin; married David Crews, son of David Crews, and his first wife. David Crews, senior, died in Madison County, Ky., in 1821. Second wife, Mildred. In his will he names his children by his first wife, Mary Newland, Mildred Bell, Jeremiah Crews, Elijah Crews, David Crews, Nancy McQueen, John Crews, deceased and Rody; by his second wife, Andrew Crews, Temple Crews, Anna Crews, Sophia Crews and China Crews." Of the children of Elizabeth Maupin and David Crews, were:

1. David Crews; married Malinda Maupin. (See Sec. 1-4.)
2. James Crews; married Mary Maupin. (See Sec. 1-6.)

Section 3. Patsy Maupin; married William Dinwiddie, Jan. 30, 1800.

Section 4. Susannah Maupin; married David Gentry, July 28, 1804. (See Part III, Chap. 46, Sec. 2.) They went to Missouri, and raised a large family of children.

Section 5. Delilah Maupin; married William Dulaney, May 10, 1804. They went to Missouri. She died July 10, 1814, and he died July 20, 1815. They left these children:

1. James Dulaney.
2. Betsy Dulaney.
3. Jane Dulaney.
4. William Dulaney.

For whom their grand-father, Daniel Maupin, was guardian. (See note at foot of Chap. 14, of Part I.)

Section 6. Polly Maupin; married Richard Cornelison, Oct. 11, 1810.

Section 7. Sally Maupin, born March 17, 1797; married Joseph Dulaney, Feb. 8, 1812, and died in Monroe County, Mo., Sept. 17, 1834, children in part:

1. Daniel Maupin Dulaney; married Jacintha Maupin, daughter of Joel Maupin and Mary Maupin (whose maiden name was Maupin) his wife.
2. William H. Dulaney, born Jan. 9, 1818, in Howard County, Missouri.
3. Garland Maupin Dulaney, born Nov. 8, 1827; married March 21, 1848, to Miss C—— M. Stevens, and lived at Moberley, Randolph County, Mo., and had children.

Section 8. James Maupin; married Elizabeth Banta, Feb. 24, 1820. They finally settled in Missouri.

Section 9. John Maupin; died single, Jan. 31, 1822.

Section 10. Martin Maupin; died July —— 1824.

Section 11. Talitha Maupin; married Jefferson Gates, Jan. 2, 1826.

The children of Daniel Maupin and Margaret McWilliams his second wife, are named in the coming sections numbered 13 to 23, inclusive:

Section 13. Cynthia A. Maupin, was born in Madison County, Ky., June 30, 1806. She married Thomas E. Gates, May 11, 1827; she died Jan. Jan. 24, 1851, leaving one daughter, towit:

1. Bettie Gates; married William F. Elmore, son of James Elmore, of Madison County, Ky., Dec. 27, 1846, they had two sons:
   1. Thomas Elmore, went to Texas, (reported dead.)
   2. James Carroll Elmore, went to Texas, (reported dead.)

Section 14. George Washington Maupin, was born in Madison County, Ky., Dec. 10, 1807, and he married Mary Walker, May 20, 1828, she was born June 18, 1812, and died Feb. 3, 1844, by whom he had ten children; she died in 1844, and George Washington Maupin married the second time, Susan E. Haley, June 17, 1840, who bore him six children.

GEORGE W. MAUPIN.

Washington Maupin, was a most extraordinary man—the country, in his day and generation never produced a shrewder, better business man. He was blessed with a strong mind, well balanced and splendid judgment, with a good physical constitution and other gifts. Although his education was limited, he was simply a power in the land. Apparently, he made money without extraordinary exertion, and accumulated a good estate, owning broad acres of Kentucky blue grass land, and large tracts in the south and elsewhere. Was ever charitable and free in bestowing gifts to poor people, and especially little poor children. He was indeed fond of children, and rarely passed a poor, needy urchin, without giving it a piece of money, in consequence of which the children all liked him, and he was very popular in his scope, which was indeed broad. The hospitality of his home, plain and unassuming was noted. Nearly every one knew, or knew of, Washington Maupin. He had almost a national reputation. Was fond of the hound and the chase, and none knew better how to get the best efforts of his dogs than he, and he procured the finest imported breed of dogs that could be had regardless of price, but he made his sport in the chase profitable. He seemed to have untiring energy, and for endurance, he could not be excelled.

He was at one time elected by the voters of his county to represent them in the Legislature, but that office did not suit his fancy, and he resigned. He lived for a time in his earlier life in the State of Missouri, but preferring his native state returned to Kentucky, and spent his remaining days in Madison County. His whole life was an active one. He died in 1865, thus ending the career of a most noble, generous, kind, charitable, brave, true and respected man. The memory of whom will remain in the mind of each acquaintance of his, as long as one of them survives.

He furnished five gallant sons: Caldwell, Arch, Seth, George and Joel, to the southern cause, in the Civil War, who enlisted in the company (E) of Captain Robert Bruce Terrill, (their cousin) of the 11th Kentucky Cavalry, Colonel D. Waller Chenault, under the command of the noted daring raider, General John H. Morgan. Of whom, Seth and George, were Lieutenants, and Joel, corporal. Lieutenant Seth Maupin fell severly wounded at the battle of Mt. Sterling, Ky., which wound ultimately caused his death, his captain was badly wounded in the same engagement.

Corporal Joel Maupin was wounded in the Green River fight.

At Greasy Creek, Lieutenant General Johnson's Brigade, was cut off by the enemy, from General Morgan's command, and the general called for some young man, to volunteer to perform the dangerous and seemingly almost impossible feat of carrying a message through the lines of the enemy to Johnson, informing him of the situation, and how to act to save himself and men, and the young corporal Joel Maupin, (who was only fifteen or sixteen years of age when he enlisted in the cause) stepped forward and volunteered his services, saying "I am your boy," which offer was accepted by the general, who patted him on the shoulder, and commending him for his daring and bravery, gave him the message, and sent him on the mission of delivering same, with scarcely a ray of hope that he would return alive, but young Maupin, nothing doubting, and undaunted, with as good a horse as the country could produce, presented to him by his father when he entered the army, mounted his fleet stud—well spurred—and with all the swiftness of his charger, dashed through the lines of the enemy, with the enemy's bullets flying around him thick and fast, but most miraculously he went through unhurt, and delivered the message to Johnson, which resulted in the saving of Johnson and his men from being captured. And he returned safely to General Morgan with the news of the accomplishment of his mission and received the praises and plaudits of the General and his whole command for his brave and heroic act. First wife's children:

1. James W. Maupin; died a bachelor.

2. Caldwell C. Maupin; married Dorcas K. Maupin his first cousin. (See Sec. 20-1) He was a gallant confederate soldier. and died soon after the war, issue:

   1. Archibald Maupin; died in infancy.

3. Archibald Maupin; killed on the streets of Richmond, by a shot from a gun, in a fight to which he was not a party, after having made a gallant soldier in the service of the confederacy in the Civil War.

4. Seth W. Maupin; died from the effects of a wound received in battle at Mt. Sterling, during the Civil War, having gallantly served as a soldier of the Southern Confederacy.

5. George W. Maupin, was a brave and gallant soldier in the Confederate Army, served one term as Jailer of Madison County, married Fannie Stivers. His children:

1. Jennings Maupin; married Miss Mattie Turpin.
2. Alexander Maupin; died when a young man, single.
3. William Maupin; married Miss —— Lakes.
4. George W. Maupin; died young.
5. Stone Walker Maupin.
6. Jessamine Maupin; died in infancy.

6. Joel W. Maupin, enlisted when less than sixteen years old in the Confederate Army, and did valiant service till captured on the Ohio raid, and imprisoned; married first Edna Maupin his first cousin, (See Sec. 20-8) issue:

1. Archibald Maupin; married Maud Riddell. (He died.)
2. Walker Maupin.
3. Wallace Maupin.

Joel Maupin, married for his second wife, Lou Davis. They live at Kingston, Madison County, Ky.

7. Cynthia Maupin; died in childhood.
8. Mollie Maupin; died in infancy.
9. Worth Maupin; died in infancy.

Second wife's children:

10. Anna T. Maupin; married her first cousin, Socrates Maupin. (See Sec. 16-2.) Now live in Lafollette, Tenn.
11. Mattie G. Maupin; married Joseph W. Bales, (two terms sheriff of Madison County,) no issue. They now live in Lexington, Ky.
12. Florence Maupin; married Dr. C. J. Bales, issue:
    1. Samuel Worth Bales; dead.
    2. Cathline Bales.

    They now live in Richmond, Ky., Dr. Bales is a member of the Board of Health.
13. Alexander T. Maupin; killed, was never married.
14. Richard W. Maupin; died a bachelor.
15. William Fleming Maupin; died when a youth.

Section 15. Leland D. Maupin, was born July 6, 1809, was a prominent farmer of Madison County, Ky., and represented the County in the State Legislature in 1849. He died May 14, 1868. He was married three times, first to Eliza Broaddus, June 16, 1831, second to Elizabeth Jane Moore, June 15, 1837. and third to Martha R. Hurst. His last wife was an excellent woman; (as was also his other two wives); died in Madison County, Ky., at her son, Julian's Nov. 19,, 1906. Children of his first marriage:

1. John Daniel Maupin; married first Sarah Rayburn, and second Mary R. Walton June 2, 1849, issue of first marriage:
    1. Mary Maupin; married first Mr. —— Cline; killed on railroad. And second Mr. —— Potts.
    2. Emma Maupin; married —— ——.
    3. Leland D. Maupin.
    4. Anna Maupin; married —— ——.

Children by his second marriage to Elizabeth Jane Moore:

2. Brutus Maupin; married Amelia Terrill; died at Harrisville, Missouri.
3. Waller L. Maupin; married Theodocia Rice, issue
    1. Levi Maupin.
    2. Rice Maupin.
    3. Land Maupin.
    4. Charles Maupin.

5. Janie Maupin.
6. Frank Maupin.
4. Leland D. Maupin; married Lizzie B. Moore. Issue:
1. Addie G. Maupin; married J. Walker Covington.
2. to 5. Four children died in infancy. L. D. Maupin and wife live in Madison County, Ky.

Children by his third and last wife, Martha R. Hurst:
5. Jasper Maupin; killed, was never married.
6. Julian Maupin; married Lizzie Hunt. They live in the Elliston precinct, Madison County, Ky. Mr. Maupin is a farmer and trader, issue:
1. Blanch Maupin.
2. John C. Maupin.
3. Amber Maupin.
4. Sarah N. Maupin.
5. William Maupin.
6. Julian H. Maupin.
7. Lizzie Cathleen Maupin.
7. Breckinridge Maupin; married Lucy Terrill. He is a farmer. (See Sec. 17-2-3.) Issue:
1. Jasper L. Maupin.
2. Lavinia Maupin; married Alexander Parrish, issue:
1. John Parkes Parrish.
3. Louisa Maupin.
4. Martha Maupin.
5. Terrill Maupin; dead.
6. Leland Maupin; dead.
7. Daniel Maupin.
8. Cathaline Maupin.

They live near Kingston, Madison County, Ky.
8. Annie Rebecca Maupin; married Owen Walker Hisle, issue:
1. Armer Hisle.
3. Rosa Lee Hisle; dead.
4. David Irvine Hisle.
5. Owen Walker Hisle.

Mrs. Anna Hisle is dead, and her husband married again Miss —— Ford. He and his family live about one mile east of Richmond, Ky. (Since going to press Mr. Hisle has died.)
9. Milton Maupin; died young.
10. Rosa Lee Maupin; died.

Section 16. Daniel C. Maupin, was born Jan. 15, 1811, and died Jan. 16, 1865. He married Nancy J. Walker, Jan. 5, 1831. He was a prominent and highly respected farmer of Madison County, Ky., and had the name of being as clever and honest a man as lived in the County. Their children:

1. Dr. John W. Maupin, a prominent physician and farmer of Madison County, Ky.; married Sarah Campbell. They live on Silver Creek, in Madison County, Ky., issue:
issue:
1. Caldwell Maupin.
2. John Maupin.
3. Nancy Maupin; married Bean Allen.
4. Carrie Maupin; married William Faris.
2. Socrates Maupin, a respectable and popular citizen and farmer of Madison County, Ky., until of recent date, he moved to Lafollette, Tennessee; he married his first cousin, Annie T. Maupin, (See Sec. 14-7) issue:
1. Hattie Maupin; married William West.
2. Annie Maupin; maried Dr. Hugh Bennett Kincaid.

3. Marshall Lee Maupin.
4. Ewing Maupin; married Miss Julia Riddell.
5. Susan May Maupin; married George F. Crawford.
6. Bayard Dabney Maupin.
7. Socrates Maupin, Jr.
8. Kate Thomas Maupin.

3. William King Maupin, was a man of remarkable good sense and sound judgment, and a gentleman in the full meaning of that word, exceedingly conscientious, kind hearted and true. A brave, faithful and intrepid confederate soldier and scout. In 1862, he piloted General E. Kirby Smith's Army, through the Kentucky mountains into Madison County, when the battle of Richmond was fought, in which the first cannon was planted on the farm of his uncle, George Washington Maupin, known as the Hart land, on Hay's Fork. He was captured in Morgan's famous raid into Indiana and Ohio, and lay in prison at Camp Douglas. He died soon after the war, having never married.

4. Sarah Maupin; married Archibald W. Kavanaugh. (See Part VII, Chap. 11, Sec. 3.)

5. Sidney Maupin, was a soldier in the Confederate Army. After the war went to Missouri and married Mrs. Fannie Osborn.

6. Julia Maupin; single.

7. Harriett Maupin; married Caldwell Campbell, issue:
   1. Mary Campbell.
   2. Daisy Campbell; married James Deatherage.
   3. Anderson Campbell, went to Louisville and married.

8. Nancy Maupin.

9. Franklin Maupin; married Ophelia Francis, no issue. Live south of Richmond, Ky., on a farm and is a quiet substantial citizen, attends strictly to his own affairs, and is scrupulously honest.

10. Josephine Maupin; married Preston Beatty, issue:
   1. Horace Beatty.
   2. Frank Beatty.
   3. Cecil Beatty; married Nancy Elkin, have a son.
   4. Lila Beatty.
   5. Harry Beatty.

11. Emma Maupin.

12. Harry Maupin; married in Missouri; live in the state of Texas.

Section 17. Parthenia W. Maupin, was born Aug. 5, 1812; married Wiliam T. Terrill, Nov. 10, 1829, she was a kind hearted, pious christian woman, and well beloved by her kith and kin, and others who knew her. Children:

1. John C. Terrill, was an attorney at the Richmond Bar. An officer in the Confederate Army, during the Civil War, General John H. Morgan's command; died many years ago.

2. William C. Terrill; married Louise Browning, issue:
   1. Lewis C. Terrill; married Dora Hunter, children:
      1. Lewis C. Terrill.
      2. Tempest Terrill.
      3. Grover C. Terrill.
      4. Mary Terrill.
   2. Lucy H. Terrill; married Breckinridge Maupin. (See Section 15-7.)
   3. John Browning Terrill; dead; married Malissa Fisher, issue:
      1. Herbert B. Terrill.

4. Parthenia W. Terrill; dead; married Robert Yates. Children:
1. Mae Yates; married C. E. Clifft.
2. Ethel Yates.
5. William C. Terrill; married Lizzie Duncan, (See Part VII, Chap. 5,) children:
1. Ora Terrill.
2. Bennett H. Young Terrill.
6. Robert Bruce Terrill; married Bessie Devore. Children:
1. Rodes Terrill.
2. J. Browning Terrill.
3. Elizabeth Bales Terrill.
4. Louise Terrill.
5. William Sullivan Terrill.
7. Joe M. Terrill; married first Annie Witt, and second May Witt. Children of fiirst marriage:
1. Gordon Terrill.
2. Ruby Terrill; dead.
3. Infant; ; dead.
Children of second marriage:
1. Annie Witt Terrill.
3 Daniel Maupin Terrill; married first Pattie Francis, (See Part 1 Chap. 13, Sec. 3,) and second Mattie Kavanaugh, (See Part VII, Chap. 5, Sec. 7,) he had no children by his last wife. His first wife's children are:
1. Arthur Terrill; married Nancy Settle.
2. Helen B. Terrill.
3. Ruth C. Terrill; married Bailey Rosson, of Tennessee.
4. Ula Lee Terrill.
5. Johnnie Frances Terrill, a daughter.
4. Captain Robert Bruce Terrill, was Captain of Company E, 11th Kentucky Cavalry, Colonel D. Waller Chenault, General John H. Morgan's command, Confederate Army, Civil War, and was badly wounded in battle at Mt. Sterling, Ky. In 1868, was elected clerk of the Madison Circuit Court, which office he filled for a term of six years. He married Amelia Miller. (See Part I, Chap. 15, Sec. 2.) Their children:
1. Mabel Terrill; married Vernon Riggs of St. Louis, Mo.
2. Ethel Terrill; married Edwin Rugg, of Cincinnati, Ohio.
Captain Terrill was a brave soldier, a polite, elegant gentleman, now living at the confederate veterans home, Pewee Valley, Kentucky.

Section 18. Eliza Ann Maupin, was born June 20, 1814, she married Chisel Gooch, Feb. 18, 1830, children:
1. Arzela Gooch; married —— —— Williams.
2. Cornelius Gooch; married Mahala Jane Golden, Sept. 18, 1855. Has a son:
1. William Gooch.
3. Thomas Gooch.
4. Remus Gooch.
5. Rachel Gooch.
6. Henry Gooch; married —— Woolery, his oldest child saw her great, great grand-father, William Witt.
7. James Gooch.
8. Nancy Gooch.
9. Lucy Gooch.
10. Laura Gooch.

Section 19. William M. Maupin, was born July 16, 1816; married Margaret Ann Stapleton, of Fayette, Mo. They settled in

Glasgow, Mo., in 1856. Mr. Maupin was an extensive trader in live stock, of fine breed. Their children.

1. Robert D. Maupin; married Martha Smith. Their children:
   1. Cleve T. Maupin; married Mary Eliza Roberson, no children.
   2. Bettie Maupin; married Samuel Edwards, issue:
      1. Richard Dale Edwards.
   3. R. Lee Maupin; married Fannie Neale, no children.
   4. Agnes Maupin; married Fred Besgrove, their children:
      1. Frederick Besgrove, twin.
      2. Forest Besgrove, twin.
      3. Anice Besgrove, twin.
      4. Agnes Besgrove, twin.
      5. Keith Besgrove.
      6. Alfra Besgrove.
      7. Rose Besgrove.
   5. Rosa Maupin.
   6. Martha Maupin.
   7. Mary Blanche Maupin.

   The three latter are single, and keep house for their widowered brother, Cleve Maupin.
2. Mary Eliza Maupin; married William H. Crews. (See Sec. 1-4-1.)
3. Joseph C. Maupin; married Alice Major. Their five children:
   1. Margaret S. Maupin.
   2. Major Maupin.
   3. Dorsey Maupin.
   4. Jane Maupin.
   5. Dorcas Maupin.
4. Parthenia Maupin; married William B. Miller. Their three children:
   1. William Yates Miller; married Wilmoth L. Tindel. Their three children:
      1. Mildred Miller.
      2. Paul Tindel Miller.
      3. William Y. Miller.
   2. Annie C. Miller; married W. J. Crews. Their three children:
      1. Elliot Crews.
      2. Odell Crews.
      3. Irvine Crews.
   3. J. Earl Miller; married Obie Watson. Their one child:
      1. Lida Miller.

   W. B. Miller, was a son of James Miller, son of Lewis Miller, whose wife was Miss Yates, natives of Madison County, Ky., but emigrated to Missouri.

Section 20. Thomas Jefferson Maupin, was born May 10, 1819; married Jane W. Lackey, Oct. 23, 1845, was a prosperous farmer and prominent citizen of Madison County, Ky. Their children:

1. Dorcas K. Maupin; married Caldwell C. Maupin, her first cousin. (See Section 14-2.)
2. Mattie Maupin; married Dudley Cohn, (or Chorn.)
3. Alice Maupin; married ——— ———.
4. Susan Maupin; married Dudley Cohn, after the death of her sister, Mattie.
5. Lewis Maupin; married Rosa Dunn.
6. Mary Maupin; married ——— Cohn. (or Chorn.)
7. Margaret Maupin; married Ollie T. Terrill. They live in Garrard County, Ky.

8. Edna Maupin; married Joel W. Maupin, her first cousin, (See Sec. 14-6) she died and Mr. Maupin married again Lou Davis.

Section 21. Nancy Maupin, born Jan. 16, 1822, married James Roberts Aug. 27, 1842, she died May 25, 1881. Their children:

1. Edwin Roberts, was a soldier in the confederate army, he married first Kate Rhodus, issue:
    1. Cleveland Roberts.
2. Elizabeth Roberts; married Humphrey Kindred, children:
    1. James Kindred, went to Missouri and married.
    2. Sallie Kindred, went to Missouri and married.
    3. Charles Kindred.
    4. Nora Kindred, went to Missouri and married.
3. Howard Roberts; died.
4. Margaret Maupin Roberts; died Aug. 14, 1863.
5. Cynthia Roberts, born Aug. 24, 1847. died Feb. 21, 1891; married Charles Moore, issue:
    1. Forest Moore.
6. Thomas Jefferson Roberts; married Mary Davis, children:
    1. Bessie Roberts.
    2. Nannie Roberts.
    3. Mary Roberts.
    4. Parthenia (Thancy) Roberts.
    5. Thomas Jefferson Roberts.
7. Charles Roberts; married Mollie Rhodus, issue:
    1. Roy Roberts.
8. Daniel Roberts; married Georgia Gash. Children:
    1. Claud Roberts.
    2. Jesse Roberts.
    3. Ernest Roberts.
    4. Charles Roberts.
9. Parthenia (Thancy) Roberts; married Hezekiah McKeehan. Children:
    1. Howard McKeehan; died.
    2. John McKeehan.

    They live near Kingston, Madison County, Ky. Mr. McKeehan, is a highly respected citizen of his community.
10. John Roberts; died Dec. 10. 1880.
11. William Roberts; married Lou Davis. Children:
    1. Gracey Roberts.
    2. Jennie Roberts.
    3. James Enos Roberts.

Section 22. Thomas Howard Maupin, born May 15, 1823; married his relative, Elizabeth J. Maupin April 27, 1848, (See Chap. 2-B.) Children:

1. Thomas Green Maupin; married Mary Todd, issue:
    1. Thomas Lee Maupin; married Miss Barclay.
2. Clay S. Maupin.
3. William Maupin; died in infancy.
4. Daniel Maupin; married Joan Gooch, issue: Three girls and a boy.
5. Millard Maupin.
6. Margaret Jane Maupin; married Dr. James McWilliams. Children:
    1. John McWilliams; married Mary Parrish.
    2. Cleve McWilliams; married Thomas Powers.
    3. Jane McWilliams; married Dillard Anderson.
7. Jesse Maupin; married Bettie McWilliams.

Section 23. Mary E. Maupin, born May 18, 182-; died March 29, 1836.

CHAPTER 13.

MARY MAUPIN.

(Named in Chapter 3, Section 8.)

Article 1.—Mary Maupin, a daughter of Daniel Maupin, senior, of Albemarle County, Va., and Margaret Via his wife; married Matthew Mullins, of Goochland County, Va., where they settled, lived and died. (See The Mullins Family of Albemarle, Part VIII, Chapter 14.) .His father was a Welchman.

Matthew Mullins was a sergeant in the Revolutionary Army in Captain William Croghan's Company of the fourth, eighth and 12th, (consolidated) Regiment of Foot, commanded by Colonel James Woods, and he and two sons, hereinafter named were with the Virginia Militia in the French and Indian War in 1758. Their children:

Section 1. William Mullins, served in the French and Indian War in 1758, and in the Revolution, and was killed in battle. He married ——— ——— and left two children:

1. —— Mullins; died in infancy.
2. William Mullins, emigrated to Madison County, Ky., where he married Nancy (or Mary) Woods, June 18, 1801. In about 1812 they emigrated to Missouri and they died there leaving two children:

Section 2. John Mullins, served in the French and Indian war in 1758, died in Virginia unmarried.

Section 3. Gabriel Mullins, was a soldier of the continental army, in the Revolutionary struggle. He married Rachael Ballard, daughter of Francis Ballard, a brother to Bland Ballard, senior, of Shelby County, Ky. They emigrated from Virginia to Madison County, Ky., about 1790, and afterwards moved to, and made their home in Pendleton County, Ky., issue:

1. Stephen Mullins; married Miss ——— Riddell of Pendleton, County, Ky. She died without issue, and Mr. Mullins married his second wife, Miss ——— Thrasher, and had a number of children.
2. Reuben Mullins.
3. Richard Mullins.
4. Fountain Mullins.
5. Mary Mullins; married Peter Rush, emigrated to Indiana and settled in Rush County, where are many of their descendants.
6. Frances Mullins; married Mr. ——— McRay, emigrated to North, Missouri.
7. Tinsley Mullins.
8. Patrick Mullins.
9. Elizabeth Mullins.
10. ——— Mullins.

Section 4. Matthew Mullins, was a private soldier in the Revolutionary Army, enlisted in Albemarle County, Va., in 1780, and was discharged in 1781. He served under Colonels Richardson, Innis and Lindsey, was at the battles of Jamestown, and siege of Yorktown. He married in Virginia, Sarah Clark. They emigrated to Madison County, Ky., in 1791, where he died in 1836, in the 77th year of his age. He received a pension for war service, issue:

1. Lavinia Mullins; married William Hogan of Madison County, Ky. Nine children were born to them.

2. Peggy Mullins; married Mr. —— Richardson. Her husband died leaving her with one child; dead; and she married the second time Calloway Young.

Section 5. Richard Mullins; married in Virginia, Mary Clark, they emigrated to Madison County, Ky., issue:

1. Hudson Mullins; married —— —— and moved to Indiana.

2. Susan Mullins; married Mr. —— Gillispie, and had children, one daughter:

1. Peggy Gillispie; married Mr. —— Boggs, of Madison County, Ky.

His wife died and Richard Mullins, married for his second wife, Susan Woods, a daughter of Adam Woods of Madison County, Ky., Oct. 3, 1797. (See Part II, Chap. 7, Sec. 9.) They emigrated to Missouri and Richard Mullins lost his life by drowning about the year, 1825.

Section 6. Margaret Mullins; married Jeremiah Yancey, of Albemarle County, Va., issue:

1. Charles Yancey; married Miss —— Field, in Virginia, whom he survived and married a second wife —— —— Among his children were:

1. Jeremiah Yancey, Jr.

2. Ralph Yancey.

2. Iechonias Yancey; married a sister to the second wife of his brother, Charles Yancey, and left issue.

3. Robert Yancey; married Miss —— Rozelle. They went to Missouri, where they died, issue:

1. Jeremiah Yancey.

2. Charles Yancey.

3. Clarissa Yancey; married William Rodes, of Virginia. (See Part III, Chap. 3, Section 7, E. 1.)

4. —— Yancey, a daughter.

4. Joel Yancey; married Miss Martha Rodes in Virginia, they emigrated to Barren County, Ky. Joel Yancey was a very cultured man, was state senator from Barren County, Ky., 1816-20, and represented that county in the Lower House of the Kentucky Legislature, 1821-31. (See Part III, Chap. 3.)

5. Mary Yancey; married David Rodes in Albemarle County, Va., and they had five children.

6. Elizabeth Yancey; married John Woods of Virginia and they left children.

Section 7. Jane Mullins; married Benjamin Clark, of Albemarle County, Va. They emigrated to Madison County, Ky., where she died in 1844, in the 90th year of her age, leaving ten children:

1. William Clark; married Catherine Sweeney, of Madison County, Ky. Had three children, one of whom:

1. Susan Clark; married William Wilson of Lexington, Ky., and a son, married Miss Wickliffe of said city.

2. —— Clark.

3. —— Clark.

2. David Clark; married Miss —— Robinson, of Madison County, Ky. They had six children.

3. Sarah Clark; married Samuel McMahon, of Madison County, Ky. They emigrated to Missouri, and they had seven children.

4. Susan B. Clark; married William Woods, of Madison County, Ky., Aug. 13, 1801. (See Part II, Chap. 7, Sec. 1.) They emigrated to Missouri and there left numerous descendants.

5. Elizabeth Clark; married John Martin of Madison County, Ky., and had four sons. She survived her husband, and married again Mr. —— Heathman.

Richard Clark; married Miss Gordon, of Madison County, Ky., and left issue.

7. Lucy Clark; married Thomas S. Bronston, senior, of Madison County, Ky., and they had ten children, among them, towit:

1. Mary Jane Bronston; married first Samuel Black, and second Newton Dale.

2. Samira Bronston; married Dr. James Baker, of Abbeville, District, South Carolina.

1. Sallie Bronston; married Thomas S. Bronston, (Little Tom,) issue:

1. Charles J. Bronston, an eminent and learned lawyer, formerly commonwealth's attorney of the Tenth Judicial District of Kentucky. Now a resident of the City of Lexington, Ky. He was a delegate from Fayette County to the late Constitutional Convention.

4. Lucy Bronston; married David K. Best, formerly lived in Madison County, Ky.

6. Mary Ann Bronston; married William Smith Collins. (See Part VI, Chap. 8, Section 1.)

7. Emma Bronston; married Lewis E. Frances.

8. Henrietta Bronston; married Dr. Robert C. Chenault. (See Section 9-11-8 of this chapter.)

9. Thomas C. Bronston; married Mattie McCreary. (See Part VI, Chapter 2, Section 9, note.)

10. Jacob S. Bronston; married first Sarah Black, (See Part III, Chap. 5, Sec. 4-12) and second, Carrie Evans.

8. Robert Clark; died, unmarried.

9. Mary Clark; married Dudley Webster of Madison County, Ky., and left issue:

1. Ben Webster; married Rhoda A. Gilbert, Nov. 17, 1846. (See Chapter 8, Section 3.)

10. Woodson Clark; married Mary Green, of Madison County, Ky. This family emigrated to Putnam County, Indiana.

Section 8. Mary Mullins; married Lewis Gillispie. They lived in Madison County, Ky. Had no children. She lived to be more than 90 years old.

Section 9. Elizabeth Mullins; married William Chenault in Albemarle County, Va., in 1770. He was a son of Felix Chenault, and Miss D'Aubigne (Dabney) his wife. Felix Chenault was a son of Hugo Chenault. Hugo Chenault was a son of Estienne (or Stephen) Chenault the pioneer, the Chenaults were French Huguenots. William Chenault, was born in 1749, was a Revolutionary soldier in Capt. Henry Terrill's Company of Colonel Josiah Parker's 5th Virginia Regiment of the Continental Army, and he spent the winter of 1778-8, at Valley Forge, was in Washington's march in pursuit of the British in 1778, from Valley Forge through New Jersey to New York City, just after the evacuation of Philadelphia by the enemy. Was in the battles of Stillwater in 1777, before the surrender of Burgoyne at Saratoga, Brandywine and Germantown.

At the close of the war, he settled in Albemarle County, but in the fall of 1786, they emigrated to Madison County, Ky., and settled near where the city of Richmond is, on a farm purchased of Josiah Phelps. He died Dec. 30, 1813. His will bears date July 23, 1803, probated Jan. 3, 1814, in Madison County, Kentucky Court. "A." After locating in Madison County, he placed his membership with the Tates Creek Baptist Church, of which Elder Andrew Tribble, was then pastor, but thereafter removed his membership to the Dreaming Creek, or Mt. Nebo Baptist Church of which Elder Peter Woods was then pastor. His deposition is of record in deed book-D-page 550. He was a signer of the Albemarle Declaration of Independence April 21, 1779.

"A" The executors of his will were his sons, David, William, and Anderson.

They had eleven children, viz:

1. Garland Chenault, born and died in Virginia in infancy.
2. Waller Chenault, born and died in Virginia, in infancy.
3. John Chenault, born and died in Virginia in infancy.
4. David Chenault, born in Albemarle County, Va., Sept. 30, 1771; married in 1793, to Nancy Tribble, daughter of Elder Andrew Tribble. Jonied the Baptist Church at Mt. Nebo, in Madison County, Ky., about two miles north east from Richmond, on a prong of Otter Creek in 1795, and was baptized by Elder Peter Woods. Was ordained to the work of the ministry, and his work commenced during the great revival of 1800-3.

He had only a common school education, but was blessed with a strong intellect, good judgment, and the gift of the Holy Spirit. Was for twenty years a Justice of the Peace of the County, an extensive farmer, and accumulated a considerable fortune. For a period of more than fifty years, he served four churches as pastor, besides preaching much through the mountains of Kentucky, even down to old age. He preached at Unity, Cane Spring Lulbegrud, Log Lick, White Oak Pond, Mt. Taber, Stoner's Branch and Union. He died May 9, 1851, in the faith of God's elect. The fruits of his marriage were ten children:

1. Cabell Chenault, born July 25, 1795; died March 1881, married Emily Mitchell of New Castle, Ky, issue:

1. Robert Chenault; married Josephine Prewitt Cavens of Fayette County, Ky., in 1854, she died in 1872, and he married his second wife, Sallie Prewitt, of Jessamine County, Ky. In 1861, he went South, and joined the confederate army. Issue of the first marriage:

1. John Cabell Chenault, born April 21, 1855, was a country merchant in 1876, educated for the law, in the Law Department of Central University, admitted to the Richmond Bar in 1878, appointed Police Judge of Richmond, Ky., in 1881. Elected the two succeeding terms, elected Judge of the Madison County Court in 1884, re-elected in 1886 and 1890. Was a strong candidate for the Democratic nomination for representative in the Legislature in 1895, but was defeated. In Dec. 1884, he married Eleanor B. Oldham. (See Part VI, Chap. 17, Sec. 7.)

2. Thomas A. Chenault; married Mary Duncan, of Madison County, K . (See Part VII, Chap. 9, Sec. 3-2-2.) He died leaving a widow and children.

3. David Chenault; married Susan Elmore of Mercer County, Ky. He died in Richmond, Ky., leaving a widow (who is now dead) and two children.

4. Daniel M. Chenault, lawyer, Richmond, Ky., married first Ida White, whom he survived and married second, Elizabeth Reid.

5. William Tandy Chenault; married Minnie Turner, of Shelby County, Ky., now living in Jessamine County, Ky.

Issue of second marriage:

6. Emma Chenault; married Eli Bean Evans, of Clark County, Ky., now in New Mexico.

7. Robert Earl Chenault; married Galbreath.

2. Nancy Chenault; married John W. Huguely, of Madison County, Ky., Aug. 30, 1843, they moved to Boyle County, Ky., where they both died, issue:

1. John A. Huguely; married Miss Cromwell, of Lexington, Ky.

2. Cabell Huguely; married Miss —— Roberts, of Boyle County, Ky.

3. Jacob Huguely; married Miss Robinson, of Boyle County, Ky.

3. Elvenie Chenault; married William Shearer, of Madison County, Ky., Dec. 23, 1851; both dead, issue:

1. Nannie Shearer; married O. T. Wallace, of Garrard County, Ky. (See Part IV, Chap. 4, Sec. 1-g.)

2. Ann Shearer; married James Burnsides of Garrard County, Ky.

4. Elizabeth Chenault; died young.

5. Sallie Chenault; died young.

6. David Chenault, was a confederate soldier in Colonel D. Waller Chenault's Regiment, taken prisoner on the Ohio raid, and confined in Camp Douglas, made his escape, recaptured. He married Mary Bullock of Illinois in 1865, and lives on the eastern outskirts of Richmond, Ky., issue:

1. Cabell Chenault; married Ann Crutcher, now living in Tucumcari, New Mexico, owns a big cattle ranch. Farmer and stockman, and interested in the bank.

22. Bessie Chenault; married James Elmore, of Mercer County, Ky., living near Point Leavell, Garrard County, Kentucky.

3. Charles Chenault, at home with his parents, lately moved to Tucumcari, New Mexico.

7. Cabell Chenault, joined the confederate army in 1862; died in the service at Monticello, Ky., was a handsome man, and brave soldier.

8. Anderson Chenault, joined the confederate army at 19 years of age, was captured on General Morgan's Ohio raid, escaped from Camp Douglas, recaptured and tried at Louisville, Ky., as a rebel spy, but was released. In 1866 he married Bettie Fogg, of Woodford County, Ky., and settled down to farming in Madison County, Ky., saved and accumulated a fine estate and died, issue:

1. Agnes Chenault; married Caswell Goff. Had one child, and died and her child died.

2. Samuel Chenault; died.

3. Christopher Fogg Chenault; married Nannie Moberley Hume. (See Part I, Chap. 13, Sec. 7.) He is engaged in farming and other enterprises near Richmond, Ky.

4. Jeptha Chenault, a farmer near Richmond, Ky.

5. Emily Chenault; married Clifton Shropshire, of Fayette County, Ky.

6. Elijah A. Chenault; died.

9. Jeptha Chenault; married in 1874, to Lavinia Estill of Madison County, Ky. (See Part VI, Chap. 14, Sec. 8.) He died leaving issue:

1. Estill C. Chenault; married Brutus J. Clay, of Bourbon County, Ky.

10. Harvey Chenault, a farmer, stockman, trader, etc., of Conway, Ky., died since going to press.

2. Joyce Chenault; married Captain James Munday.

3. David Chenault; married Oct. 25, 1827, Louisa Quisenberry, born Sept. 29, 1811, issue:

1. John Chenault, 1830-96, settled in Dallas County, Texas. Served through the Civil War, in the confederate army.

2. Colby Chenault, 1831—— served with Tennessee troops in the confederate army, in the Civil War.

3. David Chenault, 1833, was a confederate soldier in the Tennessee line during the Civil War.

4. James Chenault, 1834, also a confederate soldier in the Civil War, with Tennessee troops.

5. Harvey Chenault 1837, a confederate soldier in the Civil War, with Tennessee troops.

6. Sallie A. Chenault 1839; married Mr. —— Guthrie.

7. Nancy Chenault, 1844; married Mr. —— Martin.

8. Lucy Chenault 1847; married Mr. —— Barry.

9. Frances Chenault, 1841; married Mr. —— Tyree.

10. Milton Waller Chenault 1849; married and had eight children.

11. Maria Louisa Chenault 1851; married Mr. —— Barry.

12. William Chenault, 1853.

13. Millard Filmore Chenault, 1856.

4. Harvey Chenault, 1802-1843; married March 30, 1826, to Ann McCord Douglas (1810-1891). Mrs. Ann Chenault married secondly Dr. William R. Letcher, Oct. 2, 1850. Issue:

1. David Chenault; (1827-1869) married Pattie Tribble, daughter of Dudley Tribble, senior, of Madison County, Ky., Jan. 31, 1850.

2. Eliza Jane Chenault. (1830-1834.)

3. William Chenault. (1832-1854.)

4.Matilda Chenault; (1835-1884) married John R. Blackwell.

5. Harvey Chenault (1838-1858.)

6. Thomas Douglas Chenault; (1840-19-) married Carlisle Chenault. (See 5-1-5-below and Part III, Chap.)

7. John Chenault. (1842-1843.)

5. Sallie Chenault (1804); married Duke Simpson.

6. William Tandy Chenault (1807); married Virginia Quisenberry, and settled in Montgomery County, Ky., issue:

1. Joel Chenault; married Elizabeth Gay.

2. David Waller Chenault; married Emma Reid.

3. Nancy Chneault; married William Bridgeforth.

4. B. F. Chenault; married Bell Anderson.

5. John Wesley Chenault; married Bettie Robinson.

6. Annie Chenault; married George T. Fox.

7. William Tandy Chenault.

7. Waller Chenault (1809-1843); married Berlinda McRoberts, Nov. 17, 1835. No issue.

8. Anderson Chenault; (1812-18--) married Margaret Kavanaugh Oldham of Madison County, Ky. (See Part VI, Chap. 27.)

9. John Chenault; (1815-1843) unmarried.

10. Nancy Chenault (1819—); marrried Alexander Tribble, Oct. 26, 1843, whom she survived and she married again, H. Clay Broaddus; both died at Richmond, Ky. (See Part VII, Chap. 7, Sec. 1.) No issue by either marriage.

5. William Chenault, (1773-1844) born in Albemarle County, Va., married Susannah Phelps, daughter of Josiah Phelps, of Madison County, Ky. Represented Madison County in the Kentucky Legislature in 1822, issue:

1. Waller Chenault, served in the Kentucky Legislature, in 1848; married Talitha Harris, Oct. 30, 1833. (See Part III, Chap. 48, Section 8,) issue:

1. William O. Chenault; married first Caledonia Miller, May 11, 1856, (see Part I, Chap. 14,) and he married second Lucy Gilbert, no issue of last marriage.

2. Elizabeth F. Chenault; married Joseph Brinker, July 12, 1855.

3. Joseph Chenault, captain in Colonel D. Waller Chenault's company of confederate cavalry. Fell in battle at Horse Shoe Bend in 1863, unmarried.

4. Susannah Chenault; married William (Wagoner) Miller. (See Part I, Chap. 14.)

5. Carlisle Chenault; married Thomas Douglas Chenault. (See 4-6 above.)

6. Christopher D. Chenault; married first Florence Dillingham, whom he survived and married again Sallie Gibson Humphries, of Woodford County, Ky. Now residents of Lexington, Ky. (See Part III, Chap. 48, Sec. 8.)

7. Waller Chenault, was a physician in charge of the Anchorage Insane Asylum. He married Sallie Webb, of New Castle, Ky., died leaving a son:

1. Waller Chenault, a resident of Madison County, Ky.

8. Nancy Chenault; married Dr. George W. Evans. She died and Dr. Evans married Mary Spencer Smith. (See Part II, Chap. 11, Sec. 5, and Part III, Chap. 48, Sec. 8.)

9. Overton Harris Chenault; married Lida McCann, Lexington, Ky. (See Part III, Chap. 48, Sec. 8.)

10. Laura Chenault; married P. H. Eastin of Fayette County, Kentucky.

11. Ella Chenault; married William D. Watts of Fayette County, Ky. (See Part III, Chap. 48, Sec. 8.)

2. Nancy Chenault; married first Samuel B. Taylor, March 15, 1827, and second Reuben Munday, Oct. 31, 1832. The latter was a Colonel in the Federal Army, Civil War.

Issue of the first marriage:

1. Susan Ann Taylor; married James A. Harris of Madison County, Ky., who settled in Lincoln County, Ky., near Stanford. (See Part III, Chap. 31.)

2. Mary Munday; married Dr. ——Bronaugh, issue:

1. Reuben Munday Bronaugh; married —— ——

3. William Chenault; died single. Represented Madison County, in the Lower House of the Kentucky Legislature, in 1840. State Senator 1840-6, Constitutional Convention 1849, Presidential Elector 1849.

4. Josiah Phelps Chenault; married Narcissa Oldham, Oct. 29, 1832. (See Part VI, Chap. 14, Section 4.)

5. Elizabeth Chenault; married Samuel Bennett, Dec. 11, 1834. (See Part III, Chap. 47.)

6. Susan Chenault; married David D. Oldham, Feb, 8, 1837.)See Part VI, Chap. 14, Sec. 1.)

7. David A. Chenault; married Sallie Ann Smith, June 4, 1851, no issue.

6. Mary Chenault; married Thomas Todd, of Madison County, Ky., emigrated to Missouri, and settled in Calloway County, left issue.

7. Jane Chenault; married Josiah Jones, and they lived and died in Madison County, Ky., leaving issue.

8. Elizabeth Chenault; married Christophĕr Hardwick of Henry County, Ky., and both died there, leaving issue.

9. Sarah Chenault; married John Samuels, of Henry County, Ky., and died there without issue.

10. Nancy Chenault; married Thomas Brown, of Henry County, Ky., she died in 1854, leaving ten children.

11. Anderson Chenault, 1788-1854; married first in Henry County, Ky., to Emily Cameron, (1796-1836) leaving eight children. His second wife was Mrs. Nancy Harris, of Madison County, Ky., widow of Overton Harris, Aug. 3, 1837. (See Part III, Chap. 48.) Issue of first marriage:

1. Elizabeth Chenault, 1816-1831.

2. John Samuel Chenault, 1818-18—; died single.

3. Dr. William J. Chenault, 1820-1846. In 1845, he enlisted in the Mexican War, in Captain J. C. Stone's Company of Humphrey Marshall's first Kentucky Cavalry. Died in camp near Port Lavacca, Texas, April 17, 1846.

4. Mary B. Chenault; married Elias Burgin, of Madison County, Ky., Dec. 5, 1839, issue:

1. Elizabeth Burgin; married James P. White.
2. Mary Burgin.
3. Lucy Burgin.
4. Nancy Burgin.
5. William A. Burgin; married Joyce Munday.
6. ——- Burgin; died in infancy.

5. David Waller Chenault; (1826——) married Tabitha Phelps, no issue. Served through the Mexican War as subaltern of Captain J. C. Stone's company, of Colonel Humphrey Marshall's first Kentucky Regiment of volunteer cavalry, in which capacity he displayed marked military talent and ability. After the war he returned to Madison County, Ky., and engaged in farming. In the Civil War, when General Braggs forces were in Kentucky, he was commissioned Colonel, and recruited a full regiment of cavalry from the counties of Madison, Clark and Estill designated first as the seventh,, afterwards the 11th Kentucky volunteer confederate cavalry, under the command of General John H. Morgan. He was killed in battle at Green River Bridge, Kentucky, July 4, 1863.

6. Anderson Tifney Chenault (1829——); married first Ann V. Williams, whom he survived and second, Dec. 31, 1896, Mrs. Pattie Parrish, no issue by either marriage. He represented Madison County in the Kentucky Legislature 1867-9, and 1887-1888.

7. Emily Cameron Chenault, 1832; married Oct. 14, 1847, James Francis Quisenberry, whom she survived, issue:

1. Emily Alice Quisenberry, 1848—; married June 21. 1870, Joseph Addison Hinkle, native of Tennessee, and ex-confederate soldier, was captured at Ft. Donelson, and imprisoned at Camp Douglas. They settled in Louisville, Ky., issue:

1. Emma May Hinkle, 1871; married, 1894, N. F. McDonald, of McKenzie, Tennessee.

2. James Marvin Hinkle, 1873, went to Texas.

3. Lewis Rogers Hinkle, 1880, died in McKenzie, Tenn., in 1887.

2. Anderson Chenault Quisenberry, born Oct. 26, 1850. Compiler of genealogies of the Quisenberry and other families,

married March 1, 1879, Miss Corinna Broomhall, of Springfield, Ohio, born Oct. 3, 1858, issue:

1. Adelaide Corinna Quisenberry, born July 10, 1881.
2. James Francis Quisenberry, born July 10, 1886.
3. Colby Broomhall Quisenberry, born Dec. 16, 1888.
4. Florence Emily Quisenberry, born Jan. 8, 1895.

3. Waller Quisenberry, born Jan. 12, 1853; married Dec. 12, 1894, Emma Lisle, of Clark County, Ky., issue:

1. A daughter, born Sept. 17, 1896.

4. James Francis Quisenberry, Jr., born Jan. 23, 1855; died Feb. 4, 1880; unmarried.

8. Dr. Robert Cameron Chenault (1831-1894); married Henrietta Bronston, (See Section 7) issue:

1. Emily Chenault; married Asa Runyon, whom she survived, with a son and a daughter, she is an M. D., at Richmond, Virginia.
2. Lucy Chenault.
3. Mary Chenault; married Aitchison Alexander Bowmar, of Versailles, Ky., and she has a daughter.
4. Pearl Chenault; married Dr. Silas A. Evans, proprietor of High Oaks Sanitarium at Lexington, Ky., an institution established by her father, Dr. R. C. Chenault.
5. Robert Chenault; single.

Let it be stated that seemingly nearly every one of the numerous branches springing from the first Gabriel Maupin, who landed on American soil, for many generations had a son, Daniel, and many of them a son, Gabriel, and in fact down to the present generation some bear the name Daniel, resulting in several Gabriels and many Daniels, and among them occured frequent intermarriages, the lapse of time, breaks and losses in the family records, and other circumstances, so complicate the lines that at this date it is very doubtful, if an absolute correct trace of all the lines can be followed by any one, unless favored with ample means, time, inclination and a great deal of laborious research and thought. Therefore it is very probable, some errors herein occur. But in the main the families springing from Daniel and his wife Margaret Via, through their children, Daniel, who married Elizabeth Dabney, John, who married Frances Dabney, Mary, who married Matthew Mullins, can be easily traced and it is believed that so far as we have gone into these branches, and dealing with them, the record herein made is substantially correct.

Note: The Ballard Family of Albemarle County, Va.

As early as 1738, Thomas Ballard, obtained a patent for 320 acres of land, near the foot of Piney Mountain. His descendants became numerous, all having large families, occupying farms in the stretch of country between Piney Mountain and Browns Cove. Thomas Ballard, died in 1781. He married —— —— His children were:

1. Thomas Ballard; died in 1804. He married — — . His children were:

1. John Ballard; married Elizabeth Thompson daughter of Roger Thompson. (See Part VIII, Chap. 7.) He died in 1829. Their children were:

1. Edward Ballard; married Elizabeth Gentry daughter of George Gentry, and Elizabeth his wife. They emigrated to Madison County, Ky., and were the parents of:

1. Austin Ballard, late of Madison County, Ky., who married Lucy Martin, daughter of William Martin and Winifred, his wife. (See Part III, Chap. 5, Sec. 4.)

2. John P. Ballard, late of Madison County, Ky., who married Joicy Jane Permilia Ann Sarah Douglas Karr, Nov. 26, 1833.

3. George Ballard, late of Madison County, Ky., who married Lavinia Moberley.

And others.

2. James Bell Ballard; married Fannie Jarman, a daughter of William Jarman and Sarah Maupin his wife. (See Chap. 4.) Their children:

1. Dr. William J. Ballard.
2. John Garrard Ballard.
3. Thomas Houston Ballard.
4. James Dabney Ballard.
5. Edward Powers Ballard.
6. David Nimrod Ballard.
7. Pleasant Palestine Ballard; married Mary Francis, a daughter of Thomas Francis, April 16, 1840, now living in Richmond, Ky., at the age of nearly four and a half score years. In an early day, long before the civil war, held the office of Justice of the Peace, sheriff of the county, States assessor and census-taker during the Civil War. For a number of years was in the United States Internal Revenue Service. Has been a wonderfully popular man in the county, and especially strong in his party, being attached to the Republican party, but now old and feeble. His wife long since dead. (Mr. Ballard recently died, nearly 90 years old.)
8. Tiberius Bell Ballard; married, first, Martha Jane Heatherley, June 18, 1840, and secondly ——— ———
9. Mary Frances Ballard; died young.
10. Elizabeth Catharine (Kirtie) Ballard; married first, Wiliam Harris, and secondly John K. Harris, brother to her first husband, Dec. 29, 1853. She is yet living in Madison County, Ky., staying most of the time with her daughter, Mrs. J. W. Stivers at Kingston.

3. David Ballard.
4. John Ballard.
5. Nicholas Ballard.
6. William Ballard.
7. Wilson Ballard.
8. Elizabeth Ballard; married Pleasant Jarman, son of William Jarman and Sarah Maupin his wife.

2. James Ballard, belonged to the Light Infantry, 1794-1802. He married Ann Rodes, a daughter of David Rodes. He died in 1853. (See Part III, Chap. 3.) Their children were:

1. Garland Ballard.
2. Thomas Ballard.
3. David Ballard.
4. Susan Ballard; married Thomas L. Shelton.
5. Selina Ballard; married Thomas Bohanan.
6. Judith Ballard; married Nimrod Day.
7. Frances Ballard; married Porter Cleveland.
8. Sophia Ballard; married Hudson Oakes.
9. Mary Ballard; married William Thompson. (See Part 8, Chapter 7.)

3. Ann Ballard; married Mr. Bruce.
4. Mary Ballard; married Mr. Davis.
5. Lucy Ballard; married Joseph Harvey.
6. Elizabeth Ballard; married Frost Snow.
7. Martha Ballard; married Thomas Petit.

2. Wiliam Ballard; married Miss Jarman, a daughter of William Jarman, and lived below Mechum's Depot. He was a signer of the Albemarle Declaration of Independence of April 21, 1779. Their son:

1. John P. Ballard, moved to Richmond, Va., and founded the Ballard House, formerly one of the most popular in the place.

3. John Ballard.

4. David Ballard.

5. Bland Ballard; married Frances Shifflett. He died in 1809. Had a family of five sons and ten daughters. He donated the ground on which the old Ivy Creek Methodist Church was built. (The father of the Indian fighter, bearing the same name, Bland, senior, was twice married but the names of his wives are unknown. He was the father of the pioneer hunter, scout and Indian fighter, Captain Bland W. Ballard. His father Bland, senior, was killed by Indians in 1788, at the little Fort on Tick Creek, a few miles east of Shelbyville, his son Benjamin was shot. His son, Captain Bland W. Ballard used his rifle with telling effect, killing a number of the indians, what relation to this subject, Bland, who married Frances Shifflett, we do not know.)

6. Samuel Ballard.

7. Ann Ballard; married Gabriel Maupin. (See Chap. 2.)

8. Frances Ballard.

9. Susan Ballard; married William Petit.

PART VI.

CHAPTER 1.

1. GENEALOGICAL TABLE OF THE OLDHAM FAMILY. 2. EARLY MARRIAGES IN MADISON COUNTY, KY., OF THE OLDHAM NAME GLEANED FROM THE FIRST MARRIAGE REGISTER OF THE COUNTY COURT. 3. ITEMS CONCERNING THE NAME OLDHAM.

—Genealogical Table.

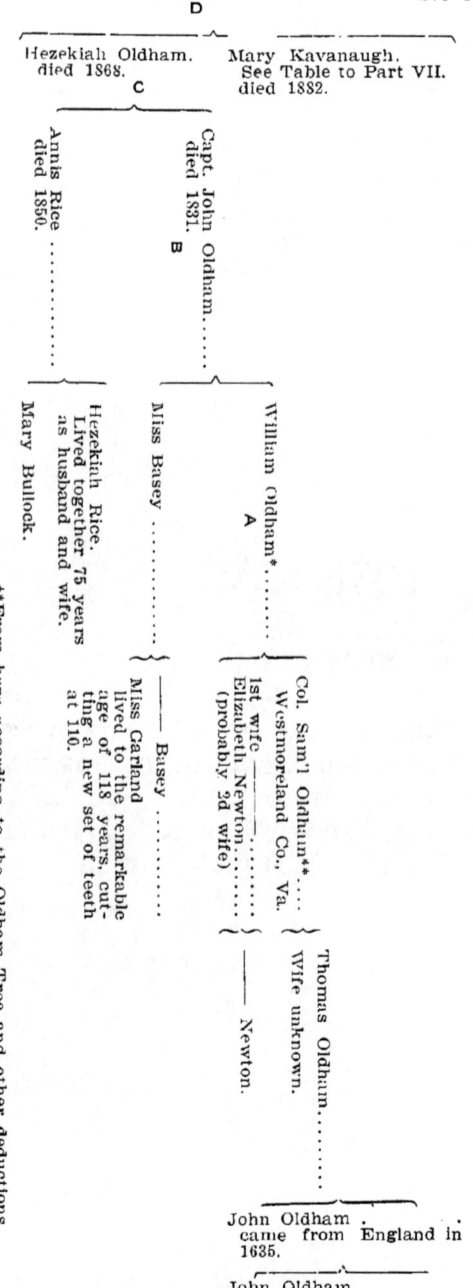

Katherine Oldham
wife of
Wm. Harris Miller.
See Tables to Pts. I & VII

Wm. Kavanaugh Oldham
died 1899.
D

Jacintha Catherine Brown
See Table to Part VIII.
died 1880.

Hezekiah Oldham.
died 1868.
C

Mary Kavanaugh.
See Table to Part VII.
died 1882.

Capt. John Oldham......
died 1831.
B

Annis Rice ....
died 1850.

William Oldham*........
A

Miss Basey ....

Hezekiah Rice.
Lived together 75 years
as husband and wife.

Mary Bullock.

Col. Sam'l Oldham**....
Westmoreland Co., Va.

1st wife ——— ....
Elizabeth Newton.........
(probably 2d wife)

——— Basey ....

Miss Garland
lived to the remarkable
age of 118 years, cut-
ting a new set of teeth
at 110.

Thomas Oldham..........
Wife unknown.

——— Newton.

John Oldham . . .
came from England in
1635.

John Oldham,
of Plymouth, came from
England in 1623.

**From here according to the Oldham Tree and other deductions.
*Traditionary.

A

1. Jesse, m Elizabeth Simpson. Chap. 3.
2. Maj. George. Chap. 2, Sec. 2.
3. Moses, m Mary Rice. Chap. 2, Sec. 3.
4. Conway. Chap. 2, Sec. 4.
5. James. Chap. 2, Sec. 5.
6. Richard, m Ann Pepper. Chap. 6.
7. Captain John, m Annis Rice. Chap. 13b.
8. William. Chap. 2, Sec. 8.
9. Judith, m Fisher R. Bennett. Chap. 2, Sec. 9.
10. Elizabeth, m ——— Pepper. Chap. 2, Sec. 10.
11. Miss, m ——— Battershell. Chap. 2, Sec. 11.

B

1. Abner, m Hannah White. Chap. 14.
2. Absalom, m Polly Challis. Chap. 15.
3. Hezekiah, m Polly Kavanaugh. Chap. 16.
4. Caleb, m 1 Milly Covington, 2 Abigail Moberley. Chap. 31.
5. Polly, m James Grubbs. Chap. 33.
6. Sallie, m 1 Thomas Moberley, 2 Jack Moore. Chap. 34.
7. Nancy, m Jesse Grubbs. Chap. 36.
8. Elizabeth, m William Fisher. Chap. 35.
9. John Rice, m 1 Jane Reid Moberley, 2 Mrs. Ferguson, nee Hedges. Ch. 37.

C

1. Othniel Rice, m Sydonia Noland. Chap. 17.
2. Sallie Ann. Chap. 16, Sec. 2.
3. Ann Rice, m James Noland. Chap. 18.
4. William Kavanaugh—Jacintha Katherine Brown. Chap. 19.
5. Thomas H., m Nancy E. Smith. Chap. 26.
6. Susan Kavanaugh. Chap. 16, Sec. 6.
7. Hannah Woods, m Hyman G. Bush. Chap. 16, Sec. 7.
8. Margaret, m Anderson Chenault. Chap. 27.
9. Charles Kavanaugh, m Susan C. Duncan. Chap. 28.
10. Abner, m Josephine Embry. Chap. 29.
11. Mary Elizabeth, m Captain William Tipton. Chap. 30.
12. Hezekiah. Chap. 16, Sec. 12.

D

1. Ann. Chap. 19, Sec. 1.
2. Mary Kavanaugh, m Col. James P. Eagle. Chap. 20
3. Burlington. Chap. 19, Sec. 3.
4. Katherine, m William H. Miller. Chap. 21.
5. Margaret, m John Doty. Chap. 22.
6. A daughter. Chap. 19, Sec. 6.
7. William Kavanaugh, m Lillian Munroe. Chap. 23.
8. Kie, m Caroline Weeden. Chap. 24.
9. Dr. Ira Brown, m Mary Newland. Chap. 25.

Article 2.—Early Marriages, in Madison County, Ky., gleaned from the first marriage register of the County Court:

Oldham Anna—Harris, William, Feb. 4, 1790.
Oldham Hezekiah—Oldham, Frances, Nov. 26, 1795.
Oldham Moses—White, Ann, Nov. 10, 1796.
Oldham George—Todd, Sarah, Sept. 21, 1797.
Oldham, Samuel—White, Polly, Aug. 8, 1797.
Oldham, Presley—Moore, Elizabeth, June 7, 1798.
Oldham, Presley—Wills, Mary, Feb. 18, 1802.
Oldham, Elizabeth—Harris, Barnabas, —— 19, 1803.
Oldham, Richard—Reid, Patsey, Jan. 26, 1803.
Oldham, James—Merritt, Didamah, Dec. 1, 1803.
Oldham, Abner—White, Hannah, Dec. 1809.
Oldham, William—Gilbert, Sally, Oct. 19, 1809.
Oldham, William—Wilkerson, Annal, June 29, 1812.
Oldham, Hezekiah—Kavanaugh, Polly, Oct. 7, 1813.
Oldham, Caleb—Moberley, Abigail, April 21, 1814.
Oldham, James--Douglas, Nancy, June, 4, 1814.
Oldham, Richard—Mary Ann Park, Sept. 4, 1834.
Oldham, Wade, H—Arthusa Jane Yates, Feb. 20, 1834.
Oldham, Othniel R—Sydney Noland, May 17, 1838.
Oldham, Dawson—Caroline Smith, Nov. 22, 1842.
Oldham, Thomas H—Nancy E. Smith, May 6, 1847.
Oldham, Hiram D—Emily Biggerstaff, Feb. 3, 1848.
Oldham, Thomas—Sarah Harris, Aug. 14, 1849.
Oldham, Wink—Catherine Brown, May 11, 1851.
Oldham, Hezekiah—Jane Tillett, Sept. 21, 1854.
Oldham, Charles K—Susan Duncan, July 31, 1856.
Oldham, Abner—Josie Embry, June 15, 1859.
Oldham, Hezekiah—Eliza Olds, Oct. 20, 1859.
Oldham, Napoleon—Susan Ann E. Prunty, Jan. 23, 1862.
Oldham, J. P.—Jael F. Hume, Dec. 20, 1864.
Oldham, Richard—Minerva Ross, Nov. 9, 1865.
Oldham, Clifton—Hulda F. Scrivner, Feb. 12, 1868.
Oldham, Patsey—Barnes, Jesse, Dec. 9, 1817.
Oldham, John—Floyd, Elizabeth, Oct. 20, 1818.
Oldham, Ursley—Jackson, Hancock, March 8, 1821.
Oldham, Richard—Williams, Sally, Nov. 2, 1824.
Oldham, Hannah—Biggerstaff, John, Aug. 19, 1824.
Oldham, Enoch—Bentley, Harriet, Jan. 20, 1825.
Oldham, William—Moberley, Susan, Oct. 30, 1826.
Oldham, Willa—Sutton, John, Nov. 15, 1827.
Oldham, Frances—Barnes, Turner, Sept. 11, 1828.
Oldham, Armilda—Haley, Frances, Feb. 5, 1829.
Oldham, Patsey—Park, John, April 20, 1830.
Oldham, Sophia—Woods, James, June 17, 1830.
Oldham, Alex R—Reid, Miriam, Sept 15, 1831.
Oldham, John R.—Moberley, Jane, R., Jan. 13, 1831.
Oldham, Milton—Harris, Agnes, M., Feb. 3, 1831.
Oldham, Miriam—Brooks, Jeremiah, V., April 12, 1833.
Oldham, Napoleon—Sally Ann Karr, Nov. 29, 1836.
Oldham, Junius—Mary M. Hisle, Feb. 4, 1868.
Oldham, Joseph F—L. Ann Ellison, Nov. 26, 1868.
Oldham, Charles—Candice Howard, Oct. 12, 1896.
Oldham, Sallie—David G. Martin, May 21, 1874.
Oldham, Rufus—Sallie Knight, April 22, 1894.
Oldham, Ann P—Jonathan Cox, Oct. 2, 1833.
Oldham, Ann—Lawson Talbott, Jan. 3, 1837.

Oldham, Elizabeth—Sanford Feland, Jan. 19, 1837.
Oldham, Mildred—William G. Bush, Nov. 23, 1838.
Oldham, Mary Ann—Richard J. Dejarnatt, Aug. 15, 1839.
Oldham, Miranda—William W. Peacock, Sept. 16, 1840.
Oldham, Malvina—George Shackelford, Oct. 22, 1829.
Oldham, Narcissa—Josiah P. Chenault, Oct. 29, 1832.
Oldham, Sophia—Temple Burgin, Dec. 26, 1836.
Oldham, David—Susannah Chenault, Feb. 8, 1837.
Oldham, Elizabeth—Joel Karr, Feb. 17, 1837.
Oldham, Frances, Ann—Bryant Searcy, Nov. 8, 1837.
Oldham, Eliza E—Josiah G. Lipscomb, Aug. 13, 1844.
Oldham, Sallie Ann—William Arvine, Feb. 13, 1845.
Oldham, Marium—John A. Mize, Nov. 22, 1843.
Oldham, Juliett—Jeremiah Broaddus, Jan. 13, 1848.
Oldham, Hannah—Hyman G. Bush, March 30, 1848.
Oldham, M. A—S. B. Tipton, April 3, 1851.
Oldham, Louisa—Jonathan T. Estill, July 24, 1849.
Oldham, Pauline—Peter Ellis, Jan. 3, 1851.
Oldham, Dorinda—William Willis, Dec. 23, 1851.
Oldham, Polly—Relsy Harlow, Dec. 13, 1820.
Oldham, Ann R—James Noland, Jan. 9, 1837.

Article 3.—Items Concerning the Name Oldham.

Section 1. From the Oldham Daily Standard, published in Oldham, England, of date Wednesday, Nov. 8, 1905. "The story of Oldham." How did it originate? A question from over sea.

"We have received the following letter from Mrs. Kate Oldham Miller, of Richmond, Ky., U. S. A.:—

"If you find it in your power, and convient to do so, will you give me some account of the origin of the name of your town? My ancestors for some generations have lived in the United States of America, but they were of English extraction, and I am endeavoring in a blind sort of way to learn something of the English branch of the family. If you can forward this communication to some one who can probably give me some information about the Oldham family, and if anything is known of the migration of some of them to America, and who they were, I shall esteem it a great favor. Should you prove yourself so kind as to become interested to this extent on my behalf, please lay the blame for your trouble on the name of your thriving town, which persists in getting into the papers on this side of the waters from time to time."

"On enquiries this (Wednesday) morning we learn on the authority of Mr. Samuel Andrew, the well known antiquary that it is merely a matter of conjecture what the origin of the name Oldham is. It was spelt in various ways. "Oldom," being one of the oldest forms. There is no connection between it and the words "Old Hamlet." There can be no doubt Oldham itself supposing it to mean an old hamlet, carries one back into "hams" and "tuns" as seen in the names of Birmingham, Wrexham, Sandringham, and other places. The name "Oldham" leads one to suppose it is of Saxon origin. Nobody can tell exactly what "old" means, except that it was the centre of the old town. History records that the town itself was originally surrounded by seven holy crosses, which showed that the circuit enclosed belonged to an ancient order of knights, the Knights of St. John of Jerusalem. Within these crosses there were certain old privileges of British origin such as "the traces of the open field," which would in itself go to show that Oldham existed before the Saxon Conquest, and therefore might inherit its name from the prefix "old" and the affix "ham" joined together.

Perhaps some of our readers will be able to trace the writers family genealogy."

Section 2. John Oldham, an English Satirical Poet, born at Shipton, Gloucestershire, Aug. 9, 1653; died at Holme Pierpoint, Dec. 8, 1683. He wrote against the Jesuits, and was called the English Juvenal.

Section 3. John Oldham, (first American ancestor) came from England on the Fortune and landed at Plymouth in 1623, and was murdered by the Pequod or Narragansett Indians in the Narragansett Bay, near Block Island, in 1636. His two sons, John aged 12, and Thomas aged 10, at the time they came over from England on the Elizabeth and Ann in 1635, were with him at the time and were held by the Indians as captives, and were given up under the terms of treaty with the Narragansett Indians, made afterwards. (See Chapter 38.)

Section 4. William Oldham. In June 1787, a military expedition under Major (Lt. Colonel) William Oldham upon the waters of the Wabash. He was one of the first Justices of the Peace of the Jefferson County Court. He was commanding a regiment under Governor St. Clair at the time of the Governor's defeat, Nov. 14, 1791, and fell in that battle with the indians. Oldham County, Ky., was named for him.

Section 5. Captain John Oldham.

At the organization of the first Circuit Court of Estill County, Monday June 20, 1808, in the 17th year of the commonwealth the Hon. Samuel McDowell,, Judge in the seat came—Stephen Trigg and John Oldham, Esquires, who severally produced certificates of their qualification as assistant judges of said court, holding commissions from Christopher Greenup, Esquire, Governor of this Commonwealth, and were duly seated and acted as such Judges.

The Clerk Ro. P. Clark holding certificate of his quafification as clerk, signed by Ninevah Edwards, Caleb Wallace and George M. Bibb, Judges of the Court of Appeals, attested by Achillis Sneed, clerk, C. A.

Oct. 19, 1812, John Oldham's Ferry across the Kentucky River near the mouth of Falling Branch, was established.

Captain John Oldham carried the first drove of one thousand head of hogs from Madison County, Ky., over the mountains to South Carolina, herding them every night. He built the first brick dwelling house in Estill County.

Section 6. Absalom Oldham, was the first sheriff of Estill County, his commission from the Governor bearing date March 17, 1808.

Section 7. Hezekiah Oldham, at February term 1810, of the Estill County Court, was appointed third inspector of hemp, flour and tobacco, at Water's inspection. Hezekiah Oldham at the solicitation of Major McClannahan of the Richmond branch of the old Northern Bank of Kentucky, went from Richmond, Ky., to Louisville with wagons and teams and a negro servant and hauled thousands of dollars of gold, two wagon loads, with goods and gold from Louisville to the Richmond branch of said bank, and there safely delivered the gold, this occured way back in an early day; before the day of railroads, when transports were by wagons and team, the country sparsley settled.

It was indeed a hazardous undertaking. The bank officials at Louisville calling aside Major McClannahan, said "You are taking a murderous risk, it cannot be possible that you mean to trust this gold without guard through one hundred and twenty miles of the country, much of the road running through a wild unsettled wilderness in the hands of this one white man, and his negro slave. McClannah laughingly replied, "We will risk it, there is nothing between here and Richmond that can tempt, corrupt or overpower that man, he will not be turned from the integrity of his purpose, and will defend the last dollar with his life. On the way the precious load was left in apparent carelessness, though the secret eye of Mr. Oldham was never off of it, and no one suspected otherwise than that he was carrying a load of ordinary goods or provisions to the interior as was common in those days.

Section 8. Zerah Oldham, on 16th day of Nov., 1815, qualified as constable of Estill County, with Absalom Oldham and Alexander Collins, as his securities.

Section 9. Members of the Kentucky Legislature:

In the House of Representatives:

Absalom B. Oldham, from the County of Estill 1819.
Judge, John P. Oldham, from the County of Jefferson 1828.
Abner Oldham, from the County of Madison 1843. (C)

Section 10. Jesse Oldham.

"Twetty's Fort, or the Little Fort, built March 26, 1775, about five miles from Richmond, 132 feet over one mile south west from Estill's old station in Madison County, Ky., on a small branch of Taylor's Fork (of which no printed accounted was had until the publication of Collin's late Kentucky History.) Deposition of Jesse Oldham on file in suit in the Circuit Court, says that it was built the day after the indian attack, before the break of day, upon Boone and Twetty's company about 100 yeards from Boone's Trace, in square form, about six or seven feet high, of logs, as a protection against surprises or sudden attacks of the indians, was not covered and the wounded bodies of Captain William Twetty and his ward, young Felix Walker, were removed into it, and there nursed.

On the second day after it was built Capt. Twetty, who was shot in both knees, died and was buried in the fort, and the company remained to nurse young Walker until April 1, (1775) and part of them probably until April 6, (1775) when he was well enough to be removed to Boonsborough." The fort was never finished, nor again occupied as a fort, but allowed to rot down and disappear. For six years, was one of the best known and most noted localities in what is now Madison County.

Section 11. Office of Ro. L. Mitchell, clerk Superior Court, Caswell County.

Yanceyville, N. C., Jan. 10, 1906.

Dear Sir:—Yours to hand, I find only three Oldhams names mentioned on our records, Elizabeth Oldham, wife of Jesse Oldham, who had property willed her by Mary Simpson in 1798. Susannah Oldham, who had property willed her by Mayfield Hensley in 1801, and Mary Oldham's children willed property by John Rice in 1804. I find where no Oldham willed any property. I hope that the above may be of some service. Sorry I can't give more. I am yours truly,

R. L. Mitchell, Clerk.

Section 12. Clerk's Office Circuit Court, Prince William County, E. Nelson, Clerk.

Manassas, Va., Jan. 15, 1906.

Dear Sir:—Yours received, and after a careful examination I am unable to give you but little information. I find in 1770, Dec. 5, Wiliam Oldham, conveyed to James Tyler, a tract of land in this

County, 109 acres. In 1762, William Oldham conveyed to Foushee, a tract of land in same County, and the name of William Oldham is the only one I find on our records. I am sorry I can do no better for you, but the war played havoc with our record. Yours truly,

E. Nelson."

Section 13. Office of Fanquier Circuit Court, John R. Turner, Clerk, A. R. Bartenstien, Deputy Clerk.

Warrenton, Va., Jan. 9, 1906.

W. H. Miller, Esquire.

Sir: Your letter of the 6th inst., at hand. This County's Records commence in 1759, and I suppose that the name Oldham was an English one, who left here prior to the cutting off of the County, from Prince William County. A. R. Bartenstien.

Section 14. Major William Oldham, born near Brookstown, in Madison County, Ky., in 1802. (See Chap. 13 a Section 1.) He emigrated to Texas in the early thirties, and bought a Mexican title to a large body of Brazos River bottom land. In 1842 Major Oldham, his relative Thomas Oldham, (See Chap. 39, Sec. 3), and "Big Foot" Wallace (See Part 4, Chap. 1, Art. 3, Sec. 37) were of a company of Texans who chased a very superior force in point of numbers of Mexicans across the Rio Grande into Mexico with the result as graphically told in the sketches set forth in Chapter 13 a, Section 1. He was a Major in the Mexico-Indian-Texan wars.

Section 15. Mary Oldham, maid from England came over in the Fortune Nov. 1621, accompanied by Wybram Panties and Elizabeth Neil. On the Fortune were also, William Bassett, Englishman of Cecil Lecht, accompanied by Roger and Edward Goddard. Bassetts Bans were published first with Mary Butler on the 19th day of March 1611, but she died before the first publication, and he soon found however another mate July 29. (Story of Pilgram Fathers, as stated by themselves page 164.)

The allotsments—The Falls (by lot) of the grounds which came in the Fortune according as their lots were cast March 1623. These 50 acres were located on both sides of Willoughbysbrooke:

Mary Bassett adjoining Rodger, 1 acre.
John Oldham, and others joined with him 10 acres.
Thomas Tilden 3 acres.
Cuthbert Culbertson 6 acres.
Ausbury Anistable, 4 acres.
Richard Warm 5 acres.
Edward Bangs, 4 acres.
Stephen Tracey, 3 acres.
Thomas Clark, 1 acre.
Robert Barbell, 1 acre.
Robert Radcliffe, beyond the swamp and stony ground, 2 acres.

These about James Hobs hole:—Nicholas Snow, Anthony Dix, Martha Pierce, servants, Edward Holmes, Frances Palmer, wife of William Palmer, 1 acre. Jonathan Pratt and Phineas Pratt, 2 acres. These lie on east side of town towards Eel River. (Story of Pilgram Fathers page 388.)

Section 16. John Oldham, discovered the Black Lead mines, of Stonebridge, Conn. (North East, G. and H. R., Vol., 2, page 236.) See Section 3.

Section 17. Richard Oldham, of Cambridge, was here as early as 1650, and was first resident on the north side of the river, and died Dec. 9, 1655. His wife was Martha, daughter of William Eaton of Watertown, by whom he had two sons, Samuel and John. His widow married Thomas Brown Oct. 7, 1656. (Pages His. of Cambridge.) See Chapter 38.

Section 18. The Freeman's Oath was required of every one who desired to become a member of the Colony of Massachusetts. This oath was taken by:

John Oldham, May 1631. (Col. Rec. Vol. 1, page 73-4.)
Richard Oldham, May 7, 1651. (Col Rec. Vol. 4, page 75.)
Samuel Oldham, son of Richard May 7, 1673. (Col. Rec. Vol.-- page 242.)

Section 19. List of counties, towns, etc., bearing the name Oldham, found on Map:

England— Oldham. (City.)
Virginia— Oldhams.. (Town.)
Kentucky— Oldham County.
Oldham. (Town.)
Oldham's Landing, Oldham County.
Ohio— Oldham. (Town.)
Texas— Oldham County.
South Dakota—Oldham. (Town.)

CHAPTER 2.

THE OLDHAM FAMILY.

Article 1.—It is believed that all persons in the colonies prior to the Revolution who bore the name, were of kin, save such as may have acquired the name by adoption.

The family is of an heroic race, old Saxon, as the name implies "Aldholm," litterly "Oldhome." The "Ald," was translated "Old" which was correct, while "holm" for "home" was translated "ham" an old English law term, from which "hamlet" is derived, according to some philologers.

The name came into England with the Saxons more than fourteen hundred years ago, and into this country more than two hundred and eighty years ago, when Captain John Oldham came to the shores of Connecticut.

Mr. Patterson, Professor of Philosophy and President of the State Agricultural College at Lexington, Ky., a philologist, gives as the meaning of the name Oldham as Anglo-Saxon, and means "Oldhome," the Anglo-Saxon for 'home," being "hame," the "e" was dropped in the course of time. Oldhams were on this side of the water as early as 1621. Mary Oldham maid, came over from England in the Fortune in Nov. 1621. John Oldham of Plymouth, New England, came to Plymouth in 1623, and was murdered by the indians in his Shallop, in Narragansett Bay, off the coast of Block Island in 1636.

The family tradition is "that in the early part of the eighteenth century, three Welsh brothers came to America and settled in different sections of the colony of Virginia, branches subsequently running southward, and settling on the Dan and Yadkin Rivers in North Carolina, and some in South Carolina many later on emigrating to Kentucky." This tradition is somewhat at variance with other accounts, Family Trees, etc., of other branches of the Oldham family, running their lineage back to John Oldham, who came from London, England, in 1635, and settled in Virginia. Such early emigrations of course did not prevent subsequent ones. In the last days of the seventeenth and the first days of the eighteenth century a flood of emigrants came into America from England and elsewhere, and settled in the colonies. Many of them stopped for a time in Pennsylvania and more northerly parts, and moved southward to Virginia and other parts of the country.

The impressive family tradition that the three Oldham brothers came and settled in Virginia cannot be easily erased from the minds of our branch of the family, who, when speaking of their ancestors, the same is the uppermost thought with them. "And that the youngest of said brothers was William, who was only a youth ten or twelve years of age when he came, and was raised to maturity by his oldest brother, and that he married Miss Basey, and settled on the Patomac River.

Our parent William K. Oldham ,son of Hezekiah Oldham and Mary Kavanaugh his wife, now deceased, repeatedly said "that all the Oldhams in the United States were kin, for they all sprang from three Oldham brothers, who came to America a long time ago, and that one got separated from the other two, and was lost sight of."

The impressions on the minds of the living members of our branch as to the names of the two brothers of William are vague, and uncertain, some think their names were "John and Edward," some 'John and Richard," some "Edward and Richard," and some "John and Moses."

An extract from Paignes History of Cambridge, kindly furnished by Samuel Oldham, Esquire, of Zanesville, Ohio, reveals one Richard Oldham, in Cambridge as early as 1650, and was first resident on the south side of the River, and died Dec. 9, 1655. His widow whose maiden name was Martha Eaton, married Thomas Brown Oct. 7, 1656. (His children appear in Chapter 38.)

Diligent search, enquiry and investigation has been made, and correspondence had with Court clerks of various counties of Virginia, North Carolina and other places, and with many other persons, without discovering any other Richard Oldham, than Richard of Cambridge, until coming down through the years to the Richard Oldham who was born March 1, 1745, in the section of Prince William County, Va., that was cut off to form the County of Fanquier, and who was a Revolutionary soldier in the North Carolina line, and subsequently settled in what is now Estill County, Ky., where he died in 1834, a pensioner then for Revolutionary service. And next, Richard Oldham, who was also, a Revolutionary soldier, first a Lieutenant, then Captain and then Major, and who died in Madison County, Ky., in 1836, then a pensioner and was known as "Ready Money" Richard Oldham, (See Chap. 4.) And next Major Richard Oldham, (son of Lieutenant, Colonel William Oldahm who fell at at St. Clairs defeat) born in 1787, was Major in the war of 1812, and died in 1835. Since there has been many Richard Oldhams, nor, has any Moses Oldham been found, till the Moses, son of William, of Prince William County, Va., who was a Revolutionary soldier in the North Carolina line, who removed from Caswell County, N. C., to Montgomery County, Tenn., where he was living in 1804. Since there has been several Moses Oldhams.

Tradition in the absence of record evidence is better than nothing, but, at best, is apt to be incomplete, full of error, and not very minute in detail. In the family tradition at least three generations probably have been lost sight of, and omitted from the reckoning.

The Oldham Tree, printed in Chapter 41 sets forth Lieutenant Colonel William Oldham, who fell in the battle of St. Clairs defeat Nov. 4, 1791, (wife Penelops Pope) as a son of John Oldham and Ann Conway his wife, and the said John, as a son of Colonel Samuel Oldham and Elizabeth Newton his wife, of Westmoreland County, Virginia. The tradition held by the descendants of Captain John Oldham, who died in Estill County, Ky., in 1831, is that William Oldham, who lived in Prince William County, Virginia, in 1745, the father of Captain John Oldham, aforesaid was the uncle of Lieutenant Colonel William Oldham, aforesaid.

If the Tree, and the tradition aforesaid be true, which the writer is unable to confute, then beyond any question William Oldham, of Prince William County, aforesaid, the father of Captain John Oldham was a son of Colonel Samuel Oldham and Elizabeth Newton his wife, of Westmoreland County, Va., whose lineage according to the Oldham Tree, runs back to the youth, John Oldham, who was brought from London, England, in the Elizabeth and Ann in 1635, who was a son of John, of Plymouth.

Colonel Samuel Oldham's home was in Westmoreland where he died. Lieutenant William Oldham left Berkeley County, Va., and settled at the Falls of the Ohio in Kentucky; the children of William Oldham of Prince William, moved to Caswell County, North Carolina and part of them, from North Carolina to Kentucky.

It is apparent that several of the Oldham family owned lands in the Counties of Lancaster and Chester, Pennsylvania, some of them lived and died in Chester County, leaving wills. (See Chapter 38.)

The Elizabeth and Ann brought over from England to America in 1635, two youths John Oldham, aged twelve years and Thomas Oldham, aged ten years.

Richard Oldham of Cambridge, Mass., was there as early as 1650, and was most certainly a brother to the youths, John and Thomas. The trio were certainly sons of John Oldham of Plymouth; some histories state that they were. John Oldham of Plymouth in 1629, or 1630, returned to England, and he was in England in 1635, the year said boys were brought over; they would not have been brought at their tender ages, in all probability, if their parents or nearest relative had not been coming or already here.

John Oldham of Plymouth was killed by Indians the next year after the youth's arrival in America, and History states that "his two sons were held captives by the Indians." These two sons were certainly John and Thomas, and he had them in his trading vessel (Shallup) with him, at the time he met his death. If the Tree is correct, the youth John had a son, Thomas, (wife's name probably Rachael Butcher) and this son Thomas Oldham, was the father of Colonel Samuel Oldham, of Westmoreland County, Va., aforesaid. (See Chapter 39 and 41.)

It appears from the records of Prince William County, Va., that one William Oldham owned land in that County prior to 1762, and until 1770; he probably owned the land there, several years prior to the former date. In 1762 he was in said County and conveyed to one Foushee a tract of land in said County, in 1770, he was in said County and surveyed and conveyed to James Tyler, one hundred and nine acres of land in the same County. He may have left Prince William about this latter date. It is probable that his wife had been dead a number of years. Were the records in tact, probably more complete data could be obtained, but the war played havoc with the records of Prince William County, as well as of other Counties of Virginia.

In his application for a pension for service in the Revolutionary war, whilst a resident of Estill County, Ky., Richard Oldham states that "he was born March 1, 1745, in Fauquier County, Va.," but at that date Fauquier County had not been organized, and his birth occured in Prince William, for Fauquier County was carved out of Prince William and her records do not antidate the year 1759. When the application was made, it was Fauquier, and it was a very natural statement for Mr. Oldham to say "he was born in Fauquier." Estill County, Ky., was not established till 1808. Mr. Oldham settled on that soil in 1795, and now we say he settled in Estill County, and call himEstill County Richard Oldham.

William Oldham, of Prince William aforesaid could not have been Lieutenant Colonel William Oldham, mentioned above, who settled at the Falls of the Ohio, for the latter was born June 17, 1753, according to the record in his family Bible held by his widow, after his death, and was only nine years old when the deed was made to Foushee in 1762, and only seventeen years of age when the deed was made to James Tyler in 1770. He was not old enough at either date to legally transact business.

It is hoped that in the near future the clear facts may be brought to light by enquiring minds and many of the present perplexities removed. The wife of William Oldham of Prince William tradition says, was Miss —— Basey, and the children born to them are set forth in the following sections, towit:

Section 1. Jesse Oldham; married Elizabeth Simpson, settled in Caswell County, North Carolina, emigrated from there to Kentucky and settled on Otter Creek, near Boonsborough, in Madison County, where he died in 1814, of whom more is said farther on in this chapter as well as in Chapter 3.

Section 2. Major George Oldham, of Lees Legion. He probably settled in Barnwell District, South Carolina. The state of Virginia granted him 2666 2-3 acres of land, June 16, 1807, for war service.

Section 3. Moses Oldham; married Mary Rice, a sister of John Rice, who died in Caswell County, North Carolina in 1804, and by his will devised property in Tennessee, to thee children of his deceased sister Mary, wife of Moses Oldham then living in Montgomery County, Tennessee. For further history of this subject see Chapter 39.

Section 4. Conway Oldham, was a soldier in the Revolutionary war, and made claim to the United States Congreses for such service. The State of Virginia granted to Conway Oldham 4000 acres of land for services in the Revolution from April 1877, to Nov. 11, 1782. Another Conway Oldham, was second Lieutenant and was killed at Eutaw Springs Sept. 8, 1781. They both served in the Virginia line.

Section 5. James Oldham. The tradition is that he came to Kentucky and settled in what is now Estill County, Ky.

Section 6. Richard Oldham, born March 1, 1745, in what was in 1759 Fauquier County, Va., which County was cut out of Prince William County. He married Ann Pepper in North Carolina, and died in Estill County, Ky., in 1834. Of whom more is said further on in this Chapter as well as in Chapter 6.

Section 7. Captain John Oldham, born Nov. 10, 1757. He married Annis Rice, daughter of Hezekiah Rice and Mary Bullock, in Caswell County, North Carolina, Feb. 24, 1783. He died in Estill County, Ky., Nov. 17, 1831, on the Kentucky River just below the mouth of Drowning Creek. Of whom more is told in this chapter, as well as in Chapter 13 b.

Section 8. William Oldham. The tradition is that he was a soldier of the Revolution, and emigrated to Kentucky and settled at the Falls of the Ohio, and at the first sale of lots of Louisville, was a purchaser, and was prominent in the early separatists conventions held at Danville. If so, there may have been two William Oldhams who settled at the Falls.

Section 9. Judith Oldham. It is said that she married Mr. Bennett in North Carolina.

Note: "One Fisher R. Bennett, wife Judah, acquired lands on the Kentucky River in Madison County, Ky., where they were living in 1806. In Oct. of that year they conveyed sixty acres of land to Carroll Eades of Clark County, Ky., and Fisher R. and Richard Bennett conveyed land to John Bennett.

Notes: In 1799, Sarah Bennett conveyed land to her son, Peter H. Benneet. Her will was probated Oct. 7, 1816, naming her children: 1. Ann Beennett. 2. Sarah Bennett, the wife of Mr. Rice, (their two youngest children being, Taletus Rice, Nancy Rice.) 3. Polly Bennett, wife of Charles Anderson. 4. William Bennett, wife Nancy. 5. Susannah Bennett, wife of Thomas Pussley. 6. Peter H. Bennett. 7. John Bennett (had four children, the oldest, Elizabeth Bennett. (At this date there were two John Bennetts in Madison County, Ky., one of them was a son of the testator, Sarah Bennett.) 8. Nancy Bennett, the wife of Mr. Rayburn. By reference to Chapter 39, it will be seen that Moses Oldham, had a daughter Sallie, wife of Mason Bennett, probably the testatrix Sarah.

In 1803, Elijah Bennett and wife Patsey conveyed land to Thomas Thorpe.

Moses Bennett's will was probated Oct. 2, 1843. He sold home he bought of John Maupin, lies about five miles north east of Richmond, on the great road that leads from Richmond to the mouth of Muddy Creek, and is now owned and occupied by James Noland as a home. His children in the will:

1. Patsey Bennett.
2. Lenuel D. Bennett. Whose son:

   1. Dr. H. J. Bennett, now living near Silver Creek, south west of Richmond on the Lancaster Road.
3. Sophia Bennett, wife of Mr. —— Ross.
4. Sabrnia Bennett, the wife of Dr. Edmund R. McCreary, they were married Nov. 15, 1832, and were the parents of:

   1. Hon. James B. McCreary, formerly Governor of Kentucky, State Legislator, Speaker of the House, United States Congressman, United States Senator, serving on many important Committees. Noted politican and statesman, was also a Major, and promoted Lieutenant Colonel in the Confederate Army in the Civil War. Of whom his men were fond, with whom he would divide his blanket and bread. He married Miss Hughes.
   2. Mattie McCreary; married Thomas C. Bronston. (See Part V, Chap. 13, Sec. 7-7-9.)

Section 10. Elizabeth Oldham, tradition says she married Mr. Pepper, in North Carolina.

Section 11. Miss —— Oldham; married Mr. —— Battershell. "Mr. Thompson B. Oldham, born in 1819, now living with his daughter near Burgin, Ky., says: "When a young man I was travelling through the Mountains of Eastern Kentucky and stopped at a house and the land-lady informed me that she was kin to me, and said her mother Mrs. Battershell, was a sister to my grand-father, which I did not know, but when I returned home I related this to my Aunt Betsy Fisher, and she said "yes, my father had a sister to marry a Battershell, who the family lost sight of, and knew not what had become of them.

The greater part of our branch of the family went from Virginia and settled on the Dan and Yadkin Rivers in North Carolina, principally in Caswell County. They all left that country about the same time, probably about the year 1789. Moses went to Montgomery County, Tenn., Major George, probably to Barnwell District, South Carolina, and the others, save probably, Conway, to Kentucky. A note from the clerk of the Caswell Superior court follows: "Yanceyville, North Carolina July 31, 1906." I hand you herewith a list of all transactions of record in our Court, it seems that the Oldhams all left here about one time. R. L. Mitchell. (Clerk.) The list towit:

"A grant from State Governor, Richard Caswell, to——
George Oldham, 1779.
Jesse Oldham, 1779.
Moses Oldham, 1779.
Richard Oldham, 1782.
George Oldham, 1783.
Richard Oldham, 1783.

"Deed from Jesse Oldham and wife Elizabeth to Tyre Harris, 1783.
George Oldham to John Williams, 1787.
Richard Oldham to George Barker, 1787.
George Oldham to William Bruette, 1788.
Richard Oldham to George Barker, 1789.
Jesse Oldham and wife Elizabeth to Thomas Hornbuckle, 1787.
Jesse Oldham and wife Elizabeth to Thomas Bruette, 1787.
Moses Oldham to Thomas Foster, 1789.
James Oldham to Dudley Ballard, 1787.
Moses Oldham to Daniel Buford, 1791.

"April Court 1810. Then I find a power of attorney that is written as follows: "That we Moses Oldham of Montgomery County, Tenn., husband of Mary Oldham, deceased, sister of John Rice, deceased, George Oldham, Jesse Oldham, Moses Oldham, Joel Oldham, Sallie Bennett and husband, Mason Bennett, Liddy Branthy and husband, Abram Branthy, Conway Oldham and Elisha Oldham, by their father, Moses Oldham, have constituted and appointed Solomon Debow lawful attorney to make choice of certain parcels of land in Tennessee, and elsewhere devised to us by John Rice deceased."

Evidently this family were closely related to the Conway family. So many of them naming a son Conway, would lead one to think so.

Conway, Jesse, Moses, Richard, James and Captain John, enlisted in the Revolutionary army, the four latter from Caswell County, N. C., in the line of said state, and served during the remainder of the war. George was a Major of Lee's Legion. John first served as an ensign and then Captain in 1777, he was in General Gates Command, when defeated at Camden, South Carolina, Aug. 16, 1780, by the British under Cornwallis, in said battle the standard bearer was shot, and Captain Oldham seized the standard and bore it till the defeat of his commander. He was after this placed in the command of General Nathaniel Green, in which he remained till the war closed. He was in the battles of Cowpens Jan. 17, 1781, Guilford

Court House, March 15, 1781, Eutaw Springs, and witnessed the defeat and surrender of Lord Cornwallis at Yorktown. His service stretched over a period of more than four years. Richard was in Captain John's Company, under Colonel Moore, and Captain John was his brother, as shown in his application for a pension. He served for more than four years.

After the close of hostilities, and before the ratification of the treaty of peace, Captain John Oldham married as above stated in Caswell County, North Carolina, where a number of his children were born. Jesse was married a long time before the war, and had a number of grown children, and several married ones, when he came to Kentucky from the Yadkin River with Colonel Daniel Boone, and was with Colonel Boone and Captain William Twetty at Twetty's Fort, or the Little Fort, when attacked by the Indians as related in Chapter 3. He assisted in the construction of the Fort at Boonsborough in 1775, in which year he raised on Otter Creek not far from the Fort, a crop of corn, among the first crops raised in Kentucky soil by white men, and returned to North Carolina, entered the army, and after the war brought his family to Boonsborough, and established his home near the fort, where he lived till his death in 1814.

Ready Money Richard Oldham, (the subject of Chapter 4) served in the same war, lived near Jesse, and died there June 17, 1836. Abner Oldham, son of Captain John, was born in Caswell County, Dec. 2, 1783, and was twelve years old when his father moved to Kentucky. (See inscription on his tomb.) For military records, see Chapters 4-6-and 13 B, and 38.

The supreme court records of Caswell County show that Elizabeth Oldham, wife of Jesse Oldham, was willed property by Mary Simpson in 1798; that Susannah Oldham was willed property by Mayfield Heresly in 1798. She was probably the wife of one of the Oldham brothers, George Conway, James or William, and that the children of Mary Oldham, wife of Moses Oldham, was willed property by John Rice in 1804. This branch of the family is traced from Fauquier or Prince William County, Va., to Caswell County, North Carolina, and from there to Kentucky and Tennessee; probably some of them drifted further south and to other parts.

Jesse, Richard, senior, Conway, James Moses and Captain John, were all in the battle of Guilford Court House, so also, was Major George of Lee's Legion, and on the night of that battle was born, Eda, or Edith, the daughter of Jesse Oldham, who came with the family to Kentucky, and died near Boonsborough, many years ago, unmarried. During the battle an older daughter sat in the window of their home, and listened to the cannonading and the roar of small arms. These incidents were often told in the family, and there are some yet living who knew Edith, and remember hearing her tell them.

Mr. Thompson B. Oldham, of Burgin, Ky., son of Abner Oldham, the oldest living of the name in this section says, that his father all through his life, repeatedly told him as well as other members of his family that 'Lieutenant, Colonel William Oldham, was his (Abner's) father's first cousin," this would make them sons of brothers, and that Abner's grand-father was named "William."

Richard Oldham was born March 1, 1745. Jesse was many years older than Richard. Captain John was born, Nov. 10, 1757, and Lieutenant Colonel William Oldham, was born June 17, 1753, they were contemporaries, and the family believes their relationship was as above stated.

According to some authorities Isaac Oldham who was in Captain John Vanmeter's Company of Pennsylvania Rangers from 1778 to 1783, was the father of Lieutenant, Colonel William Oldham, killed at Governor St. Clair's defeat, Nov. 4, 1791. That Isaac Oldham by his first wife had three children, viz: William John and Sarah, and that the three moved to Kentucky and settled in Louisville and Lexington, and that William was the Lieutenant Colonel, who was killed as stated, but this would seem improbable because the will of Isaac Oldham, was not probated till 1821, thirty years after the death of the said Lieutenant Colonel. It is certainly unusual for a testator to devise anything to a child who has had no existence for so long a time.

One William Oldham, other than said Lieutenant Colonel, lived in Lexington and owned a cotton factory there as late as 1825, and one John Oldham, died in Madison County, in 1801, and another was in Russellville, Ky., at a later date as shown below.

Notes of some Oldhams whose lineage we have not traced:

John Oldham was living on Muddy Creek in Madison County, Ky., where he died in 1801, the clear implication is from the order appointing Samuel Elliot administrator of his estate, and that part thereof within the State of Kentucky, that he owned property in another state. John Harris was the surety on the bond. Daniel Miller, Henry Harris, Samuel Dent and Joshua Dillingham, appraisers who were all residents of Muddy Creek, and most of them came from Virginia if not all, and from Albemarle County.

In 1807, one John Oldham, then in Russellville, Ky., held a power of attorney from William McBane, to sell and convey a section of land on Red River in Robertson County, Tenn., recorded in the Fayette County Court.

William Oldham, earlier than 1825, wife Lucretia E. owned and occupied property on Main street and Town Fork of Lexington, and a cotton factory and house, and lot of ground, which factory he sold in 1825, to Drake and Gullivan, and in 1829, he sold other property to Edward Oldham, and bought of Abram Clay four acres on the south side of the Boonsborough road in Fayette.

William B. Oldham and wife Sallie Elliot, lived in Clark County, Kentucky in 1820.

James Oldham, was a contractor for erecting the buildings of the University of Virginia, in Charlottesville, and he built the woodwork of the first pavillion on the Doric Order, for the University with the four adjoining dormitories on West Lawn, which work brought him to the County, where he was induced to settle, and in 1828, purchased from the trustees of Benjamin Hardin, land on the Staunton Road, immediately east of Mechum River Depot, where he kept for several years, a house of public entertainment. His wife was Mary Gamble, daughter of Henry Bambel. He died in 1843. (Rev. Edgar Woods, his of Albemarle.)

Edward Oldham, wife Mary, prior to 1821, and to many years after 1836, lived in and near Lexington, Ky., and they had a son, Edward, and Rev. William Abner Oldham of Nortonville, Kansas, who once lived near Lexington, knew old man Edward Oldham when he saw him, and his son, Edward intimately.

Lieutenant Edward Oldham, of the Flying Company, second mounted batallion in the Revolution, married Mary Enson.

(From Notes by Mr. Sam Oldham.)

It will be noticed that the wife of each, was named Mary.

Newport Oldham, died in Montgomery County, Ky., in 1820,

his estate was appraised by Alexander Collins, William O. Jameson and William Morris, Oct. 20, 1820.

Samuel Oldham, wife Daphney, prior to 1832, and later than 1840, lived in and near Lexington, Ky., and owned property there.

In 1835, Samuel Jull, executed a bill of sale to his grand son, Samuel Oldham of Lexington, Ky., of a negro man Levin, and a negro woman, Harriet.

Samuel Oldham in 1838, on the Clark County record conveyed his interest in the real and personal estate of John Talbott.

Clark is an adjoining County to Fayette.

See list of early marriages in Madison County.

The County of Caswell, North Carolina, was named in honor of Governor Richard Caswell, who granted lands to the Oldhams in 1779 to 1783.

James Oldham. His children (and perhaps himself) settled at Oldham's Landing in Oldham County, Ky. We have not traced his lineage back. Attention is called to the fact, that Moses Oldham died in Montgomery County, Tenn., in 1867, and in his will devised property to the heirs of his deceased son, James K. Oldham. (See Chap. 39, Article 2, Note.)

The subject James Oldham; married ——— ——— and died leaving three children, two sons and one daughter, viz:

1. Uriah Wright Oldham, was Captain of Company F. 9th Kentucky cavalry of the Union forces of the Civil War. He married Mary Conway. He and his brother, Andrew Jackson Oldham engaged as partners in merchandise at Oldham's Landing until 1873. Uriah Wright Oldham, whilst on a business trip in Tennessee was murdered near Johnson City said state, for his money, which brought the partnership to a sudden close. After this occurrence, his widow Mrs. Mary Conway Oldham, with two children moved to Carroll County, Ky., and she and her daughter are now residing at Carrollton, Ky. The two children, viz:

1. Dr. James P. Oldham, born 1863, at Oldham's Landing, Oldham County, Ky. He graduated in Medicine in 1886, from the State College of Kentucky, and located in Little Rock, Arkansas, where he practiced his profession two years. His health becoming impaired, for the improvement of same, in 1888, he removed to San Antonio, Texas, where he now resides, practicing his medical profession. In 1891, he married Mollie Graham. They have one child, viz:

1. Violet Oldham, born 1892.

2. Carrie Oldham, born in 1865, at Oldham's Landing, now living with her mother in Carrollton, Ky.

2. Andrew Jackson Oldham, was partner of his brother, Uriah Wright Oldham, in the merchantile business at Oldham's Landing, until 1873, the year his brother was killed.

3. Harriet Oldham; married Harrison Land. They had a number of children, and emigrated to Illinois.

(For additional notes see Chapter 38.)

Westmoreland County, Va., the home of Colonel Samuel Oldham, born 1686, died 1759 or 1762, borders on the Potomac just above its junction with the Chesapeake Bay, and across the River lies Maryland. Some sixty odd miles in a straight line north west of Westmoreland, is Prince William County, on the Patomac with Fauquier, formerly a part of Prince William, the home of William Oldham, adjoining and Berkely—the former home of Lieutenant Colonel William Oldham, lying a little west of north of Prince William.

The southern boundary line of Pennsylvania, binds Virginia and Maryland on the north.

Lancaster, with Chester adjoining it on the east, and York on the west, are Pennsylvania Counties, the Susquehanna which flows into the Chesapeake Bay, separates York and Lancaster, these three Counties all touch the northern boundary of Maryland, and are on Chesapeaks waters.

In the County of Chester, Robert Oldham owned land in 1707, (some say Bucks) however he died in Nottingham Township Chester County in 1749, wife Mary, daughter of Jos ph White and Elizabeth his wife. They had daughters and sons, Edward and Robert.

The following owned lands in Chester County, Pennsylvania: Joseph Oldham 1754, Robert Oldham 1765 to 1774, and John Oldham 1765 to 1769. About 1750, Thomas Oldham (Junior) being suffixed because his father had the same given name, died in Chester County, and his widow Mary, qualified as administratrix of his estate. In 1756, another Thomas Oldham, father of the one above named, styled senior, died in East Nottingham, his will mentioning his wife Rachael, (daughter of Zacharias Butcher) and daughters, and these sons, towit:

1. Thomas Oldham, who was dead in 1750, and his widow Mary was administrator as above stated. They had a son:
   1. Thomas Oldham, (probably the owner of York County lands in 1779 to 1783.)
2. William Oldham, who was dead, widow Sarah.

Thomas Oldham owned lands in York County, Pa., 1779 to 1783.

,The following owned lands in Lancaster County, Pennsylvania: Edward Oldham 1735, William Oldham 1747, Thomas Oldham 1749 and Nathaniel Oldham 1749.

The above settlements were all on waters tributary to the Chesapeake Bay, and these people were all of the same stock. Proper investigation would make discoveries that would throw a flood of light on the trace and make clear the relationship. The North Carolina family who emigrated from the waters of Chesapeake Bay, run back to the same original Anglo-American ancestor. The kinship of the family has been recognized by all its branches in the multiplication of the Johns, Thomases, Josephs, and Richards. The name of Robert did not come into the family until after the marriage of Thomas Oldham, son of Thomas to Mercy, daughter of Robert Sproat. The name Samuel, seems to have been brought from England, for it has been a name common in every branch of the family in the states. The name Isaac, was given by Thomas to his second son, and has been continued in all branches of the family. A full notation of the given names of the family would show this distinctly. (See closing part of Chapter 38.)

Matters of interest may be found in Brook's History of Medford, Winsor's History of Duxbury, Paige's History of Cambridge, Savage's Dictionary, third volume, Bond's History of Watertown, and Frathingham's History of Charleston.

Captain John Oldham (of Plymouth) was the first representative 1634, of Watertown to the General Court of Massachusettss.

In 1632 he and John Masters were appointed to advise with the Govenor and his assitants about raising public stock. John Oldham with John Dowil, obtained from John George a grant for a tract of land embracing most of the territory of the present cities of Charleston, Cambridge, Summerville and a part of Watertown. (See Frothingham's History of Charleston.) The grant was not valid, and the General Court granted Mr. Oldham a farm of 500 acres in Watertown April 1, 1634, which was long known after his death as the "Oldham farm."

The theological differences between Rev. John Syford and John

Oldham with the Plymouth colonists terminated in 1627, by the exclusion of Syford, Oldham, Roger Williams and some seventy others of the colony. The Plymouth Colonists who came over from Holland in 1621 were Congregationalists, whilst Syford, Oldham and others were church of England people. Oldham and Syford went to Nantasket, thence with Conant to Cape Ann, their home in 1628, well reconciled with Plymouth, but Oldham never returned as a settler of that colony. (See Chap. 39.)

The fireside stories in the family are that Mrs. Basey, the mother of the wife of William Oldham of Prince William County, Va., was before her marriage Miss Garland, and that she lived to the remarkable age of one hundred and eighteen years, and cut a new set of teeth when one hundred and ten years old. And that Hezekiah Rice and Mary Bullock, (parents of Annis Rice the wife of Captain John Oldham) lived together as husband and wife, seventy five years.

Mr. Samuel Oldham an intelligent, honorable, and venerable gentleman of Zanesville, Ohio, has taken many notes and had favored us with interesting and instructive letters, data and scraps of history, to whom our sincere thanks are tendered. (Se Chap. 38.)

We here present copy of a letter written by Warren S. Ely, Genealogist and Librarian, Bucks County Historical Society, to Samuel Oldham, Esquire of Zanesville, Ohio, which Mr. Oldham furnished the writer, to-wit:

"Doylestown, Pa., 10-10-1907. Samuel Oldham, Esquire, Zanesville, Ohio. Dear Sir: The bond of Jonathan Oldham administrator of the goods, rights and credits of John Oldham, late of Cheshire, in the Kingdom of England, merct, (merchant) with Philip Andrew as surety, is dated Aug. 22, 1698. The grant of the letters in Book A, page 265, begins: "Whereas John Oldham, late of Cheshire, in ye Kingdom of England, lately dyed intestate, as in affirmed, having whilst he lived, and at the time of his decease, goods, rights, credits, etc., in divers places within ye province of Pennsylvania, and territories thereto annexed, whereby the power and authority to grant letters of administration devolved upon us etc.

Letters granted to Jonathan Oldham Aug. 22, 1698. The "Inventory of ye estate and chattels, rights, wares, and merchandises of John Oldham, late of Cheshire, in ye Kingdom of England merchant, deceased, as it was shown to us ye appraisers. Afterwards upon ye 23rd day of Aug. 1698, by Jonathan Oldham, ye administrator, consists chiefly of dry goods in rolls, etc., showing that he was a merchant, as stated in the bond and letters of administration. It also included his purse and apparell.

I found no settlement of the accounts of Jonathan Oldham as administrator, nor did I, by diligent search, find any transfer of real estate to, or from either John, or Jonathan Oldham. **

I obtained the original papers in the estate, but they consisted only of the inventory above quoted and the bond. Unfortunately there are no Orphan's Court papers of Phil. County, in existence that I am aware of until a much later period than this

Respectfully Yours,
Warren S. Ely.

It seems beyond question that the intestate John Oldham, described in Mr. Ely's letter, was the youth John Oldham, who came over in the Elizabeth and Ann in 1635, when 12 years of age, who would have been 75 years old in 1698.

CHAPTER 3.

JESSE OLDHAM.

(Named in Chapter 2, Sectoin 1.)

Article 1.—Jesse Oldham, a son of William Oldham and Miss —— Basey his wife, was born probably in Prince William County, Va.

He moved to North Carolina before the Revolution, and lived for a time on the Yadkin River, not a great distance from Guilford Court-House. He married Elizabeth Simpson. In 1798, Martha Simpson a resident of Caswell County North Carolina died, and in her will devised property to Elizabeth Oldham, wife of Jesse Oldham. (See Chap. 1, Sec. 11.) Jesse Oldham came to Madison County, Ky., in the early part of the year 1775, with the company of Colonel Daniel Boone, and Captain William Twetty, and was with them when attacked by the Indians before day break, March 25, 1775, in which battle Captain Twetty was so seriously wounded that he died and Felix Walker was painfully wounded, but recovered His deposition which was filed in the Court states that "Twetty's Fort, or the Little Fort, was built March 26, 1775, about five miles from Richmond, (and 132 feet over one mile south west from Estill's old station in Madison County, Ky.,) on a small branch of Taylor's Fork. That it was built the day after the Indian attack before the break of day, upon Colonel Boone's and Captain Twetty's Company, about 100 yards from Boone's Trace, in square form, about six or seven feet high, of logs, as a protection against surprises, or sudden attacks of the indians, was not covered, and the wounded bodies of Captain William Twetty and his ward, young Felix Walker, were removed into it, and there nursed.

On the second day after it was built Captain Twetty who was shot in both knees, died, and was buried in the fort, and the company remained to nurse young Walker, until April 1, (1775), and part of them, probably until April 6, (1775), when he was well enough to be removed to Boonsborough.

Jesse Oldham, after the death and burial of Captain Twetty, and when young Walker had sufficiently recovered to be moved, went with him to Boonsborough, about the 6th of April, and he assisted in the building and completion of the Fort at Boonsborough, which work was not completed until June 14, 1775, and he made one of the force of the defenders of the fort against the besieges made by the indians.

Jesse Oldham was one of the men, who raised the earliest crops of corn in Madison County, Ky. He raised corn in 1775, on Otter Creek, not far from the Boonsborough Fort—of the very first crops raised in the Boonsborough settlement, as shown by depositions—and probably no earlier crops were raised in Kentucky soil by white men. It seems that after coming to Kentucky in the company of Colonel Daniel Boone, Jesse Oldham returned to North Carolina and he and one or two of his sons, enlisted in the Revolutionary Army in the North Carolina line. He and his son, and his brothers Captain John Oldham, Richard, Conway, James and Moses and Major George Oldham, the latter of Lee's Legion, were all in the battle of Guilford Court House.

Jesse Oldham died in Madison County, Ky,. in 1814, having first made and published his last will and testament, bearing date Jan. 28, 1814, probated April 4, 1814, and recorded in will book B. page 38, which will is in the following words and figures, towit:

"In the name of God, amen. I, Jesse Oldham, of Madison County, and State of Kentucky, being in my perfect senses, do make and ordain this my last will and testament. First: I give and bequeath my soul to Almighty God, that gave it, and my body to be buried by my executors in a christian like manner, and as touching such worldly goods as it hath pleased God to bless and endow me with, I give and dispose of in the manner and form following:

Item—I give and bequeath to my daughter, Amy Burton, one shilling sterling, and no more.

Item—I give and bequeath unto my son, Richard Oldham, one shilling sterling, and no more.

Item—I give and bequeath unto my daughter, Mary Ann and George, one shilling sterling, and no more.

Item—I give and bequeth unto my daughter, Anna Harris, one shilling sterling, and no more.

Item—I give and bequeath unto my son, Tyre Oldham fifty pounds, Kentucky currency, and no more.

Item—I give and bequeath unto my daughter, Frances Oldham, one shilling sterling, and no more.

Item—I give and bequeath unto my daughter Sally Burton, one shilling sterling, and no more.

My will and desire is that Jesse Oldham, Elias Oldham, Eady Oldham, Nathaniel Oldham and John K. Oldham, those five last mentioned children, shall have all the residue of my estate, to be equally divided amongst them, both real and personal estate is my will.

Lastly, I appoint my son, Jesse Oldham, and my son Nathaniel Oldham, my whole sole executors, of this my last will and testament.

In witness whereof I have set my hand, seal, this 28 day of Jan. 1814. JESSE OLDHAM. (Seal.)

Signed and sealed in the presence of:—
Daniel Williams.
Frances Hally.
Nancy (X) Hally, Betsy Hally.

N. B. The words "to be" was interlined before signed.

At a Court held for Madison County on the fourth day of April 1814, this writing was proven to be the last will and testament of Jesse Oldham, by the oaths of Daniel Williams and Frances Hally two subscribing witnesses thereto, and ordered to be recorded, and the same has been done accordinly. (B page 38.) Teste, William Irvine, Clerk.

Jesse Oldham had grand-children when he came to Kentucky He was indeed, one of the brave Kentucky pioneers and frontiersman, and deserves grateful commemoration of the good, patriotic people of the grand old commonwealth, he helped to settle, and especially Madison County, where his early conspicious part was played, and whose soil contains his bones. Much more could be said of this noble character. The children mentioned in the will:

Section 1. Amy Oldham; married Mr. Burton.

Section 2. Richard Oldham, the individual described in Chapter 4, who married first Ursley Williams, and second Patsey Reid, his father, Jesse, must have been considerably older than his brothers, and this son, must have been also, the oldest child of Jesse, and he possibly was very young when he joined the army, which was often the case, for it took the young and the old to overcome the British. (See Chapter 4.)

Section 3. Mary Ann Oldham.

Section 4. George Oldham.

"One George Oldham, on the 21st of Sept. 1797, married Sarah Todd, in Madison County, Ky."

"A County Court order of April 5, 1803, shows George Oldham entitled to fifty acres of land on the east side of Drowning Creek, in Madison County, Ky.," (now Estill) where they lived, his wife Sarah, was a member of Viney Fork Baptist Church.

Section 5. Anna Oldham; married William Harris in Madison County, Ky., Feb. 4, 1790. (See Part III, Chap. 44.)

Section 6. Tyre Oldham his wife, was Nancy —— He acquired lands in Madison County, Ky., as early as 1798, and made several deeds to lands in said county, in which his wife, Nancy joined, and his name appears on the Clark County records of 1807. He removed to Falmouth, Ky., at least, Mr. Thompson B. Oldham says so.

Section 7. Frances Oldham; married in Madison County, Ky., November 26, 1795, her cousin Hezekiah Oldham, son of Richard Oldham, of Estill County, and Ann Pepper his wife. (See Chapter 7.)

Section 8. Sally Oldham; married Mr. Burton.

Section 9. Jesse Oldham.

Section -0. Elias Oldham.

Section 11. Eda (Edith) Oldham, remained a maid, was born in Guilford, North Carolina, the night of the battle, in which battle her father, brother and uncles were engaged. She died in Madison County, Ky.

Section 12. Nathaniel Oldham. He married in Estill County, Kentucky., March 6, 1811, Peggy Sparks, who bore him one child, and died, and on Aug. 7, 1814, he married Dosha Spence in Madison County, Ky. (See Chapter 5, for further particulars.)

Section 13. John K. Oldham. The records show that he owned considerable real estate on Otter Creek and the Kentucky River, in Madison County, Ky., and that his wife was Nancy. His name appears on the Fayette records Nov. 15, 1833. He also removed to Falmouth, Ky.

Note: Mr. Thompson B. Oldham of Burgin, Ky., is authority for the following statements, viz:

"Jesse Oldham and his wife Elizabeth Simpson, had a grand-son, towit:

Williamson Oldham who went from Kentucky to Tennessee. He studied law, and was licensed to practice and moved to Arkansas, and became Judge of the Supreme Court thereof, and subsequently removed to Texas, and was a very distinguished lawyer and politician. "Judge Oldham use to correspond by letter with Abner Oldham. (father of Thompson), of Madison County, Ky., and in one of his letters he wrote "tell Aunt Edith, she is the only woman in Kentucky who I can say spoiled the Judge of the Supreme Court of Arkansas."

Additional sketch, furnished by Mrs. Rebecca J. Fisher, President of the William B. Travis Chapter Daughters of the Republic of Texas, Austin, Texas: Capital. 'State Librarian."

WILLIAM S. OLDHAM..

William S. Oldham, was born in Franklin County, Tenn., on June 19, 1813, and was a descendant of an old Virginia family. At the age of thirteen years, he opened a school in mountains of Tennessee, in order to procure means to continue his education. Having followed this calling two years, he obtained a situation in the office of the District Clerk of Franklin County. Judge Nathan Green directed his study of law. In 1836, he removed to Fayetteville, Arkansas, where he formed a partnership with S. G. Sneed.

At Fayetteville, Mr. Oldham soon established an eminent reputation, and in 1842, was speaker of the Arkansas House of Representatives, in 1844, he was chosen almost unanimously by the Legislature an associate Justice of the Supreme Court of Arkansas, and held that position until the fall of 1848, when in consequence of ill health he resigned, in contemplation of making his future home in Texas.

In the spring of 1849, he removed to Texas, and located at Austin, ** in 1858, the Legislature of Texas passed an act authorizing the Governor to receive proposals for the preparation of a digest of all the general statute laws of the state. The contract for preparing this digest was awarded to Messrs. Oldham and White.

In 1861. Judge Oldham, was strongly in favor of secession. He was chosen a member of the Provisional Congress, at Montgomery, and was subsequently elected a senator in the Congress of the Confederate States and held that position until the close of the war.

At the close of the war Judge Oldham, retired to Mexico. Upon the fall of the empire in 1866, he went to Canada. He returned to Texas, and having settled in Houston, devoted himself exclusively to the practice of his profession. He was stricken with typhoid fever and died with that disease at Houston, on the 8th day of May 1868. The Bench and Bar of Texas, by James D. Lynch, pages 254 to 261.

CHAPTER 4.

RICHARD OLDHAM.

(Known as "Ready Money Richard Oldham."

See Chapter 3, Section 2.

Article 1.—Richard Oldham, son of Jesse Oldham, and Elizabeth Simpson, his wife, and to distinguish him from others with a similar name, was called and known as "Ready Money Richard Oldham," he having at all times money on hand and ready, probably suggested the name.

He married in North Carolina, Ursley Williams, a daughter of Henry Williams. A report made Oct. 20, 1807, by J. Pitman, Robert Tevis and John Wilkerson, commissioners appointed on the motion of Richard Oldham, of the division of negroes of Henry Williams, decesaed, that were in the hands of said Oldham, to be divided between the children of Richard Oldham and first wife, Ursley, shows the following allotment of same:

To Elizabeth Harris, Simon and Solomon $475, she to pay $20.

To Goodman Oldham, Isaac $400, he to receive $55.

To Nancy Oldham, Jacob and Fanny, $500, she to pay $45.
To Patsey Oldham, Jane and Sarah, $450, she to receive $5.
To Nuty (Ursley) Oldham, Peter and Rose, she to receive $5.

Richard Oldham's wife Ursley, having died, on the 26th day of July 1803, he married again Patsey Reid, daughter of Alexander Reid. "April 8, 1809, John Newman and Nancy, (late Nancy Reid) executed to the heirs of Alexander Reid, deceased, deed to 1-3 of all land of said heirs, of Alexander Reid, deceased, except 300 acres, tract on Cumberland River in Knox County, Ky., called the Flat Lick tract, what Newman and wife agree to take for their third. Two of the heirs, Richard Oldham and Goodman Oldham agree signed: John P. Newman, Nancy Newman, Richard Oldham, for himself and John Reid one of the heirs, Goodman Oldham, John P. Newman, gdn for Polly and Hannah Reid "wits: Overton Harris, John Oldham and James Smith."

Ready Money Richard Oldham, served it seems in the Revolutionary war, and the war of 1812, certainly in the latter. He was an officer of the Kentucky Militia from 1808 to 1821. He was first Lieutenant May 3, 1808 of the seventh Infantry, Captain Dec. 1, 1809, Major of the seventeenth Infantry April 19, 1814, honorably discharged June 15, 1815, was of the Kentucky State Militia March 9, 1819, honorably discharged June 1, 1821. He went from Virginia to Caswell County, North Carolina. Thence after the Revolution to Madison County Ky., and settled on Otter Creek, and ecquired considerable real estate on Otter Creek, and the River adjacent to Bonsborough, his home was near that of Jesse Oldham, his father. He was a prosperous man financially. He died on his estate June 17, 1836, his will dated April 13, 1835, was probated July 4, 1836. the anniversary of the declaration of independence. His sons, Alexander R. Oldham and Jesse Oldham and his widow Patsey, qualified as executors.

The following record also appears: State of Kentucky, Madison County, Sct., November Court 1836. Satisfactory proof was this day made in open court by the oaths of Nathaniel Oldham, and James Woods, that Richard Oldham, late a pensioner of the United States, departed this life on the 17th day of June 1836, and that the said Richard Oldham was the identical person named in one original certificate now here shown to the Court bearing date the 26th day of Jan. 1833, and signed by Lew Cass, secretary of war, granting to the said Richard Oldham, a pension of $80 per annum, and numbered 4708, and it was further proven to the satisfaction of the Court that Patsey Oldham is the widow of said Richard Oldham, and that she is now living."

Patsey Reid Oldham the widow, went to Platte County, Mo., where some of her children were living. The children of the first marriage to Ursley Williams were:

Section 1. Elizabeth Oldham; married first Barnabas Harris in 1803, (See Part III, Chap. 45) second, Mr. Clark.

Section 2. Goodman Oldham, acquired land in Madison County, one purchase was from Moses Wallace in 1814. He removed to Falmouth, Ky.

Section 3. Nancy Oldham; married Overton Harris. (See Part III, Chapter 48.)

Section 4. Patsey Oldham; married Jesse Barnes, in Madison County, Ky., Dec. 9, 1817. They went to Missouri in 1837-8. Their children:

1. Sidney Barnes; married Lucinda Moberley Nov. 9, 1854.

2. Richard Barnes.
3. Minerva Barnes; married Mr. Smith, went to Tennessee.
4. Clifton Barnes.
5. Caleb Barnes.
6. Dudley Barnes.
7. Thomas Barnes.

Section 5. Ursley (Nuty) Oldham; married Hancock Jackson March 8, 1821.

Children of the second marriage to Patsey Reid:

Section 6. Alexander Reid Oldham; married Miriam Reid Sept. 15, 1831. They went to Munroe County, Mo.

Section 7. Sophronia Oldham; married James Woods June 17, 1830, they emigrated to Munroe County, Mo.

Section 8. Milton Oldham; married Agnes M. Harris Feb. 3, 1831. (See Part III, Chap. 44, Sec. 2.) They went to Missouri.

Section 9. Frances Oldham; married Turner Barnes Sept. 11, 1828. Their children:

1. RichardBarnes, went to Missouri.
2. Patsey Oldham; married William Dailey, went to Illinois.
3. Rachael Barnes; married Mr. Barnes.
4. Mary Barnes; married Elias Barnes, Junior.
5. Samuel Barnes; married Miss Todd.
6. Thomas Barnes; married Miss —— Gill.

Section 10. Louisa Oldham; married Richard M. Harris. (See Part III, Chap. 44) they went to Platt County, Mo.

Section 11. Jesse Oldham, went to Munroe County, Mo., when a single man, married Miss —— Cotton.

Section 12. Polly Ann Oldham; married Richard Dejarnatt Aug. 15, 1839. They went to Van Buren County, Mo.

Section 13. Overton Harris Oldham, went to Platt County, Mo., before he was grown, where he died unmarried.

Section 14. Richard B. Oldham, was a little boy when he went to Platt County, Mo., and died unmarried.

Section 15. Talitha Oldham; married Alpheus Ellington. Went to Platt County, Mo. Of their children were:

1. Mary Ellington; married Overton Harris. (See Part III, Chapter 10, Section 1.)

2. Amelia Ellington; married William Hayden Harris. (See Part III, Chapter 10, Section 5.)

CHAPTER 5.

NATHANIEL OLDHAM.

(Named in Chapter 3, Section 12.)

Article 1.—Nathaniel Oldham, a son of Jesse Oldham and Elizabeth Simpson his wife, married Peggy Sparks March 6, 1811, in Estill County, Ky., and his second wife Dosha Spence in Madison County, Ky., Aug. 7, 1814, and settled on Otter Creek, where he spent his days.

He was born in North Carolina. The fruits of this union were the children named in the coming sections: By first wife:

Section 1. David Oldham; married —— ——. He left Madison County, Ky., and remained away a period, when he returned with his wife and family, having then a daughter nearly grown, and lived in said County a short time only, when he removed to the state of Missouri, and further history of him has not been procured.

Children of second wife:

Section 2. Dawson Oldham; married Caroline Smith Nov. 22, 1842, issue:

1. Sanford Oldham; married Zerilda Neale, issue:
   1. Smith Oldham.
   2. James May Oldham, now deceased, married Jessie Royce.
   3. Annie Neale Oldham; dead.
   4. William Dawson Oldham; dead.
2. Sallie Oldham, now deceased, married Robert G. Tribble, issue:
   1. Alexander Tribble; married —— ——
   2. Carrie Tribble; married Garth Cuddy.
   3. Annie Tribble; dead.
   4. Dudley Tribble; married Gertrude Patterson, issue:
      1. Eugene Tribble.
      2. Robert Tribble.
   5. Alice Tribble.
3. Mary Oldham; dead.
4. Nannie Oldham.
5. James Oldham; married Blanch Hyeronymus, issue:
   1. Mary Oldham.
6. Carrie Oldham.
7. Alice Oldham.

8. William Smith Oldham, conducting a large furniture and undertaking establishment in Richmond, Ky. He married June 9, 1899, Mary Pattie, daughter of Dr. Coleman D. Pattie and Miss Emma Crockett his wife. Dr. Pattie was a confederate soldier in the civil war, under the command of General John H. Morgan, enlisted when only fifteen or sixteen years old, and was captured in the Ohio Raid made by his bold commander, and lay for 19 months a prisoner of war in Camp Douglas. Freedom was offered him provided he would take the oath of allegiance to the Federal Government, which he declined to take, because he had vowed to support the confederacy. Finally he with others was taken to Virginia for exchange, but in a short time General Robert Lee, surrendered his army, which virtually ended the war, and Dr. Pattie returned from Virginia to his Kentucky home, and afterwards located in Richmond, Ky., and was for a number of years the leading druggist of the city. Now holds a

position in the Citizens National Bank, and has made a host of friends. The children of William Smith Oldham and Mary Pattie his wife:

1. Coleman D. Oldham.
2. Emma Crockett Oldham.

Dawson Oldham was a substantial farmer of Madison County, Ky., a quiet good citizen, who attended strictly to his own business, and raised a nice family of sons and daughters.

Section 3. Hirom D. Oldham; married Emily —— Biggerstaff February 3, 1848, issue:

1. Rosebell Oldham; married James Roberts.
2. Melissa Oldham; married Eugene Land.
3. William Oldham married —— Davis.
4. Nancy Oldham; married James Veal.

Section 4. Emarine Oldham.

Section 5. Elizabeth Oldham; married —— Giles, issue:

1. Losada Giles; married —— Barnes.

Section 6. Eady (M. A.) Oldham; married S. B. Tipton, April 3, 1851.

Section 7. Dorinda Oldham; married William Willis Dec. 23, 1851, issue:

1. Mary Willis; married Samuel Dejarnatt.
2. Dr. Thomas Willis; married —— ——
3. Emma Willis.

Section 8. Sanford Oldham, the oldest child of the second marriage. He went to Tennessee, and died when a young man.

CHAPTER 6.

RICHARD OLDHAM.

(Known as Richard Oldham of Estill County.)

(Named in Chapter 2, Section 6.)

Article 1.—Richard Oldham, a son of William Oldham of Prince William County, Va., and Miss —— Basey his wife, was born in a section of Prince William County, Va., that was embraced in Fauquier, that was formed in 1759, out of Prince William on the first day of March 1745.

This subject was a soldier in the Revolutionary army, he enlisted in Caswell County, North Carolina in the North Carolina line, in the company of Captain John Oldham, his brother, as a letter in the following form shows, towit:

"O. W. and N. Division, 3-525.
M. B. H. Department of the Interior
Inv. File, 14053 Bureau of Pensions,
Rev. War. Washington, D. C., Dec. 21, 1905.

Madam:—

In reply to your request for a statement of the military history of Richard Oldham* a soldier of the Revolutionary war, you will find below the desired information as contained in his application for pension on file in this bureau:

Date of Enlistment or Appointment	Length of Service	Rank	Officers Under Whom Service Was Rendered.		State
			Captain	Colonel	
1777	3 months	Private	‡John Oldham	Moore	N. C.
†Shortly after.	3 months	Private	John Oldham	Not stated	N. C.
	3 months	Private	John Oldham	Not stated	N. C.

*Referred to as Richard Oldham, Sen

‡Soldier's brother.

†Battles engaged in—Guilford Court House.

Date of application for pension, Aug. 14, 1832. His claim was allowed.

Residence at date of application, Estill County, Ky., there in 1833.

Age, born March first 1745, in Fauquier County, Va.

Remarks: No family data.

Very Respectfully,
V. Warner, Commissioner.

Mrs. Kate Oldham Miller,
Richmond,
Madison County, Kentucky."

Richard Oldham, married Ann Pepper of North Carolina, and about 1795, he emigrated from Caswell County, North Carolina, to Kentucky, and settled on the Kentucky River, or Red River above the mouth of the latter, which location was included in Estill County, when it was established in 1808. Here he spent the remainder of his life, and from this home he drew the pension for his service in the Revolutionary war.

On the 18th day of Aug. 1834, in the Estill County Court, his son Zerah Oldham, qualified as administrator of his estate.

Stephen Collins Oldham, son of Zerah Oldham born in 1815, is now living in Austin, Texas, having passed his ninety first birth day, and having celebrated his sixty sixth wedding day, the 24 day of Dec. 1905. The children of Richard Oldham and Ann Pepper his wife, are set forth in the coming sections 1 to 10 inclusive, towit:

Section 1. William Oldham, born April 23, 1777, probably in North Carolina. He emigrated to Kentucky about 1800, and settled on Muddy Crek in Madison County, where he was married Oct. 19, 1809, to Sallie Gilbert, daughter af Samuel Gilbert, and whom he survived, and on the 30th day of Oct. 1826, he married the second time Mrs. Susannah Anderson Moberley, (nee Reid) widow of Benjamin Moberley. A fuller account of whom will be found in Chapter 11, and also in Part II, Chapter 48, Section 2.

Section 2. Zerah Oldham; married Amelia F. Collins, Dec. 24, 1839. History of whom will be found in Chapter 40.

Section 3. Hezekiah Oldham. He married his first cousin Frances Oldham, daughter of his uncle Jesse Oldham and Elizabeth Simpson his wife, Nov. 26, 1795, (See Chap. 3, Sec. 7) and settled on Otter Creek, not far from Boonsborough. History of whom will be found in Chapter 7.

Section 4. Samuel Oldham; married Polly White, Aug. 8, 1797. History of whom will be found in Chapter 12.

Section 5. Moses Oldham: married Ann White Nov. 10, 1796. History of whom will be found in Chapter 13 A.

Section 6. Richard Oldham. He married in Madison County, Ky., Nov. 2, 1824, Sallie Williams. He settled in Montgomery County, Ky., and was known as Montgomery County Richard Oldham. Their children were:

1. Nancy Oldham: married first Samuel Baldwin. They had no children, she married second George Hazelrigg, the father of Judge James H. Hazelrigg, late Judge of the Kentucky Court of Appeals, and had:
    1. Ida Hazelrigg.
    2. Duck Hazelrigg.

George Hazelrigg died, and his widow Nancy married a third husband.

2. Thomas Oldham: died unmarried.
3. Marion Oldham; married Miss —— Tipton, and emigrated to Missouri.
4. Miss Walker Oldham: married Matt Anderson.
5. John Oldham.
6. William Osborne Oldham.

Either 5 or 6 married Miss Hainline.

7. Miss —— Oldham: married Mr. —— Green.
8. Miss —— Oldham: married Benjamin Cockrill. At one time a state senator.

Section 7. Ann Oldham; married Joseph Collins, Sept. 14, 1809. History of whom will be found in Chapter 8.

Section 8. Milly Oldham: married Josiah Collins, a minister, who left the old Baptists in the times of the reformation and went with what is styled the Christian Church. History of whom will be found in Chapter 9.

Section 9. Edith Oldham: married Jesse Cobb, of Estill County. History of whom will be found in Chapter 10.

Section 10. Miss —— Oldham: married Mr. —— McLean. They emigrated to Missouri.

CHAPTER 7.

HEZEKIAH OLDHAM.

Of Otter Creek.

(Named in Chapter 6, Section 2.)

Article 1.—Hezekiah Oldham, a son of Richard Oldham of Estill County, and Ann Pepper his wife, came from North Carolina to Madison County, Ky., in about 1795, and where on the 26th day of November 1795, he married his first cousin Frances Oldham, a daughter of his uncle Jesse Oldham, and he settled on Otter Creek, where he ever after lived. (See Chap. 3, Sec. 7.)

He died in 183--, after first making and publishing his will, which is of record in the County Clerk's office. His children are named in the coming sections:

Section 1. Celia Oldham; married Nathaniel Williams, of Madison County, Ky., to whom were born:

1. William Williams; married Emilly Parrish, the issue of this union being:
   1. Taylor Williams; married —— Dozier, and went to Illinois.
   2. William Albert Williams; married —— Taylor.
   3. Mollie Williams; married S. P. Goode.
   4. Abner S. Williams; died young.
   5. Julia Williams; married Samuel Shearer, junior.
2. Julia Ann Williams; married John H. Parish, Sept. 15, 1842.
3. Tandy Williams; married Mary Butner.
4. Nathan Williams, Jr., married Mildred Oldham. (See Sec. 5-1.)
5. Daniel Williams; married Mary Jordon, issue:
   1. Merrett Williams, now in Oklahoma.
6. Miriam Williams; married John Reid. (See Part II, Chap. 21, Section 4-5.)
7. Naomi Williams; married James L. Hazelwood.
8. Celia Williams; married Joseph Reid. (See Part II, Chap. 21, Section 5-10.)
99. Amanda Williams; married first ——Wright and second Campbell Wilmore.

Section 2. Elizabeth Oldham; married Joel Karr Feb. 17, 1837, had a son:

1. Hezekiah Karr.

Section 3. Hezekiah Oldham. (Married Jane Tillett Sept. 21, 1854, and Eliza Olds Oct. 20, 1859.)

Section 4. Frances Ann Oldham; married Bryant Searcy Nov. 8, 1837, issue:

1. Elias Searcy; married Jennie Golden.
2. Mollie Searcy; married Samuel Alezander.
3. Charles Searcy; married Ellen Gillen.
4. Elizabeth Searcy; died young.
5. Nathaniel Searcy.
6. Alonzo Searcy.
7. George W. Searcy; married —— Morris.
8. Belle Searcy; married Waller Grimes.
9. Sally Searcy.
10. James Searcy.
11. Jack Searcy; died young.
12. Celia Searcy; died young.

Section 5. Edmund B. Oldham; married Jarene Hill, and had a daughter:

1. Mildred Oldham; married her cousin, Nathan Williams, Jr. (See Section 1-4.)

Section 6. Sally Ann Oldham; married William Arvine, Feb. 13, 1845. William Arvine and his wife made their home on Station Camp Creek, in Estill County, Ky. Their children:

1. John William Arvine, never married. Post Office, Dallas, Wyoming.
2. Sarah Frances Arvine; married James Coffman, living in Cross Plains, Texas. Their children:
   1. William Coffman; married Ethel Wood, live in Ada, Indian Territory.
   2. Kentucky Blanche Coffman; married William McGowan, live at Cross Plains, Texas.
   3. Lula Olive Coffman; married J. R. Nation, live in Quannah, Texas.

4. Etta Coffman: married John Baum, live in Dressi, Texas.
5. Laura Coffman: married Scott Gilbert, live in Cross Plains Texas.

3. Edwin Taylor Arvine: married Martha Scott, daughter of Dr. Scott, of Blue Banks, Estill County, Ky., and live on Station Camp Creek. Their children:

1. Homer Arvine: married Margaret Campbell, of Estill County, Ky.
2. Mittie Arvine: married Clay Moores, of Estill County, Ky.
3. Algin Arvine; single of Station Camp.
4. Hubert Arvine; single, of Station Camp.
5. Raymond Arvine; single, of Station Camp.
6. Flora Arvine.
7. Ninnie Arvine.
8. Sallie Arvine.

4. Thomas Christopher Arvine, lives in Sherman, Texas.

5. Joseph Carter Arvine; married —— ——
They live in Sherman, Texas.

6. David Chenault Arvine: now dead: married Miss —— Newton. Their children:

1. Thomas Arvine; dead.
2. Nannie Arvine; married Dr. —— ——

7. Andrew Jackson Arvine; married Mary Westman, live in Cottonwood, Texas. Their children:

1. Christopher (Major) Arvine; single.
2. Lula Arivne; married James Richardson, live in Sabannah, Texas.
3. Minnie Arvine: married —— —— live in Cottonwood, Texas.
4. Joe Arvine.
5. Sis —— Arvine.
6. Effie Arvine.

And four others, names unknown.

8. Owen Walker Arvine; married Malinda Kelley. They live on Station Camp Creek, in Estill County, Ky. Their children:

1. William Arvine: maried —— ——
2. Nannie Arvine; married John William Carson. They live in Hamilton, Ohio, issue:
    1. Albert Carson.
    2. Cyrus Carson.
    3. John M. Carson.
    4. Mollie Carson.
    5. Lena Carson.
    6. Kate Carson.

9. Nancy Ann Arvine: married Thomas J. Million, of Madison County, Ky., a son of Esquire Green B. Million, late a wealthy citizen of said County, and number of years one of most efficient and best qualified Justices of the Peace. Thomas J. Million died in Richmond, Ky., May 20, 1906. He had been an invalid for a number of years, and his good wife and daughters faithfully and untiringly admistered unto his wants to the end. He bore his afflictions with patience and fortitude, and died the triumps of a living faith. He had been a farmer, and was for a time in the Internal Revenue Service. His brother Elza Million, served one term as Judge of the Madison County Court, elected by the voters of the County. Their children:

1. Isabella Million.
2. Anna Million; married Jacob McCord, son of Andrew McCord. Have one child:

1. Mary Catherine McCord.
3. Green B. Million.
4. Mary A. Million; married O. G. Gray, a tobacco grower. They live at Newby in Madison County, Ky.
5. Emma Lou Million.
6. Elizabeth Million.

Section 7. Willa Oldham; married John Sutton, Nov. 15, 1827.

Section 8. Jackson Oldham; single; (died.)

Section 9. Nathaniel Oldham; died single.

Section 10. Enoch Oldham; married Harriet Bentley, Jan. 20, 18825. He went to Missouri, and entered a section of land and put out 150 acres in walnuts, which was afterwards known as Oldham's Grove.

Section 11. Nathan Oldham; married Rebecca Spence.

CHAPTER 8.

ANN OLDHAM.

(Named in Chapter6, Section 3.)

Article 1.—Ann Oldham, a daughter of Richard Oldham of Estill County, and Ann Pepper his wife, came from North Carolina to Kentucky with her father, and on the 14th day of Sept. 1809, in Estill County, was married to Joseph Collins.

The fruits of this union were the children named in the coming sections:

Section 1. Williaam Smith Collins; married Mary Ann Bronston, a daughter of Rev. Thomas Bronston and Lucy Clark his wife. (See Part V, Chap. 13, Section 7.) Mr. Bronston was a prominent citizen of Madison County, and died in Richmond, Ky., some years since. In his younger days he was an active business man and farmer. Five children were born of this union:

1. Joseph Collins; married Mary Embry, to whom were born:
   1. Thomas B. Colins; married —— Lackey.
   2. Mary Belle Collins; married James Arbuckle.

Mr. Collins enlisted in the Confederate Army Sept. 10, 1862, in the Company of his brother Captain Thomas B. Collins, (being Company F, 7th, afterwards, the 11th Kentucky Cavalry, Colonel Waller Chenault's Regiment, under that gallant commander, noted raider, and intrepid General John H. Morgan, and held the rank of Sergeant. He now holds a certificate as a member with the rank of Sergeant, of the Confederate Veterans Association of Kentucky, bearing date Dec. 19, 1892. This subject is a prominent citizen of Richmond, Ky., and handles fancy horses.

2. Thomas Bronston Collins, was born near Richmond, Ky., Oct. 4, 1842; died in Paris, France, April 12, 1869. A scholar and patriot, graduating with honors at Bethany College, Va., he was one of the first to espouse the Southern cause, entering as private in the Buckner guards. Afterwards Captain of Company F, Kentucky Cavalry, was with Zollicoffer, when that gallant officer was killed at the battle of Mill Springs, Ky. An exile from his native land, he attended the Medical College at Brussels, after which he completed his studies in Paris, and practiced in the hospitals of that City, where he contracted disease of the lungs, which resulted in his death.

"Your own proud and heroic soil,
Shall be your fitter grave,
She claims from war, her richest spoil,
The ashes of her brave."

He raised a Company of Madison County men, Feb. 10, 1862, of which he was captain, known as Company F, 7th, afterwards the 11th Kentucky Cavalry, his Colonel was D. Waller Chenault, under the command of General John H. Morgan. He was a brave and efficient officer, received a wound in the thigh at the battle of Greasy Creek. At the battle of Cynthiana, Ky., he became separated from General Morgan's Command. His war record from that time on, is better told in the language of his own statement, made at Montreal, Canada, Nov. 14, 1864, whilst a prisoner. His statement exhibits the bold, daring, fearless and true spirit of the man, which was made on the occasion of his arrest, proceedings and trial in the Canadian Court for his extradition to the United States. From the Canadian authorities he subsequently made his escape, and went to Nova Scotia, from there to Germany, thence to Paris, France, and there whilst engaged in the study and practice of medicine, was taken sick and died, thus bringing to a close the career of a most noble, chivalrous and brave young man. From there his remains were brought to Richmond, Ky., and interred in the beautiful Richmond Cemetery, and his grave properly marked by a monument. Here read his statement:

"The St. Albans Raider. Statement of the Prisoner:

Montreal, Nov. 14, 1864.

The Prisoner's Voluntary Statement.

All the prisoners made statements.**

Statement of Thomas B. Collins:

"I am a native of Kentucky, and a commissioned officer of the army of the Confederate States, now at war with the so-called United States. I served under the command of General John Morgan, and became separated from it at the battle of Cynthiana, Ky. Having eluded the Yankees, I joined Lieutenant (Bennett H.) Young, afterwards at Chicago, knowing it to be my duty to my Government, as well as to myself, never to desert its cause, I owe no allegiance to the so-called United States, but am a foreigner, and a public enemy to the Yankee Government. The Yankees dragged my father from his peaceful fireside and family circle and imprisoned him in Camp Chase, where his sufferings impaired his health and mind, and my grand-father has been banished from Kentucky by Brute Burbridge. They have stolen negroes and forced them into their armies, leaving their women and children to starve and die. They have pillaged and burned private dwellings, banks, villages, and depopulated whole districts, boasting of their inhuman acts as deeds of heroism, and exhibiting their plunder in the Northern Cities as trophies of Federal victories.

I have violated no laws of Canada or Great Britian, whatever I done at St. Albans, I did as a confederate soldier acting under Lieutenant Young. When I left St. Albans I came to Canada for protection. I entered an hotel at Stanbridge, unarmed and alone, and was arrested and hand-cuffed, by a Canadian Magistrate, Whitman, assisted by Yankees. He had no warrant fo my arrest nor had any sworn complaint been made to him against me. About $9,300 was taken from me when I was arrested, part Confederate booty, lawfully captured and held by me as such, and part of my own private funds. I ask the restoration of the money taken from me, and my discharge as demanded by the rules of International law. The treaty under which my extradition is claimed applies to robbers, murderers, thieves and forgers. I am neither, but a soldier, serving my country in a war commenced and waged against us by a barbarous foe, in violation of their own Constitution,—in disregard of all the rules of warfare as interpreted by civilized nations, and christian peoples, and by Yankees too wise to expose themselves to danger, while they can buy mercenaries, and steal negroes to fight for them—who, while prating of neutrality, seduce your own people along the border to violate the proclamation of your August Sovereign, by joining their armies and leave them when captured by us to languish in prisons in a climate unwholesome to them, and in which they are almost sure to die. If I aided in the sack of the St. Albans banks it was because I knew the pocket nerve of the Yankees to be the most sensitive, and they would suffer most by its being rudely touched. I cared nothing for the booty, except to injure the enemies of our country. Federal soldiers are bought up at the rate of $1,000, a head, and the capture of $200,000, is equivolent to the destruction of 200 of said soldiers, I therefore, thought that the expeditions would pay. "I guess" it did, in view of fact also, that they have wisely sent several thousand soldiers from the "bloody front" to protect exposed points in the rear. For the part I took, I am ready to abide the consequences—knowing that if I be extradited to the Yankee butchers my Government can avenge, if not protect his soldiers.

(At the conclusion of the above statement there were loud bursts of applause from all parts of the Court.)

After the battle of Wild Cat, and General E. Kirby Smith's march through Kentucky, and the battle of Richmond Aug. 30, 1862, Captain Collin's Company was organized and went out from Kentucky with General Smith's army, and joined the command of General Morgan. His company was composed of eighty of Madison County's boys, as brave and daring spirits as ever shouldered a musket. Morgan's raid into the States of Indiana and Ohio—in which was nearly every one of Collins' company, was never surpassed for endurance, dash and daring, being in the saddle twenty one days, without rest or sleep, save the sleep gotten while mounted and marching along—the poor creatures upon which the soldiers were mounted eating only what was handed by the rider whilst in motion.

The following names appear on the Muster Roll of Captain Collins Company, most of the company having enlisted at Richmond, Ky., Sept. 10, 1862, towit:

"Thomas B. Collins, Captain, J. F. Oldham, first Lieutenant, R. J. Park, second Lieutenant, C. H. Covington, third Lieutenant, James Tevis, first Sergeant, James Caldwell, second Sergeant, Thomas Dejarnett, third Sergeant, W. B. Benton, fourth Sergeant, S. C. Broaddus, first Corporal, Robert Caldwell, second Corporal, Alex R.

Fife, third Corporal, Robert Miller, fourth Corporal, Thomas Oldham, Farrier, James Miller, Blacksmith, I. Asbill, Henry Benge, John Benton, Van Benton, T. C. Broaddus, George Butler, Jake Bronston, Peter Beck, James Cosby, James Coulter, Charles Covington, Joseph Collins, (Orderly), James Cochran, W. G. Coldiron, Joel Embry, John Hutchison, Elihu Hall, Wiley Horn, William Grubbs, Anderson Harris (killed at Greasy Creek) David Gillner, Joe Jones (wounded at Greasy Creek), Meredith Jones, M. B. Judy, Jacob Kurtz, Archibald Kavanaugh, J. B. Mize, Travis Million, Owen McKee, James Norman, Presley Oldham, Richard Oldham, James Oldham, Samuel Meeks, Thomas Portwood, Ben Price, Silas Pearce, Robert Rownan, James R. Sims, John Semonis, Andrew Turpin, Samuel Turpin, Harris Thorpe, Granville Troxelle, Durrett White, Daniel White, Joseph Watts, William Wielder, Alex Woods, (died Nov. 13, 1862), C. T. Wright, O. R. Oldham, Robert Hume, Sam Embry, T. D. Carr, J. H. Boggs, James Jones, James Grubbs, Joshua Brooks, Napoleon Brooks, Richard Brooks, John Cornelison, A. J. Dudley, David Irvine, Harvey Ellison, Silas Baxter, Sam Berry, William Berry, Charley Coley, Thomas Hamilton, (died at Camp Douglas, Sept. 27, 1863.)

3. Lucy Collins; died.

4. William Joel Collins, a substantial farmer of Madison County, Ky., had a host of friends and was very popular. He married Ree Phelps, a daughter of Peter T. Phelps, Esquire. Their children were:

1. Peter Phelps Collins.
2. William Smith Collins; dead.
3. Charles Bronston Collins; dead.
4. M. A. Collins. (A physician.)
5. Joseph Jacob Collins.

5. Jacob S. Collins, an influential citizen of Richmond, Ky., Ex-Mayor of said City, an energetic and shrewd business man. Now Democratic candidate for sheirff. He married Kate Marshall, a daughter of Rev. —— Marshall. To whom were born, two sons and two handsome daughters, towit:

1. Marshall Collins.
2 Lucile Collins
3. Mary Ann Collins.
4. William Joe Collins.

Section 2. Leannah Collins; married Zach. Crews.

Section 3. Milton P. Collins, never married, lived and died in Madison County, Ky., leaving a good estate.

Section 4. Joel Collins. He and his brother Joseph, were twins, and he married Mary Beeler Oldham, they had no children. He lived and died in Madison County, Ky., leaving a good estate.

Section 5. Joseph Collins, a twin to his brother Joel, died in his infancy.

Section 6. Sally G. Collins; married William G. Watts, they had no children. (See Part 1, Chap. 14, Section 8.)

Section 7. Mariam F. Collins; married Robert Yates Aug. 1, 1844, to whom were born:

1. Leannah C. Yates⅛ married Joseph Gibbs, issue:
   1. Lucy Gibbs; married Robert Patton.
   2. Alex Gibbs; married Bessie Rayburn.
2. Margaret Ann Yates; married William H. Bates, have issue.
3. William Yates, went South, and married.
4. Milton P. Yates; married Florence Stivers, issue:
   1. Owen Yates.

5. Sallie Yates; died in her infancy.
6. Jacob Collins Yates; married Nannie Crooke, issue:
   1. John Yates.
   2. Margaret M. Yates.
   3. Sally Proctor Yates.
   4. Miriam Yates.
   5. Susan Yates.
   6. Benjamin F. Yates.
   7. William Yates.
   8. Nanie Kavanaugh Yates.
   9. Josephine Yates.

(See Part III, Chapter 26, Section 5.)

Section 8. Ann Collins; married Ed Cornelison Feb. 18, 1847, issue:

1. Ann Cornelison; married John Roberts.
2. Joseph Collins Cornelison, went to Iowa, married —— ——

Section 9. Patsey Collins; married George W. Park, a successful and excellent farmer of Madison County, Ky. To this union were born:

1. Collins Park; died young.
2. Samuel R. Park; married Almira Butner, have issue.
3. Annie Park; married John Francis Wagers, issue:
   1. Minnie Wagers.
   2. Pattie Wagers; married Matt Cohea.
   3. Georgia Wagers.
   4. Frankie Wagers.
4. Curtis F. Park; married Julia Rice, issue:
   1. Joe Park, twin to his brother James.
   2. James Park, twin to his brother Joe.
   3. Curtis Park.
   4. George Park.
   5. Smith Park.
5. Joel Collins Park; married Lucy Downey Embry, see Part I, Chapter 9, Section 3. To them were born:
   ,1. Mary Beeler Park; married —— ——
   2. Embry Park; married —— Alexander.
   3. Susan Park.
   4. Patsey Park; married Thomas Irvine Miller. (See Part I, Chapter 13, Section 4-4.)
   5. Curtis Hume Park.
   6. George Park.

CHAPTER 9.

MILLY OLDHAM.

(Named in Chapter 6, Section 4.)

Article 1.—Milly Oldham, a daughter of Richard Oldham of Estill County, and Ann Pepper his wife, came with her father from North Carolina to Estill County, Ky., she married Josiah Collins, a brother to Joseph Collins, the husband of her sister, Ann.

Her husband Josiah Collins was ordained by the old Baptist Society as a minister of the Gospel. When the great reformation divided the church he went with the reformation and died in that faith. He spent his life in Madison County, Ky., and preached in the County and out of it, and solemnized the rites of many marriages. The fruits of this union were the children named in the coming sections:

Section 1. Joel Collin;s married —— Foster.

Section 2. Jeremiah V. Collins; married first Frances B. Reid, daughter of Jack Reid Aug. 1. 1839, and second —— Lane.

Section 3. William Collins, never married.

Section 4. Louisa Collins; married first Starling Woods, and second Wilson B. Stivers, issue of first marriage:

1. Lou Woods; married Hr. William L. Hockaday.
2. —— Woods; married Congrave Green.

Section 5. Pauline Collins; married Richard Davis, March 16, 1826.

Section 6. Ann Collins; married first Joseph Huls, issue:

1. America Huls; married first Talton Embry, and secondly Thomas Huls.

Mrs. Ann Huls; married second Webber H. Sale, issue:

1. Collins Sale; married —— ——
2. Shelton Sale; married —— ——
3. Thomas Sale. W. H. Sale and his wife now live in Texas, and are aged.

Section 7. Milly Collins; married Robert M. Watts, March 28, 1845. (See Part I. Chap. 14, Section 8,) issue:

1. Green Watts.
2. Doc Watts.
3. Fannie Watts.
4. Tennis Watts.

Section 8. Albert Collins; married in Clark —— Oldham.

CHAPTER 10.

EADY (EDITH) OLDHAM.

(Named in Chapter 6, Section 7.)

Article 1.—Eady (or Edith) Oldham, a daughter of Richard Oldham of Estill County, Ky., and Ann Pepper his wife, was born in North Carolina, about the year 1773, and came with her parents to Estill County, Ky.

She married Jesse Cobb, and settled on the Kentucky River in said County. He represented Estill County in the Kentucky Legislature in 1826. The fruits of this union were the children named in the coming sections:

Section 1. Anne Cobb; married James A. Merrill.

Section 2. Debora Cobb; married James White.

Section 3. Mildred Cobb; married William Wilson, the parents of Alexander P. Wilson, now deceased, Pleasant Wilson, now deceased, and Mrs. Campbell Williams, the mother of Alex Williams of College Hill, Madison County, Ky.

Section 4. Bettie Cobb; married Thomas Baldwin, issue:

1. Jesse Baldwin; married Sallie Park, issue:

1. Thomas E. Baldwin, a prosperous farmer of Madison County, Ky., married Ellen Collins, issue:

1. Mary Baldwin; married Ensign or Lieutenant Colonel, Carlo Britton, United States Navy.

2. Lena Baldwin; married William H. Shanks, of Stanford, Ky. Democratic candidate for Representative in the Legislature.

3. Olivia Baldwin.

4. Thomas Baldwin.

2. Bettie Baldwin; married John W. McPherson, issue:

1. Richard McPherson.

2. Thomas McPherson; died.

3. Pattie McPherson, a trained nurse.

4. John McPherson; married Grace Atherton.

5. Jesse McPherson.

6. Annie McPherson, a stenographer.

7. William McPherson.

8. Harry McPherson.

2. Samuel Baldwin; married Nancy Oldham, a daughter of Richard Oldham and Sallie his wife. (See Chap. 6, Sec. 3.) They had no children. Samuel Baldwin died, and his wife married the second time Mr. Hazelrigg, and there were two children of this union:

1. Ida Hazelrigg.

2. Duck Hazelrigg.

Mr. Hazelrigg died, and the said Nancy married her third husband.

Section 5. Mary Cobb; married John Stofer of Montgomery County, Ky., Jan. 29, 1824. Children:

1. Albert Stofer.

2. William Stofer; married Miss Corrington.

3. Richard Stofer; married Miss Corrington.

4. Silas Stofer; married first Miss Turner, and second, Miss Donald of Fleming.

5. Susan Stofer; married James Roberts.

6. Bettie Stofer; married Warren Mitchell, they went to Kansas.

Section 6. Henry Cobb; married Sally Simmons, issue:

1. Elizabeth Cobb; married William Q. Covington.

2. —— Cobb; married William W. Park.

3. Mary Cobb; married William Willis.

4. Sally Cobb; married Harry Crawford.

5. Henry Cobb; died unmarried.

Section 7. John Cobb; married Betsy Eldridge. (or Moore.)

Section 8. Samuel Cobb; married (Adaline Hanks.

One Samuel Cobb; married Parmelia Ann Park Feb. 14, 1838.

Section 9. William Cobb; died when only four or five years old.

Section 10. Nancy Cobb, was blind, and died at 12 years of age.

Section 11. Jesse Cobb; married Eliza Park Nov. 1, 1842, to whom were born:

1. Mary Cobb; married Cyrus Park.
2. Rhoda Cobb; married Joel T. Embry, issue:
   1. Charles Embry.
3. Milly Cobb; married Robert Caldwell.

Jesse Cobb's wife died and he married her sister Tabitha Park Feb. 14, 1850, to whom were born:

1. Winnie Cobb; married John C. Caldwell.
2. Pattie Cobb; married James A. Harding.
3. Minerva Cobb; married Charles E. Colyer.
4. Lilly Cobb; married William L. Blanton.
5. Jesse Cobb. The present efficient and polite clerk of the Madison County Court. Now serving a second term. He married Ella Elmore, the parents of a very interesting family of children, now living in Richmond, Ky., formerly a citizen of Estill County.
6. Ida Cobb; married C. D. Munday.
7. Richard C. Cobb; married Sally Elizabeth Thorpe. (See Part I, Chap. 13, Section 1-10.)

Jesse Cobb, the father of the above two sets of children was a prominent farmer of Estill County. His farm being on the Kentucky River, near the mouth of Drowning Creek, where he lived and died. His last wife now 1905, lives in Madison County, with her children.

Section 12. Richard Cobb; married Minerva Park Feb. 8, 1842, and moved to Lincoln County, where he became a prominent and successful farmer. He was born in 1818. His wife was born May 4, 1822, and they were married Tuesday February 8, 1842. The fruits of this union were:

1. Sallie Winifred Cobb; married Thomas Phelps, a rich farmer of Madison County, Ky., and a clever man.
2. Elizabeth Cobb; married Nathan H. McKinney, of Lincoln County, Ky.
3. Carlisle Cobb; died in her infancy.
4. Kate Cobb; married Harrison T. Bush, issue:
   1. Richard C. Bush, attorney at law.

   Mrs. Bush died and her husband married Bettie Harris, of Lincoln County. (See Part III, Chap. 31, Section 6.)
5. Mary Cobb; married William H. Hocker.
6. Florence Cobb; married John H. Myers.
7. Ettie Cobb; married Joseph H. McAlister.
8. Richard Cobbb; married Tabitha Taylor Phelps.

Jesse Cobbs, senior, died June 1, 1836, aged 67 years, and his wife, Eady (Edith) died June 23, 1836, aged 63 years.

CHAPTER 11.

WILLIAM OLDHAM.

(Named in Chapter 6, Section 7.)

Article 1.—William Oldham, a son of Richard Oldham of Estill County, and Ann Pepper his wife was born in North Carolina April 23, 1777.

He came to Madison County, Ky., about 1798, and married first Sallie Gilbert, a daughter of Samuel Gilbert Oct. 19, 1809, and settled and lived on Muddy Creek in Madison County, Ky. His wife having died he married secondly, Oct. 30, 1826, Mrs. Susannah Anderson Moberley (nee Reid) widow of Benjamin Moberley, deceased. (See Part II, Chap. 48, Sec. 2, and Part VI, Chap. 6, Sec. 8.) The children of the first marriage, towit:

Section 1. Wade Hampton Oldham; married Arthusa Yates, Feb. 20, 1834. Their children:

1. William Oldham, when a boy became entangled in the gear on a horse and was killed.

2. Joseph F. Oldham, was first lieutenant in Captain Thomas B. Collins's Company F 7th, afterwards the 11th Kentucky Confederate Cavalry. Colonel D. Waller Chenault, General John H. Morgan's command, and was captured on the Ohio and Indiana raid. After the war he married Lydia Ann Ellison, a daughter of Amos Ellison, Nov. 26, 1868, and sold goods for many years at Speedwell, afterwards on the Red River road, two and a half miles south of Waco, and then moved to Union City, where he was a merchant till his death. His widow lives in Richmond, Ky. He had one son:

1. Joseph H. Oldham, Jr., married Miss Lena Hackett, Nov. 22, 1898, a resident of Richmond, Ky.

3. Richard Oldham; married Minerva Dolly Ross, Nov. 9, 1865.

4. Oscar Oldham, went to Beattyville, Ky., and married —— — He was a soldier in the Federal Army.

Section 2. Elizabeth Oldham; married Sanford Feland Jan. 19, 1837. They emigrated to Missouri.

Section 3. Minerva Oldham; married Jeremiah V. Brooks, April 12, 1833, and died leaving two children:

1. Sallie Brooks.
2. J—— Brooks.

Section 4. Miranda Oldham; married Mr. William W. Peacock, September 16, 1840.

Section 5. Ann P. Oldham; married Mr. Jonathan Cox, Oct. 2, 1833.

Section 6. Mariam Oldham; married first Mr. John A. Mize Nov. 22, 1843, and secondly Thomas H. Blakemore March 27, 1851. Had by the first marriage a son:

1. William Oldham Mize, a lawyer, up in the Hazel Green section.

Section 7. Milly Oldham; married William T. Bush Nov. 23, 1838. They had:

1. Sallie Bush; married Rufus Moberley.
2. John Bush, went into the army. Know nothing further of him.
3. Miss Bush; married Little William Oldham, son of Richard Oldham and Mary Ann Park his wife. They emigrated to Texas. (See Section 10.)
4. Miss —— Bush.

Section 8. Sallie Oldham.

Section 9. Patsey Oldham; married Ichabod Moberley. (See Part 6, Chapter 31-7.)

Section 10. Richard Oldham; married Mary Ann Park, Sept. 4, 1833. Their children:

1. Wade Oldham, went to Illinois and married.

2. Eli Oldham; married Miss —— Sams. Had a daughter:
   1. Temperance Oldham, went to Clark County, and married, and now lives there.
3. Samuel Gilbert Oldham; died in the army.
4. Napoleon B. Oldham; married Miss Susan Ann Elizabeth Frunty Jan. 23, 1862.
5. William Oldham; married Miss Bush, and emigrated to Texas. (See Section 7.)
6. George Oldham; married Miss Dillingham, daughter of Elihue Dilingham, of Missouri.
7. Junius B. Oldham; married Mary M. Hisle Feb. 4, 1868. They emigrated to the West and now live in —— Oklahoma. They had:
   1. Richard Oldham. And others.
8. Winnie Oldham; married Munroe Lackey, she died leaving a son:
   1. Richard Oldham Lackey, now a merchant of Richmond, Ky.

Children of William Oldham and Mrs. Susannah Anderson Reid Moberley his wife:

Section 11. Armilda Caroline Oldham; died Aug. 20, 1832, at the age of five years, and nine days.

Section 12. Amanda Oldham; died Oct. 12, 1850, at the age of 17 years, 9 months, and 6 days.

Section 13. Juliet Oldham, born March 10, 1835; married Jeremiah Broaddus Jan. 13, 1848, (See Part I, Chap. 13, Sec. 3,) a prosperous farmer of Madison County, Ky., who became the owner of her father's homestead, on Muddy Creek, where they both lived and died and were buried, she died April 13, 1893, and her husband married the second time, Caroline Harris, (See Part III, Chap. 14, Section 4,) but no issue:

The children of Juliet and Jeremiah Broaddus:

1. Andrew J. Broaddus; married Hannah Oldham. (See Chap. 26, Sec. 3.) Has been County Assessor of Madison, elected by the Democratic vote, is a farmer. Their children:
   1. Thomas O. Broaddus; married Milly Moberley.
   2. Pearl Broaddus; married George Park.
   3. Mattie Broaddus; married Alexander Turpin.
   4. Nannie Broaddus; married George Gentry.
   5. Alma Broaddus; married Jacob Gentry.
   6. Andrew Goff Broaddus.
   7. Tobe Hackett Broaddus.
   8. Grover Cleveland Broaddus.
   9. Everett Kavanaugh Broaddus.
   10. Laura Etta Broaddus; died.
2. William Oldham Broaddus; married Emma Hill, daughter of Elba Hill, of Madison County, Ky., emigrated to the West. Their children:
   1. Allie Broaddus; died in infancy.
   2. Lillie Broaddus; married Mr. Phinx.
   3. Susan Broaddus; married Mr. Smith.
3. Susannah Broaddus, born April 6, 1853, died Aug. 9, 1878, the wife of H. Clay Chambers, leaving these children:
   1. John Chambers; married Florence Willoughby.
   2. Julia Chambers; married Hugh Duncan. (See Part VII, Chapter 9, Section 3.)
   3. Jeremiah Chambers; married Sarah Taylor, daughter of John Gidion Taylor.

4. Elbridge C. Broaddus; married Georgia Thorpe, daughter of George H. Thorpe and Elizabeth Yates his wife. (See Part III, Chapter 13, Section 1.) Their children:

1. Bessie Broaddus; married Rufus K. Moberley.
2. Juliet Broaddus; married Harvey Green.
3. Hume Broaddus.
4. Muggie Broaddus; married Charles L. Moberley.
5. Emma Broaddus.
6. Edgar Broaddus.
7. Wilson Broaddus.
8. Curg Broaddus. (A daughter.)
9. Caroline Broaddus.
10. Eva Broaddus.
11. A son, unnamed, died shortly after birth.

5. Jeremiah Broaddus; married Kate Oldham. (See Chapter 28, Section 4.) Their children:

1. Estille (Stella) Broaddus.
2. Leonard Broaddus.
3. Abner Broaddus.
4. Verna Broaddus.
5. Susan Broaddus.
6. Julian Broaddus.
7. Bessie Lee Broaddus.
8. Willie Broaddus.
9. Marietta Broaddus.
10. Jeremiah Broaddus.
11. A child died in infancy.

This family emigrated to Indiana.

6. Grace Broaddus; married first Dr. Coleman C. Christopher, and secondly William D. Bonny. Had children by both husbands. Children of the first marriage:

1. Lena Christopher; married George Ogden.
2. Mary T. Christopher.
3. Lizzie Sue Christopher.
4. A child died in infancy.

Children of the seocnd marriage:

5. Lucile Bonny.
6. —— Bonny.
7. —— Bonny.

7. Julietta Broaddus; married Tobias Hackett, and left these children:

1. Bazzie Hackett; married Lewis Roberis, went to Cuba.
2. Lula Hackett.
3. May Hackett, a son.
4. Willie Hackett.

8. Eva Broaddus; married Lee Todd. Their children:

1. Robert Todd.
2. Clarence Todd.

9. Elizabeth Broaddus, born Dec. 26, 1869, died April 9,

1. Charles Parkes.

10. Mattie B. Broaddus, born April 8, 1855, died May 26, 1860.

11. Lycurgus Broaddus; married Maym Douglas. They emigrated to Missouri. Their children:

1. Beatrice Broaddus.
2. Sue Frances Broaddus.

William Oldham died Sept. 26, 1849, aged 72 years, 5 months, and 3 days, and his wife Susannah Anderson Reid Moberley Oldham, died May 13, 1851, at the age of 63 years, 5 months and 16 days

CHAPTER 12.

SAMUEL OLDHAM.

(Named in Chapter 6, Section 8.)

Article 1.—Samuel Oldham, a son of Richard Oldham of Estill County, and Ann Pepper his wife, was born in North Carolina, and immigrated to Madison County, Ky., prior to 1797, and settled on Otter Creek, where he was married to Polly White August 8, 1797.

He emigrated later on to Missouri. Their children:

Section 1. Milly Oldham; died when about twenty years old.

Section 2. Schuyler Oldham, was with Walker in his fillibustering expedition, and was killed in Nicaragua.

Section 3. Hannah Oldham; married John Biggerstaff Aug., 19, 1824.

Section 4. Napoleon B. Oldham; married Sallie Ann Karr Nov. 22, 1836.

Section 5. Ann Oldham; married Lawson Talbott Jan. 3, 1837.

CHAPTER 13. A.

MOSES OLDHAM.

(Named in Chapter 6, Section 6.)

Article 1.—Moses Oldham, a son of Richard Oldham of Estill County, Ky., and Ann Pepper his wife, came from Caswell County, North Carolina about 1795, and settled in Madison County, Ky., on Otter Creek, within a few miles of Boonsborough.

On the tenth day of Oct. 1796, in the last named County, he was married to Ann White. This family subsequently emigrated to Missouri. The tradition is that Moses Oldham before leaving for the West, occupied most of his time in flat boats on the Kentucky, Ohio and Mississippi rivers, buying all kinds of produce and supplies, and floating same to New Orleans, where he would dispose of his stock and crafts, and walk back to Kentucky, through the wild country—the tramp requiring many days of hazard and peril, but being hardy and courageous, the same was his delight. The children born to them were, viz:

Section 1. Major William Oldham, was born at the home on Otter Creek in Madison County, Ky., in 1802. After growing to manhood he owned and lived on a farm near Brookstown, in said County containing three or four hundred acres, and Abner Oldham, a first cousin, and brother-in-law to his father, was his nearest neighbor, and Abner's son Thompson B. now living remembers William Oldham well, and has heard Ibsan tell of his visits to the home of his brother, William, in Texas, and of their wonderful exploits. William Oldham was a trader on a large scale, while a resident of

Kentucky, and in the early thirties formed a partnership with K. G. of Clark County, and they went to New Orleans with a large number of negro slaves, having sold the greater portion, Oldham entrusted the money for them with his partner to bring home, whilst he remained to make sale of the rest. When Oldham returned home he found that his partner had gambled the money away and mortgaged his property to his father, and left the debts (for the price of about 200 negroes) for Oldham to pay. Oldham held what money he had, and in about 1835, went to Texas, and bought a Mexican claim of three leagues of land, in the Brazos river bottoms, leaving his farm near Brookstown in Madison County, Ky., which his partner's father managed to have applied to the payment of a debt he claimed the partnership owed him.

Thomas B. Oldham remembers seeing the drove of about 100 of the slaves, including men, women and children pass his house starting for the south.

William Oldham was never married. After going to Texas he served on the frontier, and in the wars with the Mexicans, and held the rank of Major, and his name was made famous on account of his part in border warfare.

At the out break of the Mexican war, many recruits were raised in Madison County, Ky., and went to the war, among them Waller Chenault (afterwards Colonel in the Confederate army, who fell in battle in 1862), while passing through Texas, Captain Chenault was taken sick and stopped at Major Oldham's home, was taken in, and there lay sick a long while and was kindly treated and cared for free of charge. Major Oldham told Captain Chenault, that when land got up so he could get something for it, he would sell enough and return to Kentucky and pay his debts. He owned a large tract of land on the Brazos river, lying twelve miles east from Caldwell, Burleson County, Texas, and his sister had also a large tract adjoining.

Major Oldham and a relative Thomas Oldham, (mentioned in Chapter 39) and Big Foot Wallace, (mentioned in Part IV, Chapter 4, Section 4-4) were in the Maier Expedition graphically pictured in the clipping from the St. Louis Globe Democrat. Upon reaching the river near the town of Maier, Thomas Oldham, G. B. Eurath, and ten other comrades were detailed to remain in camp and care for the horses, while the rest of the Texans crossed the river to see about provisions etc., and the fight ensued in which the Mexicans were repulsed, and the hand-ful of Texans took possession of a large building in which they forted, the Mexicans surrounded them and sent a flag of truce, saying they had 1000 more men and demanding surrender of men and arms, promising that the Texans should be fed and well treated.

In the mean time, two of the company of Texans, Chalk and Sin Clair had hid behind a bunch of cane near the out side corner of the building and soon made their escape and went to the river and hailed the boys left to care for the horses to bring over the boat, the boys asked "Who are you?" the response was "Chalk anl Sin Clair." The boat was hurried over, and just as they landed back on the Texas side with Chalk and Sin Clair, the Mexicans called to them to bring over the boat, but no satisfactiory answer being given when asked "Who are you?" the boys knocked holes in the boat and sank it, and hurried to camp, mounted their horses, each leading a horse, and started for home chased by the Mexicans, who followed for several days, some days being in sight all the day. Major Oldham became a prisoner in the hands of these cruel Mexicans. At Matamoras they planned to escape. When their dinner was brought to them, Cameron jumped in the door, and waived his hat, and all broke out, knocking the guards down and capturing their guns and escaping, followed by the Mexicans. Not knowing the country they soon starved out for water as well as bread, and all except Major Oldham and one comrade (name not recalled) surrendered again to the Mexicans. Oldham and his comrade took to the mountains and climbed and crawled in the hot sun in sight of the enemy for two days without water to quench their thirst and to cool their parched tongue and lips. His comrade wanted to give up, but Major Oldham said no, I had as soon die in the mountains as to be murdered by the Mexicans. They crossed over the mountains and found water and rested and started for home, and for three weary months without blankets and sufficient clothing and destitute of food, only as they found it in the mountains and on the prairies and often without water to the point almost of famishing. One day after they had done without water for two or three days, down in a deep gulch they found some damp sand into which they scratched and found water. His comrade would drink a little and Major Oldham would pull him away, and then he would get down to it, and drink as long as he could hold a drop, but their stomachs were in such feeble condition as not to retain the water at first, they took it turn about and stayed with the water till their thirsts were thoroughly quenched. Looking up they saw bees working out of a hole in the bank of the gulch into which they dug with their knives and fingers and got all the honey they could wrap up in a green deer hide they had, and there they camped for the night. After reaching the border of Texas they called at a Mexican ranch, hoping to get something to eat, but found no one at home. Winter was approaching and the shirt of his comrade was worn out, plenty of clothes and blankets were hanging on the fence, Major Oldham took a blanket, but his comrade, a very conscientious man, refused to take anything, until rather compelled by the Major to take a shirt. That night very severe weather set in and they came near freezing. To Major Oldham his comrade said that "the Lord sent the cold on them because they stole the blanket and shirt," but the Major always thought their lives were saved by taking them, and that the cold weather was coming any way.

In 1866, Joseph Alexander McMurry now living in Valley Mills, Texas, went to Burleson County to close up some business for his father, and stopped and stayed over night with Major William Oldham, he was then living on his farm with his old slaves, who had not left him. He had cut a new set of teeth, his eye sight had come back, and he could see as good as ever he could, and his hair, eye brows and beard had turned black. Major Oldham was buried in the Austin City new Cemetery. The record of his interment shows, "1868," June 22, Major William Oldham, 66 male, killed by fall from Bluff of River." John Eckels lived near Major Oldham. The Major had a sister, Arzela, married Robert Eckels in Madison County, Ky.

The following clipped from the St. Louis Globe Democrat:

"Harrowing Lottery of Death."

Prisoners of Mier captured by Mexicans. Drew from a pot of beans to know if they should live.

(St. Louis Globe Democrat.)

History has no other story to tell like the story of Mier. When the historian lives who can write of Mier as McCauley wrote of the defenders of Londonderry, the republic of letters will possess another immortal, and when the artist lives whose genius will be equal to the task of reproducing the scene of "The Lottery of Death," the eyes of all the world will be turned upon the Lone Star, and all tongues will mention the names of the heroes of Mier in tones of wonder and admiration.

But one of the famous three hundred who furled the flag of the Lone Star, where Mexican gore choked the gutters is now alive, John Rafus Alexander, nearly 90 years of age, totally blind and very deaf, sits upon the porch of his comfortable home near Round Mountain in Blanco County, Texas. "Where the latch string has hung on the out side for more than half a century," ever willing and eager to tell the story of old wars, and fight over the battles of the land he loves so well.

Mier was an affair ignored by early historians. Many suspected improper motives and shameful conduct on the part of some of the leaders, while others openly charged General Fisher with cowardice. In the fall of 1842, General Woll, at the head of a Mexican army, made a dash across the Rio Grande, and by forced marches through a country that had been deemed impracticable for military operations, he suddenly appeared at the gates of San Antonio. The defenseless city was easily captured, and after making prisoners of the Supreme Court and many prominent citizens, the venturesome General sought to return to Mexico greatly encumbered by spoils. The Texans sprang to arms, and enraged to frenzy by the massacre of Dawson's men, after they had surrendered, they threw themselves upon the retreating Mexicans at the Salio, and slaughtered them until they were saved by flight and night. Allowing the retreating army no time to rest or sleep, the mad Texans harassed it night and day, until the Mexicans, famished and bleeding were driven into the Rio Grande. There General Summerville disbanded the Texan army and ordered the men, volunteers, to return to their homes. Unfortunately there were several soldiers of fortune in the camp. Here was the material for the occupation of such men. Some of them had led ragged batallions across the Pyranees, others had defended barricades inthe streets of Paris; and another group, of which General Fisher was Chief, had been mixed up with the annual revolutions in Mexico. The cry of "On to Mexico!" was raised, and the drums beat for recruits in the camp. The spirit of war was uppermost in the minds of the disappointed men who saw the Mexicans struggling away with spoils, and the blood of comrades on their hands. Old Mars was loose, and the orators made the enraged Texans hear the God of war striking his shield and promising them victory. Three hundred of them seized their arms, and shouting the battle cry "On to Mexico!" they embarked on the Rio Grande under the command of General Fisher. They carried the town of Mier by storm, and obtaining possession of a row of adobe buildings that commanded the plaza(they held the place through the dawning hours of a Christmas morning, and all Christmas day they fought as their comrades had fought at the Alamo, and San Jacinto. Three hundred against three thousand. The Texans understood the situation. They knew that Ampulia was coming by forced marches with 1,700 infantry and a train of artillery. They ought to have retired, but the soldiers of fortune promised them victory. "Stand to your guns, boys," they said, "and we will lead you to the palace of Santa Anna, where you can open the dungeons of Perote, and release your comrades and run your arm to your elbows into the treasure of the Montezumas."

On the morning of the 26th the earth trembled beneath the roar of cannon, and grape shot fell upon the 300 like hail. Big Foot Wallace, Captain Cameron and Major Oldham looked toward the river, hoping to see a way of retreat. They saw long lines of infantry with fixed bayonets and cannon in every street. "Another Alamo," Wallace made the exclamation, and as the three returned to the firing line muttering, "Yes, another Alamo," Fisher fell. Again and again the Mexican infantry charged across the plaza and often a whole regiment was held at bay or driven back by the handful of Texans. Great breaches were made in the walls by solid shot, and sharp-shooters swarmed on the housetops. Every charge had been repulsed, the streets were thickly strewn with the dead, and blood was flowing in the gutters when the Mexican General made a demand for a surrender of the place.

"I was standing near a window" says Mr. Alexander, "when Major Oldham called my attention to General Fisher and three Mexican officers, who were having a parley in the street. After a moments absence, Oldham turned to me, saying, "why John, the d—m coward is talking of surrendering." Yells of rage and despair drowned all other noise. Some said we were betrayed, others said that Fisher was not wounded at all. They called him a traitor. A dozen men were making speeches at once. I remember well that Big Foot Wallace said "Don't talk to me of Mexican mangnanimity, it means fill us with beans one day, and bullets the next." General Fisher's hand was bloody, but he could not have been badly hurt, for he kept on his feet. "Before we realized what had happened, General Fisher and a part of the army was moving out of the building under the protection of a white flag. All semblance of discipline was lost. Soldiers crowded about the officers asking for orders. Only a few moments passed and there were not more than a dozen armed men in our works. "I hated to surrender, but Oldham said, "Boys, I guess we had better go with the rest and hope for a chance to make a break."

"While we were stacking over arms, the Mexican officers treated us with the greatest courtesy, promising that we should soon be sent back across the Rio Grande." The Mier prisoners were first sent to Matamoras, under a strong guard. They arrived famished foot sore, and perfectly sensible of the fact that the Mexicans intended to violate every term of the capitulation.

While staggering through the streets of Matamoras with their bleeding feet, bound in rags, and their swollen tongues black and cracked protruding from their mouths, Major Oldham happened to see a friend of his boyhood standing upon the sidewalk, the man was a wealthy traveler and he proved to possess a heart of gold. Touched by the wretched plight of his old friend and his comrades, he instantly poured $100 in gold into Major Oldham's hands. A few hours afterward he visited the dirty prison where the heroes of Mier were confined and distributed $1,000 amongst them. Mr. Alexander has forgotten the name of this noble man, but he said Oldham's children who live in Burleson County will remember it.

The betrayed prisoners were next started on their long march toward the dungeons of Perote. "We were always talking of making a break," said the old veteran, "but all of our plans failed. We passed through Monterey and Saltillo, and 75 miles beyond, at the haciendo Del Salado, the galling yoke had worn to the quick. The Texans were familiar with stories of the horrors of the gloomy dungeons of Petrote, and brave men with tears in their eyes, declared that they would rather die fighting the cruel guards than to tamely go on to vaults of darkness, where death by starvation and torture surely awaited them. "The day was dawning at the Salado, "says Mr. Alexander," when I went out to stir up the camp fire. Brave Major Brenham—after whom the town of Brenham was named—and young Lyon sat there. Brenham said "I am covered with scars that I got in the dungeons of Perote. They will know me and shoot me the moment we get there." Lyon stepped to the door. He said "it is too late, that red-cap company are mounting their horses." "Brenham sprang to the door and seized one of the guards and Lyon downed another. The break had been preconcerted, but I did not know it. A wild yell "Liberty or Death!" was on every lip. Big Foot Wallace, Oldham and Cameron were first to spring at the throats of the Mexicans. Brenham and Lyon were both killed. Each of us singled out a cavalryman, and about half secured arms and horses at once. The cowardly guards were paralyzed with terror, and they fled, or surrendered on the spot. We secured cartridges and rations and $1,400 in silver and galloped away from the haciendo Del Salado. If we had been governed by the advice of Wallace, Cameron and Oldham and kept the highway we could have defied pursuit and easily reached the Rio Grande. We followed the road for 75 miles, and we camped and cooked dinner almost in sight of Saltillo. Here many of the men became alarmed and they broke away into the mountains. The triumverate of braves galloped among the startled Texans, storming, threating and warning them of the danger of plunging into the barren wastes, and limitless solitudes, where there was neither water nor food, but all to no purpose. For days and days they wandered, famished and ready to drop dead from hunger and thirst. Some opened the veins in the necks of their horses and sucked the blood, others threw themselves upon the ground and digging at the roots of cactus, they pressed the damp earth to their parched lips. In this condition they were captured by the humane General Mexia. He was so deeply touched by the wretched condition of the wanderers that he made his soldiers give them water and food on the spot.

Santa Anna ordered Mexia to have every tenth man shot, but the brave, generous soldier refused to have anything to do with such an inhuman piece of butchery. The monster of ingratitude had no difficulty in finding a butcher. In the twilight, when the tired prisoners of Mier sat about the camp fires of the haciendo Del Salado, talking of home and friends so far away, a brute appeared amongst them with an earthen jar in his hands, by his side stood an officer, little less beastly in look, who told the prisoners to prepare for the lottery of death. A few words were spoken. It was whispered that those who drew death here, would escape the horrors of Perote. There were 159 white beans in the jar, and 17 black ones. Brave Cameron advanced with his head erect, and the firm, proud step of one going to battle. "Well, boys," he said if we must draw, I will do it first. He drew life. The brave scout was doomed for Santa Anna had him shot some days afterward. The poor fellows who drew black beans were pushed in a group under a black flag. Their courage did not fail them. Two brothers drew together, one was lying sick on a cot. The sick boy drew life, but he put his arm about the neck of his brother, and when he drew death, the two noble boys exchanged beans. Those who stood near heard the whispered words, "you know I have got consumption, go home and take care of mother."

That terrible night 159 Texans sat with their faces buried in their hands. They could hear the volleys of musketry that closed the earthly career of their brave, patriotic comrades and many of them registered vows that were not forgotten when war raged over Mexico a few years later.

John Rufus Alexander, Major Oldham and seven others escaped into the mountains. Oldham was a born leader, possessing the courage and endurance of a Spartan. Alexander was young, strong and brave. These two stuck together, and after enduring incredible hardships, traversing parching plains and the inhospitable solitudes of rugged mountains for 300 miles without meeting a single human being, they finally reached the land of the Lone Star, where they threw their living skeletons upon the soil so dearly bought, and wept for joy. The other seven perished or were recaptured. The prisoners of Mier were thrown into the dungeons of Perote. Some were yoked together and made to draw carts on the streets of the city of Mexico.

Santa Anna's wife, an angel, saw them, and their misery touched her tender heart. She visited their gloomy prison and with her delicate hands she soothed the brows of the sick. She gave them little luxuries—luxuries to them—and she unlocked the chains of many. When this angel of mercy was lying upon her death bed, she called her cruel husband to her side, and made him promise "to send the poor Americans to their home." He kept his word.

In 1844 Big Fooot Wallace led the last remnant of the prisoners of Mier across the Rio Grande, and many got down on their knees and kissed the land they had helped to buy with blood and tears.

I spent two nights and a day with this venerable old hero. "We had a hard time," he said "to wrest this fine land from the Indians and Mexicans, and make it a safe place for the countless thousands who now possess it. I am proud of my share."

Section 2. Conway Oldham; died unmarried.

Section 3. Ibsan Oldham; died unmarried.

Section 4. Leonidas Oldham, emigrated to Missouri and married ——— ——— in that country.

Section 5. Jerusha Oldham; married William Thompson, son of Lawrence Thompson, and Kizziah Hart his wife, a daughter of Nathaniel Hart, who was killed by Indian's at his home on Otter Creek, just above Boonsborough, within 150 yards of where stands the brick house he built, and a short distance from the old log house built by Jesse Oldham.

Section 6. Armilda Oldham; married Frances Haley Feb. 5, 1829.

Section 7. Arzela Oldham; married Robert Eckels.

CHAPTER 13 B.

CAPTAIN JOHN OLDHAM.

(Named in Chapter 2, Section 9.)

Article 1.—Captain John Oldham, a son of William Oldham and Miss Basey his wife, was born in Prince William County, Va., Nov. 10, 1757.

He was a Revolutionary soldier enlisted in Caswell County, North Carolina, was soon promoted to the rank of Captain and was Captain of a company in 1777. He was in General Gates' command, when said General was defeated at Camden, South Carolina, Aug. 16, 1780, by the British under Cornwallis. In this battle the Colonial Standard bearer, was shot down, and Captain John Oldham seized the standard, and bore it till the final defeat of his command.

After this battle he was in the command of General Nathaniel Green, until the close of the war. He was in the battles of Cowpens Jan. 17, 1781, witnessed the defeat of Lord Cornwallis, and he was in all the battles participated in by General Green's command, after entering same, stretching over four years service. Here is a letter from the Hon. V. Warner, Commissioner of Pensions:

"Old War and Navy Division. 3-1883. M. B. H.

Department of the Interior
Bureau of Pensions.

Wid. File 8492,
John Oldham. Washington D. C. Dec. 22, 1905.
Revolutionary War.

Madam:—

Referring to the above noted claim, you are advised that neither John Oldham, nor his widow, Annis Oldham, ever applied for a pension on acount of his service in the Revolutionary war, but that on June 12, 1852, their son, Hezekiah Oldham, for himself and brothers and sisters, applied for what ever pension, was due their father and mother, giving the following data:

John Oldham was born Nov. 10, 1757, and served three months as ensign, and Captain in Colonel Moore's Regiment, North Carolina line; he was in the battles of Camden, Compens and Guilford Court House, he died in Estill County, Ky., Nov. 17, 1831.

He married Annis Rice, born March 4, 1759, on Feb. 24, 1783, in Caswell County, North Carolina; she died in Estill County, Ky., March 14, 1840. The children's claim was allowed

Children: Abner, born Dec. 2, 1783, Absalom, born May 28, 1785. Hezekiah, born April 10, 1787, Caleb, born June 1, 1789, Mary, born May 22, 1791, married James Grubbs, Sarah, born May 14, 1793, married Thomas S. Moberley, Elizabeth, born June 15, 1795, maried William Fisher, Nancy, born Dec. 10, 1797, married Jesse Grubbs, John Rice, born July 14, 1801.

Grand-children: David D. Narcissus, married Josiah P. Chenault, Sophia, married Temple Burgin, Helen M., Thomas B., Miranda. Louisa, married Jonathan Estill (children of Abner) Othniel R, son of Hezekiah, John M. (P.), son of Caleb.

Very Respectfully,
V. Warner, Commissioner.

Mrs. Kate Oldham Miller,
Richmond, Madison County,
Kentucky."

Annis Rice the wife of Captain John Oldham, was a daughter of Hezekiah Rice and Mary Bullock his wife, of Caswell County, North Carolina, the said Mary Bullock was a sister of James Bullock, who settled near Walnut Hill in Fayette County, Ky. The Bullocks around Lexington descended from said James Bullock.

Hezekiah Rice and Mary Bullock, lived together as man and wife seventy years. (See slip at foot marked "Rice.)

In 1795, Captain John Oldham, his wife, and at that time six children Abner, Absalom, Hezekiah, Caleb, Mary and Sally moved from Caswell County, North Carolina to Kentucky, and he preempted a large tract of land, in what was then Clark, now Estill County, Ky., on the Kentucky River, near the mouth of Drowning Creek, and purchased other lands, and became the owner of lands on both sides of the River, in both Madison and Estill Counties.

Other children than those last above named, were born in Kentucky. Estill County was established in 1808, and at the organization of the first Circuit Court thereof on Monday June 20, 1808, in the seventeenth year of the Commonwealth, Judge Samuel McDowell in the seat as presiding Judge, Stephen Trigg and John Oldham, Esquires who held commissions from the hand and seal of Christopher Greenup, Esquire, Governor of the Commonwealth of Kentucky, as assistant Judges of said Court, bearing date Feb. 18, 1808, produced their separate certificates of qualification and were duly seated as assistant Judges, and Captain John Oldham held the office of Judge a number of years. His ferry across the Kentucky River near the mouth of Falling Branch, was established Oct. 19, 1812, by order of the court.

Captain John Oldham at an early date, after becoming a resident of Kentucky drove from his home over the mountains to Charleston, South Carolina, the first drove of hogs (1,000 head) that had been driven from Kentucky to the South—which he had to herd every night—there being no lot or pound along the route in which to confine the hogs. His young son Hezekiah (Kie) being with him to assist in the drive, which was a considerable undertaking, walking and driving 1000 hogs, through the wilderness from Kentucky to South Carolina. Afterwards he carried many droves to the Southern markets. His sons, Kie and Caleb, for many and many years, after growing to manhood and being thrown on their own resources, made it a practice every fall, to drive hogs through to the South, and became noted drovers, buying up all the hogs in the country that were for sale.

The first brick house in Estill County, was a dwelling built by Captain John Oldham. He was a man of wonderful nerve, energy and endurance, very prosperous and just.

After settling in Estill County, Captain John and his brother Richard Oldham, and his neighbors, joined in a successful effort to procure a school teacher. He wrote to a relative in Wales to send him a man qualified to teach school, in response a Mr. Hutchison, a learned English and Latin scholar, came from Wales, to the home of Captain Oldham in Estill County, and there taught the children of Captain Oldham and others and his oldest sons Abner and Absalom became good English as well as Latin scholars. Hutchison remained in Kentucky till his death, and taught school at other places.

Captain John Oldham whilst he lived would make no application for a pension for service in the Revolution saying "he was opposed to the pension law and would not accept its benefits, that it was the rightful duty of every patriotic citizen to defend the liberties of his country—that the soldiers in time, received their regular pay for service," and he held that "this sacred duty was degraded by the pension law."

In his day the farmers wintered their hogs on mast. One season the acorns were scarce in Captain Oldham's neighborhood, and he drove his hogs up on Station Camp Creek to mast, and left his two oldest sons, Abner and Absalom, to look after and take care of the hogs, the boys made their camp, under a shelving rock of the cliff, in front of which they placed a log; they had with them two good bear-dogs. "Ring and Rover," and guns, the dogs however, were afraid of panthers. One night the boys went hunting, and the dogs treed a bear up a big poplar tree, they both fired their guns at the bear, and the bear tumbled out, one of the balls having struck behind the shoulder, bruin was badly wounded but not dead, the boys ran upon it, one with a knife, the other with an axe, and they soon dispatched the bear, skinned it and swang the meat upon some high forks, out of reach of the wolves, which were plentiful. On returning to camp, their father was there, with corn meal with which to make Johnny Cakes, and meat and salt; they brought the bear meat, and skin into camp. The next night a panther, scenting the blood of the bear, was attracted thereby to the camp, the noise made by the panther awakened Captain Oldham, who spied the creature by the bright camp fire shinning its eyes, and presenting and resting his gun over the log in front of the rock-house camp, he took deliberate aim between the eyes, fired and dropped the panther dead, which was also skinned; the boys then had a bear skin and a panther skin to help soften their bed. When Captain Oldham returned home he took a quantity of the bear meat with him.

On another occasion Captain Oldham mounted his horse with his gun in hand and dogs following, and went from his home across the river to the Madison side in search of his horses, one of which was a bell horse, shortly his dogs came running back to him with their hair all turned up the wrong way, bristling with fright; holding his gun ready to shoot, Captain Oldham suddenly rode up near to an old she panther with two very young ones. He hastily fired and killed the old one, and tied her behind his saddle across his horse and captured the young ones alive, and tied them firmly to a sapling, leaving the string long enough for them to move about, expecting to return and get them after finding his horses, he found his horses and did return, but behold, the two young panthers had climbed the sapling and hanged themselves over a limb by the string and had died from strangulation.

Before his death which occured Nov. 7, 1831, Captain John Oldham made and published his last will and testament which bears date the second day of Aug. 1831, and was probated at the February Term of Court 1832, and recorded in will book B, at page 14. The will is in the following language:

"The last will and testament of John Oldham, Senior, who being of sound mind, and disposing memory, do make and ordain and constitute this my last will and testament:

It is my desire that my body be committed to the earth in decent, christian burial, with a hope that my soul will enter that rest prepared for those that believe in the name of the Lord, Jesus Christ at the resurrection of the dead.

Item: First, I will and desire that my beloved wife Ann, have the house and farm attached to it of four hundred acres, also, all the household and kitchen furniture, or as much as she thinks proper to keep, one new ox cart, and four oxen, and as many of the farming utensils as she may think proper to keep, and as much stock of every kind, as she may think it will be necessary for her to have to live on, such as horses, cattle, sheep hogs, etc. I also, give to my wife the following negroes, towit: Charles, Harry, Cebried, George, Huston and Nance.

Item: Second, I will and bequeath to my daughter Polly Grubbs, a negro girl named Aggy.

Item: Third, I give to my daughter Betsy Fisher, a negro girl named Dafney.

Item: Fourth, I give to my daughter Sarah Moberley, a negro boy, named Stephen.

Item: Fifth, I give to my daughter Nancy Grubbs, a negro boy named Elijah.

Item: Sixth I give to my son Abner Oldham, a negro boy named Caleb, worth $350.00.

Seventhly—It is my will and desire that the negro boy named Daniel that lived with my son Absalom, be given to my grand-son John Oldham, son of my son Absalom, when he arrives at the age of twenty one years, and until my grand-son arrives of age, it is my will and desire that said boy remain with my son Absalom's family for the purpose of assisting in raising and taking care of the family.

Eighthly, I give to my son Hezekiah, a negro man named Sam, worth $425.

Ninthly—I give to my son Caleb Oldham, a note I hold on the Walker's for $425. If said note should not be collected and made use of in my life time, and should the money be made use of in my life time, I give him a negro girl named Ruth worth $350.

Tenthly—I give my son John R. Oldham, a tract of land of two hundred acres in Madison County, known by the name of Kelley place, also a black boy named Bob.

It is also my will, and desire that all my black people not disposed of in this my will, that my executors get disinterested men and have them valued, and that my children then divide them at their valuation. Also it is my wish that my executors sell the two tracts of land I have of one hundred acres each known by the Stillhouse place, and Stinson place, on the river above Major Alexanders, and that one hundred acres be added to each place, of the land I purchased of Allen, and sold with said tracts, also all the property left on the place, after my wife has taken what she wants out of it, I wish sold for what it will bring and the money arising from said sales, I wish equally divided between my children, and the parts that will be going to my son Absalom and Polly Grubbs. I wish the money to be left in the hands of my executors to be applied by them to the educating of their children, and should there be more than sufficient for that purpose, I wish it divided among their children. It is also my will and desire that after my wife's death, the negroes herein left to her, be valued as named before, and divided among my children, as the other negroes named, except it is my wish that Harry and his wife, be not separated, but go together.

It further is my wish that at the death of my beloved wife, that the place she lives on together with the stock of every kind and descripion, be sold to the highest bidder, and the proceeds thereof to be divided equally among the heirs as before named. It is my further wish upon the division aforesaid, that my daughter Betsy Fisher be charged fifty dollars for the child the woman had when I gave her to them, but not giving her the child. I wish her to keep the child and pay fifty dollars, which I wish to be deducted out of the money that may be going to her. It is my further will and desire that should my son, Caleb, not receive the bond for the money, but have to take the negro girl Ruth, that he receive seventy five dollars in money. Also that my son Abner Oldham receive seventy-five dollars in money to make their negroes of equal value with Hezekiah and John R. Oldham's, said $75, to each of them to be paid out of the proceeds of the sale of property, before any division made, then the balance to be divided. It is my further will and desire that should I have any other property real or personal not named in this my will to be disposed of and the money equally divided as before mentioned, between my heirs.

It is further my will and desire that my sons Abner Oldham and John R. Oldham, be my executors to carry into effect this my last will and testament, with such powers as conferred on them by this will, and particularly desire them, my said executors to carry this into effect agreeable to my wishes named in this my will.

In testimony whereof, I have hereunto set my hand and affixed my seal this second day of Aug. 1831. The words "Dafney" on the first page and "Daniel" on the second interlined before signed.

JOHN OLDHAM (Seal.)

Witnesses:
Robert Clark.
Benjamin Straughan.
Joel White.

Estill County, February Court 1832. The foregoing last will and testament of John Oldham, was produced in court, and proven by the oaths of Robert Clark and Joel White, subscribing witnesses thereto and ordered to be recorded. Attest: Robert Clark Clerk.

The inscriptions on the tombs to the graves of Captain Oldham and his wife are as follows:

"Sacred to the memory of Captain John Oldham, a patriot of the Revolution, who was born Nov. 10th, 1757, and died Nov. 17th, 1831."

"Sacred to the memory of Annis Oldham, wife of Captain John Oldham, born March 4, 1757, died March 14, 1840."

The inventory of the widow Annis Oldham's personal estate bears date March 31, 1840.

Captain John Oldham died in 1831, and his wife Annis Rice Oldham, died March 14, 1840. To Captain John Oldham and Annis Rice his wife, were born the children named in the coming sections:

Section 1. Abner Oldham; married Hannah White. The subject of Chapter 14.

Section 2. Absalom Oldham; married Polly Challis. The subject of Chapter 15.

Section 3. Hezekiah Oldham; married Polly Kavanaugh. The subject of Chapter 16.

Section 4. Caleb Oldham; married first Milly Covington, second Abigail Moberley. The subject of Chapter 31.

Section 5. Polly Oldham; married James Grubbs. The subject of Chapter 33.

Section 6. Sally Oldham; married first Thomas Moberley, second Jack Moore. The subject of Chapter 34.

Section 7. Nancy Oldham; married Jesse Grubbs. The subject of Chapter 36.

Section 8. Elizabeth Oldham; married William Fisher. The usbject of Chapter 35.

Section 9. John R. Oldham; married first Jane Reid Moberley, second Mrs. Ferguson (nee Hedges.) The subject of Chapter 37.

Note—Rice.

About the year 1763, Hezekiah Rice purchased from John Michie land near the Horse Shoe of the Rivanna, in Albemarle County, Va., which land Michie had purchased from John Henry, father of the great Orator, Patrick Henry. In the said year 1763, Hezekiah Rice and his wife Mary conveyed this land back to John Michie.

William Rice of Halifax, married Jean Walker, daughter of Thomas Walker and Margaret Hooper his wife.

The above named Hezekiah Rice, evidently discended from

Thomas Rice, who was born in England, of Welsh parents and was an early adventurer into Virginia April 29, 1693. Obtained a patent for land in Kingston Parish, Gloucester County, Va., the land being due unto him by and for the importation of one person into the colony, and was deeded 1200 acres of land in Hanover County, on both sides of Cub Creek and Dirty Swamp. In the latter part of his life Thomas Rice owned a small plantation in the lower part of what in 1824, was Hanover. Here he left his wife with nine sons and three daughters, and went to England to receive a fortune, which had been left him, but never returned. The sailors reported that he died at sea, but it was supposed that he was assassinated. No return was ever made of his property and his family were left in a destitute condition. The major part of the family moved some thirty miles further up the country where they procured a small plantation and raised numerous families. Among those who moved North was William Rice of Culpeper, who was among the early settlers, who came sometime before Culpeper was organized. July 29, 1736, he acquired 400 acres of land in the Forks of the Rapid Ann, in the County of Orange. His will bears date Feb. 9, 1780, probated April 17, 1780. His children were:

1. Richard Rice.
2. John Rice; married Mary Finney, moved to the Shenandoah Valley, bought a large tract of land, and built on it and went back, and removed to Rockingham where he died in 1804.
3. Benajah Rice.
4. Hannah Rice.
5. Ann Rice, the wife of John Graves.
6. Sarah Rice, the wife of Edward Graves.

The apostle of Kentucky, David Rice, was a nephew of said William Rice, and David Rice a brother to Benjamin was a lawyer of Bedford County, Va., and John Holt Rice (a son of Benjamin) was a D. D. and the first pastor of Richmond Memorial Church, and Professor of Theology in Union Theological Seminary, Va., and once Moderator of the Presbyterian general assembly, and another son of Benjamin namely, Benjamin Holt Rice, was a professor in Princeton. Many of the Rice family have been, and are lawyers, ministers of the Gospel, and doctors of medicine.

In the old days the Welsh manner of spelling the name was "Rhys," though even then when written in English was often spelled "Rice." (Notes on Culpeper of Dr. Slaughter, by Raleigh T. Green.)

John Rice died in Caswell County, North Carolina, in 1804, leaving a will, by which he deeded property to the children of Mary Rice, the wife of Moses Oldham, and sister to John Rice.

CHAPTER 14.

ABNER OLHAM.

(Named in Chapter 13, Section 1.)

Article 1—Abner Oldham, a son of Captain John Oldham and Annis Rice his wife, was born in Caswell County, North Carolina, Dec. 4, 1783, and came with his parents to Madison County, Ky., in 1795, he then being a lad twelve years of age, his father rode over a large section of Kentucky and settled on the Kentucky River in what was in 1808, embraced in the organization of Estill County.

Abner went to school to the Welsh school teacher, Mr. Hutchinson and was learned in the English branches, as well as a good latin scholar. In December 1809, he married Miss Hannah White of Madison County, and acquired in time considerable real estate on the Kentucky river, and the waters of Otter Creek, in the latter County, and made his first home on the waters of Muddy Creek and moved from there to a farm on the Kentucky river about one mile above the present town of Ford, and four miles above Boonsborough, where he lived and died. He made many trips to New Orleans in flat boats, with tobacco and other productions, and walked back from there on seventeen different occasions.

He and his brother Kie, went with their father and assisted in carrying the first drove of one thousand hogs from Kentucky through the woods and over the mountains to the Southern market. Abner on his own account often bought up large droves of hogs, and carried them to the Carolina markets. He dealt extensively in all sorts of live stock and produce, and drove many horses to the Eastern country, New York, Pennsylvania and other states, and was a very active business man.

He represented Madison County in the Kentucky Legislature in 1843, and died June 15, 1852, and his mortal remains were interred in the Richmond Cemetery, the following inscription appears on the tomb stone to his grave:

> "Abner Oldham, born in Caswell County, North Carolina, Dec. 2, 1783, removed with his father to Madison County, Ky., in 1795, where he resided until his death June 15, 1852."
>
> On another side of the stone are these words:
>
> "In his character, frank and decided, he discharged with marked fidelity, his duty to his family, his friends and his country, indulging a fondness for reading, he became one of the most intelligent farmers in the county, which he represented creditably and faithfully in the Legislature."

His varied interests, and work and callings in the day in which he lived required for success, nerve, endurance, perseverance and grit. All of these qualities he possessed in a remarkable degree.

On one occasion he shipped and went himself to New Orleans with a large quantity of bacon and tobacco, and finding no market in New Orleans for his bacon, he reshipped it to Cuba, where he went, and stayed in Cuba some time, two or three months, and there sold his bacon and made good money on it. On this trip he was gone from home some four months or more. Children were born to him and his wife in the following order:

Section 1. Ulysses Oldham; died at twelve years of age.

Section 2. David D. Oldham, was born on Muddy Creek, in

Madison County, Ky., in Jan. 1812. He was a fine humored, jovial fellow, was not very fond of reading, was very fond of jokes and fun. Was a farmer of Madison County, a number of years, and moved to Fayette County, and was a farmer in that County till his death about 1890 at the age of seventy eight years. He married Susan Chenault Feb. 8, 1837. (See Part V, Chap. 13, Section 9.) Their children:

1. Ann Oldham, the oldest child, was born in Madison County, Ky.; married Caleb Manor Wallace, son of Samuel, son of Judge Caleb Wallace. (See Part IV, Chap. 5, Sec. 1.) Their children:

   1. David Manor Wallace; married Miss —— Williams of Fayette County, Ky.
   2. Henry Buford Wallace; unmarried.
   3. Susan Wallace; married Waller Marshall, of Lexington, Ky.
   4. Annie Wallace; married Robert Nash, of Lexington, Ky.

2. Rev. William Abner Oldham, was born in Madison County, Ky., —— 184-. He was educated at the State University in Lexington, Ky. He is a regular ordained minister of the Christian Church. A Christian gentleman, of fine standing, not only in the church of his choice, but with all who know him. He is not very tall, but of very heavy and stout build. He emigrated to Missouri, and now lives in Nortonville, Kansas. He attended the Kentucky and Madison County Home Coming in 1906, where he met greeting with greeting, of his many relatives and friends of his younger days. He married Miss Talitha Evans of Fayette County, Ky., his home county before his emigration therefrom Westward. Their children:

   1. Susan Oldham; married John W. Harris of Boone County, Mo., but now a banker in Nortonville, Kansas. (See Part III, Chap. 37, Sec. 1.) Mr. Harris, was a son of John W. Harris and Ann Mary McClure, his said father was a son of Overton Harris and Mary Rice Woods.
   2. Mary Frazier Oldham; married H. J. Groves of Kansas City Mo.
   3. William Abner Oldham Jr.; married Ann Miles of Kansas City, Mo.
   4. Silas Evans Oldham, of Kansas City, Mo.
   5. Lila Oldham: married J. T. Wallace of Carthage, Mo.

Section 3. Narcissa Oldham, was born in Madison County, Ky., she married Josiah P. Chenault, of the same County, Oct. 29, 1832. (See Part V, Chap. 13, Sec. 9.) They had seventeen children five of them died in their infancy, viz:

1. Hon. William Chenault, an eminent and learned lawyer of the Richmond Bar, was born in Madison County, Ky. He married Miss Ann Givens, of Boyle County, Ky. He was one of the founders of the Filson Club, and died June 2, 1901, at Colorado Springs in the state of Colorada, where he had gone seeking a health resort. No more fitting tribute can be paid to his memory than to insert here the remarks of Hon. Reuben T. Durrett, President of the Filson Club, at a memorial meeting of the club held in Louisville, Ky., Oct. 7, 1901. Mr. Durrett said:

"It was a beautiful custom of the ancient Athenians to collect the remains of those who lost their lives in battle, and to inter them at the public expense in a suburban cemetery of Athens, with a funeral oration setting forth their virtues. In a similar manner, the Filson Club, honors her dead members by memorial meetings in their behalf, with obituary notices of them to be preserved among her archives.

'In the list of names of deceased members for commemoration at this memorial meeting, is that of William Chenault of Richmond, Ky. He was one of the founders of this club, and it seems fitting that I, as its President, should speak of him on this occasion. In this room on the 15th day of May, 1884, Mr. Chenault and myself, with eight others met and organized the Filson Club. The names of these ten founders were Richard H. Collins, John Mason Brown, George M. Davie, William Chenault, Bazil W. Duke, James S. Pirtle, Thomas W. Bullett, Alexander P. Humphrey, Thomas Speed and Reuben T. Durrett. Of these, the first named four, Richard H. Collins, John Mason Brown, George M. Davie and William Chenault, have died and the remaining six are all of the Founders of the Club left among the living. They have been spared to see the original ten members swell to four hundred, and to see sixteen quarto volumes of valuable historic matter published by the club, while a seventeenth volume is in course of publication. It was the custom during the first years of the club, to assign to members subjects on which to prepare papers to be read to the club. At the second meeting in 1884, Mr. Chenault was appointed to prepare a paper on Isaac Shelby, and his two administrations as Governor of Kentucky. This he did, and a noble paper it was. He went over the first administration from 1792 to 1796, and the second from 1812 to 1816, and pointed out the different messages, and the different laws, which not only met the exigencies of the time, but helped to shape the future policy of the new state. He then took up the military career of Governor Shelby and presented him as a young soldier in the battle of Point Pleasant in 1774, when the first guns of the American Revolution were fired at the Indians as the advanced guard of the British. Next he presented him in the battle of Kings Mountain in 1780. When, with his bold and hardy transmountaineers the army of Ferguson were destroyed and the drooping hopes of the patriots raised to the anticipation of their assured independence. And, lastly, he presented him in the war of 1812, when almost having reached his three score years and ten, he mounted his horse at Frankfort, and rode with his conquering Kentuckians to the River Thames in Canada, where the British under the infamous Proctor, were routed and the second war of the Revolution practically brought to an end. And finally he took up the private life of Governor Shelby, and presented him on his farm, known as Traveler's Rest, in Lincoln County, Ky., raising better corn and wheat and flax and tobacco and finer horses and cattle and sheep and hogs, than any body else. He even went into the working room of Mrs. Shelby and displayed the wheels on which the yarn was spun and the loom on which it was woven into cloth for the clothing of the whole family. At a subsequent meeting he was appointed to prepare and read a paper on education in Kentucky. This he read at the December meeting in 1885. It covered the whole field of education from the teacher and pupil of the log cabin, praticed by the pickets of the fort, to the present system, in which the teacher is employed by the state and the pupil taught free. Those early Fort-Schools, in which letters and figures marked on boards with charcoal, were used, instead of books, were vividly presented, and the hearer could almost see Mrs. Cooms at Harrodsburg and Mr. Doniphan at Boonsborough, using such charcoal boards in their classes. This paper on education was so thoroughly and admirably done, that the Hon. Z. F. Smith, published it in his History of Kentucky, and thus gave it a permanent place in our literature.

William Chenault was a native of Madison County, Ky., where he was born in 1835. His ancestors were Huguenots, who had fled from the Province of Languenoc, in Southern France to avoid persecution, on the revocation of the Edict of Nautes. They escaped to England and from there came to Virginia about the year 1700. In 1786, his father Josiah Chenault came to Kentucky and settled at no great distance from Boonsborough in Madison County.

(This last statement in regard to Josiah Chenault is erroneous. Josiah Chenault was a son of William Chenault and Susannah Phelps, the latter a daughter of Josiah Phelps, the said William Chenault, born in 1773, was a son of William Chenault and Elizabeth Mullins. Josiah's father and grandfather, both named William, came from Albemarle County to Madison County, Ky., in the fall of 1786, before the second William was married and certainly Josiah was not at that time born.)

Here William was born and educated in the schools of the County until he was old enough, and advanced enough for college. He was then sent to Dartmouth College, in New Hampshire, where he was graduated in 1856. He then studied law in Richmond, Ky., and so rapidly learned the law, that at a time when most students are only prepared for cases before magistrates, he had mastered the science and was offered the chair of professor in the law department of the university of Louisville. This position he accepted and taught law classes with marked ability for some eight years or more. At length his health began to fail, and he longed for the fresh air and green fields of his native place. He resigned his chair in the law school and returned to Richmond, where he formed a law partnership with the Hon. John Bennett, which existed at the time of his death.

Mr. Chenault was not only a profound lawyer, but had made fame in other branches of learning. He had read many books in various departments of knowledge, and was a man of broad culture. Outside of his profession, however, he was probably best equipped in history. Born as he was and reared as he was, near the old historic Boonsborough, it is possible that, that gave something of an antiquarian tinge to his historic taste. Although Boonsborough had vanished before his day, he knew where every cabin and picket stood, and could point out the locality of every tree behind which an indian had hid while firing at the fort. He knew the names of the men, women and children who had inhabited the fort, and could relate the details of every conflict they had had with the Indians. His knowledge of Boonsborough, however, did not bound his historic learning. He knew everything and every body in Madison County, and had mastered every history of Kentucky, from Filson in 1784, to Smith of the present day. He was, also, familiar with the best histories of the United States and of other countries.

William Chenault was a modest, unpretending gentleman, of the good old school of Virginia and Kentucky. Though studious and retiring in his nature, he was fond of his friends and of their company, He always had time, and was never too weary to help the young members of the bar, and was equally generous and kind in imparting literary and historic knowledge to those in search of them. He was an exemplary christian, and there was no blemish on the bright escutcheon of his moral character. He had a strong and brilliant mind, which enabled him to take hold of the philosophy of the law, and he depended more upon the broad principles of legal science than he did upon individual cases. He was a public spirited citizen and did telling work, in securing a branch of the Louisville and Nashville Railroad for Madison County, and in locating Central University at Richmond.

During the last few years he suffered from a paralytic affliction, which left him with such trembling hands, that he could illy use his pen. In the hope of a restoration to health, he went to the Hot Springs of Arkansas, but found there no relief. He then went to Colorado Springs in the distant state of Colorado, where his sufferings were ended in death on the 2nd of June 1901.

"In the death of William Chenault, the Filson Club, has sustained a great loss, and so has the County of Madison, and the state of Kentucky."

Mr. Chenault was somewhat deficient in his chirography and on occasions when the subject matter had for the time slipped his memory, it required his deepest thoughts for him to read what he had penned, which was sometimes a source of amusement to the Court and Bar. When some brother lawyer would ask the Court for a rule against Mr. Chenault to put his pleadings in writing that can be read.

It is well remembered that on one occasion when the writer was in the clerk's office early one morning, Mr. Chenault came in and threw down on the table the petition in an old case, which was in his own hand-writing, and said: "M—, I wish you would make me a copy of this petition," and he immediately stepped out, and as soon, the writer went to work to copy it, which called for a close scrutiny and much study, finishing the work as best he could the copyist certified. "The foregoing is as true a copy as I can make from the original." In the evening Mr. Chenault came back and said "M" did you copy that little petition for me?" When the copy as made was handed him, which he opened and looked at, and then remarked: "That is all right, I had no idea you could copy it, the reason I wanted you to copy it, I could not read it myself," and then he shouted, jumped and laughed in a manner that could have been heard a considerable distance, and his actions peculiar only to himself, were very amusing, and that copy no doubt is among the papers of that old case today. (Walton v Jones.) Mr. Chenault would sometimes tell this. He was a fine man. He and his wife had one child:

1. Isabella Chenault; married William Argo. (See Part VII, Chapter 5, Section 2.)

2. Ulysses O. Chenault; died unmarried, he was the first born, and should have been metioned first.

3. Abner Oldham Chenault; married first Miss Reynolds, and secondly Lillie Thompson.

4. Professor Jason Chenault; married Ellen Thompson. He died in 1896.

5. Lavinia Oldham Chenault; married Dr. Thomas B. Montgomery, of Lincoln County, Ky.

6. Susan Ann Chenault; married James Miller, of Lincoln County, Ky. She is now a widow living in Ardmore, now the state of Oklahoma, lately Indian Territory. (See Part I, Chapter 8, Section 7.)

7. Helen Chenault; unmarried.

8. Waller Chenault; married Mary Hudson of Lancaster, Mo. They now live in Fort Scott, Kansas.

9. Ed Chenault; married a lady of Blanford. They now live in Fort Scott, Kansas.

10. Reuben M. Chenault; married Miss Lipscomb. They live in Fort Scott, Kansas.
11. Josiah P. Chenault; married Ellen Lowe.
12. Robert D. Chenault; died.
13. David Chenault; died.
14. Anna Chenault; died.
15. Mary Ann Chenault.

Section 4. Sophia Oldham, born May 22, 1816, died; Jan. 18, 1879; married Temple Burgin, Dec. 26, 1836. He was born Oct. 20, 1805, and died May 8, 1884. They had twelve children, towit:

1. Lucy Jane Burgin, born Oct. 7, 1837; died June 20, 1819.
2. Narcissa Burgin, born July 11, 1839, married Abraham Smith, Aug. 14, 1857. They had two children, towit:
    1. Florence Smith, born Dec. 25, 1858; died Nov. 3, 1875.
    2. Mary E. Smith, born April 23, 1860; died Sept. 20, 1877.
3. Hannah Burgin, born May 29, 1841, lives with her brother John, in Burgin, Kentucky.
4. Lavinia Burgin, born June 20, 1843, died Feb. 19, 1844.
5. Ulysses Burgin, born Jan. 2, 1845; died May 18, 1849.
6. Helen Burgin, born Jan. 10, 1847; died May 28, 1849.
7. Ada Burgin, born Feb. 1, 1849; married J. M. Curd Sept. 3, 1872. They had three children, towit:
    1. Lillian Curd, born Aug. 10, 1873; married Everett Elliott March 19, 1902.
    2. Wallace Curd, born June 25, 1875; died May 8, 1876.
    3. Temple Curd, born Aug. 31, 1877.
8. Dickey Burgin, born Feb. 3, 1851; died Feb. 3, 1852.
9. Preston Burgin, born Jan. 25, 1853; died April 3, 1901; married Eugenia Starks Nov. — 1883. They had five children:
    1. Ann S. Burgin, born April 12, 1887.
    2. Sophia T. Burgin, born Sept. 3, 1888.
    3. Florence E. Burgin, born March 6, 1891.
    4. Ike S. Burgin, born April 2, 1896.
    5. John Burgin, born July 3, 1897.
10. Alice Burgin, born July 1, 1857, lives with her brother John.
11. John Burgin, born Aug. 22, 1860, was a good lawyer, and at one time practiced law in Independence, Mo., he and his unmarried sisters, live together in Burgin, Mercer County, Ky.
12. Sallie Burgin, born April 26, 1862; died Feb. 16, 1881.

Section 5. Thompson B. Oldham, born in Madison County, Ky., — day of 1819. He married Nancy Phelps, a daughter of William Phelps and Margaret Poindexter. He was a farmer of Madison County, Ky., till 1854, when he moved to Montgomery County, Ky. He was for a number of years United States Storekeeper and gauger. His second wife was Mrs. Nancy Phillips nee Farrell. He is now a widower and lives with his daughter Mrs. F. M. Combs in Burgin, Ky. The children of the first marriage:

1. Cordelia Oldham; married Smith Hansford, and their home is in Harrodsburg, Ky., where Mr. Hanford is engaged in merchantile business.
2. William Phelps Oldham, hardware merchant, coal dealer and book-keeper for Oldham brothers in Mount Sterling, Ky. On the 28th day of Nov. 1905, at the age of 60 years, he married Nancy Smith.
3. Margaret Phelps Oldham; married M. S. Tyler, a lawyer of Shelbyville, Ky.
4. Louisa Estill Oldham; married J. B. Mitchell, a farmer near Lexington, Ky., issue:

1. Susan Mitchell, now in Tokio, Japan.

5. Lavinia Oldham, a missionary sent by the Christian Church to Tokio, Japan.

6. Eliza W. Oldham; married F. M. Combs, a farmer near Burgin, Ky., with whom her father makes his home.

7. Sallie Oldham; married F. H. Reppert. They live in Silverton, Ohio.

Section 6. Helen Oldham; died at the age of thirty four; unmarried.

Section 7. Miranda Oldham; married Charles Rogers. Their children:

1. Abner Rogers; married —— —— and they live in Mount Sterling, Ky., and have a number of children.

2. Charles Rogers; unmarried, of Lexington, Ky.

3. John Rogers; married Miss —— Williams, of Midway. They live in Versailles, and are in fine fix, and have children.

4. Jennie Rogers, lives with her brother John, in Lexington, Kentucky.

Mrs. Miranda Rogers; died about four years ago.

Section 8. Louise Oldham; married Jonathan Estill July 24, 1849. (See Part III, Chap. 3, Sec. 7.) Their home was on little Muddy Creek, in Madison County, Ky., here they lived on a farm for a number of years, when they bought property in Richmond, known as the Holloway property, and moved thereto and lived for several years, and returned to the farm, where Mr. Estill died a a few years since, his wife having died first. Their children:

1. Laura Estill, became the second wife of Lewis E. Francis, she is now a widow, no issue.

2. Lavinia Estill; married first Jeptha Chenault, secondly Mr. Cunningham, and third Mr. John Cunningham of Bourbon County, Ky. Her last two husbands were brothers, but no issue from either. Issue of the first marriage:

1. Estelle Chenault; married Mr. Brutus J. Clay.

3. Wallace Estill; married Anna Chenault.

4. Hattie Estill; died young.

Mrs. Lavinia Oldham Estill often accompanied her father to Frankfort, during the meetings of the Legislature, of which he was a distinguished member. She was a gracious, refined, accomplished woman, of brilliant intellect, an interesting conversationalist and attractive in the best society.

Section 9. Lavinia Oldham; died in 1843, at the age of about fourteen years.

CHAPTER 15.

ABSALM OLDHOAM.

(Named in Chapter 13, Section 2.)

Article 1.—Absalom Oldham, a son of Captain John Oldham, and Annis Rice his wife, was born in Caswell County, North Carolina May 28, 1785.

He came with his parents to Clark, now Estill County, Ky He married his first cousin Polly Challis, the 16th day of March 1812. The said Polly Challis was a daughter of John Challis and Milly Rice his wife, born Dec. 15, 1798, died July 24, 1880.

The said Milly Rice Challis was a sister to Annis Rice the wife of Captain John Oldham, the mother of the subject. Estill County was established in 1808, and Absalom Oldham was the first sheriff of the County holding his commission from Christopher Greenup, Esquire, Governor of the Commonwealth bearing date March 17, 1808. He represented Estill County in the Kentucky Legislature in 1819. His home was on the Kentucky River, below and near the mouth of Drowning Creek on the opposite side from said Creek, where he died the 8th day of Feb. 1831. Absalom Oldham received a good English education from the Welsh teacher Hutchinson, learned also, Latin. The fruits of his marriage were the children named in the coming sections:

Section 1. Rufus King Oldham, a citizen of Estill County. He died a bachelor, born Aug. 19, 1818; died June 16, 1881.

Section 2. Absalom Oldham; married Sarah A. Williams (1) whose mother died recently at the century mark. He lived in Estill County till the death of his wife, when he broke up house-keeping and came to Madison County, and now lives with his daughter Mrs. Combs. The children born to him and his wife, were:

1. Mary Elizabeth Oldham; married Samuel G. Jackson.
2. William Oldham; married Effa Tribble.
3. Lottie Oldham; married Obediah Curry.
4. Maggie (Milly) Oldham; married William W. Combs.

Section 3. John C. Oldham; married Nancy Skinner, issue:

1. Clifton Oldham; married Hulda F. Scrivner Feb. 12, 1868.
2. William Oldham; married —— Troop. (Indiana.)
3. Rufus Oldham; married first Lou Hamilton, secnod Sally Knight April 22, 1874.
4. America Oldham; married John Eckly.
5. Kate Oldham; married Henry B. Rose.
6. Amanda Oldham; married Emet Wells.
7. Henry Oldham; married Della Azbill.
8. John Oldham.
9. Olivia Oldham; married William C. Griffith.
10. Laura Oldham; married Frank Pelsue.
11. Nancy Oldham; died young.
12. Frances Oldham; died young.

Section 4. Milly Oldham; married John B. Stone, born July 25, 1825; died Jan. — 1856, issue:

1. Mary Stone; married Rufus Moberley.
2. Josephine Stone; married first Henry Howard, second Henry Sewell.
3. Jefferson Stone; married first Ann Thornburg, second Matt Jones.
4. Dean O. Stone; married Jael Thornburg.

Section 5. Dean Swift Oldham; died in 1857.

Section 6. Walker Oldham, born Feb. 4, 1832, died Sept. 19, 1834.

(1) Sara A, the wife of Absalom Oldham Jr., was a daughter of William Williams and Lotta Finnell his wife, the latter was born Dec. 11, 1804, and died Sept. 11, 1905, living to the remarkable age of 100 years and 9 months.

CHAPTER 16.

HEZEKIAH OLDHAM.

(Named in Chapter 13, Section 3.)

Article 1.—Hezekiah Oldham, a son of Captain John Oldham and Annis Rice his wife, was born in Caswell County, North Carolina April 10, 1787.

He came to Kentucky with his parents in 1795, and on the 7th day of Oct. 1813, he married Mary Kavanaugh of Madison County,

HEZEKIAH OLDHAM.

MARY KAVANAUGH.
Wife of Hezekiah Oldham.

who was born April 29, 1798, she being in the sixteenth year of her age. Mary Kananaugh was a daughter of William Kavanaugh and Hannah Woods his wife. (See Part VII, Chap. 8, Sec. 3.) Hezekiah Oldham died July 13, 1868, and his wife died Sept. 10, 1882.

At the February Term 1810, of the Estill County Court, he was appointed third inspector of hemp, flour and tobacco at Water's inspection. His education consisted in only knowing how to read, write and cypher. He went to school to Hutchison. Hezekiah Oldham was a farmer on a large scale, being the owner of 2500 acres of land and a dealer in all kinds of live stock, and farm products, tobacco, etc., raised on his own farm tobacco in large quantities in his earlier life, and would buy up all the hogs for sale in the country around for the southern market, which would be driven through to the South. And ship tobacco in flat boats from his landing on the Kentucky River to New Orleans market, to which metropolis he made several trips, and would dispose of all, and return home through the country, getting rides when he could, much of the way back made on foot, for want of other modes of travel.

The story goes that one year, he raised a large crop of tobacco, and bought up all the tobacco in the country, and made ready for its shipment to New Orleans, and the low stage of the water prevented the shipment and he held the tobacco till the next year and added to it his new crop and other purchases, and went and carried his cargo of flat boats to New Orleans and there disposed of it all, and strapped $12,000 in belts around his person and started on foot home, catching rides on the way as he could, and arrived safely at home with the money, the proceeds of his stock.

Besides the farm, field and stock dealing, he was the proprietor of and conducted the business of running trains of wagons, often from eight to sixteen horses attached to one wagon, and at places requiring it the teams would be doubled, as was often necessary which business he personally superintended and managed, being out in the night and exposed to all sorts of inclement weather, hauling pig iron from the Kentucky Mountain furnaces and iron works, salt from Goose Creek salt works, and goods from Cincinnati and Louisville to Richmond and various other interior towns, these were the activities of a past age, but necessary in that day. He was well known and trusted over a large portion of Kentucky and in the South. Nearly every one knew of Kie Oldham and his personal acquaintances were legion. Although having been dead for nearly forty years still the memory of this noted man and his character exists in the minds of the people and there can scarcely be found a person twenty years of age who cannot relate something of his life. His career extended from a period reaching back near to the close of the Revolution to some years after the close of the civil war, within which space transpired many important and noted events, such as the war of 1812, the Mexican and the Civil War, Indian wars, in different parts, the Louisiana and Spanish purchases and other grants to the nation, and wonderful improvements in farming implements, machinery of all kinds and modes of transportation, etc., which he witnessed from a primitive to a most improved state. Through him was handed down to his children and from his children to their children the account of his grand-father William Oldham and the traditions related in Chapter 2, and the losing sight of Edward, and of his uncles and aunts, (brothers and sisters to his father, Captain John Oldham) whom he knew the story of whom has been given from parent to child to the present generation, and is believed by the descendants. When a boy Mr. Oldham, the subject, accompanied his father with the first drove of hogs from Kentucky to the South Carolina market. (See Chap. 1, Item

HYMAN C. BUSH.

HANNAH WOODS OLDHAM,
Wife of Hyman G. Bush.

7.) To Hezekiah Oldham and Mary Kavanaugh his wife the children named in the coming sections were born:

Section 1. Othniel Rice Oldham, born June 8, 1817; married Sydonia Noland. The subject of Chapter 17.

Section 2. Sally Ann Oldham, born Feb. 14, 1819; died in her infancy.

Section 3. Ann Rice Oldham, born Jan. 1, 1820; married James Noland. The subject of Chapter 18.

Section 4. William Kavanaugh Oldham, born Nov. 11, 1821; married Jacintha Katherine Brown. The subject of Chapter 19.

Section 5. Thomas H. Oldham, born Oct. 25, 1823; married Nancy E. Smith. The subject of Chapter 26.

Section 6. Susan Kavanaugh Oldham, born March 11, 1826; died in her infancy.

Section 7. Hannah Woods Oldham, born Jan. 3, 1828, she married Hyman G.Bush March 30, 1848, she had no children.

Section 8. Margaret Oldham, born Oct. 25, 1829; married Anderson Chenault. The subject of Chapter 27.

Section 9. Charles Kavanaugh Oldham, born Sept. 24, 1834; married Susan C. Duncan. The subject of Chapter 28.

Section 10. Abner Oldham, born Sept. 14, 1837; married Josephine Embry. The subject of Chapter 29.

Section 11. Mary Elizabeth Oldham, born March 29, 1840; married Captain William Tipton. The subject of Chapter 30.

Section 12. Hezekiah Oldham, born Oct. 1, 1843; died in his infancy.

CHAPTER 17.

OTHNIEL RICE OLDHAM.

(Named in Chapter 16, Section 1.)

Article 1—Othniel Rice Oldham, a son of Heegkiah Oldham and Mary Kavanaugh his wife, was born in Madison County, Ky., June 8, 1817.

OTHNIEL RICE OLDHAM

On the 17th day of May 1838, he married Sydonia Noland, a daughter of Capt. John Noland, senior, May 17, 1838, and lived and died in Madison County, Ky., March 7, 1900, in the 84th year of his age. He was a farmer. In the great Civil War of 1862, he enlisted in the confederate army, Captain Thomas B. Collins Company F. 7th, afterwards 11th Kentucky cavalry, Colonel D. Waller Chenault, General John H. Morgan's command. Two of his sons being in the same army. He was a kind hearted good man, and had many friends.

An incident of his army life was, that he and his cousin and comrade Thomas M. Oldham, on a certain occasion whilst stationed at Monticello, were granted leave of absence, and bethought themselves, to make their way to their homes in Madison County to see their wives and children, but on the way, in Lincoln

County, were intercepted, arrested and carried to Cincinnati and there imprisoned, tried and sentenced as spies to suffer the penalty of death, but through the interposition and persistent efforts of a lady, who afterward became the wife of Rev. Milton Elliot, aided by General Speed S. Fry, their lives were spared, and they finally released , by taking the oath of allegiance and fidelity to the United States Government, when they returned home to their families. They ever afterwards when the occurance was referred to would remember their friends and benefactors, and speak kindly of them, and held themselves in readiness to do any act of kindness within their power for them. The children of Othniel Rice Oldham and Sydonia Noland his wife are named in the coming sections:

Section 1. James William Oldham, never married, died a bachelor. He enlisted in the confederate states army in Captain Thomas B. Collins' Company F. 7th, afterwards 11th Kentucky cavalry, Colonel D. Waller Chenault, General John H. Morgan's command. Was captured on General Morgan's Indiana and Ohio raid at Cheshire Ohio, and carried to camp chase, thence to Camp Douglas where he remained confined in prison eighteen months. He was a deputy sheriff of Madison County under the sheriff, his brother-in-law N. B. Deatherage 1878-82.

Section 2. Hezekiah Oldham, was born in Madison County. He also enlisted in the confederate states army, under the command of General Morgan, and was wounded in the fight at Pine Mountain Sept. 8, 1862, when Captain Jesse, commanding two companies of confederates, went into an ambuscade of Federal soldiers. He died shortly after retiring from the army service, having never been married.

Section 3. Mary Oldham; married Nathan B. Deatherage shortly after his return from prison at Camp Douglas, having been one of General John H. Morgan's raiders and captured on the Ohio raid, they were sweethearts before the war. She died without issue, and her husband married her first cousin Mary Noland. Mr. Deatherage was twice elected sheriff of Madison County, holding the office two terms, and made an excellent sheriff.

Section 4. Charles Oldham; married Candice Howard Oct. 12, 1876. To whom were born:

1. Sydney Oldham;; married —— Handy.
2. Chambers Oldham.
3. Mary Oldham.
4. Othniel Oldham; died Dec. 13, 1906.
5. James Thomas Oldham.
6. Nettie Oldham.
7. Emma Oldham.
8. John Chenault Oldham.
9. Anderson Oldham.
10. Gertrude Oldham.

Section 5. Thomas Shelton Moberley Oldham, a prosperous farmer of Madison County, Ky., married Kate Baumstark. To whom were born:

1. Mary Earl Oldham.
2. Sidney Oldham, killed in his infancy by the kick of a horse.

Section 6. Temperance Chambers Oldham, became the second wife of David G. Martin, whose first wife was her cousin Sally Elizabeth Oldham. (See Chap. 32, Section 1, and Part III, Chap. 35, Section 1.) They had no children.

JOHN CABELL CHENAULT.

Section 7. Eleanor Bird Oldham; married Judge John C. Chenault, Judge of the Madison County Court two terms 18—, and prior thereto was Judge of the Richmond Police Court 18—. He is a practicing attorney at law of the Richmond bar, and late proprietor and Editor of the Richmond Climax. (See Part V, Chap. 13, Section 9.) To them were born:

1. Anderson Sidney Chenault; died young.

2. Joseph Prewitt Chenault.

3. John Cabel Chenault.

4. Nannie Evans Chenault; died in her infancy.

CHAPTER 18.

ANN RICE OLDHAM.

(Named in Chapter 16, Section 3.)

Article 1.—Ann Rice Oldham(a daughter of Hezekiah Oldham and Mary Kavanaugh his wife, was born in Madison County, Ky., Jan. 1, 1820.. She married James Noland, a brother to her brother Othniel's wife Jan. 9, 1837.

To whom were born a number of children and she was left a widow, and when advanced in years, she followed her children to Missouri where she died. Their children are named in the coming sections:

Section 1. Mary Eleanor Noland.
Section 2. Ann Rice Noland; married John Foster.
Section 3. John Noland; married Belle Garner.

ANN RICE OLDHAM.
Wife of James Noland.

Section 4. Margaret Chenault Noland; married James Fox.

Section 5. Othniel Noland.

Section 6. Nathan Noland.

Section 7. Mary Noland; married John Gaines.

Section 8. Abner Noland.

Section 9. Temperance Chambers Noland; married James Gaines.

Section 10. William Noland.

Section. 11. Hezekiah Noland.

Section 12. Nannie Noland.

And four other children who died in their infancy, and names unknown.

CHAPTER 19.

WILLIAM KAVANAUGH OLDHAM.

(Named in Chapter 16, Section 4.)

Article 1.—William Kavanaugh Oldham, a son of Hezekiah Oldham and Mary Kavanaugh his wife, was born in Madison County, Ky. Nov. 11, 1821.

He married March 11, 1851, Jacintha Catherine Brown, a daughter of Ira Benajah Brown, and Francis Jarman Mullins his wife of Albemarle County, Va. (See Part VIII, Chap. 14, Sec. 7.) Mrs. Oldham died July 10, 1880. He died May 20, 1899, in the 78th year of his age. He was for many years a leading and successful stock farmer of Madison County in the blue grass section of Kentucky, and was known as a man of incorruptible manners and integrity, his

WILLIAM KAVANAUGH OLDHAM.

JACINTHA CATHERINE BROWN.
Wife of Wm. K. Oldhnm.

course was unquestioned, but conservative and wise in his dealings with men, he made few enemies, and numbered his friends by the score.

He was a large slave owner and out spoken in his allegiance to the Southern cause, but never joined the army, or was at any time connected with military service. He possessed a rare fund of humor, and a large sympathy with human nature, and these traits kept his heart young, and preserved the sparkle in his eye which made him the favorite of young and old alike. He never sought to injure an enemy, nor ever betrayed a friend. The children of William Kavanaugh Oldham and Jacintha Catherine Brown his wife are named in the coming sections:

Section 1. Ann Oldham, born June 30, 1852; died July 2, 1856, from injuries received by a fall from a horse.

Section 2. Mary Kavanaugh Oldham, born Feb. 4, 1854; married Colonel James Philip Eagle. The subject of Chapter 20.

Section 3. Burlington Oldham, born Nov. 8, 1855; died Jan 8, 1856.

Section 4. Katherine Oldham, born Dec. 5, 1856; married William Harris Miller. The subject of Chapter 21.

Section 5. Margaret Oldham, born March 1, 1859; married John Doty. The subject of Chapter 22.

Section 6. A daughter not named, born in 1864, and died the day after her birth.

Section 7. William Kavanaugh Oldham, Jr., born May 29, 1865; married Lillian Munroe. The subject of Chapter 23.

Section 8. Kie Oldham, born Jan. 17, 1869; married Caroline Weenden. The subject of Chapter 24.

Section 9. Dr. Ira Brown Oldham, born March 2, 1871; married Mary Newland. The subject of Chapter 25.

CHAPTER 20.

MARY KAVANAUGH OLDHAM.

(Named in Chapter 19, Section 2.)

Article 1.—Mary Kavanaugh Oldham, a daughter of William Kavanaugh Oldham, senior, and Jacintha Catherine Brown his wife, was born in Madison County, Ky., Feb. 4, 1854, married Jan. 3, 1882, to Colonel James Phillip Eagle, of Lonoke, Arkansas, the marriage occuring at the home of her father in Madison County, Ky.

After their marriage Colonel Eagle and his wife, went to the state of Arkansas, where they lived the remainder of their days, residing for a numebr of years on Colonel Eagle's cotton plantation in Richwoods, Lonoke County. Colonel Eagle was a prominent minister of the Missionary Baptist Church, served several times as President of the Southern Baptist Convention, a large and influential organization. Was a large cotton planter, and in his adopted state, Arkansas, having been born in Tennessee from which he moved with his parents when a youth, he was very prominent and influential and popular, having been elected several times to the Arkansas Legislature from Lonoke County, and speaker of the House of Representatives. Was twice elected Governor of the State, administering the affairs of state with signal ability, and statesmanship, creditably to himself and to the people. When elected Governor, he and his wife left their country home in Richwoods and moved to Little Rock, the Capital of the state, where they acquired a nice, commodious and handsome mansion, richly furnished with everything needful for their comfort and pleasure, including an excellent library of rare books. They had no children. They travelled a great deal. All their earthy wants were bountifully supplied.

On the 15th day of Feb. 1903, (Sunday morning) at their mansion Mrs. Eagle departed this life in peace with her God, surrounded by her loving husband and her sisters and brothers, honored and respected by the people, of her adopted state, and hosts of friends and admirers scattered over the United States and elsewhere, for she had acquired National reputation by reason of her connection with the Congress of Women, Worlds Columbian Exposition, Chicago, U. S. A., 1893, to which she was elected a delegate from the State of Arkansas, and was Chairman of the Committee of Congresses, of the Board of Lady Managers and Editor in two large volumes of the Congress.

Colonel Eagle was never well after the death of his wife, which was a severe shock to him. He wrote a beutiful book of Memoirs of his wife after her death (which is referred to), had a handsome and costly monument erected in the cemetery at Little Rock to himself and wife while he lived.

On the —— day of —— 1904, he passed peacefully away, at his Little Rock home. After a great funeral concourse his remains were buried by the side of his wife's in the Little Rock Cemetery. He was a hard student and obtained the major portion of his education after arriving at manhood. He served through the Civil War of 1862, in the army of the confederate states, enlisting as private promoted to the rank of Colonel. He gave much to churches and charities, the latter days of his life especially being consecrated to the cause of his redeemer. The press published much concerning the works and lives of this couple.

CHAPTER 21.

KATHERINE OLDHAM.

(Named in Chapter 19, Section 4.)

Article 1.—Katherine Oldham, a daughter of William Kavanaugh Oldham, and Jacinth Katherine Brown his wife, was born in Madison County, Ky., Dec. 5, 1856, and at her father's home near Richmond, Ky., on the 27th day of Feb. 1884, she was married to William Harris Miller. (See Part I, Chap. 13, Sec. 8.)

She was educated for the most part at home under private tutors, but was graduated from the Richmond Female Seminary of Kentucky. She has given several years of her life to teaching select schools. While she does not claim to be an author, she has from time to time published short articles in periodicals that have always elicited favorable comment. She has been for many years a member of the Regular Baptist Church. Quoted from Ex-Governor James P. Eagle's Memoir of his wife:

"From Mrs. Kate Miller of Richmond, Ky., came the following lines as a tribute to her departed sister:

The frost of death is on her brow,
  The waxen hands lie still and cold;
And over eyes of softest blue
  The eye-lids' jetty fringes fold.

Sweet thoughts seem poised upon the lips,
  Half smiling so like life they are,
But light and thought have closed their doors
  In brighter lands they wander far.

The chiseled image, fair and white,
Holds not the spirit fairer still,
But all within is night and death,
And waits death's mission to fulfill.

'Tis but the alabaster vase,
Which holds our cherished rose in bloom;
The fragrance still we have, but she
Now spreads her leaves in larger room.

What though the tears from grieving hearts,
Well up and flood our heavy eyes,
Our sorrow still is full of hope.
We know she lives in paradise.

What though the curtain darkly falls
And hides our friend from living view;
Whate'er the clime where she abides,
We know her loving, leal and true.

That which we had we still will claim,
Nor will we count our treasure lost;
Sweet commune still with her we'll hold,
Nor count the tears our parting cost.

Nor hours, nor days, nor weary years,
Can from our lives her life efface;
And somewhere in the halls of time,
We'll meet and greet her face to face.

For all events are garnered grain,
If we God's laws but understood,
And days of care, and nights of pain,
And death and sorrow work for good.

Nothing is lost in wisdom's plan,
Through toil and tears we reach the goal;
Toward that divine event we move,
Which solves the mystery of the soul."

No children were born to William H. Miller and Katherine Oldham his wife.

CHAPTER 22.

MARGARET OLDHAM.

(Named in Chapter 19, Section 5.)

Article 1.—Margaret Oldham, a daughter of William Kavanaugh Oldham and Jacintha Catherine Brown his wife, was born in Madison County, Ky., March 1, 1859.

She married John Doty of Madison County, Dec. 16, 1884. (See Part VII, Chap. 11, Sec. 1-6.) They lived on a farm near Richmond, a number of years and then moved to town a few years ago, to educate their children, where they acquired property and now live. Mr. Doty owns a farm near the town. The children born to them are named in the coming sections:

Section 1. Wiliam Kavanaugh Doty, born Saturday Jan. 30, 1886, 11 o'clock A. M.

Section 2. John Doty, born Tuesday Oct. 18, 1887, at 1 o'clock P. M.

Section 3. Eagle Doty, born Wednesday Jan. 8, 1890, at 3 o'clock A. M.

Section 4. Mary Doty, born Oct. 30, 1891, at 6:30 o'clock.

Section 5. Hezekiah Doty, born Oct. 10, 1893.

Section 6. A daughter, an infant died; born Sept. 21, 1894.

Section 7. Oldham Doty, born June 10, 1899.

Section 8. Margaret Doty, born Sunday Sept. 21, 1902.

Mr. Doty was born November 25, 1852.

CHAPTER 23.

WILLIAM KAVANAUGH OLDHAM, Jr.

(Named in Chapter 19, Section 7.)

Article 1.—William Kavanaugh Oldham, Jr., a son of William Kavanaugh and Jacintha Catherine Brown his wife, was born in Madison County, Ky., May 29, 1865.

He obtained most of his education at the common schools of Madison County and Central University at Richmond. At about the age of seventeen he and his younger brother Kie left Richmond on horse back, and rode through the country to Lonoke, Arknasas, where he has since made his home, and there became superintendent and manager of the cotton plantation of his brother-in-law Ex-Governor James P. Eagle, which position he held as long as Governor Eagle lived, and managed the affairs to the entire satisfaction of Mr. Eagle. He now owns a good landed estate in Lonoke County. He married Lillian Munroe, a daughter of Wellington Munroe, of the town of Lonoke, on the —— day ——

Hon. WM. K. OLDHAM, Jr.

Mr. Oldham recently received at the hands of the Democratic party of his County of Lonoke, the nomination as a candidate for a seat in the Lower House of the General Assembly of the State of Arkansas, and was elected.

After the adjournment of the thirty sixth session of the Arkansas Legislature of 1907, the Daily Arkansas

Democrat published with other things in its editorial colums, the following:

"Hamiter and Oldham brothers leaders in past Legislature. "Senator John H. Hamiter, Senator Kie Oldham, Pulaski, and Speaker Alllen Hamiter, of Lafayette, and Representative Oldham of Lonoke, made their influence felt upon Legislature in the State General Assemgly. Each one extremely popular in his sphere.

So far as the records show there has never been a session of the Arkansas Legislature in which there has been two sets of brothers, one each in the senate and the house, until that which recently adjourned. In the thirty sixth there was senator John H. Hamiter in the South wing, and Speaker, Allen H. Hamiter, in the House, and Senator Kie Oldham in the South and Hon. W. K. Oldham in the house. This condition is said to have never existed before. The two senators represent the same County, Pulaski. The tenth senatorial district composed of Pulaski, and Perry Counties is represented by two Little Rock attorneys, Hon. John H. Hamiter and Kie Oldham. But in the House the other brothers represent widely divergent counties. Mr. Oldham represented Lonoke County, lying to the east of Pulaski, while Speaker Hamiter was elected from Lafayette County, but represented the state at large in his position as presiding officer of the House.

"Hon. W. K. Oldham in the House was rarely on the floor, but the opponents of bills he favored never for once forgot he was there. Representative Oldham is one of the most unique characters of the past General Assembly. Such intense love for a brother is rarely seen as that of Will Oldham for Senator Oldham. Always mindful of the physical necessities and comforts of his distinguished brother Mr. Oldham was noted by all with whom he came in contact. And on Legislative matters he was a power to be considered at all times. Never pushing himself into the fight. but standing at all times ready to defend his position, or yet to make the attack if necessary. Mr. Oldham won for himself a position high in the regard of his fellows.

As chairman of the Insurance Committee, Mr. Oldham occupied a most important and interesting position. When the various insurance measures came up for discussion, he was always ready to give data regarding any feature of the questions, all were guaranteed of a fair and impartial hearing. While Mr. Oldham favored the passage of a bill which would relieve the situation so far as insurance was concerned, the opponents of this were always allowed to be heard and the arguments were listened to with deep attention.

The repeal of the feature of the Anti-Trust law which affects insurance companies, was the biggest matter coming before the Insurance Committee. Some time was spent in discussing the bill. United States Senator Jeff Davis appeared before the committee and fought the bill. But the committee recommended that the bill pass, and it passed. This is one of the few committees whose recomendations was not reversed by the House, nor the senate.

Hon. William K. Oldham came to Arkansas in 1885, from Madison County, Ky. His whole life has been spent on a farm, and he is one of the most sucessful planters in Lonoke County. He was educated at Central University inRichmond, Ky. He and Senator Kie Oldham of Pulaski are brothers and have been associated in business since they came to Arkansas. It has been noticed that they have been constantly together when the general assembly was not in session. Mr. Oldham was in the race for Representative only nine days. This is his first political venture, but his services in the House have demonstrated that he was one of the strongest men on the floor. His power was felt by the opposition during the pendency of the Argenta bill, the Lee-Browning bill, and upon the occasion of his bout with his colleague, Hon. Joseph B. Reed, over the repeal of the four-wire fence law which applies to their County.." (See Chapter 24 following.) The fruits of this marriage are the children named in the coming sections:

Section 1. William Kavanaugh Oldham, (3rd) born in Lonoke County, Arkansas.

Section 2. Lillian Munroe Oldham, born in Lonoke Coutny Arkansas.

Section 3. Mamie Katherine Oldham, born at Pettus, Lonoke County, Arkansas, Nov. 10, 1906; died since going to press.

CHAPTER 24.

KIE OLDHAM.

(Named in Chapter 19, Section 8.)

Article 1.—Kie Oldham, (called Kie) a son of William Kavanaugh Oldham and Jacintha Catherine Brown his wife, was born in Madison County, Ky., Jan. 17, 1869, when a youth went with his elder brother William, each on horse back, from Richmond to Lonoke, Arkansas, in which state he has since made his home, and where he completed his education, at a Baptist College at Texarkana, and afterwards graduated in a school of law.

His profession being that of a lawyer. Was private secretary to Governor Eagle, whilst Governor of that State. Was attorney for various tribes of Ute Indians representing them in causes pending in the United States Court of Claims, for damages for indian depredations, and depredations of others against the Utes, and he went over the western states and territories taking depositions in the cases, and in which cases he was very successful. He was also, attorney for Cuban American Claimants in causes pending in the United States Tribunals for damages caused by the Spanish-American war, which the United States in their treaty with Spain in some manner assumed the liability, and spent from the fall of 1903, till the summer or fall of 1904, on the island of Cuba, taking depositions in the cases, which are as yet undetermined.

HON. KIE OLDHAM.

He married Caroline Weeden, a daughter of Captain William Weeden of Waubaseeka, Arkansas, and he owns a home in Little Rock, the Capital of the State of Arkansas, where they live. No children have been born to them. Mr. Oldham recently received from the Democrats of the senatorial District in which the City of Little Rock is, the nomination as a candidate for State Senator, and was elected. (See Part 6, Chap. 23.)

The Arkansas Daily Democrat, further said:

"Kie Oldham was born in Madison County, Ky., in 1869. He is a son of Wiliam Kavanaugh Oldham and Jacintha Kate Brown, the former a native of Kentucky, and the latter of Virginia. He is a brother of Mrs. James P. Eagle, and of the Hon. W. K. Oldham, Representative from Lonoke County. He came to Arkansas in 1884. He graduated from Ouachita College in 1889, and in 1893 entered the University of Virginia, completing his law studies in June, 1894. He was admitted to the bar Oct. 3, 1894, since which time his home and law office have been in Little Rock. His most conspicuous service in the Senate was rendered in the passage of the bill providing for the re-annexation of Argenta to Little Rock, in the passage of the Fellow Servant Bill, which bears his name, and as chairman of the joint committee on the State Capital.

Senator Oldham has been considered to be one of the leading members of the upper house. His hundreds of friends regretted exceedingly his determination to not stand for the Lieutenant Governorship. As chairman of the State Capital Committe, Senator Oldham came into close contact with the greatest proposition brought to the attention of the General Assembly. In that position as presiding officer of this committee, he displayed the best in the man. Careful, conservative, yet energetic, and possessed of a determination to get at the heart of every point presented, he was of invaluable aid to the committee, and incidentally to the state of Arkansas. Senator Oldham is one of the most beloved members of the senate. While he fought strenuously many measures which came before the upper body, he never for once lost the high esteem of every member.

In the Argenta re-annexation fight, he was a moving spirit. And at the same time he desired the right to be done, and to give every interest and person a fair hearing. When the Lee-Browning bill came up for discussion, Senator Oldham was found battling for the business interests of the state and each have but further endeared him to the people.

CHAPTER 25.

DR. IRA BROWN OLDHAM.

(Named in Chapter 19, Section 9.)

Article 1.—Dr. Ira Brown Oldham, a son of William Kavanaugh Oldham and Jacintha Catherine Brown his wife, was born in Madison County, Ky., March 2, 1871.

Went to the common schrools of said County, and Central University at Richmond, and graduated in a medical school at Louisville, and received a diploma, and located in Madison County, where he practiced medicine a number of years. till the autumn of 1903, when he moved to the growing city of Muskogee, Indian Territory, and there acquired property, and settled for the practice of his profession.

Shortly after graduating in medicine he was married to Mary Newland, a daughter of Elder, A. Christopher Newland, of Lincoln County, Ky. The fruits of this union are the children named in the coming sections:

Section 1. Elizabeth Oldham.

Section 2. Kate Oldham.

Section 3. Ira Brown Oldham.

Section 4. Philemon Oldham.

Section 5. Mary Oldham: born ——; died Oct. 19, 1906, in Muskogee, Oklahoma.

Section 6. Newland Oldham, born in Muskogee, Indian Territory Aug. 8, 1907.

CHAPTER 26.

THOMAS H. OLDHAM.

(Named in Chapter 16, Section 5.)

Article 1.—Thomas H. Oldham, a son of Hezekiah Oldham and Mary Kavanaugh his wife, was born in Madison County, Ky., Oct. 25, 1823, and was a farmer.

He married Nancy E. Smith, May 6, 1847, and they raised a family of children, his wife died June 9, 1809, aged 40 years, and Mr. Oldham, married a widow Mrs. Bettie Edmonson, nee ——

THOS. H. OLDHAM.

NANCY E. SMITH.
Wife of Thos. H. Smith.

but there was no issue of this union. In his latter days Mr. Oldham moved to Lexington, Ky., where he died. His remains were buried in his grand-father's old burying ground on the Kentucky River.

The children born to him and his first wife are named in the coming Sections:

Section 1. Eliza Oldham; married first Strother Anderson, of Montgomery County, whom she survived, and married the second time James Elam. Children by first husband:

1. Maud Anderson.
2. James Anderson.
3. Wayne Anderson.

Section 2. Humphrey Oldham; married Sallie George, of Montgomery County, where he has lived since he arrived at maturity. To whom were born:

1. Joel Oldham. (son.)

Section 3. Hannah Oldham; married Andrew J. Broaddus of Madison County. (See Chapter 11, Section 3-1.)

Section 4. John Oldham; remains single.

Section 5. Anderson Oldham; married Nannie Peelman, issue:

1. Claude Oldham.
2. Nannie Oldham.
3. Eliza Oldham.

Section 6. Laura Oldham; married Brutus Kavanaugh Duncan. (See Part VII, Chap. 9, Sec. 3-2, and Chap. 31, Sec. 1-4-a.)

CHAPTER 27.

MARGARET OLDHAM.

(Named in Chapter 16, Section 8.)

Article 1.—Margaret Oldham, a daughter of Hezekiah Oldham and Mary Kavanaugh his wife, was born in Madison County, Ky., Oct. 25, 1829.

She married Anderson Chenault, and they moved to Montgomery County. Mr. Chenault was a prosperous farmer of said County. Mrs. Chenault was left a widow a number of years ago, and still occupies the old homestead, she and her brother Abner are (1905) the only surviving children of Hezekiah Oldham. (See Part V, Chap.)

Her children are numbered in the coming sections:

Section 1. William O. Chenault; married Belle Moss, issue:

1. Anderson Chenault; married Miss Bayless, of Lexington, Ky. He died since going to press.
2. William Chenault.
3. Waller Chenault.
4. Charles Chenault.
5. Samuel Chenault.

Section 2. Nannie Chenault; married John Woodford, issue:

1. Thomas Chenault Woodford.
2. Catesby Woodford.
3. William Woodford.
4. Lucy Clay Woodford.
5. Margaret Woodford; married —— Gay, issue:
   1. Callie Gay.
   2. John Gay.
   3. Nannie Gay.

Section 3. Waller Chenault; died a bachelor.

Section 4. Anderson Chenault; married Josephine ——. He died in Tampa, Florida in 1904.

ANDERSON CHENAULT.

MARGARET K. OLDHAM.
Wife of Anderson Chenault.

Section 5. Mollie Chenault; married James Bogie, issue:

1. Anderson Bogie.
2. James Bogie.
3. Edward Bogie.
4. Joseph Bogie.
5. Arabella Bogie.
6. Margaret Bogie.

Section 6. Margaret Chenault; married —— Deering, issue:

1. Mary Woodford Deering.
2. Chenault Deering.

Section 7. Lucy Chenault; married Bishop Clay.

CHAPTER 28.

CHARLES KAVANAUGH OLDHAM.

(Named in Chapter 16, Section 9.)

Article 1.—Charles Kavanaugh Oldham, a son of Hezekiah Oldham and Mary Kavanaugh his wife, was born in Madison County, Ky., Sept. 24, 1834.

He married Susan Duncan, a daughter of William Duncan and Catherine Hume his wife, July 31, 1856. (See Part VII, Chap. 9, Section 2-4.) When the Civil War came on he enlisted in the Confederate States Army, and was a Lieutenant in Company F. 7th afterwards 11th Kentucky Cavalry, Colonel D. Waller Chenault, General John H. Morgan's command. After the war in 1870, he

CHARLES K. OLDHAM.

SUSAN CATHERINE DUNCAN.
Wife of Charles K. Oldham.

was elected sheriff of Madison County, and re-elected in 1872. Afterwards was Marshall of Richmond. Was in the United States Internal Revenue service during Mr. Cleveland's last Presidental administration. His children are named in the coming sections:

Section 1. William Duncan Oldham, a wealthy merchant of Richmond, Ky., married Mary Ferrill, issue:

1. Fhenal Oldham.
2. Harrel Oldham.
3. Abner Ferrill Oldham.
4. Lonsil Oldham; died in infancy.

Section 2. Charles Kavanaugh Oldham, a wealthy merchant of Mount terling, Ky., married Bessie Baumstark.

Section 3. Abner Oldham, a wealthy merchant of Mount Sterling, married Minnie Patton, issue:

1. William Oldham.
2. Charles Oldham.
3. Abner Oldham.
4. Susan Catherine Oldham; died in infancy.

Section 4. Kate Oldham; married Jeremiah Broaddus. (See Chapter 11, Art. 2, Section 3-6.)

CHAPTER 29.

ABNER OLDHAM.

(Named in Chapter 16, Section 10.)

Article 1.—Abner Oldham, a son of Hezekiah Oldham and Mary Kavanaugh his wife, was born in Madison County, Ky., Sept. 14, 1837.

He married Jospehine Embry, a daughter of Elder Allen Embry and Samiramus Moberley his wife, June 15, 1859. (See Part VII, Chapter 4, Atricle 2, Section 2-1-f.) He was a soldier in the Confederate Army, General John H. Morgan's command. He was Deputy Sheriff while his brother Charles was high Sheriff of Madison County 1870-4. Afterwards Chief of Police and Marshall of Richmond. Later on removed to Lexington, Ky., and was on the police force there, and became chief. Afterwards was elected Justice of the Peace, which office he has held a number of years, and still (1905) holds. He and his sister Margaret Chenault are the only survivors of Hezekiah Oldham's children. The children born to Abner Oldham and Josephine Embry his wife, are named in the coming sections:

ABNER OLDHAM.

JOSEPHINE EMBRY.
Wife of Abner Oldham.

Section 1. Thomas Oldham; died when a young man.

Section 2. Abner Oldham; died before his maturity.

Section [illegible] L[illegible]a Oldham; married P. F. F[illegible]n, and they live in Lexington, Ky. They have no children

Section 4. Allene Oldham, lives in Lexington, Ky., she married William Montague. Their children:

1. Thomas Montgaue.
2. William Montague.
3. Mary Josephine Montgaue.

Section 5. Charles Oldham; married Marrie Hammond. He is a real estate agent at Lexington, Ky. Their children:

1. Hammond Oldham.
2. Dorothy Embry Oldham.

Section 6. Marie Oldham, lives at Lexington, Ky.

Section 7. Embry Oldham, lived at Lexington, Ky., unmarried. He died there Aug. 9, 1906, age 23 years, his remains were brought to Richmond, Ky., and buried in the cemetery. The floral tributes were beautiful and grand. Elder Blake said "Embry Oldham was one of the finest, and best young men of Lexington."

CHAPTER 30.

MARY ELIZABETH OLDHAM.

(Named in Chapter 16, Section 11.)

Article 1.—Mary Elizabeth Oldham, a daughter of Hezekiah Oldham and Mary Kavanaugh his wife, was born in Madison County, Ky., March 29, 1840.

Capt. WILLIAM B. TIPTON.

MARY ELIZABETH OLDHAM.
Wife of Capt. W. B. Tipton.

She married Captain William B. Tipton of Montgomery County, Ky. After their marriage Mr. Tipton enlisted in the Confederate States Army, holding the rank of Captain. After the war they spent the remainder of their days in Montgomery County. Captain Tipton was also a Mexican war veteran. Their children are named in the coming sections:

Section 1. Kavanaugh Tipton; married Anna Russell. He was killed whilst with a possee, in the act of arresting a criminal.

Section 2. Elizabeth Tipton; married Howard Wilson. Mr. Wilson was killed in the same manner as his brother-in-law Kavanaugh Tipton, but on a different occasion.

CHAPTER 31.

CALEB OLDHAM.

(Named in Chapter 13, Section 4.)

Article 1.—Caleb Oldham, a son of Captain John Oldham and Annis Rice his wife, was born in Caswell County, North Carolina, June 1, 1789.

CALEB OLDHAM.

He came to Kentucky with his parents in 1795. He was a wonderfully energetic man. In his vigorous manhood was an extensive trader and farmer, and for a number of years carried annually to the Carolina market great droves of hogs, which were driven through on foot, and before age crept upon him was a prosperous man. His home was on Muddy Creek, some two miles south of Elliston, below the mouth of Hickory Lick, which he purchased by deed Sept. 22, 1817, of Garland Collins and Elizabeth his wife, and on March 8, 1844, Caleb Oldham deeded land to Christopher I. Miller, he had purchased of Collins. He married Milly Covington, a daughter of Robert Covington, senior. (See Part VII, Chap. 18, Section 1, f.) To whom was born:

Section 1. Martha B. (Patsey) Oldham, who married Elder John M. Park April 20, 1830. She died July 8, 1851. Elder John M. Park, was born Nov. 30, 1806, and died Nov. 3, 1877, but after his wife's death Elder John M. Park, married Mary Harris, a daughter of Judge Christopher Harris and Sally Wallace his wife. (See Part III, Chapter 34, Section 1.) To John M. Park and Patsey Oldham his wife, were born:

1. Ann Eliza Park; married Joseph Scrivner Dec. 21, 1848, issue:
   1. Thomas Scrivner; married Kate Ambrose.
   2. Irvine Miller Scrivner; married Emma Wallace. (See Part IV, Chapter 11, Section 1.)
   3. Ree Scrivner; married Jonah Wagers.
   4. Pattie Scrivner; married Jeff Wagers.
   5. Jeff Scrivner; married first Miranda Wagers, and secondly Lou Warford.
   6. Susan Frances Scrivner; married Abe Kelley.
   7. Burnam Scrivner; married Kate Prather.
   8. Bettie Scrivner; married James Cosby.
   9. Joe Scrivner; married Mattie Wagers.
   10. James Scrivner; died at 19 years of age.
2. Milly Park; married James Anderson Wagers Nov. 1, 1855, she died leaving issue:
   1. John Wagers; married Mattie White, live in St. Joseph, Missouri.
   2. William Wagers; married Lou Tudor, live in Bloomington, Illinois.
3. Robert Jefferson Park, was a Lieutenant in the Confederate States Army, Captain Thomas B. Collins Company F., 7th, afterwards 11th Kentucky Cavalry, Colonel D. Waller Chenault, Gen-

eral John H. Morgan's command. He married Eliza Christopher, and died in Lexington, Ky., leaving issue:

1. John Mills Park.
2. Nettie Park.
3. D. Park; married Eliza Broaddus. (See Chap. 11, Sec. 13.)
4. Horace Park.
5. Mattie Park.
6. Ida Park.

4. Mary Park; married Archibald Kavanaugh Duncan. (See Part VII, Chap. 9, Section 3-2.)

5. Talitha Park; married Anderson Wagers, lately husband of her sister Milly, she died leaving issue:

1. Laura Wagers; married Solomon Kelley.
2. Archibald Wagers; married Mary Fowler.
3. Flora Wagers; married Elliot Campbell.
4. Park Wagers; married Miss Shepherd, emigrated to Missouri.
5. Hubert Wagers.
6. Mary Wagers.
7. James Wagers.

6. Fanny Park; married L. Morton Scrivner, she died leaving issue:

1. Forest Scrivner; died young.
2. Eva Scrivner; married Henry Rayburn.
3. Herbert Scrivner; married Bessie Rayburn.
4. Harry Scrivner; married Rachael McCord.
5. Alma Scrivner; school teacher.
6. Sue Scrivner; school teacher.
7. Nettie Scrivner, clerk in her brother's store ,at Winchester, Kentucky.

Article 2.—After the death of Milly Covington wife of Caleb Oldham, Mr. Oldham, on the 21st day of April 1814, married Abigail Moberley, a daughter of John Moberley, senior, the said John Moberley senior's children were:

1. Benjamin Moberley; married Susannah A. Rend.
2. Abigail Moberley; married Caleb Oldham.
3. Nancy Moberley; married Larkin Hume.
4. Viney Moberley; married George Ballard.
5. Susan Moberley; married Daniel Gates Oct. 10, 1822.
6. Ichabod Moberley; married Patsey Oldham, daughter of William Oldham.
7. Thomas Moberley; married Sally Oldham. (See Chap. 35.)
8. Richard Moberley; married Betsy Shelton. (See Part VII.)
9. William Moberley; married Dianna Field.
10. John Moberley; married ——, Morris.
11. Polly Moberley; married James L. Brassfield, cousin to James E. Brassfield.
12. Tabitha Moberley; married James E. Brassfield.

The children of Caleb Oldham and Abigail Moberley his wife, are named in the coming sections:

Section 2. Malvina Oldham; married George Shackelford Oct. 22, 1839, issue:

1. Caleb Oldham Shackelford, St. Louis, Mo.
2. Clara Shackelford; married John W. Ockerson. They live in St. Louis, Mo., they have no children.
3. Maggie Shackelford; married John Beach, no issue.
4. Cecilia Shackelford; married John Thompson.

Section 3. Shelton Oldham; married first Eliza Drake, and second time, Mrs. Sarah P. Lewis a widow, who after Shelton Oldham's death, married Josiah Lipscomb, former husband of his sister Eliza Oldham.

Section 4. Thomas Moberley Oldham. The subject of Chapter 32.

Section 5. William Moberley Oldham; married Anna Robinson, issue:

1. John Baldwin Oldham; married Katie Pitman, no children.
2. Ella S. Oldham; married J. K. Daughters, no children.
3. Mary R. Oldham; married William M. Wood, no children.
4. Will Dowell Oldham; married Alice J. Bronston, children:
   1. Edwin B. Oldham.
   2. William Dowell Oldham.

Section 6. Eliza E. Oldham; married Josiah G. Lipscomb, Aug. 13, 1844. Josiah Lipscomb afterwards married the widow of Shelton Oldham. Eliza Lipscomb, left seven or eight children.

Section 7. Elizabeth Oldham; died young.

Section 8. Pauline Oldham; married Peter T. Ellis Jan. 3, 1851. To whom were born:

1. Hezekiah Ellis; died unmarried.
2. Walter Scott Ellis, went South and married.
3. Sanders Ellis, went South and married.
4. Sallie Ellis.
5. George Ellis.
6. Anna Ellis; died.
7. Mary Ellis.
8. Ada Ellis.
9. Nannie Ellis; died.

This family of children all emigrated to South Carolina.

Section 9. Diannah Oldham, went to Missouri, married Dr. Robertson.

Section 10. Mary Oldham; died in her infancy.

Section 11. John Preston Oldham, was a soldier in the Confederate States Army, Captain Thomas B. Collins Company F. 7th, afterwards 11th Kentucky Cavalry, Colonel D. Waller Chenault, General John H. Morgan's command. He married Jael F. Hume, Dec. 20, 1864. (See Part III, Chap. 21, Sec. 4.) Their children:

1. Mary Oldham; married Meredith Hayden. Had one child:
   1. — — Hayden.
2. Sallie Oldham.
3. Margaret Oldham.

CHAPTER 32.

THOMAS MOBERLEY OLDHAM.

(Named in Chapter 31, Section 3.)

Article 1.—Thomas Moberley Oldham, a son of Caleb Oldham and Abigail Moberley his wife, was born in Madison County, Ky., the — day of —— 18—.

He married Sarah Overton Harris, a daughter of Judge Christopher Harris and Sallie Wallace his wife, the 14th day of Aug. 1849. (See Part III, Chap. 36, Sec. 1, Art. 1.) When the Civil War came on he enlisted in the Confederate States Army, Captain Thomas B.

THOMAS MOBERLY OLDHAM.

SARAH OVERTON HARRIS.
Wife of Thomas Moberly Oldham.

Collin's company F. 7th, afterwards 11th Kentucky Cavalry, Colonel D. Waller Chenault, General John H. Morgan's command. (See Chap. 18, for sketch or incident of the subject, and his cousin and comrade Othniel R. Oldham.) The children of this subject and his wife are named in the coming sections:

Section 1. Sally Elizabeth Oldham, born 1852 April 20; married David Gentry Martin May 26, 1874. She was born in 1852, and died Jan. 9, 1892. After her death Mr. Martin married her cousin Temperance Oldham, daughter of Othniel R. Oldham and Sydonia Noland his wife. (See Chap. 17, Section 6, also Part III, Chap. 36, Section 1.) No living issue.

Section 2. Joseph Christopher Oldham, born June 17, 1858; married Mattie Williams, daughter of W. Thomas B. Williams, late a farmer, capitalist, and banker of Irvine, Ky., March 15, 1800. No living issue.

CHAPTER 33.

POLLY OLDHAM.

(Named in Chapter 13, Section 5.)

Article 1.—Polly Oldham, a daughter of Captain John Oldham, and Annis Rice his wife, was born in Caswell County, North Carolina May 22, 1791.

She came to Kentucky with her parents in 1795, and on the day of —— 18—, was married to James Grubbbs. To whom were born the children named in the coming sections:

Section 1. Amanda Grubbs; married John P. Dillingham, and died shortly after her marriage.

Section 2. Miss —— Grubbs; married Mr. —— White, a son of Joel White.

Section 3. Miss —— Grubbs; married Mr. White, a son of Joel White.

Section 4. John Grubbs; died at the age of about twenty years.

Mr. James Grubbs; died—day—18—,and Polly Oldham Grubbs, his widow married Jack Moore.

CHAPTER 34.

SALLY OLDHAM.

(Named in Chapter 13, Section 6.)

Article 1.—Sally Oldham, a daughter of Captain John Oldham and Annis Rice his wife, was born in Caswell County, North Carolina May 14, 1793.

SALLIE OLDHAM.
Wife of Thomas Moberly.

She came to Kentucky with her parents in 1795, and on the 8th day of Feb. 1816, was married to Thomas Moberley, a brother to Abigail Moberley, the second wife of Caleb Oldham. (See Chap. 31.) Thomas Moberley was a soldier in the war of 1812. They moved to Montgomery County where they made their permanent home. To them were born the children named in the coming sections:

Section 1. Caleb Oldham Moberley; married Eliza Taylor, issue:

1. Sallie Moberley; single.
2. Bessie Moberley; single.
3. Lin Moberley; married Miss —— Garrison.
4. Minnie Moberley; single.

Section 2. James Moberley; married Fannie Whitseil, issue:

1. Nellie Moberley.
2. Thomas Moberley.
3. Grace Moberley.
4. —— Moberley.

Section 3. America Moberley; married Andrew Fesler, (his second wife), issue:

1. Thomas Fesler.
2. Henry Fesler.

CALEB CLDHAM MOBERLY.

Section 4. Julia Moberley, married William Sidener (both dead.) Issue:

1. Julia Sidener: married T. G. Cunningham. Issue:

1. Thomas Cunningham.

Section 5. Parthenia Moberley; married James Moore. They live in Missouri.

Section 6. Martha Moberley; married Mr. —— Stone. No issue.

CHAPTER 35.

ELIZABETH OLDHAM.

(Named in Chapter 13, Section 7.)

Article 1.—Elizabeth Oldham, a daughter of Captain John Oldham and Annis Rice his wife, was born in Estill County, Ky., June 15, 1795.

ELIZABETH OLDHAM.
Wife of Wm. Fisher.

She married William Fisher, April 25, 1815, and moved to Montgomery County, Ky., where they spent their remaining days. William Fisher was a soldier in the war of 1812. They left issue:

Section 1. A daughter, killed when four or five years old.

Section 2. Pauline Fisher; died at twenty years of age, unmarried.

Section 3. Jefferson Fisher; died before he was twenty one years old.

Section 4. John Fisher; married an Ohio lady.

Section 5. James Fisher; married in Fayette County.

Section 6. William Fisher, went to Missouri and married Ann Oldham his cousin, daughter of John Oldham and Jane Reid Moberley. (See Chapter 37, Section 1.)

CHAPTER 36.

NANCY OLDHAM.

(Named in Chapter 13, Section 8.)

Article 1.—Nancy Oldham, a daughter of Captain John Oldham and Annis Rice his wife, was born in Estill County, Ky., Dec. 10, 1797.

She married Jesse Grubbs Dec. 24, 1818. He was in the war of 1812, and they moved to Montgomery County, Ky., where they made their home and spent their remaining days. Their children:

NANCY OLDHAM.
Wife of Jesse Grubbs.

Section 1. Joel H. Grubbs; married Mary Green. Their children:

1. Jesse Grubbs; married ——— ——— of Lexington, Ky. He died there in January 1906.

2. Thomas Grubbs; married Rose Armstrong, daughter of the old miller at Lexington, Ky., where they now live.

3. Nannie Grubbs; married Julius Arterburn of Mt. Sterling, Ky. They are both dead. Her husband was deaf, and was worth a half million dollars, issue:

1. Mary Arterburn; married Mr. Hudson of Louisville, Ky.

Section 2. Mary Grubbs; married Andrew Fesler. Their children:

1. John Fesler, who died recently. He married first Miss Crain, and secondly, Virginia Barlow. Children of the first marriage:

1. Lula Fesler; married M. C. Clay, of Mt. Sterling, and died. Issue:

1. Elizabeth Clay.

Children of the second marriage:

2. Andrew Fesler; married ——— ———, lives in Goldfield, Nevada.

3. Joel Fesler; married ——— ———, lives in Pittsburg, Pa.

4. Florence Fesler; married Mr. ——— Stevens, of Cincinnati. She is a practicing dentist in that City.

5. Fontaine Fesler, lives in California.

6. Milton Fesler.

2. Joel H. Fesler; married Lucy Jameson, live in Mt. Sterling, Kentucky, no issue.

Section 3. John Grubbs; married Minerva T. Stoner, daughter of Washington Stoner, who was a son of the old pioneer Michael Stoner, whose wife was a daughter of George Boone, brother to Colonel Daniel Boone, the founder of Boonsborough. Mr. Grubbs died without issue, and his widow Minerva T. Stoner Grubbs, married secondly, General Richard Williams, a brother to General John S. (Cerro Gordo) Williams. Washington Stoner's wife was Miss Tribble, his cousin, a daughter of Peter Tribble (son of the pioneer preacher, Andrew Tribble) and wife, Mary Boone, daughter of George Boone.

Section 4. Thomas Higgason Grubbs; married Mary Eliza Jarman, in Madison County, Ky., she was a daughter of Edward B.

Jarman and Judith Waddy Maupin his wife. The said Judith being very young, left school in Charlottesville, Albemarle County, Va., to marry. After the marriage, Mr. Jarman and his bride made their home in Madison County, Ky., and there raised their family, and died honored and respected by the people with whom they mingled. (See Part V, Chap. 3, Sec. 5.) Their children:

1. Charles D. Grubbs, a practicing attorney of the Mt. Sterling Bar; married Mary W. Hazelrigg. Their children:
   1. Hazelrigg Grubbs.
   2. Thomas Grubbs.
2. Jesse Edward Grubbs; married Allie W. Graves. He is a merchant in Winchester Ky.
3. Catherine Chapman Grubbs; married H. R. Prewitt, State Insurance Commissioner.
4. Virginia W. Grubbs; married Harry G. Hoffman. In insurance business in Mount Sterling, Ky., issue:
   1. Mary Louise Hoffman.

Section 5. Sarah Elizabeth Grubbs; married William H. Winn, now deceased, was a member of the Mt. Sterling bar, and Judge of the Montgomery County Court. Their children:

1. John G. Winn, a member of the Mt. Sterling bar, and President of the Montgomery National Bank. He married Catherine Prewitt, a daughter of Richard Hickman Prewitt, of Fayette County, Ky. Their children:
   1. Richard Prewitt Winn.
   2. John Jacob Winn.
2. Mary Winn; married Andrew T. Lockridge, now deceased, late a lawyer of Mt. Sterling, Ky., issue:
   1. Harry Winn Lockridge.
3. Jessie L. Winn; married R. W. Deering, Dean of Western University at Columbus, Ohio, chair of German, issue:
   1. Dorothy Deering.
4. Pierce Winn, cashier of the Mt. Sterling National Bank; married Agnes T. Catlett, childless.
5. Robert Hiner Winn, one of the leading attorneys at law, of Mt. Sterling, Ky. He married Miss Elizabeth M. Turney, of Bourbon County, Ky. No issue.
6. Nell Winn; married David Underwood Lipscomb. Wholesale Hardware Merchant, Nashville, Tennessee, and an elegant gentleman, issue:
   1. Sarah Lipscomb.

CHAPTER 37.

JOHN RICE OLDHAM.

(Named in Chapter 13, Sec. 9.)

Article 1.—John Rice Oldham, a son of Captain John Oldham and Annis Rice his wife, was born in Estill County, Ky., July 14, 1801.

JOHN RICE OLDHAM.

He married Jane Reid Moberley Jan. 13, 1831. (See Part II, Chap. 48. Sec. 2.) They emigrated to Missouri and made their home in Columbia or Independence. His wife died and Mr. Oldham married again Mrs. Ferguson nee Hedges. Children of the first marriage:

Section 1. Ann Oldham; married her cousin William Fisher. (See Chap. 35, Section 6.)

Section 2. Miss —— Oldham; married Joe Phelps in Missouri.

Issue of the second marriage:

Section 3. David D. Oldham, a detective in Kansas City, Mo.

CHAPTER 38.

1. LETTERS FROM SAMUEL OLDHAM, ESQUIRE, OF ZANESVILLE, OHIO, WITH NOTES FURNISHED BY HIM FROM "BROOK'S HISTORY OF MEDFORD," "PAIGNE'S HISTORY OF CAMBRIDGE." "HISTORY OF SCITUATE, MASSACHUSETTS, BY DEAN." "SAVAGES DICTIONARY," "BOND'S HISTORY OF WATERTOWN." 'SMITH'S MEMORIAL," "VIRGINIA DOC. 1830," "PENNSYLVANIA ARCHIVES," "EAGLE'S PENNSYLVANIA GENEALOGIES," ETC., WITH SUMMARIES THEREFROM.

1. The very pleasant and instructive correspondence with Samuel Oldham Esquire of Zanesville, Ohio, has brought forth many interesting letters from him, enclosing notes, and much information concerning the early Oldhams of Massachusetts, Pennsylvania and elsewhere. The lack of space forbids the presentation herein of all his letters in full, and summaries only of the notes are presented.

Omitting personal matter, some of his letters and extracts from some, with summaries follow:

Zanesville, O., Nov. — 1905.

Mr. W. H. Miller, Richmond, Ky. My dear Sir: Your favor of the 16th inst at hand and carefully noted. At the outset, let me say, that Captain John Oldham and Lieutenant Colonel, William

Oldham, killed at. St. Clair's defeat, Nov. 4, 1791, were full brothers, and Sarah Oldham, who married William Merriweather, was the full sister of both. and they were the children of Isaac Oldham by his first marriage. By Isaac Oldham's second marriage, there were eleven children five sons and six daughters, fourteen in all, who grew to be men and women. The children of the first marriage, to-wit: William, John and Sarah Oldham settled in Louisville and Lexington, Ky. The children of the second marriage: James, Thomas, Isaac, Alline, Mary, Elizabeth, Catherine Esther and Robert. settled in Ohio, Hannah in Missouri. Samuel the youngest, born in 1792, remained on the home place in Virginia until his death, March 1876.

Isaac Oldham, the father, was past fifty years of age when the Revolution begun; he was born in 1726, and died on what he calls his plantation in Ohio County, Va., in 1821. I will quote you a paragraph from his last will and testament, which was proven in Court, Ohio County, Va., at the September term A D 1821. "I give and bequeath to my son William Oldham, the sum of one dollar; my daughter Sarah, one dollar; my son John, one dollar, also, to my son, James the sum of one dollar, in addition to what they have previously received. I am not able to say what had been previously given to the children William, John and Sarah, but James, who was the eldest child by the second marriage received in 1799, a deed for one hundred acres of land Middle Wheeling Creek, Ohio County, Va. That there had been some settlement of the interests of the children named before their going to the south is doubtless true, as shown by the will. I can't say, who was the mother of William, John and Sarah, nor can I tell you where the birth place of Isaac was.

Samuel Oldham, who died in Louisville, in 1823, was the brother of Isaac Oldham, and not the brother of Colonel William Oldham, as stated in some genealogies that have been complied.

Note: Mr. Thurston's Tree, sets forth Lieutenant Colonel William Oldham, killed at St. Clair's defeat, Samuel Oldham, who died in Louisville in 1823, and Winifred Oldham, who married Colonel John Neville, as brothers and sister, and children of John Oldham and Ann Conway. (Writer.)

He was a resident of Frederick or Jefferson County prior to the formation of Berkely County in 1770, but was included in Berkely when that County was formed. Adam Stephens was the first sheriff of that County, (Berkely) and Samuel Oldham was one of the sureties on the bond, which was in the sum of one thousand pounds current money, and the default to our Sovereign Lord, King George, the third. Daniel Morgan was another surety on the bond. John Neville was one of the Justices approving the bond. John Neville, was the second sheriff of Berkely County. He married Winifred Oldham. He was a Colonel in the Revolution in the Virginia line. At the end of that struggle, he removed to Pittsburg, Pa. Was United States Marshall, during the whiskey insurrection in the five Western Counties of Pennsylvania, and had his dwelling burned by the rioters. Both himself and wife died and were buried at Pittsburg, Pa. The wife of General Neville was as I have stated Winifred Oldham, the sister of Samuel Oldham, of Berkely County, Va., the same who died at Louisville, Ky., in 1823, and the sister of Isaac Oldham. "Allspaugh in his Annals of the West, states that General Daniel Morgan, and Lieutenant Neville were brothers-in-law. If that statement is true then General Morgan, married an Oldham. Samuel Oldham was one of the sureties on General Neville's bond as sheriff of Berkeley County, and between the years 1772 and 1782, the time he removed to Louisville, Ky., his name is on some nine legal instruments on record in Berkeley County, Virginia.

Isaac Oldham's military record in the Revolution from 1778, to 1783, was in Captain John Van Meter's company of Pennsylvania Rangers. (See Pennsylvania Archives 3rd series, Vol. XXIII, p. 228-319.) This company was raised in Westmoreland County, Pa. William and John served in Captain Nelson's company of Independent Riflemen, which was raised in Westmoreland County, Pa. This company was raised for service in Canada, but when at Ticondaroga to join Montgomery, by a resolution of the Continental Congress, attached to the third Pennsylvania Regiment, Colonel Wayne commanding, and afterwards to the fifth Pennsylvania, Colonel Johnson, commanding. After Nelson had been retired from the service John Oldham became the Captain of the company and William who had been Ensign, was promoted to a Lieutenant. William was never Captain of this company, unless it was by brevet. John continued Captain until his resignation.

John Oldham—Captain Oldham's company, formerly Nelson's company, was an independent one, and was by resolution of Continental Congress, March 24, 1777, attached to the fifth Pennsylvania, Colonel Francis Johnson commanding. He was commissioned the 27th of Sept. 1776, and retired from the service Jan. 1, 1781. William Oldham was first Lieutenant. (See Penn. Archives second series Vol. X.) William Oldham of Pennsylvania was first Lieutenant of Nelson's company, Independent Rifles of Westmoreland County Pa., from Jan. 30, 1776, to Jan. 1777. Was Lieutenant Colonel commanding the militia force under Governor St. Clair and was killed at St. Clair's defeat, near Fort Recovery Ohio, Nov. 4, 1791.—Pennsylvania Archives second series, Vo. X, p. 62—.

Isaac Oldham, made many trips by flat boats or Kentucky "Broadhorns," between 1783, and 1800. On one of these trips the convoy of boats was attacked by the savages, when some forty miles above Louisville. The first fire of the Indians on the arched roof of the boats resembled a hail storm from the glancing balls. All the boats escaped, except Greathouse, which was captured, landed and destroyed, those on board taken captives from whom nothing was ever head (of them.) On the arrival of the other boats at Louisville, a detachment of cavalry was sent in pursuit of the Indians, but without avail. Many incidents of the early settlements and of kindred I have heard from my father, but as I was only a boy of less than sixteen at the time of his death they made but little impression upon me. As the matter now stands I am one of the three or four of the second generation whom can say Isaac Oldham was their Grand-Father. ** Respectfully,

SAMUEL OLDHAM.

Extract from Samuel Oldham's letter of Dec. 16, 1905:

"Samuel, who was the uncle of William, John and Sarah, settled at Louisville, where he resided until his death in 1823. Did Sarah go to Louisville with Samuel? I think she did, for neither William or Captain John were married until after they settled in Kentucky. William according to all authorities married Penelope Pope. ** The date of Sarah's marriage to William Meriweather is inaccurately stated. The Virginia Historical Magazine Vol. VII, p. 103, does not give the date of the marriage. The Tree of William Oldham's descendant, fixes the date as 1788. Did the Oldham's I have named, or any of them engage in business, Merchantile or Manufactory, at the fall of the Ohio? (Note: One William Oldham owned a cotton factory in Lexington, Ky., as late as 1825, writer.) If they did the County records would throw some light on the matter. I think they did, and my reason for thinking so, is from the fact that grand-father, Isaac Oldham, made several trips to Louisville, both before and after William's death. These trips were made on Kentucky "Arks" or "Broadhorns," as these flat boats were called. **

"The settlement with William, John and Sarah, as shown by grand-father's will, may have been made after they went to Kentucky, or it may have been made before,, but that it was made the will itself shows, which is of record in Ohio County, Va. The fact that William, John and Sarah, were the children of Isaac Oldham, is known to numbers of Isaac Oldham's great grand-children. Of the grand-children, only six remain, Thomas and J. R. Smith of Dallas, West Virginia., the former 88, the latter 86, years of age. Mrs. Mary Armstrong, aged 75 years, the youngest child of Samuel Oldham, the youngest son of Isaac Oldham. He died in 1884. Mrs. Armstrong has grand-father's Bible, I think. My brothers, my sister and myself, are the only grand-children of Isaac Oldham and the nieces and nephews of William, John and Sarah Oldham."

Notes enclosed with Mr. Sameul Oldham's letter of Dec. 25, 1905, showing the names of Oldham, who owned land in Pennsylvania. 150 to 200 years ago, etc.:

"Robert Oldham in 1707, 100 acres in Buck County Pa.

"Edward Oldham in 1735, 150 acres in Lancaster County, Pa.

"Thomas Oldham 1749, 100 acres in Lancaster County, Pa.

"William Oldham 1747, 40 acres in Lancaaster County, Pa.

"Nathaniel Oldham 1749, 100 acres in Lancaster County, Pa.

"Joseph Oldham 1754, 150 acres of land.

"Robert Oldham, owned land in Chester County, in 1765-1776-1768-1769-1774.

"John Oldham, owned land and was taxed in Chester County, Pa., in 1765-66-67-68--69.

"Thomas Oldham, owned land and was taxed in York County, in 1779-1780-1782-1783.

"George Oldham, granted 26662-3, acres by Virginia, June 16, 1807.

"Conway Oldham, had 4000 acres given by Virginia Nov. 11, 1782.

In Pennsylvania:

"William Oldham, Captain Oldham, John Oldham, all received compensation for depreciated pay, and hence served in the army 1775-1783. (Pa. Archives second series Vol. XIII, p. 176.)

Conway Oldham, James Oldham, Jesse D. Oldham, John Oldham, Moses Oldham, Richard Oldham. All made claim to the United States Congress for Revolutionary services.

Richard Oldham, North Carolina and Kentucky, served in the Revolutionary Army, first Lieutenant seventh Infantry May 3, 1808. Captain Dec. 1, 1809, Major 17th Infantry April 9, 1814, honorably discharged June 15, 1815. M. S. K. 9th March 1819, honorably discharged June 1, 1821. (His Register U. S. Army, by Hitman, Clerk, in Adj't General Office.)

Richard Oldham 1744-1833. Served as private in North Carolina Militia. He was a pensioner from Estill County, Ky, where he died. (Lineage Book D. A. R. Vol. XV, p 14036.)

Major Richard Oldham, born May 13, 1787, was an officer in the United States Army, where he attaained the rank of Major, in active service at New Orleans, in 1812-1814. He married Eliza Washington Martin, daughter of Major Thomas Martin. Major Richard Oldham resigned from the army and settled in Louisville, Ky., where he was elected Jailer and died in 1835. He had eight children. (Tree of William Oldham.)

From Samuel Oldham's letter of Jan. 6, 1906:

** "I hand you with this a copy of the official bond of Adam Stephens, the first sheriff of Berkely County, Va. You will notice that one of the Oldham's is one of the sureties on this bond,. Aside from this interesting fact, the Daniel Morgan name as one of sureties, was the famous Revolutionary officer of that name. His grave is in the old cemetery at Winchester, Va. **

"My father Robert Oldham, has been asleep more than fifty years, yet, I, when a boy, (I am now more than seventy years) heard my parents talk over incidents, mention names and places, the remembrance of which has aided me much in the quest I have been making."

(Furnished by Miss Henshaw, Martinsburg, Va.)

Bond referred to in letter:

"Copied from the official records of Berkely County in Martinsburg, Va., where Adam Stephens and his bondsmen, swear their allegiance to the King of Great Britian. "Stephens to the King:

"Know all men by these presents that we Adam Stephens, Samuel Oldham, William Hencher (Henshaw), George Cunningham, Archibald Shearer, George Stogden, George Briscoe, Daniel Morgan and Henry Newkirk, are held and firmly bound and constituted to our Sovereign Lord King George, the Third, in the full and just sum of one thousand pounds, current money of Virginia to be paid to our said Lord the King, his heirs and successors, to which payment well and truly to be made, we bind ourselves, executors and administrators each and every one of them jointly and severally openly by these presents, and sealed with our seals, this 19th day of May 1772.

The condition of the above obligation is such, that whereas, the above bound, Adam Stephens is constituted and appointed sheriff of the County of Berkely delivered by a commission from the Governor, under the seal of the Colony dated the 18th day of April 1772, therefore, the said Adam Stephens shall well and truly collect and receive all officers fees, and dues put into his hands to collect, and truly account for the pay of the same to the officres to whom such fees are due, respectively and at such times as are prescribed by law, and shall well and truly execute, and due returns make of all presents, precepts to him directed, and pay and satisfy all sums of money and tobacco, by him received, by virtue of any such process, to the person or persons to whom the same are due, his or their executors, administrators or assigns and in all other things shall truly and faithfully perform the said office of sheriff during the time of his continuance therein, then the above obligation to be void, otherwise to remain in full force and virtue.

Adam Stephens. (Seal.)

Samuel Oldham (Seal) George Stogden. (Seal.)
George Cunningham (Seal) George Briscoe. (Seal.)
William Henshaw (Seal.) Daniel Morgan. (Seal.)
Archibald Shearer (Seal.) Henry (X) Newkirk. (Seal.)

At a court held for Berkely County May 19, 1772, this bond is acknowledged by the parties thereto and ordered to be recorded.

Test: Will Drew Clerk of Court.

Gentlemen, Justices, John Neville, Robert C. Willis, Robert Stephens, Goodue Swift, William Patterson."

From Samuel Oldham's letter of Feb. 4, 1906:

"I have a copy of the Tree of William Oldham, and will say to you as I wrote to Mr. A. V. Oldham of Louisville, that from William Oldham down the Tree is highly creditable.** The value of the Tree as a record depends upon the intermarriage and offspring of Colonel Samuel Oldham and the widow Elizabeth Newton, whose maiden name was Elizabeth Stark. There is nothing to show where either Samuel Oldham or the widow Elizabeth Newton resided at the time of their marriage. That they after marriage settled in Westmoreland County, Va., and continued to reside there until their death, I have no doubt, but I would like very much to know where this marriage of Colonel Samuel Oldham and the widow of Captain Thomas Newton took place, and where Colonel Samuel Oldham resided prior to the marriage.

It is stated in the Tree, that the offspring of this marriage was John Oldham, born in 1705. "The William and Mary's Quarterly, Vol. IX, page 249, says that Elizabeth Oldham, was the daughter of Nephemiah Stark. She married, first, Captain Thomas Newton, and married, in 1728, Colonel Oldham; she was the step-daughter of Major Andrew Gilson, and conveyed her part of the land by patent to her mother. In the deed she calls Willougby Newton "my son and heir." Geneologists have made searching enquiries about this John Oldham, but he has not been found. It would seem that the marriage of Colonel Samuel Oldham, and the widow Newton, took place in 1728; how could John Oldham born in 1705, be the child of Elizabeth Oldham, and why did she call Willoughby Newton her son and heir, if John Oldham, her son and heir, had an existence at all? It is said in the Tree, that this John Oldham married Ann Conway. Hayden says Ann Conway married Robert Emons in 1729. With Colonel Samuel Oldham's marriage with the widow of Captain Newton in 1728 and John Oldham's birth in 1705, and Ann Conway's marriage to Robert Emons in 1729, we may dismiss the subject without further comment.** "In William Oldham's Tree, no mention is made of Samuel Oldham's birth place, or from whence he came when he settled in Louisville, he was simply a brother of William. Sarah Oldham is made the daughter of Samuel. In the Virginia Historical Magazine Vol. VII, page 103, "Sarah Oldham married William Merewether, was born in 1757-8, and died in 1814." No statement of her parentage is given.

From letter of Samuel Oldham, of April 6, 1906:

"Mrs. Armstrong is the only child of uncle Samuel living, and as her father died in 1876, and as grand-father called it in his will, Mrs. Armstrong probably knows a great deal about the Oldhams. In a conversation with her some two years ago, I said to her: "The descendants of Captain John and Colonel William do not think that Isaac Oldham, was the father of John and William. To this she replied "but he was." In this matter of investigating the genealogies of the Oldham family I have no purpose or interest to subserve only the truth, that is what I am seeking, and have kept steadfastly in view.** I have a note from Mr. John Baxter of Oklahoma City, O. T., who is the grand son of Isaac Oldham, and his wife, Sarah (Marling) Oldham, in which he says: "Two or three brother's came from England, and settled in South Carolina, they afterwards removed to Vermont, and then settled in Lancaster County, Pa. I remember hearing my grand-father say that he was born in Bedford County, Pa., in 1779. That Isaac Oldham bought and improved a farm near West Alexander in Virginia. That two half brothers left home and went to Kentucky, near Lexington, who had no correspondence with the rest of the family, on account of differences in politics during the Revolution. Two sisters married and settled in Baltimore and one sister lived in Pittsburg. If your grand-father was not one of the two, or three brothers who came from England, he was born and married in Vermont. If the two brothers who went to Kentucky belonged to that generation, their names were John and William. The sister of Isaac Oldham at Pittsburg, was doubtless Mrs. Neville, who was the sister of Samuel Oldham at Martinsburg." Here is another note, this is from Mr. J. T. Oldham, the grand-son of Thomas Oldham, the second son of Isaac Oldham and his wife Sarah (Anderson) Oldham, born 1777, married Miss Nancy Davis of Virginia in 1797. Mr. Oldham's home is in Cambridge, Guernsey County, Ohio.

"My great grand-father and his family came from New Jersey, and settled in Western Pennsylvania, and Ohio County, Va. My grand-father came to Ohio from Washington County, Pa. The members of the family who came to Ohio from Western Pennsylvania and Virginia were Isaac, Thomas (the writer's grandfather), James and Robert. Samuel remained in Virginia.** There were two half brothers who migrated to Kentucky—Colonel William Oldham, killed at St. Clair's defeat, was one of them, he was a half brother of my grand-father." A note from Mrs. Florence Jones of Reynoldsburg, Ohio, a grand-daughter of Isaac Oldham, and his wife Sarah (Marling) Oldham, says: "I can't answer your questions in regard to your grand-father, except that he was twice married." I am of the opinion that Isaac Oldham's first wife died and was buried in Frederick County, Va. The second wife was Miss Sarah Anderson. It is insisted that this marriage took place at Bedford County, Pa. This wife, my grand-mother, was the sister of Colonel William Anderson of the Revolution, she was also, a sister of Mr. C. Anderson a Magistrate of Allegheny County, Pa. Colonel William settled in Washington County, Pa., where he resided until his death.

Isaac Oldham the third child of Isaac Oldham, and his wife Sarah (Anderson) Oldham, married Miss Sarah Marling of Haper's Ferry, Va. Once a year for many years after this settlement in Ohio 1807, (the Indians had not gone away yet under the Greenville Treaty) she would make a trip to her old home to the Ferry on horse back."

From Samuel Oldham's letter of May 26, 1906:

"In the way of Oldham names I will give you those of my father's family: Sarah, Isaac, Eliza, John, Robert, Ann, William, Robert, Martha Ann, Samuel, Thomas and Phoeba. You will notice that Robert is mentioned twice. The first Robert died in infancy. All those I have named have crossed over the river, but Samuel, Thomas and Phoeba. The children of my grand-father's family as mentioned in his will were: William, John Sarah, James, Elizabeth, Thomas, Isaac, Catherine, Hannah, Esther, Alline, Mary Robert and Samuel."

Note—Mr. Samuel Oldham of Zanesville, states that there was but one Captain John Oldham in the Continental Army, which is error. There was Captain John, of the Pennsylvania Rifles, and Captain John, of the North Carolina line, who after the war settled in Estill County, Ky., where he died. (Writer.)

Samuel Oldham's letter of August 28, 1906:

"I have been in quest of information in regard to Robert Oldham, who is mentioned in Pennsylvania Archives as having purchased land in Buck's County, Pa., in the year 1707. Mr. Warren S. Ely, of Doyleston, the Librarian of Buck's County Historical Society, is making the quest for me. In a recent note from him he says "The reference of Dr. Hayden, in regard to Robert Oldham, is to Pennsylvania Archives, second series page 483, of Vol. XIX, it reads as follows: "10-2-1707. "Sold Robert Oldham 100 acres of land joyning on William Hentley for £20, to be paid in 12 months, with interest Rent as Hentley." "It a minute of the commissioners of property and interest in minute book "G." The sequel to it is found on page 396, of the same volume, under date of June 30th. 1705, which reads as follows: "William Hentley desiring to purchase 200 acres at the head of Peter Dix's land, beyond Brandywine, joining on Thomas Withers, agrees to pay £40 at a shilling per cent rent. Granted, provided Joel Bailey, may also be accommodated with the like, if he desires it, on the same terms. He is to pay £20 in three months and the rest first month 1705, with fifteen months interest, if he can sooner. "The application of Joel Bailey for the 200 acres above referred to is found on page 347, and was held in abeyance, because it was ordered, that the land be sold, very sparingly for the future in the County of New Castle, or there abouts. "Joel Bailey was of Chester County, near Robert Pyles.

"All these items show that the grant of Robert Oldham was in the lower part of Chester County near the line of New Castle, Delaware, and was without doubt, the same 70 acres and 40 acres, held respectively by Robert Oldham and John Oldham 1765-1778, in East Nottingham, township, Chester County, referred to in my last letter, and a memorandum you have among Dr. Hayden'n notes. "Why Dr. Hayden should have conceived that the land was in Buck's County, I cannot understand, it was probably merely a suggestion not followed up by research. Anyhow, your quest should be in Chester County.

"Your Isaac Oldham, if of this line, was more probably a grand son of Robert Oldham of 1707, than a son. The land appears to have been partitioned off between a Robert and a John, prior to 1765."

"The probate records of Chester County, show the following:

"Will of Robert Oldham, Nottingham Township."

Dated Aug. 3, 1742, proved April 17, 1749, Will Book "C" page 124. Wife, Mary, son Edward, and daughter Mary Good, 5 shillings each; daughter Eleanor Walliston a cow, son Robert, my plantation, on which I have long lived, containing 150 acres, he to maintain my wife Mary, during her life. Son Robert sole executor, signed, Robert Oldham Witnesses—John Boggs, Robert Whitiker and Samuel Thomson."

Will of John White, Nottingham.

Book "A" page 371. Dated Oct. 13, 1731, proven May 18, 1732. Wife Elizabeth, plantation during widowhood, then to son Joseph, who is to maintain his sister Sarah White during her life; daughter Mary Oldham five shillings. Wife Elizabeth and John Ruddell executors.

"Robert Oldham, witness to will of Hugh Morgan, dated July 28th, 1727, proved April 6, 1728."

"Letters of Administration on estate of Thomas Oldham, senior, of Chester County April 20, 1750, to widow Mary Oldham."

"'Will of Thomas Oldham of East Nottingham, dated Feb. 3rd. 1756, proved March 1756. Book "D" page 35. Wife Rachael, one third of real and personal estate; Mary, widow of deceased son, Thomas, and their son Thomas five shillings each. Sarah, widow of son William, five shillings each; Lacy Rawles, husband of deceased daughter Mary five shillings; daughter Martha, wife of Joshua Littler (John Littler, son of Joshua, born Wilmington, Delaware, 12-26-1739, married Sarah Staples, born 5-27-1746, her daughter Sarah Littler born 4-20-1739, married James Gilpin) daughter Susannah, wife of Daniel Brown; daughter Hannah, wife of Thomas Barrett. Executors, son-in-law, Thomas Barrett, and friend William Churchman. Witnesses: William Churchman, James Hamell, George Churchman. Letters of administration to Thomas Barrett, only.

"Will of Rachael Oldham, East Nottingham, dated May 23rd, 1761, proved Dec. 13, 1762. Son, Simon Taylor; son Joshua Litter; grand-daughter Rachael, wife of Elisha Brown, and Thomas Barrett, residue of estate. Witnesses, Mordicia James, Micajah James, David Brown."

"Will of Zachariah Butcher, of East Nottingham, dated Aug. 18, 1754, proved Dec. 4, 1755, "P" page 25. Daughter Sarah Butcher, £5; executors to sell real and personal estate, and divide the proceeds among my children, viz: Mary, Elizabeth, Margaret, Susanna, Rachael, Hannah, Sarah. Executors of estate, Robert Oldham, and daughter Mary. Witnesses, Samuel Gilpin, Joseph Gilpin, Samuel Gilpin, Jr."

"Will of Mary Butcher, East Nottinghaf, dated Nov. 3rd, 1766, proved Jan. 29, 1767. All my title to ¾ of tract of land formerly belonging to my father Zachariah Butcher, to be conveyed and proceeds to sisters, Margaret Collett, Susanna Passmore, Rachael Oldham, Hannah Butcher and Sarah Day. Executor, sister Hannah Butcher."

"Will of Neal Cook, Nottingham, "B" page 27. Dated Feb. 14, 1737-8, proved May 29, 1738. Sons John and Daniel one shilling each, son Cornelins, 136 acres, on Buck Creek, Maryland where I formerly lived; son William, 100 acres at lower end of said tract, he paying to my grand-daughters, Katherine and Elizabeth Cook, £5 when of age. Daughter Katherine Wallistein, daughter Mary Ruddell, grand-daughter Ann Ruddell, Catherine McKeeb, son-in-law John Ruddell, William Rutledge a sorrel mare. Executors, wife Ann. Witnesses, Thomas Scott, William Oldham, John Ruddell."

"Edward Oldham, (probably eldest son of Robert Oldham) of Nottingham, Chester County, his wife Mary White had a warrant of survey for 150 acres of land in Lancaster County Feb. 4, 1735-6. (See Pennsylvania Archives Volume XXIV, page 495.) This land was doubtless in that part of Lancaster which then extended to the "Setting Sun," laid off in Cumberland in 1750. Bedford laid off out of Cumberland 1771, and Westmoreland out of Bedford 1773. This would place Isaac, if son of Edward, and grand son of Robert, where you first found him. There is no will of Edward Oldham in Lancaster County, but he may have died in Cumberland prior to the organization of Bedford 1771.** "I believe Edward was old enough to be the father of Isaac born 1726.

"The Oldhams all left Chester prior to 1800.

"Find nothing of Robert and Rachael Oldham, after that date.

"I have assumed that Mary, wife of Robert Oldham senior, was Mary White, mentioned in the will of Joseph White in 1732, but this is possibly a violent presumption, as the Mary White Oldham there mentioned may have been the widow of Thomas Oldham, Jr., to whom letters of administration were granted in 1750, though not very probable, possibly as Thomas Oldham, the father mentions only one child of his deceased son Thomas in 1756. Mary was probably not married to Thomas Jr., as early as 1732." You will notice that these notes do not account for a John Oldham who was a land owner in Nottingham 1773 to 1789, or some where there. (See my former letter.* Dr. Hayden's notes."*)

"I still hold that if you are a descendant of Robert Oldham, Isaac was a grand son. There is hardly room to doubt that Robert's sons were old enough to have a child born in 1726.

"Did you ever hear of the Thomas Oldham, seems contemporaneous with Robert, in the same Township?"

Mr. Miller, I send you these extracts** with the hope that at least they may be interesting.** You will see that the location of the Oldhams mentioned in Mr. Ely's notes was Chester County, Pa., New Castle, Delaware, and in Maryland.

Yours with kind regards,
Samuel Oldham.

Notes included in Samuel Oldham's letter of Jan. 28, 1907:

"John Oldham, 1600-1636. Born in England A D 1600, emigrated to Plymouth in 1623. In 1624, he and an Episcopal minister named John Lyford, conspired against the government of Plymouth, and dispatched letters containing charges aganist the established authorities to England. The plot was detected and Oldham was banished from the Colony, although he later became reconciled with the inhabitants, and rendered them some service. Settling in Massachusetts Bay Colony, he became a man of prominence, and was Deputy from Watertown to the first General Court of Magistrates of Massachusetts. In 1636, while he was on a trading expedition his pinnace was treacherously captured near Block Island. His murder was the immediate cause of the famous Pequod War. (International Encyclopedia.) It proved that the murderers were chiefly Block Island Indians, with a few of the Narragansetts, who then governed that Island. It was supposed, seeing these Indians with Mr. Oldham, that they were in the plot, as some of the Narraganset Sachems were found to be. Those who escaped crossed the sound to the Pequod Indians and were protected by them. The Governor and Council of Massachusetts determined to demand satisfaction of the Narragansett and Pequods, for their crimes, and ninety men having volunteered to form an expedition, Captain Endicott was appointed to command them, and they first visited the Narragansetts. These Indians submitted to the terms, gave up the sons of Mr. Oldham, promised good behavior for the future. The Pequods however, would do nothing, and Captain Endicott was ordered to take possession of Block Island, kill the men recross the sound, to the Pequod Country. (Dwights History of Connecticut.)

In confidence of their fidelity (Pequods) John Oldham** went in a small bark to trade with the natives of Block Island, and they murdered him, but spared his two boys, and two Narragansett Indians who were of his company. The murderers were discovered by a crew of small vessel, one Gallup, master from Connecticut which happened to come upon them soon after the fact. Gallup had with him, only one man and two boys, and no arms except two muskets and two pistols. Although the deck was full of Indians who had guns, swords, and yet they were not much used to them, they made but little resistance and when he boarded the vessel they jumped into the sea, and many of them were drowned. He found Oldham's body not cold, his brains beat out, and his hands hacked off. (Winthrops History of Massachusetts, Volume 1, page 160.) This occurred in the year 1636.

John Oldham murdered by the Indians, who came aboard his vessel to trade in 1636. This event brought on the Pequod war. He came to Plymouth in 1623, associated with Lyford in 1624, and sat up a separate worship on the sabbath (Church of England) intending to alter—perhaps assume the Government. He afterwards lived at Hull, and Cape Ann, and represented Watertown in 1634.

In 1633, with Hall and others he traveled from Dorchester to a place on the Connecticut River, now called Windsor. This exploration led to its settlement. (Drakes History of American Biography, page 160.) In 1624, John Oldham and Lyford, the minister of New Plymouth stirred up a faction there and were banished from that Colony. They began a settlement at Nantasket. The same year some belonging to Dorchester in England sent over fishermen and made necessary provision for a fishery at Cape Ann, and Rogers Conant, who with the rest (80 in all) to Nantasket, was appointed their overseer. A grant was made by one of the Georges, it is not said which, to Oldham and others of part of Massachusetts Bay, (five miles square) which occasioned some dispute with them and the Massachusetts grantees. (History of Massachusetts by Thomas Hutcherson Vol. 1, page 15.) Rogers Conant while contemplating a voyage to the New World, the company who promoted the planting of New P'lymouth were seriously divided. Such lack of harmony had existed two years, and appears to have had its rise from a difference of opinion as to ministration of Civil and Ecclesiastical affairs in the Colony. They all knew that the disciples of John Robinson who had come hither, brought with them the platform of Congregationalism, animated by the inherent principles of liberty. This so far prejudiced their minds that they thwarted the favorite purpose of himself and people in London to unite with their friends at Plymouth in the great mission of religion and philanthropy. In the mean while, not ashamed to incur the odium of not being careful of the spiritual wards of the Colonists they obtained another in his stead. The person chosen was John Lyford, who had been a minister in Ireland. He came on a ship which arrived in March 1624. At first he rendered himself agreeable to the emigrans and provided for them. It was soon discovered that he and John Oldham were carrying out the design of the dissatisfied members of the company in England by plotting as Bradford states both against our church and government, and endeavored to overthrow them.

The Governor made himself acquainted with the policy, but kept it secret. When, to use his own language, Lyford and his few accomplices with factions part of the adventurers sent, adjudging their party strong enough to rise up, oppose the government and church, draw a company apart set up for themselves, and he could administer the sacraments to them by his Episcopal calling. In reference to this subject Hubbard remarks that individuals who came over with Lyford affirmed that a principal why he and his supporters were treated as enemies by Governor Bradford and his council was their antipathy against the way of separation, wherein those at Plymouth had been trained up under Mr. Robinson. The same author further observes that some of them sorrowing do affirm upon their own knowledge that the first occasion of the quarrel with them was the baptizing of Mr. Helton's child, who was not joined to the church at Plymouth.

This attepmt at Revolution was so much in accordance with the design of the council for New England to crush out congregationalism in the plantation of Plymouth, and in every other which might be settled within their jurisdiction, the conviction forces itself on our minds that the advocates in London co-operated with that respectable body. The effort made by this clergyman and his followers, was their exclusion from the Colony. Among those so rejected was Roger Conant, who it appears came over in the same vessel with Lyford. (N. E. H and G R. Volume 2.)

Conant took up his abode at Nantasket, at which he resided for more than a year, unmolested, in the fine exercise of his religious persuasion. The Dorchester Company in the spring of 1624 received leave from the Plymouth Colony proprietor, a patentee of Cape Ann, to settle emigrants on the latter station. In compliance with the decision of their company John Humphrey their treasurer, notified Conant that they had elected him Governor, and would commit unto him the charge of all the affairs, as well fishing, as planting. At the same time, John Oldham who had been banished from Plymouth for zealous endeavors to carry out the plans of Lyford there, was invited to superintend the fur trade with the Indians, but he declined--Conant accepted. He was accompanied by Lyford, who was employed to preach for the colonists, was put under the authority of his friend and parishoner. Though Lyford and Conant were so favorably situated still their former difficulty at Plymouth was warmly agitated in England among the proprietors of the plantation. One part of them in a numerous assembly for discussing the subject employed John White a Lawyer of London, the other engaged the Rev. Thomas Hooker. The conclusion was adverse to the case of Lyford, still his advocates being two thirds of the adventurers forsook Governor Bradford, and his supporters with heavy responsibil ities. (N. E. H and G. R. Volume 2, page 236.)

Hugh Peters and John Oldham: Hugh Peters returned to London by May 11, 1629, when he attended a Court of assistants who were convened to hear the proposition of Oldham in the charter of the Massachusetts Company. As to the manner of its being granted was suitable evidence of the royal party of England to overthrow the liberties of congregationalism in New Plymouth and crush their budding everywhere they may appear. (N. E. H and G R. Vol. 5.)

Mary Oldham. Of those who came over in the Fortune Nov. 1623, the first of those was William Bassett. His bans were published first with Mary Butler on the 19th of March 1611, but she died before the first publication. He soon found however another mate July 29. Aug. 13, William Bassett, Englishman of Cecil Lecht, accompanied by Rodger and Edward Goddard; Mary Oldham, maid from England, accompanied by the General Court of the colony on the 22 day of May 1627, the name of the wife of William Bassett is given as Eliabeth Bassett as there were two names mentioned in his family. (Story of the Pilgrim fathers as told by themselves.)

The Falls (by lot) of the grounds which came in the Fortune according as their lots were cast March 1623. These 50 acres were located on both sides of the Willougsbybrooke. Mary Bassett adjoining Rodgers 1 acre, John Oldham and others joined with him 10 acres, Thomas Tilden 3 acres, Cuthbert Culbertson 6 acres, Anthony Armsable 4 acres, Richard Warne 5 acres, Edward Bangs 4 acres, North side; Stephen Tracy 3 acres, Thomas Clark 1 acre, Robert Bartlett 1 acre, Robert Radciff, beyond the swamp and stony ground 2 acres. These about Hobs hole, Nicolas Snow, Anthony Dix, Robert Wallene, North, Martin Pierce, his servants Edward Holmes 1 acre, Frances Palmer, wife of William Palmer 1 acre, Jonathan Pratts and Phenix Pratt 2 acres. These lie on the east side of town towards Eell river. (Story of the Pilgrim fathers.)

John Oldham's boys: May 14, 1635. This underwritten are to be transported to New England in the bargue Elizabeth and Ann, Rodgers, Captain. Mr. and Mrs. Thomas Peters have brought certificates from the minister of Parish of their confirmation to the order and discipline of the Church of England. Richard Sampson, tailor, aged 28 years, Thomas Alsop, 20 years, Robert Stanley, 22 years, John Oldham 12 years, Thomas Oldham 10 years, etc. (New England Historical and Genealogical Register Vol. XIX.)

John Oldham discovered the Black Lead Mines at Stonebridge, Connecticut.

Joseph Oldham. In the record of the first Church of Scituale, now the First Unitarian Church of Norwalk, Mass., of those who had been baptized by Guiluline (William) Witheral pastor of the church since his election to office in 1645, are these:

Oct. 3, 1658, Mary, daughter of Thomas Oldham.

Jan. 6, 1660, Thomas ye soune of Joseph Oldham.

(N. EE. G and H. R. Vol. for 1903.)

Richard Oldham was found indebted to the estate of Nathan Sparrowhawk, on appraisement of the property in 1647. (N. E. G and H. R. Vol. VII, page 173.)

The Freeman's Oath. Under the charter of Massachusetts Colony, none were regarded as freemen or members of the body politic, except such as were admitted by the General Court and took the Freeman's oath. This Court was continued in existence until by the second charter the Colony was transformed into a province. The names were orally stated then written down by the clerk, hence the various ways of writing Oldham.

"I. A. B and C., being by the Almighty's most wise dispensation became a member of this body consisting of the Governor, Deputy Governor, assistants and commonality of the Colony of Massachusetts in New England, do freely and sincerely acknowledge that I am justly and lawfully subject to the government of the same, and do accordingly submit my person and estate to be protected, ordered and governed by the laws and constitution thereof, and do faithfully promise to be from time to time obedient and conformable thereunto, and to the authority of said Governor and assistants and their successors, and to all such laws, orders, sentences and decrees as shall be lawfully made and published by them, or their successors. And I will always endeavor, in duty I am bound, to advance the peace and welfare of this body or commonwealth to my utmost skill and ability. And I will to my best power and means seek to divert and prevent whatsoever may tend to the ruin and damage thereof or any of the said Governor, Deputy Governor, or assistants or any of them or their successors, and will give speedy notice to them or some of them, of any sedition, violence, treachery, or other hurt, or evil which I shall know, hear or vehemently suspect to be plotted or intended against the commonwealth or the said government established. And that I will not at any time suffer or give consent to any council or attempt that shall be offered, given or attempted, for the impeachment of said Government, or making any change or alteration of the same contrary to the laws and ordinances thereof, but shall do my utmost endeavor to discover, oppose and hinder, all and every such counsel and attempt. So help me God." Taken before the General Court, by: John Oldham, May 1631, Richard Oldham May 7, 1651, Samuel Oldham, of Cambridge, May 7, 1673. (Colonial Records.)

Marriages:

Thomas Oldham of Scituale, Mass., and Mary Witheral Nov. 25, 1656.

Joseph Stitson and Hannah Oldham, both of Scituale, Mass., Nov. 6, 1668.

Thomas Oldham and Mary Sproat, both of Scituale, Mass., Nov. 6, 1683. (N. E. G and H. R.)

Sarah Oldham, daughter of Richard North, 1650-1664. Ann Bates, was daughter of Sarah Oldham. Frances wife of Richard North was daughter of Ann Oldham 1668-69. (N E Gand H R. Vol. VI, p 208.)

Grace Oldham and Anthony Eames Dec. 11, 1724.

Abigail Oldham, daughter of Deacon Samuel, and Abigail Oldham, was born Sept. 30, 1709, and married in Charleston, Mass., May 16, 1734 to Samuel Sumner, she died prior to 1750. (N E G and H R. Volume IX page 30.)

Caleb Oldham, of Scituale and Berthune Stephens married in Marshfield, October 21, 1724.

The Oldhams and Governor Bradford:

In the genealogy of Governor Bradford's family it is shown

(36)

that Elisha married Hannah Cole. 2 Bersheta Le Brook Sept. 7, 1718, who survived her husband and married secondly Joshua Oldham, of Pembroke, Mass.,—253. Desire married Major Watterman Cleft—254, VII. Hannah Elephalt, who married Prince Heas, Aug. 8, 1751, and lived in Duxbury; she died Jan. 11, 1756, aged 26. He married second Mrs. Oldhams. (N. E. G and H. R. Volume IV, p 238.)

Chart
by
Samuel Oldham

nas Oldham.
rn Circa, 1680, died in Nottingham Township, Feb. 16, 56; married 1st, at Chester, ., meeting of Friends (Pa.), out April, 1704, Susannah w, who died prior to 1728; rried 2nd, July 3, 1728, chael ( ) Littler, widow of nuel Littler, who died July 1762.

Mary Oldham.
d. April 21, 1724; m. May 21.7, Lacy Rowles.

Thomas Oldham, Jun.
b. ——; d. Feb. 13, 1749-50; m. 1727, Mary White, daughter of Jos. White, of Nottingham.

Martha Oldham.
b. ——; d. ——; m. 1st, Nov. 11, 1736, Jos. Underhill; m. 2d, prior to April 21, 1750, Jas. Swinton.

Susannah Oldham.
b. ——; d. ——; m. Nov. 11, 1736, Daniel Brown, of Cecil County, Md.

William Oldham.
b. ——; d. — 1749; m. June 10, 1736, Sarah Dix, dau. of Nathan Dix, of Nottingham, Chester County, who married 2d, 1751, —— Morris; removed to Tyrone Township, York County, 1746.

Hannah Oldham.
b. ——; d. ——; m. Nov. 29, 1739, Thomas Barrett, who was executor of her father's will, 1756.

Deborah Oldham.
b. ——; d. ——; m. Nov. 9, 1733, Joshua Littler, son Sam'l and Rachael, the latter second wife of her father.

Thomas Oldham.
b. ——; d. prior to 1772; m. Rachael Butcher.

Thomas Oldham*
John Oldham*
Susannah Oldham*
Martha Oldham*
Joseph Oldham||
Deborah Oldhamo
Anne Oldhamo
Hannah Oldhamo
Rachael Oldhamo

Children of William

Nathan Oldham.
Est'mt survey 110 a. land in "White Barrens" in East Nottingham, Chester County, April 23, 1759.

Isaac Oldham.
b. about 1739 or 1740; d. ——; m. in Menalien Township, York County, Pa., Oct. 20, 1762, Mary Younger; joined church 1768, and removed from these parts.

Rachael Oldham.
certificate to North Carolina, 1768.

Thomas Oldham.
b. ——; d. ——; m. in York Co., Oct. 13, 1779, Rebecca Blackburn, dau. of Thos. Blackburn; removed to Cumberland Co., Pa., 1800.

*All of age 1772.
||Above 14 yrs. 1772.
oUnder 14, 1772.

"John Oldham, who came from England to America in the Fortune and landed at Plymouth in 1623, it seems had three or four sons who came to America, viz: John, Thomas and Richard, and probably Joseph, that his son:

1. John Oldham came to America from England in the Elizabeth and Ann in 1635, at the age of twelve years, and was the next year captured by the Indians at the time his father was murdered. He married —— —— and probably was the merchant who died in 1698. (See Chap. 41.) He may have had other children than Thomas (as above indicated). His son:

1. Thomas Oldham, married —— —— and had children, (but whether the same Thomas, who died in Chester County, Pa., in 1756, is unknown.) He had probably other children than Samuel. His son:

1. Colonel Samuel Oldham, born about 1680, perhaps married more than once, however the case may be, he married Elizabeth Newton, and died in Westmoreland County, Va., 1759-62. (See Chap. 41.) Of his children were:

1. William Oldham; married Miss —— Basey, whose mothers maiden name was Garland. (See Chap. 2.) He lived in Prince William County, Va., or the section thereof which was cut off into Fauquier County in 1759. Their children were:

1. Jesse Oldham; married ElEizabeth Simpson. (See Chapter 3.) z
2. Major George Oldham. (See Chap. 2, Section 2.)
3. Moses Oldham; married Mary Rice. (See Chap. 39.)
4. Conway Oldham. (See Chapter 2, Section 4.)
5. James Oldham. (See Chap. 2, Section 5.)
6. Richard Oldham; married Ann Pepper. (See Chap. 6.)
7. Captain John Oldham; married Annis Rice. (See Chapter 13b.)
8. William Oldham. (See Chap. 2, Sec. 8.)
9. Judith Oldham; married Fisher R. Bennett. (See Chapter 2, Section 9.)
10. Elizabeth Oldham; married Mr. —— Pepper. (See Chapter 2, Section 10.)
11. Miss —— Oldham; married Mr. —— Battershell. (See Chapter 2, Section 11.)

2. John Oldham; married Ann Conway. (See Chapter 41.) Children, viz:

1. Conway Oldham. (See Chapter 41.)
2. Miss —— Oldham; married Lawrence Ross. (See Chap. 41.)
3. Miss —— Oldham; married Mr. —— Barton. (See Chapter 41.)
4. Miss —— Oldham; married Mr. Rector. (See Chapter 41.)
5. Winifred Oldham; married Colonel John Neville. (See Chapter 41.)
6. Samuel Oldham. (See Chapter 41.)
7. Mary Ann Oldham; married Major Abraham Kirkpatrick. (See Chapter 41.)
8. Lieutenant Colonel William Oldham; married Penelops Pope.

(The above table is made from notes furnished—the Oldham Tree—and tradition proof.)

2. Thomas Oldham, of Duxbury, Cooper Scituale, came to America from England in the Elizabeth and Ann, in 1635, at the age of ten years, and the next year, he and his brother John, were with their father in his trading shallop on the Narragansett Bay, when their father was murdered and the two boys taken and held captives by the Indians. He was a land owner in Scituale in 1650, and lived near King's Landing. He married Mary, daughter of Rev. William Wetheral of Scituale Nov. 20, 1656, and died in 1711. Children given in another place in this Chapter following.

3. Richard Oldham of Cambridge, born in England was in Cambridge as early as 1647, and took the Freeman's oath in 1651. He was first resident on the south side of the river, and died Dec. 9, 1655. His wife was Martha, daughter of William Eaton of Watertown. She married again Thomas Brown Oct. 7, 1656. The children of Richard Oldham, are set forth in another place in this Chapter following.

In Cople Parish Westmoreland County, Va., in the grave yard, is the tomb of Mrs. Elizabeth Oldham, who died in 1759 in her 72 year. And the tomb also of Samuel Oldham, was a vestryman of the Church Cople 1755, with this inscription:

"Samuel Oldham, of Westmoreland County. Faithful friend. Departed this life on the — day of April 1759, in the 72 year of his age.

Thomas Oldham, of Duxbury, Coper, Scituale, (1643) the youth who came from England in 1635 in the Elizabeth and Ann, and a brother of John, his fellow passenger, was a land owner in Scituale in 1650, his home was probably near King's Landing. He married Mary Witheral, daughter of Rev. William Witheral of Scituale Nov. 20, 1656. He died in 1711. Their children were:

1. Mary Oldham, born Aug. 20, 1658, baptized Oct. 3, 1658.

2. Thomas Oldham, born Oct. 30, 1660, Scituale. He was administrator of his fathre's estate. He married Mary Sproat, daughter of Robert Sproat in 1683, and removed to the Two Mile. His descendants are in Pembroke. Their children:

    1. Mary Oldham; married Andrew Newcombe of Eastham.
    2. Desire Oldham; married Samuel Tilden 1717.
    3. Joshua Oldham, 1684, twin.
    4. Mary Oldham, 1684, twin.
    5. Sarah Oldham.
    6. Hannah Oldham.
    7. Grace Oldham.

3. Sarah Oldham.

4. Hanah Oldham.

5. Grace Oldham.

6. Isaac Oldham, born about 1670, of Scituale, married Mary or Hannah Keene, of Duxburg, daughter of Josiah Keene, of Pembroke, Nov. 21, 1695, went to Pembroke in 1703, had one son and two daughters:

    1. Isaac Oldham; married Mary Stetson. Children:
        1. Isaac Oldham.
        2. Hannah Oldham.
        3. Deborah Oldham.
        4. David Oldham; married Deborah Baker, of Pembroke, had a son:
            1. Aurora William Oldham, born Jan. 24, 1779, married Nov. 3, 1824, Jane Miller Smith, born April 13, 1804, only child of Captain Miller and Jane (Stockbridge) Smith his wife. He died March 5, 1865. She died June 26, 1789.

Children:
1. Jane Reid Oldham, born Oct. 1825.
2. Miller Smith Oldham, born Dec. 1827.
3. Georgiana M. Oldham, born Aug. 1830.
4. Henry Williams Oldham, born Aug. 1832.
5. Mary Barker Oldham, born Nov. 1834.
6. Ellen Smith Oldham, born Nov. 1836.
7. George Barker Oldham, born July 1839.
8. Charles J. Oldham, born Oct. 1841.
6. Emma Frances Oldham born Dec. ,1843.
10. David S. Oldham, born Aug. 1845.

5. Jonathan Oldham; married Patience Clapp, of Scituale. Children:

1. Joseph Oldham; married Grace Tilden of Marshfield. Children:
1. Joseph Oldham; dead.
2. Jonathan Oldham; married Eunice Faxon, had:
1. Clara Oldham.
2. Loving Oldham.
3. Eunice Oldham.
3. Grace Oldham.
6. Mary Oldham.
7. John Oldham.
8. Daniel Oldham.
9. Lydia Oldham.
10. Ruth Oldham.
11. Able Oldham, of Winchester, N. H.
2. A daughter, name not given.
3. A daughter, name not given.
7. Ruth Oldham.
8. Eliza Oldham.
9. Lydia Oldham, 1679.

All born before 1679. (Windsor's History of Duxbury.)

Robert Oldham, of Nottingham Township, Chester County, Pa., will bears date Aug. 3, 1742, probated April 17, 1749, son Robert, sole executor. Wife, Mary. Children:
1. Edward Oldham.
2. Mary Oldham, the wife of Mr. Good.
3. Eleanor Oldham, the wife of Mr. Walliston.
4. Robert Oldham, given plantation on which his father had so long lived, containing 150 acres in Nottingham Township, Chester County, Pa., he to maintain testator's wife during her life.

d Thomas Oldham, Jr., of Chester County, Pa. Letters of administration granted to his widow Mary Oldham April 20, 1750.

e Thomas Oldham, Sr., of East Nottingham, Pa., will dated Feb. 3, 1756, probated March 1756. Thomas Barrett and William Churchman, executors. Wife Rachael, given one third of real and personal estate, she was a daughter of Zachariah Butcher. Their cihldren:
1. Thomas Oldham, deceased, widow Mary (? White.) Son:
1. Thomas Oldham.
2. William Oldham, deceased, widow Sarah.
3. Mary Oldham, deceased, late wife of Lacy Rawles.
4. Martha Oldham, wife of Joshua Littler. Children:
1. John Littler, born in Wilmington, Del., 12-26-1739; married Sarah Staples, born 5-27-1746, her daughter;
1. Sarah Littler, born 4-20-1769; married James Gilpin.
5. Susannah Oldham, wife of Daniel Brown.
6. Hannah Oldham, wife of Thomas Barrett.

f Rachael Oldham, of East Nottingham, widow of Thomas Oldham, will bears date May 23, 1761, probted Dec. 13, 1762. Children:

1. Simon Taylor.
2. Joshua Littler; (son-in-law) married her daughter Martha.
3. Thomas Barrett; (son-in-law) married her daughter Hannah.

Grand-daughter of Rachael:

1. Rachael, wife of Elisha Brown.

g Zachariah Butcher, of East Nottingham. Will bears bears date Aug. 18, 1754, probated Dec. 4, 1755. Robert Oldham and daughter Mary, executors. Children:

1. Mary Butcher, who subseqquently died leaving a will (of East Nottingham) bearing date Nov. 3, 1766, probated Jan. 29, 1767, executrix, sister Hannah Butcher. Her sisters devisees, towit: Margaret Collett, Susanna Passmore, Rachael Oldham, Hannah Butcher and Sarah Day.
2. Elizabeth Butcher.
3. Margaret Butcher; married Mr. Collett. (After 1754.)
4. Susanna Butcher; married Mr. Passmore. (After 1754.)
5. Rachael Butcher; married Thomas Oldham.
6. Hannah Butcher (subsequently executrix of her sister Mary's will.)
7. Sarah Butcher; married Mr. Day. (After 1754.)

h Joseph White, of Nottingham. Will dated Oct. 13, 1731, probated May 18, 1732. Wife, Elizabeth, given plantation during widowhood. She and John Ruddell, executors. Children:

1. Joseph White, plantation of testator, after cessation of widowhood of testator, he to maintain his sister Sarah White, during her life.
2. Sarah White.
3. Mary Oldham (probably the wife of Robert Oldham, above whose will bears date 1742.

i Neal Cook of Nottingham. Will dated Feb. 14, 1737-8, probated May 27, 1738. Wife Ann executrix, witnesses: Thomas Scott, William Oldham and John Ruddell. Children:

1. John Cook.
2. Daniel Cook.
3. Cornelius Cook, 136 acres on Buck Creek, Maryland, where testator formerly lived.
4. William Cook, 100 acres at lower end of said tract.
5. Katherine Wallistien.
6. Mary Ruddell, husband John Ruddell, issue:
   1. "Ann Ruddell." Grand-daughter of testator, other grand-daughters, viz:
      "Katherine Cook."
      "Elizabeth Cook."
      "John Ruddell."
      "Katherine McKeek."
   er's sons-in-law:
      "John Ruddell."
      "William Rutledge."

j Edward Oldham had a warrant of survey for 150 acres of land in Lancaster County, Feb. 4, 1735-6, (Pa. Archives, Vol. XXIV, p 495) doubtless in the part of Lancaster County which then extended to the "Setting Sun," laid off in Cumberland in 1750. Bedford was cut out of Cumberland in 1771, and Westmoreland out of Bedford in 1773. There is no will of Edward Oldham in Lancaster

County. He may have died in Cumberland, before the organization of Bedford in 1771.

The Oldhams all left Chester County, Pa., prior to 1800.

Edward Oldham's grant of 150 acres was in the Forks of Octaron Creek.

k Isaac Oldham, born in 1726, died on his plantation in Ohio County, Va., in 1821. His will was probated at the Sept. term 1821. He was in the Revolutionary war, in Captain John Van Meter's Company of Pennsylvania Rangers from 1778-1783. He was twice married first to —— —— and second to Sarah Anderson, sister to Colonel William Anderson. Children of his first marriage:

1. William Oldham (who Mr. Sam Oldham, of Zanesville, O., states was the Lieutenant Colonel who fell in Governor St. Clair's defeat in 1791, and who married Penelope Pope, and settled in Louisville, Ky., but it is differently stated in the Oldham Tree, by R. C. B. Thurston of Louisville, Ky.) Note: Lieutenant Colonel William Oldham was killed in 1791, 30 years before Isaac Oldham's will was probated.
2. John Oldham, settled in Kentucky.
3. Sarah Oldham; married William Merriwether (according to Mr. San Oldhams) and settled in Kentucky.

Children of the second marriage to Sarah Anderson:

4. James Oldham, settled in Ohio.
5. Thomas Oldham, settled in Ohio.
6. Isaac Oldham; married Sarah Marling, settled in Ohio.
7. Alline Oldham, settled in Ohio.
8. Mary Oldham, settled in Ohio.
9. Elizabeth Oldham, settled in Ohio.
10. Catherine Oldham, settled in Ohio.
11. Esther Oldham, settled in Ohio.
12. Robert Oldham, settled in Ohio; married —— —— Had:
    1. Sarah Oldham; dead.
    2. Isaac Oldham; dead.
    3. Eliza Oldham; dead.
    4. John Oldham; dead.
    5. Robert Oldham; died in infancy.
    6. Ann Oldham; dead.
    7. William Oldham; dead.
    8. Robert Oldham (again); dead.
    9. Martha Ann Oldham; dead.
    10. Samuel Oldham, now living in Zanesville, Ohio.
    11. Thomas Oldham, yet alive.
    12. Phoebe Oldham, yet alive.
13. Hannah Oldham, settled in Missouri.
14. Samuel Oldham, born in 1792, remained on the old homestead of Isaac Oldham in Ohio County, Va., till his death in March 1876.

l Richard Oldham, of Cambridge, (perhaps son of John of Plymouth,) (See Chap. 1, Sec. 2 and 17, and Chap. 2.) born in England. Freeman in 1651, was here as early as 1650, and was first resident on the south side of the river, and died Dec. 9, 1655. He married Martha Eaton, daughter of William Eaton of Watertown. His widow married Thomas Brown Oct. 7, 1656. His children:

1. Samuel Oldham; died between July 13, 1727, and June 10, 1728. He was a Freeman in 1690. He married Hannah Dana, daughter of Richard Dana Jan. 5, 1671, and had:
    1. Samuel Oldham, born 1672, died Jan. 14, 1673.
    2. Samuel Oldham (again), born Jan. 15, 1673, died Aug. 24, 1675.

3. Hannah Oldham, born March 25, 1676; died July 9, 1676.
4. Andrew Oldham, born April 22, 1677; died July 12, 1677.
1. Nathaniel Oldham, born —— died May 3, 1678.
6. Mary Oldham, born June 1, 1679; married James Reid, mentioned in will of July 13, 1727.
7. Hannah Oldham, born Oct. 10, 1681; married Amos Gates May 19, 1703, mentioned in said will.
8. Ann Oldham, born —— living in 1727, unmarried, mentioned in said will.

2. John Oldham, of Cambridge, (son of Richard first) born about 1652. He was a Freeman in 1690, and was selectman from 1694-1714; died Oct. 14, 1719, aged 67 years. He married Abigail Wood July 22, 1675, and had a second wife Elizabeth, who survived him. His children of the first marriage:

1. John Oldham, born July 20, 1676; married Mendenhall Parkes Nov. 1, 1720. He died between March 7, and July 9, 1733. His wife Mendenhall married Joseph Fessenden Dec. 6, 1733. His children:
   1. John Oldham, born Dec. 17, 1720; married Miss Chadwick June 2, 1743. He died, and his wife administered on his estate Feb. 21, 1757. His children:
      1. Abigail Oldham, born March 18, 1743, died May 26, 1744.
      2. Sarah Oldham, born July 30, 1746.
      3. Susanna Oldham, born March 11, 1748-9.
      4. Abigail Oldham, (again) born 1752.
      5. John Oldham, born Nov. 1, 1754.
   2. Samuel Oldham, born Aug. 26, 1722.
   3. Mary Oldham, born March 20, 1727.
   4. Abigail Oldham; died unmarried Oct. 20, 1743. (named in will.)
   5. Jonathan Oldham, named in will.
   6. Elizabeth Oldham, named in will.
2. Abigail Oldham, born Nov. 28, 1679; married Captain Samuel Frothingham, of Charleston, Mass., Nov. 3, 1708. (Poage's History of Cambridge, etc.)

John Oldham of Duxbury, married Eliabeth Chandler in 1779, died June 19, 1832, at 78 years of age. Children:

1. Elizabeth Oldham, born Jan. 6, 1780.
2. John Oldham, born March 1, 1782, removed to Pembroke.
3. Chandler Oldham, born Jan. 25, 1784.
4. Thomas Oldham, born April 25, 1786.
5. Anna Oldham, born March 15, 1789.
6. Hannah Oldham, born Feb. 14, 1792.
7. Sally Oldham, born June 17, 1794.

Peleg Oldham, borther to John Oldham of Duxbury, married Ann Simmons. (Windsor's History of Duxbury.)

In 1802 Squire Boone and wife Jane, conveyed land on Silver Creek in Madison County, Ky., to Basset Prather, Obediah Newman and Polly Meriwether, heirs of George Meriwether, deceased, of Jefferson County, Ky. In 1815, George Wolfscale, of Wayne County, Ky., conveyed land on the same creek to James R. Williams and wife Fannie, Obediah Newman and wife Martha Woods Newman, John H. Cox and wife, Polly, heirs of George Meriwether, deceased, of the County of Jefferson. In 1813 Obediah Newman, and wife Martha K., James R. Williams and wife Fannie, John H. Cox and wife Polly, heirs of George Meriwether of Jefferson County, Ky., conveyed Silver Creek lands to James Reid of Madison County, Ky., James Bigham, Jesse Clarke's heirs John Reid and Joseph Hiett by separate deeds.

In 1809 an agreement was executed between John Newman and wife Nancy, late Nancy Reid, and Alexander Reid's heirs, whereby one third of all the lands of said heirs except 300 acre tract on Cumberland River, in Knox County, called the Flat Lick tract, Newman and wife take for their third. (Signed) John P. Newman, Nancy Newman. Richard Oldham, for himself and John Reid one of the heirs. Goodman Oldham, John P. Newman, guardian for Polly and Hannah Reid. Witnesses: Overton Harris, John Oldham, James Smith.

Since going into the hands of the printers, the following notes have been received from Samuel Oldham Esquire of Zanesville, Ohio, which are presented as written by him:

"Thomas Oldham and Susannah Few, declared their intentions of marriage at Chester monthly meeting 12' 28' 170¾. Robert Barber and Joseph Coburn, Elizabeth Job, and Hannah Barber to enquire.

1-27-1704. They appear the second time and receive permission.

4-27-1709. A certificate reequested for Thomas Oldham to Concord. Thomas Vernon and Nicholas Fairlamb to enquire.

This meeting orders Elizabeth Fishborn and Hannah Barber to make enquiry concerning Susannah Oldham's life and conversation, in order for a certificate.

5-25-1709. A certificate signed for Thomas Oldham.

At Concord monthly meeting 9-14-1709, Thomas Oldham of Nottingham produced a certificate from Chester.

Mary Oldham, daughter of Thomas of Nottingham, and Lacy Rawles, of Nottingham, were married 3-21-1724, at Nottingham meeting.

At New Garden monthly meeting 9-25-1727, Nottingham complains of Thomas Oldham, son of Thomas for marriage out of meeting.

10-30-1727. Thomas Oldham Jr., hath given a paper condemning his marrying a wife by license before a Justice.

Thomas Oldham, of Nottingham, and Rachael Littler, widow of same place were married 5-3-1728, at Nottingham meeting.

Deborah Oldham, daughter of Thomas of East Nottingham, and Joshua Littler son of Samued, deceased, of same place, married 9-9-1733, at East Nottingham meeting.

Susannah Oldham, daughter of Thomas of East Nottingham, and Daniel Brown, son of William deceased, of Cecil County, married 9-11-17?, at East Nottingham meeting.

Martha Oldham, daughter of Thomas, of East Nottingham, and Joseph Underhill, son of John, of Cecil County, married 9-11-1736, at East Nottingham meeting.

Hannah Oldham, daughter of Thomas of East Nottingham, married 9-29-1739, at East Nottingham meeting. (Name of gentleman omitted.)

Thomas Oldham; died 2-16-1756. Rachael Oldham died 7-22-1762, formerly wife of Samuel Litter.

At New Garden monthy meeting 11-7-1767, Thomas Oldham a young lad placed apprentice, produced a certificate from Warrington dated 6-14-1766.

He received a certificate back to Warrington 7-4 1778.

Robert Oldham was a witness to will of Hugh Morgan of Nottingham 7-28-1727.

Joseph White of Nottingham, in will March 13, 173½, mentions his daughter, Mary Oldham, and gives her 5 shillings.

William Oldham, a witness to will of Neal Cook, of Nottingham, Feb. 24, 173⅞.

Will of Robert Oldham of Nottingham, joyener, dated Aug. 3, 1742, proved April 17, 1749. To son Edward and daughter Mary Good 5 shillings each. To daughter Eleanor Walliston one cow, to son Robert my plantation I have long lived on, containing 150 acres, he to maintain wife, Mary, during life. Executor. Signed, R. - -. Witnesses: John Boggs, Robert Whitker, Samuel Thomas.

Thomas Oldham Jr., intestate. Letters to Mary Oldham April 29, 1750.

Zachariah Butcher, of East Nottingham, yeoman, in will Aug. 18, 1754, gives his daughter Rachael Oldham 40 shillings and a share of the reversions, and appoints his son-in-law Robert Oldham one of his executors.

Will of Thomas Oldham of East Nottingham, dated 2-3-1750, proved March 2, 1756, to wife Rachael, one third of the estate real and personal. To Mary widow of son Thomas, and to their son, Thomas, 5 shillings each. To Sarah, widow of son William, and to Lacy Rawles, husband of daughter Mary, deceased, 5 shillings each. To daughter Martha, wife of James Scivinton, 5 shillings each. To daughter Susannah, wife of Daniel Brown, and daughter Hannah, wife of Thomas Barrett, all remainder of estate, real and personal. Executors: son-in-law, Thomas Barrett, and friend, William Churchman. Witnesses: William Churchman, James Hamil, George Churchman. Letters to Thomas Barrett—the others renouncing.

Will of Rachael Oldham, of East Nottingham, dated 5-23-1761, proved Dec. 13, 1762. To son Simon Taylor 5 shillings, to son Joshua Littler 5 shillings. All remainder of estate to granddaughter Rachael, wife of Elisha Brown, and Thomas Barrett. Executors Thomas Barrett and Elisha Brown.

Mary Butcher of East Nottingham in will 10-3-1766, mentions her sister Rachael Oldham, also her father Zachariah Butcher, deceased.

John Oldham, late of Cheshire, England, died intestate. Letters granted Aug. 22, 1798, to Jonathan Oldham. (Phila. Registry.)

Deed 18-3mo. May 1750. Thomas Oldham, blacksmith, of East Nottingham, to Thomas Oldham his grand-son, of the same place farmer, recites that John Churchman Jan. 1, 1730, conveyed to Thomas Oldham, blacksmith 250 acres in Nottingham.

Thomas Oldham, blacksmith, now, for 10 shillings conveys to his grandson 150 acres of this including the great meadow adjoining land of his son, Thomas, deceased, the house wherein the grantor resides and all buildings, but reserving use thereof during life. No survey is given. (Deed Book H, page 2.)

Mortgage 13-7th mo. 1750, Thomas Oldham, farmer to Edward Oldham, of Chester County, the above land for £10. (Deed Book J, 70.) Satisfied Aug. 24, 1754.

Mortgage, 19-4mo., 1754. Thomas Oldham, Jr., and Mary his wife of East Nottingham, to Jeremiah Brown, Jr., of West Nottingham, for £100 messuage and 250 acres conveyed to him by his grandfather, Thomas Oldham May 10, 1750. No survey, except bounded on south by the street and land of Rowland Rogers, and on the East by John Hill, on North and West by James Brown, John Churchman and John Oldham. (Deed Book T-166.)

A warrant was granted April 10, 1707, to Robert Oldham for 100 acres near Brandywine, next adjoining to land laid out to William Huntly, and upon the same terms. This was surveyed in Kennett on the 8th day of March 1707.

A survey of 150 acres at Nottingham was made for Thomas Oldham April 17, 1716.

A survey of 307 acres in Nottingham was made for Robert Oldham Dec. 8, 1720.

A warrant was granted Feb. 4, 1735-6, to Edward Oldham for 150 acres of land in Lancaster County.

A warrant was granted June 6, 1747, to William Oldham for 40 acres in Lancaster County, perhaps on what became York County and later Adams County.

A warrant was granted Feb. 23, 1749, to Thomas Oldham of Chester County for 100 acres in West Nottingham, next to his other land, and George Pomroy. By virtue of this warrant there was surveyed May 31, 1750, 141 acres, 50 perches, and allowance, patented as 141 acres. This was adjoining and on the North side of the line of the first survey of Nottingham. The draft shows Thomas Oldham on the South.

A warrant was granted April 23, 1759, to Nathaniel Oldham for 50 acres more or less, in East Nottingham, next Robert Sheppard, and the widow Scott. In pursuance of this warrant a tract of about 110 acres, and allowance was surveyed by John Churchman May 15, 1759, in the White Barrens.

Nathaniel Oldham was probably the oldest son of William and Sarah (Dix) Oldham, maternal grand-father Nathan Dix.

At Orphan's Court Oct. 8, 1751, William Owen and Mary his wife, the administratrix of Thomas Oldham, the younger, deceased, appeared pursuant to a citation granted out of Register's Office for the making the accounts of their administration on said estate, but they not being in readiness, therefore ordered that they appear at next Orphan's Court and make up their accounts, etc.

Dec. 17, 1751. On petition of Thomas Oldham, Elisha Gatchell, the younger, Thomas Oldham and John Oldham, are appointed guardians of Deborah, Hannah, Ann and Rachael Oldham, children of Thomas, under 14 years of age.

Dec. 15, 1752. On petition of Joseph Oldham, son of Thomas, deceased, George Churchman is appointed guardian.

June 16, 1772. On petition of John Oldham, one of the sons of Thomas Oldham, late of East Nottingham, who died intestate a writ of partition is granted the children being, Thomas, John, Susannah, Martha, Deborah, Joseph, Anne, Hannah and Rachael, of whom Thomas is entitled to two tenths.

Sept. 15, 1772. The sheriff makes a return of a division on Aug. 18, 1772, by a jury composed of Mordecia, James, Timothy Kirk, Elisha Gatchell, Archibald Job, John White, David Brown, John Pugh, Samuel England, Johsn Churchman, Benjamin Willson, and Benjamin Chandler. It appeared that John Oldham had bought the two shares of his sisters Susannah, Martha and Deborah, also, half of his brother Joseph's share, and there was laid out to him 8 acres, 60 perches, including a dwelling house, and some improvements. Hezekiah Rowles had purchased the rights of Hannah and Rachael, and received 34 acres, 89 perches. Anne Oldham's share, was 16 acres, 67 perches. John Oldham's part was on a road leading toward Chester, and next West of land of David Poe, late of Thomas Oldham, senior.

"The 23rd of ye 12 mo. 1749, Feb. 1750, an inventory of ye estate of Thomas Oldham, Jr., deceased, ye 13 inst. The appraisers were Elisha Gutchell, Jr., and Rowland Rogers. The items indicate a blacksmith, amt. $223, 14 s, 4½ p. Bond of Mary Oldham, widow, $500; sureties, Edward Oldham and Messrs. Brown. No account filed.

Inventory of Thomas Oldham taken 2-24-1756, by John Chuchman and Mordicai James, L 104-18-8. No account filed. (Dates prior to 1752 are old style.

Oldham.

Warrington Monthly Meeting.

Nathan Oldham produced a certificate 11 16-1747-8, for self, wife and children, from East Nottingham, dated 10-20-1746, and addressed to Sausbury Monthly meeting, from which Warrington was recently separated.

Sarah Oldham complained of 4-15-1751, for marriage out of meeting. Perhaps widow of William. Sarah Mains appeared 5-20-1751, and made satisfaction for her misconduct.

Rachael Oldham received a certificate to New Garden, North Carolina, 10-21-1758.

Isaac Oldham and Mary Younger, both of Manallin Meeting, declare intention of marriage 9-11th and 10-9th-1762.

Isaac Oldham of Menalen Township, County of York, Province of Pennsylvania, and Mary Younger of the Township, County and Province aforesaid, were married 10-20-1762, at Menalen Meeting. James and Mary Magrew or McGrew, signed as the nearest relative.

Thomas Oldham received a certificate to Kennet, 2 mo-8-1766. (This appears to have been taken to New Garden.)

Isaac Oldham, of Menallin Meeting 1-10-1767, hath been so unstable as to be baptized or sprinkled with water, 12-12-1767. He offers something which is not satisfactory, 5-7-1768. He is disowned.

Mary Oldham, wife of Isaac, hath complied with the form of water baptism, and justifies her conduct therein—disowned, 10-8-1768.

Thomas Oldham produced a certificate from New Garden 11-7-1778, dated 7-4-1778.

Thomas Oldham and Rebekah Blackburn declare intentions of marriage 9-11and 10-9-1779. Thomas Oldham of Manallen Township in the County of York, son of William Oldham, deceased, of Tyrone Township in the said County, and Rebekah Blackburn, daughter of Thomas Blackburn of Manallin Township, married 10-13-1779, at Manallin Meeting. Manallin Meeting was established in 1782 by division of Warrington.

Thomas Oldham produced from Menallin 11-9, dated 10-14-1782, with wife, Rebekah and children William and Alice.

Thomas Oldham of Newberry Meeting 7-9-1785, requests certificate to Menallin for self and children William, Alice and Thomas, which is granted 8-13-1785.

James Garretson of Newberry Meeting received a certificate to Dunnings Creek [illegible]-8-1806, to Mary Alice Oldham.

Oldham—Taxables in Chester County, Pa. The year in which taxes were paid in East Nottingham, Chester County, Pa.:

Thomas Oldham, 1718,'19,'20,'21,'22,'23,'24,'25,'26,'30,'32,'34, '35,'37,'39.

Thomas Oldham Jr., 1729,'32,'34,'35,'37,'39,'40,'47,'49,'53.

1. Robert Oldham, 1720,'21,'22,'24,'25,'26,'30,'34,'40,'47,'49,'50, '53,'54,'56,'58,'60,'62,'63.

2. Edward Oldham, 1724,'25,'26,'29,'30,'32,'34,'35,'37,'39,'40, '47,'49,'50,'53,'54,'56,'57,'58,'59.

William Oldham, 1730,'40.

Mary Oldham, wiodw 1750.

John Oldham, 1750,'53,'54,'56,'57,'58,'60,'62,'1763.

Zebulan Oldham, 1753.

Nathan Oldham, 1758,'1760,'1762,'1763.

1. This includes both Robert Oldham, Sr., and Robert Oldham Jr.

2. This was eldest son of Robert Oldham senior.

I have not given the amount of tax paid, only the year in which it was paid.

3. Son of Thomas, senior, went to Tyrone 1746, there was no assessment for Nottingham before 1719.

Robert Oldham, senior, and his family were not friends. Thomas senior, and his descendants all were Quarkers.

Mr. Ely says: "Hardly think Robert Oldham, was a brother to Thomas, as he does not seem to be a Quaker, though he may have married out and lost membership prior to settlement in Nottingham. Do not think they descended from John Oldham, of Virginia 1635, but from John Oldham, late of Cheshire, England, on whose estate letters of administration were granted to Jonathan Oldham, at Philadelphia Aug. 22, 1698." This John Oldham ought to be investigated thoroughly. He was old enough to have been the John Oldham, who is said to have come to Virginia from England in 1635."

CHAPTER 39.

MOSES OLDHAM.

(Named in Chapter 2, Section 3.)

Article 1.—Moses Oldham, a son of William Oldham of Prince William County, Va., and Miss —— Basey his wife, was born in Virginia, probably in Fauquier County, which was carved out of Prince William embracing the old home of William Oldham in the new County.

He served as a soldier in the Revolutionary army, and made claim to the United States Congress for said service. He and several of his brothers emigrated from Fauquier County, Va., prior to the Revolutionary war, to Caswell County, North Carolina, where he was married to Mary Rice, a sister to John Rice who died in Caswell County about the year 1804 and devised property to the children of his sister Mary, and her husband, Moses Oldham, his said sister then being dead. Moses Oldham was then living in Montgomery County, Tenn, and was living there as late as 1810, in which year, he as the husband of Mary Rice, deceased, sister of John Rice, deceased, and their children, executed a power of attorney to Solomon Debow, of record in the clerk's office of the Supreme Court of Caswell County, in which the names of the children are set forth towit:

Section 1. George Oldham.

Section 2. Jesse Oldham.

Section 3. Moses Oldham. His grand son, Joseph Alexander McMurry, of Valley Mills, Texas, writes that "he thinks he came to Texas from Rutherford County, Tenn., in 1839. He once lived in Davidson County, Tenn., also at one time in Missouri. He married first —— —— To whom two sons were born. He married for his second wife Christiana Tarpley. She died about 1853, and was buired on the old home place, where Moses Oldham settled in 1839, three miles east of Caldwell, Burleson County, Texas. Moses Oldham remained on this place with his negroes until 1860, his health gave way, and his son-in-law Joseph -- McMurry, brought him home with him where he died in 1861, (Miss Lillye Oldham of Brymer, Texas, writes that "Moses Oldham died at Robinson, McLennon County, Texas,") (His son Moses was buried in Robinson Cemetery, six miles south of Waco,) and was buried on the old home place, of Joseph McMurry, now owned by Joseph Alexander McMurry, where his father settled in 1855, who says he often heard his mother speak of Moses Oldham's brothers and especially of Con, her uncle, a very wealthy bachelor, who sometimes would partake too freely of mountain dew, which would make him feel very rich, when he would scatter handfuls of money all around the streets to everyone, which his friends would gather up and return to him when he sobered. His grand son Edward M. Oldham, of Brymer, Texas, remembered hearing his parents speak of their uncle Abraham Branthy.

The father of the subject, Moses Oldham, whose name was also Moses, came to the new country of Tennessee from North Carolina. He and his sons and negroes went out a long way from the settlements into the cane brakes and located, and begun clearing up a farm—sowed a large patch in turnips—winter came on—provisions gave out—excepting the turnips, and they were too far out to take oxen and carts back to the settlement for the necessary provisions—wild meat and turnips was their dependence until crops were made, or until winter broke, and one was appointed each day to hunt game until a goodly supply was laid in. Moses seemed to be the most expert hunter, and when meat was scarce, he at one time went hunting for many successive days, when the snows were deep—several days went by without any success—coming in at night with feet frozen in his moccasins, he would roast turnips and poltice his feet with them to draw out the frost, and make ready for the next days hunt—the meat being entirely out—nothing but turnips to eat; so he and his dog, a small fice, started out in the morning plodding through the snow, not knowing whether he would find any meat that day or not, but he had not gone more than a mile before his little dog ran to a large fallen tree and began to bark,—a very large fat bear who had made his bed on the opposite side of the log reached his head over to see what the trouble was—the little dog caught him by the nose and held his hold till Mr. Oldham put a rifle ball in his head, then returned home, got the oxen and cart and hands, and went and brought in his meat.

Moses Oldham the subject of this sketch, was with Jackson at New Orleans in the battle with the British, and when his army horse died, he had him buried, saying the buzzards should not pick that horse's bones. He enlisted as a private in Captain Archibald McKinney's company of Colonel Robert H. Dyke's regiment of Tennessee volunteer cavalry, war of 1812. The muster roll of that organization on which his name appears, has remarks showing that he enlisted Sept. 24, 1813, honorably discharged Dec. 10, 1813, served two months and twenty five days, was allowed eight days for travelling 120 miles from Fayetteville to Franklin Court House, Williamson County after his discharge.

He re-enlisted Sept. 28, 1814, as a private in Captain Richard Tate's company second (Williamsons) regiment, Tennessee mounted volunteer gun men, in the same war, to serve to April 27, 1815, and the roll on which his name appears shows that his service expired May 2, 1815, (serving seven months and five days) and that he was allowed pay for traveling eighty miles from Nashville in Davidson County place of residence to Fayetteville, Lincoln County, where he was mustered into service.

The following is a copy of a receipt now held by Edward McKinney Oldham, of Brymer, Texas:

"Received this eighth day of Feb. 1817, from Moses Oldham the sum of four dollars, twenty cents, for the direct tax of 1816, upon the property of Moses Oldham in the County of Williamson in the fifth collection district in the state of Tennessee. Nich P. Perkins.

Dollars, 4.20 Collector of the Revenue for the fifth collection district of the state of Tennessee."

The children of Moses Oldham, and —— —— his first wife were, viz:

1. Ebenezer Oldham, who lived and died in the state of Missouri.
2. John Oldham; married first Polly Tarpley (or Gant). He emigrated to Kentucky, went from Kentucky to Missouri, and in Dec. 1840, in company with his brother-in-law, Mr. —— McMurry, removed to Texas. He had a number of children by his first wife, but all are dead. His second wife was Miss Jane Reid, daughter of Jacob and Matilda Reid. When he moved to Texas, he took the remainder of his father's negroes with him. The children of his second marriage to Jane Reid,—all dead save one—were, viz:

   1. Edward McKinney Oldham, the only child now living was born in Texas, —— —— He married Nov. 28, 1878, Hepcy Katherine Clark. Their home is in Brymer, Burleson County, Texas, and Mr. Oldham is now the Post Master of Brymer. He has heard his father speak of his (father's) uncle, Abraham Branthy, (the husband of his Aunt Lydda Oldham) and that his grand-mother Oldham's maiden name was Mary Rice. The children born to Edmund McKinney Oldham and Hepcy Katherine Clark his wife, were as follows, viz:

      1. Lanna Oldham; married George Bell Ransom Feb. 10, 1905.
      2. Leona Roberta Oldham; married J—— C—— Garrison August 17, 1905.
      3. Leona McMaudia Oldham.
      4. Thomas Nugent Oldham.
      5. Lillye Oldham, now living with her father in Brymer, Texas.

   2. Moses Oldham; died single.
   3. Thomas Oldham; died single.
   4. Milton Oldham; married Bettie White.
   5. Lucy Oldham; died single.
   6. Samantha Oldham; married Samuel Harvey.
   7. Emily Rice Oldham; died when quite small.

The children of Moses Oldham, and his second wife Christiana Tarpley, were, viz:

8. Thomas Oldham, lived in Texas. He was a comrade of his relative Major William Oldham, of Burleson County, Texas, in the Mier expedition described in Chapter 1, Section 14, and in Chapter 13a Section 1. He was fitted out with horse and arms for the expedition by his brother-in-law —— McMurry; his brace of pistols were single barrels, about ten inches long, carrying an ounce ball. When his company of Texans reached the river near the town of Mier, Thomas Oldham, G. B. Eurath, and ten others were detailed and left in camp to care for the horses, the rest of the Texans crossed the river to see about provisions, when the fight ensued in which the Mexicans were repulsed, and the Texans took possession of the large building as told in Chapter 13a section 1. Thomas Oldham married Miss Nancy Leeper. In 1861, he enlisted in the Confederate Army, Colonel Allen's

regiment, and died in the service at Pine Bluff, Arkansas, in Dec. 1862, or January 1863, leaving two sons, and two daughters, viz:

1. William Oldham. He is a typical Oldham, and lived an old bachelor's life, until recently he married a young girl — ——. His home is in Hamilton County, Texas, and his wealth is estimated at two hundred and fifty thousand dollars.

2. James F. Oldham. He is an engineer on the railroad, and lives in Enis, Ellis County, Texas.

3. Catherine Oldham; married Mr. —— Bodenheimer. They live in Lampassas, Lampassas County, Texas.

4. Miss —— Oldham; married Mr. —— Austin, who is the partner of her brother William Oldham. They live in Evant, Coryell County, Texas.

4. Moses Oldham, the youngest boy, another pure blood Oldham, married —— —— and raised three sons, and two daughters. He enlisted in the Confederate army in 1861, company K, 15th Texas Infantry. He was with his regiment in all its hard fought battles, sometimes bare-footed, and half naked. Once he had to charge through a Cherokee Rose Hedge bare footed, in pursuit of the enemy, and soon found one who had no use for his boots, and he shod himself. He was killed by a stroke of lightning in 1882, and his remains were buried in Robinson Cemetery, six miles south of Waco, Texas. His children, viz:

1. John Oldham; married —— —— and lives at Albany, Shackelford County, Texas. He had a daughter:

1. Miss —— Oldham; married —— —— and they were living between Waco and Cameron, when last heard from.

2. William Oldham, lives at Albany, Shackelford County, Texas.

3. Lee Oldham, lives, also, at Albany.

4. Miss —— Oldham; married —— —— and they live in McClennon County, Texas.

5. Miss —— Oldham; married —— —— They also live in McClennon County, Texas.

5. Elizabeth Oldham; married Joseph —— McMurry. Mr. McMurry and little family, with his brother-in-law John Oldham and his family in December 1840, emigrated from Missouri to Texas, bringing with them the remainder of the negroes of their father Moses Oldham, and they settled in Burleson County, and were pioneers of that section of the new country of Texas. They both died in Texas, and were buried in Robinson Cemetery, six miles south of Waco, where also two sons and two daughters are buried. The children born to them were, viz:

1. Joseph Alexander McMurry, born in Burleson County, Texas, four miles east of Caldwell Nov. 20, 1843, married May 29, 1867, (first) Mary Ellen Cutbirth, who was born Aug. 27, 1842, her mother, Anna Cutbirth was a descendant of Colonel Daniel Boone, the world renowed Kentucky pioneer, she died within the month of November 1906, in Texas, in the ninety first year of her age. Mrs. Mary Ellen McMurry died Oct. 29, 1884, and on the 8th day of Dec. 1889, Joseph Alexander McMurry married again Mary Elizabeth Preston, who was born in Ohio County, Ky., her mother was a Condit. (or Conduit) descended from the Conduits who came over in the Mayflower, and she has recently received a book of the genealogy all the way down to herself. No children have been born of the second marriage. Mr. McMurry's youngest living daughter remains with him and is an accomplished young lady, and a sweet music-

ian. He raised an orphan girl named Lillye, who is now clerking in the largest dry goods establishment in Valley Mills. Mr. McMurry was born and raised at a time when kin and good friends were appreciated. His parents reached Texas, when every man and woman had to help the other, all had to stand hand in hand for each others protection. He was born and largely raised on the frontier—schools were scarce, and he received only a limited education, he learned something of reading, writing, arithmetic and spelling. He moved to Valley Mills, Bosque County, Texas, several years ago, for two reasons, one was, he was unable to do much work on the farm, the other was, to educate his children. With a partner he engaged in merchandizing—they were driven to the wall by hard times and big credit, and he thinks unless the wheel of fortune makes a phenominal turn in his favor, he will be a hopeless bankrupt the balance of his days. We pray for the wheel to make the turn. Of the first marriage the following children were born, viz:

1. Roxie Alice McMurry, born Jan. 12, 1869, died March 7, 1872.

2. Samuel Lee McMurry, born April 6, 1871, he lives with his father.

3. Anna Elizabeth McMurry, born Oct. 30, 1873; married Mr. —— Blankenbeckler, they live in Stamford, Texas.

4. Mary Emily McMurry, born March 22, 1876, she married Mr. —— McElhannon. They live ten miles from Valley Mills and her husband is selling goods for McNeil Brothers.

5. Eva Matilda McMurry, born Nov. 30, 1878, she is an accomplished young lady, living with her father.

6. Martha Barnett McMurry, born Aug. 5, 1881, died June 22, 1884.

7. Joseph William McMurry, born Oct. 21, 1884, lives with his father.

2. Samuel McMurry; married Fannie Posey, she died in 1861. Mr. McMurry enlisted in the confederate army, and died in the service leaving one son, viz:

1. Joe McMurry, living now in Melano, Texas.

3. Moses William McMurry; married —— —— and they live at Roscoe, Nolan County, Texas. They had four children:

1. Mr. ——— McMurry, his oldest son, died recently. A fine young man, just passed his twenty first birthday, liked by all who knew him and was superintendent of his Sunday School.

4. George W. McMurry; married —— —— They live at Mulock, Hansford County, Texas. They have four sons about grown and a baby boy.

5. John McMurry; married —— —— and died leaving five children.

6. Stonewall Jackson McMurry, is a Presbyterian minister. He married —— —— They live in Ft. Worth, Tarrant County, Texas. He is Pastor of the Presbyterian Church in North Ft. Worth. They have four children:

7. Ann Eliza McMurry; married first —— —— and second Mr. —— Wilkinson, she lives at Lawn, Taylor County, Texas, twenty miles south of Abiline, and has three children.

8. Emily McMurry; married Mr. —— Mullins, she died leaving five children, all married, except the youngest, a boy.

9. Nannie McMurry; married Mr. —— Tate, she died leaving a daughter and a son:

1. Nannie Tate, now grown, living in Seattle, Washington.

2. Nolly Tate.

6. Nancy Oldham; married twice, first Mr. —— McEwing, who died in Tennessee leaving her with one child, and second Pleasant Thop, and raised a large family, and died at Thop's Spring's in Hood County, Texas, three years ago. The issue of her first marriage was:

1. William J. McEwing, living in Aspermont, Stonewall County, Texas.

The issue of the second marriage, in part:

2. James Thop; married —— —— and lived in Hood County, Texas, has been bed ridden for ten years with rheumatism. His young son:

1. Henry Thop, took an overdose of morphine and died. James Thop's daughters are all married and scattered.

7. Emily Oldham; married William Holmes (or Haines) in Tennessee, and they emigrated to Texas in 1839, and she died at the home of her brother-in-law, Mr. McMurry in Burleson County, Texas, about 1847-8. One daughter:

1. Emily Holmes (or Haines) married Mr. —— Conner. They live at Eagle Lake, besides other children, they have:

1. Mollie Conner, an accomplished well educated young lady.

8. Samantha Oldham; married Nathaniel Shields. They lived in Bell County, Texas. Mr. Shields died leaving her with four children, and she subsequently married John Nesbitt, she died near Devilla, Texas, about 1868. Issue of her first marriage:

1. Bettie Shields, lives between Cameron and Rockdale.
2. Richard Shields, lives between Cameron and Rockdale.
3. Mary Shields; married Mr. —— Bryant. They live in Coryell County, Texas.

9. Catherine Oldham; married Neville Gee, she died in Burleson County, Texas, in 1857, leaving one child:

1. Jane Gee, now the wife of Beverley Porter.

10. Eliza Oldham; married Parham Posey, she died about 1858, leaving a son, and a daughter:

1. James Posey.
2. Adaline Posey.

Section 4. Joel Oldham, mentioned in the power of attorney from Moses Oldham and his children by Mary Rice his wife, to Solomon Debow. (See Chap. 2, Section 9, Note.)

Section 5. Sallie Oldham; married Mason Bennett, mentioned in said power of attorney. (See Chapter 2, Section 9, note.)

Section 6. Liddy Oldham; married Abraham Branthy, mentioned in said power of attorney. (See Chap. 2, Sec. 9, Note.)

Section 7. Conway Oldham, mentioned in said power of attorney.

Section 8. Elisha Oldham, mentioned in said power of attorney.

Article 2—Note: Moses Oldham; we may say unquestionably a grand-son of Moses Oldham and Mary Rice his wife, set forth in the beginning of this Chapter 39, (and son of either George, Jesse, Joel, Conway or Elisha, who were sons of Moses Oldham and Mary Rice aforesaid) owned in his own name, and also in partnership with Thomas F. Pettus and P. C. Hambough, large bodies of land in the Counties of Montgomery and Williamson, Tennesssee, and in Arkansas and Mississippi, besides a handsome personal estate, which he disposed of by will bearing date May 5, 1867, and probated the same year, and of record in the clerk's office of the County Court of

Montgomery County, Tennessee, in which his children, legatees of the will are set forth as follows, viz:

1. James K. Oldham, deceased, heirs given one share.
2. Minerva Louisa Oldham, wife of Mr. —— Clardy, given one share.
3. John Rice Oldham's deceased, heirs given one share. Of whom, his son:
   1. Moses Oldham, given testators watch, by whom he is styled his grand-son, son of his son, John Rice Oldham.
4. Mary Jackson Oldham; married B. K. Gold, given one share besides $5,000 in money. The testator nominated his son-in-law B. K. Gold, executor, to act without security in carrying the will into effect, a manifestation by the testator of the utmost confidence in his son in-law.

CHAPTER 40.

ZERAH OLDHAM.

(Named in Chapter 6, Section 2.)

Article 1.—Zerah Oldham, a son of Richard Oldham of Estill County, Ky., and Ann Pepper his wife, was born Feb. 12, 1781, in Caswell County, North Carolina, and came with his parents to Kentucky about 1795, when the subject was about sixteen years of age.

He married Amelia F. Collins, about 1807, a daughter of Stephen Collins and Catherine McIntosh, his wife. Amelia was born Oct. 4, 1791. The 16th day of November 1815, Zerah Oldham qualified as constable of Estill County, Ky., with Absalom Oldham and Alexander Collins as sureties. August 11, 1834, he qualified as administrator of his father's estate. He owned lands in Clark County, Ky., as early as 1821, and as late as 1830. He was living in Montgomery County, as early as 1836, and as late as 1839.

On the 26th day of March 1836, in said County he, as administrator executed a deed to Jesse Cobb (his brother-in-law.) Zerah Oldham emigrated to Missouri, where he died about 1843-4, and his wife died in the same state about 1874-5. The children born to them were as named in the following sections, 1 to 10 inclusive:

Section 1. Eliza L. Oldham, born Oct. 8, 1808; married John Whitseil, of Lees Summit, Missouri.

Section 2. Evaline C. Oldham, born Feb. 24, 1811, she died in Kentucky, unmarried.

Section 3. Richard Oldham, born Sept. 4, 1813. He emigrated to Missouri, with his father, but returned to Kentucky, and married Sabra —— and died in Montgomery County in 1854, leaving a will, probated at the October Term of Court 1854. He may have had other children, but those appearing on the Court records were:

1. Benjamin F. Oldham.
2. Alexis M. Oldham.
3. Sarah Ann Oldham.

4. William Edward Oldham.

At the date the will was probated, the three last named children were minors, and Burrell S. Tipton was appointed by the Court, their guardian.

Section 4. Stephen Collins Oldham, was born Nov. 3, 1815, in Estill County, Ky., upon a farm near Red River, a tributary of the Kentucky, and not far from a village called from a newly started industry "Iron Works." On Christmas Eve, Dec. 24, 1839, about three miles east of Independence, Missouri, at the home of his bride's father, Samuel Shortridge, he was married to Susan Ann Shortridge, who was born Jan. 6, 1823, on a farm in Bourbon County, Ky., about eight miles from Mt. Sterling, and three from North Midddleton. Amelia F. Collins, the mother of Stephen Collins Oldham, was a daughter of Stephen Collins and his wife, Catherine McIntosh, as above stated and was born Oct. 4, 1791. Stephen Collins was from Virginia—one of the fire side traditions of the family was Catherine's story of how when a girl she helped to mould bullets for the men who were fighting in defense of Boonsborough, during its seige by the Indians. There was a large family of Amelia's brothers and sisters, among whom were Joel Collins, of Oxford, Ohio, Josiah Collins, a preacher, and Joseph Collins, both of Madison County, Ky., and James Collins of Sangamore County, Illinois.

Mr. Oldham lived on the farm, where he was born till about five years of age, when the family moved to Clark County, Ky. Of the Estill County home, few recollections are preserved, but among them is one of the home in which they lived being blown down by a hurricane, and of seeing the logs of the house, and the corn from the crib scattered over the field. The house stood, about a half mile from Red River. On the removal of the family to Clark County, they settled about twelve miles from the town of Winchester and eight or nine from Mt. Sterling, but after a few years and when the subject was about the age of ten, they moved across the line into Montgomery County, on a farm about seven miles from Mt. Sterling, which continued to be their home till they emigrated to Missouri in 1839. The Montgomery County farm, was a tract of fertile land on the North Fork of Lulbegrud Creek, but broken and in places rocky, some of it was finely timbered, including a maple forest from which as a part of the winter labors of the farm they made the sugar supply of the family. They raised chiefly corn, marketed by fattening hogs, which used to be driven south in the fall to market in South Carolina and Georgia. The house stood on a hill sloping toward the north east, to a spring and was about a mile and a half from the Creek. It was a comfortable two story building, with two rooms and a gallery below, and two above. Here Mr. Oldham grew to manhood, in the ordinary life of a country boy of the period. His first school teacher was in Clark County—one Joe Hornback, and he attended two winter schools in Montgomery County. A better opportunity was afterwards afforded him for a while when at fifteen years of age he spent over a year with his uncle Joel Collins, of Oxford, Ohio. Mr. Collins was secretary of Miami University at that place—the alma mater of so many distinguished western men, and though not prepared to enter the University, young Oldham had here for a short time the advantage of a good school. He joined the Christian Church at the age of twenty, being baptized by Elder John Smith, a pioneer preacher distinguished for his eloquence and ability, and whose memory has been lovingly preserved to our times, under the homely nick name of "Raccoon John Smith." With this church his wife afterwards in her twentieth year, united, and the family life has been throughout the whole course one of modest, but deep and trustful piety. To have led through every trial for seventy years the life of a consistent and devoted christian is the lot of few. In the fall of 1836, Mr. Oldham then just of age, went to Independence, Jackson County, Mo., where he remained and worked about a year, and where he cast his first vote, which was with the whig party. He then returned to his father's home in Kentucky, and there remained till the fall of 1839, when the entire family removed to Missouri. They travelled of coure in wagons, crossed into Ohio, and journeyed west across Indiana and Illinois. In the latter state they overtook and joined one evening a party of several families from an adjoining County of Kentucky, and bound for the same destination, who had camped for the night in a wood at the edge of a prairie. Among them were Samuel Shortridge and family of Bourbon County, Ky. They were not previously acquainted but being from adjoining Counties, knew each other by reputation, like most Kentucky pioneer families living in the same part of the state. In the family of Samuel Shortridge was a daughter, Susan Ann Shortridge, then in her seventeenth year, and the journey across the Western prairies together was only the beginning of a longer one in which as husband and wife, these two of the emigrgants have since gone on together for sixty seven years. (Xmas Eve 1906). The parties travelled in company across Illinois, separating in the western part of the state. The Bourbon County party went by way of St. Louis, while the Oldhams crossed the Mississippi at Alton.

West of the River they came together again, and finished the journey in company to their destination. Independence, Jackson County on the western border of Missouri. The trip they describe as a delightful one, the weather was pleasant, the roads good, both families were accompanied by their negro servants—for both were slave owners—who relieved them of the hardest of the labors of the camp, and march, and the free gypsy life of the road was little hardships to pioneers.

Susan Ann Shortridge Oldham, was born on a farm in Bourbon County, Ky., about eight miles from Mt. Sterling and three from North Middleton. Her mother died when Susan Ann was about four years old, and her father married a second wife, Mary Bryan, daughter of Jonathan Bryan, living near Winchester, Clark County, Kentucky.

Of her grand parents Susan Ann can give only the names of her father's mother, Nancy Shortridge, and her mother's father William Yates, of Montgomery County, Ky. Kindred are remembered of the names of Shortridge, Hedges and Owens, whose relationship cannot be definitely stated. Of the brothers of Samuel Shortridge—one John Shortridge, a widower lived with him, George William and Charles, lived at some distance. Of his sisters, Susan Harris, Nancy, wife of James Hedges, and Polly, wife of William Butler, all lived near; Mrs. Hopper lived in Henry County, Ky., and Betsy, wife of George Shortridge, a cousin, lived in Indiana. Jesse Yates, a brother of Sarah Yates, lived near Mt. Sterling, was a man in good circumstances, and had several sons.

Arriving at Independence, in November, Samuel Shortridge purchased and settled on a farm about three miles east of that place, and here on Christmas Eve, 1839, his daughter Susan or Ann, as she was usually called, was married to Stephen Collins Oldham, whose family had settled about a mile and a half west of the town. The young couple, remained at the Shortridge home that season, but the next fall set up house-keeping in a home of their own, about a mile and a half south east of Independence. Two years were spent in this first home, the following two upon a farm purchased from Mr. Shortridge, between Mill Creek and Blue, near the present Kansas City, which was then not even a village. The place proved malarious and unhealthful, and they bought and removed to another about five miles south of Independence, in a rich prairie country, but then called the "condemned land," because it was thought that it could not be settled for lack of timber. They resided there six or seven years. Trade was opening with the south west at this time, and Independence was the starting point for wagon trains carrying merchandise from New Mexico, over the old Indian haunted Santa Fe trail. Mr. Oldham engaged in this business in connection with his brother-in-law, Ben Thompson, and made the trip to Santa Fe in 1848, returning by the same route and being absent about four months. Another trip was made by Mr. Thompson. Another removal now took place, to a farm purchased in Cass County—the new home was about three miles from the Kansas line—nine from Harrisonville the County seat, and about a mile from a village called Morristown, near the present town of Freeman. The farm was a fine body of land of 160 acres, about 40 in timber, the rest prairie. Their first house here was a log cabin—later they built a comfortable frame house, and had an excellent orchard, and good improvements.

In 1851, soon after moving here Mr. Oldham ventured again on the toilsome and perilous, but fascinating business of the Santa Fe trail. This time he was absent seven months, going to El Paso, and returning on horse back through Texas, by way of San Antonio, and Austin. For ten years peace and prosperity smiled upon the Cass County homestead. But darker days were at hand. The storm which in 1861, gathered over the country from sea to sea, hung no where with blacker terrors than over the Missouri and Kansas border. Mr. Oldham (like most of the Whig party) was attached to the Union, but his feelings were not shared by the family.

Samuel, his eldest son was early in the ranks of the Southern Army. Morristown the neighboring village, was occupied by the forces to which he was attached and their pickets were posted in the yard of the homestead. In October 1861, the position was attacked by a Federal force, from Kansas under Jamison. The family fled during the fight to Pleasant Hill, returning in a few days long enough to gather up their household effects they turned their backs on the home, which they were to occupy no more. Going to Jackson County they rented the Brookin place about six or seven miles south of Independence, a farm on which they raised the next year a fine crop. On the first of October following, they were required to move on a few days notice under what is known as the "Ewing Order." This ruthless decree issued on August 25, 1863, by the commander of the department in retaliation for the raid upon Lawrence by Quantrill's guerrillas required the removal of every family living within three miles of the border Counties of Missouri, within fifteen days, from its issuance and converted this rich and once prosperous country into a desert. A yoke of steers belonging to their land-lord (their own had been carried off) was hitched to an old abandoned wagon, into which Mr. Oldham had hastily fitted a tongue—the only remaining horse "Big Shoulder," left to them, because so worthless that no one would take him, was harnassed to an old buggy, and leaving everything they possessed, the fugitives found refuge in Charitan County, sheltering themselves and six children in an old tobacco barn on the Ellington place, three miles from the village of Roanoke, and twelve from Glasgow. Here they passed the winter.

In the spring they rented the Williams place in the same neighborhood. The next year they moved again, starting to go to Illinois, but stopped in Marion County, Mo., near Palmyra, and about twelve miles from Hannibal. There upon a farm known as the Young place, Mr. Oldham made a crop the last year of the war. In the fall of 1865, they returned to Jackson County. Here on February 23, 1866, while stopping at the home of their sister, Mrs. Thompson, the second son William, a youth in his eighteenth year was killed by the accidental discharge of a pistol. They rented again this year the Brookin place, and here rejoiced to welcome back their first born. Samuel returned in safety from the thousand perils of four years service in Shelby's Confederate Cavalry, from which he brought back nothing but a name among his comrades for steady courage, in the face of every form of danger and indomitable cheerfulness under every extremity of hardship. The Cass County farm Mr. Oldham had been compelled to sell during the war for the little which it would bring in such troublous times.

With his family of young and helpless children he found himself stripped of everything, but courage and constancy. In the fall of 1866, the reunited family sought a new home in the south west. They moved in wagons through the Indian Territory to Fannin County on the Northern border of Texas, where they lived for the seven years following. An incident of the journey through the territory, which threatened to make misfortune complete was the loss from the wagon of the satchel containing the little hoard remaining for the sale of their property. A vigorous pursuit and seach succeeded in reclaiming it from the hands of a wayfarer who had picked it up. Their homes were, Dr. Smith's farm on Red River, one year, Bonham, one year, the Harris place, three miles east of Bonham, one year, the Rowland place seven miles east of Bonham and near the present town of Dodd City, three years, and the Beasley place in the same neighborhood, one year.

The first venture in the new state had proved unfortunate. The Smith farm was in the Red River bottom—unusual floods swept away a larg part of the crop, and the malarial sickness incident to such a season and locality was severely felt. But having reached their worst, and left little prospect of becoming other than a tenant farmer, matters begun to mend, somewhat, under the steady force of economy and hard work. Railroads had not yet penetrated the country, and the employment of wagoning to the nearest market, the town of Jefferson in Eastern Texas, gave fairly profitable returns in the intervals of farm labor. The school maintained at Bonham by Rev. Charles Carlton an eminent and inspiring teacher, to whom education in Texas is under obligations, gave opportunity to the elder children to complete a fragmentary education obtained under great difficulties. In the fall of 1873, Mr. and Mrs. Oldham and their family now reduced to three daughters and two sons, removed to Cook County, Texas, taking a small farm north of and just out side the limits of the town of Gainesville, which belonged to their son-in-law E. H. Crenshaw. This they occupied two years. In the fall of 1875, they moved into the town of Gainesville. In September 1876, they moved to Sherman, Texas, which was then the home of their daughters Mary and Ann. They had reached the time of life when the incidents of a family history are no longer the births and marriages which add to its number, but the sadder chronicle which tells how, from love's shining circle the gems drop away." Mr. Queen the son-in-law, had died on June 27, 1875, their son James S. Crenshaw died at Sherman on Feb. 17, 1878. It was nearly twenty years before they were called to mourn another break in the family circle, Samuel the oldest son, died at Bonham Sept. 27, 1897.

In Sherman for the first time since the storm of the Civil War had left them houseless fugitives, they found themselves in enjoyment of their own home. Mr. Oldham purchased a residence on South Travis street. Soon there were only himself and wife to claim shelter, for the youngest son had left to begin the successful winning of his way in the world, but the home was still a gathering place for children and grand-children. None of these however had remained in Sherman, and in 1887, they sold their home, and built a new one in the neighboring town of Denison, near to that of the daughter Ann, who with her husband, had become resident of that place. Here they dwelt for the following ten years. They were of the sort that never lacked for good neighbors, and the familiar, but loving title of Grand-pa, and Grand-ma Oldham was bestowed by all who knew them.

In 1896, a "hazard of new fortune," called Mr. Wilkinson and his wife to the State Capitol at Austin. The parents were strongly urged to abandon house-keeping and make their home with them and consented to do so. Here they have passed tranquilly the years succeeding. On the third of Nov. 1906, Mr. Oldham celebrated his ninety first birth day. Much of the time during each year has been spent in visits to their other children. Their life's work is done. The recording angel need drop few tears over the page. It is an honorable, a manly, and a womanly record, of which the children's children's children whom they see about their knees, may justly feel proud. Their lot has been toilsome and obscure. They have known hardship and grief, but they have wronged no one, and have helped many. They have eaten the bread of their own labor, and have owed no man. They have hated none, and have loved and been loved by many. Most of all, they have done their service in the world as those who believed it to be a training for immortality and they await in Christian faith the words, "Enter thou unto the joy of thy Lord." In short it can be recalled, how often has been heard the casual enquiry about this family coupled with the words "The best people I ever knew." The children born to them were as named in the following sub-sections 1 to 9 inclusive, viz:

1. Samuel Zerah Oldham, born about a mile and a half south east of Independence, Mo., Dec. 24, 1840, the first wedding anniversary of his parents. He was early in the ranks of the Southern Army, Shelby's forces, in the Civil War, as detailed in the foregoing sketch of his father. While living at Bonham, Fannin County, on the northern border of Texas, Feb. 7, 1869, he was married to Ellen Moore. He died at Bonham, Sept. 27, 1897, His family still live at that place.

2. Sarah Oldham, born Aug. 3, 1843, on the farm between Mill Creek and Blue, near the present Kansas City, which was then not even a village.

3. Mary Amelia Oldham, born Nov. 4, 1845, on the farm about five miles south of Independence, Mo., in a rich prairie country, but then called the "condemned land," because it was thought it could not be settled for lack of timber. While living at the Rowland place in Fannin County, Texas, she married July 29, 1869, to E. H. Crenshaw. They made their home in Sherman, Texas, where Mr. Crenshaw died Feb. 17, 1878.

4. William Shortridge Oldham, born Dec. 22, 1848, on the prairie farm five miles south of Independence. In his eighteenth year, he was killed by the accidental discharge of a pistol, whilst the family were stopping with his aunt Mrs. Thompson, in Jackson County, Mo.

5. Ann Maria Oldham, born in their log cabin home in Cass County, Mo., about three miles from the Kansas line--nine from Harrisonville, the County Seat, and about a mile from a village called Morristown Aug. 18, 1852. At the home in Gainesville,

Texas, Nov. 4, 1875, she was married to A. E. Wilkinson, a distinguished lawyer of Sherman, Texas. Afterwards they became residents of Denison, Texas. In 1896, a "hazard of new fortune," called Mr. Wilkinson and his wife to the state capitol at Austin, where they now live. Mr. Wilkinson was Judge of the Supreme (State) Court, and is now Vice President of the Texas Bar Association.

6. Eliza Catherine (Kate) Oldham, born in the Cass County, (Mo.) home, Feb. 19, 1855. Whilst living on the E. H. Crenshaw farm near Gainesville, Texas, March 31, 1874, she was married to Joseph P. Queen, a young merchant of Gainesville. Mr. Queen died June 27, 1875, and his widow on the 6th day of April 1880, was married the second time to S. H. Noland, a merchant of Sherman, Texas. Their home is now in Dallas.

7. Medora Bell (Dora) Oldham, born in the Cass County (Mo.) home Oct. 27, 1857. At the home in Gainesville, Texas, Sept. 20, 1876, she was married to Charles E. Edwards, of Gainesville. They and their descendants remain residents of Gainesville.

8. James Simeon Oldham, born in the Cass County (Mo.) home, Oct. 29, 1859, died at Bonham, Texas, Aug. 24, 1877.

9. O. L. Oldham, born June 19, 1864, on the Williams place near the village of Roanoke and about twelve miles from Glasgow Mo. He now resides at Dallas, Texas, where he is a hardware and implement merchant. Dec. 22, 1899, he was married to Annie Bond, of Brownsville, Tenn.

Section 5. Epaphroditus C. Oldham, born July 8, 1818; died unmarried in Pitt County, Mo.

Section 6. James S. Oldham, born May 8, 1821; died in California, where he left a family.

Section 7. Catherine Oldham, born —— 1823, married Ed. Hickman of Independence, Mo.

Section 8. Sally Ann Oldham, born —— — 1826; married Josiah Collins, were living at Lee's Summit, Mo., up to the time of Mr. Collins' death in 1904.

Section 9. Albert Oldham, born —— — 1829, still living in Independence, Mo.

Section 10. Joel Oldham, born —— — 1831; died in 1896 in Boise City, Idaho.

CHAPTER 41.

Oldham Family Tree.

By R. C. Ballard Thurston, May 1899.

I. John Oldham, came from England in March 1635, and settled in Virginia. I have learned very little of him or his sons, but a correspondent thinks that a celebrated family of that name in Maryland is descended from him. He is supposed to have settled in what afterwards became Westmoreland County, Va., but only from the fact that one of his grand-sons lived there. I have not learned the name of his wife, and know of only one son.

II. Thomas Oldham, nothing is known of him, except that he left a son:

III. Colonel Samuel Oldham, born 1680, died 1762; married Elizabeth Newton, born 1687; died 1759. He had estate in Westmoreland County, where he is supposed to have lived and died, leaving several children. His title, Colonel, is supposed to have been derived from his rank in the County militia.

John Newton, the emigrant came from Virginia about 1650-60, probably with a first wife and three sons, was in Westmoreland County in 1672; married second time between 1673 and 1677, Rose —— who was the widow of first John Tucker, and second Hon. Thomas Gerrard, both of Westmoreland County. He was Master and Mariner. His will was dated Aug. 19, 1695, probated July 1699, in which he mentions a son John, and his four children (one of whom was named William) a son Joseph and his three sons, and a son Benjamin, and his daughter all by the first marriage, and by the second marriage, son Gerrard, daughter Elizabeth (who married Thomas Willoughby) and a son Thomas, all the second set were apparently single in 1695. The Elizabeth Newton who married Colonel Samuel Oldham, was most likely a daughter of either John or Benjamin Newton, by the first set, but this is a matter for investigation.

In Bishop Meade's work "Old Churches," etc, of Va. Vol. 2 pages 151, etc. on Cople Parish, Westmoreland County, he speaks of Welmington,, the family seat of the Newtons, and says: "In the same grave yard is the tomb of Mrs. Elizabeth Oldham, wife of Colonel Samuel Oldham, who died in 1759, in her 72nd year." I know the name of only one son:

IIII. John Oldham, born in Westmoreland County in 1705, died ——— — ———; married Ann Conway. The only Conway named Ann, mentioned by Hayden in his Virginia Genealogies who could have married John Oldham, was the oldest child of Edwin Conway, third of Lancaster County, as he was born in 1681, and married Ann Ball in 1704, and their child Anne, was probably born about 1705, but she married Robert Edmunds June 10, 1729. Hayden asks "Did she marry second 1752, Thomas Chinn?"

The only dates I have for the births of the children of John Oldham and Ann Conway are 1736 and 1753, so I think it most likely that she was the daughter of Edwin Conway third, and did not marry Thomas Chinn in 1752. (Note: It will be noticed that William Oldham of Fauquier County, Va., who married Miss Basey, had a son Conway, and the name "Conway" was continued for generations; several of his grand-children and great grand-children were named Conway.) They had eight children:

1. Conway Oldham, second Lieutenant 12th Virginia regiment in Revolution Dec 1776, first Lieutenant April 2, 1777, transferred to eighth Virginia Sept. 3, 1778, Captain in 1780, and killed at Eutah Springs South Carolina Sept. 8, 1781, unmarried.

2. A daughter, who married Mr. Lawrence Ross of Fauquier County, Va., and left two sons Presley and Neville Ross.

3. A daughter, who married Mr. —— Barton.

4. A daughter, who married Mr. Rector, and had two sons Presley and Neville Rector.

5. Winifred Oldham, born 1736, died 1797; married Aug. 24, 1754, Colonel John Neville in Virginia. (See Sec.)

6. Samuel Oldham; died in 1825; married twice and settled in Kentucky. (See Sec.)

7. Mary Ann Oldham; married Major Abraham Kirkpatrick. See Section.)

8. Lieutenant Colonel William Oldham, born 1745, according to Miss Keys, but June 17, 1753, according his widows family bile. Killed at St. Clair's defeat Nov. 4, 1791; married Miss Penelope Pope of Louisville. (See Section.)

IIII 5. Winifred Oldham, according to the notes I have, was the fifth child and born in 1736. This I think must be a mistake, she was probably the first child, I am satisfied that the eighth child was born 1753, or rather the eighth child that lived, for there may have been one or more, who died in infancy, this would make 17 years between Winifred andthe eighth child known.

Again, if I am right in supposing that her mother was the Anne Conway, (daughter of Edwin Conway, third) who married Robert Edmunds, in 1729, she must have married second John Oldham, not later than 1735. According to Miss Keys Winifred, was born 1736 ,died 1797, married at the age of 18 on Aug. 24, 1754, in Virginia, General John Neville, of Pittsburg, Penn., where both of them are buried, in the old Presbyterian Church Yard. General Neville was Colonel of the second or third Virginia Regiment in the Revolution and was brevetted General after the war. Was Marshall of the District of Pennsylvania during the whiskey insurrection, when his home was burned by a mob, led by a Breckinridge. Miss Keys says, "I think there is a connection with the Neville family further back than the marriage of Winifred Oldham and General or rather Colonel Neville of Pittsburg.

Presley as a given name occurs in the Oldham family prior to the time of marriage of Winifred and John Neville. Presley is a Neville name, as Colonel John Neville, had a brother Presley, also a grand-nephew Presley Neville Pepper, who was the grandfather of Paul Cain, of Louisville, Ky. They had but two children, according to Miss Keys, who claims to have a complete record of their descendants:

1. Presley Neville.
2. Amelia Neville; married Major Isaac Craig, of the Revolution.

IIII 6. Samuel Oldham, moved to Jefferson County, Va., (now Kentucky) where the old minute book shows that he took his oath of office as Magistrate Aug. 7, 1787, and appeared as security for his brother, William Oldham, who had been appointed sheriff on Sept. 3, 1786. He married at Louisville, but such records do not anti-date 1784. He left a will on record at Louisville, dated Sept. 4, 1820, a codical to which is dated Jan. 23, 1823, probated Feb. 10, 1823, and recorded in will book 2, page 214, in which he mentions his wife Ann, and all his children except John, the husband of each of his daughters except 1 and 7, they probably being dead at the time. He left his son, Conway trustee for several of his married daughters and his son Henry in whom he seems to have had but little confidence. He therefore died early in 1825. Samuel Oldham married first Jane Cunningham, and had one child:

1. Sarah Oldham, born 1772, died 1830, married William Merriwether, Virginia History May, Oct. '97, Volume and 198. The license was issued May 22, 1788, but there was no return. They were ancestors of Mr.s Udolpho Snead of Louisville, Ky.

Samuel Oldham; married second Ann Lipscomb, and had ten children :

2. Nancy Oldham; married Thompson Taylor, license issued Feb. 15, 1796, and return made Feb. 18, 1796.

3. Conway Oldham; married Frances Ross, license issuel Dec. 26, 1800, return made Jan. 1, 1801, by Henry Pottorff. He left a will dated Nov. 25, 1825, a codicil to which was dated Nov. 8, (probably an error for 28) 1825, probated Dec. 8, 1825, and

recorded in will book 2, page 308, at Louisville, Ky. He mentions his wife, Frances, two of his children as married and the other as single:

3-1. Nancy Oldham; married Frederick Herr, license issued Feb. 3, 1821, return made Feb. 4, 1821, by James Vance.

3-2. Susan Oldham; married John Herr, Jr., license issued and return made by Ben Allen April 10, 1822.

3 (3-12) Samuel, Presley, Mary, Ann, Conway, Fiturah, Elizabeth, Martha and William Levi Oldham, all single 1825.

4. William Oldham; married Elizabeth Field. The license was issued for him and Betsy Field, daughter of Reuben Field May 1, 1806, and return made May 6, 1806, by James Vance. He left a will dated Feb. 25, 1826, probated April 3, 1826, and recorded in will book 2, page 319, at Louisville, Ky. He mentions having inherited a farm from his father, Samuel Oldham, also his wife Elizabeth, who "shall keep all my children that are not married together," but does not mention their names. Among the marriage records I find the following whom I take to be his children:

4-1. Elvise Oldham, (daughter of William Oldham) and Jefferson Overstreet, license issued and return made by Richard Corwin, March 18, 1825.

4-2. Moses Oldham, and Elizabeth C. McDaniel, daughter of Elijah and Sarah McDaniel, license issued July 1, 1824, return made July 4, 1824, by P. S. Fall.

5. Patsey Oldham; died single.

6. Henry Oldham; married Elizabeth —— and lived 20 miles south of Louisville, Ky., on Salt River, no record of his marriage here.

7. Winifred Oldham. On Nov. 22, 1809, a marriage license was issued to Winny Oldham, daughter of Samuel Oldham and Carver Mercer, the return was made Nov. 26, 1809, by Nathan H. Hall.

8. Elizabeth Oldham; married Levi Tyler of Louisville, Ky. The license was issued and marriage return made Oct. 4, 1810, by Joseph Oglesby. They certainly had one son:

8-1. Henry Tyler; married Miss Rebecca Gwathney, and had a large family. One of them was recently Mayor of Louisville.

9. Mary Oldham. On Feb. 12, 1815, a license was issued for Polly Oldham, daughter of Samuel Oldham, and Walter Powers, but no return was made, though she is mentioned in her father's will, as the wife of Walter Powers.

10. John Oldham; died in infancy.

11. Amelia Oldham; married Charles L. Harrison, license was issued May 15, 1817, and return made May 16, 1817, by D. C. Banks. They certainly had three children, whom the writer has known:

11-1. Kate Harrison; married William McDowell Bent, of Louisville, but died without issue.

11-2. Amelia Harrison; married Thomas Speed of Louisville, but now of Asheville, North Carolina.

11-3. Julia ? —— Harrison; married Harry Dumisdel, of Louisville.

IIII 7. Mary Ann Oldham; married Major Abraham Kirkpatrick of the Revolution and had two sons, and three daughters according to my mother's notes, but only three daughters are mentioned by Miss Keys:

1. Mary Ann Kirkpatrick; married Dr. Joel Lewis.

2. Amelia Louisa Kirkpatrick; married Judge Shaler, of Pittsburg, Penn.

3. Elizabeth Kirkpatrick; married Christopher Cowan.

IIII 8. Lieutenant Colonel William Oldham, was born 1745, according to Miss Keys, his widow's family Bible, however, states he was born, June 17, 1753, and is probably correct, for he was a young man at the outbreak of the Revolution, serving as first Lieutenant in Nelson's Independent Pennsylvania Rifle Company from Jan. 30, 1776, to Jan. 1777. The Jefferson County, Va., (now Ky.) Minute Book, contains the following references to him:

"April 6, 1784, William Oldham, was present at a meeting of the Justices of the Peace, he being one of them.

"April 10, 1784. Ordered to take a list of the tithables at the Falls of the Ohio, and other points.

"May 4, 1784. Present at a meeting of Justices of the Peace.

"July 6, 1784. Ordered to appraise the estate of George Meriweather.

"Nov. 3, 1784. Appointed Deputy Surveyor.

"August 12, 1785. Produced his commission as Justice of the Peace, and of Oyer and Terminer.

"Sept. 6, 1785, appointed Deputy Surveyor.

"Nov. 2, 1786, recommended for Major.

"Nov. 8, 1786, recommended for Lieutenant Colonel.

"Dec. 6, 1786, took oath as Major.

"Feb. 5, 1788, recommended for Lieutenant Colonel.

"May 7, 1788, present at a meeting of Justices of the Peace.

"Sept. 2, 1788, produced commission as sheriff, gave bond, with Samuel Oldham as surety and took oath of office.

"Sept. 3, 1788, judgment of the Justices that the admission of William Oldham to the office of sheriff was premature and his bond was surrendered.

"Oct. 7, 1788. Produced commission as sheriff and took oath, etc. He married on July 24, 1783, Miss Penelope Pope, born Feb. 12, 1769, died Sept. 16, 1821, (daughter of Colonel William Pope and his wifee Penelope Edwards of Louisville.)

He was Lieutenant Colonel in command of the Kentucky militia when he was killed at St. Clair's defeat on Nov. 4, 1791, and sent home to his wife, his gold watch and chain, which he had on when he fell mortally wounded. His will was dated Sept. 6. 1791, probated Dec. 6, 1791 and recorded in will book 1, page 29, at Louisville, Ky., which I quote as follows: I leave to my wife, Penelope the tract of land on Chenowith Run, and negro man Bosen, with household furniture and one third part of all my stock forever. Also during her widowhood, I leave to her Gilbert and Violet. The residue of my estate both real and personal I bequeath with the two negroes that I leave my wife Penelope, during her widowhood to be equally divided between my four children John, Richard, Abigail, and William Oldham, excepting a preemption of 400 acres near Butler's Lick," etc. etc., appointed Richard G. Anderson, Richard Taylor and Jacob Funk, Gents, executors, witnessed by George Pearce. His widow afterwards married Henry Churchill, whose youngest brother married her daughter, Abigail.

(Note:—Mr. Samuel Oldham of Zanesville, Ohio, in his letter, recorded in this volume, states that Samuel Oldham, who died at Louisville, Ky., in 1823, and his sister Winifred Oldham, the wife of Colonel John Neville, were brother and sister to Isaac Oldham, (his grand-father) and were not a brother and a sister to Lieutenant Colonel William Oldham, who was killed at St. Clair's defeat, November 4, 1791. He also states that Lieutenat Colonel William Oldham, was a son of said Isaac Oldham, by his first marriage, but it will be noticed that Isaac Oldham's will in which he makes bequest to his son William, was not probated till 1821, thirty years after the death of Lieutenant Colonel William Oldham.) (Writer.)

His children were:

1. Judge John Pope Oldham, born Feb. 28, 1785. (See Sec.)
2. Major Ricahrd Oldham, born March 13, 1787. (See Sec.)
3. Abigail Oldham, born May 1, 1789 .(See Section.)
4. William Oldham, born -- 1791, before his father started on the campaign in which he lost his life, but the child died young, aged about four or five years.

III-8-1. Judge John Pope Oldham, born Feb. 28, 1785, left a will on record at Louisville, Ky., will book 3, page 216, but I did not examine it. He was for many years Judge of the Circuit Court at Louisville, Ky., and one of the most prominent and highly respected citizen. His wife was Miss Malinda Talbott, daughter of Dr. Talbot of Huntsville, Alabama. She lived to an extreme old age, surviving her husband, and all her own children, leaving a will recorded at Louisville, Ky., in will book 9, page 349, but I did not examine it. They had four children, but I do not know the order in which they were born:

1. William Oldham; died without issue.
2. Talbot Oldham; died without issue.
3. Sophia Oldham; married Hon. Judge Bullock, of Louisville, and had only one child:
   3-1. John Oldham Bullock; married Miss Loraine Turner, of Wheeling, Va., (now West Virginia,) and had four children:
      1. Horace Bullock; died in childhood.
      2. Edward Bullock, born 1850; died 1891, without issue, was law partner of his step-father Ex-Governor Bowman, of Parkersburg, West Virginia.
      3. Talbott Bullock, City Attorney, of Parkersburg, W. Va.
      4. John Oldham Bullock; married and was once assitant Post Master at Parkersburg, where his mother lived 1898.
4. Susan Oldham, born 1816, died 1870; married Horace Hill (See Sec.) a merchant of Louisville, Ky., and had twelve children:
   1. Sophie Hill; died in childhood.
   2. Elizabeth Hill; died in childhood.
   3. Horace Hill, born 1839, died 1869.
   4. John Oldham Hill; married Miss Mary Zenora, of Louisville, and had four children:
      4-1. Antonine Hill; died in childhood.
      4-2. Sally Shannon Hill, born 1868; died 1886.
      4-3. Susan Oldham Hill; married George Mulligan and lived in Louisville, Ky.
      4-4. Marie Hill; single; lives in Louisville, Ky.
   5. Linda Hill; married Barry Coleman of Louisville, Ky., had eleven children:
      5-1. Thomas Coleman; married Louisa Aycock of Texas, has one child:
         1. Linda Hill Coleman.
      5-2. Linda Coleman; died in childhood.
      5-3. Dora Coleman; died in childhood.
      5-4. Sue Coleman; died in childhood.
      5-5. Horace Coleman; married Mary Richardson and live in St. Louis, Mo
      5-6. Sophie Coleman; single; lives in San Francisco, Cal.
      5-7. Barry Coleman; born 1871; died 1891, without issue.
      5-8. Evan Coleman; died in childhood.
      5-9. Ethel Churchill Coleman; married Waller Bonner of Texas, two children:

1. Lucy Hill Bonner, born 1895.
2. Georgie Bonner, born 1896.

5-10. Dupont Coleman; single lives in San Francisco, Cal.

5-11. Lucy Given Coleman; born 1886, lives in San Francisco, California.

6. Fannie Smith Hill; married Clarence Howard Barnes of of Lexington, Ky., one child:

1. Emily Clarence Barnes.

7. Sue Hill; married first Garret Marshall, and second William B. Dick, both of Louisville, and had two children:

7-1. Horace Hill Marshall; died in childhood.

7-2. James Melton Marshall, of Louisville, Ky.

8. William Prather Hill, died in 1869, without issue.

9. Lucy Hill; single.

10. Churchill Hill; died in childhood.

11. Lila Hill; married William P. Lee of Louisville, Ky., had three children:

11-1. William P. Lee Jr., of Louisville, Ky.

11-2. Linda Lee, a young lady in society in Louisville.

11-3. Jouett Lee, a young lady in society in Louisville.

12. Leonare Hill, living in St. Louis, Mo.

IIII-8-2. Major Richard Oldham, born March 13, 1787, was an officer in the United States Army, where he attained the rank of Major, was in active service in New Orleans in 1812-14; married Elise Washington Martin, daughter of Major Thomas Martin (first commandant of the Newport, Kentucky barracks, and one of the original members of the order of the Cincinnati) and his wife, Susan Washington Ledbetter, who was a descendant of Colonel John Washington, the great-grandfather of General George Washington. Major Richard Oldham resigned from the army and settled in Louisville, Ky., where he was elected Jailer, and died in 1835. He had eight children:

1. Jane Oldham; married William Wetmore, of New York, and had five children:

1-1. Florence Wetmore; married William Rassourne of Tennessee and had children..

1-2. Mary Wetmore; married Mr. Porter of Tennessee.

1-3. Oldham Wetmore; married Miss Oglesby, of New Orleans.

1-4. John Wetmore.

1-5. Leona Wetmore; married Paul Jumon of New Orleans.

2. William Henry Oldham; deceased.

3. Thomas Martin Oldham; deceased.

4. Catherine Oldham; deceased; married John Edgerton of Ohio, one child:

4-1. Emma Edgerton; married John K. Bell of New Orleans.

5. John Pope Oldham; deceased, had two children:

5-1. Emma Oldham.

5-2. Sulie Oldham.

6. Penelope Abigail Oldham; married William A. Violet of New Orleans, La., and had five children:

6-1. Atwood Violet, cotton Broker at No. 30-32 Broad Street, New York City; married Miss Olga Quantrill of New Orleans, La., and had four children:

1. Thomas Violet.
2. Olga Violet.
3. Atwood Violet.
4. Quantrill Violet.

6-2. Ella Violet.

6-3. Lily Violet.

6-4. Edwin R. Violet.

6-5. Margueritte Violet; married Charles B. Whelen of Philadelphia, Pennsylvania, and has two children:

1. Violet Whelen.
2. Charles S. Whelen.

7. Mary Oldham; married John B. Robertson of Nashville, Tennessee, five children:

7-1. Elenora Robertson; married Dr. William Poe, of Baltimore, Md.

7-2. Paelix Robertson.

7-3. William Frank Robertson.

7-4. Minnie Robertson; married Mr. Jones of Arkansas.

7-5. Penelope Robertson; married Mr. John Simpson of Arkansas.

8. George W. Oldham; married Miss Miller of Louisville, Ky., one child:

8-1. Alfred Violet Oldham; single, and clerk of the City Court at Louisville, Ky. (To whom the writer is indebted for a copy of this Tree.)

IIII-8-3. Abigail Oldham, born near Louisville, Ky., May 19, 1803, when she was but little more than fourteen years old, and died at their place, Spring Grove July 5, 1854, and was buried in the family burying ground now near the southern limits of the City. Had sixteen children:

1. Mary Eliza Churchill, born April 14, 1804; married Charles William Thruston, of Louisville, Ky., May 27, 1824, and died Feb. 9, 1842, see Section.

2. Penelope Pope Churchill, born Aug. 14, 1806, died July 26, 1812.

3. Julia Ann Churchill, born Aug. 12, 1808, died Aug. 6, 1821.

4. Armisted Ludwell Churchill, born Oct. 27, 1810; died May 1873; married Rebecca Catlett, and had five children:

4-1. Samuel Churchill, of Bobnoster, Mo., married twice, and had children.

4-2. George Churchill; died in infancy.

4-3. Letitia Churchill; married ——— ———

4-4. Henry Churchill; married twice, and had children.

4-5. Fannie Emily Churchill; married Dr. Calmes, and live in Arkansas.

5. Samuel Bullitt Churchill, born Dec. 6, 1812; married Amelia C. Walker, of St. Louis, Mo., June 14, 1836, and died at Louisville, Ky., May 14, 1890, was in the Legislature, and at one time Lieutenant Governor of the state, was twice Secretary of State for Kentucky, had eleven children.

6. William Henry Churchill, born Sept. 14, 1814; married twice first Miss Kate Clarke, daughter of Dr. William Clarke ,of Louisville, but she died soon after without issue. He then married second Julia Williams, widow of Clarence Prenticee who survived him but had no issue.

7 Abigail Prather Churchill born March 9, 1817. married Meriweather Louis Clark, Jan. 9, 1834. He was an officer in the United States Army, in the Mexican War, where he served with distinction and later a General in the Confederate Army. He was a son of General and Governor William Clarke of the Lewis and Clarke expedition, to the north west in 1804-6. A General in the United States Army, in the war of 1812, and Territorial

Governor of Missouri. She died Jan. 10, 1852, leaving seven children:

7-1. William Hancock Clark; married in New York City, and now living in Washington, D. C.

7-2. Samuel Churchill Clark; deceased.

7-3. Mary Eliza Clark; deceased.

7-4. Merriweather Lewis Clark; married Miss Mary Anderson of Louisville, Ky., was President of the Louisville Jockey Club and later a widely known Judge at many race courses, committed suicide at Memphis, Tenn., April 22, 1899, leaving a widow and three children:

7-5. John O. Fallon Clark; deceased

7-6. George Rogers Clark; deceased.

7-7. Charles Jefferson Clark; deceased, married Miss Lena Jacob of Louisville, Ky., and had two daughters.

8. John Churchill, (baptized John Pope Rowan Churchill) but dropped the middle name later in life, born March 20, 1819; married twice, first Mrs. Selena Gray Lawrence on March 2, 1858, by whom he had one son. His wife died Feb. 23, 1859, and he married second Miss Ermina (Lena) Nicholas, on Nov. 11, 1890, by whom he also had one son. He died March 21, 1897, leaving a widow and one son:

8-1. William Henry Churchill, by first marriage, born Dec. 2, 1858, and died Aug. 2, 1859.

8-2. John Churchill, by second marriage, born Sept. 19, 1891, when his father was over 72 years old, and is still living.

9. A son born July 2, 1821, died 14th same month, unnamed.

10. Emily Ann Churchill, born Sept. 7, 1822; married March 31, 1842, Mr. Hampden Zane, of Wheeling, W. Va., but is now a widow, living in Louisville, Ky. Had three children:

10-1. Abigail Churchill Zane, born Feb. 9, 1843; died.

10-2. Mary Eliza Zane, born June 27, 1844; married George R. R. Cockburn, of Toronto, Canada. Mr. Cockburn was for some years President of the Upper Canada College, and was a member of the Canadian Parliament. They had two children:

10-2-1. Hampden Zane Churchill Cockburn, born Nov. 19, 1867, and now a lawyer at Toronto.

10-2-2. Emily St. Aubert Cockburn, born April 1, 1871; married Mr. Thomas Tate of the Canadian Pacific Rail Road, and now living at Montreal, Canada, one child:

10-2-2-1. Winifrede Tate, born about 1892.

11. General Thomas James Churchill, born March 10, 1824, served as Lieutenant in the United States Army, during the Mexican War, where he was complimented for bravery, etc., before he was made a prisoner. Was Major General in the Confederate Army and later Governor of Arkansas. He married Miss Annie Senir, and settled at Little Rock, Arkansas. Had six children:

11-1. Abby Churchill, born March 25, 1854, died aged about twenty.

11-2. Samuel Churchill, born May 17, 1856, married Kate Hooper, daughter of Dr. Hooper, a surveyor of distinction in the Confederate Army, and has three children:

11-2-1. Thomas J. Churchill.

11-2-2. Marie Churchill.

11-2-3. Hooper Churchill.

11-3. Ambrose Sevier Churchill, born Dec. 24, 1858; died in infancy

11-4. Juliette Churchill, born Jan. 20, 1861; married W. Ralph Goodrich of Little Rock, who died soon after, no children.

11-5. Daily St. Aubert Churchill, born Aug. 29, 1865; married Mr. John Calef, but has no children.

11-6. Mattie Johnson Churchill, born Jan. 11, 1868; married Mr. Edward Laughorne of Virginia, but now living in St. Louis, Mo., where they have two children:

11-6-1. Annie Sevier Laughorne.

11-6-2. Thomas Churchill Laughorne.

12. Charles Thruston Churchill, born Jan. 10, 1826; died March 20, 1865; married Miss Susan Churchill Payne on March 21, 1850. They were closely relaated as their mothers were half sisters and her maternal grand-father, Henry Churchill, was an elder brother of his father, Samuel Churchill. They lived at Elizabethtown, Ky., and had seven children:

12-1. William Henry Churchill, born Jan. 1, 1851; married Miss Maggie Talbott, of Jefferson County, Ky., in Oct. 1875, and had one daughter. (His first wife obtaining a divorce from him for non support, and afterwards married Joshua F. Bullitt Jr., of Louisville, Ky., but now of Big Stone Gap, Va.) He married second Miss Clara Irvine, and died in New Orleans, La., Oct. 12, 1892. No issue by second marriage:

I. Elizabeth Farr Churchill, born Feb. 1877, and lives with her mother at Big tone Gap.

12-2. Hampden Zane Churchill, born Jan. 30, 1853, formerly lived at Little Rock, Arkansas, but now live sat Elizabethtown, Kentucky, single

12-3. Mary Payne Churchill, born Oct. 1855; died 1856.

12-4. Abby Oldham Churchill, born Aug. 1857; died in infancy.

12-5. Samuel Thomas Churchill, born March 28, 1862, died Sept. 24, 1868.

12-7. Charles Thruston Churchill, a posthumous child, born July 20, 1865, single and living in Louisville, Ky.

13 & 14. Twin sons, still born, Aug. 23, 1827.

15. Isabella Penelope Pope Churchill, born July 21, 1829, married Mr. Altrens J. McCreary, and died Feb. 14, 1861, without issue.

16. Julia Maria Preston Pope Churchill, born Sept. 30, 1833, married Nov. 17, 1857, Dr. Luke P. Blackburn, late Governor of Kentucky, she is now a widow, and resides with her sister, Mrs. Lena, in Louisville, Ky., had no issue.

III-8-3-1. Mary Eliza Churchill, born April 14, 1804, married Charles William Thruston, of Louisville, Ky., May 27, 1824, and died Feb. 9, 1842. They had four children:

1. Samuel Churchill Thruston, born March 10, 1825; married Sept. 17, 1850, Miss Kate Keller of Louisville, but was killed by lightning at his farm on Green River Kentucky, April 26, 1854. They had no issue.

2. Frances Ann Thruston, born Nov. 30, 1826; married Andrew Jackson Ballard of Louisville, Ky., April 27, 1848, and died at Vienna, Austria, April 30, 1896. (See Sec.)

3. Mary Eliza Thruston, born Feb. 8, 1829; died May 22, 1835.

4. O'Fallon Thruston, born Feb. 21, 1831; died Dec. 9, 1832.

III-8-3-1-2. Frances Ann Thruston, born November 30, 1826; married April 27, 1848, Andrew Jackson Ballard, of Louisville, Ky., who was for many years clerk of the United States Court, at Louisville. She died of pneumonia at Vienna, Austria, April 30, 1896. Had five children:

1. Charles Thruston Ballard, born June 3, 1850, a prominent business man of Louisville, Ky., a member of the firm of Ballard

and Ballard, Millers, and twice President of the Board of Trade; married April 28, 1876, Miss Evaline Modest (Mina) Breaux, daughter of Colonel Gus A. Breaux, of New Orleans, La. They had eight children:

1-1. Abby Churchill Ballard, born Feb. 16, 1872, to be married June 1, 1899, to Mr. Jefferson Davis Stewartt, of Louisville, Ky.

1-2. Emille Lock Ballard, born Sept. 18, 1880, and died Dec. 10, 1886.

1-3. Mary Thruston Ballard, born Nov. 25, 1882; died Feb. 5, 1894.

1-4. Charles Mym Thruston Ballard, born Nov. 28, 1886.

1-5. Gustave Breaux Ballard, born Oct. 7, 1888.

1-6. Fannie Thruston Ballard, born April 30, 1890, one of twins.

1-7. Churchill Ballard, twin to last; died Feb. 18, 1891.

1-8. Mim Breaux Ballard, born June 24, 1895.

2. Bland Ballard, born Oct. 29, 1851; died Aug. 15, 1892.

3. Abigail Thrustion Ballard, born June 24, 1853; died at Mantone, France April 2, 1874, but is buried by her mother in Cave Hill Cemetery, Louisville, Ky.

4. Samuel Thruston Ballard, born Feb. 11, 1855, a prominent business man of Louisville, Ky., and a member of the firm of Ballard and Ballard, Millers, married Jan. 25, 1883, Miss Sunshine Harris, daughter of Mr. Theodore Harris, Banker, Louisville, Ky. They had four children:

4-1. Mary Harris Ballard, born April 28, 1884.

4-2. Theodore Harris Ballard, still born Sept. 14, 1886.

4-3. —— Ballard.

4-4. —— Ballard.

PART VII.

CHAPTER 1.

1. GENEALOGICAL TABLE OF THE KAVANAUGH FAMILY. 2. EARLY MARRIAGES IN MADISON COUNTY, KY., OF THE KAVANAUGH NAME GLEANED FROM THE FIRST MARRIAGE REGISTER OF THE COUNTY COURT. 3. ITEMS TOUCHING THE KAVANAUGH NAME.

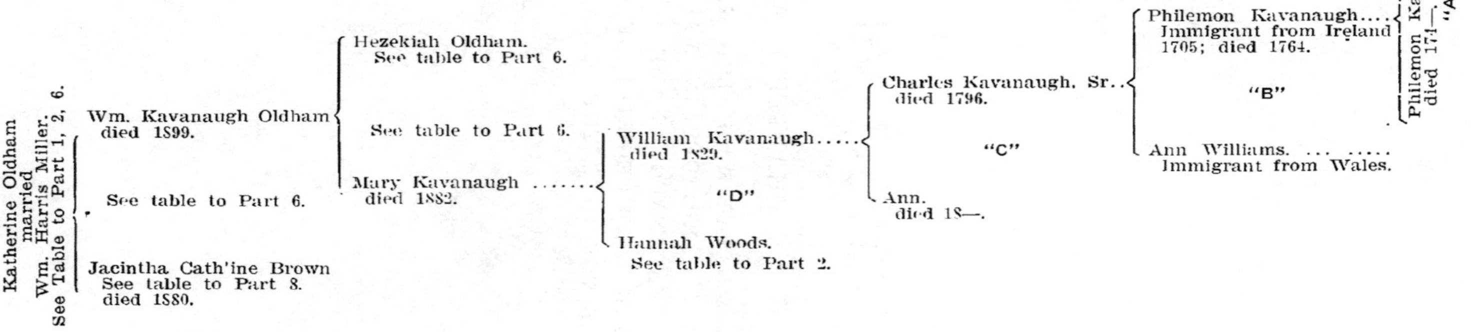

Katherine Oldham
married
Wm. Harris Miller.
See Table to Part 1, 2, 6.
Wm. Kavanaugh Oldham
died 1899.
See table to Part 6.
Jacintha Cath'ine Brown
See table to Part 8.
died 1880.
Hezekiah Oldham.
See table to Part 6.
See table to Part 6.
Mary Kavanaugh ....
died 1882.
William Kavanaugh.....
died 1829.
"D"
Hannah Woods.
See table to Part 2.
Charles Kavanaugh, Sr..
died 1796.
"C"
Ann.
died 18—.
Philemon Kavanaugh....
Immigrant from Ireland
1705; died 1764.
"B"
Ann Williams. ... .
Immigrant from Wales.
Philemon Kavanaugh.
died 171—.
"A"

A

1. Charles. Chap. 2.
2. Philemon, m Ann Williams. Chap. 2. "B"

B

1. Charles, m Ann . Chap. 3. "C"
2. Benjamin. Chap. 2. Sec. 2.
3. Williams, m Mary Harrison. Chap. 2, Sec. 3.
4. Philemon. Chap. 2. Sec. 4.
5. Anna. Chap. 2. Sec. 5.
6. Mary. Chap. 2. Sec. 6.
7. Miss, m William Covington. Chap. 2, Sec. 7.
8. Sarah. Chap. 2. Sec. 8.

C

1. Philemon, m Elizabeth Woods. Chap. 4.
2. Mary, m Joseph Ellison. Chap. 7.
3. William, m [illegible] Woods. Chap. 8. "D"
4. Charles, m Fr[illegible]s Chap 13.
5. Joel, m Peter Woods. Chap. 11.
6. Sarah Ann, m James Mills [illegible]. Chap. 15.

D

1. Susan, m Isaac Duncan. Chap. 9.
2. Annie, m Andrew Briscoe. Chap. 10.
3. Polly, m Hezekiah Oldham. Chap. 8, Sec. 3.
4. Sallie, m Charles English. Chap. 8, Sec. 4.
5. Philemon, m Patsey Gilbert. Chap. 16.
6. Charles, m Peggy Warren. Chap. 11.
7. Archibald, m 1 Miss Baxter, 2 — Winchester. Chap. 8, Sec. 7.
8. Nicholas, m Jane Wallace. Chap. 12.
9. William, m Betsy Freeman. Chap. 8, Sec. 9.

Article 2.—Early marriages in Madison County, Ky., gleaned from the first marriage register of the County Court.

Kavanaugh, Susannah—Duncan, Isaac, Sept. 24, 1795.
Kavanaugh, Ann—Briscoe, Andrew, Feb. 25, 1796.
Kavanaugh, Ann—Estill, Benjamin, June 12, 1794.
Kavanaugh, Mary—Ellison, Joseph, Sept. 1, 1787.
Kavanaugh, Nicholas—Wallace, Jane, Jan. 12, 1817.
Kavanaugh, William—Miller, Elizabeth, June 13, 1798.
Kavanaugh, William—Booten, Ruth, Sept. 21, 1815.
Kavanaugh, Polly—Oldham, Hezekiah, Oct. 7, 1813.
Kavanaugh, Charles—Warren, Peggy, July 3, 1817.
Kavanaugh, Elizabeth..Argo, James, Aug. 6, 1818.
Kavanaugh, Hannah—Cox, Benancy, March 19, 1833.
Kavanaugh, Sarah Jane—Asa Carter, June 29, 1837.
Kavanaugh, Hannah Ann—Volney Doty, Sept. 2, 1841.

Article 3.—Items touching the Kavanaugh name. (From Court Records, and Histories.)

Section 1. Charles Kavanaugh, Senior.

In the Madison County Court, June 24, 1788. 'O'rdered that it be certified that satisfactory proof was made to this Court, that

Charles Kavanaugh, Senior, is the elder son of Philemon Kavanaugh, deceased, formerly of Culpepper County."

July 22, 1788. "Odered that Charles Kavanaugh, Senior, be exempted from personal service, on any public road, etc. September 16, 1790. "The Rev. Charles Kavanaugh, (Senior) produced credentials of his being in regular communion with the Methodist Society, and took the oath of fidelity to the Commonwealth. Whereupon, the said Charles Kavanaugh is licensed to celebrate the rites of matrimony on his entering into bond in the clerk's office, conditioned as the law directs.

October 4, 1796. Charles Kavanaugh, seniors's will was probated, etc.

Section 2. Charles Kavanaugh, Junior, (son of above.)

In Madison County Court, Feb. 27, 1787. "On motion of Charles Kavanaugh, Junior, it is ordered that his ear mark, towit: A crop in the right, and hole in the left ear be recorded."

October 6, 1789, Charles Kavanaugh (Jr.) produced his commission as Captain of Militia, etc.

October 2, 1792. Authorized to celebrate the rites of marriage—being in regular communion with the Methodist Church.

Section 3. Rev. Charles Kavanaugh.

In Madison County Court, March 5, 1795. "Rev. Charles Kavanaugh produced credentials of his being in regular communion with the Methodist Church."** etc., took oath and authorized to celebrate the rites of matrimony agreeable to the forms and customs of the said church.

Section 4. Philemon Kavanaugh.

In the Madison County Court, Sept. 25, 1787. Administration on his estate to Archibald Woods, and Thomas Shelton, and the same persons appointed guardians to William Kavanaugh and Ann Kavanaugh orphans of Philemon Kavanaugh, deceased.

Dec. 2,1794. Inventory and appaisment of his estate was returned and ordered to be recorded.

Section 5. Rev. Williams Kavanaugh.

In the Madison County Court, Jan. 3, 1797. "On the motion of the Rev. Williams Kavanaugh, who produced credentials of his ordination, and also, of his being in regular communication with the Methodist Church, he took the oath of fidelity to the Commonwealth. Whereupon he entered into and acknowledged bond as required by law, and he is hereby authorized to celebrate the rites of matrimony agreeable to the forms and customs of the said Church, between any persons to him regularly applying therefor within the State.

Section 6. William Kavanaugh. (Son of Charles, Senior.)

In the Madison County Court, June 7, 1790, William Kavanaugh, produced his commission as Lieutenant of Militia."

Nov. 2, 1790. William Kavanaugh produced his commission as Captain of Militia."

Section 7. William Kavanaugh.

In the Madison County Court, May 3, 1802. It was noted on the order book. "That William Kavanaugh is entitled to 150 acres of land in Madison County, on the head waters of the North branch of Round Stone, a North Fork of Rockcastle by virtue of his having improved same, etc."

Section 8. Rev. Hubbard Hinde Kavanaugh. Was Superintendent of Public Instruction for the State of Kentucky 1839-40, and editor of a temperance paper at Maysville 1841, and one of the most noted and talented Bishops of the Methodist Episcopal Church. (C)

Section 9. George W. Kavanaugh, was a membeer of the Kentucky Legislature in the House of Representatives from the County of Anderson 1843-50. (C)

Section 10. Jean Baptiste Cavaignac, a French Revolutionist, born at Gorden in 1762, died in Brussels March 21, 1829. In 1792, he was elected to the National Convention where he voted for the death of Louis XVI. As commissioner to the army in Lor Vendee, and afterwards to that in the Pyrances, he gave evidence of energy and talent. He took part in the Thermidonans against Robespierre, and was sent on a third mission to the army of the Rhine, and Moselle.

On the (1st Prairial) May 20, 1795, he commanded the troops who vainly attempted to protect the convention against the insurgents. On ('the 13 Vende Maire) Oct. 5, he was assistant to Barras, and Bonaparte in repelling the attack by the sections. For a short time he was a member of the Council of 500. In 1806, he entered the service of Joseph Bonaparte at Naples, and was continued under Murat. In 1815, during the hundred days, he was prefect of the Somme. On the second restoration he was expelled from France, as a regicide, and took up his residence in Brussels, where he lived in obscurity. (Amer.-Cyclo.)

Section 11. Eleonore Louis Godefroy Cavaignac, son of Jean Baptiste Cavaignac, born in Paris, in 1801, died May 5, 1845, was a French Journalist. He was one of the most popular leaders of the Republican party, during the revolution and the reign of Louis Philippe. He distinguished himself in the Revolution of July, but upon the elevation of Louis Philippe to the throne he took part in the conspicracy for the overthrow of the new dynasty and was several times arrested and put on trial. After the out break of April 1834, he was arrested and sent to prison but escaped July 13, 1835, and retired to Belgium. In 1841, he returned to France and became one of the editors of the Reforme, the most violent of the opposition journals. (Amer.-Cyclo.)

Section 12. Louis Eugene Cavaignac, a brother to Eleonore Louis Godefroy Cavaignac, a French General, born in Paris Oct. 15, 1802, died at his country seat Chateau Ournes, department of Sarthe, Oct. 28, 1857. He was educated at the polytechnic school, entered the army as sub-Lieuteant of Engineers, took part in the French expedition to the Mona, and was appointed Captain in 1829. On the Revolution of 1830, he declared for the new order of things, but soon entered the association national, an organization of the opposition, for which he was, for a while, discharged from active service. In 1832, he was sent to Africa. Being entrusted in 1836 with the command of Tlemcan, he held this advanced fortified post for three years against the assaults of the Arabs. In 1839, by reason of impaired health he asked to be placed on leave, he was then a Major. A few months later he returned to Africa, where his defense of Cherchell was no less brilliant than that of Tlemcan. In 1840 he was promoted Colonel of the Zouaves, and in 1841, he was made Brigadier General and Governor of the Province of Oran. On the Revolution of February, 1848, he was appointed Governor General of Algeria, and promoted to the rank of General of division. The same year he was elected to the constitutionaal assembly and was allowed to leave Algeria to take his seat as a representative. He reached Paris two days after the disturbance of May 15, and was immediately appointed Minister of war. In a few weeks 75,000 regular troops were gathered within the walls, while 190,000 national guards were ready to support them against the threatened rising of the working classes. Yet the insurrection broke out on the dissolution of the Atitier Nationaux. On June 22, barricades were erected in the most central parts of the city. Cavaignac concentrated his troops in order finally to bear on the principal points with irresistable force. The assembly having invested him with dictatorial powers, the struggle commenced June 23, and was continued with internicine fury for seventy hours, resulting in a complete victory for the government. On June 29, Cavaignac resigned his dictatorship, and he was unanimously elected chief of the executive power. He declined several propositions to make him President for four years without recourse to an election. The election for President took place Dec. 10, and out of 7,327,345 votes, Cavaignac received but 1,448,107. After the Coupdetat of Dec. 1851, he was arrested and sent to the castle of Ham, his name being placed at the head of the list of the proscribed. Having been set at liberty he lived for a time in retirement in Belgium, and when he returned to France, resided mainly at his country seat in the department of Sarthe. In 1852, he was elected to the Legislative body, but refused to take the oath of allegiance to the Emperor. In 1857, he was again chosen by the electors of the third district of Paris, but again refused to take the oath. This was the last public act of his life. One morning as he was leaving the house to visit a friend he suddenly expired in the arms of an attendant without uttering a word. (Amer.-Cyclo.)

Section 13. Julia Kavanaugh, a British authoress, born in Thurles, Ireland, in 1824, died Oct. 28, 1877. She early went with her parents to France, where she was educated. In 1844, she took up her residence in London. She published in 1847, a tale for children, entitled "The Three Paths." This was followed by "Madeleine," (1848), a story of peasant life in France, and in 1850, by a series of historical sketches, "Woman in France in the Eighteenth Century." In 1851, appeared "Nathalie," a novel in which the scene is also, laid in France. Among her other works are: "Women of Christianity, exemplary for Piety," (1852) "Daisy Burns," (1853) "Grace Lee," (1854) "Rachael Gray," (1855) "The Hobbies," (1857) "Adele" 1858) "French women of Letters," (1861) "English women of Letters," (1862) "Queen Mab," (1863) "Sybil's second Love," (1869) and "Sylvia" (1870). (Amer.-Cyclo.)

Section 14. Kavanaugh, name of a Lake in Michigan.

CHAPTER 2.

THE KAVANAUGH FAMILY.

Article 1.—In the County of Cavan, or Kavan, Province of Ulster, Ireland, was a Church and school of the name Kilkaavan, at which Daniel Kavanaugh was educated, and he was the first to bear the sur-name "Kavanaugh," the suffix "augh" meaning "of." The name is spelled commencing with either the letter "C" or letter "K," but most frequently with the latter.

On November 5, 1688, King James II, of England upon the landing at Torbay of William Prince of Orange with fifteen thousand

(15,000) men, and who had the support or sympathy of the greater portion of the population of the Country fled to France where he was received by Louis XIV, and provided with a large allowance from the public treasury by the said Louis, and the palace of St. Germain as a residence. In 1689, he went to Ireland, where he was royally received, and he made endeavors to regain the throne, but the mental superiority of William Prince of Orange, with the fleets of Holland and England at his command, thwarted James Second's hopes, and he returned to France, and a portion of the Kavanaugh family went with him to France, and one of the name fled to Prussia. In the history of Napoleon is named a member of the Prussian Court, Kavanaugh, who doubtless descended from the Irish refugee to Prussia. He seemed to have ideas and convictions peculiarily his own, and was a conspicuous and noted personage of said Court, who readily made known his position on any question, or his objection to any measure, somewhat a family characteristic to this day.

Louis Eugene Cavaignac (Kavanaugh) of France, a son of Jean Baptiste Cavaignac, and who was prominent in the affairs of state in the time of Louis Phillipe, was born in Paris, Oct. 15, 1802, the same year that Bishop Hubbard Hinde Kavanaugh of Kentucky was born. Jean Baptiste Cavaignac was one of the deputies of the convention during the Revolution of 1793. No man of his times was more distinguished than General Louis Eugene Cavaignac, who died in 1857. He was, no doubt a descendant from the Kavanaugh, who went with King James II, from Ireland to France. When the French Republic was established, he received nearly one and a half million votes for the Presidency.

The family tradition is, that three brothers left Ireland together. One of them stopped in England, and the other two came to America. General Kavanaugh who commanded Queen Victoria's army in India, had a like family tradition, his paternal ancestor having settled in England, while two of that ancestor's brothers went to America. The General belonged to the same original stock (see Life and Times of Kavanaugh, by Redford.)

The two brothers who came to America were Charles Kavanaugh and Philemon Kavanaugh, who were sons of Philemon Kavanaugh, and it is firmly believed that their father Philemon, also came. Their immgiration was about 1705. The said Charles Kavanaugh held the title to forty thousan dacres of land in what was then Essex County, Va., the tract extended westward and above the Beverly line up Muddy Run to Judge Field's mills across by Poor Town to Gibson's mills on Mountain Run, a portion of which he bequeathed to his daughter Mildred and has never been out of the Yancey family, and is this day owned by Benjamin M. Yancey, a great grand-son of Lewis Davis Yancey and his wife, the said Mildred Kavanaugh and by their great, great grandson, James William Yancey, the latter's place "Arlington." And upon this vast estate the two brothers Charles and Philemon Kavanaugh settled in 1710,. This land was doubtless a grant from the Crown of England. Although the title was vested in the said Charles, his brother, Philemon had an equitable undivided moiety thereof, at least he thought he had, reasoning from the wording of a clause or item in his will made in 1764, namely:

"My will and desire is, that one "moyaty" of that land whereon my brother, Charles Kavanaugh lives, be sold by my executors, and that my said brother make lawful deed to the purchaser for the same, and the other "moyaty." Remaining I give my right thereof to my said brother, to him and his heirs forever."

Conclusive evidence that the testator, Philemon, considered that he owned half of the land, and had a right to dispose of same, and that his brother Charles was entitled to the other half, and that he recognized the fact that the title was in his brother Charles, who was requested by the will to pass the title by deed to the purchaser the half testator desired to be sold.

Orange County was cut out of Spotsylvania in 1734, and Spotsylvania was carved out of Essex, and in 1748, Culpeper County out of Orange, the Kavanaugh settlement and possessions being thereby thrown into the County of Culpeper, which was named in honor of Thomas Lord Culpeper, Governor of the Colony of Virginia, 1680-1683.

Not being sufficiently advised, the statement is not made positive that Philemon Kavanaugh, senior, the father of the two brothers, Charles and Philemon came to America, but the belief that he did is based upon the facts disclosed by the Court Records of Culpeper County, extracts from which are hereinafter presented from said records it appears that said Charles Kavanaugh, for years prior to 1750, was executor of the estate of Philemon Kavanaugh, deceased, (his father) and the will was most probably probated in the Court of one of the other Counties named, as formed prior to the formation of the County of Culpeper. An examination of the records of the Courts of those several Counties would doubtless reveal the truth of the mattter. Would Philemon Kavanaugh, senior, have lived and died testate in Ireland, or some foreign land in his day and time, when there were no railroads, no telegraphic and telephonic communications, and when it took a month to cross the ocean, and appointed a son residing in far away America, executor of his estate? One would think not. He certainly was a resident of America at the time of his demise, and perhaps, it was by the terms of his will that the title to that large landed estate was vested in his eldest son Charles.

For some reason or other, said Charles Kavanaugh did not hold the position of executor, to the end, but prior to 1750, was supplanted as such, by the appointment by the Court, of Thomas Slaughter and W. Green as administrators de-bonis non, of Philemon Kavanaugh, senior, in his room and stead, which office they held for a time, and in 1750, they made a settlement before commissioners of the Court of their accounts, and were succeeded by James Pendleton, who in 1759, made a settlement before commissioners, Robert Green and Gabriel Jones of his accounts.

It seems that it was many years from the death of Philemon Kavanaugh, senior, before his estate was finally settled. Said Charles Kavanaugh had a wife, but who she was is in the dark, and he raised if not more, one child, a daughter:

1. Mildred Kavanaugh, who became the wife of Lewis Davis Yancey. Mr. Yancey about the year 1710, settled in the part of the Country that in 1749 helped form the County of Culpeper, and they had a daughter:

   1. Elizabeth Yancey, to whom Philemon Kavanaugh, senior, gave one hundred acres of land on Muddy Run.

In 1642 five Welchmen, John Yancey, Charles Yancey, William Yancey, Joel Yancey and Robert Yancey, came to Virginia, with Sir William Berkely, afterwards Governor, and settled in the James River country. From one of these four last named emigrants (Yancey) from Wales, sprang Lewis Davis Yancey, who settled as aforesaid in Culpeper County, Va., about 1710, or rather in what was subsequently Culpeper County. He married Mildred Kavanaugh, daughter of Charles Kavanaugh, of Irish parentage. Mr. Yancey died and was buried on the estate, the portion now owned by his great grand-son James William Yancey, known as "Arlington." The children of the emigrant John Yancey were:

1. Charles Yancey; married Miss Dumas, issue:

1. Captain Charles Yancey (1741-1841) of Louisa County, married Mary Crawford. Their children:

1. Ann Yancey.

2. Elizabeth Yancey; married Joseph Kimbrough. Their children:

1. Dr. William Kimbrough.

2. Unity Kimbrough; married Colonel Edmund Pendleton.

3. Sarah Kimbrough; married Peter S. Barrett.

4. Maria Kimbrough; married Bickerton Winston, moved to Kentucky.

5. Captain Charles Yancey Kimbrough; married Mary P. Honeyman.

6. Elizabeth Kimbrough; married Dr. L. M. Legin.

7. Susan H. Kimbrough; married Robert H. Anderson.

3. Unity Yancey.

4. Louisa Temperance Yancey.

5. Robert Yancey.

6. Mary Yancey.

7. Rhoda Yancey; married Rev. William Crawford.

8. Joel Crawford Yancey.

9. Benjamin Yancey.

10. William Crawford Yancey.

2. Rev. Robert Yancey, was ordained by the Bishop of London at his palace in Falham, in Middlesex, July 25, 1768, as an Episcopal Priest, there being no Bishop in this country under the Colonial Government. On his return from England, he accepted the parishes of Tellotston and Trinity in his native country in 1774. He was the first who preached in that section of the country, the doctrine of Universal redemption. He married Ann Crawford, daughter of David Crawford. Their children:

1. Betsy Yancey 1795.

2. Major Charles Yancey, 1770-1857, born in Trinity Parish, Louisa County, Va., removed to Buckingham County. He was known throughout the state, as the 'Wheel Horse of Democracy," and also, had the sobnquet of "Duke of Buckingham." He married Mary Spencer. Their children:

1. Mary Chambers Yancey; married Coloned John Horsley, of Nelson County.

2. Frances Westbrook Yancey.

3. Elizabeth Ann Yancey; married first Robert Williams of New York, and secondly Richard Morris of Gloucester, Virginia.

2. Leighton Yancey; moved to Rockingham County.

3. Bartlett Yancey; moved to North Carolina.

The children of the above named Lewis Davis Yancey, and Mildred Kavanaugh his wife were:

1. Elizabeth Yancey, who was given one hundred acres of land on Muddy Run by Philemon Kavanaugh, as before stated.

2. John Yancey; married ——— ——— and settled in Rockingham County. His children:

1. Layton Yancey, was Lieutenant in first Continental Dragoons in the Revolutionary Army. He married Fannie Lewis. Their children:

1. Layton Yancey,.

2. Colonel William Burbridge Yancey; married first, Mary Smith and secondly, Mary Gibbons. His children:

1. Dianna Smith Yancey; married George Oliver Conrad of Harrisonburg.
2. Captain Thomas L. Yancey; married Margaret Newman.
3. Edward S. Yancey; married Fannie Mauzy.
4. William Burbridge Yancey. Captain of Peaked Mountain Greys, Civil War. He married Victoria Winsborough.
5. Charles Albert Yancey; married Julia Morrison, of Cumberland, Md.
6. Mary Frances Yancey.
7. Margaret J. Yancey; married Joseph N. Mauzy.
8. Dr. Layton B. Yancey; married Virginia Hopkins, of McGaheysville, Va.
9. John Gibbons Yancey; married Bennett Bradley, of Harrisonburg.

3. Charles Yancey; married Lucinda Moyers. Their children:
1. Charles Yancey.
2.Elizabeth Yancey; married Mr. —— Hudson.
3. Ann Yancey; married Thomas Hamsberger.
4. Columbia Yancey.
5. Fountain Taliaferro Yancey.

4. John Yancey.
5. Albert Yancey.
6. Thomas Yancey.
7. Fannie Yancey; married William Price, of Standardsville.
8. Clarissa Yancey; married William Rodes, son or Captain Jack Rodes and Francina Brown his wife, of Albemarle County, Va. (See Part III, Chap. 3, Sec. 7, and Part V, Chap. 13, Section 6.)
9. Maria Yancey; married Mr. —— Grans.
10. Louisa Yancey; married Thomas Garth.

2. Ludwell Yancey.
3. John Yancey.
4. Fannie Yancey.
5. Polly Yancey.

3. Richard Yancey; married —— —— His children:
1. Henry Yancey.
2. Elizabeth Yancey; married Mr. Story.
3. Judith Yancey; married Daniel Field.
4. Agatha Yancey; married Benjamin Pendleton.

4. Charles Yancey; married 1740, Miss Powers, of Eastern Virginia. Their children:
1. Kesia Yancey; married George Freeman, went to Kentucky.
2. Ann Yancey; married Geeorge Doggett, North Carolina.
3. William Yancey; married Miss Stone.
4. Thomas Yancey; married 1799, Sarah Mitchell. Their children:
1. Charles Yancey; (1801-1867) married Miss Withers, moved to Tennessee.
2. John William Yancey; (1803-1894) married 1834, Jane Terrill. Their children:
1. William T. Yancey; married Nannie Stevenson. Their child:
1. William Yancey.

3. Elizabeth Yancey; (1806-1841) married William Wiggington. Their children:

1. Sallie Wiggington.
2. Edmonia Wiggington; married Henry Field.
3. Benjamin Wiggington; married moved to Missouri.
4. Susan E. Wiggington.

4. James Powers Yancey; (1804-1884) married 1845, Mary Coons. Their children:
1. James William Yancey; married Florence Miller. Their children:
1. Ethel Yancey.
2. James Yancey.
3. William Yancey.

5. Benjamin Yancey, born 1809; married 1839, Catherine Banks, daughter of Dr. William Tunstall Banks, of Madison Court House. Their children:
1. Pamelia Somerville Yancey; married Captain Joseph D. Brown. Their children:
1. Mary Catherine Brown; married Rufus T. Carpenter. Their children:
1. Stacey Harris Carpenter.
2. Joseph Daniel Carpenter.
3. Ellie Florence Carpenter.
4. Frank Hill Carpenter.
5. Leslie Pamelia Carpenter.

2. Lila Banks Brown; married Thomas M. Henry, attorney at law, of Pittsburg, Pa. Their children:
1. Lucy Maxwell Henry.
2. Pamelia Brown Henry.
3. Josephine Henry; married J. Benjamin Flippin, of Cumberland County. Their children:
1. Sue Gray Flippin.
2. Elise Josephine Flippin.
3. Majorie Pamelia Flippin.

4. Benjamin Armistead Henry; Married Frances Todd Faunt Le Roy, of King and Queen County. Their children:
1. Virginia Faunt Le Roy Henry.
2. Joseph Daniel Henry.
3. Juliet Faunt Le Roy Henry.

5. Andrew Edward Henry.
6. Gertrude Pamelia Henry; married John Banister Sparrow of Danville, Va., now living in Martinsville.
7. Florence Armistead Henry; married Oliver G. Flippin, of Cumberland County.

2. Edward Duke Yancey.
3. Dr. Charles Kavanaugh Yancey.
4. Mary Crimora Yancey; married John W. Payne. Their children:
1. Mary Catherine Payne.
2. Emma Carson Payne.
3. Fannie Keith Payne.
4. Crimora Yancey Payne.

5. Sallie Thomas Yancey; married John W. Payne.

6. Kesia Ann Yancey; (1812-1881) married Edward Lightfoot.
7. Susan Yancey.

5. Philip Yancey; married ——— ——— His children:
1. Lewis Yancey; married ——— ———
2. Philip Yancey.

3. Richard Yancey.
4. Iechunias Yancey.
5. Archillis Yancey.
6. Robert Yancey.
7. Kavanaugh Yancey.
8. Polly Yancey; married James Menifee.
9. Delpha Yancey; married Henry Menifee.
10. Mary Ann Yancey; married William Johnson.

6. Robert Yancey, was a Captain in the Revolutionary Army. He married Miss Holliday.

7. James Yancey, was a Major under General Green, in the Revolutionary Army. After the war he settled in the western part of South Carolina and practiced law. He married Miss Cudworth, of Charleston. Their children:

1. Benjamin Cudworth Yancey; married Caroline Bird, daughter of Colonel William Bird, of the "Ariary," Warren County, Georgia. Their children:

1. William Lowndes Yancey, the 'Oroator of Secession," "fire eater," as he was termed in the invective of those days. He married Sarah Caroline Earle, daughter of George Washington Earle, of Georgia. Their children:

1. Colonel William Earle Yancey; married ——— ———. His children:

1. Virginia Yancey; married Mr. ——— Besson.
2. Ellen Yancey; married Hon. W. H. Skaggs.
3. Mary Yancey; married Charles Preston Lewis.
4. Martha Yancey.
5. Eva Cubet Yancey.
6. William Lowndes Yancey.
7. Benjamin Cudworth Yancey.
8. Dalton Huger Yancey.
9. Goodloe Harper Yancey.
10. Miss ——— Yancey; married John L. Harrett.

2. Benjamin Cudworth Yancey.

8. Lewis Yancey; married Henrietta Faver, (daughter of John Faver, who died in 1783). Their children:

1. George Yancey.
2. Garland Yancey.
3. Mary Yancey; married Thompson Tutt.
4. Ibly Yancey; married Lewis Tutt.

9. Nancy Yancey; married Mr. Nalle.
10. Miss ——— Yancey; married Mr. Nalle.

A Mr. Yancey a descendant, married Elizabeth Jeffries, (daughter of James Jeffries who died in 1805.)

The above data of the Yancey family taken from Dr. Slaughter's notes on Culpeper, complied and published by Raleigh Travers Green, with his consent.

The immigrant Philemon Kavanaugh, brother of Charles, died in Culpeper County, Va., in 1764, having made and published his last will and testament, which bears date Feb. 6, 1764, and probated March 16, 1764, and in these words and figures:

"In the name of God, Amen. I, Philemon Kavanaugh, being weak and low, but of sound mind and memory, and calling to mind the mortality of man, that all men must die, I do, therefore, constitute and appoint this my last will and testament, revoking all other will or wills, and as to my worldly goods that it has pleased God o bless me with, my desire is, that they may be disposed of in the nanner following, towit:

Imprimis: I render my soul to God, who gave it, and I desire ny body be decently buried in a Christian like manner, at the "dis-ression" of my executors, hereinafter named.

Item—My will and desire is that one "moyety" of that land, whereon my brother, Charles Kavanaugh, now lives, be sold by my executors, and that my said brother do make lawful deed to the purchaser, for the same, and the other "moyety" remaining, I give my right thereof to my said brother, to him and his heirs forever.

Item—I lend to my loving wife, Ann Kavanaugh, the land and plantation whereon, I now live during her natural life, or widowhood, and at her deceease or day of marriage, I do give the said land to my son Benjamin Kavanaugh, to him and his heirs forever.

Item—I lend all the residue of my estate, after paying all my just debts, to my said wife, Ann Kavanaugh, for during her natural life, or widowhood and at her decease, or day of marriage, my will and desire is that my said estate, with the money arising from the sale of the above mentioned land, be equally divided amongst all my children.

I do constitute and appoint my loving wife, Ann Kavanaugh an executrix, and my loving friend, William Williams, executor of this my last will and testament. Revoking and disannulling all other will or wills, legacies or bequeaths whatsoever. In witness whereof, I have hereunto set my hand, and seal this sixth day of February in the year of Our Lord, one thousand seven hundred and sixty four. PHILEMON KAVANAUGH. (L S)

Signed, sealed and published in the presence of:

Charles Kavanaugh.

Charles Yancey.

Ann Kavanaugh.

At a Court held for the County of Culpeper on Friday the 16th day of March 1764, this last will and testament of Philemon Kavanaugh, deceased, was exhibited to the Court, by Ann Kavanaugh and William Williams the executors therein named and was proved by the oaths of Charles Yancey, and Charles Kavanaugh, witnesses thereto, and ordered to be recorded. And on the motion of the said executors, certificate is granted them for obtaining a probate thereof, in due form, they having sworn to the same and given bond and security according to law.

Teste: ROGER DIXON, Clerk.

A copy Teste, W. E. Coons, Clerk."

At the time the will was drawn, the testator's brother Charles Kavanaugh, was living on the land named in the will, one moiety of which testator directed to be sold, and for his brother to make deed to the purchaser, and his right to the other moiety to go to his said brother, and he was evidently one of the witnesses to the will.

In 1764, the inventory of the personal estate of the testator Philemon Kavanaugh, was returned to the Court amount 108L, 15 S.

The said Philemon Kavanaugh, who died in 1764, married Ann Williams, a Welch woman, she qualified as an executrix of his will. In 1756, eight years prior to the death of said Philemon Kavanaugh, Ann Kavanaugh gave by deed to her daughter Sarah Kavanaugh, then only fourteen years old, a negro girl named Venus, at that time only eight years old. So far as learned the children of Philemon Kavanaugh were:

Section 1. Charles Kavanaugh; married Ann — - — They emigrated and settled in Madison County, Ky., a more complete account of whom is given in Chapter 3.

Section 2. Benjamin Kavanaugh, to whom his father devised the old home place, after the death or marriage of his widow.

Section 3. Williams Kavanaugh; married Mary Harrison. They also emigrated and settled on the waters of Muddy Creek in Madison County, Ky., a more complete history of whom, is given in Chapter 17.

Section 4. Philemon Kavanaugh, for whom James Pendleton was guardian.

Section 5. Anna Kavanaugh, James Pendleton of Culpeper County, Va., was also, her guardian, perhaps she married Adam Woods. (See Part II, Chap. 7, Sec. 5.)

Section 6. Mary Kavanaugh. The said James Pendleton was her guardian too.

Section 7. Miss Kavanaugh, a daughter, whose given name was probably Frances, married Mr. Covington, whose given name was perhaps William, of whom more will be found in Chapter 18.

Section 8. Sarah Kavanaugh, for whom the said James Pendleton was guardian a number of years, and afterwards, until her maturity her father Philemon Kavanaugh, was appointed, qualified and acted as her statutory guardian. She was born in 1742, and her guardian made his final settlement in 1763.

Prior to 1752, the said Sarah, her brother, Philemon and her sisters Anna and Mary, were minors, the said Sarah the youngest, just ten years old, had received legacies from the estate of their grand father Philemon Kavanaugh, deceased, through the executor, their uncle Charles Kavanaugh, and James Pendleton of Culpeper County was appointed their guardian and in 1752, filed his account as such amount 66 L 4 S. He made a settlement of his accounts in 1753, the assets consisting of negroes, and other personal property. The same year, another settlement amount 37 L 15 S 10¾ d, and in 1754 amount 76 L 12 S 11 d, and between 1754 and 1758, it seems that the wards, excepting Sarah, had arrived at the age of maturity, and her father had been appointed and qualified as her guardian in place of Mr. Pendleton, and in 1758, he showed in his account as guardian, that he then had the negro girl Venus, at that time ten years old, belonging to his ward, the said Sarah, which girl was given her by her mother Ann Kavanaugh in 1756. In 1759, said guardian showed to the Court, that he had the same girl 11 years old, and in 1761, 13 years old, and in 1762, the guardian charged one years board, £3 and clothing £3, and credited by hire of the said girl, 11 years old £3, and in 1763, made his final settlement showing that the negro girl was then 15 years old, his ward being then twenty-one years old. Although further on in this work it appears that Charles Duncan married Sarah Browning—it is however, probable that he was twice married, it is evident that the subject Sarah Kavanaugh married Charles Duncan the year she arrived at the age of 21 years (1763), and many years thereafter (about 1784), moved to and settled in Madison County Ky., on the waters of Muddy Creek where she died in 1824, and was buried in the Duncan Grave Yard, on the farm now owned by our County Clerk, Jesse T. Cobb. The inscription on the tomb: "Sarah Duncan, born 1742, died in 1824, in the 82nd year of her age." Showing that she was 21 years old in 1763, the year of the final settlement of her guardian, and the County Court records show that Robert Covington was her son-in-law.

Abstracts, etc., from the records of the Culpeper (Virginia) Court, showing transactions of the Kavanaugh's made and furnished December 21, 1905, by W. E. Coons, Esquire, Clerk of said Court.

"Kavanaugh Family."

"Lewis Davis Yancey, settled in Culpeper County, about 1710, and married Mildred, daughter of Charles Kavanaugh, of Irish parentage, who owned 40,000 acres of land in this county.

"Culpeper County was taken from Orange County in 1749, and Orange County from Essex in 1734.

1752, Will book A, page 68.

"James Pendleton, guardian of Philemon, Anna, Mary and Sarah, filed his account, amounting to £66 4s.

1753, Will book A, page 83.

"James Pendleton, guardian settled his account for the same children, that came from the estate of Philemon Kavanaugh and came through the hands of Charles Kavanaugh, executor, and consists of negroes and other personal property.

1753, Will book A, page 84.

"James Pendleton, guardian, settled hs accounts for same children amounted to £37, 15s 10¾d.

1750, Will book A, page 86.

"Thomas Slaughter and W. Green settled administrator's account before the Court, of Philemon Kavanaugh, £444, 3s 7d.

1754, Will book A, page 106.

"James Pendleton guardian of same children settled his account amounting to £76, 12s 11d.

1758 Will book A, page 177.

"Philemon Kavanaugh, guardian of Sarah Kavanaugh, showed in his account settled before the Court, that he held a negro girl named Venus, 10 years old, belonging to said Sarah.

1759 Will book A, page 192.

"James Pendleton, administrator of Philemon Kavanaugh, deceased, had his account settled before Robert Eastham, Robert Green and Gabriel Jones, commissioners of the Court, which amounted to £218 12s ¼d.

1759 Will book A, page 189.

"Philemon Kavanaugh, guardian of Sarah Kavanaugh, shows that he has the same negro girl now 13 years old.

1762 Will book A, page 288.

"Philemon Kavanaugh, guardian of Sarah Kavanaugh, charges one year's board £3, and clothing £3, and credited by hire of said negro girl 11 years old £3.

1763 Will book A, page 346.

"Philemon Kavanaugh, guardian of Sarah Kavanaugh, settled his account showing that said negro is now 15 years old.

1764 Will Book A, page 366.

"Inventory of the estate of Philemon Kavanaugh, was filed, amounting to £108, 15s.

"Granters in deeds."

Deed Book A, page 489, 1753, Charles Kavanaugh and Ann his wife, made a deed to Robert Coleman, for 1000 acres, being the land given by Philemon Kavanaugh to Elizabeth Yancey, daughter of Lewis Davis Yancey on Muddy Run.

Deed book B, page 346, 1755, Charles Kavanaugh deed 400 acres of land on Muddy Run, to John Connor.

Deed book B, page 468, 1756, Ann Kavanaugh gav negro Venus to her daughter Sarah Kavanaugh.

Deed book C, page 17, 1756, Philemon Kavanaugh gave a bill of sale to Thomas Brown, Junior for three negroes.

Deed book C, page 595, 1761, Charles Kavanaugh and Ann his wife, gave deed of trust to Davenport Burkett on 481 acres of land being land devised to him by his father Philemon Kavanaugh.

Deed book D, page 354, 1763, Philemon Kavanaugh to John

Greer, bill of sale on one negro and one handkerchief for £45.

Deed book F, page 55, 1768, Charles Kavanaugh, gave power of attorney to William Brown.

Deed book N, page 200, 1786, Philemon Kavanaugh's executors deeded 100 acres of land to Richard Pettinger.

Deed book R, page 504, 1791, Philemon's executors deeded 21 acres of land to Peter Vandyke.

Deed book S, page 4, 1791, William Strother, executor of Philemon Kavanaugh of Woodford district Kentucky, sold 26 acres of land to Robert Yancey.

Deed book T, page 421, 1797, Ann Kavanaugh, Joseph Ellison and Mary his wife, William Kavanaugh and Hannah his wife, Charles Kavanaugh and Frances his wife, Peter Woods and Jael his wife, James Moores and Sarah Ann his wife, and all of Madison County, Ky., deeded 127 acres of land to Iechunias Yancey, and at the same time, they deeded 240 acres of land to Richard Henry Yancey, and also 96 acres to William and Major Yancey.

CHAPTER 3.

CHARLES KAVANAUGH, Senior.

(Named in Chapter 2, Section 1.)

Article 1.—Charles Kavanaugh, senior, a son of the immigrant from Ireland, Philemon Kavanaugh and Ann Williams, a Welch woman his wife, was a Methodist Episcopal preacher, and his wife was named Ann.

He and his family within the period 1775-1787, came from their old home, where their father died in 1764, in Culpeper County, Va., and settled in Madison County, Ky. His children, at the time were grown, at least, most of them were, when he died in 1796, he had grand children.

The following is the wording of an entry found in Order Book A, of the Madison County Court, of date June 24, 1788, towit: "Ordered that it be certified that satisfactory proof was made to this Court that Charles Kavanaugh, senior, is the elder son of Philemon Kavanaugh, deceased, formerly of Culpepper County."

On the 16th day of Sept. 1790, he produced to the County Court credentials of his being in regular communion with the Methodist Society and took the oath of fidelity to the Commonwealth etc., and was authorized to solemnize the rites of marriage.

He performed much service of this kind in Kentucky, and especially in Madison County. He died in Madison County in 1796, for his will bearing date Oct. 13, 1795, was probated Oct. 4, 1796, and recorded in Will Book A, page 125, which is in the words and figures as follows, towit:

"Charles Kavanaugh's Senior Will."

In the name of God, Amen, the thirteenth day of October in the year of our Lord one thousand seven hundred and ninety five.

I, Charles Kavanaugh, senior, of Madison County, and State of Kentucky, being of perfect mind, and memory, thanks be to God, for the same, and calling to mind the mortality of my body, and knowing that it is appointed for all men once to die, do make and ordain this my last will and testament, that is to say principally and first of all, I give and recommend my soul to God, who gave it, as for my body, I recommend it to the earth to be buried in a Christian like manner, at the discretion of my executors, nothing doubting, but at the general resurrection I shall receive the same by the Almighty power of God, and as touching such worldly estate as I am possessed with I give, divide and dispose of the same in manner and form following, that is to say:

First: I desire my tract of land lying on the Kentucky River below the mouth of Drowning Creek be divided in quantity and quality, between James Mills Moore and Charles Kavanaugh Moore and Elizabeth Mills Moore, his two children, that the said James Mills Moore have one half of the said tract of land, of the first choice—having regard to quantity and quality, as above mentioned, and the said Charles and Elizabeth his children, the other half of the said tract of land. Provided further, that if the said land, or any part of it, should be lost by a prior claim or other means, the loss shall not fall on the remaining part of the estate. However, if a loss should take place of a part of the land, it shall be equally proportioned between said Moore and his two children, according to the quantity first given.

Item—Whereas, I have a law suit depending for a certain tract of land and the rents thereof in Culpeper County, and State of Virginia, which if I should gain, I desire my executors William and Charles Kavanaugh and Peter Woods, or whoever goes into transact the business, after being paid for their trouble out of what is recovered, shall deliver the balance with all the rest of my estate into the hands of my wife, Ann Kavanaugh during her life, then the whole of the estate at her death to be equally divided beween my five children, viz: Mary, William, Charles, Jael and Sarah Ann. I give and bequeath to the heirs of my eldest son, Philemon Kavanaugh, the sum of five shillings sterling and no more, as I have already given the said Philemon such parts of my estate as I intended, and I do hereby utterly revoke and disannul all former testaments, wills and legacies by me in any way made before this time—ratifying and confirming this and no other to be my last will and testament. In witness whereof, I have hereunto set my hand and seal, the year and day above written. CHARLES KAVANAUGH, Senior (L S.)

Signed, sealed, published, pronounced and declared by the said Charles Kavanaugh, as his last will and testament in the presence of:

Will Irvine.
Is. Hockaday.
William Fox.

At a Court held for Madison County on Tuesday the 4th day of Oct. 1796, this will was proved to be the last will and testament of Charles Kavanaugh, deceased, by the oaths of William Irvine, Isaac Hockaday and William Fox, witnesses thereto, and ordered to be recorded. Teste: Will Irvine, Clerk.

Oct. 4, 1796. The last will and testament of Charles Kavanaugh senior, deceased, was proved by the oath of William Irvine, Isaac Hockaday and William Fox, witnesses thereto, and ordered to be recorded. And on the motion of Peter Woods, and William Kavanaugh, the executors therein named, a certificate is granted them for obtaining a probate thereof, in due form they having first made oath and together with Daniel Maupin and Eusebus Hubbard, their secureties entered into and acknowledged their bond in the penalty of £500, conditions as the law directs." His children are named in the coming sections:

Section 1. Philemon Kavanaugh; married Elizabeth Woods. The subject of Chapter 4.

Section 2. Mary Kavanaugh; married Joseph Ellison Sept. 1, 1787. The subject of Chapter 7.

Section 3. William Kavanaugh; married Hannah Woods. The subject of Chapter 8.

Section 4. Charles Kavanaugh; married Frances —— The subject of Chapter 13.

Section 5. Jael Kavanaugh; married Petter Woods. The subject of Chapter 14.

Section 6 Sarah Ann Kavanaugh; married James Mills Moore The subject of Chapter 15.

Charles Kavanaugh, Sr., of Madison County, then Vi|rginia, on the 27th day of May 1788, executed a power of attorney appointing his trusty and well beloved son, William Kavanaugh, his true and lawful attorney to sue, and be sued, to grant, bargain, sell and convey his lands and other property in the County of Culpeper, and to transact all kinds of business for him. There after, and after his death, and probate of his will, his widow Ann, and his children legatees. Mary and her husband Joseph Ellison, William Kavanaugh and Hannah his wife, Charles Kavanaugh and Frances his wife, Jael and her husband, Peter Woods, Sarah Ann and her husband James Moore, of the County of Madison and State of Kentucky on the 23rd day of Oct. 1797, united in deeds conveying to Richard Henry Yancey, Iechumas Yancey, William Yancey and Major Yancey, of the County of Culpeper, State of Virginia, certain lands in the latter named County to which Charles Kavanaugh, senior, held the title, which deeds recite "that whereas Charles Kavanaugh, senior, late of the County of Madison and State of Kentucky for divers good causes and considerations him moving duly made and appointed his son, the aforesaid William, his true and lawful attorney with power to sell and convey land to him belonging in Culpeper County and State of Virginia, and make a complete title thereto; the said Charles Kavanaugh duly made and published his last will and testament in writing and of record in the County and State first above mentioned in which the following beqquest of the said land to his wife Ann aforesaid for life and remainder to his five children Mary, Wiliam, Charles, Jael and Sarah Ann, and the said Mary and Sarah Ann and Jael intermarried with the said Joseph, Peter and James."**

The deeds were signed and acknowledged by all of the parties of the first part, save Frances, the wife of Charles Kavanaugh.

Charles Kavanaugh, Junior and Frances his wife, were in Rutherford County, Tenn, Sept. 15, 1815. (See deed to James McMullen, L page 18.)

CHAPTER 4.

PHILEMON KAVANAUGH.

(Named in Chapter 3, Section 1.)

Article 1.—Philemon Kavanaugh, the elder son of Charles Kavanaugh, Senior and Ann his wife, was married in Virginia to Elizabeth Woods.

They came to Madison County, Ky., prior to 1787, at least on the 25th day of Sept. 1787, appears an order of the Madison County Court (A p 62) granting to Archibald Woods and Thomas Shelton, (borthers-in-law and the latter having married Elizabeth the widow) letters of administration on the estate of Philemon Kavanaugh, deceased, and John Miller, Hale Talbott, James French and Stephen Hancock were appointed appraisers, and on the same date Archibald Woods, and Thomas Shelton were appointed guardians to William (Woods) Kavanaugh, and Ann Kavanaugh, orphans of Philemon Kavanaugh, deceased.

Let it be noted here that Philemon Kavanaugh married Elizabeth Woods, a sister to the said Archibald Woods, and Archibald Woods had married a sister to the said Thomas Shelton, and after Philemon Kavanaugh's death, the said Thomas Shelton married Philemon Kavanaugh's widow, the said Elizabeth. (See Part II, Chap. 7, Section 12.) Philemon Kavanaugh died at least nine or more years prior to the date of the death of his father. His children are set forth in the coming sections:

Section 1. William Woods Kavanaugh. The subject of Chapter 5.

Section 2. Ann Kavanaugh. The subjejct of Chapter 6.

Article 2—As beforesaid, after the death of Philemon Kavanaugh, his widow Elizabeth Woods Kavanaugh, married Thomas Shelton who was a pioneer Baptist preacher, and a brother to Mourning Shelton, the wife of Archibald Woods. (See Part II, Chap. 6, Sec. 12), and children of William Shelton and Lucy Harris his wife. (See Part III, Chapter 3, Section 6.) The children of Thomas Shelton and Elizabeth Woods Kavanaugh his wife:

Section 1. Susan Shelton; married Thomas Reid, July 29, 1806. (See Part II, Chapter 21, Section 1.)

Section 2. Betsy Shelton; married Richard Moberley March 3, 1802. They came from Albemarle County, Va., and married in Madison County, Ky., where they settled and made their home on Muddy Creek, near the present village of Elliston, and where they lived and died

Note: Rev. Edgar Woods in his history of Albemarle mentions the names of the children of William Shelton, whose first wife was Lucy Harris, as follows, towit: "William Harris Shelton, Mourning, the wife of Archibald Woods, Elizabeth the wife of Richard Moberley, Dabney Shelton, Sarah Shelton, Lucy Shelton, the wife of Elliot Brown, Agnes Shelton, Weatherston Shelton and Thomas Shelton." and further states that "the first three migrated to Kentucky." If Rev. Edgar Woods is correct, in his statement then Elizabeth or Betsy, the wife of Richard Moberley, was not a daughter of Thomas Shelton. Attention is called to the fact, confirmed by the Court records that the marriage of Betsy Shelton and Richard Moberley took place in Madison County, Ky., March 3, 1802, and not in

Albemarle, and also, to the fact that their only son, was named Thomas Shelton Moberley. It does seem from all the circumstantial evidence and published statements heretofore made, that she was a daughter of Thomas Shelton. Archibald Woods married Mourning Shelton in 1773, a daughter of William Shelton and Lucy Harris, twenty nine years prior to the marriage of the said Betsy and Richard Moberley.

The children of Betsy Shelton and Richard Moberley, were:

1. Samiramus Moberley; married Elder Allen Embry, a Baptist preacher Feb. 13, 1824. Mrs. Embry died leaving issue, and Elder Allen Embry married again Oct. 22, 1844, to Mrs. Nancy Dudley, and again Sept. 27, 1858, to Mrs. Susannah Hume nee Miller, and again to Miss —— Renfroe. (See Part I, Chapter 9.) The children of Samiramus Moberley and Elder Allen Embry, were:

1. Ann Elizabeth Embry; married John F. Burnam April 28, 1841, issue:

1. Allen Embry Burnam; married Julia Burnam, of Bowling Green, Ky.

2. Richard M. Embry; married Elizabeth Hull of Fleming County, Ky. Their children:

1. Samiramus Embry; married William Hull.

2. Susan Embry; married Mr. —— Rash of Fleming County, Ky.

3. Thomas Embry.

4. Sarah Embry; married —— ——

3. Leonidas Embry; married Mrs. Nannie Embry nee Hood, widow of his brother William, and had:

1. Richard Embry, a lawyer of California, Missouri.

4. William R. Embry; married Nannie Hood. Their children:

1. Irene Embry.

2. Ann Embry.

3. William Embry.

4. Allen Embry. And three other children, names not furnished.

5. Lucilla Embry; married Francis M. Hampton Sept. 14, 1852. Their children:

1. Bettie Hampton; married Joseph Hedden, of Shelbyville, Ky. They now live in Mt. Sterling, Ky.

2. Franky Hampton.

6. Talton D. Embry; married firstly America Huls, and secondly a Jessamine County lady. He had a son of his first marriage:

1. Allen Embry.

7. Dr. Gideon Embry; married Bettie Smith of Irvine, Ky., where their home is, and where Dr. Embry practices medicine, issue:

1. Maude Embry.

8. Josephine Embry; married Abner Oldham. Their home was for a number of years in Madison County; they finally moved to Lexington, Ky., and Mr. Oldham has been a Justice of the Peace there a number of years. (See Part VI, Chap. 29.)

2. Nancy Moberley; married Ambrose F. Dudley Sept. 11, 1827. They lived and died in Madison County, Ky. Their children:

1. Mary E. Dudley; married Nathaniel Hart.

2. Ambrose J. Dudley; married Susan Gilbert, issue:

1. Gilbert Dudley; married —— ——

2. Lucy Dudley; married David Doty. (See Chap. 11, Sec. 1.)

3. Bessie Dudley, teacher in the Caldwell High School, Richmond, Ky.
4. Gordon Dudley.
5. Herndon Dudley.
6. Charles Dudley.

3. Thomas P. Dudley; married Mary Gentry. He was killed by runaway of horse he was driving attached to buggy, issue:
1. Richard M. Dudley.
2. Ambrose J. Dudley.
3. Sallie Dudley; married Jonah Wagers.
4. William Dudley.
5. James Dudley.

4. Samira E. Dudley.

5. Rev. Richard M. Dudley; married first Bettie Thompson, of South Carolina, and second Miss Hinton of Bourbon County, Kentucky. He was until his death, Chief Officer of the Georgetown Baptist School, and a prominent minister of the Baptist Church.

Mrs. Nancy Dudley; married the second time Elder Allen Embry, October 22, 1844.

3. Thomas Shelton Moberley, was a practitioner of medicine, and an extensive farmer, capitalist and large land holder. He married Nancy Lipscomb March 5, 1844. They had a son:

1. Thomas Shelton Moberley, Jr., the noted handler, breeder and raiser of short horn cattle of Madison County, his herd winning the prize and wearing the blue string at the World's Fair or Great Columbian Exposition, Chicago, where cattle were shown from all parts of the world. He married Ida Brassfield. Their children:
1. Geneva Moberley; died when approaching womanhood.
2. Neville Moberley; married Jean Amsden.

Section 3. Lucy Shelton; married Jonathan Estill July 25, 1798. The Circuit Court records, (Clay vs Estill) deed book A, page 329, June 1838, mentions Jonathan Estill's heirs, towit:
1. James Estill.
2. Benjamin Estill.
3. John Estill.
4. William Estill.

And other unknown heirs.

Note: Early marriages of members of the Shelton family in Madison County, Ky., some of whom were children of Thomas Shelton and Eliazbeth Woods Kavanaugh:

Shelton, George, married Elizabeth Miller Nov. 15, 1795.
Shelton, Lucy—Jonathan Estill July 25, 1798.
Shelton, Elizabeth—Richard Moberley March 3, 1802.
Shelton, Susan—Thomas Reid July 29, 1806.
Shelton, Hannah—John H. Bray Dec. 24, 1807.
Shelton, Elizabeth—Edward Bray March 5, 1812.
Shelton, Polly—Richard Bray Dec. 30, 1814.
Shelton, Polly—William Carr March 1, 1814.

CHAPTER 5.

WILLIAM WOODS KAVANAUGH

Known as Big Bill Kavanaugh

(Named in Chapter 4, Section 1.)

Article 1.—William Woods Kavanaugh, known as Big Bill Kavanaugh, a son of Philemon Kavanaugh and Elizabeth Woods his wife, was born in Culpeper County, Va., Nov. 9, 1776, and came to Madison County, Ky., prior to 1787, for on the 25th day of Sept. 1787, by an order of the Madison County Court, his step-father, Thomas Shelton, and his uncle Archibald Woods, were appointed guardians to him and his sister Ann, as well as administrators of his father's estate.

How long at that time, he had been in Kentucky, the writer does not know. Information has been furnished by members of the family that his father Philemon Kavanaugh, was killed by Indians on the Wilderness Road, from Virginia to Kentucky.

In the will of Charles Kavanaugh, Sr., of Madison County, Ky., his grand-father referrence is made to the two children of his eldest son Philemon, then deceased, giving to each five shillings. These two children at the date of said will were about grown. He married in Madison County, Ky., June 13, 1798, Eliabeth Miller, a daughter of Colonel John Miller and Jane Dulaney his wife. (See Part I, Chapter 14, Section 6.) They moved to Franklin County, Tenn.

He was drowned Dec. 14, 1814, while attempting to swim the Tennessee River on horse-back, the stream at the time being much swollen by heavy rains. His numerous descendants are in the Counties of Madison and Garrard, Kentucky, Franklin and Lincoln Counties, Tenn., and elsewhere. Their children:

JOHN MILLER KAVANAUGH

Section 1. John Miller Kavanaugh; born Dec. 31, 1799, in Madison County, Ky. He went to Tennessee. On the tenth day of Dec. 1822, he was married in Franklin County, Tenn., to Samiramus Shelton Woods, daughter of William Woods and Mary Harris his wife. (See Part II, Chap. 10, Sec. 3, and Part 3, Chap. 9,) she died Sept. 16, 1841. Their children:

1. Elizabeth Kavanaugh of Lincoln County, Tenn., she married Mr. —— Turner, and lived in said County. Their children:
    1. James Henry Turner.
    2. Sue Lou Turner.
    3. —— Turner, a son.
2. William Kavanauugh.
3. Robert Kavanaugh.
4. Thomas Kavanaugh.
5. Mourning Kavanaugh.
6. Margaret Kavanaugh.
7. Mary Jane Kavanaugh, the second wife of Major Thomas G. Miller. (See Part I, Chap. 14, Sec. 10.)

Section 2. Elizabeth Woods Kavanaugh, born July 14, 1801. She married in Madison County, Ky., Aug. 6, 1818, James Argo, and they settled on Paint Lick Creek, in Garrard County, Ky. Their children:

1. Nancy Argo; married Dr. C. T. Spillman.
2. Amelia Jane Argo; married James Adams.
3. Robert Argo, was twice married. His second wife was Margaret Henderson. Their children:
   1. William Argo; married Isabella Chenault. (See Part VI, Chap. 14, Section 4.)
   2. John Argo, went to Colorado.

Section 3. Philemon Kavanaugh, born May 29, 1803. He married Margaret Palmer. Their children:

1. Dulaney Kavanaugh.
2. John Kavanaugh.
3. Samiramus Kavanaugh.
4. Amelia Kavanaugh.
5. Sophia B. Kavanaugh.

Section 4. Amelia J. Kavanaugh, born June 2, 1805, she married James Graham Denny, a prominent farmer of Lincoln County, Ky. Their children:

1. William Kavanaugh Denny, formerly a citizen of Garrard County, Ky., afterwards a merchant of Richmond, Ky. When he left Richmond, went to a farm in Garrard County, near old Paint Lick Church. He now makes his home in Virginia. [Died since going to press.] He was twice married, his first wife was Miss—— Moran, his second wife was Miss Kate Basket nee Smith. Had one daughter by his first wife:
   1. Lizzie Denny; married Filmore Arbuckle.

   Had also one daughter by his second wife:
   2. Willie May Denny; married Isaac Steinberger of Virginia. Their children:
      1. Sarah Van Meter Steinberger.
      2. —— —— Steinberger.
      3. - —— —— Steinberger.
2. Alexander R. Denny; married Pauline Lackey. Their home was in Garrard County, Ky. Their children:
   1. Mattie Denny; married James Duncan.
   2. Sallie Denny; married Jesse Hocker, of Stanford, Ky.
   3. Cabel Denny; married Ada Farra.
3. Archibald K. Denny; married first Belle Givens, and secondly Pattie Givens. His home was in Garrard County, Ky. Children by his first wife:
   1. Richard Denny.
   2. James Denny.
   3. Logan Denny.

   Child by his second wife:
   4. Belle Denny.
4. James Denny; married Mary Beatty. They live in Garrard County, Ky. Their children:
   1. William K. Denny.
   2. Alexander R. Denny.
   3. Samuel Murrell Denny.
   4. Marshall Kavanaugh Denny.
   5. Kate Lee Denny.
5. Sallie Denny; married Dr. —— Bosley.
6. Lizzie Denny; married Finley Denny, of Kansas City, Mo.
7. Maggie Denny; married Isaac Pearson, of Harrodsburg, Ky. Their children:
   1. Amelia Pearson; married Mr. —— Cooper, of Lebanon, Kentucky.

2. Jack Pearson.
3. Clarence Pearson.
4. Charles Pearson.

8. Amelia Denny; married Philip Cooper, of Lebanon, Ky.

JANE MILLER KAVANAUGH.
Wife of Capt. John K. Faulkner and John W. Walker.

Section 5. Jane Miller Kavanaugh, born Oct. 20, 1809. She married first, General John Faulkner, of Garrard County, Ky., and secondly, John W. Walker, a very prominent citizen of Garrard County, Ky. Children of the first marriage:

1. Margaret Faulkner; married William White, of Madison County, Ky., she married secondly Rev. Robert J. Breckinridge, and thirdly Rev. Robert L. Breck. There were no issues of the last two marriages. Children of the first marriage:

1. John F. White; married Lizzie Field, daughter of Ezekiel H. Field.
2. Jennie White; married John Duncan Goodloe. (See Part II, Chap. 11, Section 6.)
3. George D. White; married his cousin Jennie Faulkner. (Sub Sec. 5, below.)

2. Mary Faulkner; married William Lusk. Their children:

1. George Lusk; married Georgia Miller.
2. Jennie Lusk; married Rev. Hervey MacDowell, live in Pass Christian, Mississippi.
3. Faulkner Lusk.
4. William Lusk.
5. Eliza Lusk; married Lewis L. Walker.

3. Colonel John K. Faulkner, was a Colonel in the Federal Army, in the Civil War. He married Elizabeth Bell. Their children:

1. Jennie Faulkner; married her cousin George D. White.
2. Pattie Faulkner; married James Engleman.
3. John K. Faulkner; died single.

4. Lizzie Faulkner; married George Denny, a farmer of Garrard County, Ky. Had no children.

Children of the second marriage of Mrs. Jane Miller Kavanaugh Faulkner and John W. Walker:

5. W. Stephen Walker, a well known and prominent citizen of Garrard County, Ky. He married first Belle Denny and secondly Frances Terrell. Had one daughter by his first wife:

1. Lizzie Walker; dead; married Mr. —— Bowlin.

Children by his second wife:

2. John Walker.
3. Ed Walker; dead.
4. Toles Walker; married Maud Moffett.
5. Archibald Walker.
6. Margaret Walker.
7. Robert Walker.
8. Belle Walker; died single.

6. Ed H. Walker; married Lizzie Woods. (See Part II, Chap. 20, Section 3.) Their children:

1. Mary Walker.
2. Woods Walker; married Sallie May.
3. Ed Walker; dead.
4. Jane Walker.
5. Mattie Walker.
6. Margaret Walker; married Luther Gibbs, issue:
   1. Elizabeth Gibbs.

7. Wade H. Walker; married Florence Moran. Their children:
   1. Dr. Frank Walker.
   2. Estille Walker.

8. Jennie Walker; married Rice McClain. Had one child:
   1. Jennie McClain; married Givens Terrell.

9. Archibald Kavanaugh Walker; married first Miss Sabra Owsley, daughter of Dr. John Owsley, of Lincoln County, Ky., and secondly, Susan Francis, daughter of Joseph Francis. Children by his first wife:

   1. Isabel Walker.
   2. John Walker, served as a soldier in the war with Spain, and died since the war.
   3. Walter Walker; married ———
   4. Ed Walker.
   5. Stephen Walker.

   Chilren of the second marriage:

   6. J. Wade Walker.
   7. Thomas Walker.
   8. Joseph Walker.

Section 6. Dulaney Miller Kavanaugh, born May 15, 1811, died single.

ARCHIBALD W. KAVANAUGH

Section 7. Archibald Woods Kavanaugh, born July 13, 1813, was an influential citizen and substantial farmer of Garrard County, Ky. He married Dorcas Lackey, a daughter of William Lackey and Miss Wilson his wife. Their children:

1. William Kavanaugh, was at one time elected Clerk of the Garrard Circuit Court, served one term. He married Jemima Royston. Their children:
   1. John Kavanaugh; dead.
   2. Jennie Kavanaugh.

2. Archibald Kavanaugh, a well to do farmer of Garrard County, Ky. He married Eda Francis. Their children:
   1. Edna Kavanaugh.
   2. Martha Kavanaugh.
   3. Joe Kavanaugh.
   4. William Kavanaugh.
   5. ——— Walker Kavanaugh.
   6. Benjamin Hudson Kavanaugh.

3. Lizzie Kavanaugh; married John Lewis Francis, a farmer residing a mile and a half east of Richmond, Ky., on his farm, his father's old home. Their children:
   1. Dorcas Francis, a school teacher, holding a first class certificate.
   2. Archibald Kavanaugh Francis.
   3. J. Lewis Francis.

4. Amelia Kavanaugh, now living with her sister Mrs. J. Lewis Francis, unmarried.

5. Mattie Kavanaugh; became the second wife of Daniel M. Terrill, late a farmer of Madison County, Ky. (See Part V, Chapter 12, Section 17.) She is now a widow living in Richmond, Kentucky.

6. Susan Kavanaugh; married Benjamin F. Level, issue:
   1. William Kavanaugh Level; married Minnie Arnold, issue:
      1. William Kavanaugh Level.
      2. Clay Level.
   2. John Y. Level.
   3. Dorcas K. Level.
   4. Susan Frances Level.
   5. Benjamin F. Level.
   6. Archibald K. Level.

7. Dulaney Kavanaugh; died single.

William Woods Kavanaugh, named at the head of this Chapter, was living in Franklin County, Tenn., June 15, 1811, as appears from a power of attorney he executed to Robert Miller, his brother-in-law, of record in the clerk's office of the Madison County Court, in deed book H, page 139. After his death his widow, Elizabeth Miller Kavanaugh, married Thomas Kennedy Nov. 9, 1820.

CHAPTER 6.

ANN KAVANAUGH.

(Named in Chapter 4, Section 2.)

Article 1.—Ann Kavanaugh, a daughter of Philemon Kavanaugh and Elizabeth Woods his wife, came from Culpeper County, Va., to Madison County, Ky., prior to the year 1787.

On the 25th day of Sept. 1787, her uncle Archibald Woods, and her step-father Thomas Shelton, were appointed guardians for her and her brohter, William Woods Kavanaugh, as well as administrators of her father's estate. Her grand-father Charles Kavanaugh, Sr., of Madison County, Ky., in his will, gave the two children of his eldest son Philemon, five shillings each, (being this subject Ann, and her said brother.) In the order of Court appointing guardians the wards are styled "Orphans of Philemon Kavanaugh, deceased." On the 12th day of June 1794, in Madison County, Ky., she was married to Benjamin Estill. Their children:

Section 1. James Estill; married —— ——. Their children:
1. Horatio H. Estill.
2. William Kavanaugh Estill.
3. Isaac V. Estill.
4. Robert G. Estill.
5. James W. Estill.
6. Benjamin Estill.
7. Elizabeth A. Estill; married Philip Baldwin.
8. Tantha Estill; married Boone Davis.
9. Cornelia C. Estill; married Mr. —— Tunnel.

10. Rachael W. Estill; married Robert Mullens. Their children:
   1. Fannie M. Mullens.
   2. Ardora A. Mullens.
   3. Jemima E. Mullens.
   4. Isaac Mullens.
   5. Leland Mullens.
11. Fannie E. Estill; married Mr. —— Cobb. Their children:
   1. Mary V. Cobb.
   2. Cora E. Cobb.
   3. Fannie J. Cobb.
   4. James A. Cobb.
   5. Rhoda Cobb.
   6. B. Cobb.
12. Annetta B. Estill.
13. Sallie M. Estill.

Section 2. Susan Estill; married William Timberlake. Their children:

1. John Timberlake.
2. James E. Timberlake.
3. Mary Timberlake; married Mr. —— Wright.
4. Annie Timberlake.

Section 3. Martha Estill; died childless.

Section 4. Philemon Kavanaugh Estill; married —— —— .

Section 5. Benjamin Estill; married —— —— died childless.

Section 6. Rachael Estill; married Richard Timberlake. Their children:

1. John Timberlake; married Mary A—— ——, and he died, and his widow became the second wife of Peter W. Estill. (See Section 9.) Children of John Timberlake and Mary A —— his wife:
   1. Lucy Timberlake.
   2. Annie Timberlake.
   3. Estill Timberlake.
2. Benjamin Timberlake.
3. Ellen Timberlake; married Mr. —— Younger.

Section 7. Jonathan P. Estill; married Judith Rogers. Had one son:

1. Richard Estill; died at about the age of twenty years.

Section 8 Sarah Estill; married John McPherson. Their children:

1. John W. McPherson, was a gallant soldier in General John H. Morgan's command, of the Confederate Army, and was captured on Morgan's Ohio and Indiana raid in 1862, and imprisoned at Camp Morton, Indiana. In removing the prisoners from said prison to Camp Douglas, Illinois, John W. McPherson and Robert D. Miller jumped from the train of cars and made their escape together. (See Part I, Chap. 13, Sec. 2.) John W. McPerson married Bettie Baldwin. (See Part VI, Chap. 10, Sec. 4.)
2. William Kavanaugh McPherson.
3. Sallie McPherson; married James Rice.

Section 9. Peter W. Estill; married first, Sarah Cochran Oct. 7, 1852, she died childless, and he married again Mary A. Timberlake, widow of John Timberlake, son of Richard Timberlake and Rachael Estill his wife. (See Section 6.)

Section 10. Wallace Estill; married —— —— Had one son:

1. Wallace Estill; married —— —— Their children:

1. Robert W. Estill.
2. Ben D. Estill; married Julietta —— Their children:
   1. Clarence Estill.
   2. Alice Estill.
   3. Laura Estill.

CHAPTER 7.

MARY KAVANAUGH.

(Named in Chapter 3, Section 2.)

Article 1.—Mary Kavanaugh, a daughter of Charles Kavanaugh, senior and Ann his wife, came from Culpeper County, Va., to Madison County. On the first day of September, 1787, she was married to Joseph Ellison.

Mr. Ellison was born Jan. 11, 1758, and died May 7, 1830. She was a legatee of her father's will, and she and her husband on the 23rd day of Oct. 1797, joined with the other heirs in the deeds conveying to the Yanceys lands in Culpeper County. Mr. Ellison and his wife lived and died in Madison County, Ky. His will bears date Dec. 4, 1814, and was witnessed by Christopher Harris and Harvey Beatty. He owned considerable land and a number of negro slaves. In his will he made provision for his wife Mary, and his two children and their husbands. Their children:

Section 1. Nancy Ellison, born Sept. 5, 1788, died Dec. 6, 1837. She married Nicholas Hocker, who was born Jan. 11, 1782, and died Dec. 6, 1854. They were members of Viney Fork Baptist Church. Nicholas Hocker in his day, was one of the most substantial citizens and farmers of Madison County, their children:

1. Joseph Ellison Hocker, born April 23, 1805, moved to Seneca, Kansas. On the fifth day of Dec. 1831, he married Elzira Brassfield, daughter of James E. Brassfield and Tabitha Moberley his wife; she died, and on the fifth day of Jan. 1832, he married the second time ——— ——— His children, viz:
   1. Ann Maria Hocker; married Joseph Lipscomb Oct. 7, 1853. Their home was in Los Angeles, California.
   2. Mildred Hocker, home Los Angeles, California.
   3. Mary Hocker; married Mr. —— Williams; home Dever, Colorada.
   4. Clara Hocker.
   5. George Hocker.
   6. Nicholas Hocker; home was in Arizona.
   7. James Hocker.
2. Alfred Hocker, born Feb. 16, 1807; died Sept. 15, 1808.
3. Elzira Hocker, born May 28, 1809; died July 24, 1852. She married George W. Broaddus, a Baptist preacher Dec. 11, 1828, issue:
   1. Henry Clay Broaddus; married first Elizabeth Bush, and second Mrs. Nancy Tribble, issue of first marriage:
      1. George W. Broaddus; died when a school boy.
      2. Pleasant Bush Broaddus; married Hallie Simmons, no

issue. Elected by Democrats, and now sheriff of Madison County, Kentucky.

3. Hyman G. Broaddus; died young.
4. Jennie Broaddus; married Presley F. Stillings.
5. Elvira Broaddus; married Christopher Harris Park. (See Part III, Chap. 34, Sec. 2, and Part VI, Chap. 31, Sec. 1.)
6. Bessie Broaddus; married John T. Embry. (See Part I, Chap. 9, Section 3.)
7. Cora Lee Broaddus; married Thomas M. Wells.

2. Mary A. Broaddus; married Lewis C. Haggard Sept. 6, 1855, issue:

1. Powhatan Haggard.
2. Walter Haggard.
3. Dixie Haggard.
4. George Haggard.
5. Joseph Haggard.

3. James Broaddus; died.

4. Mildred Broaddus; married William F. Berry, issue:

1. Clay Berry.

5. Martha Broaddus; married first Thomas Burgess, and second Isaac Newton Hill, issue of second marriage:

1. Pattie Hill.

6. William Andrew Broaddus; married Cassie Woods. Had one child, died in infancy, and they are both dead.

7. Thomas Miller Broaddus, author of "Broaddus Complete Family Record." He married Alice Dejarnatt. They live in Shawnee, Oklahoma. Mr. Broaddus has been clerk of the Court there for a number of years, issue:

1. Clay Broaddus.
2. Nicholas Broaddus.

4. George W. Hocker, born June 19, 1811; died April 4, 1830.
5. James Hocker, born Nov. 22, 1813; died June 18, 1814.
6. James D. Hocker, born Sept. 1, 1815; died April 18, 1840.
7. Nicholas Hocker, born March 5, 1818; died July 31, 1843.
8. William K. Hocker, born June 5, 1820; died Mrach 28, 1897. He married first Miss Sallie Feris, second Virginia Brown, daughter of Ira Benajah Brown and Frances Jarman Mullins Nov. 5, 1846. (See Part VIII, Chap. 14, Section 3.) He married the third time Irene Faris. Issue of first marriage:

1. Ellen Hocker; died young.

Issue of second marriage to Miss Brown:

1. Fannie Hocker; married Samuel Shanks, a wealthy citizen of Lincoln County, Ky., issue:
   1. Ella Shanks; married Thomas Rice.
   2. William Hocker Shanks; married Lena Baldwin. (See Part VI, Chap. 10, Sec. 4, and Part VIII, Chap. 14.)
   3. Frances Shanks; married William Tate.
2. Nicholas Hocker; died of small pox in 186—.
3. Mary Brown Hocker; married Samuel Calhoun Roan of Mississippi. Had four or five children, all died in infancy, and she died, and Mr. Roan married again.
4. Nannie Hocker; married Lewis Simpson, a stirring business man, now at Waco, Texas, connected with the large lumber firm of William Cameron and Co. Since going to press they have moved to Quannah, Texas, running a large lumber establishment. Issue:
   1. Lewis Simpson.
   2. Nannette Simpson.

3. Lucy Simpson.
4. Miss Willie Simpson.

5. Lucy Hocker; married Dr. Powhatan Trueheart, a noted physician of Sterling, Kansas, issue:

1. Marion Trueheart, a practicing physician, now in partnership with his father at Sterling, Kansas.
2. Virginia Trueheart.

6. Jennie (Virginia) Hocker; married Charles Beckett, a stockman of Kansas City, Mo., and has a ranch in Texas, issue:

1. Harry Beckett, attorney at law.
2. Frances Beckett.

7. Miss Willie Kavanaugh Hocker, lives at Wabasecka, Ark., a highly educated and accomplished lady.

9. Martha Ann Hocker, born Aug. 28, 1822; married William Lackey, a substantial citizen of Lincoln County, both highly respected and regarded; died at Stanford, Ky., issue:

1. Samuel E. Lackey; married Susan Alexander, and lives at Gallatin, Tenn. (See Part I, Chap. 14, Sec. 10-6-a.)
2. Nicholas Hocker Lackey; died a bachelor.

10. Mary Jane Hocker, born Feb. 21, 1825; died Jan. 25, 1905. She married Colonel Thomas Woods Miller June 1, 1841. (See Part I, Chap. 12.)

11. Robert Harris Hocker, born Sept. 8, 1827; died Oct. 19, 1843.

12. Jael Woods Hocker, born Feb. 27, 1831; married first Joel Gentry, and second Richard Gentry, brother to her first husband. (See Part I, Chap. 14, Sec. 2.) Issue of first marriage:

1. Nicholas Hocker Gentry of Sedalia Mo.
2. Ella Gentry; married Mr. Morrison. They live in Denver, Colorado.

Issue of the second marriage:

3. Mary Gentry; married Mr. Walburn, of New York City.
4. Richard Gentry, now dead, but he left three children.
5. Nannie Gentry; married Mr. Estill, of Sedalia, Mo.

Jael Woods Hocker, the wife of Joel Gentry and the widow of his brother Richard Gentry, is still living, she resides in Sedalia, Mo., on South Broadway. (See Part I, Chap. 14, Section 2-3.)

Section 2. Jael Ellison, born September 14, 1795; married Robert Harris. For further particulars see Part III, Chap. 17.

CHAPTER 8.

WILLIAM KAVANAUGH.

(Named in Chapter 3, Section 3.)

Article 1.—William Kavanaugh, a son of Charles Kavanaugh, Sr., and Ann —— his wife, was born in Culpeper County, Va.

He married Hannah Woods, a daughter of William Woods and Susannah Wallace his wife. (See Part II, Chap. 6, Sec. 11, and Part IV, Chap. 2, Sec. 2.) They came to Madison County, Ky., some time prior to 1787. William Kavanaugh was the trusted and well beloved son who went with a power of attorney from his father to

Yancey's. He was a legatee of his father's will, and one of the executors thereof, and he and his wife Hannah joined in the deeds in 1797 to the Yanceys.

October 5, 1790, he was recommended as a Lieutenant of militia and qualified as such Nov. 2, 1790. June 7, 1791, qualified as Captain of militia. In deed book C, page 346, is recorded a bond for title to 100 acres of land from Michael Wallace to him, dated March 3, 1795, reciting that said Kavanaugh had raised a cabin on said land. On the 31 day of August 1815, by deed (L page 78) he conveyed this bond to his son William Kavanaugh Jr., the title to which land was afterwards perfected in his son.

There is found (D page 102) April 7, 1791, a deed from John Reid to Archibald Woods and William Kavanaugh, to 400 acres of land on Muddy Creek being a pre-emption to include his mill seat and improvements, and (E page 396) Jan. 4, 1803, a deed from Thomas Mosely of Montgomery County, Ky., attorney in fact for John Guerant of Buckingham County, Va., to William Kavanaugh of Madison County, Ky., to 1000 acres of land on the head branch of Rockcastle. Sept. 15, 1817, he conveyed to his son-in-law Andrew Briscoe, (M page 143) 158½ acres of land on Muddy Creek.

He died in 1829, for his will dated March 15, 1823, was probated November 2, 1829, and recorded (E page 21) in which he appointed his son Charles Kavanaugh and William Goodloe executors thereof—Goodloe did not qualify and Charles Kavanaugh qualified and acted as sole executor. Therein he sets free certain negro slaves, and gave certain negroes land on Owsly's Fork. His wife Hannah having died and he having again, towit: on the 21, day of Sept. 1815 married Mrs. Ruth Booten. No issue however by this marriage, he in his will made bequests to his wife, Ruth, and special bequests to his son, Archibald and to two grand-children, a son and a daughter of his son, Nicholas Kavanaugh, deceased, and his daughter Susannah Duncan. His other property he directed to be divided equally between his children named in the will. His son William was not mentioned in the will, but testator many years before had deeded to said son the bond on Michael Wallace for the hundred acres of land.

In April 1784, William Kavanaugh, senior, was one of a party of scouts composed besides himself of Samuel Estill, Harris Massie, John Woods, Nicholas Proctor, John Mitchell, William McCreary, Azariah Martin and others, who left Estill's Station in pursuit of an Indian camp near the mouth of Station Camp Creek, and passed the Little Picture Lick, at or near the Bue Banks, where the Indians had blazed trees and painted pictures on the blazes with black and red paint.

The second wife of William Kavanaugh, senior, Mrs. Ruth Booten, was the widow of Favis Booten, and a daughter of Samuel Estill, and her daughter Mary Ann Booten, had married Thomas Harris, a son of Christopher Harris and Elizabeth Grubbs his wife, (See Part III, Chap. 12, Sec. 2,) and after Thomas Harris died, his widow Mary Ann, married Joel Embry, and among her Embry children was a son Thomas Harris Embry, named for her first husband, but this son was not a blood relative of her first husband.

William Kavanaugh's five sons, Philemon, William, Nicholas, Archibald and Charles, all served as soldiers in the war of 1812. There were no issues of the second marriage.

The children of William Kavanaugh senior, and Hannah Woods his wife were: (It is not claimed they are set forth in the order of birth.)

Section 1. Susannah Kavanaugh; married Isaac Duncan Sep. 21, 1795. The subject of Chapter 9.

Section 2. Annie Kavanaugh; married Andrew Briscoe, Sept. 25, 1796. The subject of Chapter 10. (See Part IV, Chap. 18, Sec. 2.)

Section 3. Polly Kavanaugh; married Hezekiah Oldham, Oct. 7, 1813. For further account see Part VI, Chapter 16.

Section 4. Sallie Kavanaugh; married ? Charles English. They went to Missouri.

Section 5. Philemon Kavanaugh; married Patsey Gilbert, a daughter of Samuel Gilbert. The subject of Chapter 16.

Section 6. Charles Kavanaugh; married Peggy Warren, a daughter of the old pioneer Thomas Warren, July 3, 1817. The subject of Chapter 11.

Section 7. Archibald Kavanaugh; married first Miss Baxter, and secondly Miss Winchester. He settled in Lexington, Mo. He was a soldier in the war of 1812. He raised a large family of children, among them were:

1. Colonel Charles Baxter Kavanaugh. Held the rank of Colonel in the United States Army. He went as a soldier with Donethen to California. His home was in Lexington, Mo.
2. A son; died at Santafe, New Mexico.
3. Phinis Ewing Kavanaugh, of Lexington, Mo.
4. ? Hannah Kavanaugh; married Benancy Cox, March 19, 1833.

Section 8. Nicholas Kavanaugh; married Jane Wallace, a daughter of Michael Wallace, and Jane Bratton his wife, Jan. 12, 1817. (See Part IV, Chap. 7, Section 2.) The subject of Chapter 12.

Section 9. William Kavanaugh. He was not mentioned in the will of his father, but owned and occupied one hundred acres of land, near Richmond, Ky., which his father on August 31, 1815, (L page 79) gave and conveyed to him, or rather gave him a bond for a title thereto, of Michael Wallace, which was afterwards perfected in said son, William Kavanaugh, Jr. He married Betsy Freeman, and moved to Anderson County, Ky., a number of years prior to the year 1832. On the 3rd of Feb. 1832, he and his wife Betsy, then living in Anderson County, conveyed said land to Edmund L. Shackelford. (Deed book — page 234). Their children were:

1. Ann Maria Kavanaugh; married William Whittington, formerly the husband of her deceased sister Susan Adela. Their children:
    1. Paul Whittington; died in infancy.
    2. Silas Whittington; died in infancy.
    3. Ann Adela Whittington; died in infancy.
2. Hon. George W. Kavanaugh. Formerly was Judge of the Anderson County Court. He represented Anderson County in the State Legislature in the years 1843 and 1850. He was a very popular and influencial citizen of the County. He married Miss Russel Wills. Their children:
    1. Caroline Kavanaugh; died unmarried.
    2. Elizabeth Kavanaugh; married George Phillips of Lebanon, Ky. She is now a widow and lives in New York City, and has one grown son:
        1. Roy Phillips.
    3. George Breckinridge Kavanaugh; died in early manhood, unmarried.
    4. Russel Kavanaugh; died unmarried.
    5. John Anderson Kavanaugh; married —— ——. He had no children.

3. Susan Adela Kavanaugh; married William Whittington. Their children:

1. Mary Adela Whittington, late of Daughter's College, Harrodsburg, Ky. She was one of the best educators, and most entellectual of her time. After she graduated she taught school all the remainder of her life, dying at the age of forty years past. Her remains were buried at Harrodsburg, and a monument erected by her pupils marks her grave. She was of the best product of the Kavanaugh family.

4. Araminta Kavanaugh; died young.

5. Charles Nicholas Kavanaugh; married Lucy Erwin Lillard. Their children:

1. Mary Kavanaugh; died in infancy.

2. Aileen Kavanaugh; married Dr. J. W. Gilbert, of Lawrenceburg, Ky. Their children:

1. Emma Gilbert.

2. William Kavanaugh Gilbert; died at the age of sixteen years.

3. Dr. John Whittington Gilbert.

4. George Hubbard Gilbert.

5. Roberts Gilbert; died in infancy.

6. James Freeman Gilbert.

3. Dr. Charles William Kavanaugh; married Susan Mary Mullins. Their children:

1. Charles Nicholas Kavanaugh.

2. A child; died in infancy.

3. A child; died in infancy.

Mrs. Kavanaugh died and Dr. Charles William Kavanaugh, married the second time Rhoda Caldwell. Their children:

4. Aileen Gilbert Kavanaugh.

5. Lucy Emrin Kavanaugh.

6. Dandrige Whitfield Kavanaugh; married Harriet Taylor. Their children:

1. Mary Edna Kavanaugh; died in infancy.

2. Ann Elizabeth Kavanaugh; died in infancy.

3. Dandrige Whitfield Kavanaugh; died unmarried.

7. Hubbard Hines Kavanaugh; died in infancy.

8. Thomas Archibald Kavanaugh; died leaving no children.

CHAPTER 9.

SUSAN KAVANAUGH.

(Named in Chapter 8, Section 1.)

Article 1.—Susan Kavanaugh, a daughter of William Kavanaugh and Hannah Wood his wife, came with her parents from Culpeper County, Va., to Madison County, Ky., prior to 1784.

On the 24th day of Sept. 1795, she married Isaac Duncan. (See The Duncan Family Chapter 18). They settled in Madison County, and raised a number of children:

Section 1. Philemon Duncan.

Section 2. Browning Duncan.

Section 3. William Duncan, born in Madson County, Ky., Nov. 24, 1799. He married Catherine Hume. She was born March 7, 1798, she died Feb. 17, 1840. William Duncan married second Betsy Hume, sister to his first wife. His second wife had no children:

Children of the first marriage:

1. George Hume Duncan: married Matilda Boyd, June 28, 1855, now owns and lives on the original Williams Kavanaugh farm on Muddy Creek. Their children:

1. William Duncan; married Susan Taylor.

2. June Duncan: married Mrs. Myrty Duncan, widow of his brother Harry.

3. John Duncan.

4. Lizzie Duncan; married William Terrill. (See Part V, Chapter 12, Section 17.)

5. Harry Duncan: married Myrty Tipton. He died and his widow married his brother June Duncan.

6. Hugh Duncan: married Juliet Chambers. (See Part VI, Chapter 11, Section 11.)

2. Archibald Kavanaugh Duncan, born April 24, 1835; died March 29, 1890. He married Mary Park, daughter of Elder John M. Park and Patsey Oldham his wife, who was born Feb 16, 1840. (See Part VI, Chap. 31, Sec. 1.) Their children:

1. Brutus Kavanaugh Duncan, born April 8, 1860; married Laura Oldham, daughter of Thomas H. Oldham and Nancy Smith his wife. (See Part VI, Chap. 31, Sec. 1, and Chap. 27, Section 6.) Their children:

1. Chenault Kavanaugh Duncan, born April 6, 1886.

2. Helen Ellis Duncan, born April 13, 1884.

3. Charles Duncan, born Feb. 1, 1896.

4. Archibald Kavanaugh Duncan, born April 24, 18—.

2. Mary Mills Duncan, born March 31, 1865; married Thomas Chenault. (See Part VI, Chap. 31, Sec. 1, and Part V, Chap. 13, Section 9.) Their children:

1. Archibald Cravens Chenault.

2. David Waller Chenault.

3. William Kavanaugh Duncan; died an old bachelor.

4. Susan Catherine Duncan; married her cousin Charles Kavanaugh Oldham. (See Part VI, Chap. 28.)

5. Caroline Duncan; married Shelton Harris. (See Part III, Chapter 14, Section 1.) Had one child that died in infancy.

CHAPTER 10.

ANNIE KAVANAUGH.

(Named in Chapter 8, Section 2.)

Article 1.—Annie Kavanaugh, a daughter of William Kavanaugh and Hannah Woods his wife, came from Culpeper County, Va., to Madison County, Ky., and on the 25th day of Feb. 1796, she married Andrew Briscoe, a son of Captain William Briscoe, and Elizabeth Wallace his wife. (See Part IV, Chap. 18, Sec. 2.)

The said Andrew Briscoe, was a legatee of his father's will, of record in the Clerk's office of the Madison County Court. On the 15th day of Sept. 1817, was the owner of and living on land on Muddy Creek, adjoining Colonel Barbee Collins, etc., see deed from his father-in-law William Kavanaugh, M. page 143. He went to Lexington, Mo., with his family.

CHAPTER 11.

CHARLES KAVANAUGH.

(Named in Chapter 8, Section 6.)

Article 1.—Charles Kavanaugh, a son of William Kavanaugh and Hannah Woods his wife, was born on the — day of —— 17—.

He owned and occupied valuable property near Richmond, Ky., where he lived; was an extensive farmer, owned a number of negro slaves, handled blooded horses, such as the noted Gray Eagle stock, at one time regarded as the best. He was exceedingly energetic and nervy. He was a soldier in the war of 1812. He was married to Peggy Warren, Jan. 3, 1817, and to them were born a number of children and his wife died and he lived a widower a great many years and died about the close of the civil war in 186—, was an ardent democrat, and strong out spoken southern sympathizer. Their children are named in the coming sections:

Section 1. Hannah Ann Kavanaugh; married Volney Doty the 2nd day of Sept. 1841, to whom were born:

1. Charles Kavanaugh Doty, was a soldier in the Confederate States Army of the Civil War of 1862, in General John H. Morgan's command. He married Mrs. Susan Sparks nee Turley, issue:
   1. Mary Doty; married Jesse Tudor.
   2. Edgar Doty.
2. Boyle Doty, was a Confederate soldier in General John H. Morgan's command, and was captured on the famous Ohio raid, and imprisoned at Camp Chase, and removed to Camp Douglas, where he was confined for eighteen months. He died in Madison County in 190— a bachelor.
3. Taylor Doty. Lives near Fort Worth, Texas. Has never married.
4. Azariah Doty, was killed in a combat in Richmond, Ky., after the close of the Civil War, in 1867-8, between Harris, Kavanaugh, etc., on one side and Paris, etc., on the other.
5. Maggie Doty; died when a young lady.
6. John Doty, born in Madison County, Ky., Nov. 25, 1852. He married Margaret Oldham, a daughter of William Kavanaugh Oldham and Jacintha Catherine Brown his wife, the 16th day of December 1884. (See Part VI, Chap. 22.) He owns valuable property in Richmond, Ky., and a good farm near the town. He moved to town some years since to educate his children, the issues of the marriage are:
   1. William Kavanaugh Doty, born Saturday Jan. 30, 1886, at 11 o'clock a. m.
   2. John Doty, born Tuesday, Oct. 18, 1887, at 10 o'clock a. m.
   3. Eagle Doty, born Wednesday Jan. 8, 1890, at 3 o'clock a. m.
   4. Mary Doty, born Oct. 30, 1891, at 6.30 o'clock a. m.
   5. Hezekiah Doty, born Oct. 10, 1893.
   6. A daughter, born Sept. 21, 1894, lived only a short period.
   7. Oldham Doty, born Jan. 10, 1899.
   8. Margaret Doty, born Sunday, Sept. 21, 1902.
7. Volney Doty, born 185—; married Nannie Kavanaugh, a daughter of his uncle Archibald W. Kavanaugh and Sarah Maupin his wife. (See Section 3.) Many years ago, they moved to Texas, and they live not a great distance from Fort Worth. To them were born:
   1. Maggie Doty; married Ernest Rout.

2. Sallie Doty.
3. Eunice Doty.
4. Lizzie Doty.
5. Lena Doty.
6. Virgie Doty.
7. Volney J. Doty

8. Archibald Kavanaugh Doty, born in Madison County, Ky., in 185—. He married Elizabeth Francis, a daughter of John W. Francis and Susan —— his wife, to whom were born:

1. Susan Doty.
2. Russel Doty.
3. Archibald Doty.
4. Geneva Doty.

9. David C. Doty, was born in Madison County, Ky., 18—. He married Lucy —— Dudley, a daughter of Ambrose J. Dudley and Susan Gilbert his wife. He was elected a magistrate of the County, and whilst such, was assassinated in the night time at his own barn, by a gang of negro thieves and desperadoes—only one of the gang paying the penalty on the gallows at Richmond under a judgment of the Circuit Court of the County. (See Chap. 4, Section 2.) He left these children:

1. Gordon Doty.
2. Dudley Doty, a daughter.

10. Robert E. Lee Doty; married Arie Lackey, they live now in Madison County, Ky., near Richmond. (See Part I, Chap. 14, Section 11.) To them has been born:

1. Robert Doty.
2. Hannah Doty.
3. Emma Doty.
4. Elizabeth Doty.
5. Malcom Doty.

11. Thoams J. Doty, twin to Elizabeth Doty; married first Mary Kavanaugh, a daughter of Archibald W. Kavanaugh, and Sarah Maupin his wife. (See Section 3-3.) To whom were born:

1. Lizzie Doty.
2. Archibald Doty; died at six months of age.

Thomas J. Doty's wife died and he married her sister Ophelia Kavanaugh. (See Sec. 3-4.) No issue. Both of his wives were his first cousins. He lives in the Indian Territory.

12. Elizabeth Doty, twin to Thomas J., died young.

Section 2. Susan Kavanaugh; died young.

Section 3. Archibald Woods Kavanaugh, was born in Madison County, Ky., and was a soldier in the army of the Confederate states, in the Civil War of 1862. After the war, in the fight at Richmond, in which his Nephew Azariah Doty, was killed, he received a severe wound. He married Sarah Maupin, a daughter of Daniel C. Maupin and Nancy Walker his wife, (See Part V, Chap. 12, Sec. 16-4), and he was for a number of years a popular and highly respected citizen of Madison County, Ky., where most of his children were born, but for a number of years he has lived in the west in the State of Kansas, Post Office Vinton, now living there, and is upwards of 78 years of age. The following children were born to him and his wife:

1. Nannie Kavanaugh; married Volney J. Doty, her first cousin. (See Section 1-7.)

2. Maggie Kavanaugh; married Ben Lesert, to whom were born:

1. Willie Lessert.
2. Wade Lessert.

3. Susie Lessert.
4. Fay Lessert.
5. Clemmie Lessert.
6. Harry Lessert.
7. ——— Lessert.

They live in Indian Territory.

3. Mary Kavanaugh; married Thomas J. Doty, her first cousin, to whom were born: (See Section 1-11.)
   1. Lizzie Doty.
   2. Archibald Doty.
4. Ophelia Kavanaugh; married and became the second wife of her cousin Thomas J. Doty, formerly the husband of her sister Mary. (See Section 1-11). No issue.
5. Jennie Kavanaugh; married Samuel Waldschmidt, to whom were born:
   1. Sallie Waldschmidt.
   2. Bena Waldschmidt.
   3. Margaret Waldschmidt.
   4. Frank Waldschmidt.

They live in Kansas.

6. Charles Kavanaugh; married Dana Stagnor, issue:
   1. Archibald Kavanaugh.
   2. Anne ——— Kavanaugh.
7. William Kavanaugh; married Dana Kavanaugh, the widow of his brother Charles, no issue. They live in Kansas.
8. John Kavanaugh.

Section 4. Humphrey Kavanaugh, was born in Madison County, Ky. He never married. After the close of the Civil war, he was severely wounded in the fight in the town of Richmond, in which his Nephew Azariah Doty was killed, and was moved to the house of James Shaw, Sr., on his father's land, and one night whilst sitting propped up in bed near and in front of a window to his room, a fatal shot fired through the window by an unknown assassin ended his life. He was a soldier in the Mexican War.

CHAPTER 12.

NICHOLAS KAVANAUGH.

(Named in Chapter 8, Section 8.)

Article 1.—Nicholas Kavanaugh, a son of William Kavanaugh and Hannah Woods his wife, was born in Madison County, Ky.

On the 12th day of Jan. 1817, he married Jane Wallace, a daughter of Michael Wallace and Jane Bratton his wife, (see Part IV, Chap. 7, Sec. 2,) and went to Missouri. He was on an occasion captured by the Indians and held captive some time, and made run the gauntlet, which he did, and knocked some of the savages down, and secured his liberty. He died and his widow married again Mr. Canole. Nicholas Kavanaugh was a soldier in the war of 1812. On the 18th day of March 1817, (M page 85) he and his wife Jane, conveyed to William Kavanaugh the interest of his wife in the lands of her deceased father, Michael Wallace, lying in or adjacent to the town of Richmond, Ky. Their home was in Lone Jack, Jackson County, Mo. When his father died in 1829, Nicholas Kavanaugh, was dead, but how long he had been dead, no evidence is at hand, he left a son, and a daughter, who were made special bequests by their grand-father William Kavanaugh, in his will, but he failed to set forth in the will the names of these two grand-children. The name of the son was probably:

Section 1. Malcolm Kavanaugh.

The son mentioned in William Kavanaugh's will, supposed.

Section 2. Miss —— Kavanaugh, a daughter mentioned in Wililam Kavanaugh's will.

The Hannah Kavanaugh who married Benancy Cox, March 9, 1833, was probably the daughter of Nicholas Kavanaugh.

We have been unable to gather any data concerning these two children of Nicholas Kavanaugh and Jane Wallace his wife.

CHAPTER 13.

CHARLES KAVANAUGH, Jr.

(Named in Chapter 3, Section 4.)

Article 1.—Charles Kavanaugh, Jr., a son of Chares Kavanaugh Sr., and Ann —— his wife, was born in Culpeper County, Va.

As early as or prior to 1787, being then a grown man, he came from the place of his birth to Madison County, Ky. In the first Order Book (A) of the Madison County Court, at the date Feb. 27, 1787, appears this entry:

"On motion of Charles Kavanaugh, Jr., it is ordered that his ear mark towit: A crop in the right, and a hole in the left ear, be recorded." October 6, 1789, he "produced his commission and qualified as Captain of militia. Oct. 2, 1792, he was authorized to celebrate the rites of matrimony being in regular communion with the Methodist Church. His wife was named Frances, for he joined as one of the grantors in the deeds to the Yanceys of Culpeper County, Va., as one of the legatees of his father's will in 1797, in which deeds his wife's name appears to be Frances, and other deeds show that her name was Frances, and he evidently married before immigrating to Kentucky.

It seems from Court records, that this Charles Kavanaugh, Jr., his uncle Williams Kavanaugh, and his cousin Charles Kavanaugh, a son of said Williams went from Madison County, Ky., to Tennessee, prior to 1804, for it is found of record that the two latter acknowledged deeds as early as 1804, in Smith County, Tenn., to lands in Madison County, Ky. If he had any children, they are unknown to the writer at this time. Charles Kavanaugh, Jr., and Frances his wife were residents of Rutherford County, Tenn., Sept. 15, 1815. See deed to James McMullin (L page 18).

CHAPTER 14.

JAEL KAVANAUGH.

(Named in Chapter 3, Section 5.)

Article 1.—Jael Kavanaugh, a daughter of Charles Kavanaugh, Sr., and Ann —— his wife, was born in Culpeper County, Va., she came to Madison County, Ky.

She married Peter Woods, a son of William Woods and Susannah Wallace his wife. (See Part II, Chap. 6, Sec. 3, and Part IV, Chaptr 2, Section 2.) Peter Woods was a noted pioneer Baptist preacher. They remained some time in Madison County, Ky., where he did much preaching of the gospel, and solemnized very many marital rites. He moved to Tennessee, thence to Boone County, Mo., and they spent their remaining days in Missouri. He died in Cooper County in 1825.

It is said that he raised a large family, but at this time the writer is unable to give the names of his children. His wife Jael, was a egatee of her father's will and she and her husband in 1797, joined in the deeds to the Yancey's of Culpeper County, Va.

CHAPTER 15.

SARAH ANN KAVANAUGH.

Named in Chapter 3, Section 6.)

Article 1.—Sarah Ann Kavanaugh, a daughter of Charles Kavanaugh Sr., and Ann —— his wife, came from Culpeper County, Va., to Kentucky with her parents and her husband, James Mills Moore, who she married in Virginia.

They setted finally on the Kentucky River, near the line between Estill and Madison on land given them by Mr. Kavanaugh. Sarah Ann Kavanaugh and her husband James Mills Moore, and two children which they had at the time her father prepared his will in 1795, Charles Kavanaugh Moore and Elizabeth Moore were legatees of his will. They owned at one time lands on Otter Creek, which they sold in 1797 and 1798. They had at least three children named in the coming sections:

Section 1. Charles Kavanaugh Moore, a legatee of his grandfather's will, descendants of whom are now on the Kentucky River and scattered over Madison and Estill Counties.

Section 2. Elizabeth Moore, a legatee of her grand-father's will, and who it appears married a man named Guthrie and went to Green County, Ky., for on Aug. 6, 1799, her father James Moore conveyed to her, as Elizabeth Guthrie and her sister Lyddia Moore 82 acres of land in said County, and one negro boy, Nase. (D page 637.)

Section 3. Lyddia Moore, born after the date of her grandfather's will. At least her name was not mentioned in the will, she evidently went to Green County, Ky., with her sister Elizabeth Guthrie.

CHAPTER 16.

PHILEMON KAVANAUGH.

(Named in Chapter 8, Section5.)

Article 1.—Philemon Kavanaugh, a son of William Kavanaugh and Hannah Woods his wife, was a soldier in the war of 1821.

He married Patsey Gilbert and lived a number of years in Madison County, Ky., and moved to Morgan County, Mo., three of his children were living March 11, 1839, and one of them in Madison County, Ky. His wife was a daughter of Samuel Gilbert. She was a member of the Baptist Church at Viney Fork. The names of his children are found in deed book X, page 514 in a power of attorney given by Charles Kavanaugh for himself and his infant brothers and sisters to his brother Samuel G. B. Kavanaugh, to sell their interest in their Mother's (Fatsey) land given them by William Oldham and Susannah his wife, (See Part VI, Chap. 6, Sec. 8, and Chap. 11, of same Part, and Part II Chap. 48), and are set forth in the coming sections:

Sectiona 1. Charles Kavanaugh, in 1839, was living in Morgan County, Mo.

Section 2. Samuel G. B. Kavanaugh. In 1839 was living in Madison County, Ky., and was attorney in fact for his brother Charles, in his own right, and as guardian for three of his younger brothers and sisters. It seems that his wife's name was Mary Shrites, and that they moved to Clark County, Ky., the records of the Clark County Court reveal the name Samuel G. B. Kavanaugh and his wife Mary Shrites, and in 1904, the names of the heirs of Samuel Kavanaugh appear on the records of said Court as follows:

1. Lela Kavanaugh, wife of Charles Bates.
2. Jeff Kavanaugh.
3. Will Kavanaugh, wife, Mattie.
4. Taylor Kavanaugh, wife, Minnie.

Section 3. Rhoda Kavanaugh, emigrated to Missouri.

Section 4. Nicholas Kavanaugh; died unmarried.

Section 5. Susannah Kavanaugh.

Section 6. Philemon Kavanaugh, emigrated to Missouri.

Section 7. Sallie Jane Kavanaugh; married Asa Carter June 29, 1837. Mr. Carter died and Mrs. Sallie Jane Kavanaugh Carter married again Dr. Edy, or Eddy.

CHAPTER 17.

WILLIAMS KAVANAUGH, Sr.

(Named in Chapter 2, Section 3.)

Article 1.—Williams Kavanaugh, Sr., a son of Philemon Kavanaugh, immigrant from Ireland and Ann Williams his wife, immigrated from Wales, according to the history entitled "Life and Times of Kavanaugh."

.. Bishop Hubbard Hinde Kavanaugh, was born in Virginia, and came to Kentucky in 1775. He settled in Madison County, on the waters of Muddy Creek, a little south of what is now the village of

Waco, where George H. Duncan who has Kavanaugh blood in his veins now lives. He was born in 1744, old style. His wife was born Feb. 1, 1744, and was Mary Harrison, daughter of Mr. Harrison an immigrant from England to New England, and who moved and settled in Virginia, and Miss Johnson his wife, Mr. Harrison and two brothers who came with him to Virginia each lived to be very old.

In the Madison County Deed Book D, page 71, a deed dated August 2, 1796, from Williams Kavanaugh and Mary his wife to Charles Kavanaugh, to 88 acres of land on Muddy Creek is recorded, and in the same book page 141, a deed from the same grantors to Jesse Morrice to 50 acres of land on Muddy Creek, being part of the tract on which the grantors then lived. On Jan. 13, 1802, Williams Kavanaugh and Mary his wife had moved to Tennessee, and were residents of Smith County, in said State. See deed to Joshua Townsend, E. page 398.

The above subject was a minister of the Methodist Episcopal Church, but from Bishop Kavanaugh's account left that society and joined another society, and as the Bishop has given a lucid account of him, it is unnecessary here to attempt to say more, except to name such of his children as we are able: (See Chap. 1, Item 5.) Among his children were:

Section 1. Rev. Charles Kavanaugh came from Culpeper County Va., to what was afterwards Madison County, Ky., and on March 5, 1795, was authorized by the County Court to solemnize the rites of marriage, and his uncle Charles and cousin Charles Jr., had been granted similar licenses. He was in Smith County, Tennessee, May 30, 1804, (see deed to Joseph Proctor, E page 725,) and Williams Kavanaugh, Sr., resided at that time in the same Couny. In making the deed aforesaid it does not appear that this Charles Kavanaugh, had any wife.

Section 2. Williams Kavanaugh, Jr., as shown by the Bishop's history, was born near the dividing line between Virginia and Tennessee, August 3, 1775, whilst his parents were moving to the District of Kntucky from Virginia. On March 29, 1798, he was married to Hannah Hubbard Hinde, daughter of Dr. Thomas Hinde, and Mary T. Hubbard his wife. Mary T. Hubbard, was a daughter of Benjamin Hubbard, an English merchant.

Mrs. Kavanaugh died at the residence of her son-in-law John Stevens in Madison County, Ky., June 11, 1852, her husband, the Reverend Williams Kavanaugh, Jr., having died Oct. 16, 1806. In 1799, Thomas Hinde deeded to him 138 acres of land in Clark County, Ky. (See Deed Book No., 4, page 350.) Their children:

1. Thomas Williams Kavanaugh, was born in Clark County, Ky., Jan. 5, 1799. He entered the United States Army, and was commissioned first Lieutenant. He died May 29, 1823, unmarried.

2. Leroy Harrison Kavanaugh, was born May 29, 1800. He married Rachael Martin, and died at Mt. Carmel, Ill., in Nov. 1864. He was deeply pious, and remarkably zealous. He removed to Mt. Carmel, Ill., where he exerted a wide influence. The community—all his friends—erected a handsome monument to his memory.

Will K. Kavanaugh, of St. Louis, Mo., a very prominent man in the affairs of the city, and quite wealthy, is a grand-son of Rev. Leroy Harrison Kavanaugh.

3. Hubbard Hinde Kavanaugh. "Old man Eloquent," was born Jan. 14, 1802. He was twice married, first to Margaret C. Green, and secondly to Martha Lewis, nee Richardson. He left no off spring. He was very prominent in the Methodist Episcopal Church, and became one of the most noted, talented and influential Bishops of his day and generation. He died at the parsonage of

the Methodist Church in Columbus, Mississippi, Wednesday morning, March 19, 1884. For further particulars, see "Life and Times of Kavanaugh, by Redford."

4. Mary Jane Kavanaugh, born Nov. 16, 1803. She married John Challen, of Lexington, Ky., and died April 18, 1863. They moved to Waverly, Illinois.

5. Benjamin Taylor Kavanaugh, born April 23, 1805. He married Margaret Lengenfelter April 23, 1827. He became a Methodist minister, and was a gifted man, of fine intellect, studied medicine, and was a professor in a medical college. The University of Missouri. He was appointed editor of the St. Louis Advocate. In 1861, he joined the Southern Army, under General Price, and was Chaplain for two years. He was then appointed missionary for the army by Bishop Payne, and served to the close of the war. He also served as surgeon and physician in the army as occasion required. Dr. Benjamin T. Kavanaugh was the author of "Electricity, The Motor Power of The Solar System," and other books. He was also editor of "The Huston (Texas) Masonic Mirror," some years. By many he was regarded as the equal (if not his superior) of his brother the Bishop. He died in Mount Sterling, Ky., in 1866. They had three children:

1. Mary Kavanaugh; married Mr. Mendenhall, of Philadelphia. They had two children:

1. Ada Mendenhall, last heard from was living in Texas.

2. Williams Mendenhall, last heard from was living in Texas.

2. Thomas Hinde Kavanaugh, Dr., died of yellow fever in Texas, 1867.

3. Julia Kavanaugh; died of yellow fever in Texas, in 1867.

6. William Barbour Kavanaugh, born Oct. 17, 1807. He was a posthumous child. He married Nov. 16, 1831, in Clark County, Ky., Susan Ann Evans, the marriage was solemnized by the Rev. Edward Southgate. He was also a minister of the Methodist Church, and a gifted speaker, an extremely close logical reasoner, and often in fights of oratory equalled his brother, the Bishop. He was a profound thinker, and a great reader. He was many times presiding Elder in Kentucky, and had aslo, the charge of a District, when he was transferred to the California Conference. He and his wife Susan Evans, had eleven sons, ten of whom grew to manhood, honored and respected citizens wherever found. He died in 1888. Their children were:

1. Peter Evans Kavanaugh; married first Mary Le Compte, daughter of Congressman Joseph Le Compte, of Henry County, Ky., and second Miss Lawson, of Shelby County. Children of the first marriage:

1. Margaret Kavanaugh; married —— —— and lives in Franklin County, Ky.

2. Elizabeth Kavanaugh; married —— —— and lives in Franklin County, Ky.

3. Luke Kavanaugh. Post Office Pots grove, Franklin County, Ky.

4. Joseph Kavanaugh; married —— —— and lives in Franklin County, Ky

5. Martha Kavanaugh; married —— —— and lives in Franklin County, Ky.

Children of the second marriage:

6. Barbour Kavanaugh.

7. John Lawson Kavanaugh.

8. Alice Kavanaugh.

2. Charles Williams Kavanaugh, was a lawyer of Newport, Ky., and died unmarried at about the age of forty years.

3. Hubbard Hinde Kavanaugh; married Miss Anna Kimbrough, of Alabama, during the Civil War. He had entered as student at Alabama University, was appointed chaplain to a regiment, but acted as aid-de-camp to Colonel ——, was always seen on his cream colored horse in the midst of the fray, either carrying orders, or attending the wounded, he never knew what fear was. After the war General Fayette Hewitt at Frankfort, Ky., had him appointed chaplain of the Penitntiary, where he did a wonderful work among the convicts—had great influence over them. He died several years ago, while still serving in this capacity. Their children:

1. Judge William M. Kavanaugh, of Little Rock, Arkansas, is one of the most brilliant young men of the state. Has filled many important offices; is now President of the Southern Trust Company, with a capital of $500,000—and in the last few months his friends announced him as candidate for then next Governor, but he has declined to run, and his name has been withdrawn, he seems to have a brilliant future before him, and as far as intellect is concerned it is assured. He maried Miss Ida Floyd, of Clarksville, Arkansas, they have fine young children.

2. Frank Kavanaugh, is assistant State Librarian at Frankfort, unmarried.

3, Emma Kavanaugh; married Clarence Gayle. They live in Frankfort, and have four young children.

4. Susan Kavanaugh; married Earl Rogers, of Frankfort, Ky. They have four young children.

5. Josephine Kavanaugh; unmarried, residence with her Mother in South Frankfort, Ky.

4. Robert Hord Kavanaugh, served as first Lieutenant during the Civil War, on the Confederate side, afterwards married Miss Margaret Nolan, of Pendleton County, Ky. They had five children who lived with their mother at Boston Station, Ky. Lieutenant Kavanaugh died in about 1881.

5. Marcus Henry Kavanaugh; married Miss Mary Poynter. They had two sons, only one living with his father at Falmouth, Ky., his mother died when this living son was a baby:

1. Will P. Kavanaugh.

6. Sydnor Kavanaugh; married Miss Elizabeth Applegate, she died leaving five young daughters, who live with their father at Fort Thomas, Ky.—one lately married.

7. Thomas S. Kavanaugh, was more like his distinguished Uncle Bishop H. H. Kavanaugh, both in physique and intelect than any of the family. He married Miss Anna Poynter, and early in the eighties (80's) removed from Pendleton County, Ky., to Jefferson County, Arkansas, where until the time of his death in 1899, he was a manufacturer of shingles and hard wood lumber. He was one of the most congenial of companions, and had that ready Irish wit so apt in repartee. He had the grasp of large affairs in his hands, but his sudden death ended it all. He left one son, who lives in Pine Bluff, Arkansas, with his widowed mother. The children born were:

1. Miss —— Kavanaugh, the only daughter died in 1904.

2. Edwin Mark Kavanaugh; married Miss Ida Bunn, daughter of Dr. Dudley Bunn, and they have two little daughters:

1. Vivian Kavanaugh.

2. Anita Kavanaugh.

8. James Barbour Kavanaugh, a brilliant young lawyer; died in his twenty first year; unmarried.

9. Richard Kavanaugh; married Lilla Richardson. Mr. Kavanaugh is dead, his widow and two unmarried daughters live in Louisville, Ky.

10. Joseph Kavanaugh; died when three years old in Newport, Ky.

11. Edward T. Kavanaugh; married Mattie McClannahan. They live near Falmouth, Ky. Their children:

1. Mary Evans Kavanaugh; unmarried.
2. Hiram Kavanaugh; unmarried.

CHAPTER 18.

MISS —— KAVANAUGH.

(Named in Chapter 2, Section 7.)

Aticle 1.—Miss ——Kavanaugh, a daughter of Philemon Kavanaugh and Ann Willams his wife, married Mr. Covington, and they were the parents of a number of children born in Culpeper County, Va., several years prior to the Revolutionary War, of whom Robert Covington, who married Mary Duncan, as hereinafter stated, was one.

One Thomas Covington, died in Culpeper County, leaving a will bearing date December 5, 1756, probated Jan. 15, 1767. He lived on, and owned property in the town of Culpeper, and had a wife, Jael, and daughters and sons.

(November 19, 1764, the Court appropriated to Thomas Covington in full satisfaction for repairing the church, vestry-house, deal-post and six trenches, 700 lbs., of tobacco, besides 3500 lbs., already received.)

1. Ann Covington; married John Faver, son of John Faver, (who died about 1783) and Isabella his wife.
2. Sarah Covington; married Mr. Tutt.

His sons were perhaps:

3. Mr. —— Covington; married Lucy Strother.
4. Mr. —— Covington; married Mildred Strother.

He had a brother Richard. The said Lucy and Mildred Strother were daughters of John Strother (who died in 1795) and Mary his wife.

One William Covington, died in Culpeper County, in 1783-4, leaving a number of children, just below named, among them a son, Robert, and about 1797, one Frances Covington (no doubt his widow) owned land on Muddy Run, adjoining William Covington, deceased, and others. The children of William Covington, who died in 1783-4:

1. Eleanor Covington; married Robert Hensley.
2. Guzzel Covington; married —— Cooper.
3. Elizabeth Covington.
4. Robert Covington.

It is more than probable that the given name of the Miss Kavanaugh, at the head of this chapter was Frances and that her husband was William and that the Robert Covington, below named, who married Mary Duncan was their son, the same as the Robert Covington, folowing the figure 4 above.

The mother of the Robert Covington who married Mary Duncan, is known to have been a Miss Kavanaugh of Culpeper County, Va., and Doctor Slaughter's notes on Culpeper give the name of only one Robert Covington, towit: Robert, a son of the William Covington, who died in 1783-4, as above shown.

1. Robert Covington, evidently a son of William Covington and Miss ? Frances Kavanaugh his wfe; married Mary Duncan, a daughter of Charles Duncan and Sarah Browning (or Sarah Kavanaugh) his wife.

Robert Covington was born in Culpper County, Va., Jan. 3, 1760, and died in Madison County, Ky., Aug. 10, 1847, and his said wife was born in Culpeper Nov. 10, 1764, and died in Madison County, Ky., March 8, 1841, and their remains were buried in the Duncan Grave Yard, on Muddy Creek, the farm now owned by Jesse T. Cobb. Their marriage occurred in Culpeper County in 1782.

The records of the Madison County Court show that Robert Covington was a soldier in the Revolutionary Army, and held a pension sertificate which is there recorded, and that he drew a pension for said service. After the war they moved from Culpeper County, Va., and settled on Muddy Creek, about two miles south of what is now the village of Elliston, in Madison County, Kentucky in 1792, where he acquired land and owned lands, and where they both died at the dates aforesaid. Their children were:

1. William Covington, born July 31, 1783, in Culpeper County, Va., died in Madison County, Ky., Aug. 26, 1869. He married Edith Moberley, a daughter of Benjamin Moberley, issue:

1. Milton C. Covington (1812-1853) married Paulina Dillingham, (born 1815) Jan. 22, 1833, issue:

1. Mary Lizzie Covington, 1834-1869; married M. H. Benton, issue:

1. Sallie Benton, 1868———.

2. William Henry Benton, 1867.

2. Milly Ann Covington; married William Benton, issue:

1. Hon. James M. Benton, attorney at law, and at present Judge of the Circuit Court, for the Judicial District of which the County of Madison forms a part. He married Bessie Smith, a daughter of Dr. Curren C. Smith and Sallie Short Goodloe his wife. (See Part II, Chap. 11, Section 5.)

3. William Jep. Covington 1835; married Mary Ann Estes, they live in Clay County, Mo., issue:

1. Minnie Estes; married 1885 James A. Metheny.

4. Martha J. Covington, 1839——; married 1859, Thomas J. Scrivner, issue:

1. Paulina Scrivner, 1860; married George McQuery, issue:

1. William Jefferson McQuery.

2. James Henry McQuery.

2. William Henry Scrivner, 1862; married Ettie West, 1882.

3. John Milton Scrivner, 1865.

4. Annie Scrivner.

5. Edward H. Scrivner.

5. Amanda M. Covington, 1842; married 1865, Elihue Polk Benton, born 1844, issue:

1. Lena Benton, 1867.
2. Mattie Ann Benton, 1872.
3. Bessie Benton, 1880-1882.
4. Fannie Kate Benton, 1882.

6. Robert Henry Dillingham Covington 1846; married 1869, Fannie Quisenberry, 1853, of Clay County, Mo., issue:

1. Sarah Paulina Covington 1878.
2. Mattie Covington 1879-1880.
3. Henry Leslie Covington 1880.
4. Annie Meadow Covington 1881.

7. John M. Covington 1849; married 1874 Ella D. Moberley, 1854, issue:

1. Ruth Wilmot Covington, 1877.
2. Benny Milton Covington 1883-1884.
3. Willie Taylor Covington, 1882.

8. Ben Elihue Covington, 1852; married 1879, Folka Brooks, of Jessamine County, Ky., issue:

1. Paulina Covington, 1880, twin.
2. Betsy Covington, 1880-1880, twin.
3. A daughter; died 1882.
4. Johnnie Covington, 1883.
5. James Conner Covington, 1885.

2. Jeptha M. Covington, 1816; married first Oct. 31, 1839, Sallie Ann Cruze. 1823-1840, married secondly May 26, 1842, Mary Scudder, 1823-1879, issue by second wfe:

1. Sallie A. Covington, 1844; married 1863 Allen H. Brock, 1843, issue:

1. Albert C. Brock.
2. Jeptha F. Brock, 1865.
3. John Milton Brock, 1867.
4. William Asa Brock, 1870.
5. Mary F. Brock, 1873.
6. Nancy E. Brock, 1875.
7. Infant Aug. 8, 1877.
8. Annie L. Brock, 1878.
9. Thomas H. Brock, 1880
10. Allen H Brock, 1883.

2. Lavinia Edith Covington, 1846; married 1873, Thomas H. Benton, 1848-1881, issue:

1. Ann Eliza Benton, 1876.
2. Charles L. Benton, 1878.

3. Lucy F. Covington, 1848; married 1873, Eli Pearson 1851, issue:

1. Mary Catherine Pearson.
2. Scudder Pearson, 1875.
3. Milly Pearson, 1877.
4. Sallie Frances Pearson, 1879.
5. Jonathan Dudley Pearson, 1882.

4. William Rufus Covington, 1850-1882; married Normanda J. Boain 1857-1880, issue:

1. Robert Conner Covington, 1874-1875.
2. John W. Covington, 1876.
3. Mary Eliza Covington, 1878.

5. Milton Conner Covington, 1853; married 1876, Lucy Garrett, 1859-1885, issue:

1. John William Covington, 1877.

2. Nannie Christopher Covington, 1879.
3. Dora Covington, 1880-1880.
4. Mary Lucy Covington, 1881.
5. Ida F. Covington, 1883; died 1883.

6. Rebecca E. Covington, 1855-1856.

7. Angemima C. (Kitty) Covington, 1858-1885; married 1876, Jonathan P. Moberley, 1854, issue:

1. John Christopher Moberley.

8. Mary Mildred Covington, 1860; married 1881, John Dozier, 1858, issue:

1. Leota Dozier, 1882.
2. James Dozier, 1884.

9. Paulina Covington, 1863--1863.

10. Nancy H. Covington, 1864; single.

3. Milly D. Covington, 1818; married Nov. 3, 1836, Benjamin Simpson, 1810-1862, issue:

1. Sarah E. Simpson, 1837; married James Allen.
2. Mary L. Simpson, 1839-1846.
3. Julia F. Simpson, 1841; married Dudley Berryman.
4. Eliza A. Simpson, 1843; married first Mr. Gilmore, second Mr. Krunk, third Mr. Haggard.
5. Paulina M. Simpson, 1845; married James, (son of Cyrus) Benton.
6. Mary E. Simpson, 1846; married Albert Coleman.
7. William F. Simpson, 1848; married Paulina G. Gilmore.
8. James I. Simpson, 1850; married Adeline Belle.
9. Lucy L. Simpson, 1852; married —— Haggard.
10. Milton C. Simpson, 1854.
11. Coleman S. Simpson, 1856-1859.
12. Jeptha R. Simpson, 1858.
13. Harriet D. Simpson, 1861; married Nichols.

4. William Q. Covington, Oct, 15, 1820-1906; married March 6, 1845, to Elizabeth A. Cobb, 1828. (See Part VI, Chapter 10, Section 6.) Issue:

1. Robert H. Covington, 1845; married 1866, Patrai Hisle, 1857, issue:

1. Mattie Rea Covington, 1867.
2. James Walker Covington, 1870; married Addie G. Maupin. (See Part V, Chapter 12, Section 15.)
3. William Quinn Covington.

2. James M. Covington, 1848-1850.

3. Martha E. Covington, 1851; married 1869, Willis Hisle, issue:

1. William M. Hisle, 1869.
2. Samuel Hisle, 1872.
3. Elizabeth Louise Hisle, 1883.

4. Mary M. Covington, 1853; married 18— Charles L. Searcy, issue.

1. Edith L. Searcy, 1884.
2. Elizabeth Searcy, 18—.

5. Milton C. Covington, 1856; married 1879, Mary Jett, issue:

1. Bessie Covington, 1880.
2. Lula W. Covington, 1885.

6. Coleman W. Covington, 1861-1861.

2. Sallie Covington, born and died in Culpeper County, Va.
3. Eliabeth Covington; married John Stanley.
4. Milly Covington; married Caleb Oldham. (See Part VI, Chapter 31.)

5. Lucy Covington; married Joseph Hensley, issue:
  1. Polly Hensley; married —— Level, issue:
    1. Robert M. Level.
    2. Lucy Level; married —— Kilchner.
    3. Woodson Level.
    4. Frances M. Level; married —— Farsin.
    5. Mary E. Level; married —— Hammond.
    6. Julia Level.
  2. Samuel C. Hensley; married —— —— issue:
    1. Martha J. Hensley; married —— Gibson.
    2. William Hensley.
    3. Joseph Hensley,
    4. Milly O. Hensley; married —— Black.
  3. Elia Hensley; married —— Vermillion, issue unknown.
  4. Martha Hensley; married —— Higgason, issue:
    1. Willis H. Higgason.
    2. Millie B. Higgason.
  5. J. M. Hensley.
  6. Robert Hensley.
  7. Joseph D. Hensley.
  8. William W. Hensley.
  9. Lucy A. Hensley; married William M. Thomas. (See Part III, Chapter 5, Section 4.)
  10. Harriet Hensley; married —— O'Neil.
6. Polly Covington; married Henderson Ogg, issue:
  1. William C. Ogg; married first Ann Allen, second Mrs. Eliza Berry. (See Part III, Chap. 44, Sec. 1.) Issue of by first marriage:
    1. Mary Jane Ogg; married William C. East.
    2. Ann Ogg; married Samuel Griggs.
    3. Nannie Ogg; married Shelby Jett.
  2. Coleman C. Ogg; married —— ——
  3. Robert Ogg; married —— ——
  4. —— Ogg.
7. Charles Covington; married Rachael Lackey, 1819, issue:
  1. Charles Covington; married.
  2. Nancy Covington; married —— Ronan.
  3. Elizabeth Covington; married —— Riley.
8. Coleman Covington; married Matilda Duncan. He was a prominent man, and represented Madison County in the Kentucky Legislature in 1855-7. They had no children.
9. Robert Covington; married Ann Eliza Harris, daughter of Judge Christopher Harris and Sallie Wallace his wife. (See Part III, Chapter 9.)

Note—The Duncan Family of Culpeper, and

The Browning Family of Culpeper.

From Dr. Slaughter's notes, enlarged and revised by R. T. Green.

1. William Duncan, will dated Feb. 24, 1781, probated Oct. 15, 1781. Children
  1. Charles Duncan.
  2. James Duncan.
  3. Rawley Duncan.
  4. William Duncan.
  5. John Duncan.
  6. Joseph Duncan.

7. Annie Duncan; married —— Roberts.

The will was witnessed by Wiliam Hughes, William and Shadrack Browning.

2. William Duncan, wife Rosanna. Will dated May 17, 1790, probated Sept. 20, 1801. Children:

1. William Duncan.
2. James Duncan.
3. Frederick Duncan.
4. Benjamin Duncan.

3. Robert R. Duncan, wife Ann, will dated June 7, 1788, probated Oct. 21, 1793. Children:

1. Robert Duncan.
2. Charles Duncan.
3. Sammy Duncan.
4. Joseph Duncan.
5. John Duncan.
6. Gollup (or Gallup) Duncan.
7. Phillis Duncan; married John Barbee, and they had:
   1. A daughter; married Enoch Bradford.
8. Ann Duncan; married Thomas Pope.
9. Mary Duncan; married first Joseph Hackley, second Thomas Grinnan.
10. Rosa Duncan; married James Jett.
11. Lavinia Duncan; married John Lightfoot.

4. James Duncan; wife Mary, Aug. 17, 1801. Had children:

1. Sally Duncan; married —— Yancey.
2. Mary Duncan.
3. George Duncan.
4. Francis Duncan.
5. Joseph Duncan.
6. Liney Duncan; married —— Johnston.
7. Lucy Duncan; married —— Threlkeld.
8. Elizabeth Duncan; married —— Rout.

5. James Duncan's estate was divided in August 1819, by George Duncan, John D. Browning and Bryant O'Bannon, Commissioners. He lived on Thornton River. His children were:

1. Lewis Duncan.
2. Michael Duncan.
3. James Duncan.
4. Lucy Duncan.
5. William Duncan.
6. Hiram Duncan.
7. John Duncan.

John Browning, born in England in 1594, came to Vriginia in 1622, in the ship "Abigail," and served in the house of Burgessees in 1629.

William Browning, came to Virginia in 1623, in ship "Bona Nova." (See Hatter's list of American emigrants.)

It is supposed that the Virginia Brownings descended from one or both of the above named, but the line of descent cannot be directly traced.

The Brownings appeared in Virginia soon after the settlement of the Colony.

Francis B)rowning settled near Gain's Cross Roads, now Rappahannock, in 1735. He came probably from Caroline County, about that time. One Thomas Browning came to Culpeper, but returned to Caroline.

1. Francis Browning; married Miss Lloyd of Maryland, and they had the following children:

1. Francis Browning; married Frances Norman. (See Section two following.)
2. Nicholas Browning; married Sarah Washburn.
3. John Browning; married Miss Demorest.
4. Jacob Browning; married Elizabeth Bywaters.
5. Mary Browning; married Courtney Norman.
6. Ruth Browning; married William Duncan.
7. A daughter; married —— Turner.

2. Francis Browning; married Frances Norman, (named above 1-1.) and had these children:

1. Shadrock Browning; married Polly Route.
2. Charles Browning; married Mollie Strother.
3. William Browning; married Milly Roberts.
4. James Browning; married Miss Deane, and moved to Kentucky.
5. Reuben Browning; married Ann Hickman, and moved to Kentucky.
6. John Browning; married Elizabeth Strother.
7. Isaac Browning; married Eliabeth Browning, a daughter of Joshua Browning, a Captain in the Virginia State line.
8. Francis Browning; died in the Revolutionary Army.
9. Mollie Browning; married James Duncan.
10. Sarah Browning; married Charles Duncan, probably a son of the first William. (See Section following:)
11. Asenith Browning; married Benjamin Duncan.

CHARLES DUNCAN.

Reference 2-10 above.

Charles Duncan; married Sarah Browning, as shown in the above items 2-10. He was no doubt a son of the first William Duncan, herein before named who died in 1781. Whether Charles Duncan came to Kentucky, it is not known, but Sarah Duncan his wife came, and it is reasonably certain that he came. However, she was left a widow and lived and died on Muddy Creek, in Madison County, Ky., and was buried in the Duncan Grave Yard, located on the farm, now owned by Jesse T. Cobb, and the stone tablet to her grave has on it this inscription: "Sarah Duncan, born 1742, died 1824, in the 82nd year of her age." (See Chap. 2, Sec. 7, for statement.)

Her husband Charles Duncan had been dead many years. (20-25 years.) They had the following children:

1. Mary Duncan, born in Culpeper County, Va., Nov. 10, 1764, where she married Robert Covington, and they came to Madison County, Ky., about 1792, as shown in the beginning of this Chapter, in Section 6, she died March 8, 1841, as herein before stated.
2. Nimrod Duncan; married in Culpeper County, Va., in 1797, to Lucy Brownig.
3. William Duncan; married first —— —— second Sallie Collins, a daughter of Thomas Collins of Madison County, Ky., Feb. 21, 1825.
4. Charles Duncan; married Margaret Woods, of Madison County, Ky., Dec. 17, 1795, and second Maryan E. ——
5. Shadrack Duncan; married Eliabeth Williams of Madison County, Ky., August 4, 1803.
6. Isaac Duncan; married Susannah Kavanaugh, daughter of William Kavanaugh, and Hannah Woods his wife, of Madison County, Ky., Sept. 21, 1795, their children are set forth in Chapter 9.
7. John Duncan; married in Madison County, Ky., first Fannie Lloyd, No .v 9,8115, and second Jane Owing, March 10, 1825.

8. Milly Duncan; married Jaret Phelps. They settled on Tates Creek in Madison County, Ky.

(See Below.)

9. Henry Duncan.

10. —— Duncan, a daughter; married Eli Simmons. Had:

1. Josiah P. Simmons; married Patsey Phelps Jan. 18, 1830, raised a family and died in Madison County, Ky.

2. George P. Simmons; died single. He went to California during the gold fever, and accumulated a nice estate, and returned to Madison County, Ky., where he died. Will dated Jan. 28, 1870, probated Feb. 24, 1870, bequests to his brothers and sisters and to Susan, wife of Amos Deatherage.

3. Sallie Simmons; married Henry Cobb.

4. Eliabeth Simmons; married Noah Hatton. Had a daughter Mattie Hatton.

5. Thomas Simmons.

6. Madison Simmons.

11. Zachariah Duncan.

Madison County Record.

Jarrett Phelps, will bears date Jan. 23, 1851, was probated June 2, 1851, wherein he names his wife Milly and children:

1. George Phelps.

2. A daughter; married William Stone. In the will styled his son-in-law William Stone, father of W. J. Stone, late Governor of Mo., and United States Senator.

3. Elizabeth Phelps; married —— Turner.

4. Susan Phelps; married —— Grosheart.

5. Charles D. Phelps.

6. Sally Ann Phelps; married Wiley Embry, Jan. 14, 1827. The parents of:

1. Joel W. Embry, living on Barnes Mill pike in Madison County, Ky., whose daughter:

1. Zenarda Embry; married Matt Arbuckle.

From "Notes on Culpeper County.

Dr. Slaghter's, St. Mark Parish." With permission of R. T. G.

Marriages:

Browning, Sarah, daughter of Francis Browning and Frances Norman his wife, married —— Duncan, year not stated.
Browning, George, married Millian Covington, 1809.
Browning, Mollie—James Duncan.
Browning, Asenith—Benjamin Duncan.
Browning, Lucy—Nimrod Duncan, 1797.
Browning, Elizabeth—Benjamin Duncan, 1793.
Covington, Peggy—Dan Brown, 1794.
Covington, Millian—George Browning, 1809.
Covington, John—Elizabeth Griffin, 1819.
Covington, Mary—William Deatherage, 1817.
Covington, Lucy—Gallup Duncan, 1805.
Duncan, Gallup—Lucy Covington, 1805.
Duncan, Charles—Sarah Browning.
Duncan, James—Mollie Browning.
Duncan, Benjamin—Asenith Browning.
Duncan, James—Dorcas Butler, 1797. (Daughter of Spencer Butler who died in 1818.)
Duncan, Fred—Sarah Hallard, 1797.

Duncan, Edmund—Harriet Dulaney, 1812.
Duncan, George—Hannah Brown, 1810.
Duncan, Nimrod—Lucy Browning, 1797.
Duncan, Benjamin—Elizabeth Browning, 1793.
Duncan, William—Lucy Bywaters, 1789.
Duncan, William C.—Catherine Hughes, 1823.
Duncan, Seney—Allen Johnson, 1793.
Duncan, Elizabeth—John Routt, Jr., 1794.
Duncan, Mary—George Strother, 1798.
Duncan, Lucy—Dan Threlkeld, 1790.
Duncan, Charles—Elizabeth Dillard, (daughter of George Dillard, died 1790).
Duncan, Benjamin; married Susannah Hawkins, daughter of Matthew Hawkins, died in 1820, and Bettie, his wife).
John Dillard; died in 1808, wife Ann, and left property to:

Peggy Duncan.
Mary Duncan.
Elizabeth Duncan. (1)
Sally James Duncan.
Lucinda Duncan.
Priscilla Bowman.
Ann Carter.

All daughters of his sister Lizzie Duncan, the wife of Charles Duncan, above stated.

From Madison County, Ky., Records.

Benjamin Duncan's will, dated Nov. 5, 1796, probated Dec. 5, 1796, wife Elizabeth. Children:

1. John Duncan.
2. Samuel Duncan.
3. Eliabeth Duncan; married —— Arnot.

John Duncan's will dated Aug. 21, 1848, probated Oct. 7, 1848, wife Lucy (White). Children:

1. Malinda Duncan; married William Harris. (See Part III, Chapter 37.)
2. Emily Duncan; married Harry Goodloe. (See Part II, Chap. 11, Section 6.)
3. Susan Duncan; married John Hart.
4. John A. Duncan.
5. Livia (Olivia); married Octavus Goodloe. (See Part II, Chapter 11, Section 10.)
6. Elizabeth Duncan; married ? —— Taylor.

Gabriel Duncan's will bears date April 11, 1843, probated May 5, 1845, wife Mary. Children:

1. Elizabeth Duncan; married Williams. Children:
   1. Susan Williams.
   2. Eliabeth Wiliams.
2. Nancy Duncan; married —— Edge.
3. Patsey Duncan; married —— Batterton.
4. Anderson Duncan.
5. Polly Duncan; married —— Bennett, had children.
6. Charlotte Duncan; married —— Hainline.

John Phelps will, dated —— probated Aug. 7, 1798. Children:

1. Nancy Phelps.
2. Rody Phelps.
3. Patsey Phelps.
4. Cary Phelps.
5. John Phelps.
6. Sarah Phelps.
7. Sally Phelps.
8. Milly Phelps.

9. Betsy Phelps; married —— Willis.
10. Thomas Phelps.
11. Shadrack Phelps.
12. Magdalin Phelps; married —— Stapp.
13. Philip Phelps.

Sally Phelps will, dated Sept. 8, 1838, probated Dec. 1, 1828, daughters:

1. Cynthia Phelps.
2. Nancy Phelps.
3. Catherine Phelps.

Josiah Phelps, will dated June 17, 1835, probated July 6, 1835. Present wife Martha. Children:

1. Jarrett Phelps.
2. Thomas Phelps.
3. Susan Phelps; married William Chenault. (See Part V, Chapter 13, Section 9, and Part VII, Chapter 18.)
4. Nancy Phelps; married —— Baker.

Samuel Phelps will, dated Jan. 24, 1849, probated June 7, 1852, wife, Tabitha. Children:

1. Peter T. Phelps.
2. Nancy B. Phelps; married —— Jones.
3. Samuel B. Phelps.
4. Ann Tabitha Phelps.
5. Marcus A. Phelps.
6. Thomas Phelps. (See Part VI, Chap. 10, Section 12.)
7. Josiah Phelps.

See the Moberley family.

Excerpt from History, by the late William Q. Covington, of Madison County, Ky:

"Robert Covington, was born in Culpeper County, Va., July 3, 1760. His mother was a Kavanaugh, related to Bishop Kavanaugh, recently deceased. He married Mary Duncan in Culpeper County, Va., who was born November 10, 1764. They came to Madison County, and settled near Richmond, where they remained but a short time, then bought and moved to what is known as "the old Robert Covington farm," three miles south of Waco, part of which was then heavy cane brake, and there were indians in the County. On that farm they spent most of their lives.

Robert Covington was in the war of the Revolution. The old Church Register of Viney Fork shows that Robert Covington and Mary Covington his wife, joined the United Baptist Church at Viney Fork second Saturday in September 1798, and Robert Covington was dismissed by letter second Saturday in December 1826. He then took membership at Bethel on the Big Hill pike, Mary his wife, was dismissed by letter June 2nd, Saturday 1828. Robert Covington died August 10, 1847, aged 87 years, 7 months and 7 days. Mary his wife, died March 8, 1841, aged 76 years, 3 months and 28 days. They were buried on the William Duncan old farm 1¼ miles south of Elliston (now owned by Jesse T. Cobb,) tomb rocks to memory.

The Moberley Family.

At an early day, three brothers, John Moberley, Benjamin Moberley and Edward Moberley, came from South Carolina and settled in Madison County, Ky.

John Moberley, the oldest, built the old stone house one mile east of Speedwell; he married Miss Jenkins, raised twelve children and lived to see all of them married. He and his wife were buried on a hill west of and near Crooksville. Their children:

1. Benjamin Moberley; married Susannah Anderson Reid. (See Part 2, Chap. 48, Sec. 2, and Part VI, Chap. 31, Sec. 1.)

2. John Moberley; married Miss Patsey Morris, June 20, 1815.

3. Thomas Moberley; married Sallie Oldham, daughter of Captain John Oldham. (See Part VI, Chapter 34.)

4. William J. Moberley; married Miss Dianna Field, of Richmond, Ky., Dec. 21, 1830.

5. Ichabod Moberley; married Patsey Oldham, daughter of William Oldham and Sallie Gilbert his wife. (See Part VI, Chap. 11, sug. Part VI, Chap. 31, Sec. 1.)

6. Richard Moberley; married Betsy Shelton March 3, 1802, and lived and died at the old residence the Dr. Thomas Shelton Moberley farm, near Eliston. (See Part II, Sec. 4, Part III, Chap. 3, Sec. 6, and Part VI, Chap. 31, Sec. 1.)

7. Nancy Moberley; married Larkin Hume. (See Part VI, Chap. 31, Sec. 1, and Part I, Chap. 9.)

8, Lavinia Moberley; married George Ballard, Sept. 23, 1819. (See Part I, Chap. 9.)

9. Abigail Moberley; married Caleb Oldham. (See Part VI, Chapter 31.)

10. Polly Moberley; married James L. Brassfield May 22, 1806.

11. Tabitha Moberley; married James E. Brassfield May 29, 1806.

12. Susan Moberley; married Daniel Gates Oct. 10, 1822.

Benjamin Moberley (1) was born in South Carolina March 4, 1760. He came to Madison County, Ky., and settled on Tates Creek. He married his first cousin Lavinia Meadows, a first cousin to preacher Andrew Tribble, progenitor of the Tribble families of Madison County, Ky. She was born April 13, 1760, and died Aug. 23, 1844. Her father John Meadow, lived to be one hundred and three years old, and it was a current saying among his neighbors, that he was never known to be angry. Benjamin Moberley built the old log house, 1¼ miles south of Speedwell. He and his wife lived and died in that house.

He died September 7, 1838, aged 78 years. His father, Benjamin Moberley, died at the age of 75 years, his wife was a Miss Price. Benjamin Moberley and Lavinia his wife, and his brother John and his wife, were members of the Church at Viney Fork, in 1798, joined by letter second Saturday in May and helped constitute the Church at Bethel in 1813. They were pious, orderly members and troubles in their own or sister churches were referred to these two brothers. The children of Benjamin Moberley and Lavinia Meadow:

1. Ephraim Moberley, born June 7, 1785; married Elizabeth Cruz, August 15, 1805.

2. Edith Moberley, born June 19, 1787; married William Covington.

3. Jason Moberley, born June 26, 1791.

4. John Moberley, born Sept. 30, 1793; married Eliabeth Baugh, January 2, 1816.

5. Elizabeth Moberley, born April 23, 1796; married Hiram Quinn.

6. Benjamin Moberley; born April 21, 1798; married Julia Simpson.

7. Simeon Moberley, born —— married Artimesa Banta, March 9, 1826.

"True merit and honest worth are recognized in our country, without much regard to ones blood, notwithstanding it has been said "blood will tell." Many of noble parentage have fallen into disrepute, while others of ignoble birth have risen to eminence and distinction. It is on this account, perhaps, the people of the United States have neglected to keep record of their lineage, or ancestry, more than two or three generations, hence few are able to tell who their great grand-parents were, or more than that at most. But on entering into conversation with the old, who we find knew something of our forefathers, we find ourselves much interested, and sometimes feel humiliated that we know so little of our ancestry. For this reason I have made an effort to gather some information concerning the ancestry of my father and mother, and their descendants. Many family and other records have been over hauled, and yet, the information is very limited and imperfect; but I present what I have been able to gather, in the hope that it may prove of some interest to the present and more to the rising generations. ** If this information herein given appears partial in some instances, I have only to say, I have given such facts as I could get."

PART VIII.

CHAPTER 1.

GENEALOGICAL TABLE OF THE BROWN FAMILY.
1½. EARLY MARRIAGES IN MADISON COUNTY, KY.
2. ITEMS CONNECTING THE BROWN NAME WITH EVENTS.

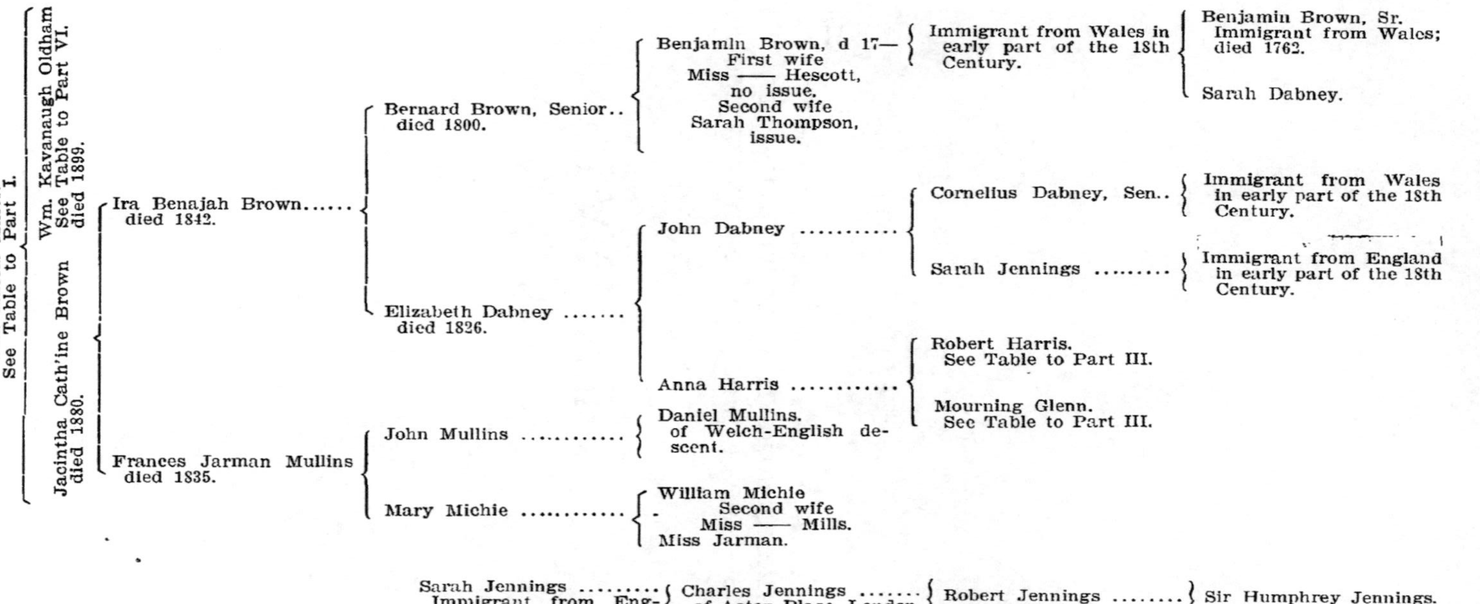

married
Wm. Harris Miller.
See Table to Part I.
Wm. Kavanaugh Oldham
See Table to Part VI.
died 1899.
Jacintha Cath'ine Brown
died 1880.
Ira Benajah Brown......
died 1842.
Frances Jarman Mullins
died 1835.
Bernard Brown, Senior..
died 1800.
Elizabeth Dabney ....
died 1826.
John Mullins ....
Mary Michie ....
Benjamin Brown, d 17—
First wife
Miss —— Hescott,
no issue.
Second wife
Sarah Thompson,
issue.
John Dabney ....
Anna Harris ....
Daniel Mullins.
of Welch-English descent.
William Michie
Second wife
Miss —— Mills.
Miss Jarman.
Immigrant from Wales in early part of the 18th Century.
Cornelius Dabney, Sen..
Sarah Jennings ....
Robert Harris.
See Table to Part III.
Mourning Glenn.
See Table to Part III.
Benjamin Brown, Sr.
Immigrant from Wales; died 1762.
Sarah Dabney.
Immigrant from Wales in early part of the 18th Century.
Immigrant from England in early part of the 18th Century.
Sarah Jennings ....
Immigrant from England.
Charles Jennings ....
of Acton Place, London.
Robert Jennings ....
of England.
Sir Humphrey Jennings.
of England.

Article 1½—Early marriages in Madison County, Ky., gleaned from the first marriage register of the County Court:

Brown, Washington—Jane McQueen, May 26, 180?.
Brown, Thomas—Rachael Pursley, June 23, 1796.
Brown, Joseph—Eliabeth Ellison, June 9, 1795.
Brown, James—Hannah Pursley, March 31, 1795.
Brwon, Henry—Rebecca Roberts, Feb. 23, 1797.
Brown, Edward—Sarah Hoy, Nov. 29, 1797.
Brown, Robert—Ruth Brown, July 10, 1794.
Brown, Benagah—Judith Brown, Nov. 25, 1810.
Brown, James—Anna Clark, June 25, 1810.
Brown, Joseph—Jemima Turner, Dec. 3, 1811.
Brown, John—Ann Hamilton, 1813.
Brown, Peggy———Park.
Brown, Jane—David Gillispie, June 30, 1810.
Brown, Thomas—Nancy Chenault, 1813.
Brown, Edward—Janey Campbell, Aug. 8, 1815.
Brown, George—Polly Wilson, 1811.
Brown, Thomas—Hannah Hogan, Jan. 19, 1819.
Brown, Charles—Tabitha White, Sept. 17, 1818.
Brown, Elias—Susan Mauzy, Jan. 1, 1824.
Brown, Roswell—Eliza Morrison Jan. 9, 1823.
Brown, Hugh—Peggy Sappington, May 13, 1824.
Brown, Thomas—Amelia Estill, Aug. 16, 1842.
Brown, John D.—Mary Ann Smith, March 15, 1860.
Brown, B. H.—Pattie B. Roberts, Sept. 12, 1866.

Article 2.—Items connecting the Brown name with events (from Histories Collins and others.) (Sometimes spelled "Brown" and sometimes 'Browne.")

Section 1. Beverley Brown. A member of voluteer state dragoons under Captain William Garrard's command, of Major James V. Balls squadron in the service of the United States, was killed in action December 18, 1812, as shown by entry on muster roll. (c)

Section 2. Daniel Brown and others in the summer of 1776, were improving in the bottom immediately above the mouth of Lawrence Creek, in Mason County. (c)

Section 3. Hugh Brown, was one of the seven first Justices of the Peace who organized the County Court of Allen County, April 10, 1815. (c)

Section 4. James Brown, was one of Captain James Harrod's company of thirty one men, who in May 1774, came down the Monongahela and Ohio Rivers and up it to the mouth of Landing Run Creek, now Oregon, in Mercer County, east of Salvisa, thence across to Salt River near McAfee's Station, and up that River to Fountain Blue, and to the place now Harrodsburg. (c)

Section 5. Henry B. Brown was associate Editor and publisher from May 1, 1842, to May 1, 1845, of the Maysville Eagle. Afterwards representative in the Ohio Legislature from Cincinnati, and prosecuting attorney of that City. (c)

Section 6. Captain James Brown, was Captain of a company of mounted Kentucky volunteers in the service of the United States against the Wiaw Indians under the command of Brigadier General Charles Scott, mustered in at the rapids of the Ohio June 15, 1791, by Captain B. Smith, first United States Regiment.

John Brown was a member of the same company.

Section 7. Hon. John Brown, was born at Staunton, Va., Sept. 12, 1757, was a distinguished statesman of Kentucky, and a representative in the old Congress from the District of Kentucky 1787 to 1791, and continued in the United States Senaee till 1805. Was one of the many subsribers to the proposals for establishing a society to be called "The Kentucky Society for Promoting Useful Knowledge" December 1, 1787, and one of the directors of the first bank of Kentucky chartered in 1807, and one of five commissioners under the act of January 31, 1814, to contract for building new Court House at Frankfort. He died at his residence at Frankfort, August 28, 1837. (c)

Section 8. Hon. James Brown, a brother of the Hon. John Brown was a distinguished lawyer of Kentucky and a cotemporary at the bar of Henry Clay and others. (c)

Section 9. Dr. Preston W. Brown, a brother to Hon. John Brown, was a graduate of the School of medicine in Philadelphia, and favorably known to the profession as a successful practitioner of medicine in Kentucky. He died in Jefferson County in 1826. (c)

Section 10. Dr. Samuel Brown, a brother to Hon. John Brown, was the first to make use of vaccination as a preventative for small pox in Lexington, Ky., prior to 1802. He was a graduate of Edinburg, and was very distinguished for his medical writings, and for many years filled with great credit to himself and usefulness to the institution the chair of Professor of Theory and Practice of Medicine, in the Transylvania University. He died in Alabama. (c)

Section 11. John Mason Brown was a distinguished Kentuckian. Under the act of Feb. 2, 1869, was one of nine commissioners to improve the state house. (c)

Section 12. Major Brown in August 1792, raised a company and commenced a vigilant search for marauding indians who had committed depredations on the Rolling Fork of Salt River. Falling on their track he pursued and overtook them when a brisk skirmish with them ensued, the indians were killed and the others fled, one of Major Brown's company was killed and two wounded. (c)

Section 13. Rev. O. B. Brown, was a hearsay witness to the killing of Tecumseh by Colonel Johnson. (c)

Section 14. Hon. John Young Brown, a distinguished lawyer and statesman, was elected several times to Congress, and Governor of the state in 189—. (c)

Section 15. Browns Spring of Chalybeate water near Crab Orchard. Boonsborough in Oldham County. Brownsburg, in Washington County. (c)

Section 16. Exhibit of members of the Legislature:

In the Senate—

George I. Brown, of the County of Jessamine, 1829-34.
Scott Brown, of the County of Franklin 1873-7.

In the House of Representatives—

Archibald C. Brown, of the County of Shelby, 1855-7.
E. A. Brown, of the County of Christian 1863-5.
Erasmus O. Brown, of the County of Meade, 1855-9.
George N. Brown of the County of Pike, 1849.
George P. Brown, of the County of Laurel 1850.
George I. Brown, of the County of Jessamine 1824-1850.
George W. Brown, of the County of Jessamine 1829-1832.
Henry O. Brown, of the County of Harrison 1824.
James S. Brown, of the County of Owen, 1835-1841.

Jefferson Brown, of the County of Warren, 1849.
John Brown, of the County of Boone, 1813.
Peter Brown, of the County of Washington, 1833.
Preston Brown, of the County of Woodford, 1802.
Samuel M. Brown, of the County of Jefferson, 1825
Thomas D. Brown, of the County of Hardin, 1841-844-7.
Thomas Brown, Jr., of the County of Henry, 1849.
Thomas S. Brown, of the County of Floyd, 1862-3.
William Brown of the County of Christian, 1859 61.
William Brown, of the County of Jessamine, 1873.
William Brown, of the County of Harrison, 1809.
William W. Brown, of the County of Morgan, 1851-5.
Richard J. Browne, of the Coutny of Washington, 1862-3. (c)

Section 17. Aaron V. Brown, represented Tennessee in the United States Congress, as a Democrat 1839-45. Was Governor of said State 1845-7, and Post Master General in Buchanan's Cabinet 1857-9. (Appleton's Cyclo.)

Section 18. Benjamin Grats Brown, was member of the Missouri Legislature 1852-8. Edited the Missouri Democrat 1854-9. Commanded a brigade during the Civil War. Represented Missouri in the United States Senate as a Republican 1863-7. Was Governor af said state in 1871, and taking an important part in the Liberal Republican movement, was Liberal Republican and Democratic candidate for Vice President on the ticket of Horace Greely in 1872. (Id)

Section 19. Charles Broeden Brown, was the first American to adopt Literature as a profession. He wrote topics of the times, and published six successful novels, which were unsurpassed until the appearance of Cooper's works. (Id.)

Section 20. Henry B. Brown, born in 1836, a Michigan Jurist, was appointed Judge of the United States District Court for the Eastern District of Michigan, in 1875, and associate Justice of the Supreme Court of the United States in 1890. (Id)

Section 21. Jacob Brown, had been a militia general in New York, when the war of 1812 called out his abilities. He gained a victory at Sacketts Harbor in 1813. Was made Major General in the regular army and in 1814, won the victories of Chippewa and Lundy's Lane. In 1821, he succeeded to the command of the army as General in chief. (Id)

Section 22. John Brown, of Providence Rhode Island, a rich merchant led the party which destroyed the Jasper in 1772. He was delegate from Rhode Island to Congress 1799-1801. (Id.)

Section 23. John Brown of Massachusetts, aided in the capture of Ticondaroga, and took Fort Chambly in 1775. Served under Montgomery at Quebec. In 1777, he captured Ticondaroga together with large supplies. (Id.)

Section 24. John Brown, noted, ardent, and uncomprising abolitionist 1800-1859, executed at Charleston, Va., Dec. 2, 1859, became a hero in the songs of the Northern Armies. His life was written by F. B. Sanborn. (Id)

Section 25. Nicholas Brown, of Providence Rhode Island, a successful merchant. Was a liberal benefactor of R. I. College, which in 1804, changed its name to Brown University in his honor. (Id.)

Section 26. Joseph Emerson Brown, born 1821, had risen to prominence as a lawyer, when he became Governor of Georgia, which office he held from 1857-1865, including the Civil War period. In the Civil War he took an active part, seizing Forts Pulaski and Jackson. At the beginning of 1861, he advocated earnest resistance—though several times opposed by President Davis. He was chief justice of the Supreme Court of the State and United States Senator 1881-1891, and died in 1894. (Id)

Section 27. Robert Brown, introduced the separatist doctrine, was a clergyman of the Church of England, of Norwich until 1580, when he began proclaiming against the discipline and ceremony of the Church. His followers were called Brownites. The Pilgrims were largely influenced by the Separatist doctrines. The Pilgrim fathers were Brownites. (Id)

Section 28. Ford Madox Brown, an English painter, born at Calais, France in 1821. He studied his art in Belgium and Paris, and sent two cartoons to the competition in Westminster Hall in 1844, and a cartoon and frisce in 1845. After visiting Italy, he painted "Wycliffe reading his translation of the Scripture," and in the following year exhibited "King Lear," and the "Young Mother." He produced in 1851, at the royal academy a large painting of Chaucer reading his poetry at the Court of Edward III, "Christ washing Peter's feet," exhibited in 1852, gained the prize of the Liverpool Academy in 1856. One of his latest works is entitled "The English Fireside." (Id)

Section 29. Goold Brown, an American Grammarian, born in Providence, Rhode Island March 7, 1791; died at Lynn, Mass., March 31, 1857. He was a teacher for over twenty years in the City of New York. His "Institutes of English Grammar," appeared in 1823. In the same year, he also published "First Lines of English Grammar.' His "Grammar of English Grammars," was the most extensive and complete grammar of the English language, and has continued to stand in high repute. A revised edition which he had just completed at the time of his death appeared in 1857. (Id)

Section 30. Henry Kirke Brown, an American Sculptor, born at Lynden, Mass., in 1814. He produced the first bronze statue ever cast in this country, and completed several well known works in marble: "Hope," the "Pleiades," the "Four Seasons," the statue of General Nathaniel Greene, in the Capital at Washington. A statue in bronze of Dewitt Clinton, the equestrain statue of Washington in Union Square, New York, the statues of Lincoln in Brooklin and New York, and an equestrain statue of General Scott in Washington. (Id.)

Section 31. Hugh Stowell Brown, an English Clergyman, born at Douglas, Isle of Man in 1823; doubting some of the doctrine of the established church, he joined the Baptist denomination and was a popular lecturer. (Id)

Section 32. John Brown, an English author, born at Rothbury, Northumberland Nov. 5, 1715. His works were extensive. (Id.)

Section 33. John Brown, a Scottish Biblical Critic, born in Perthshire, about 1722; died at Haddington, June 19, 1787. He learned the Italian, Spanish, German, Duth, French, Arabic, Persian, Syniac and Ethiopic languages. His principal works are: "A Dictionary of the Bible," " A Self Interpreting Bible," and a "History of the British Churches." (Id)

Section 34. John Brown, a Scottish Physician, founder of the Brenonian System, born in Borwickshire in 1735, died in London, October 7, 1788. (Id)

Section 35. John Brown, a Scottish divine, born near Whitburn, Lentethgowshire, July 12, 1784; died Oct. 13, 1858, was ordained pastor of the Burgher Congregation at Beggar in 1806. In 1821, removed to Edniburgh, and was chosen professor of dentistry in 1834. As a preacher he was among the first of his day. (Id)

Section 36. John Brown, a Scottish Author, (son of the divine mentioned in Section 35) born in Beggar, Lanarkshire, in Sept. 1810. (Id.)

Section 37. John Newton Brown, D. D., an American Clergyman and author, born in New London, Conn., June 29, 1803; died in Germantown, Pa., May 15, 1868. (Id)

Section 38. Rawdon Brown, an accomplished English Scholar, whose researches have revealed better knowledge of the career of John Cabot. (Id)

Section 39. Robert Brown, a British Botanist, born at Montrose, Dec. 21, 1773; died in London, June 10, 1858. (Id)

Section 40. Sir Samuel Brown, an English Engineer, born in London, in 1776; died March 15, 1852. (Id)

Section 41. Samuel Brown, a Scottish Chemist and Poet, born at Haddington, February 23, 1817; died in Edinburgh, Sept. 20, 1856. (Id)

Section 42. Tarleton Brown, an American Soldier, born in Barnwell District, South Carolina, in 1754; died in 1846. He served throughout the Revolutionary War. Obtained the rank of Captain, and left interesting memoirs of his experience, containing much original information concerning the events in the two Carolinas of the time. (Id)

Section 43. Thomas Brown, (called "Tom") an English Satirist, born in Shropshire in 1663; died in 1704. (Id)

Section 44. Thomas Brown, a Scottish Philosopher, born at Kirkmabrick, near Dumfries, Jan. 9, 1778; died at Brompton, near London April 20, 1820. (Id)

Section 45. William Lawrence Brown, a Scottish Theologian, born at Utreaht, Holland, where his father was pastor, Jan. 7, 1755; died May 11, 1830. (Id)

Section 46. Charles Farrar Browne, an American Humorist, born at Waterford, Maine, April 26, 1834, died at Southampton, England, March 6, 1867. (Id)

Section 47. Edward Harold Browne, an English Bishop, born in 1811. (Id.)

Section 48. Frances Browne, an English poetess, born at Stanortar, County Donegal, June 16, 1818. (Id.)

Section 49. George Browne, Count, a Russian General, born in Ireland, June 15, 1698; died at Riga, September 18, 1792. (Id)

Section 50. Hablot Knight Browne, an English Artiste, known by the psuedonyme of "Phiz," born in 1815. (Id)

Section 51. Henrietta Browne, (the pseudonyme of Sophie de Bouteiller Madame Desauex) a French Artist, born in Paris in 1829, a great grand-daughter of the Irish General Browne, who settled in France, after the battle of Culloden, 1746, and the daughter of the Count de Bouteiller a Breton Nobleman, of much musical and administrative talent, by his marriage with the widow of the Italian composer, Benincore. (Id)

Section 52. Isaac Hawkins Browne, an English poet, born at Barton, on Trent, in 1706, died in 1760. (Id)

Section 53. John Ross Browne, an American traveller and author, born in Ireland, in 1817. While he was a child his father emigrated to America, and settled in Kentucky. (Id)

Section 54. Mary Ann Browne (Mrs. James Gray), an English poetess, born at Maidenhead, Thicket Berkshire, Sept. 24, 1812; died in Cork, January 28, 1846. (Id)

Section 55. Simon Browne, an English Theologian, born at Shipton Mallet, Somersetshire in 1680; died in 1732. (Id)

Section 56. Sir Thomas Browne, an English physician and author, born in London, Oct. 19, 1605; died at Norwich Oct. 19, 1682. (Id)

Section 57. William Browne, an English poet, born at Tavistock, Devonshire, in 1590; died about 1645. (Id)

Section 58. William George Browne, an English traveller, born in London in 1768; died in Persia in 1813, educated at Oxford, travelled in Egypt, and attempted to explore the interior of Africa, but was stopped in Darfoor, where he was detained as a captive for thrree years. He published "Travels in Africa, Egypt and Syria," in the years 1792-8. He afterwards undertook a journey through Persia, but on the way from Tabris to Teheran was murdered by banditti. (Id)

Section 59. Notes from Madison County Court Records:

Nicholas Brown, will dated and probated in 1813, commences with these words: "Being called on in a campaign under the command of General Green Clay to go to fight the British in Canada, do make this my last will and testament." He states that he is a son of Caleb Brown, and names as his brothers and sisters: Edward Brown, Henry Brown, John Brown, Hugh Brown, Caleb Brown and Peggy Park. And names his uncle Hugh Brown as executor.

One Nicholas Brown, August 22, 1809, bought land on the east fork of Otter Creek, from William West, which he and his wife Sarah, afterwards conveyed to H. and L. Searcy.

Caleb Brown, March 6, 1807, bought land on Silver Creek, of N. Durbin. His children were:

1. Nicholas Brown, whose will was probated in 1813.

2. Edward Brown; married Nov. 29, 1797, Sarah Hoy, and Aug. 8, 1815, Janey Campbell. In 1817, processioners made report of his land. Feb. 10, 1808, Edwin Brown, bought land on Otter Creek, of Andrew Tribble. In 1811, Edward Brown and Sarah his wife, were conveyed part of the George Boone preemption on the east side of Tates Creek, by Polly Ballew and others. Feb. 1813, Edward Brown was conveyed land by Andrew Tribble on Otter Creek.

3. Henry Brown; married Feb. 23, 1797, Rebecca Roberts. In 1790, Henry Brown bought land on the south of Reid's Mill of James Dozier's executor. Jan. 10, 1800, bought land of George McCormack. April 15, 1814, bought land on Otter Creek of Joshua Wheeler. Oct. 29, 1796, Henry Stephenson Brown and John Brown, sons of Caleb Brown, bought land on Otter Creek, of Leonard Dozier.

4. John Brown; married Ann Hamilton in 1813. (John Brown, Jr., Aug. 1, 1789, bought land on Speeds fork of Sugar Creek, of Robert Henderson.) John Brown July 5, 1796, bought land on Otter Creek, of Thomas Clay, and Nov. 15, 1798, of H. Laughlin on Otter Creek. John Brown Jan. 3, 1805, of Garrard County, bought land of Green Clay on Drowning Creek.

5. Hugh Brown; married Peggy Sappington, May 13, 1824. November 20, 1809, C. Newland executed a power of attorney to Hugh Brown. May 7, 1814, John Sappington, executed to Hugh Brown, a power of attorney, (probable the uncle, spoken of in the will of Nicholas Brown.)

6. Caleb Brown, chose James Sappington, who qualified as his guardian in 1819.

7. Peggy Brown; married Mr. Park ——-

John Brown, Nov. 18, 1788, bought land on Paint Lick Creek, of David Maxwell. John Brown, Sept. 27, 1809, bought land on Station Camp, of Robert Herndon.

John Brown in 1794, was exempted from paying County levy. John Brown died in 1802, wife Euphan, and William Riley and Nicholas Brown, qualified as administrators. His infant children:

1. Eleanor Brown.

2. James Brown.

(James Brown; married Anna Clark, in 1815.)

3. Michie Brown.

David Brown of Jefferson County, Aug. 25, 1795, executed a power of attorney to his brother John Brown of Madison County.

John G. Brown of Greenbrier County, Va., Jan. 29, 1801, was deeded 4695 acres of land, on Station Camp and Drowning Creek.

John G. Brown of Ohio County, Ky., March 18, 1814, conveyed to Jesse Craven lands on Station Camp, and Chasning Creek.

Benajah Brown, appears as early as 1787, and married Judith Brown, November 25, 1791.

Thomas Brown, appears as early as 1787, and married Rachael Pursley, June 23, 1796.

Thomas Brown; married Nancy Chenault in 1813. (See Part V, Chapter 13, Section 9.)

Thomas Brown bought lands of Higgason Grubbs Oct. 3, 1807.

James Brown, appears as early as 1788; married Hannah Pursley March 31, 1795.

James Brown, bought land on Otter Creek, of Robert Tevis, in 1795.

James Brown, bought land on Muddy Creek of John Blachard, June 6, 1804.

Joseph Brown, appears as early as 1790; married Elizabeth Ellison June 9, 1795.

Joseph and Robert Brown, bought land on Paint Lick Creek, of Robert Henderson August 5, 1794. They bought land on Paint Lick Crek of Michael McNeily Dec. 30, 1797.

Samuel Brown appears as early as 1790, bought land on the Kentucky River of John Crooke, July 9, 1801, and Aug. 1, 1803, on Drowning Creek of John Crooke, and April 1805, on said River of Elisha Witt. Robin Brown, April 22, 1788, bought land on Speed's fork of Sugar Creek, of James Knox (probably a brother to Jesse Brown, above). Robert Brown, married Ruth Brown, July 10, 1794.

George Brown, December 10, 1795, bought land of Innis Henry. He and his wife Elizabeth May 19, 1796, conveyed land on the east fork of Otter Creek to John Conley. George Brown; married Polly Wilson in 1811.

William Brown, bought land of Sherwood Harris June 5, 1792, and December 17, 1807, on Otter Creek of Owen Herndon, and March 1, 1808, of Thomas Townsend two slaves, and April 7, 1812, of the Trustees of Richmond lot no., 8, on the south side of Main Street. (May 4, 1796, William Brown and wife Margaret, of Fayette County, conveyed land on Silver Creek to Alex Gaston.

William Brown's will dated 1814, probated 1816, wife Elizabeth. She and testator's neighbor, William Goodloe, executors: witnesses: Josiah Gentry, Caroline Hix and Adam Caplinger, issue:

1. Polly Brown; married John Miller, Feb. 9, 1804. (See Part I, Chapter 14, Section 5.)

George Brown in 1826, qualified as administrator of William Brown's estate.

Brightberry Brown, of Albemarle County, Va., Nov. 3, 1789, executed a power of attorney to Robert Rodes to receive lands from William Hoy's heirs, etc.

Joshua Brown, Jan. 5, 1794, bought land on Silver Creek of Elisha Green, and Aug. 10, 1815, bought land on Silver Creek of Caleb Brown Jr., deed signed by "Caleb Brown, Honor Brown."

Charles Brown, Oct. 4, 1796, bought land on Paint Lick of John Brown, and October 19, 1809, of John Arnett on Silver Creek. He and his wife Henrietta, March 5, 1810, conveyed land on Silver Creek to John Hume.

Charles Brown: married Tabitha White, Sept. 17, 1818.

Elias Brown, Dec. 16, 1807, bought land of James Holman. He married Susan Mauzy, January 21, 1824.

Bazel Brown, of Fairfield County, Ohio, June 4, 1816, executed a power of attorney to his son:

1. Bazel Brown.

John H. Brown, Presbyterian minister in 1829, was authorized to solemnize the rites of matrimony.

Section 60. List of Counties, towns, etc., bearing the name, found on map:

Maine—
- Brownsfield.
- Brownville.
- Brownsville Junction.

New Hampshire—
- Brown Brook.

Vermont—
- Brown Lake.
- Brownington Lake.
- Browns River.
- Brownington.
- Brownington Center.
- Brownsville.

Massachusetts—
- Browning Pond.
- Brown.

New York—
- Brownson.
- Brownsville.

Pennsylvania—
- Brownfield.
- Brownhill.
- Brownlee.
- Browns L-22.
- Browns P-5.
- Brownsburg.
- Brownsdale.
- Brownstone.
- Brownsville N-6.
- Brownsville No. 3, O-30.

Florida—
- Brown.

Louisiana—
- Brown.
- Brownlee.

North Carolina—
- Brown Creek.
- Brown Mountain.
- Brown's Store.
- Brown's Summit.
- Brownsville.
- Brownstone.
- Brown.

Alabama—
- Brownley Creek.
- Brown's Creek.
- Browns.
- Brownsboro.
- Browns Creek P. O.

Tennessee—
- Brown.
- Brownlow
- Brownsboro.
- Browns Chapel.
- Brownsville.

Ohio—
- Brown County.
- Brownhelm.
- Brownhelm Station.
- Brown Run.
- Browns.
- Browns (2).
- Brown's Mills.
- Brownsville.
- Browntown.

Arkansas—
- Brown Creek.
- Brown 9-5.
- Brown K-14.
- Brownstown.

Michigan—
- Brown County.
- Brow[illegible]
- [illegible]
- Brown's Mills.
- Brown's Siding.
- Brownsville.

Minnesota—
- Brown County.
- Brownsburg.
- Brownsdale.
- Brownsville.
- Brownton.
- Brown Valley.

Texas—
- Brown County.
- Brownings.
- Brownsboro.
- Brownsville.
- Brownwood.

New Jersey—
- Brown Mills.
- Brown Mills Junction.
- Browntown.

Maryland—
- Browningsville.
- Brownsville.

Delaware—
- Brownsville.

Virginia—
- Browns.
- Brownsburg.
- Browns Cove.
- Browns Store.
- Browntown.

West Virginia—
- Brown.
- Brownstown.
- Brownsville.

South Carolina—
- Brown.
- Brownell.
- Brownsville.

Georgia—
- Browns.
- Brown's.
- Brown's Bridge.
- Brown's Crossing.
- Brownsville.
- Browning.

Mississippi—
- Brown's Creek.
- Brown's Bayon.
- Browns Creek P. O.
- Brownsville.
- Brownsville 2.

California—
- Brownell.
- Browns Valley.
- Brownsville.

Kentucky—
- Browning.
- Brownsboro.
- Brown's Cross Roads.
- Brown's Grove.
- Brown's Valley.
- Brownsville.

Indiana—
- Brown County.
- Brownell.
- Brownsburg.
- Brownstown.
- Browns Valley.
- Brownsville.
- Brown.

Illinois—
- Brown County.
- Browning.
- Browns.
- Brownstown.
- Brownsville.

Wisconsin—
- Brown County.
- Brown's Siding.
- Brownsville.
- Browntown.

Iowa—
- Brown.
- Brownville.

Missouri—
- Brown Branch.
- Browning.
- Brownington.
- Brownsdale.
- Brown Springs.
- Brown's Station.
- Brownwood.

Kansas—
- Brown County.
- Brownell.
- Brownsville.

Indian Territory—
- Brownsville.

Nebraska—
- Brown County.
- Brownlee.
- Brownson.
- Brownville.

Wyoming—
- Browns Springs.

Utah—
- Brown Cliffs Mountain.
- Browns Cliffs.

Washington—
- Brownsville.

Colorado—
- Browns Creek.
- Brown.
- Brown (2.)
- Brown's Canon.

Nevada—
Brown Knobs.
Browns D-6.
Browns A-8.
Oklahoma—
Brown.
South Kakota—
Brown County.
Brownsville.
Montana—
Brown Mountain.
Brownes.
Browning.
Oregon—
Brownsboro.
Brownsville.
Browntown.

CHAPTER 2.

THE BROWN FAMILY.

Article 1.—The Brown family herein are of English origin, Anglo-Saxon. The original head of the American branch, Benjamin Brown, in the early part of the eighteenth century came from Wales, and settled temporarily in Hanover County, Va., subsequently he moved to Albemarle County, Va., and settled in Brown's Cove, the place where he made his permanent home, called Walnut Level or Trinidad, which is now owned by his descendants, the Auburn family.

Rev. Edgar Woods in his history of Albemarle states "that the Browns of Brown's Cove, were a Hanover family. Its head Benjamin and his oldest son Benjamin, patented a large area of land in Louisa County, both before and after its establishment in 1742. They began to obtain grants in Albemarle, also, soon after its formation. From 1747 to 1760, they entered more than six thousand acres on both sides of Doyles River. **Benjamin died in 1762, leaving eleven children: Benjamin,, William, Agnes, Barzellia, Benajah, Bernard, Bernis, Bezaeel, Brightberry, Elizabeth, the wife of John Price and Lucretia, the wife of Robert Harris.

Benjamin Brown was a clergyman in the Revolutionary Army, a member of Light Horse Harry Lee's troop. Two of his brothers, Brightberry and Bezalul Brown, were captains in the same service, and another brother Bernard Brown was also, a soldier of that army, whose principal duty was to carry dispatches for General Washington from New York to Charleston, South Carolina, and was chosen for that service because of his wonderful powers of endurance and his trust worthiness, and of whom (it is told) General Washington said, "he could make his trips quicker than any other man, in the service he had tried."

The Brown family ranks among the first families of Virginia and have ever held that position since Virginia has been their home. From their early settlement, their prominent part in public affairs, the high character generally prevalent among them, and the lasting impress they have made on the natural scenery of the country is one of the most noted in its history. (Rev. Edgar Woods.)

Benjamin Brown, died at his home, Trinidad in Brown's Cove, in 1762. His first wife was a Miss Hescott, a Welch lady, no children were born of this union. He married the second time Miss Sarah Thompson, born in 1724, she died in 1815, at the age of ninety one years. Their children were:

Section 1. Bernard Brown, Sr., married Elizabeth Dabney, daughter of John Dabney of Albemarle, and Ann Harris his wife. (See Part III, Chapter 3, Section 7.) A more complete history of whom is given in Chapter 3 .

Section 2. Bezaeel Brown, was Captain of a company of Virginia troops in the Revolutionary Army. He married Polly Thompson, a sister to Nathaniel Thompson. He was formerly a Magistrate of Albemarle County, and was sheriff of the County in 1805. Their children:

1. William T. Brown: married Mary Ann Jarman, daughter of James Jarman. (See part V, Chap. 4, note). He died in 1877. Their children:

DR. WM. E. BIBB.

MARY S. BROWN.

1. Lucy Brown; unmarried.
2. Sarah Brown; married John R. Early.
3. Mary S. Brown; married Dr. William E. Bibb.
4. Captain Bezaeel Brown; single.
5. J. W. Brown; single.

2. Captain Bezaeel Brown; married Elizabeth Price in 1817. Their children:

1. George Brown: married Harriett Golding. Their children:
   1. Lucien L. Brown.
   2. Virgil Brown; dead.
   3. Mary Brown; single.
   4. Wilmes Brown; single.
   5. Sallie Belle Brown; married Faunt Kemper. Their children:
      1. Helen Kemper; married Mr. Arles.
      2. Mary Kemper; married Mr. Miller.
      3. Margaret Kemper; single.
      4. Agnes Kemper; single.
2. W. W. Brown; married Miss Sprinkle.
3. Mary Frances Brown; married Waller Harris. (See Part III, Chap. 3, Sec. 4, and Part VIII, Chap. 11, Sec. 7.)
4. Francis Brown.
5. Erastus R. Brown; married Miss Harper, went West.
6. Aldretus P. Brown; married Emily Scott.
7. Cornelia Brown; married Dr. J. W. Poynts.
8. Columbia Brown.
9. Oscar Brown, went to Texas.

10. Mattie A. Brown.

11. Lucy T. Brown; married first Ham Michie and second J. D. Garth. Issue of first marriage:

1. Fannie Michie.

Issue of second marriage:

2. Lizzie Garth; single.
3. Allie Garth; single.
4. Charles Garth; single.
5. Mattie A. Garth; married Rev. J. J. Laferty. Their children:
    1. Annie Laferty; married Mr. Cates.
    2. George Laferty; married Miss Lay.
    3. Dr. Walter Laferty; married Miss Tally.
    4. William Laferty; married Miss Owens.
    5. Edward Laferty; married Miss Taylor.
6. Sarah Garth; married Buck Autrim. Their children:
    1. Columbia Autrim; married Gus Brown.
    2. Price Autrim; married Miss Constable.

3. Elizabeth Brown; married Jesse Garth. Their children:

1. Bezaleel Garth; married Miss Gillum. Their children:
    1. James Garth; died in the Confederate Army.
    2. William Garth; also died in the Confederate Army.
    3. John Garth; single.
    4. Mary Ann Garth; married Ira B. Brown.
    5. Lou Garth; single.

2. Brightberry Garth; married first Miss Graves of Madison County, and second Jane Early. Issue of first marriage:
    1. Virginia Garth; single.
    2. Martha Garth; married first Calvin Garnett. Their children:
        1. Henry Garnett.
        2. Robert Garnett.
        3. Virgil Garnett.

Issue of second marriage of Brightberry Garth to Jane Early:
    3. Virgil Garth.
    4. Miss Garth; married Mr. Brown in Texas.

3. William Garth; married Miss Early. Their children:
    1. George Garth; married Victoria Nicol.
    2. Howard Garth; married Malinda Wayland.
    3. Joseph Garth.
    4. Bettie Garth; married Addison Buckner.
    5. Kate Garth; married Mr. Harrison, went west.

4. Thomas Garth; married Louisa Yancey. Their children:
    1. Jesse Garth; single.
    2. Lewis Garth; married Fannie Plunkett.
    3. Yancey Garth; married Mary Parrott.
    4. Junius Brutus Garth; married Mollie Durrett.
    5. Bettie Garth; married William Rout.
    6. Lucy Garth; married Richard Yancey.
    7. Portia Garth; sinlge.
    8. Texas Garth; single.
    9. Jane Garth; single.
    10. Miss Garth; married Mr. Nicol, went south.

5. Sarah Garth; married Mr. Goodman. Their children:
    1. Clay Goodman.
    2. Sidney Goodman.
    3. Green Goodman.

6. Polly Garth; married Mr. Sumner, no issue.

4. Lucy Brown; married her cousin Reuben Dabney Brown, son

of Bernard Brown and Elizabeth Dabney his wife. (See Section 3, and Chapter 3, Section 3, and Chapter 6.)

5. Sarah Brown; married Charles Parrott. Their children:

1. B. B. Parrott; married Julia Ann Stephens, of Orange. Their children:

1. Mattie Parrott; single.
2. E. Rossar Parrott; single.
3. Mary Parrott; married Yancey Garth. Issue:
   1. Charles Garth.
4. William H. Parrott; married Lizzie Beckers. Their children:
   1. William Parrott.
   2. Lucy Parrott.
   3. Ernest Rossar Parrott.
5. G. B. Parrott; married Sallie Catterton. Their children:
   1. Fannie Emory Parrott.
   2. Bledsoe Parrott.
   3. Ethel Parrott.
   4. George Parrott.
   5. Stanley Parrott.
   6. Baby Parrott.

2. W. T. Parrott; married Frances Thompson. (See Chap. 7, Section 7.)

3. C. H. Parrott; married Martha Brown. (See Chap. 11, Section 4.) Their children:

1. W. H. Parrott; married Faith Thomas. No children.
2. Soonie Parrott; single.
3. C. C. Parrott; single.
4. Lizzie Parrott; married Captain Marcellus Kemper. Their children:
   1. Pearre Kemper.
   2. Frank Eugene Kemper.
   3. William Kemper; dead.
   4. Tribble Kemper; dead.
   5. Mary Kemper; single.
   6. Fannie R. Kemper; married W. B. Bibb. Their children:
      1. Ellis Bibb.
      2. Charles Bibb.
      3. Kemper Bibb.
      4. Nannie Bibb.
      5. Eugene Bibb.
      6. Mary Elizabeth Bibb.

4. N. B. Parrott; married Mrs. G. W. Early, nee Alice Stownels of Prince William County. Their children:

1. Lucy Parrott; single.
2. Nettie Parrott; married Fray Yeager; no issue.
3. Sudie Parrott; single.
4. Lizzie Parrott; single.
5. Edward Parrott; single.
6. Charles Parrott; married Lucy Stephens; no children.

5. Lucy E. Parrott.

6. Columbia M. Parrott; married N. E. Early. Their children:

1. Edward T. Early; married Anna Norwood of South Boston, issue:
   1. James William Early.
2. Sallie Bettie Early, not married.
3. Jane Early; married Edwin Blakely. Their children:
   1. Ovall Blakely.
   2. Sudie Blakely; married T. P. Moyers, no issue.

3. Bettie Blakely; married C. D. Shackelford.
4. Lutie Early; singlge.
5. Doc Early; single.

7. Sarah Parrott; married Livingston Stephens. Their children:

1. Sarah Hulett Stephens; single.
2. Mary Lucy Stephens; married J. M. Moyers, no issue.

6. Mary Brown; married Dr. Charles Brown, and she lived to be ninety two years old. (See Chap. 3, Sec. 6, and Chap. 9.)

Section 3. Brightberry Brown, was Captain of a company of volunteer cavalry, in the Revolutionary Army. He married Susan Thompson, sister to the wife of his brother. Bezaleel. He died in 1846, at the age of eighty four years. Their children:

1. Horace Brown, lived at the head of the Cove, just beneath Brown's Gap and his home, on account of the bracing air, quiet seclusion and generous fare, was a favorite resort of the Methodist preachers during the heat of summer.

2. William Brown; married Susan Fretwell. They had a son:

1. Strother Brown; married —— —— and had a son:
1. Orville Brown.

3. Edmund Brown; married Theodocia Michie (see Chap. 14.) They had a son:

1. Marshall Brown.

4. Nimrod Brown; married Susan Brown, daughter of Reuben D. and Lucy Brown. (See Chap. 8, Section 11.) They had a son:

1. Reuben Brown.

5. Clifton Brown; married first Sarah Brown and second Bettie Brown, both daughters of Bernard Brown Jr., and Miriam Maupin his wife. (See Chapter 8, Sec. 6, and 7.) No issue of the second marriage. Children of the first marriage:

1. Tazwell Brown; married Isabella Brown, went South.
2. William A. Brown, killed at Williamsburg, Va.
3. Dr. T. H. Brown; married Miss Carpenter. Their children:
   1. DeWitt Brown.
   2. Lula Brown.
   3. Sallie Brown.
   4. Virdie Brown.
   5. Edward Brown.
   6. Bernard Brown.
4. Susan Brown.
5. Virginia A. Brown.

6. Brightberry Brown; married Harriet Rollins. Their children:

1. Jacquelin Brown.
2. Isabella Brown; married Tazewell Brown.

7. Mildred Brown; married Thomas H. Brown. (See Chapter 3, Section 7, and Chapter 10.)

8. Amanda Brown; married George Brown, son of Reuben D. Brown and Lucy Brown his wife, (see Chap. 6, Sec. 1, also Sec. 2, of this Chapter.) Their children:

1. Llewellyn Brown, killed in Confederate Army.
2. George Brown, killed in Confederate Army.
3. William Brown, killed in Confederate Army.
4. Reuben Brown.
5. Clifton Brown.
6. Benjamin Brown.
7. Susan Brown; married John Chenault.
8. Lucy Brown; married Mr. —— Adams.
9. Sarah Brown; married Mr. —— Adams.
10. Charles Brown, killed in Confederate Army.
11. Amanda Brown.

Section 4. **Bernis Brown,** (See Chap. 16) was one of the early Methodist preachers in the County of Albemarle, entering the ministry some years before the close of the eighteenth century. He was a signer of the Albemarle Declaration of Independence April 2, 1779. He married Henrietta Rodes, a daughter of John Rodes and Sarah Harris his wife. (See Part III, Chapter 3, Section 7.) He died in 1815. Their children:

1. Sarah Brown; married Thomas Jones.
2. Henrietta Brown; married John Ruff.
3. Ann Brown; married John Dickerson.
4. Bernis Brown; married ——— ——— emigrated to Saline County, Mo., and was one of her pioneers, and a very prominent man of the County. He was County Judge, County Surveyor, and held other important offices. His wife died leaving him with twelve children. Some one was talking to a handsome widow about him, and she said "I have no objection to the Judge, but I have to the jury."
5. Tyre Brown, the subject of Chapter 16.
6. Benjamin T. (Long Thompson) Brown; married Lucy Ann Richards. She lived to be ninety five years old. Their children:
   1. Bernie Brown; married Bettie Imbodin.
   2. James R. Brown; single.
   3. Jefferson Brown; married Florence Carter.
   4. Lucien Brown; married Miss ——— Michie.
   5. Lucy Brown; single.
7. Elizabeth Brown.
8. John R. Brown; married Candice Hall, no issue.

JUDGE BURNIS BROWN.

Section 5. Francina Benajah Brown; married Mary Jarman, a daughter of Thomas Jarman. (See Part V, Chap. 4, Sec. 1.) He sold his Albemarle property and moved to Buckingham. Their children:

1. Beverley Brown.
2. Miletus Brown.
3. Garland Brown; married Patsey Bransford. Children:
   1. Jack Brown.
   2. Martha Brown.
   3. Sallie Brown.
4. Katie Brown.
5. Patsey Brown.
6. Sallie Brown; married James Jarman. (See Part V, Chap. 4, note.) Their children:
   1. Mary Ann Jarman; married Colonel William T. Brown. (See Section 2, and Chapter 4.)
   2. Miletus Jarman; married Miss Hansberger. Their children:
      1. Robert Jarman; died single.
      2. Henry Jarman; died single.
      3. Clotilda Jarman; married J. W. Rodes. (See Chap. 4.)
      4. Etta Jarman; married Mr. Bethum.
      5. Mary Kitty Jarman; married Marion Brown.
      6. Sarah Jarman; married Dr. Thompkins. Their children:
         1. Mattie Thompkins.
         2. Kate Thompkins.

3. Robert Thompkins.
4. Samuel Thompkins; married Miss Thompkins.

Section 6. Barzellia Brown, sold out in Albemarle and emigrated to Shelby County, Ky., in 1809.

Section 7. Lucretia Brown; married Robert Harris, and emigrated to Surry County, North Carolina. (See Part III, **Chap. 3,** Section 2.)

According to History of Albemarle by Rev. Edgar Woods, Benjamin Brown had the following children besides the above mentioned:

Section 8. Benjamin Brown, the eldest. He and his brother William were executors of their father's will, and had their portion and residence in Hanover and Louisa.

Section 9. William Brown, was co-executor with his brother Benjamin of his father's will, and their homes were in Hanover and Louisa.

Section 10. Agnes Brown.

Section 11. Elizabeth Brown; married John Price.

CHAPTER 3.

BERNARD BROWN, SENIOR.

(Named in Chapter 2, Section 1.)

Article 1.—Bernard Brown, Senior, a son of Benjamin Brown, the immigrant from Wales, and Sarah Thompson his wife, was born in Albemarle County, Va., Jan. 28, 1750; was married to Elizabeth Dabney, daughter of John Dabney of Albemarle and Ann Harris his wife, June 22, 1773. (See Part III, Chapter 3, Section 7.) Elizàbeth Dabney was born June 18, 1751.

Bernard Brown as mentioned in Chapter 2, was a soldier in the struggle for American Independence, whose duty was to carry dispatches for General Washington, from New York to Charleston, South Carolina, and was chosen for that service because of his trust worthiness, and extraordinary powers of endurance, of whom his General said "that he could make the trip quicker than any other person in the service of whom he had knowledge." He was a practicing attorney at law of Albemarle County, and represented clients in Kentucky, as proof of this latter statement on the fourth of December 1801, Daniel Maupin, Sr., a resident at that time of Madison County, Ky., by deed of record gave to his son John Maupin, fifty pounds he had collected, that was in the hands of Bernard Brown of Albemarle County, Va., who was his acting attorney at law. Bernard Brown was killed by the fall of a tree Feb. 26, 1800, and his wife lived twenty six years thereafter, and died July 21, 1826, at the age of seventy five years and thirteen days. His home was at the foot of Bucks Elbow, not far from White Hall in Albemarle County, Va. Their children are named in the coming sections:

Section 1. Francina Brown, she married Captain John (or Jack) Rodes, a son of John Rodes and Sarah Harris his wife. (See Part III, Chapter 3, Section 7.) The subject of Chapter 4.

Section 2. Robert Thompson Brown; married Betsy Crenshaw. The subject of Chapter 5.

Section 3. Reuben Dabney Brown; married his cousin Lucy Brown. The subject of Chapter 6.

Section 4. Lucy Brown; married Nathaniel Thompson, a brother to the wives of her uncles Bezaleel and Brightberry Brown. The subject of Chapter 7. (See "The Thompson Family of Albemarle.")

Section 5. Bernard Brown, Jr., married Miriam Maupin, a daughter of Daniel Maupin and Martha Jarman, his first wife. (See Part V, Chapter 4, Section 2.) The subject of Chapter 8.

Section 6. Dr. Charles Brown; married his cousin Polly Brown. The subject of Chapter 9.

Section 7. Thomas Harris Brown; married his cousin Milly Brown, she died and he married Lucy Goodman. The subject of Chapter 10.

Section 8. Bezaleel Brown; married Betsy Michie. The subject of Chapter 11.

Section 9. Benjamin Hescott Brown; married Judith Fretwell. The subject of Chapter 12.

Section 10. Sarah Brown; married her cousin Colonel Beverly A. Brown. The subject of Chapter 13.

Section 11. Ira Benajah Brown; married Frances Jarman Mullins. The subject of Chapter 14.

Section 12. Asa Brightberry Brown; married his cousin Maria Brown. The subject of Chapter 15.

CHAPTER 4.

FRANCINA BROWN.

(Named in Chapter 3, Section 1.)

Article 1.—Francina Brown, a daughter of Bernard Brown, Sr., and Elizabeth Dabney his wife, was born in Albemarle County, Va., May 24, 1775.

She married as aforesaid, Captain John (or Jack) Rodes, a son of John Rodes and Sarah Harris, his wife. (See Part III, Chap. 3, Sec. 7, E.) She died the third day of May, 1846, at the age of 71 years, leaving these children:

FRANCINA BROWN.
Wife of Capt. Jack Rodes.

Section 1. William Rodes; married Clarissa Yancey. He lived 80 years.

Section 2. Sydney Rodes; married Powhattan Jones

Section 3. Ryland Rodes; married Miss Virginia Woods.

Section 4. Sarah Rodes; married first James Payne and second Samuel Woods. (See Part II, Chap. 25, and Part III., Chap. 3, Sec. 7.)

Section 5. John Rodes; married Mrs. Ann Morris nee Durrett, widow of William Morris, no issue.

Section 6. Lucy Rodes; married — Newlands and went west.

Section 7. Jacintha Tazewell Rodes, daughter of Captain John Rodes and his wife Francina Brown, and a granddaughter of Bernard Brown and his wife Elizabeth Dabney, and a great grand-daughter of Benjamin Brown and his wife Sarah Thompson, married first, Captain John Massie Smith, of Nelson County, Va., and second, Captain James M. Harris of Nelson County, Va. By her first marriage she had six children, hereinafter named, and by her second marriage, she had three children hereinafter named, nine in all, towit:

1. Robert Hardin Smith; married Mary Ann McCue. They had six children, viz:

1. Bettie Jacintha Smith; married Dr. Jacob Pinckney Killian, their children are:

1. Lelia Killian; married Dr. John Fleming.
2. Alda Killian; single.
3. Irma Killian; single.
4. Kenneth Killian; single.

2. Ida Massie Smith; married William Henry Turner. Their children are:

1. Robert Emmett Turner.
2. Mary Massie Turner.
3. William Henry Turner, Jr.
4. Dorothy Ida Turner.
5. Virginia Eliabeth Turner.

3. James Emmett Smith; married Grace Lee McLellan. Their children are:

1. McLellan Smith.
2. Mary Virginia Smith.
3. Ruth Birney Smith.

4. John William Smith; married Ruth Lawrence Heywood.

5. Virginia Alice Smith; married Harry Thomas Autrim. Their children are:

1. Thomas Houston Autrim.
2. Robert Emmett Autrim.
3. Mary Virginia Autrim.
4. Frank Templeton Autrim.
5. Katherine Taylor Autrim.

6. Marianna Robinette Smith; married her cousin Edward Massie Smith.

2. William Henry Smith; died aged thirty three years, never married.

3. Bettie Massie Smith; married her cousin Charles Rodes. They had three children, viz:

1. William Smith Rodes; married Mattie M. McCue, no issue.
2. Alice Jacintha Rodes; married John Montgomery. They have eight children.
3. Robert Clifton Rodes; died single.

4. Charles Thompson Smith, an old bachelor, a very lively, active proposition, in that class of social outlaws, now sixty nine years old, and living at Harlan, Ky. Charles Thompson Smith was twenty-three years old when he volunteered in the First Greenbriar Cavalry Company under Captain Robert B. Moorman, in the spring of 1861, being a slender youth, run down from close study, in health and flesh, and weighing only one hundred and twenty pounds, and was found, in consequence, unfit for infantry service, and was furloughed to go home to arrange his business affairs, and to get horse and other equipments.

Rejoining the army he was one of a portion of his company sent hastily to Rich Mountain to aid in the relief of Colonel Pegram, then engaged with the Federal or United States Military forces, but before reaching their destination the Confederates had been defeated. On the excursion when his horse was jumping a fence, Smith was thrown violently out of the saddle, receiving a twisting violent wrench of the left loin, severely straining it and displacing a muscle of the back; an injury from which he has never thoroughly recovered. Upon examination by Dr. W. L. Barksdale, of Hinton, West Virginia, at that time Surgeon of the company, the hurt was pronounced a permanent one, and he was furloughed indefinitely, and advised to remain as quiet as possible. In the early fall of 1861, young Smith started back to the army, but before reaching it, General Robert E. Lee had disbanded the company, giving as his reason, that "It contained too much valuable recruiting material to be kept in the service as a company." This wise step resulted in the raising of several cavalry and other companies from Greenbriar County for the Confederate Army.

First Lieutenant, F. W. M. Feamster, gave testimony of the faithful picket duty, rendered by this young soldier, at Laurel Hill. He says "I was ordered to select reliable men, and during the night I visited the pickets every four hours, I always found Smith at his post, which was regarded as a very critical and dangerous position."

After the injury spoken of Charles Thompson Smith re-entered the Confederate service, as employee of Captain J. C. Deane, Quarter Master of the 59th Regiment of Virginia Infantry. In 1862 at Nags Head, he was promoted by General Wise to the rank of Captain, on his staff, and in charge as acting Quarter Master of the Regiment. During the land battle at Roanoke Island, notwithstanding he was a non-combatant, he took the rifle gun of private John Hanna, who was ill, and founght under Captain F. M. Imboden, in the thickest of the fight, reloading and shooting so often that the gun got so hot (thus contracting the bore) that it could not be recharged. After the surrender General Reno, U. S. A., remarked that " Smith was the first Quarter Master he ever saw in a fight." At this critical point in the battle Adjutant Blocker, owing to the effect of heavy canonading, became too sick for duty, and Lieutenant Frank Anderson of said Regiment ordered Smith to act as Adjutant in Lieutenant Blocker's place until the battle ended. For six hours the battle raged and in spite of the fearless display of gallantry by the officers, and personal bravery of the private soldiers, it ended in Confederate defeat, because of the overwhelming numbers against them. During this engagement Smith was struck by a spent ball which did no damage and in no other of five fights and skirmishes in which he engaged, did he receive a gun shot wound during the war.

Being paroled as a prisoner of war, Charles Thompson Smith engaged in the manufacture of salt at Saltville, Va., from 1862 until 1865. Released from parole in the fall of 1863, he rendered valuable service to the Confederates as a soldier in protecting this most important salt furnishing point to the Confederacy, and to the people of the state. On one most dangerous mission riding thirty miles in the night in extremely cold and stormy weather, and through the enemy's lines as courier to take a special message from General Breckinridge for reenforcements to save the salt works from capture. He was shot at many times and barely escaped death and capture by General Stoneman's forces. In response to that message, the same night, with Smith as guide, General Bazil W. Duke was sent to the rescue, in command of a selected cavalry force, which stampeded the enemy back into Kentucky, thus saving the great salt works from destruction.

After the war with depleted health and fortune, but with true Southern courage, Smith applied himself to the affairs of civil life. His fidelity, business aptitude and tact were displayed to the public, first in the office of sheriff, which he twice held under bond of $90,000. His legislative talent and qualifications were manifested during one term in the House of Delegates and three terms in the Senate successively, in which service he signally demonstrated his natural ability and enviable sagacity in recognizing and grasping the new and living issues of the times, which required the exercise of fine statesmanship, to shape them into laws. The Legislative Journals and statutes of Virginia show that his name as a skillful legislator and valuable public servant is united indelibly with the history of the commonwealth as the author of more legislation perhaps since the war, than any other faithful legislator, and mainly of legislation which affects and protects all classes and vocations, of men and women. His Post Office address at this time is Harlan, Ky.

5. Frances Rodes Smith; died single, aged thirty five years.

6. John Massie Smith, born August 29, 1843; married May 21, 1867, Nellie Timberlake.

The three brothers, Charles Thompson Smith, Francis Rodes Smith and John Massie Smith, went out of college into the Confederate Army. Hence their educations were not completed as far as was intended, the Civil War having practically ruined them financially. But John as he is called in the family is what the people of his native and adopted counties esteem as a leading citizen, intelligent gentleman, and consistent member of the Baptist Church.

John Massie Smith was only in the seventeenth year of his age when he entered the Confederate Army. This brave young patriot was on repeated occasions selected by his Colonel and other officers to perform daring and desperate duties, and therefore was recommended for promotion, but he modestly declined, mainly because of his youthful age, saying that he was "satisfied with the honor of being a private in the ranks of his company," and as such surrendered, having fought in thirty battles. He is at this time a leading citizen of Albemarle County, Va. He is well beloved for his many fine traits of character. He lives at Shadwell, three miles east of Charlottesville, in Albemarle County, on the Chesapeake and Ohio Railway. He is very found of his kin. His wife died many years ago, and he has not married again, nor is he likely to do so. He and his wife were the parents of five children, viz:

1. Rosa Bibb Smith; married Dr. John B. Turpin, no children.
2. Edward Massie Smith; married his cousin Mamie A. R. Smith, no children. They live at Shadwell, with their father John Massie Smith.
3. Sallie W. Smith, single, lives with her father and brother Edward.
4. Nellie Timberlake Smith; married John B. Greenway, no children. Mrs. Greenway died aged twenty one years.
5. Charles Thomas Smith; died in infancy.

Children by the second marrigae of Jacintha Tazewell Rodes and Captain James M. Harris of Nelson County, Va., viz:

7. James Clifton Harris; married Bettie Smith. They had six living children:
   1. Massie Harris.
   2. Lila Harris.
   3. Bettie Harris.
   4. Charles Thomas Harris.
   5. Edward Harris.
   6. Daisey Harris.
8. Lizzie Woods Harris, never married.
9. Mary Alice Harris; married her cousin William Clifton Harris, issue one child, viz:
   1. Lizzie Jacintha Harris; married Professor William Knox Tate. They have four children, viz:
      1. William Knox Tate, Jr.
      2. Mary Alice Tate.
      3. Lillian Jacintha Tate.
      4. Helen Rodes Tate.

Note—John Massie Smith Esquire, of Shadwell, Va., has the coat of arms of the Rodes, Dabney and Crawford families. John Rodes his great, great grand-father married Mary Crawford.

"The Crawford Family of Virginia."

From the Times despatch, Genological column:

"Arthur in his dictionary of names speaks of the name of Crawford as assumed by the proprietor of the land and barony of Crawford in Lenarkshire, Scotland. The extreme ancestor of the ancient family of Crawford, in Scotland, was Reginald, youngest son of Ataw, the fourth earl of Richmond. He accompanied David, the first to the North and received extensive grants of land in Strath Clueys at Clydesdale, where his immediate descendants adopted the name of Crawford. The name itself was first spelled "Craufurd," being Gaeltic, signifying "the pass of blood" from "Cru." bloody, and "furd" a pass, or way, as commemorative, probably of some great conflict with the aboriginees.

John Crawford of Scotland, born about 1600, died about 1676, emigrated to Virginia about 1643. He was a lineal discendant from Quintin Craufurd, of Kilburney, on the West Sea of Scotland.

David Crawford, the only son of John, was born 1625, and came to America with his father, settling in St. Peter's (afterwards St. Paul's) parish in New Kent. John Crawford the emigrant, was the youngest son of Earl Crawford of Scotland, about the middle of the seventeenth century. He settled first in James City County, afterwards moving to New Kent, and later being in Hanover Couny, when that was formed. The wife of David Crawford (1) is not known. Their children were: 1st. Eliabeth, born 1650, married

Nichoals Merriwither, second, a daughter, who married a Mr. McGuire, and removed south, 3rd, Captain David Crawford (II) born 1662, died Sept. 1762, 100 years of age. He married Eliabeth Smith who died at 101 years. These are the great, great grand-parents of Robert H. Smith, William H. Smith, Bettie Massie (Smith) Rodes, C. T. Smith, Frances Rodes Smith, John Massie Smith and James Clifton Harris, Lizzie Harris and Mary Alice Harris, children of Jacintha Tazewell Rodes, by her first marriage to Captain John Massie Smith, and her second marriage to Captain James M. Harris All of Nelson County, Va., near Greenfield Post Office.

Captain David Crawford, first lived in Hanover County, with his wife; in their old age moved to Amherst, now Nelson County.

The fourth child of David Crawford (1) was John, who died December 13, 1639.

The children of Captain David Crawford (II) and his wife, Eliabeth Smith Crawford, were:

1. David (III), born 1697; married Ann Anderson, died in Amherst County 1766.
2. Elizabeth, born 1699; married James Martin, and settled in the forks of Rockfish River, Amherst County.
3. John, born March 1701; married Mary Duke.
4. Mary, born March 3, 1703; married John Rodes. (See Part III, Chap. 3, Sec. 7.) John Rodes and Mary Crawford Rodes were the great great grandparents of the children of Jacintha Tazewell Rodes by her first marriage to Captain John Massie Smith, and her second marriage to Captain James M. Harris.
5. Judith, born 1705; married Joseph Terry.
6. Michael, born 1707; married —— ——

Captain David Crawford, son of David (1) grand-son of John (1) lived in the fork of the North and South Anna Rivers in Hanover County. In 1758, some two or three years after his son David (III) had moved to Amherst, he moved and settled on Rockfish river on the south side near the road, passing over "Duke's Gap," and near the foot of "Round Top" Mountain, about one mile north of "Stony Battle," being a remarkable part of the road, where vast walls of rock are rolled up each side of the road like giant walls.

As Captain of a troop of cavalry in 1714 he proclaimed George (1) King.

Captain David Crawford was buried in the forks of Stony Battle road, about one hundred yards west of the spring in Nelson County, east of the "Three Ridge" Mountain at the base, being one mile west of the house owned by Ryland Rodes.

David Crawford, son of Captain David Crawford was Commodore Vandebilt's great, great, grand-father. Mrs. Vanderbilt was Miss F. A. Crawford of Mobile, Alabama.

David Crawford (III) (son of David (II) David (1) John (1) married Ann Anderson. Their children were thirteen in numbr:

1. Susanna. 2 John, 3 Elizabeth, 4 David, 5 Joel, born Oct. 16,1736, fa'her of Hon. William Harris Crawford, 6 Charles, 7 Sarah, 8 Mary, 9 Nathan, born Oct. 16, 1744, died 1833, and married his first cousin, Judith Anderson, in 1768, grandparents of Mrs. John W. Dickinson and Mrs. John B. Coles, of Greenfield in Nelson County. Their father was Nelson Crawford, son of Nathan; 10 Peter, 11 Nelson, 12 William, 13 Ann.

The Nathan Crawford farm is now 1881, owned by Samuel Woods.

The children of Captain John W. Dickinson and his wife Judith Anderson Crawford Dickinson were:

1 Judith Anderson; married her first cousin Henry Washington Martin, 2 Henry W., 3 Fannie Coles, married Dr. Dold of Augusta County. Rev William Crawford of Louisa County, Va., wrote in his

family Bible, William Crawford, was the son of Nathan Crawford, who was the son of David Crawford, who was the son of John Crawford a Scotchman, who came to this County in the seventeenth century, and is supposed to have been killed during Bacon's war with the Indians. Rev. William Crawford was the grand father, and his son Hon. Robert Leighton Crawford, the father of Mrs. F. A. Crawford Vanderbilt, second wife of Commodore Cornelius Vanderbilt.

The Hon. William Harris Crawford, only child of Hon. Joel Crawford and his wife Fannie Harris Crawford (see Part III, Chapter 3, Section 11), was born in Nelson County, Va., Feb. 24, 1772, and was taken to South Carolina in 1774. In 1783 the family again removed to Columbia County, Ga., where his father died five years later. He was elected to the State Senate in 1802. In 1807 he was elected to the United States Senate. During this canvass he fought a duel with Peter L. Van Alen, a lawyer, and his antagonist fell mortally wounded. He also fought another duel with George Clarke, and was himself severely wounded. He was re-elected to the United States Senate in 1811. When Vice President Clinton was disabled by sickness, Mr. Crawford was chosen President of the Senate protem. In 1813 President Madison offered him the appointment of Secretary of War, which he declined. He accepted however, the post of Minister to France, where he remained two years. In 1815, he asked a recall, and while still on his voyage was appointed Secretary of War. In 1816 he was appointed to the Treasury Department, and remained in that office during President Monroe's administration until 1825, when he was honored the same position in John Q. Adam's cabinet, bu declined it. Mr. Crawford returned to his home at the end of Monroe's term in 1825, and in 1827 was made Judge of the Northern Circuit of Georgia, which he held up to his death, which occurred in Elbert County, Ga., Sept. 10, 1834, aged 62 years.

The arms for Crawford, which have been sacredly handed down from the first John Crawford in Virginia are given in Burke's English Peerage, as for Crufurd of Scotland, described as follows: Arms Quarterly—first and fourth gules, a fesse ermine, third and third azure, a chevon between three cross—patees, or, crest, an ermine, (or weas) argiue. Motto: Sine labi nota (Nothing without labor.)

Section 8. Frances Rodes: married Garland Brown. He was living at 84 years.

Section 9. Virginia Rodes: married Captain Wilson C. Smith.

Section 10. Tyre Rodes.

CHAPTER 5.

ROBERT THOMPSON BROWN.

(Named in Chapter 3, Section 2.)

Article 1.—Robert Thompson Brown, a son of Bernard Brown, Sr., and Elizabeth Dabney his wife, was born in Albemarle County, Va., Jan. 16, 1777, he and his brother Reuben Dabney Brown, were twins.

He married Betsy Crenshaw. Of this union were born children. They emigrated to Sumner County, Tennessee.

CHAPTER 6.

REUBEN DABNEY BROWN.

(Named in Chapter 3, Section 3.)

Article 1.—Reuben Dabney Brown, a son of Bernard Brown, Sr., and Elizabeth Dabney his wife, was born in Albemarle County, Va., Jan. 16, 1777, he and his brother Robert Thompson Brown, were twins.

He married his cousin Lucy Brown, daughter of Bezaeel Brown. Of this union were born these children: (See Chap. 2, Sec. 2.)

Section 1. George Brown: married Amanda Brown. (See Chap. 2, Section 3-8.)

Section 2. Brightberry Brown; married ——— ———

Section 3. Llewellyn Brown.

This whole family moved from Albemarle County, Va., to Sumner County, Tennessee.

CHAPTER 7.

LUCY BROWN.

(Named in Chapter 3, Section 4.)

Article 1.—Lucy Brown, a daughter of Bernard Brown, Sr., and Elizabeth Dabney his wife, was born in Albemarle County, Va., Nov. 7th, 1778.

She married Nathaniel Thompson, son of William Thompson. She died Feb. 16, 1852, at the age of eighty one years. Their children and descendants are set forth as follows, towit:

Section 1. Edmund J. Thompson; married Fannie Hill. Their children, towit:

1. Marietta B. Thompson; married first John Clopton, and second Jerry Martin, she left no children.
2. Martha F. Thompson; married Jerry Martin, issue:
   1. Fannetta Martin; married Charles Cosby.
   2. Lizzie Martin; married William Field.

Section 2. Bernard Brown Thompson; married Mary Ann Chapman, issue:

1. Bettie Thompson; married E. B. Brown. Children:
   1. Sallie Brown.
   2. Mary Brown; married first James Early (no issue), second B. Gates Garth. Children:
      1. Lizzie Garth.
      2. Edwin Garth.
      3. Burwell Garth.
      4. Randall Garth.
      5. Bernard Garth.
      6. Hunter Garth.
      7. Ruby Garth.
   3. Bernard A. Brown; married Mosie Pollard. Children:
      1. Mamie Brown; married Rowland Latham
      2. Terry Brown; single.

BERNARD THOMPSON

3. Lutie Brown; married Joab Durrett, no living issue.

Section 3. Lucy Brown Thompson; married William T. Chapman, she lived to be ninety one years old. Their children were:

1. J. T. Chapman; married Fannie Blakely, no issue.
2. N. B. Chapman; married Fannie Shearman, issue:
   1. Hon. John S. Chapman; married Sallie Davis.
   2. Thomas J. Chapman; married Gertrude Plunkett.
   3. Bettie Chapman; single.
3. William S. Chapman; married Mary Shearman, no living children.

Section 4. Mary Dabney Thompson; married James E. Chapman. Their children:

1. Mary Chapman; married first Dr. Mallory, no issue; second, Smith W. Brown of Buckingham. No living children.
2. N. T. Chapman; married Bettie Rodes. Their children:
   1. Willietta Chapman; married Mr. Wells.
   2. T. R. Chapman; married Georgia Woods
   3. Edmund T. Chapman; married Lizzie Beckwith, issue:
      1. Beckwith Chapman.
      2. Edmund Thompson Chapman, Jr.
3. Fannie M. Chapman; married Dr. Finks Catterton.
4. Lucy Ann Chapman; unmarried.
5. Virginia Chapman; married Bernard Chapman, issue:
   1. James Waggoner Chapman.
   2. William Chapman.
   3. Lilla Chapman.
   4. Fannie Chapman; married Mr. —— Head.
6. Sarah J. Chapman; married Thomas A. Chapman, issue:
   1. Mary Buford Chapman.
   2. Charles Chapman.
   3. Lizzie Chapman.
7. James Chapman, never married.

Section 5. Bettie Thompson; married Joab Early. She lived to be eighty years old. Their children:

1. William T. Early; married Elizabeth Michie, issue:
   1. Everetta Early; married —— —— died leaving a son:
      1. N. E. Early; married C. N. Parrott, issue:
         1. E. T. Early; married Anna Norwood, had a son:
            1. James W. Early.
         2. Sallie B. Early; single.
2. N. E. Early.
3. Susan Early; married Thomas Eddins, no issue.
4. Nancy Early; married Dr. Thomas Shearman, no issue.
5. Jane Early; married Edwin Blakely. Children:
   1. Orville Blakely; married —— Landrum.
   2. Sudie Blakely; married T. P. Moyers, no issue.
   3. Bettie Blakely; married C. D. Shackelford, issue:
      1. Lutie Shackelford; single.
      2. Doc Shackelford; single.
6. Lucy Early; married Peter Durrett. Children:
   1. Bettie Durrett; married Davis Eddins, issue:
      1. Thomas C. Eddins; married Miss —— Graves, issue:
         1. Lucy Eddins; married Frank Gibbs.
         2. Elijah Eddins; married Lottie Cole. Children.
   2. Joab Durrett; married Lutie Brown, no living issue
   3. Clingman Durrett; married Miss Brooking, issue:
      1. Child; married Eddins.
   4. William Green Durrett; married in the South.
   5. Judge Robertson Durrett; married Miss —— Yancey.

6. Nathaniel Durrett; married Mary Thomas, no issue.
7. Alice Durrett; married Thomas Graves.
8. Mollie Durrett; married Junius Brutus Garth.
9. Lucy Durrett; married John Graves, no issue.
10. Bernard Durrett; married Bearer.

Section 6. Mildred Thompson; married James Early. Their children:

1. John R. Early; married Sarah Brown, issue:
   1. James W. Early; married Willie Koiner, issue:
      1. Marie Early.
   2. N. B. Early; married Sudie Brown, daughter of H. N. Brown. Their children:
      1. Nimrod Early.
      2. Mary Early, twin.
      3. Lucile Early, twin.
      4. N. B. Early, Jr.
   3. Sallie Early; married Garrett Martin. Their children:
      1. Fannie Martin; single.
      2. Nellie Martin; married Dr. Everett.
      3. Lula Martin; married Mr. —— Coleman. Have a daughter:
         1. Virginia Coleman.

WILLIAM T. PARROTT.

FRANCES THOMPSON.
Wife of William T. Parrott.

Section 7. Nancy Frances Thompson; married William T. Parrott, of Albemarle County, Va. Their children:

1. Eliazbeth Parrott; died in infancy.
2. Charles Parrott; died young.
3. C. B. (Boots) Parrott, killed in the battle of Hatcher's Run, March 3, 1865. He belonged to Pickett's Division of the Confederate Army.
4. William N. Parrott, was a non commissioned officer in Pickett's division of the Confederate Army, but of a different regiment and brigade from his brother, C. B. Parrott, who fell at Hatcher's Run. However, William N. Parrott was engaged and wounded in the same battle. He was wounded also in Picketts celebrated charge at Gettysburg. He was of Kempers old brigade, composed of the 1st, 7th, 11th. 17th, and 24th, Virginia, and was in the second battle of Manassas. Kemper was

then in command of three brigades, acting as Major General. Colonel D. M. Corse, being the ranking Colonel, placed him in immediate command of the Kemper Brigade, who made at a critical moment one of the most brilliant movements ever witnessed on a battle field, when Kemper's old Brigade, with Colonel Skinner, on old Fox, his sorrel horse, in the lead wielding his sword with deadly effect, and William N. Parrott hard by, took a five gun battery and four regimental flags.

Mr. Parrott seems to bear a charmed life, being survivor of many hair-breadth escapes, which would be enough to kill an ordinary man. If the Confederate soldiers had all been as hard to kill as he, President Davis would never have gone to Fortress Munroe. This veteran, like Achilles, must be only vulnerable in the heel, as that is about the only part of his body which has escaped injury. He began at the early age of six years to court death by getting himself, unwittingly in the way of a large tree that was being felled—the whole top of the tree falling over him, pinning his body to the ground, and costing him about a pound of flesh and skin. On twelve different occasions his life seemed to hang by a thread, and some of his experiences were thrilling in the extreme, his injuries including broken arms, broken collar bone, broken ribs, broken legs, dislocated hips, and bruises and strains innumerable. On three occasions he was caught under falling timber. Once thrown from a horse, rebreaking a leg, and climbing upon his horse, rode in that condition a distance of fifteen miles to his home. He was once thrown from a wagon, and reeled around the wheel. He was in eighteen regular battles—including Picketts gallant charge at Gettysburg, besides numerous skirmishes, of the Civil War. He was in the very hotbed of the war, and was shot twice by a cannon and twice by a musket, and was in the wreck of the Fat Nancy in 1888, between Washington and Charlotte, North Carolina, when the train went through a trestle sixty feet high, mashing the car into kindling wood, sustaining at that time the most critical injuries—one leg was broken in three places, the other leg hurt, still worse in the hip, two ribs broken, both elbows nearly broken, and his whole body fearfully mashed, and bruised, still he survived. How he has retained his hold upon life, is one of the miracles of God's providence. He calls himself a stack of patched up bones—really he looks now, at an advanced age, as though he might stand several more knocks.

The Thompsons and Parrotts can battle long,
  The Dabney blood runs red and strong.
They all awake at the call of the drums.
  The blood of the Browns to the rescue comes,
They marshal their forces at his call,
  Who takes this fortress must fight them all.
K. O. M.

W. N. Parrott's father is now, ninety four years old, with his mind in perfect tact.

William N. Parrott; married first his cousin, Bettie Cobbs, she lived only fourteen months after their marriage, left no children. He married second, Bettie J. Whitlock, of Richmond, Va. Their home is in Charlottesville, Albemarle County, Va. His last wife recently died. They had four children, viz:

1. Blanch Brown Parrott; married her cousin Charles B. Hopkins. They have only one child:

1. Ethel Hunter Hopkins, now five years old. (1906.)
2. Eva Pressley Parrott; died young.
3. Nathaniel Edward Parrott; died young.
4. Lizzie Hampton Parrott; died young.
5. Sallie M. Parrott; married John S. Hopkins. Their children:
1. Charles B. Hopkins; married his cousin Blanche Brown Parrott.
2. J. W. Hopkins.
3. E. B. Hopkins.
4. Fannie Hopkins; married W. B. Nuttycomb, an Englishman, a good man. Their children:
1. William Nuttycomb.
2. Wallace Nuttycomb.
4. Hopkins Pearre Nuttycomb.
6. Lucy Parrott; married Dr. Finks Catterton, she died at the birth of her first and only child, so did the infant.
7. Edmund James Parrott; died young.
8. Fannie Parrott; died young.
9. Nannie H. Parrott; single.
10. Ida Parrott; died with fever; unmarried.
11. Bernard T. Parrott; married his cousin, Sallie Brown, daughter of Horace Brown.• Their children:
1. Bessie Parrott; died when about twenty years old.
2. Horace Edward Parrott; unmarried.
3. Charles B. Parrott; married Lizzie Chapman, no issue.
4. George W. Parrott; unmarried.
5. Bernard Thompson Parrott; unmarried.
6. Nathaniel I. Parrott.
7. Lucy F. Parrott; unmarried.
8. Emory B. Parrott; unmarried.
9. Sallie Brown Parrott.
10. James Nimrod Parrott, burned to death when young.

Section 8. Nancy F. Thompson.

Note: The Thompson Family of Albemarle.

Joseph Thompson, was one of the original Justices of the Peace of the County, and the first sheriff. His home was in the bounds of Fluvanna, near Palmira. He died in 1765. His wife's name was Sarah. Their children:

1. Captain Roger Thompson, was a Captain in the Second Virginia of the Army of the Revolution. In 1737, Roger Thompson, Jr., patented nearly 300 acres of land on Fosters Creek in the Stony Point neighborhood.

2. George Thompson, was a Lieutenant in the State militia in the Revolutionary War.

3. Leonard Thompson, was a Lieutenant in the State militia in the Revolutionary War.

4. John Thompson, was first Lieutenant in the seventh Virginia of the Revolutionary War. In 1737, one John Thompscon, perhaps this person, entered more than 500 acres of land on the South Fork of the Rivanna, and in 1739 one hundred and twenty acres more, a short distance above, on Mormans River, thought to be a brother of Captain Roger Thompson, who died in 1838.

5. William Thompson; married Elizabeth Davis. Their children:
1. Roger Thompson; married Miss Crenshaw. Their children:
1. Nathaniel Thompson, Jr., married Temperance Crenshaw, daughter of William W. Crenshaw. He gave the land on which Wesley's Chapel was built, and died in 1835.

2. William Thompson; married first Mary Ballard, and second Betsy Ward. (See Part V, Chap. 13, note.)
3. Nicholas Thompson.
4. Susan Thompson; married William Ward.
5. David Thompson; married Dolly Crenshaw.
6. Mary Thompson; married Richard Franklin.
7. Elizabeth Thompson; married John Ballard. (Note to Part V, Chapter 13.)
8. Sarah Thompson; married Samuel Ward.

2. Nathaniel Thompson; married Lucy Brown. He died in 1874. (See Chapter 3 and 7.)
3. William Thompson, went to Tennessee.
4. Frances Thompson; married David Crenshaw, went west.
5. Mildred Thompson; married Nicholas Crenshaw, went west.
6. Susan Thompson; married Captain Brightberry Brown. (See Chap. 2, Sec. 3.)
7. Bettie Thompson; married Joab Early.
8. Polly Thompson; married Captain Bezaleel Brown. (See Chap. 2, Sec. 2.)
9. Lucy Thompson; died single.
10. Nancy Thompson; died single.

In 1776 Waddy Thompson, of Louisa, came to the County of Albemarle. His first wife Elizabeth Anderson, daughter of Nelson Anderson, of Hanover, having died, he married in Albemarle, his second wife, Mary Lewis, daughter of Robert Lewis and the widow of Samuel Cobbs. (See Part V, Chap. 5, Sec. 2.) He died in 1801, and his last wife in 1813. Children of the first marriage:

1. Nelson Thompson, received from his father 250 acres of land south west of Stillhouse Mountain, which he sold in 1794, to Thomas Garth, Sr. He then bought on Beaver dam, of Hardware, where he died in 1798.
2. Anderson Thompson.
3. David Thompson, moved to Woodford County, Ky.
4. Waddy Thompson, moved to Rockingham County.
5. Susan Thompson; married David Rodes, being his second wife, she married the second time James Kerr. They remained in Albemarle, and kept for a time the Swan Tavern. Mr. Kerr did in 1822, and she died in 1847.
6. Lucy Thompson.

Children of the second marriage:

7. Ann Thompson; married first John Slaughter, and second Philip Grafton. Children of the first marriage:
    1. Mary L. Slaughter.
    2. Waddy Thompson Slaughter; married Frances Ballard, and was living in New York in 1823, where he was Post Master, and owner of a tan yard, the most lasting monument of the place, which he bought from Nathaniel Landcraft, and sold to James Lobban.
    3. Robert L. Slaughter.
8. Mary Thompson; married James Poindexter.
9. Susan Thompson; married Jesse Davenport.
10. Mildred Thompson; married James Scott.
11. Judith Thompson; married William Poindexter.

A piece of cotton fabric, now (1906) one hundred and fifteen years old, presented by W. N. Parrott to his cousin, Mrs. Kate O. Miller made of cotton grown by William Thompson (great, grandfather of Willam Parrott) on his plantation in Albemarle County, and which his daughter Elizabeth Thompson, carded, spun and wove, into muslin, of such a delicate texture, that upon the completion of the whole piece of twelve yards, it was passed through an ordinary finger ring; she made the muslin (from which the piece was cut) into a dress gown which she wore on the occasion of her marriage to Captain James Early of Green County. The goods being as fine and soft and delicate as the product of the latest equipped mills, of the present day. The degree of skill exercisd in the weaving of same, was simply wonderful, and shows that the ladies of one hundred years ago, were as prettily gowned, as the belles of today. By an accident a hole was burned in the gown, and a darn which was put in it at the time is so perfectly done that today it is extremely difficult to detect the original from the substituted threads. The dress is in possession of Mrs. John R. Early of Earlysville. The Early House, has been in the possession of the family for one hundred and thirty years—the fifth generation now occupying it. It was built by Mr. Early's great, great, grand-father, Mr. Richard Durrett.

A sample of another piece of ancient cotton cloth stamped and called calico, was presented by Mr. Parrott to Mrs. Margaret O. Doty, which is a quaint relic of a fabric woven one hundred years ago, from cotton grown on the estate of Captain Nathaniel Thompson of Albemarle. The plain white cotton cloth was taken to Louisa Court-House, where the crudest kind of stamping was done, the two colors, red and black, showed only on one side. After the stamping process, the cloth was called calico. About this bit of cotton, hangs a tragical story of nearly a century ago. The cloth was cut and made into a wrap for an infant—one day the child while being carried in the arms of a servant, was let fall, and sustained injuries from which it died, the tiny victim of the slave's carelessness—had the child lived he would have been a great uncle of W. N. Parrott.

CHAPTER 8.

BERNARD BROWN, Junior.

(Named in Chapter 3, Section 5.)

Article 1.—Bernard Brown, Junior, (called Barney), a son of Bernard Brown, Senior, and Elizabeth Dabney his wife, was born in Albemarle County, Va., March 15, 1781.

He married Miriam (or Elmira) Maupin, a daughter of Saddler Daniel Maupin and Mrs. Hannah Harris his wife. (See Part V, Chap. 4, Section 2.) He died in 1828. Their children:

Section 1. Smith Brown; married Martha Brown, she died and he married again Mary Chapman.

Section 2. James Brown; married Kate Ford.

Section 3. Bernard Brown; married ——— ———

Section 4. Allen Brown; married Mary Koogler.

Section 5. Sidney Brown; died unmarried.

Section 6. Sarah Brown; married Clifton Brown. (See Chap. 2, Section 3.)

Section 7. Bettie Brown; married Clifton Brown, her cousin. (See Chapter 2, Section 3.)

Section 8. Pyrenia Brown; married Tilman J. Maupin. (See Part V, Chapter 4, Section 4.)

Section 9. Thompson Brown; married Sarah Brown.

Section 10. Francis Brown; married Miss Adams.

Section 11. Susan Brown; married Nimrod Brown. (See Chap. 2, Section 3.)

Section 12. George Brown; married Amanda Brown. (See Chap. 2, Sec. 3.)

CHAPTER 9.

DR. CHARLES BROWN.

(Named in Chapter 3, Section 6.)

Article 1.—Doctor Charles Brown, a son of Bernard Brown Senior, and Elizabeth Dabney his wife, was born in Albemarle County, Va., May 3, 1783, died 1879, aged 96 years.

He married his cousin Polly Brown, daughter of Bezaleel Brown. (See Chapter 2, Section 2.) He was a doctor of medicine of the old school, an honest, upright and intelligent man, and lived four and a half score years. He lived in Charlottesville, till 1822, when he moved to a farm on the waters of Ivy Creek, which he bought from Crenshaw Fretwell and on which his son Ezra still lives.

DR. CHARLES BROWN.

POLLY BROWN.

Charles Jennings and William Jennings of Acton Place, London, were sons of Sir Humphrey Jennings of England. William died a bachelor, leaving a large estate worth many millions. His brother Charles had an only child, a daughter Sarah Jennings, who came to America and settled in Virginia where she became the wife of Cornelius Dabney, and died leaving a number of children, and Bernard Brown, Senior, married a daughter of her son John, (see Part III, Chapter 15, Article 2,) her numerous descendants and representatives became heirs to said fortune. Dr. Charles Brown being one of the many heirs. Some efforts had been made to secure the same, but without success.

Dr. Brown being a man of fine character, intelligence, influence and strong convictions for the right, became very much interested, and encouraged by many of the heirs undertook the task of gaining the estate, with liberal assistance from interested persons, and worked hard in the case for years, and made some two or three trips to England in this behalf—one of them being made after he was past four score years of age, but his efforts were in vain—the estate was too large to be permitted to leave England.

Having many blood relatives in Madison County, Ky., in his old age, he made some two visits to see them. We remember one of his visits to our grand-father, Christopher Harris (prior to April 1871,) (the date of grand-father's death), when he was 80 years old, past, and Dr. Brown was five years his senior—they talked of the fortune, of old times, of old Virginia folk, etc., and the two old men had a jolly time together and highly entertained one another. He left some valuable notes in the hands of Captain Micajah Woods of Charlottesville, Va. To Dr. Charles Brown and his wife were born these chiildren:

Section 1. Bezaleel Ira Brown; married Mary Ann Garth. Had a daughter:

1. —— — -: married Oscar Early.

Section 2. Ezra M. Brown; married Sally Tilman. He was living when 71 years old.

Section 3. Charles Thomas Brown; died a bachelor.

Section 4. Algernon Brown; married a lady in Mississippi.

Section 5. Oswin Brown; died single.

Section 6. Bettie Brown; married William H. Jones, and raised a family of ten boys, and no girls.

Section 7. Elvira Brown; married Mr. —— Ayers, of Mississippi.

CHAPTER 10.

THOMAS HARRIS BROWN.

(Named in Chapter 3, Section 7.)

Article 1.—Thomas Harris Brown, a son of Bernard Brown, Senior, and Elizabeth Dabney his wife, was born in Albemarle County, Va., April 16, 1785.

He married his cousin Milly or Mildred, a daughter of Brightberry Brown (see Chap. 2) who died, and he married Lucy Goodman. He left the follwing named children, but not advised as to which wife was their mother:

Section 1. Eliza Dabney Brown; married Lewis Campbell.

Section 2. Suky Brown; married Benjamin Childress, she was living at 75 years of age.

Section 3. Lucy Ann Brown; married Richard Noel.

Section 4. Parthenia Brown; married William Haydon, issue:

1. Parthenias Haydon; married Kate Gentry, a daughter of Nathan Gentry and Samantha Brown, his wife; she lived to the age of 82 years. (See Chap. 14, Sec. 6, and Part V, Chap. 10, Sec. 4.)

Section 5. Lavinia Brown; married John Holbrook.

Section 6. Emaline Brown; married William G. Fretwell, she ived 85 years.

Section 7. Robin Brown; married —— Crenshaw.

CHAPTER 11.

BEZALEEL BROWN.

(Named in Chapter 3, Section 8.)

Article 1.—Bezaleel Brown, a son of Bernard Brown, Senior, and Elizabeth Dabney his wife, was born in Albemarle County, Va., September 22, 1787.

He married Betsy Michie, a daughter of John A. Michie, and died April 20, 1825, leaving these children:

Section 1. William Dabney Brown; died a bachelor.

Section 2. Addison Brown; died young, having never married.

Section 3. John Augustus Brown; married Columbia Brown, a kinswoman.

Section 4. Martha Brown; married C. H. Parrott, a brother to William T. Parrott, father of Captain William N. Parrott of Charlottesville, Virginia. (See Chap. 2, Sec. 2.)

Section 5. Cynthia Brown; married her kinsman, Colonel William Harris Brown.

Section 6. Angeline Brown; married Dr. George Kemper.

Section 7. Mary Frances Brown; married Waller Harris. (See Part III, Chapter 3, Section 4, a 4.)

CHAPTER 12.

BENJAMIN HESCOTT BROWN.

(Named in Chapter 3, Section 9.)

Article 1.—Benjamin Hescott Brown, a son of Bernard Brown, Senior, and Elizabeth Dabney his wife, was born in Albemarle County, Va., March 12, 1790.

He married Judith Fretwell, daughter of Hudson Fretwell. Of this union were born these children:

Section 1. William Bernard Brown; married Belle Clayton, issue:

1. James Brown; married first —— Weston, second —— —— no issue. The last heard of they were in the Klondyke Country.

BENJAMIN HESBOTT BROWN.

JUDITH FRETWELL.
Wife of Benjamin Hescott Brown.

2. Amanda Brown; married Dr. —— McMahon, issue:
   1. Bernard McMahon.

3. Jennie Brown; married —— McCullough, no issue. He trades in mules in the Sandwich, or Hawaiian Islands. His wife frequently goes with him on these trips.

Section 2. Thomas Brown; died young.

Section 3. Charles Wesley Brown; married Venia Spurgeon, issue:

1. Mollie Brown.
2. Benjamin Brown.

Section 4. Iurenia Brown; married Sampson Wright. They had no children.

Section 5. Virginia Brown; married Alexander Blake. Their children:

1. John Blake.
2. Mary Blake; married Joseph Wolfskill.
3. Maggie Blake; died at eighteen years of age.
4. Joseph Blake; married —— ——, they had a child, when six months old weighed forty pounds.

Section 6. Betsy Brown; married Mr. —— Richardson. Their children:

1. Lilburn Richardson.
2. Miss —— Richardson.

Section 7. Francina Brown; married Mark Long. Their children:

1. Charles Long; unmarried.
2. Gus Long; unmarried.
3. Minnie Long; unmarried.

Section 8. Velunia Ann Brown; married John Ingraham. Their children:

1. Fannie Ingraham; married Mr. —— Holmes. Their children:
   1. Lizzie Holmes.

Mr. Holmes died and his widow Fannie, married Mr. McNamara.

2. William Ingraham; married —— ——
3. Octavia Ingraham; married Mr. —— Martin. Their children:

1. Joseph Martin; died unmarried.
2. Lizzie Martin; married Mr. Hudson.

Section 9. Elvenie Brown; married Mr. — Griggs. Their children:

1. William Griggs; married —— —— Had no children.
2. Archilles Griggs; unmarried.
3. Mattie Griggs; married —— ——
4. Horace Griggs; married —— ——

CHAPTER 13.

SARAH BROWN.

(Named in Chapter 3, Section 10.)

Article 1.—Sarah Brown, a daughter of Bernard Brown, Senior and Elizabeth Dabney his wife, was born in Albemarle County, Va., June 6, 1792.

She married her cousin Colonel Beverly A. Brown son of Miletus Brown, of Buckingham County. (See Chap. 3, Sec. 10.) She died May 2, 1852. Their children:

Section 1. Edwin Brown; married Bettie Thompson.

Section 2. Virginia Brown; died, unmarried.

Section 3. Emaline Brown; married Alexander Mosely. Children:

1. Emma Mosely.
2. Beverly Mosely; married Miss Miller.
3. Mary Mosely; died single.

Section 4. Lucy Frances Brown; married first John Hawthorne, and secondly, John Holbrooke. Children of first marriage:

1. Sallie B. Hawthorne; married Cornelius Hayden.
2. John T. Hawthorne; married Jennie Harris.

Section 5. Sarah Brown; married Vernon Cobbs. Children:

1. Bettie Cobbs; married W. N. Parrott. (See Chap. 7, Sec. 7.)
2. Virginia Cobbs; married C. B. Brown, no issue.
3. Lucy Cobbs; married Richmond Nolly. Children:
   1. Pearly Nolly.
   2. George Nolly.
4. George E. Cobbs.

CHAPTER 14.

IRA BENAJAH BROWN.

(Named in Chapter 3, Section 11.)

Article 1.—Ira Benajah Brown, a son of Bernard Brown, Senior, and Elizabeth Dabney his wife, was born in Albemarle County, Virginia June 5, 1794.

He and his brother Asa Brightberry Brown, were twins. He married Frances Jarman Mullins, daughter of John Mullins and Mary Michie his wife. (See note "The Mullins Family of Albemarle.") His wife was born December 1st, 1798, and died May 23, 1835, and

Ira Benajah Brown, died Feb. 25, 1842. After his wife's death, he married again Mary Caruthers, of Rockbridge County. He lived only a short while after his second marriage. The children of the first marriage:

DR. ROBERTS AND WIFE, MARY ELIZABETH BROWN.

Section 1. Mary Elizabeth Brown, born in Albemarle County Va., January 17, 1818. She died Aug. 1, 1854. She married Dr. —— Roberts. Their children:

1. Frank Roberts, went to Illinois; married —— ——
2. Fannie Roberts; married Mr. —— Bradford.
3. William Roberts; married Mintie Knox. They live in California.
4. John Roberts; died in Alton prison during the Civil War.
5. Dr. Brown Roberts; married —— —— and died in Laddonia, Missouri.

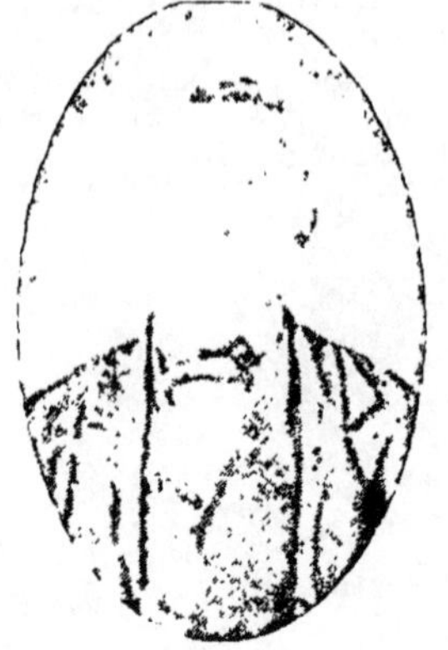

BURLINGTON DABNEY BROWN.

MARY ANN HARRIS.
Wife of Burlington Dabney Brown.

Section 2. Burlington Dabney Brown, was born in Albemarle County, Va., May 17, 1820. He died April 26, 1886. He married Mary Ann Harris, daughter of Ira Harris and Sarah Lewis his wife. (See Part III, Chapter 3, Section 4.) They emigrated to Missouri. Their children:

1. Hugh Hescott Brown, born April 7, 1846. He married Mary Ann Metier.
2. Ira Lewis Brown, born March 2, 1848.
3. Linn Roy Brown, born Nov. 5, 1849; died March 22, 1850.
4. Frank Brown; married Bettie French. They live in Jefferson City, Missouri.
5. Harry Brown; married Virginia Ann Bishop. They live in Clarenden, Arkansas.
6. Ralph Brown.
7. Hattie Brown; married Samuel Hatcher. They live in Auxvassa, Missouri.
8. Nettie Brown; married Dr. E. A. Lofton, of Laddonia, Mo.

Section 3. Virginia Frances Brown, was born in Albemarle County, Va., Dec. 17, 1822. She married William Kavanaugh Hocker, of Madison County, Ky. (See Part VII, Chap. 7, Sec. 1.) Their children:

1. Fannie Hocker; married Samuel Shanks, of Lincoln County, Kentucky. Their children:
    1. Ella Shanks; married Thomas Rice. They live in Stanford, Ky., no issue.
    2. William Hocker Shanks; married Lena Baldwin, daughter of Thomas E. Baldwin and Ellen Collins his wife. (See Part VI, Chap. 10, Sec. 4, and Part VII, Chap. 7, Sec. 1.)
    3. Frances Shanks; married Wiliam Tate. They live in Stanford, Kentucky.
2. Nicholas Hocker; died near Lonoke, Arkansas, of small pox, a few years after the war.
3. Mary Brown Hocker; married Samuel Calhoun Roan. To them were born some four or five children, but they all died in infancy. Mrs. Roan has been dead many years.
4. Nannie Hocker; married Lewis Simpson. Their home is in Waco, (since removed to Quannah), Texas. (See Part VII, Chap. 7, Sec. 1.) Their children:
    1. Lewis Simpson.
    2. Nannette Simpson.
    3. Lucy Simpson.
    4. Willie Simpson (daughter.)
5. Lucy Hocker; married Dr. Powhatan Trueheart, and are residents of Sterling, Kansas. Dr. Trueheart is a noted and distinguished physician. Their children:
    1. Marion Trueheart, a physician.
    2. Virginia Trueheart.
6. Jennie Hocker; married Charles K. Beckett. Their residence is in Kansas City, Mo. Their children:
    1. Harry Beckett; a practicing attorney-at-law in Portland, Oregon.
    2. Frances Beckett.
7. Miss Willie Kavanaugh Hocker, a first class school teacher of Wabaseeka, Arkansas, a cultured and refined lady.

Section 4. James Landon Brown, born in Albemarle County, Virginia, June 22, 1824; died June 7, 1852.

Section 5. Sarah Ann Brown, born in Albemarle County, Va., March 1, 1826; died May 1, 1846.

Section 6. Samartha Susan Brown, born in Albemarle County, Va., March 21, 1828. She died March 30, 1896. She married James Nathan Gentry. Their home was in New Hope, Va. Their children:

1. Sallie Gentry.
2. Mary Michie Gentry.

JAMES NATHAN GENTRY.

SAMANTHA SUSAN BROWN.

Wife of James Nathan Gentry.

3. Jennie Gentry; married Charles Firebaugh. Their children:
   1. Lee Firebaugh.

They live in St. John, Kansas.

4. Fannie Gentry; married H. G. Barnhardt. Their children:
   1. Walter Barnhardt.
   2. Gray Barnhardt.
   3. Ruth Barnhardt.
   4. Myrtle Barnhardt.
   5. Nathaniel Barnhardt.
   6. Frank Barnhardt.

5. Kate Gentry; married W. Parthenias Haydon. (See Chap. 10, Sec. 4.) Their children:
   1. Clyde Haydon.
   2. Nathaniel Haydon.
   3. Mary Haydon.
   4. Willie Haydon.
   5. Ira Brown Haydon.
   6. Robert Lee Haydon.

They live in Fluvanna.

6. Angeline Gentry. She is a first class school teacher, an accomplished lady, a splendid stenographer, now holding a lucrative position in Richmond, Va. A fine scribe, and the only person known to the writer who can write as well with one hand as the other and make two correct copies at once of the same paper.

7. Gertrude Gentry; married W. T. Weller. Their home is in Augusta County, Va. Have a daughter:
   1. Margurite Weller.

8. Pattie Gentry; married G. F. Barger. Their home is in Kansas.

Section 7. Jacintha Catherine Brown, was born in Albemarle County, Va., August 10, 1830. She married William Kavanaugh Oldham, of Madison County, Ky., March 11, 1851. (See Part VI, Chap. 16, Sec. 4, and Chap. 19). She died June 10, 1880.

Section 8. Angeline Mildred Brown, was born in Albemarle County, Va., Oct. 9, 1832. She married March 16, 1853, Charles

Warner Harris, son of Ira Harris and Sarah Lewis, his wife . (See Part III, Chap. 3, Sec. 4.) They went to Missouri, where her husband died. After which Mrs. Harris came to Kentucky, and lived for a number of years, with her sister Mrs. William K. Oldham, in Madison County. Her friends were all who knew her. She married a second time, John Harris Miller, son of James Miller and Frances Harris his wife, of Lincoln County, Ky. (See Part I, Chap. 8, Sec. 5). In which County she died. By the last marriage she had no children. The children of her first marriage were:

1. Mary Howell Harris, born Sept. 15, 1854; died Jan. 12, 1857.
2. Charles Lee Harris, born July 24, 1857, a bright and promising young man, who acquired a splendid farm, within a few miles of Stanford, Lincoln County, Ky., and seemed to be prospering in his occupation, when he was stricken with a fatal disease and died, highly respected by his fellows, young and old.

Section 9. A female child; unmarried, born Feb. 28, 1835; died in a short while.

THE MULLINS FAMILY OF ALBEMARLE.

John Mullins, a son of Daniel Mullins, of Welch and English descent, married Mary Michie, daughter of William Michie and his wife, who was a Miss Jarman. They had, besides other children, three daughters, towit:

1. Frances Jarman Mullins; married Ira Benajah Brown, as stated in the beginning of this Chapter.
2. Mary Ann Mullins; married Anderson Hughes, of Flurvanna County, Va.
3. Bettsy Mullins; married Thomas Gentry, her first cousin, who was a son of Josiah Gentry and Nancy Mullins his wife. Thomas Mullins represented the County in the Legislature, he had a son:
    1. Curran Gentry, who lived in Iowa near to his relative, William Mullins.

Several years ago, there was a Doctor Ira Mullins, who lived in Dickerson County. He, it is thought, subsequently went to Texas.

THE MICHIE FAMILY OF ALBEMARLE.

The first of the name to settle in Albemarle County, Va., was John Michie, a Scotchman, who bought land near the Horse Shoe of the Rivanna, from John Henry, father of the great Orotar, Patrick Henry, which he subsequently sold to Hezekiah Rice, and repurchased the same from Rice in 1763. Where John Michie died in 1777, and was buried in the Horse Shoe on Mechums River, and the land is still occupied by his descendants. His children:

1. John Michie; died before his father.
2. Robert Michie.
3. James Michie.
4. Patrick Michie, made his home south west of Earlysville, between the Buck Mountain Road, and the south fork of the Rivanna. His wife was named Frances. He died in 1799. Their children:
    1. Nancy Michie; married Joseph Goodman.
    2. James Michie.
    3. Elizabeth Michie; married Thomas Maupin. (See Part V, Chap. 2, B.)
    4. Sarah Michie; married William G. Martin.
    5. Martha Michie; married Richard Davis.
    6. Susan Michie; married William Michie.

7. Mary Michie; married John Maupin. (See Part V, Chap. 2-6.)

8. David Michie.

9. Susan Michie; married ? William Michie.

5. William Mchie, became a large land holder in the Horse Shoe, of the Rivanna. He purchased in 1793, from Lewis Webb, of New Kent, two thousand and ninety acres in one tract. He established on the Buck Mountain Road, the public house, which has since been known as Michie's Old Tavern. He was appointed a Justice of the Peace, in 1791, served as sheriff in 1803, and died in 1811. He was twice marriel. His first wife was Miss Jarman, and his second wife was Ann Mills, thought to be a daughter of David Mills. (He was a signer of the Albemarle Declaration of Independence April 21, 1779. Chillren of his first marriage:

1. John A. Michie, was appointed a Justice of the Peace in 1807. He married Frances Jarman, daughter of Thomas Jarman, and diel in 1827. Their chillren:

1. Frances J. Michie.

2. Ann Michie.

3. Sarah Michie.

4. Elizabeth Michie; married Bezaleel G. Brown. (See Chap. 3, Sec. 8, and Chap. 11.)

5. Theodosia Michie; married Edmund Brown. (See Chap. 2, Sec. 3.)

6. John E. Michie.

7. James Michie, was appointed a Justice of the Peace in 1816. Served as sheriff in 1843. His home was on the North Fork of the Rivanna, south of Piney Mountain. He died in 1850. He married Frances Garth, daughter of Thomas Garth, Jr. Their children:

1. Mary Elizabeth Michie; married William T. Early.

2. Virginia Michie.

3. Susan Michie.

4. Adaline Michie.

5. Dr. J. Augustus Michie.

6. Thomas Michie.

7. Theresa Michie; married Lucien Michie.

8. Alexander H. Michie.

9. Henry Clay Michie.

8. William Michie.

9. Robert Michie.

10. Jonathan Michie; married Miss Michie, sister of Thomas J. Michie, of Staunton, Va. Their children:

1. John P. Michie.

2. Margaret Michie; married Dr. Theodore Michie.

3. Frances Michie; married Dr. R. N. Hewitt, of Campbell County.

4. Thomas Michie.

5. Chapman Michie.

6. Franklin Michie.

11. Mary Michie.

12. Martha Michie.

2. Mary Michie; married John Mullins (see above 'The Mullins Family of Albemarle.")

Children of the second marriage of William Michie to Ann Mills:

3. William Michie; married Susan Michie, thought to be the daughter of Patrick Michie and Frances his wife. Their children:

1. Dr. James W. Michie.

2. David Michie.
3. Frances Michie.
4. David Michie, enterprising and thrifty.
5. Lucy Michie; married Benjamin Richards.
6. Sarah Michie; married Christopher Wood.
7. Mary Michie; married Mr. Woods.

The two latter couples, and their brother Robert Michie, lived in Louisa County.

James Michie Jr., commonly called "Bean Jim," was a son of one William Michie. His residence was at Longwood, west of Earlysville. He died in 1847. He married Eliza Graves, of Rockingham. Their children:

1. Dr. Theodore Michie; married Margaret Michie.
2. Octavius Michie.
3. Joseph Michie.
4. Lucien Michie; married Theresa Michie.
5. Oran Michie.
6. Claudius N. Michie.
7. Eugene Michie.
8. Catherine Michie; married William A. Rogers.
9. Cornelia Michie.
10. Virginia Michie.

CHAPTER 15.

ASA BRIGHTBERRY BROWN.

(Named in Chapter 3, Section 12.)

Article 1.—Asa Brightberry Brown, a son of Bernard Brown, Senior, and Elizabeth Dabney his wife, was born in Albemarle County, Va., June 5, 1794.

He and his brother, Ira Benaiah Brown, were twins. He married his cousin, Marie Brown, daughter of Garland Brown, of Buckingham County. (See Chap. 3, Sec. 12.) He died Jan. 30, 1839. Their children:

Section 1. Martha Brown.
Section 2. Bernard Brown; married Susan Brown.
Section 3. Bettie Brown; married Samuel Woodson.
Section 4. Thomas Ally Brown.

CHAPTER 16.

TYRE BROWN.

(Named in Chapter 2, Section 4, Sub. Sec. 5.)

Article 1.—Tyre Brown, a son of Rev. Bernis Brown and Henrietta Rodes his wife, was born in Brown's Cove, Albemarle County, Va., June 13, 1793.

He married Sarah Nicholas, of Rockingham County, Va.

In this connection is set forth, "Family History of the Browns, by Mrs. M. Virginia B. Osburn, (of Richmond, Mo.,) towit:

"On the east side of the Blue Ridge Mountains in Albemarle County, Va., there is a beautiful Cove in the Mountains called

"Brown's Cove." Here is where the ancestors of our family came to from over the water, and were among the early settlers of Old Virginia. I visited this place from the West, when I was a young lady, in 1877. It was early in April, but the grass was green, and the weather fine. Spring had already come to that balmy section. I entered on horse back, in company with my cousins, a daughter and two sons of my great uncle, Thompson Brown. We stopped at first at the large white house, of a relative, who received us with great hospitality. This farm was adjoining the old ancestral home of Bernis Brown. We stayed over night and rested with this relative after over ten miles ride, and in the morning crossed the fields, and approached the old Brown home from the rear. The path we followed was the one made by the negroes, long ago, as they passed from one plantation to another on their nightly peregrinations. Many a 'possum and 'coon had they carried along this path, and, no doubt, many a chicken from neighboring roosts. The fence was made of rails, low, and in many places falling down. The old country had not yet had time to recover from the effects of the Civil War. We crossed the fence several times before we arrived at the foot of the slight eminence upon which the house was built, and was a prominent feature of the place. How often out in Missouri, I had heard my dear aunt Julian, speak of this spring, and wish for a drink from it!. She lived at this place with her uncle Thompson Brown, after the death of her parents. Once I heard her say "I never expect while I live to be able to go back and see that old spring again, but when I die, I hope I may be permitted to flit by there before I leave this world." Now here I stood by the side of this famous spring, and how shall I describe it? The ground around it was worn hard and smooth, and by its side, shading it, stood a tremendous old knarled oak tree. A large nail was driven into this oak upon which hung a gourd, and out from beneath a huge lime stone rock, there flowed into a large stone basin, a crystal drink fit for the gods! The house was old and unpainted. A conspicious feature of the place, was the great old oak trees in the yard. I had never before seen such oaks. In my far away West, where I had grown up, I had seen taller, knarled, scarred old looking ones Mistletoe grew, and hung in great green bunches from the bark of these trees, giving them a strangely beautiful appearance. As I stood out under these ancient oaks ("under the mistletoe" for the first time in my life) I cannot find words to express the feeling that came over me, as I viewed the scene around. Upon enquiry I found that the scars on several of the trees were caused by bullets. The Old Browns were fond of their guns, and the target for the shooting match was often placed upon these trees.

I never knew the history of the family father back than my great grand-father. Long years ago, this home right at the foot of the Blue Ridge—this old home—with its crystal spring and rippling water, its noble oaks, and swinging mistletoe, was the abode of a Methodist preacher, and that preacher, was my great grandfather, Bernis Brown. My great, great, grand-father, had a large family of sons, and they were called the "B. Browns," because, they were all given names with B., Bernis, Brazil, Bradbury, and Benjamin, are some of the names, and to this day these names are found among their descendants, but out of this large family, there is only one which mainly interests me, and that one is my great grand-father, Bernis. He was the Democrat, while the rest of his brothers were whigs. He also, was the preacher in the family. A few rods from the house at Brown's Cove, upon a little knoll, he lies buried in the family burying ground. I went and stood by his grave during that memorable visit and noticed it was kept in good repair. A plain granite slab, with his name carved upon it marks his grave. His wife was laid beside him, and two large sassafras trees stood near, like sentinels guarding them. I have never heard anything about his preaching. The cause of this, I suppose, is that my father was not a religious man. However, about two years before my father died, he talked to me for the first time, about his grand-parent, and related an interesting incident which reflects honor upon him, and shows that his heart was right. I do not think that my father had ever mentioned this to any one else. It was kept a secret, from the first on account of the turbulent state of affairs in Virginia at that time, and no historian got hold of it. The brothers of Bernis Brown being of the opposite political party were not entrusted with this secret, so that their descendants know nothing about it to this day. The incident is this: Bernis Brown was an intimate friend of Thomas Jefferson. In the spring of 1781, during the Revolutionary War, Thomas Jefferson, who was then Governor of Virginia, fearing the British might capture the State Archives, which were then at Monticello, entrusted them secretly to Bernis Brown to take care of and conceal. He took them out to his home at Brown's Cove, and with the assistance of an honest old mountaineer packed them upon the backs of mules and took them up over the "Black Rocks" in the Blue Ridge Mountains, not far from his home, and concealed them in a cave. The friends of Jefferson knowing that Monticello was in great danger of being invaded by the British, would come to him and ask anxiously about the state archives, and to them all the great man would only say "never mind, they are safe." The invading army did get to Monticello, but failed to get their booty. The father of Democracy escaping on horse back, and the archives safe in the hands of his staunch Democratic friend. The secret was well kept, and to this day no historian has ever known that Bernis Brown, once had charge of and saved the Archives of Old Virginia.

My grand-father Tyre Rodes Brown, was born in Brown's Cove, Albemarle County, Va., June 13, 1793. He was an educated man and a teacher. He married Miss Sarah Nicholas, of Rockingham County, Va., and lived after his marriage on his farm on North River, near Weyers Cave, Va. Their children were a follows:

Section 1. Madison Nicholas Brown, born in Browns Cove, Albemarle County, Va., March 21, 1815. He married Mary Sewell Hopkins, daughter of Philip Hopkins of Staunton, Va., and niece of Colonel Joseph Mauzy, on St. Valentines Day 1844. He died Dec. 17, 1780, and his wife Feb. 6, 1896; issue:

1. Mary Virginia Brown; married Mr. Morris Osburn, Dec. 6, 1881. Home Richmond, Mo. One son was born of this union:

   1. Worth James Osburn, who is now twenty four years old, and a professor of mathematics at Central College, Fayette, Mo. He graduated from Central College and took the Master's Degree from Vanderbilt University before he was twenty-one. He was assistant teacher of mathematics at Vanderbilt the year after he was graduated from there, and is now making a success of college work.

2. Thomas Jefferson Brown; married Miss Clemmie Rust, who died and left two little girls:

   1. Pocahontas Rust Brown.
   2. Kate Strother Brown.

These two girls were educated at Stephens College, Columbia, Mo., and are now living with their father on the old home farm at Lone Star.

3. Julian Catherine Brown; married Mr. Alfred T. Irvine of

Saline County, Mo., and died March 8, 1875, a few weeks after the birth of a fine son, whom she named:

1. Brown Houston Irvine. This son was drowned while bathing in Salt Fork, Saline County, Mo., when about twelve years of age.

4. Frances Elizabeth Brown; died when a child June 19, 1861.

5. Tyre Brown, a fifth child, and second son, was born at "Lone Star," Ray County, Mo., Jan. 31, 1860, and died Sept. 23, 1893. He married Miss Sallie Rust. Three sons were born of this union:

1. Roger Q. Brown.
2. Rust B. Brown.
3. Richard Tyre Brown; died at about six years of age.

Section 2. Julian Henrietta Rodes Brown, born on North River, Rockingham County, Va., April 7, 1818. She married Charles Carthrae.

Section 3. Sidna Eliazbeth Brown, born on North River, Rockingham County, Va., May 18, 1821. She married Addison Carthrae.

My aunts Julian and Sidna spoke of my father, the eldest, in the most affectionate terms—calling him "Brother,"—and always looked up to him with the greatest respect. Dear Aunt Julian has often told me of the times she would go with him in a boat out on the river fishing. Some times they would go at night, she carrying the pine torch. But, alas! alas! the blow came to this happy family. Typhoid fever, that dread scourge, struck them, and completely annihilated the home. The father died Dec. 29, 1835, the mother the next day, and both were buried together.

Then nearly all of their slaves died at that time of the same disease, leaving the three bright, interesting children, suddenly, without father, mother, colored servants or home. The three aged respectively twenty, seventeen and fourteen were not only left without father, mother, kind old servants, and all that made home, home, but they were each torn apart, and put into the wide, wide world. How hese homeless orphans must have suffered, and how lonely and homesick they must have been away off from one another!

Julian went to live with her uncle, Thomas Brown, who then lived at the home of her grand-father Bernis, in Brown's Cove. Sidna went to live with an aunt, and my father, Madison, came to McGaheysville, not far from his broken home, and secured a position as clerk in the merchantile house of Colonel Mauzy, a wealthy and prominnt man of that village. At this place my father first met my mother, Miss Martha Sewell Hopkins, daughter of Philip Hopkins, of Staunton, Va., and niece of Colonel Mauzy—a pretty motherless girl under the care of her uncle and aunt. Here for several years these two young people—she four years his junior, met at the same table and of evenings made sweet music together, he on the violin, and she accompanying him on the piano. Is it any wonder that thse two fragmerts of broken homes should have fallen in love with one another? They were married Feb. 14th, (St. Valentine's Day) 1844, and soon went to house-keeping at a small place on "the pike," now called "Mauzy," about seventeen miles from McGaheysville, where my father went into the merchantile business, in partnership with Richard Mauzy, son of Colonel Joseph Mauzy.

My father's two sisters had long been settled on rich farms in Saline County, Mo. Sidna having married Mr. Addison Carthrae and started immediately for the West, her sister accompanying her. They left Virginia Sept. 9, 1839. A short time after they were in Missouri, Julian married Mr. Charles Carthrae, brother of her sister's husband.

Several months previous to my father's marriage he visited his isters and also, his uncle Bernis Brown, who also lived in Saline County, and was so much pleased with the State, that he became anxious to make it his home, but it was hard for my mother to consent to leave all of her relatives and friends and so they tarried in Virgniia after their marriage. But years moved on, and a time come, when the dream of Missouri was to be realized. Four children were then born into the family, Mary Virginia, Thomas Jefferson, Julian Catherine and Frances Elizabeth, and my mother became convinced that Missouri was a better place in which to raise them. So it was for her husband's and children's sake she made the splendid self-sacrifice of leaving everything else, that was dear to her, to brave "the unknown." It was in the spring of 1854, they parted with their old friends forever and started with us on our long journey Westward. We spent the first summer in Saline County, Mo., with my father's relatives, and in the fall settled upon the farm my father had bought in Ray County, Mo., which he named "Lone Star."

"Richmond, Mo., Jan. 10, 1907.—Mr. W. H. Miller—:

Enclosed you will find a portion of my sketch of the Browns, which contains the data you have asked for. As my work will not be published, you are welcome to do as you please with this part of it. I can assure you it is truthfully given as far as I know. I beg to say also, that the incident about Bernis Brown and Thomas Jefferson in Revolutionary times is true history and not mere tradition, as my father was very truthful and exact in his statements. The "additional data" I have thrown hastily together for you, but you can dispense with it if you choose. The family records of Benjamin Brown's family here have been lost, so I can tell you nothing about them, Very Truly,

M. Virginia B. Osburn."

SUPPLEMENT.

1. DELANEY. 2. TATES CREEK, DREAMING CREEK, VINEY FORK, AND BETHEL CHURCHES. 3. ITEMS FROM ANNALS OF AUGUSTA COUNTY, VIRGINIA, EXHIBITING MILLERS, McDOWELLS, WALLACES, WOODS, AND OTHERS AMONG THE FIRST SETTLERS—THE ESTILLS AND REIDS A LITTLE LATER. 4. REFERRING TO ROBERT HARRIS, THE IMMIGRANT FROM WALES, HIS SON WILLIAM, ETC. 5. REFERRING TO ROBERT HARRIS, WIFE NANCY GRUBBS; REV. CHRISTOPHER HARRIS, WIFE ELIZABETH GRUBBS; JAMES HARRIS, OF ALBEMARLE, WIFE MARY HARRIS; HIGGASON GRUBBS, WIFE LUCY HARRIS; JAMES BERRY, WIFE SARAH GRUBBS, AND OTHERS. 6. REFERRING TO SUSAN WOODS AND HUSBAND, ASHBY SNELL, AND DAUGHTER NORA, AND LEWIS PINDELL, AND SON, GOVERNOR XENOPHEN OVERTON PINDELL, OF ARKANSAS. 7. HEZEKIAH RICE AND MARY BULLOCK, HIS WIFE. 8. JUDGE JAMES HARRIS, OF BOONE COUNTY, MO., AND SABRA BROWN JACKSON, HIS WIFE, MENTIONED IN PART III, CHAPTER 37, SECTION 2. 9. KAVANAUGH, ANNA.

1.—Delaney.

This family was founded A. D. 1677, by Carmac Cas, son of Olliol Ollum, King of Munster, and Sabia, daughter of Con Kead Caha, King of Ireland. The ancient name was Deaghlabhairb, meaning "proper in speech." Their possessions lay principally in the Counties of Clare and Roscommon. They were also Chiefs of Tuath-on-Toriadh, and a clan of much note in Upper Ossory, Queens and Kilkenney.

(Extract from Rooney's Irish Families.)

Until recent date the name was spelled "Delaney," and so found spelled on the early records of Virginia and Kentucky. Now it is often spelled "Dulaney." In this book the modern form is used in spelling the name.

2.—Tates Creek, Dreaming Creek, Viney Fork and Bethel Churches.

The Tates Creek and the Dreaming Creek Churches, both of the Old School Baptist order and discipline called "United," were among the very first, if not the first, churches constituted in Madison County, Kentucky. Another very old church of the same faith and order was Viney Fork, located on Muddy Creek where the village of Speedwell is, which was constituted to-wit: On January 22, 1797, eighteen persons in fellowship met and appointed messengers to visit Tates Creek and Dreaming Creek, asking for help; and on February 26 they reported to an adjourned meeting, Bros. Andrew Tribble and Isaac Newland, from Tates Creek, and Bros. Peter Woods and Christopher Harris, from Dreaming Creek, and on March 20, 1797, adopted a Church Covenant and Rules of Decorum, and at a meeting second Saturday in August, 1797, agreed to build ie Viney Fork Stone Church House, and to call Bro. Christopher arris, as pastor for the church, and on second Saturday, October, 797, Bro. Harris answered the call to preach for them, and he id his wife joined that church the same day.

The following were among the members received from its or- anization to 1845:

allew, Thomas
Susannah
Mary
Nancy
Fannie
George W.
Lydia
urnam, Henry and wife
Sarah
rown, Jane
William
Betsy
Matilda
reckinridge, Eave
James
roaddus, Edward
Mary
George
Elvira
Mary Ann
Clay
Cynthia
Elizabeth
Mildred
Nicholas H.
ollins, Elizabeth
Garland
Sarah
William
Mildred
William
James
Sallie
William
ovington, William
Robert and wife
Mary
Elizabeth
adlebough, Sybil
William
Didamah
ews, Betsy
Jael
David
Betsy
Charles
uncan.
Lucy
William
owden, Elizabeth
illingham, Joshua

Ellison, Joseph and wife
Mary
Elizabeth
Nancy
Elizabeth
Gilbert, Samuel
Jennie
Susannah
Gentry, Nancy
Benajah
Harris, Christopher and wife
Elizabeth
Higgason
Thomas
Margaret and John, (husband and wife)
James
Didamah
Holman, Sarah
Henderson, Sarah
Sarah
Lucy
Lavisa
Sally
Hocker, Nancy
Elvira
Hocker, Nicholas
Mildred
Jennings, Thomas
Rachael
William
Delina
Jacob
John
Elizabeth
Jameson, Martha
Elizabeth
Jones, Isom
Delaney
Kavanaugh, Patsey
Logan, Elizabeth
Moberley, John and wife Nancy
Lavinia
Richard
Edith
Mary
Ephraim
Benjamin, Jr.
Abitha (Tabitha)
Elizabeth
Elizabeth

Miller, Betsy
Lewis
Mary Jane
Maupin, Susannah, 1st Cooper, (wife of Overton)
Susannah
Susan
Newland, Mildred
John
Oldham, Sarah (wife of George)
Munday, Reuben and wife Nancy
Phelps, William
Polly
Park, Polly Ballew
William
Rea, Elizabeth
Reid, John and wife Anne
Shelton, Elizabeth
Thorpe, James
Zachariah
John
Rebecca
Josiah
Nancy
Mourning
Peggy
Dodson
James
Nancy
Susan
Sinthy Ann
Fannie
Peggy
Tribble, Peter
Ann
Woods, Anderson and wife, Elizabeth
Elizabeth
Wallace, Lida
Enfield
Stephen
William
Yates, Joshua
John
Margaret
John
Rebecca
Elijah
Mattie
Joshua
Hannah

Rev. Geo. W. Broaddus, then a member of the Old School Baptist Church at Viney Fork (at said church meeting house) was ordained as a minister of the Gospel the second Saturday, April, 1845, by a presbytery composed of Moses Foley, David Chenault (from Cane Spring), Nelson C. Alspaugh, Moses B. Willis and Jonas D. Wilson. Bro. Moses Foley was Moderator and Anderson Chenault, Clerk, and Elder Broaddus was called to the pastorate of the church, which he accepted for six months. About this period the church drifted into the ways of the Missionaries, and soon became identified with that denomination.

The Bethel Church of Old School Baptists, located on Hays Fork of Silver Creek, on the Big Hill road, near the present village of Kingston, and six or seven miles south of Richmond, Ky., was constituted second Saturday in October, 1813. Elder Christopher Harris, Moderator.

The following names appear among the members enrolled (those marked * were organizing members), to-wit:

Beatty, Edmund and wife*
Brassfield, James
Tabitha
Mary
Burnam, John
Lucinda
Covington, William
Robert
Edith
Collins, Garland*
Francis, Edith
Gates, Cynthia
Harris, Margaret
Susannah
Moberley, John*
Moberley, Benjamin, Sr.*
Edward
Susan*
Elizabeth*
Martha
Richard
Lavinia*
Benjamin, Jr.*
Nancy*
Oldham, Susannah
Price, Moses M.*
Catherine*
Searcy, Nancy
Wolverton, Thomas, Elder
Anna

The last meeting held there by the Old Baptists of which there s any record, was on the third Sunday in June, 1872; preaching y Elders James J. Gilbert and John M. Park.

. Items from the Annals of Augusta County, Virginia, by Joseph A. Waddell:

The business of the people of Augusta was transacted at Orange Court House until December, 1745, when the Court of Augusta was rganized.

The battle of Bothwell Bridge in Scotland was fought June,22, heir escape, made their way to Ulster, and from them many of the heir escape ,made their way to Ulster, and from them many of the eople of Augusta County have descended. An appendix to the old Scotch Book, called "A Cloud of Witnesses," says: "Anno 1679, of he prisoners taken at Bothwell were banished to America two undred and fifty who were taken away by Paterson, a merchant of eith, who transacted for them with Provost Milns, Laird of Barton, he man that first burnt the Covenant, whereof two hundred were lrowned by shipwreck at a place called "The Mulehead" of Darness, near Orkney, being shut up by the said Paterson's order beneath he hatches,—fifty escaped." The Bothwell prisoners were herded ike cattle for many months in Grayfriar's Church Yard. Edinburgh without shelter, half-clad and half-starved. Those who refused to ake the oath of allegiance to the persecuting Government were sentenced to banishment. The list of these men reads like a muster-roll of Augusta County people; including the familiar names of Anderson, Brown, Campbell, Miller, Reid, Walker, etc. Among the prisoners who survived the shipwreck and escaped to Ireland were Thomas Miller, John Martin, and others.

As far as known the country now embraced in Augusta County, was never entered by white people until the year 1716. However, in 1710, some portion of the valley of Virginia had been seen from the top of the Blue Ridge by Europeans. Governor Spotswood in a letter to Council of Trade, London, Dec. 15, 1710, says: "A company of adventurers found the mountains not above a hundred miles from our upper inhabitants, and went up to the top of the highest mountain with their horses, tho they had, hitherto, been thought to be unpassable."

It would seem that the adventurers looked into the valley from the mountains in the neighborhood of Balcony Falls. This portion of the valley was then entirely uninhabited. The Shawnee Indians had a settlement in the lower valley, at or near Winchester, and parties of that tribe frequently traversed this section on hunting excursions, or on warlike expeditions against Southern tribes; but there was no Indian village or wigwams within the present limits of the county. The first passage of the Blue Ridge, and entrance into the valley by white men was made by Governor Spotswood in 1716. Starting from Williamsburg, leaving coach, and taking horse, at Germanna, a small frontier settlement, where he was joined by others of his party, a company of Rangers, and four Meherren Indians, comprising in all about fifty persons, they journeyed by way of the Upper Rappahannock river, and after thirty six days from the day they left Williamsburgh, scaled the mountain at Swift Run Gap, descended on the western side into the valley and encamped on the bank of the Shenandoah river. Proceeding up the river and finding a place where the river was fordable, crossed it, and there on the western bank, the Governor formally "took possession for King George the First, of England." (George I died and was succeeded in June, 1727, by his son, George II.) In commemoration of this expedition Governor Spotswood sought to establish the order of "Knights of the Golden Horse-shoe."

In 1727, Robert Lewis, William Lynn, Robert Brooks Jr. James Mills, William Lewis, and Beverley Robinson, for making discoveries of land among the mountians, and desirous of taking up some of those lands petitioned the Governor and Council for six years' time to seat the same.

The first permanent settlement by white people was made by natives of Germany in 1726, on the Shenandoah river, a few miles below the present village of Port Republic.

William Beverley, son of Robert Beverley, the Virginia Historian, and grand-son of Robert Beverley, who commanded the Royal forces at the time of Bacon's Rebellion, was a lawyer of Essex County 1720-1740; member of the House of Burgesses, and of the Governor's Council, and County Lieutenant of Essex, died March, 1755, his only son, Robert, then a minor. Said William Beverley in a letter of April 30, 1732, claimed the land by right of discovery and survey, and says "he has already sold some of it to a Pennsylvania man"; but the colony of sturdy Dutchmen were ahead of Mr. Beverley, having settled several years before near Massannutting, who in pettion to Governor and General Council claimed five thousand acres they purchased of Jacob Stover for a great sum of money, upwards of four hundred pounds.

Among the petitioners was Adams Miller.

Fifty-one white people were settled on nine plantations on the Shenandoah near Massannutting Mountain in 1733; the settlement was made in 1729; previous to 1729, there were some, although very few, white inhabitants there. Among the few white inhabitants previous to 1729 was Adam Miller. He resided at and owned the place now known as Bear's Lithia Springs, near Elkton. The certificate of his naturalization issued under the hand of Governor Gooch, March 13, 1741, set forth that he was a native of Sherstien in Germany, and had lived on the Shenandoah for 15 years next before the date of the paper. Showing that Adam Miller, came to the valley as early as 1726. It is probable that Jacob Stover's title to the property was established, as Gabriel Jones and Thomas Lewis, who bought lands in 1751, and made their homes on the Shenandoah derived their titles indirectly from Jacob Stover, the deed to Mr. Jones sets forth that Stover had obtained by patent a grant of five thousand acres.

Besides the German Colony, the early settlers of Augusta were of the Scotch-Irish race, and up to the time of the Revolutionary War, very few persons of any other race came to live in Augusta.

At a Council of war held by order of the Governor at Augusta Court House July 27, 1756, one of the points on the frontier where the Council unanimously agreed that a fort should be constructed for the protection of the inhabtants, was at Captian John Miller's on Jackson's Creek, twenty miles from Trout Rock.

George Crawford, son of Patrick and Sally Crawford, and to whom his father left the plantation on which he resided, was born October 1, 1754, married Nancy Winter, daughter of William and Ann Boone Winter, the latter the aunt of Daniel Boone, the Kentucky pioneer. Hannah Winter, a sister of Mrs. Crawford, married Henry Miller, the founder of Miller's Iron Works on Mossy Creek Augusta County.

All the children of George and Nancy Winter Crawford, were daughters, viz:

1. Nancy Crawford, wife of John Miller.
2. Hannah Crawford, wife of Henry Miller.
3. Sally Crawford, second wife of James Bell.

4. Jane Crawford, wife of Franklin McCue.
5. Martha Crawford, wife of Peter Hanger.
6. Polly Crawford, wife of James Bourland.
7. Rebecca Crawford, died unmarried.
8. Margaret Crawford, wife of James Walker.

The Biographers of the celebrated Daniel Boone, state that he came from Pennsylvania on an excursion to Augusta in 1748-9, with his cousin Henry Miller. The latter returned to the county and built on Mossy Creek the first Iron Furnace in the valley.

February 23, 1744, Peter Scholl and others of Smiths Creek (now Rockingham) petitioned the court, setting forth that they were required to work on a road thirty miles distant from their plantations, and praying for a new road near home, which was granted.

Peter Scholl, was one of the first Justices of Augusta in 1745, and probably the same Peter Scholl, who was living in Kentucky in 1776, intimately associated with Daniel Boone, and spoken of as Boone's nephew-in-law.

Thomas Miller was a member of the 7th Regiment led by Captain Robert Gamble, when Stony Point was taken from the enemy July, 15, 1779. General Charles Lee declared the storming of Stony Point the most brilliant achievement he was acquainted with in history.

John Gratton, one of the Church Wardens of Augusta parish in 1774, was a Scotch-Irish Presbyterian of the old Covenanter's faith and practice, noted for his love of David's Psalms in long metre, and his long prayers at family worship. He settled on North river, now in Rockingham County, and built the first good flour mill in the valley.

One of his daughters became the wife of Colonel Robert Gamble; another the wife of Samuel Miller, son of Henry Miller, the founder of the Iron Works on Mossy Creek in 1774.

The political convention which met in Staunton July 15, 1832, that recommended Mr. Clay for the presidency, placed Samuel Miller, of Augusta, on the electoral ticket nominated by the convention.

Henry Miller, the founder of the Iron Works having died, his administrators, Samuel Miller, and John M. Estill, advertised for sale Sept. 6, 1811, the furnace and forge, with 8,000 acres of land, (supposed to be the most valuable property of the kind in Virginia).

At the Session of the County Court of Augusta, Oct. 16,1793, the Court ordered the sheriff to erect a gallows at the forks of the roads leading from Staunton to Miller's Iron Works, and to Peter Hanger's, and that same be considered as the place of execution of all condemned persons in the future, which may by law be executed by the sheriff of Augusta.

William Miller was a musician in Captain John C. Sower's Company in 1813.

David Miller was a sergeant in Captain Alexander R. Given's Company in 1813.

In 1818, the Rev. John McCue, who had filled a large space in the County of Augusta, was thrown from his horse and killed one Sabbath morning while on his way to Tinkling Spring Church. He was a good man, when so inclined could tell comic stories in a manner irresistably laughable. His sons were James A., John, and Franklin McCue, long prominent citizens of Augusta. Dr. William McCue, of Lexington, and Cyrus McCue, a lawyer, who died young. His daughters were Mrs. Matthews, Mrs. Potterfield, Mrs. McDowell, and Mrs. Miller.

The Harrisonburg and Warm Springs Turnpike, chartered in 1830, passed by Miller's Iron Works.

As early as 1734 Michael Woods, an Irish immigrant, with three sons and three sons-in-law, came up the valley and pushed their way through Wood's Gap (now called Jarman's), and settled on the eastern side of the Blue Ridge. His sons-in-law were Peter, William, and Andrew Wallace. Samuel Wallace, (brother of the latter trio) removed to the Caldwell Settlement, now Charlotte County, married Esther Baker, and was the father of Caleb Wallace, a distinguished man in Kentucky, born in 1742.

During the Revolutionary War officers were sometimes transferred from one regiment to an other. In a list of officers on the establishment of eight regiments, found among the papers of Colonel Robert Gamble, after the battle of King's Mountain, which occurred October 7, 1780, James Woods (grandson of Michael Woods) was Colonel of the Eighth, Robert Gamble, a Captain, and John McDowell and Henry Bowyer, Lieutenants of the same regiment. Captain Andrew Wallace, (grand-son of Michael Woods,) and Thomas Bowyer of the Eighth are entered as having been killed at King's Mountain. On the old army list it is stated that Captain Andrew Wallace was killed at the battle of King's Mountain. Foote states however, that he was killed at Gulford. He says, Captain Andrew Wallace from near Lexington was in the regular service and had always shown himself a brave man. That morning he expressed a mournful presage that he would fall that day; in the course of the action he sheltered himself behind a tree, with some indications of alarm; being reproached, he immediately left the shelter and in a moment received his death wound.

Thomas Lewis' home in 1746 was probably at his father's on Lewis' Creek, about two miles northeast of Staunton; Michael Woods resided east of the Blue Ridge in Albemarle; the road or path between the homes of Lewis and Michael Woods was through Woods' Gap. The Journal of Thomas Lewis (the first Surveyor of Augusta County) of the expedition of himself and others in 1746 to establish a part of the line of Lord Fairfax's grant,states; "that Colonel (Peter) Jefferson, (father of the President late County Surveyor, and County Lieutenant of Albemarle) and Mr. Brooke set off for home on Saturday Nov. 15.; on Monday the 17, most of the men being discharged, the horses, tents, etc., were set up at auction at Captain Down's, and on the same day Mr. Lewis took leave of the Gentlemen Commissioners, and started home, he arrived at Michael Woods about two o'clock, and crossed the Blue Ridge, that evening, spent the night at Samuel Gay's and reached home on the 19th having been absent two months and nine days."

The first County Court of Botetourt was held February 14, 1770, and John Bowyer was one of the Justices and Richard Woods was appointed and qualified as sheriff. and James McDowell and James McGarvack as his deputies, or under sheriffs. On the third day of the term Andrew Woods was among the members recommended to the Governor for appointment as additional Justices.

Ann Poage, daughter of Thomas Poage Sr. married Major Archibald Woods, of Botetourt, March 5, 1789, who was a son of Mrs. Martha Woods, daughter of Robert Poage Sr. Major Woods removed to Ohio County and died in 1846. His son, Thomas Woods, who was cashier of the North Western Bank of Virginia at Wheeling, was the father of the Rev. Edgar Woods of Pantops Academy, Albemarle.

Joseph Bell of the Stone Church family was in 1781, an agent for buying cattle and on Feburauy 24, wrote to the Governor in regard to the difficulties, the farmers were unwilling to sell to the State on credit and under orders from Colonel (James) Woods, he had seized many cattle. Attorneys paid to do so, pronounced the proceedings illegal and he expected to be sued. He said, however, "Good Whigs perform their duty with most punctuality."

Under ordinance passed by the State Convention in July, 1775, providing for the organization of Minute Men, the Commissioners from the Counties of Buckingham, Amherst, Albemarle and Augusta, composing a district, met on the 8th of Sept., 1775, at the house of (Colonel) James Woods, (son of Colonel John Woods, and Susannah Anderson, of Albemarle) in Amherst, now Nelson.

Samuel McDowell was one of the commissioners from Augusta.

Virginia furnished fifteen regiments of regulars, known as the Continental line. James Woods was the original Colonel of the Twelfth regiment, and Charles Lewis of the Fourteenth, (Colonel James Woods, about the year of 1795, removed to Kentucky and settled on Paint Lick Creek in what is now Garrard County. His wife was Mary Rice.)

The first Session of the County Court of Rockridge was held April, 7, 1778, at the house of Samuel Wallace. John Bowyer, and Samuel McDowell, were two of the first Justices present. Among the other Justices commissioned was Andrew Reid. Andrew Reid, being appointed clerk was sworn in. Among other County Officers who qualified were: Samuel McDowell, Colonel; John Bowyer, Lieutenant, and James McDowell, County Surveyor.

In 1782, the Marquis of Chastillux, a French officer, traveled extensively in Virginia. The Marquis and his party forded South river where Waynesborough now is, and put up for the night at a little inn kept by Mrs. Teaze, or Teas, a daughter of Colonel John Reid, son of Thomas Reid, who came from County Down Ireland. Thomas Reid was a brother of John and Andrew Reid, the latter the father of the Rockbridge family.

Mary Cunningham, was born in or a little before the year 1747, having been baptized in that year, by the Rev. John Craig. After attaining womanhood, she became the wife of Robert Reid, son of John Reid, "of the Kingdom of Ireland," as he is described in the payment of an old suit; he was a tavern keeper and the owner of seven hundred and forty acres of land adjoining the town of Staunton and a house and lot in town. In the evening of the first Sunday in December, 1775, the young preacher, McMillan rode from the Stone Church, with Mrs. Reid and lodged at her house. Mr. Reid died in October, 1787, intestate and without issue. His estate escheated to the commonwealth, subject to the widow's dower interest, but in 1789, the Legistature passed an act granting the property to Mrs. Reid. Mr. Reid, however, had a brother, John Reid, and two half sisters, Mrs. William Reid, and Mrs. William Buchanan, and the descendants of one, or more of those relatives, after Mrs. Reid's second marrige, brought suit to recover the property but were unsuccessful.

Spottsylvania County had jurisdiction over the lands of the valley from the date of the first settlement, 1726-1732, till 1734, when Orange County was constituted. After the latter date, for some years the valley was a part of Orange. The County Court of Orange was opened January, 21, 1734, and among the Justices included in the commission of the peace issued by Governor Gooch was Benjamin Borden, a native of New Jersey, and agent of Lord Fairfax in the lower valley, who obtained from Governor Gooch a patent dated Oct. 3, 1734, for a tract of land in Frederick County, which was called Borden's Manor, and was promised 100,000 acres on the James river, west of the Blue Ridge, as soon as he should locate a hundred settlers on the tract. Borden and Beverley were indefatigable in introducing settlers from Europe. Borden's Tract was south of Borden's Manor, and in the present County of Rockridge, The first settlers on the tract were Ephraim McDowell and his family. His daughter, Mary Greenlee related in a deposition taken in 1806, the circumstances under which her father went there. Her brother, Jas. McDowell, had come into Beverley's Manor during the Spring of 1737, and planted a crop of corn near Wood's Gap, and in the fall her father, her brother, John, and her husband and herself came to occupy the settlement. Before they reached their destination, and after they had arranged their camp, on a certain evening at Linnville Creek, (now Rockingham) Borden arrived, and asked permission to spend the night with them, being on his way to his Tract from his Manor in the lower valley. He informed them of his grant and offered them inducements to go there. The next day they came on to the house of John Lewis, and there it was finally arranged that the party should settle in Borden's Tract.

Ephraim McDowell was then a very aged man, and lived to be over one hundred years old; when a youth of sixteen was one of the defenders of Londenderry. He and his family located on Timber Ridge, orginally called "Timber Grove", being attracted by the forest trees on the ridge, which were scarce elsewhere in the region.

Borden offered a tract of one hundred acres to any one who should build a cabin on it, with the privilege of purchasing more at fifty shillings per hundred acres. Each cabin secured to him (Borden) a thousand acres.

Mrs. Mary Greenlee, in her deposition, related that an Irish girl named Peggy Millhollen, a servant of James Bell, dressed herself in men's clothes and secured five or six cabin rights.

Samuel and Richard Woods, were among the settlers in Borden's grant. Borden obtained his patent Nov. 8, 1739. He died the latter part of 1743, in Frederick, leaving three sons, Benjamin, John, and Joseph, and several daughters.

The next spring his son Benjamin appeared in Rockbridge (as it is now) with authority under his father's will to adjust all matters with the settlers on the grant. He had been in the settlement, however, before his father's death.

Mrs. Greenlee says: "Benjamin Borden, Jr., * * * proved to be an upright man, and soon won the confidence of the people." The saying "As good as Ben Borden's bill" passed into a proverb. He married Mrs. Magdalene McDowell (originally Miss Woods, of Rockfish, daughter of Michael Woods and Mary Campbell, his wife) widow of John McDowell, who was killed by Indians in December, 1742, and by her had two daughters, Martha and Hannah. Martha became the wife of Robert Harvey; Hannah never married.

Benjamin Borden, Jr., died of small-pox in 1753. His will was probated in Augusta County Court Nov. 21, 1753. The executors were John Lyle, Archibald Alexander, and the widow, Magdalene. Mr. Lyle declined to serve. His personal estate was large. Mrs. Magdalene Borden contracted a third marriage with Colonel John Bowyer.

Michael Bowyer and several sons of French Huguenot descent were among the early settlers of Augusta County. Michael Bowyer died prior to 1761. His sons, viz:

Thomas Bowyer moved to Botetourt, and in 1780-1 was a Captain in the 8th Virginia Regiment, Continental line. Afterwards Major, and died childless in 1785.

John Bowyer, settled in Borden's Tract in 1753, when quite a young man, and at first was a school teacher. He soon married Mrs. Magdalene Woods-Borden, as stated, and became independent In 1763, at Augusta Court he qualified as Captain of Militia, was one of the first Justices of Botetourt in 1770. In 1781 was Colonel of Rockbridge Militia, and went with his command to lower Vir-

inia on the occasion of Arnold's invasion. He died near Lexing-
on, Virginia, in 1806, leaving no issue, and is remembered as
eneral Bowyer.

William Bowyer, was a merchant in Staunton from 1766 to 775, and maybe longer. In 1772 was a member of the vestry of ugusta parish and a church Warden in 1777, and as Lieutenant-olonel of Militia, commanded a body of men sent to re-enforce eneral McInbosh, on the Ohio River in August, 1776, and was ieutenant-Colonel of Colonel Sampson Matthews' regiment in the xpedition to lower Virginia in 1781, and was Sheriff of Augusta in 784. He had a daughter who married Mr. — Miller, ancestor of he late Fleming Bowyer Miller, of Botetourt.

Michael Bowyer, qualified as Lieutenant-Colonel of Militia at ugusta Court in 1763, and was a member of the vestry in 1773, nd of the County Committe in 1775. Early in the Revolution he ad a store in Fincastle which he left in charge of his nephew, Henry owyer, to join the army.

On the 28 February, 1739, John McDowell, whose history is iven in Part II, Chap. 4, Sec, 1, which will not be repeated here, ith his wife Magdalene (Woods,) his son, Samuel McDowell, and ohn Rutter, his servant, came from Great Britian in the year 1737, o dwell in the Colony and settled in Borden's Tract. He had two ons, Samuel, and James, and a daughter, Martha, wife of Colonel eorge Moffett.

Samuel McDowell was born in 1733. In 1773 he was a member f the House of Burgesses from Augusta County and was, it is easonably certain, Captain of an independent company of Rangers t the battle of Point Pleasant in 1774. In 1775-6, he, and Thomas ewis represented Augusta County in the State Convention. When ockbridge County was formed in 1777, he became a citizen of that ounty, his residence being there. In 1781 he commanded the attallion of Rockbridge Militia at the battle of Gulford. In June f the same year he was sworn in at Staunton as a member of the overnor's Council, Governor Nelson qualifying the same day at the ame place. At the close of the war in 1783, Samuel McDowell emoved to Kentucky with his wife and nine younger children eaving two married daughters in Virginia viz: Mrs. Andrew Reid, hose husband was the first clerk of Rockridge County Court, and ather of the late Samuel McDowell Reid, of Lexington. The ther daughter, Sally, the first wife of Judge Cabel Wallace of Charlotte County, afterwards of Botetourt, who was first a Presby-erian minister, then a lawyer, who removed to Kentucky and be-ame a Judge of the Court of Appeals of Kentucky.

Samuel McDowell, was one of the three Judges of the first Kentucky Court. President of nine Conventions which met at Danville Ky. between December 27, 1784, and July 26, 1790, and also of the Convention which framed the first Constitution of Kentucky in 1792. He died in 1817 aged 84 years. His son Dr. Ephraim McDowell, studied medicine with Dr. Humphrey, in Staunton Virginia; completed his professional education in Edinburg Scotland, and was very eminent as a surgeon. Amonw the numerous descen-dants of Judge Samuel McDowell were General Irvine McDowell, of the U. S. Army, General Humphrey Marshall, and the wife of James G. Birney, the Liberty Candidate for President of the U. S. in 1840 and 1844. The wife of Judge Samuel McDowell was Mary McClung whose brother, John McClung, was the father of William McClung, who removed to Kentucky and became a distinguished Judge. He died in 1815. His wife was a sister of Chief Justice Marshall, and his sons, Colonel Alexander K. McClung and Rev. John A. McClung, D. D., were highly distinguished.

A brother of Judge McClung, the late Mr. Joseph McClung lived until his death on Timber Ridge.

James McDowell, son of John McDowell and Magdaline Woods had one son James McDowell, Colonel in the war of 1812, father of the late Governor James McDowell.

Martha McDowell, daughter of John McDowell, and Magdaline Woods, married Colonel George Moffett, son of John Moffett and Mary Christian, his wife. Colonel Moffett was born in 1735. He lived on the Middle river farm, owned for many years past by the Dunlap family, called Mount Pleasant, and built the stone dwelling house still on the place. He was not only prominent during the Indian Wars, and the Revolution but was so, also, in civil affairs, having been a Justice of the Peace, an Elder of the Presbyterian Church, and one of the first trustees of Washington College, Lexington, Virginia. He was a man of commanding presence and eminently religious. He died in 1811, aged seventy-six years, and was buried in Augusta Church grave yard. His children were: John Moffett, James McDowell Moffett, Samuel Moffett, William Moffett, Mrs. General McDowell of Kentucky, Mrs. Colonel Joseph McDowell of North Carolina, Mrs. Kirk of Kentucky, and Mrs. James Cochran of Augusta County, Virginia.

James McDowell Moffett was the father of the late Mrs. John McCue, and Mrs. Cochran was the mother of John, George M., and James A. Cochran.

Robert McDowell proved his importation May 22, 1740, in the Orange Court.

Prior to 1745 there were no courts and court days except at Orange Court House beyond the mountain. No lawyers resided in this bailiwick till 1753, when we find Gabriel Jones, the King's Attorney, residing on his estate near Port Republic. But the sturdy Scotch-Irish people pressed into the country and by the year 1745 the Andersons, Bowyers, Bordens, Breckinridges, Browns, Campbells, Lewises, Millers, Moffetts, McDowells, Pilsons, Poages, Prestons, and others abounded in the settlement.

On the 30th of July, 1742, the inhabitants of Borden's Tract petitioned Governor Gooch to commission John McDowell, Captain of Militia. George Moffett, James McDowell, three Andersons and others were signers of the petition.

On the 27th of November, 1742, the inhabitants of Borden's Tract petitioned for a road to Woods Gap and the Court ordered that the road be cleared from James Young's through Timber Grove.

The military force of Augusta in the fall of 1742 consisted of twelve companies of about fifty men each. William Beverley was County Lieutenant, James Patton, Colonel, and John McDowell was one of the Captains. All grown men were enrolled regardless of age. Ephraim McDowell, then an old man, was a member of his son John's company, and among the privates were sundry Irvines and Millers. David Logan and Robert McDowell belonged to Captaine Cathrey's company.

John McClannahan, Jr., son of John McClannahan, and Margaret Ann Lewis, his wife, moved to Kentucky in 1807, returned to Virginia on business, and died in 1815, probably at Lewisburg. He inherited from his father the land on which Lewisburg is built. His wife was Mildred Maupin, of Williamsburg. They had seven children, only two of whom lived to maturity and married, viz:

John Gabriel McClannahan, married Eliza McClung, of Greenbrier, and died in 1838.

Virginia McClannahan, married Captain John Gantt, of the U S. Army, and their only son:

N. B. Gantt, was living in Louisville in 1890. Mr. Gantt wrote "that his grandmother, Mildred Maupin McClannahan, related that she had often heard her mother-in-law say that at the time her husband (the first John McClannahan) died the fort was beseiged by Indians, and as she sat by his bed she heard their whoops." In her prayer book is this entry: "June 30, 1774, that fatal day," probably the day of her husband's death.

Note.—Likely the above named John Gabriel McClannahan was named in commemoration of his two grandfathers, John McClannahan and Gabriel Maupin, and his mother, Mildred Maupin McClannahan, a daughter or grand-daughter of the first Gabriel Maupin, the French Huguenot immigrant, and Marie Spencer his wife; most probably the daughter of their son, Gabriel Maupin, who was also an immigrant.

Gabriel Maupin, Senior, died testate, and it is an old story that he in his testament gave his son, Daniel Maupin, only a French crown, because he married contrary to his father's wishes.

Daniel Maupin married Margaret Via, and raised a large family of sons and daughters, whose descendants are of the best families of Virginia and elsewhere. Several of Daniel Maupin's sons served in the Indian Wars and protecting the frontier before the Revolution against the Indians, and also in the Revolutionary War.

Daniel Maupin died testate in Albemarle County, Va., in 1788. His descendants have a record as soldiers hard to surpass. A great number of them were in the Civil War, mostly in the Southern army, and their blood was spilt on nearly every battlefield in Virginia and Maryland, as well as on other fields.

William Ramsey, Samuel Carrithers and Hugh Barclay were part of the jury empannelled May 14, 1778, to try Mary Walker for "speaking words maintaining the power and authority of the King and Parliament of Great Britain over the Colonies of America," whom they found "guilty," and the court sentenced her to close "gaol" four days and a fine of 15 pounds and 10 shillings.

Wallace Estill, of Irish descent, was born in New Jersey in 1707. His first wife was Marcy Bowdy. After the birth of five children he removed with his family to Augusta County, between 1744 and 1747, and a sixth child was born in Augusta.

Benjamin Estill, the second son of Wallace Estill and Marcy Bowdy, was born September 20, 1735; married in Augusta Kitty Moffett. He was a Justice of the Peace in 1764 and afterwards removed to the Holston. His sons were: Captain John M. Estill, of Long Glade, Augusta County, and Judge Benjamin Estill, of South West Virginia.

Wallace Estill married a second time, Mary Ann Campbell of Augusta: By this marriage he had nine children, among them: James Estill, born November 9, 1750, and Samuel Estill, born September 10, 1755.

James Estill married in Augusta, Rachael Wright, and removed to Greenbrier. Before the year 1780, he removed to Kentucky, and settled at Estill's Station, in the present County of Madison, and fell at the battle of Little Mountain with Wyandotte Indians in March 1782.

Samuel Estill the younger brother of James, married Jane Tess or Teas, and also emigrated to Kentucky. He was celebrated in his youth as an Indian fighter, and for his great size in his latter years, at the time of his death weighing 412 pounds.

At an early day the people living on the East side of the Blue Ridge were called Tuckahoes, from a small stream of that name, while the people living on the West side were called Cohees, from their common use of the terms, "Quoth he, or she" for "Said he, or she."

4.—Referring to Robert Harris, the Immigrant from Wales, and his son William, who married Temperance Overton, of Part III, Chapter 2.

Some entertain the belief, and may be correctly, that Robert Harris came from Wales to Richmond, Virginia, and was employed in the tobacco house of one Rice, who soon died, and Robert Harris married his widow, Mary, who was a daughter of William Clayborne, Secretary of the Virginia Colony, and that William was born in Virginia. His father having engaged in the tobacco business, probably led William to be a tobacconist.

5.—Note referring to Part III, Chapter 3, Section 4, Sub-section 5, and Chapters 6 and 12.

In Part 3, Chapter 3, Section 4, Sub-section 5, in setting forth the children of James Harris and Mary Harris, his wife, it is stated that Lucy Harris married Thomas Grubbs; the authority for said statement appears on page 221 of Rev. Edgar Woods' History of Albemarle County, Virginia. Notwithstanding, it would seem that said Lucy Harris married Higgason Grubbs and immigrated with her husband to Madison County, Kentucky, confirmed by facts hereinafter stated.

The statements appearing in Part III, Chapters 4, 6 and 12, and possibly elsewhere in said Part, that "Two sons of Christopher Harris and Mary Dabney, his first wife, married daughters of Higgason Grubbs," and that "Robert Harris married Nancy Grubbs, daughter of Higgason Grubbs," and that "Christopher Harris (Rev.) married Elizabeth Grubbs, daughter of Higgason Grubbs," are erroneous in so far as saying they were "daughters" of Higgason Grubbs; the truth of the matter is they were sisters of Higgason Grubbs. This mistake was not discovered till since going to press.

The records of the Madison County Court show that "Lucy" was the name of the wife of Higgason Grubbs. Quoting from deed recorded in D. B. I., p. 250, date July 9, 1812: "I, Higgason Grubbs, of Madison County, and State of Kentucky, do hereby relinquish all claim as husband to my wife, Lucy Grubbs, daughter of James Harris, deceased, of Albemarle County, Virginia, by virtue of a will made by James Harris aforesaid, which gives to said Lucy Grubbs one-sixth of certain negroes he lent to his wife, Mary Harris, during her widowhood or lifetime," etc.

Higgason Grubbs had numerous land transactions, probably more than any other man in the county in his active days save General Green Clay. He married in Virginia and immigrated to Madison County, Ky. at a very early day in its settlements, and whilst Kentucky was a part of Virginia, and known as Kentucky County. He was here prior to 1781, and remained till his death in 1830. His wife Lucy survived him only a short while. Higgason Grubbs established, it seems, two forts in the present County of Madison: Grubbs' Station, on Tates Creek, two miles west of Hoy's Station, in 1781, and Grubbs' Station, on Muddy Creek, prior to October, 1792. (Col. His.)

Miss Lizzie Berry has a wonderfully good mind and retentive memory, and has taken great interest in her people, and genealogy and knows a great deal about her ancestors, and the old pioneers of the county, much she got from her father, (Major James Berry,) who never forgot anything in his life, and knew the pedigrees of people of his nativity better than most any one, and his daughter's statements are entitled to much weight and credit.

The following sketch was furnished by Mr. Charles S. Grubbs, of Louisville, Ky., of the law firm of Grubbs & Grubbs (Chas. S. and Rodman Grubbs), office Kenyon Building, 216 Fifth Street:

HIGGASON GRUBBS.

Higgason Grubbs was one of the early and prominent settlers of Madison County, Kentucky. He came into the state from Virginia about the time of the exodus from Albemarle and other counties, about 1780, having prior to his removal to Kentucky intermarried with Lucy, daughter of James Harris, of Albemarle County, Virginia. He was an extensive dealer in lands, and while, possibly, living in Lincoln County a few years, he seems to have been, with this exception, a resident of Madison County until his death, June 30, 1830. (He lived a while in Estill County.)

The records of Lincoln, Madison, and other Counties, principally Madison, disclosed many transactions relating to the purchase or sale of lands, or to the defense or prosecution of suits growing out of the question of title. He came into Kentucky from Virginia, and from Albemarle County.

The earliest record indicating his presence in Kentucky is found in the shape of a deposition in Madison County, Kentucky, given on the 14th day of March, 1801, in which he locates a corner tree on a survey, he testifies that in October, 1780, he and Jesse Copper, while buffalo hunting camped at the root of a beech tree, which bore the initials "H. G." and "J. C." and the figures "1780." He testifies that the initials were put on this tree at the time named; and that the tree is the one called for in the Shelton survey.

In the same suit Jesse Copper testifies that "he and Grubbs had gone buffalo hunting from the Station where James Hendrick's now lives."

On July 9, 1812, (D.B.I. p. 249.) Madison County, Higgason Grubbs relinquished all claim as the husband of Lucy Grubbs, daughter of James Harris, deceased, of Albemarle County, Virginia, under the will of James Harris.

Collins History of Kentucky Vol. II, p.521, states that Grubbs Station, Madison County Kentucky, was settled by "Captain" Higgason Grubbs, before October, 1781.

In the case of Grubbs vs Lipscomb, Madison Circuit Clerk's office Book B.p. 442. Aguilla White testifies that he removed from Grubb's Station in the spring of 1783. Cradlebough (William) testifies that Grubbs' Station was also called Hancock Station, and was on the waters of Tate's Creek.

His prominence in the early settlement of the state is shown by this synopsis of his public life:

1. 1787. One of the Trustees of Boonesboro, appointed by Governor of Virginia to supply place of first trustee who refused to act, the appointment being made under "Act to explain and amend the Act for establishing the town of Boonesbrough, Madison County Kentucky," (Virginia Legislature 1779,) passed December 29, 1787. Hennings Statutes. Vol.XII. p.603. See, also Hennings Vol.XII. p.37, 240, and 788.

2. Member from Madison County Kentucky, of Convention in Danville 1787-88.

3. 1790. Member Virginia Legislature from (Madison Co. Ky.) Counties formed in 1792, into State of Kentucky. (His name appears

frequently in Journal of the House of Delegates Commonwealth of Va. Session began Monday October 18, 1790.)

4. 1792. Member and representative (Madison Co.) '1st. Constitutional Convention.

5. Member House Representatives (Madison Co.) Ky. 1792-1796, 1797, 1978, 1801, and 1802. He seems to have retired from public life about this time, probably being compelled to do so by reason of the necessity of looking after his private interest in lands, which seem to have been the subject of more or less litigation growing out of conflicting titles. The records of Madison County disclose this fact and it would seem that in his later years he lost much, if not all, of his estate which he had acquired in his earlier and more prosperous days.

6. Grubbs' Station, Madison County Kentucky, settled by Captain Higgason Grubbs before October, 1792. (Collins History of Kentucky.)

Higgason Grubbs seems to have been an only son, but he had the following sisters, some of whom, at least, removed to and lived in Madison County, Kentucky.

1. Elizabeth, married Christopher Harris.
2. Nancy, married Robert Harris.
3. Mary, married —— Moore.
4. Hennie, married Andrew Ray (Rea.)
5. Lucy, married Thomas Gooch.
6. Sally, married James Berry.
7. Annie, married William Boone.
8. Susan, married —— Bartow.

In Virginia History and Biography Vol.VIII.p.212, descendants of Daniel Maupin, Albemarle County, Va. it is shown that Andrew Rea, married Henrietta Grubbs.

Thomas Grubbs, the oldest son of Higgason Grubbs, died in Montgomery County Kentucky, many years ago, but the family tradition is that he was born in Virginia.

In addition to Thomas Grubbs, Higgason Grubbs had four sons and one daughter, all of whom were born in the State of Kentucky, and died residents of this State.

John Grubbs one of the sons, married his cousin, Lucy Gooch, and the only daughter married —— Barnes.

Besides a member of patents issued in Kentucky, the records Richmond, Va. show the following patents were issued to Higgason Grubbs.

Higgason Grubbs, assignee of John Jackson, Book G. p. 247, 100 acres 1781.

Higgason Grubbs, assignee of Samuel Baldwin, Book G. p, 252, 200 acres.

Higgason Grubbs, assignee of Wm. Hancock, Book G. p, 250, 100 acres.

Higgason Grubbs, assignee of Jesse Copper, Book G. p. 275, 100 acres.

Higgason Grubbs, assignee of Green Clay, Book W. p, 268, 400 acres.

Higgason Grubbs, assignee of Green Clay Book W. p, 466, 1300 acres.

Higgason Grubbs, assignee of Samuel Clements, who was assignee of Samuel Walnut, Grant L. Henry, June 2, 1784-15. 400 acres.

John Higgason of New Kent Co. Book 10 p, 63, 122 acres. 1712. John Higgason, Book 410, p, 536, 2037 acres. 1716.

Higgason Grubbs seems to have acquired the title of "Captain," and while it is posible he was connected with some of the early military bodies that came into the state, no evidence is found of his being a Commissioned officer. He was a surveyor and the records of MadisonCounty, Kentucky, show that he was a man of education, as he wrote a good hand, spelled accurately, and in many instances in giving depositions and preparing legal documents these documents seem to have been in his own hand writing, and were carefully and well drawn. Attached hereto are two extracts, one from the Richmond Climax, a paper published in Madison County, which were written by William Chenault, now dead. One of these articles speaks of "William Grubbs, a pioneer and father of Higgason Grubbs."

In Gleanings Virginia History, Boogher, the name Grubbs appears at the following points:

Page 23, reference is had to Henning Vol. 7 p, 226.
Page 25, Albemarle County, Henning Vol. 7 p, 22.
Page 27, Thomas Grubbs.
Page 38, Vol. 7- -200 Henning, Jacob Grubbs.
Page 116, Richard Grubbs.

In St. Peter's Parish Register, New Kent Co. Va. the Vestry Book has this entry: "1754, Anne, daughter of Hensely and Susannah Grubbs, born October 6, baptized November 10, 1758. Susannah, daughter of Hensely and Susannah Grubbs, born May 15, baptized June 18."

We observe supra, two sisters of Higgason Grubbs, married a Harris, and he had a nephew, Hensley Harris, well known in Southern Kentucky, where he died some years ago. Hensley seems to have been a family name, but are not advised where the name Higgason comes from, except, it is an old Virginia name, found in York and other Counties, where Captain Robert Higgason, and others of the same name were well kown.

In the Library of Congress, Manuscript Division, Vol. 8 page 1067, and Vol. 9 page 1128, will be found letters of James Grubbs to James Munroe, who was evidently of Virginia.

There is also, in the Library of Congress a pamphlet of the Grubbs family of Pennsylvania and Delaware, some of whom removed into Virginia. This family was the immediate descendants of John Grubbs, who immigrated from England, 1677 and settled at Grubbs' Landing, Delaware, 1681. Judge Ignatius C. Grubbs, of Wilmington, Delaware, is a descendant of this line, and has given considerable attention to the family history both in America and England. While the families are each, possibly, of the same origin, English, no connection between the two has so far been made.

In England the name is Grubb and Grubbe, but there seems to be no definite explanation why another branch spell the name "Grubbs". Possibly the accidental changing of the old English final "e" to "s".

Extract from the Climax:

Visiting His Old Home.

"James William Parrish, Esq. of Winchester, came over last week to meet the few remaining friends of his boy-hood. He was born in Madison, but left here half a century ago. His father was Samuel Parrish, who came from Lexington about 1817, and married a daughter of Captain James Berry, who was wounded in the battle of Little Mountain, in which Captain James Estill was killed and brought to Boonsborough on the back of the slave Monk.

Capt. Berrys wife was a daughter of William Grubbs, a pioneer, and sister of the distinguished Higgason Grubbs, who represented Madison County in two famous Separation Conventions at Danville, also in the Constitutional Convention of 1792, and was representative in the first Legistature which convened at Lexington, and Elector of the first Senate, an office that perished with the first Constitution. Mr. Grubbs' daughter married Squire Boone Jr. nephew of the immortal Daniel, and father of Major Levi D. Boone, of Chicago. Mrs. Parrish's brother was Major James Berry, formerly Post-Master of Richmond. Mr. Parrish and the late Thomas Parrish of the Foxtown vicinity were brothers.

He has many attachments for his old home. When a young man, he boarded at the "Widow's Inn," a hotel kept by two widows in what is now the Dellingham, or Climax building. Mr. Parrish is hale and hearty. He was accompanied by his nephew, Mr. J. A. Parrish, better known as Captain Jack 2:08¾.—Richmond Climax.

From a series of articles by William Chenault, now deceased, which appeared in Richmond (Ky.) Register:

"In the fall of 1791, Captain Higgason Grubbs built a station six miles east of Madison Court House and moved a few families to that place. A crop was raised here in the summer of 1792, but the inhabitants left the station for a short time in the summer through fear of Indians, and returned again in the same fall. A convention was called at Danville, on the 2nd of April, 1792, to make a Constitution for the new State of Kentucky about to be admitted into the Union on the 1st of June of that year. Madison was represented in this Convention by Thomas Kennedy, Joseph Kennedy, Thomas Clay, Higgason Grubbs, and Charles Kavanaugh. The pro-slavery clause of the Constitution was the main issue before the Convention. All the delegates from Madison were for the clause, except Charles Kavanaugh, the pioneer Methodist minister, who recorded his vote against pro-slavery feature of the Constitution. He was true to the teaching and doctrines of the pioneer Methodists of the County that no man should purchase a slave except in case of mercy and humanity.

In May, 1792, Isaac Shelby was chosen Governor, not by the people but by forty electors chosen by the people. The electors chosen for Madison County were William Irvine, Higgason Grubbs, and John Miller. Our first Senator was, also, elected by the forty electors, and their votes gave the position to Thomas Kennedy.

A contest soon arose over the location of the Capital of the state and Boonesboro made quite an effort to obtain the prize. On the 30th of August, 1792, the citizens of the county subscribed $8,166.67 in money and 18,550 acres of land to secure the permanent location of the Capital at Boonesboro. The two largest subscribers were Gen. Green Clay, and Judge Thomas Clay. The first gave $1,000 in money and 10,000 acres in Madison County land. The second gave 3,000 acres of land in same county. Liberal sums were donated by John Holder, William Bush, William Calk, William O'Rear, D. Bullock, Robert Clark, Jr. Robert Clark, Sr. John Moore, John Wilkerson, James McMillan, James French, Robert Elkin, William Hayes, Henry Haynes, Peter Evans, Ebenezer Platt, Higgason Grubbs and many others.

On the first day of June 1792, the District of Kentucky became the State of Kentucky. Governor Shelby appointed David Gass, John Miller, James French, and Robert Rodes as the new Judges of the Court of Quarter Sessions. John Snoddy, Archibald Woods, Joseph Kennedy, Adam Lewis, Thomas Kennedy, and Moses Dooley were made Justices of the Peace with power to hold County Court.

John Boyle, the old pioneer Justice, who had roamed the County with Daniel Boone, sold out his farm near Estill Station and moved to the Western end of Madison in the present County of Garrard. With John Kincaid, of Milford, he had followed the flag of Gen. George Rogers Clark, in his expedition against the Kaskaskia and Vincinnes in 1778 and 1779, and was one of the sufferers from the robbery of Daniel Boone at Painter's Fork in 1781. His friend Joseph Kincaid, had already fallen on the bloody battle field of Blue Licks where he was a soldier in the same company with Ezekiel Field, the father of the well known merchant of Richmond.

The pioneer element of the County was beginning to yield other influences. The sway of military men was yielding to that of the farmer, the teacher and the professional man. The way was beginning to be opened for the coming of Barnabas McHenry and John Finley, to the County and their influences as teachers in the County was long to be felt upon the rising young men of the County and State at large." (Signed) W. C.

As furnished by Miss Mary Elizabeth (Lizzie) Berry, (daughter of James H. Berry, and Emily S. Fox, his wife) of Speedwell Madison County, Kentucky. William Grubbs and wife, Susan Hearne, came to Kentucky from Albemarle County, Virginia, about the year 1775, and made claim to land. He died in a few days after he came to Kentucky, and was buried at Bryan's Station. After his death his wife and ten children came to Madison County.

"Sarah Grubbs, daughter of William and Susan Hearne Grubbs, married James Berry. Her mother's maiden name was Hearne. Her only brother was:

Higgason Grubbs, who married Lucy Harris, of Albemarle County, Virginia.

Her sisters:

1. Elizabeth Grubbs, who married Christopher Harris, a preacher.
2. Nancy Grubbs, who married Robert Harris, brother of the above Christopher Harris.
3. Mollie Grubbs, married Robert Moore.
4. Susan Grubbs, married John Moore.
5. Annie Grubbs, married Squire Boone, Baptist preacher.

(Court records show "Nancy Grubbs" married William Boone, August 16, 1789.)

6. Lucy Grubbs, married Thomas Gooch.
7. Hennie Grubbs, married Andrew Ray (Rea).
8. Fannie Grubbs, married Joshua Barton.

Daughters of Sarah Grubbs Berry (and husband, James Berry):

1. Annie Berry, married Thomas Turner.
2. Nancy Berry, married Edwin Berry.
3. Susan Berry, married Samuel Parrish.
4. Elizabeth Berry, married Christopher Harris. (See Part 3, Chapter 28.)

Her sons:

5. William Berry, died single.
6. James H. Berry, married Emily S. Fox.

(Children of James H. Berry and Emily S. Fox his wife:)

1. Mary Elizabeth Berry, single.
2. James Thomas Berry, married Elizabeth daughter of Isaac Hill. Mr. Berry is now Deputy Assessor of Madison County, Ky., which position he has filled at intervals for the last forty years or more, and is now a canidate for the office of assessor.
3. Susan Berry, died a number of years ago.
4. Nannie Berry, married James M, Hendren, late Justice of the peace of the County, now a merchant at Speedwell.
6. George Berry, died several years ago.

JamesBerry, (the pioneer) was a son of Thomas Berry, and his wife (I think a Bocock, don't know for sure.)

James Berry, had two brothers, Garret, and Thomas. Don't know who either married. Also two sisters:

Bettie Berry, married —— Frazier.

Pattie Berry, died single.

Children of Higgason Grubbs and Lucy Harris:

1. William Grubbs, married ————.

2. John Grubbs, married Miss Lucy Gooch. (He married four or five times.)

3. Thomas Grubbs, married Katie Howard.

4. James Grubbs, married Nancy Oldham. (See Part VI, Chapter 33.)

5. Jesse Grubbs, married Nancy Oldham. (See Part VI, Chapter 36.)

6. Lucy Grubbs, married —— Barnes. (Parents of the late Colonel Sidney M. Barnes, of the Federal Army in the Civil war, who resided at Irvine, Ky., and Thomas H. Barnes, formerly Clerk of the Madison County Court, one of the very best of scribes, well remembered by many of the old residents of the County.)

These are all I know, there may have been more.

The aforesaid J. Thomas Berry, past 76 years of age, very active, and now Deputy Assessor, says his grandparents, James and Sarah Berry, were in the fort on Shallow Ford Creek, and William Berry, their oldest child, was born in said fort some time in 1783. Said fort was established on the farm now owned by Jacob S. White. His father, James H. Berry, was born December 6, 1802, and died July 2, 1879. Nineteen years between his birth and that of his oldest brother, William, who died on Shallow Ford within a mile and a half of the place of his birth, in the fall of 1857. His grandfather, James Berry, was wounded in the thigh in the battle of Little Mountain with Wyandotte Indians, in which his captain, James Estill, was killed, and Mr. Berry was carried off the battlefield on the back of the slave negro Monk. William Watts Moore, who died a few months ago, past 94 years of age, was a son of Reuben Moore and Nancy Watts, his wife, and a grandson of one of the Moores who married Miss Grubbs above stated, sister to Sarah Berry. Joseph Warren Moore, who married Margaret Frances Harris (See Part III, Chap. 3) was a brother to Wm. W. Moore.

June 21, 1812 (D. B. I, p. 76) Higgason Grubbs and wife Lucy, conveyed by deed to Nancy Moore, late wife, now widow, of Reuben Moore, fifty acres of land on the waters of the East Fork of Otter Creek.

On November 14, 1831, (D. B. No. 1, p. 423) John Moore and Milly, his wife, and Henry Watts and Elizabeth, his wife, late Elizabeth Moore, children and heirs of Nancy Moore, deceased, also heirs of George Moore, deceased, of Calloway County, Missouri, conveyed to Silas Tribble the land on East Fork of Otter Creek, being same land that was on the 21st day of June, 1812, sold and conveyed by Higgason Grubbs to Nancy Moore, now dead.

Marriages of Record:

William Boone—Nancy Grubbs, August 16, 1789.
John McCord—Jennie Reid, March 23, 1797.
Thomas Grubbs—Katy Howard, November 28, 1798.
Joseph Moon—Fannie Reid, May 21, 1799.
Joseph Boone—Nancy Moon, August 28, 1814.
Nicholas Kavanaugh—Jane Wallace, January 12, 1817.
Lucinda Woods—Paul Dantic, June 17, 1819.

6.—Note referring to Part II, Chapter 20, Section 6, and Part III, Chapter 40, Section 4.

Susan Woods, married Ashby Snell. Their daughter Nora Snell, married Levins Pindell, of Arkansas City, Ark. whose son:

1. Xenophen Overton Pindell, is now the acting Governor of Arkansas, while Governor Little is hopelessly ill. He is known as Ove Pindell, and X. O. Pindell.

The Memphis Commercial Appeal mentions him in nearly every issue.

7.—Note refering to Hezekiah Rice and Mary Bullock his wife. (See Part VI, Chapter 13b, Note)

Mrs. Luella Duncan Curlee, wife of Shelby H. Curlee, now of 5724 Chamberlain Avenue, St. Louis, Mo., and a grand-daughter of Martha Rice, and William Clifton, and a great-grand-daughter of Hezekiah Rice, and Mary Bullock, furnishes the following data:

"The first Rice record given, Nathaniel Rice, as Secetary of the Province in 1731. He was not the Emigrant, but thus far we have not found the Emigrant, but hope to locate before we cease our inquiry. His son:

Hezekiah Rice, married Mary Bullock. Hezekiah Rice was a delegate to the Hillsborough Convention, August 21, 1775, from Orange County, North Carolina, which County was afterwards divided into the two Counties of Orange and Caswell.

Hezekiah Rice was Lieutenant in Continental Army 1775, Captain November 28, 1776. His war record is established and will be given by the War Department, Washington, D.C. or in the History of the Continental Army of North Carolina. The D. A. R. Chapters and State Historical Societies have gotten together some very good work on this subject.

Hezekiah Rice and his wife, Mary Bullock, had:

1. Ann, (Annis) married Captain John Oldham. (See Part VI, Chapter 13b.)

2. Joel Rice, married and has descendants in North Alabama.

3. John Rice, and his brother, Elisha were killed by the Indians near Clarksville, Tennessee on their return to North Carolina from Memphis Tennessee. John Rice, had been given a land grant of 5,000 acres of land on the bluff, or what is now the City of Memphis; the grant was made April 5, 1787. Rice Bullock's land grant was made December 31, 1784.

Nathaniel Rice's land grant was made December 31, 1784.

George Rice's land grant was made December 31, 1784.

John Rice, was at the Halifax Cenvention 1776, from Orange County, North Carolina. He was the brother of Martha the wife of William Clifton.

4. Elisha Rice, was killed by the Indians as related above in 3.

5. Martha Rice, married William Clifton; she and her husband and four children, born in North Carolina, removed to Huntsville, Alabama, prior to 1816, in which year the first deed to them was recorded.

6. Williamson Rice, married and has descendants in North Alabama.

8.—James Harris, of Boone County, Missouri.

(See Part III, Chapter 37, Section 2)

Overton Harris, and his wife, Mary Rice Woods, came to the territory of Missouri from Kentucky in the year 1817, settling in what is now known as Boone County, and of which County Overton Harris was the first sheriff and was subsequently County Judge.

JAMES HARRIS.

They had six children, James, the subject of this sketch, being the second child. He was born in Boone County, May 17th, 1818, and died in the same county, July 11th, 1881. He was given such an education as was afforded by the common schools of Missouri at that day and was one of the first graduates of Bonne Femme Academy. He later studied the art of surveying, and was at one time Deputy United States Surveyor and surveyed many of the public lands in Missouri and Arkansas preparatory to bringing them into market. He was elected several times to the office of County Surveyor of Boone County, the duties of which position he discharged with great credit to himself and satisfaction to the people. In 1858 he was elected as Boone County's representative in the State Legislature and in 1866 was elected County Court Judge, which position he held for twelve years. Colonel W. F. Switzler in writing of his official services in the Columbia Statesman says that "to Judge Harris more than to any other man is Boone County indebted for its excellent credit and fair name among the various Counties of the State." During the Civil War Judge Harris, although a slave owner and in close social and buisness relations with the South, was an outspoken Union man maintaining from the first and throughout the struggle that the government of our fathers should be kept as one and inseparable forever.

Judge Harris united with the Bonne Femme Baptist Church August 8, 1839, and was a member of this one congregation for nearly forty-two years. As a Baptist, his influence was known and felt throughout the entire State. He was one of eight men to give $5,000 each to found a school of theology at William Jewel College. He was one of the organizers and founders of the Baptist Female College at Columbia, Missouri, now known as Stephens College, and from its foundation and continuously up to the time of his death was one of its trustees and most loyal friends.

On December 5th, 1848, Judge Harris was united in marriage with Sabra Brown Jackson, daughter of Judge Wade M. Jackson of Howard County and niece of Clayborne Jackson, at one time governor of Missouri. Mrs. Harris died at the home of her son David H. Harris in Fulton, Missouri, on December 29th, 1903. To this marriage there were born fourteen children, as follows:

1. Elizabeth (now deceased), who married Capt. Hiram C. Pierce.
2. Mary, who died in infancy.
3. Sallie, who married Macon Bradley.
4. John Sterling, (now decased) who married Sarah Hall.
5. Overton, who married Luella Dollarhide.
6. Wade Jackson, who married Nettie Baker.
7. Julia Stone, who married Joseph W. Johnston.
8. Anna May, (now deceased) who married Samuel M. Baker.
9. Margaret Bass, who married John T. Trimble.
10. David Hickman, unmarried.
11. Louise Hickman, who married Robert L. Holland.
12. Susan Duncan, who married R. Stockton Dorsey.

13. James Howard, unmarried.
14. William Boone, unmarried. (Two latter twins.)

9.—Kavanaugh.

Mrs. Anna Poynter Kavanaugh, of 916 14th Avenue, Pine Bluff Arkansas, writes:

Philemon I, eldest son of Col. Charles I, second son of Sir Moroch Kavanaugh, having been deprived of their estates in Ireland by the Cromwellian treaty, emigrated to France in 1691, and the two sons, about 1705, came to America. Col. Charles Kavanaugh, whose regiment fought at Derry (violating the treaty of Limerick), returned from America to France, leaving his brother Philemon in Virginia.

Charles II, eldest.

Philemon II, married Ann Williams, second marriage, and had two sons.

Charles III.

Williams.

Philemon II arms are those of his father and Sir Moroch Kavanaugh, thus:

"Ar. two lions pass. gu. in base, 2 crescents of last. Motto: Sciothchain. Agus Fairsinge, "Peace and Plenty."

SUPPLEMENT No. II.

ELDER TYREE CRAWFORD HARRIS AND WIFE, LAVINIA HUGHES. REFERRED TO IN PART III, CHAPTER 10, SECTION 10.

Tyree Crawford Harris was the son of Tyree Harris and Sallie Garland, of Boone County, Mo., and was the tenth of thirteen children. He was born in the year of our Lord 1824.

TYREE CRAWFORD HARRIS.

From childhood he was naturally very delicate. Although no marks of any settled disease were visible, yet he was unable to perform any hard physical labor. Possessing a playful and gentle disposition, he was a great favorite among his early companions—rarely, if ever, known to be out of humor, or in the least to become irritated, as was common with boys of his age. He never used profane language, or engaged in gross wickedness of any kind.

In early youth, Tyree Harris possessed extraordinary sprightliness; at the age of six years he commenced school, and with uncommon aptness he comprehended, as with instinct, every probilem presented to him. Though the schools of that day were greatly inferior to what they are now, yet his progress was remarkable. At the age of thirteen fears were entertained of his early decline with consumption; but by such exercise as suited his inclination his health was restored.

In October, 1839, he attended the regular monthly conference of the Baptist Church at Mt. Gilead, in Howard County, Mo., and under the faithful preaching of Elder Thos. Fristoe, he, for the first time, clearly saw himself a helpless sinner before God. He went home the same evening in deep distress, with a clear view of the depravity of the human heart. But ere long the burden was removed: and delivered from the thraldom of sin, through faith in the Lord Jesus Christ, his soul was enabled to rejoice in His redeeming grace and dying love.

At the regular meeting of the Bethlehem Church, in Boone County, in November following, he was received into fellowship by experience and baptism, by that faithful servant of God, Fielding Wilhite. His prayer at the water will never be forgotten by those who were present. His whole soul was drawn out in the most earnest melting appeal and supplication to the Divine throne, that young Tyree Harris might be qualified to dispense the word of life and become an eminent minister of the gospel. He commenced the exercise of public prayer with great acceptance. In December, 1841, the church granted him license to preach, which he did, to the astonishment of multitudes who heard him. Shortly after this, Rowland Hughes of Howard County, learning the future promise of young Tyree Harris, and hearing him on one occasion himself, proposed to take him into his family and complete his education, which he did to the satisfaction of all concerned. He was educated in Boonville, under Professor Kemper.

His youthful appearance, together with his bold and earnest manner, his untiring zeal, his eloquent and pungent appeals from the pulpit soon won for him the name of the "boy preacher."

His style was forcible, attractive and popular; his manner easy and graceful; his voice sweet and mellow. With a clear, strong mind, he possessed great vivacity of thougt and versatility of style. Fluency of speech and lively imagination were combined to make him a "bright and shining light." His manner, both in private and public, in the pulpit and out of it, was such as to make him popular both with the church and the world.

In December, 1843, he assisted in the constitution of the first Baptist Church in the city of Boonville; and in August following he commenced his labors with this church as their regular pastor. Though young, he commanded an influence for good and attracted great congregations, and soon succeeded in building a large and commondious house of worship. Under his minstry his church enjoyed a high degree of prosperity; members were added almost monthly by experience and baptism, until they became a large and influential body.

With the brethren in Boonville he spent the prime of his short life. This people loved him dearly. The name of Tyree Harris is still fresh in the menory of those who enjoyed the labors of this eminent divine. Whilst in the field he also for a time preached for the churches at Big Lick and Nebo, in Cooper County, and after eight years of successful toil he left a large church and took charge of the congregation in Fayette in 1851.

In 1852 he commenced his labors as pastor of the church in Columbia, Mo., where, by his distinguished pulpit efforts and his Christian and gentlemanly deportments, he endeared himself to a large circle of admiring friends and acquaintances.

During his pastorate here he was also president of the Columbia Female Academy. And under his able superintendence the institution flourished beyond a parallel at that time. He canvassed the state in behalf of the institution, presenting the claims of female education; and his eloquent appeals met a liberal response, for around him were gathered 125 young ladies from all parts of the state.

In 1853 he was called to the chair of English Literature in William Jewell College, but did not accept the position.

In 1854 he was called to take charge of the Female College at La Grange, in Georgia, but did not accept.

After two years of arduous toil in the pulpit and schoolroom, he was called to and accepted the care of the Baptist church in Lexington, Mo. He entered upon his labors in this field with renewed ardor and zeal, and determined to spend his life with the people of God there. He was soon attacked with typhoid fever, and in two months after he entered upon his duties there he was called to his reward.

His wife's maiden name was Lavinia Hughes.

Bro. Harris was considered by all who knew him as the ablest and most promising young man in the state. View him as a man, as a minister of the New Testament, and hear his earnest appeals from the sacred desk, and you would mark him as a man of no ordinary talent. As pastor, he was kind, affectionate and prayerful; as a reasoner, clear and forcible; and as a speaker he had strength, beauty and eloquence. Possessing these rare gifts, he was successful in all his labors on earth, and now, whilst his works do follow him his memory is fragrant in the hearts of many.

ERRATTA

Index

Page 7—"Blythe, Lucy—Wm. E. Simmons"; should be "Simms".
"Bodwin"; should be "Bodine".
"Bound"; should be "Bond".
"Booten Falitha"; should be "Talitha".
"Bordiue"; should be "Borden".

Page 10—"Brown, Algerson"; should be "Algernon".
"Brown, Benjamin Hescott—Judith Frehrell"; should be "Fretwell".

Page 12—"Brown, John R.—Candica Hall"; should be "Candice".

Page 13—"Brown, Sorah"; should be "Sarah".

Page 15—"Burnsides, John—Fanuie Ballnor"; should be "Ballew".
"Bush, Elizabeth—C. C. Broaddus"; should be "H. Clay Broaddus".
"Caldwell Loody"; should be "Lovely".

Page 18—"Chenault, Sallie—Due Simpson"; should be "Duke Simpson".
"Chenault, Wm. O.—Belle Mass"; should be "Moss".
"Christopher, Florince"; should be "Florence".
"Christopher, Grace, Mrs.—Wm. D. Bomey"; should be "Bonny".

Page 20—"Cochran, Sarah—Peter Al. Estill"; should be "Peter W. Estill".
"Cole, Lewis K. — Tabitha Covington"; should be "Talitha".
"Collins Lunuah"; should be "Leannah".

Page 21—"Combs, M. F.—Elijah W. Oldham"; should be "Eliza".
"Conrcy, Edward B."; should be "Edward".

Page 22—"Cox, Levi Preston—Mary Belle Wools"; should be "Woods".

Page 24—"Dabney, Mary—Thomas Mirror"; should be "Minor".

Page 25—"Deering—Jessie S. Ulinn"; should be "Winn".

Page 26—"Doty, Charles K.—Mrs. Susan Suarks"; should be "Sparks".

Page 27—"Dulaney, Walliam H.—Tabitha Harris Bordine"; should be "Talitha".
"Dull, Loura"; should be "Laura".

Page 28—"Duncau, Malon B.—Donndy Cornelison"; should be "Dorindy".

Page 29—"Ellington, Annilia"; should be "Amelia".

Page 32—"Field, Deanna"; should be "Dianna".

Page 35—"Gentry, Overton—Lulinda Reid"; should be "Lucinda".

Page 36—"Gillum, Miss—Bezanel Garth"; should be "Bezaleel".

Page 38—"Grubbs, Thomas—Lucy Harris"; should be "Grubbs, Higgason".

Page 39—"Hall, Mr.—Mrs. Polly Gubert"; should be "Gilbert".

Page 42—"Harris, Lucy—Thomas Grubbs"; should be "Higgason Grubbs".

Page 44—"Harris, Sidney—* * Miss Mary Jane Miller"; should be "Mrs. Mary Jane Miller".
"Harris, Susan—Nicholas Bunley"; should be "Burnley".

Page 46—"Henning, Mr.—Hargaret McKee"; should be "Margaret McKee".

Page 48—"Hopkins, Mary—Lutton T. Woods"; should be "Luther T. Woods".

Page 49—"Hume, mma—Thos. Thorpe"; should be "Hume, Emma"

Page 50—"Jarman, Cathensie"; should be "Catherine".

Page 52--"Jones, Josiah—Jaru Chenault"; should be "Jane".
Page 55- "Keblinger, W. J.—Mary Garman"; should be "Mary Jarman".
Page 63—"Mannie, Sallie—Foster Harris"; should be "Manning".
Page 64-—"Martin, Saniera"; should be "Samira".
"Martin, Saniera"; should be "Samira".
Page 66—"Maupin, Dorcas K.—Caldwell C."; should be "Caldwell C. Maupin".
Page 68—"Maupin, Josephine—Pheston Beatty"; should be "Preston Beatty".
"Maupin, Kittie—George L. Burkhatter"; should be "Burkhalter".
Page 69—"Maupin, Robert- Miss McGehu"; should be "McGehee".
"Maupin, Nancy- -Thos. Stagour"; should be "Stagner".
Page 72--"Michie, Lucien—Theresa Hichie"; should be "Michie".
Page 74--"Miller, John Thos.—Annie Elkin"; should be "Anice".
Page 75—Miller, Laura Frances—J. H. Hoastman"; should be "Horstman".
Page 77—"Mills, Menan—Fannie Jopett"; should be "Jouett".
Page 78—"Mizo, John A." etc., should be "Mize".
Page 78- "Moberley, Simeon—Arthisa Banta"; should be 'Arthusa'
Page 79—"Moore, Elizabeth—Prisley Oldham"; should be "Presley".
Page 80—"Murrell, Betsy—Janus Reid"; should be "James Reid".
Page 81—"Noland, John—Belle Garnis"; should be "Garner".
"Noland, Margaret C.—James Fax"; should be "Fox".
Page 82—"Oldham, Chas.—Caudice Howard"; should be "Candice"
Page 84—"Oldham, Mary Jackson—B. K. Gola"; should be "Gold".
Page 85—"Oldham, Polly Ann—Richard Dyarnatt"; should be "Dejarnatt".
"Oldham, Richard * *—Arsley Williams"; should be "Ursley".
"Oldham, Sam'l Zerah—Ellea Moore"; should be "Ellen".
Page 88—"Paxton, Janus"; should be "James".
Page 91—"Pullins, Wm.—Minerva Halman"; should be "Holman".
"Quisenberry, James F.—Emily CCrenault"; should be "Chenault".
"Quisenberry, Brownhall"; should be "Broomhall".
Page 92—"Rea, Jemima—Richard Bickitt"; should be "Beckett".
Page 96--"Rogers, Martha Mendricks"; should be "Hendricks".
Page 97—"Scrivner, Eva—Henry Raybarn"; should be "Rayburn".
Page 98—"Searcy, Charles M."; should be "Charles L."
"Shackleford, Margaret—Robert Haven"; should be "Hann".
Page 101—"Smith, Carraline"; should be "Caroline".
"Snodgrass, James Wods"; should be "James Woods".
Page 102—Cpeller, B. Jane"; should be "Spiller".
"Stamper, Austin—nna Wingate"; should be "Anna".
Page 109—"Walker, Menry"; should be "Henry".
Page 111—"Wallace, Caleb B., of Bogle;" should be "Boyle".
Page 112—"Wallace, Thomas Quirk—Carrie Hugleton"; should be "Carrie J. Congleton".
Page 113- "Watts, Margaret—Austin Bordman"; should be "Boulware".
Page 114--"Whiteman, Enuriel"; should be "Emuriel".
Page 115--"Williams, Lrsley", etc.; should be "Ursley".
Page 116—"Wood, Twoin"; should be "Wood, Turner".
Page 118—"Woods, Elizabeth—John M. Sarroll"; should be "Carroll".
"Woods, Elizabeth—George Pasell"; should be "Paull".

Page 119—"Woods,, John, of Honkston Co."; should be "Hinkston Co."
"Woods, Louisa—S. Calin Baker"; should be "S. Colin".
Page 120—"Woods, Michael—Lizzie Mussirley"; should be "Messerley".
Page 121—"Woods, Slity," etc.; should be "Woods, Suity".
Page 122—"Worthington, Mamie—James"; should be "James Stone."
Page 125—"Crawford, F. A., Miss—Com. Cor. Anderbilt"; should be "Vanderbilt".

Book Proper

Page 13—13th line from top "Sunny County"; hould be "Surry".
Page 15—19th line from top "Thomas Stayour"; should be "Stagner".
Page 19—In caption, the figure "4" should be placed before "A Brief History of Culpeper County, Va."
Page 20—26th line from bottom, "Bossie's Trace"; should be "Boone's Trace".
Page 26—14th line from bottom, "Copart"; should be "Cozart".
Page 28—7th line from battom, "Station Creek"; should be "Station Camp Creek".
Page 39—14th line from top, "Fuvanna"; should be "Fluvanna".
Page 45—Gen. Table, C-3, "Gen. John Waller"; should be "Gen. John Miller".
Page 46—"Miller, Cynthiana—James Parges"; should be "Parkes".
Page 47—"Miller, Chas. Irvine—Tolika Harris"; should be "Chris Irvine Miller, and Talitha Harris".
"Miller, Caledonia—Ulm. O. Chenault"; should be "Wm. O. Chenault".
"Chenault Alaker"; should be "Chenault Waller".
Page 50—"Park, Ann Eliza—Joseph O. Scrivner"; should be "Joseph Q. Scrivner".
Page 51—Sec. 4, "Col. Nichilis Miller"; should be "Nicholas".
Page 54—"Daniel Miller, from County of Madigson"; should be "Madison".
3d line from bottom, "Eskill"; should be "Estill".
Page 83—4th line from bottom, "girds"; should be "birds".
Page 107—3d line from bottom, "Edward Oldham"; should be "Edward Broaddus".
Page 149—11th line from top, "dreamy"; should be "dreary".
Page 185—Chap. 4, "Albermarle"; should be "Albemarle".
(This same mistake occurs in many other places, especially in Part II, Chapters 6, 8, 12, 13, 14, 17, 19, 20, 21, 22, 27, 29, 34, 36, and 37, and so forth.)
Page 199—Sec. 11, "Missouri County"; should be "Madison County"
Page 221—Sub-sec. 6, "Woods Elavin O'Rear"; should be "Slavin".
Page 253—Gen. Table C, "James—Susannah Gass"; latter name should be omitted.
Page 261—21st line from bottom, "Susannah Gass" should be omitted here, as she was the wife of one James Harris, but probably not the subject.
Page 262—5th line from top, "One"; should be "Some".
The note on this page should have been placed immediately below Sec. 3 on page 263.
Page 263—Under the date "Oct. 1, 1814," the word "deceased" instead of the word "deed" should follow "Benjamin Harris".

Page 265—5th line from bottom, "Ann Gamison"; should be "Garrison".
Page 269—Sub-sec. 5, "Lucy Harris married Thomas Grubbs"; should be "Higgason Grubbs".
Page 273—Sub-sec, 4-2-1, 25th line from top, "Patter Harris"; should be "Pattie Harris".
Page 276—Chap. 4, 22d line from bottom, "sisters" should be substituted for "daughters".
Page 277—19th line from bottom, letter "I" between "Sr." and "Will" should be omitted.
Page 278—Art. 3, caption "emoing"; should be "coming".
Page 279—Sec. 12, "Susannah Gass, daughter of David and Sarah Gass," was the wife of one James Harris, but probably not the subject.
Page 287—Chap. 6, word "sister" should take the place of the word "daughter" after the name "Nancy Grubbs".
Page 295—Chap. 12, word "sister" should be put in the place of word "daughter" after the name "Elizabeth Grubbs".
Page 299—Below Sec. 7 this should be omitted, to-wit: "3. Georgia Thorpe, married Elbridge Broaddus", as this belongs in another place.
Page 304 Chap. 16, the date of the death of Margaret Maupin Harris should be "1855" instead of "1858".
Page 305—3d line below "Obituary," the figure "4" instead of "24" should precede the word "days".
Page 309—Top line "Robert Coyler"; should be "Robert Colyer".
Page 311—Sec. 4, Chap. 23, "Perry"; should be "Peery".
Chap. 24, Secs. 1 and 2, "Pem Winn"; should be "Pen Winn".
Page 322—Chap. 35, Sec. 7, date "1870" should be "seventies".
Chap. 36, Sec. 1, the words "and died" should be placed after the name "David G. Martin".
Page 324—Sec. 2, James Harris. See Supplement.
Page 333—Sec. 1, Sub-sec. 9-5, "Bettie Arvine"; should be "Belle".
5th line below caption, "Hartleg"; should be "Hartley".
Page 336—"Elizabeth Harris—Ariah Davis"; should be "Azariah".
Page 337—Chap. 46, Sec. 1, "Reuben Eastus Gentry"; should be "Reuben Eustice Gentry".
Page 341—Chap. 47, Sec. 1-7, "Walter Bennett"; should be "Waller Bennett".
Page 347—Chap. 47, caption, the words, "data furnished by Hon. Willis Overton Harris" should be in parenthesis.
Page 350—"Wallace, Ella—Cov, Robert"; should be "Cox, Robert".
Page 353—21st line from top, "head" instead of "hand" should be between the words "His" and "was".
Page 369—Sec. 10, "Edward B. Conroy"; should be "Edward Conroy" here, as well as in the index.
Page 372—Sec. 9-1, "Ethel Payne"; should be "Estill Payne".
Page 376—2d line from top, "Andrew"; should be "Adam".
Page 376—Sec. 5, "he fell in battle" should follow the word "when"
Sec. 6, the figure "6" instead of "4" should follow the word "Chap."
Page 377—1st line at top, "he fell in battle" should be omitted here and placed as above indicated in Sec. 5 of the preceding chapter.
Page 393—28th line from top, "sons of Daniel"; should be "descendants of Daniel".
Page 395—B. Thomas Maupin was probably a son of Jesse Maupin of Chapter 3, Sec. 7.
Page 405—2nd line from top, "Jean Ra"; should be "Jean Rea".

Page 451—27th line from top, figures "22"; should be "2".
Page 462—"Oldham, Wink"; should be "Oldham, Wm. K."
Page 471—32d line from top, "He sold home"; should be "His old home".
Page 473—31st line from top, "Heresley"; should be "Hensley".
Page 483—Sec. 9-2, "Patsey Oldham"; should be "Patsey Barnes".
Page 489—Sub-sec. 9, 8th line from bottom, "in" should be placed after the word "died".
Page 495—Sec. 4-1, "Hr. William L. Hockaday"; hould be "Dr. Wm. L. Hockaday.
Page 500—Sub-sec. 9, after "April 9" should follow "1892, the wife of Dee Park; issue:"
Page 502—14th line from tob, "Thomas B. Oldham"; should be "Thompson B. Oldham".
Page 505—31st line from top, "over" after "stacking," should be "our".
Page 520—After Sec. 8-4, "Mrs. Lavinia Oldham Estill"; should be "Louise Oldham Estill".
Page 530—6th line from top, "holds"; should be "held".
Page 534—Chap. 25, 1st line below caption, "schrools"; should be "schools".
Page 542—Art. 2, "Susannah A. Rend"; should be "Reid".
Page 551—20th line from bottom, "head" after "ever" should be "heard".
Page 557—10th line from top, "Nottinghaf"; should be "Nottingham".
Page 580—Chap. 40, Sec. 1, "Whitsell"; should be "Whitsitt".
Page 599—C. 6, "Moon"; should be "Moore".
Page 626—Chap. 8, in the bottom line after the word "to" is omitted the following words, which should be added, to-wit: "Culpeper County, Virginia, after March 27, 1788, and made sale of lands and other property there belonging to his father to the".
Page 646—Bottom line date "8115" should be "1815".
Page 664—9th and 13th lines below caption, "Bezaeel" and "Bezalul"; should be "Bezaleel".
Page 666—Sec. 2, "Bezaeel Brown"; should be "Bezaleel Brown".
Page 678—Chap. 6, 1st line below caption, ,"Bezaeel Brown"; should be "Bezaleel Brown".
Page 700—After "9" in the caption the name "Anna" should not have appeared here.
1. Delaney, date "A. D. 1677"; should be "Anno 177".
Page 703—The 11th line from top should be omitted, being a repetition of the line above it.
In 9th line from top, and after "June 22," should be inserted "1769. Some of the prisoners taken in that battle and who made".
Page 709—32 line from top, "Gulford"; should be "Guilford".
10th line from bottom, "Amonw"; should be "Among".
Page 713—25th and 30th lines from top, "Copper"; should be "Copher".
Page 714—27th line from top, "Bartow"; should be "Barton".
13th line from bottom, "Copper"; should be "Copher".
Page 717—Between the 5th and 6th lines from bottom, Section 5 was omitted, which should be inserted, to-wit: "5. Lucy Berry, married William H. West, merchant and farmer of Speedwell, Madison County, Ky."
9th line from bottom, "canidate"; should be "candidate"
Page 718—7th and 8th lines from bottom, "Moon"; should be "Moore".

INDEX.

Figures indicate as follows: first, Part; second, Chapter; third and fourth, Section.

ADDENDA

LIBRARY OF CONGRESS
0 003 216 884 A

Printed in the USA
CPSIA information can be obtained
at www.ICGtesting.com
LVHW020832021023
759799LV00076B/113